P9-DHE-800

GUADALCANAL

GUADALCANAL ★★★

Richard B. Frank

RANDOM HOUSE New York

Library of Congress Cataloging-in-Publication Data

Frank, Richard B.
    Guadalcanal/by Richard B. Frank.
       p.   cm.
   ISBN 0-394-58875-4
    1. Guadalcanal Island (Solomon Islands), Battle of, 1942–1943.
I. Title.
D767.98.F73 1990
940.54'26—dc20   90-8265

Maps by William J. Clipson

Manufactured in the United States of America
24689753
First Edition

*To the memory of
my father,
George R. Frank
1917–1988*

PREFACE

"There are two Guadalcanals: the battle and the legend," wrote George McMillan, the accomplished historian of the 1st Marine Division. Guadalcanal, of course, was more than a battle. It was a six-month campaign marked by seven major naval engagements, a score or more clashes ashore, the almost daily cut and thrust of air combat, and a dozen encounters between planes and ships, only one of which earned the dignity of a title. For most of its course it teetered in precarious balance with first one side and then the other gaining the advantage. The attitudes of the most senior American political and military officials plummeted from ill-founded optimism to resignation to humiliating defeat. No campaign in World War Two saw such sustained violence in all three dimensions—sea, land, and air—where the issue hung in doubt so long.

If its intrinsic attributes made the struggle for Guadalcanal special, it was its context that made it a legend. The Pacific War began for the United States at Pearl Harbor, a humbling of national pride, quickly followed by a mortifying succession of defeats—Guam, Wake, Bataan, and Corregidor—that rubbed salt into the original wound. All of this capped over a decade of buffeting of the United States and the western democracies economically and militarily to a degree that shook the normally resilient American self-confidence to its core. The fact that these defeats came at the hands of a race once viewed with a special affection, and later with a special loathing, added to the sting and injected a raw visceral edge to the attitudes of the American participants and population.

It is more the legendary than the inherent qualities of the Guadalcanal campaign that assured it a large niche in both wartime and postwar culture. When James Jones composed his vivid combat novel *The Thin Red Line,* he set it on Guadalcanal, in part because of its strong autobiographical bloodline, but perhaps more because, as he said,

   . . . what Guadalcanal stood for to Americans in 1942–3 was a very special thing. To have used a completely made up island would have been

to lose all of these special qualities which the name Guadalcanal evoked
for my generation.

The campaign triggered a stream of works of vastly varying quality
by historians. In the forefront of these efforts stand three accounts.
The first in chronology, length, and literary quality is Samuel Eliot
Morison's depiction of Guadalcanal in the last portion of Volume IV
and all of Volume V of his masterly *History of United States Naval
Operations in World War II.* The next two works appeared in the
1960s and complement each other. These are Samuel Griffith's *The
Battle of Guadalcanal* and Thomas G. Miller's *The Cactus Air Force.*
Griffith made a distinguished contribution to the campaign as a
Marine officer, and his contacts with Japanese participants added
important new information to the body of history. Miller swelled the
public record with many facts, insights, and anecdotes about the
aerial struggle over the island, largely from the American perspective.

In view of this trio of works the reader should well demand, as
indeed was demanded of this writer early in his efforts, why another
book about Guadalcanal? The answer to this question is twofold.
First, this account differs in its approach from Morison, Griffith, and
Miller. As admirable as these three works may be, each author
adopted the perspective of one of the three dimensions of the struggle. Morison, of course, centers on the naval aspects; Griffith on the
ground and particularly the Marine contribution; Miller on the core
of the air campaign from August to November 1942. This account
presents the first entirely balanced study of the Guadalcanal campaign apportioning fair weight to all three dimensions—land, sea,
and air.

The pursuit of balance led directly to the second distinguishing
aspect of this book. On the American side, principal reliance has
been placed upon primary source material, including both official
reports and a judicious selection of contemporary personal and journalistic works. In addition, the declassification of certain records
during the last decade has yielded important new information on
radio communications intelligence matters that appear here for the
first time. However, the bulk of the new material that emerges in
detail for the first time in these pages for English-speaking readers
originates from the Japanese side. Previous accounts of this campaign drew largely from a series of monographs prepared shortly
after the war by Japanese officers. In general, these monographs were
brief and prepared from limited records. A decade later the Japanese

initiated a comprehensive history of the war. This project resulted in a massive outpouring of work totaling 101 densely detailed volumes. Of this series, four volumes pertain to the efforts of the Imperial Army and Imperial Navy on, above, and around Guadalcanal. It is the information from these volumes that permits for the first time an examination of the campaign balanced in regard to both its three dimensions and its two sides.

Certain conventions have been honored and others broken in this narrative. Rather than litter each page with a sprinkling of footnotes to snag the eye, sources are presented at the end of the book referenced to page and keyed to specific passages. Those who wish to scrutinize the basis for the assertions in this work will find the documentation there. Moreover, at the many junctures where this writer encountered factual contradictions in the records, the basis for the final choice is explained in the notes. This technique has also been employed to address certain points of concern to specialists rather than to the general reader.

The interests of accessibility have also led to certain deviations from technically precise nomenclature. As explained in the text, literal translation of organization titles in the Imperial Navy has been eschewed in favor of the United States Navy system for simplicity. For similar motives, though with more reluctance, Japanese aircraft are identified by the system adapted by the United States as the campaign ended. This method has become so thoroughly ingrained in postwar usage in the United States and is so familiar to such a large body of readers that an insistence on technical accuracy would sacrifice too much in the way of clarity. For the same reason, Japanese names are rendered in western style, given name first and surname second, rather than the reverse that is proper Japanese usage.

Although this is not a study of military and naval technology of the period, it is frequently quite impossible to explain both what happened and why it happened without reference to the virtues and vices of certain weaponry—notably aircraft, torpedoes, and radar. Similarly, there has been no flinching from a discussion of tactical doctrine when it intimately tied to the course and outcome of the battles recounted here.

There is one other important feature of the design of this work of which the reader is forewarned. A conventional campaign study focuses on a finite geographical locale with logical borders and then rotates the perspective in some ratio between the two opposing sides. The Guadalcanal campaign does not fit neatly into this mold. The Japanese viewed the Solomon Islands and New Guinea as a unified

Southeast Area for which they appointed dual Army and Navy commanders headquartered at Rabaul. As a result of a compromise at the highest command levels in the United States, the Pacific theater was divided into two major strategic commands: Admiral Chester W. Nimitz's Pacific Ocean Area and General Douglas MacArthur's Southwest Pacific theater. The partition line of these commands runs both literally and figuratively through this account, with New Guinea squarely in General MacArthur's bailiwick and the Solomons shared between the two commands. The campaigns involving the eastern tip of New Guinea and Guadalcanal were contemporaries in time and competitors for resources on both sides. Although these endeavors were geographical neighbors and were connected in important respects at the operational level, space forbids a comprehensive discussion of both in one book. Therefore this account is confined geographically to the environs of Guadalcanal and the perspective is alternated between the Japanese and the Americans on and around Guadalcanal and their respective superior commanders.

ACKNOWLEDGMENTS

★ ★ ★

Since I began working on this narrative in October 1977, many individuals have made contributions that have materially improved its accuracy and quality. My thanks must first go to H. C. "Chris" Merillat, a veteran of the campaign and author of two distinguished books on Guadalcanal, *The Island* and *Guadalcanal Remembered.* He shared with me not only his insights and private diary, but more important, he was also an unfailing source of moral support through the many years this account was in preparation.

Next, I wish to recognize Don Cyril Gorham and Y. ("Tommy") Tamagawa who assisted me in acquiring copies of the Japanese Self Defense Agency history volumes pertaining to the Guadalcanal campaign and in locating for me Bunichi Ohtsuka as a translator. Bunichi proved to be an inspired choice as he is fluent not only in two languages, but also reads the elaborate and arcane style of writing prevalent in Japan before and during the war in which much of the text of the Defense Agency series appears. He also enthusiastically worked the irregular hours my schedule permitted and did so with good humor and courtesy. I am now happy to count him among my friends.

The development of new friends proved to be a major delight of this project. Among these are John Lundstrom and James Sawruk. To students of the Pacific war, John is recognized as the leading authority on strategy and air operations in 1942 through his two books, *The First South Pacific Campaign* and *The First Team.* He not only has a commanding knowledge of the American documentary sources and unexcelled contacts with veterans of the struggle, but he also has studied the original Japanese air unit reports. He is working on a sequel to *The First Team* that will cover naval air combat from the battle of Midway to December 1942. Besides most unselfishly sharing with me with the fruits of his own research, he read and skillfully critiqued drafts of this narrative. Jim Sawruk is a researcher par excellence who has discovered and explored previously overlooked documentary source material and is an expert in naval aircraft deployment, operations and losses. He has also diligently pursued veteran contacts and filled in large voids in the record on many points, notably PBY and B-17 operations, in addition to resolving questions concerning the loss of at least three ships.

No serious history of the Pacific war can be written without the assistance of the excellent service department historical centers and the National Archives located in the Washington, D.C., area. My thanks must go to all of the staff of these organizations who have assisted me. Several of them, however, merit special recognition. Mr. Robert Cressman, who is an old friend, works at the Ships History branch of the Naval Historical Center. He not only shared his considerable knowledge of this period, but also kept a sharp lookout during the course of his work for material that would benefit my narrative. He located many nuggets of information that I otherwise would never have seen. He also contributed his considerable editorial skill to reviewing and improving early drafts of this narrative. Mr. Mike Walker also went above and beyond the call of duty to take my rudimentary descriptions of information I needed and translate them into wonderfully apt, and often quite obscure, source material. Dr. Dean Allard, now the director of the Naval Historical Center, extended his encouragement for many years, and most graciously took time out of his very busy schedule to review my manuscript.

The staff at the Marine Corps Historical Center likewise provided outstanding support, but I must particularly single out for thanks Benis Frank and that very gracious lady, Joyce Bonnett. At the National Archives, Mr. John Taylor showed me why he is an institution there in his knowledge of many areas, particularly radio intelligence.

My very special friends Gregory Embree and Lieutenant Colonel Dennis Fontana not only kept faith in my efforts for many years, they also cast sharp editorial eyes over my scribblings and much improved the final product. George McGillivray, a veteran of the campaign, also provided encouragement and assisted my understanding on many points concerning the 7th Marines and maps. William Clipson turned my simple sketches into a fine collection of maps. My agent, Robert Gottlieb, achieved more with my manuscript than I had ever dreamed. My very thoughtful editor, Robert Loomis, demonstrated why he is at the top of his profession and spurred me to my best efforts.

Virginia, April 1990

CONTENTS

PREFACE   vii

ACKNOWLEDGMENTS   xi

CHAPTER 1   STRATEGY, COMMAND, AND THE
             SOLOMONS   3

CHAPTER 2   PLANS, PREPARATIONS, AND
             APPROACH   32

CHAPTER 3   THE LANDING   59

CHAPTER 4   THE BATTLE OF SAVO ISLAND   83

CHAPTER 5   FIRST DAYS ASHORE   124

CHAPTER 6   THE TENARU   141

CHAPTER 7   THE BATTLE OF THE EASTERN
             SOLOMONS   159

CHAPTER 8   TWO WEEKS OF SPARRING   194

CHAPTER 9   THE BATTLE OF EDSON'S RIDGE   218

CHAPTER 10   REINFORCEMENT AND
             REASSESSMENT   247

CHAPTER 11   BATTLES ON THE MATANIKAU   267

CHAPTER 12   THE BATTLE OF CAPE ESPERANCE   292

CHAPTER 13   THE "HIGH-SPEED CONVOY"   313

CHAPTER 14   THE BATTLE FOR HENDERSON
             FIELD   337

CHAPTER 15   THE BATTLE OF THE SANTA CRUZ
             ISLANDS   368

CHAPTER 16   RETREATS AND ADVANCES   404

CHAPTER 17   THE NAVAL BATTLE OF
             GUADALCANAL, PART I: THE
             BATTLE OF FRIDAY
             THE THIRTEENTH   428

CHAPTER 18   THE NAVAL BATTLE OF
GUADALCANAL, PART II: CONVOY
AND CAPITAL SHIP ACTIONS   462

CHAPTER 19   THE BATTLE OF TASSAFARONGA   493

CHAPTER 20   THE DECEMBER DECISION   519

CHAPTER 21   THE FINAL OFFENSIVE BEGINS   540

CHAPTER 22   THE FINAL OFFENSIVE CONTINUES   559

CHAPTER 23   OPERATION "KE"   577

CHAPTER 24   SUMMARY AND REFLECTIONS   598

APPENDIX 1   FORCES ARRAYED FOR THE
LANDING   619

APPENDIX 2   ORDER OF BATTLE OF THE
17TH ARMY   631

APPENDIX 3   ALLIED NAVAL CASUALTIES   637

APPENDIX 4   LOSSES OF PRINCIPAL AIRCRAFT
TYPES   645

A NOTE ON SOURCES   647

NOTES   651

GENERAL INDEX   767

INDEX OF MILITARY UNITS   789

GUADALCANAL

1

STRATEGY,

COMMAND, AND

THE SOLOMONS

"Now comes the adult's hour"

STRATEGY AND COMMAND: THE RISE OF COMINCH

The Japanese aircraft that destroyed the Pacific Fleet's battleships at Pearl Harbor transformed American naval tactics, strategy, and command. Sheer necessity ordained the new tactics centered on the fast carriers and their planes. The new strategy emerged tentatively as the offspring less of necessity than of political dictates and their military corollaries. It resulted in an unanticipated major commitment to the South Pacific, initially in a defensive posture aptly described by John Lundstrom as the First South Pacific Campaign. In a subsequent phase of this commitment, the South Pacific became the arena for the first American offensive of the war with the landings on Guadalcanal in August 1942. This phase may be appropriately labeled the Second South Pacific Campaign, and its tumultuous opening stages are the subject of this narrative.

The campaigns in the South Pacific, however, may not be regarded as simply the inevitable products of inexorable political and military logic. Events created a milieu, and others, notably President Franklin D. Roosevelt, made important contributions, but the South

Pacific strategy was forged principally by one man, Admiral Ernest Joseph King. Here the strategy and command changes resulting from Pearl Harbor intersected, for the Japanese attack completed the remarkable resurrection of King's career.

In 1942, King attained his sixty-fourth birthday and completed his forty-first year as a naval officer. His father was a seaman, a bridge builder, and finally a foreman in a railroad repair shop. Drawn to his father's workplace, young Ernest absorbed the complexities of gears and lathes and the simple unpretentiousness of the workmen. After graduating fourth in a class of eighty-seven from the Naval Academy, King pursued a career remarkable for its versatility, with important work in surface ships, submarines, and naval aviation. He completed all his assignments with distinction, for the brain beneath his balding pate was agile with technical matters and he possessed a prodigious memory.

Besides intelligence and dedication, one other pillar supported King's professional reputation: his toughness. He regarded exceptional performance of duty as the norm and evinced insensitivity or even callousness to his subordinates, upon whom he also frequently exercised his ferocious temper. But if King proved harsh with subordinates, he was no toady to superiors. Those who fell short of King's standards found he could be hostile, tactless, arrogant, and sometimes disrespectful or even insubordinate. As a junior officer this conduct earned him more than a healthy share of disciplinary actions. He defined the span of his concerns beyond his career when he once commented, "You ought to be very suspicious of anyone who won't take a drink or doesn't like women." King, the father of seven, was deficient in neither category.

Though a latecomer to naval aviation at age forty-eight, King took command of the carrier *Lexington* in 1930 as a captain. More assignments in aviation followed promotion to flag rank, culminating in the duty of Commander Aircraft, Battle Force of the Pacific Fleet as a vice admiral. In March 1939, King reckoned himself among the handful of the seventy-four serving flag officers seriously competitive for the job of Chief of Naval Operations, the top uniformed position in the Navy. Crushed when the assignment went to Admiral Harold R. Stark, King thought his career was finished. Reverting to rear admiral's rank, he soon received orders to report to the General Board—an advisory body composed of senior admirals awaiting retirement who, it was hoped, on this "twilight cruise" would deliberate selflessly and objectively on matters ranging from strategy to ship characteristics.

After a period of despair, King told one visitor, "They're not done with me yet, I will have another chance." The path back to the mainstream of the Navy began with his fortuitous assignment as the escort officer on a tour of the fleet for Charles Edison, the Secretary of the Navy. King next headed a study ("the King Board") that both diagnosed and recommended remedies for serious deficiencies in fleet antiaircraft armaments. Edison, impressed by King's conspicuous ability, wrote President Roosevelt that the Navy needed a shaking-out of "peace-time psychology" and that the one man who could do it was Rear Admiral Ernest J. King.

Admiral Stark also recognized King's talents, but the man who provided an essential thrust to King's comeback was Adolf Hitler. The middle of 1940 found the German dictator the sole master of most of Western Europe and anxious to bring England to heel by cutting her Atlantic lifeline. Franklin Roosevelt, hemmed by neutrality laws and isolationists in Congress, was no more than a coauthor of American foreign policy, but as Commander in Chief of the Armed Forces his writ ran larger and he resolved to use the United States Navy to aid embattled Britain. He immediately confronted a problem in fleet organization and deployment. The great bulk of American naval power lay concentrated in the Pacific, and in the now critical Atlantic, United States naval presence consisted of a modest collection of old and heterogeneous vessels used primarily for training—or as one waggish admiral commented, for "showing the flag at flower shows for local politicians." Roosevelt conceived a far more aggressive role for this squadron, a "Neutrality Patrol," and after the original commander, Rear Admiral Hayne Ellis, failed to display zeal commensurate with Roosevelt's expectations, the President replaced Ellis with Ernest King. In January 1941, in a surprise move, the Navy was divided into three major commands: Atlantic, Pacific, and Asiatic. King took the helm of the Atlantic Fleet and regained the pinnacle of power.

Nine days after Pearl Harbor, King learned that Admiral Chester W. Nimitz would become the new Commander in Chief Pacific Fleet (CINCPAC) and King would assume the position of Commander in Chief U.S. Fleet. Moreover, although Stark was retained for a time as Chief of Naval Operations, King would be the effective commander of all United States naval forces. The new job was acceptable, but not the old acronym, CINCUS, pronounced "sink us." The new acronym would be King's alone: COMINCH.

King, a keen student of both sea and land warfare, like all senior officers was thoroughly conversant with the body of strategic plans developed between the wars. Each of these plans bore the color code of the potential adversary: Black (Germany), Red (United Kingdom), and Orange (Japan). In the Pacific, the United States viewed the defense of the Philippines as the central problem and Japan as the chief threat. The Joint Board, composed of Army and Navy officers, formulated several plans that ultimately called for the Army garrison in the Philippines to hold the entrance of Manila Bay until succored by a relief expedition convoyed by the Navy, which intended to carve its way across the Central Pacific through the Marshall and Caroline islands, known as the Mandates, as Japan held them as mandates under the League of Nations. The American sailors anticipated that the climactic moment of the relief would be a great sea fight by opposing fleets of battleships in the mold of Jutland.

The advent of Hitler's Germany and his alliance with Italy and Japan raised the specter of war against multiple enemies. This lead to the "Rainbow" series of war plans, i.e., multiple colors, of which "Rainbow Five" (or officially WPL-46) was in effect at the time of Pearl Harbor. The fundamental premise of this plan was concentration on defeating Germany first with the Pacific theater in the strategic defensive. Upon assumption of his duties as COMINCH, King found the Pacific Fleet under restrictive orders to protect only the area east of the 180th meridian (basically the International Date Line) and to stop the Japanese only at Samoa and Palmyra islands. This would concede key South Pacific islands to the Japanese, and by the time Nimitz officially replaced Admiral Husband E. Kimmel as CINCPAC on December 31, he found new orders from King: the Pacific Fleet would first cover and hold the line Hawaii-Midway and maintain communications with the West Coast; and secondly, and "only in small degree less important," the fleet would protect the sea lanes from the United States to Australia, chiefly by covering and securing the line Hawaii-Samoa with an extension to the Fiji Islands at the earliest practical date.

King issued these new orders from "Arcadia," the code name of the first joint conference with the British after formal American entry into the war. The Churchill-led delegation arrived in Washington anxious to find out whether the Americans still intended to honor the "Germany First" principle not only embodied in "Rainbow Five," but also certified as the American aim during secret Anglo-American staff conferences in 1941. The visitors gained quick assurance that American policy remained constant, and the written agreement produced at "Arcadia" reaffirmed this principle. This

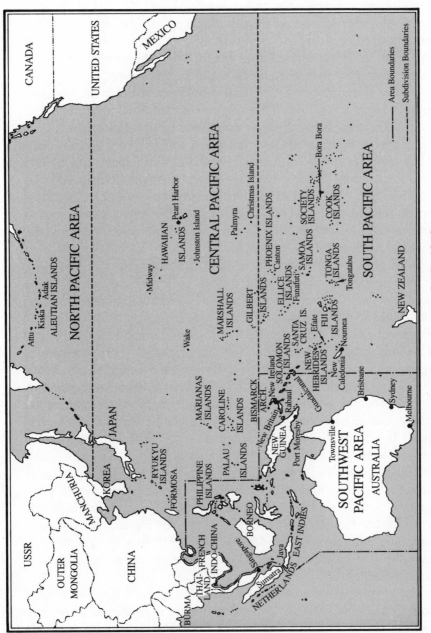

Pacific Ocean Areas, April 18, 1942

carefully vague paper also called for "maintaining only such positions in the [Pacific] theater as will safeguard vital interests," without defining what constituted "vital interests." At King's insistence, the agreement also authorized the seizure of "vantage points" from which an offensive against Japan could be developed.

Even as the conferees toiled, however, Japan struck with astonishing speed over a vast area. This surge prompted two important steps. First, "Arcadia" created a new command to link the disparate national forces fighting against the drive for the Netherlands East Indies through the Philippines and Malaya. This became the ABDA Area (American, British, Dutch, Australian), and British General Sir Archibald Wavell added it to his already long résumé of thankless duties. Second, and of great future import, the Americans agreed to make a definite commitment to the South Pacific area to secure the sea lanes to Australia.

During the first five months of 1942, American Army, Army Air Forces, and Navy planners skirmished by voice and pen over the island garrisons required to defend the elongated supply routes to Australia and New Zealand. Each service interpreted the "Arcadia" agreement exactly along the lines of how it planned to fight the war as a whole. On the one extreme stood the Army Air Forces, begrudging every plane and man sent to the Pacific and wedded to the theory of victory through strategic air bombardment. From its viewpoint, Germany combined the virtues of being not only the most dangerous enemy, but also the one immediately assailable. From bases in England, B-17s and B-24s could reach most of the Reich, whereas no prospect existed of gnawing at the industrial heart of Japan for many months or years. To Army aviators the dispersion of scarce air units through theaters other than Northern Europe would achieve no strategic purpose and invited defeat in detail. Although not independent like the Royal Air Force, the Army Air Forces enjoyed near autonomy and carried considerable heft, for it was recognized that the buildup of air power would have to "precede any form of decisive offensive action."

The naval leadership occupied the other pole. While the British wrongly suspected them in general and King in particular of rabidly favoring absolute priority for the war in the Pacific, American admirals considered a passive defense in the Pacific neither acceptable nor necessary. They wanted strong reinforcements sent to the Pacific forthwith, even at the temporary expense—as they saw it—of the European theater. Navy strategy foresaw a buildup of garrisons, both land and air, on a series of islands along the shipping routes from San

Francisco and Hawaii to Australia and New Zealand. These would both defend the supply routes and provide forces for limited offensives.

Army leaders, including the Army Chief of Staff, General George C. Marshall, shared views much nearer those of the Army Air Forces than of the Navy. Although Army strategy surfaced early, it received its clearest expression in a master war plan prepared under the direction of Brigadier General Dwight D. Eisenhower in February 1942. Assuming the safety of the continental United States and Hawaii from direct attack, the Army planners advanced three prerequisites for a successful conclusion of the war: maintaining the United Kingdom, active Soviet participation in the war, and the security of the Middle East and India to prevent a junction of the Germans and Japanese. They classified only as "highly desirable" the security of Alaska and the supply lines to Australia and Burma. As for the South Pacific, Eisenhower's team expected the Japanese to capture the oil-rich Netherlands East Indies and therefore saw the only remaining objective in the theater as the purely defensive task of maintaining communications with Australia. Consequently, a minimum of forces would be assigned to the Pacific because of the limitations of shipping, equipment, and trained troops. Maximum effort would be concentrated for the accumulation of forces in the United Kingdom for an invasion of Europe as soon as possible. "We've got to go to Europe and fight," wrote Eisenhower, "we've got to quit wasting resources all over the world—and still worse—wasting time."

Given these conflicts among the American services, it is not surprising that the selection of forces and bases necessary to guard the lines of communications to Australia emerged not in one single coherent plan, but rather after a series of individual battles. Navy orders sent Marine reinforcements to strengthen Samoa, and the Army quickly promised and delivered two small contingents for the atolls of Canton Island (1,500 troops) and Christmas Island (2,000 troops), situated south of Palmyra on the route to Samoa. King's first tentative step toward developing a position in the South Pacific produced an essential refueling base at Bora-Bora. The obvious strategic importance of New Caledonia, with its valuable nickel and chrome deposits, won the dispatch of 17,000 men of an ad hoc unit subsequently designated the Americal (for "Americans in New Caledonia") Division.

The garrisoning of New Caledonia and Bora-Bora marked the extension of the defense line into the South Pacific and created the first strains on Army resources. As Navy planners demanded more island strongpoints, their Army counterparts steadily insisted that no more than a minimum of islands be secured and that none should receive more than the minimum garrison to defend it. Despite the avowed priority for Europe, the exasperated soldiers noted that almost all the forces sent overseas in the first six months of the war went to the Pacific. They put their foot down to a Navy proposal on February 5 to erect a base at Funafuti in the Ellice Islands intended as an outpost to cover the Fijis and Samoa and as a link toward the Solomons.

Meanwhile, in late January, the Japanese advance interjected political factors strongly tilting debate in favor of King's campaign to expand efforts in the South Pacific. After the fall of Rabaul on New Britain on January 23, the British predicted that the next Japanese targets were the Fijis and New Caledonia; they voiced a call for the defense of the area by the Pacific Fleet. The Australian government was thoroughly alarmed, as its four best divisions were overseas, three in the Middle East and one in Malaya. Already on January 21, Australian Prime Minister John Curtin informed Churchill that two Australian divisions must be returned to defend their homeland. Curtin's demand threatened to ripple broadly across Allied strategy, for withdrawal of the Australian divisions would jeopardize Allied prospects in the Middle East and their movement and replacement would pose enormous shipping problems. Churchill appealed to Roosevelt for aid, and the President intervened directly in strategic planning to authorize thickening defenses in the South Pacific even at the expense of Europe. On February 15, the President declared that the United States would assume responsibility for the defense of New Zealand, and the same day orders were cut sending the American 41st Infantry Division to Australia. Three days later, Roosevelt informed Churchill that the United States would detail troops to Australia and New Zealand so that those governments would be willing to keep their divisions in the Middle East.

On February 20, President Roosevelt assured Prime Minister Curtin that the United States was in the best position to reinforce Australia and New Zealand and pointed out that the United States Navy was already deploying to defend the area. The latter reference alluded to two recent actions of King in furtherance of his developing campaign in the South Pacific. On January 24, King appointed Rear Admiral Herbert F. Leary commander of the new ANZAC Area and charged him with the job of shielding the waters around Australia and New Zealand. More important, on King's initiative a carrier group formed around *Lexington* headed for the South Pacific at the end of January. Curtin was not mollified. On March 4 he asked for two more divisions to take the place of one Australian and one New Zealand division now slated to stay in the Middle East. Churchill seconded this request, which Roosevelt met, and within a few days preparations began to sail the American 32d Infantry Division to Australia and the 37th Infantry Division to New Zealand.

One additional factor, less explicit but no less potent, lurked in the background of this series of political decisions by President Roosevelt. Intellectuals and military planners might find Hitler's Germany the supreme threat to American values and security, but the average citizen regarded Japan with "unbridled fear, hatred, and distrust," thanks to Pearl Harbor. The bulk of the American people would never have understood, or tolerated, a policy of virtual idleness in the Pacific during long months of buildup for a decisive offensive in Europe.

Japanese moves imperiling Australia and the South Pacific stamped squarely on a vital nerve that not even the most cold-blooded American Army planner could ignore. The single most important determinant of Western Allied capabilities from Pearl Harbor to 1944 was what Churchill labeled "the shipping stranglehold." Simple arithmetic revealed that the same amount of merchant-ship tonnage that would transport two men to the Southwest Pacific could move five men to England, and it actually required less cargo capacity to keep those five men fighting. Once political leaders decided that Australia must be held, the Japanese thrust into the South Pacific menaced the whole global strategy by threatening to impose an intolerable strain on shipping resources. Thus the combination of political factors and the threat to shipping resources created powerful winds that enabled King to sail American strategy out of the doldrums of a minimal commitment to a passive defense of the South Pacific.

King continued to shift major American naval units toward the South Pacific by ordering two heavy cruisers and four destroyers sent to the Samoan area. On February 15, the day Singapore fell, King directed that the carrier group formed around *Yorktown* steam to the vicinity of Canton Island. Doubts about the emphasis on the South Pacific area were not confined to the American Army and Army Air Forces. Both the commander and staff of the Pacific Fleet also challenged the wisdom of sending major forces to the south. They regarded these redeployments as threats to compromise the official chief mission of the Pacific Fleet: to protect Hawaii. On practical grounds the lack of adequate naval bases raised disturbing questions about the fate that might befall any major fleet unit damaged in the South Pacific. Only gradually were Nimitz and his staff won around to enthusiastic support for King's scheme.

On February 18, King broached to the Army a proposal to establish a garrison at Tongatabu in the Tonga Islands, the chosen site of an advanced naval base, and at Efate in the New Hebrides. This set off alarm bells in the War Department, for it was suspected to be the first step toward the initiation of a major offensive in the Pacific. Consequently, on February 24 General Marshall asked King for more information on the project. King responded to Marshall's inquiry on March 2, candidly admitting that the purpose of establishing the line of island bases was not only to protect the lines of communication to Australia but also to set up "strongpoints" from which to initiate a "step-by-step" advance through the New Hebrides, Solomons, and Bismarck Archipelago. Such an offensive, he pointed out, would deflect the Japanese advance from Australia and draw Japanese forces away from India. He could accept restriction of Army troop requirements to those for Efate and Tongatabu, but he refused to remain on the defensive.

President Roosevelt convened a meeting to discuss Pacific strategy on March 5 with the newly formed Joint Chiefs of Staff, composed of Marshall, King, and General Henry H. Arnold, Chief of the Army Air Forces. King presented his views very much along the lines of his March 2 memorandum, which he summarized as: hold Hawaii, support Australia, drive northward from the New Hebrides. Marshall and Secretary of War Henry L. Stimson pressed for a commitment to an early cross-Channel attack from England to France. Roosevelt affirmed the need to hold Australia and, typically, seemed to give the nod to King's proposed strategy.

Despite the apparent agreement of the President with King's views, dispute continued within the Joint Chiefs of Staff as to whether future commitments were to be made to the Pacific at the expense of the buildup in Europe. Circumstances now aided King's opponents, for the Soviets, whose recent counteroffensive had bogged down, urged major action to aid them. Churchill seconded the Soviet agitation. At a meeting of the Joint Chiefs of Staff on March 16, Marshall and Arnold outvoted King and reconferred official sanction on the strategy of a rapid buildup of forces in Europe with the restriction of reinforcements to the Pacific at "current commitments." They also granted approval for bases at Efate and Tongatabu, but this effectively ended the deployment of Army troops to defend the lines of communication to Australia at 41,000, supplemented by 15,000 marines. King yielded to this general plan to avoid alienating Marshall and thus risking the adoption of the even more radical Army Air Force plan of no reinforcement at all to the Pacific.

On March 26, Rear Admiral Richmond Kelly Turner, chief of the War Plans Division, prepared a memorandum for King pointing out: "It is a far different matter attempting to establish advanced bases in the Solomons than in the islands heretofore occupied." Turner detected no sign the Army would change its mind and release more troops and aircraft for the defense of the South Pacific. "Even worse," he added, he doubted that Arnold was providing the aircraft strengths already approved. His gloomy assessment concluded that there appeared to be no way the Navy could conduct a successful offensive in the current situation. Turner urged King, however, to appoint a commander for the South Pacific and provide him with amphibious troops.

Turner's recommendation concerning the South Pacific reflected the resolution of the fundamental question of command arrangements in the Pacific during March, though to no one's complete satisfaction. The Japanese thrust to Java not only gutted the short-lived ABDA Command but also created a natural dividing line between the Asian continent and Australia and the rest of the Pacific Ocean. Logic might seem to point to the desirability of placing the entire Pacific theater under one commander, but such a step ran aground on the shoals of irreconcilable conflicts between the American Army and Navy. The enormous national popularity and seniority of General Douglas MacArthur made him the obvious choice for such a command. But the naval leaders, with King in the forefront, properly objected to consigning a vast natural naval theater to an Army officer whose recent performance left them unimpressed. In turn, however, no naval officer was acceptable to the Army over MacArthur.

On March 9, the Joint Chiefs of Staff adapted essentially a Navy plan for command in the Pacific. MacArthur became commander of the Southwest Pacific Area, composed of Australia and the area to the northwest, including the Philippines. The ANZAC Area was abolished and its commander, Admiral Leary, and his ships became the nucleus of MacArthur's naval forces. The rest of the Pacific fell under Nimitz, who now wore two hats, one as Commander in Chief Pacific Fleet (CINCPAC) and the other as Commander in Chief Pacific Ocean Area (CINCPOA). MacArthur and Nimitz would receive orders through their respective service chiefs, Marshall and

King, who in turn acted as executives for the Joint Chiefs of Staff, which held ultimate jurisdiction over all matters pertaining to strategy, subject finally to decisions of the American-British Combined Chiefs of Staff on grand strategical policy and "related factors."

The Joint Chiefs split the Pacific Ocean Area into North, Central, and South Pacific subcommands, with boundaries at 40 degrees north latitude and the equator. Nimitz retained direct command of the first two, but King informed him that a separate commander would be appointed for the South Pacific Area. King requested Nimitz to nominate an officer for this position, adding the comment that Nimitz need not confine his consideration to officers now under his command. This was an oblique reference to the fact that the candidate would have to be a senior admiral who could pass muster with Secretary of the Navy Frank Knox. Although Knox abstained from interfering in assignments of admirals outside the Navy Department itself, he adamantly refused to elevate any of the top-ranking officers he deemed implicated in the disaster at Pearl Harbor. For the position of South Pacific Commander, Nimitz put forth his commander of the Pacific Fleet battleships, Vice Admiral William S. Pye, who had held the same post under Admiral Kimmel. As the relief for Pye, Nimitz proposed Rear Admiral Robert L. Ghormley, then in London, with the postscript that, in the alternative, he could accept Ghormley as the new South Pacific commander. Although Pye was one of his few intimate friends, King promptly selected Ghormley for the new command.

Robert L. Ghormley was fifty-nine years old in 1942 with a service career including sea duty in destroyers and battleships and many important staff assignments culminating in the key job of chief of the War Plans Division in 1938 and 1939. He served from 1940 until summoned for his new post as the Special Naval Observer in London. Physically large, Ghormley also possessed a dominating intellect widely respected in the small world of professional naval officers. The absence of other conspicuous traits may help explain his flair for diplomacy. Though genial and well liked by his subordinates, he was reserved and socialized little.

On April 18, 1942, Lieutenant Colonel James Doolittle led sixteen B-25s from the deck of the carrier *Hornet* in a raid on Japan that was virtually the first glimmer of good news to the angry and humiliated American public. In Washington that same day, King issued terse orders to Ghormley that the latter recalled as follows:

You have been selected to command the South Pacific Force and South Pacific area. You will have a large area under your command and a most difficult task. I do not have the tools to give you to carry out that task as it should be. You will establish your headquarters in Auckland, New Zealand, with an advanced base at Tongatabu. In time, possibly this fall, we hope to start an offensive in the South Pacific. You will then probably find it necessary to shift the advanced base as the situation demands and move your own headquarters to meet special situations. I would like for you to leave Washington in one week if possible.

There was no hiatus in the struggle over strategic planning in April while King and Nimitz chose the commander for the South Pacific area. On April 1, President Roosevelt received what became known as the "Marshall Memorandum," which essentially called for a definite choice between security in the Pacific and an early offensive in Europe. Marshall believed prompt American action was essential to prevent defeat of the Soviet Union and the United Kingdom. He asked for priority to a plan whose trio of components became known by their code names: "Bolero," a buildup of troops and aircraft in Europe that would stop the dispersion of resources to the Pacific; "Sledgehammer," a limited offensive on the European continent in 1942 to aid the Soviet Union; and "Round-up," a major invasion of Europe set "very tentatively for April 1943."

Marshall recognized that British endorsement of his plan would powerfully affect the President's attitude, so he flew to London in April to rally British support. On arrival he found the British extremely—but justifiably—anxious over rampaging Japanese carriers in the Indian Ocean. The British began by asking for the United States naval and air units to shore up their position, but when Japanese intentions merely to raid and not to land became clear, they gave assent to Marshall's scheme. Events showed the British considered Marshall's plan unrealistic about Allied capabilities to test cases with the German Army on the European continent in 1942, but this episode marked the end of British interest in expanding Allied efforts in the Pacific.

While Marshall visited London, King and his planners were not idle. On April 16, Turner presented a four-phase "Pacific Ocean Campaign Plan." Phase one would be a buildup of forces and positions in the South and Southwest Pacific to secure the area and to prepare for an offensive against the Japanese. The second phase was a combined offensive by American, New Zealand, and Australian forces through the Solomons and New Guinea to capture the Bismarck Archipelago and the Admiralty Islands. During the third phase, the Marshall and Caroline islands would be conquered and become sites for advanced fleet and air bases. The final phase would witness an advance into the Netherlands East Indies or the Philippines, "whichever offers the more promising and enduring results." With King's approval this became the basic Navy war plan for the Pacific.

Turner's design clearly traced its lineage to the strategy carefully incubated between the wars for a Central Pacific advance commencing with operations in the Marshall and Caroline islands. Now, however, this was to be preceded by a thrust in the South and Southwest Pacific areas that had not figured at all in prewar calculations. Two fundamental considerations undergirded this shift. First, the depth of the Japanese advance created unanticipated political demands to secure the areas proximate to Australia and New Zealand. Second, the old plans had been forged around a Jutland-style battleship engagement as the centerpiece of strategy. Now air power had ascended from a key component to the principle determinant of strategy. For the first eighteen months or more of the war, the United States Navy would operate with only seven fleet carriers (one unsuited for Pacific operations). These carriers were too few and individually too valuable to risk in providing sustained air cover for an offensive. Thus the Allies required an area where a step-by-step advance could be mounted under the umbrella of land-based aircraft, and from the positions held in the spring of 1942, only the Southwest and the South Pacific fitted these specifications.

Even before he submitted his master Pacific war plan, Turner was aware that he would be the commander of the Amphibious Force for the South Pacific. He described his new assignment as an "opportunity packed billet," and Turner, a man of "corrosive ambition," possessed a keen eye for opportunity. Fifty-seven years old in 1942, he had a lean, straight frame and a face dominated by dark threatening eyebrows. Wire-rimmed glasses gave him a schoolmasterish air in keeping with both his heritage (he was the son of a schoolteacher) and his gratingly didactic manner. After an early career in surface ships, Turner became a naval aviator, but he was not an intimate member of the air fraternity. From his earliest days in the Navy, he proved himself a tireless worker, nearly incapable of delegating work, and his staff found he used them as an extra set of hands rather than as an extra set of heads. Others described him frequently as irascible, if not actually mean, and determined, "a hard man to deal with if you were contrary to his ideas." Like many men of stellar intellect, he displayed little patience for beings of lesser endowments. Turner carried the Navy's standard in strategic policy battles in 1942 with planners from the other services and presented King's views well, but with such an acid tongue that eventually General Marshall demanded his ouster for the sake of interservice harmony. King could hardly have failed to see a great deal of himself in Turner.

The first week of May brought a final Presidential decision on the question of whether the United States should accept immediate hazards in the Pacific in order to prepare for future offensive action in Europe in 1942. Although only recently Roosevelt had once again appeared to be waivering toward greatly augmented efforts in the Pacific, he now reaffirmed his order that "Bolero," the European buildup, take pride of place among American priorities. During the remainder of May, Admiral King used the developing threat of a massive Japanese attack on Midway, detected by radio intelligence, to attempt to pry loose more forces for the Pacific, but to little avail.

Although May saw Nimitz maneuvering skillfully to draw his carriers back from the South Pacific to defend Midway, on the 28th he took the time to respond to multiple prods from King for some kind of aggressive action. As will be seen, on May 3 the Japanese captured Tulagi in the southern Solomons and Nimitz proposed a strike on that location by the appropriately named 1st Marine Raider Battalion. This move would have the dual purpose of unbalancing the Japanese and blunting their drive to the southeast. MacArthur quickly objected to the move on the grounds that he was already thinking "hit and stay" and he possessed no forces to hold Tulagi. Moreover, he believed a Japanese regiment garrisoned their southeasternmost bastion. Instead of a raid, he advocated a northward drive beginning with the occupation of the New Hebrides and Santa Cruz islands. Likewise, King disdained the Tulagi plan. He too looked for a more substantial operation in the view of the growing Allied strength in the area. Despite the cutoff of further reinforcements, by the end of June, MacArthur's Southwest Pacific theater would field three and one-half divisions while in Ghormley's South Pacific theater there would be the Americal Division at New Caledonia, the 37th Infantry Division en route to the Fijis, a regiment each at Efate and Tongatabu, and most important, the 1st Marine Division training for amphibious warfare in New Zealand. The raid proposal died quietly, but the dangling Japanese position in the southern Solomons would not be forgotten.

STRATEGY AND COMMAND—JAPANESE

Soldiers of the Imperial Army ironically shared with their American counterparts a repugnance for involvement in the Pacific theater in general and the South Pacific in particular. As in the United States, the naval service propelled the nation into the Solomons, though in another parallel, there was intraservice debate over the wisdom of such a distant expedition. The evolution of strategic thinking and the chain of decisions that placed Japanese bases in the Solomons in the spring and summer of 1942 can be comprehended only in the context of the peculiar Japanese command structure, prewar planning, and the role of two critical personalities, Admiral Isoroku Yamamoto and Vice Admiral Shigeyoshi Inoue.

In 1941 the military dominance of Japan's political institutions reached its final form with the appointment of General Hideki Tojo as Premier. The Emperor, though both divine and the head of state, exercised little influence over the actual management of the government, and still less over the armed forces. As head of the government, Tojo presided over a cabinet that included serving officers as ministers of the Army and Navy. These ministers, however, bore responsibility only for administrative and logistical matters. The real locus of power rested in Imperial General Headquarters, which was subdivided into Army and Navy sections. In 1941 and 1942, General Hajime Sugiyama was the Chief of the Army General Staff and Admiral Osami Nagano was the Chief of the Naval General Staff.

Grand strategical plans were the official prerogative of Imperial General Headquarters, and these were usually codified in written agreements, signed by Sugiyama and Nagano for their respective services. These written compacts, termed Central Agreements, emerged after frequently fractious debate, for the basic outlooks of the Imperial Army and Navy were as different as east and west. The soldiers remained oriented westward to the Asian continent and thus toward China and the Soviet Union. They were, in fact, obsessed with the Soviets and viewed them as the most likely and dangerous foe. The more cosmopolitan Navy looked to the east across the Pacific and saw the United States and its fleet as its most likely opponent. Both services recognized Japan's dependence on supplies of raw materials from the south, especially oil from the Netherlands East Indies, but the Army loathed the thought of committing its main force in that direction for fear of Soviet adventures.

A marked divergence in war planning flowed naturally from these fundamental differences in perspective. The Army envisioned a war of three stages: first, attack on the Philippines and the Southeast Asian area to expel the American, British, and Dutch colonists; second, shaping of the resources of the new territories into more military sinew; and third, extraction of most forces from crippled China and the launch of a massive onslaught to settle accounts with the Soviet Union. The Army consigned defense of the Pacific to the Navy with minimal Army support.

The Imperial Navy foresaw a two-phase war commencing with a rapid strike south for the resource areas followed by a redeployment to the east to repel the inevitable American counterblow anticipated in the Central Pacific via the Marshall and Caroline islands. Strategists of both services agreed, however, that the war would be limited in scope and that Japan, after seizing its objectives, would negotiate a peace after utilizing the power of defense and her interior lines to exhaust her opponent. This policy carried the stamp of historical validity through her victories over China and Russia during the last of the nineteenth century and the early years of the twentieth.

With the situation in China stalemated, Japan's German ally at flood tide, and her relations with the United States in precipitous decline, 1941 saw Imperial General Headquarters contemplating war in deadly earnest. The plan that emerged provided for two "operational stages." The First Operational Stage was divided into three parts:

Part I: Attacks on the Philippines, Malaya, Borneo, the Celebes, Timor, Sumatra, and Rabaul

Part II: Converging attacks on Java from east and west, coupled with the invasion of southern Burma

Part III: Conquest of the remainder of Burma followed by the pacification and defense of the new areas comprosing the "Greater East Asian Co-Prosperity Sphere"

The Second Operational Stage encompassed the seizure of eastern New Guinea, New Britain, the Fijis, Samoa, the Aleutians, Midway, and "strategic points in the Australian area."

Although Admiral Nagano held the central post in the Imperial Navy, actual command of the great bulk of its fighting power lay vested in Admiral Isoroku Yamamoto, the highly popular commander of the Combined Fleet. The husky son of an impoverished samurai of one of the losing clans in Japan's complex civil wars, Yamamoto stood as a full admiral known for a famous snappy salute.

Yet he was plain-spoken, without a whiff of pomposity, and could be a "mischievous devil" in the words of one officer who knew him well. A graduate of Eta Jima, the Imperial Japanese Naval Academy, Yamamoto recognized early the potential of aviation, and he had commanded the great carrier *Akagi* and then a carrier division. His brilliant career included study at Harvard and a tour as naval attaché in Washington, where he learned to respect American industrial power and developed an affinity for football and poker. This latter came naturally, for he loved gambling, and an American observer might have found it significant that in the Japanese game of Shogi, Yamamoto favored "rush tactics"—a bold thrust at the very outset of the game to achieve decisive results.

Yamamoto became Commander in Chief of the Combined Fleet in September 1939. He directed five mobile fleets with the principal warships of the Imperial Navy and three area fleets responsible for specific geographic locales. The administrative titles and the principal combatant types in each of the mobile fleets were: 1st Fleet (battleships), 2d Fleet (cruisers), 3d Fleet (carriers), 6th Fleet (submarines), and 11th Air Fleet (land-based fighters, bombers, and patrol planes). Each of these fleets was also known by an operational title reflecting something of its anticipated role during wartime: Main Body (1st Fleet), Advanced Force (2d Fleet), Striking Force (3d Fleet), Advanced Expeditionary Force (6th Fleet), and Base Air Force (11th Air Fleet). The area fleets included the 4th Fleet (operational title: South Seas Force), based in the Mandates and deploying an assortment of old light cruisers, destroyers, submarines, auxiliary vessels, and land-based air flotillas. The similarly outfitted 5th Fleet (operational title: Northern Force) covered the northern Pacific approaches to Japan.

When presented with the master war plan of Imperial Headquarters in 1941, Yamamoto and his staff refused to confine themselves to the role of executing strategy fashioned in Tokyo. Yamamoto was convinced that his one true objective was the United States Pacific Fleet, which embodied the single most potent force arrayed against Japan. Worse yet, the "Two-Ocean Navy Act" authorized by a frightened American Congress in 1940 threatened to make the Pacific Fleet overwhelmingly stronger. From Yamamoto's fertile brain and his gambler's instincts for "rush tactics" came Operation "Z": a decisive blow against the Pacific Fleet at Pearl Harbor by Japan's six biggest carriers at the opening moment of hostilities. The audacity of this plan, and the major reason for its success, was that it not only rejected dogma on the likely course of the war within both the Imperial and United States navies but also stood on its head Japan's traditional strategy of waiting for her enemy's main forces to come to her. Yamamoto overcame resistance to his plan on the Naval General Staff with a threat to resign, a clear indication of the informal power he wielded, and all other Japanese operations were timed around the Pearl Harbor strike.

There is one other Japanese naval officer who contributed significantly to war planning in general and the move into the South Pacific in particular. This man was Vice Admiral Shigeyoshi Inoue, commander of the 4th Fleet or South Seas Force. Very "air-minded," as befitted the former chief of the Aeronautical Department, Inoue was a pungent commentator on Japanese politicians and military men, who he said,

> . . . both underestimated America's natural strength and the spiritual strength of its people, particularly its women. They had a childish notion that since women had such a powerful say there, it wouldn't be long before they started objecting to the war.

As the commander responsible for absorbing the expected American counterthrust in the Mandates, Inoue quickly pointed out in preliminary planning that Rabaul lay only 700 miles from the main Japanese bastion in the Central Pacific at Truk, and that by striking north from Rabaul, the Allies would outflank the whole main Japanese defensive position built around the Marshalls. This argument struck home and resulted in the addition of Rabaul to the basket of locations Inoue was to gather during the First Operational Phase with Guam, Wake, and Makin in the Gilberts.

But Inoue also believed that safeguarding Rabaul demanded the seizure of positions on New Britain, Lae and Salamaua on eastern New Guinea, and Tulagi in the southern Solomons. By holding fortified airfields in these locations, the Japanese could meet Allied attacks by shuttling aircraft from base to base. Inoue lacked authorization to snatch these additional locations during the First Operational Stage, and more important, he had few ships under his command and none bigger than some vintage light cruisers. For assault forces and garrisons in his far-flung command, Inoue had a few units of Special Naval Landing Forces (Japanese naval infantry)[1] and the only Imperial Army unit allocated to the area, the "South

---

[1]Sometimes erroneously referred to as "Japanese Marines," these units were a peculiar Japanese hybrid, more like permanent organizations of sailors in landing parties than like units of soldiers specially trained in amphibious warfare.

Seas Detachment." This was a brigade-sized unit of about 5,000 men built around the 144th Infantry Regiment and commanded by Major General Tomitaro Horii.[2] With Horii's troops, Inoue seized Rabaul on January 23 from its small Australian garrison with air support by part of Vice Admiral Chuichi Nagumo's carrier Striking Force.

By the time Rabaul fell, the Japanese were sweeping rapidly toward success in all phases of the First Operational Stage with such giddy ease that the high command began its binge with "Victory Disease" (senshobyo). The symptoms of Victory Disease, overextension and dispersion of forces, became manifest in both the Naval General Staff and the Combined Fleet during the first quarter of 1942. On January 29, the Naval General Staff approved the extension of Japan's defensive perimeter outward from Rabaul by the seizure of Lae, Salamaua, Tulagi, and Port Moresby on the southeastern end of New Guinea. Securing Port Moresby was crucial in Inoue's view not only as one of his net of air bases to defend the area, but also because in Allied hands it would permit B-17 attacks on Rabaul and beyond, while in Japanese hands it would allow deep reconnaissance into the Coral Sea. This latter was vital because the Japanese had recognized before the war that the Allies might press their counterattack through the triangle of Port Moresby, Rabaul, and Tulagi as an alternative to the obvious avenue across the Central Pacific.

Lae and Salamaua fell easily to Inoue on March 8, but two days later a devastating raid by aircraft from the carriers Lexington and Yorktown sank or damaged thirteen of the eighteen vessels in Inoue's command. This little-heralded action generated results vastly disproportionate to forces involved. Beyond the serious depletion of available resources, the attack shocked Inoue and Horii with the recognition that American carriers roamed unchallenged in the South Pacific. They temporarily postponed the attack on Port Moresby and requested carrier support before embarking on further conquests.

Inoue's urgent plea for carrier backup moved his operations from a local matter into the realm of strategic policy, where debate raged over how Japan should exploit her incredibly easy successes. The notion that Japan must remain on the offensive was taken as a matter

[2]General officer ranks in the Imperial Army were major general (shosho), lieutenant general (chujo), general (taisho), and field marshal (gensui). Thus a major general in the Imperial Army was the equivalent to a brigadier general in American practice.

of faith, and the Naval General Staff began to eye eliminating Australia as a base for an Allied counterattack. These fantasies were quickly extinguished by the Imperial Army, which curtly informed the naval planners that Japan had neither ten or twelve spare divisions nor the shipping capacity to capture and hold Australia. The Navy Section of Imperial General Headquarters then studied a series of operations to isolate and neutralize Australia by cutting its supply lines. They proposed the "FS" Operation to seize New Caledonia, the Fijis, and Samoa about June or early July, after the rescheduled Port Moresby–Tulagi operation.

The stunning success of the Pearl Harbor attack and other early operations sent Yamamoto's prestige to lofty heights and did nothing to diminish the enthusiasm of the commander and staff of the Combined Fleet for setting strategic policy. These brilliant triumphs, however, clouded judgment at the Combined Fleet as well as in Tokyo. For the first half year of the war, Nagumo's sextet of fleet carriers were trumps in the Pacific because of both the numbers of embarked aircraft and the superlative skill of their air crews. It is therefore amazing in retrospect, and damning of Yamamoto's stewardship, that after the Pearl Harbor strike they never again operated together. From December onward, the Striking Force always lacked one or two of the original six carriers because of diversions to support distant but simultaneous operations and the need for upkeep and repair. Of these operations, the sortie of Nagumo with five carriers into the Indian Ocean squandered precious time and caused a wastage of planes and pilots for only ephemeral results.

Yamamoto continued to believe that his objective remained the Pacific Fleet, and especially its carriers, which advertised their potential in a series of raids in February and March from the Marshalls to Marcus. He reasoned that a plunge into the South Pacific must be deferred until he could force a conclusive sea clash before the Americans could build and assemble a new fleet. He therefore proposed to attack Midway with the real object of bringing on a decisive battle on terms highly favorable to Japan. In a final showdown in Tokyo between April 2 and 5, Yamamoto won his way, again by threatening to resign if his plan was not ratified. To accommodate Inoue, in the interval between the Indian Ocean raid and Midway the carriers *Zuikaku* and *Shokaku* would support the seizure of Port Moresby and Tulagi.

Thanks to recent scholarship by John J. Stephan, we now know that Yamamoto's Midway plan represented only part of a still larger design to capture Hawaii. Yamamoto possessed perhaps the most unclouded understanding among senior Japanese officials of the implications of the immense imbalance in military potential between Japan and the United States, and he refused to gloss over this chasm with wishful thinking about how superior "spiritual power" would enable Japan to overcome these material disparities. Yamamoto recognized, in Stephan's words, that "Japan's only hope against such a formidable adversary lay in bold military action followed by skillful diplomacy." Hawaii fitted Yamamoto's prescriptions precisely: militarily, it would serve as bait to trap the Pacific Fleet and its carriers; politically, with its 400,000 American inhabitants, it would be "the lever that Tokyo would use to exert pressure on Washington to end the war." Vehement opposition in the Imperial Army to this scheme abruptly collapsed after the April 18 Doolittle raid. Following this, the Imperial Army got into step with Yamamoto's thinking and issued orders to three divisions to begin preparations for an assault on Hawaii. After his planning triumph, and recognizing the high stakes on the Midway effort, Yamamoto wrote to a friend: "The 'First Operational Stage' of Operations has been kind of a children's hour and will soon be over, now comes the adult's hour. . . ."

The rescheduled operation to capture Port Moresby and Tulagi began satisfactorily when a small unit of ships and men seized Tulagi on May 3. But the next day one of Inoue's nemeses, the carrier *Yorktown*, lashed this detachment, sinking a destroyer and three small auxiliaries and damaging two other ships. The confused encounter that followed between May 7 and 8, christened the Battle of the Coral Sea, cost the Japanese the new light carrier *Shoho*, while the Americans lost the heavy carrier *Lexington*, a fleet oiler, a destroyer, and sixty-six planes. However, not only was Port Moresby saved, the Japanese paid for their tactical success with seventy-seven planes and heavy damage to the carrier *Shokaku*. The combination of damage to *Shokaku* and aircraft losses kept both big Japanese carriers out of the Midway operation, in which they might have proved invaluable.

A Japanese bomb maimed *Yorktown* but she scurried north to Pearl Harbor, where an army of workmen patched her up in two days to meet the Japanese off Midway with her sister ships *Enterprise* and *Hornet*. With the Imperial Navy's plans brilliantly forecast by American code breakers, Admiral Nagumo's unsupported Striking Force stumbled into an ambush and lost four carriers with 250 aircraft and many irreplaceable aircrews plus a heavy cruiser. In the vastly unequal exchange, the Americans were permanently deprived of the services of *Yorktown*, a destroyer, and 147 ship- and shore-based aircraft. The Battle of Midway stands as a turning point marking the end of the Japanese strategic offensive in the Central Pacific and Yamamoto's bid to create favorable conditions for a successful end to the war by offensive action. But Midway did not make Japan's loss of the war by any means inevitable. The Combined Fleet, save for its carriers, was nearly intact, Japan's air arms were diminished but still very deadly, and her army was, if anything, stronger than it had been in December 1941. Moreover, the Americans were thousands of miles from any point posing a mortal danger to Japan.

THE SOLOMONS ARENA AND THE COAST WATCHERS

The Battle of the Coral Sea ended the First South Pacific Campaign. With Japanese extension into the Central Pacific checked at Midway, the strategists on both sides began laboring on what would become the Second South Pacific Campaign, which would dominate the middle phase of the Pacific War. Before recounting the evolution of the opposing strategies for the new campaign, it is appropriate to sketch the important natural and man-made features of the theater as they existed by June 1942.

To the north of the continent of Australia lies the great island of New Guinea, which serves as a glacis for the continent from blows aimed from the north. Due east of the center of New Guinea is the Bismarck Archipelago, whose main islands are New Ireland and New Britain. Extruding from the northern end of New Britain is the Gazelle Peninsula, housing Rabaul, the best harbor in the region. From Rabaul it is only 640 miles north to Truk, the main Japanese base in the Central Pacific, and the coast of New Guinea is only another 440 miles farther south—"next door" by Pacific standards.

Stretching southeast from the curved joining of New Ireland and New Britain are the Solomons, a group of several hundred islands of assorted sizes with a total land area of 18,600 square miles. The main islands are aligned like a set of footprints with Bougainville, Choiseul, Santa Isabel, and Malaita marking the northerly set of impressions and Vella LaVella, New Georgia, the Russells, Guadalcanal, and San Cristóbal as the imprints of the other foot to the south. At their northern tip, the Solomons are only 5 degrees south of the equator, and the group stretches a total length of about 675 miles. They are largely volcanic in origin and lie within the world's wettest area. The difference between the "dry season" of the southwest monsoon from April to October and the "wet season" of November to March is not always readily noticeable to the inhabitants.

The significance of Rabaul in 1942, apart from its magnificent harbor, rested with the fact that it also provided terrain amenable to airfield development. The Solomons offered few other potential airfield sites, but another one existed at Buka off the northern end of Bougainville, and a third lay on the northern coast of Guadalcanal. Ninety miles long on its predominant northwest-southeast axis, Guadalcanal averages about 25 miles in width. A mountain chain commands the center of the island with the highest peak reaching 7,000 feet. On the south side of the island, the precipitous fall of the land to the coast and shielding reefs make ships unwelcome. Apart from the mountains, the majority of Guadalcanal is characterized by erosion-contorted ridgelines crosshatched in a haphazard fashion, damp and humid beneath a dense, multilayered surface of rain forest. Centuries of the same erosion, however, have created a coastal plain on the northeast side of the island with many sandy beaches between Aola and the Matanikau River. Here coconut plantations and huge verdant fields and occasional ridges covered with tall, razor-sharp cogongrass predominate over the denser growth along the streams and in the defiles. The watercourses consist of a few usually shallow but rambunctious rivers or creeks that knife down from the mountains with swirling energy. A second and distinctly different watercourse is in the form of placid ribbons of water in the flatlands meandering to the sea; they are essentially small lagoons. While most streams have numerous fords inland, some become relatively deep near the coast and form obstacles to men or vehicles. But the majority, including even some of the larger bodies of water tracing their origins into the interior, end at the juncture with the ocean in sandbars that afford crossing sites.

In 1941, the Australian Territory of New Guinea exercised political control of Bougainville and Buka. The remainder of the Solomon Islands fell under the British Solomon Islands Protectorate, headed by a resident commissioner. William S. Marchant held this post at the capital of Tulagi, a modest island hanging off the southern coast of Florida Island. Marchant presided over a population of 500 Europeans, 200 Chinese, and 94,700 natives. These latter are dark, nearly black-skinned, woolly-headed Melanesians who speak over forty dialects; some of them until recent times had a distinct taste for "big pig"—human flesh. The colonizers and assorted missionaries provided not only political unity to the area, but also a common language in pidgin English. The natives had survived for centuries on

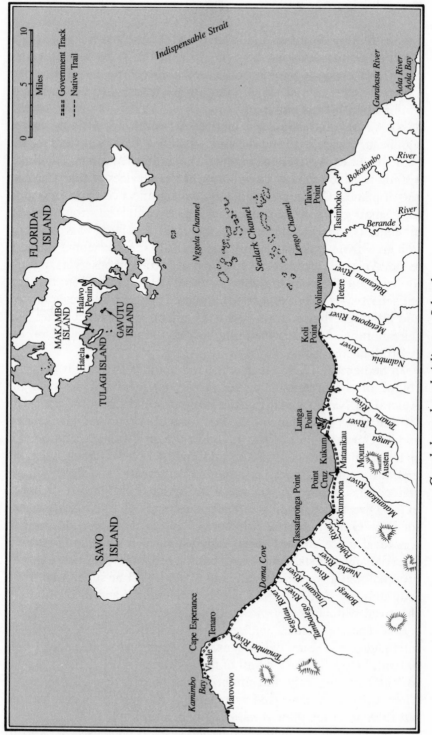

Guadalcanal and Adjacent Islands

simple hunting, farming, and fishing, and the colonialists added only slight economic development. The principal business activities were copra and coconut plantations, dominated by the Lever Brothers Company, and interisland shipping, largely controlled by the Burns-Phillips South Seas Company.

As we have already seen, neither Australia nor Britain proved significant forces to defend the area. In early 1942 a twenty-four-man detachment of Australians manned the unfinished airstrip at Buka; a similarly sized unit at Tulagi boasted the services of four Catalina patrol planes. Of far greater long-term significance than these pitifully small garrisons of trained soldiers was a select group of local inhabitants who became known as the coast watchers. This organization grew from experience in World War I that underscored the need to rim Australia's enormous coastline with trained observers, mainly to detect the presence of raiders or other forms of transient belligerent activity. By 1939 the service numbered 800, mainly local officials, and although the program had been extended to New Guinea and the Solomons, the overwhelming bulk of the personnel were on the Australian mainland.

In September 1939, Lieutenant Commander Eric Feldt assumed charge of the organization. He proved an ideal link between the Australian Navy (which ran the program) and the coast watchers, for Feldt was a graduate of the first class of Australian naval cadets and a veteran of World War I, and in the interwar years he worked as the civilian warden of Wau Gold Field on New Guinea. There he met and came to understand the temperamental and fiercely independent "islanders." Upon recall to service, Feldt joined the office of the Director of Naval Intelligence and took charge of intelligence for New Guinea and the Solomons. He regarded these locations as a natural fence and set about establishing coast-watching stations like so many pickets. Feldt expanded the program to include a picked group of non-government staff, and by mid-1941 he supervised sixty-four stations. Feldt also saw to the development and distribution of the coast watcher's key piece of equipment, his teleradio.

The coast watchers confined their activities almost entirely to intelligence work, not fighting, as reflected in their code name, "Ferdinand," after the pacific bull of the children's story. Their role was to "sit circumspectly and unobtrusively and gather information." They were never conceived as a clandestine espionage organization, but their situation altered radically with the arrival of the Japanese. Any civilian on a Japanese-controlled island who used a radio to transmit intelligence data would be a spy and subject to summary execution. Although the coast watchers were issued military ranks and badges, few deemed it likely that the Japanese would treat them as prisoners of war. Feldt hoped that some of his carefully recruited and supplied men would continue to broadcast, and he was not disappointed. Coast watchers in areas under Japanese domination became highly dependent upon native loyalty, which would not be taken for granted nor assumed to be perpetual. "The native," wrote Feldt, reflecting contemporary views, "is a realist in matters of race. Since he first came into contact with other peoples he has always been subject to them and had developed the habit of looking to whoever is most potent for direction." A few, such as those at Buka Passage, immediately switched allegiance to the Japanese, but in a great tribute to the decency of the local colonial officials and missionaries, the vast majority remained loyal. The Melanesians served willingly as porters for the coast watchers' radios and stores, and some quite voluntarily gathered valuable information during hazardous spying missions to Japanese bases.

Of the many stations set up by Feldt and still operating after the Japanese overran the Solomons, six became critical. On the northern tip of Bougainville near the Buka Passage was Jack Read, an assistant district officer who had a dozen years' experience in the islands but had reached Bougainville only in November 1941. On a hill near Buin at the southern tip of Bougainville was the short, bespectacled Paul Mason, who had spent twenty years in the area. Mason, noted Feldt, looked less like the sort of hard-bitten character popularly imagined for a coast watcher than any other Caucasian in the area, "missionaries not excepted." District Officer Donald Kennedy established himself on a plantation at Segi Point on New Georgia. Feldt described Kennedy as a middle-aged man who projected "a natural aura of command"; his native assistants viewed him as from the mold of Captain Bligh.

The three stations on Guadalcanal reflected the diverse sources from which coast watchers were drawn. Feldt sent Pay Lieutenant Donald S. MacFarland, an Australian naval reservist called up in 1941 from his job as a buyer for a dry goods store, to work with resident commissioner Marchant. When Marchant moved his headquarters to Malaita, MacFarland remained on Guadalcanal on Feldt's orders and linked up with a tubby but knowledgeable plantation manager, Kenneth D. Hay. When the Japanese approached, they moved their base of operations to Gold Ridge, an elevation 15 miles inland. At the western end of the island was the station of F. Ashton "Snowy" Rhoades, the son of a prosperous Sydney family

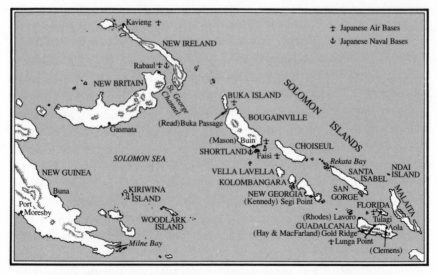

The Solomons and the Coast Watchers, August 1942

who had fallen on hard times and ended up as the manager of the Burns-Phillips plantation at Lavoro. Lean and grizzled, Rhoades looked the very model of a proper coast watcher.

At Aola along the eastern portion of the northern coastal plain was district officer Martin Clemens. His aplomb and build bespoke his Cambridge education and athletic inclination. After Marchant, who was overwhelmed by the situation, removed to Malaita, Clemens maintained order in the area. He reasoned that the Japanese were sure to pay a visit to Aola as the local seat of government and prepared a fallback position in the hills where he could both maintain observation of the coast and retain contact with his native supporters and intelligence agents.

Clemens heard the code words "Steak and Eggs" on his radio on May 1 signifying the rapid evacuation of Tulagi by its tiny garrison following a heavy air raid. On May 3 the Japanese landed at Tulagi and the small adjacent islands of Gavutu and Tanambogo. The following day the attack of *Yorktown*'s planes cheered Clemens and the locals. MacFarland reported on the results of the attack, and ten days later Clemens picked up a downed American torpedo bomber crew that he eventually slipped back to the New Hebrides. But the Japanese also captured a native medical practitioner on Savo after *Yorktown*'s attack, and, threatened with execution, he disclosed the names and several locations of coast-watching stations on Guadalcanal. Native loyalty, however, thwarted Japanese efforts to capture Clemens and his colleagues.

On May 28, Clemens learned of a brief visit by two Japanese launches to the north coast of Guadalcanal. He suspected they came seeking some of the cattle on the Lunga Plain to supplement their rations. More patrols appeared to collect cattle, and a few of the visitors went for gallops on horses. Others vandalized the buildings of the Lever Brothers plantation near Lunga Point, suggesting they were not considering a permanent occupation.

In reality these visits carried more import than Clemens guessed. As early as May 18, Captain Shigetoshi Miyazaki, the commander of the seaplane-equipped Yokohama Air Group stationed at Tulagi, reported that Guadalcanal was amenable to the installation of an advanced air base. An inspection party confirmed Miyazaki's judgment on May 27. After the check in the Coral Sea and the defeat at Midway, the Imperial Navy General Staff authorized the "SN" Operation to strengthen the outer perimeter of Japan's advance by constructing airfields at key strategic points on the Papuan peninsula, the Louisiade Islands, and the Solomons. On June 13, the Naval General Staff elected to place an air base on Guadalcanal. Two more parties on June 16 and 19, the latter headed by Admiral Inoue, toured the area of the island about the Lunga Plain.

The first body of Japanese reached Guadalcanal on June 8 and pitched tents in businesslike rows. A vessel debarked more men and supplies, and the Japanese commenced erecting a wharf. On the afternoon of June 20, heavy clouds of smoke lingered over the plain as the Japanese began burning grass. Clemens, MacFarland, Hay, and Rhoades speculated by radio and native runner on the activity. On July 6 a twelve-ship convoy anchored off the wharf and disgorged men and equipment that the coast watchers deduced was for airfield construction. The new arrivals included 1,350 men of the 13th Construction Unit under Captain Kanae Monzen and 1,221 men of the 11th Construction Unit of Commander Tokunaga Okuma. Clemens and his colleagues would have been amazed to discover that the day before the Japanese convoy arrived, Ernest J. King and Chester W. Nimitz knew the Japanese intentions and King was already planning to make Japanese tenure on Guadalcanal short.

2

PLANS,

PREPARATIONS,

AND APPROACH

"Tulagi and adjacent positions"

FROM MIDWAY TO "WATCHTOWER"

The stunning triumph at Midway propelled American planners at all levels into a flurry of schemes to exploit the victory. The first and rashest of these emanated from MacArthur on June 8: give him a division of amphibiously trained troops with two carriers in support and he would take Rabaul and hurl the Japanese back 700 miles. This clarion call fell on the surprisingly receptive ears of both Army and Navy staff officers in Washington and even aroused the interest of General Marshall. The Chief of Staff, however, counseled that the Navy would have to agree on the operation, and Navy pens quickly pricked MacArthur's bubble. Fundamentally, the admirals refused to entrust precious carriers to MacArthur's command, and on practical grounds they found the prospect of operating carriers in the reef-studded Solomons, flanked with enemy air bases, disquieting. The Navy registered its objections and countered with a plan that envisioned a more gradual approach with the seizure of intermediate air bases as a prerequisite to an assault on Rabaul.

On June 24, MacArthur parried the criticism of his plan by declaring that his original message only sketched his intentions. Naturally, he pointed out, the capture of bases in the Solomons and along the north coast of New Guinea would be necessary preliminaries to seizing Rabaul. Contemporary plans at this headquarters, however, plotted a "gradual" approach of from fourteen to eighteen days! Nonetheless, this message focused discussion on the question of command, since an ostensible consensus existed that the climb back to Rabaul must be one rung at a time.

That same day, June 24, an impatient King directed Nimitz to prepare to capture "Tulagi and adjacent positions." The next day King stressed to Marshall the need to seize the initiative before the "golden opportunity" presented by the victory at Midway slipped from their grasp. COMINCH recommended an attack about August 1 to capture the Santa Cruz Islands and positions in the Solomons with the ultimate objective of New Guinea and New Britain.

On June 26, Marshall presented the case for endowing command of the offensive in MacArthur. Acknowledging that simple lines drawn on the map earlier that year were not absolutely controlling, Marshall argued that MacArthur's position and knowledge would enable him best to coordinate Allied efforts. King replied in writing the same day. He began by pointing out that in Europe, where the major forces engaged would be ground troops, King had acceded to Army command. In phrases that became progressively less tactful, King stated that naval and amphibious forces predominated in the Pacific and command should therefore be Navy. In fact, he asserted, the operation "could not be conducted any other way." In a further slap at the Army and MacArthur, King promised to proceed "even if no support of Army forces in the Southwest Pacific is made available." Underlining this threat, King directed Nimitz on June 27 to prepare for operations on the premise that only Navy and Marine units would be available.

Marshall restrained himself from a reply in kind to this provocative missive. Not so MacArthur, who threw one of his more remarkable tantrums of the war. While he did not see King's letter to Marshall, he did read the message from King to Nimitz, and CINC-PAC's response listing some of MacArthur's own air and naval units among the lineup of forces for the attack. As if that were not enough, the general discovered King again communicating directly with MacArthur's naval commander, Admiral Leary, in flagrant breach of the chain of command. On June 28, MacArthur presented these facts to Marshall as a bill of particulars proving that Navy ambitions extended to the "general control of all operations in the Pacific theater." If the Navy succeeded, he believed the Army would be reduced to the subsidiary role of providing occupation forces at the disposal of the Navy under command of Navy or (worse yet) Marine Corps officers. MacArthur insisted a master plan lay behind these moves, which he had uncovered "accidentally" when he was Chief of Staff of the Army, for the Navy to gain complete control over national defense and to reduce the Army to a training and supply organization. MacArthur vowed he would take "no steps or action with reference to any component of my command" except under direct orders from Marshall.

MacArthur's intemperate signal arrived just as a series of conferences and messages in the last two days of June finally produced a commander and a specific directive for the offensive. Initiating the move to compromise, Marshall wrote to King emphasizing that all hands agreed on the need for haste. He also informed King, as he had MacArthur after the latter's outburst of June 28, that "regardless of [the] final decision as to command, every available support should be given to the operation." During a face-to-face meeting, King proffered a solution to the impasse: Ghormley to command the Tulagi operation under Nimitz with MacArthur to lead the rest of the campaign against Rabaul. Marshall dutifully passed this to MacArthur, who again found it wanting from the standpoint of "coordination"—with obvious implications as to who would be the best coordinator.

On July 1, Marshall countered with an offer that skillfully blended King's proposal with modifications designed to meet MacArthur's objections. The campaign would be divided into three parts. Task One would be the seizure of Tulagi and the Santa Cruz Islands under Nimitz on August 1. For this operation MacArthur would surrender 1 degree of longitude along the eastern border of his command, thereby placing the southern Solomons in the South Pacific Area. Task Two would be the capture of Lae, Salamaua, and the northeast coast of New Guinea, and Task Three would be the attack on Rabaul and adjacent positions in the New Britain–New Ireland Area. MacArthur would have the reins for Tasks Two and Three, but the Joint Chiefs of Staff would reserve for themselves the right to determine when command would pass. Remarkably, the Joint Chiefs of Staff never formally approved this plan. Rather King and Marshall adapted it on July 2, acting without consultation with General Arnold, with one change: to Task Two they added the remainder of the Solomon Islands. Resigned in the face of this directive, on July 6 MacArthur pledged his full support to the plan and offered the use of his naval forces for Task One, code-named Operation "Watch-tower." The overall plan was christened "Pestilence."

On the same day the compromise plan met approval, two other thorny problems found resolution: King consented to the creation of an Army commander for that service's activities in the South Pacific, and Major General Millard F. Harmon was appointed to this job from his position as Chief of Air Staff. Parochialism and personalities had rendered Army-Navy cooperation in the Pacific less than opti-mal, but Harmon proved a felicitous choice. He exercised consis-tently sound judgment and maintained uniformly excellent relations with the Navy. At the same time, Marshall and Nimitz resolved the divisive issue of heavy bomber employment in the Pacific by creating two mobile air forces, available for operations anywhere in the Pacific, under control of the Joint Chiefs.

To brief Nimitz on these vital decisions, King flew to San Fran-cisco for a meeting beginning July 3. Turner attended their first meeting, and he received the welcome news that three carriers in-stead of two would support the landings. Turner asked for a diver-sion timed for about ten days before the landing to garner Japanese attention, and here is an appropriate point for a digression on the fruits of this request. Eventually American commanders mounted three feints to help Task One, all of which proved ill-starred. In the northern Pacific, a group of cruisers and destroyers conducted a bombardment of Kiska on August 7 after fog thwarted and collisions marred two earlier attempts. Light cruiser *Boise* aborted her raid on the Japanese picket boat line east of the home islands after she broke radio silence in an attempt to recover lost float planes. Stormy seas nearly terminated the 2d Raider Battalion's hit-and-run attack on Makin on August 17–18 in a fiasco that might have included the capture of President Roosevelt's son James. The Americans hoped that the British Eastern Fleet in the Indian Ocean would stage a feint, but King explained at San Francisco that the inadequacies of attack planes on the Royal Navy's carriers made the Admiralty reluctant to expose its flattops as required for a convincing threat to the Japanese southwestern flank. In the end the British contributed a demonstration in the Indian Ocean using some ships and radio deception. None of these ventures discernibly affected the Japanese.

Amazingly, Guadalcanal had still not been specifically earmarked as a target. On June 27, Nimitz directed the seizure of an airfield site in conjunction with the assault on Tulagi, but he specified no loca-tion. Turner recommended adding Guadalcanal to the operation for an airfield site on July 3, but on the afternoon of July 5, American radio intelligence concluded the Japanese had landed airfield construction troops on Guadalcanal.[1] That same day in conference, King and Nimitz temporarily deleted the Santa Cruz Islands from Task One and substituted Guadalcanal. Fortunately, from the start the staff of the unit selected to make the landing, the 1st Marine Division, had planned to land substantial forces on Guadalcanal. The new target was prophetically code-named "Cactus."

DOUBTS AND DOUBTERS

Admiral Ghormley arrived in Noumea on May 18 and immediately displayed his considerable diplomatic skills by defusing an explosive local political situation prompted by the imperious actions of General de Gaulle's local representative, Contre-Amiral Georges d'Argenlieu, who had ousted the popular but Vichyite Governor Sautot. On only his sixth day in his new command, orders reached Ghormley on June 25 to prepare to seize "Tulagi and adjacent positions." The admiral immediately concluded he was far from ready for such an undertaking. His problems began in his own headquarters. Delays of hours or days separated Ghormley from incoming messages, because of his inexperienced and small signal complement. His tiny staff lacked any expertise in amphibious operations, save for one Marine officer. Deliberate planning may have been impossible in any event for lack of time and a marked deficit in information. What little intelligence was available came from old charts and maps of the area, and Ghormley derived his only current information on the Japanese situation from the reports of high-flying pilots, aerial photos, and the clandestine radios of the handful of coast watchers on Guadalcanal. He had no major naval units under his direct command.

The question of air power overshadowed all other calculations. Ghormley, who controlled no carriers, suffered deficiencies in both suitable aircraft and even rudimentary bases from which to operate them. By August 7, the South Pacific theater contained a total of 282 aircraft (land-based and seaplanes) under Rear Admiral John S. McCain, a wizened, shrewd, fifty-eight-year-old aviator whose bulging jaw gave him a resemblance to the cartoon character Popeye. This seemingly formidable number, though, was highly deceptive. It

[1]Because of the International Date Line, local time in the Solomons was July 6 as given in Chapter 1.

included such biplane antiques as the Royal New Zealand Air Force Singapore flying boats and Marine SBC-4 dive-bombers. The vast watery expanse of Ghormley's domain resulted in many of his planes being parceled out to defend an elongated arc of bases covering the lines of communication to Australia. Of the complement of seventy-nine P-39s and P-400s[2] and forty-nine Grumman F4F Wildcat fighters, the first two lacked altitude performance and all lacked the range to operate over the southern Solomons from the available bases. Indeed, of McCain's 282 planes, only the thirty-two B-17s of the 11th Bomb Group, led by a determined and skillful commander, Colonel LaVerne "Blondie" Saunders, could effectively conduct a combat mission over the southern Solomons from their bases at Espíritu Santo and Efate, respectively 590 and 715 miles from Guadalcanal. Saunders's planes "doubled in brass" as search planes with twenty-eight PBY Catalina flying boats and eighteen Lockheed Hudsons.

A want of airfields complemented the lack of aircraft. By the landing date all the aircraft in the South Pacific would be nested on seven widely scattered islands. The closest of these to Guadalcanal was Espíritu Santo, and its creation is an excellent example of the abrupt mounting of "Watchtower." Nimitz approved the occupation of the island in May; however, with defensive considerations still dominant, he forbade the construction of an airfield until there was an adequate garrison to defend it. Ghormley declined to shift troops from rear bases for this purpose both for lack of shipping and for fear of exposing vital lines of communication to Australia. Permission to build the field came only on July 3, and the very next day Nimitz ordered it made ready for B-17s by July 28.

Espíritu Santo became the first job in the South Pacific assigned to the newly arrived "Seabees" of the 3d Naval Construction Battalion. They swarmed onto the island and began to fell trees, but these skilled workers soon began to drop nearly as fast themselves from malaria. Medication and determination in equal doses saw the task accomplished in time for the first B-17 to land on the appointed day. Even with this new base 125 miles closer to the target area, there remained a chronic shortage of replacement planes, crews, spare parts, engines, and the mechanics to wrestle with the available aircraft.

Burdened with such somber thoughts, Ghormley traveled to Mel-

[2]P-400 was the designation of a modified, export version of the Bell P-39.

bourne for a conference with MacArthur on July 8. The general's ruminations on the campaign proved to be almost identical to the admiral's. They identified the key problem as gaining and maintaining air superiority over the landing area to protect the assault shipping. MacArthur doubted that his fliers could interdict Japanese air and naval attacks from Rabaul. Nimitz's carriers could furnish protection, but they might have to denude the transports to safeguard themselves. MacArthur and Ghormley fretted over performance shortcomings in their collection of land-based fighters, and both discounted the likelihood of surprise in view of the depth of Japanese air reconnaissance.

More disturbing still was the marked change in the situation with respect to enemy air power. Airfield development at Kavieng, Rabaul, Lae, Salamaua, Buka, and Guadalcanal would enable the Japanese to bring overwhelming aerial might to bear on any Allied forces venturing into the Solomons. Citing all of these factors, MacArthur and Ghormley radioed the Joint Chiefs of Staff: "The initiation of this operation at this time without a reasonable assurance of adequate air coverage during each phase would be attendant with the gravest risk. . . ." Not content to rest there, they went on to challenge the entire strategy of a step-by-step approach and offered their opinion that the attack should be delayed until sufficient forces could be gathered to push through to Rabaul in one continuous movement.

The joint MacArthur-Ghormley message triggered umbrage among both Army and Navy planners in Washington. Admiral Turner's replacement as chief of the War Plans Division, Rear Admiral Charles M. Cooke, noted acidly that when confronted with a concrete plan, MacArthur was balking at a much more modest sally than the leap to Rabaul for which he had so recently sounded his trumpet. To Navy planners the Japanese buildup called for speed, not delay. At this same moment, however, radio intelligence indicated that the Allies were not alone in considering a South Pacific offensive.

RADIO INTELLIGENCE: INTENTIONS VERSUS TENDENCIES

On May 26, during the halcyon days of cryptanalysis prior to the Battle of Midway, it was authoritatively estimated that 60 percent of Imperial Navy signal traffic was being intercepted and 40 percent of those messages read, though the recovery from the typical message

averaged only about 10–15 percent. Two days later the Imperial
Navy at long last changed its major operational cryptographic system from the version called JN-25b by American intelligence officers
to JN-25c, and American code breaking entered an eclipse that
shrouded virtually the entire Guadalcanal campaign. The only rays
of light came from fragmentary reading of individual messages and
from a few lesser codes which remained accessible. Important among
the latter was that of the harbormaster at Truk, who dutifully reported the arrivals and departures of warships to Tokyo—and to the
major Allied radio intelligence staffs at Pearl Harbor, Melbourne,
Washington, and Ceylon.

Intelligence officers anticipated such interludes of drought in
cryptanalysis before the war and prudently prepared to garner information from traffic analysis, the other main branch of radio intelligence. Traffic analysis is the derivation of intelligence from the
external characteristics of a communications system and encom-
passes a spectrum of techniques ranging from the crude to the highly
sophisticated. Simple direction finding, or locating a radio transmitter, and hence a unit, by triangulation from two or more listening
stations maintained for that purpose, occupies the coarse end of the
scale. Nearly as rough is the measure of volume. Watchful American
analysts plotted the density of radio transmissions throughout the
Japanese Empire and drew inferences about the concentration of
forces and interests. Careful monitoring of the patterns and rhythms
of Japanese radio activity also offered clues. For instance, the sudden
cessation of radio traffic by a group of units pointed to the imposition
of radio silence, a common prelude to an operation, while the lack
of signal traffic from a single vessel hinted that it was docked or in
transit. Analysts charted Japanese radio frequency selection, because
the Imperial Navy persisted in using certain characteristic frequencies for carrier communications. Notably, Japanese carrier aviators
aloft on training flights in home waters habitually chatted on the
same frequencies. Intelligence officers discerned this practice and
used it to locate enemy carriers that themselves issued no radio
traffic. Another and more sophisticated technique in this category
was the identification of individual enemy radiomen by their particular "fist," or keying style, which is as distinctive as fingerprints. The
association of a radio operator with a particular ship greatly simplified the tracking of that vessel.

More fruitful still could be the external characteristics of the
encrypted messages themselves. Each message carried a heading
specifying the originator and addressees as well as routing instruc-

tions. This information appeared either in plain language or could be readily unshackled from simple codes, and careful scholarship enabled American experts to derive significant information from what they could read. Of course, the messages concealed the originators and addressees with call signs, and typically the Japanese utilized as many as 20,000 warship call signs at any given time, with major units employing up to seven separate calls. But sleuths working in Pearl Harbor, Melbourne, Washington, and Ceylon adeptly stripped away these masks. A serious flaw in Japanese communications practice eased this feat. Each originator attached a sequential serial number to its coded messages, but the Japanese failed to accompany a change of call signs with skips in the sequence of the serial numbers. Thus a comparison of the serial numbers on the new messages with the prior sequences could compromise the new call sign. This practice offered another gift to analysts, who linked multipartite messages by their sequential serial numbers. Japanese communicators erroneously sought security in multipartite messages by varying the call signs of the originators and addressees in each signal, but actually they only managed to compromise alternate calls.

Once analysts recognized a unit's call sign, they could make important deductions from the message headings and their fluency in Japanese radio procedure. Broadly speaking, Imperial Navy signal traffic darted along about 200 radio circuits with individual administrative and command messages moving up a chain of command to the nearest shore station, which then made an "umbrella" broadcast with powerful transmitters to all addressees in its region. Messages destined for addressees in other regions contained routing instructions for relay to the appropriate communications zone. American analysts called each of the fleet command circuits a "mother," and each "mother" had certain "chickens" under its radio "wing." At lower levels the same principles applied, so radio intelligence experts could ferret out Japanese task organization and deployment by observing the interchange of messages between certain headquarters and particular units. This process, termed "association," formed the bedrock of traffic analysis.

The message routing instructions also proved nuggets of intelligence. The channeling of messages for a ship or command to a particular communications zone presented an obvious inference. In a more subtle application of this technique, if message headings showed a visit by the chief of staff of the 3d (carrier) Fleet to the headquarters of the 4th Fleet, analysts could reasonably deduce that operations of the carriers in that locale were being planned. More remarkable still, knowledge of call signs and Japanese communication procedure could even enable American experts to track a ship maintaining radio silence, since messages for the ship contained routing instructions indicating the order of the ship's transit of communications zones, e.g., Tokyo, Saipan, Truk, and Rabaul.

Careful development of expertise into the patterns of Japanese organization and operations, what the analysts called "tendencies," paid large dividends when combined with radio intercepts. Analysts recognized that certain units habitually operated with the Japanese carriers, for example Cruiser Division 8, *Tone* and *Chikuma.* By following the whereabouts of these cruisers, the location of the carriers could be surmised. Similarly, the regular scrutiny of Japanese destroyer movements yielded insight on the deployment of major units, which never sailed without escort, and convoy routes.

After May 28, the Japanese progressively tightened their communications security with more frequent changes in the cryptographic system, multiple changes of call signs, the use of cover calls (i.e., a headquarters using the call sign of another unit), the scrambling or elimination of sequential numbers on secret messages, and the adaptation of certain communications procedures resembling those employed by the U.S. Navy. At first intelligence officers feared this stemmed directly from a monumental breach in the secrecy of cryptanalysis activities by the *Chicago Tribune* newspaper, which published an article after the Battle of Midway revealing extensive advance knowledge of Japanese plans. The story strongly implied the compromise of Japanese secrets by espionage or code breaking. Walter Winchell widened the breach by denouncing the *Chicago Tribune* for revealing the Navy's success against Japanese codes in two of his popular radio broadcasts, then a Congressman blurted out on the floor of the House of Representatives, "Somehow our Navy had secured and broken the secret code of the Japanese Navy." When the Japanese next changed their main operational cryptographic system in August, American and British anxieties became acute that Germany and Italy also might start doubting their communications security. Yet to this date we have no clear evidence that this change was occasioned by knowledge of these security lapses rather than simply by growing prudence.[3]

---

[3]Other examples of indiscretions included published comments by Prime Minister Curtin after the Battle of the Coral Sea that there would be plenty of warning of any renewed Japanese

Lest the reader gain the impression that Japanese communications were an open book, it must be emphasized that traffic analysis required thousands of messages. Just the interception in readable form of the hundreds of daily signals in the distinctive Japanese Morse code posed a formidable task. Moreover, it could be easily frustrated by nature or by security measures such as low-power transmissions, or, for ships at anchor, land lines. Further, as invaluable as traffic analysis could be, it lacked the reliability of cryptanalysis. The latter delivered the enemy's intentions while the former gave only his "tendencies" in the form of hypotheses which could only be "proved or disproved by the passage of time." Finally, possessing information and acting on it are two different things. Delays in disseminating radio intelligence information, code-named Ultra, could lead to frustration, and the relay of critical Ultra signals from Pearl Harbor to the South Pacific required an average of about two hours.

Using the above methods of traffic analysis with dashes of cryptanalysis, intelligence officers assembled evidence of aggressive Japanese designs in the South Pacific. By July 3, units identified at Rabaul included the 8th Base Force, the 25th Air Flotilla, the 5th Sasebo Special Naval Landing Force, fifteen warships, and a dozen transports. A profusion of messages revealed merchantmen from all over the Empire carving wakes toward Rabaul, and heavy communications traffic between Army headquarters at Rabaul and Davao suggested imminent troop movements. Analysts soon associated more headquarters, such as that of the 17th Army, with the Rabaul-Bismarcks area, and between July 18 and 29, they divined that the 8th Fleet, a new organization, would be taking over the southern area, with the 4th Fleet restricting itself to the Mandates. A step-up in Japanese radio intelligence activities indicated an effort to fix the location of Allied forces as a prelude to active operations. The focus of all radio activity in the Japanese Empire appeared to be Rabaul.

Besides these general signs, two key indicators of Japanese offensive intentions emerged in July. The shift of submarines to the region suggested the creation of a typical Japanese submarine scouting line, a harbinger of other enemy attacks. But the massing of air units at Rabaul portended unmistakable belligerent designs. This preliminary had presaged virtually every important Japanese movement of

---

attack on Port Moresby and a U.S. Navy Department press release later during the Guadalcanal campaign indicating a major Japanese offensive was underway in the Solomons area that CINCPAC headquarters said "practically tells the [Japanese] that we are reading their mail."

the war. Only the continued presence of the carriers in home waters implied some interval before the attack. The impact of these straws in the wind on Admiral King seems clear. He wanted to hit first.

Against this background of pessimism from MacArthur and Ghormley and urgency based on radio intelligence, the Joint Chiefs met on July 10. Marshall, exasperated by British foot-dragging over an offensive in northern Europe, made the conference memorable by speaking heatedly of reversing the "Germany First" strategy in favor of concentration of the American effort on the war against Japan. Had British observers been present, their eyebrows would have lifted appreciably when King displayed no great enthusiasm for this fundamental shift in priorities. Perhaps even more remarkably, this gathering represented the first formal consideration of the Solomons attack by the full Joint Chiefs of Staff. Without much recorded discussion, the Chiefs drafted a signal for Ghormley and MacArthur. They fully appreciated "the disadvantages of undertaking Task One before adequate forces and equipment can be made available for the continuance without interruption of Tasks Two and Three," but they believed "that it is necessary to stop without delay the enemy's southward advance" and they did "not desire to countermand operations already underway." The dispatch went on to ask MacArthur and Ghormley to itemize specifically additional forces not prospectively available "but absolutely essential to the execution of Task One." Faced with this intransigence, on July 11 Ghormley replied that he could carry out Task One with the forces in hand provided MacArthur could interdict Japanese aerial activities in the New Britain–New Guinea–northern Solomons area. Events shortly proved that the general could not.

POST-MIDWAY JAPANESE PLANS AND PREPARATIONS

On June 11, Imperial Headquarters "postponed" execution of the "FS" Operation to grab New Caledonia, the Fijis, and Samoa, and a month later quietly canceled these ambitious plans. To the Imperial Navy, the key factor was the loss of 400 ship- and land-based aircraft at Coral Sea and Midway, which far exceeded current or prospective production. In the view of the Imperial Army, however, the strategic initiative still rested with Japan. On June 12, the Army Section of Imperial General Headquarters directed that the 17th Army under Lieutenant General Harukichi Hyakutake mount an overland attack on Port Moresby by scaling the Owen Stanley Mountains forming the backbone of the Papuan peninsula.

One provision in the now abandoned plans for the "Second Operational Stage" that survived was the creation of the new 8th Fleet. Its operational title, Outer South Seas Force, reflected the mission of guarding conquests in the South Pacific, while the 4th Fleet (now the Inner South Seas Force) reverted primarily to the mission of defending the Mandates. Guiding the new fleet would be Vice Admiral Gunichi Mikawa, an intelligent, soft-spoken sailor of broad experience who enjoyed the confidence of the Naval General Staff. He had commanded the escort of Nagumo's carriers during their rampage from Pearl Harbor to the Indian Ocean.

Even though the new fleet's area of responsibility was significantly less than originally envisioned, the forces assigned to Mikawa were not large. Besides his fleet flagship, heavy cruiser *Chokai,* the admiral controlled Cruiser Division 6 with Japan's four most senior heavy cruisers, Cruiser Division 18 with three of Japan's oldest light cruisers, two destroyer divisions with eight middle-aged destroyers, and Submarine Squadron 7 with five boats.[4] Further, Mikawa lacked jurisdiction over the air units at Rabaul, which remained under Vice Admiral Nishizo Tsukahara, commander of the 11th Air Fleet.

Mikawa expressed concern over the vulnerability of his area to Tokyo on July 21 in a request for more destroyers. Two days later he predicted to the Combined Fleet an American descent on Guadalcanal before the Japanese established an air base there. These musings apparently created no particular ripples at Imperial General Headquarters, which firmly believed that the Allies would mount no serious counterattack before 1943. Imperial Headquarters noted reports of the landing of American marines on an unidentified Pacific island (actually New Zealand), convoy sailings, airfield construction,

---

[4]The Japanese grouped battleships and cruisers generally by threes and fours into *sentai* or squadrons. They identified *sentai* by numbers, but not ship types. Originally, battleships composed *Sentai* 1 to 3 and cruisers *Sentai* 4 and up. Likewise they gathered eight to sixteen destroyers into *suirai sentai,* which translates as torpedo squadron or flotilla. By mid-1942, numbering of the *suirai sentai* ran from 1 to 6 and 10 (though 6 was disbanded in July), and each usually had an old light cruiser as flagship. For purposes of clarity, this narrative will ignore strict Japanese terminology and employ American-style nomenclature. Thus *Roku Sentai* becomes Cruiser Division (Crudiv) 6 and *Roku Suirai Sentai* becomes Destroyer Squadron (Desron) 6. The Japanese, like their American counterparts, broke their destroyer squadrons down into two to four *kuchiku tai* or destroyer divisions (desdiv), each with nominal strength of four ships. Normally ships of the same class composed cruiser and destroyer divisions.

and increased radio activity in the South Pacific, but perhaps because it is natural to interpret enemy actions in reference to your own designs, they construed Allied activities as representing reinforcements for the defense of Australia and New Guinea. The establishment of Ghormley's new South Pacific Command passed undiscovered.

Mikawa reached Truk on July 25, and there one of his trusted staff officers, Commander Toshikazu Ohmae, sketched the results of a preliminary scrutiny of the situation as a picture of disunity, weakness, and lack of interest. Ohmae found the 17th Army riveted on its New Guinea mission and unconcerned about the Solomons. The 25th Air Flotilla and the 8th Base Force, jointly charged with local defense, neglected to cooperate. Although an airfield on Guadalcanal would be ready for operations in early August, neither the 25th Air Flotilla nor its parent 11th Air Fleet knew where the aircraft would come from to occupy it. The former command anticipated withdrawal for refitting shortly and evinced a palpable lack of concern about future operations in the area. During the 25th and 26th, Mikawa conducted meetings with the staff of the 4th Fleet. When the newcomers expressed concern about a possible Allied attack on Guadalcanal, the 4th Fleet staff scoffed at this notion as "absolutely" out of the question.

Mikawa journeyed to Rabaul, arriving on July 30. The 8th Fleet staff applied themselves immediately to reinforcement operations to New Guinea, but soon found their attention diverted back to Guadalcanal. Starting on July 31 and each day for the next week, the B-17s of the 11th Bomb Group began a pre-invasion "softening-up" campaign with bombing raids by two to eleven planes. This cost one Flying Fortress and crew in a ramming attack by a Japanese float plane on August 4. Apprehension at 8th Fleet headquarters grew on August 5 when the Special Duty Group (Radio Intelligence) at Imperial Headquarters suggested that increased Allied radio activity might presage a hostile operation in the South Seas Area. The 8th Base Force's own radio unit also noted a change in the enemy communications pattern, and an 8th Fleet staff officer later claimed that he reviewed the details of the intercepts and concluded that the target must be Guadalcanal. On August 6 the native laborers on Guadalcanal working on the airfield suddenly fled into the jungle. The report of this—dismissed as an example of native fecklessness—got into the air to Rabaul, but gained no more heed than any of the other hints of the storm gathering over Guadalcanal.

"THE OLD BREED"

"It is urgently necessary that an amphibious force be stationed in the South Pacific," wrote King on April 29 in an order creating the South Pacific Amphibious Force. The sharp edge of the organization would be the new 1st Marine Division, commanded by a new major general, Alexander Archer Vandegrift. He was fifty-five years old in 1942, of sturdy build with a hard jaw ending in a dimple underlining his handsome face. His soft voice carried the liquid drawl of his Virginia birthplace. Seasoned by a rich medley of duties in a career that already spanned thirty-four years, Vandegrift's thinking consistently revealed a quick grasp of the essentials in any professional challenge. As a protégé of the legendary General Smedley Butler, he understood that the most important element in war is man. Imbued with a sure comprehension of human nature, Vandegrift displayed expert judgment of officers and men. His quiet exterior radiated determination, and he was gifted with a naturally optimistic outlook. The tensile strength of both these latter qualities would be severely tested at Guadalcanal.

The 1st Marine Division then represented a title, not a tactical unit. It had undergone a simultaneous process of disintegration and reorganization thrice within the past year and most recently had been wrecked in late March by orders to prepare a regiment for shipment to Samoa. Vandegrift selected the 7th Marines,[5] and since he believed this unit would likely face combat shortly after its arrival, as indeed it would have without the victory at Midway, he ruthlessly stripped other elements in the division of many of their most experienced officers and noncommissioned officers to fill to the brim the ranks of this regiment. Carrying the cream of the embryo division as well as much scarce equipment, it sailed from Norfolk on April 10, 1942.

Five days later, Vandegrift received instructions to move his division on May 1 to New Zealand, where it would become the Landing Force of the South Pacific Amphibious Force. He greeted these

---

[5]In American practice, U.S. Marine Corps regiments are conventionally referred to as, for example, the 7th Marines rather than as the 7th Marine Regiment. Under the then-current "D-series" organization tables, a rifle regiment numbered 3,168 men, divided into a headquarters company, a weapons company, and three 933-man rifle battalions. Each rifle battalion fielded a headquarters company of 111 men, a weapons company of 273 men, and three rifle companies, each of 183 men. Three rifle regiments, an artillery regiment, and numerous support units made up a Marine division of nominally 19,514 men.

orders with mixed emotions. Although on the one hand glad to be headed for the combat theater, Vandegrift on the other hand fully comprehended the incomplete status of his division's training. Of his three infantry regiments, one had just been detached with no indication of when, if ever, it might return to the division. The 5th Marines had already been picked over to form the 1st Raider Battalion and to fill out the 7th Marines. However, it at least had conducted tactical exercises since December 1941. Reconstituted from a cadre status only in March, the 1st Marines stood in a much lesser state of readiness, although it was blessed with very strong leadership at regimental and battalion level. Each battalion of the 5th Marines and one of the 1st had exercised at the prophetically named Solomons Island, Maryland, amphibious training facility in March and April.

The proficiency of the divisional artillery regiment, the 11th Marines, with its weapons, mostly 75mm pack howitzers, was a bright spot. The division incorporated a full panoply of support units, including one battalion each of light tanks and amphibian tractors. Much of the marines' equipment tended to the dated, if not obsolete. While the Army standardized on the excellent M-1 Garand semiautomatic rifle in 1936, the marines on Guadalcanal carried the same M-1903 Springfield bolt-action rifle their fathers made famous in France in 1917. Vandegrift knew the division stood well short of "a satisfactory state of readiness for combat," but General Thomas Holcomb, Commandant of the Marine Corps, assured him of no combat assignment before January 1, 1943. Holcomb's source was impeccable—Admiral King.

The division's ranks, rapidly swelled to full strength, divided almost entirely into two categories. Young, mostly under twenty, recent enlistees in post–Pearl Harbor fever formed the vast majority. They joined for a variety of reasons that included prominently the elite reputation of the Corps and the general belief that, as the recruiting posters boasted, the marines would be first to fight. None donned the forest green seeking safety or comfort. These new marines were of generally high caliber, for, as the official United States Army history of World War Two ruefully acknowledged, the Marine Corps and the Navy secured a very disproportionate share of the men best fit for combat service.

The other group was by contrast small in number, but, like a drop of dye in a gallon of water, they gave the whole division an unmistakable hue and they stamped a nickname on the division: "the Old Breed." One of their own officers, Lieutenant Colonel Samuel B. Griffith, colorfully described them:

. . . first sergeants yanked off "planks" in navy yards, sergeants from recruiting duty, gunnery sergeants who had fought in France, perennial privates with disciplinary records a yard long. These were the professionals, the "Old Breed" of the United States Marines. Many had fought "Cacos" in Haiti, "bandidos" in Nicaragua, and French, English, Italian, and American soldiers and sailors in every bar in Shanghai, Manila, Tsingtao, Tientsin, and Peking.

They were inveterate gamblers and accomplished scroungers, who drank hair tonic in preference to post exchange beer ("horse piss"), cursed with wonderful fluency, and never went to chapel ("the Godbox") unless forced to. Many dipped snuff, smoked rank cigars or chewed tobacco (cigarettes were for women and children). They had little use for libraries or organized athletics . . . they could live on jerked goat, the strong black coffee they called "boiler compound," and hash cooked in a tin hat.

Many wore expert badges with bars for proficiency in rifle, pistol, machine gun, hand grenade, auto-rifle, mortar and bayonet. They knew their weapons and they knew their tactics. They knew they were tough and they knew they were good. There were enough of them to leaven the Division and to impart to the thousands of younger men a share of both the unique spirit which animated them and the skills they possessed.

The first echelon of the division, composed of the division headquarters, the 5th Marines, and some divisional units, filed aboard the transport *Wakefield* at Norfolk while longshoremen loaded two cargo ships with the division's equipment and supplies necessary to set up a new base. The *Wakefield* sailed on May 20, passed through the Panama Canal, and arrived in Wellington on June 14. The second echelon of the division, under the assistant division commander, Brigadier General William B. Rupertus, contained the 1st Marines and the remaining divisional elements. It journeyed by rail to San Francisco and sailed from that port in June aboard a mixed group of eight vessels.

As the first echelon stretched their legs, set up a new home, and tried to develop a deeper basis of alliance with the local female population, Ghormley summoned Vandegrift and a few of his key staff officers to Auckland on June 26. The normally affable admiral brusquely informed them of the proposed attack to seize and defend "Tulagi and adjacent positions," plus Ndeni in the Santa Cruz Islands. For these tasks Vandegrift would have his truncated division, the 1st Raider Battalion, the 1st Parachute Battalion, and the 3d Defense Battalion. To replace the 7th Marines, the 2d Marines of the 2d Marine Division would sail from San Diego to join the 1st

Marine Division at sea en route to Guadalcanal. D-Day was set as August 1, only three weeks after the expected arrival of the second echelon at Wellington.

As neither Vandegrift nor any member of his staff had the vaguest idea about the nature of the objective or the Japanese forces presumably ensconced there, the obvious first step in preparations was the gathering of intelligence on terrain, landing beaches, climatic conditions, and enemy dispositions. Time proved so short, though, that certain irrevocable decisions had to be made before essential features of the target were known. Vandegrift enjoined the strictest secrecy and wrapped the guise of "landing exercises" around all the preliminary preparations.

A Wellington daily, the *Dominion,* shattered equanimity on the operation's security on July 4 with a New York–datelined article by Major George Fielding Eliot stating, "The only way to take positions such as Rabaul, Wake Island and Tulagi, is to land troops to take physical possession of them." The paper went on to help its readers by pointing out:

> It may be significant that the censor passed the news of the arrival of the completely equipped expeditionary force of American Marines at a South Pacific port recently, as marines are not usually sent to bases where action is not expected.

Eliot concocted his article from nothing more secret than a map of commonly known Japanese positions, but he spread consternation among American officers.

This scare did not halt the assembly of information, but the ready catalogue of facts on the objective area proved slim. These numbered a few photos of Tulagi Harbor and conventional small-scale hydrographic charts, dating from the early part of the century, brief Army and Navy intelligence summaries, the *Pacific Islands Yearbook,* and assorted Royal Navy and British Colonial Office records. Vandegrift offered to dispatch a team of officers and men to Guadalcanal to contact Martin Clemens and gather firsthand information, but Ghormley vetoed this sensible idea as "too dangerous." The only direct scrutiny of Guadalcanal by the marines prior to the landings came on July 17 when Lieutenant Colonel Merrill B. Twining and Major William McKean hitched a ride aboard a B-17 from Port Moresby on a photographic reconnaissance flight. They quickly redirected their gazing to the shapes of three float Zeros curling upward from Tulagi to intercept. Their brief observations and the photo-

graphs revealed no extensive beach defenses protecting Guadalcanal's northern coast.

The quest for information took other officers to Noumea and
Auckland while the Division Intelligence Officer, Lieutenant Colonel
Frank Goettge, winged to Melbourne on July 1 for a week's stay with
a side trip to Sydney. Besides examining the slender archives available at MacArthur's headquarters, Goettge contacted the Australian
armed forces and commercial firms such as Lever Brothers and the
Burns-Phillips South Seas Company. He also interviewed many
planters, traders, civil servants, and ship's officers with knowledge of
the target area. Eight of his informants, hastily commissioned in the
Australian services, joined the division as guides, pilots, and advisers.

The most vital task facing Goettge during the pre-landing phase
was the provision of maps and aerial photos. No complete topographic map of Guadalcanal existed, and despite Goettge's best efforts the marines *never* possessed a really satisfactory map during the
entire campaign. A Navy hydrographic chart of the Tulagi-Gavutu
harbor area, corrected to 1910, was modified by drawing on details
from recent photos and information from the newly acquired guides.
For Guadalcanal, tracing from photos produced a rough, uncon-
trolled sketch "map" of the area from Aola to Lunga Point and
extending about 2.5 miles inland. The marines sent urgent requests
for more photos, particularly of Guadalcanal. Colonel Charles A.
Willoughby, MacArthur's intelligence officer, ordered a thorough
coverage of Guadalcanal and Tulagi. By July 20 a controlled mosaic
of the Lunga Beaches was ready in Australia, but the boxes containing this photomap were improperly addressed and lost in Auckland.

The arduously gathered intelligence was skimpy and all too frequently wrong. The most conspicuous error rested in the estimate of
Japanese strength. Although analysts provided an almost complete
count of Japanese warships, thanks largely to radio intelligence, they
placed the number of Japanese aircraft at Rabaul and Tulagi at 150,
whereas the actual total on the landing date stood near 100. Even this
surpassed the enumeration of Japanese in the Guadalcanal-Tulagi
area. The 1st Marine Division figured the garrison at 8,400, while
Admiral Turner reduced this to 7,124. Ghormley pegged Japanese
strength on the objective at 3,100. The actual count was 3,457, of
whom 2,571 were on Guadalcanal.

Standard doctrine prescribed that planning proceed downward
through each command level, but the orderly sequence of planning
became another casualty of the hasty mounting of "Watchtower."
Ghormley issued his plan on July 16 calling for the landings in the

Guadalcanal-Tulagi area followed immediately by the seizure of Ndeni in the Santa Cruz Islands. He gathered all the water- and land-based aircraft in the theater into one command designated Task Force 63 under Rear Admiral McCain. He placed all the seaborne forces headed for Guadalcanal and Tulagi under the direction of Vice Admiral Frank J. Fletcher, whose Expeditionary Force was also known as Task Force 61.

The 1st Marine Division should have published its plan last, but in fact issued its plan on July 20 calling for a simultaneous attack on Guadalcanal and targets in the Tulagi area. For these tasks the division was split into two unequal parts. The Guadalcanal Group, totaling about 11,300 men under the direct command of General Vandegrift, contained Combat Group "A" composed of the 5th Marines reinforced (Colonel Leroy P. Hunt), Combat Group "B" with the similarly configured 1st Marines (Colonel Clifton B. Cates), and a Support Group with the remaining divisional elements under the division artillery commander, Colonel Pedro A. del Valle. Their principal objective was the airfield near Lunga Point. The second part of the division was the Northern Group built around four rifle battalions totaling about 3,000 men under the assistant division commander, Brigadier General Rupertus. They would seize Tulagi and the twin islands of Gavutu-Tanambogo.

Admiral Fletcher, the Expeditionary Force commander, did not release his plan until July 28. He divided his armada of eighty-two vessels into an Amphibious Force under Turner and an Air Support Force under Rear Admiral Leigh Noyes. The latter contained three carrier groups with Fletcher directly in command of the *Saratoga* Group, Noyes in charge of his own *Wasp* Group, and Rear Admiral Thomas C. Kinkaid flying his flag in *Enterprise*.

Turner arrived in Wellington on July 17 and sailed five days later for Guadalcanal. He wisely accepted the 1st Marine Division plan as the basis for his own, but immediately established an irritant in his relations with Vandegrift by insisting that two battalions of the 2d Marines be kept as a reserve under Turner's command for the Ndeni operation. On July 19, Rear Admiral Victor A. C. Crutchley RN (VC) arrived in Wellington with Task Force 44, nicknamed "MacArthur's Navy," of three Australian and one American cruiser and the majority of what would shortly be nine destroyers. Turner's operations plan, issued on July 30, divided the transports into two groups for Guadalcanal and the Tulagi area and split the warships into several fire support groups, a minesweeping group, and a screening group, with the last under Admiral Crutchley.

The most glaring fault in these plans was the command arrangement. Ghormley chose to exercise his leadership from a moored flagship in Noumea, for reasons we will presently explore. This left Fletcher as the senior officer afloat off Guadalcanal, and he opted to remain in his flagship, *Saratoga*. What would prove to be a crucial lapse was that if Turner wished to get an air search of an area, he would have to ask Fletcher to ask Ghormley to order McCain to perform it.

The gathering of intelligence and the drafting of plans constituted only part of the formidable problems facing Vandegrift and his officers; loading was even more of a challenge. The marines designed and executed the transfer to New Zealand as an administrative move from one base to another, not with a view to immediate deployment to combat operations. As a result, all the ships had been commercially rather than "combat" loaded. The former method emphasizes cramming the most into each hull, while the latter method is profligate of space but essential for a landing, since the cargo is loaded in the reverse order of that in which it will be needed. (Colonel Hunt explained to some correspondents that "the essence of combat loading is not to put the toilet paper on top of the ammunition.") Many ships' cargoes would have to be unloaded, sorted, and then reloaded. Wellington's limited port facilities, the five-berth Aotea quay, enormously complicated the situation. Marine commanders immediately recognized that the first echelon would have to be loaded at once to clear the quay for the second echelon, due in on July 11.

The bespectacled division supply officer, Colonel Randolph M. Pate, controlled the continuous five-ring circus from a small office on the quay. He quickly calculated that there would not be nearly enough space on the available shipping to accommodate the miniature army under Vandegrift's command. The drastic program of streamlining started with the individual marine; each man would take only that needed to "actually live and fight." All excess clothing, bedding rolls, and company property was stored. Some nonessential units or parts of units were left behind, together with 75 percent of the heavy vehicles. Pate slimmed supply stocks from the prescribed ninety days to sixty days and pared ammunition reserves to ten units of fire.[6]

Each ship was assigned teams of 300 marines under a field officer to work around the clock to empty, sort, and reload; sometimes all

---

[6]A unit of fire is the theoretical expenditure rate for each weapon for one day.

three actions were in progress simultaneously on the same ship. New Zealand provided thirty flatbed trucks to supplement the division's organic transport and the expert advice of Major W. W. Horton. To the disgust of the marines, the leaders of the New Zealand dock unions insisted on regular tea breaks and refused to work their crews at all in the inclement weather that arrived with a "southerly" concurrently with the second echelon. The police summarily ordered them off the docks and, except for a few operators of special loading machinery, all the labor was leatherneck.

The quay afforded only limited shelter, and the cold driving rain that pelted the marines as they worked melted the flimsy cardboard packaging of many supplies, washed the labels off cans, and caused the sodden cartons to split open and spill their contents on the ground. The quay resembled a wet beehive with supplies being manhandled by bent figures glistening with rain. Water accumulated on the stone-covered surface of the dock until it became a marsh with dunes of cornflakes intermingled with paper pulp, clothing, candy bars, cigarettes, and ration cans. This scene became the strongest memory many marines would retain of Wellington, and morale slumped.

Despite the best efforts of the second echelon, it became clear that loading would not be completed in time for the scheduled landing date. Vandegrift and Ghormley believed there was no option but to ask for a delay, and King granted a dispensation to August 7. Finally on July 22, the first clear day in three weeks, the vessels bearing the 1st Marine Division sortied in single file from Wellington.

During the frenzied preparations to launch "Watchtower," Marshall, King, and Harry Hopkins flew to London in July at President Roosevelt's direction for the purpose of securing British concurrence on a plan of campaign that would get American troops into action against Germany in 1942. The British stood obdurately against "Sledgehammer," a limited landing on the European continent. Under Presidential pressure, the American delegation agreed to commit the United States to a seaborne assault on North Africa in the fall. This plan carried the evocative title of Operation "Torch"; it also carried full priority over "Watchtower," to the extent that the latter was soon dubbed Operation "Shoestring."

RENDEZVOUS AND REHEARSAL

On July 26, rendezvous was made off Koro Island in the Fijis. That afternoon Admirals McCain, Kinkaid, Turner, Crutchley, key members of their staffs, and General Vandegrift climbed *Saratoga*'s accommodation ladder to meet Fletcher for the only pre-landing conference of the major commanders. In a critical error of judgment, Ghormley decided he lacked the time to travel to this important meeting and in his stead sent his chief of staff, Rear Admiral Daniel J. Callaghan. As Fletcher's operations plan only reached Ghormley in September, he thus deprived himself of complete information as to the intentions of his subordinates for the first American amphibious assault of the war, apart from the disturbing contents of Callaghan's notes.

Vice Admiral Frank Jack Fletcher, the fifty-seven-year-old Expeditionary Force commander, presided over the gathering. As a carrier commander since the start of the war, Fletcher possessed an unexcelled but mixed combat record dogged by misadventures credited by some to bad luck and to others, including King, to ineptitude. Nimitz, however, did not find Fletcher's conduct wanting and, indeed, urged Fletcher's promotion to vice admiral on a reluctant King, thus securing Fletcher's position as Expeditionary Force commander. Fletcher appeared fatigued from the strain of long sea command—since the start of the year he had been on the ocean for 154 of 207 days—and the battles of the Coral Sea and Midway. To Vandegrift he looked nervous. The new vice admiral also proved disconcertingly uninformed about the landing plans.

Most of the conference dealt with logistics and was "animated," to quote one participant, or acrimonious in the view of another. Fletcher wasted no time before bluntly indicating his lack of faith in the prospects of success for "Watchtower." None too subtly, he implied the venture was Turner's brainchild and thus the ill-conceived product of one who lacked combat experience. The stormy meeting hit gale force when Fletcher asked Turner how long unloading would require. About five days, replied Turner, whereupon Fletcher declared he would withdraw the carriers after two days to avoid air counterattacks. With his temper inflamed, Vandegrift interposed to announce that the days of landing a small number of marines and leaving were past; this was a permanent occupation by a full division. Fletcher relented to the extent of promising to stay for three days. Admiral Callaghan scribbled detailed notes revealing his concern over Fletcher's skittishness about the operation, but he did not invoke his authority as Ghormley's representative. When briefed by Callaghan, Ghormley's reaction was to suggest operating the carrier fighter planes from Guadalcanal if the airfield was ready, and if not, to protect the beachhead from Efate with some of McCain's Wildcats, using belly tanks supplied from the carriers. The latter scheme foundered on practical problems, and Ghormley did not insist on the former or that Fletcher remain to cover the unloading.

Ghormley's passive response to Fletcher's fiat represented the first symptom of a disease that would plague the SOPAC commander. In part it may have reflected Ghormley's command personality, but in large measure it stemmed from the role Nimitz allocated to him. After their May 1942 conference, Ghormley recorded his understanding of the command position granted him by Nimitz:

> The Commander-in-Chief, Pacific Fleet would order Task Force Commanders to report to the Commander South Pacific Force for duty. The Commander South Pacific Force would direct the Task Force Commander to carry out his mission (as given by the Commander-in-Chief Pacific Fleet). The Commander South Pacific Force would not interfere in the Task Force Commander's mission unless circumstances, presumably not known to the Commander-in-Chief Pacific Fleet, indicated that specific measures were required to be performed by the Task Force Commander. The Commander South Pacific Force would then direct the Task Force Commanders to take such measures.

Under this prescription, Ghormley would not determine the missions of the task forces assigned to his theater and would be even more restrained from interferring in their tactical execution. Nimitz seemed to suggest a modification of this arrangement when he signaled King on June 27 concerning the seizure of Tulagi that "Ghormley will be placed in full command of the operation." If Ghormley believed this message expanded his authority, he was quickly disabused of this notion.

King appended to his July 2 message describing Tasks One through Three the comment that he assumed Ghormley would be task force commander for Task One, "which he should command in person in the operating area." This appeared to grant Ghormley a much more active role than the May directive provided, but Nimitz spoke again on July 9 designating Ghormley task force commander for Task One and placing him "in strategic command in person" in the operating area, which was defined as "initially" the New Cale-donia–New Hebrides area. Nimitz's comment that "I have full con-fidence in your ability to carry this operation to a successful conclusion" looks odd when juxtaposed with the fact that that phrase "strategic command" did not admit of the exercise of close tactical oversight, nor did the defined operating area initially include the southern Solomons. On July 31, Ghormley announced he would command the theater from the tender *Argonne* at Noumea. Neither King nor Nimitz objected to this arrangement.[7]

What then did Nimitz have in mind when he plainly circum-scribed Ghormley's role? Did Nimitz lack confidence in Ghormley from the outset? Or did Nimitz see the very great gamble represented by the operation and wish to entrust direct command to his most seasoned subordinate commander while closely monitoring the situa-tion from his headquarters? There is no direct evidence on Nimitz's underlying rationale, but he must carry responsibility for effectively making Fletcher the commander for Task One.

Ghormley's fundamental problems as COMSOPAC extended even beyond the nature of his authority to the very priority and purpose of "Watchtower." The original mission assigned to Ghormley was the defense of the sea lanes to Australia and New Zealand. The Joint Chiefs of Staff defined the purpose of "Pesti-lence" as the seizure and occupation of the New Britain–New Ire-land–New Guinea area to deny it to the Japanese. No one informed Ghormley that this new mission took priority over that originally assigned, nor did he assume it did. To the contrary, throughout the campaign and in his subsequent writings, Ghormley always insisted that "Watchtower" ranked *second* in priority, and he conducted himself accordingly. Moreover, he seems to have been confused about the very purpose of the seizure of Guadalcanal. Was it an

[7]There is one other message in this series that warrants passing mention. On July 11, Ghormley requested that special efforts be made to forward to him all intelligence, as he would be "afloat" in the near future. In ordinary usage "afloat" could mean aboard *Argonne* sitting in Noumea harbor, but in the context of this message, it suggests Ghormley expected to be in circumstances more demanding on communications than a quiet harbor berth. This raises the possibility that Ghormley actually planned to take charge of the Expeditionary Force, much as Spruance and Halsey did later in the war. In this light it is interesting to note that at the Koro conference Fletcher privately informed Callaghan that he was pleased to be in tactical command as he had assumed Ghormley would exercise that function. It may be further conjectured that Nimitz recognized Ghormley's intent to assume tactical command and expressly ruled out this course of action. The fact that a message of this nature was not preserved would not be unprecedented in Nimitz's dealings with his admirals.

offensive move to take the war to the Japanese with its air base, or was it a defensive move to deny the Japanese a base with which to threaten Allied positions to the south? The former dictated the rapid buildup of Guadalcanal's airfield, while the latter, which seems to be the objective as Ghormley perceived it, permitted more modest efforts.

CINCPAC selected Koro by map for the rehearsal with security as the preeminent consideration. As an advanced reconnaissance party from the Amphibious Force discovered, the reef conditions made landings difficult, if not impossible, and very hazardous to the irreplaceable landing craft. Turner elected to go ahead with the rehearsal, but canceled it after only about one-third of the marines actually landed. The transport crews gained valuable practice in deploying the boats and debarking the marines. The exercise uncovered the unreliability of the boat engines, and at Vandegrift's insistence boat pools were organized. The multiple failures in the exercise were sobering, and one Marine officer recalled that the only time he saw Vandegrift dejected during the entire campaign was at Koro. Turner and Vandegrift consoled themselves with the old saw that a bad rehearsal foreshadows a good performance.

During the waning hours of July 31, the fleet coiled itself into an antisubmarine disposition and set sail for Guadalcanal.[8] As the official Marine Corps history would dryly comment: "Seldom has an operation been begun under more disadvantageous circumstances." King catapulted "Watchtower" off at a velocity that mocked all conventions and under conditions that affronted a fair portion of the principles of war. The theater commander and his principal subordinates were confused about the objective of the enterprise; in Ghormley's case this prevented him from achieving economy of force in his dispositions, particularly with respect to aircraft. Unity of command had been forfeited by the division of the Pacific into two theaters in March, but its practical consequences emerged clearly with "Watchtower," not least with respect to massing all air strength in the region to cover the expedition during the critical assault phase. Moreover, the selected instruments for conducting the landings consisted of approximately 19,000 marines—such was the rush that a certifiable count was never made—of a hybrid, half-trained division and a hastily fabricated Amphibious Force led by an admiral who arrived

----

[8]The complete task organization for the Expeditionary Force, its supporting air forces, and all relevant Japanese forces is contained in Appendix 1.

at the eleventh hour before sailing. Finally, the sheer audacity of taking the strategic offensive may be gleaned from the following table of naval strengths:

	Carriers (Heavy/ Light/Escort)	Battleships (New/Old)	Heavy Cruisers	Light Cruisers	Destroyers (New/Old)	Submarines
American						
Total:	5/0/3	5/10 = 15	17	25	195	128
Atlantic:	1/0/2	4/3 = 7	3	9	52/27 = 79	40
Pacific:	4/0/1	1/7 = 8	14	13	59/21 = 80	88
Japanese	4/4/2	2/10 = 12	17	20	67/39 = 106	62

Note: The discrepancies in the American figures with regard to light cruisers and destroyers between totals and Atlantic/Pacific distribution reflects ships unassigned (either in conversion or new vessels working up) or those otherwise assigned.

It took a week[9] to reach the destination, and during the last hours of the voyage Admiral Turner thought of the words of the well-known military critic Captain B. H. Liddell Hart, who wrote in 1939:

A landing on a foreign shore in the face of hostile troops has always been one of the most difficult operations of war. It has now become almost impossible. . . .

[9] On August 4, 1942, destroyer *Tucker* steamed into a defensive minefield at Espíritu Santo and sank. Her skipper, Lieutenant Commander W. R. Terrell, was exonerated when an investigation showed that *Tucker* had never been informed of the minefield. American accounts of the Guadalcanal campaign have normally omitted *Tucker* from loss figures, as her demise came three days before the official start of the campaign. However, I believe that the transit time of the assault force should be considered as part of the campaign, and *Tucker*'s loss came at a principal base in the theater.

3

THE LANDING

"The invincibility of a refined technique"

THE FIRST DAY ON GUADALCANAL

As dawn of August 7 washed Lunga Plain in first light, the men of the 13th Construction Unit awoke and began their routines of ablutions and breakfast. Their commander, Captain Kanae Monzen, expected visitors this day—two staff officers from Rabaul to discuss deployment of planes to Guadalcanal; preliminary exchanges had suggested the first aircraft would arrive on August 16. This may have pleased Lieutenant Commander Norinaga Okamura of the 11th Construction Unit. For weeks he had urged vehemently that the island needed an air unit. Okamura's men still lay mostly abed when at 0614 the rush and roar of shells sundered the morning stillness. From his perch on Guadalcanal's mountainous spine Martin Clemens gazed out in joyful wonder at the size of the Allied Fleet, the greatest yet assembled for an amphibious assault.

Eight months to the day had elapsed since Japan struck Pearl Harbor without warning. Now, the Allies achieved complete surprise by a combination of good planning and good luck. The Expeditionary Force set a course west by south after departure from Koro designed to resemble that of a convoy headed for Australia. At noon on August 5 at a point south of Rennell Island, bows swung to point due north for the final run to Guadalcanal. Providence then smiled upon the Allies. Heavy clouds and rain blanketed the sea on which the assault convoy and the carrier groups advanced, cloaking their approach. Japanese search planes from Rabaul and Gavutu either did not penetrate the weather front or failed to see the armada as it plowed north at a stately 12 knots.

Leaving the carriers to gambol southwest of Guadalcanal, the assault convoy rounded Cape Esperance in the early hours of August 7 as the skies cleared and the moon rose. There it split into two groups. The Tulagi-bound transports, Group "Yoke," headed north around Savo Island while the much more numerous Guadalcanal transports, Group "X-ray," glided through the channel south of Savo. To all hands topside the sun's radiance disclosed Guadalcanal's dominant blue-green mountains shading into softer greens and browns as the coral ridges, grassy plains, and coconut plantations emerged from the night. At first sight—before the island gathered its sinister reputation—Admiral Turner thought it looked beautiful. The heavy cruiser *Quincy* heralded this first blow of the great Allied counteroffensive with a salvo, and very shortly other ships joined in raking Lunga Point, the site of suspected coastal batteries, with gunfire. At the same time 16 Grumman F4F-4 Wildcats from *Wasp*'s VF-72[1] swooped down to destroy all seven of the large four-engined Kawanishi H6K4 ("Mavis")[2] flying boats and likewise torch all eight of the Nakajima A6M2-N float Zeros ("Rufes") of the Yokohama Air Group moored off Halavo. An interisland schooner loaded with gasoline became a flaming orange beacon under the cumulative impact of destroyer gunfire and a strafing fighter.

The Guadalcanal group reached their transport area 4.5 miles from the shore at 0651 and Turner set Zero Hour for 0910. At the traditional order of "Land the Landing Force," boats swung out and cargo nets cascaded down the high sides of the transports as anxious

---

[1]In American naval usage, fighter squadrons were designated VF, scouting squadrons VS, bombing squadrons VB, torpedo squadrons VT, and patrol squadrons VP. V is the designator for heavier-than-air machines to distinguish them from blimps.

[2]This narrative will note the formal designation of Japanese aircraft upon their initial introduction followed by the code name ("Mavis," etc.) used by the Allies from about November 1942. Thereafter, identification will be by the code name, with the exception that the well-known popular term "Zero" will be employed in lieu of the code names "Zeke," "Hamp," and "Rufe" for the various models of the Mitsubishi A6M Type "O," Carrier Fighter.

groups of marines jostled forward to descend to the bobbing landing craft. The newly organized boat pools worked admirably; all boat formations crossed the lines of departure promptly and moved in good order toward the beach. The Marine report noted proudly that the landings proceeded "with the smoothness and precision of a well rehearsed peace-time drill."

Vandegrift premised his attack plan on the notion that there were 5,000 Japanese on the island including an infantry regiment of 2,100 men. He believed Lunga Point sheltered the bulk of the Japanese, but native reports placed a detachment near Koli Point building another airfield. The Marine general chose to land on a 1,600-yard-wide strip of white sand designated Beach Red, approximately midway between these points and 6,000 yards from Lunga Point. Combat Group "A" (the 5th Marines, Reinforced, less the 2d Battalion) would seize a beachhead. Combat Group "B" (the 1st Marines, Reinforced) would then pass through them and strike out for the "grassy knoll," actually Mount Austen, which the guides described as the dominant terrain feature near the airfield.

At 0910 the 1st Battalion, 5th Marines (Lieutenant Colonel William E. Maxwell) scrambled over the sides of their landing craft—

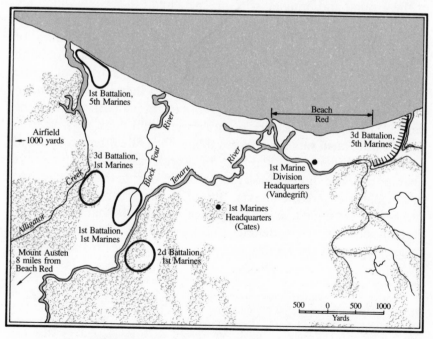

Guadalcanal Landings and Advance, August 7, 1942

most of these early models lacked ramps—and waded ashore on the right half of Beach Red. The 3d Battalion soon joined them and together they swiftly staked out a 2,000-yard-long and 600-yard-deep beachhead. As the marines had hoped, there was no opposition, and buzzing observation planes from the cruisers reported few signs of life around Lunga Point. Marine officers remained skeptical; they still expected a stiff fight. The 1st Marines followed in a column of battalions and once ashore struck out on an azimuth of 260 degrees to secure the "grassy knoll." Colonel Cates immediately saw that this was a mountain, not a "knoll," and that it lay much farther inland than anticipated. Just behind the beachhead the 1st Marines hit the tangled banks of the southeastern tributary of the Tenaru River.[3] They breasted it by driving an amphibian tractor into the streambed and laying prefabricated bridging material across it. Once over the Tenaru, the marines filtered through a coconut plantation but promptly ran into Guadalcanal's rain forest for the first time and began their education in jungle warfare.

The lords of Guadalcanal's jungle were the great hardwood trees that soared up to 150 feet and had girths as much as 40 feet across. Their straight trunks sprouted only high branches that formed a "sunproof roof." Their massive flared roots snaked across the surface of the ground and mingled with creepers and other vines which lay like thick trip wires while other leafy vines festooned the trunks of the trees. The eye could penetrate only a few feet into the foliage of the jungle floor, composed of varicolored plants, bushes, ferns and at least eleven kinds of thorns. Catcalls from squadrons of exotic birds in the upper canopy mocked marines as they exhausted themselves and dulled machete blades trying to chop a path through the tangle. Sheltered in the dark bramble were wild dogs, pigs, lizards, and gigantic bush rats the size of rabbits. Fish filled the streams and crocodiles slithered in and out of watercourses and mangrove swamps near the shore. Much more troublesome to the marines than this menagerie were the insects. Butterflies remarkable for their size and beauty abounded, as did gaggles of mosquitoes that hummed as they dispensed malaria, dengue, and lesser fevers. The sour odor of decay permeated the steamy stagnant air, for beneath the lushness

---

[3]The identity of the various watercourses between Beach Red and the Lunga River became the subject of considerable confusion during the campaign. The maps on pages 27 and 61 show the correct names. At the time of the landings, the marines believed Alligator Creek was the Tenaru River and the Tenaru was the Ilu River. Some accounts indicate the southeastern tributary of the Tenaru south of Beach Red was Ilu Creek.

omnipresent rot made the yellow clay earth porous. Even the sturdi-
est-appearing trees sometimes presented only facades for gutted in-
teriors that disposed them to topple randomly on the unwary.
Everywhere there was dampness. At Tulagi the British recorded an
average of 164 inches of rain per year; at times it fell in torrents as
if some celestial spigot had been opened.

Laden with heavy packs and accouterments, and debilitated by the
long sea voyage on board the jammed transports, the 1st Marines
slowed to about three hours per mile. The want of a real map compelled a compass course that led them repeatedly over the twisting
Tenaru, further detaining them. Meanwhile the 1st Battalion, 5th
Marines commenced a cautious advance from Beach Red along the
shore toward the mouth of Alligator Creek that no order nor exhortation from the regimental commander could hurry. As with the 1st
Marines, though with less excuse, control soon broke down as some
units pressed ahead while others tiptoed carefully forward "as if they
were about to encounter the entire Imperial Army," in the disgusted
words of Vandegrift. Regimental commanders lost contact with their
battalions; battalions groped for each other and their companies. One
marine on the flank of a column simply disappeared. Perhaps fortunately the leathernecks encountered no Japanese.

Trouble of a different character was also brewing back on the
beach. Grounded landing craft littered the surf, while just beyond,
and sometimes in the water as the tide rose, rested a jumble of boxes,
crates, and barrels. A short distance offshore other landing craft
idled awaiting a parking place on the beach. This scene became a
subject over which a great deal of ink was shed as to the respective
responsibilities of the Navy and the Marines. The fundamental bot-
tleneck was the inability of the overwhelmed Marine shore party,
roughly 300 men from the 1st Pioneer Battalion, to unload landing
craft as rapidly as the transports filled them and sent them ashore.
The situation became chaotic after the destroyer minesweepers verified the absence of mines in the inshore waters and the transports
closed the beach before noon, thereby shortening the boat trips. The
commander of the transports, Captain Lawrence F. Reifsnider, directed each ship to detach fifteen sailors to help ashore, but this was
not nearly enough. The sight of some idle marines cracking coconuts,
swimming, and lounging around the beach enraged transport officers. Vandegrift fielded only five infantry battalions to subdue the
garrison lurking somewhere on Guadalcanal, and he naturally and
properly had no desire to detach one of his maneuver units for
stevedore work with a battle in prospect. Some of those apparently

unemployed marines were in fact the trailing elements of units headed inland. But there were also a goodly number of support troops whose idle hands were not occupied with critical tasks, and who could have partly, but not completely, alleviated the beach congestion. The Japanese afforded relief for the beach party by halting unloading for three and a half hours with an air raid.

AIR RAIDS, AUGUST 7

From Tulagi a flood of plain-language transmissions began at 0652, reporting the presence of twenty ships attacking Tulagi and then, with increasing urgency, bombing, shelling and landing preparations. At 0805, Radio Tulagi proclaimed, "We pray for enduring fortunes of war," and pledged a fight "to the last man." Thereafter it fell silent. For many hours these messages granted Nimitz his only evidence of Allied progress.

Though surprised by the attack, the Emperor's lieutenants quickly acted to answer the prayers of the Tulagi garrison. Admiral Yamamoto ordered a "decisive counterattack." Vice Admiral Nishizo Tsukahara, commander of the 11th Air Fleet at Tinian, announced that he was flying to Rabaul to assume command of the area and would bring with him all of the Misawa Air Group's Mitsubishi G4M1 ("Betty") attack planes.

At Rabaul on this morning sat thirty-two Bettys, twenty-four long-range A6M2 Model 21 Zeros ("Zekes"), fifteen shorter-range A6M3 Model 32 Zeros ("Hamps"), sixteen Aichi D3A ("Val") divebombers, and two Nakajima J1N1 ("Irving") reconnaissance planes, while four Mavis flying boats floated in Simpson Harbour. By coincidence, Rabaul hosted a special concentration of planes gathered to launch a major attack this morning on the new Allied air bases at Milne Bay on New Guinea. For this purpose the bellies of twenty-seven Bettys bulged with bombs. Rear Admiral Sadayoshi Yamada, commander of the 25th Air Flotilla, required no prompting on the need for action. He barked orders for the bombers to set out immediately without pausing to change their loads from bombs to the even more deadly torpedoes. The Bettys would be escorted by eighteen of the twenty-four available long-range Zeros of the crack Tainan Air Group, whose roster sparkled with three of Japan's leading fighter aces, Saburo Sakai, Hiroyoshi Nishizawa, and Toshio Ota. A group of nine Vals lacked both a Zero escort and the range for a round trip to Guadalcanal. Japanese officers advised pilots of fuel-short Zeros and dive-bombers to make for the crude airstrip at Buka off the northern tip of Bougainville. More realistically, they sent a destroyer and a Kawanishi H8K "Emily" flying boat to Shortland off the southern end of Bougainville to create a predesignated ditching area for Val crews.

Led by scout planes to snoop for the American carriers, the Bettys took off at 0930 followed at intervals by the Zeros and the Vals. As the twin-engine attack planes streaked south they passed over coast watcher Paul Mason on Buin, who signaled at 1037: "From S.T.O. 24 bombers headed yours." Stations in Melbourne and Pearl Harbor rebroadcast this warning to the invasion fleet. Aboard the Australian heavy cruiser *Canberra* the crew was informed that the day's menu included lunch at 1100 and an attack by enemy planes at noon.

One of the Zeros turned back, leaving fifty-three aircraft headed south to challenge the American toehold on Guadalcanal. Two Mitsubishi products, the Betty and the Zero, spearheaded this attack, just as they had since the start of the war. Within each Betty's cigar-shaped fuselage studded with gun positions rode seven men of the 4th Air Group. Their versatile mount could perform high-level bombing or sea-level torpedo attacks and possessed the range of a B-17 while yielding only a modest speed advantage at altitude to the Grumman F4F-4. The lack of armor protection for the crew and of self-sealing covering for the huge fuel load of 1,294 gallons carried in the wings, however, seriously offset these capabilities. Although the Betty's official designation was Type One Land Attack Plane, its propensity to disintegrate in a ball of flame with only one hit in the fuel tanks led the crews to wryly call them "Type One Lighters" or "Flying Cigars."

Weaving above the Bettys were the fabled Zeros. More than any other achievement, the Zero first shattered the stereotype of the Japanese as mere imitators. It was the offspring of a brilliant design team under Jiro Horikoshi who extracted inspiration from a specification demanding a seemingly impossible blend of agility, speed, and range. Their labors produced a sleek low-wing monoplane that incorporated such original features as an all-around-vision canopy, control-wire elasticity to improve high-speed handling, and a downward twist of the wingtips to lower stall speed. The Zero possessed markedly superior climb, acceleration, and maneuverability over the Grumman F4F, besides being generally superior in speed. Although sometimes overlooked, one of its cardinal virtues was its combat range of over 1,200 miles with a drop tank, which made it the world's first single-engine strategic fighter plane. The A6M2 Model 21 needed every inch of this range to reach the 565 miles from Rabaul to Guadalcanal and return. The Japanese retained the Model 32 Zeros for the defense of Rabaul because their slightly more powerful engines weighed more, consumed more fuel, and displaced some fuel capacity, thereby reducing their range about 25 percent, and thus below the minimum requirement for sorties to the lower Solomons. For purposes of this narrative, the Model 32 variants will be styled the "short-range" Zeros, though this term is meaningful only in comparison to the extraordinary performance of the Model 21.

All this excellence was not without cost. The Achilles' heel of the Japanese aircraft industry was power-plant development, and no type of aircraft is so dependent upon engine selection as a fighter. Jiro Horikoshi fitted the Zero with the Nakajima Sakae Type 12, but the Sakae delivered only 950 horsepower, while the Wildcat's Pratt & Whitney R-1830 delivered 1,200 horsepower. Given this disparity, Horikoshi recognized that the only way to endow his creation with superior performance was to make it aerodynamically cleaner and markedly lighter. He therefore initiated rigorous drag-reduction and weight-control programs, the latter including the use of new light-weight metals, and he reduced the safety factor in structural members. As a result of these efforts the Zero came out fully one-third lighter than the Wildcat. By western standards the Zero was very lightly built, and Horikoshi believed that weight considerations alone precluded the fitting of armor to protect the pilot and installation of self-sealing fuel tanks. It is also instructive to recall that the Zero's 1937 specification did not demand armor or self-sealing fuel tanks, nor did any other nation incorporate these features at that time, but by 1942 all major combatants except Japan had so fitted their aircraft. These omissions rendered the Zero dreadfully vulnerable, and one other technical shortcoming grossly impaired the Zero's battle effectiveness: the standard radio proved ineffective, and on this day, as on most others, the Zeros of the 11th Air Fleet headed for Guadalcanal flew without radios.

One of the clear lessons of World War Two is that a nation's air power depends as much upon a plentiful supply of well-trained airmen as it does upon the qualities of its aircraft. In this sphere, though, Japanese traditionalism and short-sightedness created a crippling handicap. The Imperial Navy's air service entered the war with only about 3,500 pilots. They were the products of a feudalistic prewar training scheme designed to nurture a very few pilots who would overcome superior enemy numbers by their superb skill, like the samurai warriors of old, or what one Japanese officer dubbed the "premise of the invincibility of a refined technique." For example, the class that future ace Saburo Sakai joined in 1937 comprised only seventy of the 1,500 applicants. Besides the academics and athletics that marked aviation instruction all over the world, the Japanese training syllabus incorporated such feats as hanging by one arm from an iron pole for ten minutes, swimming underwater for a minimum of a minute and a half, somersault dives from high diving boards to the ground, and brutal wrestling matches where the losers could face dismissal. Only twenty-five men graduated in Sakai's class, a typical rate of attrition. These rigors instilled fierce pride in the graduates, and early victories against Allied air forces seemingly confirmed the view that quality counted more than quantity. Eight months of war had inflicted serious losses among the front-line air groups that contained the cream of the naval air crews through steady attrition as well as the hemorrhages at Coral Sea and Midway. But the survivors, both carrier-based and land-based, still presented the sharpest edge of Japan's defense.

Despite the coast watcher's advanced warning, a breakdown in the complex flying schedules organized by Admiral Noyes left only twelve instead of the planned twenty-four Wildcats stacked over the landing area to meet the Japanese. Compounding this problem, an erroneous vector sent a division of four Wildcats of *Enterprise*'s VF-6 away from the air battle altogether. The Wildcat would win no aerodynamic or beauty contests, with its square-cut wings set in a portly fuselage. On the ground its main landing gear extruded from the forward fuselage, giving the plane a look aptly compared to that of a knock-kneed bumblebee. It was not without virtues, including a quicker rate of roll and better control at high speed, and a faster dive than the Zero, largely because of the Wildcat's greater mass. Its wing-mounted sextet of fast-firing .50 caliber machineguns could easily destroy a Zero. When the roles were reversed, as they frequently were, the rugged Wildcat proved resistant to the Zero's armament of two rifle-caliber machineguns and a pair of slow-firing 20mm cannon. In contrast to the the Tainan Air Group's large roster of polished veterans, a substantial majority of tyros from recent training courses leavened with a cadre of combat veterans filled American cockpits.

At 1315, the Bettys arrived, but heavy cloud disrupted their aim and all their bombs thundered harmlessly on the sea. They encountered eighteen Wildcats in two installments. First appeared the remainder of the original contingent of defenders: eight Wildcats from *Saratoga*'s VF-5. Lieutenant James J. Southerland got in among the bombers and expended his ammunition in a pair of runs, hitting two planes heavily. Five Zeros jumped the other three members of his division, shooting down two Wildcats while the third escaped with forty-nine holes. The second VF-5 division split, with two battling the escort while the other duo tackled the bomber formation, lacing at least two Bettys with .50 caliber fire before escorting Zeros shot them both down. Only one of the pilots of the four downed Wildcats survived.

Lieutenant Southerland tried to disengage, but three Zeros barred his path, and Saburo Sakai soon joined them. Southerland executed brilliant defensive moves against four opponents, but Sakai gradually gained position astern, using the Zero's superior maneuverability to inflict fatal damage on the Wildcat. Just before he bailed out, Southerland surveyed the condition of his mount, which by now must have been hit well over a hundred times:

> Flaps and radio had been put out of commission. . . . The after part of my fuselage was like a sieve. She was still smoking from [an] incendiary [hit] but not on fire. All of the ammunition box covers on my left wing were gone and 20mm explosives had torn some gaping holes in its upper surface. . . . My instrument panel had been shattered, my rear view mirror was broken, my plexiglass windshield was riddled. The leakproof tanks have apparently been punctured many times as some fuel had leaked down into the bottom of the cockpit even though there was no steady leakage. My oil tank had been punctured and oil was pouring down my right leg and foot.

Southerland marveled that his Wildcat "still perform[ed] nicely in low blower, full throttle and full low pitch." This account should illustrate fully what the adjective "sturdy" means when it is inevitably coupled to any description of the Grumman F4F Wildcat.

Sakai had just rejoined his comrades after dispatching Southerland's Wildcat when a bullet came whizzing through his canopy, missing his head by inches. The amazed Sakai glanced back to find that the round came not from an enemy fighter, but from an SBD dive-bomber. The Dauntless from Wasp's VS-71 quickly became Sakai's sixtieth victim. The rash pilot, Lieutenant Dudley Adams, survived; his gunner was not so lucky. Spotting what looked like another flight of Wildcats, Sakai and another pilot dove in astern of them only to discover at the last moment that they were Dauntlesses. The SBD gunners of Enterprise's VS-5 and VB-6 unleashed a barrage of fire that smashed Sakai's canopy and creased his skull. Recovering from the stunning blow to the head, Sakai discovered he was blind, his left side was paralyzed, and his tattered Zero was plummeting seaward. After pulling out of the dive, he wiped the blood from his face and found he had lost his vision in his right eye; the loss turned out to be permanent. The head wound soon began to transmit waves of pain through his body, and the loss of blood acted as a potentially lethal anesthetic. Sakai fought the stupor by striking himself on the wound to produce excruciating jolts of pain. In one of the epic flights of the war, Sakai, with just one eye, one arm, and one leg, nursed his crippled plane back over the 565 miles to Rabaul.

The second contingent of Wildcats to intercept the raid, ten aircraft of *Enterprise*'s VF-6 belatedly launched to defend the transports, entered the fray as the bombers withdrew and pursued them as far as New Georgia. Four of these Wildcats fell to Zeros, but three of the pilots were recovered. In the course of all these exchanges three Bettys fell and two ditched or crash-landed. Two Zeros failed to return.

The nine Japanese dive-bombers arrived about 1500 and used clouds skillfully to achieve attack positions. They managed only one hit, on destroyer *Mugford*'s afterdeck house; it knocked out two 5-inch guns and killed nineteen men while wounding thirty-two more. Sixteen Wildcats jumped the Vals and later claimed to have splashed more than were present. Five of the dive-bombers fell to fighter guns and the remaining four ditched on the way back; only three crews survived.

This first clash over Guadalcanal, which cost 50 percent of the participating Wildcats, added proof, if any were needed, of the marked superiority of the Zero in a dogfight. The Japanese fighter pilots expected stiff opposition and were not disappointed. Sakai graded Lieutenant Southerland as the most skillful antagonist he had ever encountered. But the main object of the attacks—the disruption of the landing—was signally not achieved. Five Bettys, nine Vals, and two Zeros had been expended with most of their crews in exchange for one nonfatal hit on a destroyer. One of Japan's greatest aces was out of the campaign on the first day. It was an omen.

After moving his command post ashore in the afternoon, Vandegrift assembled his regimental commanders. For the next day's operations the Marine general ordered Colonel Cates to reorient his advance to head directly toward the airfield, whither the 5th Marines would also proceed along the shore. Cates was able to contact only one of his battalions to change its orders during the night. After dark the situation became so chaotic on Beach Red, despite its extension to the west, that unloading was suspended altogether at 0242.

Twilight found the 1st Marines one mile from their start point, dispersed and exhausted. The 1st Battalion, 5th Marines drew up at long last at Alligator Creek, 2 miles west of Beach Red, and set up a perimeter defense for the night in anticipation of a Japanese assault. No attack developed, though it was not due to a want of aggressiveness on the part of the Japanese. The surprise morning bombardment irretrievably scattered the sleeping 11th Construction Unit and many men from other units. But Captain Monzen rallied a body of stalwarts and led them southeast to seek battle in the dark. They became lost in the jungle and returned before making contact with the marines. Monzen's men may have puzzled at the not too distant popping of rifle fire in the direction of the suspected American positions.

This was the first night ashore for the young marines, and the hostile physical surroundings mixed with the unease generated by the proximity of the enemy and that most primitive of emotions, fear of the dark. Describing the feelings of men on nights like this, Private Robert Leckie wrote:

> It was darkness without time. It was an impenetrable darkness. To the right and left of men rose up those terrible formless things of my imagination, which I could not see, but I dared not close my eyes least the darkness crawl beneath my eyelids and suffocate me. I could only hear. My ears became my being and I could hear the specks of life that crawled beneath my clothing, the rotting of the great tree which rose from its three cornered trunk above me. I could hear the darkness gathering against me and the silences that lay between the moving things. I could hear the enemy everywhere about me, whispering to each other and calling my name. I lay open mouthed and half-mad beneath that giant tree. I had not looked into its foliage before the darkness and now I fancied it infested with Japanese. . . .

The night reverberated with shouts of "Halt!" and the snaps and rips of rifle and machinegun fire. After his conference with Vandegrift, Colonel Cates tramped back to his command post making as much noise as possible and using a flashlight to try to reassure nervous marines that he was not Japanese. One marine still took a shot at the colonel, but Cates recorded, "Luckily he was an artilleryman and he made a clear miss." Not so fortunate was a young Navy corpsman who got up to relieve himself; at dawn he lay in white-faced death.

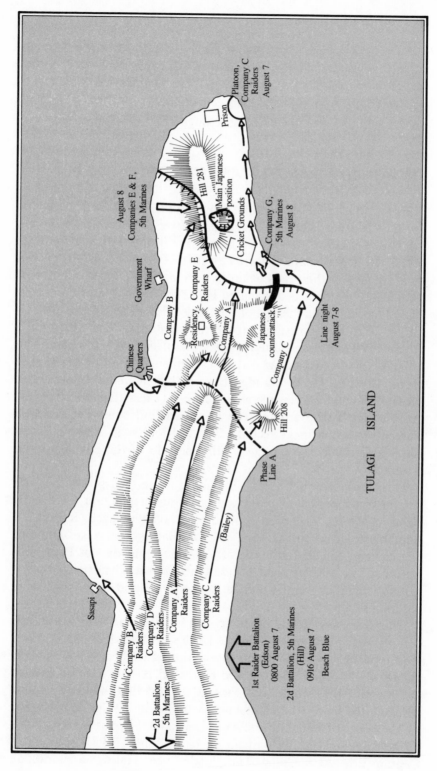

Battle for Tulagi, August 7–9

Little word reached Vandegrift about the landings on Tulagi and Gavutu-Tanambogo during August 7. At 0007, August 8, he received an alarming message from Brigadier General Rupertus that the 1st Raider Battalion had suffered 22 percent casualties while the 1st Parachute Battalion had lost a staggering 50–60 percent.

TULAGI AND GAVUTU-TANAMBOGO

Tulagi is an island about 2 miles long and half a mile wide lying just south of Florida Island. A ridge rising over 300 feet above the sea marks the northwest-southeast axis of the island. About two-thirds of the way down from the northwest tip of Tulagi the ridge is broken by a ravine and then rises again in a triangle of hills, the southeasternmost of which was designated Hill 281 after its elevation in feet. The island had been the seat of the British Solomons Islands Protectorate, and governmental structures, including the Governor's House or Residency, dotted the southeast end of the island. The Japanese garrisoned Tulagi with a detachment of the 3d Kure Special Naval Landing force totaling about 350 men under Commander Masaaki Suzuki. Aerial reconnaissance revealed that the strongest defenses on Tulagi fronted the northeast and southeast beaches. Therefore, the marines selected a 500-yard-long strip of shore (Beach Blue) about midway on the southwest side of the island for the assault.

Transport Group "Yoke," including three transports, four destroyer-transports, and one cargo ship under Captain George B. Ashe in *Neville,* anchored about 5 miles off the beach. Rupertus's Landing Force comprised the 1st Raider Battalion; the 1st Battalion, 2d Marines; the 2d Battalion, 5th Marines; and the 1st Parachute Battalion. Vandegrift picked these units for what he expected to be a tough fight, as they were the best-trained and most aggressive battalions available.

The island terrain and the hydrographic situation required a fairly complicated plan. After elements of the 1st Battalion, 2d Marines secured flanking positions on Florida, the 1st Raiders would land on Tulagi at H-Hour to be followed by the 2d Battalion, 5th Marines, and together they would seize the island. Gavutu-Tanambogo would be assaulted by the 1st Parachute Battalion at H plus four hours.

The honor of being the first American assault troops to step ashore in the Solomons fell to Company B, 1st Battalion, 2d Marines under Captain Edward J. Crane. They landed near Haleta on Florida at

0740 to secure a promontory which commanded Beach Blue, but found no Japanese present. The rest of their parent battalion (Lieutenant Colonel Robert E. Hill) waded ashore on Florida's Halavo peninsula east of Gavutu-Tanambogo for like purposes and identical results. At precisely H-Hour, 0800, the boats bearing Companies B and D of the Raiders grounded offshore on the coral and the embarked marines sloshed ashore, sometimes slipping and tearing cloth and flesh on the spiny coral heads. Unlike their comrades on Guadalcanal, they traveled light. "Don't worry about the food," their commander, Lieutenant Colonel Merritt A. Edson, told one company commander. "There's plenty there. Japs eat, too. All you have to do is get it." The Japanese did not have the narrow beach under observation, because immediately behind it the heavily wooded ground rose steeply. The leading companies pushed straight across the island from the beach with Company B securing Sasapi and then wheeling right while Company D faced right immediately after cresting Tulagi's spine. The second wave brought in Companies C and A. The latter scaled the ridge to tie into the right flank of Company D at the crest and Company C extended the Marine line to the southwest shore. In an arrowhead formation the Raiders swept down the island to Phase Line A, where the first resistance confronted Company B from outposts in the former Chinese quarters. In the scuffle a young doctor was killed and the Company D commander was wounded. Meanwhile the 2d Battalion, 5th Marines (Lieutenant Colonel Harold E. Rosecrans) landed on Beach Blue by 0916, releasing Company E of the Raiders from the chore of securing the beachhead. Elements of the new battalion combed the northwest end of the island but found no Japanese.

When the Raiders tried to move beyond Phase Line A, Company C butted immediately into heavy opposition from concentrated machinegun fire on the southwest side of the spine around Hill 208. In the course of overcoming this opposition, the company commander, Major Kenneth D. Bailey, was wounded after he dashed forward to the top of a Japanese cave and from there kicked cover from the embrasure. With grenades and small-arms fire Company C overpowered all resistance and then resumed the advance with Company A until they reached a spot where the ground fell away steeply to a small flat field—in tranquil times the cricket grounds. One platoon of Company C felt its way down the shore to the southeast tip of the island, but the remainder of the marines halted.

The fighting marked the initial encounter with the tactics for which the Japanese became well known. They entrenched strongly in cleverly constructed dugouts and tunnels, and the marines discovered the coral cave impervious to anything but a lucky hit from naval guns or bombing. Japanese defensive tactics included allowing the point of a unit through unmolested to ambush the main body and making plentiful use of sniper harassment, though the marines deemed Japanese marksmanship poor—"If they had been good shots," said Major Justice Chambers, "few of us would have survived." The garrison anchored their resistance in the ravine west of Hill 281 and on the steep slopes of that hill. It became apparent that this nest could not be overcome before nightfall, so the marines hastily prepared for defense. The Raiders' line rested on the high ground overlooking the cricket field with Companies B (with attachments from Headquarters Company), E (Weapons), A, and C shoulder to shoulder from left to right. Company D and the 2d Battalion, 5th Marines backstopped the line.

During the night the Japanese mounted savage counterattacks and drove a wedge between Company C and Company A, cutting off the former from the other Raiders. Knots of men from the 3d Kure Special Naval Landing Force hurled themselves against the newly extended flank of Company A in an attempt to crumble the Marine line but were repulsed. Small groups and individuals infiltrated to the Marine command post at the Residency and made five separate attacks on it between 0030 and 0530. Some of them broke into the building only to find that the marines had abandoned it; these Japanese were wiped out at dawn. In the first light, Company A emerged from their positions to find twenty-six dead Japanese within 20 yards of the defensive line.

Three thousand yards east of Tulagi are the twin islands of Gavutu-Tanambogo, joined by a 500-yard-long causeway. Each of the islands is dominated by a hill rising precipitously from the otherwise level ground. The mound on Gavutu rose to 148 feet above the sea and thus was named Hill 148; its counterpart on Tanambogo was likewise christened Hill 121. The islands are surrounded by coral reefs that precluded approach except from the east. The net effect of the terrain and hydrographic situation was to channel attackers into a narrow funnel dominated by high ground on two sides. The Japanese garrison under Captain Shigetoshi Miyazaki numbered 342 men of the Yokohama Air Group operating a seaplane base on Gavutu, 144 men of the 14th Construction Unit, and fifty men of a platoon from the 3d Kure Special Naval Landing Force. Of these 536 men, only

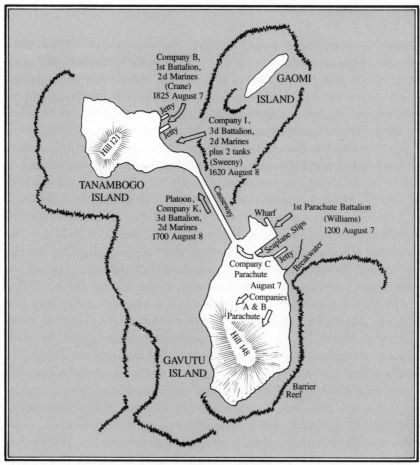

Gavutu-Tanambogo

the last-named platoon was trained specifically for ground combat, but lengthy training was hardly necessary to defend these islands.

Rupertus slated the 1st Parachute Battalion under Major Robert H. Williams to take Gavutu and Tanambogo. Mustering only 397 men, including the attached Navy medical personnel, the parachutists were outnumbered by the defenders. A military rule of thumb is that high ground dominates low ground, so Major Williams planned to take Gavutu first and then Tanambogo. The division order specified an attack at H-Hour plus four, long after the garrison could be expected to be alert, because of a shortage of landing craft and an underestimation of the defensive possibilities of the islands. In retrospect a surprise attack in the dark might have made the battalion's task easier, though nothing would have made it simple.

As soaked and seasick parachutists watched from their boats on the long run in from the east, an impressively furious bombardment from the light cruiser *San Juan* and destroyers *Monssen* and *Buchanan* rocked Gavutu, but the flailing lasted only five minutes.

Dive-bombers from *Wasp* then pelted the island for double that time. Neither of these batterings did much harm to the defenders, although they did knock out an 80mm gun on Hill 148. Either by design or because of the heavy pre-landing bombardment, the defenders allowed the first wave of landing craft laden with Company A to beach without resistance. The naval bombardment tossed huge chunks of concrete into the path of the boats, forcing most to veer to the right from the intended touchdown on the seaplane ramp and to deposit the marines on a concrete dock. The first wave pushed inland about 75 yards, but the Japanese rallied and from Hills 148 and 121 placed a withering fire on the attackers. The following two waves churned through water flecked by heavy fire from machineguns and rifles and suffered some casualties in the boats. As Company B in the second wave and Company C in the third wave debarked, they found the dock swept with machinegun fire, and in these few minutes about one man in ten was hit. The fusillade riddled the battalion command group, killing two staff officers and wounding the battalion commander. Major Charles A. Miller succeeded to command. The battalion command post and the aid station huddled in the partly demolished Lever Brothers store, just off the dock, whose walls were continually perforated by gunfire.

Although the loss of many leaders and the dense fire created confusion, the parachutists achieved part of their mission, for two reasons. First, every man in the battalion understood the plan of attack; second, the junior enlisted men displayed ample initiative and courage. Company C established a firing line facing Tanambogo to assist the attack by suppressing fire from that quarter. Individuals and small groups from Company B, with assistance from some members of Company A, moved out at 1400 to take Hill 148. This they seized, and they made their position on the island tenable, though by no means secure. Unfortunately, a request for air support resulted in the belated appearance of some SBDs, which attacked Hill 148 shortly after the marines surmounted it, causing several deaths and injuries. The Japanese flag flying there was removed immediately afterward and the Stars and Stripes fluttered above it for the first time about 1800.

With the coming of night the wounded, who had lain exposed all day, were recovered and evacuated to *Neville*. During the sodden night several Japanese swam to Gavutu from Tanambogo and were shot as they were believed to be trying to infiltrate Marine positions. Later it appeared that some of these men may have been laborers attempting to surrender. But other dim figures in the night who were undoubtedly Japanese sallied from caves and dugouts to engage the parachutists. With heavy casualties, Gavutu still unsecured, and Tanambogo yet to be taken, Major Miller requested reinforcements.

When this appeal reached Rupertus, he had in hand Company B, 2d Marines fresh from its morning mission on Florida. Although advised against it, Rupertus decided to send Company B alone to subdue Tanambogo. Captain Crane shuttled his boated command to Gavutu, where Miller told him Tanambogo contained only a few snipers. Armed with this misinformation, Crane set out for the northeast shore of Tanambogo with five boats to attempt a landing about 1845. Unfortunately, the naval gunfire support ignited a huge gasoline fire that illuminated the approaching landing party. Heavy gunfire greeted the boats, causing severe casualties among the exposed Navy crewmen. When a bullet felled the coxswain of the third boat, it sheered out of line, followed by the remaining two boats. Only two boats reached shore, and Crane, recognizing his position as untenable, reembarked the wounded and all but a dozen men, with whom he returned via the causeway to Gavutu about 2400.

The failure of Crane's assault impelled Rupertus to request reinforcements, and this prompted Turner to release both the remaining battalions of the 2d Marines from reserve. The 2d Battalion, 2d Marines headed to Tulagi, where the attack resumed in the morning. Companies E and F of the 2d Battalion, 5th Marines advanced over the top of Hill 281 to the southwest side of the island, trapping remaining defenders. American mortars and machineguns played over the area until 1500, when the Raiders and Company G of the 2d Battalion, 5th Marines pushed through the ravine blasting the Japanese out of their strongpoints.

Although organized resistance ceased, the fighting continued for four days. In American eyes, the Japanese fought with astonishing tenacity. Each man battled until killed and each machinegun crew fought to the last man, who usually took his own life. The Japanese caves and dugouts could not be cleared by grenades, which were frequently thrown back. The marines possessed no flamethrowers or bangalore torpedoes, and the only tank that came ashore threw a track. But within the ranks of the Raiders was a Marine Gunner named Angus Goss to whose ears "an explosion was the sweetest music conceivable." During the morning of August 8 he and a crew improvised pole charges, and tactics were fashioned on the spot. About noon the blasting of the remaining Japanese positions began. Demolitions men screened by smoke slithered forward with a charge while machinegunners sprayed the mouth of the cave. Shrieks signaling the end of the occupants often accompanied the muffled sound of the detonations. The emotions of the Japanese listening to this process from adjacent positions can only be imagined.

Only three Japanese surrendered on Tulagi, and they reported that about forty of their number had escaped to Florida by swimming. These latter only postponed their fate, as Marine and native patrols hunted them down relentlessly during the next two months. Prisoners confessed that the garrison had taken to caves at the outset, believing that a raid was in progress; only later on the afternoon of August 7 did the defenders begin to organize resistance. In contrast to 347 of 350 Japanese who perished on or around Tulagi, of the roughly 2,400 Marine attackers, the 1st Raiders lost thirty-six killed and fifty-two wounded, the 2d Battalion, 5th Marines suffered six dead and eighteen wounded and the 2d Battalion, 2d Marines lost two killed and five wounded. Adding one dead and one wounded from the 1st Pioneer Battalion brings total losses to forty-five killed and seventy-six wounded.

The other reinforcing battalion, the 3d Battalion, 2d Marines (Lieutenant Colonel R. G. Hunt), was directed to land on Gavutu and then use boats to attack Tanambogo. Hunt's companies began landing at 1015, and Company L assisted the parachutists in exterminating Japanese resistance on Gavutu. Another tragic bombing incident cost Hunt's marines four killed and eight wounded. Sniping and machinegun fire from Tanambogo continued to hinder the marines, who methodically proceeded to treat the caves and dugouts in which the Japanese crouched with twenty cases of TNT. One of the leaders in this close and dangerous work was Captain Harry L. Torgerson of the parachutists, a blond giant who had his trousers removed by one blast.

At 1500, *San Juan* shelled Tanambogo, and thirty minutes later Hunt ordered the attack. *Buchanan* steamed into Gavutu Harbor at 1600 and pounded Tanambogo at short range. At 1615, two tanks under Lieutenant R. J. Sweeny landed, followed within five minutes by Hunt's Company I. The tanks split, each with its cluster of supporting riflemen, with one rumbling south and the other east to assault the slopes of Hill 121. One tank drew ahead of its infantry as it attacked a pillbox and suddenly Japanese—led by Captain Miyazaki and the remaining officers of the Yokohama Air Group— swarmed around it. The Japanese disabled the vehicle and then set it afire with flaming rags and gasoline, killing two of the three-man crew. The sole survivor came out feet first through the driver's hatch, whereupon a frenzied mob seized and severely beat him. Many of his tormentors were oblivious to a hail of fire from the lagging Marine riflemen, and the next day forty-two slain Japanese lay around the hulk of the tank. Lieutenant Sweeny's own tank performed much useful work, but the lieutenant was killed. At 1640 a platoon of Company K assaulted across the causeway. By 2100 Tanambogo was "secured," though with many Japanese still in its bowels; these died the next day in blasted caves or savage close-range fighting with knives and bayonets.

Nearly one in five of the Parachutists fell, with thirty killed and forty-five wounded of the original 397. Total Marine losses on the twin islands reached seventy killed and eighty-seven wounded of about 1,300 men committed. The attackers seized twenty prisoners, but this number included fifteen laborers, who, unlike their brethren on Guadalcanal, apparently actively fought beside the combat troops. The rest of the garrison died defending the two islands, save about forty who reached Florida only to be hunted down, so ultimate Japanese fatalities on Gavutu-Tanambogo came to 516.

Counting seven sailors lost among the supporting naval vessels, a total of 122 Americans died to secure Tulagi, Gavutu, and Tanambogo; total Japanese casualties came to about 863. The struggle for these isles was a preview of what the island war in the Central Pacific would be like from Tarawa to Iwo Jima. The 1st Marine Division report of this action is equally applicable to all that followed:

> . . . the combat assumed the nature of a storming operation from the outset, a soldier's battle, unremitting and relentless, to be decided only by the extermination of one or the other of the adversaries engaged. Soldierly behavior was manifest wherever the enemy was encountered.

GUADALCANAL, THE SECOND DAY

On the morning of August 8, ground crews at Rabaul tended to the twenty-nine operational Bettys, nine of which had arrived only the day before from the Misawa Air Group, and fifteen long-range Zeros. Admiral Yamada ordered another strike with all available aircraft to sink the American carriers. At 0800, twenty-seven torpedo-laden Bettys lumbered aloft with all fifteen Zeros. Five reconnaissance planes fanned out ahead of the strike group, but again failed to pinpoint the American flattops, so the attack group turned for Guadalcanal. En route, the Japanese flew over the aerie of Jack Read, and at his warning the transports got underway. The crafty Japanese air group leader evaded Wildcats waiting over Savo by a wide swing to the north and then a diving turn to emerge at treetop level over Florida. Abruptly the twenty-three Bettys that completed the flight without mechanical difficulty burst out of the east in several groups to charge the fat transports just before noon.

The only three *Enterprise* Wildcats that managed to engage the enemy formations before they achieved attack positions claimed one Zero and three Bettys, but the Japanese suffered grievously at the hands of the ship's gunners. The Bettys rippled the sea surface from an altitude of only 20 to 40 feet in accordance with tactics that brought success early in the war against weak antiaircraft defenses. But now the Japanese aviators faced more heavy guns guided by sophisticated fire-control systems and, more important a proliferation of the deadly 20mm antiaircraft machineguns. On her last sortie in December 1941 the British battleship *Prince of Wales* carried only seven of these weapons, but now twelve or so adorned each of the sluggish transports, and from some vessels came a further barrage of automatic rifle and submachinegun fire.

Plane after plane burst into flames and pancaked or cartwheeled into the sea, but one Betty succeeded in putting a torpedo into the starboard bow of destroyer *Jarvis,* killing fifteen men and causing severe damage. Another Betty in its death dive smashed with a "blood-red" burst of flame into the superstructure of transport *George F. Elliot* at 1203. The transport began to blaze, and a ruptured fire main and a premature abandonment by a sizable portion of the crew hindered the fire-fighting effort. Eventually, destroyer *Hull* scuttled her in shallow water. *Elliot*'s losses are unclear; at least seventeen sailors and marines died. Only five of the attacking Bettys fluttered back to Rabaul, where the crewmen entered exorbitant claims of sinking and damaging Allied ships. Two of the escorting Zeros likewise failed to return. No American aircraft fell in this raid. In just two days the Japanese had expended thirty-six aircraft in attacks on Turner's transports. American losses totaled nine Wildcats and one SBD in combat and five Wildcats, two PBYs, and two B-17s operationally.

Ashore, Vandegrift defined the line of the Lunga River as the Marine objective for August 8. Colonel Cates redirected one of his battalions of the 1st Marines toward the new objective, but it still found heavy going in the dense growth. After excavating a trail to the lower slopes of Mount Austen on August 8, Cates's two remaining battalions retraced their path to the shore and marched down the beach to the new line.

The 5th Marines enjoyed much more favorable terrain, consisting of flat coconut plantations along the shore, but its movement remained hesitant. After a personal reconnaissance by Vandegrift in a jeep ahead of the lines that drew rifle fire at only one point, the regiment moved somewhat more briskly under the direct supervision of Colonel Hunt. The leading elements crossed the main bridge over the Lunga and at about 1500 encountered the first scattered resistance at Kukum. Thus it was well into the afternoon before the first green-clad figure stepped onto the plain where the deserted airstrip waited. The 1st Marines seized this vital piece of real estate by 1600.

Near Lunga Point amazed marines scanned the evidence of Japanese energies during the occupation. There were three antiaircraft batteries, ammunition dumps, radio stations, a refrigerating plant, an air compressor plant, vehicles, and stacks of supplies. Most of this booty was entirely intact, for neither the former owners nor the bombardment had caused significant damage. A number of trees lay toppled across a few of the tents and buildings in which the Japanese had lived and worked. Only a few corpses were found. The personal effects of many men littered the camps. Cups and bowls of rice, meat stew, and prunes sat at deserted tables as if the diners were to return momentarily. Some beds were neatly made, others disheveled. Canteens, mosquito nets, hats, shirts, and the distinctive two-toed *tabi* boots were spilled haphazardly, betraying their owners' hasty and disordered departure. The failure of the Japanese to put up any formal organized resistance around the airstrip is as baffling now as it was to the marines then. Not least of the discoveries was a copy of the current version of the main Japanese naval code—what the Americans called JN-25c—but yet another change in the Japanese cryptographic system by midmonth largely nullified this coup. The marines also seized an example of one of Japan's first radars, a shore-based air search model, which Turner loaded on a transport to take back for study.

By nightfall the two Marine regiments pressed up on the line of the Lunga and prepared for their second night on Guadalcanal.

The triumph of the marines on Tulagi, Gavutu-Tanambogo, and Guadalcanal vindicated the toiling of Marine and some Navy officers to create a practical modern doctrine of amphibious warfare during the interwar era when the name Gallipoli alone was deemed sufficient proof that such operations were foredoomed. These officers broke the daunting complexity of this maneuver down into its parts and found ingenious solutions to a myriad of difficulties. Clearly there remained serious areas of weakness, the most glaring of which was unloading.

The naval bombardment and bombing doctrine also contained major flaws; neither was effective, and the admirals would not learn until Tarawa that only carefully aimed and adjusted fire would destroy the rugged log, coral, or concrete structures in which the Japanese burrowed.

Within the 1st Marine Division these first operations exposed deficiencies in planning, patrolling, coordination, communications, control, and fire discipline. Some of these problems could be attributed to equipment, such as the pathetic radios, and much of the rest cannot have greatly surprised Vandegrift in light of the state of training of the division. Already some leaders had been tried and found wanting from platoon to regimental level, notably in the hesitant advance along Guadalcanal's coast. Overall, however, there was much to be proud of in the manner in which the green division had successfully executed its difficult mission.

As darkness enveloped the marines for their second night on the island the situation appeared well in hand. By dawn of August 9, they learned that these moments were short-lived on Guadalcanal.

4

THE BATTLE

OF SAVO ISLAND

"A fatal lethargy of mind"

TWO NAVIES

The Battle of Savo Island initiated a series of night gunfire and torpedo actions that became the hallmark of naval warfare in the Solomons for the next sixteen months. This first clash resulted in the most humiliating defeat suffered by the United States Navy in World War Two, and it stands as a prime example of the power of surprise in war. The proximate causes of this disastrous engagement were the astute maneuvers, designed to gain and exploit surprise, of a skillful Japanese admiral and a long chain of erroneous judgments and assumptions by his Allied counterparts. But the root causes of the thrashing at Savo—and much American woe to follow—lay in prewar strategic and tactical philosophies and their technical progeny.

At the center of the strategy distilled in the interwar years by planners in both the Imperial Japanese and United States navies stood a battleship-dominated fleet action that both sides expected to be joined in the vicinity of the Philippines. The Japanese, in fact, referred to this as the Decisive Battle Doctrine. Under the governing naval treaties, fifteen United States battleships would trade salvos with nine Japanese.[1] American strategists calculated the power of a battle line as the square of its numbers, thus giving themselves a better-than-two-to-one (225 versus 81) superiority. To extract the maximum advantage from their preponderance of big guns, the Americans intended to fight the decisive battle at long range in limitless, sunlit visibility.

Of probably equal importance to the character of the United States Navy in 1942 were its history and traditions. The trouncing of the Spanish fleet at Manila Bay and Santiago in 1898 represented the only modern American major surface actions. The U.S. Navy enjoyed no tradition of night battle and, unlike the British, did not extract the conclusion from World War One that a major navy must be prepared equally to fight by night and by day. Although the training schedules of U.S. warships included frequent night battle practice, artificialities and limited scale sapped their realism. Further, events in 1940 and 1941 seriously diluted even this expertise. Established crews became pools regularly raided for drafts to man the new ships commissioned under the expansion program. Moreover, President Roosevelt's Atlantic "Neutrality Patrol" precluded much training. For instance, the cruiser *Vincennes,* a Neutrality Patrol veteran, had last fired a night battle practice in February 1941. Finally, the Japanese held the initiative for the first seven months of war, which bestowed on them a major practical advantage. They were able to keep their cruiser and destroyer divisions largely intact, while a series of exigencies forced American commanders to constantly break up normal tactical groupings.

Japanese expertise in the art of night fighting grew from seeds of strategic theory in the fertile soil of the traditions of the Imperial Navy. Equally adept with sums, the Imperial Navy's strategists declined to present their outnumbered fleet for annihilation according to an American script. The Japanese foresaw a preliminary phase to the Decisive Battle, a phrase they aptly labeled the Attrition Battle. They intended to begin whittling down the size of the American battle fleet at long range first with their submarines. But the Imperial Navy also prepared to inflict further losses on the American battle fleet as it passed the Mandates with very-long-range twin-engine

---

[1]Principally, these were the Washington (1922) and London (1930) naval treaties that set the famous or infamous 5-5-3 ratio of capital ships between the U.S., the U.K., and Japan. The Japanese actually deployed ten "treaty" battleships at the outbreak of the war after refurbishing *Hiei,* supposedly "disarmed" under the Washington agreement.

torpedo bombers. For this purpose they developed the Mitsubishi G3M ("Nell") and the Betty, both with exceptional range, 1,864 miles in the case of the Betty, while carrying one torpedo. These planes demonstrated their worth by sinking the British battleship *Prince of Wales* and the battle cruiser *Repulse* in December 1941, and their presence would have an important, if indirect, effect at Savo.

Once the fleets approached close at hand, Japanese destroyers and cruisers would endeavor to torpedo more battle-line units under the cloak of darkness before the Decisive Battle. These tactics ideally suited the traditions of the Imperial Navy, which had employed nocturnal torpedo attacks with success in both the Sino-Japanese War of 1894–95 and the Russo-Japanese War of 1904–6. During the interval between the world wars, Japanese cruisers and destroyers honed their skills in realistic, large-scale night combat exercises. Reflecting the intensity of this training, sailors of the Imperial Navy proudly boasted in a song that their weeks contained no weekends, only two Fridays and two Mondays.

The development of weapons and equipment naturally followed from the strategies and tactics of each navy. For the Japanese these included an array of superior night battle equipment, including excellent optics, flashless powder, pyrotechnics, and, most important, torpedoes. The Imperial Navy recognized the performance advantages offered by an oxygen-fueled (rather than air-fueled) torpedo after World War One. Development work between 1927 and 1933 culminated in the matchless Type 93 61cm (24-inch) "Long Lance" torpedo. Its efficient, nearly wakeless power plant propelled the outsized 1,090-pound warhead for the unheard-of range of 22,000 yards (11 nautical miles) at 49 knots or 40,000 yards at 36 knots. Its American contemporary, the Mark XV 53cm (21-inch) torpedo, could deliver its smaller warhead a mere 6,000 yards (3 nautical miles) at 45 knots or 15,000 yards at 26.5 knots. Much more serious from the American viewpoint was one other characteristic of the Mark XV: it seldom exploded even after a direct hit. Three crucial defects bedeviled the Mark XV—the faulty depth-setting mechanism that caused the torpedoes to run far under their targets; the supersecret Mark VI magnetic influence exploder (designed to detonate the warhead beneath the hull of the target) that frequently either failed to work at all or caused the torpedo to explode prematurely, and the flimsy contact exploder that was often crushed rather than activated by impact with the target.

Torpedo performance not only determined the effectiveness of classes of ships, it also exerted important influence on ship characteristics and tactics. The Japanese could reckon on scoring hits with the Type 93 at ranges undreamed-of in the western navies. They mounted this superb weapon on the great majority of their cruisers and destroyers and provided spare torpedoes and quick reload apparatus so that their ships generally carried, and could actually use, twice as many torpedoes in one action as the simple number of launching tubes would indicate.[2] Japanese tactical doctrine emphasized the use of the Long Lance by all ships equipped with torpedoes in preference to gunfire. By contrast, the U.S. Navy viewed the gun as the master of the torpedo and followed a tactical doctrine stressing movement to effective gunfire range, which was assumed to be outside the danger area from Japanese torpedoes. Although American destroyers carried torpedoes, no American heavy cruiser and only a few light cruisers mounted torpedoes in 1942. At Savo the United States Navy would get its first taste of Japanese expertise in night battle in the Solomons and of the Long Lance.

MIKAWA'S REACTION

Even before the first radioed yelps from Tulagi indicated whether a raid or a major landing was in progress, Admiral Mikawa decided audaciously to counterattack with his surface units despite the presence of American carriers. About 0830 he signaled orders to assemble his flagship, *Chokai,* and the four heavy cruisers of Cruiser Division (Crudiv) 6 at 1300 for a tentative night attack on enemy ships off Guadalcanal. American radio intelligence intercepted this message, but it resisted decoding until August 23, long after its priceless value vanished. Initially, Mikawa omitted the light cruisers *Tenryu* and *Yubari* of Crudiv 18 from his order of battle, as he believed them to be more of a liability than an asset in view of their age and the state of their training. But the senior staff officer of Crudiv 18, Commander Tamao Shinohara, insisted on their participation with such élan and stubbornness that Mikawa finally agreed to enroll them. No choice burdened Mikawa as to destroyers; various

---

[2]The Japanese also possessed 24-inch air-fueled torpedoes of lesser performance fitted to their oldest light cruisers, like *Nagara,* and at least some *Fubuki* Class destroyers. These carried either 761- or 827-pound warheads at only 38 or 43 knots for 10,900 yards.

duties claimed all but elderly *Yunagi*, which joined the Striking Force.[3]

While awaiting the arrival of Crudiv 6 with four of his heavy cruisers from Kavieng—where they had been kept out of reach of Allied aircraft—Mikawa kept his staff busy. The admiral sent four of the five boats of Submarine Squadron 7 hastening south to Guadalcanal to attack Allied shipping; he also sought to reinforce the defenders at Guadalcanal and Tulagi. Seventeenth Army headquarters offered confident assurances that it could easily expel the Americans from the lower Solomons. The Army officers admitted, however, that they could release no troops for such a task without approval from Imperial Headquarters. Undaunted, Mikawa energetically gathered a unit of 519 sailors with rifles and machineguns and embarked them on *Meiyo Maru* and *Soya,* a supply ship. They set sail to aid their embattled countrymen screened by minelayer *Tsugaru* and two small escorts. At 1255 on August 8, Mikawa recalled the small convoy when the formidable dimensions of the American landing became clear. Just after midnight that night, while retracing their course, they stumbled upon twenty-three-year-old *S-38* (Lieutenant Commander Henry G. Munson) at a point about 14 miles west of Cape St. George. Munson managed to torpedo *Meiyo Maru,* which took 373 men down with her.[4]

During the morning of August 7, Mikawa and his staff also contemplated the dangers and opportunities the Striking Force might meet. The presence of American carriers and the absence of reliable charts posed formidable hazards. The Japanese hoped the 25th Air Flotilla would deal with the enemy carriers, while the commander of the 8th Base Force assured Mikawa that a battleship could take passage down the New Georgia Sound. Other concerns came from the ad hoc and unbalanced character of the Striking Force. The four ships of Cruiser Division 6 constituted an experienced team, but none of the other ships in this scratch force had worked together before. Some found the lack of destroyers disquieting. None of these factors deterred Mikawa from taking direct command of the venture to thwart the Allied offensive at its outset. About 1430, a jaunty Mikawa broke out his flag in *Chokai* and

[3]Mikawa's unit apparently enjoyed no official title. It will be referred to in this account as the Striking Force, following the practice of the United States Naval War College Analysis.

[4]Although the ancient "S" boats were trying to their crews, they were fitted with the older but much more reliable Mark X torpedoes with simple contact exploders that worked.

steamed out of Rabaul's Simpson Harbour. As Mikawa's Striking Force cantered south at 1937, they rushed over *S-38*, the day before her encounter with *Meiyo Maru*, too close for the submarine to fire torpedoes.

Dawn on August 8 found Mikawa eager for the answers to a pair of questions: where were the American carriers and what were the Allied dispositions and strength around Guadalcanal? Only aerial reconnaissance could quickly secure this information. Rabaul-based aircraft continued on the 8th, as they had on the 7th, to search vainly for the American carriers artfully concealed beneath clouds southwest of Guadalcanal. But on the 7th the aviators from Rabaul did find twenty-seven transports and several destroyers off Guadalcanal as well as three heavy cruisers, thirteen transports, and several destroyers off Tulagi.

To complement the efforts of the land-based planes, Mikawa decided to launch a search with his own cruiser float planes. He chose a patch of sea east of Bougainville for this purpose, carefully selected to mask his intent and evade carrier plane attacks, yet near enough to close Guadalcanal on the night of August 8–9. Three planes headed east for what proved to be a fruitless examination of the waters north of the Solomons that cost one plane to a *Wasp* SBD, while *Aoba*'s plane chugged south to scout the landing area. To further conceal his designs from Allied patrol planes, Mikawa dispersed his ships over a wide area after the float planes departed. This precaution proved prescient, for at 1020 lookouts sighted a Lockheed Hudson. Mikawa immediately ordered a 90-degree turn by all ships to confuse the plane, which disappeared obligingly at 1036, just as recovery began of the pair of survivors of the first three planes. With this task completed, Mikawa had begun to assemble his flock at 1100 when *Chokai* spotted another aircraft low on the horizon. The admiral thought this was the same Hudson, and when it approached at 1110, *Chokai* shooed it away with a few main battery salvos. Believing the Striking Force had been detected, Mikawa and his staff anxiously awaited the arrival of more Allied planes. To their relief, however, none appeared.

At noon *Aoba*'s plane returned from a very successful bit of snooping off Guadalcanal. Its crew tallied fifteen transports with one "battleship," four cruisers, seven destroyers, and one ship that resembled an "auxiliary carrier" off Lunga Point. Near Tulagi they counted two heavy cruisers, twelve destroyers, and three transports. Remarkably accurate, except for the nonexistent "battleship" and "auxiliary carrier," this intelligence confirmed the intriguing picture of a divided

Allied force. Still troubled about the location of the carriers, Mikawa broke radio silence to again ask the 25th Air Flotilla if they had been sighted, but he received no reply. The admiral and his staff estimated that there were no carriers within 100 miles of Guadalcanal and that they posed no danger unless the Striking Force made its approach too early. At 1300 he headed south at 24 knots and at 1600 left Bougainville Strait and entered New Georgia Sound. Mikawa's decision was bolder than he knew. His course threatened to place the Striking Force in range of three American carriers.

At 1642, Mikawa signaled his battle plan. The Striking Force would penetrate the passage south of Savo, torpedo the enemy units off Guadalcanal, sweep toward Tulagi to attack with gunfire and torpedoes, and withdraw by the passage north of Savo. The attack would start at 0130 so that the Striking Force would be beyond a 120-mile radius from Savo, and thus well away from retaliation by carrier planes, before sunrise. In view of the confined waters and the inexperience of his ships in operating together, Mikawa selected an elementary line-astern formation with 1,300 yards between vessels to allow each ship to individually employ its guns and torpedoes. For recognition purposes each cruiser hoisted white streamers, twenty-three feet long and three feet wide, on each side of the main yardarm; *Yunagi* displayed smaller streamers in the same position.

During the calm voyage down the New Georgia Sound, Mikawa's radiomen eavesdropped on a great deal of American carrier plane traffic, but as the sky darkened, the chatter trickled out, indicating the planes were now on board their ships. Sunset came at 1816, and at 1830 all ships jettisoned topside inflammables. As befitted an admiral of a service modeled on the Royal Navy, at 1842 Mikawa sent a Nelsonian signal to all ships:

> In the finest tradition of the Imperial Navy we shall engage the enemy in night battle. Every man is expected to do his utmost.

ALLIED PREPARATIONS

To secure the landing area against surface-ship or carrier-plane attack, Allied admirals devised a multilayered defense. They expected early detection of approaching ships by long-range search aircraft from both the Southwest Pacific and the South Pacific theaters. Carrier aircraft could supplement these patrols and constituted a formidable threat to any Japanese ship venturing toward Guadalcanal. Picket destroyers, equipped with radar, ostensibly guaranteed that no hostile task force could near Savo Island at night without the alarm being sounded, and a close screen of cruisers and destroyers provided a final and potent line of defense. Yet, within forty-eight hours Mikawa turned all these planes to ashes.

The air search plan fashioned hastily prior to the landing followed the theater boundary lines with the sectors generally west of 158 degrees west longitude the responsibility of MacArthur and the area east of that line the province of Ghormley. Royal Australian Air Force Lockheed Hudson twin-engine reconnaissance planes flown from Milne Bay on New Guinea performed the relevant Southwest Pacific search duties. In the South Pacific theater, the slow and vulnerable Navy PBY Catalinas drew sectors to the north and northwest, likely approaches for major fleet units from Truk, thus exploiting their range advantage over the B-17s of the 11th Bomb Group. Rear Admiral McCain, boss of all the aircraft in the theater, flew his flag in seaplane tender *Curtiss* at Espíritu Santo, which from August 5 played host to Patrol Squadron 23 (VP-23). From August 6, the old and small seaplane tender *McFarland* operated five VP-11 and two VP-14 Catalinas from Ndeni in the Santa Cruz Islands, while the modern small seaplane tender *Mackinac* set up a refuge on August 8 for nine PBYs of VP-23 at Maramasike Estuary, Malaita. Twenty of the thirty-two B-17s of the 11th Bomb Group also drew search duty. With much faster cruising speed than the PBYs, and the armament and armor to defend themselves, the B-17s prowled the sectors to the west, including New Georgia Sound, where contact with fighters was frequent. Both types of aircraft had ASE radars with the nominal range of 15–25 miles, when they worked. The search scheme is illustrated in the map below.

Not everyone was satisfied with the search plan as originally proposed. Fletcher requested that aircraft covering New Georgia Sound reach the end of their sectors at dusk and probe back on their return leg with radar to prohibit an enemy task force from sneaking down the sound after the dawn search. Turner, also seeing this natural avenue of approach, asked McCain on August 7 for a special search of the sector from 290 to 318 degrees from Malaita (which covered Mikawa's path), adding: "Southwest Pacific is responsible for this sector, but I consider a morning search by you is necessary for adequate coverage."

The concern over the air search plan proved well justified. On the 7th, Mikawa evaded the regular search planes, but Southwest Pacific B-17s raiding Rabaul saw Crudiv 6 and reported it as four cruisers

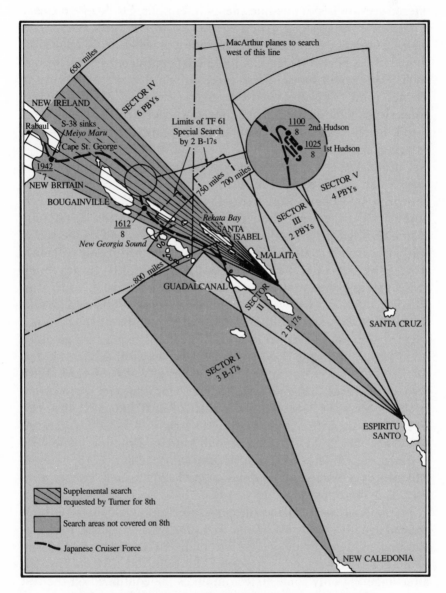

Mikawa's Approach and McCain's Air-Search Plan

and one destroyer 25 miles north of Rabaul on a westerly course. A second B-17 contact placed six unidentified ships in St. George's Channel on course southeast. Later that day, *S-38* sent a dispatch announcing that two destroyers passed over her at 1942 followed by three heavy cruisers at "very high speed" on course 140 degrees. The B-17 sighting reports of clusters of ships off a major Japanese base offered scant clues of possible enemy intentions, but *S-38*'s message possessed substance. A group of men-of-war sprinting southeast raised a number of possibilities, including a strike at Guadalcanal, though the reported strength of the enemy contingent argued against such a belligerent move. These three contact reports did not reach Turner until 0700 on August 8. *S-38*'s warning did not unduly concern the admiral and his staff, for, in theory, no enemy task force could reach Guadalcanal without first being detected by Allied search planes.

Unfortunately for the Allies, on August 8 the holes in the air search net identified by Fletcher and Turner proved amply wide enough to let Mikawa wiggle through. The weather impeded several South Pacific theater flights, including those in Sector II, the only sector through which Mikawa passed. The right half of the sector was not searched at all and the left half to a distance of only 650 miles from Espíritu Santo, 100 miles less than scheduled. In any event these planes would not have found Mikawa, because, exactly as Fletcher foresaw, Mikawa entered the area about 1700, roughly nine hours after the morning flights reached the limits of their patrol. McCain and his staff failed to honor Fletcher's request for an afternoon search of Sector II on August 8, an inexplicable lapse in view of the contact reports on August 7, especially that of *S-38*. With respect to Turner's request on August 7 for a special search from Malaita, after the war McCain's chief of staff indicated that two B-17s from Espíritu Santo scoured the area on August 8 with negative results to a point 315 miles beyond Malaita. But these planes flew a dawn search and reached its extremity about 1215, missing Mikawa by a tantalizing 60 miles, or perhaps fifteen to twenty minutes of flying time.

In the Southwest Pacific theater a different catalogue of failures yielded equally disastrous results. Standing orders required the Hudson that sighted Mikawa at 1025 to make an immediate report and to maintain contact until relieved. The pilot did neither. Instead, after lingering only some sixteen minutes, he continued on the rest of his mission before returning to Milne Bay. There he imparted news of seeing two destroyers, three cruisers, and two "gunboats or seaplane tenders" at 1025 in position 5°49′ South, 156°7′ East, on course 120 degrees, speed 15 knots. The pilot of the second Hudson that approached Mikawa at 1100 recounted upon his return that he found two heavy and two light cruisers, one small unidentified ship, and one cruiser similar to the British *Southampton* Class at 5°42′ South, 156°5′ East. He gave neither a course nor a speed. There were incredible delays in transmitting these two sightings to those who needed to know, Turner and Crutchley. Bobbing along in routine fashion over intricate communications channels, these urgent contact reports reached the former about 1900 and approximately 2130 respectively. By then Turner had what looked like an even bigger problem on his hands.

It will be recalled that at Koro Fletcher unveiled his intention to withdraw the carriers on August 10. Now, on the afternoon of August 8, he learned that the Japanese had employed upwards of "40" twin-engine torpedo bombers against the transports during the noon hour. The loss of *Lexington* at Coral Sea and *Yorktown* at Midway, primarily to Japanese torpedoes, made Fletcher understandably apprehensive about the safety of his carriers; but this alone does not justify his next acts. After confirming that the Japanese aircraft brandished torpedoes, Fletcher proposed to Admiral Noyes that the carriers withdraw immediately; Noyes readily assented to this recommendation. At 1807 Fletcher advised Ghormley and Turner:

> Fighter plane strength reduced from 99 to 78. In view of large number of enemy torpedo planes and bombers in this area, I recommend the immediate withdrawal of my carriers. Request tankers be sent forward immediately as fuel running low.

Thirty minutes later, Fletcher turned Task Force 61 to course 140 degrees, the initial maneuver in an evolution designed to take the carriers farther out of harm's way to the southeast during darkness before reversing course to achieve a new dawn operating position to support Turner on August 9—unless Ghormley sanctioned his withdrawal.

Ever since this decision—an undoubted turning point in Allied fortunes—critics have loaded barbed challenges, even scorn, into questions and hurled them at Fletcher like so many javelins. Why did Fletcher fail to consult Turner as well as Noyes before proposing a withdrawal? Even with enemy torpedo planes about, was there any sign that the carriers had been detected or that they could not continue to hide beneath the clouds southwest of Guadalcanal ("with no more severe consequences than sunburn," according to Samuel Eliot Morison)? If torpedo planes threatened the speedy carriers, did they not imperil even more the plodding transports the carriers were supposed to protect? If fighter plane strength stood at seventy-eight, wasn't this still only one less than the total available at the start of the Battle of Midway? Where lay Fletcher's concern for his role as

Expeditionary Force commander? Unfortunately Ghormley ascribed the retirement to a shortage of fuel in a message to Nimitz on August 9 and the impression stuck in some quarters that low oil bunkers represented the sole, or the primary, reason for Fletcher's conduct. This interpretation became a tool to further taint Fletcher's decision, as it later emerged that the carrier groups possessed sufficient fuel to operate for several more days.[5]

Years later Fletcher replied, in part, to his critics. He accented the facts that his command represented 75 percent of the remaining American fleet carriers with no reinforcements due until 1943, and that the Japanese could potentially soon put four carriers in the Solomons area to his three. Fletcher pointed out warnings of Japanese submarines approaching the general area, and he acknowledged that the superiority of the Zero over the Wildcat—and by implication the effectiveness of the defense of the carriers—weighed heavily on his mind. (In this context, it will be recalled that half the Wildcats in combat on August 7 were shot down.) Finally, he asserted that he remained bound by Nimitz's letter of instructions issued before Midway, which adjured him to be governed by the principle of the calculated risk, meaning that he should accept battle only where he found prospects of inflicting more damage that he would receive. Under this formula Fletcher's carriers could not duel with land-based torpedo bombers with the likelihood of inflicting a greater loss than they could suffer. These thoughts help explain but do not alter what Fletcher's signal on the evening of August 8 leaves clear: he regarded the preservation of the carriers as more important than any of his other duties, including his responsibility as Expeditionary Force commander to oversee the success of the landings and to protect the irreplaceable assault shipping and Vandegrift's marines.

As darkness fell on August 8, Kelly Turner faced some tough decisions, and it is only fair to view them in their contemporary context. Two days of air attacks had deprived Turner of a transport and damaged a pair of destroyers; he could expect more of the same on the 9th, now without protective air cover. Messages from Nimitz,

[5]The Naval War College Analysis shows that Fletcher's destroyers were 75 percent full in TG 61.1.1 (the *Saratoga* Group), approximately 42 percent full in TG 61.1.2 (the *Enterprise* Group), and 44 percent full in TG 61.1.3 (the *Wasp* Group). The cruisers were all 50 percent or more full and the carriers remained in good shape with the lowest, *Enterprise*, with fuel for three more days of operations.

warning of orders for Japanese submarines to attack shipping off Tulagi, diverted Turner's attention to that threat. Direction finder bearings traced the submarines' approach, and on the 8th there was a false alarm over the sighting of a submarine in the transport area. Other information available included radio intelligence reports locating *Chokai* and *Aoba* at sea and placing Crudiv 6 in the Rabaul area and Crudiv 18 in the Solomons. Radio intelligence analysts also learned that the 8th Fleet commander was at sea, suggesting the initiation of a major Japanese operation, but this choice bit of information was not broadcast in time to help Turner on the night of August 8.

Turner lacked another key piece of news for timely digestion. Inexplicably, only at 2333 on August 8 did McCain's headquarters issue notification of the incomplete South Pacific searches on August 8, particularly in New Georgia Sound. Ironically, although the scheduled reconnaissance would not have found Mikawa in any event, knowledge of gaping holes in the coverage might have prompted an enhanced state of readiness in the screen this night. Further, plans existed for supplemental coverage by the carriers on request if McCain's efforts failed, but, of course, without notification *Enterprise,* the duty carrier, only launched the customary 200-mile afternoon search. Two of the fourteen pilots extended their flights to 260 miles on their own initiative, while the other twelve went to 220 miles. Once again fortune blessed the Japanese, for had one of the latter pilots pushed on to 260 miles he would have found Mikawa in Bougainville Strait.

What Turner could review on the evening of August 8 was the Hudson contact reports, and characteristically he plotted them personally. The first sighting totaled seven ships and placed them neither in nor on a course for New Georgia Sound. Further, it gave a speed insufficient to reach Guadalcanal that night. Inexperience with the vagaries of aircraft contact reports led Turner to accept too readily the pilot's description of the presence of two "seaplane tenders" in the Japanese task force. A seaplane tender possessed neither the speed to reach Guadalcanal that night nor other characteristics to make it a likely candidate for fighting a night surface battle. The second report placed six ships about 7.5 miles north and west of the first location approximately thirty minutes later. This fitted consistently with about a 15-knot rate of advance. Piecing the two reports together, Turner concluded the Japanese planned to set up a seaplane base at Rekata Bay on Santa Isabel Island from which to launch torpedo plane attacks on the 9th, and that the second contact evidenced the return to Rabaul of part of the escort of the "seaplane tenders." Based upon this assessment, Turner requested McCain to attack Rekata Bay at dawn.

In view of the information actually available to Turner on August 8, his judgment appeared, and still appears, quite reasonable. When events proved this estimate egregiously wrong, Turner would be castigated on two mutually exclusive counts. One group of critics charged provocatively that Turner actually knew or should have discerned Mikawa's designs but did nothing. In response to this, it need only be pointed out that the contact reports were not susceptible to such an unequivocal interpretation. Moreover, whatever his faults, nothing in Turner's character or conduct suggests that idleness would be his response to such a threat.

The second school of criticism taught that Turner fell into the sometimes subtle, but always perilous, error of sifting raw intelligence for likely enemy intentions rather than possible enemy capabilities. Turner countered this argument by asserting that to demand more foresight from him would require that he multiply the reported Japanese strength by a factor of three or four and then intuit the complete failure of the day's aerial reconnaissance effort, including the special search he requested. But the admiral's mistake rested not in a want of clairvoyance. Turner possessed far too much competence as a naval officer to overlook the Japanese capacity to stage a night surface attack, and he acknowledged as much when he took the time to review Crutchley's screening plan in the evening of August 8. His real error resided in failing to follow the fundamental principle of identifying the most dangerous enemy capability and guarding against it. In this case Turner would have substantially discharged his direct responsibility, and just possibly averted a large measure of the disaster that followed, by personally warning the screen that the contact reports that day might well presage an attack that night. Such a caution might have gone far to dispel the mind-set so evident this night that an attack by Japanese surface forces was improbable.

Fletcher's withdrawal prompted Turner to call a meeting with Vandegrift and Crutchley to review the situation, an action that generated unfortunate consequences. Although a discussion of the disposition of the screen must be deferred, one important point must be noted here. At Turner's summons, Crutchley proceeded to the meeting in *Australia* rather than by small boat, for understandable reasons of speed and safety. At 2055 Crutchley directed Captain Bode of *Chicago,* the next senior officer, to take charge of the Southern Group of Allied cruisers, with a postscript explaining the purpose of his departure and adding that he might or might not return. Crutchley blundered fatefully in neglecting to inform either Rear Admiral Norman Scott or Captain Frederick Riefkohl, the commanders of the other two cruiser groups, of his absence. As a result of this error, both Scott and Riefkohl continued to assume all night that Crutchley remained in charge of the Southern Group. Accelerating the unraveling of command arrangements in the screen, Captain Bode decided not to have *Chicago* take station ahead of *Canberra,* the customary place for the senior ship, because he expected Crutchley to return and wished to avoid night maneuvering. By this choice Bode substantially deprived himself of the ability to control his group in the action that followed.

On boarding Turner's flagship, Vandegrift observed that while he felt exhausted, the two sailors looked ready to pass out. Turner explained the situation and his tentative decision to withdraw, finding that Crutchley shared his conclusion about the intentions of the "seaplane tenders." An alarmed Vandegrift graded his men on Guadalcanal as in "fair shape," but desired a firsthand check of developments on Tulagi. Anticipating this request, Turner had the destroyer-minesweeper *Southard* standing by to bear Vandegrift to Tulagi. With the understanding that Turner would await his report before finalizing the decision to withdraw, the general departed at midnight.

Upon reboarding *Australia,* Crutchley elected not to return to the Southern Group, because this would involve night maneuvering and because he thought "but a few hours" remained until the screen would reform at 0500. Instead, he posted his flagship inside the destroyer screen of the Guadalcanal transport area. He turned in without notifying any of his subordinates or Turner of his whereabouts.

As the Allied commanders conferred, the screening force carried out its patrols for the second night in accordance with the plan devised by Crutchley and approved by Turner. Crutchley's scheme reflected the vexing problem presented by the complicated geography, the diverse threats, and the fact that unloading continued in two widely separated locations. The eastern approaches to the transport areas off Tulagi and Guadalcanal are, from north to south, the Naggela, Sealark, and Lengo channels. To the west, conical Savo

Island squats between Florida and Guadalcanal, creating two entrances to Savo Sound, a 10-mile-wide gap to the north and a roughly 7-mile-wide entry to the south. As the 100-fathom curve runs within 1,200 yards of Savo's shores, even heavy ships could steam quite close at night and gain concealment from the island's 1,673-foot peak. Intelligence reports placed eleven Japanese cruisers, thirteen destroyers, two seaplane tenders, and fifteen submarines in the Solomons. Eight to ten motor torpedo boats and possibly some midget submarines were thought to be in the Guadalcanal area. Thus, Japanese capabilities included either a major attack or a light raid by surface forces.

Crutchley arranged his dispositions with the chief goal of containing any enemy threat before it could reach the transports. He viewed the eastern approaches as unlikely routes for a major attack, but fine avenues for destroyers or motor torpedo boats. Therefore, he sealed off these portals with Rear Admiral Norman Scott's task unit of light cruisers *San Juan* and H.M.A.S. *Hobart* and destroyers *Monssen* and *Buchanan.* Having deduced that the western approaches represented the greater peril, Crutchley stationed his flagship and the bulk of his cruisers and destroyers there. Ideally, the best counter to an attack would be a single concentration of his six cruisers. The thoughts troubled the British admiral, however, that if he stationed his ships together west of Savo a palpable danger existed that an enemy task force could slip by without being detected, and if he placed his concentrated ships east of Savo there still remained the risk that the enemy could steal past unobserved, with the added hazard that an engagement would then be in waters uncomfortably close to the transport areas. The lack of a joint tactical doctrine in his mixed-nationality command, and of a common voice radio, presented serious practical obstacles to a single formation. In addition, the admiral's experience had led him to conclude that groups of more than four heavy ships were unwieldy at night.

In Crutchley's mind, splitting the cruisers into two groups and placing one in the northern and the other in the southern passage around Savo would guarantee the interception of an enemy attack on the transports from the west. Crutchley retained direct command of the Southern Group, including heavy cruisers *Australia, Canberra,* and *Chicago.* These ships, and their screen of destroyers *Bagley* and *Patterson,* were old teammates and shared a joint operating procedure. They patrolled their sector by steaming at 12 knots on a line approximately 12 miles long running northwest-southeast, reversing course about every hour. Heavy cruisers *Vincennes, Quincy,* and

Astoria and destroyers *Helm* and *Wilson* composed the Northern Group. Captain Riefkohl of *Vincennes,* the senior cruiser skipper, maneuvered his group in a box patrol, steaming at 10 knots and changing course every thirty minutes.

Crutchley, who had never met the cruiser captains in the Northern Group, placed these ships together on the grounds that they were all American and would share a common doctrine. He neglected to ensure that the groups understood each other's patrol plan, and thus neither could be certain of the other's whereabouts at any time. Crutchley issued very vague instructions for repelling a night surface attack and failed to conduct tactical exercises en route to Guadalcanal. He did specify a rendezvous to the northwest of Savo where destroyers would gather to mount mass torpedo attacks, but this provision hung contingent on forewarning from air search.

Crutchley divided his remaining strength of nine destroyers between two roles. Groups of three and four destroyers respectively afforded antisubmarine screens to the Guadalcanal and Tulagi transport groups. The remaining two destroyers, *Blue* and *Ralph Talbot,* stood watch as pickets west of the Southern and Northern groups respectively. The SC radars they mounted, like all early radars, demanded a great deal of art from their operators to achieve maximum performance. A secret U.S. Fleet Bulletin in March gave the ranges of the SC radar as 4 to 10 miles, but few officers fully appreciated at this time how the proximity of land could drastically reduce even this performance. Under Crutchley's plan, each picket roamed a 6.5-mile patrol line, unsynchronized with the other, so that a large gap could develop in their coverage. Turner approved this plan, but like many flag officers in 1942, he knew very little of the recently introduced radar, and he relied on the assurance of a staff officer that 12 to 14 miles represented the effective range of the sets. In the aftermath of the battle the one error Turner admitted freely was that it would have been much better to assign four ships to the picket line instead of two.

With the two transport groups and the screen separated by distances of 15 to 20 miles, Turner split his flag officers so that one oversaw each group. Turner remained with the Guadalcanal Transport Group and Scott patrolled in the vicinity of the Tulagi Transport Group. This left only Crutchley with the screen. No flag officer was available for the Northern Group, and experience later showed it was not realistic to expect a captain to both fight his ship and control a task group. The only flag officers off Savo this night would be Japanese.

COMPOSITION OF FORCES

1. JAPANESE
Striking Force
Vice Adm. Gunichi Mikawa

HEAVY CRUISERS:

Chokai	Capt. Mikio Hayakawa
Cruiser Division 6	Rear Adm. Aritomo Goto
Aoba	Capt. Yonejiro Hisamune
Furutaka	Capt. Araki Tsutau
Kako	Capt. Yuji Takahashi
Kinugasa	Capt. Masao Sawa

LIGHT CRUISERS:

Cruiser Division 18	Rear Adm. Mitsuhara Matsuyama
Tenryu	Capt. Shinpei Asano
Yubari	Capt. Masami Ban

Screen

DESTROYER:

Yunagi	Lt. (sg) Okada Seiichi

2. ALLIED
Task Force 62
Rear Adm. Richmond K. Turner
Task Group 62.6 (Western Screen)
Rear Adm. Victor A. C. Crutchley RN (VC)

Radar Pickets

DESTROYERS:

Blue	Cdr. Harold N. Williams
Ralph Talbot	Lt. Cdr. Joseph W. Callahan

Southern Group: Rear Adm. Crutchley

HEAVY CRUISERS:

H.M.A.S. *Australia*	Capt. H. B. Farncomb RAN
H.M.A.S. *Canberra*	Capt. Frank E. Getting RAN
Chicago	Capt. Howard D. Bode

DESTROYERS:

Bagley	Lt. Cdr. George A. Sinclair
Patterson	Cdr. Frank R. Walker

Northern Group: Capt. Frederick L. Riefkohl

HEAVY CRUISERS:

Vincennes	Capt. Riefkohl
Quincy	Capt. Samuel N. Moore
Astoria	Capt. William G. Greenman

DESTROYERS:

| Helm | Lt. Cdr. Chester E. Carroll |
| Wilson | Lt. Cdr. Walter H. Price |

Task Group 62.4 (Eastern Screen): Rear Adm. Norman Scott

LIGHT CRUISERS:

| San Juan | Capt. James E. Maher |
| H.M.A.S. Hobart | Capt. H. A. Showers RAN |

DESTROYERS:

| Monssen | Cdr. Roland N. Smoot |
| Buchanan | Cdr. Ralph E. Wilson |

An indication of the material superiority of the Allies can be gleaned from the following table:

	Guns						Torpedo Tubes	
	8″	6″	5.5″	5″	4.7″	4″	24″	21″
Allied:								
Cruisers	52	8	—	48	—	20	—	32
Destroyers	—	—	—	32	—	—	—	111
Japanese:								
Cruisers	34	—	10	—	20	—	44	6
Destroyers	—	—	—	—	4	—	—	6

Note: The Allied total includes Admiral Scott's ships but not the destroyers with the transport groups. The ships of Crudiv 6 and *Chokai* carried one reload for each of their eight 24-inch tubes = 40 extra "Long Lances." *Yubari,* which may or may not have mounted the Long Lance, carried spare torpedoes for her four 24-inch tubes but apparently had no fast-reloading capacity, and the same applies for the 21-inch tubes on *Tenryu* and *Yunagi.*

THE BATTLE SOUTH OF SAVO, 0143–0150

An ally awaited Mikawa off Savo, the weather: a moonless, overcast sky with patches of light mists floating above the smooth sea, particularly to the northeast of Savo. On this night, as on most others, rainsqualls clustered over Savo about 2330 and then drifted slowly southeast in ragged formations, opening and closing corridors of visibility from north to south. These cloud curtains exerted an important affect on the battle, and Mikawa skillfully capitalized on those around Savo to cloak his approach.

About 2100 the exultant 25th Air Flotilla signaled that the day's aerial onslaught had sunk three cruisers, two destroyers, and nine transports and left other ships aflame. This erroneous news bolstered Mikawa's confidence and convinced him he now possessed material superiority. At 2312 his ships catapulted four float planes to scout the area and provide flare illumination. These aerial scouts soon reported three Allied cruisers south of Savo. At 2400 the Japanese stood to battle stations and increased speed to 26 knots. The Striking Force assumed battle formation with *Chokai* leading *Aoba*, *Kako*, *Kinugasa*, *Furutaka*, *Tenryu*, *Yubari*, and *Yunagi*. Although it was

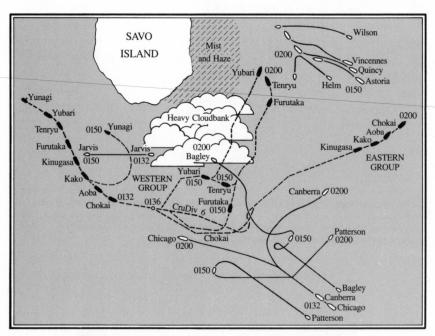

Battle of Savo Island, 0132–0200, August 9

a very atypical arrangement for the Imperial Navy, Mikawa prudently consigned the pair of light cruisers and his sole destroyer to the rear of the column in view of his doubts about their training and the inexperience of his ships in operating together.

Only three minutes after sighting Savo at 0050, *Chokai*'s vigilant lookouts spotted *Blue* steaming slowly across the path of the Striking Force from right to left at the range of 10,900 yards (over 5 miles). Mikawa calmly chopped speed to 22 knots to reduce wakes that might betray his presence and nudged *Chokai*'s bow left to enter by the northern passage. Oblivious to the many guns trained on her, *Blue* reversed course at the northern end of her patrol line and began to open the range to the south. As she did so, *Chokai*'s alert lookouts spied a "destroyer" off the port bow. This was in fact a small, wandering interisland schooner, not *Ralph Talbot*. Nonetheless, Mikawa reacted to the report and ordered right rudder to head again for the southern entrance. The entire Striking Force passed, leaving the two destroyer watchdogs quiet on either hand.

This was the first time—but far from the last—in the Solomons that ships of the Imperial Navy detected their opponents by visual means before radar discovered their presence. The primitive radars in use at this time suffered drastic reduction of already limited detection ranges because of echoes from landmasses, a phenomenon not well understood by Allied commanders, who were apt to repose excessive confidence in their electronic eyes. By contrast, the Japanese sought and achieved maximum performance from optics by utilizing specially selected lookouts equipped with outsized binoculars. At a more human level, on this night fatigue dulled the Allied lookouts and radar operators, and neither group had any idea if or where the Japanese might appear. On the other hand, Mikawa's lookouts were fresh and had the vital advantage of knowing where to look for Allied ships.

Mikawa shaped a series of courses to pass just outside the 100-fathom curve and to hide in the folds of low clouds around Savo. At 0133 he ordered "All ships attack" and increased speed to 30 knots. At about this time *Yunagi* became detached from the Japanese column. According to her skipper's account, *Yunagi* lost sight of the ships ahead of her and at the same time the lamp on the compass failed. *Yunagi* hauled out to the west, presumably to avoid an untimely encounter with her consorts or her enemies.[6] At 0134, look-

---

[6]Other Japanese versions state she was detached to cover the picket destroyers and because she lacked the speed for a steady 30 knots.

outs on *Chokai* saw a "cruiser" to port. This actually was the destroyer *Jarvis,* crippled by a Betty's torpedo in the noon attack, limping off on a solitary retirement from the area. Pressing his luck to the maximum, Mikawa held fire despite the close range. The disciplined ships in *Chokai*'s wake followed the example of the flagship, though *Furutaka* seized the opportunity to slash unsuccessfully at *Jarvis* with torpedoes. *Jarvis* remained mute, probably because her radios had been destroyed in the air attack. Two minutes later, anxious eyes on *Chokai* distinguished three "cruisers" slightly off the starboard bow at an actual range of 12,500 yards. Mikawa came left to course 120 degrees and ordered "Independent firing." *Chokai*'s commander, Captain Hayakawa, cried in a powerful voice, "Torpedoes fire to starboard," and at 0138 four Long Lances plopped into the water just as lookouts on the flagship sighted *Vincennes* to the northeast at the incredible range of 18,000 yards. *Chokai* broke the misty silence at 0143 with a salvo at *Canberra,* and soon thereafter aircraft flares blossomed over the transports off Guadalcanal, betraying the Southern Group in pale light.

Aboard the Allied screening ships this night, weary sailors and their exhausted officers sought rest. In their lassitude they ignored signs of Mikawa's approach. *Ralph Talbot* afforded the first clue at 2345 when she identified a cruiser-type float plane (one of Mikawa's scouts and illuminators) low over Savo heading east toward Tulagi. She broadcast on the TBS:

"WARNING! WARNING!
PLANE OVER SAVO HEADED EAST."[7]

In yet another communications failure, neither *Ralph Talbot* nor a relay ship could get this bit of news to Turner. *Blue, Patterson, Vincennes, Quincy,* and some others received the message, but only on board *Patterson* did it bring the skipper to the bridge.

Ralph Talbot's message reached neither cruiser in the Southern Group, for they lacked TBS radios. As this group steamed at a leisurely 12 knots up the northwesterly leg of their patrol line at 0143, the lookout in *Canberra*'s crow's nest faintly made out a ship

---

[7]TBS (Talk Between Ships) was a very high frequency (VHF) voice radio for tactical communications. It combined the virtues of speed and security, as its low power limited its range and thus the danger of enemy eavesdropping.

dead ahead only 4,500 yards distant, probably *Chokai* emerging from the cloud banks around Savo. For *Canberra* the action was fleeting but devastating. The bridge watch called Captain Getting and the navigator, but less than half a minute later lookouts spotted torpedo tracks as two ships materialized on the port bow only a few thousand yards away. As flares silhouetted *Canberra*, *Chokai* commenced firing, and *Furutaka* quickly followed suit with her guns and four torpedoes. About 0144, *Aoba* added her gunfire and released three torpedoes at *Canberra*; two minutes later *Kako* joined in with firing at both *Canberra* and *Chicago*.

The helmsman put *Canberra*'s wheel over to starboard to unmask the main battery, a maneuver that also physically barred the direct route to the Guadalcanal Transports. Within the space of four minutes, before *Canberra* could fully man or train out her main battery, she sustained twenty-four hits from the five ships that marked her as a target. An early hit, probably from *Chokai*, killed the gunnery officer and mortally wounded the captain. Other hits knocked out both boiler rooms and thus all power for armament, pumps, and fire-fighting equipment. Shells splintered the 4-inch gun deck and scythed down the crews before more than a few, if any, shots could be fired. The torpedo tube crews fared no better. Other shells entering low on the port side perforated the hull and exited below the waterline to starboard, causing a list that soon increased to 30 degrees.[8] By 0150, *Canberra* was coasting to a halt with a bonfire amidships. No contact report could be sent because there remained no electric power for the radios.

Chicago observed the flash of what may have been *Furutaka* firing torpedoes at *Jarvis* about 0142 or 0143 and then sighted aircraft flares about 0143. Two minutes later she saw *Canberra* swing hard to starboard. The watch on *Chicago* failed to grasp the reason for this abrupt maneuver despite the fact that three or four ships were firing

---

[8]Whether a torpedo hit *Canberra* during the action is much disputed. Her executive officer, Commander J. A. Walsh, and some of her survivors insisted she was. In particular, one seaman recalled in 1973 seeing a huge hole in her starboard side when he abandoned ship. Her navigator, Lieutenant Commander Mesley, did not believe a torpedo struck *Canberra*, and an Australian Board of Admiralty investigation agreed, citing various technical arguments that, in kind, Admiral Crutchley challenged. Samuel E. Morison believed she was, but the exemplary Naval War College Analysis concluded she was not. This writer tends to doubt *Canberra* suffered torpedo damage, if only because he is not aware of any other case where a single Long Lance torpedo struck a ship and there remained any doubt in her survivors' minds about the fact.

at *Canberra*. Two ships—"dark objects" in *Chicago*'s report—now appeared between *Patterson* and *Canberra* and a third had emerged to the right of *Canberra* when, at 0146, lookouts sighted a torpedo to starboard. Hardly had *Chicago*'s wheel spun hard to starboard when it was abruptly reversed to avoid two torpedoes spotted to port. This turn served to separate *Chicago* from *Canberra*. At about 0147 one torpedo from *Kako* erupted against *Chicago*'s starboard bow, heaving a column of water as high as the foretop and transmitting a shock wave that damaged the main battery director. A second torpedo thudded nastily against the machinery spaces but failed to explode. Even the Long Lance was not infallible.

Captain Bode reached his bridge and saw a "destroyer" (actually *Furutaka*) to port in a position to launch torpedoes, so he kept *Chicago*'s mangled bow pointed west. Despite the taunts of numerous muzzle flashes, *Chicago*'s gunnery department could not fix its sights on any targets. A pair of star shell salvos discharged to remedy this problem ended in futility when not one of the shells functioned properly. Just before 0148 a shell pierced the starboard leg of the mainmast and exploded over the forward funnel, scattering shards that wounded thirteen men, two fatally. Still groping for her enemies, at 0149 *Chicago* observed *Patterson* locked in action with some Japanese ships. *Chicago* joined in with her 5-inch battery, probably scoring a hit on *Tenryu* that killed twenty-three and wounded twenty-one. As the battle drew away from her to the northward, *Chicago* swept her port side with two searchlights that revealed only empty open sea. Inexplicably, Captain Bode kept *Chicago* standing to the west as the battle ebbed south of Savo. Worse—much worse—he sent no report of his encounter.

Captain Bode gave no orders to his destroyers, but both tangled individually with Mikawa. About 0144, *Bagley*'s lookouts glimpsed several ships. She heeled hard left to fire her starboard torpedoes, but the firing bearing passed before the crews could set the primers in the warheads. Her skipper kept her spinning left to bring her port torpedoes to bear. At 0149, *Bagley* fired four torpedoes, probably at Crudiv 18, *Furutaka* and *Kinugasa*. All missed. *Bagley*'s commander then chose to steer west to screen the entrance south of Savo.

Mikawa's descent found only *Patterson* of the Southern Group properly alert, with her skipper, Commander Frank R. Walker, already on the bridge. She sighted a ship at 0146, probably *Furutaka*, close in to "Savo," yet again more likely the cloud bank. Two qualities conspicuously absent elsewhere this night characterized

Walker's reactions: alacrity and intelligence. Sounding General Quarters, he tried to notify *Canberra* and *Chicago* by blinker light while immediately sending a radio message:

"WARNING! WARNING! STRANGE SHIPS ENTERING HARBOR."

Walker immediately turned to port and yelled the order to fire torpedoes, but by mischance a crashing roar of *Patterson*'s guns swallowed the command before the torpedo officer could hear it. Demonstrating a firm understanding of the vital importance of a contact report, Walker personally repeated the warning over the TBS. He then noted a torpedo bubbling by the starboard quarter, compliments of *Furutaka*. *Patterson* began a gun duel with *Tenryu* and *Yubari,* using her searchlight to illuminate her foes and zigzagging to avoid their fire. At 0148 an enemy shell knocked out the two after 5-inch guns, started a fire, and left ten killed and a like number wounded. The Japanese thought they had sunk her, but Walker's bluejackets smothered the blaze and one minute latter *Patterson* was again hurling 5-inch defiance at *Tenryu* and *Yubari.* With his fighting blood up, Walker spurned his screening mission to keep *Patterson* pressing after a group of Japanese cruisers heading east; his gunners took a 5-inch bite out of *Kinugasa* at 0156. At 0210 Walker received a message to head for the destroyer rendezvous and broke off his pursuit.[9]

Having demolished the Southern Group in about seven minutes, Mikawa was setting his sights on the Northern Group when his column split unintentionally into two jaws. Following *Chokai* in a gradual turn to 050 degrees started at 0144 were *Aoba, Kako,* and *Kinugasa.* These four ships became the Eastern Group of Japanese cruisers. At 0148, *Chokai* cast a quartet of torpedoes toward *Vincennes* at the range of about 12,000 yards. One minute later Mikawa turned prows to 069 degrees to engage the Northern Group. Meanwhile *Canberra* lurched across the original Japanese track, forcing *Furutaka* to swerve hard to port at about 0147½.

Crudiv 18 may have initiated a turn northeast on their own at 0144, or perhaps they saw *Furutaka*'s course change and followed

---

[9]This message was from Admiral Crutchley, who had decided to summon unengaged destroyers to *Australia* to mass for a torpedo attack. However, signalers garbled the coded coordinates of the rendezvous, and four destroyers, including *Patterson,* dashed off for the prearranged rendezvous northwest of Savo.

her. In either event, these three ships now became the Western
Group of Japanese cruisers. At 0155 they changed course to 020
degrees to use torpedoes on the Northern Group and *Furutaka*
announced their presence by illuminating *Quincy* and opening fire.
By this time *Quincy* and her sisters were in a desperate situation.

THE BATTLE NORTH AND EAST OF SAVO, 0150–0230

At 0140, three minutes before *Chokai*'s guns opened the action,
Vincennes led the Northern Group into a turn at the southeast
corner of their box patrol. On all three cruisers the captains lay
asleep in their sea cabins just off the bridge, and the crews stood at
Condition Two, a reduced state of readiness to give them a respite.
After plotting the day's sighting reports, Captain Riefkohl, the group
commander, calculated that a Japanese striking group could attack
Guadalcanal that night, and he admonished the watch on *Vincennes*
to exercise extreme vigilance. He failed, however, to pass his
thoughts or his warnings to *Quincy* or *Astoria,* and he still assumed
that Crutchley was with the Southern Group.

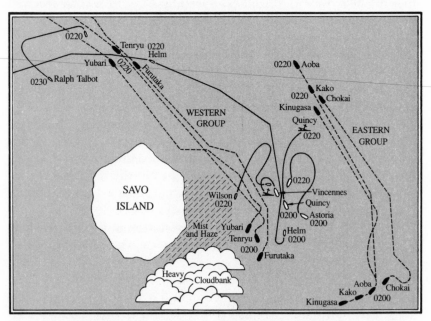

Battle of Savo Island, 0200–0230, August 9

At 0144 the watches on all three cruisers felt underwater explosions—Japanese torpedoes detonating at the end of their runs, another clue of Mikawa's presence—but all of them passed this off as an antisubmarine action by the Southern Group. At 0145 watch standers saw flares and *Vincennes, Quincy,* and *Wilson* noted gunfire to the south. With painful slowness they began to stir from their languor. On *Vincennes* a summons brought Captain Riefkohl to the bridge. The cloud curtains to his south granted him no view of stricken *Canberra* or *Chicago* or hostile heavy cruisers. All he could see was gun flashes from *Patterson*'s scuffle with *Tenryu* and *Yubari.* Riefkohl rightly assessed these as smaller naval guns, for indeed all these ships mounted only 5-inch or 5.5-inch guns. He received no contact reports or orders from the Southern Group, and although *Vincennes* received *Patterson*'s warning, no one informed Riefkohl. He therefore appraised the situation as a Japanese light unit in battle with the Southern Group. Reasoning that this might be a decoy to lure him away from the northern passage, Riefkohl decided to increase speed to 15 knots but to let the situation develop.

Riefkohl still waited at 0150 when shutters snapped open on three searchlights to the southeast and powerful beams of light fastened themselves to *Astoria, Quincy,* and *Vincennes.* He thought this was the Southern Group inadvertently illuminating him, and he asked over the radio for the lights to be extinguished. Only when shells began to fall about his ships did Riefkohl grasp the awful truth.

When *Chokai*'s light latched onto *Astoria,* Admiral Mikawa noted with pleasure that her guns were still trained in, or so he thought, and he ordered "Commence fire." Just before 0151 the flagship issued her first salvo at *Astoria,* while *Kako,* either just before or just afterward, let fly with rapid, accurate salvos at *Vincennes. Aoba* placed third in opening fire, but first in hitting her target, *Quincy.* The unhurried Japanese gunners expertly felt for deflection and then reached for range, and very soon all three scored heavily. The gunnery officer of *Kako* could see fires gnawing at the vitals of the American ships through rents in their hulls made by Japanese shells, and Commander Ohmae, Mikawa's chief of staff, could plainly discern through his binoculars the decks of American vessels alive with running figures. But after 0155, Mikawa's once-neat column formation further disintegrated. *Chokai* changed course to 028 degrees at 0158 and then came to 059 degrees one minute later, probably because Mikawa perceived the danger that the two groups of Japanese ships would fire into each other. Admiral Goto on board *Aoba* ignored this last maneuver of the Striking Force flagship and kept his ships on a more northerly course. *Chokai* began to fall off on the starboard hand of Crudiv 6 and soon steamed into trouble.

In the rear of the American column and slowest to wake to the impending danger was *Astoria*. In 1939, under Richmond K. Turner, she had borne the ashes of Japanese Ambassador Hiroshi Saito to Japan in a goodwill gesture which prompted a Japanese poet to write:

> The spirit, incarnate, of friendship and love
> Deep in the Heart of history.
> The record of the human world, full of changes and vicissitudes.
> The people of Japan, where cherries bloom,
> In future far away
> Will never forget their gratitude to the *Astoria*.

"Changes and vicissitudes" caused the Japanese to overlook their gratitude this night, but they were materially aided by the bridge watch on *Astoria*.

Astoria was neither at nor going to General Quarters when illuminated. By chance, Lieutenant Commander William H. Truesdell, her diligent gunnery officer, was already at the main battery director when he observed flares and then *Chokai*'s first salvo. He twice requested the bridge to sound General Quarters, but the supervisor of the watch, Lieutenant Commander James R. Topper, failed to act. As *Chokai*'s second salvo fell, Truesdell hesitated no longer, and *Astoria*'s main battery gave voice. This swiftly brought Captain Greenman to the bridge. Incredibly, Lieutenant Commander Topper still dawdled and only ordered "Stand by to sound General Quarters," but the quartermaster, Quartermaster Third Class A. Radke, had seen and heard enough; he sounded the general alarm.

Captain Greenman arrived on the bridge just as Truesdell loosed *Astoria*'s second salvo. Roused from an exhausted sleep, with no information on the situation and with his ship already in action, Greenman demanded: "Who gave the order to commence firing?" Lieutenant Commander Topper responded that he hadn't given the order or authorized the sounding of General Quarters. In a calm voice the captain said: "Topper, I think we are firing on our own ships. Let's not get excited and act too hasty. Cease firing!" Immediately after Topper agreed that *Astoria* might be firing at her friends, a bridge talker relayed a message from Truesdell as: "Mr. Truesdell said, 'For God's sake give the word to commence firing!'" At the same moment Greenman witnessed salvos splash by *Vincennes* and *Quincy*. He ordered fire resumed with the enigmatic words:

"Whether our ships or not, we would have to stop them." Four precious minutes had been squandered in getting *Astoria* set to fight, and only one minute later a salvo from *Chokai* started a fire in the hangar and the boat deck, making her an easy target.

Chokai began to score many hits, and for ten minutes after 0200 *Astoria* took a terrific concentration of fire from *Aoba, Kako, Kinugasa,* and *Chokai.* A cascade of hits from the foremast aft severed communications, wiped out fireroom number one, disabled most guns, and ignited blazes large and small throughout the midships section. Dense black smoke from the fires overhead and hits forced the abandonment of the other engineering spaces. By 0211, *Astoria*'s course bent around to 185 degrees, but four minutes later power flickered out and the bridge lost steering control. The gunnery officer arrived to advise the captain to evacuate the bridge because of the danger of a fire in the 1.1-inch clipping room overhead, and at 0216 Greenman ordered all hands gathered on the bow. Glancing out, he saw a searchlight and bellowed down for turret II to fire on it. The communications officer, Lieutenant Commander Walter B. Davidson, climbed into the turret and coached it onto *Kinugasa*'s light. *Astoria*'s last salvo missed *Kinugasa* but sailed beyond her to smack Mikawa's flagship in her foremost main battery turret, killing or wounding fifteen men. As the Japanese fire ceased, *Astoria* glided to a halt with flames consuming her amidships.

Of all the Allied ships near Savo this night, *Quincy* impressed the Japanese the most, but paid a terrible price for her valor. During the ninety minutes before the battle, her radar picked up one of Mikawa's planes and some crewmen heard it, but everyone disregarded this hint. In the two minutes before sounding General Quarters, *Quincy* sailors observed flares burst over the transport area, heard *Patterson*'s warning, and saw gunfire to the south. That was enough for *Quincy*'s bridge watch, and as the General Quarters alarm rang, Captain Moore stepped out to the bridge. When searchlights stabbed out at the three American cruisers, Moore flashed *Quincy*'s recognition lights and then, in short succession, received two orders over the TBS: increase speed to 15 knots and fire on the searchlights. Moore gave the word to commence firing, but *Quincy*'s main battery was not ready.

Aoba landed the first of many shells on the fantail just before 0153 and shortly afterward riddled *Quincy*'s bridge. Among other hits, one sheared off the bases of 5-inch cartridge cases in the fuze pots on gun number four, causing them to "burn like roman candles," killing all hands on the left side of the gun. Just before 0155 a shell smashed a float plane in the well deck and sprayed flaming gasoline that ignited the other four SOCs. Bellows of flame exploded aft with a whoosh, and soon the boat deck was crackling too.

At 0155, *Furutaka* switched on a searchlight and assailed *Quincy* from port, as shortly did *Tenryu*. By 0200, *Quincy* found herself in a crossfire from the west and east and unable to return the fire of the Western Group of Japanese cruisers because of hits that jammed turret III in train. Moore apparently realized he was being overtaken on both sides by columns of Japanese ships, and in order to avoid collision with *Vincennes*, he gallantly conned *Quincy* out of the American column almost straight at the Eastern Group while exhorting his gunners, "We are going down between them—give them hell!" To Japanese eyes, *Quincy*, afire from amidships aft, lurched out of the American formation as if to ram with her forward guns firing "with great spirit."

Japanese admiration for *Quincy* and her captain did not detain them from punishing her with concentrated gunfire, and at 0204 *Quincy* shuddered as two torpedoes from *Tenryu* slashed open her port side. Staggering forward, *Quincy* fired a salvo—probably at *Kako*—that arched over that ship to score on *Chokai*. One projectile hit near the aircraft crane with only minor damage, but two or three others passed only about 20 feet aft from where Admiral Mikawa stood and bored into *Chokai*'s chart room, killing or wounding thirty-six men and turning the flagship's charts to embers. Shortly after 0210, another hit on *Quincy*'s bridge snuffed out the life of almost everyone there and mortally wounded Captain Moore. One by one, all communications circuits failed and guns were silenced by hits or fires. At 0216 the ship whipped again as a torpedo from *Aoba* struck her on the starboard side aft, and about the same time the Eastern Group ceased firing at the obviously sinking *Quincy*.

As the flames receded from around the main gunnery control position, Lieutenant Commander Harry B. Heneberger, the gunnery officer, sent his assistant, Lieutenant Commander John D. Andrew, down to the bridge to ask for instructions. Andrew reported:

When I reached the bridge level, I found it a shambles of dead bodies with only three or four people still standing. In the Pilot House itself the only person standing was the signalman at the wheel who was vainly endeavoring to check the ship's swing to starboard to bring her to port. On questioning him I found out that the Captain, who at that time was laying [sic] near the wheel, had instructed him to beach the ship and he was trying to head for Savo Island, distant some four miles on the port quarter. I stepped to the port side of the Pilot House, and looked out to find the island and noted that the ship was heeling rapidly to port, sinking by the bow. At that instant the Captain straightened up and fell back, apparently dead, without having uttered any sound other than a moan.

As *Quincy* slid to a halt, Heneberger, nominally seventh in line of succession and soon to be the senior surviving officer, climbed down from his gun control position past carnage-strewn platforms to the main deck. With the ship twisting to port and sinking, he ordered that the few remaining rafts and life nets be placed into the water. *Quincy* foundered, bow first, rolling to port at 0238, the first of many ships that would soon give these waters the name Iron Bottom Sound.

The searchlight that illuminated *Vincennes* found Captain Riefkohl still awaiting orders or information from Admiral Crutchley. When *Chokai*'s first salvo kicked up geysers, *Vincennes* replied with a spread of star shells. *Kako*'s premier salvo resolved Riefkohl's remaining doubts. He ordered open fire, but shortly thereafter *Vincennes* suffered her initial hits from *Kako*'s main and secondary batteries, including one in the hangar that turned her five planes into torches. Seeing the Eastern Group of Japanese cruisers about to pass astern of *Astoria,* threatening the unusual maneuver of crossing his column's T from astern, Riefkohl ordered speed increased to 20 knots and the helm put over 40 degrees to port.[10] *Vincennes'* gunners slapped a hit on *Kinugasa*'s steering gear with their second salvo, causing the Japanese cruiser to begin to wobble about in the wake of her sisters. It also made the Japanese cruiser snap off her searchlight, but this little availed *Vincennes,* for her fires amidships served as beacons to Japanese gunners. As Riefkohl swerved his ship radically to starboard, he asked for 25 knots at 0155, but one of *Chokai*'s torpedoes permanently belayed this order when it walloped *Vincennes* on the port side forward.

Furutaka and *Tenryu* administered more torment to *Vincennes* at

---

[10]"Crossing the T" is a naval term for a situation in which a favorably placed column of ships is broadside, or in the position of the cap of a T, to a second column of ships approaching, or steaming away, at a 90-degree angle, in the position of the stem of the T. The column at the cap is tactically much favored because it can fire full broadsides at the enemy column, which can only reply with its forward or after guns.

0200, and shortly after 0203 *Vincennes* again wallowed as a torpedo from *Yubari* detonated in number one fireroom, extinguishing all life there. The gun deck by now was a charnel house of silent smashed guns attended by still figures. The gunnery officer, Lieutenant Commander Robert L. Adams, arrived on the bridge to inform the captain that there were no guns. Riefkohl then tried to conceal his ship with smoke, but there remained no surviving engineers in a position to carry out his orders. Still believing some of the ships firing on him might be friendly, Riefkohl ordered a new set of colors hoisted. Strangely, this was followed by a several-minute respite, but at 0213 *Chokai*'s searchlight beam again grasped *Vincennes* and for three minutes more hits sprinkled her hull and decks before the pummeling ceased permanently. Riefkohl passed the word to abandon ship at 0230, and *Vincennes* went hissing to her grave at 0258.

On *Vincennes*' starboard bow at the start of the action was destroyer *Wilson*. She saw the searchlights stab out and then observed the spouts of Japanese shells falling around the American cruisers. *Wilson* opened fire on *Kako*'s searchlight, and then shifted her aim successively to *Aoba* and *Chokai* without success. Her gun flashes provoked counterfire from *Chokai* and *Tenryu*, but she suffered only a few scratches from shrapnel.

A general masking of senses stymied *Helm* as much as *Wilson*. When the Japanese opened fire, *Helm*'s skipper could see the falling shells but not the firing ships. At 0152, *Helm* received Riefkohl's order for his destroyers to attack, which *Wilson* never got, and commenced stalking a strange ship to the southwest until a bolt of lightning revealed her as *Bagley*. Reversing course, Commander Carroll noted his cruisers now being illuminated from the east. Charging in to help, he passed between *Vincennes* and *Quincy*, narrowly avoiding a collision with *Wilson*. At 0210, *Helm* received a message that was believed to order destroyers to the predesignated rendezvous off Savo and proceeded there.

The twin Japanese tentacles curled to the northeast and soon found *Ralph Talbot* in their path. As this destroyer stood down the southwest leg of her patrol line at 0210, *Yunagi* briefly illuminated her from the south, disclosing *Ralph Talbot* to the Western Group of Japanese cruisers, which had begun their retirement at 0208. *Tenryu* snapped open a searchlight on *Ralph Talbot*'s port side at 0216 and began to fire at the American with *Furutaka*. Together they managed only one hit on *Ralph Talbot*'s number one torpedo tube mount. Lieutenant Commander Callahan divided his actions between his hopes and his fears: he flashed *Ralph Talbot*'s recognition lights while announcing his identity over the TBS, and simultaneously increased speed and zigzagged. The Japanese checked their gunfire, but *Tenryu* kept a searchlight screwed to *Ralph Talbot*.

Callahan observed a vessel passing astern at 0218 and brought *Ralph Talbot* right to bear guns and torpedoes. *Yubari* illuminated her and opened fire with *Furutaka*. In quick succession *Yubari* scored five hits that disabled the gun and torpedo controls, knocked out the radar, and hit the wardroom, killing fourteen, including the ship's doctor. In vain retaliation, *Ralph Talbot* got away one torpedo in local control, using *Yubari*'s searchlight as a point of aim. The enemy fire suddenly subsided as the Western Group got the order to retire, and at 0232 the illumination finally snapped off. Very fortunately, a rainsquall hid the listing and slowing *Ralph Talbot* as straight-shooting *Yubari* swept by only a mile away. After a brief power failure, *Ralph Talbot* crawled in close to Savo, where she effected repairs.

It will be recalled that *Yunagi* peeled out of the Japanese column prior to 0143. As she headed west she sighted and trailed *Jarvis*. *Yunagi* closed the range near enough to see the gaping hole in *Jarvis*'s side and opened fire at 0155, later claiming she had inflicted serious damage. She also launched torpedoes that failed to score. After five minutes *Yunagi* went to look elsewhere, perhaps because *Jarvis* proved tougher than expected. *Yunagi*'s only other contribution this night was the momentary illumination of *Ralph Talbot*.

At 0216, Mikawa consulted his staff. Although the Striking Force had suffered only trifling damage and still possessed about 60 percent of its shells, the unit was in serious disarray and had expended about half the torpedoes. Mikawa and his staff estimated that it would take about two hours to reassemble and put about for the transport anchorages, leaving only about one hour until daylight. They assumed the American carriers must be hastening northeast for a dawn attack. The fresh example of what American carrier planes could do to cruisers in the fate of *Mikuma* and *Mogami* at Midway left the Japanese properly fearful of the results of such an attack.[11] If they departed immediately they still anticipated an air attack, but it would find the Striking Force already 120 miles up the New Georgia Sound—and they might tug the American flattops within range of

---

[11]*Mikuma* was sunk; *Mogami* was severely damaged and required many months to repair.

Rabaul's torpedo planes. Finally, they were confident that a great victory had been won, and they had been assured by the Army that driving out the stranded Americans would pose no great problem. At 0220 Mikawa ordered a retirement.

If Mikawa felt content with his accomplishment, some of his captains distinctly did not. During the swing around the Northern Group, Captain Sawa emptied *Kinugasa*'s starboard torpedo tubes at the transports 13 miles away off Tulagi. He secured no hits but displayed a keen strategic sense in the heat of battle. Now as Mikawa ordained a withdrawal, Captain Hayakawa of *Chokai* importuned the admiral without success to renew the attack to sink the transports.

By 0340 the Striking Force had reassembled. At dawn the formation shuffled into an antiaircraft disposition, and topside all hands turned eyes skyward. Meanwhile Commander Ohmae gathered the reports of all ships and, after some judicious deflating of claims, concluded that they had sunk five Allied cruisers and four destroyers. At the same time, officers totaled damage within the Striking Force. *Chokai* enumerated six 8-inch hits and four 5-inch hits, including several duds. Her operations room was wiped out, her number one main battery turret was out of action, the aviation crane was damaged, and many minor nicks testified to machinegun hits. *Aoba*'s torpedo tubes were blackened from a fire, and *Kinugasa* showed the effects of hits in the number one engine room and the port steering compartment, resulting in a flooded storeroom. Machinegun fire had dented other ships, and *Aoba* and *Kako* were each short one plane and crew.

When no air attack developed, at 0958 Mikawa detached Crudiv 6 without escort for Kavieng via Bougainville Strait while the other ships made for Rabaul. Tokyo released the first news of the battles in the Solomons this day and claimed Allied losses came to one battleship, five cruisers, four destroyers, and ten transports. The news agency Domei crowed, "British and American naval strength has been reduced to that of a third-rate power." But as Crudiv 6 triumphantly approached Kavieng on the morning of August 10, it encountered one of the humblest units of the American fleet, the submarine *S-44* (Lieutenant Commander John R. Moore), which exacted the first retribution for Savo. Despite the presence of a plane overhead, Moore closed the range to a mere 700 yards and fired four torpedoes. Three of these weapons disemboweled *Kako* at 0910, and she sank five minutes latter. Her sisters managed to pick up all but seventy-one of her crew, including fifteen wounded. On this sour note they entered Kavieng at 1811.[12]

AFTERMATH AND ASSESSMENT

When the Japanese whirlwind passed, *Canberra* lay motionless with a sharp list and fierce fires amidships. Her crew struggled to organize bucket brigades, toss ammunition over the side, and flood magazines. About 0300, *Patterson* hove into view, but exploding ammunition on *Canberra* compelled the destroyer to keep her distance for over an hour. After securing alongside to port, *Patterson* sent over four hoses and a hand pump. With the aid of a rainsquall, the flames were being tamed when Admiral Turner directed at 0500 that *Canberra* be destroyed if she could not accompany a retirement scheduled for 0630. With fires preventing access to engineering spaces, Samuel E. Morison aptly described this message as a "death warrant." Commander J. A. Walsh, *Canberra*'s executive officer, halted salvage efforts and ordered "Abandon ship" at 0515. This was delayed when *Patterson* cast off to confront a radar contact which had encroached to within 3,000 yards. When *Patterson* obtained no answer to a trio of challenges, she clicked on a searchlight. This was too much for jumpy gunners on *Chicago,* who fired despite orders to the contrary, and *Patterson* replied in kind with three salvos. Fortunately, both ships missed. Commander Walker of *Patterson* thought the stranger's silhouette looked familiar, so he flashed the emergency identification signal. Captain Bode of *Chicago* grumbled it was the wrong signal, but reined in his gunners.

Patterson returned to secure alongside *Canberra* aft as *Blue* snug-

---

[12]Total Japanese casualties were distributed as follows:

	Killed	Wounded
Chokai	34	48
Kinugasa	1	1
Tenryu	23	21
Kako (torpedoed August 10)	71	15
Total:	129	85

Losses on *Kako* include one civilian. These figures apparently do not include the crews of three float planes that were lost, which would probably add six more to the list of killed.

gled up on *Canberra*'s bow. The cruiser's able-bodied men refused to budge until all the wounded were clear. After the living left, Turner gave *Selfridge* the job of burying *Canberra*. In a pathetic display of the qualities of American torpedoes, *Selfridge* fired four torpedoes at the stationary target, securing only one hit; three others ran under without exploding. She then pounded the hulk with 263 rounds of 5-inch. When thus engaged, *Ellet* appeared and mistook *Selfridge* for Japanese. In another example of frayed nerves, *Ellet* loosed a few shells at *Selfridge* before identities were established. *Ellet* then completed the task of scuttling *Canberra* with one torpedo. *Canberra* sank at 0800, and her popular captain, who was scheduled for promotion to admiral in a few months, died later that day.

In the two hours after the battle passed by *Astoria*, Captain Greenman collected nearly 400 men on the bow. The first lieutenant mobilized bucket brigades, which began to make some headway, but they could not dampen a severe fire in the wardroom and the officers' quarters. Unbeknownst to the men on the bow, a second group of survivors totaling about 150 men had assembled on the stern. According to the ship's chaplain, M. J. Bouterse, they "sat dumbly expectant, beyond fear or hope or any feeling." Galvanized by the executive officer, Commander F. E. Shoup, this group also fought fires, while keeping turret III manned and ready against the return of the Japanese. The sound of a gasoline pump forward about 0400 gave the first intimation of life there to Shoup. He began to think *Astoria* could be saved, as the 3-degree list was stable and the chief engineer expressed optimism about regaining power. A little divine encouragement came about 0400 when a drenching rainsquall rendered considerable assistance to the fire fighters. Half an hour later, *Bagley* skillfully came alongside in a bow-to-bow "Chinese landing." But the fires below continued to spread, and it was correctly doubted that the forward 5-inch magazine had been flooded. Captain Greenman feared the blaze would reach the magazine before the crew reached the fire; he ordered off the bow party. Within fifteen minutes *Bagley* took aboard the wounded and then the able-bodied.

As *Bagley* backed off, a flashing light from *Astoria*'s stern attracted her, and at 0545 she came alongside aft. After a brief huddle with Shoup and the chief engineer, Greenman organized and spearheaded a salvage party of 325 men. They mounted energetic efforts to fight fires, plug holes, and, most important, get steam up, but the boilers could not be coaxed into life and water began to ship through holes in the hull, causing the list to increase. The fires around the wardroom could not be quelled, and many small explosions occurred as the ship's list increased to 10 degrees. A much heavier explosion in the forward 5-inch magazine occurred about 1100. Within half an hour water began lapping through the holes on the second deck. At 1205, Greenman ordered the men off, and ten minutes later *Astoria* lay wearily on her port side and sank by the stern, twisting to port.

Fletcher's carriers reversed course to the northwest at 0100 while awaiting Ghormley's verdict on the retirement. The first flash reports of the battle reached some ships in the task force about 0300, but apparently not *Saratoga*. Shortly before 0330, Ghormley ratified the withdrawal, and thirty minutes later the task force put about to the southeast once again. Captain Forrest Sherman of *Wasp* asked Admiral Noyes three times to request permission from Fletcher for *Wasp*, whose air group was specially trained in night operations, to dash north with a few well-fueled destroyers to attack the Japanese; but Noyes refused each time to forward the request to Fletcher. According to Fletcher, he was not shown any reports of the battle until between 0500 and 0600 that morning. One or two members of his staff entreated the admiral to go back, but Fletcher rebuffed them with the comment that if he were Japanese, he would relish such an opportunity to get the American carriers with land-based air power. Fletcher kept *Saratoga*'s bow pointed southeast.

Admiral Turner observed the aircraft flares and the gunfire. At 0145 the Guadalcanal transports stopped unloading, and all got underway five minutes later. Commendably, the transports milled around for several hours without either collision or an exchange of gunfire between friends, despite the poor visibility and the temptation to imagine enemies near at hand. Still without word from Vandegrift on the state of unloading at Tulagi, Turner faced up to a crucial decision. Aware that the cargo discharge was far from complete and without information on the surface action, except for the absence of an attack on his transports, he displayed his mettle by deciding to stay for another day of unloading without air cover. He informed Fletcher of his decision at 0641 and added a last plea for air support from the carriers. Fletcher never stopped his gallop from the guns, and Turner got his answer at 1415 when he intercepted a signal from Fletcher to Ghormley by which Fletcher effectively abdicated the role of Expeditionary Force commander to Turner.

During the morning hours, Turner gradually became aware of the disaster to his screen, including his old ship, *Astoria*. Unloading halted upon receipt of a coast watcher report at 0840 of a group of Japanese bombers headed south. The passage of several hours without an attack left all hands puzzled.

Equally mystifying was the disappearance, without a trace, of the destroyer *Jarvis,* and only after the war did research disclose the link between these two events. After her fight with *Yunagi, Jarvis* continued her solo retirement and was seen by *Blue* at 0250.[13] After daybreak a *Saratoga* pilot spotted *Jarvis,* but Japanese eyes saw her too. At 0945 a 4th Air Group plane reported *Jarvis* as a "battleship" 90 miles southwest of Tulagi. Other planes radioed that the transports remained in the landing area. Admiral Yamada, commander of the 25th Air Flotilla, anticipated contact with the American carriers this day and at 0740 mounted a strike with sixteen Bettys of the Misawa Air Group and fifteen Zeros. Presented with a choice of targets, Yamada elected to send his planes after the damaged man-of-war rather than after the plebeian transports. At 1240, under cover of strafing fighters, the torpedo planes attacked and sank *Jarvis* about 130 miles southwest of Savo. In her last fight *Jarvis* clawed down two of the Misawa Group planes and damaged four others, one of which was written off in a crash landing. No doubt some men were left in the water when *Jarvis* sank, but they had slim chance of survival. No distress signal was received, and Lieutenant Commander Graham had jettisoned all boats and rafts the day before to lighten his severely damaged ship. Under the remorseless brassy sun the survivors drifted for a few days in their life jackets until claimed by delirium and death.

Turner's gamble did not fully pay off as alerts for air attacks haltered the tempo of unloading, except at Tulagi, where sailors and marines achieved remarkable progress between midnight and the afternoon of August 9. As the day faded, Turner gathered his depleted task force, and near sunset he sailed for Noumea. The marines were now alone.

Mikawa won a spectacular, if flawed, victory. His decision to pit his ill-assorted surface-ship Striking Force against a materially stronger foe backed by aircraft carriers was stunningly aggressive. Yet he complemented his audaciousness with adroit maneuvers designed to ensure surprise. Bolstered by faith in the supremacy of the Imperial Navy in night combat, Mikawa said later that once the dangerous approach phase passed and Savo loomed ahead he was confident of

---

[13]Turner sent a message directing *Jarvis* to leave by the eastern passage and for *Hovey* to accompany her. Lieutenant Commander Graham of *Jarvis* either ignored the order or, more likely, never got it.

victory. Certainly the Japanese never displayed their skill at this form of naval warfare to greater advantage than on the night of August 8–9, 1942. To these professional attributes of Mikawa and his crews must be added a generous supply of luck, as Mikawa himself acknowledged, for almost all the good fortune this night flowed to the Japanese.

Mikawa's failure to destroy the transports, ostensibly the object of his mission, constituted the flaw in the victory and invoked Yamamoto's ire. There can be little doubt that destruction of the transports by Mikawa, or by Yamada's airmen on the morning of August 9, would have ended the campaign shortly in ignominious defeat for the Allies. In elaborating on the decision to withdraw after the war, Commander Ohmae offered the view that the Decisive Battle doctrine underlay Mikawa's calculations. One of its sacred tenets was that the destruction of the enemy's surface fleet automatically brings a constriction of his command of the sea. It was only in 1944, when it was too late, that the Imperial Navy understood that air power could invalidate this axiom. Even without the elimination of the transports, Mikawa snatched the initiative from the Allies. It was up to Imperial Headquarters to exploit the golden opportunity he had conferred upon his country.

The United States Navy reacted swiftly, if sometimes questionably, to this debacle. Prompt notification went to the next of kin of the 1,077 Allied servicemen killed, and on August 20 the Australian government revealed the loss of *Canberra*. [14] But the U.S. Navy con-

---

[14]Allied losses were divided as follows:

	Killed	*Wounded*
Canberra	85	55
Chicago	2	21
Vincennes	342	257
Quincy	389	147
Astoria	235	190
Ralph Talbot	14	16
Patterson	10	14
Total	1077	700

Totals include seventeen marines killed and thirty-six wounded on U.S. cruisers. Losses on *Canberra* include one U.S. Navy officer. The losses on *Jarvis*, if any, are unknown, as she was lost the next day with all hands, 233. Her only survivors were six wounded men transferred from the ship after the torpedoing on August 8. Material losses included fifteen SOCs and probably two Seagull V float planes aboard the lost cruisers.

firmed only the sinking of one unidentified cruiser and concealed its other losses from the public for as long as possible on the grounds that this kept useful information from the Japanese. This rationale could not encompass the need of American Army planners to know of the defeat, but they also remained in the dark until October, when the full losses were publicly announced in conjunction with the news of a victory.

Like Pearl Harbor, the Battle of Savo Island triggered a special investigation. The Secretary of the Navy ordered Admiral Arthur J. Hepburn to conduct an inquiry, and he was joined by Commander Donald J. Ramsey. They flew out to the Pacific, where they interviewed Turner and Crutchley and as many senior officers as possible. Upon return to the United States they also interviewed Captains Bode and Riefkohl. Shortly after his interview, Captain Bode took his own life.

Admiral Hepburn's thorough report offered crisp conclusions: "The primary cause of this defeat must be ascribed generally to the complete surprise achieved by the enemy." As the reasons for the surprise he listed:

(a) An inadequate state of readiness on all ships to meet a sudden night attack.
(b) The failure to recognize the implications of the presence of enemy planes in the vicinity prior to the attack.
(c) Misplaced confidence in the capability of the radar pickets.
(d) Communications failures which resulted in the lack of the timely receipt of vital enemy contact information.
(e) A lapse in both communications and doctrine to timely warn that practically no effective reconnaissance had been flown covering the enemy approach during the day of August 8.

To these he added:

> As a contributory cause . . . must be placed the withdrawal of the carrier groups on the evening before the battle. This was responsible for Admiral Turner's conference, which in turn was responsible for the absence of the *Australia* from the action. It was furthermore responsible for the fact that there was no force available to inflict damage on the withdrawing enemy.

In assessing responsibility, Hepburn stated that there lay a "twilight zone" between culpable inefficiency and "more or less excusable error of judgement," and found censure definitely warranted only for Captain Bode. While obviously impressed with Admirals Turner and

Crutchley, Hepburn noted the failures of the SOPAC air search, but failed to recommend action against McCain. Hepburn also faulted Riefkohl's leadership, but hindsight suggests that Riefkohl was far more sinned against than sinning. Of Crutchley's failure to notify his subordinates or Turner of his whereabouts, which does not fall within the ambit of an error of judgment, Hepburn said nothing.

When the report reached Admiral Nimitz, he rearranged and expanded the list of causes of the complete surprise achieved by Mikawa: communications weaknesses; failures of the various air search plans; failure of the search planes that saw Mikawa to track him; erroneous estimate of the enemy's intentions; overdependence on radar; failure to respond to the presence of enemy planes; lack of flag officers in the cruiser forces engaged; and, finally, the "probability that our Force was not psychologically prepared for action."

It was mid-1943 before the Hepburn report arrived at the office of Admiral King. Captain G. L. Russell performed the initial review and, after a shrewd analysis, recommended that the matter be considered closed. "It does not necessarily follow," he wrote, "that because we took a beating somebody must be the goat." With that sentiment King agreed—in this case.

There is one final and timeless moral to be drawn from Savo that Turner, after reflection on the battle, phrased thus:

> . . . The Navy was still obsessed with a strong feeling of technical and mental superiority over the enemy. In spite of ample evidence as to enemy capabilities, most of our officers and men despised the enemy and felt themselves sure victors in all encounters under any circumstances. . . . The net result of all this was a fatal lethargy of mind which induced a confidence without readiness, and a routine acceptance of outworn peacetime standards of conduct. I believe that this psychological factor as a cause of our defeat, was even more important than the element of surprise.

This lethargy of mind would not be completely shaken off without some more hard blows to Navy pride around Guadalcanal, but after Savo the United States Navy picked itself up off the deck and prepared for the most savage combat in its history.

5

FIRST

DAYS ASHORE

"There is considerable room for doubt"

SETTLING IN

We must now go back to pick up the story of the marines ashore on the morning of August 9, as Turner learned of the Savo disaster and decided to withdraw. Apprised of this turn of events, Vandegrift gathered his principal subordinates near Alligator Creek in a driving rain in a scene he described for his biographer thus:

> Singly or in pairs they straggled to my CP [command post], the colonels, lieutenant colonels, and majors on whom so much depended. They already were a sorry-looking lot with bloodshot eyes and embryonic beards and filthy dungarees. They were tired. They did not talk much as they slumped to the wet ground under the coconut palms and huddled over their knees against rain hissing on a pathetic fire. Some smoked, others sipped black coffee from aluminum canteen cups and swore when the hot metal touched chapped lips. Most of them watched the beach and the parade of small boats landing survivors whose semi-naked bodies black from burns and oil of the sunken ships claimed the ministrations of our doctors and corpsmen. Even as they watched, the cruiser *Chicago,* her

bow shot away, limped past transports busily hoisting landing craft to their decks.

The picture of the overall situation could be divided roughly in two. One part constituted confusion—no marine knew the exact score in the naval battle. The other part rested on facts offering little in the way of assurance: only a fraction of the supplies and virtually none of the heavy equipment had been landed. Vandegrift told his key officers candidly of the pullout of the carriers and the imminent departure of the transports. Then, after directing them to pass this news to the men, Vandegrift summoned the traditions of the United States Marines Corps, for which tough spots are no novelty, and told his deputies to also inform the division that this would be no Bataan or Wake Island. Next Lieutenant Colonel Gerald Thomas, the operations officer, laid out the three immediate tasks confronting the division: form a defense perimeter around the airfield, move the supplies within that perimeter, and finish the airfield.

In the circumstances literally changed overnight, Vandegrift perceived the security of the airfield as his mission, pending a favorable turn in the naval and air situation. His experienced eye identified the most menacing Japanese move as a counterlanding across beaches at Lunga Point to retake the still-incomplete airstrip. The hasty departure of the transports left 6,075 marines in the Tulagi–Gavutu–Tanambogo area, including six infantry battalions, while there were only five infantry battalions among the 10,819 marines left to defend the much larger area on Guadalcanal. Moreover, Turner's transports bore away 1,800 men, mostly from the 2d Marines. The limited rifle strength on Guadalcanal dictated an elementary defense plan: stop any landing at the water's edge. Vandegrift anchored the right or eastern flank of the beach defenses at Alligator Creek with a short extension inland of 600 yards on the west bank. The line traversed the shore west to a point 1,000 yards southwest of Kukum where it meandered inland a brief distance along the first low hills in the coastal strip. The 5th Marines (less the 2d Battalion on Tulagi) held the western half of the 9,600-yard-long beach defense line. The eastern half of the line, from the interunit boundary of the Lunga to Alligator Creek, became the jurisdiction of the 1st Marines, less its 1st Battalion. With four battalions on line, Vandegrift's reserve on Guadalcanal comprised only the 1st Battalion, 1st Marines and a tank company. The southern half of the oval perimeter amounted to another 9,000 yards of dense jungle broken only by the Lunga and some coral ridges covered by tall grass. Artillery and support units bivouacked by the Lunga and the ridges to provide a rudimentary defense for this inland portion of the Marine enclave. Annoying infiltration by snipers and small parties soon led to the creation of a continuous line of outposts.

The scarcity of picks, axes, and shovels and a lack of any mines inhibited fortification of the beaches. Only eighteen reels of barbed wire had been landed, but the marines stripped wire from cattle fences on the Lunga plain to provide a thin barrier at points of likely danger. The defenses consisted of a continuous cordon of weapons emplacements and foxholes, backed by mortars with the bulk of the infantry detailed to reserves. Two battalions of 75mm pack howitzers (2d and 3d Battalions, 11th Marines) and one of 105mm howitzers (5th Battalion, 11th Marines) were dug in south of the airfield where they could rain shells at any point on the perimeter.

Elements of Colonel Robert H. Pepper's excellent 3d Defense Battalion added an important dimension to the above arrangements.[1] Pepper's men dug in a battery of 90mm antiaircraft guns emplaced north of the airstrip so deeply that when the barrels were depressed, the guns were completely below ground level. They sprinkled antiaircraft machineguns about the airstrip.

The available supplies lay piled on Beach Red, 3 miles from the new perimeter and totally exposed to land, sea, or air attack. Fortunately for the marines, no Japanese commander seized this opportunity. Using a procession of American and captured Japanese trucks over engineer-maintained bridges and roads, as well as amphibian tractors and lighters offshore, the marines segregated their supplies into dispersed dumps within the perimeter in four days of concentrated labor.

At the same time the marines inventoried their captured Japanese supplies and equipment, which included almost every conceivable item needed by a military force: arms, ammunition, food, clothing, transportation, tools, and building materials. Japanese food commanded particular interest among the hungry marines—tins of fruit, milk, seaweed, a tasty sliced beef in soy sauce, crabmeat, bountiful

---

[1]Prewar planning called for the seizure of advanced fleet bases in the Pacific, and the unique Marine defense battalions were created to provide them with antiaircraft and coastal defense. There were several tables of organization for these units, but generally each controlled three batteries (twelve guns) of 90mm or 3-inch antiaircraft guns, thirty .30 caliber and sixteen to thirty .50 caliber machineguns, and six to eight coast defense guns ranging from 5-inch to 7-inch. The defense battalions lacked infantry components. Pepper's coast defense batteries had not been landed.

rice, and even candy. Mechanically adept hands speedily put to use a dozen Chevrolet-type trucks with a fair-sized quantity of Japanese fuel. The division quartermaster gathered another type of Japanese fuel—sake and beer—but not before the unofficial distribution of a goodly amount. On final count, quartermasters reported four units of fire and perhaps seventeen days of food. The latter was calculated on the two-meals-a-day schedule that went into effect August 12.

While establishing the defense perimeter and moving supplies occupied most of his marines, Vandegrift rightly saw the completion of the airfield as the key to long-term survival. An unfinished gap of about 180 feet occupied the center of the field; engineers estimated it needed 6,700 cubic feet of earth fill. The marines possessed none of their heavy earth-moving equipment, except one angle-bladed bulldozer of the 1st Pioneer Battalion engaged with other duties. The engineers surmounted this challenge by mobilizing the captured Japanese construction equipment: six road rollers, four generators, six trucks, about fifty handcarts for hauling dirt, about seventy-five hand shovels, a quantity of explosives, and two exotic-looking gasoline-powered locomotives—dubbed the Toonerville Trolley—that pulled hopper cars for earth moving.

Turner's parting promise of aircraft by August 11 underscored the need for speed. Using Japanese explosives and hand shovels to loosen dirt from a small hill adjacent to the runway, the engineers transported the fill to the gap with the hopper cars and the trucks. There a Japanese air compressor tamped the earth down to prevent settling. By August 12 the runway reached 2,660 feet, and by August 18 it stretched the full 3,778 feet. Only 150 feet wide, the field ran east to west, with the west end very near the Lunga and the east end about a mile from the mouth of Alligator Creek. It was surfaced with dirt or, at best, gravel, for no metal matting had been landed. Engineers improved the approaches by blasting away dense growths of trees, some with trunks 30 feet in diameter. They improved and added to the dispersal and servicing areas begun by the former owners. But the field still lacked taxiways, revetments, and a drainage system when, on August 12, it was named Henderson Field after Major Lofton Henderson, a Marine squadron commander lost at Midway. That same day it received its first American aircraft, Admiral McCain's personal Catalina amphibian flown by his aide, Lieutenant W. S. Simpson. Upon inspection, Simpson declared the field fit for fighters. On the trip out, he transported two wounded men, thus establishing the prime means for medical evacuation.

Despite their hard work, the marines regarded these first days in the Solomons as a relatively pleasant interval in view of the ordeals ahead. In their idle moments marines found outlets for leisure activities as diverse as the taste and background of the 16,000 men ashore. As always with Americans, most individuals gave top priority to souvenir hunting. Some wrote letters on Japanese rice paper while others traded Japanese occupation scrip for Japanese cigarettes. One sergeant started a flower-arranging class, using as his text a beautifully illustrated Japanese book. At the higher echelons, Merritt Edson found time to read a few hours a day from an English translation of *A Short History of Japan.* He added cultural refinement to his mess with Japanese records played on a liberated Victrola.

Second only to souvenir hunting as a pastime was spreading the latest scuttlebutt. The naval battle became topic number one, and many continued to consider it an Allied victory despite mounting evidence to the contrary. A near second was the date on which they would be relieved by the "doggies"—a rather derisive label in the Marine lexicon for Army troops. The marines looked upon themselves as elite assault troops who in the natural order of the universe should be withdrawn to prepare for the next attack, perhaps in Australia or New Zealand, where the grateful citizenry would properly acknowledge the new South Pacific heroes.

Two incidents afforded comic relief. The marines held as an article of faith that no Japanese soldier could get his tongue around an English *L.* Thus passwords ran to the likes of "polyglot," "Lilliputian," and "bilious." A few nights after the landing a small party of Japanese, or perhaps some starving laborers or overactive imaginations, provoked a good deal of indiscriminate firing near the airstrip. While it was not a unique episode in these first anxious nights ashore, the marines remembered it because fervent cries of the password by endangered leathernecks filled the night. It became ever afterward known as "Hallelujah Night." The second incident involved the 200–300 head of cattle that, with the wire removed from their fences, roamed the perimeter as a kind of mobile food dump. Inevitably a Japanese bomb started a stampede. Respecters of neither rank nor dignity, the terrified bovines crashed straight through the command post of the 1st Marines, leaving a wake of destruction. It was one of the most bizarre episodes of the war in the South Pacific.

No Japanese aircraft appeared on August 9, and those overhead on the following day did not bomb. Six Zeros strafed on the 11th, and three bombers dribbled bombs into the jungle west of the perimeter on the 12th. Almost daily raids about noon became a feature of the next week, and although they achieved little material damage, the

Japanese airmen leached away at the defenders morale. The bombers initially attacked at only 10,000 feet, but when a battery of 90mm antiaircraft guns got into action the bombers flew at a more respectable 25,000 feet. The engineers obtained their first practice at filling craters when eight visitors on the 18th left several holes in the newly extended runway. More ominously, on the 15th the marines captured woven baskets released by Japanese aircraft with food, ammunition, and a message that translated: "Help is on the way! Banzai!"

The Imperial Navy had other ways to remind the marines of their isolation. On the 12th, two Higgins boats and a tank lighter left Guadalcanal on the inaugural run of a communications and mail service to Tulagi. As they neared Tulagi the black shape of an I-boat rose from the choppy waters and white-clad submariners scampered to the deck gun in plain sight of horrified marines ashore. The boats strained to maximum speed, but soon the leading Higgins boat began spewing blue smoke and lost way. The coxswain of the other Higgins boat laid his craft alongside the now crawling leader and its passengers tumbled over. Shots from the submarine boxed in the overloaded boat ahead and astern as it surged forward. The boat's future looked bleak, but then suddenly four water spouts bracketed the I-boat. The Marine pack howitzer battery responsible for the splashes, Battery E, 11th Marines, further demonstrated its accuracy with a second volley that appeared to score a hit. The Japanese crewmen scrambled below and their boat dived. By day and night the sub and her sister, presumably *I-122* and *123,* now collectively dubbed "Oscar" by the marines, surfaced to toss shells into the perimeter. On the 13th when one insolently popped up in broad daylight to prepare to fire, a few rounds from 75mm half-tracks caused her skipper to think better of the plan.

Vandegrift prescribed vigorous patrolling with the dual purpose of securing the perimeter and locating the original Japanese garrison so it could be destroyed. Some confusion arose initially from scattered daily contacts with partially armed and uniformed orientals, who proved to be Korean laborers. Called "termites" by the marines, some of these individuals surrendered. Many more, abandoned by their Japanese masters, probably starved to death in the jungle.

When probes from the 5th Marines ran into firm resistance at the Matanikau River on August 9 and 10, First Sergeant Steven Custer, enlisted leader of the division intelligence section, decided to take a combat patrol to gather more definite information on the Japanese concentration. Coincidentally, a Japanese sailor had been captured. His interrogators found him surly, but with the benefit of some alcoholic tongue lubricant, he sputtered out the possibility that others in his group might be induced to surrender. Lieutenant Colonel Frank Goettge, the division intelligence officer, quickly pieced this comment together with a tale that a white flag had been seen west of the Matanikau, and elected to lead the patrol himself. From a straight combat mission, the patrol was recast by the prospect of capturing a few prisoners and by a humanitarian concern to gather the Korean laborers in the bush. It finally numbered twenty-five men, including many key members of the division and the 5th Marines intelligence sections and Lieutenant Commander Malcolm Pratt, the surgeon of the 5th Marines.

Having secured Vandegrift's reluctant permission for this venture, Goettge led the patrol out by boat from Kukum after dark on August 12, to a fate that remains unclear. It seems probable that the party came ashore too close to the Matanikau. As Goettge stepped into the brush off the beach with the talkative sailor on a leash, a burst of shots killed them both. With the patrol pinned down on the beach and quickly decimated, command devolved upon Captain Wilfred Ringer, who sent a runner for help. The messenger regained Marine lines near dawn, exhausted and badly cut up from the swim and crawl over coral. Two other men who escaped as the Japanese overwhelmed the last of the patrol soon joined him. One of these latter individuals recounted a lurid tale of seeing the glint of swords or bayonets as the Japanese hacked to death wounded marines. When the news reached Colonel Hunt, he dispatched his reinforced Company L, which landed west of Point Cruz and swept back without contact. Neither the patrol nor subsequent investigation adduced definite information on the fate of all the men who went with Goettge, but tidal graves, a few helmets, and Dr. Pratt's empty medical bag seemed to supply the answer.

Later events suggested the Japanese sailor was probably telling the truth as he knew it. Japanese battle ethics did not admit of surrender, so instruction in this eventuality was scarce to nonexistent. Consequently, those Japanese prisoners who talked were considered reliable sources of information. The "white flag" was most likely only a regular battle flag that, by coincidence, was furled to conceal its central red disk. Lieutenant Colonel Edmund J. Buckley from the 11th Marines got the job of trying to reconstruct the division intelligence section.

For thirty-six years this story seemed bad enough, but then new facts disclosed its potential for far more than a local disaster. The missing included the Japanese interpreter for the 5th Marines, Lieutenant Ralph Corry, who performed consular work in Japan before the war. But Corry more recently had labored at breaking Japanese codes in Washington, D.C. Unsatisfied with this personal contribution, he volunteered for more active service and somehow gained permission to join the 1st Marine Division. Had he been captured and compelled to talk, the effects would have been incalculably great on the conduct of the war in the Pacific.

On the morning of August 15, Marine sentries were startled to see two marching files of scantily clad natives approaching the perimeter from the east led by a tall, bearded white man in bush hat, ragged shirt and trousers, and a pair of immaculately shined oxford shoes. The leader proved to be Captain Martin Clemens, the official representative of His Majesty's Government. Some of his native police accompanied Clemens, and the chief of his scouts, Sergeant Major Jacob Vouza, joined him shortly. Vandegrift quickly accepted Clemens's offer of his services and those of his loyal followers, who provided an invaluable source of intelligence and guides. Eventually Clemens divided the island into five districts, each with its company of scouts. Clemens's scouts proved the bane of the Imperial Army on Guadalcanal, much as the coast watchers were the bane of the Imperial Navy in the Solomons.

Near dusk of August 15, for the first time since Turner's withdrawal, vessels wearing the Stars and Stripes stood into Lunga Roads. These were the elderly destroyer transports *Colhoun, Little, Gregory,* and *McKean.* Sent by Ghormley's order, they carried the seeds of an air base in the form of fuel, munitions, tools, and spare parts. They also landed Ensign George W. Polk and 110 men of "Cub One."[2] Unlettered in the required skills but willing, these men would perform yeoman efforts in fueling and arming the first aircraft. Stepping ashore too was Lieutenant Colonel Charles H. Hayes, an old hand at running primitive airstrips. He carried a letter from Admiral McCain promising aircraft by the 18th or 19th.

On August 16, destroyer *Oite* dropped the first Japanese reinforcement of Guadalcanal at Tassafaronga Point: 113 men of the 5th Yokosuka Special Naval Landing Force under a Lieutenant Takahashi. Captain Monzen acknowledged their arrival and two days later signaled Rabaul that he had gathered about 100 fighting men and approximately 328 workers in the area 1,100 yards west of Lunga

---

[2]"Cub" was the code name for specially organized advanced fleet fuel and supply bases of intermediate size. An explanation follows below in the text.

Point, though he admitted another 1,000 workers remained scattered in the jungle. That night in an ominous new tactic the Imperial Navy afforded the marines their first taste of being on the receiving end of naval gunfire. Three destroyers fired a post-midnight salute at both Tulagi and Guadalcanal.

FIRST ACTION ON THE MATANIKAU

After Goettge failed to return from his patrol, Vandegrift began contemplating a strike at the enemy concentration west of the Matanikau. Recognition that the potential profit from any operation with substantial forces beyond the perimeter had to be weighed against the risk of jeopardizing the security of the airfield tempered his aggressiveness. Thus, a week elapsed before Vandegrift found that the balancing of these factors permitted the 5th Marines to set out for the first battle on the Matanikau. Three companies each drew a separate role: Captain William B. Hawkins's Company B would occupy Japanese attention with an attack across the sandbar at the mouth of the Matanikau; Company L under Captain Lyman D. Spurlock would envelop the defenders' position by crossing the Matanikau well inland and advancing north on the west bank of the river; and meanwhile, Captain Bert W. Hardy's Company I would be boated to the west of Kokumbona to foreclose escape in that direction.

On August 18, Spurlock's company initiated the operation by advancing to a crossing point on the Matanikau about 1,000 yards inland, killing ten Japanese en route. At dark they nestled down on the west side of the river. During the afternoon, Hawkins's men ambled to a point close to the river mouth. On the morning of August 19, a Marine artillery preparation greeted the Japanese at the Matanikau with the sunrise. Hawkins's men found the enemy at the sandbar would not budge, and Spurlock discovered the jungle gave way only slightly more easily than the Japanese to his front. Almost immediately, small-arms fire from a ridge several hundred yards to the west raked Company L, felling a platoon leader; Lieutenant George H. Mead, Jr., the company's executive officer, took charge of the platoon, but he too was killed.

Spurlock deftly wheeled his platoons to fend off Japanese trying to obstruct his advance by fire and small probes from the west while making steady, if slow, progress north through dense growth. It was

1400 before Company L began to spread a net around Matanikau village. Spurlock, hearing Japanese voices chattering and yells of "Banzai," which confirmed reports from scouts of an impending enemy charge, quickly adjusted his front so that when some of the Japanese suddenly boiled into a clearing with fixed bayonets, hot lead delivered with devastating accuracy at short range met their cold steel. A firefight with the remaining dug-in defenders rattled until 1600, when the marines entered the village to find sixty-five dead Japanese. Company L counted its losses at four dead and eleven wounded.

Company I contributed nothing to this attack, but its day was nonetheless full of adventure. Accompanied by Lieutenant Colonel William J. Whaling, the executive officer of the 5th Marines, the boats laden with Company I departed Kukum at 0430. They attracted rifle and machinegun fire from the coast, and as they made their way farther west, the Japanese destroyers, which lingered after their bombardment, flung salvos in their direction. The company landed successfully and rooted out the Japanese in Kokumbona village, driving the surviving defenders into the hills at a cost of one fatality. Company I then returned by boat to Kukum at 1700. The newly arrived Lieutenant Takahashi claimed credit for driving Company I back into the sea and boasted of capturing three landing craft and one machinegun.

This first battle of the Matanikau inflicted some losses on the Japanese, but proved of no great import to the campaign. It harbored lessons about terrain and control difficulties as well as a caution about excessively complicated schemes of maneuver, but the Marine command failed to grasp these fully. On the credit side, Company L acquitted itself very well in carrying the objective alone. The daylight bayonet charge—squandering strength far better invested in a coordinated defense—revealed the Japanese propensity for what the marines dismissed as the "tactically dramatic." Japanese preference for the offense would be shortly demonstrated on a much grander scale.

"NOT MUCH OF ANYTHING HAS BEEN DONE"

Dogged by erratic communications, Admiral Ghormley gained his first inklings of the Battle of Savo Island from Fletcher. COMSOPAC responded by ordering the Ndeni operation suspended, if it was not already underway, and by authorizing Fletcher and Turner to withdraw. Not until Turner's arrival in Noumea on the 14th did Ghormley learn details of the landing and the disaster off Savo.

Ghormley's sources are not clear, but on the morning of August 9 he warned Turner and Vandegrift of a Japanese counterlanding force en route to Guadalcanal. To confront this threat, he asked MacArthur on the 10th to dispatch some submarines to prowl the Solomons, and two days later he requested air strikes on the shipping concentration at Rabaul. MacArthur explained he possessed no spare undersea craft, but ordered his bombers to Rabaul. Ghormley's petition to Nimitz for submarines produced another rebuff. On the 11th, Ghormley formally charged Fletcher with the task of protecting the landing area and its lines of communications. That same day, Vandegrift radioed his first situation report and requested another regiment.

At Nimitz's headquarters the intelligence staff culled hints from Japanese communications as to the dimensions and source of any reaction to the landing. These nautical detectives noted the use of a special code, the general pattern of radio traffic, messages to the harbormaster at Truk requesting berthing space for major units, and partial decodes of signals revealing the transfer of planes from other ships to the big carriers *Shokaku* and *Zuikaku* and light carrier *Ryujo*. From these strands they wove together a picture of the assembly of a Japanese task force, including carriers and battleships, for a mission in the vicinity of the Solomons. On the 12th, CINCPAC predicted the arrival of a major contingent from the Combined Fleet in the South Pacific within a week to ten days.

During the first days of "Watchtower," Ghormley received some rations of good news. On the day of the landing, Nimitz announced he was sending the *Hornet* group south to replace the *Wasp* group. After Savo, Admiral King hastened the movement of the new fast battleship *South Dakota* to the Pacific and also informed Nimitz that the War Department had empowered General Harmon to divert aircraft en route to Australia for use in the South Pacific if they could be more effectively used by Ghormley.

On the 15th the Joint Chiefs of Staff proclaimed to Ghormley their belief that Task One was substantially accomplished and that it was time to prepare for the early execution of Task Two, involving the seizure of Lae, Salamaua, and the northeast coast of New Guinea. In his reply on the 17th, Ghormley sought to correct what he mildly termed a "misconception" of the situation by stating that no further advance was possible without air and ground reinforcements. Lacking these, he bluntly told his superiors, a reasonable doubt existed that the marines could hold Guadalcanal.

General Harmon likewise attempted to inject reality into thinking in Washington. The failure to provide for the rapid exploitation of Henderson Field, as manifested by the lack of aviation engineers with the landing force or the necessary equipment and supplies, generated his concern over Navy management of "Watchtower." In a letter to Marshall he wrote:

> The thing that impresses me more than anything else in connection with the Solomons action is that we are not prepared to follow up. . . . We have seized a strategic position from which future operation in the Bismarcks can be strongly supported. Can the Marines hold it? There is considerable room for doubt.

The theme of doubt about "Watchtower" that Ghormley played for his superiors all too rapidly began to infect their views of COM-SOPAC himself. Ghormley reacted to the shelling of Vandegrift's marines by submarines and then destroyers via a request to Fletcher to detach cruisers and destroyers to sweep the waters off Lunga Point. Fletcher demurred on the grounds that communications difficulties made it inadvisable to send on nightly sweeps portions of his already thin carrier escorts. Ghormley did not press the point. By the 19th, the CINCPAC daily operational summary reflected impatience with the situation, noting that "since the initial landing not much of anything has been done by our Task Forces."

THE SUPPLY SNARL AND THE ARRIVAL OF MARINE AIR GROUP 23

The absence of both supplies and aircraft threatened the survival of the marines no less than the presence of more Japanese on Guadalcanal. Moreover, it is fitting to address these topics now because it was only *after* the marines pushed ashore that senior officers fathomed the full dimensions of these potentially lethal defects. The supply problem transcended the immediate tactical factors and lay rooted in prewar neglect, the hasty launching of "Watchtower," and poor staff work. Routine fleet exercises in the interwar period failed to accustom commanders to grappling with complicated logistical problems. Although considerable attention and practice had crafted a doctrine of amphibious assault, little searching thought and no realistic practice had been afforded in conducting a sizable landing from crude bases 6,000 miles from the United States. A gross failure in Washington to appreciate the time required to move supplies in the South Pacific or to construct airfields and bases was compounded by plain ignorance of the general physical layout of the theater and its stark primitiveness.

The tropical climate, rough terrain, and absence of harbors or transportation facilities guaranteed the difficulty of any supply activity in the South Pacific, but fundamental errors in the initial logistical arrangements for Ghormley's command compounded these obstacles. In April the Army set up its supply line to run directly from San Francisco, and, lacking resources at Pearl Harbor, the Navy soon followed suit. No coordination of supply activities existed, and soon both services were requisitioning separate shipping for the long Pacific hauls to the same destinations. The most important of these would be the advanced base for the South Pacific theater, but the situs of this facility changed no fewer than three times in the course of the campaign. King originally favored Tongatabu in the Tonga Islands, but when Ghormley flew out to his new command the immensity of the theater and its distance from the United States sobered him. Upon arrival in Auckland he proposed that it become the advance base for Task One. Auckland lay 5,680 miles from San Francisco, 1,100 miles more than Tongatabu, and 1,825 miles from Guadalcanal.[3]

Those who viewed the situation from maps might well question the soundness of Ghormley's choice. Ghormley, however, grasped that distance alone was not the sole element affecting the movement of supplies. Cargoes jammed into scarce shipping at San Francisco had to be unloaded, sorted, and stored upon arrival in the South Pacific. This required deepwater harbors equipped with berthing, lighterage, warehouses, cranes, and stevedores. Only Auckland enjoyed these attributes. Espíritu Santo and Efate (and, of course, Guadalcanal) boasted no such refinements. Noumea possessed a three-berth Grand Quay and a single-berth Nickel Dock, but few other qualities of a major supply base. Thus directing a ship to a port forward of Auckland would not necessarily expedite the movement of its cargo to the marines; in fact, quite the reverse could be true.

---

[3]By way of contrast, it is worth noting that only 3,500 miles separates New York City from Liverpool or Casablanca, major bases for operations in the European and Mediterranean theaters respectively.

Washington planners did foresee the need for specially equipped units to create advanced bases. They organized detachments code-named "Lions" for large advanced fleet bases and "Cubs" for intermediate fuel and supply bases. During his preliminary planning in Washington, Ghormley vainly asked for one of each. Further pleas for such essentials as naval construction battalions, building materials, and even a mere dozen civil engineers were only grudgingly answered. No Lions would reach the South Pacific in 1942, and when the first Cub arrived in the theater in Noumea, it did so without its assortment of desperately needed lighterage and pontoons.

Noumea, the ultimate advanced base, dramatically displayed the fruits of the failure to appreciate the logistical problems of the South Pacific theater. Shipping directors ignored its estimated twenty-four-ship-per-month capacity, and by September 23 the harbor contained eighty-six ships. They, in effect, became substitutes for nonexistent warehouses. When these idle vessels arrived alongside Noumea's docks, more horrors unfolded. Some lacked the rig to lift deck cargo like 20-ton radar units, thus leaving the contents below the blocked hatches inaccessible. Yet no heavy cranes were available before October. In other cases, cargoes for Brisbane had been loaded above those for Noumea and vital items could not be readily located, for many ships carried manifests identifying their load as merely crates of machinery or dry goods. A shortage of labor and transportation left tons of unmarked and unsorted stores stacked helter-skelter around the port exposed to the weather and pilferage. Each service separately unloaded its ships, and both sometimes only partly discharged a ship and returned it to anchor.

Army cooperation presented one of the few bright spots in this collage of mismanagement. General Patch formed a provisional port company on his own for Noumea and added more laborers. He clothed survivors of Savo in Army garments, and when Vandegrift requested machetes for jungle movement, Harmon modified and forwarded to Guadalcanal some of the 20,000 cavalry sabers that had somehow found their way to Noumea.

Moving supplies the 1,100 miles from Noumea to Guadalcanal—a distance equal to a trip from New Orleans to New York City—was fraught with more dangers and difficulties. R4Ds (Navy DC-3s) of VMJ-253 lugged critical items, like fuel, and evacuated most of the wounded. Ghormley requested two squadrons of these aircraft, but the second arrived only in late October. The absence of cargo-handling facilities at Guadalcanal compelled the valuable transports equipped with their own landing craft to haul supplies on the final dangerous leg to the marines. This practice had an extremely important effect on the Navy's tactical capabilities. Because of the limited ability of the marines to literally manhandle supplies, the transports could be sent up only in twos or threes, thus generating severe strains on the scarce destroyer resources available to Ghormley for escorts. This escort duty fractured all division and squadron integrity, with highly deleterious consequences in the night surface actions around Guadalcanal.

The appalling dangers in the logistical situation and its reflections on the direction of the war at the highest levels were readily evident to Assistant Secretary of the Navy James Forrestal, who toured the theater in September. He confided to Ghormley that if the American people learned of the true circumstances, there would be a "revolution" at home.

Without local air cover, the regular movement of transports to Guadalcanal remained academic. General Harmon complained to General Arnold that "the plan did not have as its first and immediate objective the seizure and development of [Guadalcanal] *as an air base.*" But this charge is too broad. In their initial situation estimate on July 6, the CINCPAC staff recognized the importance of stationing air units in the target area as soon as a landing field could be readied. The real crux of the dilemma rested in identifying and forwarding the squadrons to be based at "Tulagi and adjacent positions." Fighters with high-altitude performance stood as the foremost requirement, which in practical terms meant Wildcats, and these could come from only three sources. Fletcher's carriers each owned a squadron of the Grumman fighters, but he would not countenance even temporary basing of a portion of these on Guadalcanal. Ghormley possessed a total of forty-nine shore-based Wildcats, but he believed he must retain these to defend his other island responsibilities. More mundanely, a recommendation from Turner on July 21 that two of Ghormley's Marine fighter squadrons be placed on standby to "immediately . . . proceed by air" to Guadalcanal upon completion of a landing strip served to disclose that all the South Pacific Wildcats lacked the range to reach Guadalcanal from the existing land bases without belly tanks, and despite diligent efforts by Admiral McCain, the necessary parts and modifications could not be carried out before the need became acute. The Marine squadrons under Nimitz in Hawaii constituted the third possible source for Wildcats, and in the event became the backbone of the initial air garrison for Guadalcanal in the shape of the first echelon of Marine Air Group 23 (MAG-23).

Nimitz refused to part with any of these squadrons before August 1 for a very good reason: they desperately needed training. Formed as recently as May 1 at Ewa Field on Oahu, MAG-23 consisted of two fighter (VMF-223 and VMF-224) and two dive-bomber (VMSB-231 and VMSB-232) squadrons. The fighter squadrons began their tutelage on obsolete Brewster F2A-3 Buffaloes, and the bomber outfits got the Douglas Dauntless SBD-2s, a model recently discarded from the front-line carrier service. In July, with an alert to the squadron commanders of a "special mission," the fighter squadrons exchanged their Buffaloes for full complements of the Grumman Wildcat F4F-4s, the latest Navy fighter, while the dive-bomber units acquired the SBD-3, which enjoyed armor and self-sealing gas tanks. To fill out their rosters, Captain John L. Smith's VMF-223 and Captain Robert E. Galer's VMF-224 split two groups of newly assigned pilots: one composed of the latest graduates of flight school and fighter training, and the second an assortment of pilots who had survived the slaughter of the defending Marine fighters at Midway by the nimble Zeros. Major Richard Mangrum of VMSB-232 was issued ten newly minted pilots, most of whom had never dropped a bomb. In the next three to four weeks, Smith and Mangrum put their charges through the most intensive indoctrination they could devise, with emphasis on bombing and gunnery. Ready or not, nineteen VMF-223 F4Fs and twelve VMSB-232 SBDs were loaded on board *Long Island,* the prototype "auxiliary escort carrier" converted from a merchant ship hull, which sailed southwestward on August 2.

En route, *Long Island*'s skipper notified Ghormley of the woeful state of training of Smith's pilots. The problem passed to McCain, who directed Smith to exchange a dozen of his novice airmen for an equal number of the more experienced pilots of VMF-212 on Efate. The detour to Efate meant that *Long Island* did not reach a position 190 miles from Guadalcanal off the southern tip of San Cristobal until the afternoon of August 20. A combination of a short flight deck and light winds necessitated catapulting each plane, a first for most of the pilots. When Lieutenant Colonel Charles L. Fike, executive officer of MAG-23 and leader of the echelon, took the last F4F off, he joined the others, who had all successfully become airborne, and set course for Guadalcanal.

As the afternoon gave way, the ears of the marines prickled with the distant drone of aircraft motors. The last eleven days had taught them a basic lesson on air power: aircraft, unless employed in massive numbers in small areas, could do surprisingly little damage against dug-in troops; but they could create disruptions, and the morale of even the most determined men suffered appreciably from the feeling of impotence before enemy air superiority. This time, however, when the sounds became shapes they were unmistakably those of sturdy Dauntlesses and the portly Wildcats. Marine eyes feasted on the glint of white stars as Mangrum's SBD swooped low over the crude runway. The dive-bomber leader then set his plane down with a swirl of dust and alighted to have his hand personally pumped by General Vandegrift. The following crews were somewhat taken aback by the wild joy of their hosts, who tossed helmets in the air and cheered. Old campaigners like Cates and Vandegrift noted that a good many youngsters shed tears and were not ashamed to admit their own eyes were moist too. By the formidable reckoning of Lieutenant Colonel Gerald Thomas, no episode in the eventful campaign gave such a fillip to Marine morale as the arrival of the first American planes. It came none too soon, for in less than twelve hours the American hold on Henderson Field would be tested.

6

THE TENARU

"One stroke of the armored sleeve"

IMPERIAL PLANS

Thus far, the Japanese reaction to the Allied landings had been based solely on the initiative of the local commanders and limited to the air and sea resources at hand. Vandegrift's marines toiled to prepare a perimeter because military logic dictated that Japan's next step would be to counterattack by land to take advantage of the Savo victory and quickly recapture Guadalcanal. This would both secure bases for further moves and deal the Allies the sort of psychological blow that most Japanese strategists were banking upon to force a peace settlement ratifying Japan's conquests.

To work out a joint plan to deal with the new situation, members of the Army and Navy Sections of the Imperial General Headquarters convened a series of liaison study meetings. The first of these assemblies, on August 7, reached a tentative consensus that the landings represented no more than a "reconnaissance in force." Current estimates of American capabilities heavily influenced this appreciation, particularly limited U.S. Navy carrier strength. This erroneous view of the enemy situation was excusable in the case of the Imperial Army. The Imperial Navy supplied their soldier colleagues with inflated claims of American carrier losses while concealing the destruction of four Japanese flattops at Midway. Since Allied possession of the airfield would inhibit prospective operations in the Southeast Area, however, it was decided that no time would be wasted in arranging moves to expel the invaders if they should be so unwise as to linger.

The chief of the Operations Division of the Army Section, Lieutenant General Shin'ichi Tanaka, found the "reconnaissance in force" interpretation suspect. He recalled intelligence reports of the sortie of a large convoy from San Francisco in mid-July and of the relocation of MacArthur's headquarters to Brisbane. This information suggested to Tanaka a major Allied jab of which the Guadalcanal landing might be a part. His suspicions gathered substance as the first amplifying reports from Rabaul arrived. Attacking aircraft on August 7 placed over thirty transports off Guadalcanal, prompting the 8th Fleet to estimate that one division was ashore. The 17th Army staff worked from the same source of information, but divided sharply over both Allied intentions and strength. Some members concurred with 8th Fleet officers on a divisional scale landing, but Colonel Hiroshi Matsumoto insisted that American dependency upon "the amenities" required twenty transports to carry only one regiment. The first message from 17th Army to Imperial General Headquarters allowed the attackers only twenty transports, but added that the escort included one aircraft carrier, one battleship, four cruisers, and fifteen destroyers. The 17th Army also requested permission to use part of an infantry brigade to meet the new threat while reaffirming its intention not to alter its plan to attack Port Moresby.

When reconvened on August 8, the Imperial Headquarters liaison study group revised its estimate to reflect these reports pointing to a major Allied move. By August 10, the Navy identified the unit at Guadalcanal as a well-equipped Marine division. Clearly, any attempt to recapture Guadalcanal would meet heavy opposition and marshaling units for a counterattack would have to be the first step in a Japanese riposte.

On August 10, in the usual Japanese fashion, Admiral Nagano and General Sugiyama issued a Central Agreement incorporating the liaison study group's conclusions for future operations in the New Guinea and Solomons theater. Like the 17th Army, Imperial Headquarters still deemed Port Moresby to be the centerpiece of Japanese designs in the theater. The new Central Agreement, however, amended the mission of Lieutenant General Hyakutake's 17th Army. Originally, Hyakutake was to "leapfrog" the 18th Army and take Port Moresby. Under his new orders, Hyakutake would immediately retake Guadalcanal and Tulagi with forces made available to the 17th Army consisting of Major General Kiyotaki Kawaguchi's 35th Infantry Brigade and 4th and 28th Infantry Regiments, called the Aoba and Ichiki Detachments respectively. Of these units the 35th Brigade was in the Palaus and the Aoba Detachment was in the Philippines. Immediately available was Colonel Kiyoano Ichiki's detachment with its shipping at Guam. With fatal effect, Ichiki's availability merged shortly with a downward revision in the estimate of Allied strength and the colonel's own headstrong character.

On the 11th the pilots of six Zeros returned from low strafing swoops over Guadalcanal to affirm American strength, thus buttressing the estimate that Guadalcanal held a division of marines. Also in the first days after their arrival, submarines *I-122* and *I-123* provided their fish-eye views of doings ashore. The report of *I-123* contained details that should have alerted Imperial Headquarters to the presence of major units ashore, but like the Allies, the Japanese possessed only marine charts or maps of very small scale, which were inadequate for plotting *I-123*'s revealing observations. The picture of marines swarming over a patch of Guadalcanal barely coalesced before it was discarded. On the same day that the new Central Agreement was signed, the Japanese military attaché in Moscow signaled Tokyo that "well-informed" but indiscreet Soviet sources had divulged vital information on their ally's Pacific venture: the American troops had the limited mission of destroying the airfield and withdrawing, their morale was low, and they were in no condition to conduct sustained operations. This interesting tidbit of intelligence bemused American code breakers, but it afforded no solace to the 17th Army, which was not informed of its existence. Moreover, its influence on decisions at Imperial Headquarters is unclear, as much more concrete evidence of Allied weakness shortly came to hand.

A sweep by Imperial Navy destroyers on August 11 and 12 confirmed the absence of Allied naval forces, and, apart from daily reconnaissance flights by B-17s, the Japanese detected no Allied air activity in the Guadalcanal area. It is possible that staff officers interpreted submarine reports of boats moving from Guadalcanal to Tulagi as a withdrawal, and read an account of the Goettge disaster as proof of Allied weakness ashore. However, the key piece of intelligence came on August 12. On that date a senior staff officer of the

8th Base Force, Lieutenant Commander Matsunaga, rode one of three bombers dispatched to Guadalcanal. Not surprisingly, from a perch over 10,000 feet above Lunga Point he failed to see many marines frolicking around the airfield and only a few boats in the water. From these observations he concluded that the main body of troops had been withdrawn. Unfortunately for Japan, Matsunaga's superiors weighed his report in accordance with his rank and position rather than in keeping with its intrinsic value. Thus, by the 13th, Admiral Nagano imparted to the Emperor that the Americans on Guadalcanal were quiet, and although the size of the landing remained unclear, Imperial Headquarters believed that the remaining forces were not large because of the losses off Savo and the withdrawal of the transports.

Reflecting the downward revision in the estimate of American strength—and foreshadowing a fatal policy of piecemeal commitment—on August 12, the vice chief of the Army General Staff, Lieutenant General Moritake Tanabe, radioed a strongly suggestive message to Hyakutake:

> The scope of operations for the recapture of strategic points in the Solomon Islands will be decided by the Army Commander on the basis of his estimate of the enemy situation. General Headquarters believes that it is feasible to use the 35th Infantry Brigade and Aoba Detachment if the situation demands. However, since tactical opportunity is the primary consideration under existing conditions, it is considered preferable, if possible, to recapture those areas promptly, using the Ichiki Detachment and Special Naval Landing Forces.

Despite the surfeit of confidence at Imperial Headquarters mirrored by Tanabe's message, a few staff officers harbored misgivings over the small size of Ichiki's unit and already envisioned resupply difficulties. Among the pessimists was Colonel Susumu Nishiura, the chief of the Administrative Division of the Army Section. When he learned of the plan to send Ichiki on alone, he recalled the disaster of Nomonhan against the Soviets[1] and later follies in China, where inadequate forces were committed time after time. The decision so disturbed him that he called on Premier and Defense Minister Tojo, for whom he had worked as a staff secretary. Tojo heard him out, but refused to intervene—the decision rested with General

---

[1] In July and August 1939, the Red Army thoroughly trounced units of the Imperial Army in a clash along the Manchurian-Mongolian border near the village of Nomonhan. Japanese losses reached 17,000, including 8,440 killed. This event was a shock to the Imperial Army.

Sugiyama, declared Tojo. Nishiura then went directly to Sugiyama, whose pithy reply to the colonel's protests was: "The orders have been issued. They cannot now be rescinded."

At 17th Army Headquarters, planning for Ichiki's employment occupied August 12 and 13. The chief of staff, Major General Akisaburo Futami, reckoned American numbers at 7,000 to 8,000 and hesitated to send Ichiki alone. Brasher spirits among the staff argued that an opportunity to quickly eject the invaders lay at the fingertips of the 17th Army and depreciated Futami's estimate of American strength. They urged immediate dispatch of Ichiki to answer the Navy's request for troops. In any event, they believed Ichiki could forestall completion of the airfield. As for Ichiki's weakness, they asserted that within ten days he could be reinforced by the 35th Infantry Brigade. Futami found Rear Admiral Munetaka Sakamaki, the chief of staff of the 11th Air Fleet, also favored the bolder thrust with Ichiki. Futami had barely decided to send Ichiki ahead when he was handed the message from Tanabe suggesting just that course of action.

A radio message summoned Ichiki to Truk, where Colonel Matsumoto of the 17th Army delivered his orders. The written directive advised Ichiki that the Americans' strength was unknown but they appeared quiescent. As of August 13, the airfield remained unused. The mission of the 17th Army was defined as a quick attack to destroy the American lodgment in the Solomons; Ichiki's role was to recapture the airfield if possible, and if not, to occupy a position on the island and await reinforcements. For this purpose a spearhead of 900 men under Ichiki would proceed to the island immediately and land at Taivu Point (22 airline miles east of Lunga Point). As a diversion, a detachment of about 250 Special Naval Landing Force troops would be placed ashore at Kokumbona, to the west of the American perimeter.

A former instructor at the Imperial Army's Infantry School, Kiyono Ichiki held repute as an expert infantry tactician and all-purpose firebrand. His distinguished record included command of rifle units in China; indeed, as a mere company commander his impetuous actions led to the "Marco Polo Bridge Incident" in 1937, which ignited Japan's enduring war in China and is often marked as the beginning of World War Two.[2] After Pearl Harbor, his 28th

---

[2]With tensions already high between Japan and China, in July 1937 Imperial Army units stationed in occupied Manchuria launched "maneuvers" into clearly Chinese territory. Ichiki's

Infantry Regiment enhanced a reputation gained in the Russo-Japanese as an elite assault unit through a series of amphibious assaults. He had been slated for the landing on Midway before disaster struck the Japanese carriers. Ichiki firmly shared the widely held view in the Imperial Army at this time that night attacks with swords and bayonets—the traditional tactic of the Imperial Army—would easily secure success against American forces.

Matsumoto supplemented Ichiki's written orders with a briefing. If Ichiki's initial attack failed, he should occupy a position near the airfield and launch repeated night assaults to preclude completion of the airstrip. Matsumoto later claimed he warned Ichiki that there might be as many as 10,000 troops on Guadalcanal and to avoid frontal attacks. The cautionary effect of Matsumoto's words may have been dispelled when he added that the Americans were possibly intent on withdrawal. Although Hyakutake's orders left room for discretion after arrival on Guadalcanal, Ichiki announced to Matsumoto that he would attack the airfield on the second night after the landing. His men would carry only 250 rounds of ammunition per man and seven days' rations, partly because of the restrictions imposed by their transportation, but equally reflecting Ichiki's serene confidence. Ichiki further illustrated his unbounded optimism by asking if he could also occupy Tulagi, but Matsumoto advised him to wait for Kawaguchi's brigade. At the conclusion of their conversation, Ichiki expressed his gratitude for being awarded this mission after being denied the opportunity to emblazon his name in fame at Midway.

Getting Ichiki to Guadalcanal became the first task assigned to Rear Admiral Raizo Tanaka, commander of Destroyer Squadron 2 and recently designated "Commander Reinforcement Group" in charge of moving troops and supplies to Guadalcanal. On the evening of August 15, the 8th Fleet instructed Tanaka to transport Ichiki's First Echelon of 900 men from Truk to Guadalcanal and land them on the night of August 18–19. Ichiki's Second Echelon, totaling about 1,100 men, and supplies were to move in two transports escorted by Tanaka's flagship, the old light cruiser *Jintsu,* and two aged destroyers converted to handle landing craft and reclassified as *Patrol Boat 34* and *Patrol Boat 35.* They would be joined by

company penetrated to what westerners referred to as the Marco Polo Bridge across the Hu River and skirmished with Chinese units. A series of escalations followed that culminated in full-scale war.

Patrol Boat 1 and *Patrol Boat 2* (of similar origins) escorting *Kinryu Maru* with the 5th Yokosuka Special Naval Landing Force embarked. This second echelon would land in the vicinity of Taivu Point on the night of August 23–24.

At 0700 August 16, Ichiki and the First Echelon departed from Truk in six destroyers. The task organization was as follows:

Ichiki First Echelon

Detachment Headquarters	164
Battalion Headquarters (2d Battalion, 28th Infantry)	23
1st to 4th Infantry Companies (105 men each)	420
Machinegun Company (8 heavy machineguns)	110
One Platoon Battalion Gun Unit (2 70mm guns)	50
Engineer company (1st Company, 7th Engineer Construction Regiment)	150
Total	917

Transport Unit
Capt. Torajiro Sato

Desdiv 15	*Kagero*
Desdiv 4	*Hagikaze, Arashi*
Desdiv 17	*Tanikaze, Hamakaze, Urakaze*

Sato's destroyermen deposited Ichiki and his troops at Taivu Point by 0100 on August 19. Infused with their leader's confidence, Ichiki's men began their march westward toward the airfield. They trudged approximately 9 miles to Tetere, where they slipped into the jungle to rest and to avoid detection at 0630 on August 19. From the direction of Tulagi they heard the sound of guns.

These muffled blasts represented the leisurely shelling of Tulagi by *Kagero, Hagikaze,* and *Arashi,* which had been detailed by Tanaka to guard the landing area. While they were thus occupied, three B-17s passed overhead releasing sticks of bombs. Three of these scored direct hits on *Hagikaze*'s stern that killed thirty-three of her crew and wounded thirteen. Tanaka ordered her to withdraw from the area under the escort of *Arashi; Kagero* remained alone to watch the area.

BRUSH VERSUS SHIBUYA

American radio monitoring intercepted the dispatch sent to Ichiki in the Saipan communications zone diverting him to Truk. The contents of the message stayed elusive, but analysts marked Ichiki as an addressee. Careful listening detected Ichiki's arrival in Truk and revealed an association of his unit with Destroyer Squadron 2. On the 17th, based upon these or other messages, Nimitz issued an alert warning that the Japanese intended to reoccupy Guadalcanal and Tulagi. He identified the forces detailed for the attack as a unit of the Special Naval Landing Forces under the escort of *Jintsu* and some destroyers with other warships in support, including the heavy cruisers of Cruiser Division 6. Nimitz also listed in the enemy order of battle a special shock unit, originally destined for Midway and now being lifted from Truk to Guadalcanal—Ichiki. The exact date of the attack was unknown, but it was estimated to be possible as early as August 20.

At this time Vandegrift lacked the high-grade cryptographic systems required to monitor CINCPAC's intelligence broadcasts directly. Consequently, critical information was forwarded in ad hoc fashion to Guadalcanal, notably via message drops by reconnaissance planes or orally to Vandegrift or a few key staff officers by way of pilots flying round trips to the island. The August 17 warning reached Vandegrift—how is a mystery—but it lacked any hint at the site of the landing.

On August 12, a few engineers began a hike to the Tetere area to survey for a possible airfield site; this caused the first chance contact with Ichiki. A rifle platoon under Lieutenant Joseph Jachym afforded an escort. While they were passing through Tetere on the 13th, a Catholic priest informed them of rumors of an enemy force farther east along the coast. Lieutenant Jachym prudently chose to return to the perimeter with this news and, if necessary, take a larger force to verify it. His report was pieced together with a story from Clemens's scouts of a Japanese radio station at Gurabasu. To destroy this detachment and its radio, early on the 19th Captain Charles H. Brush hit the trail with a patrol of about sixty men drawn from Company A, 1st Battalion, 1st Marines. About the same time Ichiki sent ahead a thirty-eight-man patrol of his own under a Captain Shibuya to set up a communications point near the Alligator Creek.

About noon, as Brush's men prepared to halt for rest and food, native guides warned them of the approach of some Japanese—

Shibuya's men advancing with negligible security precautions. Brush hastily launched an attack that checked the Japanese from the front while Lieutenant Jachym hooked around the Japanese left flank with a part of the command. In a firefight lasting just under an hour, the marines killed all but five of the Japanese, the survivors escaping into the bush, at a cost to Brush of three killed and three wounded. Setting out local security, Brush moved among the bodies of four Japanese officers and twenty-nine men, noting they wore the star insignia of the Imperial Army instead of the chrysanthemum of the Imperial Navy. The fresh condition of their clothes bespoke their recent arrival on the island, and the large amount of communications gear betrayed the presence of a larger unit. Brush examined a map that disclosed in startling detail that the Japanese knew the Marine line on Alligator Creek extended but a short distance inland. Brush gathered papers and diaries and made for the perimeter.

Word reached Ichiki about 1630 of a clash between Captain Shibuya and an estimated company of American troops. The colonel rushed forward one company to help and followed it shortly with his entire command. By 1700 he learned of the virtual annihilation of Shibuya's party. Without pause for reflection on this disaster, Ichiki pressed ahead and did not halt until 0430 the next morning after he crossed the Nalimbu River.

Brush reentered the perimeter flush with his story and a haul of papers, diaries, and the map. Translations of the diaries confirmed that their late owners belonged to a regimental unit which had sailed from Guam. None of the documents told Vandegrift what he most needed to know: the size, location, and intentions of this Japanese force. The map not only illustrated the line along Alligator Creek, but also accurately depicted the Marine artillery positions near the airfield.[3] Vandegrift now faced the first of a series of difficult choices he would have to make in the defense of Guadalcanal. Some staff officers urged him to unleash the only reserve battalion to grapple with the approaching Japanese force. But lacking clear information as to the enemy strength and intentions and worried about being left without a reserve in the event of a simultaneous attack from the west or the sea, Vandegrift wisely decided to await the Japanese within the perimeter.

---

[3]How the Japanese acquired this information is unclear. Samuel B. Griffith linked it to the later discovery of Japanese observation posts on Mount Austen offering panoramic views of the perimeter, but the Japanese account suggests that such posts were not established at this time. Possibly the information came from aerial photographs, but this is far from certain.

ICHIKI ATTACKS

Like the Battle of Bunker Hill (which was fought on Breed's Hill), the Battle of the Tenaru River is an action passing under an alias. Martin Clemens and the natives called the watercourse anchoring the eastern end of the Marine beach defenses Alligator Creek after its formidable inhabitants—which were in fact crocodiles. Whatever its name, it was not a flowing stream, but rather a tidal lagoon that emptied into the sea only in the monsoon or after a storm. No more than 100 feet wide at any point, it was separated from the ocean by a sandbar that varied in width from about 25 to 50 feet and rose about 10 feet above the "Tenaru." The west bank was slightly higher than the east bank, and the position near the mouth resembled an embryonic castle with the tidal lagoon for a moat and the sandbar for a drawbridge. This castle, however, wanted for ramparts to the south or rear.

On August 20, Lieutenant Colonel Edwin A. Pollock's 2d Battalion, 1st Marines manned the west bank of Alligator Creek from a point about 1,000 yards inland north to the sandbar. From the corner formed by the sandbar and the beach, the 2d Battalion's line turned sharply west, where it linked up with positions of its sister 3d Battalion. The arduous work of clearing vegetation to extend the line 3,500

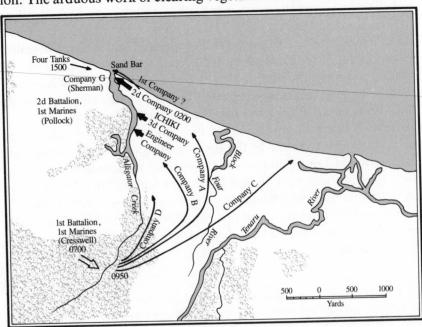

Battle of the Tenaru, August 21

inland had begun, but had progressed little by this date. On the sandbar near the west bank, the marines strung a single-strand barbed-wire fence. Dug-in machineguns covered the sandbar, and because Alligator Creek approached the sea at an oblique angle, "upstream" guns could rake the bar and the point of land on the east bank. An extra supply of canister ammunition sat next to a 37mm gun sited to sweep the bar. One platoon of Company G (Captain James F. Sherman) and two platoons of the 1st Special Weapons Battalion, about 100 men in all, occupied the emplacements by the sandbar. Early-warning antenna in the form of outposts and small patrols routinely stood watch on the east bank at night, but despite Brush's patrol and other warnings, the fall of darkness on August 20 triggered no special alert among Pollock's marines.

Meanwhile at 1200 on August 20, Ichiki gathered his commanders and issued his attack plan. With little regard for the Marine dispositions, he essentially ordered a march down the beach culminating in an assault with the initial objective of capturing the old camp of the 11th Construction Unit between Alligator Creek and the Lunga. Once secure on the first objective, Ichiki anticipated fanning out detachments to seize the airfield and a position on the Lunga. A patrol of engineers would depart first to sniff for crossing points on Alligator Creek, with the main body moving out after dark at 2000. The order of march would be three rifle companies with the battalion headquarters leading the detachment headquarters, the machinegun company, and the battalion gun platoon, the remaining rifle company and the engineer company in the rear. From his plan and movement order it is evident that Ichiki expected to pierce the Marine perimeter easily, or, as he put it, with "one brush of the armored sleeve."[4]

It was pitch-dark as Ichiki's men approached Alligator Creek. Marine outposts on the east bank reported hearing voices and metallic sounds and were withdrawn, together with a patrol that observed a white flare. About midnight, a sentry at the point fired at a shape that failed to answer his challenge. Rifle fire began to sputter lightly across the torpid lagoon, probably at the engineer patrol and Ichiki's van. Life on the perimeter featured nightly minor affrays with small enemy parties, and at first these omens attracted no particular attention.

---

[4]From a Japanese saying dating to the days of the samurai warriors, who wore armored garments. The American historian Gordan Prange indicated it had a colloquial meaning loosely equivalent to "We'll mow 'em down!"

Ichiki reached Alligator Creek shortly after 0030 and consulted with the leading company commander and Major Kuramoto, the battalion commander. The colonel ordered an assault across the sandbar by a strong detachment under the covering fire of other troops. About 0200 a green flare arched over the mouth of the lagoon, signaling the start of a headlong charge by the 2d Company—about one hundred men—over the sandbar. Quivering battle cries drowned the sound of sand crunching beneath scores of boots. In the eerie green light, marines could see a dark bobbing mass of men bearing down on their positions. The Marine line ignited with muzzle flashes, and many attackers crumpled and fell on the bar under the hail of rifle shots, bursts of machinegun fire, and the hellish breath of 37mm canister. Leaving a thick wake of dead and dying, the hurtling column reached the west side of the bar, where the barbed-wire fence broke its momentum scarcely 30 yards in front of the Marine emplacements. The leaders gingerly examined the obstacle, which some thought electrified, as the survivors closed up to the wire. More toppled before the fence, but Ichiki's men were not considered a shock unit without a cause. Snipping or flattening the barrier, a final few—some brandishing bayonets in their hands like swords—swirled into the Marine fighting holes to engage in hand-to-hand combat.

For nine months, Allied units had sometimes bolted to the rear abandoning duty and dignity when confronted by shrieking Japanese infantry like Ichiki's veterans. Pollock's marines were grass-green, but resolute—for all they knew it was always supposed to be like this. Stories of courageous and desperate struggles by individual marines abounded, but one episode involving the three-man crew of a machinegun near the focal point of the breakthrough entered American folklore. The gunner, Private John Rivers, of Indian stock, slammed hundreds of rounds into the onrushing phalanx until a bullet struck him in the face and killed him. Even as he died his devoted fingers squeezed the trigger for another 200 rounds. Corporal Lee Diamond then fired the gun until wounded in the arm. His place was taken by Private Albert A. Schmid, who fired until an exploding grenade flung him from the gun. Hot fragments pierced both of Schmid's eyes and blinded him, but he crawled back to his post and fought on with a pistol.

Ichiki ordered attacks by the 1st and 3d Companies, but they made no progress. A bold group of Japanese managed to swim Alligator Creek and set up a machinegun in an abandoned amphibian tractor. Their fire or grenades silenced the 37mm gun that had wrought havoc on the bar. Observing from a position only a few yards behind the firing line, Lieutenant Colonel Pollock measured the progress of the battle and, seeing the penetration at the sandbar, ordered forward another platoon of Company G in a counterattack. Within the hour, the line was restored and all the attackers who had vaulted the wire were dead.

With his main assault blunted, Ichiki now tossed in his machinegun company and his battalion guns. Their fire searched for the Marine positions on the far bank but did not establish fire superiority, for Colonel Cates request for artillery support had been answered. Ranging shots and then a concentration of 75mm shells from the 3d Battalion, 11th Marines fell on the sandbar within 100 yards of the Marine line. Acting then on his intuition, Cates shifted the fire to the point of land on the east bank, apparently creating disorder among Ichiki's men there, who may have been gathering for another try at the bar. Evidently in an attempt to turn what was hoped to be the open beach flank of the stubborn marines at the bar, Ichiki or one of his officers dispatched another company to try to infiltrate through the surf. The marines detected this group, and as they wheeled to spring up the beach their assault was first raked with machinegun fire and then smothered by artillery. Leaving a few men and machineguns very close to Pollock's line, Ichiki's main body withdrew to a coconut grove about 200 yards from the sandbar. A firefight rattled on the rest of the night.

The din of the battle awoke men all over the perimeter, including the newly arrived aviators, who wondered if every night on Guadalcanal was like this. From a distance Martin Clemens observed tracers ricocheting into the sky and the pink glow created by the intense firing which silhouetted the palm trees by Alligator Creek. A call summoning him to Pollock's command post terminated Clemens's sight-seeing. There he found his chief scout, Sergeant Major Vouza, desperately wounded but insistent on telling his story. Sent out the day before on a scouting mission, Vouza had decided to stop by a village to drop off a small American flag presented to him by the marines. When he arrived in the village he discovered a party of Japanese. They readily divined from the flag that Vouza's enthusiasm for Japan's Great East Asia Co-Prosperity Sphere was well controlled. His situation became decidedly worse when he recognized one of his captors. This was a sinister individual Vouza knew as Ishimoto, who had now discarded the guise of an itinerant carpenter and shipwright he had maintained around Tulagi before the war in favor of a Japanese uniform.

Ishimoto identified Vouza and began to interrogate him. When Vouza proved uncommunicative, his captors tied him to a tree, pounded him with rifle butts, and finally jabbed bayonets into the flesh of his chest and arms. Vouza remained silent, so, with one final slice of a blade across the neck, they left him to die. Regaining consciousness hours later, he chewed through the grass ropes that bound him and stumbled toward the Marine perimeter to bring a warning. Weakened by blood loss, Vouza finally crawled on all fours a distance of about three miles through the battle area. Completing his own story, he gasped out a description of the size and equipment of the Japanese unit he had seen. As Clemens held his hand, he finished by dictating a long dying message to his wife before he collapsed. Whisked to a hospital and pumped full of blood, Vouza staged an amazing recovery. Within two weeks he was afoot and soon was once again on patrol. Vandegrift awarded Vouza the Silver Star Medal, but conferred a much rarer honor by appointing him a Sergeant Major of the United States Marine Corps.

THE DESTRUCTION OF ICHIKI

At daybreak Ichiki showed no signs of withdrawal, perhaps mindful of his orders to gain a position near the airfield, but made no further efforts to attack. The coming of daylight resolved the situation for Vandegrift and Thomas, who had been worried that Ichiki's attack might be only a part of a larger plan for coordinated assaults from other directions, particularly the west. Now Thomas expressed their intent: "We aren't going to let those people lay up there all day." He, Cates, and Lieutenant Colonel Lenard B. Cresswell devised a plan to envelop Ichiki by passing Cresswell's reserve battalion (1st Battalion, 1st Marines) with a platoon of light tanks across Alligator Creek inland to encircle and destroy the Japanese near the sand spit. Vandegrift readily assented, and before 0700, Cresswell's men crossed the dry bed of Alligator Creek well inland, but the terrain prevented the tanks from following. Cresswell detached Company D at the east bank to bar a breakout to the south and pushed on to the east with the rest of his command. At 0950 his companies swung north, crossing their line of departure. On Cresswell's right, Company C reached the coast first and isolated a Japanese platoon, which reacted with what the Marine report labeled the "customary bayonet charge." Following another custom created by Spurlock's men on the Matanikau, Company C broke the attack with fire and then closed in to kill the survivors. Leaving Company C in an eastern blocking position, Cresswell pushed west with Companies A on his right and B on his left, encountering little opposition until he compressed Ichiki into a triangle by the mouth of the lagoon.

All morning long, Pollock's men laced the Japanese positions east of Alligator Creek with mortars and picked off unwary Japanese as if on a rifle range. They now heard gradually increasing volleys of rifle fire and bursts of machineguns, including the distinctive far gurgle of Japanese Nambus, as Cresswell's marines closed the trap. Soon the marines on the west bank saw the squat figures of Japanese soldiers darting among the rows of coconut trees—some dashing out onto the beach, where they were felled. Attempts by some of Ichiki's men to escape to the east were thwarted, and one group that broke through ran into Company C. Strafing aircraft pounced on a few who took to some boats.

Colonel Cates authorized the platoon of light tanks that had been standing by to make a reconnaissance of the beach on the east side of Alligator Creek. As correspondent Richard Tregaskis watched, four of them churned across the bar about 1500, and then on the initiative of the platoon leader, Lieutenant Leo B. Case, swerved and plunged into the coconut grove,

> ... their treads rattling industriously. We watched these awful machines as they plunged across the spit and into the edge of the grove. It was fascinating to see them bustling amongst the trees, pivoting, turning, spitting sheets of yellow flame. It was like a comedy of toys, something unbelievable, to see them knocking over palm trees which fell slowly, flushing the running figures of men from underneath their treads, following and firing at the fugitives. It was unbelievable to see men falling and being killed so close, to see the explosions of Jap grenades and mortars, black fountains and showers of dirt near the tanks, and see the flashes of explosions under their very treads.

Lacking anti-tank guns, many Japanese died bravely confronting the tanks with grenades or magnetic anti-tank mines. One tank suddenly lurched to a stop when an explosion broke a tread. The other tanks huddled protectively around it and rescued its crew, and then resumed ravaging the grove. When they returned to the east bank, Vandegrift wrote, "the rear of the tanks looked like meat grinders."

To the surprise of observers on the west bank, who thought the tanks had cleaned out the coconut grove, firing accelerated as they began to see the taller shapes of Cresswell's men filtering through the trees. About 1630, recognizing the hopelessness of his situation, Ichiki burned the regimental colors and committed suicide.[5] Singly and in small groups the survivors tried to flee in the only direction available—the sea. Those not cut down on the beach were systematically shot as they tried to swim away. By 1700, cautious groups of Cresswell's men closed up to Alligator Creek and the victors assumed the battle was over. Marines began to stride over the sandbar and into the grove to gawk at what they had wrought and collect souvenirs, while corpsmen moved among the bodies hoping to preserve any remaining life. But a number of Ichiki's men chose to use their last breaths to try to take an American with them. They shot a few marines, and one Nipponese sergeant startled Lieutenant Colonels Twining, Pollock, and Cresswell by discharging an automatic pistol in their faces—without effect—and then blowing off the top of his own head. The marines saw this as final evidence of Japanese treachery; their answer was simple and direct. Lining up on the banks of Alligator Creek, riflemen set corpses twitching with round after round while other marines moved into the grove and along the beach with pistols ensuring that all of Ichiki's men joined their commander in death.

During the battle one Japanese soldier surrendered, and twelve wounded members of the Ichiki Detachment, including one officer, were captured; only two unwounded survivors became prisoners of war. Marine losses totaled forty-four dead and about seventy-one wounded, including three each in Brush's patrol. In sundry postures of violent death on the sandbar and in the grove, nudging each other in the surf or half-buried and washed of their gore by the tide, were at least 777 Japanese. The marines captured ten heavy and twenty light machineguns, 700 rifles, twenty pistols, two 70mm guns, twelve flamethrowers (never used in the battle), and a considerable quantity of demolition equipment. They were particularly happy to relieve Ichiki's men of a large number of much-needed shovels.

By the standards of World War Two, the miscalled Battle of the Tenaru River was a small action, but it was much more important than the mere numbers of men engaged would indicate. In the after-

---

[5]This is the version of Colonel Ichiki's death related in the Japanese Defense Agency history. One Japanese survivor reported he last saw Ichiki during the night walking forward to the front line, a trip from which the colonel did not return to this survivor's knowledge. This is entirely plausible and perhaps would explain the paralysis that seems to have gripped the detachment after the failure of the night attacks.

math of Japan's total defeat in 1945 it is difficult to recapture the psychological atmosphere of August 1942, but the blitz starting on December 7 created a myth of Japanese invincibility. Unsettling questions arose from many quarters about the ability and willingness of the sons of democracy to stand up to the offspring of the totalitarians, even from Churchill, who privately wondered about his own troops after the surrenders at Singapore and Tobruk. For the marines the "Tenaru" indisputably demonstrated the mortal character of the Japanese soldier.

But the psychological products of the battle had a darker side. The failure of all but a tiny number of Ichiki's men to surrender and their last attempts to kill marines in the act of providing succor came as a shock, even to Vandegrift, who wrote to Holcomb a few days later:

> General, I have never heard or read of this kind of fighting. These people refuse to surrender. The wounded wait until men come up to examine them . . . and blow themselves and the other fellow to pieces with a hand grenade.

If Japanese strategists hoped this willingness to die to virtually the last man would cause the westerners to blanch at the brutal implications of such battle ethics, the actions of the marines as the sun set on August 21 would have given them food for thought. If the Japanese wanted to fight to the death with no quarter asked or given, the marines were ready to oblige them fully.

The immolation of Colonel Ichiki and his unit reveals a great deal about their commander and the Imperial Army. Even granting that Ichiki was misinformed about the numbers and the morale of the marines, he recklessly committed himself to attack with but half his unit before he personally set foot on Guadalcanal. The destruction of Shibuya's patrol should have injected some prudence into his conduct and afforded an honorable reason to change his plans and take advantage of the flexibility Hyakutake's orders allowed. Ichiki sealed his fate by disdaining reconnaissance and ignoring key information concerning the open inland flank of the marines for a frontal assault into prepared positions. But the disaster was not solely due to the character or professional shortcomings of Ichiki, for his contempt of American infantry units was shared by most officers in the Imperial Army at that time. Admiral Tanaka commented: "This tragedy should have taught the hopelessness of 'bamboo spear' tactics," by which he meant the blind faith that an "invincible" Japanese spirit would overcome superior Allied firepower. Perhaps even deeper than the arrogance built on easy triumphs and fanciful theories lay the code of the Japanese warrior, Bushido. As a distinguished marine who fought on Guadalcanal, Samuel B. Griffith, expressed it:

> . . . part of what happened at the Tenaru can perhaps be traced to the willingness of the Japanese in the moment of desperation to embrace with stoicism what fate had clearly ordained. To die gloriously for the Emperor in the face of insurmountable odds was the ineluctable duty and indeed the subconscious desire of many Japanese soldiers.

Between August 22 and 29 the survivors of Ichiki's command drifted back to Taivu Point, some looting native gardens along the way. By the latter date, 128 men had assembled, including those originally left at Taivu after the landing. On the 22d a radio message informed the 17th Army that Ichiki's detachment had been "almost annihilated at a point short of the airfield." Officers at the headquarters of the 17th Army, the 8th Fleet, and the 11th Air Fleet initially greeted this signal with disbelief. Not until the 25th did these officers accept a dispatch sent by Lieutenant Sakakibara, a communications officer in the Ichiki detachment, and recognize the extent of the disaster. By then the second naval battle of the campaign had been fought.

THE BATTLE OF

THE EASTERN

SOLOMONS

"The enemy planes are directly overhead now!"

A CONVOY AND THE COMBINED FLEET

Even as Ichiki performed the ultimate act of atonement for his failure, his Second Echelon and the 5th Yokosuka Special Naval Landing Force were already at sea packed aboard a three-transport convoy. Those soldiers topside could see the prominent bridgework and four funnels of the light cruiser *Jintsu,* flagship of Rear Admiral Tanaka, and the low shapes of eight destroyers ahead and to the flanks. Tanaka led the convoy out of Truk on August 16 and began what developed into an intricate dance of alternating lunges toward and away from Guadalcanal. Tanaka's maneuvers were intimately connected to those of the Combined Fleet, but the linkage was not mutual.

Admiral Yamamoto assembled two large task forces comprising four battleships, four carriers, one escort carrier, sixteen cruisers, one seaplane carrier, and thirty destroyers for duty in the South Pacific. These vessels had almost all been undergoing upkeep, repair, or training after Midway, but the biggest overhaul was in the area of tactics. As recently as the June clash, Japan's twelve battleships occupied the hub of fleet organization and plans. Now eight of them remained behind and the other four played a clearly subordinate role, thus finally resolving the contradictions since the start of the war between the theoretical and actual relationships of the Imperial Navy's carriers and battleships. A newly conceived battle array revealed the extent of this metamorphosis. The bulk of the cruisers of the 2d Fleet or Advanced Force would be placed 110 to 150 miles ahead of the carriers, where they might finish off enemy ships crippled by carrier plane attacks, but where they also would serve as a magnet for attacking American aircraft.

The costs and the lessons of Midway also prompted a reorganization of the remaining carriers and their air groups. There now would be just two fleet carrier divisions, each nominally composed of one light and two heavy carriers. The light carrier was to afford local cover for the carrier division, freeing the full clout of the big carriers for attack missions. Simultaneously, the aircraft complements of the carriers were reshuffled. The two large carriers of Carrier Division 1, *Shokaku* and *Zuikaku,* would each operate twenty-seven fighters, twenty-seven dive-bombers, and eighteen torpedo planes. The attached light carrier *Ryujo* would carry only fighters and torpedo planes, twenty-four of the former and nine of the latter. This represented an increase in the total plane complements of the two big carriers, achieved through adding fighters and dive-bombers though at the cost of some torpedo planes. These complements reflected recent experience and new tactics that called for the vulnerable torpedo planes to be held in reserve until initial attack groups of fighters and dive-bombers damaged the enemy. To augment the air search capabilities of the Combined Fleet and to free carrier planes for other roles, the battleships and cruisers accompanying the carriers would mount more float planes.

The Imperial Navy needed time to implement these changes and to conduct training in the new tactics, but Admiral King's insistence on an early offensive denied the Japanese a respite. In the haste of sailing for the Solomons, the staffs of the 3d Fleet or Main Body (which contained the carriers) and the 2d Fleet or Advanced Force consulted but briefly. They intended to use a pause at Truk for detailed planning, but, inexplicably, Admiral Kondo sailed his Advanced Force before Admiral Nagumo's Main Body arrived. The two fleets rendezvoused at sea at 0700 on August 21, and then split again to head south separately. The only clear point of agreement was that defeating the American carriers held first priority; defending the reinforcement convoy stood at a distant second.

Admiral Fletcher's Task Force 61, with three carriers, one battle-ship, seven cruisers, and eighteen destroyers, loitered in the waters off the southeast end of the Solomons, just out of range of Japanese search planes from Rabaul. Twice daily the Americans cast 200-mile-long nets of search planes, but as at Coral Sea and Midway, they anticipated punctual warning of the approach of Japanese flattops from radio intelligence. This time, however, the wizards of radio intelligence worked largely from traffic analysis, whose gossamer linkages produced only misty outlines of Japanese intentions and maneuvers.

On August 16 some analysts correctly interpreted the radio silence of the 3d (Carrier) Fleet or Main Body as a sign that it had sailed—a view not universally shared. The Pacific Fleet intelligence summary for August 17 placed *Shokaku, Zuikaku,* and *Ryujo* in home waters, though it acknowledged that they were expected to steer south shortly, as in fact they had been heading for twenty-four hours. At 0000 on the 18th, the Japanese changed all major call signs, tempo-rarily snuffing out the most fruitful source of insight from traffic analysis. Two days later the Pacific Fleet intelligence officer placed all Japanese carriers in home waters and rated a sortie by Carrier Division 1 as a "slight possibility." But on this same day, traffic analysts announced that the headings in messages dated August 11 and 13 appeared to give the organization of a carrier task force under the 1st Air Fleet (an alternative title for the 3d or Carrier Fleet) and a surface combatant task force under the 2d Fleet commander.

Correctly delineating Japanese task organization certainly repre-sented an important accomplishment, but projecting Japanese move-ments proved to be a more difficult feat. On August 21, the radio intelligence station in Melbourne suggested that the Japanese carrier task force was already at Truk based upon the routing of a single message to one of the units of the task force, *Chikuma,* to the Truk communications zone. Reinforcement for that conclusion material-ized in similar message routings to the chief of staff and the commu-nications officer of the carrier task force. But doubts about the accuracy of Melbourne's call-sign recoveries and the routing of liter-ally dozens of other messages to the carrier fleet through the Tokyo communications zone strongly contradicted that surmise. The Pacific Fleet intelligence officer offered his opinion that "unless [Jap-anese] radio deception is remarkably efficient, this force remains in the homeland." The next day, August 22, confirmation of the call signs and routing of messages for Cardiv 1 to Truk prompted the Pacific Fleet intelligence officer to swing to the stance that a carrier task force with *Shokaku, Zuikaku,* and possibly *Ryujo* was either in the Truk area or between Japan and Truk, and that a 2d Fleet task force was either at Truk or en route Truk to Rabaul. But the CINC-PAC intelligence summary was distinctly more muted in its conclusions. According to this message, there existed "no positive indications" to confirm the departure of Japanese carriers from home waters, but the "possibility of undetected departure" of *Shokaku, Zuikaku,* and *Ryujo* "subsequent to 16 August should not be disregarded."

While the Americans were baffled about the location of the Japanese carriers across the Pacific, the Japanese were perplexed about the exact location of the American flattops known to be somewhere east or southeast of Guadalcanal. On August 20 flying boats from Shortland spotted two American carriers, one the escort carrier *Long Island,* the other a fleet carrier, about 250 miles southeast of Guadalcanal. Orders went promptly to Tanaka to head northwest with his charges to keep them out of the jaws of American carrier planes. Early the next day the Japanese correctly interpreted the fragmentary last words of a Mavis reporting it was under air attack (by *Wasp* SBDs) as demonstrating the presence of a carrier. The 11th Air Fleet mounted a strike of twenty-six Bettys with thirteen Zeros in escort to get this worthy target. They failed to find a carrier, and on the return trip the escort went to Guadalcanal to look for trouble. They found it in the form of four Wildcats led by Captain John L. Smith, the commander of VMF-223. At around 1207 the Marine planes engaged all thirteen Zeros near Savo Island. The Japanese pilots believed they found no fewer than thirteen Wildcats in the air and claimed four shot down for "sure" plus two "probables." Their marksmanship was superior to their math and they holed every one of the American fighters. The one flown by Technical Sergeant John D. Lindsey glided back to Guadalcanal to make a dead-stick landing, and its carcass became the charter member of the Henderson Field "bone heap"; another damaged F4F never flew again. Ground observers thought they saw a plane splash, and Captain Smith, who fired his guns but made no claim, was credited with one of the Zeros. In fact, no Japanese plane was lost in this action. Such was the formidable reputation of the Zero fighter that the mere survival of these four pilots caused the morale of the squadron of tenderfoot marines to zoom.

On August 21, industrious Japanese search planes also detected a small convoy of two freighters and a "cruiser" steaming toward Guadalcanal. These were actually the cargo ships *Fomalhaut* and

Alhena, bearing much-needed supplies and squired by the destroyers *Blue, Henley,* and *Helm.* The ingredients for a nautical skirmish were mixed when Admiral Mikawa ordered the destroyers *Kawakaze* and *Yunagi* to make a nocturnal interception of the Americans off Guadalcanal and, at almost the same time, Admiral Turner directed *Blue* and *Henley* leave the convoy and steam ahead to keep Japanese reinforcements away from Guadalcanal. Bad weather prevented *Yunagi* from keeping her appointment, but Commander Kazuo Wakabayashi of *Kawakaze* pressed on alone.

The Americans placed their faith in radar to penetrate the black void of a moonless and overcast night, while the Japanese trusted to their lookouts. Once again, Japanese eyes excelled American radar. At 0355, *Blue* was 600 yards ahead of *Henley* when she simultaneously picked up a radar and sonar contact on a high-speed vessel only 5,000 yards away. *Blue* maintained her course and speed while training guns and torpedoes on the target. Suddenly at 0359 the orange-red glow of a torpedo hit sheering off *Blue*'s stern pierced the darkness. The half-ton warhead ripped away *Blue*'s steering gear, paralyzed her propellers, and left nine of her crew dead and twenty-one wounded. This was but one of six Long Lances launched by *Kawakaze,* which expeditiously darted away; the Americans surmised that a motor torpedo boat had hit *Blue. Henley* waited upon her sister until dawn, which revealed *Blue* immobilized but afloat.

This same dawn found the Japanese fleet commanders pondering fragments of information. News of Ichiki's failure disturbed them less than confirmation that Henderson Field now hosted American planes. Their concern would have increased a little more had they learned that five P-400s of the U.S. Army Air Force's 67th Fighter Squadron reached Guadalcanal this day. The Combined Fleet proposed that Ichiki's Second Echelon be delivered posthaste to Guadalcanal by destroyer transports to snip the sprout of American air power at the root. Admiral Tsukahara found the 17th Army objected strongly to this proposal. The destroyer conversions could not haul the soldier's artillery, and the senior Army officers, who as of this date still disbelieved reports of Ichiki's defeat, remained confident that he would soon hold the airfield. The 8th Fleet also pointed out that a landing on the 24th as planned would be impossible in view of the time required for the destroyer transports to sail from Shortland, rendezvous with the transports, and then steam to Guadalcanal.

The news of American planes on Guadalcanal and the presence of American carriers somewhere southeast of the island understandably made Tanaka worry about the safety of his transports. Before noon on August 22 he posed the obvious question: who would provide direct air cover for his ships? Tanaka's query exposes a serious weakness in Japanese planning. Moreover, the answer to his signal illuminates rickety Japanese command arrangements. Tanaka's immediate superior, the 8th Fleet, promptly asked the 11th Air Fleet for planes for Tanaka, but Admiral Tsukahara preferred to support the convoy by offensive rather than defensive means. Weather foiled a strike group he dispatched to Guadalcanal this day, and the admiral resolved to try again the next day. Tsukahara proposed that Nagumo's carriers assume responsibility for direct air cover over the convoy on the 24th. The Combined Fleet believed that the Japanese carriers must be held in reserve to deal with their American counterparts and that a strike on Guadalcanal would probably betray their location. Some Japanese officers may have suffered uneasy feelings as the situation developed a semblance to Midway, with the Japanese carriers being called upon to neutralize the air strength of an island outpost with American carriers poised on their flank. The product of these various concerns emerged as an awkward compromise that matured over the next thirty-six hours. If the morning of August 24 passed without detection of the American carriers, the Japanese carriers would afford cover for the convoy. Until then Tanaka, now back on course for Guadalcanal, would do without air support.

The weather on the 23d again shielded Guadalcanal, and Tsukahara's fliers returned with their bombs. Search planes lofted during the day from Japanese carriers and the Advanced Force located no American vessel, but no doubt existed as to the proximity of American carriers. Japanese submarines thrived in the waters to the southeast of Guadalcanal, and both *I-17* and *I-11* sighted carrier planes, three of which attacked *I-17*. The Japanese task forces, however, proved less elusive, for an American plane found the Advanced Force. To keep the whereabouts of his carriers veiled, at 1825 Nagumo swung the Main Body to head north, and Kondo perforce followed suit.

The sighting of Kondo's ships came late in an already busy day for American aviators. Routine search missions from *Enterprise* found three surfaced submarines carving high-speed wakes pointed south. To knowledgeable officers this immediately raised the possibility that they were part of a typical Japanese submarine scouting line for a major task force. At 0950 one of McCain's ubiquitous Catalinas spied Tanaka's convoy 250 miles north of Guadalcanal and began to shadow it. Without air cover, the Japanese admiral could only direct cold fury at the pesky plane. The Catalina report stirred Fletcher to lash out after a fortnight's inactivity. At 1510, *Saratoga* stuck her bow into the wind and peeled off thirty-one SBDs and six TBFs. In the interval, Tanaka's plight won him permission to once again turn back. The PBY witnessed his course change, but, in the first of a series of maddening communications failures, its report did not reach Fletcher until that night. The *Saratoga* strike group under her air group commander, Commander Harry D. Felt, ran into a partition of sullen gray clouds punctuated by rainsqualls and performed very well in just retaining its cohesion. Unable to find the convoy in the murk, Felt led his group to Guadalcanal, where they put down after dark in a landing pattern enlivened by machinegun fire from the Japanese or "doubting marines."

With food and ammunition in short supply, the situation on Guadalcanal looked grim upon the PBY report of an approaching convoy, presumably bearing substantial Japanese reinforcements. After some soul searching, Vandegrift decided to risk all of his small air force to hit the convoy. At 1630 he watched as nine SBDs and twelve F4Fs took off, uncertain whether he would see any of them again. The same amalgamation of clouds and rain forced the less experienced Marine fliers to turn back. After their return, Vandegrift moved among the dejected airmen offering consolation despite the strain in his own face.

About the time the Marine aviators were returning, Fletcher was making a crucial decision. At 1700, radiomen copied the latest radio intelligence estimate from Pearl Harbor. It located *Shokaku, Zuikaku,* and *Ryujo* at Truk, but placed no carriers south of that point. No American plane had seen a Japanese carrier to indicate otherwise, and Fletcher did not find as much significance in the presence of a convoy and in the submarine sightings as did some of his subordinates. Concluding that battle was not imminent and under orders from Ghormley to release a carrier to refuel, Fletcher detached the *Wasp* Group for refueling. At sunset, *Wasp* headed south, transporting two valuable cargoes: sixty-two aircraft of a well-trained air group and the best chance in 1942 for the United States Navy to have potentially decisive quantitative superiority in a carrier action.

The twilight hours witnessed a decision on the fate of the destroyer *Blue. Henley* had commenced to tow her at daylight on August 22, first toward Lunga and then toward Tulagi. This change proved fatal. Her twisted stern plates made *Blue* an exceedingly recalcitrant tow, and darkness of August 23 found her still some distance from the haven of Tulagi harbor. With a report of approaching enemy warships in hand, the Squadron Commander proposed that *Blue* be scuttled, and Admiral Turner concurred. *Blue* sank at 2221.

On Guadalcanal the *Saratoga* airmen bedded down with their planes as best they could. Many sampled the emergency rations in their survival kits, while all through the night the laborious process of refueling the planes by hand went forth. The marines could offer little besides coffee, but the Japanese provided entertainment. Admiral Mikawa sent the destroyer *Kagero* to sweep the waters of Iron Bottom Sound; she thus became the indirect agent of *Blue*'s demise. *Kagero* arrived off Lunga Point at 2330 and tarried long enough to throw a few shells at the marines and their guests before departing. At the same moment that *Kagero* approached Lunga Point, Tanaka pointed the prows of his ships once again on course 160 degrees for Guadalcanal.

THE CARRIER BATTLE OF AUGUST 24

At 0600 on August 24, the Japanese Main Body and Advanced Force set course 150 degrees and bent on 20 knots. *Shokaku, Zuikaku,* and *Ryujo* carried 171 planes; the two available American carriers carried 154. The Japanese trio readied seventy-three Zeros, but the American pair countered with only fifty-seven Wildcats (the two F4F-7s were unarmed photographic reconnaissance planes). For dive-bombing the Japanese relied on fifty-four Aichi D3A1s, code-named "Val" by the Allies. The Val spread a graceful pair of elliptical wings, but its fixed, spatted landing gear ("pants down" in the American vernacular) disfigured its aerodynamic pulchritude. The sixty-eight available Douglas SBD-3s were beloved for their simple, sturdy design and viceless flying characteristics. The manufacturer quoted a maximum speed of 250 mph, but actual speed in service was less, and the speed that counted most—when lugging a bomb—pegged at an agonizing 130 knots. The Japanese conducted torpedo and horizontal bombing in the Nakajima B5N2 ("Kate"), by now obsolescent and highly vulnerable. The forty-four Kates sitting on Japanese flight decks still retained a deadly sting, because they brandished a reliable torpedo that packed a 450-pound warhead. The two American torpedo squadrons counted on hand twenty-nine of the new Grumman TBF Avengers, a typical product of its manufacturer endowed with angular wings, a husky fuselage, and great strength. Armor plating, self-sealing gasoline tanks, and a unique turret gun

COMPOSITION OF FORCES

1. JAPANESE
Combined Fleet
Adm. Isoroku Yamamoto
in battleship **Yamato**
at Truk

BATTLESHIP:

Yamato   Capt. Gihachi Takayanagi

ESCORT CARRIER:

Taiyo

DESTROYERS:

Desdiv 7(-)   Capt. Kaname Konishi
  Akebono   Lt. Cdr. Minoru Nakagawa
  Ushio   Cdr. Yoshitake Uesugi

Third Fleet (Main Body)
Vice Adm. Chuichi Nagumo
in **Shokaku**

HEAVY CARRIERS:

Carrier Division 1   Vice Adm. Nagumo
  Shokaku   Capt. Masafumi Arima

Strike Group Commander: Lt. Cdr. Mamoru Seki
27(26)   Zeros   Lt. Hideki Shingo
27(27)   Vals   Lt. Cdr. Seki
18(18)   Kates   Lt. Cdr. Shigeharu Murata

  Zuikaku   Capt. Tameteru Notomo

Strike Group Commander: Lt. Sadamu Takahashi
27(25)   Zeros   Lt. Ayao Shirane
27(27)   Vals   Lt. Takahashi
18(18)   Kates   Lt. Shigeichiro Imajuku
(First figure authorized; second figure available 24 August)

Screen

DESTROYERS (From Desron 10):

Desdiv 10   Capt. Toshio Abe
  Kazegumo   Cdr. Masayoshi Yoshida
  Yugumo   Cdr. Shigeo Semba
  Makikumo   Cdr. Isamu Fujita
  Akigumo   Cdr. Shohei Soma
From Desdiv 16
  Hatsukaze   Cdr. Kameshiro Takahashi
Unattached
  Akizuki

Close Support of Carriers (Vanguard Force)
Rear Admiral Hiroaki Abe
in **Hiei**

BATTLESHIPS:

Battleship Division 11	Rear Admiral Abe
Hiei	Capt. Masao Nishida
Kirishima	Capt. Sanji Iwabuchi

HEAVY CRUISERS:

Cruiser Division 7	Rear Admiral Shoji Nishimura
Kumano	Capt. Kikumatsu Tanaka
Suzuya	Capt. Masatomi Kimura
Cruiser Division 8(-)	
Chikuma	Capt. Keizo Komura

Destroyer Squadron 10
Rear Admiral Satsuma Kimura in **Nagara**

LIGHT CRUISER:

Nagara	Capt. Toshio Naoi

DESTROYERS:

Desdiv 4	Capt. Kosaku Ariga
Nowaki	Cdr. Magotaro Koga
Maikaze	Cdr. Seiji Nakasugi
From Desdiv 17	
Tanikaze	Cdr. Motoi Katsumi

Detached Carrier Strike Force
Rear Admiral Chuichi Hara
(Commander CruDiv 8)
in **Tone**

LIGHT CARRIER:

Ryujo	Capt. Tadao Kato

Strike Group Commander: Lt. Kenjiro Notomi

24(23)	Zeros	Lt. Notomi
9(9)	Kates	Lt. Binichi Murakami

HEAVY CRUISER:

Tone	Capt. Yuji Anibe

DESTROYERS:

Desdiv 16	Capt. Kiichiro Sato
Amatsukaze	Cdr. Tameichi Hara
Tokitsukaze	Cdr. Giichiro Nakahara

Second Fleet (Advanced Force)
Vice Admiral Nobutake Kondo
in **Atago**

HEAVY CRUISERS:

Cruiser Division 4	Vice Admiral Kondo
Atago	Capt. Matsuji Ijuin
Maya	Capt. Shunsaku Nabeshima
Takao	Capt. Bunji Asakura
Cruiser Division 5	Vice Admiral Takeo Takagi
Myoko	Capt. Teruhiko Miyoshi
Haguro	Capt. Tomoichi Mori

Screen
Destroyer Squadron 4
Rear Admiral Tamotsu Takama in **Yura**

LIGHT CRUISER:

Yura	Capt. Shiro Sato

DESTROYERS:

Desdiv 15	Capt. Torajiro Sato
Kuroshio	Cdr. Tamaki Ugaki
Oyashio	Cdr. Tokikichi Arima
Hayashio	Cdr. Kiyoshi Kaneda
Desdiv 9	Capt. Yasuo Sato
Minegumo	Cdr. Yasuatsu Suzuki
Natsugumo	Cdr. Moritaro Tsukamoto
Asagumo	Cdr. Toru Iwahashi

SEAPLANE CARRIER:

Carrier Division 11(-)	
Chitose	Capt. Seigo Sasaki
	7 Jakes, 15 Petes

Standby Force
(Not at sea)

HEAVY CARRIER:

Junyo	Capt. Shizue Ishii

Support Force
Capt. Teijiro Yamazumi

BATTLESHIP:

Mutsu	Capt. Yamazumi

DESTROYERS:

Desdiv 2	Capt. Masao Tachibana
Harusame	Cdr. Masao Kamiyama
Samidare	Cdr. Takisaburo Matsubara
Murasame	Cdr. Naoji Suenaga

Southeast Area Commander
Vice Admiral Nishizo Tsukahara

Eighth Fleet (Outer South Sea Force)
Vice Admiral Gunichi Mikawa

Close Cover Force
Admiral Mikawa

HEAVY CRUISERS:

Chokai	Capt. Mikio Kayakama
Crudiv 6	Rear Admiral Aritomo Goto
Kinugasa	Capt. Masao Sawa
Aoba	Capt. Yunejiro Hisamune
Furutaka	Capt. Araki Tsutau

Convoy Escort Force
Rear Admiral Raizo Tanaka

Destroyer Squadron 2
Admiral Tanaka in **Jintsu**

LIGHT CRUISER:

Jintsu	Capt. Torazo Kozai

DESTROYERS:

Desdiv 24	Capt. Yasuji Hirai
Suzukaze	Cdr. Kazuo Shibayama
Kawakaze	Cdr. Kazuo Wakabayashi
Umikaze	Cdr. Nagahide Sugitani
From Desdiv 15	
Kagero	Cdr. Minoru Yokoi
From Desdiv 17	
Isokaze	Cdr. Shunichi Toshima
Desdiv 30	Capt. Shiro Yasutake
Yayoi	
Mutsuki	Cdr. Hatano
Uzuki	

Transport Force

TRANSPORTS:

Kinryu Maru, Boston Maru, Daifuku Maru
Embarking 1,500 troops of Ichiki's Second Echelon and the 5th
   Yokosuka Special Naval Landing Force.

PATROL BOATS:

No. 1, 2, 34, 35

Sixth Fleet (Advanced Expeditionary Force)
Vice Admiral Teruhisa Komatsu
(at Truk)

SUBMARINES *(Actually at sea in Solomons area):*

Submarine Squadron 1
Rear Admiral Shigeaki Yamazaki
in **I-9**

I-9	Cdr. Akiyoshi Fujii
Subdiv 2	Capt. Hiroshi Imazato
I-15	Cdr. Nobuo Ishikawa
I-17	Cdr. Kozo Nishino
I-19	Cdr. Takaichi Kinashi
Subdiv 4	
I-26	Cdr. Minoru Yokota
Subdiv 15	
I-31	
I-33	

Submarine Squadron 7
Rear Admiral Setsuzo Yoshitomi
in **Jinjei** *at Rabaul*

Subdiv 13	Capt. Takeharu Miyazaki
I-121	Lt. Cdr. Yasuo Fujimori
I-122	Lt. Cdr. Sadatoshi Norita
I-123	Lt. Cdr. Makoto Nakai
Subdiv 21	Cdr. Tsutau Fujimoto
RO-34	Lt. Cdr. Masahiko Morinaga

Submarine Squadron 3
Capt. Hanmazu Sasaki

I-11	Cdr. Tsuneo Shichiji
Subdiv 11	
I-174	
I-175	

Eleventh Air Fleet
Vice Admiral Tsukahara

25th Air Flotilla (5th Air Attack Force)
Rear Admiral Sadayoshi Yamada

Tainan Air Group	Zeros
2d Air Group	Zeros, Vals
4th Air Group	Bettys
Yokohama Air Group	Mavis
14th Air Group	Emily
(Detachment)	

26th Air Flotilla (6th Air Attack Force)
Vice Admiral Seizo Yamagata

6th Air Group (Detachment)	Zeros
Misawa Air Group	Bettys
Kisarazu Air Group	Bettys

(Estimate strength as of August 24: 51 Zeros, 41 Bettys, 9 Vals, 2 Irvings, 8 Mavis, 3 Emily = 114 aircraft)

---

2. AMERICAN

Pacific Fleet
Admiral Chester W. Nimitz

South Pacific Area, South Pacific Force
Vice Admiral Robert L. Ghormley

Task Force 61 (Carrier Groups)
Vice Admiral Frank J. Fletcher

Task Force 11
Admiral Fletcher

CARRIER:

Saratoga		Capt. DeWitt C. Ramsey
Saratoga Air Group:	1 SBD-3 (Dauntless)	Cdr. Harry D. Felt
VF-5	28(27) F4F-4, 1 F4F-7 (Wildcat)	Lt. Cdr. Leroy C. Simpler
VB-3	17 SBD-3	Lt. Cdr. Dewitt W. Shumway
VS-3	15 SBD-3	Lt. Cdr. Louis J. Kirn
VT-8	13 TBF-1 (Avenger)	Lt. Cdr. Harold H. Larsen

Screen
Rear Admiral Carleton H. Wright

HEAVY CRUISERS:

Minneapolis	Captain Frank J. Lowry
New Orleans	Captain Walter S. Delany

DESTROYERS:

Destroyer Squadron 1
Captain Samuel B. Brewer

Phelps	Lt. Cdr. Edward L. Beck
Desdiv 2	Cdr. Francis X. McInerney
Farragut	Cdr. George P. Hunter
Worden	Lt. Cdr. William G. Pogue
MacDonough	Lt. Cdr. Erle V. E. Dennett
Dale	Lt. Cdr. Anthony L. Rorschach

Task Force 16
Rear Admiral Thomas C. Kinkaid

CARRIER:

Enterprise   Capt. Arthur C. Davis

Enterprise Air Group:	1 TBF-1	Lt. Cdr. Maxwell F. Leslie
VF-6	29(28) F4F-4	Lt. Cdr. Louis H. Bauer
VB-6	17 SBD-3	Lt. Ray Davis
VS-5	18 SBD-3	Lt. Stockton B. Strong
VT-3	15 TBF-1	Lt. Cdr. Charles M. Jett
Utility Unit 1	1 F4F-7	

Screen
Rear Admiral Mahlon S. Tisdale

BATTLESHIP:

North Carolina   Capt. George H. Fort

HEAVY CRUISER:

Portland   Capt. Laurance T. DuBose

LIGHT CRUISER:

Atlanta   Capt. Samuel P. Jenkins

DESTROYERS:

Destroyer Squadron 6
Captain Edward P. Sauer

Balch	Lt. Cdr. Harold H. Tiemroth
Benham	Lt. Cdr. Joseph M. Worthington
Maury	Lt. Cdr. Gelzer L. Sim
Ellet	Lt. Cdr. Francis H. Gardner
Desdiv 22	Cdr. Harold R. Holcomb
Grayson	Lt. Cdr. Frederick J. Bell
Monssen	Cdr. Roland N. Smoot

Task Force 18
Rear Admiral Leigh Noyes
(Not participating in action of August 24)

CARRIER:

Wasp   Capt. Forrest P. Sherman

Wasp Air Group:	1 TBF-1	Lt. Cdr. Wallace M. Beakley
VF-71	25 F4F-4	Lt. Cdr. Courtney Shands
VS-71	13 SBD-3	Lt. Cdr. John Eldridge
VS-72	13 SBD-3	Lt. Cdr. Ernest M. Snowden
VT-7	9 TBF-1	Lt. Henry A. Romberg

(One VT-8 TBF and one J2F were also aboard)

Screen
Rear Adm. Norman Scott

HEAVY CRUISERS:

San Francisco — Capt. Charles H. McMorris
Salt Lake City — Capt. Ernest G. Small

LIGHT CRUISER:

San Juan — Capt. James E. Maher

DESTROYERS:

Destroyer Squadron 12: Capt. Robert G. Tobin

Farenholt — Lt. Cdr. Eugene T. Seaward
Aaron Ward — Lt. Cdr. Orville F. Gregor
Buchanan — Lt. Cdr. Ralph E. Wilson
Desdiv 15 — Capt. William W. Warlick
Lang — Lt. Cdr. John L. Wilfong
Stack — Lt. Cdr. Alvord J. Greenacre
Sterett — Cdr. Jesse G. Coward

Destroyer Squadron 4: Capt. Cornelius W. Flynn

Selfridge — Cdr. Carroll D. Reynolds

Task Force 63 (Land-Based Aircraft): Rear Adm. John S. McCain

AT GUADALCANAL:

VMF-223	13 F4F-4	Maj. John L. Smith
VMSB-232	11 SBD-3	Lt. Col. Richard C. Mangrum
67th Fighter Sdn	5 P-400	Capt. Dale D. Brannon

SEARCH AND ATTACK AIRCRAFT:

11th Bomb Group	25 B-17E & F	Col. LaVerne G. Saunders
VP-11	circa 16 PBY-5	
VP-14	2 PBY-5 (plus 2 arriving August 24) total about 35 PBY	
VP-23	12 PBY-5	
VP-72	3 PBY-5	

made it very resilient. The Achilles' heel of American torpedo bombing, however, remained the slow and erratic Mark 13 torpedo.

The search radars mounted on both American carriers conferred an important advantage. These were reasonably efficient at tracking aircraft and enabled specially trained fighter direction officers to practice the still-rudimentary art of vectoring defending fighters to

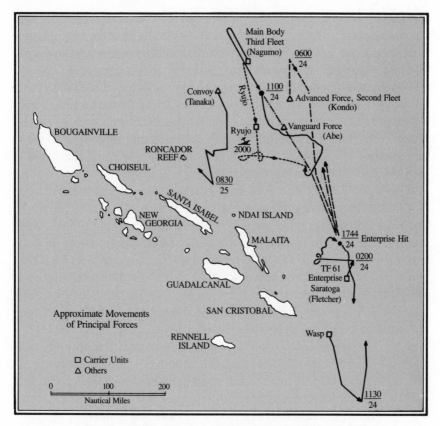

Battle of the Eastern Solomons, August 24–25

intercept enemy aircraft. By contrast, the Imperial Navy had only just equipped *Shokaku* with a radar set, and when the carrier sailed her technicians and operators had barely begun learning their trade.

The hasty departure of Nagumo's ships also disrupted the drilling of the reformed air groups. Further, the overall quality of Japanese carrier fliers had definitely diminished from the peak of proficiency evident at the start of the war. But the Americans' position was no better. Both sides had experienced heavy carrier pilot losses, and the eight squadrons aboard *Enterprise* and *Saratoga* were drafted from four prewar air groups. Many of the aviators were raw graduates of recent training classes, and the hard-eyed view of Admiral Nimitz's staff was that "pilots with experience are spread thin and those recently in battle are shaken."

As the Japanese headed south they assumed battle formation. Concern that the American carriers lurked to the east presumably prompted deployment of the Advanced Force to that side of the Japanese carriers rather than ahead as originally planned. Replacing the Advanced Force, battleships *Hiei* and *Kirishima* and cruisers *Suzuya, Kumano, Chikuma,* and *Nagara* of the carrier escort arrayed themselves in a line of bearing approximately 6 miles in front of the carriers *Shokaku* and *Zuikaku*—a far cry from the 110 to 150 miles projected. *Ryujo* had been detached at 0400 with heavy cruiser *Tone* embarking Rear Admiral Chuichi Hara and destroyers *Amatsukaze* and *Tokitsukaze.* They would cover the convoy if the American carriers remained unlocated during the morning.

During the early hours of daylight the seagoing contingents on both sides essayed search missions, which proved fruitless. A PBY gained the first contact of the day when it sighted *Ryujo* at 0935 and maintained surveillance. Other Catalinas found portions of the Advanced Force and the Main Body; none saw another carrier. Fletcher got word of the *Ryujo* contact at 0947, but after the misadventures only the day before that still left him without the services of Commander Felt's group, he cast a jaundiced eye on the PBY report and declined to order an immediate attack on the light carrier. At 0930, Felt's *Saratoga* attack group, less two Dauntlesses temporarily out of commission, took off from Guadalcanal over the watchful eyes of the enemy garrison. When the red-eyed fliers landed aboard *Saratoga* at 1105, it was with new appreciation for her civilized appointments. At 1130 the American carriers swung to a northerly heading to close the range on *Ryujo.*

With a second message on *Ryujo*'s whereabouts in hand at 1128, Fletcher elected to send off a search for other Japanese ships before committing himself against her. At 1213, *Saratoga* fighters flamed a prowling Emily. At 1239, *Enterprise* sliced off sixteen SBDs and seven TBFs to search an arc between 290 and 90 degrees true. Just over fifteen minutes later, fighters torched a Betty, this time only 7 miles from the task force.

The Wildcats prevented either Japanese plane from issuing a contact report, though Fletcher assumed the contrary. Consequently, *Ryujo* began to comply with her secondary mission at 1220 by launching a strike group for Guadalcanal. Lieutenant Kenjiro Notomi rounded up fifteen Zeros and six Kates and headed for the American toehold, while *Ryujo* scurried north to dodge any counterattack. At 1320, *Ryujo*'s attack group flickered onto a radar screen aboard *Saratoga.* Rapid plotting revealed the planes were distant 100 miles and bound for Guadalcanal. This evidence converted a still-skeptical Fletcher into a believer in the PBY contacts; he ordered

Saratoga to attack the Japanese carrier. Only twenty-five minutes after the blip appeared on her radar screen, *Saratoga* commenced flying off thirty SBDs and eight TBFs under Commander Felt. One Dauntless and one Avenger had to turn back, but the other weary pilots quickly slipped into formation and pointed their noses for *Ryujo*'s likely position.

At 1420 the *Ryujo* strike, flying recklessly low at 9,000 feet, reached Guadalcanal, where it tangled with fourteen contingents of Wildcats totaling sixteen planes and two Army P-400s. The large swirling air fight among thirty-nine planes bred two predictable results: ineffective Japanese bombing and immodest claims by both sets of fighter pilots. The marines thought they notched up nine bombers and seven Zeros while losing three Wildcats with two pilots killed and one wounded. The Zero pilots' report attained perfect symmetry: fifteen Wildcats encountered and fifteen shot down. Three Zeros and three Kates were destroyed over Guadalcanal, and one Kate crash-landed on Ndai Island, about 140 miles north of Santa Isabel. Unaware that the fighter-plane battle ended in a draw, the Marine pilots perceived it as a great victory, cutting the reputation of the Zero down to size and enormously increasing their confidence.

Shortly after 1400 a *Chikuma* float plane at long last beheld the American carriers. *Enterprise* fighters dispatched it before the crew completed a report, but the Japanese readily calculated from its time of flight and course the approximate position of the American flat-tops. More planes soared off to precisely mark the enemy location while the big carriers readied strike groups. At 1455, Lieutenant Commander Mamoru Seki of *Shokaku* led out eighteen Vals and four Zeros from his ship and nine Vals and six Zeros from *Zuikaku*. At the same time the formation headed by battleships *Hiei* and *Kirishima* began to accelerate to close the American position. Just over one hour later, at 1600, a second attack group under Lieutenant Sadamu Takahashi took off with eighteen *Zuikaku* and nine *Shokaku* dive-bombers escorted by six *Zuikaku* and three *Shokaku* Zeros. After launching these seventy-three planes the big carriers swung to the east. Seven B-17s in two groups bombed all three Japanese carriers ineffectively between 1750 and 1819, but accounted for one Zero. Heavy rain caused one of the four-engine bombers to crash on landing.

American radios now began to crackle with messages from the *Enterprise* search planes. One pair of TBFs tattled on *Ryujo* at 1410, then 198 miles from the American carriers. Because of interference between the fighter-direction and search-plane radio frequencies,

Enterprise failed to copy this message. The TBFs conducted an unsuccessful high-level bombing attack at 1428. Less luck attended another duo of TBFs. *Ryujo*'s fighters downed one (from which one crewman returned after many adventures in April 1943) and badly shot up the other. Two SBDs found the Advanced Force at 1440 bearing 347 degrees and 225 miles distant from the American carriers. They connected with a message to *Enterprise,* but were not so fortunate with their bombs in an attack on heavy cruiser *Maya.*

At 1518 the first contact report by an *Enterprise* plane on *Ryujo* finally broke through to the American task force, but it had already been eclipsed by news of bigger game. Lieutenant Ray Davis and Ensign R. C. Shaw, flying SBDs, sighted Japanese "light cruisers" and were preparing to attack them when in the distance they spotted *Shokaku* and *Zuikaku.* As they maneuvered to attack the carriers they broadcast a sighting report, but it, too, passed unnoted in the babble on the circuit. Unknown to the American pilots, *Shokaku*'s radarmen detected their approach and sent a warning to the ship's bridge. Somehow in the hurly-burly in the flagship's nerve center this alert failed to register, but lookouts shouted alarm in time for *Shokaku* to swerve suddenly, causing both bombs to miss close aboard, though they killed six men. Davis and Shaw confessed by radio the misfiring of their attack on a group of ships including two carriers, and *Saratoga* intercepted this signal at 1500. Overall the cost of the *Enterprise*'s search mission was dear. Besides the loss of one TBF recorded above, one TBF and a pair of SBDs ditched near the task force, where their crews were rescued, while another TBF crew was retrieved from the Stewart Islands.

Fletcher now stood in the awkward position of having dispatched his main punch at a Japanese light carrier when two big flattops had materialized closer at hand. The intrepid Commander Felt, however, monitored what he took as a fresh sighting of *Ryujo* at 1518 and altered course to the north for the reported position. When he found nothing there he again headed west and was rewarded at 1536 with a view of *Ryujo* and her sparse escorts.

Felt divided his attack formation so that *Ryujo* drew all fifteen Dauntlesses of VS-3 and six of VB-3's planes plus five TBFs. He earmarked the remaining seven SBDs of Bombing Three and two TBFs for the cruiser *Tone.* At 1550 the attack began, with slanting dives from 14,000 feet by a column of SBDs on *Ryujo* while the torpedo planes nosed down to the sea surface to deliver their weaponry. To Felt's chagrin, Captain Tadao Kato threw *Ryujo* into a sharp starboard turn that appeared to cause bomb after bomb to miss. After about ten bombs failed to draw visible blood, Felt countermanded his order and directed that all planes attack the carrier. He then set the example with a dive that probably scored. The Bombing Three Dauntlesses pulled up from dives on *Tone* and reoriented on *Ryujo*'s slender flight deck, claiming three hits. On recovery at sea level the SBDs found seven Zeros waiting to ambush them.

The torpedo planes under Lieutenant Bruce Harwood split into two groups to attack *Ryujo* on both bows with classic "anvil" tactics, so that no matter which way the ship turned she could not escape. But for some time the rain of bombs creating fountains of spray and smoke effectively screened *Ryujo* and compelled the torpedo planes to thrice break off their attack. It was only near the end of the dive-bombing attack that the TBFs closed in at 200 feet and 200 knots to claim one definite hit on the carrier's starboard bow and two possibles. The remaining two TBFs did not get the word to change targets and expended their torpedoes at *Tone,* without success. Although the Japanese believed that eight American planes fell in the attack, Felt's group withdrew with every plane.

Though Captain Kato asserted that no American bomb hit *Ryujo,* there is other compelling evidence of at least three bomb hits and his ship was undoubtedly absorbing water through at least one torpedo hit. Crewmen eventually subdued the greedy red tongues of her fires, but the water seepage could not be stemmed. *Ryujo*'s machinery spaces filled, leaving her with a heavy list and without motive power. One Kate launched on antisubmarine patrol just before Felt's attack made its way to Buka. The survivors of the returning Guadalcanal strike group, two Kates and twelve Zeros, plus the seven Zeros on Combat Air Patrol, all ultimately splashed down near *Ryujo;* destroyers *Amatsukaze* and *Tokitsukaze* plucked the airmen from the sea and then proceeded to take off the carrier's crew. *Ryujo* foundered at 2000 with 121 members of her complement, two Zeros, and two Kates. No American knew she was gone for sure until January 1943, when a decoded message revealed that she had been stricken from the official Navy List, a sure sign of her loss.

The word spread quickly of snoopers splashed near the task force, and consequently Fletcher's bluejackets expectantly awaited an attack. At 1602, *Enterprise*'s radar glimmered momentarily with a large unidentified flight bearing 320 degrees and distant 88 miles; this "blip" immediately disappeared. Her radar set was not designed to specifically give the altitude of air contacts—essential information for conducting an interception—but using the known characteristics of the radar wave pattern, plotters estimated the height of the flight at 12,000 feet. During the next thirty-five minutes both carriers launched more fighters, until fifty-three Wildcats were in the air. Bright-jerseyed handlers emptied flight decks of other aircraft, and radios barked orders for returning search planes to stand clear. At 1619, radar screens again blossomed with an aircraft formation, now only 44 miles distant. The altitude was again computed at 12,000 feet. At 1629, Gunner Charles F. Brewer gave a "Tallyho" upon sighting the Japanese formation bearing 300 degrees and distant about 25 miles from *Enterprise.*

Lieutenant Commander Seki split his attack unit into two groups of eighteen and nine and led them in a curve around to the north. The radar picture became completely blurred as the echoes of the Japanese planes became intermingled with those of defending fighters and returning search planes. Moreover, a breakdown of radio discipline on the fighter-direction circuit, which the controllers shared with all fifty-three airborne Wildcat pilots, rendered the task of fighter direction officer nearly impossible. After Brewer's message, a mélange of nonessential transmissions prevented the controllers from receiving information on the developing situation and from giving coherent directions. The following typified this frivolous patter:

> "Shift to high blower"
> "Look at that one go down"
> "Bill, where are you?"
> "Don't let them get away Lou"
> "Barney, just above me, hey Scope on our right side get in back of them"

Seki brought his planes in at 16,000 feet, with the result that almost all the defending Wildcats were positioned very unfavorably below and most behind the Japanese. In this extremely confused air battle, perhaps five to seven American fighters reached the nine *Zuikaku* Vals during their approach and about another ten Wildcats got among the dive-bombers during their dives. The alert Zero escort largely foiled the attempts of the remaining Wildcats to climb up to the bombers. Lieutenant Vorse's section of four *Enterprise* Wildcats had a typical experience. They sparred with Zeros while climbing to 20,000 feet. When they dove to attack the dive-bombers, the escorts again intervened to keep them away. Vorse, Ensign Francis R. Register, and Machinist H. M. Sumrall each claimed a Zero, and the ensign added a claim for an "ME-109." But Vorse was pulled from the sea astern of *Saratoga,* where he splashed after expending all his fuel. Six to eight Zeros jumped a *Saratoga* division of three Wildcats led by Lieutenant David C. Richardson. The Zeros shot down one of the Wildcats at once, but the others evened the score. Zeros also downed two of another trio of *Saratoga* Wildcats that tried to intercept the enemy dive-bombers.[1]

One of the few groups of Wildcats to engage the Vals before their dives was a three-plane *Saratoga* division led by Lieutenant H. M. Jensen. They intercepted the second nine-plane vee of Vals about 15 miles from *Enterprise,* and Lieutenant Jensen reported he flamed three before diving away to escape four angry Zeros. His two wingmen each downed two Vals, and one also claimed a Zero.

In *Enterprise*'s Fighting Six, the best and most experienced pilots headed up Wildcat divisions without regard to rank. Thus the star American performer of the day was Machinist Donald E. Runyon, the boss of a four-plane flight with two ensigns and one enlisted pilot. A cool tactician, Runyon climbed his division to 18,000 feet and placed them up-sun from the Japanese formation. He made a high-side run on a Val that exploded into flames. Trading his diving energy for altitude, Runyon ignited a second dive-bomber in a stern attack out of the sun. As he maneuvered for another attack, a Zero pounced on him from overhead. The Japanese pilot missed Runyon and then made the fatal mistake of pulling up close below and in front of his antagonist. Runyon dipped the Wildcat's nose and squeezed a burst from his six .50 caliber machine guns; the Zero blew up and flamed. Runyon made a final attack from below, on a dive-bomber, which caught fire.

Another *Enterprise* division led by Machinist D. C. Barnes plunged down with the Vals. Ensign R.A.M. Dibb shot down one dive-bomber at attitude before being chased down to the deck by a Zero. Dibb escaped in time to splash another Val. Gunner C. E. Brewer, leading the second pair of Wildcats, claimed two dive-bombers and a Zero, but his wingman, Ensign D. M. Johnson, was thoroughly shot up by a rear gunner. Four *Saratoga* Wildcats under Lieutenant R. E. Harmer attacked the first division of nine dive-bombers and registered claims for three Vals.

The two American carrier task forces stood down a southeasterly heading, with *Enterprise* about 10 miles northwest of *Saratoga.* A

---

[1]These and other air-to-air claims by the American fliers cannot be matched to the Japanese records used by this writer, which provide no details on losses. The claims are presented as recorded in American reports.

southeasterly breeze churned the sea with moderate swells. Towering altocumulous clouds blocked out four-tenths of the sky, and the sagging sun daubed ships and water in highlights and shadows while the eastern sky turned a matted blue, providing concealment for hostile planes. *Enterprise* began to work up speed to 27 knots, the maximum sustained speed of battleship *North Carolina* 2,500 yards back in her wake. Topside, gunners scanned the sky; some could see the plumes of distant falling planes. But most crewmen were sealed in interior compartments waiting and imagining events topside, hearing only snatches of reports over the communications system. *Enterprise*'s radar plot followed the approach of the Japanese strike until just before 1642 it sent the electrifying message: "The enemy planes are directly overhead now!"

Thousands of eyes scoured the zenith for sign of the Japanese, but Marine First Sergeant Joseph Schinka, in *Enterprise,* first discerned them. He ordered one of his 20mm guns to send up an accusing finger of tracers that triggered the whole task force to join with energetic, if not always accurate, fire. The Japanese intended to attack *Enterprise* with the eighteen *Shokaku* Vals while the nine *Zuikaku* dive-bombers made for *Saratoga,* but in the heat and confusion of battle—and the severe losses among the *Zuikaku* Vals—all of them chose targets in the *Enterprise* group. The tiny silver specks began to enlarge, and the onrushing Japanese dive-bombers were recorded on film by two photographers in exposed positions on *Enterprise*'s island while a third, Photographer Second Class Robert F. Read, stood calmly in her starboard after 5-inch gun gallery swinging his camera from plane to plane. Captain Arthur C. Davis on *Enterprise*'s bridge noted with icy professionalism the precise seven-second intervals between planes and that "the dives were steep estimated at 70 degrees, well executed and absolutely determined." *Portland*'s gunnery officer, who had witnessed five similar exhibitions by Japanese carrier fliers, left a different perspective. This connoisseur assessed the attack as good, but sniffed that he had seen better.

The clear sky was suddenly stained by the ugly blemishes of 5-inch bursts and divided by tracers from machineguns that wove trellises around each dive-bomber in turn. Aircraft engines whined in high-pitched protest over the furious rattle of the guns, and presently Japanese aircraft in various states of disassembly began to tumble down, trailing yellow streaks of flame. At least two of the crashing planes narrowly missed *Enterprise,* which now sliced the sea at 30 knots under full helm in the top of a giant reversed S.

The tenacious Japanese aviators toggled their bombs at 1,500 to

2,000 feet, and the first of these missed close aboard with concussive blasts that clanged the carrier's hull. Water cascaded aboard, transforming some gun tubs into wading pools. Then a bomb fell very close off the port quarter, whipping the hull and sprawling gunners to the deck in heaps as water deluged the after part of the ship. This bomb probably caused a slackening of fire that aided the following planes to draw a steadier aim. At 1644 a Japanese bomb splintered the wood flight deck at the starboard forward corner of the number three elevator, gouged down through several decks, and detonated in a petty officers' messroom, where it slaughtered thirty-five men. It left a blackened cavern filled with wisps of yellow smoke and tongues of bright flame. The flight deck bulged upward two feet over the hit, and the elevator jammed into place. Water sluiced through holes punched by fragments into a large storeroom, giving the ship slight starboard list.

Gunner's Mate William K. Powell, the chief troubleshooter for the after 5-inch guns, sprinted across the exposed flight deck to check for injury to the starboard after guns. He arrived within thirty seconds of the first hit just as a second bomb impacted only 15 feet outboard of the first in the 5-inch gun pocket he had just entered. The bomb's eruption touched off forty rounds of powder, and Powell, photographer Read, and about thirty-three others died instantly from blast, splinters, and flames.

Rolling billows of flame and smoke were curling over the stern of the speeding carrier when at 1646 a third bomb struck near the number two elevator and exploded in low order. It left a 10-foot hole in the flight deck, damaged some guns, and wounded a few men but caused no fatalities. The lens of a camera captured the precise instant of its detonation.

As the Japanese fliers muscled their planes from their dives, they skimmed along at sea level, twisting and occasionally indulging in a little strafing. One came by destroyer *Grayson* and its fire wounded eleven men, but 20mm shells riddled and splashed the plane. Other Vals found American fighter pilots seeking vengeance, and on the very fringes of the action, an SBD and a TBF pilot each claimed a Japanese plane.

While most of the Vals worked over *Enterprise,* the spacious decks of *North Carolina* attracted five of their compatriots. They discovered the battleship sailors itching for a combat test of the new generation of capital ships. Unlike her older relatives caught moored at Pearl Harbor, the new fast battleship stepped lightly at 27 knots and bristled with 102 antiaircraft guns ranging from 5-inch to .50 caliber.

North Carolina also sported a number of new gadgets for gunfire control, but at the other end of the scale from this 1942-style high technology, old salts found reassurance in familiar tools—by each 1.1-inch machinegun quadruple mount stood a sailor with a hammer and a chisel to remove jammed rounds.

North Carolina had been directing a cloud of fire over *Enterprise* when two groups of Vals singled her out, beginning at 1643. The first—probably three *Shokaku* planes—dived from the starboard bow, while a second—most likely four *Zuikaku* Vals—winged around to the port quarter. While yet another plane insolently flew by at main-deck level, these seven fountained the sea around her. One geyser close aboard the port side sent 20mm gunners sprawling and washed portions of the weather decks with a foot and a half of water. The battleship sustained only superficial damage and suffered one fatality.[2]

The attack ended in less than fifteen minutes and gunfire trickled out. The Japanese lost seventeen dive-bombers and three Zeros in roughing up *Enterprise* and one Val and three Zeros splashed before regaining their carriers. Probably about half of the dive-bombers fell to the defending Wildcats and the other half became victims of antiaircraft fire with the lion's share to gunners aboard *Enterprise*. Eight Wildcats and five pilots were lost from all causes. The confused and no doubt shaken Japanese aircrews returned to report they left two American carriers alight.

Now came "a lull in the action—the lull that every respectable battle is supposed to have," quipped Lieutenant Commander Frederick Bell of *Grayson*.

But on *Enterprise* there was no lull. Boiling up from belowdecks and scurrying across the flight deck came the assortment of ship fitters, carpenters, electricians, and ordinary seamen that composed *Enterprise*'s exceptionally well-drilled damage control parties under Lieutenant Commander Herschel A. Smith. At the scenes of the hits they began their oft-rehearsed tasks. In astonishingly little time the

---

[2] *North Carolina* observers claimed that during the carrier plane attack a group of twin-engine Japanese bombers made a high-level bombing run on the task force. Japanese records indicate that a strike of twenty-four Bettys and thirteen Zeros set out from Rabaul but were turned back by weather with no reference to an attack on American ships. Quite possibly *North Carolina* sailors mistakenly construed dogfights high overhead coincident with the dive-bombing attack as a "high level bomb attack." There is also a possibility that they saw a group of B-17s.

fires were controlled and the flight deck patched. Corpsmen tended to the ninety-nine shipmates who lay wounded to such good effect that only four would die, and they recovered the remains of the seventy-one already dead.

A pilot who viewed the starboard after 5-inch gun pocket left us this account:

> Sailors' bodies were still in the gun gallery. Most of the men died from the concussion and then were roasted. The majority of the bodies were in one piece. They were blackened but not burned or withered, and they looked like iron statues of men, their limbs smooth and whole, their heads rounded with no hair. The faces were undistinguishable, but in almost every case the lips were drawn back in a wizened grin giving the men the expression of rodents.
>
> The postures seemed either strangely normal or frankly grotesque. One gun pointer was still in his seat leaning on his sight with one arm. He looked as though a sculptor had created him. His body was nicely proportioned, the buttocks were rounded, there was no hair anywhere. Other iron men were lying outstretched, face up or down. Two or three lying face up were shielding themselves with their arms bent at the elbows and their hands before their faces. One, who was not burned so badly, had his chest thrown out, his head way back, and his hands clenched.
>
> The blackened bodies did not appear as shocking as those only partially roasted. They looked more human in their distortion.

At 1746, only one hour after the last bomb hit, *Enterprise* turned proudly into the wind at a spanking 24 knots and commenced the urgent recovery of her planes. But danger still stalked her from above and within.

Twenty-five planes were aboard at 1821 when the carrier lost steering control because of the lingering effects of the bomb hits. Two electric motors, one a standby, controlled *Enterprise*'s rudder. They occupied the steering compartment with seven men to monitor their operation. After the nearby bomb explosions, these sailors shut off all ventilation to keep out flame and smoke. Because of the fires and the machinery, the temperature in their compartment soared to an estimated 170 or more degrees. Inadvertently, a ventilation trunk was opened by remote control from above and water flooded in, shorting out the motor then in use to guide the rudder. Before the crewmen could switch over to the alternate motor, they became unconscious. With her rudder jammed hard to starboard, *Enterprise* careened through the formation, narrowly missing destroyer *Balch*. Captain Davis reduced speed to 10 knots as *Enterprise*'s hull cut little disks in the ocean.

Chief Machinist William A. Smith was the man in charge of *Enterprise*'s steering gear. He donned a rescue breathing apparatus (a self-contained breathing device) specially modified by another chief for extra endurance and plunged into the oven around the steering gear compartment. Twice he was overcome and pulled out by a safety line. On the third attempt he penetrated to the compartment and completed the switchover. At 1858, thirty-eight minutes after the casualty, *Enterprise* regained helm control.

Even as she spun in circles, *Enterprise*'s radar operators tracked another flight of Japanese planes that had been closing since 1651. This "blip" represented the second Japanese attack group, under Lieutenant Takahashi, who had aimed for an estimated position of the American carriers that proved erroneous. A corrected and accurate position report was signaled to Takahashi, but his radio operator miscopied it. Tense radar operators watched the spiking lines on cathode-ray tubes reflecting Takahashi's planes as they passed 50 miles astern of the task force, swung east on an intersecting course until due south of *Enterprise,* and then reversed course northwest at 1827. At the point they banked away, barely ten minutes' flying time separated the Vals from the helplessly circling American carrier. No Wildcats were sent to intercept, because they were all low on fuel and ammunition—which may have been fortunate, since their presence might have betrayed the proximity of *Enterprise.* The "Big E," as her sailors called her, always carried at least one guardian angel in her air group. When Lieutenant Takahashi's group arrived over their ships it was after dark. The Japanese turned on searchlights to help their planes home in, but four of the dive-bombers disappeared. One other Val ditched, but its crew was rescued.

Sunset brought a reassessment of the situation aboard the Japanese carriers. Captain Masafumi Arima of *Shokaku* wanted to continue the battle and to remain in the area to locate downed aircrews. But there were severe losses in the first attack group, and the proposed third strike was canceled. Admiral Nagumo, who had led the Japanese carriers to many victories from Pearl Harbor to the Indian Ocean and to disaster at Midway, no longer had much fire in his belly. After gathering his planes, Nagumo led the big carriers north to a fueling rendezvous. Meanwhile the two American carriers maintained a southeasterly heading into the wind, which permitted them to recover aircraft as it drew them away from the battle area.

For the American pilots the day was not yet over. Just before the Japanese attack commenced, Fletcher ordered all the remaining dive-bombers and torpedo bombers to strike the Japanese. Just before the Vals pushed over into their dives, *Enterprise* hurriedly launched her available planes, eleven SBDs and seven TBFs, with orders to attack *Ryujo*. Last away was *Enterprise*'s air group commander, Lieutenant Commander Max Leslie, who lifted his TBF off just before the bombs began to fall around his ship. *North Carolina* shot at Leslie twice and he tangled with a Japanese plane, thus understandably he failed to rendezvous with his attack group.

Similar scenes transpired on *Saratoga,* but with an unusual twist. Two SBDs and five TBFs sat perched on the flight deck as the Japanese closed. The crews had manned the planes for the purpose of moving them on the deck when the word came to take off immediately. Consternation struck the torpedo plane pilots, as only the leader, Lieutenant Harold H. Larsen, possessed all his flight gear, particularly the vital chart board essential for over-water navigation. Further, it was obvious that the mission would extend beyond darkness, and the pilots had little training in night flying. Daunted but not deterred, they took off with orders to join the *Enterprise* group. Not surprisingly, in the confusion of the Japanese attack the two small groups of American planes never linked up.

Lieutenant Turner Caldwell's eleven *Enterprise* SBDs, designated Flight 300, scoured the seas vainly for the Japanese. Fortunately, as it would develop, Caldwell elected to take them to Guadalcanal rather than search for their ship in the dark. One of the seven *Enterprise* Avengers led by Lieutenant R. H. Konig had to turn back, but the other six lumbered to the vicinity of a contact report location. There in the evening twilight they saw "high-speed wakes" and dived down to attack, whereupon they discovered the "wakes" were water breaking over Roncador Reef. Reluctantly but prudently, they jettisoned their torpedoes and returned to the American carriers, where a landing accident cost one plane.

The five *Saratoga* TBFs under Lieutenant Larsen joined up with two SBDs and set forth to find the enemy. At 1735 the Avengers stumbled upon Admiral Kondo's Advanced Force and attacked. The Japanese put up heavy antiaircraft fire and maneuvered radically as Larsen's pilots pressed home attack runs to 1,200 yards and made releases at 200 to 350 feet at 200 knots. All missed. Two TBFs alighted on San Cristóbal, from which the crews were recovered. Meanwhile Lieutenant R. M. Elder and his wingman in their SBDs found a ship they identified as the battleship *Mutsu* and commenced to dive on her. The fading light and the low clouds confounded their identification, for their target was actually the seaplane carrier *Chitose,* which circled tightly and registered indignation with her guns. The pilots claimed one hit and one near-miss. Although neither bomb scored a direct hit, the pair of near-misses sprung plates along *Chitose*'s waterline and kindled three seaplanes on her decks. The crew mastered the blaze, but the flooding spread until the port machinery spaces filled and the ship took an alarming list. Eventually this too was righted and *Chitose* set off for Truk.

In the darkness the clusters of vagabond American planes felt their way back. Long after sunset, Lieutenant Commander Leslie continued his search for the Japanese and his *Enterprise* strike group. Unable to find his charges and having made no contact himself, he finally turned back and landed aboard *Saratoga* at 2333, the last plane on either side to return to its carrier.

The last gasps of the battle were by Japanese heavy ships and submarines. Admiral Kondo took the majority of the cruisers and battleships of the Main Body and the Advanced Force purposely south to locate any damaged American ships or perhaps an unwary carrier task force and engage in night battle. From their line-abreast formation—the better to find their quarry in the dark—the Japanese fanned out float planes. One of them sighted destroyer *Grayson,* which had been detached to help American planes find their way home, and dogged her for a time. But failing to find a worthwhile target by 2400, the Japanese put about. The veritable school of Japanese submarines in the waters east of the Solomons had been ordered back and forth on various patrol lines in hopes of catching an American carrier. At 0030, August 25, *I-17* found the American carriers headed south at 20 knots, and fifteen minutes later *I-15* saw one of the groups. The commander of Submarine Squadron 1 tried to gather a posse of submarines to give chase, but the fast-stepping American ships left behind both of the boats in contact by 0200.

Thus ended the third carrier battle of the war.

THE CONVOY BATTLE OF AUGUST 25

Tanaka learned to his dismay that the weather yet again frustrated the planned 11th Air Fleet attack on Guadalcanal for August 24. After witnessing *Ryujo* galloping south at noon on August 24, Tanaka next viewed her funeral pyre. With enemy aircraft about, he sidestepped to the west with his convoy, but after dark he again headed south. Given the presence of American planes on Guadalcanal and American carriers in the seas to the southeast, the prospects for his slow transports looked bleak. He requested instructions, and at 2007 on August 24 the 8th Fleet ordered him to head northwest. But when a report reached Admiral Mikawa that Lieutenant Commander Seki's fliers had set two American carriers ablaze that afternoon, Mikawa countermanded his order and directed Tanaka to head south again at 2307. Five minutes later, Tanaka complied.

The news of two damaged American carriers was not the only erroneous piece of information the Japanese commanders based their plans upon this night. The ever watchful Japanese garrison on Guadalcanal witnessed the takeoff of *Saratoga*'s attack group during the morning of August 24. When these planes did not return, the observers on Guadalcanal leaped to the conclusion that the American air contingent had been largely destroyed and broadcast a signal to that effect. To take care of the remnants, the Combined Fleet decided to stage a destroyer bombardment and, for good measure, a bombing attack by float planes.

From Shortland, Captain Shiro Yasutake took the destroyers *Mutsuki, Yayoi,* and *Mochizuki* of Destroyer Division 30 at a sprightly pace to Lunga Point, arriving at midnight. After a fruitless sweep for shipping, they conducted a desultory ten-minute bombardment reflecting their inability to establish the location of the airstrip with their simple fire control instruments. The scattered shelling killed two marines and wounded three, but did negligible material damage. Yasutake then led his ships on a detour past Tulagi before heading for a rendezvous with Tanaka. To add to the marines' discomfort, the float planes arrived to bomb and strafe.

Retribution was on the minds of a number of dive-bomber pilots this night. At 0230, three SBDs led by the indefatigable Major Mangrum waddled off into the darkness hauling one 500-pound bomb each. They found Yasutake and dropped their bombs, without result. Three of the newly arrived *Enterprise* pilots lifted off at 0400 on a similar errand and found *Mochizuki,* operating independently to pick up stranded *Ryujo* aviators. Under the attentions of the American pilots, *Mochizuki* suffered minor damage and three wounded. One of the SBDs became lost, and its crew belatedly returned sans aircraft, which they ditched off Malaita.

Captain Yasutake graded his bombardment a failure and forthrightly signaled this fact, underscored by the presence of prowling

American planes. The Combined Fleet chose not to heed his recommendation that the landing plans be reconsidered.

Under the bright moonlight a faithful PBY found Tanaka's convoy at 0233 on August 25 and began to follow it. This plane's contact report reached Guadalcanal at 0430, placing the Japanese 180 miles to the north. Captain Yasutake rejoined Tanaka at 0740, but by that time an attack group of eight SBDs and a like number of Wildcats had been airborne for one hour and forty minutes. The Americans first vainly hunted *Ryujo* and turned back at the limit of the Wildcat's range. The escort separated and proceeded back to Guadalcanal, shooting down a Mavis search plane en route. The SBDs adjusted their return path 50 miles to the west, and at 0808 the convoy rolled up on the horizon. The five Marine dive-bombers went after Tanaka's flagship, while the trio of Navy Dauntlesses lined up on the biggest transport. There were no defending fighters over the convoy, and no antiaircraft fire impeded the dives because the Japanese initially believed the planes were "friendly." Huge plumes of water peaked around *Jintsu* from near-misses, and then Second Lieutenant Lawrence Baldinus nailed her. His bomb knifed down through the cruiser's bow between the two forward guns to explode below, where it demolished the radio room and killed or wounded a large but unspecified number of sailors. Splinters riddled the bridge, and the blast knocked Tanaka unconscious. He revived within a pall of dark smoke from fires raging below that prompted the flooding of the forward magazine. At the same time, Ensign Christian Fink from *Enterprise*'s Flight 300 plunked his bomb unto *Kinryu Maru,* igniting a fire that soon spread through the cargo to ammunition. On pullout the SBDs ran a gauntlet of float planes, and the dive-bomber gunners claimed two, though Japanese records do not confirm this.

The SBDs had begun their return flight when Major Mangrum discovered his bomb had not released. At considerable risk against the now alert defenders, he headed back to the scene and made a solo dive on *Boston Maru* that scored a near-miss off her stern. Mangrum observed *Kinryu Maru* satisfactorily afire but could not see *Jintsu.* More important, he noted the Japanese were now headed northwest, away from Guadalcanal.

Tanaka commenced picking up the pieces of his convoy. He sent Captain Yasutake's ships and two patrol boats, *1* and *2,* to aid *Kinryu Maru* while the other two transports, *Boston Maru* and *Daifuku Maru,* departed under destroyer escort to get beyond the bite of the American planes. The admiral then shifted his flag to destroyer *Kagero* and sent his former flagship north toward Truk with destroyer *Suzukaze*.

Mutsuki nosed alongside the halted *Kinryu Maru* to lend a hand, but at 1027 three B-17s droned into view overhead. Conscious of the poor record of high-flying bombers against ships, the destroyer's skipper disdained to get his vessel underway. The reward for this carelessness was a bomb that landed squarely in *Mutsuki*'s engine room, and she sank at 1140 with the loss of forty lives. The rest of the crew, including eleven wounded, were extracted from the water, at which point her sopping captain philosophized that "even the B-17s could make a hit once in a while." *Mochizuki* scuttled the blazing transport with a torpedo at 1053. At the word of the air attack, the Combined Fleet belatedly bestirred itself. The landing was canceled at 0930, and *Zuikaku* hastened south with three destroyers to afford air cover for the remnants of the now retreating convoy.

Unaware of the extent of their victory, the American planes returned to Guadalcanal to gulp fuel and gather bombs in anticipation of another attack. At 1100, coast watchers sent a terse warning of twenty-one Japanese bombers "headed yours." All but three aircraft regained the air before the Japanese arrived, but the F4Fs lacked time to heave themselves to altitude for an interception. The Japanese group of twenty-one twin-engine bombers, herded by twelve Zeros, salvoed their bombs at 1155. About forty bombs slammed to earth in a tight pattern around the field operations center, killing four men and wounding five while causing minor damage to the runway and dispersal areas. Six Marine and three Navy dive-bombers set out to make another attack on the convoy but found only empty seas littered with oil and debris at the scene of the morning's action. The Japanese were gone.

Over the next several days after the battle, the American participants counted their losses, wrote their reports, and weighed in with their opinions. Mutilated *Enterprise* needed mending at Pearl Harbor. Her crew counted seventy-five shipmates dead and ninety-five wounded—her captain thought it doubtful that bombs hitting anywhere else in the ship could have caused so many casualties—and elsewhere in the task force one man was dead and eleven wounded. Plane losses totaled eighteen from all causes (nine Wildcats, two SBDs, and seven TBFs), but after recovery efforts ended, aircrew losses amounted to only six pilots and one gunner. To these must be added the three Wildcats (with two pilots) and one SBD lost over and around Guadalcanal, as well as one B-17, one PBY, and one *Wasp* SBD, making total aircraft losses twenty-five.[3]

The reports from the carriers expounded upon the haste surrounding the assembly of the two air groups and the fact that, once embarked on a carrier, the dive-bomber and torpedo bomber pilots were afforded little practice to keep their hands in, as evidenced in the attack on *Ryujo*. There were harsh words about the ineffective fighter direction in the defense of *Enterprise,* for only about one-third of the available Wildcats engaged the Vals before or during their dives. Criticism also focused on the lack of radio discipline, but although improvements would be made in this area it could never be entirely eradicated, because it stemmed from the terrible loneliness of each pilot that compelled many to seek reassurance in unnecessary jabber. Commentators highlighted the weaknesses in communications as well as the poor functioning of the Identification Friend or Foe (IFF) equipment, which was supposed to distinguish American planes on radar screens. The Japanese were conceded to be better at air search, and it was forcefully argued that the U. S. Navy would continue to lag in this critical field until it got four-engine bombers like the B-17 that could take care of themselves in the face of fighter opposition.

The performance of the 20mm machineguns manifestly pleased the gunners. These weapons could not stop a dive-bomber or a torpedo plane from reaching its release point, but they could take a terrible toll of those pilots who pressed home their attacks. In this battle they probably accounted for half the planes downed by the ships. Tacticians disputed whether the carriers should have operated in one formation or two and extracted contrary lessons from the attack on *Enterprise.* Among those in the know on radio intelligence, the most disturbing aspect of the action was that for the first time since Pearl Harbor, the movements of Japanese carriers had not been forecast with reasonable accuracy.

Japanese lost *Ryujo, Mutsuki,* and *Kinryu Maru,* and *Jintsu* sustained major damage. An exact count of the Japanese sailors and soldiers lost is not available, but it must have exceeded the American death toll substantially. Aircraft losses totaled seventy-five: thirty-

---

[3]This lost list included one carrier TBF and one F4F, although in fact their hulks were evacuated to the United States for study of battle damage and ultimately they were rebuilt. A PBY loss occurred on August 25. The *Wasp* SBD was an operational loss on August 24. One VP-23 officer and three officers and two enlisted men of the 11th Bomb Group were killed in the B-17 crash. Total American fatalities reached ninety: fourteen officers and seventy-six enlisted men.

three Zeros, twenty-three Vals, eight Kates, seven float planes, one Betty, two Emilys, and one Mavis.[4] Much more important, although twenty-one Zero pilots survived, the Japanese recovered from all the other missing aircraft (save the four *Chitose* planes) only the crews of one Val and three Kates and several men from the Mavis.

When the last of the Main Body and the Advanced Force units reached Truk on September 7, officers examined the lessons of the battle. Many circulated complaints about communications failures, and subsequently they ascribed these to the radio frequencies in use. This could not explain, of course, the miscopied message to Lieutenant Takahashi's flight that deprived the Japanese of an excellent chance to sink *Enterprise*. The seagoing fleet fired recriminations over search and attack performance at the land-based 11th Air Fleet.

At this remove, the whole Japanese operation appears without a coherent set of objectives and deficient in coordination. The participants do not seem to have addressed the responsibility for these defects, but they loom large in retrospect. Yamamoto dispatched the most valuable units in the Combined Fleet to the South Pacific, yet he permitted Kondo and Nagumo to operate in loose confederation rather than in unity throughout the battle, as evidenced by the lack of preplanned air cover for Tanaka's convoy. If the end of the fight witnessed the strange sight of the two opposing carrier commanders steaming away from each other as if by mutual consent, Fletcher at least had a colorable reason in the evasion of a night surface battle against superior forces. What must have been painfully evident to many officers was that the Imperial Navy had come out in force but it neither crushed the American carriers nor secured the safe passage of the reinforcement convoy. There is more than a suggestion here that the shock of the Midway defeat still lingered in the minds of the Japanese commanders.

The Battle of the Eastern Solomons was unquestionably an American victory, but it had little long-term result, apart from a further reduction in the corps of trained Japanese carrier aviators. The reinforcements that could not come by slow transport would soon reach Guadalcanal by other means.

---

[4]The seven float planes were lost as follows: one *Chitose* Mitsubishi F1M ("Pete") operational and three Aichi E13As ("Jakes") by bombing on August 24; one *Chikuma* Jake to fighters on August 24; and a Jake each from *Haguro* and *Atago* to a *Wasp* SBD on August 25. An Emily also fell to *Wasp* SBDs on August 25; all other flying boat losses are mentioned in the text.

8

TWO

WEEKS OF

SPARRING

"Cactus can be a sinkhole for enemy air power"

OPERATION "KA"

Two methods of cauterizing the malignant growth of American air power on Guadalcanal were available to the Japanese after the Battle of the Eastern Solomons: attrition in the air and seizure of the airfield itself. During the following two weeks the Japanese pursued the first means vigorously while preparing for the second. The American defenders parried in the air and attempted to strengthen their grip by establishing a regular supply shuttle covered by the carrier groups.

Renewing the assault on August 26, the 11th Air Fleet sent down seventeen Bettys with an escort of nine Zeros. Thanks to a coast watcher report at 1124, a dozen Wildcats awaited them by the time they reached the airfield at 1203. Bombs ignited about 2,000 gallons of gasoline that "cooked off" two 1,000-pound bombs, to the gratification of the Japanese aviators. The Marine pilots claimed eight bombers and five Zeros at the cost of one Wildcat and its pilot. The Japanese counterclaimed no fewer than nine Wildcats and admitted the loss of two bombers which failed to return and two others that "force-landed" (often, but not always, a euphemism for write-offs). Nine bombers returned with assorted nicks, three Zeros were erased from the rolls at Rabaul, and one other limped back heavily damaged.

Bad weather turned back Japanese fliers on August 27, and the scene of action switched to the ground. With the shift of 2d Battalion, 5th Marines from Tulagi to Guadalcanal on August 21, Vandegrift fielded six infantry battalions, still too few rifles to guarantee a secure defense of the long perimeter. But the Marine command regarded waiting passively around Lunga Point as both poor tactics and corrosive to morale. Consequently, a second jab beyond the Matanikau had been planned, but it was postponed because of the sea fight. Now the mission fell to the 1st Battalion, 5th Marines under Lieutenant Colonel William E. Maxwell. Colonel Hunt's orders to Maxwell contained unrecognized ambiguity: land west of Kokumbona, sweep down the coast, *and* return to the perimeter by nightfall. Maxwell learned that artillery would fire at the mouth of the Matanikau to create a diversion while one rifle company slipped across the stream to block Japanese retreat into the jungle, but no one could give him trustworthy information on Japanese dispositions and strength.

Although close to its authorized strength of 933 men, Maxwell's battalion suffered important invisible weaknesses, both those common to other Marine battalions and one peculiar to itself. Twenty-four of the thirty-three officers had joined since April 1, thanks to wholesale transfers to fill out the 7th Marines, and recent recruits made up the great majority of the enlisted men. The long period of movement and marshaling since May 19 denied the unit opportunity to train or keep well conditioned. Maxwell was a sincere, hardworking, and energetic twenty-two-year veteran of the Marine Corps. Faced with a dearth of experience in his battalion, during training he zealously inculcated a rigid adherence to orders with lacerating critiques of errors. His policy begot obedience, but at the cost of initiative.

At 0700 on August 27, the battalion splashed ashore from boats just west of Kokumbona and found signs of Japanese presence in abandoned meals. The ground Maxwell confronted presented serious tactical challenges. Densely wooded flatlands only 200 to 300 yards wide lay adjacent to the surf, threaded by the dusty Government Track. This level ground ended abruptly in a series of parallel ridges, capped by coral cliffs, running perpendicular to the beach. Jungle-clogged ravines filled the interstices between the steep-sided ridges.

The crests of the ridges wore tall cogongrass that trapped the heat and provided no cover from the scorching sun. To guard the exposed inland flank, Maxwell placed Company C on the high ground and moved out. It quickly became apparent that over this corrugated terrain, a full company could not keep up with the rest of the battalion filtering through the growth along the shore. Maxwell recalled Company C and resumed the advance with Company B in the lead and one of its platoons on the high ground inland. The battalion progressed slowly until it reached a position where the coastal flatlands contracted to a width of less than 200 yards. There Captain Monzen's sailors sent bursts of machinegun and rifle fire and mortar blasts ripping through the leading ranks. Company D swiftly put its mortars into action, but the Japanese easily checked an effort to outflank their position to seaward.

Lieutenant Thomas Grady's platoon of Company B to the south of the expanding skirmish moved across the high ground to where it gained an excellent position to roll up the Japanese line. In the event, Grady advanced no farther, and the reasons for this failure provide a typical example of the problems of control in jungle warfare and a cautionary lesson on misdirected training. Lacking radio communication, Grady dispatched three successive runners to his company to report his opportune situation. Each of the runners, including one officer, was overcome by the heat drumming down on his helmet and collapsed, as did about twelve men in the platoon. The only message to reach Grady advised him to stand fast. Later Grady discovered this message originated from the first sergeant of Company B, who sent it only as an interim answer pending definite orders from the company commander. Grady considered launching an attack, but he deferred such action because he lacked assurance that Company D's mortar barrage would be lifted and, more important, because he was only too aware of Lieutenant Colonel Maxwell's emphasis on strict obedience to orders.

Whether more might have been done on the coastal flat is unclear, but Maxwell soon perceived that he could not overcome the Japanese opposition *and* return to the perimeter by nightfall. Maxwell viewed the latter as the controlling part of his orders, so he radioed to ask for boats to return the battalion at 1430. Division headquarters lacked appreciation of either Maxwell's situation or the terrain, but the proposal to withdraw incensed Vandegrift. He stormed over to the headquarters of the 5th Marines and ordered Hunt to take action. The colonel relieved Maxwell of command by radio dispatch and then headed for his errant battalion by boat. With the day waned too far to renew the skirmish, the battalion passed the night on high ground. During darkness the Japanese, fearing encirclement, slipped away, carrying forty wounded. At dawn the 1st Battalion swept over the scene of the fighting and counted twenty dead Japanese. Marine losses came to three dead and nine wounded.

Marine officers regarded this episode as discreditable, and most laid the onus for the failure on Maxwell. In retrospect, Maxwell faced a more difficult tactical situation than his superiors recognized at the time, and if his handling of the situation was less than deft, it was not so intrinsically poor as to warrant his dismissal, particularly in light of his confused orders and the weaknesses in his battalion that were not his fault. The evidence suggests that in Vandegrift's eyes, Maxwell's leadership became suspect because of the slow advance of his battalion on August 7 and 8, and that this incident merely validated that opinion.

While Maxwell's men fought, the Imperial Navy began a series of actions extending over the next week that would multiply Japanese air power at Rabaul. By August 29, the precipitous ebb of aircraft strength left on hand only forty-one Zeros, thirty-seven Bettys, six Vals, one reconnaissance plane, and three flying boats. Of this total of eighty-eight, only half were operational. On this same day the Japanese estimated that Guadalcanal held thirty American aircraft, a number they adjusted daily based upon pilot claims and observations of the Guadalcanal garrison—both of which sources proved suspect. A plan for substantial reinforcements was drawn up calling for aircraft to be diverted from other areas and Japan so that by September 20 Rabaul would pack ninety-three long-range Zeros, thirty-eight short-range Zeros, eighty-one twin-engine bombers, six Vals, four reconnaissance planes, and fourteen flying boats, excluding losses in the interim. Moreover, authorization was given on September 8 to commence airfield construction at Buin on the southeastern tip of Bougainville.

The consolidation and expansion of float plane activities by Admiral Mikawa complemented these developments. These aircraft performed local antisubmarine patrols, provided limited air cover, and, most important, orchestrated the nightly harassment of the Americans on Guadalcanal. The marines differentiated two types of aircraft engaged in shredding their sleep: a twin-engine plane whose distinctive motor noises led to the appellation "Washing Machine Charlie" and a single-engine float plane dubbed "Louie the Louse." Charlie's visits began later, but Louie had already made some visits. (Accounts making Louie a fixture in the night sky over Guadalcanal are exaggerated. Louie did show up with ship bombardments, which is why he is well remembered.) Initially Louie was one of the float planes from Mikawa's cruisers on special detachment. Now a total of fifty-two, drawn from three seaplane tenders and *Chitose*'s refugee air unit, unified to become the R Area Air Force under Rear Admiral Takaji Joshima. In addition to the established seaplane bases around Shortland, the R Area Air Force planned a new permanent base at Rekata Bay. However, a B-17 delayed its opening by sinking *Patrol Boat 35* bearing the base personnel on September 2, with the loss of all but fifty-two of her passengers and crew. A second attempt by *Patrol Boat 36* succeeded, and the new base opened on September 5.

Important gaps developed between these plans and their execution. The Japanese discovered, as the Americans had, that it was much easier to fly in pilots and planes than to forward the necessary ground crews, and, without mechanical nurturing, aircraft serviceability plummeted on the crude island bases. Already a sparsity of ground crews obliged 11th Air Fleet pilots to assist with maintenance. Nor was Rabaul a complete haven. MacArthur's fliers paid regular calls that produced a steady attrition of planes on the ground. Ultimately, however, the overall shortage of aircraft and crews, particularly the long-range Zeros that constituted the keystone of the air strategy, constrained Japanese aspirations. In order to immediately augment fighter strength, *Shokaku* and *Zuikaku* detached thirty Zeros (one became an operational loss) for temporary duty at Buka on August 28.

The arrival on the scene of Major General Kiyotaki Kawaguchi's 35th Infantry Brigade prompted this urgent reinforcement of air muscle. Kawaguchi's unit, originally slated to take the Fiji Islands in July during the post-Midway mop-up in the South Pacific and then proceed to New Guinea, gained a new mission after the American landing on Guadalcanal. As early as August 18, the 17th Army began penciling plans to send the main body of the brigade to Guadalcanal, Operation "KA"—an interesting reflection on the appraisal of Ichiki's chances at that date.[1]

Perhaps vain, but certainly obstinate and verbose, Kawaguchi was not without grasp. He recognized the significance of Guadalcanal, and to prove it to his soldiers he requested a suitable exhortation

---

[1]It was Japanese custom to select randomly a two-letter designator as a code name for an operation or a location. As we will see, in this case "KA" eventually came to have a distinct meaning apart from its code function to Japanese soldiers.

from the Army commander to read to the troops. On August 23 at Truk he sat down to discuss the deployment of his brigade with staff officers from the 17th Army and 8th Fleet as well as Rear Admiral Shintaro Hashimoto, the commander of Destroyer Squadron 3 detailed to escort his transports. The 17th Army staff presented Kawaguchi with orders to go directly to Guadalcanal on the transports and land on August 28. The major general quickly established that in his view, orders merely formed a handy agenda for discussion. He rightly questioned the vulnerability of his transports to American aircraft. Moreover, the general's happy experience in the Borneo Campaign, where he advanced up to 500 miles by barge, gave him a decided predilection for this means of aquatic maneuver. Instead of going directly to Guadalcanal, Kawaguchi counterproposed to take his brigade to Shortland and then leapfrog to Guadalcanal by bounds in barges. This concept won no converts in his immediate audience.

Kawaguchi sailed on the 24th, but within twenty-four hours the fate of Tanaka's convoy confirmed his fears about the transports. At 0900 on August 26, the 17th Army commanded Kawaguchi to rush 600 men directly to Guadalcanal aboard four destroyers and to take the rest of his brigade to Rabaul. A calm sea facilitated the transfer of the bulk of the 2d Battalion, 124th Infantry Regiment to destroyers *Asagiri, Amagiri, Yugiri,* and *Shirakumo,* constituting Destroyer Division 20 under Captain Yuzo Arita. The Imperial Navy accepted more and more the expedient employment of destroyers for such duties because, although each ship could carry only about 150 men or 30 to 40 tons of supplies, it could do so at very high speed at night and thus substantially evade air attack.

In the early hours of August 28, Kawaguchi reached Rabaul, and immediately the majority of the 1st Battalion, 124th Infantry embarked on three destroyers of Destroyer Division 11 for transportation to Guadalcanal. Kawaguchi pressed on to Shortland, where he verbally attacked the scheme to move his men by destroyers, and the fate of Destroyer Division 20 forcefully bolstered his objections.

Because of a shortage of fuel, the four destroyers of Destroyer Division 20 could not utilize prolonged full speed to assure a passage only in darkness within range of Henderson Field aviators. Consequently, a pair of searching SBDs located them at 1700 on August 28, 70 miles north of Guadalcanal. An eleven-plane strike group of six Marine and five Navy Dauntlesses rose from Henderson Field and found the Japanese at 1805. The SBDs split by services, and the five Navy planes selected *Asagiri* as their victim. The first bomb penetrated to the engine room. Ensign Christian Fink then drilled her with a second bomb that struck the number one torpedo tube mount. The combined bomb and torpedo warhead detonation snapped the ship in two in a spectacular explosion. Down with his flagship went Captain Arita and many others. The survivors numbered eight officers, including the skipper, 128 crewmen, and eighty-three of the approximately 150 Army passengers. The Marine pilots battered *Yugiri* with a near-miss that knocked out pairs of boilers and main battery gun mounts and left three officers and twenty-nine seamen dead and forty wounded. *Shirakumo* took a bomb or bombs which opened the forward boiler room to the sea and left the ship without power. Only two of her crew died, but sixty-two of her passengers perished. Only *Amagiri* remained unscathed. She exacted the only American loss when she shot down a strafing Marine SBD, killing its crew. *Amagiri* took *Shirakumo* in tow and headed toward Shortland accompanied by limping *Yugiri.*

The ripples of this episode extended much farther than any American conceived. Tanaka signaled at 2040 that the presence of enemy planes on Guadalcanal gave destroyer reinforcement runs slim chance of success. Captain Yonosuke Murakami, the commander of Destroyer Division 24 then en route to Guadalcanal with some of Ichiki's Second Echelon, exhibited a nonverbal amen to this view: he tacked about without orders at 1925. Murakami's backtracking infuriated Admiral Mikawa. At the 17th Army, the chief of staff, General Futami, seriously contemplated giving up further efforts to regain Guadalcanal in view of the demonstrated inability of Japan to achieve air superiority over the southern Solomons. But other staff officers refused to be disheartened and argued that final judgment should be withheld pending the outcome of the next destroyer run.

In the early hours of August 29, three Bettys harried the marines on Guadalcanal. With daylight, eighteen bombers accompanied by twenty-two Zeros of the carrier air groups mounted the main punch of the day. They crossed the Guadalcanal skies at 1155, by which time all flyable American aircraft, including ten Wildcats, were off the ground, thanks again to the coast watchers on Bougainville and New Georgia. In the ensuing scrap the marines lost no planes, but one Betty and one Zero failed to regain their bases and one damaged bomber "crash-landed" at Buka. Bombs eliminated two Wildcats and an SBD at Henderson Field, but Japanese air losses increased when B-17s visited Buka this day and damaged four Zeros on the ground. At sea a small American convoy composed of transport *William Ward Burrows* and S.S. *Kopara* neared Guadalcanal this morning and one of their five escorts, destroyer-minesweeper *Gamble,* surprised and sank *I-123.*

At 1100 on the 29th, Kawaguchi formally recommended to the 17th Army that his troops move by barge over 200 miles from Gizo Island to Guadalcanal; but before fabricating further plans, the staffs of both the 17th Army and the 8th Fleet awaited the outcome of this night's reinforcement run. Destroyer Division 11 with the majority of the 1st Battalion, 124th Infantry joined Destroyer Division 24 for the attempt, while 120 men of Ichiki's Second Echelon filed aboard *Patrol Boat 1* and *Patrol Boat 34* at Shortland for landing the following night. At 2230 on August 29, the two destroyer divisions put ashore about 450 men of the 124th Infantry and 300 of Ichiki's Second Echelon at Taivu Point with four anti-tank guns. So far so good. But the orders of Captain Murakami of Destroyer Division 24 called for a sweep for American shipping. It so happened that this night the transport *William Ward Burrows* lay helplessly aground off Tulagi. The Cactus Air Force put fourteen SBDs into the air to look for intruders and to protect *Burrows,* but they never located the Japanese on the inky sea. Nonetheless, Murakami seized the mere presence of the planes as a pretext to cancel the sweep. This failure humiliated Admiral Tanaka, and Murakami found himself without a job upon his return to Shortland.

Changing their tactics, the Japanese tried to quash the Henderson Field fliers on August 30 with a fighter sweep. Eighteen of the crack pilots from the carrier air groups passed over the coast watchers, who radioed a warning of a large formation of single-engine aircraft headed south. When the Japanese arrived at 1145, the defenders anticipated a dive-bombing attack and waited at three levels: four of the P-400s circled low over the stranded *Burrows* at Tulagi; at 14,000 feet seven more P-400s cruised, led by Captain Dale Brannon; and at 28,000 feet Captain Smith patrolled with eight Wildcats. The Zero pilots initiated the action with a climbing attack on Brannon's flight out of the clouds, downing two of the P-400s. The marines dived from overhead and caught the Japanese completely unawares. In a brief but violent battle no fewer than eight Zeros fell, and one other eventually ditched. Two of the Tulagi section of P-400s were jumped and shot down on return, making a total of four P-400s lost, but two pilots walked in. A pair of Wildcats brought their pilots home but did not fly again. The action elated the Marine pilots, who scored most of the victories, and properly so, for it was a stunning victory over some of the best pilots in the Imperial Navy.

But the battle struck a severe blow to the already sagging morale of the P-400 pilots. Their logbooks recorded many more hours of experience than Smith's men could boast, but these brave and talented men dismissively labeled their planes as "klunkers." The P-400, an export version of the Bell P-39, exemplified the sort of leftover the Army Air Forces consigned to the Pacific. It looked aggressive enough on the ground, but no amount of ground crew titillation could overcome the lack of a proper supercharging system for high-altitude operation or the absence of proper equipment to recharge its oxygen system. Its effective ceiling absolutely precluded the engagement of Japanese bombers and was suicidally low for fighting Zeros. After this day's action, the Army pilots turned to the ground support role, where the heavy armament and bomb carrying capacity of the P-400 held promise.

The Japanese had not yet shot their bolt for August 30, however, as a second group of eighteen Bettys with thirteen Zeros as escort arrived over Guadalcanal at 1510 while ground crews were refueling the Marine fighters. Two minutes later, lookouts aboard *Colhoun,* a destroyer transport in the waters off Lunga Point, spotted the Japanese formation approaching at over 15,000 feet, far above the effective range of *Colhoun*'s feeble antiaircraft armament of four 20mm guns. As the planes disappeared into clouds overhead, the ship went to full speed, but Japanese bombing accuracy was uncanny. Two bombs had hit the ship already when a string of five or six landed only 50 to 60 feet off the starboard side, with catastrophic effect: concussion toppled the foremast, uprooted one 20mm and two 4-inch guns from their mountings and blew them off the ship, pried the main engines from their bedplates, and ruptured oil lines and the fire main as the ship's boats began to flame and she settled by the stern. After two more direct hits at 1514, her captain and crew left *Colhoun* as the sea swallowed her with fifty of her complement.

At 1600 on this day of triumph and tragedy, the commander of MAG-23, Colonel William J. Wallace, arrived with the remainder of his unit: nineteen Wildcats of VMF-224 directed by Major Robert E. Galer and twelve SBDs of VMSB-231 led by Major Leo R. Smith. These replacements filled a critical need, for attrition and battle damage left the original Marine fighter squadron with but five flyable Wildcats at the end of this day.

The success of the second destroyer reinforcement shuttle, a method the Japanese soon referred to as a "Rat" (*(Nezumi)*) operation, failed to mollify Kawaguchi. He conferred with Tanaka on the 30th against the dramatic backdrop afforded by the arrival of *Shirakumo* at the end of the towline from *Amagiri*. The general refused to move a man of his brigade without further orders from his Army superiors. Nor could Kawaguchi be made to see that the essentials to success of his barge adventures off Borneo, air and sea supremacy, did not obtain in the Solomons. A frustrated Tanaka loaded the rest of the Ichiki Second Echelon, the only troops available, aboard *Yudachi* and sent her to join the patrol boats which had departed the previous day. They landed their human cargo without event that night.

Late on the 30th, new orders authorizing the movement of some of the brigade by barge rewarded Kawaguchi for his obstinacy. With this concession, 17th Army staff discerned that the barges probably could not safely pass the main American perimeter and reach Taivu Point and that Kawaguchi's brigade thus would be split and weakened. Therefore, they detailed the 2d Battalion, 4th Infantry Regiment to reinforce the main body at Taivu Point. Although the new directive stressed that only as few men as possible should advance by barge, it specified no number, and Kawaguchi interpreted it to his liking. His liking was to commission the commander of the 124th Infantry, Colonel Akinosuka Oka, to organize a barge convoy for 1,000 men.

The weather shielded Henderson Field on August 31 from Japanese bombs intended to cover the destroyer lift bearing Kawaguchi. The newly arrived pilots of VMF-224 received a rough initiation when three of their Wildcats and two pilots mysteriously disappeared during a scramble on a false alarm. Seven days later a spectral figure staggered into Marine lines in a tattered flight suit. He was one of the missing pilots, Second Lieutenant Richard Amerine, and he disclosed that his oxygen system and then his engine had failed, forcing him to bail out. He landed near Cape Esperance, 30 miles deep behind Japanese lines. Amerine cautiously started back and soon encountered a sleeping Japanese soldier, whom he killed with a rock. In the next several days he dispatched two more Japanese with the butt of his pistol and shot a fourth. With the benefit of college study of entomology, Amerine survived his week-long walk by munching on three coconuts, red ants, and snails.

The loss of three planes and two pilots on Guadalcanal was of small consequence compared to the other blow suffered by American arms this day. Dawn of August 31 found *Saratoga* steaming to the south of Guadalcanal, a position American carriers frequented in order to cover the supply routes to the Marine garrison. At 0706 the crew secured from the customary dawn battle stations unaware that their ship's distinctive profile had already been sighted by Commander Minoru Yokota of *I-26*. At 0748 a pillar of oil and water sprouted to the level of the flight deck on the starboard side abreast the island, marking the spot where a torpedo struck. The explosion flooded one boiler room, unoccupied at the time, but released gremlins within the ship's complex turboelectric machinery that brought her to a halt by 0753. Although the *Saratoga* got underway again, for most of the remainder of the day the ship experienced assorted engineering difficulties and at one point required a tow. *MacDonough* and *Monssen* pursued the culprit, but *I-26* eluded them and would make her presence known later even more painfully. During the afternoon, *Saratoga* managed to fly off twenty-one dive-bombers and nine torpedo planes to Espíritu Santo. On September 2 her fighter squadron, VF-5, flew to Efate.

The hit on *Saratoga* injured only twelve men, the worst a fractured leg, but they included Admiral Fletcher, who sustained a forehead laceration. To set *Saratoga* right required a dockyard, so the carrier began a voyage to the West Coast. With her went the wounded admiral, out of combat command for the rest of the war. Fletcher's conduct since August 7 had finally worn out the patience of even Nimitz. Some clue to Nimitz's frustration may be gleaned from the inquiries he sent to his principal subordinates during the last two weeks of August asking why the Japanese reinforcement runs were unmolested by navy surface ships or carrier planes. On August 19, Nimitz issued an extraordinary message addressed to the entire Pacific Fleet that said in part:

> Suitable targets present themselves only rarely to our guns, bombs and torpedoes. On those rare occasions our tactics must be such that our objective will be gunned, bombed or torpedoed to destruction. Surely we will have losses—but we will also destroy ships and be that much nearer to the successful conclusion of the war. We cannot expect to inflict heavy losses on the enemy without ourselves accepting the risk of punishment. To win this war we must come to grips with the enemy. Courage, determination and action will see us through.

Since common sailors and junior officers were not in a position to choose when to accept or provoke battle, the object of this prod is plain.

Frank Jack Fletcher was the most important seagoing commander in the United States Navy from May to August 1942, yet his reticence both then and after the war leaves much of his conduct enigmatic. It is easy to caricature his penchant for fueling rather than fighting, but valid grounds existed for Fletcher's caution. The whole Allied position in the Pacific rested largely on the few carriers entrusted to his command, while inferior aircraft and deficiencies in tactical refinement, radar, and radio hobbled the performance of their air groups. But when all is said and done, the record of Fletcher from Savo Island to the Eastern Solomons shows he drifted from prudence into paralysis.

Admiral Tanaka's career also took a sharp turn on August 31, when he relinquished command of the Reinforcement Unit to Rear Admiral Shintaro Hashimoto. Tanaka admitted to physical and mental exhaustion from recent grueling operations, and his squadron had suffered numerous losses. His superiors fancied he had concurred with Kawaguchi on the wisdom of the use of barges and held Tanaka accountable for the multiple failures of Captain Murakami, late of Destroyer Division 24. But unlike Fletcher, this marked an interruption, not an end, to Tanaka's tenure.

In the last hour of this eventful month of August 1942, General Kawaguchi stepped ashore on Guadalcanal from destroyer *Umikaze* to assume command of all Army units present and to prepare for an attack. With the general came nearly 1,200 soldiers delivered by *Umikaze* and seven sisters.

THE TOKYO EXPRESS

The first five days of September marked the steady accretion of Japanese troop strength on Guadalcanal, but the weather kept the airmen apart on three of these days. Four destroyers conveyed 465 soldiers to Taivu Point on the night of September 1. Three SBDs put in an appearance about 0130 and damaged *Shikinami,* which lost three soldiers killed and five others plus two crewmen wounded. One Dauntless became an operational loss. The next day, eighteen Bettys with twenty Zeros (thirteen from the carrier air groups) bombed Henderson Field about 1135, starting fires. VMF-224 assailed the formation, damaging three Bettys. The clouds hampered the escort, which returned home minus two of their number, thanks to VMF-223. No American plane was lost in this engagement. Two days later the Zeros of the carrier air groups returned to their ships, short fifteen of the thirty planes committed on August 28. On the night of September 2, two destroyers, two patrol boats, and minelayer *Tsugaru* delivered antiaircraft guns as well as soldiers. On the trip back up the channel of water between the Solomon Island chain that the Americans were beginning to call "the Slot," *Tsugaru* suffered the attentions of American airmen and lost fourteen killed and twenty wounded.

The Japanese scheduled no reinforcement run for September 3 and no air action, but the day was a significant milestone for the air campaign. After dark a Douglas R4D (as the naval service dubbed the ubiquitous DC-3) touched down on Henderson Field in the nebular glow of jeep headlights. It disgorged Brigadier General Roy S. Geiger and two staff officers of Marine Air Wing One. Above Geiger's husky shoulders sat a round face with a broad mouth and small sharp features permanently set in an expression that suggested someone within his sight was out of step. Short white hair added dignity to a countenance that would have done credit to a Roman emperor. The fifty-seven-year-old Geiger had graduated from the same 1909 class at the Parris Island School of Application for officers as Archer Vandegrift. After command of a Marine bombing squadron in World War One, he steadily progressed in rank while flying every aircraft in the Marine inventory down to the latest fighters, always commanding from a cockpit, not a desk. Geiger understood to his bones that Marine aviation existed to support the rifleman, and he made it a point to visit the front lines periodically. Stern, curt, even ruthless, some said, Geiger spared neither himself nor his subordinates. Foremost among these was his chief of staff, Colonel Louis Woods, who shared with his boss a contempt for paperwork.

Geiger and his staff set up shop in a rude one-story building erected by the Japanese on a rise northwest of the airfield. It was called the Pagoda because of its architectural style. Tactically, the situation Geiger examined held important advantages for the Henderson Field aviators. The long haul from Rabaul not only fatigued the Japanese, but also forced them into a pattern of operations the Americans could exploit. The four-hour flight from their airfields meant that the Japanese bombers must generally arrive over Guadalcanal between 1130 and 1430 to avoid dangerous takeoff and assembly in the dark or landing after nightfall. They flew down the Solomons chain seeded with coast watchers—Read and Mason on Bougainville, who usually saw them shortly after takeoff, and Kennedy at Segi Point on New Georgia, whose key alarm came with the Japanese forty-five minutes out. This provided sufficient time for all flyable aircraft to take off; the Wildcats could climb up to intercept the raiders while the other aircraft headed east to evade bombs and Zeros. Not that the Japanese enjoyed a high success rate against planes caught on the ground. The Bettys sometimes dispensed two or three 550-pound bombs that buried themselves so deeply before exploding that planes beyond 20 or 30 feet from the point of impact were only damaged by clods of earth falling back on them. More often the Japanese employed an alternate load of a dozen 132-pound instantaneously fuzed bombs per Betty that could "badly cut up" aircraft as much as 50 yards away.

An air warning radar (SCR 270) delivered by *Burrows* backed up the coast watchers. It could generally detect the large, high-altitude Japanese bomber formations at a range of 130 miles. The SCR 270 became more important as the Japanese began to take courses to avoid the coast watchers. But the radar gave only a 35- to 40-minute warning—just barely enough time for the Wildcats to gain vital altitude.

Without these warnings, Henderson Field, and ultimately Guadalcanal, could not have been defended; even with these warnings only a few minutes, perhaps a bare five to ten minutes, spelled the difference between a successful and a failed interception. And there were plenty of pitfalls to an effective interception. Rain transformed the largely dirt airfield and surrounding area into a black gooey substance that could mire a pilot trying to reach his plane, glue an aircraft to its dispersal point, or prohibit takeoffs altogether. The ruts gouged across the airstrip by the solid tail wheels of the SBDs, which acted like plows, presented more hazards to flight operations, as did potholes resulting from settling where bomb and shell craters had been filled. The climb in formation tested the two vital pieces of equipment for high-altitude operation, the oxygen system and the supercharger. These performed similar functions for the pilot and engine respectively. If either of these failed, the prudent pilot would head east to avoid combat; those who did not often forfeited their lives as well as their planes. Above 20,000 feet, the Wildcats climbed in formation at only 500 feet per minute, and the preferred altitude for an interception was 30,000 feet or better.

The marines made no attempt to vector the fighters out to intercept the Japanese at a distance, because radio communication was unreliable beyond 20 to 30 miles and the airfield was the one certain target on which the Bettys must converge. Thus to the cognoscenti of the new art of fighter direction the Cactus Air Force employed "vertical" rather than the more customary "horizontal" interception tactics. In air combat the Marine fighter pilots relied on skillful tactics largely devised by John L. Smith, newly promoted to major. The Bettys flew at 25,000 to 27,000 feet, customarily in twenty-seven-plane formations composed of nine Bettys from each of three air groups or, when there were only two Betty-equipped groups, eighteen from one and nine from the other. The twenty-seven-plane formation was shaped normally as a broad, nearly flat, vee, subdivided into three nine-plane divisions with the center one slightly ahead of the wing divisions. Each nine-plane division, in turn, was made of a trio of three aircraft vees formed into a larger vee. Zeros arranged themselves in various combinations above, below, and to both flanks of the Bettys, but their ability to coordinate their defense of the bombers was severely compromised by their lack of radios. This forced them into fairly rigid, preplanned defense by sectors around the bombers. Smith always sought to initiate the attack from a point about 5,000 feet above and ahead of the bombers. This position was not easy to achieve, because of the small speed differential between the Betty and the Wildcat at altitude.

Once in position, Smith would lead his men down in a high overhead pass, concentrating on the trailing aircraft. This presented a difficult gunnery problem in light of the rapid changes in relative position of the intercepting fighters and bombers, but his gambit offered three immense advantages. First, it placed the Wildcats in the blind spot of the coverage of the Betty's considerable defensive armament, which included a 20mm gun in the tail. Second, the bombers found it almost impossible to evade by maneuver. Third, the overhead approach coincidentally presented the Marine pilots with an excellent gunnery angle for a shot at the Betty's exceedingly vulnerable fuel tanks.

Smith taught his pupils to pull up for another pass, once past the bomber formation, if the Zeros escort had not intervened. Generally, the Americans started out in pairs, but they seldom maintained any formation after the first attack; they simply tried to stay in the same general area for mutual support. If the Zeros appeared, the Marine pilots usually dived away out of range or flew into a cloud—not very glorious, but very necessary. The speed, acceleration, and agility of the Zero made it much too dangerous to dogfight. For the Henderson Field defenders the job was to break up each raid as best they could and live to do the same thing the next day.

In these air battles the Americans enjoyed one other cardinal advantage. Because of the ruggedness of the Wildcat, the fact that the air engagements occurred over or near Guadalcanal, and the assistance of the coast watchers and Clemens's scouts with their loyal native helpers, the majority of American pilots who were shot down survived to return to duty. The converse of these factors was that only a fraction of the downed Japanese fliers survived, and fewer still returned to duty.

Marine and Navy dive-bomber crews had also developed a routine of operations, much of it inspired by Richard Mangrum, newly promoted to Lieutenant Colonel. The performance of the SBD created a 200-mile radius around Henderson Field within which attack missions could be conducted. Morning and afternoon search missions in the northwest quadrant probed for Japanese ships within this range for strike groups whose strength corresponded to the number of remaining operational SBDs. Pilots attempted to make their dive-bombing runs down the long axis of the targets, but the small size and violent maneuvers of Japanese destroyers made them exceedingly difficult to hit. Occasionally, the Dauntless pilots mounted very hazardous missions from the unlit field in the dark to hit ships just off the coast, but the Japanese quickly discovered that by not firing at the planes and by keeping their speed low to reduce wakes they could usually go undetected. It must be emphasized that the success of the SBDs must be measured not only in the number of hits actually achieved, but also in the fact that they compelled the Japanese to rely principally on destroyers for their logistical support of the ground forces on Guadalcanal.

Besides the tactical situation, Geiger faced a critical personnel situation, for the pilots of the first echelon of MAG-23 already displayed considerable strain. The reasons for this are not hard to comprehend. Combat flying is draining under the best of circumstances, and at Guadalcanal the circumstances were probably the worst any American airmen faced for a prolonged period during the war. The aircrews lived in tents in a coconut grove between the airstrip and the beach. Many slept on matting on the dirt floors of the tents, which quickly became mud in the rain. Most possessed only one set of clothes, embellished by baseball caps—blue for pilots and red for ground crews. When they bathed at all it was in the Lunga, where the opportunity was also taken to wash their garments. They consumed a diet similar to that of the rest of the garrison, heavy in captured rice, dehydrated potatoes, hash, Spam, and sausage. The only welcome item on the menu was coffee. This food generated gas during digestion that, at the reduced pressures of high altitude, produced excruciating abdominal pains. Breathing oxygen burned the body's fuel faster and made the pilots groggy. The medical officers plied them with vitamins and an occasional shot of alcohol, while their commanders tried to get them some fresh fruit.

But by far the worst aspect of the situation was that nerves stretched by repeated air battles and dive-bombing runs got no relief at night. Frequent bombardments interrupted sleep, and for long periods during the night enemy planes droned overhead dropping an occasional bomb, a practice designed to keep the Americans in foxholes for much of the night. In the opinion of one experienced pilot, aircrews could remain effective for only six weeks of this regimen. This subjective estimate was probably optimistic. Perhaps a better and objective measure is that after *Asagiri* was sunk, almost a month passed before the dive-bomber pilots next scored a direct hit on a Japanese vessel.

Geiger's prescriptions for these problems were two. First, he ordered more offensive operations, starting with flights to bomb Gizo Bay. The first of these on September 6 unfortunately cost two SBDs and crews to weather. For tortured nerves and fatigue, he offered only a stern demand that each man do all he could. On September 22 the aging general hoisted himself into an SBD and took it out to dive-bomb a Japanese position to set the example himself—and to shame the younger men.

Because of the efforts of the Cactus fliers and the lack of efforts by American admirals, a curious tactical situation arose in the waters around Guadalcanal: a change of sea command every twelve hours, creating a sort of mutual siege. By day, American ships plied the channel between Tulagi and Guadalcanal and transports arrived to unload, keeping a wary eye cocked for Japanese aircraft. At sundown all the ships flying the Stars and Stripes exited hastily to the east or sought the haven of Tulagi's harbor, "like frightened children running home from a graveyard," in the words of Samuel Eliot Morison. Shortly after darkness, Japanese men-of-war heaved into Iron Bottom Sound, which they had ruled unchallenged since August 9, with the unhappy exception of *Blue* and *Henley*. There they would favor their countrymen with rice, bullets, and soldiers and the Americans with a bombardment. These operations achieved the regularity of a crack railroad run, and disgusted marines labeled them the "Cactus Express" (soon better known as the "Tokyo Express").[2] But the Japanese did not tarry to see the namesake of their Rising Sun

[2] According to Thomas G. Miller, Jr., in *The Cactus Air Force*, p. 74, the term "Tokyo Express" was the product of a reporter, while the marines and sailors on Guadalcanal always referred to it as the "Cactus Express." Possibly the name was transformed in the press because Cactus was a code name.

banner, lest they fall under the sights of the SBDs at Henderson Field.

Admiral Hashimoto scheduled a big "Express" run for the night of September 4–5 with the threefold objective of reinforcing, bombarding, and protecting a large barge convoy, of which more anon. Light cruiser *Sendai* led eleven destroyers, six of which deposited nearly 1,000 men of the 2d Battalion, 4th Infantry Regiment and Ichiki's Second Echelon at Taivu Point to start the evening's activities. Upon completion of this chore, destroyers *Yudachi, Hatsuyuki,* and *Murakumo* steamed west to bombard Henderson Field. Their gunners commenced to limber up on the airstrip when aircraft flares began to glow to the west revealing two small ships. These were the old destroyer transports *Little* and *Gregory.* During the day they had borne elements of the 1st Raider Battalion to Savo Island to check out reports of Japanese presence, which proved false, though only by a few hours. The destroyer transports then carried the Raiders to Guadalcanal, but by the time the two ships completed their rounds for the day it was very dark and hazy. The leader of the pair, Lieutenant Commander Hugh W. Hadley, deemed an approach to Tulagi harbor too hazardous and directed his ships to steam a patrol line northwest of Lunga Point. About 0100, crewmen heard gunfire and saw gun flashes to the east and interpreted them as signs of shelling by a Japanese submarine. Both ships went to general quarters in anticipation of an antisubmarine scuffle. The American vessels were still steaming northwest at 0102 when *Little*'s radar picked up four echoes at 4,000 yards. About one minute later, aircraft flares brilliantly illuminated both ships. These were courtesy of a PBY crew who, ignorant of the presence of *Little* and *Gregory,* intended to help Marine gunners.

With only three 4-inch guns apiece, *Little* and *Gregory* were no match for modern destroyers with sophisticated fire control equipment. The Japanese illuminated both with searchlights and soon found the range, with devastating results. *Little*'s captain, Lieutenant Commander Gus B. Lofberg, tried to beach his wrecked and blazing command, but the steering gear was shot out and his ship kept twisting to seaward in her death throes. As *Little*'s crew abandoned their ship, more hits—the Japanese fired almost 500 shells at the two ships—killed both Hadley and Lofberg. *Gregory*'s suffering was in kind. The crew abandoned their blazing and sinking ship, taking with them their wounded skipper, Lieutenant Commander Harry F. Bauer. In the water Bauer ordered the two men with him to go to the assistance of another sailor. Bauer was not seen again.

The Japanese ships circled the blazing hulks, killing some survivors with their screws.

In the morning, boats from Guadalcanal picked up twelve officers and 226 men from the two crews and brought them ashore, where they huddled in small shocked groups. Losses came to twenty-two killed and forty-four wounded on *Little* and eleven killed and twenty-six wounded on *Gregory*. Admiral Turner provided the epitaph for these ships and *Colhoun:*

> The officers and men serving in these ships have shown great courage and have performed outstanding service. They entered this dangerous area time after time, well knowing that their ships stood little or no chance if they should be opposed by any surface or air force the enemy would send into those waters. On the occasion of their last trip in they remained for six days, subjected to daily air attack and anticipating nightly surface attack.

We turn now to the adventures of Colonel Oka, charged by General Kawaguchi with the mission of taking about 1,000 men to Guadalcanal in sixty-one barges. In view of Kawaguchi's treatment of his orders, there is some poetic justice in Oka's response to Kawaguchi's directives. The general commanded Oka to use Gizo Island in the New Georgia group as his point of departure; Oka took his men by ship across the Slot to the northwest coast of Santa Isabel. Kawaguchi ordered Oka to go down the southern tier of the Solomons; Oka instead proceeded down the northern tier of the Solomons. More incredibly, Kawaguchi directed him to land at Taivu Point east of the American perimeter; Oka steered his men for a landing on the western coast of Guadalcanal.

On September 3, search planes detected the barge convoy, and eleven SBDs strafed it in the morning and a second shift of seven SBDs and two Wildcats administered bullets in the afternoon. The next morning, thirteen SBDs led by Lieutenant Colonel Mangrum subjected the convoy to the same treatment. Although the Japanese had beached and camouflaged their boats, the SBD pilots holed about a third of them. The Cactus Air Force gave two encores in the afternoon in lesser strength.

These attacks necessitated repairs before Oka's men embarked upon the longest and most dangerous leg of their journey on the night of September 4–5 from San Jorge Island off the southeast end of Santa Isabel to Kamimbo Bay on the northwest coast of Guadalcanal. A low tide over the reef barred departure for two and one-half hours. When the Japanese finally got to sea at 2130, they immediately found the water filled with steep-sided waves that threw spray into the wells of the barges, and many boats began to leak badly because of the strafing. Soaked infantrymen bailed, overstrained engines started to falter, and the sea began to scatter the convoy.

The scheduled hour of landing, 0500 on September 5, passed with Guadalcanal not yet in sight. At 0620, Guadalcanal's mountains peeked over the horizon, but within twenty minutes so did the first American planes. These were two P-400s led by Captain Dale Brannon, and six Wildcats shortly joined them. The fighter pilots lined up fifteen barges for savage strafing runs. In this leading group of open craft rode Major Etsuo Takamatsu, the commander of the 2d Battalion, 124th Infantry. He inspired his men to fire back as best they could with their small arms, and they succeeded in splashing one of the Wildcats. But aircraft machineguns took a terrible toll of the huddled soldiers aboard the boats, including Major Takamatsu. The first wooden hulls touched shore at 0740. As the barges struggled to scattered locations on the coast near Marovovo, some men jumped into neck-deep water to escape the awful lashing from the planes.

As the original plan provided for the barge passage wholly in darkness, the 11th Air Fleet had programmed no air cover and the daily air raid took place too late to render relief to Oka's men. Clouds compelled twenty-seven Bettys to dump their loads away from the airstrip. Eighteen Marine Wildcats challenged the bombers and their fifteen Zero escorts, and the American aviators claimed one bomber and one fighter while losing one plane and pilot. Japanese bullets damaged three other Wildcats, one beyond repair, and wounded Major Rivers J. Morrell. Japanese records reflect the loss of one bomber and damage to six.

The initial count of Oka's men showed only 150 on Guadalcanal of the 1,000 who had set out the night before. Over the next six days, search efforts located large and small batches of Japanese soldiers at assorted points along the route, including a group of about 450 on Savo Island. During the night of September 5–6, five destroyers delivered another 370 men and provisions at Taivu Point and began the task of rounding up these dispersed detachments and shuttling them to Guadalcanal. About ninety men died in this barge expedition to Kamimbo Bay. More important, hundreds of others would not be available for the coming attack, a fact Oka was tardy to report.

GHORMLEY BESET

The last two weeks of August and the first eight days of September found Admiral Ghormley sorely pressed. His triple responsibilities to defend the Guadalcanal area, to protect the sea lanes to Australia and New Zealand, and to seize Ndeni and other points remained unchanged. Radio intelligence portrayed a massive Japanese buildup of planes, ships, and men whose purpose boded ill for Vandegrift's marines. Ghormley pleaded for commensurate resources, yet found not only that few new tools were forthcoming, but also that he was being ordered to part with some of those he already had.

The alarmingly rapid decline in the effective strength of the first Marine squadrons based on Guadalcanal prompted Ghormley on August 27 to request a program of air reinforcements and replacements based upon actual attrition, no less than 26 percent per week for fighters. On August 30, two important travelers started a chorus of voices in support of Ghormley's petitions for more aircraft. Under Secretary of the Navy James Forrestal paused in his inspection of the South Pacific to radio that the flow of planes, particularly fighters, to Guadalcanal was "imperative for the position to be held." Meanwhile, Admiral McCain paid a promised visit to Henderson Field to see conditions firsthand. He declared in simple but forceful language:

> . . . 2 full squadrons of P-38s or F4Fs in addition to present strength should be put into Cactus at once, with replacements in training to south. . . . the situation admits of no delay whatever. . . . With substantially the reinforcement requested, Cactus can be a sinkhole for enemy air power and can be consolidated, expanded and exploited to the enemy's mortal hurt. The reverse is true if we lose Cactus. If the reinforcement requested is not made available, Cactus cannot be supplied and hence cannot be held.

On September 1, Ghormley reiterated the need for more air reinforcements and observed:

> Cactus [is] not only a base of major value to the nation holding it but is [the] first foot of ground taken from an enemy who has had some cause to consider his armies invincible. . . . It is my considered opinion that at this time the retention of Cactus is more vital to the prosecution of the war in the Pacific than any other commitment.

Here Ghormley put his finger on the key point: the psychological value of holding Guadalcanal was already beginning to exceed its considerable military value.

The topic of reinforcements to Guadalcanal rested very much in front of the Joint Chiefs of Staff, but so too did other developments of a world war. Hitler's tanks threatened Stalingrad, only 50 miles separated Rommel's army from Alexandria, and the prospective invasion of North Africa retained top national priority. At the end of August the Joint Chiefs still mulled over the request for reinforcements sent by Harmon two days before the landing. The dispute in these high councils focused on fifteen air groups which General Marshall informed the British in July would be considered available for use in the Pacific because of the postponement of the second front in Europe to at least 1943, but Admiral King and the Navy planners soon learned that General Marshall did not mean exactly what he said. Upon return from London, Marshall authorized the release of only one heavy bombardment group to the Pacific. A staff committee took up the question of where to deploy the remaining fourteen air groups on August 20. A week's worth of discussion produced a consensus on where to send the planes but not when.

Armed with the series of messages from the local commanders, on September 2, King called upon Marshall for reinforcements for the South Pacific. General Arnold responded to this query on Marshall's behalf. Arnold asserted that more air reinforcements, especially fighters, could not be supplied without deducting them from other commitments approved by the Combined Chiefs of Staff. He included a chart showing the deployment of Army aircraft under Nimitz's command as of September 2:[3]

Type	On hand	En route or being prepared	Total
Heavy bombers	75	44	119
Medium bombers	24	11	35
Light bombers	7	0	7
Fighters	270	202	472

[3]These figures are not directly comparable to proposed Japanese air strength at Rabaul, because the American total included a large number of planes deployed in areas other than the South Pacific and Guadalcanal, such as Hawaii and Samoa.

Arnold insisted that short-range aircraft could not reach the area in time to assist current operations and that the fighter models assigned (which he erroneously identified as P-40s, a type not present on Guadalcanal) were adequate for the Pacific. He warned that a withdrawal of P-38s from the proposed invasion of North Africa would impose a drastic change upon, if not the abandonment of the operation. Thus while the Japanese acted vigorously to augment their air power substantially at Rabaul, the subject of air reinforcements to the South Pacific stood at an impasse in Washington.

If a niggardly allotment of planes discouraged Ghormley, he soon discovered he should be thankful for what he had. On August 28, he learned of a MacArthur request for heavy naval reinforcements. Although Ghormley retained the carriers, Nimitz directed him on August 30 to provide MacArthur with the vessels necessary to support operations on New Guinea. In early September, Ghormley released three cruisers and six destroyers of Task Force 44 back to MacArthur.

This pattern of losses rather than gains in Ghormley's resources also applied to ground units. A message advised him on August 29 that the 43d Infantry Division would reach the South Pacific in late September or early October. This proved to be an optimistic estimate, for the 43d was nearly a month late. In the interval, Nimitz ordered Ghormley on September 8 to prepare to turn over to MacArthur one regiment of experienced, amphibious-trained troops complete with shipping. Admiral Turner interceded swiftly to point out that Guadalcanal held the only troops meeting these specifications, and he labeled any withdrawal from that source as "impractical." He "respectfully" invited the attention of his superiors to "the present insecure position of" Guadalcanal attributable to the lack of adequate air and sea power, which increased dependency on ground defense. He backed Vandegrift's repeated requests for at least one more regiment to secure Guadalcanal. This message seems to have forestalled the transfer to MacArthur, but Ghormley obtained no definite instructions for some time to either cancel or ignore the orders and thus was hamstrung in his planning by the need to keep the requested forces available for transfer.

On September 7, Ghormley created Task Force 64 for screening and attack missions with an initial composition of three cruisers and about seven destroyers. Admirals King and Nimitz learned of this move at a meeting in San Francisco. The former snorted that the creation of TF 64 came "about a month late." Ghormley's superiors scrutinized operations in the South Pacific, and the list of topics reads like a bill of indictment: "calculated risks"—presumably the lack thereof—"inopportune fueling," "lack of coordination of operations," "mixing forces," the inexplicable surprise at the Battle of Savo Island, and the delay in forming Task Force 64. Was Ghormley holding up physically? Nimitz promised to check into the matter. Should Ghormley be replaced? King and Nimitz deferred this decision.

THE BATTLE

OF EDSON'S RIDGE

"This is no motley of Japs"

THE TASIMBOKO RAID

On September 5 the 17th Army offered Kawaguchi an additional infantry battalion to add to the five already present or en route to Guadalcanal. Kawaguchi, confident his 6,200 men could seize the airfield on the moonless night of September 12, rejected this proposal. In good measure, the general's assurance sprang from current Japanese intelligence estimates that persisted in grossly underestimating the number of marines on Guadalcanal. According to Kawaguchi's superiors, only 2,000 wearers of the globe-and-anchor insignia occupied the perimeter around the airfield—albeit a well-equipped body of men with fifteen planes.

While calculation of American manpower erred by a factor of about six, the innate vulnerability of the Marine situation afforded sound reason for Japanese optimism. The ability of the Marines to defend and maintain themselves hung absolutely on their use of Henderson Field; to be victorious the Japanese merely needed to deny its use, a far simpler task than physically placing their boots on it. This distinction seems to have been lost to Kawaguchi and his superiors, but not to Vandegrift, who was compelled to stretch his men along the periphery of the broad oval perimeter. Moreover, the fresh Japanese faced defenders beginning to show the debilitating effects of a month's diet short on food and rest and long on bombing and bombardment. Finally, the initiative lay with Kawaguchi to choose the time and place of attack, and the jungle canopy offered the inestimable advantage of concealment and thus surprise. The Japanese could expect to have overwhelming superiority at the point of attack, and those were the numbers that really counted.

On September 7, Kawaguchi issued his plan of attack. He immediately cast aside simplicity—the sole virtue of Ichiki's efforts—in favor of complexity. The barge convoy left the 1,000 men in the regimental headquarters and the 2d Battalion, 124th Infantry (II/124) under Oka stranded west of the American perimeter. It was impractical for them to rendezvous with the rest of the brigade, nearly 5,200 strong, currently gathered at Taivu Point east of the airfield. Therefore, Kawaguchi designated Oka's men the Left Wing Unit and slated them to attack the southwest quarter of the American perimeter.

Not content with this division of forces, Kawaguchi further split the four battalions, each about 650 strong, at Taivu so that he ended with five battalions moving along three avenues of advance. The Main Body under Kawaguchi's direct command contained three infantry battalions: 1st Battalion, 124th Infantry (I/124), led by Major Yukichi Kokusho; 3d Battalion, 124th Infantry (III/124), commanded by Lieutenant Colonel Kusukichi Watanabe; and the 2d Battalion, 4th Infantry (II/4), under Major Masao Tamura. With support units, mostly engineer and signal, they would loop down into the jungle from Tetere and storm the Marine position from the south to seize the airfield. Kawaguchi also provided for an attack from the southeast by a Right Wing Unit. This was Ichiki's Second Echelon, now christened the Kuma ("Bear") Battalion under Major Eishi Mizuno. They would puncture the American line and push north to annihilate the enemy along Alligator Creek, "thus giving repose to the departed souls of the Ichiki Detachment commander and men." An artillery unit would position its guns to the east of the Marine lines and support the attack by fire. Kawaguchi called upon the Imperial Navy to support him by a bombing campaign on September 9 and 10 and for ships to prevent the escape of the defeated and fleeing Americans. To this latter end the 8th Fleet would contribute cruisers and destroyers, while the Combined Fleet stood out from Truk on September 9 and 10 to be in position to deal with any interference by the American fleet.

Through no fault of Kawaguchi's, the sailors were erroneously informed that the assault was set for September 11. The general originally contemplated September 12 as the date for his attack, but rains on September 6 convinced Kawaguchi that the assault must be delayed to September 13. On the evening of September 7, the Imperial Navy forwarded to Kawaguchi fresh intelligence of the arrival of major American reinforcements at the Fijis, about one week's steaming from Guadalcanal. The 17th Army enjoined him to hasten his efforts, and Kawaguchi replied the next day that he would make his assault on the 12th or sooner if possible. The 17th Army rashly notified the Imperial Navy that Kawaguchi would attack on the 11th. In any event, by September 8, Kawaguchi completed the shift of almost all of his troops from Taivu to Koli Point, and he readied them to commence the approach march on September 9.

Word of the presence of Japanese east of the perimeter reached Vandegrift again through native scouts. They placed 200 to 300 enemy at the village of Tasimboko with defensive positions oriented west and along the beach. Merritt Edson and Gerald Thomas digested this news and swiftly hatched a plan to land Edson's battalion 3,000 yards beyond the Japanese concentration to take them from the rear. This scheme nearly replicated the recent Kokumbona plan, but no question lingered about the caliber of the battalion commander. Known as "Red Mike" to his men for his carrot-colored hair, Edson was quiet and reserved. When Edson did speak, listeners strained to hear his soft raspy voice, for this onetime aviator possessed a first-class command of infantry tactics. Lean and exceedingly quick on his feet, he was equally swift to recognize superior or inferior performance of duty. Beyond these martial virtues, an inner coldness marked his character. Richard Tregaskis noted that when Edson's mouth smiled his eyes did not.

The simple expedient of attaching the depleted 1st Parachute Battalion to the 1st Raider Battalion brought Edson's command up to a strength of 849 officers and men after its losses on Tulagi. Two destroyer transports, *McKean* and *Manley,* stood by to take the battalion on its expedition, as did *YP 346* and *YP 298* (the YPs were popularly referred to as "yippies" by the marines and "tuna boats" by their crews in reflection of their erstwhile civilian occupations). These four vessels could not carry all of Edson's men at once, a sobering fact for consideration when on the eve of the venture new native reports placed Japanese strength at 2,000 to 3,000. The Marine commanders, doubtful of the mathematical aptitude of Clemens's scouts, discounted these reports. While conceding some increase in Japanese strength, the division intelligence section characterized them as ill-equipped and half-starved with only "two out of ten" armed.

At 0530 on September 8, the first wave of Raiders sloshed ashore at Taivu Point. They found immediate signs of recent landings in abandoned packs, shoes, life preservers, food, and two unmanned anti-tank guns. Edson rapidly deployed his men to attack west with two companies along the coast, while a third curved inland to strike the Japanese flank from the south. About 0800, the marines contacted some of the perhaps 300 defenders in the vicinity of Tasimboko, including a battery of regimental guns landed during the night. Not all of them stood and fought. By great good fortune, just as Edson's men gained the shore a small convoy of transports *Fuller* and *Bellatrix* and their escorts steamed into view headed for Lunga, and the Japanese mistook them for a major landing force. A number of defenders fled, but the determined among them, no doubt the majority, unlimbered some guns and erected machineguns to halt the Marine advance. Soon the marines felt the concussion of muzzle blasts against their faces and heard the "furry whistle" of shells as the field guns fired at point-blank range, killing two marines and taking an arm from another. At Taivu Point, Kawaguchi ordered the artillery battery commander to meet the Marine attack with the assistance of about half a company of infantry and a platoon of engineers, and as the mutter of gunfire swelled, he sent an infantry company to guard his rear. But Kawaguchi kept the remainder of his men headed for the airfield.

Edson called for air support to meet the mounting opposition, and soon P-400s and SBDs were in action, as they had been earlier against Tasimboko. Vandegrift denied Edson's request for another battalion and suggested a withdrawal, but Edson was not one for half-finished jobs. The second lift, including the Parachutists, landed about 1130, but did not figure in the capture of Tasimboko, for Edson's original combination proved sufficient. After being out of touch for an hour during a march through swampy terrain, Company A of the Raiders regained contact with the battalion. They burst upon the Japanese from the rear, leaving clumps of defenders sprawled around their field pieces and machineguns and scattering the others. By 1230, opposition ceased, and one hour later, Edson's men entered Tasimboko to find it deserted. Under careful camouflage lay four 75mm guns, ammunition, food, medical supplies, boats, and a large radio station. While correspondent Tregaskis filled a Japanese army blanket with papers and documents, Edson detailed fifty men to jab bayonets through thousands of tins of sliced beef and crab. The rest of the supplies were destroyed or made useless. Satisfied with the destruction, Edson reembarked his command by 1700. This most successful raid cost two marines killed and six wounded; Japanese dead numbered twenty-seven. The exultant Raiders returned with pockets bulging with tins of crab and sliced beef, while twenty-one cases of beer and seventeen half-gallon flasks of sake found their way aboard the transports.

One diarist with Kawaguchi wrote: "It is maddening to be the recipients of these daring and insulting attacks." At higher Japanese headquarters the news of Edson's landing prompted much more than a flash of emotion. Some vocalized sentiment at 17th Army to have Kawaguchi about-face with his main body and deal with the new threat. But Colonel Matsumoto successfully argued that the airfield remained the crucial target, and added that—as events amply demonstrated—Kawaguchi's prickly character was such that once set on one course it was difficult to redirect him. A request to the 11th Air Fleet for retaliation produced no succor: the daily raid had already been sent to attack New Guinea, and Bettys dispatched with torpedoes that evening arrived long after the transports withdrew, though they did inflict the equivalent of a major defeat on the Cactus Air Force when an abortive attempt to intercept them cost five Wildcats in takeoff and landing mishaps. The 8th Fleet hurriedly sortied light cruiser *Sendai* and three destroyers to help, but they could not arrive until after dark. Their only accomplishment was to damage one of the YP boats used by Edson; it was destroyed the next night. The alarm even spread to New Guinea, where the Nankai Detachment halted its march on Port Moresby and marked time for several days while Japanese commanders contemplated diverting it to Guadalcanal. At Truk, the Combined Fleet ordered three light cruisers to pick up two infantry battalions of the 2d Division, totaling 1,500 men, at Djakarta and bear them to Rabaul.

Edson returned to the perimeter to announce his verdict: "This is no motley of Japs." He estimated Japanese strength at 4,000, and the translators found ready confirmation in the captured documents. Clemens's scouts, in the glow of vindication from the raid, soon brought stories of Japanese columns moving south and southwest from Tetere with natives fleeing from villages in their path. At 1st Marine Division headquarters on September 9, Gerald Thomas knew the Japanese were coming again, but the question was where? Edson drew a finger along an aerial photo and in a throaty whisper said, "This looks like a good approach." His digit traced a broken grassy ridge, barely a mile south of the airfield. This 1,000-yard-long elevation resembled an animal that had crawled south off the western end of Henderson Field just into the rain forest. At the southern end of the ridge, a knoll rising 80 feet above sea level marked the animal's head. A second knoll rose 120 feet above sea level midway along the animal's spine. Along each side of the ridge protruded spurs like legs, which prompted the Japanese to dub it "the Centipede."

Thomas and Edson presented Vandegrift with their analysis. The general found this information of more than academic interest, for just that day the new division command post opened—right on the spur forming the left rear leg of the Centipede. Over "profane" objections from his staff, Vandegrift had ordered his headquarters moved from its original location (nicknamed "impact center") on a low ridge northwest of the airfield, because its proximity to target number one virtually guaranteed a few bombs with each raid.

Perversely, the daily air raid arrived at 1115 and selected the shipping as its object. Of the twenty-seven bombers and fourteen Zeros that reached Guadalcanal, the defenses accounted for three bombers and damaged six. Five of the fifteen Wildcats intercepting the raid failed to return, as did two pilots; one other pilot was wounded. The loss of a sixth Wildcat in a takeoff accident again illustrated the serious operational hazards pilots faced on Guadalcanal. The opening of a new grass strip called Fighter One 1 mile east of Henderson Field allowed for some much-needed dispersal of aircraft. However, it soon proved almost impossible to keep drained.

One pilot missing this day was the ace Captain Marion Carl of VMF-223. He fell into the hands of friendly natives, who escorted him back to Marine lines five days later. Carl learned that in the interval his friendly rival and squadron commander, Major John Smith, raised his score to sixteen while Carl's remained at twelve. "What are you going to do about that?" queried Geiger. Carl pondered a moment and then shot back, "Goddammit, General, ground him for five days."

On September 9, the 17th Army requested Kawaguchi's views on where to land the newly arrived 3d Battalion, 4th Infantry (III/4). Though only four days before, Kawaguchi had declined a similar offer, he now asked that the battalion be debarked at Taivu Point.

But Rabaul still thought that locale was in Marine hands. Moreover, the Army staff had also begun to quietly contemplate the situation if Kawaguchi failed. In that event, they deemed it better to switch the lines of communication with Japanese forces on Guadalcanal to the northwestern end of the island. Consequently, 17th Army decided to put the III/4 ashore at Kamimbo Bay on the northwest tip of the island. Accompanying them would be Colonel Matsumoto as the advance man for the army headquarters. Imperial General Headquarters agreed that if Kawaguchi failed, the western end of the island would be the best arena for Japanese operations and so informed the Emperor.

General Kawaguchi intended not to fail, but he was learning that he had miscalculated the opposition he would face from the jungle. In his memoirs the general depicted his brigade as moving in one column toward Henderson Field, but this accurately described only the initial part of the approach march. From Koli Point his battalions advanced west and began peeling off into the jungle one by one. At the Balesuna River on September 8, the 3d Battalion, 124th Infantry (III/124) plunged inland, then west through the jungle. The next day at the Malimbiu River the 1st Battalion, 124th Infantry (I/124) angled south and a little farther west, and the 2d Battalion, 4th Infantry (II/4) pivoted left into the jungle with the brigade headquarters in its wake. The Kuma Battalion remained at Koli Point to thwart further Marine depredations until nearly midnight of September 9. Therefore, it trudged much farther west along the coast before heading inland east of the Tenaru River.

Kawaguchi's men found the advance through the jungle resembled compressing a spring—the longer you push, the harder it becomes. Soaked in sweat or bathed in rain, they plodded on, slipping where the moisture made the footing treacherous. The danger of aerial observation necessitated careful and time-consuming steps to avoid open areas by day or leaving visible tracks at any time. Encounters with Marine patrols and Clemens's scouts enlivened the latter stages of the march. On the afternoon of September 10, Japanese navigation faltered, creating an unexpected jungle traffic jam as I/124, II/4, the brigade headquarters, and the Kuma Battalion all ran into one another. The Kuma Battalion wormed off on its own course, but the other three units fell into a column. Kawaguchi was only recontacted by III/124 in the small hours of September 12.

The brigade artillerymen faced less jungle, but other difficulties balanced this good fortune. They set out from Tetere the morning of Edson's raid and suffered the attentions of American planes immediately. Their older-pattern guns could not be disassembled for movement through the jungle, compelling them to follow the coast as much as possible. Here they found the wheels of the guns swallowed by sand or sucked down by mud up to half their diameter with agonizing frequency. The carts for hauling ammunition soon burst their tires or bent their axles, and the shells then had to be wrestled forward by hand.

During the march, Kawaguchi fixed the date of attack as September 12 and so informed his subordinates. September 11 brought a double dose of bad news. The general learned the details of the devastation wrought by Edson at Tasimboko, including the loss of some artillery and the brigade's main radio. Oka finally established contact to reveal that he was still assembling his men and hoped to rally about 650 eventually. Kawaguchi's only solace remained the belief that his approach march was undetected.

When Oka gathered his much-diminished command, he decided to forward it to the position held by the Navy on the Matanikau. He made good time and met Captain Monzen at 0740 on September 11. Monzen offered to add the weight of his 450 combat troops and 1,200 construction workers to the attack. During the night of September 11, Oka's prospects brightened when the III/4, 630 strong, landed at Kamimbo Bay. With time short, Oka promptly issued his plan. He would lead the regimental headquarters and two companies of II/124 toward the bridge southwest of the airfield to make an assault synchronized with Kawaguchi's at 2000 on September 12. Monzen's men would attack along the coast, and Lieutenant Colonel Wakiya's engineer boat unit would mount a noisy feint. First, however, Wakiya's barges were to transport the fresh III/4 to the Matanikau to support Oka's attack. But the frequent strafing attacks of the Henderson Field fliers disabled so many of the barges that the III/4 had to move on foot and thus failed to arrive in time to join the attack.

Small patrol encounters increased in frequency until it became almost impossible to penetrate areas to the east of the perimeter, and native scouts brought word of Kawaguchi's columns snaking west from Tetere. Few hours remained to change Marine dispositions, but enough to hastily complete the extension of the right flank along Alligator Creek and then southwest. On the morning of September 10, following a breakfast of sodden rice and dehydrated potatoes, the Raiders and Parachutists ambled toward the ridge south of the airfield. Edson explained the move as an effort to find a quiet spot away from the bombs falling on the airstrip. Before his men could complete their march, a raid of twenty-five Bettys and fifteen Zeros arrived at 1212. Eleven Marine Wildcats took off, but only five of VMF-223 made contact. They accounted for three Bettys: two shot down and one ditched. This success cost one Wildcat and its pilot; after this raid only eleven flyable Wildcats remained of the forty-four flown in since August 20.

Sitting at Espíritu Santo was *Saratoga*'s experienced VF-5. Doctrine prescribed that the specially trained carrier pilots be reserved for duty aboard the flattops, but Guadalcanal desperately needed fighters with high-altitude performance, and in the South Pacific only the Wildcat met this requirement. Admiral Nimitz stepped in to authorize Ghormley to use the homeless carrier planes as he saw fit. For inexplicable reasons, Ghormley temporized on this offer, and initially orders went to the skipper of VF-5, Lieutenant Commander Leroy Simpler, just to ferry some of his planes to Guadalcanal as replacements. But Simpler won approval to take his whole squadron as a unit to Guadalcanal.

At ten minutes before noon on September 11 a dozen Wildcats scrambled to intercept a raid of twenty-seven Bettys and fifteen Zeros. The Wildcat pilots claimed six bombers, but only one fell, as did a single Zero. Major Galer, the commander of VMF-224, accounted for the Zero, but in turn other Zeros riddled his aircraft. After his engine quit, he ditched offshore and swam into the perimeter. Bombs destroyed a P-400 and an F4F on the ground, but these were strays.

As Edson's marines dug foxholes and cleared fields of fire with bayonets, they heard the air raid alarm heralding the Japanese approach. This generated no undue concern, since a mile separated the ridge from the customary Japanese target, the airfield. But this time the Japanese laid some of their bombs on the ridge:

> Marines who clawed a few inches deeper into their holes or flung themselves behind logs emerged shaking but safe. Those who stood, or ran aimlessly—and a few did—were killed or wounded by flying splinters.

After the last chunks of dirt flopped back to earth, chilling cries rose for corpsmen to help the fourteen wounded, but eleven marines were beyond help. The remainder suddenly knew that their "quiet rest area" must be the focus of a Japanese attack only hours or at best a few days hence. The division artillery commander, Colonel Pedro del Valle, read the portents too. He appeared on the ridge with his executive officer and saw to a survey of the ground. Del Valle's gunners labored deep into the night shifting batteries and drafting fire plans.

During this busy afternoon of September 11, Admirals Turner and McCain flew in from Espíritu Santo. At Vandegrift's command post, Turner, visibly discomfited, drew from his pocket a naval message form and silently handed it to Vandegrift. As the general read, the color vanished from his face. He then passed the message to his operations officer and chief confident, Gerald Thomas. It contained Ghormley's estimate of the situation. The Japanese were amassing overwhelmingly powerful naval, air, and ground forces at Rabaul and Truk for a major effort to retake Guadalcanal. They would begin their attack within three weeks, or perhaps as soon as ten days. To contest this onslaught, Ghormley flatly stated his forces were insufficient, and he itemized deficiencies in carriers, cruisers, destroyers, and transports. He tersely concluded that he could no longer support the marines on Guadalcanal. If he intended to shock his superiors—who had lately demonstrated an acute failure to grasp the critical nature of the situation—he succeeded. Although the message implied the admiral's moral abdication of responsibility for the fate of Vandegrift's command, Ghormley added that he was not abandoning hope. He was considering sending the 7th Marines to Guadalcanal to redress some of the odds. Thus Turner came to discuss the employment of this regiment and to clear up what Ghormley termed a "cloudy situation" on the island.

After Thomas folded the paper and stuck it in his pocket—where it stayed for the next three months—Turner produced a bottle of scotch and said, "Vandegrift, I'm not inclined to take so pessimistic a view of the situation as Ghormley does. He doesn't believe I can get the 7th Marine Regiment here, but I believe I have a scheme that will fool the Japs." Unfortunately, after these reassuring words, in the next breath Turner advanced what Vandegrift described as the "quaint notion" of sprinkling the 7th Marines in small parcels all around the island. This dispersal of forces represented Turner's solution to stopping Japanese reinforcements: put a Marine reception committee on or near every landing beach to wipe out each batch of Japanese soldiers as soon as they arrived. Even if the logistical nightmare this deployment would create could be ignored, this "ink spot" strategy contained a fatal flaw: the Japanese were already on the island in force and could just as easily annihilate isolated pockets of marines. Vandegrift vigorously urged that the 7th Marines be set ashore at the Lunga Point, where they were most needed, but this initial meeting adjourned for dinner without a decision.[1]

SEPTEMBER 12: FRUSTRATION AND FIASCO

At 1150 on the 12th a formation of Japanese bombers appeared over Guadalcanal "moving like a slender white cloud across the blue sky" and spilling bombs over the perimeter. They demolished the main radio station, ignited some gasoline, and ended the careers of three SBDs on the ground. Against the twenty-five Bettys and fifteen Zeroes, the Americans sent up twelve Marine and twenty Navy Wildcats. The interception exacted a toll of five bombers and one Zero. The newly arrived VF-5 made its presence felt, but its executive officer, Lieutenant D. C. Richardson, was wounded and another pilot sacrificed his life in a vain attempt to save his Wildcat in a dead-stick landing.[2]

Kawaguchi started the day in fine fettle. A captured American aviator disclosed that the Marine lines were strongest to the east and along the coast and weakest exactly where Kawaguchi was headed, south of the airfield. The prisoner also informed the Japanese that

[1]There is a further controversy surrounding Turner's visit and the communication he delivered from Ghormley. After the war a very distinguished officer, Merrill B. Twining, the assistant operations officer of the 1st Marine Division in September 1942 and later a full general, reported that Turner had, in fact, carried two messages. One substantially as given in the text, and a second, hand-written message, which may be interpreted as effectively authorizing Vandegrift to surrender if worst came to worst. There is no documentary or other direct support for this version of the event I could locate; however, there are several aspects of the existing record that fit with Twining's account. The surviving official message does not seem as dire as Vandegrift and Thomas recalled it, which suggests the possibility that they were combining the import of a message such as Twining described with the one that is of record. In addition, sticking an official message in a pocket permanently as Thomas recounted several times after the war would be very unusual, but tucking away a hand-written communication, especially of such content, would be highly understandable. Moreover, the failure of such a private communication to survive would not be surprising, and the reluctance after the war of Vandegrift and Thomas, the two parties most directly involved, to admit these facts to spare Ghormley humiliation bears consideration. While there can be no doubt that Twining honestly recalls the events as he reported, his account reflects so darkly on Ghormley that I am not prepared to stand upon it without at least some additional support, but I am likewise by no means inclined to totally discount it.

[2]The 11th Bomb Group sent out fifteen B-17s to attack a reported Japanese carrier this day. Because of the weather, three planes made forced landings at sea. The crews, less two men, were saved.

their approach was undetected because American pilots found it impossible to see beneath the jungle canopy. At 1225 the Kuma Battalion reported itself poised for the attack, but not all the news was good. Colonel Oka revealed he would have only two companies, not the planned two battalions, for an attack that night. The colonel promised more by the 13th, but Kawaguchi declined to postpone the assault.

A grim Admiral Turner sampled Marine cuisine in the evening. He told some correspondents that the marines would be on the island for a long time "and things will get worse before they get better." Just how much worse things would get was amply demonstrated in the next forty-eight hours.

By nightfall of September 12 the Raiders and Parachutists, now numbering about 840 men, had barely had time to string barbed wire taken from less exposed areas and dig foxholes along the new position. Edson set a boundary line down the ridge with the Parachutists to the east and the Raiders to the west. Company B of the Parachutists gripped the eastern side of the southern end of the ridge with sister Companies C and A echeloned to its rear. The frontage manned by Company B of the Raiders lapped over the western side of the ridge before submerging into the rain forest. To their right, Company C of the Raiders extended the position to near the Lunga. However, Company C's line was bisected by a small lagoon whose long axis ran parallel to the ridge and ended in an impenetrable swamp abreast the midpoint of the ridge. One platoon of Company C sat east of the lagoon and tied to Company B. The other two platoons held the area from the lagoon to the Lunga. Edson disposed Companies A, D, and E (Weapons) of the Raiders along the west side of the ridge abreast the high knoll at its midpoint. He placed his command post in a draw east of the ridge behind the Parachutists.

The thin ranks of Edson's mongrel battalion and the denseness of the jungle surrounding the ridge precluded anything like a continuous line. A series of strongpoints with fields of fire for mutual support behind a single-strand barbed-wire fence occupied the jungle frontage. To the right rear of Edson the 1st Pioneer Battalion bivouacked near the Lunga with a strongpoint on a hill just east of the river. The 1st Amphibian Tractor Battalion established a strongpoint on a hill facing to the west of the Lunga. The 1st Engineer Battalion's bivouac back stopped the left rear of Edson's battalion.

Edson was convinced a major Japanese force was coiling to his front. He planned to patrol the area the next day with the whole command to throw the Japanese off balance, and to issue the neces-

Edson's Ridge, Night of September 12–13

sary orders, he assembled his company commanders in the early evening. As this conference broke up, Edson's officers heard the characteristic chug of a Japanese float plane ("Louie the Louse") and saw a flare began to glower overhead, throwing dripping fingers of green light over Marine lines. "Louie" dropped more flares, and at 2130, *Sendai* and destroyers *Shikinami, Fubuki,* and *Suzukaze* began to cannonade the perimeter. Most of their shells fell to the east of Edson's position, but they killed three pilots, including Lieutenant Lawrence Baldinus, who had scored the hit on *Sendai*'s predecessor *Jintsu.* From Edson's lines the light sputter of firing that had been going on for some minutes began to swell into the medley of rifles, mortars, machineguns, and grenades that marked a firefight.

As the marines saw it, the crafty Japanese pushed down the east bank of the lagoonlike area west of the ridge and struck first at the vulnerable juncture of Companies B and C of the Raiders. They cut off the left-flank platoon of Company C and forced the right-flank platoon of Company B to curl back as if before a flame to protect the flank of its parent company. Seven marines went missing in this encounter, but Company B was not further molested. Another knife thrust of the Japanese sliced off the next platoon in line of Company C, east of the swamp area, while a party of Japanese working down the river imperiled the right flank of the company. During this fighting a second naval bombardment fell between about 0005 and 0050 of September 13. This time the newly emplaced 5-inch coast defense guns of Batteries B and C of the 3d Defense Battalion challenged the Japanese. They claimed one hit, but this is not confirmed by Japanese records.

The picture of the action from the Japanese side is quite different. Kawaguchi scored his brigade for a coordinated attack at 2000 aimed for the ridge; the actual execution left this plan unrecognizable. All of his assault battalions reached their assembly areas late. The I/124 attained its assembly area only two hours before the scheduled attack time. The other two rifle battalions, III/124 and II/4, stumbled into their assembly areas respectively two and three hours after the slated start time of the assault. When the three battalions, numbering 2,506 men, went forward they lost their sense of direction, almost entirely missed the ridge, and instead drifted into the low, waterlogged swath of jungle between the ridge and the Lunga. Units became lost; lost units became scattered; scattered units became intermingled. Control slipped away from Kawaguchi and his battalion commanders and it became a struggle of captains, lieutenants, sergeants, and privates against a few marines and a mass of jungle.

On the Japanese left, the I/124 advanced along the Lunga, wading the shiny, fast-flowing, chest-high waters. To the chagrin of Major Yukichi Kokusho, elements of III/124 began to entangle themselves with his men. In an effort to halt this confusion, Kokusho directed his unit to the west bank of the Lunga. By the time he restored control, only one hour remained until daylight, too late for a night attack. On the Japanese right front the III/124 advanced until it encountered the Marine line about 0100 by Japanese watches. Presumably this unit made the penetration between the Raider companies, but it could not exploit the situation because of the jungle and intense American artillery fire, which killed two company commanders. The movements of the reserve unit, II/4, cannot be reconstructed.

Kawaguchi pointed his command group at the ridge, but he too found the terrain so difficult that he sidestepped west to the Lunga and began to wade north up the streambed itself. When the depth and the flow rate became too much, the general crawled out of the water onto the east bank near dawn. There he issued orders for his fragmented command to reassemble for a new effort the night of the 13th. The muddy, wet, and mad general's exasperation was intense; he reported that "because of the devilish jungle, the brigade was scattered all over and completely beyond control. In my whole life I have never felt so helpless." His mood was not improved during the day when American bombing and shelling smashed his communications equipment.

While the Main Body endured frustration, the two Wing Units tasted fiasco. After reaching an assembly area in good time, the Kuma Battalion used its last fuel to cook food. Officer patrols failed to fix the location of the Marine lines. At nightfall the battalion set forth to do battle, but they spent the entire night thrashing in the jungle with only the distant sounds of fighting to tantalize them. At daybreak they made the mortifying discovery that their attack had misfired because their assembly area had been much farther east of the American lines than they had thought. Mismanagement also explained the absence of the Left Wing Unit from the action on this night. Colonel Oka was supposed to have set out from the Matanikau at sundown on the 11th, but for unexplained reasons he failed to begin the march with his emaciated command until 0400 on September 12. Consequently, when the sounds of battle reached him about 2200, he remained much too far from his starting position to get his men into action.

For some time during the night, Turner expressed skepticism to his Marine hosts about the authenticity of the sounds of the clash along the ridge only a few hundred yards from where he sat. But when *Sendai* and her destroyer consorts sent shells whistling over the admiral's head he put aside his doubts. The next morning he conferred with Vandegrift and Gerald Thomas at the command post of the 1st Marines, about 300 yards from the shore. "Now where do you want the 7th Marines to land?" asked Turner. Pointing to the beach, Thomas said, "That's where we want them landed, right in the perimeter." The admiral dispatched a message to this effect from Guadalcanal—with a grudging reference to the future desirability of his pet "ink spot" strategy.

After seeing Turner off, Vandegrift went to the Pagoda to reveal to his old friend and air deputy, Geiger, the contents of Ghormley's estimate. Vandegrift explained his intention to stay "come hell or high water" and, if necessary, to take his men to the hills to fight on if the perimeter could not be held. Geiger concurred and told him, "Archer, if we can't use the planes back in the hills we'll fly them out, but whatever happens I'm staying here with you."

During the morning of September 13, Edson sat on a log eating cold meat and potatoes. To his assembled lieutenants he said, "They were testing, just testing. They'll be back. But maybe not as many of them. Or maybe more. I want all positions improved, all wire lines paralleled, a hot meal for the men. Today we dig, wire up tight, get some sleep. We'll all need it." Companies A and D of the Raiders attempted to restore the original line on the battalion right flank but were brought up short.

SEPTEMBER 13: THE DECISIVE ATTACK

At Rabaul, Kawaguchi's superiors nurtured high hopes on slight information. The 12th passed with no radio contact at all with either Army or Navy units on Guadalcanal. Intercepted American radio transmissions during the night were passed through the filter of great expectations and prophesied as evidence of Kawaguchi's success. In the early morning, optimism took another surge when a plane reported sighting the prearranged signal of success—two torch fires 50 meters apart. To garner precise information, at 0630 a 17th Army staff officer soared aloft as a passenger in one of two Irving reconnaissance planes headed for Guadalcanal with nine Zeros in attendance. Before they reached their destination, eighteen new Wildcats reached Henderson Field as replacement aircraft for the two Marine fighter squadrons. Amazingly, for some hours the Japanese scouts persisted in sending reports suggesting Kawaguchi held the airfield despite the evidence to the contrary presented by twenty-eight snarling Wildcats that rose to intercept the Japanese flight. Four Zeros fell in an air battle, but the Americans lost two pilots and planes, and two other pilots were wounded.

Correspondent Tregaskis and marines on the ground obtained a thrilling view of part of this tussle:

> We saw one Wildcat . . . come diving down like a comet from the clouds, with two Zeros on his tail. He was moving faster than they, and as he pulled up out of his dive and streaked across the water, he left them behind. They gave up the chase and pulled sharply back up into the sky. . . .
>
> Many planes were dogfighting in and about the masses of cumulus clouds. I watched two planes, one chasing the other, pop out of the tower of cloud, describe a small, precise semicircle, and go back again in again.
>
> A few moments later they made another circle, like two beads on the same wire. . . . the sky resounded with the rattling of machineguns.

Right behind the reconnaissance came the usual bombing raid of twenty-six Bettys and a dozen Zeros. Because the Japanese aviators remained unsure of the situation on the ground, they droned on to Taivu Point, still thought at Rabaul to be in American hands. They dumped their loads on their helpless countrymen who had reoccupied the area, and then the Zeros went down for vicious strafing attacks. Natives later brought into Marine lines bloodstained Rising Sun flags with which the Japanese soldiers had vainly tried to identify themselves. Seven Marine and nine Navy F4Fs took off to oppose this raid. Together they knocked down a Zero and a Betty bomber and forced a second bomber to ditch, at a price of four Wildcats (one operational) and one pilot while one other Wildcat fluttered back badly damaged.

There was an American embarrassment in the air this day. In the softening light of evening, two bold float Zeros slipped in unexpectedly and shot down an SBD right over the airfield. Horrified onlookers saw the plane crash and burn, carrying the crew to their deaths. An eager VF-5 pilot, attempting to get aloft to seek revenge, washed out a Wildcat. Only ten minutes later the now aroused and itchy gunners heard another formation of aircraft approach and let fly. Fortunately they missed and were quickly quelled, for the flight comprised a dozen SBDs of *Saratoga*'s VS-3 led by Lieutenant Commander Louis J. Kirn and half that number of TBFs of *Saratoga*'s VT-8 under Lieutenant H. H. Larsen. Added to VF-5 and the eighteen new Wildcats, Guadalcanal had received sixty planes in three days.

Colonel Oka again radioed Kawaguchi on the 13th to ask for a delay to allow the III/4 to come up to buttress the attack from the southwest, but the general would brook no further delay. He directed that the decisive assault would begin at 2200 that night.

At this same time Edson prepared a surprise for the Japanese. He pulled his line back about 200 yards onto stronger ground to present the attackers with a new and unfamiliar front. The realigned front covered about 1,800 yards. Once again the Parachutists held the eastern half of the ridge with Company B facing down the ridge from just south of the high knoll. To their left in a ravine, Company C of the Parachutists, backed by its sister Company A, protected the dangling left flank. Both of these latter units were very weak. On the western slopes of the ridge hunkered Company B of the Raiders with its right flank adjoined by Company D of the 1st Engineer Battalion. Company A of the Raiders extended the line to near the Lunga and contacted the 1st Pioneer Battalion, which guarded both banks of the river. Edson held Company C of the Raiders in reserve on the high knoll in the center of the ridge with the tiny (thirty men) Company D of the Raiders to the northeast. Company E of the Raiders placed its weapons around the knoll.

Except on the ridge, Edson lacked sufficient men to form a continuous line. Small combat groups of approximately platoon strength organized at about 100-yard intervals defended the jungle and swamp area west of the ridge to the Lunga. Clear fields of fire existed only in the center along the ridge itself. Because of the obvious control problems presented by the terrain, and probably to guard against a renewal of the Japanese thrust along the Lunga, Edson detailed his executive officer, Lieutenant Colonel Samuel B. Griffith, to take charge of his right flank, including Company D of the 1st Engineers and Company A of the Raiders.

Lieutenant Colonel Merrill B. Twining from the division staff visited Edson's command during the afternoon and found the men glassy-eyed, mumbling their words and displaying the mechanical high-stepping gait that betrayed utter exhaustion. But no time remained to replace them on the line this day. The division reserve, the 2d Battalion, 5th Marines (2/5), moved to a position south of the airfield in preparation to relieve Edson on the 14th, and to be ready to reinforce his line. At the direction of Lieutenant Colonel William

Edson's Ridge, Night of September 13–14

J. Whaling, the company commanders of 2/5 prudently conducted reconnaissances of the routes they might have to take to reinforce Edson that night.

Darkness had barely settled over the ridge before the Japanese began to stir. At 1830 the first blows fell on the ridge and to the west at the junction of Companies B of the Raiders and D of the Engineers. The attackers dislodged the right platoon of Company B from the line and surrounded it for a time, but the platoon fought its way to the ridge. This effort marked the handiwork of I/124 on the Japanese left, which started forward early aiming to move along the bank of the Lunga. They surged into a 200-yard-wide gap between the two Marine companies, led by their sword-wielding battalion commander, Major Kokusho. But bravery and verve were not enough. At 2100 an American barrage dropped at the south end of the ridge, and thirty minutes later, Marine gunners laid a second barrage within 200 yards of the front line as the Japanese tide began rolling up the ridge. By 2200 a full battalion of 105mm howitzers were bucking and roaring in support of Edson, who estimated that Company B of the Raiders and two small Parachute companies—about 300 men—faced two full battalions of Japanese.

Japanese infantrymen also gathered in front of Company B of the Parachutists and began to infiltrate around the east side of the high knoll. Captain Harry L. Torgerson, the executive officer of the Parachutists, personally confirmed this latter move. He and one other officer tossed grenades into the draw in which the jabbering Japanese congregated. At 2230 the Japanese came in force. Company B of the Parachutists was subjected to an intense mortar barrage and then assaulted by a wave of infantrymen who came lunging out of the nearby jungle. The Japanese flung smoke grenades and yelled *"Totsugeki!"* ("Charge!") which to the marines sounded like "Gas attack."[3] The Marine company commander was in a tight spot. Many Japanese pummeled his front, others slithered around his left flank and rear, while the full fury of the supporting 105mm howitzer barrage crashed down much nearer than was then considered safe.

[3]The contemporary report of the 1st Parachute Battalion and H. C. Merillat's *The Island* both have the Japanese yelling "Gas attack." In his recent book, *Guadalcanal Remembered,* Mr. Merillat expressed his skepticism over attributions of English phrases to Japanese infantrymen, and offered the opinion that what sounded like "Gas attack" was really cries of *"Totsugeki."* The reader can check this thesis by noting how the syllables in the Japanese word *('tsu-geki)* have a rhythm and sound like "Gas attack," particularly if one imagines them screamed at night in a battle.

This officer decided on his own to pull back his men. Torgerson ratified this decision—the withdrawal was already in progress—and directed that both Companies B and C of the Parachutists assemble behind the high knoll, about 150 yards to the rear, from which point he hoped to mount a counterattack.

The main weight of the Japanese attack now fell on Captain John B. Sweeney's Company B of the Raiders, only sixty strong. Behind them Edson moved his command post forward to the top of the high knoll that dominated the center of the ridge. There he organized a defense with Company C of the Raiders along the south and west side of the knoll and Company A of the Parachutists on the east side. He ordered Company B of the Raiders to fall back on this position. This band of Raiders began filing rearward along the single trail atop the ridge with Companies B and C of the Parachutists.

A withdrawal at night in the face of an enemy attack ranks among the most difficult maneuvers in war. It is intrinsically confusing, and even with fresh men, control is difficult. But Edson's marines were in their sixth day of raiding, digging, and defending. Almost all functioned on nervous energy alone; some were nearly stuporous. As the Parachutists reached the rear of the knoll someone again murmured, "Withdraw"—though withdrawal had not been authorized. Some marines began to continue to move toward the airfield, an act that threatened to start a disastrous unraveling of the American line. But at this juncture appeared Major Kenneth D. Bailey of the Raiders, whose commanding presence and vivid language jerked the retreat—if not rout—up short.

What made the withdrawal possible was a curtain of bursting shells directed by the forward observers from the 11th Marines. Correspondent Richard Tregaskis heard an observer call back: "Drop it five zero and walk it back and forth across the ridge." At the division command post—where all hands (including Tregaskis) huddled on the crest of the spur under sniper fire—the voice of a battery officer was plainly audible above the raucous battle barking "Load" and then "Fire." A breathless runner brought word from Edson that the range was perfect: "It's knocking hell out of 'em." So it was. I/124 suffered many casualties from artillery and small-arms fire, and its sword-wielding commander fell dead.

But the artillery fire created one perverse effect. Major Tamura, the commander of II/4, ostensibly Kawaguchi's reserve, had advanced his battalion to an assembly area very close to the Marine lines. When the shelling of his unit became intense about 2200, Major Tamura decided not to wait for orders but to hurtle his men forward at once. He shook out the 5th and 7th Companies into a line and advanced up the ridge itself. There they smashed against Company B of the Raiders and helped to force the withdrawal. Marine fire shattered the 5th Company during its attack and pursuit. Two platoon leaders were already down when the company commander fell before the knoll on which Edson now made the final stand.

About 300 marines gripped the knoll—the last defensive position before Henderson Field—in a horseshoe-shaped line. When the commander of the 1st Parachute Battalion proved to be a "dud" at this critical juncture, Edson elevated the fiercely aggressive Captain Harry Torgerson to command. Torgerson reorganized Companies B and C of the Parachutists and then launched them in a counterattack at Edson's behest that drove forward and extended the line to the east from Company A of the Parachutists. All the while Edson moved the defensive barrage closer and again closer, but still the Japanese came.

Japanese mortars beat a tattoo on the knoll while the Marine mortars in defilade behind the rise replied in kind. As the Japanese steeled themselves for each attack, the marines pulled the pins on grenades and rolled them down the hill into the areas where Kawaguchi's men gathered. A red flare usually marked the initiation of each attack, which proved a handy reference for the American gunners. Each wave of Japanese infantry debouched from concealment and then, halting briefly to toss calcium flares, surged ahead in little knots and strings. They moved rapidly at the crouch, yelling their banzais as they leaned forward into the hill and charged face first into the ring of flame created by Marine weapons on the crest.

As they closed, showers of grenades were exchanged, each leaving a blackened spot on the grass, and frequently splinters in flesh. Marines, shrieking curses even above the din, repelled each attack mainly with grenades and machineguns, whose crews suffered severe casualties and had to be frequently replaced. Barely behind the lines and at one point in the withdrawal nearly at the front line, Lieutenant Commander E. P. McLarney and several corpsmen dressed wounds, applied tourniquets, and gave transfusions under flashlight illumination beneath ponchos to scores of bodies rent by steel.

At 0200 a Japanese mortar barrage drenched the ridge and cut the telephone-wire umbilical cord back to division headquarters essential for artillery support. Linesmen restrung wire under fire in time to get the word through at 0300 of the near-exhaustion of the supply of grenades and machinegun ammunition. A resupply was rushed forward, and once again Major Bailey was present at a crucial moment, this time crawling on hands and knees across the fire-swept ridge—his scalp grazed by a bullet that punctured his helmet—to deliver fresh grenades and ammunition. But the soul of the defense this night was Merritt Edson. A scant 10 or 20 yards behind the firing line—his clothes were pierced at the collar and waist by bullets—he controlled the battle with his rasping voice, exhorting the steadfast and excoriating those few who wavered: "Go back where you came from. The only thing they've got that you haven't is guts."

At about 0400, division headquarters began to slip in the companies of the 2d Battalion, 5th Marines to stiffen the line. They helped fend off two more attacks sent in before dawn, but not all the Japanese were stopped on the ridge. After the decimation of the 5th Company of II/4, the 7th Company continued forward, penetrating a gap in the Marine line and actually reaching the northeast side of the ridge. In this final surge, Major Tamura committed his 6th Company to make a breakthrough. As they passed through the 5th Company, nearly half the fresh unit was hit and the company commander wounded. Nonetheless, the bloodied officer pressed northeast with fifty or sixty men through the Marine position and reached the western fringe of Fighter One about 0530. There they overran a segment of the position held by Company C of the 1st Engineer Battalion and captured two machineguns. But the versatile engineers rallied with men from Headquarters Company and Company D and finally checked the Japanese for good.

With the dawn came the sound of aircraft engines as three stained and patched, but flyable, P-400s of the 67th Fighter Squadron climbed into the air to harry the Japanese with 20mm cannon and machinegun fire. They skimmed over the ridge speckled with craters, smoldering grass fires, and the debris of battle: expended cartridges, hand grenade cartons, clips, and ammunition cans with the tops ripped off. The bodies of over 500 Japanese lay like a carpet in places, sprawled in the hideous poses of violent death. In spots marines and Japanese had fallen in a death embrace, silent testimony to the violence of the battle. "With heads lolling and mouths agape, the inscrutable dead stared with glazed and sightless eyes at the morning sun," said Lieutenant Colonel Griffith. Intense retaliatory ground fire by Kawaguchi's men punctured two of the planes, which had to make emergency landings on Henderson Field.

The I/124 and the II/4 commenced their assaults nearly 1,700 strong and brought Edson's battalion to the knife edge of defeat. The attack of one more battalion would probably have brought Kawaguchi a breakthrough—and that battalion was available. Kawaguchi learned that the two assault battalions had lost nearly half their strength, but he became enraged upon discovering that the III/124 had hardly entered the action. "This powerful battalion," he angrily recalled, "the one I had counted on most, was completely mismanaged. When I heard of this I could not help shedding tears of disappointment, anger, and regret."

For some time the general could not vent his anger, for the whereabouts of both the battalion and its commander remained unknown. When Lieutenant Colonel Watanabe finally appeared, he had a dolorous tale to tell. He had set out on the 13th for Kawaguchi's headquarters with his adjutant and two orderlies. Failing to locate Kawaguchi in the jungle, they attempted to return to the battalion, but shelling pinned them down. Further, Watanabe's old war wound from Manchuria acted up and he spent the night with his small entourage trying to contact his command. Without their leader the battalion moved out of their assembly area at 1930 on the right front of the Japanese line and then fanned out at 2200. Of the entire battalion only one company apparently got into the battle. This unit probably attacked the two understrength Parachute companies and slipped around the Marine left flank, but the company sustained heavy casualties and was completely out of contact by dawn.

The main fury of Kawaguchi's attack abated at daylight, but scattered behind the high knoll lay individuals and small groups from three Japanese companies. Sniper fire ripped among the trees and tents of division headquarters, rendering any type of movement dangerous. At 0800, as a jeep crawled down the ridge bearing five wounded, a hidden machinegun suddenly riddled its occupants. Among those killed was Major Robert S. Brown, Edson's operations officer. Thirty minutes later, Captain Torgerson led the Parachutists off the ridge. Of the 397 men who stormed ashore at Gavutu on August 7, exactly eighty-six were now available to ambulate off the ridge. Companies A and B of the 1st Marines were sent on a probe of the area south of the ridge. Company A hit strong opposition and was withdrawn. Company B walked into an ambush and one platoon was virtually annihilated; the two companies lost eighteen killed.

Stock taking was in progress at the division command post when a Japanese officer and two soldiers burst from the jungle with banzais that sounded to Tregaskis like "a loud blubbering turkey gobbler's cry." The officer's sword spitted one marine, but the officer and one of his companions were shot dead. This incident occasioned the only grim humor of the battle. When the Japanese sprang from the vegetation, Marine Gunner Shepard Banta was vigorously berating a young marine for some transgression. Banta paused to shoot one of the Japanese with his pistol, and then returned to his lecture, scarcely missing a breath.

After this distraction, Vandegrift and his staff returned to a review of the situation. With their only reserve battalion committed to replacing Edson's utterly spent command, no troops remained to pursue Kawaguchi's main body. Further, the Marine command now knew of the presence of other enemy detachments. About 2200 on the 13th, the Kuma Battalion, styled the Right Wing Unit in Kawaguchi's plan, began to advance in a column toward the Marine line, whose exact location was still a mystery to the Japanese. In their path was the southeastern section of the perimeter, manned by Lieutenant Colonel William J. McKelvy's 3d Battalion, 1st Marines. McKelvy pitched his line at the edge of a patch of jungle surveying a grassy area, but his right flank was completely open. About 2330, one rifle company and the Kuma Battalion headquarters trudged into the open field fronting McKelvy's line. The Japanese encountered barbed wire and drew fire from their right. Without further ado, the leading elements charged and overran an outpost of five marines in front of Company K that the Japanese mistook for the main American line. They then assaulted the real main position of Company K, unaware that only a few score yards to the left lay an open path to the airfield. The attackers became literally entangled in the Marine wire and were beaten back, leaving the bodies of twenty-seven comrades ensnared in the fence. The dead included Major Mizuno, the battalion commander. The encounter cost four marines killed and three wounded.

At daylight the firing ceased, but Lieutenant Colonel McKelvy remained concerned that the Japanese might be waiting in the tall grass to his immediate front. At 0945, six light tanks swept the area without incident. A little later a Marine officer and an enlisted man, who had escaped from the overrun outpost, returned to report the position of Japanese machineguns on the east side of the plain facing McKelvy's battalion. The tanks set out again to deal with this menace, but committed the folly of retracing their earlier route. This time the Japanese waited with anti-tank guns that destroyed three of the tanks. Two crews escaped, but the third vehicle toppled down an embankment and overturned, entombing its occupants. A fourth tank was disabled. During the night of the 14th the Kuma Battalion made a weak attack that only succeeded in leaving five more bodies impaled on the wire, and the battalion repeated with a final spasm on the 15th, equally unsuccessful.

Even while Vandegrift and his staff assessed the situation to the south and southeast, the western prong of the Japanese attack finally made its presence known. Colonel Oka left the Matanikau position tardily at 1815 on the 13th, again for unknown reasons. He mustered two rifle companies and one machinegun company. After thrashing through the jungle all night, one rifle company attacked in daylight a Marine position on the west of the perimeter held by Company L, 3d Battalion, 5th Marines (Lieutenant Colonel Frederick C. Biebush). They were driven off with the help of a timely artillery barrage, as were several feeble attacks later in the day. The fresh III/4 halted at the Matanikau after a brush with some Americans.

At Japanese headquarters remote from Guadalcanal the hunger for news was acute but unsatisfied during the 14th. For many hours, Japanese officers obtained no information on the course of the battle, nor indeed did they know even if there had been a battle. A unit of Zeros stood by to occupy Henderson Field, while at sea major units of the Combined Fleet and 8th Fleet cruised impatiently. Three float Zeros from Rekata Bay flew down into the dawn's early light to ascertain the situation, but they only succeeded in becoming victims of VF-5. At noon one reconnaissance plane tried to penetrate the airspace over Guadalcanal with an escort of seven Zeros, one of which ditched en route. Takeoff accidents deprived the Cactus Air Force of two Wildcats—bringing to ten the number thus lost in seven days—and Japanese bullets wounded one pilot in the air battle, but VMF-223 destroyed the reconnaissance plane and VMF-224 one of the escorts. The first word from Guadalcanal this day came from Colonel Matsumoto, whose message reflected his own very deficient knowledge of events. Having landed at Kamimbo Bay with the III/4, he did not participate in any of the fighting, nor had he been in contact with Kawaguchi or Oka. Matsumoto declared that the difficulties of jungle movement had forced postponement of the attack daily from the 12th to the 13th and now to the 14th.

The last major flash of battle came in the air late in the day of the 14th. Lieutenant Takeshi Horihasi, leader of seaplane carrier *Chitose*'s air group, collected two float Zeros and seventeen bomb-laden biplane Petes for a spectacular twilight attack on Henderson Field. They approached over the mountain ridges to the south of the Marine perimeter, to be met by four VMF-224 and six VF-5 Wildcats. The American fliers claimed nine Petes and one float Zero at no cost. Actual losses included one Rufe and three Petes over Guadalcanal, while one other Pete crash-landed back at Rekata Bay, though its crew survived.

This marked the end of an air struggle since September 1 that paralleled Kawaguchi's efforts, and that was of no less importance though it had no climactic moments. American claims totaled thirty-nine bombers and twenty-one fighters. Actual Japanese losses included fifteen Bettys and ten Zeros, illustrating that the Cactus Air Force generally claimed about two aircraft for every one destroyed in aerial combat—a respectable performance given the inherent difficulties of accurately measuring the results of air battles. To the list of Japanese losses must be added one Irving reconnaissance plane and eight float aircraft, including four float Zeros, for a total of thirty-four aircraft. The contemporary Japanese records acknowledge heavy losses, particularly among bomber crews. Some air groups were exhausted, notably those of the 25th Air Flotilla that had been in action since April. Air combat and very high operational losses in the Cactus Air Force during this period reached forty-one aircraft: twenty-eight Wildcats (fifteen in air combat), eleven SBDs, and two P-400s. The Japanese also lost one flying boat, while the Americans lost four PBYs and four B-17s.

About 0830 on the morning of the 15th, Kawaguchi's long-awaited report of the battle reached Rabaul. Two officers rushed it by car to the quarters of the chief of staff of the 17th Army, but General Futami recognized its import when he saw the expressions on their faces. Kawaguchi's admission of costly failure severely shocked Hyakutake and his staff. In analyzing the causes of the defeat, 17th Army headquarters listed loss of provisions at Taivu, the ill-considered barge movement, difficulty of communication in the jungle, poor maps, and superior American firepower. The Army Section of Imperial General Headquarters added faulty intelligence, dispersal of forces, American air superiority, and the mismatch of pitting Japanese swords and bayonets against a prepared position. Still harsher were the assessments of Japanese naval officers. The chief of staff of the Combined Fleet labeled the defeat another example of the lingering intoxication engendered by the successes early in the war, for which he prescribed the antidote of "washing heads." Another of Yamamoto's key staff officers was more blunt: "The army had been used to fighting the Chinese."

Credit on the American side for defeating Kawaguchi must be shared. The Cactus Air Force contributed importantly in keeping one infantry battalion (III/4) completely out of the battle and slaughtering or dispersing nearly half of another (II/124). These men represented one-quarter of Kawaguchi's potential strength. The American fliers also forced an exhausting and time-consuming jungle march on Kawaguchi's assault units and harried the Japanese in retreat. The gunners of the 11th Marines likewise played a critical role. The 1,992 rounds of artillery fire on the night of September 13–14 by the 105mm howitzers of the 5th Battalion, 11th Marines inflicted between two-thirds and three-quarters of all of Kawaguchi's losses on the ridge and protected the withdrawal of the defenders at a desperate moment. Ultimately neither bold fliers nor expert cannoneers could have kept Japanese boots off Henderson Field without the obdurate resistance of the Raiders and the Parachutists. In recognition of his skill and extraordinary leadership, Merritt Edson was awarded the Medal of Honor. Major Kenneth D. Bailey was also awarded his country's highest honor for his inspiring contributions this night, but would not live to receive it.

Neither American nor Japanese losses in this battle can be stated with complete assurance. One contemporary report lists 111 marines killed or missing and 283 wounded in this action. However, these figures are not broken down by commands and cannot be matched to the numbers provided in the individual unit reports. According to the most authoritative sources, the Raiders suffered 135 casualties and the Parachutists 128. Of this combined total of 263, fifty-nine were killed or missing. Recorded losses in other units added another thirty-eight killed and eighteen wounded, giving a total of ninety-six killed or missing and 222 wounded. A "detailed" Japanese report sets Kawaguchi's total strength as 212 officers and 6,005 men, including the attached Kuma Battalion and the II/4. Of these, 708 (twenty-nine officers and 679 men) were killed or missing and 506 (fourteen officers and 492 men) were wounded. The loss figures are subject to considerable challenge. For example, another Japanese report states there were only about 300 men left in the II/4 after the battle of the 658 present at the start, yet the aforementioned "detailed" report gives that unit's losses as only 187 killed and wounded. Moreover, the "detailed" report clearly understates or excludes known losses aboard the destroyer transports and in the barge convoy. Thus, the true Japanese losses may well have exceeded 800 killed or missing.

For Kawaguchi's men, one ordeal ended only for another to begin. At 1305 on September 14, Kawaguchi led his Main Body out of the deadly reach of the American artillery and aircraft on the ridge. Each battalion extricated itself as best it could, but some companies remained out of touch until the 16th. At 2100 on the 15th, Kawaguchi ordered a withdrawal across the Matanikau.

All food had been consumed by the 14th, for Kawaguchi's soldiers carried only one or two days' rations from Taivu Point in anticipation of living off captured American supplies. Already exhausted and gnawed by hunger, they faced a march across the upper reaches of the Lunga in the jumble of sharp-spined ridges that constituted a part of Mount Austen, some of the most difficult terrain on Guadalcanal. Nearly every soldier was employed in carrying the wounded, who were loaded four to each tent sheet. Four of the able-bodied hefted each of these makeshift litters while a fifth man carried the party's weapons. Four more able-bodied men stood by to relieve the first group. For five or six days the columns struggled over the repetitious slippery slopes of jungle ridges and down into the sticky mud of a succession of jungle streams. Lacking "even one grain of rice" to sustain them, they ate betel nuts and weeds, while the favored few managed to kill fish with grenades.

Many wounded expired as the swaying and jolting litters opened wounds already infested with maggots. As the strength of the unwounded waned, all heavy weapons were abandoned, and then, one by one, rifles fell from weakened hands until nearly half were gone. Kawaguchi reached Kokumbona at 1400 on September 19 and met Oka and his command. Even worse trials awaited Kawaguchi's artillery unit and the Kuma Battalion. They tried to follow Kawaguchi but became lost and wandered for three weeks in the jungle, losing all their weapons and becoming severely malnourished. Had they not fortunately established radio contact on the 23d, they might all have perished.

During this ordeal of Kawaguchi's men, Imperial General Headquarters made a crucial decision. It was now apparent that the battle for Guadalcanal had become a competition to see who could reinforce the fastest, and it was more clear that at this remote island a decisive battle would be fought. Decisive forces would therefore be committed.

★ ★ ★

10

REINFORCEMENT

AND REASSESSMENT

"Our bodies are so tired they are like raw cotton"

WASP TORPEDOED, 7TH MARINES LAND

While Kawaguchi struggled for an unnamed ridge on Guadalcanal, the navies of both sides were not idle. True to his promise of September 13, Turner sortied from Espíritu Santo at 0515 the next day with five vessels bearing the reinforced 7th Marines. He set an easterly course to avoid Japanese air searches, but this thrust the convoy and the covering forces, which included carriers *Wasp* and *Hornet,* into known submarine waters. During September 14 and through the early-afternoon hours of September 15, a profusion of reports revealed at least one Japanese carrier and two battleships, plus many cruisers and destroyers, prowling in the vicinity of Guadalcanal, while additional cruisers and destroyers stood poised for Tokyo Express runs in the Shortland roundhouse. After a flying boat wearing red-disk insignia scrutinized the convoy about 1100 on September 15, Turner assumed that the shroud over American intentions had been lifted. He gauged the picture as "not reassuring," and at 1500 he resolved to withdraw temporarily to await "a more favorable

247

opportunity." But just minutes before this decision the American Navy suffered a grievous blow.

The Imperial Navy deployed nine submarines in a patrol line across the path of the American convoy as a result of aircraft sighting reports. At 1250, the sound gear of *I-19* (Commander Takaichi Kinashi) registered propeller noises. One hour later, Kinashi raised his periscope in the natural concealment of whitecaps kicked up by a 20-knot trade wind and sighted *Wasp*. The two American carriers and their escorts formed circular dispositions cruising 7 to 10 miles apart ahead of the convoy. At 1420 both task groups turned into the southeast wind for flight operations, during which *Wasp* sent aloft twenty-six of her seventy-one aircraft and recovered eleven. *Wasp* began a starboard turn at 1442 to revert to the base course of 280 degrees.

Kinashi fired six Model 95 torpedoes at *Wasp* from the range of only 1,000 yards at 1445. Ensign C. G. Durr pointed these enemy torpedoes out to Admiral Leigh Noyes and declared: "Those have got us!" Only moments after the admiral braced himself, two of the torpedoes struck the ship on her starboard side forward, with catastrophic effect. One warhead gored into gasoline stowage tanks and a second exploded abreast the forward bomb magazine; both unleashed convulsive shock waves. Planes leaped into the air like a ballet chorus and slammed back to the deck, buckling their landing gear. Spare aircraft triced to the overhead in the hangar slipped their moorings and belly-flopped onto their kin below, puncturing fuel tanks and sending rivets of high-octane peril across the decks to mingle with fuel hemorrhaging from the fractured gasoline pumping system. Instantly flames reared up on the hangar deck, where they began to revel in bombs, depth charges, and ready-use ammunition. A ceaseless series of explosions caused by air flasks in torpedoes, probably a powder magazine, and gasoline vapor racked the ship. *Wasp* took an immediate 10- to 15-degree list, and all electrical lines and fire mains in her forward half were severed.

By an incredible twist of fortune, two more American vessels in *Hornet*'s screen literally ran into torpedoes from *I-19*. Destroyer *O'Brien* avoided one torpedo with a sharp right turn, only to spot a second too close to evade. It struck *O'Brien* in the extreme bow at 1451. The ship reeled as a shock wave undulated down her keel, and when the smoke and spray cleared her lower stem gaped like a shark's mouth. But the point of impact was so far forward that it killed none of her bluejackets and wounded only two.

Like *O'Brien,* battleship *North Carolina* was executing the course change begun at 1444 when she observed *Wasp* in distress. White-caps hid the small wake of another Model 95 torpedo until at 1452 it struck the new fast battleship on the port side abreast her number one main battery turret. The explosion tore a 32-by-18-foot hole 20 feet below the waterline and lifted a churning column of oil and water to the level of the funnels. The blast distorted the roller path of turret number one while it sent a flash into the number one handling room and propelled acrid smoke into forward compart-ments, which prompted the flooding of the forward magazine as a precaution. *North Carolina* took a 5.5-degree list and lost five men, but counterflooding quickly removed the list and the tough new ship maneuvered radically as she surged forward at 25 knots.

Captain Forrest Sherman turned *Wasp* to place the breeze on the starboard bow and then went astern with her unhurt engines to keep the wind blowing the flames away from the undamaged portions of the ship and to clear burning oil on the water. Despite tempests of flame and a lethal rain of exploding ammunition, officers and men courageously grabbed hoses and attempted to fight the fire. But head work was not so impressive: someone failed to isolate the ruptured forward sections of the fire main from the intact after loops, and only a relative trickle of water could be played on the conflagration.

At 1505 a huge gasoline-vapor explosion jetted incandescent gases skyward on three sides of the island, burning Admiral Noyes about the hair and ears; Rear Admiral Norman Scott on *San Francisco* assumed Noyes was lost. About five minutes later another unusually severe eruption lifted the number two elevator from its well and dropped it askew. In the after conning station, Captain Sherman appraised the situation with his key subordinates. Although flooding presented no immediate danger, flames enveloped the forward half of the ship and the sundered gasoline tanks and forward magazines were in volcanic action. With many crewmen already dead or in-jured, there appeared to be no means to effectively fight the fire. Accordingly, at 1520 Captain Sherman made the painful decision to abandon ship. Of her crew of 2,247, rescuers saved all but 173 officers and men; the injured numbered 400, including eighty-five hospital cases. Also lost was Jack Singer, a newspaper correspondent. All but one of *Wasp*'s twenty-six airborne planes were recovered, but forty-five went down with the ship. *I-15* duly observed and reported the scuttling of *Wasp* at 2100 by three torpedoes from destroyer *Lans-downe,* as other American destroyers kept *I-19* busy avoiding eighty depth charges.

Battleship *North Carolina* departed the South Pacific for mending in a major shipyard. She was to be joined by *O'Brien,* whose story provides a long sequel to the day's events. The destroyer received temporary repairs at Espíritu Santo and Noumea for damage described in the official report as "severe flexural vibration of the ship girder"; in simple terms, her hull had been strained like a piece of tin that is bent at one point several times. During passage to Suva in the Fijis, more signs of weakness appeared, and a thorough inspection was made on her arrival. *O'Brien* departed Suva for stateside repairs, but on October 19, over one month and 2,800 miles from where she was torpedoed, the damaged destroyer's hull began buckling, and after her crew was taken off, she sank.

The loss of *Wasp,* following as it did the torpedoing of *Saratoga* on August 31 and the near-torpedoing of *Hornet* on September 6, occasioned critical inquiry by Admiral Nimitz. His report found that the carrier groups had operated in the same waters for three weeks and that they had routinely cruised at speeds imprudently low for submarine-infested waters. It was also obvious after the event that in each case the attacks came just after the carrier group turned because of flight operations and while screening destroyers raced to regain station, thus rendering their sonars ineffective. In rebuttal, Admiral Noyes presented cogent reasons for his operations and correctly pointed out that the attack on *Wasp* came in an area never before entered by the carrier groups, but Noyes would never again command carriers in combat.

After the war it became fashionable to disparage Japanese submarine operations that in the long term paid for scant gains with dreadful losses, particularly in contrast to the evisceration of Japanese trade by American submarines at relatively small cost. It is true that the Japanese clung doggedly to the prewar concept that their submarines should be employed in stalking American fleet units rather than in paring at supply lines, but the effectiveness of this policy in the first critical year of the war should not be overlooked. During 1942, when the aircraft carrier became the capital ship of both navies, Japanese submarines sank two of the six available American carriers (admittedly *Yorktown* had already been damaged, but she otherwise would have been saved) and kept a third, *Saratoga,* out of three of the four carrier battles that year. Further, in damaging *North Carolina* they put one-third of the available American fast battleships out of action at a critical stage of the Guadalcanal campaign. When *Wasp* sank on September 15, the United States Navy was left with only *Hornet* to face up to six operational Japanese carriers. This was the second golden opportunity conferred on

Yamamoto during the Guadalcanal campaign—the first being Mikawa's victory at Savo Island. The question remained how the Japanese would exploit it.

Turner still faced the immediate question of whether he could yet deliver the 7th Marines to Vandegrift. For purposes of deception, Turner maintained course with his convoy until darkness on September 15. The survivor-laden support ships with *Hornet* withdrew during the night of September 15–16 while seven Japanese destroyers landed about 1,000 men of the 1st Battalion, 4th Infantry Regiment on Guadalcanal and bombarded the marines. During the 16th, Turner reestimated the situation. He calculated that enemy ships operating off Guadalcanal on the night of September 15–16 would not be able to repeat the performance the next night and that raids by MacArthur's aircraft on Rabaul would temporarily tame Japanese air power. Most important, he received radio intelligence from Ghormley indicating the momentary withdrawal to the north of the most formidable Japanese fleet units. This information was authoritative but not certain. Thus full respect must be accorded Turner's decision at 1500 on September 16 to risk the approach to Guadalcanal without covering forces for his convoy bearing the only available reinforcements in the South Pacific.

September 16 also saw an important decision by the 8th Fleet and the 17th Army. For reasons to be explored shortly, orders were issued to immediately forward to Guadalcanal the main body of the 2d Division and a part of the 38th Division totaling 17,500 men and 176 guns. Pursuant to these orders, destroyers *Fubuki, Suzukaze,* and *Ushio,* each towing a barge, were steaming for Kamimbo when they met a twilight reception committee of thirteen SBDs and five TBFs led by Lieutenant Commander Louis Kirn. The American fliers succeeded in sinking only one barge—a poor trade for an SBD that never recovered from its dive. On the following night the destroyers *Suzanami* and *Amagiri* arrived at Kamimbo with desperately needed medical supplies and food. Although they benefited from better-coordinated air cover from the R Area Air Force, their main protector was a weather front that caused one SBD searching for them to ditch.

Turner's resolution paid off, and at 0700 on the morning of September 18, the 7th Marines and their supporting artillery unit, the 1st Battalion, 11th Marines, began landing. Rabaul learned quickly of the convoy's presence and promptly launched an air raid and dispatched light cruiser *Sendai* and four destroyers to attack the convoy. Weather deflected the airmen, and *Sendai*'s contingent arrived long after the Americans departed. Careful arrangements of manpower and cargo-handling facilities plus practice enabled the ships to disgorge 4,157 Marines, 137 vehicles, 4,323 barrels of fuel, rations, and 60 percent of the tentage of the 7th Marines by 1800. Only the loss of one patrolling SBD and its pilot to trigger-happy ship's gunners marred the proceedings. The transports embarked the survivors of the 1st Parachute Battalion plus 162 wounded Americans and eight wounded Japanese. As an added bonus this day, six TBFs of VT-8 flew in to bolster the Cactus Air Force.

After dark on September 18, destroyers *Arashi, Umikaze, Kawakaze,* and *Suzukaze* landed 170 men, four field guns, and provisions at Kamimbo. *Sendai* and her four consorts canvassed fruitlessly for the American convoy and then vented their wrath on the marines with a bombardment, to which Marine shore batteries replied without effect.

NEW JAPANESE PLANS

On September 15, the news of Kawaguchi's failure percolated up through the Japanese command channels, where it created shock and incredulity. It also galvanized staff officers of the Imperial Army and Navy into action. Within hours, thinking at Imperial Headquarters, the Combined Fleet, and the 17th Army meshed into a scheme for a concerted effort to regain Guadalcanal, and, indeed, extend Japan's holdings farther into the South Pacific. The Naval General Staff now saw Guadalcanal as the chosen site of the anticipated all-out American counterattack; it might be the decisive battle of the war. The Imperial Navy resolved to recapture Guadalcanal and girded itself to meet the total American commitment in kind by tossing in every plane and literally bringing its big guns to bear on the Marine perimeter.

The Navy Section at Imperial General Headquarters asked for the Imperial Army's views on the strategic situation and inquired if additional ground units could be spared for the Pacific. Superficially the Imperial Army sent an encouraging reply: they agreed that Guadalcanal represented an "all-out" attack; the prognosis for the Soviet-German conflict through the winter appeared such that the Imperial Army would investigate what units could be spared for the Southeast Pacific, including units from Manchuria.

At Rabaul the 17th Army and 8th Fleet forged new plans simultaneously with those in Tokyo. They resolved to place the main body of the 2d Division with elements of the 38th Division on Guadalcanal as quickly as possible. They also made the important corollary decision to halt the competing enterprise on New Guinea to take Port Moresby by overland attack. Accordingly, the Nankai Detachment drew back to the Salamaua area and Kokada to establish a strong base and to protect Buna. The 17th Army petitioned Imperial Headquarters for reinforcements, including another infantry division, a tank regiment, and many artillery, supply, and communication units.[1]

Imperial General Headquarters met this checklist of reinforcements in full, even though it involved tapping into the Manchurian reservoir. The order of battle of the 17th Army swelled by a score of units, the most important of which were the 38th Division, conquerors of Hong Kong, Sumatra, and Timor, then engaged in training for a planned attack on Ceylon, and the 8th Tank Regiment. Although these additions greatly increased the potential power of the 17th Army, they did not represent a significant fraction of the Imperial Army. They did approach the practical constraints imposed by the shipping situation.

On September 17, General Sugiyama explained to the Emperor that Kawaguchi had failed because his planned surprise attack through the jungle had collapsed in the face of a breakdown in coordination and American firepower. Sugiyama described a new scheme for an attack in October with additional forces to capture the airfield. He displayed the pervasive confidence of Imperial Headquarters by asserting that the reinforcements would make possible not only the recapture of Guadalcanal, but also further success at Rabi as an essential preliminary to taking Port Moresby and more locations in the Solomons.

During September 18 in Tokyo, planners revised the 6th and 7th Central Agreements into the 8th Central Agreement published on September 19. The new plan called for the two services to assemble reinforcements and then to cooperate in the recapture of Guadalcanal, which remained Operation "KA." The Imperial Navy would stanch the flow of American reinforcements, and to accomplish this goal the Navy pledged to commit more air units and especially to improve its airfields in the Solomons and on New Guinea. But Gua-

---

[1]Incorporated in this list were several thousand laborers to porter supplies on Guadalcanal. The 17th Army specified it wanted only Taiwanese for this role because, notes the Defense Agency history volume, it was a Japanese belief that the Taiwanese had the "strongest backs" among the subject peoples in the Greater East Asia Co-Prosperity Sphere.

dalcanal was only an appetizer under the new design; once it was consumed, other morsels would include Rabi, Port Moresby, San Cristóbal, the Russell Islands, and the Louisiades.

Coupled with the accession of many new units to the 17th Army would be a substantial increase in Hyakutake's staff, though the general would have no say in this matter. The reasons for this move were twofold. First, the existing tiny staff (only three officers) was obviously unequal to the task of managing the large expansion of units under the Army's operational control. The second reason for the change was reflected in the fact that the increase in strength to eleven officers was not accomplished by simple addition. After being briefed on Kawaguchi's failure by Colonel Matsumoto, Hyakutake's chief of staff, General Futami recorded his profound discouragement in his diary. He blamed the failure on the Navy, a sentiment shared by many Army officers at Imperial Headquarters, where the belief lingered that the Navy had compromised Kawaguchi's excellent prospects by failure to gain air superiority and by rushing him into a rash attack with a false report of an approaching convoy of enemy reinforcements. Futami did little to veil his defeatism from visiting naval officers of the 8th and Combined Fleets. He was declared "sick" and was replaced by Major General Shu'ichi Miyazaki. Colonel Matsumoto was also pessimistic, but he was shifted to become the operations officer of the incoming 2d Division. Among the additions to the staff of the 17th Army would be Colonel Masanobu Tsuji, an officer who was closely identified with Tojo and who, noted H. P. Willmott, "enjoyed an extremely unsavory reputation even in an Army hardly noted for its exacting standards of personal behavior." Tsuji's undoubted intelligence played a key role in Japan's triumph in Malaya, and he was expected to put fire into the 17th Army, which so far had not displayed much flair in the view of Imperial Headquarters.

Another officer transferred from Imperial General Headquarters with Tsuji was Colonel Norio Konuma. This officer recorded in his diary the substance of his briefings by the key figures in the Army Section of Imperial General Headquarters. These entries reveal that beneath the veneer of accommodation in the 8th Central Agreement, there remained substantial discord over the significance of Guadalcanal among the Imperial Army's policy makers.

Konuma spoke first to Lieutenant General Takushiro Hattori, chief of the Operations Section. Hattori characterized the Imperial Navy as fervently committed to recapturing Guadalcanal, but he did not agree that Guadalcanal would be a decisive battle, because the

Americans had not made sufficient logistical preparations for such an adventure. To Hattori, Guadalcanal was but one of a trio of defensive positions, along with Rabi and Port Moresby, established to protect the South Pacific, or alternatively as platforms for a campaign of attrition. He remained convinced that the main American attack could not come until 1944. As for current operations, the 17th Army's first chore was to retake Guadalcanal, preferably in early October. Hattori visualized the limit of 17th Army operations as a line including the Solomons, the Louisiades, and New Guinea. He cautioned that the Americans employed bold tactics; their defensive lines were formidable. But Hattori declined to dwell on failure— rather he was so sanguine about success that he wanted the 38th Division used for other targets, especially Rabi, perhaps simultaneously with Guadalcanal.

Konuma next spoke to General Shin'ichi Tanaka, chief of the 1st Division of the General Staff, and General Moritake Tanabe, vice chief of the General Staff. They cautioned against underestimating the Americans and emphasized the need for careful preparations with particular attention to reconnaissance of the terrain and the enemy dispositions. In Tanabe's sharply critical opinion, so far the 17th Army had failed to reflect an understanding of modern warfare and was plagued by an inclination for piecemeal commitment of forces.

The Chief of the Imperial General Staff, General Sugiyama, revealed to Konuma that he was at odds with some of his deputies. Sugiyama shared the Imperial Navy's view that Guadalcanal was the place where the war would be decided. He regarded the 17th Army as derelict in forwarding timely situation reports and as too restrained in emphasizing the difficulties they faced. He also entertained the unusual view that the 17th Army was too modest in its requests for reinforcements. Konuma should keep Imperial Headquarters better informed and endeavor to anticipate needs; he should not hesitate to ask for anything.

En route to Rabaul, Konuma stopped at Truk. There Captain Kameto Kurojima of the Combined Fleet Staff revealed that the Navy had committed almost the entire might of its air and submarine arms to the Guadalcanal area. Kurojima anticipated opening the Buin airstrip by the end of September, and he stressed the importance of shelling the airfield on Guadalcanal to safeguard Japanese reinforcements from American planes. With this array of insights, Konuma joined his colleagues on the 17th Army staff on September 20 to make detailed plans for the next attack.

LIFE ON GUADALCANAL

A comparative lull settled over Guadalcanal during the two weeks after the Battle of Edson's Ridge. This interlude affords an opportunity to describe daily existence on Guadalcanal, not only for its intrinsic interest, but also for its bearing on the coming struggles. For the Americans, two features particularly distinguish Guadalcanal from later campaigns. First, Guadalcanal came after a long run of humiliating defeats and featured a close balance of forces. Unlike troops who fought subsequent actions in the Pacific, however savage, the marines on Guadalcanal lacked the moral reserve that a long string of successes or a large preponderance of power gives to any unit.

Second, circumstances narrowed the normally large disparity in risks faced by the "support" and "fighting" units of the division. To be sure, the riflemen still confronted by far the greatest hazards: patrolling, defending his position in wild night battles, enduring sniping, priming himself for an attack. But the denizens of the "rear echelon" faced a different but serious set of dangers. The entire Marine perimeter measured about 15 square miles. At the center sat Henderson Field, the aiming point for all Japanese aviators and gunners. Since support units of the division and the flying and servicing elements of the Cactus Air Force mostly adjoined the airstrip, they suffered most from the repeated bombings and bombardments.

By mid-September the physical and emotional strain of the campaign and reduced rations had leaned the sun-bronzed flesh of Vandegrift's men. Dirt and stains clogged the weave of their tattered outer garments; socks and underwear existed mostly in memory. Filth further corrupted the already crude language until it became monotonously profane. Heretofore the absence of permanent living quarters represented the physical manifestation of the hope that the division would soon leave the island; now the receding prospects for relief produced the "great Guadalcanal housing boom." Individual marines or small groups constructed shacks or lean-tos with old crates, Japanese rice bags, palm fronds, and tree trunks. The division command post returned from its sojourn on the ridge to its former location, but the new facilities showed disturbing signs of permanence to those who thought the division had already lingered too long on Guadalcanal. The engineers built bigger and sturdier dugouts, though no structure within the perimeter was truly bombproof.

The readiness call for aviators at 0430 commenced daily life on

Guadalcanal. The hungry garrison lined up for the first of the two meals about 0700–0730. Cooks doled to the fliers, who got preferred rations, cereal—or as one pilot said, "rather thin gruel"—with limited quantities of milk, sugar, and the one welcome essential for survival, coffee. An endless stream of work maintaining weapons, building, repairing, and camouflaging, not to mention such necessities as sentry duty and patrolling, absorbed the morning hours for the bulk of the garrison.

The level of tension rose with the sun in anticipation of the nearly daily air raids between 1130 and 1400, "Tojo Time." Vandegrift habitually conducted his inspections during these hours to set an example. All over the perimeter, eyes kept flickering toward the airfield to check on the flagpole. No flag meant no alert. The hoisting of a white flag meant "Condition Yellow," bombers en route, usually about fifteen to thirty minutes out. When the black flag jerked up the pole, it signaled arrival of the raid within two to ten minutes. Men moved expeditiously to the vicinity of the nearest slit trench or shelter, but by now they were so accustomed to the bombing routine that many, despite orders to the contrary, stood erect gazing at the slow-motion evolutions of Japanese and American aircraft 5 miles high in the ether until the moment of bomb release. Colonel Clifton Cates of the 1st Marines dealt with people he spotted idling aboveground with bombers overhead in his own unique way: he fired shots from his .45 caliber pistol just over their heads. The screeching "whi-whi-whi" of falling bombs sounded much louder than the uninitiated expected, and any bomb that fell near caused violent ground tremors. Antiaircraft gunners of the 3d Defense Battalion worked methodically; their firing was a major prop to morale.

When the sky emptied of the noise of aero engines and hot shell casings ceased tumbling to the ground, a few men from all over the perimeter loped up to the ice plant, a legacy of the original Japanese garrison, adorned with two signs. The first announced:

TOJO ICE FACTORY UNDER NEW MANAGEMENT
J. GENUNG, SGT. USMC, MGR.

The second simply proclaimed: "Today's Score." After each encounter the figures for air operations were posted. Marines of all ranks felt intense pride in "their fliers," and rightly so, but the aviators stood on wobbly legs. The casualty rate leaves little room to doubt that the airmen endured the greatest stress of any group of Americans on Guadalcanal; Mangrum's VMSB-232, for example, lost six of twelve pilots killed. Lieutenant Commander Leroy Simpler, the experienced leader of VF-5, said quite simply that a man's "guts" were directly related to how rested he was. In Simpler's judgment, one week at Guadalcanal was worse than two months on a carrier.

Of course, the remainder of the garrison also experienced and showed the effects of their bleak existence. During the daylight hours those men who could slept, for sleep had become a precious commodity for all hands. Recreation consisted of an occasional bath in the Lunga River or on the beach, but the need to climb over barbed wire and the oil and debris accumulating from sunken ships diminished the charms of the latter. A letter from home (the first mail arrived at the beginning of September) or a sliver from a 10-pound ice cake were counted as treats. Seabee scientists conducted certain experiments with the fermentation characteristics of available local products, with some success. These resourceful men also turned a Japanese safe into an oven for bread and found dozens of other ways of making life more comfortable. More important, they took over responsibility for maintaining Henderson Field.

News was an important item also in short supply. Many marines thought their sacrifices were being ignored, and all ranks eagerly gathered around radios taken from wrecked planes to monitor broadcasts from San Francisco. As always, rumors substituted for hard news; by September the prize rumor was that the division would be relieved soon and go to Washington for a parade before Christmas. Souvenir collecting and selling represented the one major industry. Some marines specialized in creating phony Japanese flags or trinkets to sell to careless visitors, especially sailors—a reflection of the near-universal disgust with the Navy.

The cumulative impact of these stresses manifested itself in the blossoming of eccentricities like so many wild and varicolored flowers. As the division historian put it:

> While at the first of October every man was conscious of an almost ungovernable compulsion to show off his quirks, by the end of that month the compulsion was there without the awareness of it.

Other manifestations were less benign. For some, even periods of tedium became times to nurture what Private Robert Leckie termed a "speculative dread." Those approaching their limit displayed certain common symptoms: vacant stares from pupils that already seemed darker, larger, and rounder than normal. Such a man did not seem to understand when spoken to and his ears seemed to be hearing something in the sky. There was an unwritten rule that no one should run, since many took this as a sign of an impending air raid.

The adjustment to the proximity and possibility of death is the common feature of combat. Typical of the swiftness with which individuals moved from recognition of the speculative possibilities to the shocking realities is the experience of Private Leckie. During the afternoon of Ichiki's defeat, he went into the grove to examine his first battlefield.

> Dead bodies were strewn about the grove. The tropics had got at them already, and they were beginning to spill open. I was horrified at the swarms of flies; black, circling funnels that seemed to emerge from every orifice: from the mouth, the eyes, the ears. The beating of their myriad tiny wings made a dreadful low hum. . . . All of my elation at the victory, all of my fanciful cockiness fled before the horror of what my eyes beheld. It could be my corrupting body the white maggots were moving over; perhaps one day it might be.

One Marine officer somberly requested that the official history explicitly describe the gruesome task of burying the dead (it did not). This was no matter of mere courtesy, but necessity, for decaying flesh represented a health hazard. Moreover, it stopped the putrid stench of death, from which Leckie observed "there is no recourse but flight."

After the Battle of the Tenaru, Vandegrift wrote to General Holcomb, "The men are in good spirits and thank God still in good health." But the next month witnessed a precipitous decline in the health situation. A devastating strain of gastroenteritis that caused one death appeared about two weeks after the landing. It generally responded to treatment and lessened with improvement in camp conditions, but left its victims more susceptible to later afflictions. Poor command supervision produced some problems; in one infantry battalion entirely avoidable foot ailments rendered 159 men ineffective at one time. Medical personnel recorded the first case of dengue fever about two weeks after the landing, but not until the third week on Guadalcanal did the most important medical problem the marines would face manifest itself, one that would threaten their hold on the island as much as any Japanese attack: malaria. During all of August, hospitals admitted 900 men for malaria. Thereafter the rate exploded: September, 1,724; October, 2,630; November, 2,413;

and through December 10 another 913, bringing the total for the 1st Marine Division alone to 8,580. Although these figures included men admitted more than once, they exclude those who never received hospital treatment. With malaria came a form of secondary anemia that sapped endurance and resistance. In the South Pacific as a whole, malaria caused five times as many casualties as the Japanese. On Guadalcanal, diseases accounted for nearly two-thirds of all men who became ineffective; wounds disabled only one-quarter.

Dealing with the malaria problem required action on several fronts. Active programs belatedly went forth from September 10; a special Malaria Control Unit did not arrive until November. Atabrine was available as a prophylactic, but it was not effectively used, for two reasons. First, men heavily engaged in combat and constantly being shelled and bombed could not appreciate for some time the threat of a tiny mosquito. Second, and perhaps more important, rumors circulated freely that atabrine permanently yellowed the skin, and worse, threatened the sexual potency of users. Consequently, there was a reluctance to take the medication—it did not have the rumored side effects—and a serious failure of leadership to enforce its use.

Of the Japanese, whose suffering was greater, less is recorded. The plight of the Emperor's loyal soldiers was "indescribably wretched." Already they knew Guadalcanal as "Starvation Island," a wordplay on Ga-to, the abbreviation of the Japanese name for the island, and *gato*, written with ideographs that also mean "starvation" and "island." Rations were reduced to one-third of the normal regulation. "Rice cakes and candies appear in my dreams," wrote one member of the 17th Army. What appeared in his stomach was rice, often moldy, and soybeans, whose high nutritional value formed the only barrier between the average soldier and extinction. Another soldier wrote, "Our bodies are so tired they are like raw cotton."

The reasons for the desperate shortage of food began with bad management of an admittedly difficult logistical problem. Kamimbo was the preferred terminus for Tokyo Express runs, because it slightly shortened the exposure time of the ships and because the area around Kamimbo, unlike Tassafaronga, afforded concealment for barges during daylight hours. But the dreadful state of the coastal track meant it took two full days to move by foot from Kamimbo to the Matanikau area. Exacerbating the situation were the daily routine of armed reconnaissance patrols by SBDs and especially "the long-nosed planes," as the Japanese called the P-400s. They made movement on land "extremely difficult," and their continual attrition of barges materially effected the Japanese ability to keep their forces supplied. Moreover, American aircraft and artillery forced the Japanese to bivouac on reverse slopes down in the perpetually muddy environs of streambeds among dense foliage. This deprivation of sunlight exacted both psychological and physical costs.

The Imperial Navy was also almost criminally negligent in relentlessly forwarding troops without a commensurate increase in supplies. Tacit acknowledgment of this fact came immediately after the ridge battle, when the Tokyo Express runs suddenly shifted to large quantities of food. About 1,000 men were in makeshift hospitals because of malnutrition, malaria, and dysentery. Many died each day; few would ultimately survive. Perhaps the grimmest fate of all was that of the 11th and 13th Construction Units: they were dispersed along the supply route and told to find their own food, if possible.

NEW PLANS AND COMMANDS

On September 19 the 1st Marine Division issued a revised defense plan disposing the division's new strength of ten infantry battalions, one Raider battalion, four artillery battalions, and a small tank battalion plus support units. It established for the first time a complete perimeter defense. The line ran from Alligator Creek inland along all commanding ground to the hills and ridges west of the Lunga. It incorporated ten subsectors; three (manned by the Pioneer, Engineer, and Amphibian Tractor battalions) fronted the beach. The other seven faced inland and were parceled out two to each of the infantry regiments (the 1st, 5th, and 7th), with the remaining subsector directly under division control.

Of far greater interest than the anatomy of the defense is the thought process behind its conception. Up to this point the planning of the staff and commander of the 1st Marine Division had been thoughtful and effective, but now it showed a spark of true brilliance. They frankly admitted the new scheme represented a "cordon defense of the worst type." Since Napoleonic times, staff colleges had excoriated this type of long and thinly held line for its vulnerability to any enemy who massed his artillery and infantry against one point. The textbook solution to the problem facing Vandegrift was

a series of defensive "horseshoes" along the likely avenues of approach with reserves positioned for "defense in depth."

But Vandegrift and his staff conducted a thoroughly pragmatic
appraisal of the enemy and the terrain that led them to discard
sacrosanct principles. They regarded the strength and demonstrated
proficiency of the Henderson Field aviators as insurance against a
landing on the seaward side of the perimeter. Further, the Japanese
had twice displayed a preference for unopposed landings followed by
overland assaults. Therefore, the division staff reasoned that any new
attack would most likely come from one or more of three compass
points: east, west, or south. Vandegrift intended to meet attacks to
the east or west not at the perimeter, but at crossing points on the
Tenaru or Matanikau, where there was scope for the favored Marine
tactics of inland flanking movements or amphibious hooks. But the
terrain to the south was "so bewildering as to beggar description";
it not only made detection of an attacker by ground or air reconnaissance problematical, but also effectively prohibited an active defense
designed to stop the enemy beyond the perimeter. On the other hand,
the marines judged that simply negotiating such fine-grained rain
forest would leave an assault unit fatigued and shaken and present
an attacker with an insurmountable supply problem. Finally, there
was a professional judgment, based on recent examples, that the
Japanese displayed little imagination in their planning and entertained a faulty concept of the effectiveness of modern massed firepower.

The critical issue in defensive arrangements is usually reserves,
and here the Marine plan favored practical reality over a theoretical
elegance. The cordon defense allowed a degree of economy of force
both because it permitted unusually long frontage assignments and
because the Marine command could thin to the bone unthreatened
sectors, or in places actually contract the perimeter, to gather additional reserve units. It was also recognized that in night jungle combat the practical difficulties of movement and deployment would
preclude the timely intervention of a large conventional reserve.
Experience at the Tenaru and on Edson's Ridge engendered confidence that Japanese attacks could be defeated by even heavily outnumbered, but resolute and confident, Marine rifle units in
well-prepared positions behind barbed-wire obstacles and backed by
terrific firepower from supporting mortars and artillery. Small local
reserves stood ready in covered positions for immediate reinforcement or counterattack. Finally, no small benefit from this scheme

was that it denied the Japanese the use of their favored infiltration tactics.

Vandegrift engaged in a very bold gamble in the employment of the cordon defense, but the rearrangement of his battalions was not the only way he moved to stiffen his command. The challenges on Guadalcanal exposed a number of officers whose performance did not match Vandegrift's standards. Conspicuous among the failures were a number of senior officers, including the chief of staff of the division, Colonel Capers James, and one of Vandegrift's closest personal friends, Colonel Leroy Hunt, the commander of the 5th Marines. A September 8 request from General Holcomb for the excess senior officers created by recent promotions to be returned to the United States to help form new units afforded an opportunity to make the departure of these officers and others less painful. Vandegrift officially attributed the relief of a number of officers to this directive and announced that his policy, for reasons of "fairness," was to send home officers who had been with the division the longest. He exempted Colonel Pedro del Valle from this scheme, ostensibly because del Valle was the only trained artilleryman in his grade. In fact, Vandegrift shortly recommended del Valle for field promotion to brigadier general in recognition of the superb performance of his gunners.

Replacing James would be the newly promoted Colonel Gerald Thomas, the former operations officer and by now Vandegrift's closest confidant. Much of the division's success could be ascribed to Thomas's bright mind. Following Thomas in the role of operations officer was his brainy former deputy, Lieutenant Colonel Merrill B. Twining. Merritt Edson, who now wore the eagles of a full colonel, stood as the obvious candidate to replace Hunt based upon demonstrated performance. The movement of Edson to the 5th Marines carried with it a degree of irony. If the performance of this regiment had so far failed to match command expectations, this was partly attributable to the fact that Edson had drained many experienced and talented men from its ranks when he formed the 1st Raider Battalion. The new commander of the 1st Raider Battalion became Lieutenant Colonel Samuel B. Griffith, whom Vandegrift described as "a splendid officer." The Marine general also took the opportunity to replace a number of older battalion commanders with younger lieutenant colonels and majors who displayed aggressive spirit and conduct.

Another example of Vandegrift's pragmatic approach to problems came with the formation of a special unit. In one of the clashes with retreating elements of Kawaguchi's command, Companies A and B of the 1st Battalion, 1st Marines fell into an ambush that cost the lives of eighteen men. To Vandegrift this episode, only the latest in a series of patrolling failures, highlighted the need to cultivate men with special aptitude in jungle craft and navigation. The requirement had already been identified by William J. Whaling, the executive officer of the 5th Marines, who had formed an ad hoc unit of guides. Whaling, who had also just become one of the excess colonels for whom no regular employment existed, was the obvious nominee to lead a special unit soon christened the "Scout-Snipers." Each rifle battalion was requested to send three men, preferably one from each rifle company. These individuals generally had been avid outdoorsmen in civilian life; Gerald Thomas described them as "the weirdest characters you've ever seen" and "real Daniel Boone types."

Vandegrift found a number of tasks for the Scout-Snipers. As guides they adroitly conducted battalions or companies from one sector to another, avoiding countermarches and fatigue. They led regular patrols on normal coverage or independently patrolled difficult regions, thus materially improving this essential means of gathering tactical intelligence. They also afforded the division a method to make a close and accurate check on the positions held by all units, a difficult task in the jungle. As the Scout-Snipers grew, it became customary to send out independent patrols in groups of from five to fifteen.

Another important command change was made at this time when Admiral McCain reluctantly left his job as the commander of the South Pacific Air Forces for an important staff position in Washington. Though Vandegrift sincerely regretted McCain's departure, the able Rear Admiral Aubrey Fitch took this key aviation command. A lull in the air campaign coincided with this switch; no Japanese air raids reached Guadalcanal between September 14 and September 27. During this interval, both sides reinforced their flying units and the Japanese reorganized theirs. The headquarters of the 21st Air Flotilla (Rear Admiral Rinsosuke Ichimaru) reached Kavieng with twenty-three Bettys of the Kanoya Air Group on September 16. Nine Zeros of the Kanoya group moved on to Rabaul, which also gained twenty-one Zeros of the 3d Air Group on September 17. The next day a major restructuring placed all fighter, dive-bomber, and patrol planes under the command of the 25th Air Flotilla; all twin-engine bombers became the command responsibility of the 26th Air Flotilla. By September 20 the Japanese counted the following planes at Rabaul:

25th Air Flotilla

45 "long-range" Zeros	1 land-based reconnaissance plane
26 "short-range" Zeros	6 flying boats
5 Vals	

26th Air Flotilla

34 land-based bombers (all but three Bettys)

Total: 117

On this same date American air strength on Guadalcanal included:

36 F4F-4s	7 TBFs
25 SBDs	3 P-400s
Total: 71	

The program of air Japanese reinforcements added twenty more Bettys of the Takao Air Group on September 23 and twelve Vals (nine representing the 31st Air Group) on September 27. At this same time, all or parts of the air groups that had seen most of the action so far in the campaign (the 4th, Yokohama, Chitose) returned to Japan to re-form. During this same period the Americans added five Wildcats, eleven SBDs of VMSB-141, four TBFs, and three P-400s to the Cactus Air Force.

MacArthur's fliers continued their largely unsung contribution to the campaign with a series of night attacks on Rabaul, commencing on September 15. During the following two nights, B-17s destroyed four Bettys and three Zeros and damaged three and eight respectively. The only Japanese defense to these raids was antiaircraft fire, which Admiral Ukagi described in his diary on September 20 as "indescribably uncoordinated and unskilled." To remedy these shortcomings, experts from super-battleships *Yamato* and *Musashi* were posted to Rabaul.

On September 19, Admiral Fitch flew to Guadalcanal for a visit with Vandegrift, accompanied by Hanson Baldwin, the military affairs correspondent for the *New York Times.* Baldwin came not only to gather information but also to dispense some. He told Vandegrift that the American people labored under the false impression that the marines held most of the island, rather than the small and threatened segment they actually controlled. More startlingly, Baldwin revealed that it was common knowledge in Washington that "top officials" were increasingly alarmed over the situation and, closer to hand, Baldwin also described the deep pessimism at Ghormley's headquarters. The correspondent finally asked, "Are you going to hold this beachhead?" To this Vandegrift shot back: "Hell yes, why not?"

There was no lull in the need for the Japanese soldiers to eat. The night of September 20 found destroyers *Suzanami, Ushio, Yudachi,* and *Shikinami,* each towing a barge, on the main line for Kamimbo with ammunition and provisions. Seven Navy and three Marine SBDs under Lieutenant Commander Louis Kirn jumped *Shikinami,* putting a range finder out of action and wounding one man. Two other SBDs dispatched to attack Gizo became lost and ditched. A coast watcher picked up all but one of the four crewmen. Again reflecting the desperate need for food on Guadalcanal, on September 21, destroyers *Uranami, Shirayuki, Kagero,* and *Hamakaze* made a provision run to Kamimbo. In the clear night, American planes strafed *Kagero,* causing flooding. The aerial harassment necessitated so much maneuvering that these vessels returned to Shortland with one-third of their load of supplies.

Had Hashimoto gained his way, this would have been the last Tokyo Express run for a while, because of the growing proficiency of American planes in night attacks. But the urgent need for reinforcements and supplies compelled Destroyer Division 24 to sortie for Guadalcanal on September 24, bearing 280 men of the 4th Infantry Regiment plus construction equipment. Off Kamimbo, nine SBDs and one TBF conducted a series of attacks in which *Umikaze* and *Urakaze* sustained damage from bomb splinters that killed or wounded fourteen sailors. Although these twilight or nocturnal air-sea skirmishes seem rather tame compared to some other actions, the burgeoning potential for real disaster to the "Rat Transportation" runs as the moon moved into its full phase caused Hashimoto to cancel all further efforts for the remainder of the month. This decision provoked important alterations in Japanese plans.

11

BATTLES

ON THE

MATANIKAU

"They look just like dirty-faced little boys"

THE HIGH-SPEED CONVOY

Transforming the broad outlines of the Central Agreement at Imperial General Headquarters into detailed plans required about one week at Truk and Rabaul. Initial calculations on September 23 showed that movement of reinforcements must be complete by October 13 or 14 to permit an attack by about October 20. Naval officers envisioned the use of two means to lift the Army units to Guadalcanal: the well-tested "Rat Transportation" using twenty-seven destroyers and two seaplane carriers, and a supplementary "Ant Transportation" employing barges to lift artillery pieces too large and cumbersome for narrow destroyer decks. The planners intended to neutralize or eliminate the chief obstacle to these efforts, the Cactus Air Force, by artillery fire on Henderson Field from early October. Complementing the shelling would be an intensified series of attacks by Imperial Navy fliers scheduled to start on September 26, the projected completion date of the Buin airfield.

On September 24, Hashimoto terminated Tokyo Express runs for the rest of the month and, for reasons that will presently be seen, both completion of the Buin airfield and the "Ant Transportation" program went awry. This presented the Japanese with a serious dilemma: a buildup relying solely on the "Rat Transportation" system required a complete phase of moonless nights that would compel a one-month delay, during which the Americans could also strengthen their position. The 17th Army adamantly branded such a delay as intolerable. On September 26 the soldiers proposed movement of a substantial fraction of the reinforcements to Guadalcanal via a convoy of large transport ships. The next day, Army and Navy staff officers at Rabaul sketched a revised reinforcement scheme calling for: (1) "Rat Transportation" runs to recommence on October 1 and continue each night to October 14; (2) "Ant Transportation" to begin from Shortland that day and start delivering six bargeloads of material each night to Guadalcanal from October 1; (3) special runs on October 3 and 6 by seaplane carrier *Nisshin* with heavy artillery; (4) a stepped-up aerial offensive including night bombing of Guadalcanal; and (5) a convoy to move reinforcements directly to the 17th Army on Guadalcanal.

To explain the new plan and secure Yamamoto's approval, several officers, including Colonel Tsuji of the 17th Army, flew to Truk on September 28. Tsuji described the plight of the officers and men of the 17th Army on Guadalcanal because of lack of supplies and said they were "thinner than [Mahatma] Gandhi himself." To this Yamamoto replied: "If Army men have been starving through lack of supplies, then the Navy should be ashamed of itself." Yamamoto assented to the use of five valuable transports for the proposed High-Speed Convoy. To this plan he meshed another that antedated it by several weeks. Since early September, staff officers had mulled over the concept of using battleship guns to subdue the menagerie of American aircraft at Guadalcanal that defied efforts of Japanese aviators to annihilate them. Yamamoto now merged this proposal into the overall scheme to cover the approach of the transports to Guadalcanal.

The battleship bombardment and the High-Speed Convoy became central elements in Yamamoto's master plan. He defined the primary mission of the Combined Fleet for the October offensive as support of the recapture of Guadalcanal. The destruction of the American fleet became a secondary mission—a significant reversal of priorities from August. Timing was set around "X-Day," the date on which the buildup of Army units on Guadalcanal would be complete, tentatively fixed for October 14. "Y-Day," the anticipated date of the land offensive, was calculated as X plus six days. The battleship bombardment would be on X minus two, and the following night 8th Fleet cruisers would shell Henderson Field to ensure it remained unusable.

Imperial Navy officers tried to impress one very important point on Colonel Tsuji: once the fleet sortied from Truk, logistical considerations would limit its availability to aid the offensive to about fourteen days.

THE MATANIKAU, SEPTEMBER 24–27

The muddy Matanikau River, 5 miles west of the Lunga, became swift, deep, and unfordable near its mouth, where an alluvial sandbar partitioned it from the sea. During the last half of September, it acquired special significance for both the Japanese and American commands on Guadalcanal.

Kawaguchi entered the fourth week of September immersed in the recovery and reorganization of his command, but soon found his attention directed to simultaneously preparing to repel an American attack and mounting a thrust of his own. Japanese radio intelligence analysts suspected the Allies might shortly launch a new amphibious venture in the Solomons area and considered a landing between the Matanikau and Kamimbo to split the Japanese forces a strong possibility. When warned of this danger on September 24, Kawaguchi issued an order for the 2d and 3d Battalions, 124th Infantry (with the assistance of naval infantry), to assume positions on high ground along the coast from which to counterattack any enemy landing. The 4th Infantry Regiment was to be prepared to come under Kawaguchi's control and coordinate with Colonel Oka against a landing.

This same afternoon, increased American air activity alarmed Colonel Oka. He decided to withdraw units on the east side of the Matanikau in preparation for resisting a landing. He directed the 5th Company, 124th Infantry, sent out to bring in the Kuma Battalion survivors, to the foot of Mount Austen and pulled the 8th Company back across the river from its east-bank positions.

Toward sunset of September 24, two Japanese staff officers completed a three-day inspection trip and signaled their appreciation of the situation on Guadalcanal. They stressed that 15cm howitzers could be moved up close enough to shell the airfield effectively only by passing them across the sandbar at the mouth of the Matanikau. On the next day, September 25, Kawaguchi received instructions to seize enclaves on the east bank of the Matanikau for assembly and artillery positions. This assignment obviously conflicted with preparations to repel a landing, but before Kawaguchi could shape a solution to this contradiction he faced a threat from another quarter.

Vandegrift realized that Kawaguchi's main body had withdrawn west of the Matanikau after the Battle of the Ridge. For days thereafter the area between the Marine lines west of the Lunga and the Matanikau contained individuals and small groups of stragglers from Kawaguchi's defeated battalions. With construction of the perimeter defense in progress, Vandegrift could not spare major forces to secure the line of the Matanikau. Instead, he and his staff elected to try to dominate the area west of their lines by a series of modest operations designed to expel small bodies of Japanese and prevent large forces from establishing themselves within striking distance of the Marine perimeter.

The obvious choice for the first of such actions was the 7th Marines, who not only were fresh, but also were, in the words of Gerald Thomas, "loaded with talent." Outstanding among this talent was Lieutenant Colonel Lewis B. "Chesty" Puller, the forty-four-year-old commander of the 1st Battalion. "A chin like a bulldozer blade," as Martin Clemens said, and a barrel chest made this Virginian the very model of a Marine infantry officer, and he backed his appearance with performance. His mission was clearly exploratory: advance west astride the northern slopes of Mount Austen, cross the Matanikau, and examine the area between the Matanikau and Kokumbona. Following Puller's expedition, the 1st Raider Battalion would advance to Kokumbona to establish a temporary patrol base.

Puller's battalion, about 900 strong, moved out on September 23. Late the next afternoon his men surprised a Japanese bivouac around a "rice fire" situated on the northwest slope of Mount Austen. The marines attacked and drove them off before darkness halted the skirmish, which left seven marines dead and twenty-five wounded, eighteen of them stretcher cases. Puller radioed for assistance with his wounded and for air support the next day. Division headquarters dispatched most of the 2d Battalion, 5th Marines to Puller's aid.

The 2d Battalion, 5th Marines linked up with Puller early on September 25, and the wounded headed back under escort of Companies A and B of the 1st Battalion, 7th Marines. The rest of the force moved uneventfully west along a trail the Japanese called the Maizuru Road, and during the day the 8th Company and the 2d Battalion, 124th Regiment avoided Puller to the south. To cover the withdrawal of the 2d Battalion and the Kuma Battalion to the west

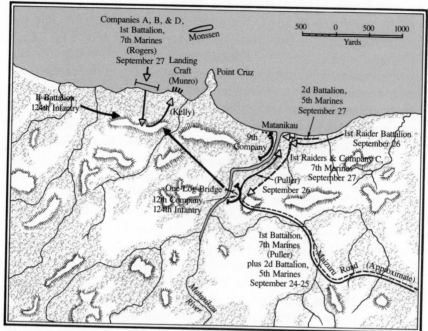

Matanikau Actions, September 24–27

bank of the Matanikau, Colonel Oka ordered his 12th Company to seize a position on the east bank of the river at the one-log bridge, a feature whose structure matched its name.

On September 26, Puller reached the Matanikau and proceeded downstream (north). About 1125 the leading elements of the 12th Company brushed with Puller's column, but neither side recognized the size of the other. Puller continued his expedition, and the 12th Company moved into Puller's wake to establish positions on the east side of the river. Farther downstream, Puller came under mortar fire from the west bank, and when he tried to cross the Matanikau near its mouth, he butted into Oka's well-dug-in 9th Company, which handily checked the marines. Bombardments from air, sea, and land impressed the 9th Company even less.

Division headquarters ordered the 1st Raider Battalion to join Puller at the Matanikau, and Colonel Edson came forward to assume command of the combined force with Puller acting as his second-in-command. A hastily devised plan called for the Raiders, with Company C of Puller's battalion, to move up the east bank of the Matanikau to cross at the one-log bridge and attack Matanikau village from the south. The 2d Battalion, 5th Marines would hold the line of the river near the bar and attack to assist the Raiders. Air and artillery support for the attacks was hurriedly scheduled.

After a sodden night, the Raiders moved out first on the morning of September 27. As they approached the one-log bridge, they came under fire from the 12th Company in well-chosen positions on the east bank, and mortar rounds began to fall on the marines from the west bank. Moving with the advance guard was Major Kenneth D. Bailey of Ridge fame. Only three days earlier, Bailey had told correspondent Tregaskis that he admired the young marines under his command so much "that when it comes to a job that's pretty rugged, you'd rather go yourself than send them." Doing just that, Bailey was killed by machinegun fire. Lieutenant Colonel Griffith, who was seriously wounded but refused evacuation, tried to slip two companies to his left to outflank the Japanese, but they too were pinned down and added more men to the growing list of casualties. At the sandbar, the 9th Company hurled back the vigorous efforts of the 2d Battalion, 5th Marines to force a crossing.

At this juncture the 11th Air Fleet put in an appearance. Although the Japanese intended to attack every day in late September, the 27th was the first day with acceptable weather. Admiral Takahashi put up eighteen Bettys (one returned early) and no fewer than thirty-eight Zeros. With a warning from a coast watcher at 1230, seventeen Marine and eighteen Navy Wildcats rose to dispute the sky. The Zero close escort became separated from the bombers by about two minutes, and in that brief interval the American pilots had a field day. Japanese accounts show two Bettys shot down and one ditched; another eleven sustained damage. Two Wildcat pilots suffered wounds, but none of their mounts was shot down. The Americans also claimed five Zeros, three by VF-5, but Japanese records confirm only one Zero loss this day.

Japanese bombs released at 1312 destroyed one SBD and two TBFs on the ground, damaged four other Dauntlesses, and left three TBFs in need of major or minor repairs. But one bomb disrupted the division headquarters signal net, multiplying the communication problems already influencing the progress of the battle on the ground. Griffith's situation report was garbled or ambiguous or both, leaving the false impression with Edson and the division headquarters that the Raiders had crossed the Matanikau and were battling on the west bank. This misconception generated orders at 1330 for the 2d Battalion, 5th Marines to renew its attack at the mouth of the Matanikau and for three companies of the 1st Battalion, 7th Marines to proceed by boat from Lunga Point to a beach west of Point Cruz to attack the Japanese from the rear.

Further Marine efforts along the Matanikau came to naught despite air and artillery support. Companies A, B, and D of the 1st Battalion, 7th Marines, under the executive officer of the battalion, Major Otho Rogers, landed near Point Cruz and pushed inland about 500 yards to the first ridgeline. Colonel Oka immediately ordered the 2d Battalion, 124th Infantry (II/124), about a mile west of the landing site, to attack and the 12th Company (facing the Raiders) to reinforce the II/124. The marines soon came under Japanese fire, and almost at once a mortar round killed Major Rogers and wounded one company commander. Captain Charles W. Kelly, Jr., assumed command as the Japanese cut them off from the beach. No radio having been brought with the landing party, the marines used white T-shirts to spell out the word "Help." Second Lieutenant Dale Leslie of VMSB-231, flying an SBD liaison plane for the division, saw and reported this message.

When Edson gained more accurate information on the situation along the Matanikau he halted the attack, despite Puller's heated objection that this would gravely endanger the landing party. Puller wasted no time in going to Kukum, where he boarded the destroyer *Monssen* and headed for Point Cruz with a group of landing craft following *Monssen* like a parade of ducks. When the landing craft headed for the original site of the landing, heavy fire greeted them, because the stranded marines had slipped further east. Lieutenant Leslie perceived the situation and guided the boats to the area where the isolated Marine unit was moving. Puller ordered Kelly to cut his way to the coast, and *Monssen* blasted a path to the beach. At this point the II/124 moved west to "reorganize" and only the 8th Company engaged Kelly's marines in a desperate hand-to-hand fight as the Japanese attempted to carry out their orders to "destroy the enemy." The resourceful Lieutenant Leslie herded some reluctant boat crews to the beach. At the shore the Japanese again placed hefty fire on the boats, and Coast Guard Petty Officer Douglas A. Munro was killed using his craft to shield the others.[1]

A count after the Marine units returned to the perimeter revealed losses of eighteen killed and twenty-five wounded in 1st Battalion,

---

[1]A posthumous award of the Medal of Honor went to Munro, the only member of the United States Coast Guard to receive this decoration in World War II.

7th Marines, sixteen killed and sixty-eight wounded in 2d Battalion, 5th Marines, and thirty-six killed and seven wounded among the 1st Raiders, bringing total casualties to sixty killed and one hundred wounded. Japanese casualties are not recorded but very likely were substantially less. Naturally the results of this action gratified the Japanese, and Colonel Oka received much credit. In his diary, General Futami labeled this the first good news to come from Guadalcanal.

In a retrospective assessment, the marines found that the operation had an improvised, purposeless flavor. It had been initiated without meaningful intelligence on the enemy situation or the terrain, and the attack was characterized by the commitment of battalions along unreconnoitered axes, beyond mutual support range, and without coordination of movements or of air or artillery support. Division headquarters ascribed the successful withdrawal of the 1st Battalion, 7th Marines to "its fighting qualities, brilliant improvisation on the part of those responsible for the movement and to the great good fortune which attended it."

The marines credited the Japanese for good handling of their forces, and of course were unaware of the fortuitous circumstance of the preparation for meeting a landing around Point Cruz based upon radio intelligence that had no direct connection with the Marine operation. The division's report of this operation, which Vandegrift signed, contained the following passage:

> The great lesson however is to be found embodied in the passage in the Field Service Regulations which warns against "drifting aimlessly into action" for in last analysis it is to be observed that this battle was unpremeditated and was fought without definite purpose other than the natural one of closing with the enemy at once and upon every occasion.

THE TOKYO EXPRESS RENEWED

On September 28 a Japanese bombing mission of twenty-seven Bettys and forty-two Zeros departed from Rabaul to strike Guadalcanal. Two of each type returned early as a result of mechanical trouble, and a coast watcher sighted the remainder at 1258. Thirty-four Wildcats met them before they reached Henderson Field in one of the largest air battles of the campaign, which produced similarly scaled claims. The jubilant American pilots all returned, though five Wildcats were temporarily out of action, and reported the destruction of no fewer than twenty-three bombers and one Zero. The actual score was much less, though still impressive: five Bettys, including the formation leader, fell near Guadalcanal, and two others crash-landed or ditched on the way back. American bullets damaged almost all of the remaining bombers. The entire Zero escort returned with four of their number scarred, but their claims of eight "sure" and five "probable" Wildcats did not counterbalance the bomber losses. The Japanese did shoot down an SBD on a radar calibration mission over the north coast of Guadalcanal. During the afternoon, the Cactus Air Force gained reinforcements when six SBDs of VS-71, late of *Wasp,* and VS-3, late of *Saratoga,* under Lieutenant Commander John Eldridge and four TBFs of VT-8 led by Lieutenant B. L. Harwood came to roost at Henderson Field.

That evening at Rabaul, Japanese aviation officers studied the result of two days of raids. The bomber crews' morale remained high, but losses in two days totaled ten of forty-two Bettys (24 percent) that reached Guadalcanal. A week of such losses would virtually wipe out the Betty units at Rabaul. Analysis singled out defective coordination between the bombers and their escorts as the primary cause of the losses, but the Japanese also gave a salute to American tactics. The Wildcats consistently went for the bombers and persistently avoided combat with Zeros. To meet the obvious demand for a change in tactics, and pending the completion of the airfield at Buin, the Japanese decided to confine their bombers to night raids and to feints to draw up the American fighters for the Zeros to engage.

The reasoning behind the new tactics again highlighted the vital importance of Buin. With Buin operational, the power of the Japanese aerial offensive would be multiplied several times. It would nearly double the number of usable fighters by permitting the employment of the Model 32 "short-range" Zeros that just lacked the endurance to reach Guadalcanal from Rabaul. Moreover, from Buin the Model 21 "long-range" Zeros would be able to greatly extend their "loiter" time over Guadalcanal. The shortened flying time would cut down on pilot fatigue and on the rigorous demands on the aircraft themselves, reflected in the increasing number of sorties aborted because of mechanical failure.

The significance of Buin had not escaped the notice of Japanese commanders. On August 31, Yamamoto ordered Buin to be completed as soon as possible, but the projected completion dates of September 17 and then September 26 slipped past. Defective design and supervision, but mainly soaking rains, caused this delay. Despite massive increases in construction troops, the field remained incomplete at the end of the month. Neither metal mats nor cut stones could overcome the soggy nature of the ground.

Based on the new tactics, the Japanese put up nine Bettys and twenty-seven Zeros for a raid on September 29. The bombers served to draw up thirty-three Wildcats before they turned back 60 miles from Henderson Field. Although the Japanese pilots claimed eleven Wildcats and one SBD, according to American records only eight Wildcats under Lieutenant Commander Simpler of VF-5 actually brushed with the Zeros. Simpler's unit lost one Wildcat and pilot, but two Zeros failed to return from the raid. On September 30 there was no raid on Guadalcanal.

The end of September brought the Chief of the Army Air Forces, General Arnold, and Admiral Nimitz to the South Pacific for first-hand scrutiny of the situation. Continual clashes at the Joint Chiefs of Staff during September on the familiar subject of aircraft for the South Pacific motivated Arnold's inspection. Outfitted with some sound advice from Marshall not to lecture but to listen, Arnold flew to Hawaii. There he found General Delos Emmons, just returned from his own trip to the South Pacific, flatly predicting defeat at Guadalcanal. On the other hand, Nimitz confidently asserted the contrary view. On September 23, Arnold reached Noumea, where he conferred with Ghormley and was appalled by the waste of shipping and obvious mismanagement of the logistical situation.

After meeting MacArthur in Australia, Arnold reached the 11th Bomb Group base on Espíritu Santo on September 27. Colonel Saunders and his uncomplaining crews impressed the Army Air Force leader, and naturally the accomplishments of the B-17s came in for examination. An assessment completed on September 20 showed 155 vessels contacted by the group's planes with a record of nineteen bombed, four hit, and only two sunk. Several elements contributed to this modest achievement, chief among which stood the fact that during the first two months of the campaign the four-engine bombers spent 78 percent of their time on search missions. Small bombing formations contracted the already low probability of hitting maneuvering ships at sea by high-altitude bombing to infinitesimal levels, and thus far on only one occasion had even four B-17s released bombs simultaneously at a single target. Obviously, the 11th Group, reduced from thirty-five to twenty-four planes by all causes by the day Arnold visited, was not sufficient. Already orders issued on September 16 directed the 72d Bomb Squadron of the 5th Bomb

Group to move from Hawaii to the South Pacific. In November two more squadrons of the group, the 23d and 31st, plus the group headquarters would reach the South Pacific.

On September 28, Arnold returned to Noumea, where his path intersected that of Nimitz, who had sensed the need for a personal examination of the situation in the South Pacific. Ghormley's habit of working in a small, sweltering office and his failure to leave *Argonne* for a month shocked Nimitz. That same day, Nimitz, Arnold, Ghormley, Harmon, and Turner conferred with MacArthur's representatives, generals Kenny and Sunderland. One by one the local officers painted a grim picture. Arnold strove to place Guadalcanal and the South Pacific in the world perspective, necessarily downplaying its importance. Arnold returned to Washington reinforced in his views that the problem in the South Pacific was not the number of available aircraft but their distribution. He later summarized his conclusions in his autobiography: "So far, the Navy had taken one hell of a beating and at that time was hanging on by a shoestring. They did not have a logistical setup efficient enough to insure success."

Nimitz proceeded from Noumea to Guadalcanal on September 30 in a B-17. The plane became lost, but one of Nimitz's staff officers, Commander Ralph Ofstie, managed to navigate the bomber to Henderson Field with a *National Geographic* map. Rain had transformed the airfield into a quagmire, affording an opportunity for Nimitz to see the problems faced daily at Guadalcanal, a fact that secretly pleased Vandegrift. The Marine general escorted his commander in chief on a tour of the perimeter, including Edson's Ridge and the hospital. That night Vandegrift explained his problems with the Japanese and with Turner.

On the morning of October 1, Nimitz decorated as many men as his supply of medals permitted before departing. An aborted initial takeoff run on the muddy field nearly proved fatal to the admiral. After a trip to Espíritu Santo, Nimitz met Ghormley again on October 2. The substance of the conference ranged over the relief of the 1st Marine Division, reinforcements for Guadalcanal, and the proper employment of carrier units. But its most important consequence was the negative impression Ghormley's physical appearance and conduct made on Nimitz.

At Pearl Harbor, Nimitz received more bad news on the intelligence situation. On September 28 the Combat Intelligence Unit issued an estimate that noted in part:

The enemy is copying our communications methods with good success. As a result we continue to be unable to read his mail [i.e., use cryptanalysis] to any great extent.

Based upon what information could be gleaned essentially from traffic analysis, intelligence officers predicted the Japanese would probably try to recapture the southern Solomons and to extend their control on New Guinea, but they could not foretell whether these operations would be sequential or simultaneous.

The poor radio intelligence situation became manifestly bleak on September 30 when the Japanese changed not simply a code, but their entire communications system. This move stripped the radio intelligence experts of many useful tools developed over a period of years for interpreting the former communication system and for a period, whose duration could not be estimated, nullified their capacity to recover call signs and hence track the movements of important fleet units, particularly the carriers.

Probably as a result of the predictions of Japanese radio intelligence experts, on October 1 aircraft of the 11th Air Fleet remained waiting quietly on the ground at Rabaul to attack American shipping expected to appear as part of a new landing operation. But the Tokyo Express again ran this night with Destroyer Division 11 (*Fubuki, Shirayuki, Hatsuyuki,* and *Murakumo*) bearing Major General Yumio Nasu, his headquarters, and men of the 4th Infantry Regiment. During an attack by five SBDs and five TBFs, *Hatsuyuki* suffered a steering casualty and turned back after transferring Nasu. Three of the TBFs became lost en route back and ditched. Although their crews were rescued, this left only one operable TBF on Guadalcanal. The remaining Japanese ships completed their landing successfully. During the night of October 1–2, a prowling B-17 hit the light cruiser *Tenryu* at Rabaul with a bomb that killed or wounded thirty men.

On October 2, the 11th Air Fleet mounted a sweep of thirty-six Zeros to fight for air superiority over Guadalcanal. Nine Bettys accompanied the mission to conduct a feint, but they became separated around Buka and returned early with nine of the Zeros. At 1230, radar detected a flight of small fast aircraft approaching Guadalcanal and twenty-two Marine and fourteen Navy Wildcats took off, too late to meet the twenty-seven incoming Zeros at altitude. The Japanese pilots extracted the full value of their height advantage and shot down six Wildcats, killing four of the pilots. The two surviving pilots were the two Marine squadron commanders. Major Robert Galer claimed two Zeros before he parted company with his riddled Wildcat near Tulagi, and Major John Smith claimed one Zero before he crash-landed his damaged plane 6 miles southeast of the perimeter. On top of these losses, two SBDs disappeared, believed to be Zero victims. The Japanese pilots returned with claims of twelve "sure" and two "probable" Wildcats plus two SBDs. American claims totaled four Zeros, but only one Zero was destroyed over Guadalcanal, while three suffered heavy damage and one lesser damage. Destroyer Division 9 (*Asagumo, Natsugumo, Minegumo, Murasame,* and *Harusame*) conducted the reinforcement run this night. Thanks to a weather front they landed their cargo of men and provisions without difficulty.

Admiral Hashimoto slated a key run of the Tokyo Express for October 3, featuring seaplane carrier *Nisshin* with nine artillery pieces, including four 15cm howitzers, and 330 men, including Lieutenant General Masao Maruyama, the commander of the 2d Division. She was scheduled to stop at Tassafaronga with destroyers *Nowaki* and *Maikaze.* Another 320 men and 16 tons of provisions would be lifted to the same destination by destroyers *Uranami, Shikinami, Makigumo,* and *Akigumo.* Destroyers *Arashio, Kuroshio,* and *Hayashio* would debark 190 men and 15 tons of provisions at Kamimbo.

To cover this very large "Express," a raid of twenty-seven Zeros and fifteen Bettys left Rabaul for Guadalcanal at 0900. Coast watcher Read signaled a warning of their approach at 1027; radar observed the bomber formation turn back at the Russells. At noon the silver specks representing Japanese fighters drifted across the blue dome over Henderson Field. The Japanese split into three sections, one of which dived to attack the airfield. Marine gunners downed one of the Zeros and a second was a write-off on its return to Rabaul, but the honors of the day went to the Marine pilots. Recognizing the shift in enemy tactics to fighter sweeps, the staff of the First Marine Air Wing stacked twenty-nine Wildcats still higher overhead. One flight of four Marine pilots led by Captain Marion Carl, to which Lieutenant Colonel Bauer attached himself, exploited their height advantage to carve up one section of Zeros, with claims running to nine enemy fighters, including four by Bauer. One Marine pilot parachuted to safety when his Wildcat was hit, and a Navy pilot crash-landed a second with a burned-out engine. Of the twenty-seven Zeros that reached Guadalcanal, nine did not return; one sustained heavy damage and three others lesser damage. During the day the Cactus Air Force added six more SBDs of VS-71 and three TBFs of VT-8 to its roster.

Nor did this raid succeed in preventing a formation of eight SBDs and three TBFs from greeting *Nisshin* and her escorts at 1725, but the Americans failed to hit. Japanese eavesdroppers overheard an alarming amount of American radio traffic, prompting antiaircraft destroyer *Akizuki* to sortie from the Shortland to cover *Nisshin* on her return. Despite the bombs of two enemy aircraft, a second relay of five SBDs rose at 2220 to challenge the Japanese off Guadalcanal. Most of these planes became lost, but Lieutenant Commander Eldridge and one other pilot found *Nisshin,* and their bombs started a leak in her engine room that compelled her to leave with two field guns and eighty men still aboard.

The next morning, seven SBDs and four TBFs found *Nisshin* and her destroyers 140 miles up the channel along the center of the Solomons the Americans called the Slot. Four of the SBDs under Lieutenant Commander Kirn dodged the escort of float planes by turning into clouds, but they lost sight of the Japanese ships as well. The TBFs attacked but enjoyed no success. In the midst of this battle a flight of 11th Bomb Group B-17s returning from a bombing mission to Buka wandered into the area. One of the Japanese observation float planes deliberately rammed a B-17. The two Japanese airmen successfully parachuted, but the Flying Fortress took its entire complement of nine to their deaths.

The Japanese sent no air raid to Guadalcanal on October 4 or 5, ostensibly because of commitments to cover a reinforcement run to Buna and *Nisshin*'s mission, but perhaps also as a result of losses on October 3. During the night of October 4–5, destroyers *Shigure, Fubuki, Shirayuki, Murakumo,* and *Ayanami* delivered 750 men and 24 tons of supplies to Kamimbo without incident.

For October 5, Ghormley scheduled a major American air offensive. He decided to risk his only carrier, *Hornet,* to hit the accumulation of Japanese shipping at Shortland, which if not the lion's den, was at least his stoop. Simultaneously, Ghormley dispatched B-17s against Buka and the Cactus Air Force against Reketa Bay. The morning of October 5, however, found the target areas roofed by the clouds of a cold front. *Hornet* launched an attack group of eighteen SBDs, fifteen TBFs, and sixteen Wildcats, but almost immediately this formation became unraveled because of overcast and three SBDs and two TBFs never joined up. Pressing in through swirls of rain and low cloud, the *Hornet* fliers claimed two float planes in the air and two more float planes as well as four of ten Mavises on the water. On retirement, *Hornet* fighters destroyed two Betty search planes. Only one of ten B-17s found Buka in the overcast, rain, and lightning that enveloped the Solomons, and the elements likewise scattered the raid on Reketa Bay; one SBD failed to return. The strike by *Hornet* did generate some beneficial fallout. The Japanese postponed the run by *Nisshin* scheduled for October 6 and for the next two days retained their planes at Rabaul awaiting an opportunity to attack the long-departed American carrier.

The Tokyo Express run of October 5 involved six destroyers bearing 650 men, two field guns, and ammunition. Nine SBDs led by Lieutenant Commander Kirn intercepted them 150 miles from Guadalcanal and heavily damaged *Minegumo*. The American aviators thought she sank, but *Minegumo* struggled back to Shortland with the aid of *Natsugumo*. Bomb splinters ventilated *Murasame*'s bow, compelling her to return also. Two further strikes totaling fifteen SBDs and three TBFs not only failed to find the three remaining destroyers but also returned minus two TBFs, from which only one crewman survived.

Close upon the heels of the failure of half the destroyers dispatched on October 5 to complete their mission came the cancellation of the "Ant Transportation" effort. The original scheme called for destroyers to tow barges from Shortland to Rendova; from there the Army-manned barges would move by night hops along a string of submarine-supported bases to Guadalcanal. The hasty mounting of the effort prevented adequate reconnaissance of routes and intermediate bases or adequate distribution of mechanics. Further, the barges proved less seaworthy than the task demanded. On October 4 the Cactus Air Force, perhaps with a clue from radio intelligence, seriously damaged one of the intermediate bases. The soldiers feared the hour of the October offensive would find the bulk of the 17th Army's firepower stranded in barges all over the lower Solomons, so on October 6 the "Ants" started back with the heavy artillery.

These derangements in the tight schedule for the buildup of forces for the October offensive prompted Hashimoto to project a shortfall of 3,000 men and many heavy weapons. Mikawa ordered the light cruiser *Tatsuta* and seaplane carrier *Chitose* to join the Reinforcement Unit on October 6. That night six destroyers, well covered by rain, landed four anti-tank guns, four regimental guns, 450 soldiers, and 150 sailors of the 4th Maizuru Special Naval Landing Force at Tassafaronga. They also managed to evacuate some wounded on the return trip. Hashimoto once again revised his plans to move 5,000 men, ten field and six antiaircraft guns, eight 15cm howitzers, and 130 tons of provisions between October 9 and 15. In recognition of these delays, on October 7 Yamamoto pushed back X-Day twenty-four hours to October 15.

THE MATANIKAU, OCTOBER 6–9

Lieutenant General Maruyama came ashore at 2000 on October 3 at Tassafaronga and the next day established his battle headquarters on the Mamura River. There he learned that of the 9,000 men who had reached the island before him, 2,000 were already dead and 5,000 were too weak to conduct offensive warfare. The survivors of whole units, such as the Kuma Battalion and Kawaguchi's artillery unit, lacked any equipment; most of the 1,000 men already hospitalized were doomed. This information shed light on one matter of pressing importance. Kawaguchi had been ordered explicitly on September 25 and again on the 28th to seize positions on the east bank of the Matanikau. But Kawaguchi, neither insensitive to the suffering of his troops nor oblivious of the danger of splitting his physically spent units, declined to execute these orders. Exasperated, on September 30 the 17th Army commanded Kawaguchi to "realize occupation of the [east] bank of the Matanikau . . . immediately." But not until three days later, i.e., the day Maruyama arrived, did Kawaguchi place one infantry company on the east side of the river's mouth.

Having assimilated this information, before noon of October 4 Maruyama directed General Nasu to supervise the occupation of artillery firing positions on the east bank of the Matanikau. Maruyama detailed the 29th Infantry Regiment to secure the coast from the Matanikau to the Poha and the 16th Infantry Regiment to concentrate between the Poha and the Mamura. Kawaguchi's exhausted 124th Infantry Regiment was to move west of the Bonegi and guard the coast. Early on October 5, Nasu ordered the 4th Infantry Regiment to place its 1st Battalion south of Point Cruz and its 3d Battalion west of the one-log bridge. Both of these units would advance one company east of the river, and the 2d Battalion would mass about two miles southwest of Point Cruz to guard the coast and back the 1st Battalion. Sunset of the following day found these battalions in position with the 3d Company, 4th Infantry Regiment on the east side of the mouth of the Matanikau.

Since termination of the unsuccessful operation on September 27, the 1st Marine Division concentrated on completion of the perimeter defenses to free troops for a large-scale offensive. In the interval, "daily bickering" between patrols confirmed enemy activity east of the Matanikau. The Marine command also discerned Japanese concentrations between the Bonegi and the Matanikau and what looked like preparations for an offensive. Vandegrift chose to strike first with the objective of seizing Kokumbona and driving the Japanese beyond the Poha. If successful, a garrison would be placed at Kokumbona to deny the enemy access to the trail complex leading to the upper reaches of the Lunga, from which the perimeter could be assaulted from the south.

The operations plan called for the 5th Marines (minus the 1st Battalion) to advance along the coast to the Matanikau and prepare to cross on order. In column behind the 5th Marines would come the Whaling Group (the Scout-Sniper detachment with the 3d Battalion, 2d Marines) and the 7th Marines (minus the 3d Battalion). These latter two units would turn inland and cross the Matanikau at the one-log bridge. Once across, the Whaling Group would attack down the first ridgeline west of the river and the 7th Marines would wheel and advance battalions abreast on successive ridgelines to the west of Whaling. The marines hoped this maneuver would trap large enemy forces around the Matanikau, and if successful, the 5th Ma-

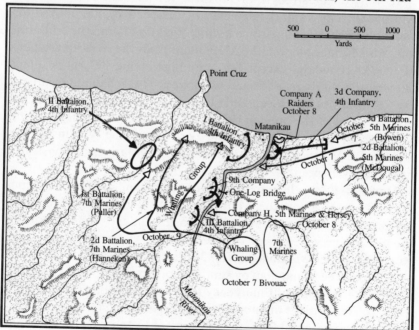

Matanikau Actions, October 7–9

rines would pass through and advance to Kokumbona. This time, division headquarters retained control of the operation and made careful arrangements for air and artillery support of the attack.

Lieutenant Colonel Julian Frisbee, the hulking executive officer of the 7th Marines, described the Marine intentions to writer John Hersey, who would accompany the attack. Concluding his explanation, Frisbee asked: "Have you ever seen men killed on the field of battle?" Hersey replied he had not. "It's possible," observed the Marine officer, "to think of dead enemy as dead animals." But as for dead marines, "they look just like dirty-faced little boys who have gone to bed without being tucked in by their mothers."

On the morning of October 7 the attack force moved forward from the perimeter at 0700 along the Government Track. The 3d Battalion, 5th Marines (Major Robert O. Bowen) made contact about 1000 with the 3d Company, 4th Infantry Regiment, approximately 500 yards east of the Matanikau. On Bowen's inland flank, the 2d Battalion (Major David S. McDougal) easily reached the Matanikau, where they secured 500 yards of riverbank and killed four Japanese incongruously washing clothes. The 3d Company yielded ground very slowly, even in the face of direct fire from 75mm guns on half-tracks.

In view of the strength of Japanese resistance, Edson asked for additional troops, and the depleted 1st Raider Battalion moved forward company by company to his aid. Nightfall found the 3d Battalion, 5th Marines holding the Matanikau from the coast to the flank of the 2d Battalion, except for one bulge about 400 yards inland housing the survivors of the 3d Company. The Whaling Group and the 7th Marines had meanwhile turned sharply south and reached bivouacs east of the one-log bridge with little opposition. To divert Japanese attention from the planned crossing of the Whaling Group and the 7th Marines, during the night the 5th Marines demonstrated near the river mouth.

During the 7th, the senior Japanese commanders remained ignorant of events along the Matanikau. At 1440, Nasu ordered an advance for the following day by both the 1st and 3d Battalions of the 4th Infantry Regiment to extend Japanese control about 1,000 yards east of the Matanikau. The 3d Battalion pushed its 9th Company across the Matanikau by sundown of October 7. The 1st Battalion did not release its "Emergency Report" on the day's action until 1700; consequently it did not reach the regimental commander, Colonel Nakaguma, until 0300 the morning of October 8. This account depicted the 3d Company holding out and the 2d Company moving to its relief. In fact, the 3d Company survivors had their backs against the Matanikau and the 2d Company's efforts to reinforce them were stymied by the complex terrain, the fast flow of the Matanikau, and heavy American fire, which killed and wounded many, including the company commander. Nakaguma commanded the 1st Battalion to check the enemy at the Matanikau and the 2d Battalion to cross to the east side of the one-log bridge to encircle the Americans along the coast after dawn. The Cactus Air Force received a major reinforcement this day of eleven P-39s, two TBFs, and two J2Fs,[2] but proved unable to stop five destroyers from landing another 600 men, two regimental guns, ammunition, and provisions at Tassafaronga that night.

Torrential rain on October 8 made all inclined areas slippery and all flat areas adhesive. Thus midafternoon arrived before the leading elements of the Whaling Group and the 7th Marines reached the crest of the ridge on the west bank of the Matanikau, a mile south of Point Cruz. During the last hours of daylight, action developed as the 3d Battalion, 2d Marines sought to clear the west bank of the river north of the crossing site and the 2d Battalion, 5th Marines (2/5) on the east bank advanced to assist them and cross the river. From this small skirmish, writer John Hersey crafted one of the classic vignettes of a small-unit action in World War Two.

Company H (Captain Charles A. Rigaud) of 2/5 descended the eastern slopes of the valley eroded by the Matanikau toward the first fork. Just before the company reached the river, there was the characteristic "high flat snap" of a single shot from a Japanese rifleman. From that moment onward, a barrage of sounds and images assaulted Hersey. Machinegun bursts punctuated a "constant fabric" of rifle fire woven with the blast of mortar shells: "a thump which vibrated not just your eardrums, but your entrails." Each roar of a mortar round was "a word spoken by death."

The men of this veteran heavy weapons company immediately comprehended that they were trapped on low ground, unable to effectively employ their principal weapons, and surrounded by the Japanese. To the Americans in the valley it appeared as if they had walked into a planned ambush. In reality, Company H simply stumbled between the 9th Company, 4th Infantry Regiment on the east bank and the rest of its parent 3d Battalion firmly ensconced on the

---

[2]The J2F was a biplane amphibian that was very useful for retrieving downed aircrew, but was not a combat plane.

west bank. The marines recognized that many of them could die in this valley and their deaths would purchase no advantage for their comrades or their country.

The eyes of the men near Hersey began to dart back along the trail down which they had entered the valley, and Hersey sensed this as the first symptom of an "epidemic" of fear. "The next sign of the growing fear," noted Hersey, "was the way men started moving around. When a mortar shell would go off nearby, they would scramble away from the vicinity to new cover, as if the thing could explode a second time."

Then as Hersey watched wide-eyed, the situation teetered toward a rout:

The marines had been deeply enough indoctrinated so that even flight did not wipe out the formulas, and soon the word came whispering back along the line:

"Withdraw."

"Withdraw."

"Withdraw . . ."

Then they started moving back, slowly at first, then running wildly, scrambling from place of cover to momentary cover.

. . . I had a hopeless desire to do something to stop the flight. It seemed wrong. . . .

[But] I couldn't do anything about it because I was caught up in the general feeling. It is curious how this feeling communicated itself. Except for a hard knot which is inside some men, courage is largely the desire to show other men that you have it. And so in a large group, when a majority have somehow signaled to each other a willingness to quit acting, it is very hard not to quit. The only way to avoid it is to be put to shame by a small group of men to whom this acting is life itself, and who refuse to quit; or by a naturally courageous man doing a brave deed. . . .

It was at this moment that [Captain] Charles Alfred Rigaud . . . showed himself to be a good officer and grown man.

Despite snipers all around us, despite the machine guns and the mortar fire, he stood right up on his feet and shouted out: "Who in Christ's name gave that order?"

This was enough to freeze men in their tracks. They threw themselves on the ground, in attitudes of defense; they took cover behind trees from both the enemy and the anger of their captain.

Next, by a combination of blistering sarcasm, orders and cajolery, he not only got men back into position: he got them in a mood to fight again.

"Where do you guys think you're going?" he shouted. And: "Get back in there. . . . Take cover, you. . . . What do you guys do, just invent orders? . . . Listen, it's going to be dark and we got a job to do. . . . You guys make me ashamed. . . ."

But the most telling thing he said was: "Gosh, and they call you marines."

Having regained control of his company, Rigaud sent a runner to the battalion commander, Major McDougal, explaining his situation and requesting permission to withdraw. Without waiting for a reply, Rigaud began to pull his men back. It was just as well—McDougal lay mortally wounded by a mortar shell.

Even before the action involving Company H, Marine commanders realized the Whaling Group and the 7th Marines could not complete the envelopment on the 8th. Therefore, they postponed the main attack for one day—reluctantly, as they feared this would enable the Japanese to redispose their forces to meet the flank attack, or to pull back out of the trap. But lacking an understanding of the actual situation, the Japanese did neither. Maruyama did not substantively intervene in the conduct of the action, and Nasu spared only enough time from future planning to exhort the 4th Infantry Regiment to hold the Matanikau and the one-log bridge. Colonel Nakaguma marched and countermarched his 2d Battalion to meet a fictitious landing along the coast.

At dusk, action flared again near the mouth of the Matanikau. The survivors of the 3d Company under First Lieutenant Ito attempted to break out of their pocket against the river and cross the sandbar. The Japanese advanced behind a smoke screen, striking Company A of the 1st Raiders. Barbed wire broke the momentum of the effort, which became a fierce, confused, hand-to-hand fight that left ten marines and thirty-six Japanese dead in Company A's positions. Very few of the 3d Company succeeded in crossing the river.

During the 8th, the Marine command received intelligence reports, probably based upon radio patterns and aerial reconnaissance, portraying the Japanese as poised to launch an all-out attempt to recapture the island. Accordingly, Vandegrift elected to terminate the operations of units west of the Matanikau the next day and withdraw them through the positions of the 5th Marines on the river. It was thought that these delays and limitations would enable the Japanese to withdraw their forces before the threatened envelopment. But Maruyama and Nasu were badly informed about the progress of the fighting over the last two days (for example, they believed a wholly erroneous report of an American landing west of Point Cruz on the 8th) and remained fixed on holding the Matanikau and recapturing positions on the east bank. Consequently, the volley of orders they issued on October 8 assured that two battalions of the 4th Infantry Regiment and the 1st Battalion, 29th Infantry Regiment remained facing the Matanikau while the 2d Battalion, 4th Infantry Regiment faced Point Cruz as Marine battalions massed to strike them in the flank and rear on October 9.

The Japanese also completed an important leadership change on October 8. During August, Admiral Tsukahara, the commander of the 11th Air Fleet, successively developed malaria and then dengue fever. He reported his ill health to Yamamoto on September 28, and the Commander of the Combined Fleet decided that Tsukahara must be replaced with the approach of a critical phase of the campaign. Accordingly, Vice Admiral Jinichi Kusaka left his job as Commandant of the Naval Academy at Eta Jima and arrived in Rabaul on this date to take charge of the 11th Air Fleet.

The Tokyo Express executed an important run on the night of October 8–9 with seaplane carrier *Nisshin* loaded with six antiaircraft guns, two 10cm howitzers, one tractor, and 180 men, and four destroyers carrying eighteen mortars and 560 men of the 4th Maizuru Special Naval Landing Force. *Nisshin* enjoyed the close escort of antiaircraft destroyer *Akizuki,* and the 11th Air Fleet scheduled two major air operations to cover her. Weather defeated the first effort, a raid on Henderson Field. The second effort involved an attempt to move fifteen Zeros to Buin to afford the seaplane carrier direct air cover, but seven of the fighters were heavily damaged on landing. Seven SBDs, four TBFs, and eleven Wildcats intercepted the Japanese vessels 140 miles from Guadalcanal and tangled with an aggressive float plane escort. The Japanese rescued two crews from three downed float planes. The Americans secured no hits and paid for their efforts with a Wildcat, whose pilot survived, and an SBD, whose crew did not.

After successfully disgorging their cargo, the Japanese ships raced 150 miles up the Slot before nine SBDs and six P-39s appeared at 0655 on the morning of October 9. The P-39 pilots claimed three of five float planes encountered and the SBD pilots one hit, not confirmed by Japanese records. One SBD failed to return.

That same morning the Marine attack jumped off under clear skies behind heavy artillery and air bombardment that caused many Japanese casualties. The Whaling Group moved handily along the ridgeline west of the Matanikau and reached the shore at the western end of the sandbar before noon. Keeping pace on Whaling's left, Lieutenant Colonel Hanneken's 2d Battalion, 7th Marines ambled down a parallel ridgeline and helped lever the surviving Japanese away from the Matanikau. Hanneken encountered resistance near Matanikau village, but a flanking movement with one company enabled him to gain Point Cruz.

On the far left, Puller's 1st Battalion, 7th Marines was echeloned back as the flank guard. Upon cresting the high ground overlooking the coast, Puller found the 2d Battalion, 4th Infantry Regiment in a wooded ravine to his front and left. Calling for artillery concentrations to his front, Puller artfully added the fire of his mortars to his left to create a "machine for extermination." Unable to withstand the rain of high-explosive shells or attack Puller through them, the trapped Japanese attempted to escape by climbing the opposite slope of the ravine. As they ran up the barren hillside, direct machinegun and rifle fire raked them, and the survivors sagged back into the ravine until the shelling drove them to repeat the attempt with the same results. Only after expending his mortar ammunition did Puller stop the action and withdraw down the coast to cross the Matanikau, as had Whaling and Hanneken ahead of him.

The cost to the marines for this highly successful three-day operation totaled sixty-five dead and 125 wounded. Although they knew Japanese losses were much more severe, the marines believed that the bulk of the Japanese forces they sought to trap escaped. In fact, the offensive mauled the 4th Infantry Regiment. An officer's diary captured later reported that the regiment lost no fewer than 690 men in this action.

As the men of the Whaling Group and the 7th Marines stepped onto the beaches near Point Cruz, a fighter sweep of twenty-seven Zeros reached Guadalcanal seeking to clear the air for another large "Express." An equal number of Wildcats and eight P-39s climbed to meet them, but in the sandwich layers of clouds the only Americans who saw the Japanese were radar operators. One Wildcat disappeared—because of oxygen failure, it was believed—but was replaced many times over when Major Leonard Davis led in twenty Wildcats of VMF-121. The Cactus Air Force also gained five more SBDs and three TBFs.

No American air strike interrupted the voyage to Guadalcanal that night of light cruiser *Tatsuta* and seven destroyers laden with 400 men of the 4th Maizuru Special Naval Landing Force and 770 soldiers, including no less a personage than Lieutenant General Hyakutake, commander of the 17th Army, and his staff. During the morning of October 10, *Tatsuta* and her five destroyers became the subject of the attentions of a strike of fifteen SBDs, six TBFs, fifteen

Wildcats, and eight P-39s, the largest yet mounted by the Cactus Air Force. Two float Zeros and two float observation planes of the R Area Air Force circling over the formation were all shot down valiantly but vainly trying to halt the American attack. Nonetheless, only destroyer *Nowaki* suffered from the unimpressive American bombing, losing eleven killed and wounded. One P-39 and one SBD were lost.

The destruction of the four float planes left the R Area Air Force without a single operational aircraft. Stretched thin by the mission of affording dawn and dusk coverage for Tokyo Express runs and by the need to guard Shortland, the R Area Air Force commenced the month of October at only 60 percent of its authorized complement of aircraft. Because float planes by their very nature are more delicate than land-based aircraft, operational strength was even less. Recorded losses for the first ten days of the month numbered eight.

Hyakutake had no sooner stepped ashore than a staff officer of the 2d Division greeted him with the stunning news of the loss of the Japanese position on the east bank of the Matanikau and the "total annihilation" of 4th Infantry Regiment. On October 10, Hyakutake established his headquarters in a valley about two miles west of Kokumbona and received more shocking reports. The Guadalcanal garrison obtained only about one-half the necessary amount of provisions, and that fact, coupled with transportation difficulties on the island, left Kawaguchi's command near death from starvation. Hyakutake immediately halted the movement of more men to Guadalcanal in favor of food and ammunition for shelling the airfield. This order did not affect the Tokyo Express run of this date, which saw three destroyers deposit another 293 mouths and ammunition at Tassafaronga.

The impact of the loss of the line of the Matanikau, and especially the assembly and artillery positions on its east bank, can scarcely be exaggerated, as they were the very crux of the operations plan for the October offensive. Seventeenth Army Headquarters emitted several signals describing the new situation and urging that the convoy be fought through regardless of whether or not an artillery bombardment neutralized American air power on Guadalcanal. Lieutenant Colonel Tsuji sent his report straight to Tokyo, where Lieutenant General Tanabe of the Operations Division of the Army Section of Imperial General Headquarters noted in his diary that the loss of the Matanikau position was a very bad omen for the October offensive.

While the major forces on both sides clashed around the Matanikau, to the east the marines launched another foray. Native reports pinpointed a radio-equipped Japanese outpost at Gurabusu, a village about 30 miles east of the Marine perimeter. Five miles west of this location at Koilotumaria were said to be a concentration of between one and two companies of Japanese survivors of actions east of the perimeter. Lieutenant Colonel Robert E. Hill of the 1st Battalion, 2d Marines on Tulagi drew the mission of destroying both these enemy positions.

At 1540 on October 9, two YP boats set out to tow eight Higgins boats loaded with four officers and 430 of Hill's men to Aola, but suffered misfortune. One Higgins boat came apart under the strain of the tow, and three sailors, one Marine officer, and fourteen men drowned. The boats arrived piecemeal between 0100 and noon of October 10, by which time Hill feared the loss of surprise. He elected to move immediately to attack Koilotumaria by an overnight march with two companies while Company C under Captain Richard Y. Stafford dealt with Gurabusu at dawn the next day.

During the early-morning hours of October 11, Stafford's company encircled the somnolent Japanese detachment at Gurabusu and in a short, one-sided battle about 0830 killed thirty-two of the garrison. Only two Japanese escaped, but one of the few return shots killed Captain Stafford. The natives identified one of the dead Japanese as Ishimoto, the former shipwright–intelligence agent who had played a major role in the Japanese occupation and the early efforts to attack the Marine position. In his exertions to win over native allegiance to Japan, Ishimoto used both verbal and more dire forms of persuasion. Evidence of the latter was found at Gurabusu in the form of the vestments, altar cloths, chalice, and patten from the Roman Catholic mission at Ruavatu. Ishimoto had summoned two priests and two nuns from the mission to Tasimboko and held them prisoner. On September 3 he had them murdered.

As a result of the unexpectedly difficult terrain, Hill's unit did not reach Koilotumaria until about 1600. By that time the Japanese there, perhaps having heard the sound of firing at Gurabusu, had fled south into the swamps. The marines killed the three Japanese present, including one officer, at a cost of one dead and one wounded. Hill returned to Tulagi on October 12, on the eve of an event every American on Guadalcanal would always remember.

12

THE BATTLE

OF CAPE

ESPERANCE

"What are we going to do, board them?"

PREPARATIONS FOR A NIGHT CHALLENGE

The early termination of the action west of the Matanikau yet again illustrated the sparsity of American forces on Guadalcanal. Admiral Ghormley saw the necessity for reinforcements; he did not see from where they would come. During his September inspection, Nimitz admonished Ghormley to "roll up" rear areas to free troops for Guadalcanal. But Ghormley remained concerned, if not obsessed, about the potentially disastrous consequences of a Japanese thrust to the sea lanes from the United States to Australia. Further, Ghormley remained under orders to seize Ndeni in the Santa Cruz Islands and inquiries from both King and Nimitz during September showed this task had not slipped from their minds. Closer at hand, Admiral Turner used his formidable powers of persuasion to incessantly advance schemes to occupy Ndeni using various combinations of Marine or Army units. Succumbing to these pressures, on September 29 Ghormley announced his intention to occupy Ndeni with part of the 8th Marines.

This decision was an alarm bell for General Harmon. On October 6 he penned a letter to Ghormley brimming with trenchant insight and prescribing a sound course of action. Harmon expressed his "personal conviction" that the Japanese could retake Guadalcanal and would do so "in the near future unless it is materially strengthened." He branded Ndeni "a diversion from the main effort and [a] dispersion of force" and emphasized: "If we do not succeed in holding [Guadalcanal] our effort in the Santa Cruz [islands] will be a total waste—and loss." The Army general urged the immediate reinforcement of Guadalcanal with at least one regiment, efforts to refine Henderson Field, and, in a tactful phrase, "the intensification, as means and conditions permit, of naval surface action in South Solomons waters."

After a conference with Harmon and Turner on the evening of October 6, Ghormley reaffirmed his intention to secure an airfield site on Ndeni, now using Army troops. But swayed by Harmon's logic, the admiral ordered immediate shipment of an infantry regiment to Guadalcanal. On the morning of October 8, the 164th Infantry Regiment of the Americal Division began loading aboard transports *Zeilin* and *McCawley* at Noumea. The transports sortied the following morning with three destroyers and three destroyer minelayers in attendance and set course to pass north of San Cristobal, thence through Lengo Passage to Lunga Roads, arriving on the morning of October 13.

Ghormley did not expect the Japanese to passively abide the approach of the convoy, so he deployed most of the available naval strength in the South Pacific in its support. Carrier *Hornet* lent air cover, and a task unit built around battleship *Washington* cruised east of Malaita shielding the right flank of the convoy. Rear Admiral Norman Scott's Task Force 64 of four cruisers and five destroyers drew the job of protecting the convoy from the west and of destroying Japanese forces moving to bombard or to reinforce Guadalcanal.

Norman Scott quietly accepted his mission, which carried with it two implicit tasks: development of a doctrine for night surface actions by cruiser-destroyer groups and revenge for the humiliation off Savo Island. Scott understood that the enemy excelled in night battle, although he was spared full knowledge of the extent of Japanese superiority: in nocturnal clashes to date they had sunk eight Allied cruisers and three destroyers without loss of a single ship. Scott recognized that he faced the twin handicaps of two decades of shortcomings in training and constant change in the composition of his task unit. Therefore he crafted a simple battle plan around the attainable rather than the desirable. His ships would steam in a column with destroyers ahead and astern of the cruisers. Destroyers would illuminate targets with searchlights as soon as possible after radar contact and discharge torpedoes at large enemy vessels and gunfire at small ones. Cruisers would open fire when they had a target without awaiting orders, and their float planes would be used to find and illuminate the enemy. If the Japanese proved strong in destroyers, the force would divide to present a smaller target to torpedoes. Scott exercised his command in these tactics and conducted a small but valuable amount of night firing practice.

The one serious deficiency in Scott's calculations was his selection of a flagship. Heavy cruisers *Salt Lake City* and *San Francisco* were nominally his most powerful units, and Scott hoisted his flag in the latter. However, the mastheads of both these vessels supported only metric-wave SC search radars of much inferior performance to that of the newer centimetric SG radars sported by both his light cruisers, *Helena* and *Boise*. To make matters worse, radio intelligence experts erroneously credited the Japanese with receivers capable of picking up radio emissions on the SC radar frequencies. Because such detection would occur well before the radars picked up return echoes from enemy ships, the advantage of the use of radar would be reversed.[1] Accordingly, Scott ordered all SC radars switched off during the approach to action and authorized the employment only of SG radars and the very narrow-beamed (and thus difficult-to-detect) fire control radars to supplement visual search for the foe. Because of the erratic performance of the SC radar, the American admiral did not regard its loss as grave, and as he was ignorant of the enormous improvement in technology represented by the SG radar, he did not switch his flag to one of his light cruisers.[2]

On October 9 and 10, Scott maneuvered his ships just beyond

[1]In very simple terms, the effective range of a radar depends upon how far out the radio wave it transmits can travel and still retain sufficient energy to "bounce back" to the radar receiver. Transmitted radio waves that fail to strike an object will continue on for a considerable distance and therefore can be picked up at great range by a suitably tuned receiver. This phenomenon is similar to the difference between the limited effective range of a searchlight and the great distance at which the light itself can be seen.

[2]Lest the reader doubt the perspicacity of Scott and his peers, it should be born in mind that the fitting of radar of any type in the United States Navy only began with six experimental sets in July and August 1940. SC radars began service with the fleet on a limited scale in the fall of 1941, and the process of general fitting of radar gained momentum only after Pearl Harbor. Thus, there had been only very restricted opportunity for any officer to develop understanding of the virtues and limitations of radar by October 1942. Moreover, as anyone who reads contemporary reports will readily see, the early sets were highly temperamental and prone to "phantom" contacts. The markedly superior SG radar sets were first fitted in April 1942, but excessive secrecy apparently masked their vast performance superiority.

range of enemy planes from Rabaul until noon before steaming north to the vicinity of Rennell Island by 1600. From there he could reach Savo Island by 2300 if the Japanese were operating that night, but on both of these days he turned back, as there was no word of enemy movements. On the 11th there was.

The multiply revised and accelerated Japanese reinforcement scheme dictated a singularly important run of the Tokyo Express on October 11. Seaplane carriers *Nisshin* and *Chitose* would lift to Tassafaronga four 15cm howitzers with towing vehicles, two field guns and one antiaircraft gun, and an assortment of ammunition and equipment, plus 280 men. Five of their six escorting destroyers would add more deckloads of troops. In a separate operation, two destroyers would escort Rear Admiral Aritomo Goto's three heavy cruisers of Cruiser Division 6. They would deluge Henderson Field with 8-inch shells fitted with antiaircraft time fuses that would burst the projectiles aboveground and thus assure a wider scattering of fragments. The Combined Fleet fondly hoped this technique would devastate the Cactus Air Force. The Reinforcement Group would reach Guadalcanal far ahead of Goto, reflecting the unreserved Japanese confidence that no American vessel would dare challenge them at night.

The protection for the reinforcement unit was entrusted to the 11th Air Fleet. Fortunately for the Japanese, the completion of the airfield at Buin barely preceded the emasculation of the R Area Air Force. Thus its role of direct air cover in the Slot could be shifted to thirty of the previously underemployed "short-range" Zeros that migrated south from Rabual. The entire operational strength of the 11th Air Fleet in "long-range" Zeros and Bettys would indirectly support the reinforcement unit with a cleverly designed two-prong attack on Guadalcanal. First, a fighter sweep would draw the Americans up for an air battle, then when the Americans landed to refuel and rearm, a second wave of fighters and bombers would catch them on the ground.

Radar picked up the first Japanese formation of seventeen fighters at 1220, enabling the Americans to get aloft eight Navy and thirty-one Marine Wildcats and a dozen P-400s and P-39s of the 67th Fighter Squadron, but the fifteen Wildcats of VMF-121 never joined up and missed the action. In the cloudy skies above the Marine perimeter the opposing fighters brushed only lightly. The main punch of forty-five Bettys and thirty Zeros lost cohesion because of the weather and arrived piecemeal barely forty-five minutes after the first wave. This proved too early to catch the Americans back on the ground. When one group of eighteen Bettys dipped below the clouds to bomb, the

VMF-223 and 224 pilots pounced on the formation, claiming eight and crippling a ninth, which was claimed by a P-39. The Japanese fighter pilots claimed two American planes, and the Americans added claims for four Zeros to the bomber toll. Actual American losses were one Wildcat and one P-39 and its pilot; Japanese records report one Betty downed and three damaged but no Zero losses.

Although the raids of the 11th Air Fleet failed to crush the Cactus Air Force, they did help keep American attack planes away from the Reinforcement Group, which sailed serenely beneath relays of Buin-based Zeros. They did not prevent search planes from finding and reporting the *Nisshin* group as two "cruisers" and six destroyers, but no American airman saw Goto. Based upon these sightings, at 1607 Admiral Scott led his ships toward Guadalcanal for an interception. At sundown, Scott sent his men to General Quarters. About this same time, a small drama transpired that illuminates the value the Japanese attached to the mission of the Reinforcement Group. In order to assure fighter cover to the last possible moment, the last flight of six Zeros was under orders to remain on station until darkness and then ditch their planes and await pickup by destroyers. These pilots executed their instructions, but five of them were not recovered.

The composition and a comparison of the opposing forces are as follows:

COMPOSITION OF FORCES

1. JAPANESE

Bombardment Group
Rear Adm. Aritomo Goto (ComCrudiv 6)

CRUISERS:

Aoba	Capt. Yonejiro Hisamune
Furutaka	Capt. Araki Tsutau
Kinugasa	Capt. Masao Sawa

DESTROYERS:

Desdiv 11 (less 2 vessels with the Reinforcement Group)
  Fubuki
  Hatsuyuki

Reinforcement Group

SEAPLANE CARRIERS:

Nisshin
Chitose

DESTROYERS:

Desdiv 9	Desdiv 11	Unattached
Asagumo	Murakumo	Akizuki
Natsugumo	Shirayuki	
Yamagumo		

2. AMERICAN
Task Force 64
Rear Adm. Norman Scott

CRUISERS:

San Francisco	Capt. Charles H. McMorris
Boise	Capt. Edward J. Moran
Salt Lake City	Capt. Ernest G. Small
Helena	Capt. Gilbert C. Hoover

DESTROYERS:

Destroyer Squadron 12: Capt. Robert G. Tobin

Farenholt	Lt. Cdr. Eugene T. Seaward
Duncan	Lt. Cdr. Edmund B. Taylor
Laffey	Lt. Cdr. William E. Hank
Buchanan	Cdr. Ralph E. Wilson
McCalla	Lt. Cdr. William G. Cooper

The armament of the two sides was as follows:

	Guns					Torpedo Tubes	
	8″	6″	5″	4.7″	3.9″	2.4″	2.1″
American							
Cruisers	19	30	32	—	—	—	—
Destroyers	—	—	20	—	—	—	25
Total	19	30	52	—	—	—	25
Japanese: *							
Cruisers	18	—	—	12	—	24	
Destroyers	—	—	—	—	—	—	—
Goto's	—	—	12	—	—	18	—
Other	—	—	30	—	8	56	—
Total	18	—	42	12	8	98	—

*Excluding the seaplane carrier, which mounted ten 5-inch guns that were unsuitable for a surface action.

It may be seen that the gunnery balance favored Scott, while the Japanese enjoyed an even more marked superiority in torpedoes.

SCOTT CROSSES THE T, 2200–2400

In obedience to their admiral's instructions, each American cruiser had forwarded all but one of its float planes to Tulagi. Just before 2200 the task force launched three of them to sift the darkness off Guadalcanal for the Japanese. Immediately after *Salt Lake City*'s plane shot from its high perch, flares in its rear cockpit burst into flame and the SOC crashed into the sea, leaving a ring of fire that glowed brilliantly for several minutes. Witnesses grimly assumed this ring marked a pyre for the crew, but they survived. Some observers anguished that the mishap had revealed the American presence, but by great good fortune, the *Nisshin* group had just passed around the mountainous northwestern shoulder of Guadalcanal and consequently failed to see the fiery warning. *Helena* did not get the word to launch her plane and jettisoned it as a fire hazard.

Tall American bow waves subsided as task force speed fell to 20 knots at 2200, and a few minutes later prows came right to round the northwest tip of Guadalcanal. The night sky was clear except for recurrent scribbles of heat lightning in the northwest quadrant. The early moonset left no ambient light, and this fact, coupled with the lack of a sea horizon and the land backgrounds, rendered visibility poor. A mild breeze originated from the southeast, and moderate swells crinkled the sea. At 2233, Scott's ships amalgamated into battle formation: destroyers *Farenholt, Duncan,* and *Laffey* leading cruisers *San Francisco, Boise, Salt Lake City,* and *Helena,* followed by destroyers *Buchanan* and *McCalla.* Scott intended to place his ships athwart the course of the approaching enemy force of "two cruisers and six destroyers" as he steamed north, and if he gained no interception, to double back to the southward to make a run along the coast "to contact the enemy, if possible before he could effect a landing, but at any rate contact him."

Unbeknownst to Scott, he had already been discovered by the Japanese. Submarine *I-26* was lurking on the surface near Kamimbo Bay about 2122 when she sighted an American "cruiser" speeding north. Commander Minoru Yokota chose to dive his boat for an attack before making a report. By the time he resurfaced and began to issue his sighting signal, time slipped to about 2341, too late to be of use. Nor was this the only potential warning the Japanese received of Scott's presence. At 2220, *Nisshin* assured Admiral Goto, then barreling down the Slot at 30 knots through a series of rainsqualls, that all was clear. At 2245, Reinforcement Group sailors disburdening *Nisshin* and *Chitose* at Tassafaronga heard Scott's float planes, but they failed to report this to the bombardment force.

At 2250, *San Francisco*'s plane reported: "One large, two small vessels, one 6 miles from Savo off northern beach, Guadalcanal. Will investigate closer." The message mixed ambiguity with a surprise— calculations based upon the earlier aircraft sighting reports indicated the Japanese ships could not reach Savo before 2300. In order to keep Savo Island a comfortable 5 miles on the starboard beam, at 2308 Scott came to course 50 degrees. At 2330 the *San Francisco* plane amplified its report to locate the hostile vessels 16 miles east of Savo and 1 mile off the beach. But at this same moment, engine trouble forced down *Boise*'s plane, leaving Scott with only one of his four intended air sentinels.

In order to remain juxtaposed between a potential enemy approach from the northwest and the three vessels already reported, at 2333 Scott directed a course change by column movement to a heading of 230 degrees. Although the decision to turn southwest at this moment proved very fortunate, a communications failure initially disguised this fortune all too well. Ironically, while the TBS radio correctly disseminated the admiral's intentions to all other ships, an intercom relay up only one deck from where Scott stood was understood by the flagship's conning party as an order for a simultaneous turn. The three van destroyers began a column movement, but a startled Captain Moran of *Boise* witnessed the flagship also begin a swing to port. Moran faced a quandary: if he executed the order as issued he would follow the van destroyers, pitching the flagship out of formation, but if he followed the flagship, the three van destroyers would be spun from the column. Moran adhered to centuries of naval tradition and followed *San Francisco*.

At about the same time that Scott ordered his course change, Goto's ships emerged at 30 knots from a two-hour passage through a long tunnel of rainsqualls. Flagship *Aoba* led the Japanese cruisers in column, followed at 1,300-yard intervals by *Furutaka* and *Kinugasa*. Destroyers *Fubuki* and *Hatsuyuki* held screening stations 3,300 yards to *Aoba*'s starboard and port bow respectively.

Unknown to Scott, the radars on two of his cruisers detected Goto minutes before he directed the course change. At 2325, *Helena* gained her first contact, and by 2332 she plotted the Japanese formation distant 27,700 yards on course 120 degrees at 35 knots. Surpris-

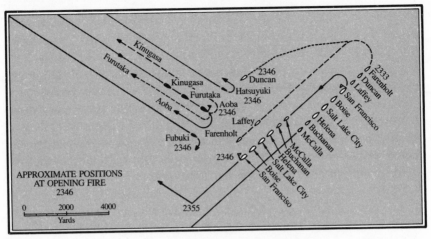

Battle of Cape Esperance, October 11

ingly, one of the much-maligned SC radars on *Salt Lake City* (whose operation violated Scott's orders) began warning of Goto at 2328. Captain Ernest Small trained *Salt Lake City*'s guns out as a precaution, but he attached such scant faith to the contact that he did not report it. As *Boise* commenced her countermarch at 2335, Goto appeared on her SG radar, but as on *Helena,* officers at first assumed that the flagship must have the contact—why else the course change?

At 2342, *Helena* reported surface vessels bearing 298 degrees true (i.e., to the northwest) and, in her radar plot, operators saw the Japanese in a T formation. This placed the Japanese on the starboard side of the now-southwesterly-steaming American formation, the opposite direction from the ships sighted near the beach. Two minutes later, *Boise* announced she had five "bogies" bearing 65 degrees. "Bogies" was a code word for unidentified aircraft, though *Boise* meant ships, and some ships did not pick up her clarifying comment that the bearing was relative, not true. The distinction was crucial: 65 degrees relative to the American column indicated she had probably the same contact as *Helena,* while 65 degrees true suggested a *third* group of enemy vessels somewhere off the port quarter to the northeast.

Not the least of those left uncertain of *Boise*'s meaning was Scott, who also suffered deep concern that the radar contacts might be the van destroyers. He interrogated Captain Robert G. Tobin, commander of Destroyer Squadron 12, in *Farenholt:* "Are you taking station ahead?" Tobin, thoroughly perplexed both about why he suddenly found himself out of formation and as to his admiral's intentions, took the query as a pointer to Scott's desires. The destroyer commander answered: "Affirmative, coming up on your starboard side," and suited his actions to his words, believing *Duncan* and *Laffey* would dutifully conform to the moves of *Farenholt*.

But at that moment *Duncan* launched a lonely charge at the Japanese formation. For several minutes before the countermarch, *Duncan*'s gunnery radar issued signs of Goto's presence. When *Duncan* turned, the contact became firm. Lieutenant Commander Taylor reached two quick conclusions: the Japanese were poised to strike the American column in its vulnerable turn, and Captain Tobin had recognized this and was jockeying *Farenholt* for a torpedo attack. Taylor acted on his instincts, and *Duncan*'s stern dug into the water as she leaped forward at 30 knots on an attack course. Lieutenant Commander Hank on *Laffey*'s bridge chose to follow *Farenholt*.

The time was 2345. *San Francisco*'s fire control radar finally located an unidentified contact only 5,000 yards to starboard, but on *Helena* no one doubted the identity of the formation closing to short range from the northwest. From somewhere on *Helena* came the provocative report "Ships visible to the naked eye," and down in radar plot an ensign impatiently demanded to the navigator, "What are we going to do, board them?" Captain Hoover could wait no longer. Although he had authorization to open fire without orders, it was only prudent to ask permission to commence fire, in view of the confusion about the location of Tobin's destroyers. Over the TBS, Hoover posed his request, using the General Signal Procedure message: "Interrogatory Roger," then he repeated it. Both times the reply came back "Roger." The admiral meant "Roger" as acknowledgment of receipt of the request, but an unqualified "Roger" also meant "Open fire" under the General Signal Procedure. Hoover exercised his option, and at 2346, *Helena*'s fifteen-gun main battery ruptured the night with flames and thunder.

The sudden ripple of gunfire up the American column caught Goto's ships unprepared and nearly unaware. At 2343, only three minutes before *Helena*'s guns spoke, Goto reduced speed to 26 knots just as *Aoba*'s lookouts made out three warship silhouettes 10,000 meters (almost 11,000 yards) away fine off the port bow. Goto thought they must be the Reinforcement Group and began sending the recognition signal. When the range spun down to about 7,000 meters, the lookouts exclaimed the shapes were enemy. While the flagship went to General Quarters, the admiral remained skeptical and ordered rudder left 10 degrees and a repetition of the identification signal. As *Aoba*'s helmsman began turning her to parallel the American course and forlorn sailors vainly flashed the recognition signal, the first American salvo smashed into her superstructure. Heavy-caliber projectiles perforated the flag bridge without exploding, but killed many men and mortally wounded Goto. Other shells disrupted all communications and demolished two 8-inch gun turrets and the main battery director.

Those shots probably came from *Boise,* whose main battery went into continuous rapid fire at *Aoba* a scant 4,500 yards distant. The Japanese flagship also initially attracted the 8-inch shells of *Salt Lake City* and *San Francisco* as well as the lighter 5-inch punches of *Farenholt,* over which the American cruisers fired. Likewise caught in the line of fire was *Laffey;* her skipper extracted her from this position by going back full emergency with his engines while swerving his vessel into the formation astern of *McCalla.* Three of *Laffey*'s guns snapped at *Aoba,* while the fourth tossed out illuminating rounds. *Helena* fired both her main and secondary batteries at ships to the right of *Aoba* that she identified as destroyers.

When the firing began, *Duncan* stood about a mile off *Aoba*'s port quarter. Lieutenant Commander Taylor noted Japanese guns still trained in as he swung his ship hard right to clear the American line of fire, but when he spotted *Furutaka* in a tempting position, Taylor reversed his helm to conduct a torpedo attack. Before *Duncan* could parallel the enemy vessel, however, it began swinging to starboard and increasing speed. *Duncan*'s guns brayed as she pursued, but the solitary destroyer quickly sustained a hit in her number one fireroom as she thrust into the waters between the two formations.

American guns were barely warm when at 2347 Scott ordered, "Cease firing our ships." Because of well-founded qualms about the whereabouts of a trio of his ships and without a radar to sort out the indistinct contours to starboard, the admiral feared the targets were not Japanese vessels but Tobin's destroyers. Scott personally visited his flagship's bridge to ensure her compliance with his order, but not all his captains heard—or cared to heed—his order, and the firing slackened but never stopped.

Once again on the TBS the admiral questioned Tobin: "How are you," to which Tobin replied he was all right.

"Are we shooting at [you]?" asked Scott.

"I do not know who you were firing at," replied Tobin.

Still not satisfied, Scott ordered Tobin's ships to flash their fighting lights. The glimmer of the appropriate small cluster of lights close off the starboard side of the flagship dispelled the admiral's doubts, and at 2351 he ordered fire resumed.

From the Japanese viewpoint, American fire hardly moderated

during this four-minute interval. *Aoba* coupled a turn to starboard with a speed increase, but hits continually rocked her, setting her alight and toppling her foremast. Only one turret in local control remained in action, and it discharged but seven shells. At 2350 she began to make smoke, which masked her fires and made some American observers think she had sunk. In her wake came *Furutaka,* which had been completely surprised when an arc of gun flashes appeared ahead. Captain Arake Tsutau immediately discerned the predicament into which Goto had stumbled with the Japanese T being crossed, and he shrewdly started *Furutaka* to port, which promised to take his ship quickly out of the deadly embrace of at least some of the American guns. But when Tsutau saw the flagship in deep distress, he gallantly turned *Furutaka* into her wake to relieve her. At 2149, *Furutaka* received many hits, and one minute later a shell struck the torpedo tubes, igniting a bright blaze that acted as a beacon for American gunners, the more so after *Aoba* began to shroud herself in smoke. Less gallantly, but more sensibly, Captain Masao Sawa immediately veered *Kinugasa* around to port as the action opened and saved his ship from damage. *Hatsuyuki* emulated this maneuver and escaped with only two hits that started a small leak.

During her firing lull, *San Francisco* tracked a ship closing to only 1,400 yards on a parallel course. This vessel, destroyer *Fubuki,* made indecipherable signals with a hooded light before she turned away only to be clutched in the shaft of a searchlight beam, revealing two white bands on her forward stack that unmistakably betrayed her nationality. Both *Boise* and *San Francisco* raked her with shellfire, as soon did most of the other American ships within range. The hapless destroyer burst into flames and began to sink.[3]

American naval officers felt great pride in the 6-inch guns on *Boise* and *Helena.* Each ship mounted five triple turrets; each turret could fire thirty or more rounds per minute. Both ships shifted aim from target to target, with devastating results. Less commendably, some of their firing was impartial. *Farenholt* found herself dangerously poised between the two formations when the battle opened. After Scott ordered the cease-fire for her benefit, her rigging snagged hits

---

[3]About 2354, *San Francisco* personnel sighted a destroyer off the starboard bow that blinkered signals and then crossed ahead and passed close aboard down the cruiser's port side. Admiral Scott reported that an American cruiser sank this vessel. The information available after the battle seemed to rule out the possibility that this "mystery ship" was either American or Japanese, and to this date the episode remains unresolved.

that sprayed fragments over her topsides, killing several men. A short time thereafter a shell, later identified as 6-inch in caliber (and therefore undoubtedly American), pierced her port side just above the waterline through an oil tank, producing a gusher of oil and water. A fragment from this hit nicked a steam line in number one fireroom, and a second hit forced its abandonment. With a 5-degree list to port, *Farenholt* retired from the action by crossing ahead of *San Francisco* and passing to the disengaged side of the American column.

About the same time that American shells drove *Farenholt* from the action, destroyer *Duncan* was curving in to launch torpedoes with her guns in full bay when shells blasted the gun director and wounded the torpedo officer after only one torpedo was away. Chief Torpedoman D. H. Boyd fired a second torpedo in local control. More shells tumbled the forward stack and torched number two 5-inch mount and its magazine. Remembering that his ship was in a cross fire, Taylor ordered the port fighting lights clicked on, but the lights no sooner came on than four shells from the direction of the American column entered *Duncan*'s hull and bridgework. With her rudder jammed hard left, *Duncan* began looping slowly clear of the battle area.

In the nine minutes remaining before midnight after Scott ordered firing resumed, all of his ships save *Farenholt* and *Duncan* joined in pummeling Goto's command, receiving only feeble return fire that did modest damage to *Boise*'s superstructure. American gunners found particularly irresistible the four vessels afire within their view: *Aoba, Furutaka, Fubuki,* and *Duncan.* Destroyer *Buchanan* launched five torpedoes at *Furutaka* about the same time as *Duncan,* and at 2358 one of them, or according to the Japanese report a salvo of shells, struck the Japanese heavy cruiser in her forward engine room. *Duncan* observers "saw" her "crumple in the middle, then roll over and disappear"; in fact, *Furutaka* collected over ninety hits above the waterline during the action and others below but kept on steaming. At 2354, Scott sent a message to Ghormley and Vandegrift: "Engaging heavy cruisers."

BOISE DAMAGED, BATTLE ENDS, 0000–0245

At midnight it seemed to Scott that "some shaking down was necessary in order to continue our attack successfully." He ordered fighting lights flashed and allowed about ten minutes to rectify his formation and then changed course to 280 degrees to pursue the enemy. "This concluded the first phase of the action," wrote the admiral.

At 0006, *Helena* and *Boise* spied torpedo wakes, compliments of *Kinugasa.* Captain Moran heeled *Boise* sharply to starboard, paralleling the wakes so that one just cleared the port bow as a second whined down the starboard side, missing the stern by about 30 yards. This was not *Kinugasa*'s last shot by any means. Both *Boise* and *Salt Lake City* employed searchlights to assist their gunners, but this also served to pinpoint their own locations. Further, *Boise*'s rapid salvos continuously bathed her in the light of her gun flashes. At 0009, *Kinugasa* began an exhibition of accurate Japanese gunnery. A typically very tight Japanese salvo pattern of 8-inch shells straddled *San Francisco*'s wake, then *Kinugasa* shifted targets to *Boise.* Captain Moran acknowledged the enemy cruiser was "shooting beautifully with twin 8-inch mounts" and straddling *Boise* forward repeatedly.

At 0010 an 8-inch shell struck number one barbette (the large armored cylindrical structure supporting a turret), jamming it and starting a smoky fire that prompted the turret officer to order it abandoned. Eleven men reached the main deck before a second 8-inch shell from *Kinugasa* penetrated the hull and exploded in the main magazine between turrets one and two. The combined detonation of the shell and exposed powder unleashed torrents of flaming gases that invaded all forward magazines, handling rooms, and gun rooms, except those of turret three, searing to death nearly a hundred men in those stations. Incandescent gases jetted from every aperture of the two foremost turrets, setting the forecastle afire and burning the men who had just emerged from turret one. "Smoke, debris, hot water and sparks flew up well above the level of the forward directors" and knocked the captain against a bulkhead. Scott feared *Boise* was lost. Moran, expecting his ship to disintegrate at any moment in one massive explosion, ordered the forward magazines flooded, but among those killed by the flames were the men at the remote flooding panel.

Two things saved *Boise* from destruction: the discipline of the men now dead in her forward magazines, whose faithful adherence to drills left only a minimum of exposed powder, and the rents in her hull from the enemy shell and the resulting explosion, which admitted an inundation of water to the core of the fire before it could ignite tons of protectively stored powder. To escape further punishment, Moran sheered *Boise* out of column to port and increased speed to 30 knots; the next enemy salvo landed short by only 50 to 100 yards.

The after 6-inch turrets continued to fire at the enemy for another two minutes before checking.[4]

Abaft of *Boise* was *Salt Lake City*. Captain Small valiantly conned his ship to interpose her between the enemy and *Boise,* and his gunners set their sights on *Kinugasa* while *San Francisco*'s guns dealt more blows to *Aoba*. In an indecisive duel, *Kinugasa* sustained perhaps a few of the only four hits she received in the action and the Japanese cruiser hit *Salt Lake City* twice. One 8-inch shell caused minor damage and the second burrowed into her framing, lost all momentum, and tumbled to the floor plates in front of a boiler. It exploded in a low-order detonation that killed one man and left others untouched only 6 feet away. This hit did cause a loss of steam that reduced *Salt Lake City*'s speed to 22 knots.

At 0016 Scott changed course to 330 degrees to press the enemy, but after a few more minutes of "desultory firing" that entirely ceased by 0020, he elected to retire, as the enemy was silenced and the American formation was "somewhat broken." He was also anxious to avoid having *San Francisco* mistaken for an enemy ship by vessels in the rear. All ships flashed fighting lights and turned to course 205 degrees to help keep identities straight. Unable to raise Captain Tobin in *Farenholt* or *Boise,* Scott sent *McCalla* to aid them. At 0044 he cautioned his command, "Stand by for further action. The show may not be over." But the main action was over.

While Scott thrashed Goto, the Reinforcement Group completed its business and retired, observed by the crew of *Boise*'s downed aircraft. Their parent ship had her forecastle fire out by 0019, but two turrets remained ablaze. Crewmen opened the hatches of one and ran hoses in, but bodies blocked the hatches of the other, so hoses had

---

[4]The shell that penetrated to *Boise*'s forward magazines was a distinctive Japanese development identified as the 91 Shiki (Type 91) AP Shell. During firing trials in 1924, Imperial Navy officers noted the particularly destructive effects of shells that landed just short of the target vessel and continued their trajectory underwater to pierce the hull. These either struck below the side armor or in lightly protected areas and caused extensive flooding. Research showed a blunt-nosed projectile gave best performance under these circumstances, so a whole family of "Diving Shells" were manufactured for every caliber from 8-inch up. (A pointed "ballistic cap" covered the blunt nose and maintained aerodynamic efficiency in flight through the air, but shattered on contact with the target or water.) So far as this writer is aware, this is the only instance during World War Two where a Type 91 shell worked as intended. American ordnance experts inspecting *Boise* figured out the characteristics of the Type 91 shell and observed that U.S. tests of this design revealed that the shell indeed maintained good underwater trajectory and possessed unusually good armor-piercing performance against light armor, but also that its efficiency was poor against any armor thickness over one-half the caliber of the shell.

The Joint Chiefs of Staff during the Guadalcanal campaign comprised, from left to right, Lieutenant General Henry H. ("Hap") Arnold, Admiral William D. Leahy, Admiral Ernest J. King, and General George C. Marshall. Leahy only joined the Joint Chiefs in July, by which time King and Marshall had ordered the Guadalcanal operation without apparent consultation with Arnold.

OPERATION WATCHTOWER

Vice Admiral Robert L. Ghormley, the first Commander South Pacific Area, a man of intellect and diplomacy, whose leadership, however, was found wanting.

Vice Admiral Frank Jack Fletcher commanded the Expeditionary Force to Guadalcanal, but his unilateral decision to withdraw the carriers marked the change in Allied fortunes.

Rear Admiral Richmond Kelly Turner (left) and Major General Alexander A. Vandegrift on the bridge of *McCawley* en route to Guadalcanal. Brilliant and dominating, Turner remained staunch through the dark hours of the campaign, but he gave the determined Vandegrift many exasperating hours.

This is the official portrait by Shugaku Homma of Admiral Isoroku Yamamoto, Commander Combined Fleet, and the Japanese leader with the best grasp of his country's strategic situation at the start of the war. At Guadalcanal, his direction faltered.

THE LANDINGS AUGUST 7–8, 1942

Marines come ashore on Guadalcanal from boats from *Barnett* on August 7, 1942.

Flames from a fuel dump burn on Tanambogo, probably in the morning of August 8, 1942. The causeway to Gavutu stretches off to the left.

AIR ATTACK, AUGUST 8, 1942

Four Bettys of the 4th Air Group make a low-level torpedo attack on American warships. The planes flew without bomb-bay doors when carrying a torpedo, hence the appearance of a notch in the belly of the planes.

NATIONAL ARCH

NAVAL HISTORICAL CENTER

This photograph illustrates how readily aviators could conclude that they were inflicting more damage than they actually were. The transport *George F. Elliot* blazes at left. The two other smoke columns, which look like they could be other stricken ships, probably represent where aircraft crashed.

A deadly Japanese 24-inch-diameter, Type 93, "Long Lance" torpedo, the finest weapon of its type in World War Two. This example was recovered from a reef off Point Cruz on Guadalcanal. It is shown here displayed outside "Main Navy," the building in Washington, D.C., where Admiral King worked.

BATTLE OF SAVO ISLAND, AUGUST 9, 1942

Vice Admiral Gunichi Mikawa, Imperial Japanese Navy, inflicted the most humiliating defeat in its history on the United States Navy.

A Japanese photographer, aboard *Furutaka*, *Yubari* or *Tenryu*, snapped this view of *Quincy* aflame and trapped by searchlight beams. *Quincy*'s outline is altered by fires and smoke. The flames to the left are presumably on *Vincennes* and the small fire or gun flash to the right is presumably on *Astoria*.

THE TENARU

Colonel Kiyoano Ichiki led the first Japanese ground reinforcements to Guadalcanal. His approach to Marine lines was discovered by native scouts, some of whom are seen here with their leader, Martin Clemens.

The fruits of Ichiki's assault: Japanese soldiers who fell on the beach in front of Marine positions west of Alligator Creek.

Sister ships *Zuikaku* and *Shokaku* formed the core of the Imperial Navy's carrier striking forces during the Guadalcanal campaign. This is *Zuikaku* on September 25, 1941.

This view captures the center of a bomb explosion at 1646 hours, August 24, 1942. The picture, looking down from the after end of *Enterprise*'s island, has often been incorrectly described as taken by Photographer's Mate Robert F. Read at the cost of his life. In reality, Read was dead when this event occurred as he was in the starboard after gun gallery, visible at the upper left, which had already been swept by bomb and powder explosions.

EDSON'S RIDGE

A marine gazes at some very shallow fighting positions scratched into a rise on Edson's Ridge. This view appears to be looking generally north and probably was taken on Hill 123. Note how the very heavy undergrowth encroaches closely on each side of the ridge.

Patrolling, like this detachment in August, was an integral part of Vandegrift's defense scheme but the quality of Marine patrols was a source of major concern. After an ambush of companies A and B, 1st Marines in the last stage of the Battle of Edson's Ridge, the Marine commander formed the Scout-Sniper detachment.

Henderson Field, the object of the entire campaign, from the southeast at the end of August. South of the far end of the field are the four hangers erected by the Japanese. Just north of the center of the field is the hill on which sits the "Pagoda" (inset), the operations center of the Cactus Air Force from August to October 13, 1942.

THE AIR CAMPAIGN

The caption of the original photograph of this Grumman F4F-4 Wildcat identifies this aircraft as the most successful of the many sent to Guadalcanal. The victory markings beside the cockpit represent the claims of the more than one pilot.

Four P-400s of the 67th Pursuit Squadron at Henderson Field. The lack of an efficient supercharger and an oxygen system incompatible with the available support equipment made these planes an insult to the brave and skilled men who flew them. To the Japanese soldiers, however, they became known as the "long-nosed planes" whose patrols made life hell for the Imperial Army.

This photograph, taken late in the campaign, shows Dauntless SBD dive-bombers at Henderson Field dispersals. The aircraft at the top right are PBYs, which were not stationed on the island in any numbers before late 1942.

Mitsubishi A6M2 Model 21 Zeros warm up on *Shokaku* on the morning of October 26, 1942, prior to take-off. Behind the Zeros are Aichi D3A1 Type 99 Vals.

This is "Aztec's Curse," a B-17F of the 11th Bomb Group in action off Gizo Island on October 5, 1942.

This November 1942 picture shows three important fliers who served on Guadalcanal. From left to right: Major John L. Smith, the commander of VMF-223; Lt. Col. Richard Mangrum, the leader of VMSB-232; and Captain Marion Carl of VMF-223.

Trailing a thin steam of smoke, a Japanese plane falls dramatically from the skies over Guadalcanal.

WASP LOST

An alert *Pensacola* photographer snapped this shot of the moment *O'Brien* was hit on September 15, 1942. *Wasp* burns in the background.

CHANGE OF
COMMAND

Admiral Chester W. Nimitz and the man he picked to be the second Commander South Pacific, Vice Admiral William F. Halsey. This photograph was taken in 1943 or 1944.

Heavy cruiser *San Francisco*, sistership of *Vincennes, Astoria* and *Quincy*, flagship at the Battle of Cape Esperance and the Battle of Friday the Thirteenth. She is seen here in December 1942 en route back for repairs. From her bridge the talented Rear Admiral Norman Scott (inset) won the Battle of Cape Esperance.

Farenholt flew the pennant of Captain Tobin at the Battle of Cape Esperance. Except for her very unusual "snakeskin" camouflage scheme, she is typical of the ships of Destroyer Squadron 12 that fought at Guadalcanal.

THE BATTLE OF HENDERSON FIELD

A marine enjoys domestic life on Guadalcanal. He cleans his Springfield M1903 rifle in front of his shelter, probably erected during the great October "housing boom." By the middle of the month, after "the Bombardment" and the "High-Speed Convoy," most marines were wondering where the fresh Japanese forces were.

The answer to the marines' question was here, on a long approach march through the dense tropical jungle south of the perimeter. This image shows typical rain forest on Guadalcanal, towering over a jeep and three marines.

The reason for the deep Japanese sweep into the jungle in October, and much grief in their efforts, was superior Marine firepower. Here is the principal weapon of the 11th Marines, a 75mm pack howitzer. The lean shape of the crewmen indicates this photograph was taken in September or October.

The Imperial Army employed the 1st Independent Tank Company in the October drive for Henderson Field. Here are five vehicles knocked out on the sandbar at the Matanikau. The tank to the left is a Type 95 light, as is the one second from right; the other three are Type 97 mediums.

THE BATTLE OF THE SANTA CRUZ ISLANDS, OCTOBER 24, 1942

This well-known shot shows a Val seconds away from crashing into *Hornet*'s island. A Kate is passing horizontally above the ship forward as aircraft strafing pelts the waters off her starboard side. Wisps of smoke on the after portion of the flight deck mark where bombs have already hit.

This image, faded and scratched, is nonetheless remarkable. The Kate boring in toward *Hornet*'s island at center has just dropped a torpedo, whose splash into the water is at the right. This weapon will strike *Hornet* at 1523 hours and finish chances of saving her.

Atlanta, a great ship, anchored in the South Pacific shortly before her loss. Visible are seven of her eight twin 5-inch guns mounts. Her sister ships included *San Juan*, *San Diego*, and the ill-fated *Juneau*.

Enterprise operating under a sky filled with antiaircraft fire at Santa Cruz. Two Japanese planes can just be made out above and forward of the ship; a third plane is splashing into the water astern. In the center of the picture is a destroyer (steaming to the left), and *South Dakota*, which has just fired.

HE NAVAL BATTLE OF GUADALCANAL, NOVEMBER 12–15, 1942

The five Sullivan brothers early in 1942. From left to right: Joseph (age 24), Francis (27), Albert (20), Madison (23), and George (28).

Washington in August 1942 in the rig she fought in at Guadalcanal and (inset) Rear Admiral Willis Augustus Lee, Jr., victor in the action of November 14–15, 1942. Behind the steel-rimmed glasses was a cool, incisive mind remarkably knowledgeable about radar.

The end of the voyage for *Yamura Maru,* a member of the November convoy. Despite her load of troops and munitions and her armament, she is still in her peacetime livery. Admiral Nobutake Kondo (inset) and Admiral Chuichi Nagumo were the principal sea-going Imperial Navy officers during the Guadalcanal campaign.

THE BATTLE OF TASSAFARONGA, NOVEMBER 30, 1942

Rear Admiral Raizo Tanaka, commander of Destroyer Squadron 2 and the Reinforcement Group at key passages during the Guadalcanal campaign. He was the victor at Tassafaronga, but, ironically, many of his own countrymen held him in less esteem than his American adversaries.

Photographs pertaining to the night actions off Guadalcanal are very rare and most are either before- or after-the-battle shots. This is *Pensacola* after the Battle of Tassafaronga. The darkened area along her waterline below the burned-out mainmast is where a torpedo struck her.

THE FINAL OFFENSIVE

These soldiers are wrestling forward supplies via the "U Pusha Maru" line up the Matanikau River. This is part of the elaborate and imaginative logistical grid that supported the 25th Infantry Division's attacks in January 1943.

Death in the tropics, in this case a Japanese soldier on January 25, 1943.

LAST SHOTS

The 78-foot Elco PT boats were the standard equipment of most American motor torpedo boat units at Guadalcanal. Here the crew of *PT 65* inspects the wreck of *I-1*.

Louisville (right) tows crippled *Chicago* on the morning of January 30, 1943. In the distance is a *Fletcher* Class destroyer.

As James Jones intimated, Guadalcanal represented a key passage for a generation raised in economic depression and political disarray. This evocative, though posed, shot shows a battle-roughened young soldier on Guadalcanal. He is presumably a member of the U.S. Army and not a marine by virtue of the fact that he grips an M-1 rifle, not an M1903 Springfield.

to be threaded up the expended case scuttles. By 0240 all fires were out and holes in her hull plugged. At 0305, *Boise* joined the task group, making 20 knots. Captain Moran felt just pride in his crew, tempered by sadness over the deaths of 107 officers and men and injury to twenty-nine others. *Farenholt,* escorted by the newly arrived *Aaron Ward,* made her way back to Noumea with three dead and thirty-six wounded.

Despite over forty hits, *Aoba* joined *Kinugasa* in retirement to the north. Goto lay mortally wounded, and his chief of staff, Captain Kikunori Kijima, succeeded to command. He told Goto he could die "with an easy mind" because two American heavy cruisers had been sunk. *Furutaka* was not so fortunate. Not quite half an hour after firing stopped, she lost power. Destroyer *Hatsuyuki* came to render assistance, but there was nothing effective for her to do. Progressive flooding from multiple hits below the waterline sank *Furutaka* at 0228 with 258 crewmen 22 miles northwest of Savo Island.

We last saw *Duncan* spinning out of the battle to the northeast. Lieutenant Commander Taylor found himself completely isolated on the bridge with raging fires ahead, behind, and below. He finally ordered the remaining bridge survivors off, by the only route now available—over the side. With the fires closing in and exploding 20mm ammunition adding its pyrotechnics, Taylor followed the executive officer over the side about 0130 and painfully watched his blazing command stagger away. Aft of number one fireroom, *Duncan* was not appreciably damaged, and her crew rallied to prevent her loss, but the flames marched relentlessly down her length. As exploding ammunition tossed debris aft, the order was given to abandon *Duncan.* The last man left about 0200.

DAYLIGHT CODA AND COMMENT

Sunrise found Scott's unit, except for *Duncan* and *McCalla,* heading for Noumea under a protective air umbrella the admiral had thoughtfully requested. Japanese search planes failed to locate him, and weather foiled a big raid of forty-one Bettys with Zero escort. *McCalla* scoured the waters lately churned by men-of-war for *Boise* or her survivors until attracted by a burning hull that could not be identified. She dropped a boat to examine the hulk at 0300 and proceeded to look for *Boise.*

The eight-man crew of the boat, under Lieutenant Commander F.B.T. Myhre, approached to within 200 yards of the vessel without being able to recognize her. From this distance Lieutenant (jg) G. T. Weems swam to a position where he could make out the large white numerals "485" representing *Duncan*'s hull number on her stern. After briefly boarding the abandoned destroyer and finding a blaze threatening her magazine, Myhre took his party off again until daylight. When the sky was light, Myhre reboarded *Duncan* to find the fire had abated, but mute evidence of its severity was readily visible—everything but the hull structure itself had melted. His small party energetically began plugging holes and moved the hand-billy pump forward to fight the remaining fire. At 1100, as Myhre's party paused to consume some well-earned rations, a sharp report followed by rumbling warned of a bulkhead collapse. By 1200 the inrush of seawater left the main deck awash and Myhre abandoned her. *Duncan* clung to life for a time but finally sank, 6 miles north of Savo Island.

As Myhre fought to save *Duncan,* aircraft and boats from Guadalcanal gave *McCalla* an edge in a competition with sharks for her survivors. Eventually 195 *Duncan* sailors survived; forty-eight of their shipmates did not. In the course of her work, *McCalla* also encountered *Fubuki* survivors. The Japanese stoutly refused thrown lines; *McCalla* sailors secured three swimmers by force. The following day, minesweepers *Trevor* and *Hovey* used press-gang tactics to compel another 108 Japanese to accept American hospitality for the duration. The Reinforcement Group rescued a further eight crewmen from *Fubuki,* making a total of 119 survivors from a nominal complement of 197.

Admiral Mikawa received word of the action at midnight. He concluded from reports that only *Furutaka* was in distress, but that the Reinforcement Group was endangered. Consequently he ordered Cruiser Division 6 to attack and destroy the enemy. In no condition to comply with this directive, *Aoba* continued trundling toward the Shortland, which she reached about 1000, and *Hatsuyuki,* bearing *Furutaka* survivors, soon joined her. The unmolested Reinforcement Group cleared the battle area, but the captain of *Nisshin* detached destroyers *Shirayuki* and *Murakumo* to tend to *Furutaka* or her survivors. He also directed destroyers *Asagumo* and *Natsugumo* to rendezvous with *Kinugasa,* which had put about to cover the withdrawal of the Reinforcement Group.

At 0700, five American planes attacked *Kinugasa,* and although she escaped damage, their efforts dissuaded her from proceeding farther south. Eleven other SBDs led by Lieutenant Colonel Cooley found *Shirayuki* and *Murakumo* at 0820. The dive-bombers scored no hits, but an oil tank on *Murakumo* began weeping oil. A second American strike group of seven VS-71 and VMSB-141 SBDs under Lieutenant Commander Kirn and six VT-8 TBFs under Lieutenant H. H. Larsen escorted by fourteen Wildcats of VMF-121 and VMF-224 under Major John Dobbin found the two Japanese destroyers 170 miles from Guadalcanal. In an expertly coordinated attack, strafing fighters deterred antiaircraft gunners, SBDs blanketed both vessels with near-misses, and a TBF managed to get a torpedo hit on *Murakumo*'s engineering spaces, leaving her without power.

Learning of *Murakumo*'s plight, *Asagumo* and *Natsugumo* hastened to her aid. Another attack group of eleven SBDs and one TBF convoyed by eight Wildcats and four P-39s found the three healthy Japanese destroyers circling their stricken sister at 1545. The strike leader, Lieutenant Commander John Eldridge, placed his bomb just aft of amidships on *Natsugumo,* and two near-misses contributed to her severe flooding. After *Asagumo* took off survivors, *Natsugumo* sank at 1627 with her captain and sixteen of her crew. Other bombs ignited fires on *Murakumo,* and after taking off survivors less twenty-two shipmates already lost, *Shirayuki* scuttled her with a torpedo.

In this action, material Japanese losses totaled one heavy cruiser, three destroyers, and at least 565 men.[5] But the most painful damage was to the pride of the Imperial Navy in its superiority in night fighting. Claims of sinking two American cruisers and one destroyer did not save Captain Kijima, Goto's chief of staff, from immediate relief. Captain Tsutau of *Furutaka* entertained the Combined Fleet staff on October 16 with an explanation of the loss of his ship. He apportioned blame between faulty air reconnaissance and the landbound staff of the 8th Fleet, which, he said, in the time-honored

[5]Japanese losses are broken down as follows:

	Killed	*Prisoners*
Furutaka	258	
Aoba	79	
Fubuki	circa 78	111
Murakumo	22	
Natsugumo	17	
Total:	454	111

cliché, did not understand the situation. The list of obvious mistakes is strikingly similar to those of the Allies at Savo Island: faulty air reconnaissance, failure to recognize clues of the enemy's presence (those float planes again), delayed communications (*I-26*'s report), and a woeful lack of readiness in every Japanese vessel—apparently not one was fully closed up for action when *Helena* opened fire. The 8th Fleet garners a portion of the blame for its plan, which let the Reinforcement Group precede Goto, creating an atmosphere of complacency over the danger of American intervention by sea. But the fundamental cause was again a "fatal lethargy of mind," this time on the part of Goto. It was his responsibility to have his ships ready for action, and it was his disbelief in his lookout's reports that enabled Scott to take him by surprise. On hearing the story of this battle, Admiral Ugaki, chief of staff of the Combined Fleet, wrote in his diary that carelessness was the Japanese undoing and that Goto should have followed the Japanese proverb "Treat a stranger as a thief."

In contrast, Scott's victory sent American spirits soaring. His initial appraisal of his captain's reports indicated three Japanese cruisers and four destroyers were sunk, but Scott added, "This estimate may be on the optimistic side," a judgment shared by Nimitz's staff. On the debit side, *Duncan* was lost, four SOCs expended, and *Boise* severely damaged, and *Salt Lake City* and *Farenholt* required the services of a dockyard. A total of 163 officers and men died.[6]

Credit must be given to the American admiral for his use of the

[6]The breakdown of American casualties is as follows:

	Killed	Wounded
Boise	107	29
Duncan	48	35
Farenholt	3	40
Salt Lake City	5	19
McCalla	0	2
Total:	163	125

Total deaths include seven marines on *Boise*.

brief interval given him to plan and prepare for battle and for his resolution in the face of the chaos about him as the battle was joined. Scott was magnanimous enough—and honest enough—to pay generous tribute to his captains for their excellent ship handling. From all quarters the splendid damage control efforts and courage of *Boise*'s crew properly drew high praise. Unfortunately, when *Boise* returned stateside for repairs a Navy publicist christened her the "one-ship fleet," a gross insult to the other ships in the action, whose names were not released for security reasons.

American reports emphasized surprise as the primary reason for Scott's success, but all hands failed to fathom fully how much this prevented an accurate assessment of Japanese skills at night fighting. Many drew dangerously false conclusions about the efficacy of American gunfire versus Japanese torpedoes. Likewise, Scott's techniques and dispositions acquired an aura from his victory that led other flag officers to follow them slavishly, with consequences that ranged from the embarrassing to the disastrous. Criticism would be leveled that Scott's formation was too densely packed and that it prohibited the effective use of the main weapon of his destroyers, the torpedo. Both of these points were true, but Scott soundly grounded his plan on the actual capabilities of his ships and their equipment at this time, which effectively prohibited sophisticated tactics. It is perhaps relevant in this regard to point out that when presented with a situation with similar features, Mikawa chose a single-column formation for the battle of Savo Island; the fate of *Duncan* and *Farenholt* illustrates the perils of a more open formation. Later faults in American tactics should not be ascribed to Scott, but to other commanders, who usually had more time to prepare, to analyze advances in skills and particularly equipment and move to more sophisticated tactics.

A junior officer on *Helena*, Charles Cook, later wrote, "Cape Esperance was a three-sided battle in which chance was the major winner." Fortune undoubtedly smiled heavily on Scott in the intricate, unintended choreography that resulted in his arrival between the two Japanese groups and the lucky misadventure of the pre-battle turn that served to place him directly in front of Goto rather than vice versa. But fortune is a patron not only of the brave, but also of the prepared. Scott deserved to win because he entered the arena girded for battle, while Goto earned his fate with his neglect. It is sobering to realize that *Furutaka* was the largest Japanese warship sunk solely by an American cruiser-destroyer group in all the battles in the Solomons during 1942 and 1943.

Just as Mikawa failed to destroy the American transports at Savo Island, Scott's night action did not impede the unloading of Japanese reinforcements, including howitzers, whose presence the marines would soon feel.

13

THE

"HIGH-SPEED

CONVOY"

"Everybody hopes we can hold on"

"THE BOMBARDMENT"

On the morning of October 13, Turner's two transports reached Lunga Roads and commenced unloading. Boats shuttled ashore 210 men of the First Marine Air Wing, eighty-five Marine replacements, and 2,850 men of the 164th Infantry Regiment. Supplies, rations, and vehicles followed the troops to add to the local inventories. The Army unit, a National Guard formation, exuded the distinctly Scandinavian character of its North Dakota recruiting area. In common with other National Guard organizations, the regiment contained few raw youths in sharp contrast to the Marine units it joined. But other characteristics that stigmatized many National Guard formations in World War Two—weaknesses in discipline and professionalism closely linked to amateurism and superannuation among the officers—had not debilitated the 164th. The superior character of the regiment reflected its vibrant leader, Lieutenant Colonel Bryant E. Moore, a West Pointer, who in the admiring words of Colonel Gerald Thomas handled his command "like a czar." In one illustrative episode, Moore swooped down on an errant company and ordered the first sergeant and company commander to exchange jobs and ranks.

Unaware of larger Japanese designs, Americans ashore viewed a double visit by Imperial "Eagles" from Rabaul as a reply to Turner's arrival, rather than what it was, the overture to the landing of their own High-Speed Convoy. The first raid of twenty-seven Bettys and eighteen Zeros eluded detection by coast watchers and was only discovered by radar when rapidly nearing the island. A total of fifty-five American fighters (forty-two Wildcats and thirteen P-39 Airacobras) scrambled at 1130. Although the P-39s could reach 27,000 feet (15,000 feet higher than the P-400s), this still placed them below the Bettys cruising at 30,000 feet. The relatively ineffective American interception forced one Zero and one Betty to ditch at a cost of one Wildcat, whose pilot survived. The first hint of something unusual came when Japanese bombardiers applied their skills not to sink Turner's transports but to put thirteen holes in the runway, with heavy damage to the metal matting. Bombs also ignited 5,000 gallons of scarce gasoline and rent twelve aircraft on the ground, including one B-17.

Only a dozen Wildcats of VMF-121 greeted the second Japanese raid—the sixty-first raid of the campaign. Captain Joseph Foss, the executive officer of the Marine squadron and an "old man" among fighter pilots at twenty-seven, led one division of four Wildcats. Foss spotted one group of Zeros, but did not see another that stalked his flight from astern. Having failed to turn on his radio, Foss was wondering why his wingmen had suddenly dived away when tracers arching over his canopy telegraphed the answer. The Japanese pilot misjudged his approach and dived below his quarry and then compounded his error by pulling up in front of the Marine pilot. In a typical honest illusion in the heat of battle, Foss believed his fire exploded the Zero, though Japanese records show all Zeros returned. Meanwhile, three other Japanese aviators scored hits that compelled a chastened Foss to glide back to Henderson Field with a windmilling propeller.[1] During the day the Cactus Air Force passed a mile-

---

[1]This episode provides an opportunity to underscore an important point. Joseph Foss, who ultimately was awarded the Medal of Honor, was, like the aviators on both sides, extremely brave and unquestionably honest in reporting what he believed he observed. The phenomenon of "over-claiming" in air battles was universal in World War Two, and reflects no moral deficiency on the part of aircrewmen, but rather the results of the ordinary distortions stemming from battle stress. This was further exacerbated by the fact that aerial combat grants

stone when Lieutenant Colonel Richard Mangrum, the inspiring leader of VMSB-232, departed from Henderson Field.

The afternoon search mission sighted a portion of the Japanese reinforcement convoy, 200 miles distant from Guadalcanal. The "High-Speed Convoy" comprised six fast transport vessels, each fitted with six to eight landing craft and strong antiaircraft batteries: the Sasago, Sakido, Kyushu, Azumasan, Nankai, and Sado Marus. These vessels carried about 4,500 troops divided among the equivalent of six battalions of infantry (the 16th Infantry Regiment, two battalions of the 230th Infantry Regiment, and 824 men of the 4th Maizuru Special Naval Landing Force), as well as one battery each of 10cm guns and 15cm howitzers, one battalion of antiaircraft guns, the 1st Independent Tank Company, and stocks of ammunition and provisions. The screen numbered eight destroyers: Samidare, Harusame, Yudachi, Murasame, Ariake, Shiratsuyu, Shigure, and the antiaircraft destroyer Akizuki, which wore the flag of Rear Admiral Takama, commander of Destroyer Squadron 4.

The approach of the convoy represented yet another innovation in Japanese plans. Originally the Imperial Navy intended to retain the vulnerable convoy at a safe distance until the 11th Air Fleet or artillery shelling neutralized American air power on Guadalcanal. But the loss of the advanced positions along the Matanikau on October 10 impelled the 17th Army to request that the convoy be forced through without reliance on army bombardment. The Navy recognized the new urgency of the situation and discarded the precondition of the confirmed elimination of the Cactus Air Force.

At 1830, at 15cm howitzer fired the first shell from a Japanese field piece to strike Henderson Field. This weapon and one peer of the 1st Battery, 4th Field Heavy Artillery Regiment squatted beneath camouflage west of the Matanikau about 2.5 miles southwest of Kokumbona, well out of retaliation range of any of the American artillery weapons ashore. As the Japanese gunners found the range and deflection, the heavy shells began to toss up dirt geysers on the western end of Henderson Field, forcing a shift of flight operations east to the fighter strip. The novelty of artillery fire following a double ration of air raids signaled to all ranks that something was afoot. Vandegrift

---

especially fleeting opportunities for accurate observation. Over-claiming is also not solely manifest in aerial combat, as many earlier passages in this narrative will illustrate.

ordered a general alert. When the last light abandoned the sky, the darkness became palpable with an impersonal brooding menace. There had been nights like this before on Guadalcanal, nights Colonel Gerald Thomas called "purple nights," but this would be the most purple night of them all.

Down from the north came Rear Admiral Takeo Kurita leading battleships *Kongo* and *Haruna,* each of which mounted eight 14-inch guns. His escort totaled nine destroyers (*Oyashio, Kuroshio, Hayashio, Umikaze, Kawakaze, Suzukaze, Takanami, Makinami,* and *Naganami*) and light cruiser *Isuzu,* flagship of Rear Admiral Tanaka. Early plans for the bombardment contemplated an even more brawny task unit of two battleships and four heavy cruisers led by super-battleship *Yamato* with her 18.1-inch guns, but considerations of maneuvering room and time resulted in the selection of Kurita's two fast (30.5-knot) battleships to pound Henderson Field into impotence. Initially, Kurita protested fervidly that the risks to his ships far outweighed the potential gains, but Yamamoto silenced these objections with a threat to do the job personally if Kurita balked.

This operation benefited from exceptionally thorough preparations. Ready for *Kongo*'s ammunition hoists stood 104 special Type 3 14-inch shells, originally designed for antiaircraft work but equally suited for bombardment of aircraft on the ground and fuel dumps. The casing of the Type 3 shell carried a modest bursting charge designed to scatter 470 individual incendiary sub-munitions over a wide swath. For precision gunfire adjustment a gunnery officer from *Yamato* squinted down from an observation post on Mount Austen, while *Kongo*'s gunnery officer donned a flight suit to lead a group of four spotter and illumination planes. Kurita's order called for firing a barrage pattern into a 2,200-meter-square area overlapping Henderson Field and the fighter strip.

The darkness brought Japanese aircraft, setting off sirens and sending the Americans back and forth from beds to dugouts and foxholes. Then at 0130 the irregular chug (like a popcorn machine, said Captain Joseph Foss) of a Japanese observation plane, "Louie the Louse," became audible. One minute later the battleships eased past the south side of Savo Island, slowed to 18 knots, and came to course 77 degrees. High in the foretops of both behemoths gunnery officers aligned range finders on a trio of reference lights twinkling along the Japanese-held coast while others below rapidly completed calculations. From the mouths of dugouts, watchers ashore witnessed "Louie" bracket Henderson Field with flares, casting pale illumination over the perimeter. At 0133½ with the range at 29,500 yards, *Kongo* belched her first salvo, followed a minute and a half later by *Haruna*.

The first rounds hit west of the runway, but Japanese gunners marched salvos back and forth across runways and parking areas as well as into the groves north of the airfields, which housed most aviation personnel. One after another, American planes, ammunition, and gasoline dumps became kindling for raging fires that within ten minutes turned the night into a garish semblance of daylight. The battleships steamed in parade formation outside the range of the Lunga Point 5-inch batteries, whose harmless barking they barely troubled to answer with their secondary armament. *Isuzu* countered the Marine guns on Tulagi. To topside Japanese sailors, the scene resembled the great Ryogoku fireworks display and provoked "spontaneous cries and shouts of excitement" that rippled over the decks.

The Americans ashore crouched within a 14-square-mile area, but only about a third of it received the bulk of *Kongo*'s and *Haruna*'s deliveries in one of the most concentrated shellings in history in terms of rapid saturation of an area. The refined Martin Clemens noted that "the ground shook with the most awful convulsions" while dust and smoke nearly solidified the very air. One later writer compared it to an explosion of "the arsenal of the underworld." The plain-spoken Captain Foss, who freely admitted he shook uncontrollably, simply said: "It seemed as if all the props had been kicked from under the sky and we were crushed beneath." One near-miss flung Vandergrift to the floor of his vulnerable dugout in a heap "without hurt except in dignity." "A man comes close to himself at such times," the general later reflected,

> . . . and until someone has experienced naval or artillery shelling or aerial bombardment, he cannot easily grasp a sensation compounded of frustration, helplessness, fear and, in the case of close hits, shock. . . .

The Japanese battleships checked fire while turning at 0213. During the lull, Navy pilot Lieutenant Frederick Mears joined about seventy men who piled into a truck to drive to the beach to escape the main impact area. "Men were yelling, even crying and trying to hide behind one another or force their way to the bottom of the truck," he recalled. When the Japanese resumed their fire, they found the conflagrations ashore obscuring all reference points, so they relied on a mechanical "shelling disc" to plot the further spread of destruction. Moreover, both ships had expended their bombardment ammunition and now used armor-piercing shells, of dubious effectiveness against a "soft" target like an airfield. One of these scored a direct hit on the command post of the 11th Marines but miraculously caused no fatalities.

At this juncture the United States Navy intervened in the form of a quartet of motor torpedo boats, popularly known as PT boats. These craft constituted the first section of Lieutenant Commander Allen Montgomery's Motor Torpedo Boat Squadron 3. They had just reached Tulagi on October 12 after a considerable delay in transit, a good portion of which was attributable to the lack of a heavy crane at Noumea to remove them from the ships that lugged them across the Pacific. Intent on preserving surprise, Montgomery resolved to withhold his vessels until a "worthwhile" target appeared, and ruefully acknowledged that on the 13th he announced they would not sortie, as originally the Japanese force was reported as "only" three destroyers or possibly one light cruiser and two destroyers, which he disdained as "too small." But when the power of the Japanese formation became plainly audible, Montgomery cleared Tulagi harbor with his four boats to engage.

In the darkness the four stubby craft soon became separated. *PT 38*, commanded by Lieutenant (jg) Robert L. Searles, fired four torpedoes, three of which malfunctioned, at a vessel identified as a "light cruiser." As *PT 38* passed only 100 yards astern of her target, Searles's bluejackets reported they felt the heat of a torpedo explosion, but this was probably only gunfire. Meanwhile *PT 60*, on which Montgomery rode and which was commanded by Lieutenant (jg) John M. Searles, Robert's brother, claimed two hits on a Japanese man-of-war, but again these were probably only gun flashes—an easy mistake to make from the low deck of a motor torpedo boat. Several boats had narrow scraps with destroyers, and *Naganami* chased *PT 60*. The American boat evaded with a smoke screen, zigzagging, and the judicious dropping of depth charges, which cooled Japanese ardor.

Although none of the American torpedoes hit, Admiral Kurita observed the gun flashes and surmised they depicted an embroilment of his screen with a submarine. Since the shelling period was near its end, he decided to terminate it five minutes early. At 0256, Japanese guns fell still and hulls began to strain as speed built up to 29 knots. During "the Bombardment"—for the Americans ashore this night thereafter spoke as if there had been no other—the two Japanese battleships fired a total of 973 shells.[2]

For the rump of the night, Japanese aircraft circled the perimeter bombing randomly, and at 0530 the Japanese howitzer, soon dubbed "Pistol Pete," began lobbing more shells onto Henderson Field to add to American discomfiture. With the first rays of daylight, men emerged with bloodshot eyes to scan a vista of devastation and commence the grim totaling: Henderson Field unusable; virtually all aviation gasoline burned; and of the Cactus Air Force's offensive punch, only seven of the thirty-nine SBDs bedded down the night before could fly and none of the TBFs. But the fighter strip and its inhabitants fared significantly better: twenty-four of forty-two Wildcats remained available as well as four of the P-400s and two P-39s. Amazingly, all this high explosive and steel killed only forty-one men of the over 20,000 present, though the dead included Major G. A. Bell and the rest of the leadership of VMSB-141. "The Bombardment" completed a withering baptism in combat in less than twenty-four hours for the 164th Infantry, which nonetheless sustained only three fatalities. The shelling also damaged the Pagoda, and Geiger, who had long suspected it was a registration point, ordered it bulldozed. The elimination of this familiar landmark and the destruction of the radio station as much as the bombardment itself created a feeling of siege.

The ecstatic Japanese witnesses of the bombardment noted fires and explosions still evident at midmorning. The 17th Army headquarters gauged the effect as equal to shelling by a thousand field guns. Based upon accounts from the 17th Army and Kurita, at 0500 on October 14, Yamamoto declared the American aircraft on Guadalcanal "suppressed" and ordered his forces at sea to head south to find and destroy the U.S. fleet.

Despite the bombardment, morning search missions departed

---

[2]Expenditures from Kurita's battleships were as follows:

	Type 3 Antiaircraft Incendiary	Type 1 Armor-piercing	Type 0 High-explosive	"Subcaliber" Modified 12-inch
Kongo	104	331	None	34
Haruna	None	294	189	21
Total	104	625	189	55

from Guadalcanal and soon delineated the main Japanese objective: six transports and eight destroyers only 140 miles distant. Vandegrift radioed: "Urgently necessary this force receive maximum support of air and surface units," and he added, "absolutely essential aviation gas be flown here continuously." But not only was American air power maimed by 14-inch shells, naval units were in no position to intervene in time. Scott's victorious task force was replenishing and could not sortie before daylight of the 15th, while the only operational carrier, *Hornet*, was refueling and, in any event, no match by herself for the entire Combined Fleet. The CINCPAC daily situation summary noted tightly that "our position is not favorable to prevent a major enemy landing."

Admiral Fitch was the one man who heard Vandegrift's cry for help and could do something about it. He ordered all seventeen available SBDs at Espíritu Santo (including eight SBDs of VB-6 under Lieutenant Ray Davis) to move to Guadalcanal immediately and the twenty Wildcats of Lieutenant Colonel Harold F. Bauer's VMF-212 to follow. But planes were useless without fuel. Fitch organized an airlift with Army and Marine Douglas transports to provide a survival diet of gasoline. Each R4D/C-47 freighted ten drums; each 55-gallon drum would keep a Wildcat in the air for one hour.

It was on Guadalcanal itself, however, that the main effort would have to be made to meet this new crisis. A false air raid alarm at midmorning left American fighters sitting on the ground refueling with gasoline drained from wrecked planes when at 1213 a raid of twenty-six Bettys dumped their bombs on the desolation of Henderson Field. The failure of the bombers or their eighteen Zero escorts to encounter airborne American aircraft did nothing to diminish Japanese confidence in the efficacy of the battleship bombardment. A second raid attacked at 1300 with twelve bombers but three fewer Zeros, only to find every flyable American fighter waiting. American claims ran to nine bombers and three fighters; Japanese records confirm the destruction of four Bettys. One Wildcat and one Airacobra fell with their pilots; bomb damage was minor.

During the afternoon one of Geiger's staff officers, Lieutenant Colonel J. C. "Toby" Munn, went to the 67th Fighter Squadron area and spoke to the assembled pilots:

I want you to pass the word along that the situation is desperate. We don't know whether we'll be able to hold the field or not. There's a Japanese task force of destroyers, cruisers and troop transports headed this way. We have enough gasoline left for one mission against them. Load your airplanes with bombs and go out with the dive-bombers and hit them. After the gas is gone we'll have to let the ground troops take over. Then your officers and men will attach themselves to some infantry outfit. Good luck and goodbye.

Twice during his talk those present ducked for Japanese shells.

The reinforcement convoy steadily closed Guadalcanal during the day with the only aircraft in sight float planes of the R Area Air Force and Zeros from the 11th Air Fleet. Nonstop exertion from first light by ground crews readied four SBDs, four P-39s, a trio of P-400s, and seventeen F4Fs for an afternoon attack. They reached the convoy about 1545, but secured no hits at a cost of one F4F. Using fuel drained from damaged B-17s, a second attack group of the same seven Airacobras and nine SBDs of VS-3 under Lieutenant Commander Kirn escorted by eight Wildcats found the convoy with the transports in two columns east of Santa Isabel at 1805. Seven of the agile biplane Petes attempted vainly to thwart the American attack. The SBD crews claimed several hits or near-misses, but only destroyer *Samidare* suffered slight damage to one gun mount and several casualties. The defenses splashed one Airacobra, and operations claimed one Wildcat and one Airacobra.

By darkness the progress of the convoy delighted General Miyazaki, the chief of staff of the 17th Army at Rabaul, and he interpreted its immunity so far as a sign of divine favor. Grasping a martial simile, he wrote in his diary, "The arrow has already left the bow." By dawn of October 15, thought Miyazaki, the outcome of the campaign would be decided.

RESURRECTION

At midnight the High-Speed Convoy gained its anchorage at Tassafaronga. Unloading proceeded smoothly without air interference, for Geiger prohibited night flying. A regular Tokyo Express run also arrived at Cape Esperance composed of light cruisers *Sendai* and *Yura,* seaplane carrier *Nisshin,* and destroyers *Asagumo, Akatsuki,* and *Ikazuchi* to deposit 1,100 soldiers and ammunition while *Shirayuki* unloaded the seeds of a midget submarine base at

Kamimbo.[3] Meanwhile Admiral Mikawa stood by to ensure the Americans enjoyed no respite. While destroyers *Mochizuki* and *Amagiri* maintained watch, heavy cruisers *Chokai* and *Kinugasa* pumped 752 8-inch shells into the American perimeter in a thirty-minute bombardment completed at 0217.

At dawn, marines and soldiers gazed west to see the masts and superstructures of Japanese transports jutting above the skyline while overhead cruised relays of fighters from carriers *Hiyo* and *Junyo* and float planes from the R Area Air Force. At 0600 a flight of six Wildcats of VMF-121 under Major Davis zoomed aloft to challenge the Japanese. While strafing the transports, Lieutenant (jg) E. T. Stover of VF-5 collided with a defending float plane. Stover returned safely with a section of Japanese wing fabric, including a portion of the insignia, snagged on his plane, but one other Wildcat failed to return.

Mechanics under Lieutenant William Woodruff worked all day on the 14th and all night readying bombers, but Mikawa's visit left only three SBDs flyable. Of this trio, one fell into a shell crater while taxiing to Fighter One—the only available runway—and a second ground-looped in another crater attempting to take off. The very determined pilot of the second plane, Lieutenant Robert Patterson of VMSB-141, insisted on trying again with the last SBD. This time he got off the ground, only to find the aircraft's hydraulics unserviceable. Nonetheless Patterson claimed a hit in a dive-bombing attack on a transport with no flaps and his landing gear extended.

Woodruff's men turned out more aircraft one by one, which immediately departed on individual attacks. The paucity of planes matched the gasoline stocks. When the fuel scavenged from damaged planes neared exhaustion, one of Geiger's staff officers remembered that Colonel Louis Woods had cached an emergency reserve—a fact the general could have discovered for himself had he read a memo in his pocket left by Woods.[4] Searches around the perimeter turned up no fewer than 465 barrels in various locations, enough for two days of operations.

In view of the rapidly mounting cost, Geiger halted the ad hoc

---

[3]Japanese midget submarines were 78 feet long and displaced about 46 tons. Each boat had a crew of two and two 18-inch torpedoes. With a radius of action of only 80 miles, they were normally transported to their operating areas by specially equipped submarines or other vessels. As on October 11, the last relay of six Zeros covering this run deliberately ditched.

[4]This story carries a commentary on military bureaucracy: Woods built up the reserve by padding expenditure reports to accelerate the forwarding of more fuel supplies.

attacks and readied a coordinated mission involving a dozen SBDs, three P-39s, a P-400, and eight Wildcats. To these twenty-four aircraft Geiger added his personal aircraft, a PBY-5A amphibian, flown by the general's pilot, Major Jack Cram. For what appeared a surely suicidal mission, ground crews slung two torpedoes beneath the high slablike wings of the Catalina. No one had ever attempted a daylight torpedo attack with a plodding, bulky PBY, nor had Cram ever dropped a torpedo in his life. Lieutenant Commander Simpler gave Cram a briefing on the technique, based on expertise derived from the fact that Simpler's brother-in-law flew torpedo planes. At about 1030 in accordance with the hastily conceived plan, the Dauntlesses slanted down in dives from the west to draw the attention of the Japanese, while Cram nosed his plane over into a steep descent from the east. The PBY's wings flexed in protest as Cram pierced the destroyer screen at 240 knots indicated airspeed—well beyond the maximum velocity the manufacturer certified as safe. Cram released both torpedoes at one transport, one of which he thought hit. Either Cram or one of the SBDs ignited a fatal fire on Sasago Maru.

The PBY banked left to make for the perimeter with Zeros and Wildcats locked in combat in her slipstream. One pursuing Zero thoroughly holed Cram's Catalina, but the Japanese pilot focused so intently on Cram's destruction that he failed to see a damaged F4F with its wheels already down in the landing pattern. One burst of .50 caliber fire from Lieutenant Roger Haberman of VMF-121 exploded the Zero, which fell in a ball of flame at the edge of the field.

Thirty minutes after Cram's attack, twenty-four Bettys executed a bombing run over the airfield, unopposed as all American fighters were otherwise committed. One Wildcat was destroyed on the ground, but antiaircraft fire winged one Betty, which ditched. By about this same time, 1100, the transports had divested themselves of almost all their cargoes of troops and heavy equipment as well as a large portion of the provisions and ammunition. The experienced crew of the Nankai Maru emptied their vessel, and she departed with destroyer Ariake at 1145, just five minutes before a raid by eleven B-17s from Espíritu Santo secured a mortal hit on Azumasan Maru. American records are skimpy, but Japanese accounts reveal that between 1315 and 1330, another American strike pounded both the ships and the materials ashore, securing a bomb hit on Kyushu Maru. Wrapped in whorls of flame, the ship was beached and became a total loss.

To Admiral Takama it appeared that the American aviators adeptly found gaps in Japanese fighter coverage and skillfully exploited the land configuration near the landing area to make surprise attacks. Their unremitting blows scattered landing craft and shore parties, and the situation became chaotic. Takama tried to communicate with his army counterpart, Major General Ito, to reassess the wisdom of continued daylight unloading, but Ito moved ashore in violation of prior agreement and could not be contacted. To evade the attacks, Takama got his ships underway and moved north of Savo to maneuver.

The low sun sharply etched the wrinkled waters at 1700 as Takama brought his ships back toward the debarkation area. Lieutenant Davis of VB-6 led four SBDs in an unsuccessful attack at 1740, but the effort offered a potent psychological demonstration of the exposed nature of the operation. At Takama's approach, General Ito signaled, "Moon bright, do not come." Accordingly, at 1742, Takama began the return journey to Rabaul with the two remaining transports. Although the riches brought by the convoy overjoyed the 17th Army, Ito's decision to cancel further unloading incensed both Army and Navy senior commanders. A 17th Army report—later proved false—that only about 20 percent of the ammunition and 50 percent of the provisions reached shore further soured interservice relations. Precise figures on the cargoes disgorged by the convoy are elusive, but the best estimate is that about 4,500 men and two-thirds or more of the supplies and equipment reached Guadalcanal.

The cost of the day's activities included three of the six transports: *Sasago, Azumasan,* and *Kyushu Maru.* During the day the R Area Air Force dispatched sixteen float Zeros and sixteen Petes while the 11th Air Fleet and Carrier Division 2 sent forty-four and thirty-six Zeros respectively for a total of 112 sorties. American claims amounted to three Zeros and one Pete; Japanese losses were actually greater—five Zeros and one Pete, as well as one Betty. American losses on October 15 totaled four SBDs with three crews, two Airacobras with one pilot, and three Wildcats (including one on the ground and one operational) and one pilot. In patrol plane actions distant from the island this day, Japanese carrier fighters downed two PBYs and their American counterparts splashed one Mavis.

To the east of Guadalcanal this same day an air attack fell on an American resupply unit. Even before Kurita's bombardment, the need to replenish the gasoline supply on the island induced the birth of a fuel-lugging expedition with destroyers *Nicholas* and *Meredith* playing shepherds for a trio of gasoline barges towed by cargo ships *Alchiba* and *Bellatrix* and motor torpedo boat tender *Jamestown.* Also in company was fleet tug *Vireo.* Orders from Ghormley at 0608 on October 16 caused all save *Meredith* and *Vireo* to turn back, and the tug took up the tow of one barge. At 1050, two Japanese aircraft attacked, and then *Meredith*'s skipper, Lieutenant Commander Harry Hubbard, received word of two Japanese ships in the vicinity. He directed his little command to put about, but it quickly became evident that no rapid withdrawal could be made at *Vireo*'s best speed of 14 knots. Consequently, Hubbard ordered her abandoned, an action distant staff officers in Pearl Harbor would label "disgraceful."

Hubbard's decision was in fact well justified, for the two aircraft already seen came from Carrier Division 1, which Yamamoto pushed into the waters east of the Stewart Islands this day looking for *Hornet*. At 1137 the Japanese launched thirty-eight aircraft (eight Zeros, twenty-one Vals, and nine Kates) to attack the various American vessels located by their scouts. About 1225, just after *Meredith* removed *Vireo*'s crew and as Hubbard prepared to sink the tug, the Japanese strike arrived. The enemy fliers required only ten minutes to plant bombs all along *Meredith*'s length and torpedo her three times. The destroyer shot down one Val and two Kates, but a Japanese destroyer picked up one Kate crew and *Grayson* recovered a second. Five Vals of a second attack group found the two American cargo ships and *Nicholas,* but succeeded only in achieving near-misses on *Bellatrix*.

After *Meredith* sank, her surviving crewmen and *Vireo*'s endured repeated strafing in the water, but this was only a foretaste of a succession of horrors. One raftload of survivors eventually reached the drifting tug and soon became separated from the others; the majority of the survivors clustered in shocked groups about the few rafts. The wounded lay in the gratings, tortured by the cruel competition between the sun that blistered their flesh and salt water that laved their burns. As the hours passed, most of the injured perished, including Lieutenant Commander Hubbard, who stoically bore terrible burns and blindness until he expired. Before death cleared sufficient room inside, the able-bodied took turns in the water clinging to the sides of the rafts, where they became the targets of savage shark attacks—one of the brutes even leaped into a raft to tear into a man. Boatswain's Mate Wesley S. Singletary of *Vireo* set a bold example for those reluctant to take their turn in the water by going over the side and pushing sharks away with his feet. When destroyers *Grayson* and *Gwin* arrived after three days and nights they found only eighty-eight men alive; 187 shipmates from *Meredith* and fifty of *Vireo* died. Ironically, *Vireo* and her barge survived.

.   .   .

American aircraft risen phoenixlike from Guadalcanal to savage the High-Speed Convoy energized Admiral Yamamoto into sending in another bombardment unit, this time heavy cruisers *Myoko* and *Maya* with Admiral Tanaka's ever-ready destroyer squadron. During the night of October 15–16, the Japanese cruisers laced the fighter strip with 926 8-inch shells while the accompanying destroyers added another 253 5-inch projectiles.

With daylight came a reckoning of the aircraft destroyed or damaged over the past three nights: six Wildcats lay in wreckage, three sat damaged but mendable; the carcasses of thirteen SBDs offered only a source of spare parts for the like number damaged but repairable, and ten other Dauntlesses needed major renewing; five TBFs were beyond salvage and the remaining three in need of major overhaul; four P-39s were destroyed; and two B-17s were beyond repair. During October 16 the Cactus Air Force flew fifty-eight sorties in seven missions to pound the landing areas, losing one SBD to ground fire. Returning pilots reported they saw "plenty" of Japanese breakfast fires. *Hornet* launched seventy-four sorties against targets at both Guadalcanal and Rekata Bay.

This day also marked a changing of the guard among the aviation units at Guadalcanal as gasoline-hauling R4Ds and C-47s evacuated the last crewmen of VMF-224 and VMSB-231. With their departure, MAG-23 finished its tour and MAG-14 took over. Lieutenant Commander Simpler also vacated Guadalcanal with the last of his pilots of VF-5. As usual, these withdrawals involved only crewmen; surviving aircraft, if any, were turned over to other units. This left only the durable pilots of the 67th Fighter Squadron of the original aerial defenders.

The intervention of *Hornet* led to her discovery by Japanese search planes, and the 11th Air Fleet dispatched a number of strikes to sink her. One of these, composed of nine Vals from Buin, failing to find *Hornet,* settled for a much less august target at Guadalcanal, destroyer-seaplane tender *McFarland.* Admiral Fitch drafted *McFarland* (Lieutenant Commander John C. Alderman), with her sister destroyer conversions *Southard* and *Hovey,* for emergency transportation of fuel to Geiger's diminished air command. *McFarland* reached Lunga Roads during the morning of October 16 carrying 40,000 gallons of gasoline and a dozen torpedoes among an assortment of ammunition. As she unloaded her volatile cargo into a barge, *McFarland* took aboard a group of 160 Navy and Marine evacuees, mostly ground crews. At 1750 the Japanese dive-bombers screamed down. *McFarland* jerked forward at her best speed and cut the barge loose while casting up her best antiaircraft barrage, which was feeble but splashed one Val. One bomb incinerated the barge, and a second missile landed amid *McFarland*'s depth charges, severing the ship's stern. Her sailors found their efforts to save their ship impeded by a handful of panicked evacuees who trampled down passageways and tried to strip crewmen of weapons and lifejackets. But her stalwart company quelled the few wayward passengers (many others helped) and stemmed most flooding as the engineers poked *McFarland*'s well-rattled machinery into 5 knots forward while keeping the port screw astern to hold her on course. With twenty-seven dead and twenty-eight wounded, *McFarland* limped into Tulagi by midnight.

Just as the Japanese attacked, Henderson Field welcomed nineteen Wildcats of VMF-212 under Lieutenant Colonel Harold F. Bauer and seven SBDs. When Bauer saw *McFarland* under attack he instantly set off to her aid, despite virtually empty fuel tanks. In full view of hundreds of men on the shore, the lone Wildcat caught the eight remaining Vals and slammed three into the sea in a few seconds. Bauer capped his performance, which would win him the Medal of Honor, by landing and giving a rousing talk that restored the morale of his fellow aviators.

During this day, Vandegrift estimated for his superiors, the Japanese convoy landed another 10,000 troops to bring Japanese strength to at least 15,000. (This considerably overstated the numbers delivered by the convoy, but was not so far off as to the total number of Japanese warriors on the island.) While he acknowledged that there were more Americans on Guadalcanal, half of them were in no condition to undertake protracted operations. Vandegrift identified two urgent steps necessary to assure the survival of his command: securing control of the sea adjacent to Guadalcanal and reinforcing the garrison by at least one division to permit offensive operations. The shock of the bombardment and the convoy resulted in the authorization for fifty Army Air Force fighters to wing to the South Pacific, and Marshall directed that one division, soon identified as the 25th Infantry Division, be readied for shipment to the South or Southwest Pacific.

Admiral Yamamoto reached into his bag of tricks for another method of bashing the Americans on Guadalcanal and ordered Carrier Division 2 (*Junyo* and *Hiyo*) to send a shipping strike in the early morning of October 17. Eighteen Zeros and eighteen Kates took departure from the two carriers in time to reach the Lunga area about 0720. But American cryptanalysts predicted the attack through a partial and corrupted break of Yamamoto's message, and eight Wildcats laid in wait for the Japanese airmen. In the ensuing air battle the defenders lost one Wildcat and pilot, but seven Kates fell over Guadalcanal and one Zero ditched. On the other hand, no American aircraft gained altitude in time to intercept a Japanese bombing raid at 1315. Nonetheless, what the Japanese called "severe antiaircraft fire" caused two Zeros and one bomber to crash-land; one Wildcat also fell. This day saw the departure of VS-3, including Kirn.

Well remembering how exposed his own supplies had been on the beaches after the August landing, Vandegrift asked for a destroyer bombardment of the Japanese convoy landing area. On the morning of October 17, *Aaron Ward* and *Lardner* flogged the coast near Tassafaronga with 1,925 5-inch shells to bolster the already strenuous efforts of the Cactus Air Force in this direction.

Although the Japanese intended the High-Speed Convoy as the last reinforcement run before the October offensive, the failure of the "Ant Transportation" (barge) program and cancellation of the seaplane carrier run on the 14th because of the intimidating presence of *Hornet* left a significant shortfall in the planned buildup. The 17th Army requested one more major effort, to include the return of the three surviving transports to complete unloading. But the Imperial Navy, mightily piqued over the decision of General Ito to cancel unloading during the night of October 15 and curbed by fuel-famished covering forces, refused to authorize more than a revival of the Tokyo Express. Further, after Japanese search planes glimpsed *Hornet* and battleship *Washington* on the 16th, the three seaplane carriers were deleted from the run, but the remaining vessels still made an impressive total: three light cruisers and fifteen destroyers. This flotilla enjoyed an unimpeded voyage to their landing areas, where they exchanged 2,159 soldiers, six field and a dozen anti-tank guns, and ammunition and provisions for sick and wounded soldiers plus transport crew survivors numbering 231 men. During this process, four destroyers warmed up their guns on the American perimeter.

Submarine *Grampus* (Lieutenant Commander John R. Craig) briefly enlivened the return trip by firing a spread of torpedoes at *Yura*. One dented plates on the light cruiser's port side forward but neglected to explode. The presence of *Grampus* constituted tangible evidence of a move to counter increasing Japanese strength in the

Solomons with an accretion of submarines. Nimitz's initial reluctance to divert submarines to the Solomons crumbled steadily during August and September until he ordered tender *Holland* to set up housekeeping at Brisbane on Australia's east coast for Submarine Squadron 2's brood of twelve submarines. From there they joined five venerable S-boats attempting to ambush the Tokyo Express or bigger game in the South Pacific.

Within days of *Grampus*'s attack the number of modern fleet submarines present or detailed to the South Pacific would be doubled to twenty-four. But initially these efforts produced very skimpy fruits: two modest merchantmen and the respectable 8,000-ton *Katauragi Maru* by *Sturgeon*. A large part of the reason for these paltry results lay in mismanagement. The officer exercising tactical direction of submarine operations in the theater, Captain Ralph Christie, positioned the boats close to the terminals of Japanese movements at Palau, Truk, and Rabaul, on the theory that they offered the densest concentration of targets. But the Japanese naturally massed their antisubmarine measures in these same environs, and Christie's dispositions forfeited the advantages of speed and mobility with which the boats could exploit code-breaking successes on Japanese merchant ship movements. In Christie's defense it must be admitted that his tactics, if staid, fitted target priorities set out by King, which placed carriers, battleships, and cruisers at the top with merchantmen, tankers, and destroyers well down the list. Christie lost none of his submarines, but *I-22* disappeared in early October. She sent her last radio message on the afternoon of October 4 and was probably destroyed by a PBY flown by Lieutenant W. King, Admiral Fitch's flag lieutenant, on October 6.

October 18 found Japanese aviators again on course for Guadalcanal in fourteen Bettys and seven Zeros. Ample early warning by Kennedy on New Georgia enabled fifteen Wildcats, drawn from the two Marine fighter squadrons present, VMF-121 and VMF-212, to seize a favorable position for an interception. The Zeros arrived early and the Wildcats shot down one in exchange for two Wildcats, whose pilots were recovered. The bombers received rough treatment, and three plummeted to destruction. One of these burst into flames under the fire of Captain Foss's guns, parted company with a wing, and spun into the water off Tulagi—but miraculously three of its crew survived without a scratch to be captured. Japanese bombs killed seven Americans and wounded eight. A fourth bomber crash-landed because of damage. The next day a sweep of nine Zeros met sixteen

Wildcats. The Zeros returned after shooting down one Wildcat, whose pilot survived. Another Wildcat and pilot became operational losses this day.

The 17th Army again asked for another run of the Tokyo Express on the 19th to lift its chief of staff to Guadalcanal. In the event, General Miyazaki did not go, but another staff officer became part of the cargo of the three ships of Destroyer Division 19, together with ammunition. They were still 175 miles out when Lieutenant Commander J. Eldridge of VS-71 found them with a dozen SBDs. Float planes harried the Americans, who scored a near-miss on *Uranami* that immobilized one shaft, forcing her to return. The remaining pair pressed on, but off Tassafaronga the relentless Lieutenant Commander Eldridge again beleaguered them with flares and bombs that caused the Japanese to abandon both landing operations and a proposed bombardment. On October 20, the Japanese sent down a morning fighter sweep of fifteen Zeros and an afternoon raid of twenty-five Zeros and nine Bettys. Clashes with defending fighters cost one Zero, but two Wildcats and one pilot were also lost.

During the forenoon of October 20, Admiral Hashimoto totaled up the deliveries of his Reinforcement Unit since October 1: 9,091 soldiers of the 17th Army plus 560 men of the 4th Maizuru Special Naval Landing Force; sixty-six guns or howitzers; nineteen mortars; twelve towing vehicles; and 160 tons of provisions. These were the fruits of ninety-two trips by destroyers, seven by cruisers, and four by seaplane carriers. On the debit side, Hashimoto listed damage to ten destroyers, three seriously. For some reason the admiral did not mention any 15cm howitzers, although he certainly landed some, and these figures do *not* include the harvest from the High-Speed Convoy, which brought the manpower total to over 14,000. The 17th Army's staff officers came up with a slightly different total: 9,372 men, eighty guns or howitzers, 4,590 boxes of provisions, and 4,115 units of ammunition of unknown type. Either set of numbers equaled big trouble for the Americans on Guadalcanal.

"THE PEOPLE'S WAR"

To senior American uniformed and civilian officials, "the Bombardment" followed by the landing of massive reinforcements moved well-founded apprehension for the security of the enclave on Guadalcanal to fear and, in some cases, despair. The desire to unmask the perilous situation of their countrymen on Guadalcanal to the public—or as some astute observers believed, to prepare the nation for a defeat—triggered a major shift in the public information policy of the United States government and the armed services during October. Ironically, while the Guadalcanal campaign molded the development of this policy, very shortly public release of information would shape the campaign.

The natural tension between newsmen and military officials is not surprising. Reporter Clark Lee spoke for many in his tribe when he accused naval officers, particularly Annapolis products, of regarding

> . . . ships of the Navy as their own private property, instead of the property of the American people. They rejected all suggestions that this was a people's war and, within reason, the people should be kept fully informed of how it was progressing.

There is little room for doubt that security considerations alone did not motivate the suppression of the shocking news about the Battle of Savo Island. The obverse side of this dispute emerges in the notes of the September conference between Nimitz and King. Nimitz complained that reporters bedeviled him and he wished them to know that he assumed the release of war news to the press meant disclosure to the enemy. To this King merely grunted that he fought that battle at least once a day. The apprehensions of senior officers burgeoned quite justly after the Battle of Midway when the *Chicago Tribune,* in a colossal display of bad judgment at the reportorial and editorial level, ran articles boasting of foreknowledge of Japanese plans that threatened to compromise Allied cryptanalytical successes against both Japan and Germany. Nor was the news blackout without success. After the war, Japanese officers would attribute part of the miscalculations leading to their failure at Midway to the lack of information on the health of American carriers through June 1942.

Control of the news was exercised by a policy of issuing only periodic, tight-lipped official communiqués and censoring correspondents in the Pacific. Faced with these inhibitions on gathering facts, newspapers resorted to "reading between the lines" of the official statements, at times with remarkable success. For example, the *New York Times* on August 23 advised its readers that the circumstances of Ichiki's arrival suggested an American naval withdrawal, and in October, when the Navy released news of Savo Island, the same paper deduced that the Japanese had achieved surprise. As early as August 26 the *Times* editorially commented that "Japan will never yield in the Solomons without a sacrificial effort to retake them."

On Guadalcanal itself, policy on this matter, like so much else that characterized the Marine effort, was governed by simple pragmatism. Vandegrift permitted correspondents to go where they liked and write what they wanted "within logical security confines." Somewhat offsetting the small size of the initial complement of newsmen, Robert C. Miller and Richard Tregaskis, was its high quality. More correspondents came as the importance of the campaign became clear, and they produced more good work, including John Hersey's superb book *Into the Valley*. Although the reporters shared the hardships of the garrison, they were not leashed by military discipline, nor were they all unadorned heroes—after the battleship bombardment one correspondent vacated the island in such haste that he abandoned all his personal effects. Worse yet, distant judges awarded an important journalism award to an individual, unesteemed by his local peers, whose "eyewitness" descriptions of night naval actions from shore observation posts remain highly dubious.

The first sign of the change in information policy about Guadalcanal in particular and, as it developed, the war effort as a whole came when the *New York Times* military affairs correspondent Hanson Baldwin returned from his trip to the island in September and censors cleared a series of his articles for publication beginning on September 27. For the first time the American people acquired a frank picture of the tenuous grasp the marines maintained on a small fraction of Guadalcanal's coastline. Baldwin underlined the significance of the campaign when he declared that the United States had "nailed the colors to the mast" over Henderson Field, and that the stakes were high, "perhaps eventual victory" in the war itself. More articles emphasizing the peril of the situation began to populate the pages of American newspapers and became the talk of radio news broadcasts. Much of it contained painful candor, as when at the end of October Baldwin wrote of the situation so far: "We have done some of it well, some of it brilliantly, some of it very badly." As a result of deserved criticism, the Navy Department changed its policy in October and, beginning with *Meredith* and *O'Brien,* commenced to announce ship losses promptly.

As the story of the struggle on Guadalcanal unfolded, the American people, no less than their leaders, intuitively grasped its epic dimensions. The *New York Herald Tribune* editorialized on October 16:

> The shadows of a great conflict lie heavily over the Solomons—all that can be perceived is the magnitude of the stakes at issue.

On this same day the *New York Times* printed an editorial that sounded ominously like a eulogy:

> . . . Guadalcanal. The name will not die out of the memories of this generation. It will endure in honor.

In the third week of October the marines and soldiers enduring on Guadalcanal monitored radio broadcasts saturated with a chorus of doomful projections on their prospects. Among those hearing these predictions there were no doubt some whose morale suffered. But the great majority remained confident and recognized, in the words of Colonel Cates, that if the situation was "no pink tea," they did not need "weak-kneed reports by some official about our precarious situation." These latter reached a peak on October 16. A reporter bluntly demanded of Secretary of the Navy Frank Knox: "Do you think we can hold Guadalcanal?" Knox's reply was not full of reckless optimism:

> I certainly hope so and expect so. . . . I will not make any predictions, but every man will give a good account of himself. What I am trying to say is that there is a good stiff fight going on. Everybody hopes we can hold on.

HALSEY TAKES COMMAND

One man who could do more than hope as Knox spoke was Chester W. Nimitz. On October 15 he read a message from Ghormley containing a cry of resignation: "My forces [are] totally inadequate to meet [the] situation." Nimitz had already exhausted the material assistance he could give Ghormley's command, but there was one other way he could influence events, and he discussed this subject with his staff on the night of October 15. Some of them noted Nimitz's normally sunny blue eyes now flashed an icy gray as he prepared to talk about what Hanson Baldwin identified as the single greatest obstacle to American success: leadership. Ghormley, said Nimitz, was an intelligent and dedicated officer, but was he tough enough to face the coming crisis, and more important, could he inspire men to feats beyond their known capabilities? The staff answered unanimously: No.

This resolved but half of the problem, for who could replace

Ghormley? Turner's name immediately surfaced, but although he was a strong leader, the marines were restive under Turner's government and there was the cloud of Savo Island over his head. Providentially just off the sick list was Vice Admiral William F. Halsey, a sailor known and admired throughout the Navy as a fighter, especially by the enlisted men. But the criteria for the job of COMSOPAC did not include personal popularity, and some senior officers suspected that Halsey's talents as a fighter and leader in close contact with the enemy would be mismatched to the role of theater commander. After some thought, Nimitz decided it must be Halsey and the next day requested King's approval. COMINCH's reply was a brutally short one word message: "Affirmative."

In retrospect, it is obvious that initially a precarious combination of responsibility without commensurate authority was thrust upon Ghormley, and that he never had more than moderate means for an immoderate task.

However sympathetically Ghormley's situation is viewed, his relief was amply justified. Contemporary explanations for Ghormely's replacement shared the common theme that he lacked aggressiveness, but this was really a symptom of his defeatism, a disease that had become rampant at his headquarters. His pessimism emerged plainly as early as his July meeting with MacArthur, but became much more profound than even the grim facts would warrant. Later King and Nimitz would attribute much of Ghormley's psychological state to the agonies he suffered from abscessed teeth, nor was this the only way Ghormley's physical condition deflated his spirit. His sense of duty led him to confine himself for months on his flagship and to deny himself recreation or exercise while he worked endless hours in a sweatbox of an office. Moreover, he became too immersed in detail, partly because his staff did not function well, and he lost sight of a point Nimitz fired at his staff: "Remember, the enemy is hurt too." Ghormley's failure to go to the conference at Koro revealed egregiously poor judgment, and during his entire tenure of command he never once set foot on Guadalcanal.[5]

---

[5]Ghormley bore the humiliation of his relief with considerable dignity, and he defended his conduct in his postwar writing by an able but largely dispassionate marshaling of facts. On one point, however, he disclosed a still-raw wound. Because of the delay in public announcement of losses at the Battle of Savo Island, the word of this painful defeat preceded the replacement of Ghormley by only a few days and left the obvious impression that the Navy held Ghormley directly responsible for the debacle. Although Ghormley carried ultimate

On October 18, Halsey arrived in Noumea, having traveled ahead of his flagship *Enterprise* to familiarize himself with the situation. A sealed envelope awaited him, which he opened to find orders to immediately take command of the South Pacific Area and the South Pacific Force. His reaction was a characteristic explosion: "Jesus Christ and General Jackson! This is the hottest potato they ever handed me!" His emotions ran from astonishment and apprehension to regret, for he had gleaned no hint of his elevation to theater commander, he knew little of the situation, and Ghormley was a friend of forty years' standing. Behind the sixty-year-old admiral was a distinguished career first in destroyers and latterly as a carrier commander. His more than medium height, broad shoulders, and barrel chest gave him a strong presence and "a wide mouth held tight and turned down at the corners and exceedingly bushy eyebrows gave his face, in a grizzled sea dog way, an appearance of good humor." He was not so impulsive as the nickname "Bull" (which was not used by his friends) suggested, but he always displayed a certain indifference to detail that looked like carelessness.

Although agreeing with Ghormley's current dispositions, within hours of taking command Halsey put his personal stamp on operations. First he simply seized a headquarters ashore from sensitive Free French officials whom Ghormley had never confronted, despite desperate conditions of crowding on *Argonne.* Within forty-eight hours he scuttled the Ndeni operation, as should have been done weeks before. But this same day Halsey was forcefully reminded of one of the sources of displeasure with Ghormley's stewardship when *I-176* torpedoed heavy cruiser *Chester* in the stretch of waters frequented by American task forces called "Torpedo Junction," in a wry play upon the title of the popular song "Tuxedo Junction." On his third day in command, Halsey decided to move the main fleet base from Auckland to Noumea, and he did not merely ask for but demanded a million square feet of covered storage space.

One simple order revealed more about his attitude than any rhetorical flourish: henceforth naval officers in the South Pacific would remove ties from tropical uniforms. Halsey said he gave this order to conform to Army practice and for comfort, but to his command it viscerally evoked the image of a brawler stripping for action and

---

responsibility as the theater commander, as we have seen he did not contribute to the errors and misjudgments underlying the disaster.

symbolized a casting off of effete elegance no more appropriate to the tropics than to war. His national popularity would endure, but later events would put his effectiveness into serious doubt. Indeed, one of his ablest subordinates would observe that by 1944 "the war simply became too complicated for Halsey." But in mid-October 1942 with his country at bay and locked in mortal combat with a relentless foe, Halsey was in his element. Within one week of taking command, Halsey sent an order to Admiral Kinkaid that would electrify the entire Navy: "Strike, repeat, strike."

14

THE BATTLE

FOR HENDERSON

FIELD

"The time for the decisive battle between Japan and the United States has come"

PLANS AND DISPOSITIONS

By October 20, Americans of all ranks on Guadalcanal were asking two questions: Where were the thousands of Japanese soldiers landed by the Tokyo Express and the mid-October convoy? And why had the Japanese failed to follow up "the Bombardment" with a major ground attack? The answer to the first of these queries remained four days distant, but the occasion for the second requires a look back at Japanese planning. At the end of September the staffs of both the 17th Army and the 2d Division concurred that the forthcoming offensive must initially be aimed at Henderson Field and the American artillery positions, and that the plan must emphasize speed, concentration, and simplicity. They disagreed, however, on the axis of the attack. Colonel Matsumoto, the operations officer of the 2d Division, advocated the coastal area; Colonel Tsuji of the 17th Army favored the heights several miles inland.

Rather than narrowing the range of disagreement, the first ten days of October injected new factors that demolished the premises for the original plan. On October 2, the Imperial Navy forwarded a report of American airfield construction at Koli Point, roughly 8 miles east of Lunga Point. The 17th Army perforce amended its list of objectives to add Koli Point, thus reinserting complexity into planning. The rival schemes of maneuver sustained a body blow between October 6 and 9 with the loss of the bridgeheads on the east bank of the Matanikau. But the fundamental reason why the preliminary designs fell into disfavor arose from the shifting appraisal of relative material strength. On October 8, the Army Section of Imperial General Headquarters pegged enemy numbers in the Solomons as one Marine division with its main body of 10,000 men on Guadalcanal; it warned that one Army division might soon swell these forces. This tabulation was woefully low. By late October there were 23,088 Americans of all services on Guadalcanal and another 4,639 on Tulagi, or a total of 27,727 in the objective area.[1]

Even though Imperial Headquarters yet again underestimated the number of Americans on Guadalcanal—this time by a factor of about two—this misinformation engended no overconfidence in the 17th Army. On the contrary, recognition of the waning Japanese striking power on Guadalcanal increasingly sobered Hyakutake's headquarters. When Hyakutake reached the island on October 10, he discovered that the five 600-man infantry battalions forming the core of Ichiki's and Kawaguchi's commands mustered scarcely the numerical strength of one. Of the five infantry battalions of the 2d Division present, the three organic to the 4th Infantry Regiment had shriveled to one-third of their authorized complement. Further, instead of enumerating its strength by battalions or batteries, the serviceable artillery was countable by individual guns: two field and two mountain pieces of 75mm plus a quartet of 150mm howitzers. To these could be added a battalion of mortars, but a severe shortage of ammunition subtracted substantially from the utility of all this heavy weaponry. Everyone who had been on the island any length of time was debilitated. Therefore, in one of his first acts, on October 11, Hyakutake ordered that the Infantry Group Headquarters of the 38th Division and the 228th Regiment (less one battalion) join the flow of reinforcements to Guadalcanal.

But even the welcome infusion of healthy riflemen could not re-

[1]Since August 7, Tulagi had served as a minor naval base and as a refueling stop for PBYs. Less by design than circumstance, it also developed into a rest area for tired rifle battalions and a reservoir for fresh ones that Vandegrift tapped occasionally. With the benefit of perfect hindsight, we may well question the substantial size of its garrison by this stage of the campaign.

dress the serious imbalance of firepower in favor of the Americans. An attack at or near the coast would amount to a brute trial of strength with scant prospect for success. Moreover, the loss of the Matanikau bridgeheads seriously diminished the odds in favor of the 17th Army. In the judgment of the planners, the reestablishment of Japanese forces on the east bank of the Matanikau would exhaust the small hoard of artillery ammunition and expend the combat power of the 2d Division to such an extent that another division would be required to attack the airfield itself.

Against this background on October 11 the chief of staff of the 2d Division, Colonel Tamaoki, and the operations officer, Colonel Matsumoto, clambered to an observation post on Mount Austen. Peering down to the south of the dusty runway of Henderson Field, they beheld patches of what they construed as clear areas in the tangled jungle carpet across Mount Austen. From this visual inspection, they inferred that Guadalcanal's interior was more accessible than they had supposed. They scrambled back to submit their findings, and Matsumoto added his opinion that no American defenses shielded the area south of the airfield. A similar journey converted Colonel Konuma of the 17th Army to the same views. Corroboration for these firsthand observations appeared to come from the gently curved, evenly spaced—and wholly spurious—form lines on a British Admiralty chart of the Mount Austen area.[2] Based upon this information, the Japanese recast the attack plan to feature a deep penetration march south of the American perimeter culminating in a surprise attack on what was surmised to be the undefended American rear. Colonel Konuma presented this design to Hyakutake, who accepted it, and on October 12 an engineer party with one company of the 124th Infantry began to create a trail.

At 0900, October 15, the 17th Army issued its formal orders. Major General Tadashi Sumiyoshi, artillery commander of the 17th Army, would distract American attention to the coastal corridor. For this purpose he would have all of the 17th Army's heavy artillery and five battalions of infantry. The 2d Division with the equivalent

[2]The Japanese employed a copy of a British Admiralty chart of Guadalcanal as their basic "map" reference. This chart was accurate as to the coastline and adjacent waters. As was customary, however, the chart did not purport to show the lay of actual inland topographic features, but contained made-up form lines designed merely to suggest inland detail. This convention was not understood by the officers of the 17th Army. Interestingly enough, the Americans also employed a copy of the same Admiralty chart as a basic reference, but did not take the form lines as a true topographic representation.

of three regiments of infantry (nine battalions) would embark on a jungle march to attack up the east bank of the Lunga to the airfield on X-Day, tentatively set for October 22. The 1st Battalion, 228th Infantry (with one company of the 38th Engineers) was christened the Koli Detachment to signify its mission of landing at that locale to occupy the mythic American airfield. This unit would land at 0200 on X-Day plus one.

That same morning, Lieutenant General Maruyama briefed a sweaty conclave of commanders as the High-Speed Convoy off-loaded. The Sendai Division would traverse the foot of Mount Austen and vault the upper reaches of the Lunga along a route styled the Maruyama Road. The order of battle divided the division's striking forces three ways. The Left Wing Unit under Major General Nasu was built around the 29th Infantry Regiment, and the Right Wing Unit under Major General Kawaguchi incorporated the 230th Infantry (with the III/124 substituting for the III/230). The Wing Units shared elements of the 3d Mortar Battalion as well as anti-tank and mountain gun units. Maruyama exercised direct control of the 16th Infantry Regiment, the division reserve. Nasu's Left Wing Unit would begin the march at 1400 on October 16, followed in order by Kawaguchi, the division headquarters, the 16th Infantry Regiment, and divisional units.

Maruyama's staff then gave their portion of the briefing. The intelligence officer, Colonel Sugita, warned that the Americans concentrated their firepower and placed outposts in front of their main positions. The operations officer, Colonel Matsumoto, announced October 20 (rather than the 22d) as the tentative attack date, presumably to encourage a rapid march. Colonel Tamaoki, the chief of staff, admonished commanders to be vigilant to preserve secrecy: no telltale smoke should utter from cooking fires, and after crossing the Lunga, soldiers should eat only crackers. In keeping with his idiosyncratic character, Kawaguchi issued a leaflet to his command on the "Spirit of the Right Wing." The gist of Kawaguchi's exhortation advised his soldiers that the enemy anchored their faith in firepower, which could be nullified by darkness and jungle, but the might of the Imperial Army rested in its bayonets. In fact, Kawaguchi afforded a précis of the 17th Army's plan that ultimately was an attempt to offset material deficiencies with the unsurpassed discipline and endurance of the Imperial Army's infantry.

Hyakutake decided to establish a centrally located advanced battle headquarters along the Maruyama Road. With Maruyama he sent emissaries, including Colonel Tsuji, who was accoutered with confidential instructions. Tsuji was counseled that although it was preferable to attack by October 20 to meet the demands of Imperial Headquarters and the Imperial Navy, it was "absolutely necessary" that the Sendai's assault be carefully readied. Therefore, if the long jungle trek detained Maruyama, the 17th Army would adjust X-Day based upon Tsuji's estimate of the necessary amount of delay. Hyakutake kept these instructions from the 2d Division's officers to encourage their efforts.

General Nasu's Left Wing stepped off as planned on October 16, accompanied by Colonel Tamaoki. A load of ammunition, including an artillery shell, and twelve days of rations bowed each soldier.[3] The gunners disassembled all their artillery pieces and hand-carried them. The Maruyama Road was a grandiloquently named small foot trail, only 20 to 24 inches wide, that tunneled through the jungle between the trees. Without accurate maps or detailed prior reconnaissance, the Japanese navigated by compass bearing, a technique that obliged them to avoid wide detours around obstacles. Many sharp-edged ridges crosshatched the division's route between the Matanikau and the Lunga, some so precipitous that men hoisted themselves upward hand over hand with vine ropes. To their dismay, Maruyama's men found the terrain even more fine-grained in the Lunga River Valley. Each day the first man would commence breaking trail early in the morning, but the last units could only begin to shuffle forward in the afternoon. Under the weight of their weapons, the artillerymen gradually sank back down the column.

On October 18, the last elements of the division began to march. Eighteen miles ahead of them, the van units reached the Lunga River. They selected a chest-deep fording point, 50 meters across, but no units crossed until after sunset to evade the glimpse of American airmen. That night Tsuji telephoned the 17th Army to report that there was no sign the Sendai's move had been discovered. He estimated that it would require four days to complete the concentration and preparations for the division's attack, thus making the prospective attack date October 22. The situation sketch the 17th Army radioed Rabaul contained a plaintive request for more air support and confessed that about one-third of the supplies landed by the High-Speed Convoy had been destroyed. Nonetheless, the 17th Army sounded an ebullient note about the future: "The victory is already in our hands. Please rest your minds."

---

[3]Later events strongly suggest the amount of food carried by the Sendai soldiers was considerably less than a twelve-day supply, and may have been more like five days' worth.

On October 19, two reports buoyed spirits in the 17th Army higher. Sugita observed the marines reinforcing the western end of their perimeter, which evinced the success of Sumiyoshi's feint, and the Imperial Navy forwarded excerpts from recent American and Allied radio broadcasts filled with gloom and doom about the situation on Guadalcanal. From these latter revelations the 17th Army took consolation for its own difficulties and extracted the conviction that American morale was rotting. By sunset of October 19, the point units of the Sendai gauged their position as 4 miles north of the Lunga ford. That night Sendai infantrymen sharpened their bayonets.

Early the next morning, October 20, the division headquarters reached the same point which Maruyama named the "Clear Water Valley." Maruyama thought he stood only a little over a mile short of the planned deployment area, 4 miles south of the airfield. In fact, the Clear Water Valley lay only 2 miles from the Lunga ford and 8 miles from Henderson Field. At noon he issued the divisional attack order, setting the time of attack as 1800 hours, October 22. The Left and Right Wings would initially advance abreast on an axis generally parallel to the east bank of the Lunga across the airfield and to the coast near the mouth of the Lunga. Following the Left Wing would be the reserve regiment under Maruyama's control. At 1300, the general ordered a concentration of the division, with strict regard to secrecy. From his battle headquarters, Hyakutake fixed X-Day for October 22 and solemnly announced: "The time of the decisive battle between Japan and the United States has come." His staff began detailed planning of how to handle the American surrender.

During the 2d Division's march, along the coast Sumiyoshi sorted his command and deftly directed a play for the edification of the American commanders. He divided his artillery array, refurbished by the convoy, into two groups; one with the fifteen available 150mm howitzers would set its sights on the airfield, and the remaining seventeen tubes (seven field and three mountain 75mm guns plus seven 100mm guns or howitzers) would support the infantry attacks. Both groupments remained constrained by the shortage of ammunition.[4] Sumiyoshi also split the rifle units in two: Colonel Oka led his 124th Infantry Regiment (less its 3d Battalion) plus the 3d Battalion, 4th Infantry, and Colonel Nakaguma controlled the two remaining

---

[4]Also available for their specialized roles were the 2d Anti-Tank Battalion and two antiaircraft battalions plus one battery.

battalions of his 4th Infantry Regiment. Sumiyoshi ordered Oka to cross the Matanikau south of the one-log bridge, occupy Mount Austen, and prepare to attack north against the American positions on the east bank of the river. The main effort would be made by Nakaguma along the coast, spearheaded by the 1st Independent Tank Company.

On the 18th, Sumiyoshi began proffering omens for an attack along the coastal front. The 150mm batteries renewed shelling Henderson Field, where operations were already at a standstill. Colonel Nakaguma's 4th Infantry Regiment turned its energies to construction and demonstrations near the coast to simulate the presence of the bulk of the Japanese forces. Colonel Oka departed Kokumbona early on October 19, crossed the Matanikau that evening, and left the Maruyama Road to swing north over craggy terrain. The Americans reacted to these scenes with intense artillery fire, prompting Colonel Nakaguma to lament, "One shot from us brings one hundred in retaliation." On October 20, Nakaguma commenced to surreptitiously gather his regiment west of Point Cruz. During the evening three tanks prickled American interest near the mouth of the Matanikau. They drew fire which wounded the platoon commander and two men and damaged one vehicle.

American commanders found Sumiyoshi's diversions persuasive because they possessed little concrete information as to Japanese intentions. A captured map suggested a three-pronged attack by a trio of divisions from east, west, and south. But no trace of Japanese forces appeared to the east, and to the south patrols found only "bands of dispirited, half starved, poorly armed stragglers and deserters." Air patrols consistently returned with negative reports. In the absence of hard evidence of enemy plans, an awareness of the vulnerabilities in American dispositions naturally flavored conjectures. The arrival of the 164th Infantry Regiment prompted revision of the main perimeter. Colonel Pepper of the 3d Defense Battalion directed the consolidated beach defenses while the rest of the perimeter was apportioned among four regimental sectors, two on each side of the Lunga. The novice 164th guarded the easternmost sector, the least likely subject of enemy activity. Its right (west) flank dovetailed into the sector held by the 7th Marines, which straddled Edson's Ridge and extended west to the Lunga. Beyond the Lunga, the 1st Marines and then the 5th Marines successively held the line. The 3d Battalion, 2d Marines was truck-mounted as the motorized divisional reserve and was buttressed by the light tanks of the 1st Tank Battalion. Each regiment held one of its battalions in reserve, but

Vandegrift appropriated two of these reserve battalions for special employment.

After the recent action on the Matanikau, Vandegrift left two battalions in an advanced battle position at the mouth of the Matanikau. The Marine command accepted this serious strain on its resources and the admitted tactical danger of such a disposition because the Matanikau outpost blocked the Government Track, the only feasible route of approach for tanks, wheeled vehicles, or artillery pieces. By mid-October a fortified "horseshoe" frowned down from the high ground along the Matanikau from the sea to the one-log bridge with flanks refused along the coast and inland; the open end of the horseshoe faced east toward the main perimeter. Defending the horseshoe was the "McKelvy Group," consisting principally of the 3d Battalion, 1st Marines (Lieutenant Colonel William J. McKelvy) and the 3d Battalion, 7th Marines. Between the horseshoe and the main American perimeter lay an unavoidable gap tenuously covered by patrols at night. This dangling detachment naturally caused much concern.

On October 21 the 11th Air Fleet commenced its program of support of the attack with a raid by twenty-five Zeros in two installments and nine bombers. In a tussle over Guadalcanal with fifteen Wildcats, one Zero and two Wildcats fell. For the Sendai Division, October 21 marked the sixth day of conflict with the jungle. Early in the morning, Japanese soldiers began what they thought would be a stealthy, but short, march to the southern threshold of the American perimeter. The riotous vegetation put a checkrein on movement, and the trailblazing party drifted off the direct course for the American positions. By nightfall, the certainty that the division had not achieved its line of departure for the attack was coupled with doubts as to when it would. Maruyama accepted a proposal from Tamaoki to move X-Day back twenty-four hours to October 23, and Hyakutake attached his apologies to the news of the postponement to Rabaul.

To retain American attention during the delay, Sumiyoshi ordered Oka to attack up the east bank of the Matanikau on the evening of October 22, and to continue his drive on the 23d to seize high ground east of the river. Sumiyoshi also saw to it that the American position on the Matanikau received a substantial dose of artillery fire around sunset of October 21.

About the time the Japanese barrage fell, General Thomas Holcomb, the Commandant of the Marine Corps, arrived at Henderson Field. During October 22, amid occasional Japanese artillery fire,

Holcomb toured the front-line positions. At 1300 a raid by a dozen Vals of the 31st Air Group with an equal number of Zero escorts enriched Holcomb's education about Guadalcanal. They went after destroyer *Nicholas* in Lunga Roads and missed; twenty-nine Wildcats intercepted and downed two of the Val raiders. Unpersuaded by this episode, the liaison officer of the 11th Air Fleet on Guadalcanal signaled his assessment that American air power had been "generally suppressed" by air attack and shelling.

During Holcomb's inspection, at a vantage point near Edson's Ridge, Vandegrift pointed to a firing lane he described as "a machinegunner's dream." Only a few miles away, Japanese engineers finished extending a trail to near the intended deployment line and the Left Wing Unit began to gather. The bulk of the division, however, remained strung out over miles of rain-soaked trails. In the evening of October 22, Maruyama reached the deployment line. The Japanese estimated they were only 4 miles south of the airfield. Although sober officers experienced serious doubts that the two wings—much less the division reserve and the artillery units—could be in position to attack the night of the 23d, Maruyama ruled out a postponement. Long after dark, Japanese soldiers continued with staggering steps to move toward the assembly area.

The 17th Army remained confident that the Sendai Division would attack on the 23d. Hyakutake directed Sumiyoshi to secure the right bank of the Matanikau as early as possible on the 23d, and the Koli Detachment to sail at noon that day. Sumiyoshi forthwith ordered a two-pronged attack for early on the 23d: Oka would crack the American line with a thrust up the east bank of the Matanikau, and then Nakaguma would jab across the river.

October 23 proved to be a day of major developments. At the urging of Holcomb, Vandegrift departed in the morning to Noumea for a conference with Halsey. In his stead, Geiger took charge of American forces on Guadalcanal. Admiral Kusaka dispatched a major raid: twelve Zeros on a fighter sweep ahead of seventeen other Zeros as a close escort for sixteen Bettys. The fighter commander of the Cactus Air Force, Lieutenant Colonel Harold Bauer, scrambled everything he had, two dozen Wildcats and a quartet of P-39s, with the admonishment "When you see Zeros, dog fight 'em." Despite the recently unfavorable fighter exchange rate, this radical shift in tactics stemmed from both growing assurance in their own prowess and the distinct impression of a noticeable decline in the average quality of the current crop of Zero pilots. The results seemed to justify Bauer's orders: claims amounted to a startling twenty-one Zeros and two bombers. On the debit side, seven Wildcats returned damaged and one VF-5 aircraft was immediately parked in the "bone heap." Captain Joseph Foss claimed four victories, but his riddled Wildcat only regained Henderson Field via a dead-stick landing. Actual Japanese losses totaled six fighters and one bomber.

Early on October 23, Japanese soldiers dropped their packs and each unit began to slice its own trail north toward the American perimeter. Scouts radiated out, but many failed to return, and those who did could only gasp that there was jungle in every direction. By now there was rust on the bayonets carefully honed on the 19th, and the physical strength wrung from each man by a week's slogging through a tightly braided jungle left most functioning mechanically. Captain Jiro Katsumata in Nasu's Left Wing scribbled in his diary:

> . . . I cannot any longer think of anything, the enemy, food, home or even myself . . . [I am] only a spirit drifting toward an undefined, unknowable world.

Without visual reference points or patrol reports on the terrain or enemy dispositions, the Japanese commanders were blindly groping when during this travail there arrived like a godsend a set of aerial photographs. The story of the production and distribution of these prints began when cameras of the 76th Army Independent Air Squadron snapped views on October 13 and 14 which revealed the presence of supply depots along the southern periphery of the American positions and fortifications along Edson's Ridge. General Miyazaki reasoned that the emplacements visible on the ridge must be part of a line of defenses in the jungle guarding the logistical facilities. He wished to take the images to Guadalcanal personally, but the Imperial Navy insisted he remain at Rabaul for coordination purposes. Miyazaki therefore had them air-dropped at Kokumbona on October 17. By this time the 2d Division had already begun its trek. Inexplicably, the photographs met with indifference, incomprehension, or both when they passed through the 17th Army Headquarters for distribution.

Kawaguchi claimed that as early as October 18, he had deduced from the photographs that strong fortifications girded the sector he was slated to attack. He believed that if he shifted his thrust to the east he would greatly enhance his chances of success. He discussed his views with Nasu, but the reaction of that officer or any other senior officer to Kawaguchi's thoughts for the next several days is not documented. By October 22, after reciting his reasoning to the ubiquitous Tsuji, Kawaguchi believed he had won a disciple to his views. Confident that Tsuji would secure formal approval to the change of plans, Kawaguchi began to redispose his men, characteristically without waiting for orders.

The murkiness of Japanese command relationships and the absence of documentation of the activities of the 2d Division Headquarters for October 23 makes important segments of this day's events misty. At noon, Tsuji reported to the 17th Army Headquarters that the enemy defenses appeared sturdy in front of the Left Wing but fragile in front of the Right Wing, and that the 2d Division had switched the 16th Infantry over to follow Kawaguchi. Whether this report represented Tsuji's information or expectations is uncertain. At the same time, Kawaguchi's hungry and exhausted men swung out to the east of Nasu's command and chopped their own new trails in absolutely trackless jungle. At 1600, Maruyama opened a message from Kawaguchi, timed 1445, which disclosed that the Right Wing was still in thick jungle, but had just reached flatter land for the first time. Its advanced reconnaissance unit had been out of touch since the day before. The two battalions of Colonel Shoji's 230th Infantry were still on the trail and only the III/124 was up with Kawaguchi. Therefore Kawaguchi would be able to attack with only one of his three battalions that night. This message followed upon news of Kawaguchi's plan to pull the axis of his attack to the east. Maruyama found this unacceptable, since it would inevitably lead to another day's delay.

By field telephone, Colonel Tamaoki, chief of staff of the Sendai Division, instructed Kawaguchi not to attempt to deviate from the original plan of attack. But the cantankerous Kawaguchi retorted: "I cannot take responsibility for a frontal attack as a unit commander." He requested Tamaoki to discuss the matter with Maruyama. About thirty minutes later a second call informed Kawaguchi that he would not have to take responsibility for a frontal attack, he was dismissed as unit commander. By seniority, command now vested in Colonel Shoji of the 230th Infantry. But an ailing Shoji protested that the relief of a commander on the eve of battle "was not the way of the samurai." All his objections won him were shouts over the field telephone from Tamaoki that these were "Orders! Orders!"

While Kawaguchi wrangled, Nasu's Left Wing Unit mustered in a position approximately 2 to 2.5 miles south of Edson's Ridge, though yet again the Japanese believed they were only a fraction of that distance from American lines. Late in the afternoon, 17th Army

Headquarters learned from Tsuji that delays would preclude Kawaguchi's Right Wing from joining an attack that night, which the 2d Division Headquarters still anticipated; that the ranks of most units were thinned by stragglers; and that only part of the 16th Infantry Regiment was in position. Tsuji added that there was still no sign that they had been detected, as the Americans were "playing tennis" beside the airfield. Although Colonel Konuma recognized that further delay would antagonize the Imperial Navy, which was already extremely disgruntled with the postponement to the 23d, and might result in entirely forfeiting support of the Combined Fleet, he balanced this against the need to mass the full strength of the 2d Division to make a coordinated attack. To allow the Right Wing to attain its position and the reserve to assemble and to prepare would require one more day. Accordingly, Hyakutake ratified Maruyama's proposal to reset the attack time for 1900 the following day—Japanese accounts consistently show Hyakutake deferring to his staff or commanders—and the necessary orders were issued in time for Yamamoto to inform the Combined Fleet at 1838 that X-Day was now October 24.

Sumiyoshi's highly successful charades along the shore to simulate the entire Japanese force continued to prosper on October 23. What made Sumiyoshi's conjuring act so compelling was the complete American failure to unearth evidence of the Sendai Division's jungle march, but this failure may not fairly be traced to simple negligence by the Marine command. Maruyama traversed totally uninhabited areas where his passage neither disturbed native villages nor crossed native trails routinely covered by Clemens's scouts. Two detachments of native scouts sent far up the Lunga River sent no reports, nor did an independent patrol from the 5th Marines. A three-day deep patrol by the skilled Scout-Snipers likewise drew a blank, and the dense jungle made the Sendai Division impervious to aerial observation. In fact, the record suggests that Maruyama's path veered much farther south than even he intended, so he inadvertently steered around any possible patrol contact.

Given the picture presented to the American command, it is not surprising to find that they successively shifted artillery positions until nine batteries were arrayed west of the Lunga. On the 23d, there was a further important realignment of the infantry battalions. For some time the Marine command had intended to eliminate the untidy grouping at the Matanikau horseshoe of McKelvy's battalion of the 1st Marines and the 3d Battalion, 7th Marines by replacing McKelvy's unit with the 2d Battalion, 7th Marines and the headquarters of the 7th Marines to gain organic unity and provide proper command facilities. As the reverse side of this choice, however, Lieutenant Colonel Puller's 1st Battalion, 7th Marines would be left alone to hold the entire 2,500-yard frontage on the southern face of the main perimeter east of the Lunga River. The risk of "singling up the line"—the borrowed nautical term for leaving one battalion to man a position designed for two—was considered acceptable in view of the negative intelligence on the enemy presence south of the perimeter.

At sunrise on October 23, Sumiyoshi's operating orders required an attack that day to support the main thrust from the south. Of Sumiyoshi's two infantry commanders, Oka was experiencing many of the same problems as Maruyama. Since swinging off the Maruyama Road on October 19, Oka had encountered exceedingly difficult terrain and only reached the northwest end of Mount Austen at dawn of October 21. During the entire day of October 22, Oka made good only a little over a half mile because of a great jungled ravine with clifflike sides. Oka accompanied his report of this fact at 0900 on October 23 with the news that he was uncertain of the location of two of his three rifle battalions that had marched somewhat to the east to seize high ground between the main American perimeter and the Matanikau horseshoe. Nonetheless, Oka pledged he would attack at 1500.

Sumiyoshi's other infantry commander, Nakaguma, organized his attack to send in the 2d Battalion, 4th Infantry (II/4) and the 1st Independent Tank Company, with the 1st Battalion, 4th Infantry (I/4) in their wake, against the Marine positions at the mouth of the Matanikau immediately after Oka initiated his assault. At 1320, Sumiyoshi instructed Nakaguma to start the attack at 1500. Nakaguma directed II/4 to prepare, but now the customary series of delays occurred. The 1st Tank Company moved to within 200 yards of the American positions by 1600, their noisy approach carefully planned and concealed by a drizzle of artillery fire that fell into the American areas during the entire day. The companies of the II/4 only commenced marching at 1700, compelling the Japanese tankers to wait. As the sunlight dwindled, miles away Tsuji telephoned his message that sparked the decision to postpone the attack another day. Sumiyoshi got word of this by field telephone in time to issue his own postponement order at 1720, but this directive failed to reach its intended recipients. Radio supplied Sumiyoshi's only means of communication with Oka and Nakaguma, and both of these latter officers were separated by the terrain not only from each other but also from their subordinate units. Word of the delay never got to Nakaguma's battalions, which attacked piecemeal.

At dusk, Japanese artillery fire suddenly swelled into a heavy barrage on the Matanikau horseshoe. "It looks like this is the night," snapped Lieutenant Colonel Twining, the operations officer of the 1st Marine Division. The clank and squeal of Japanese tanks was audible on the far bank of the Matanikau shortly before they commenced their attack. The first of the 15-ton Type 97s waddled up the coastal track to be stopped by a 37mm anti-tank gun. A second dashed out from a hidden trail and churned across the sandbar, smashing through barbed wire and crushing a machinegun position. It then reared on a stump and halted near the foxhole of Private Joseph D. R. Champagne. The nimble marine reached out and placed a grenade that ruptured the track on one side of the tank. As the tank slewed away into the surf, a half-track mounting a 75mm gun pursued and destroyed it. With the aid of flare illumination, a hail of anti-tank fire disabled the final pair of tanks, including two 7.5-ton Type 95 light tanks, in the first wave; these same weapons converted a second wave of five tanks into hulks on the sandbar. Of the forty-four men of the 1st Independent Tank Company who went into the attack only seventeen, including seven wounded, survived.

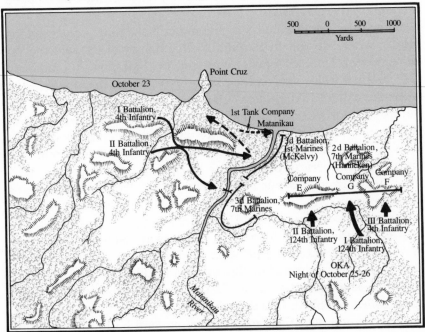

Matanikau Actions, October 23–26

The quantum increase in Japanese firepower was more than matched. The 2d, 3d, and 5th Battalions of the 11th Marines and I Battery, 10th Marines, a total of forty howitzers, heaved fire up and down preplanned range ladders about 500 yards east and west of Point Cruz. After the bombload of an SBD crumped into the base of Point Cruz, Lieutenant Colonel McKelvy requested more air support because, he cracked, it "peps the boys up." Marines could literally hear Japanese soldiers moaning and groaning beneath the pummeling. Over 6,000 rounds from Marine artillery pieces and mortars crushed the infantry attack before it really got started. Rain began to patter down at 2100, and within about an hour the marines extinguished the last embers of the attack. After a brief flurry of activity near midnight, all was quiet along the Matanikau by 0115. Losses in McKelvy's battalion amounted to only two killed and eleven wounded. Apart from the tank company, Japanese losses are not detailed but were unquestionably severe among the riflemen.

While Nakaguma's attack foundered, in Noumea Admiral Halsey presided over a conference with Vandegrift, Harmon, Patch, Holcomb, and Turner. At Halsey's bidding, Vandegrift outlined the campaign to date and current intelligence on Japanese forces. He accented the poor physical state of the malaria-riddled 1st Marine Division and the effect on morale of the constant shelling and bombing and the endless stream of Japanese reinforcements. Harmon and Holcomb seconded Vandegrift, while Turner recited an exposition of the Navy's problems and shortages—few ships getting fewer all the time. Halsey drummed his fingers on the table a moment and then, gray eyebrows bristling, he turned to Vandegrift and asked, "Can you hold?"

"Yes, I can hold," replied the Marine general, "but I have to have more active support than I have been getting."

Halsey nodded and said, "You go on back there, Vandegrift. I promise to give you everything I have."

THE SENDAI ATTACKS

At first light of October 24, the marines on the Matanikau caught sight of a long column of Japanese (obviously one of Oka's battalions) on a bare ridge to the left rear of the American position filing down into a heavily wooded ravine. Despite an application of air bombardment and artillery fire, this unit posed an obvious threat to the flank and rear of the Matanikau horseshoe. Accordingly, Lieutenant Colonel Hanneken's 2d Battalion, 7th Marines (2/7), instead of replacing McKelvy's battalion at the river mouth, deployed to a high ridge facing south which formed a natural and continuous extension of the inland flank of the horseshoe. Hanneken tied in loosely with the 3d Battalion, 7th Marines on his right (west), but a gap remained between his left (east) flank and the main perimeter.

With Hanneken gone, Lieutenant Colonel Puller stretched his single 700-man battalion to cover the entire regimental front. His 2,500-yard sector ran from east to west, first along a grassy plain southeast of Henderson Field bordered by a stretch of thick jungle, up a ridge that surfaced from the jungle on a westerly course, and then across the already blood-soaked north-south ridge that was the scene of the September battle. Puller initially thought to spread his three rifle companies evenly westward to screen his sector, but after discussion with Captain Charles Kelly, his executive officer, he instead withdrew one platoon from each rifle company and deployed them, with attached machineguns, in the positions Hanneken's battalion had materially improved about Edson's Ridge. This scheme left Puller's companies in the order A, C, B, and the composite company from east to west. The regimental commander ordered, over Puller's objection, the stationing of a forty-six-man platoon from Company A under Platoon Sergeant Ralph Briggs as an outpost on a hill 1,500 yards in front of Puller's left flank. Although the Marine command remained ignorant of danger from the south, Puller was not complacent about his assignment. He personally walked the entire line checking each firing position and ordering improvements.

Late on October 24, two startling pieces of information suddenly emerged. A man who strayed from a 7th Marines patrol reported he saw a Japanese officer studying Edson's Ridge through binoculars. A Scout-Sniper added that he had seen the smoke of "many rice fires" at a point several miles up the Lunga. But it was now too late to rearrange the American dispositions.

The two wings of the Sendai division reached what they thought was a point a little over a mile south of the airfield by 1400, at which time Maruyama set the attack for 1900. Each wing began opening a set of four trails toward the American lines through dense jungle. About 1600, sheets of rain began to rustle on the foliage; within an hour the storm intensified. Each footfall became treacherous, and in places the advancing riflemen waded down into waist-deep bogs of mud. Immediately after sunset the clouds obscured the moon and total darkness descended—units could not maintain direction and individuals could not see the man in front of them. The hour of the attack came and passed in the saturated jungle and the assault units still had not contacted the American line. But at 2100 the rain halted and, through circlets in the jungle canopy, the Japanese gazed up to light from a bright moon.

The disruptive effects of the exhaustion induced by the long jungle approach march and then the rain and darkness now enveloped the Sendai Division's assault this night in dense confusion. In theory, the Sendai Division's two wings, both composed of three rifle battalions each of about the same strength as Puller's, were hewing trails side by side toward the American line. Behind them came another three rifle battalions of the division reserve. In reality, near chaos totally obscured this scheme. The evidence strongly suggests that Shoji's Right Wing strayed onto a northeasterly course tangential to the trace of the American perimeter. One or the other of his two leading battalions, or even conceivably a unit of the Left Wing, passed within earshot of the outpost in front of Puller's line held by Sergeant Briggs at about 2130. Puller directed Briggs to withdraw to the east and reenter the main perimeter. Though some members became sepa-

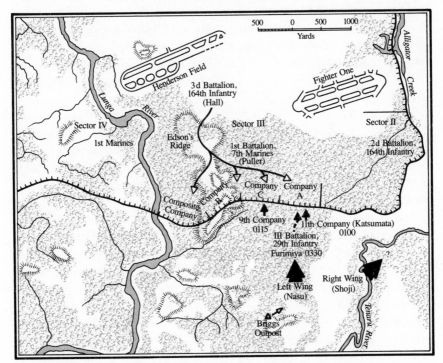

Second (Sendai) Division Attacks, Night of October 24–25

rated, Briggs moved his detachment to a clearing before the sector held by the 164th Infantry. As Briggs paused, a large body of Japanese, estimated as a battalion, passed close enough for one Japanese soldier to trip on a marine's helmet lying on the ground. The next day, Briggs led his men into American lines. Most of the missing men showed up over the next several days, and the last man turned up two weeks later. Three men remained forever unaccounted for and three others were killed and ten wounded.

Whether Shoji ever established firm control of his command is unclear, and according to some Japanese accounts, one of his battalions may have drifted to the west until it fell into the wake of the Left Wing and completely missed the action. Most likely, however, Shoji's 1st Battalion, 230th Infantry (I/230) stumbled into Puller's lines about 2200. Puller directed his men to hold their fire as long as he dared to let the outpost clear the firing area. Although the I/230 made no impression on the American perimeter, about 2200 the 2d Division Headquarters received a report that the Right Wing had overrun the defense lines and was moving into the grass clearing east of the airfield. The damp and anxious staff of the 17th Army became ecstatic when Colonel Matsumoto, operations officer of the 2d Division, called to inform them that the airfield was in Japanese hands. Matsumoto's report may well have been the product of a literally fevered misinterpretation of news reaching him, for he had a bad case of malaria, but at 0050, October 25, 17th Army signaled: "2300 Banzai—a little before 2300 the Right Wing captured the airfield."

In contrast to the marginal participation of the Right Wing, General Nasu's Left Wing definitely plunged into battle this night. Nasu's order of march arranged his three battalions in column. The leading battalion, the 1st Battalion, 29th Infantry (I/29), forged ahead shedding men and then its 3d Company along the east side of a swamp area and gradually drifting to the east. Eventually the battalion commander, Captain Kehei Nakajima, found a company from the 3d Battalion intermingled with his column. An impromptu reorganization gave Captain Nakajima this stray company and made him leader of the "right front line unit"; the 3d Battalion, 29th Infantry (III/29) gained the title, though probably not the position, of "left front line unit."

In the vanguard of the III/29 were five scouts, Captain Jiro Katsumata's 11th Company and the battalion headquarters. The scouts located the American barbed-wire defenses along a densely jungled flat east of Edson's Ridge at about 0030, October 25, and drew a nervous burst of rifle fire. Captain Katsumata strode forward and found a grass clearing bristling with barbed wire about sixty feet from the edge of the woods. The battalion commander and executive officer and the engineer platoon leader joined Katsumata, and the movement drew machinegun fire from the right and left in front of the Japanese command group. They hurriedly decided to press through between the two American machinegun emplacements before American artillery began to fall. Katsumata would use one platoon to mask the machinegun position to his left and take the rest of his company into the gap.

While the engineers began snipping passages through the wire, Katsumata brought his company forward in a quiet crawl through grass less than a foot tall. But extreme fatigue yielded erratic behavior: a few men stood up and began walking to the left; another man loosed a war cry and, despite Katsumata's orders, others took it up. This triggered the American machineguns and mortars. Most of the company snagged on the wire entanglements, and bullets, blast, and fragments killed the majority in front of Puller's Company A at about 0100.

The 9th Company was ostensibly following Katsumata's company, but it sheered considerably to the left (west). About 0115 this unit gave a great ululation and charged straight into the firing lanes of machineguns attached to Puller's Company C. Within about five minutes almost the entire Japanese company lay lifeless. The destruction of this company was mainly the work of Sergeant John Basilone's machinegun section and only the start of a long night of fierce fighting that won Basilone the Medal of Honor. By 0125, American artillery began to fall neatly along the path of the Left Wing, with devastating effect. Those who stood up were quickly chopped down by hot splinters or flattened by concussion; those who sought refuge off the trails into the jungle became lost.

By now Puller recognized that a major attack by "seasoned, well-disciplined troops" was in progress. Puller fed three platoons from 3d Battalion, 164th infantry (3/164), held as immediate reserves, rapidly into his line and requested major reinforcements. At 0200, the bulk of Lieutenant Colonel Robert Hall's 3/164 was ordered to Puller's aid. The National Guardsmen confronted as stern a test as a new unit could face: a night march along a muddy jungle trail in torrential rain to a raging battle whose dimensions were unclear, but whose ferocity was plainly audible. At 0345, Hall's battalion reached Puller's sector, and the Army commander wisely and willingly assented to allowing his untested unit to be distributed piecemeal into

Puller's line. Two companies buttressed Puller's hard-pressed left while one company went to the right. The National Guardsmen were literally led into position by the hand and dispersed along the Marine line by squads and platoons.

Through the American barrage only Colonel Furimiya, the commander of the 29th Infantry, penetrated with his headquarters and the 7th ("Color Escort") Company, but by the time he reached the front line it was nearly dawn. Coincidentally with his arrival, a heretofore lost rifle company presented itself, and the colonel directed the commander of the III/29 to take two companies and "charge." When Captain Katsumata returned wounded from an incursion into the American lines, Furimiya decided to follow him back into the enemy position.

The commander of the III/29 marshaled what men he could as a machinegun company sprayed all its ammunition from a quartet of weapons as covering fire. The American barrage clawed through the ranks of III/29, and only about 200 men reached the barbed wire, where the now unemployed machinegunners, who wielded bayonets, joined them. Perceiving that III/29 was attracting most of the enemy firepower, Furimiya led the color company with the sacred colors of the 29th Infantry in an assault to the right (east) of III/29 at 0330. Most of the Japanese died or were flung back at the wire, but over a hundred men intruded into the American positions, led by their colonel.

Just before he personally headed this onslaught, Furimiya instructed the commander of the 2d Battalion, 29th Infantry (II/29) to add the weight of his unit to the attack. By the time approximately half the II/29 had assembled, about 0400, the eastern sky was lightening. The battalion commander led two companies in an assault after sunrise, but they were checked at the edge of the jungle. About 0730, Nasu decided to withdraw back into the jungle and prepare another night attack.

The first rays of light revealed the outcome of the all-night struggle. One contingent of Japanese had carved a salient 150 yards in width and 100 yards deep in the center of Puller's line. During the hours of sunshine, the marines eradicated this toehold, recapturing two machineguns and seizing three Japanese machineguns among a litter of thirty-seven Japanese bodies. The rest of the Japanese who seeped through American lines were scattered in small isolated groups; Furimiya retained immediate control of only ten. Marine patrols killed sixty-seven of these infiltrators during the day, to add to the toll of those piled thickly along the wire. At least 300 men of the Sendai fell on the wire or within the perimeter—and artillery and mortars claimed more victims beyond the perimeter.

"DUGOUT SUNDAY"

With the Imperial Army hurling its full clout into a night attack, daylight of October 25 brought the Imperial Navy to Guadalcanal by air and also, exceptionally, by sea. As at the time of Kawaguchi's attack, early in the morning a twin-engine reconnaissance plane winged off from Rabaul to determine who held Henderson Field. This plane and its eight Zero escorts reached Guadalcanal at 0800. At that time artillery fire still interdicted Henderson Field and the preceding night's heavy rains inundated the satellite field, Fighter One. The zealous crew of the reconnaissance plane rashly chose to make a low-level inspection of Henderson Field and died in the pyre of their plane, blasted to earth by antiaircraft fire.

Meanwhile SBDs managed to lift from shell-pocked and awash runways on search flights that revealed the close investment of the island by the Imperial Navy. They found three destroyers at 0700 only 85 miles distant, though headed away from the island. Two hours later, SBDs sighted a stronger contingent at a range of 105 miles to the north-northwest on an approach course. These groups were among the five separate task units Admiral Mikawa formed to perform reinforcement and blockade missions in support of the Army attack. Reinforcement Unit A with light cruiser *Tatsuta,* minelayer *Tsugaru,* and two destroyers provided the sea lift for the Koli Detachment. Reinforcement Unit B of three destroyers stood by to forward fuel and material to put Henderson Field into immediate Japanese use. Three detachments would preclude American flight or reinforcement by sea. To the west, light cruiser *Sendai* and Destroyer Division 19 patrolled. Destroyer Division 6 (*Akatsuki, Ikazuchi,* and *Shiratsuyu*) under Commander Yusuke Yamada carried the operational title First Assault Unit and would contain the Americans at Lunga and Koli Points. The Second Assault Unit of light cruiser *Yura* and five destroyers would block to the east. This detachment was under the direction of Rear Admiral Takama, the commander of Destroyer Squadron 4, who flew his flag in antiaircraft destroyer *Akizuki.*

American planes had detected the two assault units, and their contrasting courses derived from a rapid evolution of orders during the early-morning hours. The erroneous news of the capture of the airfield prompted Mikawa at 0037 on October 25 to release his various units to carry out their diverse missions. When Mikawa learned at 0430 of the cancellation of the success signal, he recalled his units, which explains why the First Assault Unit was steaming away from Guadalcanal when observed. But at 0700, a report reached Mikawa's hands that the results of the attack on Henderson Field were unknown, and that the Army was requesting a bombardment of American artillery positions west of the Lunga. Fifteen minutes later, the liaison officer on Guadalcanal flashed a message that Lunga anchorage held an American "light cruiser." This was a flattering misidentification of one of two destroyer-minesweeper conversions, *Trevor* and *Zane*, that steamed into Lunga Roads after dawn each with two motor torpedo boats in tow.

The 8th Fleet Headquarters thought the Army was tottering on the verge of success and that perhaps only a nudge, such as a ship bombardment, would clinch the victory. Accordingly, the First Assault Unit of three destroyers drew a new assignment to conduct the shore bombardment; they put about for Lunga Point at 0815. One hour later, the Combined Fleet, monitoring these developments, directed the Second Assault Unit of *Yura* and five destroyers to join this attack. This order proved superfluous, because on his own initiative Takama had already led his vessels toward Guadalcanal.

Having discharged their tows and cargoes, *Trevor* and *Zane* were standing by—ironically anticipating a possible bombardment of Japanese positions—when they heard a radio warning of approaching Japanese warships. By 1014, lookouts sighted three enemy destroyers. Lieutenant Commander Agnew of *Trevor*, the senior officer, knew his elderly vessels, armed now only with 3-inch guns, were hopelessly outmatched. He therefore got them underway to attempt to flee via Sealark Channel. The enemy trio gave chase and, when the range measured only 5 miles, opened fire at 1027. Japanese gunners quickly found their targets and began landing shells "feet not yards" from *Trevor*'s decks. Engineers roused 29 knots from the worn machinery of *Trevor* and *Zane* (a boiler casing burned entirely through on *Trevor*), but the more modern Japanese easily closed the range so that despite a zigzag, at 1038 a 5-inch shell hit *Zane*, killing three men and knocking out a gun. Realizing he could not outsprint the enemy, Agnew decided to outdare them by turning his ships hard left into the dangerous Nagella Channel. Commander Yamada chose to attend to his bombardment mission, perhaps figuring that *Trevor* and *Zane* would become sport for Takama.

Standing in toward Guadalcanal, Yamada's vessels first dealt with tug *Seminole* and *YP-284*. Both these vessels were fresh from one of their regular domestic hauling missions of gasoline, ammunition, and a battery of artillery when they saw and were seen by the Japanese. Japanese shells killed three Marine passengers and ignited gasoline aboard *YP-284* before the "tuna boat" sank swathed in flames. *Seminole* lasted only slightly longer before she disappeared in a puddle of fire, but most Japanese shells simply punctured her flimsy hull without exploding, and only one man was lost. Following these appetizers, the Japanese destroyers commenced shelling in the Lunga vicinity, but Marine shore batteries plunked a shell into a gun mount on *Akatsuki* at 1053 that started a fire. The Japanese retired behind a smoke screen, but four Wildcats of VMF-121 then strafed them, bringing the Japanese casualty total for the engagement up to six killed and two wounded on *Akatsuki* and *Ikazuchi*.

The four Americans attracted the attention of the first contingent, eight strong, of the twenty-seven Zeros which arrived in four relays between 1000 and 1430. In the ensuing combat, Lieutenant J. E. Conger swapped fire head-on with a Zero only 1,500 feet above the sea, and then, as the Zero passed overhead, Conger rammed the enemy plane. Conger parachuted, his opponent did not, but another Zero pilot, Pilot Officer 2d Class Shirō Ishikawa, splashed down near the Marine aviator. A Higgins boat picked up Conger, who bent his rescuers from their intent to murder his seemingly helpless adversary into an attempt to provide the same service for the enemy airman. When Conger reached out to Ishikawa, the Japanese flier brandished a pistol, pushed it into Conger's face, and pulled the trigger. The weapon emitted only a wet click; it repeated the sound when Ishikawa set it against his own head. A sailor grabbed the gun and the Zero pilot was manhandled into captivity.[5]

Conger's adventure contributed only one story of this, the busiest day to date in the life of the Cactus Air Force. After the field became semidry, Wildcats continuously roared off, engaged flights of Zeros and bombers, landed, rearmed, and refueled, and took off again. A major raid of sixteen Bettys with twelve Zeros in escort reached the island at 1430; of their number, two bombers and one fighter did not return. Thirty minutes later, Japanese carrier planes put in an appearance in accordance with orders issued by Yamamoto at 1057 for

---

[5]Shirō Ishikawa spent the rest of the conflict as a prisoner of war in New Zealand. After the war, he returned to Japan for additional education and then worked in the Tokyo branch of the Chase Manhattan Bank for thirty years. In April 1990, he and Jack Conger met for the first time since their encounter in 1942.

more effort to neutralize the artillery batteries checking the Imperial Army and to get the reported "light cruiser" in Lunga Roads. At 1335, Carrier Division 2 launched twenty-four aircraft, equally divided between Zeros and Vals. These aircraft bombed at 1500, and all returned safely.

At division headquarters, Lieutenant H. C. Merillat scribbled notes reflecting the furious intensity of the air action:

1423   Condition Red. 16 bombers five miles out, at 20,000 feet altitude.
1424   Enemy planes split into 2 groups. 16 bombers coming over in a straight line.
1430   Bombs dropped along beach near Kukum.
1434   1 bomber shot down.
1435   Another bomber with motor shot out. Bombers going out.
1436   2 Zeros shot down over Field. Another bomber coming down. (5 shot down altogether)
1442   Another enemy formation coming in.
1450   Dogfights overhead.
1451   1 Zero shot down.
1452   Another flight coming in, very low, 10 miles out.
1456   Zeros strafed airfield.
1457   3 Zeros coming in, 5 miles out.
1500   9 dive-bombers over field; bombed "graveyard" of wrecked planes. (Major General Geiger chuckled when he heard what the Japanese bombers picked for a target. "Right in my bone-yard! I couldn't have picked anything I'd rather have them hit.")
1501   8 Zeros to the southwest.
1503   2 groups of enemy planes going out. A few Zeros still prowling around.
1507   6 Zeros coming in at 4,000 feet. Strafe field.
1508   3 groups of planes going out.
1516   Condition Green.

Meanwhile, as *Yura* and her five destroyers neared the center of Indispensable Strait, five SBDs led by Lieutenant Commander John Eldridge of VS-71 attacked them at 1300. Eldridge's 1,000-pound bomb struck near *Yura*'s after engine room; a 500-pound bomb smacked her decks in the same area. Another pilot near-missed Takama's flagship, *Akizuki,* immobilizing her starboard screw and flooding the after engine room. Once apprised of this attack, Mikawa canceled the bombardment mission and Takama's unit reversed course.

Takama withstood attacks without damage by three P-39s at 1415 and four SBDs at 1530, but *Yura* could not control her flooding and lost speed as her stern settled. Efforts were underway to beach the ship at 1700 when Eldridge reappeared with four SBDs, four bomb-clutching P-39s, and three Wildcats. Immediately after they attacked, six B-17s released bomb loads over the wallowing light cruiser. Either one of the P-39s or a B-17 bomb reignited fires on *Yura*. Bomb splinters thoroughly punctured *Samidare*'s starboard side and deprived *Akizuki* of a boiler. With *Yura* completely aflame, Takama ordered her crew removed. Destroyers *Harusame* and *Yudachi* scuttled *Yura* with torpedoes, and she sank at 2100.

When the Cactus Air Force added up claims for the day in aerial combat they came to sixteen Zeros and five bombers; antiaircraft fire definitely accounted for the reconnaissance plane. Japanese records confirm the destruction of ten Zeros and two Bettys. Captain Joseph Foss was again prominent with four Zeros claimed. Two Wildcat pilots survived the loss of their mounts.

During the morning and afternoon of October 25, while air and naval forces held center stage, the ground commanders on both sides reassessed the situation and redeployed their men for renewed combat after dark. The 5th Marines closed the gap between the left flank of Hanneken's 2/7 at the Matanikau horseshoe and the main perimeter. At division headquarters, Colonel Whaling faulted Hanneken's young marines for "jitterbugging"—not the dance but the contemporary Marine patois for firing without a target—but he conceded a large body of Japanese lay near—in fact, Oka's regimental-size command. Whaling also advised the placement of most troops on the line to avoid trying to move them at night along trails "knee high in mud."

It was obvious to Puller that the Japanese remained massed opposite his position. During the day the Marine and Army battalions disentwined and Puller's men resettled into the western 1,400 yards of the sector. Hall's soldiers took the eastern 1,100-yard segment facing flat jungle. The sole division reserve, the 3d Battalion, 2d Marines, waited behind Puller and Hall. Radio intelligence warned that the Imperial Army had been told to "expedite" its Guadalcanal operations and that a landing might be in the offing. At division headquarters, Lieutenant Merillat wrote in his diary: "Attempted landing tonight? Looks like this is *the* night."

Officers at the jungle headquarters of the Sendai Division recognized that many stalwart soldiers had fallen during the night, but resolved to reinforce the "success" of Furimiya, who had planted his regimental colors within the enemy perimeter. At 1300, October 25,

Maruyama informed his command that the "main force" of the Left Wing had pierced deeply into the American lines. He ordered the attack resumed after dark, and handed over control of his reserve, the 16th Infantry Regiment, and the 2d Engineer Battalion to Nasu. The 17th Army Headquarters busied itself with orders dealing with reinforcement and resupply issues: The Koli Detachment should land the morning of the 26th; The 38th Infantry Group must send one battalion to Tassafaronaga and prepare the 228th Infantry Regiment (less one battalion) to move rapidly to Koli Point; and Rabaul should initiate efforts to resupply the heavily depleted ammunition stocks.

For an hour after 2000 on October 25, such guns as the Sendai Division's artillery regiment could muster flung the small accumulation of ammunition at the positions manned by Puller's and Hall's battalions. From then until midnight a series of fights flared, principally in the area held by Hall's 3/164. To the defenders, the Japanese appeared to come on in groups of thirty to 200 under cover of machinegun fire. In the early morning of October 26, the 16th Infantry stormed forward en masse beneath a shroud of fire from heavy infantry weapons, surging against Hall's center and left with the overflow into the defenses manned by a company of the adjacent 2d Battalion, 164th Infantry. The main lunge came up the narrow artery of a trail that formed the boundary between the 2d and 3d Battalions of the 164th Infantry. But two 37mm guns of Weapons Company, 7th Marines discharging gouts of canister commanded the spout of the trail, and they wrought terrible carnage—over 250 Japanese died along this slender stretch of jungle alone. A few knots of Japanese poked through the seams in Hall's lines, but the soldiers and one company of the 3d Battalion, 2d Marines stanched this seepage and hunted down the infiltrators.

During the night the casualty list in the Left Wing multiplied. Flying steel killed Colonel Hiroyasu of the 16th Infantry as well as most of his officers and mortally wounded Nasu. But the Sendai Division again fought like a boxer with only his left fist, for the Right Wing again missed the action, for reasons that remain hard to understand. During the afternoon of October 25, Shoji received reports of an American attempt to move around his right flank. Shoji therefore pivoted two of his three battalions to cover the exposed flank, and concluded he could not attack in this posture. The 2d Division learned of this at midnight and, based upon Shoji's portrayal of the situation, approved his action. The threat to Shoji, however, was entirely imaginary.

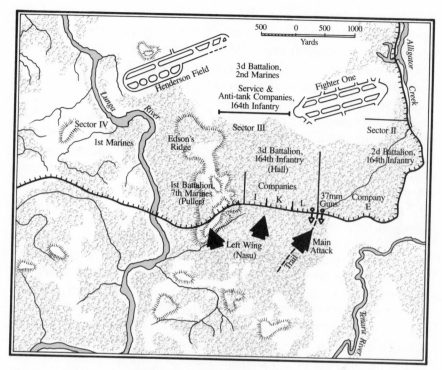

Sendai Attack, October 25–26

The Japanese did not confine their efforts this night to the area south of the airfield, for Oka finally entered the fray. The Japanese objective was an east-west saddle ridge held by Hanneken's 2/7. The Marine battalion was strung tightly across the ridge with Company F anchoring the left (east) flank on the taller of the two crests. To its right across the saddle and to the far crest extended the other two companies. On the extreme right (west) flank, one platoon detached from Company F attempted to prevent infiltration through a 400-yard gap between Hanneken and the adjacent 3d Battalion, 7th Marines. For forty minutes after 1935, Japanese artillery thumped fire across Hanneken's line, and just before midnight the thrashing of an enemy column approaching the left flank became audible.

At 0300 the Japanese struck all along Hanneken's front, but massed particularly against Company F. Japanese riflemen delivered fire from trees on the opposite heights down into the Marine positions. A machinegun section under Platoon Sergeant Mitchell Paige exacted a heavy toll, but gradually all of Paige's men became casualties, so he fired the guns alternately by himself. When one of these weapons was knocked out, Paige dashed through fire to bring up another. Despite Paige's heroism, which won him the Medal of Honor, and the skillful fire of 2/7's mortars, which dropped shells into the ravine and south slope of the ridge, at 0500 a Japanese unit, probably the 3d Battalion, 4th Infantry, scaled the steep slope and ejected the survivors of Company F from the crest.

The Japanese tenure on the ridge proved short. Major Odell M. Conoley, the executive officer of 2/7, assembled a counterattack unit composed of about seventeen men, including communications specialists, messmen, bandsmen, a cook, and a few riflemen, and led them into an attack at 0540. He was joined by elements of Company G, Sergeant Paige, and two platoons from Company C, 5th Marines. Catching the Japanese by surprise before they could consolidate their grip, the marines sent showers of grenades ahead of them and regained the ridge top, recapturing three Marine machineguns and five brought by the Japanese. By 0600 "the situation was in hand." Marines counted ninety-eight Japanese bodies on the ridge; another 200 lay dead in the ravine while blood-speckled and -streaked trails led south. Patrols dispersed small groups of Japanese who slipped through or around the porous Marine lines.

The members of the 2d Division Headquarters relied on their ears to inform them of the progress of the fighting this night. A staff officer sent forward to maintain communication did not arrive with the Left Wing until just before dawn. He immediately realized the attack had failed. With the Right Wing guarding against an illusory threat, Maruyama lacked any reserves he thought he could commit, and he notified 17th Army Headquarters—as did Tsuji—that the 2d Division could not hope to break through in its present condition. Therefore, at 0800, Hyakutake halted the attack. During the night of October 26–27 the defenders readily repulsed what they saw as several further jabs. These were actually efforts by the Sendai to recover wounded and the colors of the 29th Infantry Regiment. Over the next several days, American patrols mopped up inside the perimeter.

Once again, precise figures on losses on both sides are not readily available. A Marine report on October 26 noted that casualties for the last five days totaled eighty-six killed and 192 wounded. Puller's battalion lost twenty-six dead or missing and thirty-three wounded. The 164th Regiment suffered nineteen killed or missing and about fifty wounded. Losses along the Matanikau included fourteen killed and thirty-two wounded in Hanneken's battalion and two dead and eleven wounded in McKelvy's battalion. Aggregate American battle deaths are unlikely to have exceeded ninety.

Japanese losses were severe. The 29th Infantry Regiment reported 553 killed or missing and 479 wounded among its 2,554 men. Losses in the 16th Infantry Regiment can scarcely have been less and may well have been more—the 164th Infantry alone buried 975 bodies, though many of these must have fallen in the initial attack on Puller's battalion. Losses at the mouth of the Matanikau shredded the 4th Infantry Regiment, and over 300 more of Oka's soldiers died on or in front of Hanneken's Ridge. The estimate of the 1st Marine Division that 2,200 Japanese died is probably below the actual total.

The defeat administered a severe psychological blow to the already physically weakened members of the headquarters of the 17th Army. The headquarters staff enjoyed no privileges over the rest of the 17th Army; they lived in rain-soaked clothes, ate small amounts of rice with only rare additions of soybean paste or a few crackers, and were so debilitated that most walked with canes. In their view the failure stemmed from causes both simple and not of their own making: first, the lack of air cover, which induced the supply shortage; and second, the pressure to mount the attack without adequate preparations or rest because of scheduled fleet operations and a promise to the Emperor as to the attack date.

Commander Ohmae of the Imperial Navy afforded a quite different analysis after an inspection trip and briefing. He pointed out such obvious factors within the control of the 17th Army as the gross underestimation of the terrain difficulties, which led to severe shortages of food and medicine at the front and severe fatigue of the troops just prior to the attack; faulty assessment of enemy dispositions despite the existence of aerial photographs proving the Americans had constructed a complete perimeter defense; and a crowded list of leadership failures beginning with dissension between staff officers at 17th Army and winding through Maruyama's chronic illness (neuralgia), Kawaguchi's chronic insubordination, Oka's chronic indifference to orders, and what Ohmae branded as the sheer incompetence of Nasu and his regimental commanders ("Nasu knew nothing but charging").

Furimiya provided another perspective on the defeat. He wandered for several days inside the American perimeter, carefully destroying and hiding the regimental colors before, on October 29, directing his little band of men to try to escape. Most of them were killed, but the last man came out as late as November 2. After

Furimiya took his own life, the marines found the colonel's body and his diary, which contained, among passages in which Furimiya condemned his own failures, the following insight: "we must not overlook firepower." Finally he added in a message for Maruyama, "I am going to return my borrowed life today with little interest."

Perhaps the most instructive perspective from which to assess the performance of the American command is to consider how it would have been judged had the 17th Army's attack succeeded. We may easily imagine the very terms that would have been applied: Vandegrift and his staff would have become infamous for adapting a "discredited" cordon defense, deliberately "dangling" two battalions in an isolated and vulnerable position and "permitting" themselves to be surprised. In this light, we can fully appreciate the great credit due the Marine command, not only for an astute analysis of Japanese operational characteristics, but also for the bold willingness to risk all on the accuracy of this estimate. This is true even though the Japanese marched over 30 miles through the jungle to achieve surprise in an attack where they possessed, in theory at least, a nine-to-one superiority at the point of impact. But an integral part of Vandegrift's calculations was the exorbitant cost of such a march, which was clearly exposed by the inability of the Japanese to attack on the night of October 24–25 with more than the equivalent of one battalion—which presented itself virtually one company at a time—as well as in the sort of fog of mental fatigue which probably accounts for the way in which the Right Wing missed both night's battles. Puller's battalion deserves ample credit for its resolute stand, but its two major allies, massed artillery fire and the jungle, both figured heavily in the division's defense scheme. The degree to which the commander and staff of the 1st Marine Division let hard operational realities rather than even the hoariest of staff college teachings govern their employment of troops was further revealed on the night of October 25–26 when they deliberately chose to place reinforcements in the line itself rather than in "reserve" when such reserves would not be able to influence the battle in the conventional way.

The period of September 27 to October 26 also marked a clear phase of the air struggle over Guadalcanal. Claims by the Cactus Air Force reached 113 Zeros, seventy-two twin-engine bombers, ten Vals, and eight Kates plus three float Zeros and twenty-two biplane float types for a grand total of 228. Cactus Air Force losses aggregated 103 aircraft: forty-three Wildcats (twenty-seven in air combat), nine P-39s or P-400s (five in air combat), thirty-five SBDs (fifteen in air combat), fifteen TBFs (one in air combat), and one J2F. Losses among supporting air units included one carrier SBD (in air combat), five B-17s (three in air combat), three PBYs (all air combat), four SOCs and two Hudsons (all operational), making the grand total of losses 118 (fifty-four in air combat). Japanese losses in the 11th Air Fleet aggregated 103 aircraft from all causes: twenty-nine Bettys, sixty-three Zeros, six Vals, one reconnaissance plane, and four flying boats. Of this total all but twenty Zeros were lost in combat. To these would be added the losses of the R Area Air Force, which numbered at least sixteen float planes. Losses from the interventions by the Japanese carriers add a further twelve aircraft: one Val, two Zeros, and nine Kates. The combined total reaches 131.

Even though the marines and soldiers had held their positions against the Imperial Army, they were not fully in control of their fate. Simultaneously with the struggle ashore, at sea the navies squared off for the fourth carrier battle of the war.

15

THE BATTLE OF

THE SANTA CRUZ

ISLANDS

"Eternal vigilance or eternal rest"

JOSTLING FOR POSITION

The major portion of the Combined Fleet had maneuvered north of the Solomons since standing out of Truk on October 11. Yamamoto exercised strategic command from battleship *Yamato* at Truk, while Admiral Kondo enjoyed command of the forces at sea collectively labeled the Support Force. Carrier Divisions 1 and 2, composed of one light and four heavy carriers, formed the nucleus of this naval might.

As in August, two major commands formed the Support Force, the Advanced Force and the Main Body, but the actual disposition resembled an isosceles triangle. The Advanced Force under Kondo's direct control, two battleships, four heavy cruisers, one light cruiser, and a dozen destroyers, occupied the western corner of the triangle. This force also included Carrier Division 2, *Junyo* and *Hiyo,* very large and elaborate conversions of fast merchant liners. About 100 miles to the east of Carrier Division 2—a distance calculated to prevent one plane from seeing both carrier groups simultaneously— sailed Admiral Nagumo's Carrier Division 1 with *Shokaku,*

Zuikaku, and light carrier *Zuiho.* Their direct escort numbered one heavy cruiser and eight destroyers. Operating about 60 to 100 miles south of Nagumo, in the southeastern corner of the triangle and in a position to merit its title of Vanguard Force, stood two battleships, three heavy cruisers, one light cruiser, and seven destroyers under Rear Admiral Hiroaki Abe. The placement of Nagumo's carriers and the Vanguard Force to the east reflected the expectation that American carriers would most likely approach along that axis. To project air reconnaissance to that quarter, heavy cruiser *Chikuma* with destroyer *Teruzuki* thrust eastward and the cruiser's planes canvassed the ocean toward the sunrise on October 23. Mikawa's Outer South Seas Force of three heavy cruisers, one light cruiser, and sixteen destroyers, whose role has already been discussed, augmented Kondo's forces significantly, as did almost the full strength of the Advanced Expeditionary Force, which controlled sixteen submarines on station in the South Pacific.

In both planning and execution the maneuvers of Kondo's Support Force eschewed textbook orthodoxy, for they were not designed to isolate the American garrison on Guadalcanal prior to a ground assault. Rather, the Japanese tied the choreography of operations by the Support Force to the seizure of Henderson Field and its satellites by Hyakutake's riflemen. Pre-sailing planning called for the 17th Army to attack after sundown on Y-Day and for the Support Force to carry out a high-speed run to the south to arrive at dawn of Y plus one in positions where it could "apprehend and destroy" any American fleet units attempting to intervene. If circumstances permitted, the Advanced Force would make a foray south of Guadalcanal. In the meantime the forces at sea would conform closely to their appellation by aiding Hyakutake only at selected junctures. Thus to clear a path for the reinforcement convoy, *Kongo* and *Haruna* blasted the Cactus Air Force on the night of October 13–14, and the Support Force steered south to offer a challenge for a fleet engagement. But with only *Hornet* available, the Americans declined to become a sparring partner at those odds. Instead, they behaved like a dancing partner, keeping the separation distance constant as they waltzed south, thanks, as Admiral Ugaki correctly adduced, to the proficiency of American search planes.

Japanese aerial reconnaissance enjoyed less success. Although Imperial Navy search planes routinely located American gunnery vessel task forces near Rennell Island, their sporadic contact with American carriers entirely ended after October 16. On the other hand, Japanese radio intelligence services recognized a "powerful unit" cruising south of the Solomons as the addressee of many messages while maintaining radio silence itself. This was the *Hornet* group, but the Combined Fleet was uncertain as to its composition. These circumstances set speculation afoot in the Combined Fleet: were the units near Rennell Island bait in a subtle trap to tempt the Japanese carriers into exposing their flanks to attacks by their American peers?

From traffic patterns the Japanese deduced that another major task force sailed from Pearl Harbor about October 15. This was the newly repaired *Enterprise* and her escorts. The Japanese estimated the destination of this task force as south, and their opponents unexpectedly provided confirmation for this hypothesis. In an effort to divert Japanese attention to the Central Pacific, Nimitz sent destroyers *Lamson* and *Mahan* to raid the picket boat line off the Gilbert Islands. This ploy backfired, for rather than inducing Japanese anxiety about the Mandates, it only served to substantiate the impression that a powerful task force was steaming down to reinforce the South Pacific. The Japanese also construed the increasing number of American submarines in Solomons waters as a sign of preparations for a fleet action, and they absorbed with interest the published predictions of American officials on October 20 of the imminence of a sea clash in the South Pacific.

Of two immediate concerns looming over Kondo's Support Force, fuel came first. The operational design called for the Combined Fleet to cover both the reinforcement convoy and, one week later, the land assault during one excursion from Truk. Colonel Tsuji had been warned in late September that the Support Force could remain at sea for only about two weeks because of fuel considerations. Even this period strained the meager supplies available; oil had to be siphoned from battleships *Yamato* and *Mutsu* at Truk into tankers for transfer to vessels at sea. Moreover, the oil problem compelled Kondo to abruptly abandon his bid for a fleet action in mid-October, and the concomitant interdiction of the supply lines to Guadalcanal, to conduct refueling between October 16 and 18.

The second great concern in the Support Force was the progress, or lack of progress, of the 17th Army in preparing its attack. Only after repeated prodding did General Miyazaki announce on October 19 that Y-Day would be October 22. A penalty for dawdling at sea was exacted at 0100 of October 21, when carrier *Hiyo* suffered a fire in her engineering spaces. With her speed limited to 16 knots, too low for fleet operations, *Hiyo* retired to Truk with two destroyers. The aggressive Rear Admiral Kakuji Kakuta shifted his flag to *Junyo.* Of

Hiyo's aircraft complement, sixteen fighters and seventeen dive-bombers flew to join the 11th Air Fleet while three fighters, one dive-bomber, and five torpedo planes replaced losses on *Junyo.*

The 17th Army's calls for one and then another postponement pushing Y-Day back to October 24 dismayed the Combined Fleet. Dismay would have turned to anger had the Emperor's sailors known for sure that at 1400 on October 24, *Enterprise* finished the long dash from Pearl Harbor and rendezvoused with *Hornet,* thus partly restoring the balance of carrier air power. Command of Task Force 17, *Hornet,* and her bodyguard of two heavy and two light cruisers as well as six destroyers rested with Rear Admiral George D. Murray. Command of Task Force 16, *Enterprise,* the new battleship *South Dakota,* one heavy and one light cruiser, and eight destroyers, was exercised by Rear Admiral Thomas Kinkaid; he was also charged with tactical direction of both carrier groups as commander of Task Force 61. The unit operating in the vicinity of Rennell Island, which the Japanese repeatedly sighted, was Rear Admiral Willis A. Lee's Task Force 64, comprising battleship *Washington,* one heavy and two light cruisers, and six destroyers. Lee answered directly to Halsey at Noumea.

Japanese radio security measures succeeded in leaving Kinkaid with an equivocal picture of the tactical situation. American intelligence generated a reasonably accurate enumeration of Imperial Navy strength in the Solomons area, as this table reflects:

Carriers/ (aircraft)		Battleships	Heavy cruisers	Light cruisers	Destroyers	Submarines
Estimate	4(204)	3–4	8	6	30–40	20
Actual	4(199)	4	8	2	29	16

But as to timing, Pacific Fleet intelligence could only speculate that the decrease in the number of high-precedence and operational-type traffic as of October 19 suggested a final period of adjustment and preparation for action on a major scale. Notwithstanding the odds, Halsey solved the timing question by seizing the initiative. He issued Kinkaid taut orders bereft of timidity: "make a sweep around north Santa Cruz Islands thence southwesterly east of San Cristóbal to area in Coral Sea in position to intercept enemy forces approaching Cactus-Ringbolt [Guadalcanal-Tulagi]."

Not only did the 17th Army's delays alter the balance of sea power, they also bred other developments that sparked dissension within the Combined Fleet. During October 23, the first reset Y-Day, the Support Force pressed south to gain its predesignated positions by the dawn of Y plus one. For many hours, PBYs surveyed the Support Force before Kondo and Nagumo reversed course upon belatedly learning that the 17th Army again had canceled the attack. While the Support Force took another gulp of oil on the 24th, Nagumo's staff mulled over the probability that retracing the path taken on the 23d would virtually guarantee their early discovery, with potentially dire consequences. The staff concluded that Carrier Division 1 should try to curl north and east around the American air search net; in practical effect this meant they would be one day late in reaching the position ordered for Y plus one. This proposal prompted uproar at the Combined Fleet headquarters. In his diary Ugaki termed it "irresponsible and presumptuous" because it would both sunder the planned reconnaissance coverage to the southeast, the critical direction, and leave the Advanced Force with only *Junyo* beyond mutual support of Carrier Division 1. An order bearing Ugaki's imprimatur left no doubt that Nagumo must remain in the yoke with Kondo, but it did nothing to dispel the underlying apprehensions.

On the night of October 24–25, as the Sendai Division either ensnared itself in the jungle or impaled itself on American firepower, the Support Force sped south once again. Dawn search planes detected no enemy fleet units, but the smudgy silhouettes of Catalinas on the horizon and nearby bursts of coded radio transmissions left no doubt about the discovery of both Kondo's Advanced Force and the Vanguard Force by 1015. The latter unit successfully twisted from beneath six B-17s that dribbled bombs across the sea at 1450. The only crumb of intelligence reaching the Support Force came from the 11th Air Fleet, which yet again sighted Lee near Rennell Island. Kondo ordered Nagumo to attack Lee, but the Americans were out of range.

Kinkaid received the information he awaited at ten minutes before noon this day: two Japanese carriers on a southeasterly course 355 miles west-northwest from Task Force 61. Kinkaid aligned prows on the enemy bearing and raised speed to 27 knots. When amplifying reports from search planes failed to materialize, Kinkaid launched from *Enterprise* a dozen SBD ferrets at 1430 and, in a bold gambit, at 1520 lofted an attack group of eight Wildcats, five SBDs, and seven torpedo planes to immediately exploit any contacts. Shortly after all these aircraft vanished over the horizon, the admiral learned that the enemy had turned north, but the necessity to preserve radio silence prohibited him from notifying his fliers. The search planes returned uneventfully, but the attack group commander, in his zeal to find the Japanese, flew well beyond his orders and daylight. The night mission claimed only two lives, but water landings and a deck crash cost eight aircraft (one Wildcat, four SBDs, and three TBFs). Added to these losses were one Wildcat and three SBDs smashed in a deck crash earlier that day, so a total of twelve much-needed aircraft were pared from *Enterprise*'s brood on the eve of battle.

Without a doubt, Kondo possessed a significant superiority in aircraft for October 26. According to a post-battle return, crews for ninety-six Zeros, sixty-five Vals, and seventy-two Kates, a total of 233, were aboard his carriers. Operational aircraft numbered 199: eighty Zeros, sixty-one Vals, fifty-seven Kates, one Yokosuka D4Y1 ("Judy") reconnaissance plane. The American pair carried 163 aircraft (seventy-one Wildcats, seventy-two SBDs, twenty-six TBFs), but the operational total was less, and numbered only 136 (sixty-three Wildcats, forty-seven SBDs, twenty-six TBFs).

Besides a numerical superiority of nearly three to two, the Japanese also enjoyed a distinct qualitative advantage. *Enterprise*'s Air Group 10 represented the first of the wartime air groups formed by grafting a cadre of experienced squadron and flight leaders to the fresh products of training courses. *Enterprise*'s new tenants had trained for three months, but the mishaps in the night recovery demonstrated that enthusiasm was no antidote to inexperience. *Hornet*'s air group contained three prewar units, a former *Wasp* fighter squadron, and *Hornet*'s bombing and scouting squadrons, but the torpedo element was reformed in June from all-new personnel. The Japanese air groups contained the remaining core of superbly skilled first-line carrier fliers with which Japan had gained her victories in the months after Pearl Harbor, and as units they outmatched their American adversaries.

At 2118, as American destroyers pulled crews from the water, Yamamoto signaled that "there is a great likelihood that the enemy fleet will appear in the area northeast of the Solomons, and the Combined Fleet will seek to destroy it on the 26th."

COMPOSITION OF FORCES

1. JAPANESE

Combined Fleet
Adm. Isoroku Yamamoto
at Truk in Yamato

Support Force
Vice Adm. Nobutake Kondo

Advanced Force (2d Fleet)
Adm. Kondo

HEAVY CRUISERS:

Crudiv 4 (Adm. Kondo): *Atago, Takao*
Crudiv 5 (Rear Adm. Sentaro Omori): *Myoko, Maya*

BATTLESHIPS:

Batdiv 3 (Vice Adm. Takeo Kurita): *Kongo, Haruna*

CARRIERS:

Carrier Division 2 (Rear Adm. Kakuji Kakuta):
    Junyo

	Strike Group Commander: Lt. Yoshio Shiga	
21(20)	Zeros	Lt. Shiga
18(17)	Vals	Lt. Masao Yamaguchi
9(7)	Kates	Lt. Yoshiaki Irikiin

(First figure = authorized; second figure = operational)

Hiyo: Detached October 22 with destroyers *Isonami* and *Inazuma*

Screen
Destroyer Squadron 2: Rear Adm. Raizo Tanaka

LIGHT CRUISER:

Isuzu

DESTROYERS:

Desdiv 15: *Kagero, Oyashio, Kuroshio, Hayashio*
Desdiv 24: *Kawakaze, Suzukaze, Umikaze*
Desdiv 31: *Naganami, Takanami, Makinami*

Main Body (3d Fleet)
Vice Adm. Chuichi Nagumo

HEAVY CARRIERS:

Carrier Division 1
    Shokaku

	Strike Group Leader: Lt. Cdr. Mamoru Seki	
27(20)	Zeros	Lt. Hideki Shingo
27(21)	Vals	Lt. Cdr. Seki

| 18(24) | Kates | Lt. Cdr. Shigeharu Murata |
| 2(1) | Judys | |

Zuikaku

Strike Group Leader: Lt. Sadamu Takahashi

27(20)	Zeros	Lt. Ayao Shirane
27(23)	Vals	Lt. Takahashi
18(20)	Kates	Lt. Geichiro Imajuku

LIGHT CARRIER

| *Zuiho* | | Capt. Sueo Obayashi |

Strike Group Leader: Lt. Masao Sato

| 21(20) | Zeros | Lt. Sato |
| 6(6) | Kates | Lt. (jg) Ichiro Tanaka |

Screen

HEAVY CRUISER:

Kumano

DESTROYERS:

Desdiv 16: *Amatsukaze, Hatsukaze, Tokitsukaze, Yukikaze*
Desdiv 4: *Arashi, Maikaze*
Unattached: *Teruzuki, Hamakaze*

Vanguard Force (3d Fleet)
Rear Adm. Hiroaki Abe

BATTLESHIPS:

Batdiv 11 (Adm. Abe): *Hiei, Kirishima*

HEAVY CRUISERS:

Crudiv 7 (Rear Adm. Shoji Nishimura): *Suzuya*
Crudiv 8 (Rear Adm. Chuichi Hara): *Tone, Chikuma*

Screen
Destroyer Squadron 10
Rear Adm. Satsuma Kimura

LIGHT CRUISER:

Nagara

DESTROYERS:

Desdiv 10: *Akigumo, Makikumo, Yugumo, Kazegumo*
Desdiv 17: *Isokaze, Tanikaze, Urakaze*

Advanced Expeditionary Force
Vice Adm. Terushisa Komatsu

SUBMARINES (As of October 26):

"KO" (A) Unit: Submarine Squadron 2
    I-7
    Subdiv 7: *I-1, I-2, I-3*

Subdiv 6: *I-4, I-5*
Subdiv 11: *I-174, I-175, I-176*
I-17, I-31, I-172
"OTSU" (B) Unit: Submarine Squadron 1
I-9
Subdiv 2: *I-15*
I-21, I-24

Southeast Area Force
Vice Adm. Junichi Kusaka

11th Air Fleet
Vice Adm. Kusake

25th Air Flotilla	Zeros: 67[1]		
26th Air Flotilla	Bettys: 64		
	Val: 27		Total: 158

Plus seaplanes and float planes

[1]All strengths as of October 31.

2. AMERICAN

South Pacific Area, South Pacific Force
Vice Adm. William F. Halsey

Task Force 61
Rear Adm. Thomas C. Kinkaid

Task Force 16
Rear Adm. Kinkaid

CARRIER:

Enterprise		Capt. Osborne B. Hardison
Air Group 10:	1 TBF-1	Cdr. Richard K Gaines
VF-10:	31 F4F-4	Lt. Cdr. James H. Flatley, Jr.
VB-10:	10 SBD-3	Lt. Cdr. James A. Thomas
VS-10:	13 SBD-3	Lt. Cdr. James R. Lee
VT-10:	9 TBF-1	Lt. Cdr. John A. Collett

(Aircraft complement = probable operational total October 26)

Screen
Rear Adm. Mahlon S. Tisdale
in **Portland**

BATTLESHIP:

South Dakota   Capt. Thomas L. Gatch

HEAVY CRUISER:

Crudiv 4
    Portland   Capt. Laurence T. DuBose

LIGHT CRUISER:

San Juan   Capt. James E. Maher

DESTROYERS: Capt. Charles P. Cecil (ComDesron 5)

    Porter   Lt. Cdr. David G. Roberts
    Mahan   Lt. Cdr. Rodger W. Simpson
    DesDiv 10   Cdr. Thomas M. Stokes
      Cushing   Lt. Cdr. Christopher Noble
      Preston   Lt. Cdr. Max C. Stormes
      Smith   Lt. Cdr. Hunter Wood Jr.
      Maury   Lt. Cdr. Gelzer L. Sims
      Conyngham   Lt. Cdr. Henry C. Daniel
      Shaw   Lt. Cdr. Wilbur G. Jones

Task Force 17
Rear Adm. George D. Murray

CARRIER:

    Hornet   Capt. Charles P. Mason
    Air Group 8:   1 TBF-1   Cdr. Walter F. Rodee
    VF-72:   32 F4F-4   Lt. Cdr. Henry G. Sanchez
    VB-8:   15 SBD-3   Lt. Cdr. James E. Vose
    VS-8:   9 SBD-3   Lt. Cdr. William J. Widhelm
    VT-6:   15 TBF-1   Lt. Edwin B. Parker Jr.
(Aircraft complement = operational total 26 October)

Screen
Rear Adm. Howard H. Good (ComCruDiv 5)
in Northampton

HEAVY CRUISERS:

    Crudiv 5
      Northampton   Capt. Willard A. Kitts III
      Pensacola   Capt. Frank L. Lowe

LIGHT CRUISERS:

    San Diego   Capt. Benjamin F. Perry
    Juneau   Capt. Lyman K. Swenson

DESTROYERS: Cdr. Arnold E. True (ComDesron 2)

    Morris   Lt. Cdr. Randolph B. Boyer
    Anderson   Lt. Cdr. Richard A. Guthrie
    Hughes   Lt. Cdr. Donald J. Ramsey
    Mustin   Lt. Cdr. Wallis F. Petersen
    Russell   Lt. Cdr. Glenn R. Hartwig
    Barton   Lt. Cdr. Douglas H. Fox

Task Force 64
Rear Adm. Willis A. Lee
in **Washington**

BATTLESHIP:

　Washington　　　　　　　　　　　　　　　Capt. Glenn B. Davis

HEAVY CRUISER:

　San Francisco　　　　　　　　　　　　　　Capt. Charles H. McMorris

LIGHT CRUISERS:

　Helena　　　　　　　　　　　　　　　　　Capt. Gilbert C. Hoover
　Atlanta　　　　　　　　　　　　　　　　　Capt. Samuel P. Jenkins

Screen

DESTROYERS:

　Aaron Ward　　　　　　　　　　　　　　　Lt. Cdr. Orville F. Gregor
　Benham　　　　　　　　　　　　　　　　　Lt. Cdr. John B. Taylor
　Fletcher　　　　　　　　　　　　　　　　　Cdr. William M. Col
　Lansdowne　　　　　　　　　　　　　　　Lt. Cdr. William R. Smedberg
　Lardner　　　　　　　　　　　　　　　　　Cdr. Willard M. Sweetser
　McCalla　　　　　　　　　　　　　　　　　Lt. Cdr. William G. Cooper

Task Force 63
(Land-Based Aircraft)
Rear Adm. Aubrey W. Fitch

AT GUADALCANAL:
　F4F-4 26　　　　　P-39　6
　SBD-3 20　　　　　TBF-1　2
　P-400　6　　　　　　　　　　　　　　Total: 60

AT ESPÍRITU SANTO:
　F4F-4 24　　　　　PBY 32
　B-17 39　　　　　　OS2U　5
　Hudsons (RNZAF) 12　　　　　　　　Total: 112

SEAPLANE TENDERS:
　Curtiss
　Mackinac

AT NEW CALEDONIA:
　P-39 46　　　　　　B-26 16
　P-38 15　　　　　　Hudsons (RNZAF) 13
　　　　　　　　　　　　　　　　　　Total: 77
　　　　　　　　　　　　　　　Grand total Task Force 63: 249

THE CARRIER BATTLE OF OCTOBER 26

In 1942-vintage carrier warfare, striking the enemy first provided the formula for success, for neither side possessed the equipment or the doctrine to win on the defensive. It followed that the antagonist that found the opponent first obtained a commanding advantage. With so much depending on the work of the Support Force's search planes, Ugaki could not resist exhorting them at 2240 on October 25 to persist in search and tracking "regardless of weather and enemy planes." None of the Japanese planes, however, would begin its work much before dawn, while the night-roaming "Cats," festooned with radar antenna like whiskers, conferred a potentially vital advantage on the Americans.

By 2330 of October 25, Nagumo and his staff knew that American aircraft were in their vicinity, but they could not discern from the sightings or intercepted radio signals whether the Catalinas were shadowing Carrier Division 1 or the Vanguard Force 60 miles farther south. When destroyer *Isokaze* in the Vanguard Force dodged a torpedo dropped by a PBY at 0033, October 26, hopes grew that the carriers remained undetected, only to be dashed at 0250 when one of the large flying boats swooped over *Zuikaku* and released four bombs, which exploded about 300 yards from the carrier. This episode rearoused the fears of Nagumo's staff of a dawn rendezvous of Carrier Division 1 with a trap, and they urged a change of course. Nagumo needed no convincing, and at 0330 he abruptly veered to a northerly heading at 24 knots; forty-five minutes later the Vanguard Force did the same.

All during the night, Kinkaid kept an attack group spotted on *Hornet* in expectation of getting in the first blow, but faulty reporting and communications failure thwarted his hopes. At 0022 on October 26 a Catalina yowled a message that the "enemy" was at 07°14' South, 164°15' East, about 300 miles from Kinkaid, but she omitted the essential particulars of course, speed, and composition. Another PBY incorporated all these data in a 0310 report, but *Enterprise* failed to intercept this signal, and the other ships in the task force that did monitor the message assumed the flagship had it. The only information reaching the Japanese commanders during darkness was a 0410 signal from the liaison officer on Guadalcanal that Henderson Field remained out of the grasp of the Sendai Division.

Both sides readied search planes as first light approached, but the Japanese sowed the dawn air first. Seven float planes from the Van-

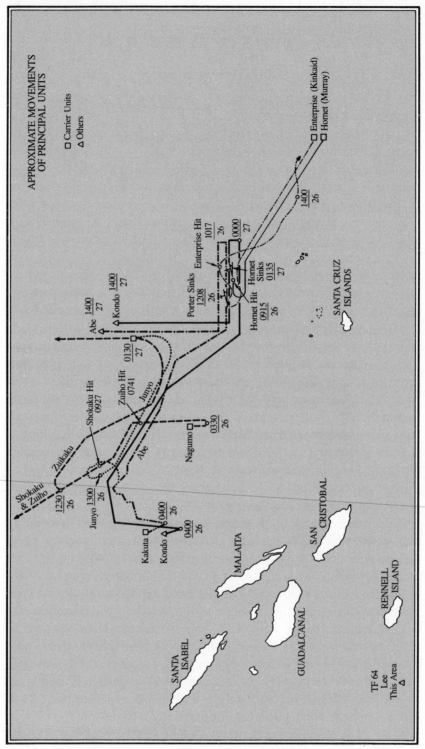

Battle of the Santa Cruz Islands, October 26

guard Force departed at 0415, well before the first hint of sun, pursued by thirteen of the swifter Kates from Nagumo's carriers at 0445. Kondo reacted to the disappointing news from Guadalcanal by reversing course to the north while "awaiting developments" in the land battle, and at 0500 he began catapulting float planes for a look astern.

Sunrise came at 0528 on October 26. Over both sides the sun contended with five-tenths to seven-tenths clouds that either lay like long brush strokes, the lowest at 2,000 feet, or gathered in the small hillocks of rainsqualls. Thirty-eight minutes before sunrise, *Enterprise* placed the southeasterly breeze over her bow and began launching a Combat Air Patrol of Wildcats and eight pairs of SBDs to cover sectors between 235 degrees and due north. In the midst of this activity, at 0512 *Enterprise* radiomen copied a relay from seaplane tender *Curtiss* of the 0310 PBY contact report, but Kinkaid assessed this information as stale. One brace of SBDs eyed one of Nagumo's precocious Kates about 85 miles out from *Enterprise*. Pressing on, this pair reported Abe's Vanguard Force at 0630 as two battleships, one heavy cruiser, and seven destroyers bearing 275 degrees from *Enterprise*, distance 170 miles, headed north at 20 knots. En route back, they again passed the same Kate or one of her friends.

The skipper of these scouts, Lieutenant Commander James R. Lee, appropriated for himself the sector that offered the most promise. There at 0650, only 200 miles on a bearing of 300 degrees from *Enterprise*, he struck the main lode, Nagumo's carriers. As Lee and his wingman climbed to attack, their radiomen flashed a contact report, which many of their squadron mates received, as well as both American carriers. While the enemy vessels made smoke and changed course, three of the twenty Zeros on Combat Air Patrol forced the two SBDs to break contact by seeking cover in some clouds after a short, inconclusive fight.

The two SBDs in the adjacent sector to the north reacted to Lee's report by heading for the enemy carriers. Zeros tackled them as they approached and pursued them from the scene. Although each SBD crew claimed a Zero, their real accomplishment was probably to clear the air for the next pair of Dauntlesses to arrive. Lieutenant Stockton B. Strong and Ensign C. B. Irvine heard Lee's report, and meticulous calculation by Strong revealed they had just enough fuel to try an attack. Aboard the Japanese vessels, lookouts glimpsed SBDs dexterously scuttling in and out of clouds to avoid pursuing Zeros, but Strong and Irvine were not seen until they were already in their dives on *Zuiho* at 0740.

Captain Sueo Obayashi reported that one of the 500-pound bombs struck his ship aft, gouging a 50-foot-wide crater in the flight deck, blasting the decks below, destroying three Zeros, and knocking out the after antiaircraft guns. Her crew stamped out fires rapidly, but *Zuiho* could neither launch nor recover aircraft, so she withdrew, escorted by two destroyers. Strong and Irvine claimed two of the angry Zeros that sniped at them on withdrawal. Another set of SBDs attacked *Tone,* without success. All of the American planes returned with combined claims of two hits on a carrier and seven Zeros. The true score, one hit on a light carrier and one Zero, was quite impressive enough.

On this morning, the Americans enjoyed no monopoly on contretemps with search planes. Plane number four from *Shokaku* found an American carrier group etched by the sunrise as early as 0612 only 200 miles southeast of Carrier Division 1. But rather than immediately divulging their discovery, the crew of this plane procrastinated while inspecting the composition of the formation. Consequently, it was 0658 before *Shokaku* received the tardy contact report from this crew, which compounded their errors by mistakenly identifying themselves as plane number one. Naturally staff officers questioned the reliability of the report, as the location did not fit the assigned sector of plane number one. Further misadventures ensued when radio difficulties prevented a *Zuikaku* plane from revealing its detection of an American carrier group and when a Judy reconnaissance plane on a shadowing mission failed to make contact because it was sent to the wrong position.

In this action, as in the Battle of the Eastern Solomons, the Japanese referred constantly to a catechism of lessons from Midway. The June battle had indelibly impressed upon them the supreme importance of hitting first in a carrier battle, so now they accepted plane four's report despite its use of an alias. Shortly after 0700, Kondo detached heavy cruisers *Myoko* and *Maya* with destroyers *Kagero* and *Makinami* to recover search planes and turned the rest of the Advanced Force on course 70 degrees at 24 knots. At 0725, Lieutenant Commander Shigeharu Murata, a strike group leader from *Shokaku,* pointed a sixty-two-plane strike in the direction of the contact report. Murata flew one of twenty *Shokaku* Kates, while *Zuikaku* contributed twenty-one Vals. The three ships of Carrier Division 1 each donated to the twenty-one-Zero escort. Two other Kates, one each from *Shokaku* and *Zuiho* (just before that ship was bombed), followed the strike group without ordnance to maintain contact. Confident that his aircrews would inflict damage on the enemy, at 0805 Nagumo ordered Abe to head for the American position.

Immediately after the first group was away, elevators began lifting a second strike from hangar to flight decks, but a quandary developed. During the night, the threat posed by prowling PBYs occasioned the disarming of all aircraft parked on hangar decks, and now handling crews completed the reslinging of bombs to nineteen Vals thirty minutes before they could remate sixteen torpedoes to their Kates. Presented with a choice between speed and coordination, the Japanese, again following the Midway catechism, unhesitatingly opted for speed. At 0810 the nineteen *Shokaku* Vals climbed away under Lieutenant Commander Mamoru Seki with five Zeros in escort. Half an hour later, Lieutenant Geichiru Imajuku gathered his 16 *Zuikaku* Kates and only four Zeros for the journey to the American carriers. One Kate from *Zuikaku* and a Val from *Shokaku* also went along in the contact-keeper role. Thus, by 0910 the Japanese had 110 planes in three organized attack groups en route to the general area of the American carriers.

In contrast to this performance, not only were the Americans late, they were also inferior in numbers, organization, and coordination. Although *Hornet* had had an attack group readied all the previous day and for most of the night, it numbered only eight Wildcats, fifteen SBDs, and six TBFs. *Hornet* began launching these at 0732, spearheaded by Lieutenant Commander W. J. Widhelm's group of SBDs armed with 1,000-pound bombs. Four Wildcats climbed skyward with the SBDs, while Lieutenant Parker's TBFs remained low at 800 feet with the other half of the Wildcat unit. All these aircraft departed at 0750—twenty-five minutes after the first Japanese strike group.

With twenty of her SBDs on search missions or local patrol, *Enterprise* could mount a strike of only eight Wildcats, three SBDs, and eight torpedo planes, accompanied by the air group commander in a ninth TBF armed only with a camera. These twenty planes began lifting off about 0747 and formed up with the SBDs leading the torpedo planes while the Wildcats split into two divisions of four, one on each bow of the strike unit; the air group commander cruised above all of them. To save time, the smaller *Enterprise* group did not try to form up with *Hornet*'s larger first strike, which was directly to port of the *Enterprise* group and about 8,000 feet above.

With unexpected dispatch, *Hornet* flew off her second strike group of seven fighters, nine SBDs, and nine TBFs by 0810, but rather than torpedoes, the TBFs each transported four 500-pound bombs, of doubtful effectiveness against large warships. This unit, with the air group commander in a tenth unarmed TBF, flowed into what amounted to a stream of American aircraft, seventy-five strong, in three main groups of dubious cohesion.

The American aircraft had advanced only 60 miles from their ships, and most were still climbing, when Nagumo's first strike appeared above headed in the opposite direction. *Hornet*'s first group passed the Zero leader unobserved, but he spotted the lower and slowly climbing *Enterprise* fliers. At 0840, nine *Zuiho* Zeros under Lieutenant Saneyasu Hiedka plunged out of the sun into the unsuspecting Americans, complacent because of the proximity of their ships and the absence of warning from radar. Symptoms of unpreparedness included the fact that not all Wildcats had their guns charged and some had not switched on their radio transmitters. Moreover, at the moment the Japanese poured down from port, Lieutenant Commander James Flatley's division of four fighters on the starboard side of the American formation was headed away in one of the weaving turns required to stay with the sluggish attack planes.

Zeros slashed into the TBF formation, scoring expertly with 20mm canon and machineguns. The plane of the squadron commander of VT-10, Lieutenant Commander John A. Collett, pitched downward with "flames gushing from [the] engine into the cockpit," as did another Avenger. Only one man from each crew survived to become a prisoner of war. The Zeros so badly damaged two other TBFs that they turned back and both ended their careers in the ocean, though the crews survived.

Lieutenant John Leppla, a hero of the Battle of the Coral Sea, led the port division of Wildcats. The sudden onslaught forced Leppla to make a split-second choice between turning to join forces with Flatley, which meant exposing the TBFs, or trying to interpose his unit between the Japanese and the torpedo planes to offer battle at severe disadvantage. He selected the latter, and it cost him his life. The Zero pilots rapidly shot down Leppla's Wildcat and two others, whose pilots become prisoners of war. The sole remaining Wildcat of this division was damaged and forced to return. When Flatley brought his division into the action, they quickly shot one of the Zeros down, to add to the two claimed by Leppla's pilots and three by TBF gunners. The Zeros molested neither the SBDs nor the air group commander in this attack, but they reduced *Enterprise*'s strike by four Wildcats and four Avengers and seriously limited its reach, because Flatley's planes jettisoned their drop tanks. "We were not sufficiently alert," admitted Flatley candidly in his report, and the moral he drew was "eternal vigilance or eternal rest." Lieutenant Hidaka lost four of his Zeros in the brief fight, and one was heavily damaged. All the rest had expended their ammunition, so they turned back, leaving the first strike group with only twelve Zeros.

Hornet's planes notified their ship of the approaching enemy aircraft, and shortly thereafter the Japanese appeared on radar screens bearing 280 degrees true, distance 60 miles. *Hornet* completed refueling seven Wildcats of the Combat Air Patrol and launched them by 0848 to join eight others. The Japanese attack group sighted *Hornet* at about 0855, but did not see *Enterprise,* then hidden in a rainsquall 10 miles to the northeast of *Hornet.* The pilots of the thirty-seven Wildcats airborne from both carriers unanimously condemned as ineffective the early fighter direction by *Enterprise:* too many transmissions containing too little information, including the vital altitude of the enemy flight, and directions given in reference to the position of ships not visible to all the American pilots. In the last stages of the Japanese approach, the *Hornet* fighter director took over and promptly placed Wildcats in the path of the enemy strike, but when the thirty-seven Wildcat pilots sighted Murata's group at 0859, about 25 miles from the task force, most found themselves looking up at the Japanese bombers, which pushed over into high-speed approaches from 17,000 feet.

Hornet swung to a northeasterly course at 0902, and her bow wave curled higher above a slight choppy sea as her engineers worked her up to about 31 knots. Her escorts tightened into a 2,000-yard-wide ring with heavy cruisers *Northampton* and *Pensacola* on her bows and light cruisers *San Juan* and *Juneau* on her quarters, plus six destroyers filling in the remaining openings. Men topside saw smoky plumes about 15 miles to the west, marking the tangle between some Wildcats, Zeros, and the leading Japanese dive-bomber unit, but the second Val detachment burst through to lead the throng of nearly twenty dive-bombers into wailing dives at 0910.

The bearing of the plunging planes swung radically as Captain Mason wildly pivoted *Hornet*'s rudder. The first two of a chain of bombs released at close range smacked into the sea abreast the bridge, followed immediately by the planes that released them, but caterwauling guns could not fend off so many resolute men. At 0912 a bomb punctured the flight deck abreast the bridge and drilled forward and down to the third deck. A few moments later, two more bombs with crisscrossing trajectories pierced the flight deck between the midships and after elevators. One slanted aft to open a blackened grotto on the third deck, and the second ripped a 7-by-11-foot hole in the flight deck, killing many men in adjacent gun batteries and on the hangar deck below. About 0914 a Val dove vertically into the ship. It caromed off the stack and smashed through the signal enclosure, where it strewed the "signal bridge with a blanket of burning gasoline," before it struck the flight deck. The remains of the plane and its crew plus an inert 550-pound bomb halted finally at the gallery deck, igniting an intense fire.

Bombs were still falling as the dark-green Kates divided into two groups to box *Hornet* to port and starboard. The torpedo planes entered long weaving glides from 6,000 feet and flared out at release altitudes of 400 to 500 feet. According to *Hornet*'s air officer, the Kates were "well spaced in azimuth and the timing was superb." In fact, the attack was not so beautifully coordinated as it appeared, for the plan called for a sequential, not a simultaneous, bomb and torpedo assault. At 0915 two torpedoes struck *Hornet* on her starboard side about twenty seconds apart. The first hit dead center on the forward engine room, crumpling four bulkheads to rip a hole 4 feet in diameter through which roared "an avalanche of oil and seawater." The second stabbed into the starboard quarter amid well-subdivided compartments, adding little to *Hornet*'s afflictions.

One of the Vals, its weapon already released, lunged in from dead astern, passed directly over the bridge, and turned left with wingtips vertical before it crashed into *Hornet* just below the port forward gun gallery. It slithered through staterooms, shedding parts and trailing flames, before toppling with the bodies of the two crewmen into the forward elevator pit.

The end of the attack at 0925 found *Hornet* halted and listing 8 degrees to starboard with fires gaining hold from the signal bridge to the fourth deck and from the forward elevator to the after end of the hangar. There was no water in the fire main where it was needed, but plenty of unwanted water in the forward engine room and two firerooms, and the carrier was minus all propulsion, power, and communications. The cost of all this was thirty-eight of the fifty-three aircraft that participated in the attack: five of the twelve Zeros, seventeen of the twenty-one Vals, and sixteen of the twenty Kates. The Japanese found some mitigation in the recovery of the crews of two Zeros, five Vals, and six Kates. In addition to losses in the strike group, one of the two Kate contact planes was missing.

As *Hornet* suffered punishment, her fliers prepared to dish it out. About 0855, her first attack group of fifteen SBDs and four Wildcats under Lieutenant Commander Widhelm spied Abe's Vanguard

Force. *Shokaku*'s radar detected Widhelm's group at 0840 when 97 miles out (the best radar performance on either side all day), and when visually identified they drew the attentions of the fourteen of the twenty-six Zeros on Combat Air Patrol. The four-plane Wildcat escort lost two of their number wrestling with some Zeros, and the other Japanese fighters found their attacks confronted by the massed fires of the SBDs expertly directed by Widhelm and his gunner. One of the Zeros succeeded in putting damaging hits into Widhelm's engine, which began issuing large streamers of smoke, but Widhelm refused to veer from his course.

The Japanese carriers rolled over the horizon about 0915, but Widhelm's engine soon quit and he spiraled down to a water landing, from which vantage point he and his gunner viewed the ensuing attack. One other SBD was shot down, and two SBDs sustained severe damage, compelling them to turn back, but the remaining eleven under Lieutenant James Vose nosed over into determined dives that scored. It was 0927 by Japanese timepieces when Vose and his mates plunged through cumulonimbus clouds to release at only 600 to 900 feet while *Shokaku* sprayed them with large and small antiaircraft fire. "I claim four direct hits on this carrier," stated Vose, and he got them. Of the thirteen SBDs that returned from this mission, five would be unfit for further service.

Half-ton bombs raked *Shokaku* from the midships elevator aft, leaving her flight deck in an alpine landscape, wrecking the middle section of the hangar deck, and rendering unserviceable all after antiaircraft guns. Near misses caused further damage, and she could not conduct flight operations, but her speed was only slightly impaired and few planes were aboard to become tinder for fires. Thanks to bitter experience at Midway, ten or so fire hoses, primed and ready, ringed the flight deck, and crewmen immediately played them upon the flames, extinguishing all fires by 1430. *Teruzuki* in the screen suffered slight hull damage and some casualties from one near-miss.

Although Widhelm repeatedly broadcast a sighting report, finicky radios prevented its reception by any of the succeeding groups of aircraft from *Hornet*. The six torpedo planes under Lieutenant Parker in *Hornet*'s first wave remained at only 800 feet, lagging gradually behind Widhelm, and never sighted the Japanese carriers. At 0915, just as Widhelm saw the enemy carriers, the torpedo planes reached the end of their planned 200-mile outward leg. After a brief search to the north and west, they split to attack *Tone*, five on one bow, one on the other, but she frustrated their efforts with heavy antiaircraft fire and abrupt turns. Of these six planes, two ditched and a Zero downed one on its return; one crew was lost.

Enterprise's small attack group enjoyed no success. Failing to sight the enemy carriers or hear Widhelm's report, the three SBDs churned the water around an unidentified "heavy cruiser." The four TBFs vainly pointed their "fish" at *Suzuya*. All the SBDs regained *Enterprise*, but two of the TBF crews found refuge on *Enterprise*'s destroyers after parting company with their planes in the water.

Hornet's second wave numbered nine SBDs and nine TBFs, plus the aircraft of the air group commander. While over Abe's much-bemused unit at 0930, Lieutenant Lynch of VB-8 heard what he interpreted as a message from Lieutenant Commander Sanchez, the leader of Widhelm's escort, indicating there were no carriers present. This message may have been an example of Japanese radio deception, but in any event Lynch decided to settle for the enemy at hand. He picked *Chikuma*, a vessel probably somewhat separated from the main formation, and commenced a skilled attack on her just before 0930. Two SBD bomb hits bracketed the cruiser's bridge, killing most men at that station. The nine TBFs added at least one direct hit on a torpedo tube mount. A near-miss that bashed in the hull, allowing water to surge into some boiler rooms, brought *Chikuma*'s casualties to an extremely high total: 192 killed, including the executive officer, and ninety-five wounded. Her bloodied captain found she could still make 23 knots; he conned her for Truk with destroyers *Tanikaze* and *Urakaze*. Had the American bombs' fuzes been set for longer delays, *Chikuma* and maybe *Shokaku* might have been sunk. Five TBF crews from *Hornet*'s second strike were rescued from the water near the American task force.

About 1000 the second strike from Carrier Division 1 was inbound looking for *Enterprise;* that carrier's group had already tasted a bizarre bit of action. One of the *Enterprise* TBFs damaged in the attack by *Zuiho*'s fighters ditched about 1,500 yards ahead of destroyer *Porter.* The landing jarred loose the Avenger's torpedo, and just as *Porter* began to move again at 1002 after picking up the plane crew, her lookouts observed the torpedo passing ahead from port to starboard. Two VF-10 Wildcats braved "friendly" antiaircraft fire to strife the circling weapon, but its second circuit terminated against *Porter*'s hull, throwing a column of water 300 feet high. This freak hit killed one officer and fourteen men and ruptured the bulkhead between both boiler rooms, leaving the destroyer with no chance of regaining any mobility on her own. Kinkaid regarded the weakening of *Enterprise*'s screen to provide a tow out of harm's way for a crippled destroyer as unsound, and on his order *Shaw* took off *Porter*'s survivors and sank her with gunfire at 1208.[2]

At 1000 the Val contingent of the second strike by Carrier Division 1 budded on *Enterprise*'s radar screen, only 23 miles distant. The Japanese saw *Hornet* dead in the water and pressed on to find *Enterprise*. Once again the fighter direction was defective: the enemy already close, the radar picture confused, the doctrine for intercept of multiple raids uncertain, and the team of fighter direction officers on *Enterprise* untried. The twenty-one Wildcats over Task Force 16 received few definite vectors and practically no altitude information and consequently were generally too low and too late to break up the attack. They picked off only two dive-bombers before the Vals pushed over.

Like *Hornet, Enterprise* was the center and guide of a ring formation, with heavy cruiser *Portland* on her port bow and light cruiser *San Juan* occupying a similar position to starboard. The latter ship boasted as many 5-inch guns, sixteen, as battleship *South Dakota* a mile and a half behind in the carrier's wake. With *Porter* and *Shaw* gone, only six destroyers remained to fill the perimeter around *Enterprise*. Eight fewer 5-inch guns supported Kinkaid's flagship than *Hornet* had, but *Enterprise* and *South Dakota* each mounted sixteen new Bofors 40mm antiaircraft machineguns, whose venomous effectiveness was about to be demonstrated.

The Vals were already well into their dives when seen at 1015, but instantly antiaircraft fire densely mottled the small patch of sky through which they dropped. Notwithstanding the absence of cloud, American observers thought the Vals discarded the steep conventional dive-bombing approach for notably shallower dives of 45 to 50 degrees. At 1017 a bomb parted wood planking and thin steel at the port forward overhang of the flight deck and continued down through the forecastle to exit the ship's structure and explode just above the troubled waters. Fragments perforated the hull and superstructure in 160 places, killing one man and wounding others, while the blast jarred the ship, tossing an SBD parked on the starboard bow over the side. Deck crews pushed another SBD over the side when fuel from its ruptured tanks threatened to stoke small wisps of flame.

Before much else could be done about the first hit, a second bomb

---

[2]I am indebted to Mr. James Sawruk for figuring out this mystery. Although the *Enterprise* pilot suspected his torpedo caused *Porter*'s loss, this remained uncertain until Mr. Sawruk pieced the whole story together, including Japanese information, which is emphatic that no Japanese submarine attacked *Porter*.

struck the flight deck just aft of the forward elevator. There the bomb split in two. The after end exploded on the hangar deck, demolishing five parked planes and riddling two spare aircraft in the overhead. The forward half continued down to the third deck to obliterate or fatally injure about forty men. A near-miss only 10 feet off the starboard side thrust a violent shock wave into the hull, causing decks to oscillate through 18 inches and bouncing parked aircraft successively to starboard until one SBD sailed over the side. This bomb also slightly damaged an engine unit and caused oil to commence squirting into the wake.

On recovery the attackers skimmed low out of the formation into a thicket of gunfire from *Enterprise*'s escorts—always more dangerous to Vals at this time than while presented with the convoluted problem of hitting a plane diving on an adjacent but radically maneuvering ship. Of the nineteen Vals in this attack group, ten, including that of Lieutenant Commander Seki, were shot down, and two more ditched. The survivors claimed one of their band crashed the carrier, a second a destroyer, and the balance secured six bomb hits on the carrier.

Slightly over twenty minutes after *Shokaku*'s Vals finished their attack, *Enterprise*'s radar emitted signs at 1135 of the approach of the other portion of the second strike group, *Zuikaku*'s sixteen Kates. Good fortune again favored *Enterprise,* as the Kates (whose departure was delayed, it may be recalled, because of an extra interval required to reequip them with torpedoes as opposed to the time required to refit the Vals in the strike with bombs) only made up about five of the thirty minutes of difference in rearming time. Thus *Enterprise* was spared exposure to the sort of coordinated attack that crippled *Hornet.* Approaching against a background of dark clouds, the Kates split to attack *Enterprise* on each bow. They evaded visual detection until within about 5 miles of *Enterprise* when one of their number burst into flames. This plane was the first victim of a Wildcat flown by Lieutenant Stanley W. Vejtasa or his wingman. Vejtasa pursued one group, perforating four with gunfire; one blew up and two others appeared to catch fire. He chased the fourth—which he thought he missed—in the clouds, but the plane dived down to plow into the forecastle of destroyer *Smith.*

At 1048 the flaming Kate crashed abreast the number one 5-inch gun. Its gasoline tanks shattered, flinging fuel that ignited and enveloped the bow. With streaks of fire somersaulting over the superstructure and the bridge muffled in smoke, Lieutenant Commander Wood dashed to the after control station with Chief Quartermaster

Frank Riduka. Finding communications out, Riduka continued to the steering engine room, where he conned the ship. Fire-fighting parties charged into the flames whipped by the ship's unchecked motion, recoiling briefly in the face of a large explosion at about 1053 that may have been the torpedo warhead. Wood threaded *Smith* through the formation to poke her fiery bow into *South Dakota*'s frothing wake. The maneuver quelched the blaze. Despite grievous wounds and casualties—fifty-seven officers and men lay dead or dying—*Smith* inspired all who saw her by maintaining station while her after guns bayed in *Enterprise*'s defense.

The group of Kates closing from the starboard bow lost some of their number to antiaircraft fire, but five made drops. Captain Hardison countered three closely spaced tracks from ahead with a sharp right turn, allowing the torpedoes to pass 50 yards off the port side; rapid reversals of the helm dodged *Smith* and a fourth wake. Meanwhile, five Kates sought to gain position to port, but Hardison presented them with *Enterprise*'s counter stern. Gunners dropped more planes in rapid succession, but one, fatally damaged, swerved to make a futile desperation release at *Enterprise*. Another plane executed an aimed release which was sidestepped easily. According to Japanese records, a total of nine Kates fell in the attack, and a tenth ditched. Of the nine Zeros accompanying both attack units, two ditched, bringing total losses in the bifurcated second strike to twenty-four of forty-four aircraft.

Immediately after the torpedo plane attack ended, *Portland* suffered a steering casualty at 1053. As the ship swung out of control to port, torpedo wakes appeared close on the starboard hand. The ship's company felt three "separate, sharp and severe jolts" at 1055 as warheads thudded harmlessly against her side. Although the torpedoes were attributed at the time to a Japanese submarine, it now appears that these were three aircraft torpedoes that inexplicably failed to explode. Only ten minutes later, *San Juan,* on the opposite side of the formation, saw a periscope, and at 1108 the light cruiser skidded sharply right to turn short of torpedo wakes approaching to starboard. These weapons, however, most likely also represented the final runs of the torpedoes released by Kates stalking *Enterprise*.

With less than an hour left of this morning, another group of Japanese planes flickered onto American radars. This was the first raid from the *Junyo* air group, led by Lieutenant Yoshio Shiga with seventeen Vals and a dozen Zeros. Airborne since 0914, the *Junyo* airmen had dipped low into their fuel supply seeking a target, but had located only the stationary *Hornet.* Shiga announced his intention to attack *Hornet*'s escorting cruisers, but officers on *Junyo* overheard his message and immediately ordered a further probe for an operational American carrier they knew was present from radio intercepts. Almost immediately, Shiga spotted *Enterprise*.

As the Vals initiated their runs at 1121 they found the American task force on the fringe of a large rainsquall with the cloud base at only 1,000 to 1,500 feet, creating a curious tactical situation: the American gunners could not see the Japanese planes until the final seconds of their dives, but the clouds forced the Japanese pilots into shallow gliding approaches to keep their target in sight. The gunners coped best with their handicap, dumping several Vals into the sea around *Enterprise*. As the carrier heeled to port under hard right rudder, one bomb skimmed off the exposed hull below the waterline and exploded approximately 8 feet from the starboard side. It shook the ship severely, opened two voids to the sea, and, coupled with previous hits, jammed the forward elevator in the up position.

Earlier damage had put *Enterprise*'s main search radar out of action, and the opening of this attack found Lieutenant Brad Williams, the ship's radar officer, endeavoring to resuscitate the unit, located on the foremast. Williams lashed himself to the "mattress-type" aerial of the SC radar to free both hands for this delicate job and labored steadily, poised between strafing bullets and answering antiaircraft fire while bombs raised geysers to his height and sent fragments whistling about him. His success was immediately clear to those in control of the radar, and a technician, eager to restore the ship's electronic eyes, switched on the power, converting the scene from one of high courage to low comedy as the aerial—and Williams—rotated majestically a dozen times before someone observed his gesticulations.

Not all the Japanese planes selected *Enterprise* for their target. *San Juan* drew the attention of several Vals, and as the cruiser heeled in a hard right turn, near-misses cascaded the sea on both sides. At 1128 a bomb struck her canted hull aft, three feet above the waterline, and punched completely through the light structure before exploding beneath the ship near the rudder. Fragments let water into three or four compartments, and the shock of the blast tripped circuit breakers, leaving the rudder jammed at full right. For thirteen minutes *San Juan* spun in circles, "breakdown" flag flapping and whistle tooting to warn other vessels of her plight.

All morning, battleship *South Dakota*'s unblooded but well-drilled gunners blasted lustily in support of *Enterprise*. Their claims for twenty-six aircraft, if considerably overstated (one was a TBF, insisted *Preston*), are one gauge of the intensity of the attacks. Although Japanese aviators noted her presence, thus far only one plane, a *Zuikaku* Kate, had attempted a deliberate run on her when it tried to convert its torpedo into a bomb, narrowly missing the battleship. But about 1129, several *Junyo* Vals popped from low clouds on the port bow to thrash the ocean astride *South Dakota*'s broad beam with 550-pound bombs. One of these planes, boring in from dead ahead, scored on the number one main battery turret. The thick armored hide of the turret left all the men inside, save the officer at the periscope, unaware they had been hit, but fragments wounded over fifty, two of whom died. One sliver of steel also caught Captain Gatch in the throat as he stood exposed outside the armored conning tower. A communications failure in shifting helm control to "Battle Two," the executive officer's station, left *South Dakota* careening out of control for one minute. When she veered at *Enterprise,* the carrier nimbly granted her the right of way. The combination of falling bombs and steering casualties during the attack of *Junyo*'s Vals caused Lieutenant Commander G. L. Sims of *Maury* to comment mildly, "During [this] attack adjacent ships seemed to change identity with marked rapidity."

Eleven of these seventeen Vals from *Junyo* failed to regain a Japanese deck, including three that ditched, and only three of the downed crewmen survived. All twelve Zeros returned, with claims for a dozen American planes. The returning airmen reported "over three" hits on a carrier plus damage to two cruisers.

As the gunfire faded again, *Enterprise* resumed the task of landing aircraft interrupted by *Junyo*'s Vals. Planes from both carriers had been circling in clusters and singles, most with fuel tanks nearly dry, many with damage and some the targets of nervous American gunners. Not only was the number one elevator jammed up, the number two elevator was temporarily stuck down, leaving a gaping hole in the flight deck and sharply shortening the landing area. Standing on the after port side platform, Lieutenant James Daniels and then Lieutenant Robin Lindsay wielded loquacious paddles guiding fifty-seven planes onto the extreme after end of the flight deck.

The last two hours before noon featured a series of orders and decisions by Kondo, Nagumo, and Kakuta. Ever hopeful to make the Japanese superiority in heavy ordnance count, Kondo directed the Vanguard Force under Abe to join him in the quest to bring the Americans into gunnery range. At 1018, Kondo made a general signal announcing his intentions to attack the enemy with his surface ships and detaching *Junyo* and two destroyers to come under Nagumo's command to coordinate further blows from the air.

Nagumo received word of the attachment of *Junyo* as he confronted a more immediate problem. Bomb damage had rendered flagship *Shokaku* temporarily deaf and mute, seriously aflame, and permanently incapable of flight operations. Thus Nagumo needed to move to another ship, ideally *Zuikaku,* to exercise effective command. On the other hand, crewmen soon restored *Shokaku*'s radio receivers, and the staff believed they were well apprised of the situation and could transmit essential signals through consorts. This analysis suggested a less urgent need to transfer the flag, and into this balance entered one other overriding consideration. With tears in his eyes, Captain Arima of *Shokaku* proposed that his ship remain in the vicinity of *Zuikaku* to help absorb further American attacks, but Nagumo's staff insisted that *Shokaku* must be preserved for future battles. Consequently, *Shokaku* began a northwesterly dash at 31 knots to clear the range of enemy carrier planes, with *Zuiho* puffing along behind at her best speed of 29 knots. *Shokaku* disdained to pause in her retirement even briefly to allow Nagumo and his staff to transfer to a destroyer, and when *Zuikaku* took up a divergent course to recover aircraft, she soon separated from the flagship. Under these circumstances, it is not surprising that upon learning of *Junyo*'s attachment to his command, Nagumo confined himself to issuing a general directive at 1140 to Kukuta to destroy the remaining "enemy *Yorktown*-type carrier." Not until 1507 did Nagumo signal his intention to switch to a destroyer and then *Zuikaku* as the situation permitted, and at 1515 he placed *Zuikaku* under Kukuta's command. In the event, a full day passed before Nagumo boarded *Zuikaku* at 1532 on October 27.

Kukuta received Kondo's 1018 order to join Nagumo, and at 1130, after recovering aircraft, he aimed *Junyo* for Carrier Division 1. Sighting masts at 1223, Kukuta pulled up *Junyo*'s sprint to maintain separation of the two remaining healthy carriers for defensive purposes while he and his staff attempted to sort out a welter of reports on American dispositions. Conflicting accounts from returning crews and shadowers left them mystified as to the number of American carriers present; the consensus was at least three, but probably more. At 1240, the distant 4th Fleet Communications Unit flashed a report that an enemy carrier lay dead in the water at 8°35' South, 166°5' East—a good fix on *Hornet.* At 1250, Kukuta turned *Junyo* to course 110 degrees, and sixteen minutes later she put a second strike group of Kates and Zeros aloft to hunt for the wounded enemy queen 260 miles distant. By that time the independently operating *Zuikaku* had been closing the American position for thirty-six minutes and preparing another attack group.

PURSUIT BEYOND DARKNESS

Brilliant individual performances like Daniels's and Lindsey's could not conceal the fact that the morning exchange of blows much favored the Japanese. At 1335, *Enterprise* completed recovery of aircraft, and Kinkaid set her on a withdrawal course of 123 degrees, rapidly putting ocean between his flagship and the Japanese as well as her sister ship. Kinkaid's report described but did not explain this action; it looked ignominious to many junior officers. His war diary listed three considerations underlying the decision to withdraw: (1) *Hornet* was out of action; (2) the extent of damage to *Enterprise* was unknown; and (3) there probably was one or more unsighted enemy carriers in the vicinity. Strangely, the list omitted the need to preserve *Enterprise,* whose survival was vital to the whole campaign. Also unmentioned was one effect of this decision—the stripping of fighter cover from the disabled *Hornet.* At 1406, *Enterprise* reestablished a Combat Air Patrol of Wildcats, and two hours later she flew off thirteen SBDs to Espíritu Santo to relieve severe congestion. For practical purposes, *Enterprise,* like *Shokaku* and *Zuiho,* exited the battle; the focus of the rest of the day's action, and on into the night, became *Hornet* and the efforts to save and sink her.

The end of the morning attack found *Hornet* listing, dead in the water, and ablaze. Destroyer *Morris* nuzzled up on the starboard side to pass fire hoses, while *Russell* and *Mustin* did likewise from port. Eager hands grasped the proffered hoses and played them on the fires already confronted by bucket brigades to such good effect that by 1000 all fires were under control, though not all were extinguished. On the hangar deck, the engineering officer, Commander Edward P. Creehan, reorganized his men to lead an attack back down into the mangled propulsion system. Within ten minutes of the torpedo hits, Commander Creehan's "Black Gang" reentered tilted, suffocating compartments under the dim twinkle of hand lanterns to commence the intricate task of locating fuel and uncontaminated feed water for the operable boilers and cross-connecting undamaged piping to thread the steam to the one functional engine unit.

Admiral Murray did not wait for *Hornet*'s engineers to regain power; just before 1000 he asked for a tow. *Northampton* maneuvered to render this service, while *Hornet*'s executive officer, Commander Apollo Soucek, supervised the rigging of the port anchor chain, a task performed by manual power alone. At 1009, as *Northampton* swiveled her stern into position to pass the towline, a lone unheralded Val from *Shokaku* swooped down over the scene and released a bomb that landed barely 25 yards off the stern of destroyer *Morris*. This prompted all of the ships alongside *Hornet* to cast off and mill around for twenty-five minutes in anticipation of other interlopers. *Northampton* returned, and by 1130 *Hornet* was moving at 3 to 4 knots at the end of a taut towline, but ten minutes later the line parted.

While Murray shifted his flag to *Pensacola* at 1145, on Captain Mason's order destroyers began taking off seventy-five seriously injured *Hornet* sailors and about 800 excess personnel. Other crewmen wrestled a line from the after elevator pit up most of *Hornet*'s length to pass to *Northampton*. At 1450, *Hornet* was again being pulled through the water at 3 knots by *Northampton* and her engineers, after many heartbreaking failures, stood poised on the verge of getting power on one shaft. Five minutes later, *Hornet* bluejackets learned of the approach of unidentified aircraft.

This was *Junyo*'s second strike of seven Kates guarded by eight Zeros, all under Lieutenant Yoshiaki Irikiin, a strike group leader from *Hiyo* now flying from her sister ship. At 1520, *Junyo*'s Kates entered their characteristic undulating dives from 6,000 feet on *Hornet*'s starboard beam. No Wildcats defended her, and she sorely missed the sixteen 5-inch guns of *Juneau* at this moment, but through a misunderstood order the light cruiser had switched allegiance to *Enterprise*. One or two torpedo-clutching Kates pointed themselves at *Northampton*, which cut the towline and presented them her stern, but *Hornet* could only spray the approaching planes with as much antiaircraft fire as her manually powered guns could dispense. This proved almost but not quite enough. Two Kates skidded into the sea. A pair of Zeros went missing and three others would ditch after the attack, but at 1523 one torpedo dropped at extremely close range struck the starboard side just aft and above the first hit. Commander Creehan preserved for us a vivid sense impression of the hit at his station one deck above, though on the opposite side of the ship from, the compartment in which the torpedo detonated:

A sickly green flash momentarily lighted the scullery compartment and seemed to run both forward toward Repair Station 5 and aft into the scullery compartment for a distance of about 50 feet. This was preceded by a thud so deceptive as to almost make one believe that the torpedo had struck the port side. Immediately following the flash a hissing sound as of escaping air was heard followed by a dull rumbling noise. The deck on the port side seemed to crack open and a geyser of fuel oil which quickly reached the depth of two feet swept all personnel at Repair 5 off their feet and flung them headlong down the sloping decks of the compartment to the starboard side. Floundering around in the fuel oil, all somehow regained their feet and a hand chain was formed to the two-way ladder and escape shuttle leading from the third deck to the second deck. . . . All managed to escape in some fashion through this scuttle . . . and presented a sorry appearance upon reaching the hangar deck.

This hit doomed *Hornet,* for it eliminated any possibility of regaining power. With the ship listing 14.5 degrees, Captain Mason passed the word to prepare to abandon ship.

At 1540 a pair of Vals appeared. One planted its bomb in the sea near *Hornet,* while the second achieved a like result near cruiser *San Diego.* These two planes represented the first wave of *Zuikaku*'s third strike of the day. They and the remaining eleven aircraft—five Zeros and six Kates—under Lieutenant (jg) Ichiro Tanaka, represented the best that Carrier Division 1 could muster after the morning raids. Captain Mason left *Hornet*'s bridge for the last time at 1550. From the flight deck he witnessed the penultimate air attack on his ship at 1555. This was *Zuikaku*'s second wave of six Kates, which executed a horizontal bombing attack that secured one hit on the starboard after corner of the flight deck, adding little to *Hornet*'s damage.

Men could scarcely stand upright when *Hornet*'s list reached 18 degrees, but *Hornet*'s heartsick crew parted from their ship in orderly fashion, Mason last at 1627. *Hornet*'s consorts were still sifting survivors from the water at 1702 when four Vals appeared. The dive-bombers and their escort of six Zeros under Lieutenant Yoshio Shiga constituted *Junyo*'s third and final effort of the day. Pushing through "severe" antiaircraft fire which damaged two Vals, they scored only a single hit on the stationary target. The bomb exploded on the empty hangar deck, sparking a fire that flared and then subsided. Rescue operations ended at 1715; dead on *Hornet* or soon to die were 118 officers and men.

During the day, terse messages from Kinkaid and Murray afforded Halsey at Noumea hasty snippets of the battle: 0949, "*Hornet* hurt"; 1300, "Am retiring southeastward . . . unable to give *Hornet* fighter coverage"; 1400, "*Hornet* in tow. No aircraft." Halsey recognized the ebb of fortune and at 1550 he ordered a general withdrawal. Nimitz added urgency to this directive when he relayed to Murray radio intelligence of powerful Japanese surface forces converging on *Hornet.* Accordingly, Murray detailed *Mustin* to scuttle *Hornet* while the rest of the task force began a high-speed retirement at 1810. *Mustin* carefully fired eight torpedoes at *Hornet* that provided another sad example of the quality of these weapons: two ran erratically, one prematured, and five hit, but only three exploded. *Mustin* advised Kinkaid of *Hornet*'s refusal to sink, and the admiral detached *Anderson* to help bury *Hornet.* Between 1915 and 1930, *Anderson* scored six hits with eight torpedoes, but *Hornet* still remained afloat.

Mustin and *Anderson*'s onerous duty attracted the curiosity of three Japanese float planes: one each from *Nagara, Isuzu,* and *Maya.* The latter two came from the Advanced Force, which gathered strength at 1740 when *Myoko, Takao,* and their two destroyers rejoined after completing their plane recovery detail. By then the Vanguard Force, including *Nagara,* stood only 12 miles north of Kondo's Advanced Force. At 1804, Kondo announced his intentions to seek a night battle and directed Kakuta to follow the gunnery units with the carriers to renew air action at dawn. This proved prescient, for one hour later Yamamoto issued an order to the same essential effect. Yamamoto added his situation estimate that the American units near the Santa Cruz Islands had lost heavily and were in disorder, which was near correct. He also erroneously believed that Lee's task unit near the Russells would probably head east to cover the crippled fleet units by the Santa Cruz Islands.

At 1851 the planes from *Isuzu* and *Maya* noted *Mustin* and *Anderson* cudgeling *Hornet* with their 5-inch guns to speed her demise. Flames gnawed *Hornet*'s soggy hull from stem to stern, but despite seven bombs, two aircraft crashes, three Japanese and nine American torpedoes, and now over 300 5-inch shells, she refused to succumb. Ugaki flashed a Combined Fleet order at 1920 to try to capture and tow *Hornet,* and cryptanalysts presented the chilling content of this message to Nimitz. At 1945, Kondo's Advanced Force pivoted to course due east and stepped off at 24 knots in an echelon formation angled to the northwest with the Vanguard Force on a conforming course still farther to the north bracketing *Hornet*'s position. Kondo unleashed Admiral Tanaka's Destroyer Squadron 2 to catch the two American destroyers.

At 2015, *Mustin*'s radar located a surface contact, but *Hornet* floated stubbornly, so the destroyers continued to pump shells into her. With *Hornet* burning fiercely and exploding, and radar disclosing the crowding of the ocean nearby, *Mustin* and *Anderson* exited the scene to the southeast at 2040, followed by a retinue of float planes. Only twenty minutes later, destroyers *Akigumo* and *Makikumo* arrived to find *Hornet in extremis.* After perusing the number 8 on her hull, each destroyer discharged two Long Lances, which finally finished *Hornet*'s agony; she sank wreathed in smoke and steam at 0135 on October 27—ironically, Navy Day in the United States.

Kondo terminated the eastward surge at 2400, turning first north, then west. Catalinas again seemed to be as much a part of the night sky as the stars, and at 0055 one hit destroyer *Teruzuki* with a bomb, killing seven of her crew, while at 0130 another dropped out of the sky to startle *Junyo* with torpedoes. Pursuant to Halsey's instructions, all the vessels wearing the Stars and Stripes under both Kinkaid and Lee took up courses for Espíritu Santo or Noumea. Their tracks crossed the ambush sites of submarines *I-21, 24,* and *15,* and all three shot off contact reports revealing the retirement. *I-24* and *I-15* also managed to spice battleship *Washington*'s path with torpedoes at 0320 and 0530 on October 27, all of which missed. During the retreat, *Mahan* and *South Dakota* collided, sending the destroyer to a dockyard for repairs.

During the 26th, Yamamoto scrutinized dispatches redolent of victory. The intelligence gleaned by the submarine pickets on the American retreat both confirmed the success of Kondo's Support Force and offered a faint chance of expanding the Japanese triumph at sea. By this time, too, the fuel situation approached crisis proportions. In light of these factors, Yamamoto directed a retirement to Truk unless the dawn search on October 27 offered profitable prospects. When search planes found only empty waters after sunrise, Kondo set course for a refueling rendezvous to the northwest en route to Truk, where anchors rattled through hawsepipes on October 30.

During the cruise to Truk, staff officers and commanders assessed the results of the battle. Certainty prevailed as to *Hornet*'s end, thanks to the opportunity to note her hull identification number, and captured aircrews corroborated the presence of *Enterprise.* But a combination of losses of squadron leaders, confused aircraft sighting reports, and an erroneous deduction from voice radio intercepts propelled the Japanese into a debate over whether three or four American flattops were present—all of which were believed sunk.[3] The carrier staffs eventually tendered reports of sinking three carriers and one each of the breeds with longer pedigrees: battleship, cruiser, destroyer, and submarine, plus one vessel "larger than a heavy cruiser." Japanese gunners and fliers volunteered claims for the destruction of seventy-nine American aircraft. Imperial General Headquarters christened this the South Pacific Sea Battle and proclaimed its fruits included the destruction of four American carriers, one battleship, and 200 or more aircraft. As will be seen shortly, these figures were not simply put out for public consumption.

No ship flying the Rising Sun flag sank, though *Zuikaku, Zuiho,* and *Chikuma* would be out of action for many weeks. But aircraft losses, and more important, aircrew losses, were severe. The Imperial Navy entered the battle with 199 carrier planes, and reported the following aircraft destroyed from all causes, including both strike participants and Zeros deployed defensively:

	Zeros	Vals	Kates	Judy	Grand total
Combat losses:	14	29	22	0	65
Lost aboard ship:	3	0	0	0	3
Ditched/operational:	10	11	7	1	29
Totals:	27	40	29	1	97

Of the 102 or so carrier aircraft that survived the day, only eighty-six remained flyable. The losses among aircrews numbered:

	Zeros	Vals	Kates
Total available:	96	65	72
Lost crews (men):	16 (16)	32.5 (65)	22.33 (67)
Percentage:	18	50	31

These 148 men included two of three dive-bomber leaders, three torpedo squadron leaders, and most section leaders. The excellence

---

[3]The Japanese monitored references to "Red Base" (*Enterprise*) and "Blue Base" (*Hornet*), which they correctly identified as carriers, but references to "River Base" deceived them into assuming it was another carrier. The identity of "River Base" is not revealed in surviving American records.

of men like Murata and Seki would never be matched by their replacements. As for the quality of the average Japanese carrier flier in this action, an interesting evaluation is provided by Commander Arnold E. True (ComDesron 2), who measured their performance against what he witnessed at Coral Sea and Midway. He observed "no diminution in the courage and daring of the individual [Japanese] pilot." Indeed, the attacks were made with "more ferocity and resolution," but True also noted "a most marked decrease in skill."

Washington promptly announced the loss of *Hornet*—too promptly, in the minds of King and Nimitz. The Americans entertained no delusions about having sunk any Japanese ships, and although the intrinsic difficulty of assessing such matters gave rise to exaggerated claims for 115 enemy aircraft, the estimate that three air groups had been rendered *hors de combat* was valid. American plane losses for October 25–27 came to eighty-one, divided as follows:

	Wildcats	*SBDs*	*TBFs*	*Total*
Combat losses:	16	4	5	25
Lost aboard ship:	8	20	0	28
Ditched/operational:	8	7	13	28
Totals:	32	31	18	81

The battle deprived the *Enterprise* air group of the pilots of six fighters and two TBFs and of three TBF crewmen; two of the fighter pilots and two TBF crewmen became prisoners of war. *Hornet*'s air group lost six fighter pilots and one each dive-bomber and torpedo bomber crew (five men), bringing total American flight crew casualties to twenty-four (twenty killed and four prisoners of war). Besides being markedly less than those of the Japanese, these losses included only one squadron commander (Lieutenant Commander Collett of *Enterprise*'s torpedo bomber unit). The ship's companies suffered 240 officers and men killed or missing. Japanese losses in this category are not compiled, but almost certainly exceeded this figure, given 192 dead in *Chikuma* and seven in *Teruzuki* and the extent of the damage to *Shokaku* and *Zuiho*.

Comments in American action reports coalesced about three areas of doctrine and tactics: air search, air attack and air defense. Scribes again conceded superiority in search and tracking to the Japanese, for though the PBYs had located the enemy first in this battle, failed or untimely communications had squandered this achievement. Had

Kinkaid received the 0310 PBY report, he might have caught the Japanese with decks full of gassed and armed planes as Spruance did at Midway. Faults in air attack flowed primarily from piecemeal commitment because of the failure of the various strike waves to join together. This stemmed from Kinkaid's explicit decision to try to hit first rather than hardest by saving assembly time—an understandable choice in the context of experience so far in the war. This problem was compounded by the failure of some squadrons of the same air group to fly together. Defects in aircraft radios garnered heaps of criticism; rightly so, for had Widhelm's sighting report been received by more following aircraft, additional damage would have been inflicted. Of the two air groups present, *Enterprise*'s Air Group 10 displayed zeal, but the more experienced and numerous (on the strike missions) *Hornet* fliers inflicted all the damage.

The subject of air defense was entwined with the circumstances of *Hornet*'s loss, a topic that spawned much bitterness. Both fighter squadron commanders, Flatley and Sanchez, wrote stinging critiques of the fighter direction failure, but Sanchez ventured even further. After personally inspecting *Enterprise*'s ad hoc fighter direction center, he declared *Hornet*'s special facility "extremely superior" in training, layout, and capabilities. From this fact he penned his conclusion that Kinkaid's failure to delegate fighter direction to *Hornet* represented either negligence or incompetence. Conceding poor functioning of fighter direction, which he attributed mainly to late detection by radar, Kinkaid tartly responded to this impudence that the real cause of the loss was "the fact that *Hornet* was dead in the water early in the action." With hindsight it seems Sanchez was probably correct that *Hornet* could have provided better fighter direction, but whether this would have saved her is problematical. It should not be overlooked that her loss was not due solely to a catalogue of American errors but was rooted, as Kinkaid suggested, in the damage caused by the initial combined dive-bomber and torpedo bomber attack, the most devastating single example of its type mounted by Japanese carrier aviators during the war.

While the American fliers anguished over their own performance, gunners expressed considerable satisfaction over their accomplishments: antiaircraft batteries may have destroyed over half of the lost Vals and Kates. Gunnery officers again noted that the heavy 5-inch guns with their elaborate radar and director systems accounted for very few, perhaps only 5 percent, of attacking dive-bombers and torpedo bombers. The new Bofors 40mm guns demonstrated their marked superiority over the older 1.1-inch quadruple mounts they replaced, and together with the proven 20mm guns, accounted for the majority of the fatally damaged planes. Kinkaid wrote: "There cannot be too many 40mm and 20mm guns on any type of ship. They knock down planes."

In his report, drafted several weeks later, Nimitz offered an assessment that has weathered the test of time:

This battle cost us the lives of many gallant men, many planes and two ships that could ill be spared. Despite the loss of about three carrier air groups and damage to a number of ships, the enemy retired with all his ships. We nevertheless turned back the Japanese again in their offensive to regain Guadalcanal and shattered their carrier air strength on the eve of the critical days of mid-November.

16

RETREATS

AND ADVANCES

"An atmosphere of tense expectation"

RETREAT OF THE SENDAI DIVISION

"An atmosphere of tense expectation was apparent in some Washington quarters" on October 26, reported the *New York Times* the next day. The apparent causes of the anxiety could be easily surmised from the war news: battles raging at Stalingrad and El Alamein as well as in the South Pacific, where the loss of *Wasp* had just been announced. The public and the newsmen remained ignorant of another cause—the fact that massive convoys bearing thousands of British and American troops destined for Operation "Torch," the landings in North Africa, were even then on the Atlantic picking their way around the U-boats that were the focus of a further key battle. Those unspecified "Washington quarters" included the White House, which bustled with the coming and going of senior officials as President Roosevelt grappled with the crisis in the South Pacific. The President created the catalyst for much of this activity with his October 24 memorandum to the Joint Chiefs, which said in part:

My anxiety about the Southwest Pacific is to make sure that every possible weapon gets into that area to hold Guadalcanal, and that having held it in this crisis that munitions and planes and crews are on the way to take advantage of our success. We will soon find ourselves engaged on two active fronts and we must have adequate air support in both places even though it means delay in our other commitments, particularly to England. . . . I wish therefore, you would canvass over the week-end every possible temporary diversion of munitions which you will require for our active fronts and let me know what they are.

Marshall and King diagnosed the urgent problem in the South Pacific as not a lack of air or ground forces but a want of shipping. Accordingly, President Roosevelt ordered twenty more ships released immediately for the Southwest Pacific on the afternoon of October 26, with the caveat that they not be diverted from tonnage earmarked for shipments destined for the Soviet Union or for "Torch."

At Imperial Headquarters in Tokyo the last five days of October witnessed the first true strategic consensus on Guadalcanal. Only now did the Army Section fully accept the view—held for some time by the Navy Section—that the fighting in the Solomons was developing into *the* decisive battle between Japan and the United States. Despite the failure of the October ground attack, Imperial Headquarters prepared confidently for another offensive, for two reasons. First, staffs in Tokyo believed that the destruction of four American carriers and a battleship at the Battle of the Santa Cruz Islands had tilted the balance of naval power decisively in Japan's favor. Second, these same officers perceived that the October attack had teetered on the very edge of success. This conviction stemmed in part from Japanese reports, but much more important, Tokyo eagerly consumed American news accounts acknowledging that penetrations of the defense lines had been restored only by counterattack, exaggerating the number of Japanese troops on Guadalcanal and emphasizing the fatigued state of the American forces on Guadalcanal, particularly the pilots. The motives behind the release of such information may have perplexed senior Japanese officers, but the contents of this news undoubtedly incited them to action.

A shocked but resolute atmosphere gripped the headquarters of the 17th Army on the morning of October 26. Even while managing the problems of immediate defeat, the staff found time to assemble a concept for another offensive. The construction of a mid-Solomons air base for use as a lever to pry back air superiority over Guadalcanal became item one in this scheme. After that essential preliminary, the 51st Infantry Division would be convoyed to Guadalcanal to join the 2d Division as the western prong of an assault about late December. The eastern prong would be the 38th Division, which would be lifted immediately to Koli Point, to which the Shoji's right wing was already moving.

The proposal to deploy the 38th Division to Koli instantly embroiled the 17th Army in a controversy not only with Imperial General Headquarters but also with its own chief of staff, General Miyazaki. The Army Section of Imperial Headquarters responded promptly to the 17th Army blueprint with a long message, the gist of which was that the essentials to success were the suppression of the enemy airfields and the proper employment of firepower. Both of these factors made "Bear Height" (the Japanese designation of the high ground just west of Henderson Field across the Lunga River) the key terrain feature of the campaign. It followed that the 38th Division must be used there. Sweetening this stern dose of advice was the offer of expedited reinforcement: the 21st Independent Mixed Brigade, promised in October, would be moved as rapidly as possible to Rabaul, for which the 51st Division was already being readied to sail. General Miyazaki not only criticized the proposed tactical employment of the 38th Division but also pointed out that establishing a major unit even farther from Shortland would needlessly complicate the logistical situation. To this hectoring, the 17th Army replied that terrain, and especially logistics, so circumscribed their firepower that they were compelled to look for other solutions. To back their assertions they offered this equation: for every ten units of resupply planned, only six were sent, only three were landed, and only two survived for consumption.

During this exchange over the airwaves, the 2d Division began its retreat. While Shoji put the bulk of the Right Wing on the trail for Koli, Tamioka, the former chief of staff of the Sendai Division, assumed command of the Left Wing with orders to bring it to the upper Lunga Valley with the rest of the division. Elements of the division fell back past Maruyama's headquarters, which remained southeast of "Centipede Height" (Edson's Ridge) until 0600 on October 28. The next day the 17th Army directed a shift of the concentration point to the upper Matanikau Valley. Some guards remained with the heavy artillery, while a few gunners searched for firing positions from which the 2d Battalion, 2d Artillery Regiment and the 20th Mountain Gun Battalion might shell Henderson Field in the near future. Far too many wounded existed for the regular medical units to tend, so each unit became responsible for the care and movement of its own sick and injured. The exertion demanded of each soldier—to propel himself, his equipment, and the wounded over the muddy jungle trail, in the penumbra of the jungle, soaked daily by rain and with few or no provisions—tested human endurance to the limit. In Lieutenant Keijiro Minegishi's diary we find this:

October 27: I never dreamed of retreating over the same mountainous trail through the jungle we crossed with such enthusiasm. . . . we haven't eaten for three days and even walking is difficult. On the up hill my body swayed around unable to walk. I can't imagine how the soldiers carrying the artillery are doing. I must take a rest every two meters. It is quite disheartening to have only one tiny teaspoon of salt per day and a palmful of rice porridge.

October 28: We had to search again for the Regimental Colors. The taste of even temporary defeat is bitter. Perhaps it is well for a soldier to sample such a thing once in a lifetime, but it's still very, very distasteful. We must win at any cost in this fight.

October 29: The sky cleared up in the morning and we saw the sun. . . . I have begun to see what seems to be malnutrition. . . . I don't know how many men must be left [behind] today.

October 30: . . . I am surprised by how food captures the mind to the degree that one is always thinking of it, I try to think of other things but can't.

November 1: . . . the company reached the Regimental Headquarters at noon and we are told we will get provisions tomorrow evening. I can hardly wait.

On the night of October 29–30, destroyers *Shigure* and *Ariake* debarked supplies and two special passengers, General Miyazaki and Commander Ohmae. Forewarned by radio intelligence, planes and PT boats skirmished with the destroyers and sent them back with a portion of their cargoes. The two important visitors joined a conference on future operations the next day at 17th Army Headquarters. In the middle of the discussion, Colonel Tsuji dramatically hobbled into the meeting. Despite a high fever from malaria, in two and a half days of continuous hiking Tsuji retraced the route of the 2d Division—a distance fresh men had taken a week to cover. He described the failure of the attack and the resulting situation in terms that put an exclamation point to the arguments of Miyazaki for the cancellation of the landing of the rest of the 38th Division at Koli. These officers scotched plans for a major landing at Koli that day.

The decision to abort the Koli operation on October 30 only prevented exacerbation of the already critical supply problem. The 17th Army figured its needs as 200 tons of provisions per day to support 30,000 men. This equaled five destroyer loads per night, or 150 in the course of a month, but the current actual rate ran at only sixty per month. Furthermore, meshing the logistical to the operational plans demanded increasing rather than simply sustaining the forces already at Guadalcanal. To this latter end, Army staff officers calculated that no fewer than forty-two transport and a hundred destroyer loads would have to reach the island in addition to the now accustomed rhythm of six destroyers every three days. Computations by naval staff officers differed somewhat from those of their Army counterparts. The 8th Fleet estimated that the movement of the rest of the 38th Division, the 51st Division, and the 21st Independent Mixed Brigade meant sea lift for 30,000 men, 300 guns, and 3,000 tons of supplies. This amount of men and material would require fifty transport or 800 destroyer and twenty seaplane carrier runs.

The bigger difference between the Imperial Army and Navy lay over the conduct, not the amount, of sea lift. The Army desired to schedule many convoys, each of a few ships. The 8th Fleet faulted this concept on the basis that it would require the prolonged suppression of the Cactus Air Force, while experience suggested two days was about the maximum period flight activities from Guadalcanal could be halted. The seamen thought it far better to dispatch one large convoy and to pave its way by increasing the 11th Air Fleet's air superiority activities and by conducting a naval bombardment. Moreover, they intended to unload the convoy only at night, which meant that the transports could disembark only about one-third of their load at a time.

After examining the 17th Army's new plan, Yamamoto commented that it was so unrealistic that success might be unattainable with such brains in charge of the Imperial Army's forces on Guadalcanal. Yamamoto's staff aimed to neutralize the Cactus Air Force with shore-based artillery, and began planning to move long-range naval guns to the island. But that offered remote, not immediate, relief, and it was the short-term options that the Combined Fleet staff commenced studying on November 4, impelled by a sense that a turning point had been reached and that now was the moment for a concerted bid for victory. Three days of labor produced an outline plan on November 7: a large convoy would lift a major reinforcement to Guadalcanal on Z-Day escorted by the 8th Fleet; beginning on Z minus three the 11th Air Fleet would wrestle for air superiority; on Z minus one the Advanced Force would take position north of Guadalcanal and the battleships *Hiei* and *Kirishima* would pound the American airfields; and on Z-Day heavy cruisers would replow the American airstrips. As for the future, the convoy would lift supplies for twenty days, during which Solomons airfield development and the positioning of long-range guns on Guadalcanal would be completed. With these augmented means the Cactus Air Force would finally be ground to impotence and a huge convoy would deliver the rest of the men and material necessary to recapture the island. Z-Day was tentatively set for November 13.

ATTACKS WEST AND EAST

In the aftermath of the October battles around Henderson Field, Halsey acted to reinforce the American hold on Guadalcanal. On October 26, however, the large transport *President Coolidge* blundered into a minefield at Espíritu Santo and became a total loss, jarring but not unhinging reenforcement plans. The sinking cost only five lives, but the 172d Infantry Regiment of the 43d Infantry Division lost all of its equipment. On October 29, Halsey pledged to Nimitz and Vandegrift that an additional beachhead would be seized on Guadalcanal at Aola, and more important, the 8th Marines would be landed on Guadalcanal shortly with an Army regiment to follow as soon as possible.

The end of October and the beginning of November witnessed a change in the composition and command of the Cactus Air Force. With the first day of the new month came the first four SBDs of Major Joseph Sailor's VMSB-132, the initial squadron of Lieutenant Colonel William O. Brice's Marine Air Group 11. The next day an R4D hauled up the first ten pilots of Major Paul Fontana's VMF-

112. These new pilots and crews found a complex of three fields: the original airstrip, now graded to 5,400 feet (3,500 of which boasted metal matting); Fighter One, now 4,600 feet of soggy rolled grass; and 3,200 feet of graded earth northwest of Henderson Field labeled Fighter Two. On the 12th, ten SBDs of Major Robert Richard's VMSB-142 and six TBFs of Lieutenant Colonel Paul Moret's VMSB-131 arrived. In the now established pattern, they replaced squadrons drained by exhaustion and losses. On November 3, surviving aircrew of VB-6 officially ended their tour, and four days later members of VS-71 did likewise.

On this occasion the cycle of rotation in the Cactus Air Force involved the top as well as the bottom. The strain of command on Guadalcanal had seriously fatigued General Geiger, both physically and mentally. During the first week of November, Louis Woods, now a brigadier general, came up to Guadalcanal to replace him. A decade younger and relatively rested, Woods was the right man for the job at hand, transformed, he quipped, from a "kindly colonel to a bloodthirsty brigadier general."

During this same period the 11th Air Fleet also shifted its composition. On October 31 this command counted on hand 158 aircraft (sixty-seven Zeros, sixty-four Bettys, and twenty-seven Vals), of which 125 were operational: forty Zeros, thirty-six Bettys (sixty counting those at the rear bases), and twenty-five Vals. That same day, sixty operational aircraft sat on Guadalcanal: thirty-four Wildcats, nineteen SBDs, and seven P-39/400s. About thirty-five operational B-17s could contribute to the defense of the island from rear bases, bringing American operational strength to ninety-five. Since the start of October, the 11th Air Fleet had lost no less than one-third of its strength, including many highly skilled crews. The dashing of the great hopes pinned on the October attack coupled with these severe losses caused a slump in morale. From October, the Imperial Navy renumbered its air groups, and in the 11th Air Fleet this process coincided with organizational changes. The 25th Air Flotilla, which had been slugging it out in the South Pacific since April, was spent. It dispatched its last sorties on November 9 and withdrew to Japan. Rear Admiral Toshinosuke Ichimaru's 21st Air Flotilla replaced it. Between November 5 and 9, fifty-one new Zeros arrived (twenty-six with the 252d Air Group), and ten Vals of the 956th Air Group reached the front line on November 10.

The R Area Air Force was effectively being rebuilt rather than simply shifting its composition. Its initial complement had been fifty-two aircraft, but by October 31 operational strength touched twenty-one aircraft. Like the 11th Air Fleet, the R Area Air Force found replacement aircraft slow to arrive and replacement crews notably younger and less adroit than the originals. On November 6, three Rufes and at least eight Petes arrived, and a week later an assortment of a dozen float planes followed.

The hiatus in air action at the beginning of November, induced by bad weather and exhaustion, was not matched on the ground. Halsey's promised reinforcements gave Vandegrift "riches beyond the dreams of avarice." These added means provided a margin for the future, so Vandegrift sought to exploit the October defensive victory. Once again attention focused on the west, this time with a twofold purpose: to drive the Japanese back beyond artillery range of Henderson Field and its suburbs once and for all; and to attempt to cut off the retreat of the enemy forces along the upper Lunga. A survey of the roster of units showed only Edson's 5th Marines available and rested, and they were reduced in numbers, so Vandegrift fetched two battalions of the 2d Marines from Tulagi to add the necessary strength. His October 30 operations order called for an attack to seize the village of Kokumbona and a drive to throw the enemy back across the Poha River. The 5th Marines would lead the attack, supported on the inland flank by the reconstituted Whaling Group, this time composed of the Scout-Snipers bonded with the 3d Battalion, 7th Marines (3/7). The 2d Marines (less the 3d Battalion) would be in reserve. The plentiful fire support included the skilled 11th Marines, Army artillery, the Cactus Air Force, and naval gunfire.

Sumiyoshi faced the Marine attack with only two threadbare regiments. Nakaguma's 4th Infantry covered the sector on the western bank of the Matanikau from the shore to the one-log bridge, beyond which Oka's mixed detachment extended the line to Mount Austen. On October 28, Oka described his command as wearied and at only half strength, so he was permitted to retain control of Nakaguma's 3d Battalion, 4th Infantry (III/4). With only two battalions in hand, Nakaguma chose to cover the entire regimental frontage with Major Tamura's 2d Battalion. Tamura spread his battalion along the Matanikau with the 7th Company near Point Cruz along the beach and the 5th Company assigned the west-bank heights, stiffened by the remnants of the Regimental Gun Company with one 75mm gun. On October 29, American stirring around the one-log bridge prompted Sumiyoshi to order the

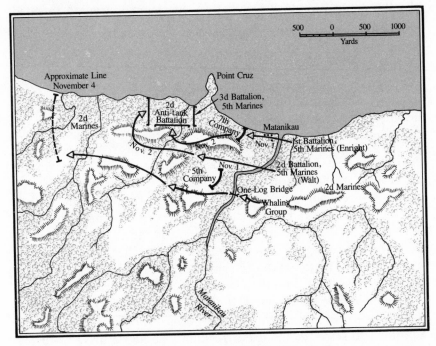

Matanikau Actions, November 1–4

reinforcement of that point. Accordingly, Nakaguma sent one company of I/4 to the high ground northwest of the bridge. The rest of the I/4 remained in reserve.

After elements of the 3d Battalion, 1st Marines patrolled and outposted the high ground just west of the Matanikau, between 0100 and 0600, on November 1, the 1st Engineer Battalion threw a trio of footbridges across the river. At 0630, to an overture by nine artillery batteries, the 2d Battalion, 5th Marines (2/5) (Major Lewis Walt) crossed Matanikau in thirty minutes with the 1st Battalion, 5th Marines (1/5) (Major William K. Enright). As aircraft, including nineteen B-17s, rained bombs on Japanese territory, the two battalions deployed with the 1st Battalion along the coast and the 2d Battalion inland. They were followed at 0800 by the 3d Battalion, 5th Marines (3/5) (Major Robert O. Bowen). Walt's 2/5 encountered very little resistance on their section of the Japanese front. This unit reached the first objective line on the ridge south of Point Cruz by 1000 and then pushed on to the second phase line by 1440. Whaling's Group strided across the one-log bridge and parallel to Walt, but farther inland, and also achieved its objective.

The story in front of 1/5 was much different. After crossing a footbridge the battalion moved forward with Company A along the shore and Company C on its left. The abrupt lash of machinegun fire and light artillery terminated their unopposed movement at 0830. In close and confused fighting, Company C butted into the main positions of the reinforced 7th Company. The Marine company suffered heavily, including the loss of three officers; it was stopped and then driven back in a counterattack.[1] Major Enright committed Company B in a gap that opened between A and C, and late in the afternoon Companies I and K of 3/5 filled an opening between 1/5 and the beach at the base of Point Cruz. Colonels Edson and Thomas and Lieutenant Colonel Twining reviewed the situation at the end of the day and decided to bypass and encircle the Japanese at Point Cruz. For this purpose, the 1/5 and 3/5 would continue to push in the sector of 1/5 while 2/5 veered north to the coast to envelop the enemy.

The lack of progress in the 1/5 sector prompted much private disgruntlement at 1st Marine Division Headquarters. This depreciation of the difficulties of the assault companies could have been rapidly cured by reading Major Tamura's diary entry this night: he simply noted his battalion had "vanished." The 7th Company, after a vigorous defense including three counterattacks, was down to slightly more than ten men, and the 5th Company counted but fifteen. The Regimental Gun Company was virtually wiped out, and its one field piece was destroyed. The 17th Army recognized the mortal peril an American breakthrough to Kokumbona would pose and sent Colonel Sugita to the scene with orders to halt the American attack at any price. But Sugita's mission appeared well beyond his means. To restore the shattered front of the 4th Infantry, Sugita deployed the 2d Anti-Tank Gun Battalion with its dozen guns near Point Cruz, and he drafted the distinctly second-line 39th Field Road Construction Unit as a fragile substitute for the riflemen he needed.

On November 2, while the Whaling Group side stepped north to take over the zone of the 2/5, thus permitting Walt's battalion to cut north to the coast just west of Point Cruz, completing the encirclement of the Japanese facing the rest of the 5th Marines. The Marine maneuvers compressed the Japanese into a draw between the coastal

---

[1]As a result of his actions on November 1 in blunting this Japanese attack, Corporal Anthony Casamento (Company D, 1st Battalion, 5th Marines) would be awarded a Medal of Honor nearly thirty-eight years later on September 12, 1980.

trail and the beach just west of Point Cruz, resulting in more cave fighting reminiscent of Gavutu-Tanambogo. Late in the day, Captain Erskine Wells of Company I led the only authenticated American bayonet charge of the campaign, which sliced through the northern portion of the enemy position to the 2/5. While the 5th Marines dealt with the pocket, the 2d Marines continued the advance. By nightfall they toed a line well west of Point Cruz.

Darkness brought a major run by the Tokyo Express. The scrubbing of a scheduled landing on October 31 freed a total of sixteen destroyers and one light cruiser to port supplies and passengers. Cruisers *Kinugasa* and *Sendai* and two destroyers lent cover. To support the Shoji Detachment then tramping toward Koli, the "Otsu" unit of five destroyers would carry 300 soldiers with two mountain guns, provisions, and ammunition to that locale. Meanwhile the "Ko" unit of eleven destroyers and light cruiser *Tenryu* freighted food, fuel, and ammunition plus 240 soldiers to Tassafaronga.

American radio intelligence intercepted preliminary signaling over this operation and extracted the outline of the scheme for five destroyers to land reinforcements at Koli on the night of November 2. The Marine command on Guadalcanal absorbed this news just after noon on November 1, but could not easily exploit it. With all the relatively rested units committed in the offensive to the west, the task of containing this new enemy threat fell upon Lieutenant Colonel Hanneken's 2d Battalion, 7th Marines (2/7), which had only begun a respite after its defensive exertions in late October. At 0650 on November 2, Hanneken's men stepped off on a forced march that carried them to the Metapona River by dusk. After dark, Hanneken traversed the exposed sandbar at the river mouth and aligned his battalion in the woods facing the beach for a distance of about 2,000 yards. They did not have long to wait.

The Ko and Otsu contingents used diverse routes in their approach, but a B-17 saw the larger unit. At 1730, Lieutenant Commander John Eldridge, the commander of VS-71, and two VMSB-132 pilots guided three SBDs out into solid overcast to try to disrupt the Japanese. About 2100, two more SBDs went on a like expedition, but of these five planes only one of the second group returned. A float plane from *Kinugasa* reported an encounter with an SBD, but neither crew was heard from again. Two SBDs disappeared, and the wreckage of two others, including Eldridge's, and the remains of the crews were found on Santa Isabel. Although the landing efforts were unhindered by aircraft, darkness and choppy seas that capsized boats retarded them at Tassafaronga. When ship-to-shore movement ended at 0130 of November 3, the destroyers retained some provisions and thirty soldiers, though sixty-five officers and men, including Commander Ohmae, had embarked for passage back to Shortland. Among those setting foot on Guadalcanal for the first time was General Takushiro Hattori, chief of the Operations Division of the Army Section of Imperial General Headquarters.

Near Koli, Hanneken's marines detected faint dark patches drifting across the bay. Signal lights, and later voices and noises, told them a landing was in progress 1,000 yards farther to the east. Over the gunwales of small boats came provisions for 2,000 men for ten days, manhandled by a company of the 230th Infantry Regiment, and a two-gun battery of mountain artillery. In the dark the marine observers thought they identified a light cruiser and small transport among the ships near the beach, suggesting a major landing. Faulty radio communications frustrated repeated attempts to report this activity.

At dawn an eight-man enemy patrol ambled up the beach and discovered the marines, at the cost of four of their number. Hanneken ranged his 81mm mortars on the landing beaches but provoked no immediate response. The lack of reaction caused Hanneken to infer he faced only an enemy battalion. At virtually the same moment that Hanneken resolved to attack, a skirmish line of "several hundred" Japanese began to advance up the beach, and 2/7 challenged this move with effective machinegun and mortar fire. But the Japanese, who actually numbered only the 300 or so landed the night before, got their mountain guns unlimbered, one in plain view on the beach, and commenced firing, while their mortars began to drop rounds on Hanneken's nearest unit, Company F.

Hanneken's situation invites comparison to that of Edson at Tasimboko, but with the important differences that Hanneken lacked contact with higher headquarters and enjoyed no air or naval gunfire support. With casualties mounting in Company F, including the commander, his mortars burning up their ammunition supply, and painfully aware of his isolation, Hanneken decided to withdraw to prevent being pinned against the coast like Ichiki. The battalion pulled back by bounds, fording the Metapona inland at a concealed crossing site rather than on the exposed sandbar. But reports of contact with Japanese to his rear convinced Hanneken that more enemy troops had been landed between his battalion and the main perimeter, so he resolved to pull back to the west bank of the Nalim-biu. From there he finally got a message through to division at 1445.

All morning the Marine command heard the muted sounds of gunfire to the east, but in the absence of news from that quarter, naturally remained riveted on the situation to the west. Between 0800 and noon, a total of five rifle companies drawn from 2/5 and 3/5 reduced the remaining Japanese enclave near Point Cruz. By noon, a desolate landscape of blocked or blasted caves and clumps of corpses marked the former location of the Japanese pocket. The marines captured a dozen 37mm guns, the equipment of the 2d Anti-tank Gun Battalion, most of which died here, and one field piece and thirty-four machineguns formerly property of the 4th Infantry Regiment. The 2/5 counted 239 dead Japanese; total enemy losses probably numbered not less than 300.

To oppose further westward American penetration, Nakaguma's 4th Infantry Regiment, which by the morning of November 3 fielded less than 500 men, received some dubious reinforcements: seventy-odd frail survivors of the Ichiki detachment and a hundred equally sapped members of the original Navy garrison. The 2d Marines, led by 1/2, with the Whaling Group again moving on the inland flank, stretched forward to a line 3,500 yards west of Point Cruz, driving the Japanese back.

In the evening of November 3, Sugita conferred with Miyazaki and Tsuji. Though malaria wracked his body, flushed his face, and obstructed his breathing, Sugita's spirit was even more sorely tried. He depicted the whole Japanese position as balanced on the edge of disaster: the front had been breached, and if the Americans pushed forward, they would cut off the retreat of the 2d Division and turn defeat into catastrophe. To this litany Sugita added that Nakaguma despaired even more about the situation and contemplated seeking death in one final charge with the regimental colors. To this Tsuji exclaimed: "Do not let them charge. If they attack all will be lost!" Miyazaki suspected that Sugita was also meditating on a similar gesture, and urged him to endure for a while longer. At the end of this huddle, Sugita, fortified by a small amount of food, wobbled off on his cane.

About this same time, General Hattori composed a message reflecting his impressions of his first hours on the island. He heard accounts of battalions crushed by one or two hours of shelling, observed the pathetic appearance of the simple soldiers as well as their officers, and witnessed for himself displays of American air mastery. In a message to Tokyo, Hattori groped for words to convey

his shock: "[the] actual situation [on Guadalcanal] is beyond imagination." A few hours sampling the lot of the officers and men of the
17th Army divested Hattori of his at times haughty disdain for the
operations of Hyakutake and his staff: the situation, confessed Hattori in another message, did not admit of conventional solutions.
Moreover, once he examined Guadalcanal firsthand, he found himself understanding and, indeed, agreeing with the plans of the 17th
Army—above all on the need to take every measure to redress the
balance of air power. His grim tidings included the conclusion that
no contribution from the 2d Division should be counted upon in the
next offensive.

What now bought time for the 17th Army that it could not purchase for itself was the unexpected and undeserved benefit of the
ill-conceived attempt to make Koli a major base of operations. Even
though Vandegrift and his staff had long since slipped the moorings
of tactical orthodoxy, the midafternoon message from Hanneken on
November 3, evidencing a substantial Japanese presence to the east,
stretched their resourcefulness. Looking at the situation map, the
operations officer, Lieutenant Colonel Twining, chuckled, "What
would the [staff] schools think of that!" Red patches representing
Japanese forces speckled the coastline from Cape Esperance east to
Kokumbona, where they touched a group of blue ovals representing
American units protruding like a tentacle from the main blue bulge
around the airfields. South of that bulge other clusters of red hovered
about the Lunga Valley. A second thin tentacle of blue extended to
the Nalimbiu, where it tapped a red spot, and even farther to the east
a new blue bulge, whose genesis will be discussed shortly, had inflated around Aola.

A document captured by the 5th Marines revealed the scheme to
land the 38th Division at Koli and buttressed the instinctive desire
to immediately smite the new threat—the marines, of course, did
not know of the abandonment of this plan. But manpower constraints tempered American pugnaciousness. Put simply, Vandegrift did not have enough troops to simultaneously push the attack
to the west, defend the main perimeter, and launch an additional
offensive to the east. The arrival of the 8th Marines the next day,
November 4, was scheduled but not assured. The certainties were
Hanneken's distress and the paramount need to guard the airfields.
Consequently, a series of orders reshuffled dispositions and missions before the sun set.

Within an hour of the receipt of Hanneken's message, Lieutenant
Colonel Puller mustered his battalion of the 7th Marines for boat

movement to reinforce his embattled sister unit. Within three hours a large-scale commitment was underway to the east: two tank companies rumbled with preparatory noises for movement down the coast to join Hanneken (but high water kept them west of the Ilu); the 164th Infantry (less the 1st Battalion) fell in to march on an inland route to the Nalimbiu; and Brigadier General Rupertus made ready to control this joint service expedition. To give the Marine and Army forces a long reach, Lieutenant Colonel Manley T. Curry's 3d Battalion, 10th Marines manhandled its 75mm pack howitzers across the rain swollen Ilu. In the interval, thirty-one assorted aircraft scrambled to tender Hanneken support. They caught the Shoji Detachment in the last legs of its march to Koli point and inflicted about one hundred deaths and injuries. Less helpfully, they also attacked Hanneken's already battered battalion and lengthened its casualty list. Shoji's men reached Koli Point, where they found 131 fever-riddled survivors of Ichiki's and Kawaguchi's efforts. They occupied a large grass clearing, whose suitability for an airstrip was evidenced by the carcasses of several crash-landed aircraft, both American and Japanese.

On November 4, action tapered off toward Kokumbona and paused along the Nalimbiu. Although the leading elements of the Sendai Division reached the 17th Army Headquarters during the day, they remained much too distant to influence events before Kokumbona, on which their survival hung. Sugita's defensive efforts did receive a major boost when the 4th Infantry Regiment regained control of its 3d Battalion, but the American offensive stood abandoned, not checked. At a conference this morning, Lieutenant Colonel Twining urged a push to the Poha—precisely what the Japanese most feared—and argued that the enemy's strongpoint at Point Cruz was their last solid defense line—as was indeed the case. But the normally aggressive Merritt Edson opposed a deep advance, invoking images of entrenched Japanese opposition in front and a dangerously open flank inland. Thomas and Vandegrift sided with Edson. With the 5th Marines and the Whaling Group recalled as part of the shuffle to meet the crisis to the east, the 1st and 2d Battalions, 2d Marines, reinforced by the 1st Battalion, 164th Infantry, briefly resumed the westward advance before halting at a point about 2,000 yards west of Point Cruz or about 4,000 yards shy of Kokumbona. If the American offensive failed to achieve its original objectives, it at least diverted scarce Japanese artillery ammunition from use in shelling Henderson Field from Mount Austen. This front passed into

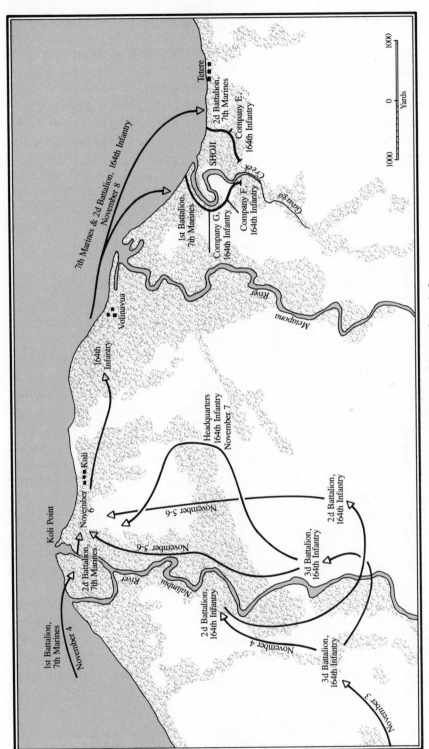

Koli Point Actions, November 4–9

relative tranquillity for the next six days, though an artillery shell killed Colonel Nakaguma on November 7.[2]

To the east, Puller's 1/7 and the regimental commander, Colonel Arthur Sims, together with Rupertus reached the Nalimbiu. There Rupertus, who as a result of a command reorganization took charge of all forces east of the Lunga, decided to await the arrival of the 164th Infantry. To fill this interval, cruisers *Helena* and *San Francisco* and destroyer *Sterett* subjected the Japanese at Koli Point to gunfire. The 164th, with Company B, 8th Marines attached, began its march by 0630, but the heat and the inland route through 7 miles of alternating gnarled swamp and parched grassy plain haltered the advance so much that the regiment drew up to the Nalimbiu only at nightfall.

During the day, orders summoned the 2d Raider Battalion to join Rupertus, but this unit had even farther to march than the 164th— and from the opposite direction. The Raiders had just reached Guadalcanal with the original mission of spearheading the singularly ill-considered effort to create a second major American perimeter and airfield at Aola. The formal responsibility for this folly rested with Halsey, but its sponsor was Turner. That essential but fractious officer retained his belief that the proper deployment of ground forces on Guadalcanal was to daub the coastline with small detachments to "mop up" the Japanese. Thus when Halsey finally canceled the seizure of Ndeni, Turner urged that the troops last earmarked for that operation be switched to Aola, where he envisioned the construction of an airfield. Accordingly, on the morning of November 4, as the 8th Marines came ashore at Lunga, Companies C and E of the 2d Raider Battalion landed unopposed at Aola to clear the way for the 1,700-man main body, including about 500 naval construction men, under Colonel W. B. Tuttle of the 147th Infantry Regiment.

A brief digression tells the story of the Aola adventure. Vigorous efforts by the Seabees to create an airfield floundered literally in swamplands. This should have been no surprise, since Vandegrift had relayed to Turner the warning of his engineers and Martin Clemens that the terrain was completely unsuitable. Vandegrift re-

---

[2]According to a captured report, on November 8 the 1st Battalion, 4th Infantry Regiment had forty-one effectives, and its sister 2d Battalion had eighty-three. The normal strength of both these battalions was 638 men. Most of these losses came in battles before November.

ported the failure of the attempt on November 22, and one week later the Aola expedition moved to the vicinity of Koli Point, where work began on another airfield.

On the morning of November 5, Rupertus instructed the 164th Infantry to cross to the east bank of the Nalimbiu and envelop the inland flank of the Japanese confronting the 7th Marines. The 3/164 breasted the swollen Nalimbiu 3,500 yards from the beach and pivoted left to advance north along the east bank with the 2/164 on a parallel path to its right rear. These units encountered light opposition from the Japanese but met heavy resistance from nature. They spent an uncomfortable night in the jungle short of the coast, which they made more unpleasant by an intramural firefight—ironically, that very day Shoji's men barely avoided a similar encounter when they finally made contact with the detachment landed on November 3.

November 5 brought an emergency run of the Tokyo Express, prefaced by the first air raid since October 30. As the American offensive toward Kokumbona crushed the defenses and threatened the existence of the Sendai Division, 17th Army sent urgent dispatches calling for the landing of reinforcements on November 4 or at least by November 5. Although an "Express" could not be marshaled for the 4th, the Reinforcement Unit compressed the runs scheduled for the 5th and 6th into the earlier date. The 11th Air Fleet attempted to assist this effort with a raid by twenty-seven Bettys and twenty-four Zeros. Heavy clouds kept honors even by hiding the Japanese formation from American fighters and the airfields from Japanese bombardiers. Antiaircraft fire destroyed two Bettys. As darkness fell, fifteen destroyers and a light cruiser closed Guadalcanal with throttles open.

Tenryu and the five destroyers of the Otsu Detachment peeled off to deliver part of the 228th Infantry Regiment at Cape Esperance. The Ko Detachment of ten destroyers stood into Tassafaronga at 2240 to land Major General Ito, commander of the 38th Infantry Group, his headquarters, and the bulk of the 228th Infantry Regiment. *PT 39,* one of four U.S. torpedo boats out this night, fenced briefly and indecisively with *Murasame.* The exchange of passengers for 206 construction workers and 142 officers and soldiers (including Kawaguchi) proceeded slowly across beaches clogged with wrecked boats. The reinforcements marched immediately for Kokumbona.

On November 6, the 7th Marines performed the tedious crossing of the flooded Nalimbiu while the battalions of the 164th slowly carved a channel through the jungle to the coast, which the 3/164 reached that night and the 2/164 the next morning. During November 7, the combined Army-Marine force pushed on to a point about a mile west of the broad mouth of the Metapona. There they dug in to defend the beach against a possible enemy landing that night. A search plane's discovery of eleven troop-laden destroyers steaming for Guadalcanal caused this precaution. These vessels were old campaigners from Admiral Tanaka's Destroyer Squadron 2 and two ships of Desdiv 10. With Tanaka chafing under orders to remain at Shortland, Captain Torajiro Sato (ComDesdiv 15) acted as conductor of this night's "Express."

To derail the Tokyo Express, the Cactus Air Force put up a typically heterogeneous strike group: seven SBDs of VMSB-132, three TBFs of VT-8, twenty-one Marine Wildcats, and nine Army P-39s of the 67th Fighter Squadron. Sato's command cruised under the protection of six Rufes and four Petes of the R Area Air Force. The float plane pilots put up a spirited fight to protect their charges, but the disparities in numbers and aircraft performance were too great. The Army pilots pounced on a group of float planes and claimed all five; the Marine pilots claimed to have picked off nine more. The actual total was all six Rufes and one Pete at a cost of one Wildcat in combat and three operationally. One of the Wildcats bore Captain Joseph Foss, a fast-rising ace, who added three float planes to his score before the rear gunner of one Pete thoroughly perforated his aircraft. Foss ditched in stormy weather but was recovered the next day. The strike group's claims widely outstripped the actual damage inflicted. The modest hull injuries and seventeen casualties on *Naganami* and *Takanami* did not deflect Sato's veterans. After depositing 80 percent of its passengers at Tassafaronga and Esperance, the "Express" picked up 497 ailing soldiers and sailors for the return trip.

By November 8, Shoji's regiment and the new reinforcements had dug in along Gavaga Creek at Tetere, about a mile east of the Metapona. While the 2/164 went into reserve, the 7th Marines maneuvered to net this Japanese detachment. During the day, dengue fever forced Rupertus to relinquish command to General Sebree and Lieutenant Colonel Puller suffered multiple wounds. Although Puller refused evacuation for some time, he was eventually forced to relinquish his command.

It was on this same day, November 8, that Halsey got the dirt of Guadalcanal on his shoes—a simple act Ghormley never chose to perform. Halsey, said Vandegrift, was "like a wonderful breath of fresh air," full of "interest and enthusiasm." The admiral talked to a great many marines of all ranks, but more important, he saw "their gaunt, malaria-ridden bodies [and] their faces lined from what seemed like a nightmare of years."

Shelling from a Japanese destroyer, one of ten of the second shift of the Tokyo Express run, the Otsu unit, interrupted Halsey's rest that night. Led by *Tenryu,* these vessels had approached Tassafaronga at 2144 when they began skirmishing with *PT 37, PT 39,* and *PT 61.* The flagship of the PT trio, *PT 61,* sustained a 5-inch-shell hit on the bow and escaped through a smoke screen, maintaining speed to keep her stem out of the water. The other two boats each fired a pair of torpedoes, and one of these struck *Mochizuki* but failed to explode.

On November 9, Vandegrift ordered that most of the 164th Infantry redeploy for commitment to a renewed western offensive. While trucks and boats shuttled the rest of the regiment and Company B, 8th Marines back to the perimeter, the 2/164th extended the lines of the 1/7 west of the creek farther inland. A pocket marked by the trace of Gavaga Creek now contained the Japanese, but the pocket had a hole in it on the southern side where a swampy creek notched the American lines. To try to patch this hole, Company E of the 2/164 was committed on the left flank of 2/7 during the night of November 9–10, but neither this company nor its sister unit, Company F on the other side of the creek, could dam a Japanese breakout. Not all the Japanese escaped, and the next day the territory under Japanese control shriveled to a clump of woods bounded by the beach and grassy fields. Two 75mm pack howitzer batteries, the newly arrived 155mm gun batteries, and aircraft pounded the remaining Japanese. Once again that night the gap to the south was not closed, and for this failure Sebree relieved Lieutenant Colonel Arthur C. Timboe, the commander of 2/164. The next day, Company G finally closed the hole, but most of Shoji's regiment escaped. The systematic extermination of the remnants in the pocket extended into November 12. American reports show 450 Japanese dead lay in their positions, and a good deal of material was destroyed or captured, including General Kawaguchi's personal effects. American losses came to about forty dead and 120 wounded.

Shoji slipped away with about 3,000 hungry and exhausted men to begin a trek to rejoin the 17th Army. They faced the frightening task of retracing their march to the Matanikau, and moreover this time they were not alone. The 2d Raider Battalion, "Carlson's Raiders," set off in pursuit. Carlson combined charisma with tactical acuity, and he organized his unit along concepts he adapted from his personal observations of the Chinese communists, from whom he also appropriated the slogan "Gung Ho," meaning "work together." He gave the marines a superb squad organization, but his mystical beliefs and his politics plainly separated him from the vast majority of his fellow Marine officers. In a classic Marine one-liner, Colonel (later Commandant) David Shoup said, "He may have been Red but he wasn't yellow."

For all practical purposes, Shoji and Carlson disappeared into the deep jungle to fight their own campaign for a month. After a major clash with elements of Shoji's command on November 11–12, Carlson relieved two of his company commanders. Thereafter, with the invaluable aid of native scouts, the Raider battalion—living on rice, bacon, tea, raisins, salt, and sugar—kept pace with Shoji's column, repeatedly falling on its trailing elements and stragglers. At the end of his expedition west across the Lunga on December 4, Carlson reported killing 488 Japanese at a cost of sixteen killed and eighteen wounded. Shoji's main body, reduced to only 1,300, reached the Lunga on November 20. Several days later he rejoined the 17th Army with only 700 to 800 survivors, of whom but twenty to thirty retained the ability to fight.

To return to the situation on November 8, as soon as Vandegrift contained the eastern threat he wheeled his forces to the west. The fresh 8th Marines (Colonel Richard H. Jeschke) and the 1/164 were grouped under the command of Colonel John M. Arthur, who brought the 1st and 2d Battalions of his own 2d Marines. Behind heavy artillery fire, they resumed the attack toward Kokumbona at 0630 on November 10. Keeping the untried 8th Marines in reserve, Colonel Arthur disposed his forces with the 1/164 on the coast, the 2/2 on its left, and the 1/2 echeloned back along the open inland flank.

By coincidence, Hyakutake had originally selected this same date for an offensive headed in the opposite direction, but he had canceled his plans when he found that the newly landed forces came to about two infantry battalions with small amounts of supplies and provisions. If insufficient for an offensive, the fresh Japanese troops proved more than adequate to fiercely dispute any American advance across the grassy coral ridges from the interleaved jungled draws and gullies. About noon, Colonel Arthur committed the 3/8 to screen a gap opening between the two battalions of the 2d Marines, but progress was slow.

After weather foiled anti-shipping strikes by Vals from November 6 to 9, on November 10 the 11th Air Fleet switched to efforts to clear the skies for Z-Day with a fighter sweep of eighteen Zeros. They drew up thirty-one American fighters, and the two sets of planes fumbled for each other between layers of cloud. The only contact came when two Wildcats brushed with a few Zeros, claiming one. Dusk found five Japanese destroyers closing the island again down the virtual rut worn in the Slot. They carried ammunition and provisions plus about 600 men, including Lieutenant General Tadayoshi Sano, commander of the 38th Infantry Division, part of his staff, and Lieutenant Commander Masatoshi Funabashi of Battleship Division 11 to act as a spotter for the bombardment. A dozen SBDs led by Major Sailor succeeded only in putting a few machinegun-bullet holes in this quintet. Three PT boats clashed briefly with the Japanese, who completed their landing activities shortly after midnight and returned with 585 sick.

On November 11 the 11th Air Fleet sent two strikes to Guadalcanal. At 0940, nine Vals and eighteen Zeros from Buin arrived and selected Turner's group of four transports and their escort as a target. The Vals damaged cargo ship *Zeilin* with a near-miss. An interception by twenty-one Wildcats produced claims of four Zeros and one Val, which did not balance the loss of six Wildcats and four pilots. Japanese pilots reported destroying twenty-five enemy planes, but they acknowledged their own losses as "great," five Vals and two Zeros. Only two hours later a raid of twenty-five Bettys with twenty-six Zeros in escort arrived to attack Henderson Field. This encounter cost three more Wildcats and two pilots as American claims ran to six bombers; one other bomber was credited to antiaircraft fire. Four Bettys were actually destroyed.

General Sano wasted no time in assuming command of the Japanese forces on the Kokumbona front. He ordered Ito to destroy the Americans west of the Matanikau and to recapture the artillery firing positions. Ito moved the II/228 (less two companies) to join the shrunken 124th Infantry near Mount Austen where they sat on the American flank. Without awareness of this building threat, on November 11 the Americans renewed the attack toward Kokumbona. Positions just beyond those achieved on November 4 had been secured by 1345 when orders came for the attack to halt and the force to retire to the Matanikau. This movement began that afternoon and was completed the next day—not without loss of some arms and equipment. Losses came to seventy-one killed or missing and 193 wounded.

To the American commanders and men involved, the withdrawal was in equal parts disheartening and inexplicable. For security reasons they could not be told the real reason for the withdrawal: the weave of reports from coast watchers, aerial reconnaissance, and radio intelligence presented an unmistakable picture of a "grand-scale offensive at Guadalcanal." Though we can fix radio intelligence as dominant in this picture, we can not do full justice to the triumph this contribution represented. The reader will recall that at the beginning of October the Imperial Navy changed its entire communications system as part of a persistent pattern of increasing radio security. On November 1 it implemented another call-sign change, and for the first week of November, American radio intelligence estimates remained notably tentative. Then on November 8 Yamamoto issued his operations order for the November attack and, in an extraordinary feat, American cryptanalysts extracted most of the key elements of the Japanese plan.

Thus when Halsey returned to his headquarters at Noumea on November 9, his staff handed him the outline of forthcoming Japanese operations: the 8th Fleet preparing to escort a large troop convoy to land at Guadalcanal on Z-Day; aircraft massing at Buin with the 11th Air Fleet under orders to begin attacks on Z minus 3; and a Japanese carrier group heading for a fueling rendezvous just north of the equator preparatory to a strike on Z minus 1. Only Yamamoto's intention to repeat the battleship bombardment of Henderson Field remained unknown. From Truk the Combined Fleet was expected to sortie with carriers *Junyo* and *Zuiho* and possibly three escort carriers, plus four battleships, five heavy and six light cruisers, and twenty-one destroyers. This lineup excluded the 8th Fleet; on November 10, a coast watcher reported the masts of sixty-one ships at Shortland, including six cruisers and thirty-three destroyers. By that same day, radio intelligence confirmed Z-Day as November 13.

Even with the considerable advantage of "reading the mail," as the CINCPAC daily summary put it, Halsey had much cause for concern. *Enterprise,* his only carrier, was still under repair and projected to be without use of her forward elevator through November 21—a serious handicap to flight operations. He also had two battleships, four heavy and four light cruisers, and twenty-two available destroyers. But Halsey did not seriously consider evading battle. To Admiral Kinkaid he sent orders to get *Enterprise* underway on the morning of November 11 and to "be prepared to strike enemy targets in [the] Cactus area."

In Washington, the "atmosphere of tense expectation" had now reached a level that would only be matched on the eve of the Normandy invasion. It was sensed there—as at the Combined Fleet— that the turning point of the campaign was at hand.

17

THE NAVAL BATTLE

OF GUADALCANAL

PART I: THE BATTLE OF FRIDAY THE THIRTEENTH

"A barroom brawl after the lights had been shot out"

CONVERGING COURSES

On the morning of November 11 in Shortland harbor, Admiral Tanaka surveyed the ungainly outlines of eleven transports aggregating 77,606 tons. Stacked in their several scores of holds stood supplies for 30,000 men for twenty days and 31,500 assorted artillery shells. Eighty-three landing craft recontoured their topsides; their decks teemed with about 7,000 khaki-green-clad soldiers in soft caps and boots. They included the regimental headquarters and 1st Battalion of the 229th Infantry and the 2d Battalion, 230th Infantry, but perhaps oddly, in view of the importance of the convoy, the majority formed a long miscellany of support units of battalion to platoon strength. The soldiers answered to Major General Suketomo Tanabe, the 2d Ship Group commander.

To provide the close escort for the convoy, Tanaka's reinforced Destroyer Squadron 2 numbered twelve vessels. The admiral and General Tanabe worked out a plan whose interesting features included a convoy speed of 10 knots and an unloading scheme that would place six of the transports at Cape Esperance and five at Tassafaronga.

The recently reorganized Combined Fleet and 8th Fleet lent distant protection of the convoy. The Combined Fleet lineup omitted carriers *Shokaku, Zuikaku,* and *Zuiho,* now en route to Japan with their heavily depleted plane groups; *Hiyo* swung at anchor because of her engineering casualty. This left only *Junyo* to afford seagoing air cover. She would sortie with Admiral Kondo, whose Advanced Force mustered the four *Kongo* Class battleships, three heavy cruisers, three light cruisers, and twenty-one destroyers. As usual, the Japanese divided their forces. Heavy cruiser *Atago,* wearing Kondo's flag, and sister ship *Takao* sailed under the label of the Main Body. *Junyo* became the pivot of the Air Striking Unit with a screen of battleships *Kongo* and *Haruna* and four destroyers. Heavy cruiser *Tone,* light cruiser *Sendai,* and destroyer *Ayanami* composed the Eastern Reconnaissance Unit. As their operational title indicated, they would project air searches to the east to protect the Japanese flank.

According to Kondo's plan, the various components of the Advanced Force would spawn another formidable bombardment unit on Z-Day minus one. Rear Admiral Hiroaki Abe would take his Battleship Division 11 (*Hiei* and *Kirishima*) to shell Henderson Field. His close screen would be afforded by Destroyer Squadron 10: light cruiser *Nagara* and destroyers *Amatsukaze, Yukikaze, Akatsuki, Ikazuchi, Inazuma,* and *Teruzuki.* Sweeping ahead of Abe's main unit would be Destroyer Squadron 4 with the flag in *Asagumo* and destroyers *Murasame, Samidare, Yudachi,* and *Harusame.* The other three vessels of Destroyer Squadron 4 (Destroyer Division 27: *Shigure, Shiratsuyu,* and *Yugure*) would stand watch in the passage between Guadalcanal and the Russells during the bombardment.

Admiral Mikawa also realigned the 8th Fleet for the November convoy operation. The Main Force would be heavy cruisers *Chokai* (fleet flagship) and *Kinugasa* and destroyers *Arashio* and *Asashio.* Heavy cruisers *Kumano* and *Maya* with light cruiser *Tenryu* would be the core of another Support Force. Their escorts would be destroyers *Kazegumo, Makikumo, Yugumo,* and *Michishio.* Rear Admiral Shoji Nishimura would take the Support Force to blast Henderson Field on Z-Day.

On the eve of this massive Japanese effort, Admiral Turner, perhaps taking a page from the Japanese book of tactics, planned to run two separate, but heavily escorted, American groups of transports to

Guadalcanal to debark over 5,500 reinforcements—and, if possible, to disrupt Japanese plans outlined by radio intelligence. Turner dispatched Rear Admiral Norman Scott with Task Group 62.4, composed of light cruiser *Atlanta* and three destroyers. They served as shepherds for transports *Zeilin*, *Libra*, and *Betelgeuse*, which gave passage to the 1st Marine Aviation Engineer Battalion, replacements for ground and aviation units, and ammunition and food. Turner himself took Task Group 67.1, loaded with the 182d Infantry Regiment (less the 3d Battalion), artillery, the 4th Marine Replacement Battalion, Navy and Marine casuals, and supplies on transports *McCawley*, *President Jackson*, *President Adams*, and *Crescent City*. Turner's hefty escort (Task Group 67.4) counted heavy cruisers *San Francisco* and *Portland*, light cruisers *Helena* and *Juneau*, and ten destroyers. It would have been still more potent, but Halsey reassigned heavy cruiser *Pensacola* and two destroyers to augment the already powerful Task Force 16, built around *Enterprise*, whose escorts originally included battleships *Washington* and *South Dakota*, cruisers *Northampton* and *San Diego*, and six destroyers. Fourteen American fleet submarines and six of the elderly S-boats patrolled South Pacific waters in support of Halsey; about fourteen I-boats performed the same service for Yamamoto.

Scott's task group took a route north around San Cristóbal that succeeded in evading submarines as planned, but not search planes. His ships sustained the attack by Vals on November 11 noted earlier, and damaged *Zeilin* retired with *Lardner* while the rest joined Turner's larger task unit for a return appearance off Lunga on November 12. Turner originally had intended to follow Scott, but two events changed his mind. First, in the forenoon of November 10, a Japanese float plane spotted Scott. Second, Turner learned *Southard* (sent ahead with *Hovey* to check for possible minelaying activity off Lunga) had encountered a Japanese submarine (*I-15*), which *Southard* sank,[1] about the same time the enemy float plane detected Scott. Turner then shaped the more customary course to pass up Sealark Channel to Lunga.

Early light on November 12 revealed the six American transports and their escort off Lunga Point. A shore battery intermittently barked at the transports and drew replies from *Helena* and later

---

[1]Postwar assessments credited destroyer *McCalla* for sinking *I-15* on November 3 at 10°15′ South, 161°50′ East and *Southard* with *I-172*. A careful review of reports and Japanese information indicates, however, that *Southard*'s success was *I-15* and that *I-172* was more likely destroyed by a VP-11 PBY on October 29 than by *McCalla*.

destroyers. As the men and material began to stream ashore, Lieutenant Commander Mitzi on Mount Austen sent back a report to Rabaul: three battleships, three cruisers, eleven destroyers, and five transports at Lunga.

Mitzi's report reached Combined Fleet Headquarters at breakfast time. Admiral Ugaki surmised the Americans would "stick around" to land their own reinforcements and try to disrupt Japanese efforts in the same vein. Ugaki mulled over sending orders for the four heavy cruisers of the 8th Fleet and Destroyer Division 27 to join Abe immediately and for the Advanced Force to prepare to follow up the next day. When he presented a memorandum along this line to the staff, the senior staff officer predicted that the Americans would "go away as usual" and it would be sufficient to have Destroyer Squadron 4 in front of Abe. Some officers predicted that the 8th Fleet would "galvanize itself" to take appropriate measures. These arguments dissuaded Ugaki from taking any action.

On Mitzi's alert, the 11th Air Fleet prepared a strike of sixteen torpedo-armed Bettys and thirty Zeros. Amply warned by coast watcher Mason and radar, Turner got his ships underway and prepared to repel an air attack as twenty Wildcats and eight P-39s scrambled. At 1405 the Japanese materialized over the green stripe of Florida's jungle and split into two groups, one swinging out to the northeast and the other banking to the southeast to bracket the transports. Turner saw the aerial jaws open and countered in the style of a matador. First, he presented the tempting broadsides of his ships like a red cape to the northeastern group. As Turner desired, the Japanese flight leader plunged prematurely into an attack before the second unit achieved position. With the first flight committed to an assault, Turner swerved his ships hard to port to offer only their narrow sterns as targets. All torpedoes missed. Meanwhile the defending fighters worked over the southeastern group. The survivors of this contingent launched a desperate attack, but individual ship movements easily combed the wakes of their torpedoes.

Brilliant colors marked this ephemeral air-sea confrontation: dappled gray ships spurting webs of glowing tracers, yellow stabs of flame from mortally stricken planes merging into black smoke before being doused in stark white geysers of spray. The inevitable result of dozens of guns attempting to track a swarm of low-flying torpedo planes among Turner's rapidly maneuvering vessels was hits by "friendly" antiaircraft fire. A 5-inch shell killed five men on destroyer *Buchanan*, wounded seven, and knocked out her torpedo tubes. A plane, already ignited by *McCawley*, bore in on *San Fran-*

cisco. Sailors manning a 20mm battery around the after control station were still firing when the plane smashed directly into their positions. The fuselage warped the splinter plating, and the wings splashed flaming gasoline over Battle Two and demolished the after fire control radar. The remnants of the Betty caromed off *San Francisco*'s superstructure and landed in the water. The one officer and twenty-three men killed included every member of three of the four 20mm crews. The wounded numbered forty-five; many, like Commander Mark Crouter, the executive officer, sustained serious burns. *San Francisco* transferred twenty-eight men to other ships for treatment, but Crouter insisted on staying aboard, a decision that shortly cost him his life.

The entire attack lasted only eight minutes, 1412–1420. American airmen reported downing seventeen bombers and six fighters, and sailors added claims for nine more bombers. In reality, eleven of sixteen Bettys and one Zero fell, at a cost of three Wildcats, whose pilots survived, and one P-39 and pilot. The fighter plane losses were more than made good that afternoon both quantitatively and qualitatively when Dale Brannon, now a major, led in the first eight of the long-sought P-38s. With other last-minute reinforcements (six F4Fs, six TBFs of VMSB-131, and ten SBDs of VMSB-142) the Cactus Air Force would number seventy-seven operational aircraft for November 13: twenty Wildcats, eight P-38s, eighteen P-39s, twenty-three SBDs, and eight TBFs. Backing them up at Espíritu Santo were two squadrons, the 69th and 70th, of Army Air Force B-26s rigged to carry torpedoes.

Even before the air-sea battle, American reconnaissance planes refined Turner's comprehension of Japanese intentions. In the forenoon radiomen logged a search plane report containing a precise count of Abe's Bombardment Unit north of the Solomons on a southerly course at a businesslike 25 knots. Another American search plane found Destroyer Squadron 4 making for its scheduled rendezvous with Abe. The detection of Tanaka's convoy just as it cleared Shortland confirmed the ultimate Japanese objective. Turner shrewdly discarded as spurious a report of a Japanese carrier south of New Georgia.

Turner placed Japanese strength at at least two battleships, two to four heavy and two light cruisers, and ten to twelve destroyers. He estimated Japanese designs to be either to attack his transports as they withdrew through Indispensable Strait or to bombard Henderson Field. No matter which of these options his powerful opponent might chose—and he had no hint from radio intelligence as to the bombardment plan—Turner knew he must face it alone, for Task Force 16 was too far south to intervene, principally because of late orders to sortie from Halsey, a lapse hard to justify given radio intelligence warning. To Turner's immense credit, he did not forsake the protection of Henderson Field in favor of his amphibious shipping, nor did he hedge his bets. He boldly elected to denude his transports of all his screening vessels save only damaged *Buchanan,* two fuel-short destroyers, and two elderly destroyer minesweepers. This yielded a task force of five cruisers and eight destroyers to stop the Japanese surface forces.

As is often the case with Turner, immediately after a large credit entry in our ledger on his performance we must add a black mark. Two rear admirals stood ready to assume command of the American unit. *Atlanta* flew the flag of Norman Scott, whose claim for command rested in the fact that he had nearly six months of sea time in his grade and in his success in a major night surface action. By contrast, *San Francisco* had worn Daniel Callaghan's flag only since October 30, when he came aboard from his former assignment as Ghormley's chief of staff, a task in which he had escaped distinction. His two weeks of sea time as a rear admiral were unlittered with any battle experience, except for the air attack that very day. But these factors seem not to have weighed heavily upon Turner, who, following rigid Navy policy, designated Callaghan as Officer in Tactical Command for the very simple reason that Callaghan had fifteen days of seniority to Scott as a flag officer.[2] In summary, Admiral Callaghan with five cruisers and eight destroyers would confront Admiral Abe

[2] According to their official biographies, Scott gained appointment as a temporary rear admiral on June 16 and acted as a task force commander from that date. His official date of rank for seniority purposes, however, was May 11. The Commander South Pacific War Diary for June 26, 1942, indicates Callaghan had been appointed a temporary rear admiral as of that date, which is consistent with the grade he held at the Koro conference. But Callaghan's official biography states his appointment as a rear admiral was on August 4 and that the appointment "is regarded for all purposes as having been accepted on the date of this letter without formal acceptance or oath of office." Callaghan's official date of rank was April 26, or fifteen days earlier than Scott's, although his date of appointment was at least ten days later. The conclusion that seniority was the basis for Turner's selection of Callaghan for command is the only rational explanation I can suggest and is fully in keeping with the firm Navy procedure of that date.

I found no information indicating either that Turner paused to reflect on whether the reflexive application of seniority was appropriate in this case in view of Scott's manifestly superior claim to command, or that Callaghan might have considered turning over tactical command to Scott. In Callaghan's case this would have been no simple matter, since he would have in effect violated a positive order from Turner. Possibly, Turner may have regarded as significant the fact that *San Francisco* had better physical facilities as a flagship. This appears to be a factor that could have been foreseen or dealt with by an exchange of flagships, scarcely an impossible feat, especially since Scott had just vacated *San Francisco* at the end of October.

COMPOSITION OF FORCES

1. JAPANESE
Bombardment Force
Rear Adm. Hiroaki Abe

BATTLESHIPS:

Battleship Division 11
Hiei   Capt. Masao Nishida
Kirishima   Capt. Sanji Iwabuchi

Destroyer Squadron 10: Rear Adm. Satsuma Kimura

LIGHT CRUISER:

Nagara

DESTROYERS:

Desdiv 6: *Akatsuki, Ikazuchi, Inazuma*
Desdiv 16: *Amatsukaze, Yukikaze*
Desdiv 61(-): *Teruzuki*

Destroyer Squadron 4: Rear Adm. Tamotsu Takama

DESTROYERS:

Asagumo (Flag)
Desdiv 2: *Harusame, Murasame, Yudachi, Samidare*
Picket Unit
(Covering the passage between the Russells and Guadalcanal)

DESTROYERS:

Desdiv 27: *Shigure, Yugure, Shiratsuyu*

2. AMERICAN
Task Group 67.4
Rear Adm. Daniel J. Callaghan

HEAVY CRUISERS:

San Francisco   Capt. Cassin Young
Portland   Capt. Laurance T. DuBose

LIGHT CRUISERS:

Helena   Capt. Gilbert C. Hoover
Atlanta   Capt. Samuel P. Jenkins
(embarking Rear Adm. Norman Scott)
Juneau   Capt. Lyman K. Swenson

Van Destroyers: Cdr. Thomas M. Stokes (ComDesdiv 10)
Cushing   Lt. Cdr. Edward N. Parker
Laffey   Lt. Cdr. William E. Hank

| Sterett | Cdr. Jesse G. Coward |
| O'Bannon | Cdr. Edwin Wilkinson |

Rear Destroyers: Capt. Robert G. Tobin (Comdesron 12)

Aaron Ward	Cdr. Orville F. Gregor
Barton	Lt. Cdr. Douglas H. Fox
Monssen	Lt. Cdr. Charles E. McCombs
Fletcher	Cdr. William M. Cole

with two battleships, one cruiser, and up to fourteen destroyers. The following table affords a comparison of the combat power of the two forces:

				Guns				Torpedo Tubes	
	14"	8"	6"	5.5"	5"	3.9"	3"	21"	24"
AMERICAN:									
Cruisers:	—	18	15	—	56	—	—	16	—
Destroyers:	—	—	—	—	34	—	—	64	—
Total:	—	18	15	—	90	—	—	80	—
JAPANESE:									
Battleships:	16	—	28	—	16	—	—	—	—
Cruiser:	—	—	—	7	—	—	2	—	8
Destroyers:	—	—	—	—	56	8	—	—	87
Total:	16	—	28	7	72	8	2	—	95

As can be seen, Abe's Bombardment Unit possessed superior gunnery power. To use one ancient, yet still illuminating, comparison, each American heavy cruiser could fire a broadside of 8-inch shells weighing 2,340 pounds; each Japanese battleship's broadside of 14-inch shells totaled 11,920 pounds. Moreover, none of Callaghan's naval rifles could pierce the main armor protection of the two enemy battleships under ordinary battle conditions. Turner believed that Callaghan's torpedo batteries would provide an equalizer against Japanese capital ships; but not only did the Japanese have more launching tubes (and one reload per tube, giving a total of 190 torpedoes), but their Long Lances worked, and the American Mark XV usually did not.

MIDNIGHT COLLISION

After chaperoning Turner's transports away through Lengo Channel, Callaghan reversed course with his task unit about 2200 and formed his battle disposition: van unit, destroyers *Cushing, Laffey, Sterett,* and *O'Bannon;* main body, cruisers *Atlanta, San Francisco, Portland, Helena,* and *Juneau;* rear unit, destroyers *Aaron Ward, Barton, Monssen,* and *Fletcher.* The distance between types was 800 yards, between cruisers 700 yards, and between destroyers 500 yards. This formation emulated Scott's at Cape Esperance, but the main reason for its selection was its amenability to the anticipated multiple course changes in these confined waters. Each change could be accomplished by movements by type divisions.

Serious flaws attended American command arrangements. First, sadly repeating the mistake at Cape Esperance, neither Scott nor Callaghan placed his flag on a ship with the superior SG radar equipment. Second, Callaghan compounded this error by placing none of the ships with SG radar, the big new destroyers *O'Bannon* and *Fletcher,* the light cruisers *Helena* and *Juneau,* and heavy cruiser *Portland,* advantageously in the column. Third, Callaghan's single-column formation essentially made Scott a supernumerary.[3]

Cushing, at the head of the American column, reentered Lengo Channel at midnight. A balmy 9-knot breeze blew from the southeast over a smooth sea. Jagged lightning slanting down over the mountains on Guadalcanal and Florida lit a partly overcast sky. To the northeast much worse weather threatened to ruin Abe's mission.

The composition of the Bombardment Unit became complete at 1530 when Takama's Destroyer Squadron 4 rendezvoused and assumed its appointed position over four miles ahead. *Yudachi* and *Harusame* formed a column to port, and *Asagumo, Murasame,* and *Samidare* took a like formation to starboard. At around 1700, Abe's ships ran into squalls and visibility plummeted. During occasional gaps, navigators spotted Nudai and Malaita islands, and Abe's vessels entered the north end of Indispensable Strait. The rain intensified

---

[3]Those aware of naval traditions may well wonder why Callaghan detailed the senior destroyer officer, Captain Tobin of Destroyer Squadron 12, to lead the rear, rather than the van destroyer contingent. The reason for this, according to a surviving staff officer, was that Callaghan anticipated executing a course reversal prior to encountering the Japanese. He intended to accomplish this maneuver by column movements of each of the two destroyer units and the cruisers, which would have placed Tobin in *Aaron Ward* at the head of the entire American formation. In the event, no such course reversal occurred before the battle.

until the wakes of escorting destroyers were barely visible from *Hiei.* At 1900, Abe issued his plan for the maneuvers during the bombardment, scheduled for 0150–0230. This scheme featured a sweep by Takama's five ships well ahead of the main body to comb the waters from Lunga Point to Tulagi for American surface or subsurface units.

At 2145 the R Area Air Force informed Abe that deteriorating weather over Guadalcanal would make aircraft spotting "next to impossible." In view of this signal and the weather about him, Abe decided that maneuvering, much less shelling, would not be possible. He opted to turn back to bide his time and await developments. Abe's command executed the turn at five minutes past midnight, but while the main body went northeast, Destroyer Squadron 4, which had already slipped out of position, headed due north and became further deranged from its screening station.

Before the first thirty minutes of November 13 passed, Abe decided to carry out his bombardment mission after new dispatches from Guadalcanal indicated improved weather. At 0038 or thereabouts, all of Abe's ships came to course 225 degrees. At 0046, Abe ordered Destroyer Squadron 4 to conduct its sweep of the waters off Lunga Point, but unknown to the admiral or his staff, the two course changes in a heavy muffle of rain clouds left Destroyer Squadron 4 not in the van, but actually behind the main body. Destroyer Squadron 4 came to course 180 degrees at 0048, and eight minutes later increased speed to 18 knots.

By 0059, when the main body assumed course 180 degrees, the formation was entirely askew. Instead of being over four miles ahead on the port bow, *Yudachi* and *Harusame* steamed substantially closer and on the *opposite* bow. The other three ships of Destroyer Squadron 4 that should have been on the starboard bow (*Asagumo, Murasame,* and *Samidare*) instead trailed off the starboard quarter. The disarray of the formation began to register at 0100 when Admiral Takama asked *Yudachi* for her position. She reported at 0106 that she could see *Nagara* broadside to port.

At 0125 the signal lights on Cape Esperance were identified. Bows came right to 140 degrees as throttlemen bled more steam into turbines to give revolutions for 18 knots. Up to this time, Abe's tactical intelligence included the following: *Hiei*'s Pete saw ten ships off Lunga at sunset; Lieutenant Commander Mitzi on Guadalcanal announced American landing operations still in progress at 1900, but after that visibility deteriorated and he could not be sure of the situation; Destroyer Division 27 issued a negative report upon reach-

ing its assigned station between Guadalcanal and the Russells at
0130; and the spotter on Guadalcanal reported no enemies aloft or
afloat off Lunga. The earlier reports caused Abe to contemplate the
possibility of encountering enemy vessels. But then he heard nothing
further and erroneously believed that Destroyer Squadron 4 was
sweeping the planned 6 to 9 miles ahead of his main body. On this
basis at 0130 Abe ordered: "Gun battle. Target airfield." Aboard
Hiei and *Kirishima,* ammunition hoists squealed and clattered as
they lifted Type 3 bombardment to the breeches of the 14-inch guns.

At this same moment, Callaghan's task force was approaching on
nearly a reciprocal course at 20 knots. As *Helena* passed Lunga
Point at 0124, her efficient SG radar displayed the first return echoes
from Abe at a range of 27,100 yards (13.5 miles). This placed the
enemy only a little over 10 miles from *Cushing.* By 0137, when the
American unit began a column movement right to course due north,
the echoes divided into three groups: the battleships and two groups
of screening vessels. But this picture was not clear to Callaghan.
Lacking a superior radar on his flagship, Callaghan resorted to the
TBS radio net to gather data on the enemy formation from those
vessels with SG radars. But his requests—and the attempts of *Helena*
and *O'Bannon* to disseminate their findings—were repeatedly interrupted by an ill-disciplined jabber of calls from other ships. The
American commander probably intended the course change at 0137
to place his column in a position to cross Abe's T, as Scott had done
inadvertently to Goto, but Callaghan achieved not a crossing but a
collision.

At 0142, Commander Stokes in *Cushing* sighted "three" Japanese
destroyers crossing ahead from port to starboard. These were *Yudachi* and *Harusame,* which also saw *Cushing* and the vessels in her
wake. Events now began to tumble, one upon another, faster than
either Callaghan or Abe could manage them.

Cushing's rudder swung to port to unmask guns and torpedoes at
the enemy vessels only 2,000 yards away. "Shall I let them have a
couple of fish [torpedoes]?" queried Stokes. Callaghan first authorized Stokes to fire torpedoes, but then ordered successively at 0145
"Stand by to open fire" and at 0147 a return to course north. These
abrupt maneuvers first west then back to due north threw the closely
spaced, fast-moving American column into a disarray that was never
put right.

The three destroyers in *Cushing*'s wake also veered left, while
Atlanta heeled sharply to port inside the destroyers ahead, and *San
Francisco* followed suit. "What are you doing?" Callaghan asked

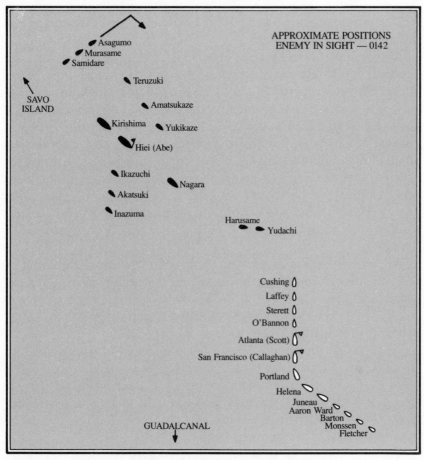

APPROXIMATE POSITIONS
ENEMY IN SIGHT — 0142

Asagumo
Murasame
Samidare

SAVO
ISLAND

Teruzuki

Amatsukaze

Kirishima   Yukikaze

Hiei (Abe)

Ikazuchi

Akatsuki   Nagara

Inazuma

Harusame
Yudachi

Cushing
Laffey
Sterett
O'Bannon
Atlanta (Scott)
San Francisco (Callaghan)
Portland
Helena
Juneau
Aaron Ward
Barton
Monssen
Fletcher

GUADALCANAL

Battle of Friday the Thirteenth, November 13

Atlanta. "Avoiding our own destroyers," replied Captain Jenkins. *Cushing* swung again to course north and sighted *Nagara* just off the starboard bow; this signified that the American formation was now aimed directly into the Japanese disposition to pass around and between the two battleships. Callaghan perceived the enemy now all about and at 0148 gave the order: "Odd ships fire to starboard, even ships fire to port."

The fastidious would later point out that Callaghan's order did not take account of the disparities in armament in the task group or the fact that some ships were already either trained on targets on the "wrong" side or had no targets on the designated side. But flawed though the order undoubtedly was, it has to be judged by the circumstances in which it was ordered. These were fundamentally that through inadvertence or mismanagement, Callaghan had brought on a close-range melee the likes of which had never happened before nor would thereafter in this war.

Abe, however, was also perplexed. *Yudachi,* uncertain of her own position, could only say the enemy was bearing toward Lunga. What enemy? What strength? Where? One minute later, lookouts on *Hiei* sang out warning of four enemy cruisers, 9,000 meters distant. To the Bombardment Unit, Abe flashed: "Probable enemy ships in sight, bearing 136 degrees." With the seconds ticking away, Captain Nishida of *Hiei* and his gunnery officer commenced an argument over whether time remained to change the main battery ammunition from bombardment shells to armor-piercing ship killers to deal with enemy cruisers. Then the lookouts on the flagship reported six enemy cruisers in the direction of Lunga and seven destroyers toward Tulagi.

Abe instructed his captains to shift target to enemy ships, and at 0145 the main body of the Japanese unit, battleships *Hiei* and *Kirishima* and their close escort of *Nagara* and six destroyers, pivoted to course 80 degrees. Although the visibility permitted firing without artificial illumination, Abe directed the flagship to use her searchlights to reveal the enemy fleet to his gunners and torpedomen and to mask the movements of the other Japanese ships. Searchlights from *Hiei* and *Akatsuki* snapped open and their beams settled on *Atlanta,* whose superstructure loomed high above the destroyers ahead of her. Down these cones of light came the first salvos of Japanese shells. The time was 0148.

Captain Jenkins of *Atlanta* sighted *Nagara* about 3,000 yards away over the tops of the American destroyers just moments before enemy searchlights from the west snared his ship. *Atlanta*'s main battery whirled back to port to fire on the illuminating ships, and she snapped out a salvo at the range of only 1,600 yards. Simultaneously *Atlanta* bluejackets spotted the right-flank Japanese trio of *Inazuma, Akatsuki,* and *Ikazuchi* firing at them. While *Atlanta*'s after guns remained on *Hiei,* her forward group rotated to the "rear" destroyer, probably *Akatsuki,* and scored damaging hits. But *Akatsuki* also managed to fire torpedoes, and one of these pierced the light cruiser's modest plating abreast the forward engine room. A series of hits from 5-inch guns, mainly from *Akatsuki* and her colleagues, and 6-inch shells from *Hiei*'s secondary battery sprinkled over *Atlanta*'s upperworks. With fires growing and way dwindling, *Atlanta*'s head began to swing around to the south, and she coasted or drifted out of the action, aflame and taking water steadily into her engineering spaces.

After these opening moments, both formations disintegrated and the battle became, in the colorful words of one American skipper, "a barroom brawl after the lights had been shot out." The surviving records are so confused and the events they describe overlap so much that a chronological account of the struggle becomes impossible. The clearest way to present the rest of the action is by following first the fate of each of the American ships in her order in the formation, and then the experience of each vessel in the Japanese contingent.

At the spear tip of the American formation, *Cushing* identified *Hiei* barely 1,000 yards to port. Despite this temptation, Lieutenant Commander Parker heeded Callaghan's orders and turned *Cushing*'s main battery on a destroyer 2,000 yards to starboard while her 20mm machineguns loosed ribbons of tracers at the enemy battleship and her torpedomen launched one "fish" to port. Japanese gunners found *Cushing* early and maimed her engineering plant. The destroyer lost headway as she bent around to starboard, and the bulk of *Hiei* reared up again, this time approaching from the starboard quarter. *Cushing* sailors discharged six torpedoes at the enemy dreadnought at a range of 1,200 yards and believed they witnessed three hits, but this was an illusion. There was no illusion concerning *Cushing*'s own condition: over ten major hits from both sides riddled her, silenced her guns, crippled her steering, and eliminated the remaining power, while enemy machineguns raked over her topsides, crumpling many of her bluejackets. After a five-minute respite, two vessels, probably *Nagara* and *Yukikaze,* passed on the starboard hand, scoring at least seven more hits on *Cushing,* which could only return 20mm fire. With *Cushing* lacking power to move or power to reply and fires gaining sway over her decks, Parker gave the order to abandon ship.

Just prior to the commencement of the action, *Laffey* made out *Hiei* and *Kirishima* off the port bow. The American destroyer spurted ahead, and her stern just passed under the overhanging stem of *Hiei* at a range John Paul Jones would have deemed close. *Laffey*'s gunners sprayed *Hiei* with 5-inch and machinegun fire, killing Captain Masakane Suzuki, Abe's chief of staff, but torpedoes fired at point-blank range failed to arm before they struck the enemy capital ship.[4] *Laffey* escaped past *Hiei,* but then, after a lull, encountered *Asagumo, Murasame,* and *Samidare.* The Japanese trio savaged

[4] All navies equipped torpedoes with a device that prevented the exploder from functioning until the weapon ran a certain minimum distance. This was designed to prevent premature detonations that could damage or sink the firing vessel.

Laffey with gunfire, and then a torpedo, probably from *Teruzuki,* removed her stern up to the after 5-inch gun. A large-caliber salvo—probably from *Kirishima*—crashed into the after boiler room and with other shells disconnected the propulsion plant and steering, while steady hits from the enemy destroyers further subtracted from *Laffey*'s combat effectiveness. Without means of containment, fires soon gained ascendancy all over *Laffey,* and Lieutenant Commander Hank gave the order to abandon ship. As she sank, *Laffey* erupted into a huge orange flaming explosion that killed many men still aboard or in the water, including Hank.

Callaghan's "odd-even" order found *Sterett,* third in column, with her guns trained to port, so she shifted over to starboard and pumped out the first of thirteen salvos at a target 4,000 yards away—perhaps *Nagara.* A hit severed helm control, and while *Sterett* struggled to steer with her engines, *O'Bannon* pulled up abreast, blanking the line of fire. *Sterett*'s gunners paused, but the Japanese did not; concentrated gunfire from port shot out the SC radar, the radio antennas, and the fighting lights. *Sterett* loosed four torpedoes and many 5-inch rounds at an enemy ship of the line to port as the range closed to only 2,000 yards. Observers on *Sterett* thought two torpedoes hit, but these were only gun flashes.

Time had slipped to 0220 by *Sterett*'s clocks when her crewmen detected a Japanese destroyer only 1,000 yards off the starboard bow. This target earned two torpedoes and a pummeling by the main armament. *Sterett* sailors thought one torpedo struck its mark, and the target sank "almost immediately." At 0227, *Sterett* received numerous hits on the port quarter that disabled the after 5-inch guns and ignited a bad powder fire that killed many men and forced the flooding of the magazines. With no remaining usable torpedoes, only half her main armament in operation, a conflagration aft, and one-fifth of her crew casualties, Lieutenant Commander Coward took his command out of the action to the east and then south. *Sterett* sustained a total of eleven direct hits, including three 14-inch bombardment type.

Last but largest of the leading quartet of American destroyers was *O'Bannon.* Her battle featured in equal measures desperate gyrations to avoid collisions with other American vessels and desperate close-range fighting. The initial fishtailing twists of the American column left *O'Bannon* lurching abruptly under a succession of rudder and engine changes to avoid embarrassing embraces with ships ahead. When an enemy searchlight fastened onto *Cushing, O'Bannon*'s gunners sent their tracers into the enemy's forward superstructure. Several rapid rudder changes to avoid *Sterett* (by 30 feet) placed *O'Bannon* astern of *Laffey* on a westerly course. A heavy cross fire enveloped both *Cushing* and *Laffey* as *O'Bannon* opened up on *Hiei*. When *Cushing* and *Laffey* dropped from sight to starboard, *O'Bannon* found herself leading the American column with an enemy capital unit a scant 1,800 yards on the starboard hand. All of *Hiei*'s batteries fired at *O'Bannon,* but every shot passed overhead. By 0156 the enemy battleship appeared well afire. *O'Bannon* fired two torpedoes, and her crew saw the enemy unit "explode" and "burning particles" fell on *O'Bannon*'s deck—yet another battle illusion. With all targets to starboard invisible, *O'Bannon* reversed course to the east, noting five burning and exploding vessels on the starboard quarter. At 0201 she swung hard left to avoid the sinking bow of *Barton,* and as she passed her sailors threw life jackets to men in the water. At 0203, shock waves from *Barton*'s tremendous death rattle caused a temporary electrical outage. After regaining power, *O'Bannon* broke off the action and headed southeast to "locate either definite targets or definite friends," said Commander Wilkinson.

Next in line were the ships bearing the two American admirals, whose fates were cruelly entwined. At opening of the action, *San Francisco* sent seven 8-inch salvos screaming after one of two destroyers on the starboard bow, probably *Yudachi*. When this target began to germinate flames and draw the attentions of other American ships, Captain Young instructed the gunnery officer to switch targets to the second destroyer. Just as the shift began, the enemy destroyer (probably *Harusame*) reversed course. What happened next is unclear. It is possible that Young mistakenly designated as a target a "small cruiser or large destroyer" on the starboard bow that, in fact, was *Atlanta*. The more likely explanation is that the crew of the main battery director trained left to follow the second destroyer, but because of their high and narrow field of vision, they failed to see disabled *Atlanta* drift into the line of fire. In either event, two full main battery salvos from *San Francisco* smashed through *Atlanta*'s superstructure. Although none of these armor-piercing shells exploded against *Atlanta*'s light plating, they set *Atlanta* "afire throughout her length" and left behind their characteristic green dye residue in ruptured compartments and mangled gun mounts. Among the many killed were Admiral Scott and three of his four staff officers.[5]

---

[5] Previous accounts of this action have attributed Scott's death to Japanese gunfire, and therefore this matter bears elaboration. The conclusion in the text is derived from Enclosure (B)

It seems clear that Callaghan witnessed this tragedy. He ordered the flagship to cease fire, but inadvertently this command was also sent as a general broadcast to the task force: "Cease firing own ships." Few ships obeyed this command. The incredulous reaction of Captain Dubose of *Portland* was typical: "What is the dope, did you want to cease fire?" Callaghan rapidly clarified his real intentions by successively broadcasting "Give her hell" and "We want the big ones! Get the big ones first!" *San Francisco* swung left to unmask her after turret and *Hiei* leveled her guns out to starboard as the two flagships passed each other at a range of only 2,500 yards. Both ships fired short initially, *Hiei*'s 14-inch bombardment shells bursting in "vivid" pyrotechnics. At the same time, both flagships were assailed by other vessels, *Hiei* by American destroyers and *San Francisco* by a cross fire from *Nagara* on her starboard quarter and *Kirishima* from port. The third salvo of 14-inch shells from *Hiei* hit *San Francisco* in the bridgework, blowing the ship's navigator, Commander Rae E. Arison, over a bulwark and down two decks, where he landed on a 5-inch gun. The feverishly engaged crew of the gun, mistakenly thinking Arison dead, "unceremoniously threw him off, hurling ejected hot cases after him." More blows from port on the bridge structure felled men on that side. Then *Hiei*'s secondary armament scored a series of hits. One shell mortally wounded Captain Young. A second shell exploded on a girder directly over the head of Callaghan, killing him and all but one member of his staff. About this same time, a hit on the auxiliary control station killed Commander Joseph C. Hubbard, the executive officer, and another shell homed into the

---

in *Atlanta*'s action report, which itemizes the location of all forty-nine known gunfire hits on that vessel. I originally studied this document with a view to discovering which Japanese vessel might have scored the hit that killed Scott. The report shows thirteen hits classed as "5.5-inch," presumably from *Nagara* or *Hiei*'s 6-inch secondary battery, including three on the bridge-works, but none in the immediate vicinity of Scott's station. *Atlanta* was also struck, however, by nineteen projectiles identified as 8-inch, undoubtedly from *San Francisco* in view of the direction from which they came and their telltale green dye. (For purposes of spotting "splashes" for gunfire adjustment when several ships are firing, bags of dye were loaded in shells to color the splashes, usually behind the windshield, the pointed cap on the shell employed for aerodynamic efficiency.) Seven of these 8-inch hits were grouped in an area measuring 6 yards high by 8 yards wide and smashed through flag plot, the passageway outside of flag plot, sky lookout, and the radio and coding rooms. The location of these hits would coincide with the position of Scott and his staff. More evidence supporting this conclusion may be found in Fletcher Pratt, *The Navy's War* (New York: Harper & Row, 1944), p. 267, which contains an account from Captain Jenkins. According to this source, after a torpedo struck *Atlanta*, one of the "big shells" killed Scott. The largest shells to strike *Atlanta* were those from *San Francisco*, for, contrary to some accounts, *Atlanta*'s report does not show any hits by 14-inch shells.

stateroom where Commander Crouter lay bandaged in his bunk and snuffed out his life.

This devastating series of hits on *San Francisco*'s control stations left only thirty-one-year-old Lieutenant Commander Bruce Mc-Candless and a young quartermaster standing in the pilothouse. McCandless found that the ship's head had come around to course south because of a steering casualty and confusion. He could have left her pointed that way out of the battle with honor intact, as *San Francisco* was heavily damaged by forty-five hits with most of her armament silenced, fires spreading from twenty-five locations, and 500 tons of water aboard. But McCandless recognized that other ships, unaware of the condition of the flagship, might follow a disengagement course. He put *San Francisco* back on course west, toward the enemy.

McCandless then made a quick inspection of the navigating bridge that revealed bodies and parts of bodies mixed thickly with scattered gear and twisted metal. Water rained down from the punctured cooling system of the 1.1-inch machineguns, and over these macabre scenes the ship's broken siren moaned. An enemy destroyer crossed ahead and passed down the port side trading blows with the port 5-inch battery.

These severe losses among *San Francisco*'s officers elevated Lieutenant Commander Herbert E. Schonland to command. Schonland, the ship's damage control officer, was belowdecks and fully occupied in keeping the cruiser "afloat and right side up," so he wisely left the conn in McCandless's capable hands. That officer kept her standing west while her surviving gunners kept up intermittent exchanges with *Hiei* and *Kirishima*. Finally, McCandless took *San Francisco* back east, skirting Guadalcanal's shore.

In the opening moments of this, her first night battle, *Portland* lashed out at a destroyer on the starboard side. Captain DuBose disregarded the cease-fire order and swung his ship from west to northerly to resume fire at an enemy "cruiser" on the starboard beam. At 0158½ a torpedo struck *Portland* far aft on the starboard side. This hit sheared off the starboard screws and bent shell plating into a most unwanted but most efficient rudder that locked the ship in a constant right circle. Just as *Portland* completed her first loop, *Hiei* slid into the line of fire and *Portland* loosed four salvos from her forward turrets at 4,000 yards, claiming ten to fourteen hits. *Portland* withheld further fire from her main battery, because other American vessels were streaming by and the situation was irredeemably confused.

With her superior radar suite, *Helena* already had a main battery
target at opening fire: *Akatsuki.* Continuous rapid fire seemed to
shoot out the enemy searchlight, but attracted return fire which did
minor but historically useful damage to *Helena*'s upperworks (one
shell stopped a clock at 0148). After pirouetting past a number of
vessels, *Helena* spied on her starboard bow destroyer *Amatsukaze*
firing at *San Francisco.* At 0204, *Helena* cut loose with both main
and secondary armament, only to check when *San Francisco* crossed
the line of fire. Meanwhile the 40mm battery sputtered at *Nagara,*
about 3,000 yards away on a diverging course. During the rest of the
action, *Helena* wove her way around a flotilla of burning and exploding ships on a plethora of courses while her gunners blasted at
retiring Japanese vessels. Five shells gouged *Helena,* but she sustained only slight damage.

The details of *Juneau*'s participation are obscure. The confusion
over the turns at the commencement of the action found *Juneau*
pulled up abreast of *San Francisco*'s starboard side. As *Juneau* maneuvered out of this position, a torpedo struck her port side in the
forward fireroom. This hit knocked out the central fire control and
may have broken her keel. With steering temporarily disabled, *Juneau* nearly collided with *Helena.* She fired few, perhaps only
twenty-five, rounds of ammunition, some of it at *Helena.* Captain
Swenson began thinking of taking her to a cove to make temporary
repairs as *Juneau* limped out of the battle area.

The rear unit of destroyers *Aaron Ward, Barton, Monssen,* and
Fletcher were ill positioned to participate at the opening of the battle,
though eager to help. *Aaron Ward,* embarking Captain Tobin, began
firing at *Hiei* at a range of about 7,000 yards. She checked fire after
about ten salvos and then at 0155 stopped and backed down to avoid
a vessel ahead, which was very likely *Yudachi.* One minute later, two
torpedoes passed under the ship from port to starboard, and then
close on the starboard side *Barton* blew up and sank immediately.
With the sea apparently clear ahead, at 0159 *Aaron Ward* rang up
18 knots and set course due north. The torpedo battery trained out
on a capital ship, probably *Hiei,* but *Aaron Ward* withheld fire
because *San Francisco* veered into close range with the enemy vessel.

After maneuvering to avoid a ship identified as *Sterett, Aaron
Ward* went to all ahead flank and took as her next target a large
destroyer or light cruiser fine on the starboard bow. The rudder was
kicked left and severe punishment dealt to this vessel. The frenzy of
firing attracted enemy searchlights from both sides, but with her
guns blasting to both beams, *Aaron Ward* fought her way out of the

illumination. During the action, *Aaron Ward* collected nine direct hits, three identified as 14-inch. Cumulatively these disabled the director, the radars, and steering control by 0225. Ten minutes later all power flickered out and *Aaron Ward* coasted to a halt.

Barton bluejackets saw enemy searchlights and gunfire ahead. She joined in the general firing at the enemy searchlights with her 5-inch guns, and about 0152 she fired five torpedoes to port. After seven minutes of combat, *Barton* stopped to avoid collision with another vessel. While she was motionless, a Long Lance slashed into the forward fireroom, and a few moments later a second hit the forward engine room. Beneath a lofty streak of flame, *Barton* broke in two and sank with amazing rapidity, carrying down 60 percent of her crew. Into the oil-stained water a pathetically few men spilled from the after topside stations and a few gun mounts.

Another witness to *Barton*'s explosive demise was *Monssen*. With her fire control radar out of action and her SC radar impassive, *Monssen* was groping for the enemy when a torpedo sliced beneath her keel and another passed ahead to hit *Barton*. Then the torpedo officer sighted *Hiei* 4,000 yards to starboard and launched five torpedoes at this target, without success. *Monssen*'s guns barked at another destroyer to port while she fired her five remaining torpedoes at a destroyer on the starboard beam. As her 20mm guns rattled at an enemy destroyer a scant quarter mile to starboard, star shells burst overhead in brilliant illumination. Were these from a "friendly" vessel? Lieutenant Commander McCombs thought so. He switched on *Monssen*'s recognition lights; they immediately attracted two searchlights and an avalanche of gunfire. In brief order thirty-seven hits, including three of major caliber, transformed *Monssen* into a flaming wreck. Her crew abandoned her about 0220.

Fletcher was the last ship in the American column, and not even her priceless SG radar could cope with the utterly confused jumble of ships ahead once the battle began. Her gunners already had their cross hairs on *Akatsuki* when that ship illuminated at the commencement of the action. But seeing *Akatsuki* blanketed by heavy fire from other ships, *Fletcher* adjusted targets to a vessel astern of *Akatsuki* that should have been *Inazuma*. *Fletcher* complied with the cease-fire order and then beheld the awesome spectacle as *Barton* "simply disappeared in fragments." Her quartermasters recorded further daunting sights: *Monssen* sinking and dropping aft on the starboard beam, medium-caliber shells raising great silvery geysers of water on both sides, and torpedoes passing under the ship, one of which broached ahead in the light of flames from *Barton*. With left rudder

Fletcher threaded her way through the littered ocean, firing at a succession of targets. Back on an easterly course, she stalked then fired torpedoes at a large vessel, whose description in *Fletcher*'s report sounds very suspiciously like *Helena.* Although *Fletcher* sailors thought the target went down after a big series of explosions, this was an illusion. Through all of this *Fletcher* sailed untouched.

The open Japanese formation affords no simple organizing guide to telling the other side of the story. But generally Abe's unit maneuvered by divisions, which therefore provides a framework for following Japanese fortunes.

In the thick of the battle from the start were the seven vessels of Destroyer Squadron 10 that formed the close screen for *Hiei* and *Kirishima.* With one exception, however, few records from this unit remain. Before *Yudachi*'s report of enemy in sight, Admiral Kimura's flagship *Nagara* cruised directly ahead of the two battleships with Destroyer Division 17 *(Yukikaze* and *Amatsukaze)* and *Teruzuki* echeloned back to port and Destroyer Division 6 echeloned back to starboard. *Nagara*'s greater bulk and distinctive three funnels assured that she passed through the sights of many American gunners, but she did not sustain major damage. Accompanied faithfully by *Yukikaze, Nagara* played a searchlight on the van of the American column, and her guns snapped at *Atlanta* and *San Francisco.* After a short swing north, *Nagara* and *Yukikaze* doubled back to the west, probably finishing off *Cushing* as they went.

Of the ships in Destroyer Squadron 10, only Commander Hara of *Amatsukaze* left us a detailed account of his vessel's participation in this battle. At the start of the action, Hara accelerated *Amatsukaze* to clear "overs" aimed at *Hiei.* Joined briefly by *Yukikaze* before that destroyer returned allegiance to *Nagara, Amatsukaze* raced down *Nagara*'s starboard side and curved in toward the American column. Flares revealed the last six vessels in the American column "moving like wraiths in the darkness," and Hara bore in and launched eight torpedoes at 0154 at a range of perhaps 3,000 yards. He saw two "pillars of fire" spring skyward, and *Barton* crumpled in the middle and vanished. At 0159—or so he claimed—Hara launched four torpedoes at a ship he identified as *Juneau,* then engaging *Yudachi.* Hara thought he secured one hit at 0202.

Hara set out to rejoin *Hiei,* the only recognizable ship in sight. En route he suddenly encountered *San Francisco,* and only by swinging the rudder hard over did he pass across the cruiser's bow and down her port side. Four torpedoes plopped from *Amatsukaze*'s tubes at the American flagship, but did not arm before they hit. The destroyer's gunners pumped many shells at *San Francisco,* aided by a searchlight Hara ordered switched on. But as in so many other cases this night, the chief beneficiaries of the searchlight were enemy gunners. This time it was *Helena* that in short order scored multiple hits, which wrecked *Amatsukaze*'s main battery director, demolished the radio room, and shot out the steering and the hydraulics for the armament. With his ship burning and circling, only the timely appearance of *Asagumo, Murasame,* and *Samidare,* which diverted *Helena*'s attention, saved Hara. *Amatsukaze* suffered a total of thirty-seven hits and lost forty-three killed, including the gunnery officer.

The last ship in the echelon to port of the battleships was the large antiaircraft destroyer *Teruzuki.* Her officers sketched fights with one enemy cruiser and no fewer than six destroyers, one of which was almost certainly *Laffey. Teruzuki* eschewed the use of a searchlight and sustained little damage.

From their original position on the starboard beam of the battleships, the three vessels of Destroyer Division 6 had pulled ahead and well off the starboard bow of *Hiei* by the moment firing began. The division leader, *Akatsuki,* was in the center of an odd left-echelon formation with *Inazuma* off her starboard bow and *Ikazuchi* on her port quarter. All three ships turned to port and may well have passed through the front of the American column ahead of *Atlanta*—at least Captain Jenkins said he saw them do so, and *Hiei* claimed that *Akatsuki* crossed her bow. *Akatsuki* used guns and torpedoes to effect on Scott's flagship, but her fate was inexorable: her searchlight drew gunfire from at least five enemy ships, and hits started fires that in turn drew more gunfire. Flights of glowing shells pursued her, enveloped her, and wrecked her. Whether she vanished beneath the sea early or lingered for a while her handful of captured survivors did not say.

Inazuma transformed the swing to port into a wide 180-degree turn, probably collected some hits, and withdrew. *Ikazuchi* pivoted through several port turns, dispensed some torpedoes, and had her forecastle gun mount damaged before she too headed northwest out of the battle.

The five ships of Destroyer Squadron 4 fought as two divisions widely separated in both distance and time. In action from the outset were van destroyers *Yudachi* and *Harusame.* Indeed, no performance this night was more remarkable than that of *Yudachi.* After crossing *Cushing*'s bow at 0142, Commander Kiyoshi Kikkawa swung *Yudachi*'s prow through a 270-degree turn to port and then, with breathtaking verve, charged straight into the American column. She fired eight torpedoes at 0155 at only 1,500 meters and claimed an enemy heavy cruiser "immediately sunk" at 0159 (apparently *Portland*) as well as a hit on a light cruiser that may have been *Juneau*. *Yudachi* passed through the jumbled American formation, probably just ahead of *Aaron Ward,* causing added confusion among the rear destroyers and forcing radical maneuvers. Heading north, *Yudachi* gave and received punishment from a series of American cruisers and destroyers at close range. Then a vessel Kikkawa thought "friendly"—good candidates are *Aaron Ward* or *Asagumo*—engaged *Yudachi,* and despite a flash of recognition lights, she sustained hits which left *Yudachi* dead in the water at 0226.

Harusame lost sight of *Yudachi* amid shell splashes at 0151. She cut a series of corkscrew turns along a northward track, using guns and torpedoes, but her actions cannot be matched to those of any other vessel.

The last Japanese vessels to engage were the remaining three ships of Destroyer Squadron 4. *Asagumo* (flag) led their column formation, followed by *Murasame* and *Samidare.* Just before the firing commenced, Admiral Takama guided them across the rear and then up the port side of Abe's battleships. Their course skimmed along the northern periphery of the melee, which probably saved them from major damage but limited their opportunities to use torpedoes. In all likelihood, this trio accounted for *Laffey* and *Monssen* and then distracted *Helena* before the American cruiser could inflict fatal damage on *Amatsukaze*. *Murasame* fired seven torpedoes at a "cruiser" and claimed three hits at 0204, sinking the target "immediately." *Asagumo* employed gunfire and torpedoes on an enemy vessel between 0215 and 0225. In return, *Murasame* sustained a hit that put one boiler room out of action and withdrew. *Samidare* also developed a "small fire," presumably from gunfire damage.

Finally, there are the two ships of Battleship Division 11. Fleet flagship *Hiei*'s searchlights enticed gunfire from almost every American vessel present. Early hits set the massive forward tower foremast alight, and with nearly every platform level trailing scarfs of flame, *Hiei* stood out even more. While none of the American ordnance available could penetrate her main armor belt, eighty-five hits punctured *Hiei*'s lighter armor and ordinary steel structures. All light antiaircraft guns were destroyed, all radio and signal communications equipment was put out of action, and all internal communications, including the control circuits for the main battery, were severed. American shells disabled the secondary battery directors, and in the confusion, *Hiei*'s 6-inch guns growled at *Asagumo, Murasame,* and *Samidare* as they sprinted past on the port side. About 0154, *Hiei* swung to port and conducted her duel with *San Francisco.* During this engagement *Hiei* suffered a critical hit aft from an 8-inch shell which jammed the rudder and flooded the steering machinery compartment.

From her position about 1,000 meters astern of *Hiei, Kirishima* ladled out fifty-nine shells from her 14-inch guns and 313 from her secondary armament. Her targets included *Cushing, Laffey,* and *San Francisco. Kirishima* separated from the flagship and headed northerly about 0154. One 6-inch shell nicked her.

On the shore, marines, sailors, and soldiers gathered on the beach, atop the coral ridges, and along the jungle fringes to watch what Lieutenant H. C. Merillat termed this "awesome melee of light and sound." Private Robert Leckie noted:

> The star shells rose, terrible and red. Giant tracers flashed across the night in orange arches. . . . the sea seemed a sheet of polished obsidian on which the warships seemed to have been dropped and been immobilized, centered amid concentric circles like shock waves that form around a stone dropped in mud.

Despite, or perhaps because of, his mismanagement, Callaghan did strike at what proved to be the most vulnerable component of the Japanese task force: Abe's nerve. From Abe's post on *Hiei*'s flag bridge, the glare of searchlights and fires masked the unfolding pattern of the battle. All he probably could discern was enemy destroyers passing at rifle-shot range, strings of enemy machinegun tracers pelting his flagship and killing his chief of staff, and the buffeting of *Hiei*'s decks under a hail of medium- and light-caliber shells. Although his ships inflicted more damage than they received, in doing so they became intertwined with the enemy and hopelessly scattered. About 0200—around the time Callaghan was killed—Abe abandoned his bombardment mission permanently.

SALVAGE AND SURVIVAL

Captain Hoover of *Helena,* unable to contact anyone senior by radio, at 0226 ordered all American ships to course 92 degrees. Despite a few shots thereafter, this message marked the end of the battle, for by now all the remaining Japanese vessels were exiting the area around both sides of Savo. The savage thirty-eight-minute encounter southeast of Savo left two American destroyers and one Japanese destroyer sunk and two American cruisers and three destroyers as well as one Japanese battleship and one destroyer disabled. Several hundred Americans and some scores of Japanese clung to wreckage in the water. Neither side expected nor gave mercy.

At 0300, *Asagumo* and *Murasame* found motionless *Yudachi* with fires raging forward. Visual inspection convinced Takama that *Yudachi* was beyond saving, so at 0317 he ordered her abandoned. Rather than taking off the crew, however, he turned his vessels north and left two boats and instructions for *Yudachi* sailors to head for Cape Esperance, about 3 miles away. This scheme was not to the taste of the commander of Destroyer Division 2, who sent *Samidare* over to pick up *Yudachi*'s crew. At 0400, 207 men from the crippled destroyer climbed over to their sister ship, which then applied her guns and one torpedo to *Yudachi*. Although *Yudachi* leaned to starboard, she did not sink.

At 0300, *Kirishima* sent the first flash report of the action. She described a "severe mixed battle" in which "both sides [suffered] considerable damage." *Kirishima* also announced the cancellation of the airfield shelling. At 0344, Yamamoto postponed the landing to the 14th; on this order Tanaka turned the convoy back toward Shortland.

Understandably, the condition of the flagship preoccupied the Japanese. Rear Admiral Kimura exercised tactical command as he enjoyed communications and Abe did not. Kimura's directives sent Destroyer Squadron 4 north with *Kirishima* while *Nagara* sought *Hiei*. At his summons, the three ships of Destroyer Division 27 plus *Yukikaze* and *Teruzuki* also joined the damaged dreadnought. On *Hiei*, crewmen smothered flames but the ship refused to answer her helm. Investigation disclosed the rudder was jammed at full right and flooding prevented access to the damaged machinery. The emergency manual steering arrangements had been shot out. Some young officers urged Captain Masao Nishida to beach *Hiei*, shell the airfield, and then move the crew ashore to join in a ground assault. Although this sort of romantically heroic gesture twanged a responsive cord in Nishida, he dispassionately recognized that the four *Kongo* Class battleships were by far the most valuable of the older types because of their speed. Therefore, every effort had to be made to preserve *Hiei*. Moreover, with her engines intact *Hiei* might yet be salvaged by getting the water out of the damaged steering compartments.

When first light inched across the patch of water between Savo and Guadalcanal, it disclosed fragments of the forces on both sides. To the east and southeast, the hulks of destroyers *Cushing, Monssen,* and *Yudachi* listed beneath smoke columns. Off Lunga Point, crippled *Portland* circled, and south of her drifted shattered *Atlanta.* Just north of Savo was *Hiei* and her retinue of attendants. After sunrise, crewmen in *Hiei*'s foretop identified an enemy vessel almost 14.5 miles away. The after turrets trained out, guns elevated, and at 0630 the first of four salvos thundered away. The report that the target sank bolstered morale on the flagship.

Hiei's cross hairs were laid on immobilized *Aaron Ward.* She began to get way on at 0618, just before *Hiei* opened fire, but power failed again at 0635. *Hiei*'s third salvo straddled, but then aircraft arrived to distract the battleship's attention. Tug *Bobolink* dragged *Aaron Ward* to the relative sanctuary of. Tulagi harbor by 0830.

Portland emulated *Hiei*'s display, but with conclusive results. The American heavy cruiser sighted *Yudachi* and sent five salvos rumbling down the 12,500 yards separating the two ships. The sixth caused *Yudachi*'s after magazine to blow up, sending her to a permanent berth in Iron Bottom Sound. When tug *Bobolink* hauled up from Tulagi, Captain DuBose sent her to help *Atlanta.* Part of *Portland*'s company accepted and tended to survivors from other ships, while another portion tried various permutations of engine combinations, anchor streaming, and boat pulls or pushes to guide *Portland* toward Lunga, but with scant progress. Finally, with *Bobolink* shoving against the starboard bow and one port screw astern and the other forward, *Portland* crawled at 2 to 3 knots to Tulagi, where she anchored at 0108 the next morning.

The end of her brief participation in the night action found *Atlanta* listing, burning, and drifting. A total of forty-nine hits had blasted armament and control stations, set blazes in the superstructure, and caused the fire-weakened foremast to topple over to port. Everywhere topside the glower of flames outlined bodies and fragments of bodies among blackened turrets, buckled decks, and crumpled bulkheads. Miraculously, Captain Jenkins was unscathed. He and the other surviving officers rallied the survivors to organize bucket brigades to control and then subdue stubborn fires, shuffle through the debris, and lighten the ship by jettisoning torpedoes, ammunition, and excess gear.

Crewmen paid out the starboard anchor to halt the drift toward the Japanese shore. Boats arrived to take off the many wounded, and then at 0930 *Bobolink* appeared, fresh from aiding *Aaron Ward.* The tug's crew administered machinegun fire to dark heads they saw poking above the waves until Jenkins begged them to cease—there were in fact many more oil-coated Americans than Japanese then struggling in the water. *Bobolink* moved *Atlanta* to a position off Kukum by 1400, but by then it had become obvious that the ship could not be saved. Though her topside was tattered above the main deck, it was the slow but relentless progress of flooding from the torpedo hit that gave *Atlanta* a 10-degree list, deprived her of power, and doomed her. With Halsey's authorization to act at his discretion, Jenkins had the rest of the crew removed and then set demolition charges. *Atlanta* sank at 2015, 3 miles west of Lunga Point. When the last of the living from *Atlanta* reached Lunga and joined the swimming survivors collected by boat, there were about 1,400 seamen from Callaghan's task force ashore.

Sleepless American airmen lifted off from Henderson Field early and were startled to find an enemy battleship northeast of Savo limping along at 5 knots. The relays of attacks began at 0615 when five VMSB-142 SBDs and four VMSB-131 TBFs assailed *Hiei,* claiming one bomb and one torpedo hit. Seven more SBDs dived on *Hiei* from 0830 to 1005 without success, followed at 1010 by the second effort by VMSB-131's four TBFs. They claimed one hit with a torpedo. At 1015, nine TBFs of *Enterprise*'s VT-10 under Lieutenant Albert Coffin opportunely appeared with six escorting Wildcats. They had been sent to reinforce the Cactus Air Force and promptly made runs on *Hiei.* In the face of spectacular webbed bursts from 14-inch Type 3 shells, the TBF crews thought they scored three hits.

At 1110, fourteen B-17s of the 11th Bomb Group released fifty-six 500-pound bombs over *Hiei,* claiming one hit, and in the hour after 1120, six SBDs attacked *Hiei* and half reported bomb hits. At 1220, six TBFs (four from VT-10) again buzzed in low at the enemy battleship and scored one certain and one more likely hit. Low clouds spoiled an attack by nine SBDs between 1340 and 1525 on *Hiei*'s escorts, but six VT-10 TBFs claimed two hits on the battleship at 1435. This brought to seventy the total number of attack aircraft sorties for the day, fifty-six divided equally between SBDs and TBFs and the balance B-17s. One TBF was a write-off from attacking *Hiei,* and weather claimed two SBDs.

During the sunlight hours, *Junyo* sent twenty-three Zeros and the 11th Air Fleet contributed twelve more to defend *Hiei.* Early in the day some of these tangled with seven Wildcats. One Wildcat was lost, but the other pilots claimed eight Zeros. Actual Japanese losses were three Zeros in combat, but no less than eight operationally due to bad weather.[6]

American radio intelligence experts read with satisfaction a series of messages on *Hiei*'s plight, but despite these attacks, morale on *Hiei* remained high and the crew struggled ceaselessly to save the ship. In the course of the day, Nishida acknowledged three bomb hits and "four or more" torpedo hits. The bombs exploded on impact, further mutilating *Hiei*'s topsides and killing crewmen, but they did not threaten the survival of the ship. The steady stream of assaults, however, foiled efforts to place collision mats over the shell holes in the steering machinery compartments so they could be pumped out.

Abe transferred to *Yukikaze* at 0815, just after signaling his plan to tow *Hiei* to Shortland with *Kirishima* that night. As the air attacks mounted in frequency and intensity, Abe decided *Hiei* could not be saved and ordered her beached on Guadalcanal at 1020, but Nishida either did not receive this order or refused to carry it out. At 1235, Abe directed that the crew be taken off when a lull in the air attacks occurred, but Nishida pleaded that his ship could still be saved, so the admiral canceled the order.

By 1530, *Hiei* visibly listed from the torpedo hits, and Abe concluded the situation was beyond recovery. Moreover, damage was mounting among the escorting destroyers, so Abe directed that *Hiei*'s crew be removed and the battleship scuttled. Despite all that had happened, Nishida retained his confidence that *Hiei* could be saved and again challenged the command, but this time Abe remained adamant. When an erroneous report reached Nishida of engine damage, he authorized preparations to abandon ship. In spite of vigorous protests from *Hiei*'s seamen, the Kingston valves were opened and the crew was assembled forward, where the roll was called. The ensign was lowered with three banzais. Pickup vessels accepted the Emperor's portrait and then the survivors, wounded first. During the abandonment, torpedo planes scored two more hits. Losses on *Hiei* came to at least 300 killed.

By 1800 the recovery of the crew was complete. But at 1838, Abe was handed a message from the Combined Fleet not to scuttle *Hiei*.

---

[6]To assist in the emergency, MacArthur released eight P-38s, which reached Guadalcanal during the afternoon, bringing to sixteen the number of these planes at Guadalcanal. They did not participate in the air attacks this day.

Abe queried this order, but Yamamoto had calculated that *Hiei*'s last service to Japan would be as a diversion for American planes as the convoy approached. When the coterie of ships that had stood by her all day departed, *Hiei*—from whose decks the Emperor had watched the last great review of the Imperial Navy—was listing 15 degrees to starboard and sinking slowly by the stern. Sometime during the night she foundered.

The sequels from the action did not all take place in the vicinity of Savo Island.

The morning after the battle found Captain Hoover in *Helena* in command of a small task group steering south for Espíritu Santo. *Helena* had destroyers *Sterett* and *O'Bannon* on her bows and *San Francisco* in column astern. Also in company was *Juneau*, which, because of steering difficulties, steamed on *San Francisco*'s starboard beam. At about 0800, *Juneau* transferred a doctor, Lieutenant Roger W. O'Neil, and three pharmacist's mates to *San Francisco* to help tend her scores of wounded.

Although the task group zigzagged, *Juneau*'s damage limited speed to about 18 knots. At 1100, from a submerged position in *Sterett*'s sector, *I-26* fired a spread of torpedoes at *San Francisco*. These missed their intended target ahead and streaked toward *Juneau*, then 1,500 yards on *San Francisco*'s starboard hand. There was no means for *San Francisco* to rapidly pass a warning, and little likelihood that in any event *Juneau* could have reacted in time. At 1103 one of the torpedoes struck *Juneau*, very near where she had been hit the night before. Lieutenant Commander McCandless described what happened:

> The *Juneau* didn't sink—she blew up with all the fury of an erupting volcano. There was a terrific thunderclap and a plume of white water that was blotted out by a huge brown hemisphere a thousand yards across, from within which came the sounds of more explosions. . . . When the dark cloud lifted from the water a minute or so later, we could see nothing of this fine 6,000-ton cruiser or the 700 men she carried.

A dreadful dilemma now confronted Hoover. Captain Lyman K. Swenson of *Juneau* was one of Hoover's closest friends, and tradition as well as humanity dictated an effort to rescue survivors. But it seemed unlikely there could be more than a handful of these under the fast-disappearing smoky marker that was the only headstone *Juneau* would ever know. *San Francisco* was too damaged and *Helena* at this critical passage was too valuable to imperil in a rescue attempt. Leaving one or both of the destroyers to pick up men from the sea would only endanger more ships and more crews. Hoover did not stop. To a passing B-17 he flashed a signal light requesting that a report of *Juneau*'s loss and the position be radioed. No attempt was made to leave spare rafts or boats.

The B-17 crew delivered the message to the operations section of the Cactus Air Force at Henderson Field, but somehow the information passed no further. Halsey learned of *Juneau*'s fate only the next day when Hoover's unit reached Espíritu Santo. Admirals Turner, Fitch, and Calhoun grilled Hoover and recommended his immediate relief. Although Hoover had performed admirably in two night battles, Halsey acted on the recommendation. In his official report Halsey found Hoover's conduct deficient on the following counts: an immediate report of the sinking should have been made, since his position was obviously known to the enemy submarine; offensive action against the submarine should have been instituted "together with, or closely followed by, rescue operations"; and compounding these failures there was the lack of any follow-up to ensure that information reached senior officers on *Juneau*'s loss so they could mount their own rescue operations. Several years later, with the perspective of hindsight, Halsey publicly stated that it had been an injustice to summarily relieve Hoover given the wrenching circumstances and Hoover's severely fatigued state. Ten days passed before a final accounting could be made of *Juneau*'s crew.

What no one who witnessed the sinking could have believed was that in a swirl of oil, 6 inches thick where *Juneau* went down, were approximately 100 to 120 men. Perhaps half had severe wounds such as absent limbs or crushing internal injuries and would not have survived in any event. Among the bobbing, oil-smeared faces was that of George Sullivan. He called for his brothers—Francis, Joseph, Madison, and Albert—but they were gone with the *Juneau*. Under the direction of the senior officer, a lieutenant, the survivors collected and tied together three rafts and seven life nets. They moved the wounded to the nets; the more fit gathered on the life rafts. With San Cristóbal visible in the distance, the able-bodied began rowing the tiny flotilla in that direction. They gained little distance, but the activity helped sustain morale. Despite their shattering experience, the survivors clung to faith in rescue in a day or so. But even after ships and planes belatedly converged to look for survivors, an erroneous position report diverted them to the wrong stretch of water.

The scenes on these rafts over the next several days were as horrific as any in the war. They are recorded here because they reflect a danger all seamen and aviators faced during the campaign, and the stories of many others who found themselves adrift perished with them. None of the trappings of civilization cushioned the survivors from the elements. With the day the sun braised exposed skin until it looked as though it had been scraped with a razor. At night the chill forced oil-soaked men to huddle together for a little warmth. Always there was the sea: it literally rubbed salt into burns and wounds, it washed away improperly secured food and water, and it swallowed men who drifted away from the rafts and nets. Moreover, the enfeebled hands of thirsty men dropped water flasks when they tried to drink, so the contents became brackish. After the third day there was no food at all, and water only when it rained.

Under this onslaught of nature, men already in many cases physically or psychologically weakened by the sinking of their ship drifted into delirium or simply gave up and died. In this fashion most men expired, but not all, for the flotilla soon attracted an escort of sharks. These chose most of their victims from men who attempted to swim toward shore or who drifted far away from the rafts. But as the sharks became emboldened, it also became dangerous near the rafts. This was demonstrated when one attacked a man as he moved from the rafts to the nets in the water. The shark gouged out his shoulder structure, including the blade, so that the arm hung by only a few strips of flesh. Somehow he pulled himself up into a net, and what happened next is told in the words of Signalman Lester Zook:

> He looked at his shipmates there and realized that he was making them nauseated, that he was driving them crazy by just being there, and the sharks were getting around close in the water because of his blood being around there and, knowingly, he pushed himself off the life nets and swam out about five or six feet and let the sharks have him rather than lay there and die like a coward and jeopardize the live[s] of his shipmates. . . .

The ultimate survivors became separated into four contingents. The senior officer permitted two seamen volunteers to take a badly wounded officer in a raft dropped by a plane on the second day and make for San Cristóbal. Fate was kind to them, for this first group of three found salvation after a seven-day voyage to the island.

The second group initially numbered twelve, including George Sullivan and Seaman Allen C. Heyn. They separated from the rest on a raft on the fourth day, but their ranks thinned rapidly. On the fifth night George Sullivan died. Finally, there remained only Heyn, who was drifting through periods of delirium, and one other man. During one interval of consciousness, Heyn realized he was grasping the upper body of his sole living comrade as a shark repeatedly attacked the man's legs and killed him. On the ninth day *Ballard* picked up Heyn.

The third and fourth contingents originally totaled twenty-seven. On the fifth day, the eight strongest men took one raft and made a last desperate attempt to reach San Cristóbal. Two of the eight men in the separate raft expired over the next two days. The senior surviving officer was with this group, but he finally cracked under the severe strain and tried to swim off, only to be killed by several sharks. Four hours later the last five men on this raft were rescued. Of the nineteen men they left on the remaining rafts, only one survived to be rescued on the tenth day in the sea.

Adding the ten men who eventually survived the ordeal in the water to Lieutenant O'Neil and the three pharmacist's mates who were transferred off the ship a few hours before she was torpedoed brings to fourteen the total number of survivors of the men who were on *Juneau* on November 13, 1942. The loss of 683 men on *Juneau* nearly doubled the number of American dead during or in the aftermath of this battle. The next-highest total was 170 (of 735) on *Atlanta* followed by 165 (of around 275) on *Barton* and 145 *Monssen* bluejackets. Other losses included eighty-six dead on *San Francisco,* seventy-two on *Cushing,* fifty-seven on *Laffey,* twenty-nine on *Sterett,* sixteen on *Portland,* fifteen on *Aaron Ward,* and one man on *Helena.* The grand total of slain American seamen came to at least 1,439, including the five Sullivan brothers and two admirals.[7]

Vandegrift signaled that "the men of Cactus lift their battered helmets in deepest admiration" to Callaghan, Scott, and their crews, and all post-battle analysis extolled the abundance of courage and perseverance on the part of all of Callaghan's officers and men. But even after acknowledging that Callaghan's unit was very much an ad hoc arrangement with no time for formal training, the professional dissection of the action turned up a depressingly long list of sins. If Callaghan had even a rudimentary battle plan, he shared it with no one who survived. In the acerbic words of Admiral William S. Pye,

[7]It must be noted that the Sullivan brothers had insisted on serving together despite urgings to the contrary from their superiors. The failure of Navy officers to absolutely order the dispersion of the Sullivans reflects the fact that no one imagined a ship as large as *Juneau* could suffer such a casualty rate. In fact, no other U.S. Navy vessel of cruiser size or larger sustained such losses in the war.

at the Naval War College: "Orders . . . such as 'Give them Hell,' [and] 'We want the big ones,' make better newspaper headlines than they do battle plans." As noted earlier, none of the principal commanders were on the ships with the best radar equipment, nor were the ships so equipped advantageously placed in the column. The utility of the formation selected was questioned, once again with the implication that a more open formation was desirable, but no one seems to have grasped the painful truth about the lack of doctrine, training, or equipment that would make the loose arrangements favored by the Japanese a practical possibility. The overreliance on the single-circuit TBS radio to try to share information and control the formation was criticized without direct comment on the serious breakdown in radio discipline after *Helena* made her initial contact report. It was also recognized that Callaghan had gained surprise but then squandered it in the six-minute delay between the sighting of *Yudachi* and the firing of the first shots—by the Japanese.

These contemporary assessments implied or directly stated that with better tactics, Callaghan could have achieved the same or better results and with fewer casualties. Maybe. With the benefit of distant hindsight it must also be recorded that given deficiencies in American weaponry, it is also possible that had Callaghan fought a more conventional battle, he might have failed to stop Abe and suffered just as heavily.

Against the American losses of four destroyers and *Atlanta* directly as a result of the battle and *Juneau* indirectly, the Japanese counted the loss of only two destroyers in the night action and *Hiei* as a result of the encounter. One Japanese report lists losses in the action of 255 missing (presumably the crew of *Akatsuki*) and 297 dead for a total of 552. It is not clear, but doubtful, that this figure includes all the losses in Destroyer Squadron 10 (forty-three on *Amatsukaze* alone, for instance), and totals as high as 450 dead on *Hiei* have been reported by officers in her complement or on *Kirishima*.

The contemporary Japanese assessments of this action highlighted the fact that Abe had been surprised and that the battle degenerated largely into struggles between individual ships. After Abe gathered the reports from his captains, he listed his accomplishments as including the sinking of five American heavy cruisers, two *Atlanta* Class light cruisers, and three destroyers plus the infliction of damage on two cruisers, six destroyers, and one motor torpedo boat. Abe was more nearly accurate in surmising that he had destroyed or damaged the entire enemy unit. Unfortunately, Abe was either ill-informed or less than candid when admitting damage to his unit. Besides the loss of *Hiei, Akatsuki* and *Yudachi,* he described *Ikazuchi* and *Amatsukaze* as suffering "slight damage," but *Amatsukaze*'s skipper declared her a "floating wreck," and the absence of *Ikazuchi* from the next stage of the battle suggests her damage was also more serious than Abe knew or reported.

The battle report of Destroyer Squadron 4 pointed out that because of their experience on the reinforcement runs, the destroyer captains were familiar with the confined waters and hence able to maneuver boldly despite the absence of a battle plan. A glowing commendation was awarded to *Yudachi*'s skipper and crew for their conduct in the action, with some forgivable overstatement of the impact of her penetration of the American line already disjointed by the maneuvers just before the battle began.

Despite the favorable material balance in the nocturnal set-to, no commendations came to Abe. Instead, he and Captain Nishida were summarily retired from the Imperial Navy.

This action stands without peer for furious, close-range, and confused fighting during the war. But the result was not decisive. The self-sacrifice of Callaghan and his task force had purchased one night's respite for Henderson Field. It had postponed, not stopped, the landing of major Japanese reinforcements, nor had the greater portion of the Combined Fleet yet been heard from.

18

THE NAVAL BATTLE

OF GUADALCANAL

PART II: CONVOY AND CAPITAL SHIP ACTIONS

"Fork in the Road"

SHELLS, THEN BOMBS AND TORPEDOES

In the early-morning hours of November 13, Halsey and Yamamoto discerned that Callaghan had deflected, if not defeated, Abe. Both admirals moved swiftly to improvise new plans. Yamamoto reset Z-Day to the 14th, causing Mikawa to order the convoy to return to Shortland. To Admiral Kondo the Combined Fleet commander issued a new set of instructions: take *Kirishima,* sweep the area off Lunga, and shell Henderson Field on the night of the 14th. Most of the vessels from Abe's unit not engaged in succoring *Hiei* or too damaged for further participation joined *Kirishima* and rendez-voused with Kondo at 2210 on November 13. By then, Kondo had formulated his plan. He would take the two heavy cruisers of Cruiser Division 4 (*Atago* and *Takao*) and *Kirishima* with suitable escorts back to Iron Bottom Sound to sweep and shell. The remainder of the Advanced Force, including *Junyo,* would hold station north of Guadalcanal, cover Kondo on his retirement, and be prepared to accept an enemy offer of a major sea fight. Yamamoto did not enjoin Kondo to include the formidable batteries of battleships *Kongo* and *Haruna* on his mission, and of their capabilities Kondo saw fit only to tap their oil bunkers to resupply other fuel-critical vessels.

Halsey was not troubled with a choice of which ships to employ to stop Japanese efforts to bombard and reinforce. By day, partly restored *Enterprise* could contribute her seventy-eight-plane air group, but with Callaghan's remnants in no state to fight, only Admiral Lee's battleships *Washington* and *South Dakota* could shield the Cactus Air Force by night. Consequently, at 1110, Halsey ordered Kinkaid to form a separate task force composed of Lee's two battleships and four destroyers. The real quandary facing Halsey was whether or not to commit Lee. Members of his staff argued cogently that it would court disaster to employ these fast capital ships in the constricted waters off Savo, where the cramped maneuvering room would negate their virtues of maneuverability and long-range fire-power and make them ripe targets for the torpedoes of an enemy talented in night fighting. Halsey recognized the logic of this, the Holy Writ of the Naval War College, but typically, he based his decision upon more visceral reasoning. As he saw it, wars are won by fighting, and for the Navy to do nothing to stop the Japanese now would "riddle" American morale on Guadalcanal.

At 1652, Halsey ordered Lee to take his unit, now designated Task Force 64, to Iron Bottom Sound to block Japanese efforts to bombard Henderson Field. This directive, however, found Task Force 16 still over 360 miles south of Savo Island, partly because of delays imposed by air operations and submarine scares, but largely because of previous instructions from Halsey to keep Task Force 16 in southerly latitudes. Kinkaid detached a destroyer to radio the chagrined South Pacific commander that Lee could not possibly reach Savo Island before 0800 the next morning.

This fumbling by Halsey and his staff at Noumea left the field clear for Mikawa to conduct a cruiser bombardment of Henderson Field in accordance with the original Japanese plan. To this end, Mikawa sortied his 8th Fleet from its anchorages at 0630 on November 13. But even before these units got underway they suffered their first casualty when one of MacArthur's planes scored a hit on destroyer *Michishio* that left her unable to sail. *Chokai,* with Mikawa's flag at the truck, served as guide for the Main Body, which also included *Kinugasa,* light cruiser *Isuzu,* and destroyer *Arashio.* Admiral Nishimura commanded the Support Force, composed of heavy cruisers *Suzuya* and *Maya,* light cruiser *Tenryu,* and destroyers *Yugumo, Makikumo,* and *Kazegumo.*

November 14 was only ten minutes old when Nishimura's Support

Force and *Arashio* separated from Mikawa northwest of Savo and steamed in to conduct a bombardment. At 0130, float planes dropped flares and the two heavy cruisers began a thirty-one-minute gunfire exercise, during which they dispensed 989 8-inch projectiles. Nishimura observed fires and some chain explosions, but he correctly reckoned the airfield still usable. In fact, he missed Henderson Field entirely and only splattered the area around Fighter One, destroying two Wildcats and one SBD while shrapnel scarred another fifteen Wildcats. Two PT boats from Tulagi contested, but did not impede, his evolutions.

Mikawa and Nishimura rendezvoused at 0750 on November 14 south of New Georgia, but they did not get away unscathed. Wrathful American aviators rose in five SBDs of VMSB-132 led by Major Joseph Sailor and three TBFs each from VT-10 and VMSB-131. Stacked above the attack planes were eight Wildcats. They found Mikawa about 0830 and returned with precise and vivid descriptions of bomb and torpedo hits that Japanese records fail to confirm. But this was only the first inning for American fliers this day.

During the night, *Enterprise* and her consorts stood northwest at high speed and at dawn lay about 200 miles south-southwest of Guadalcanal. Heavy rainsqualls kept search planes on the deck until 0608, when two SBDs headed northwest along 200-mile scouting sectors between 285 and 315 degrees. Four other pairs followed them, covering a swath on the compass through 015 degrees to 250 miles. One hour after the first launch, one SBD pilot reported ten unidentified planes about 140 miles out approaching *Enterprise.* This information was erroneous, but it caused Kinkaid to immediately launch a strike of seventeen SBDs armed with 1,000-pound bombs and ten Wildcats. Lieutenant Commander James Lee pointed this group north, anticipating that the search planes would soon flush suitable targets.

Two *Enterprise* scouts, Lieutenant (jg) Robert D. Gibson and Ensign R. M. Buchanan of VB-10, found Mikawa's cruisers and destroyers south of New Georgia at 0815. Gibson credited the Japanese with two battleships, two heavy cruisers, one possible "small carrier," and four destroyers. After shadowing Mikawa for nearly an hour and a half, sending a stream of reports, Gibson ended his vigil with a dive-bombing attack at about 0930. His bomb whistled down to strike *Kinugasa* in front of the bridge and bored deep into her vitals. Its explosion killed Captain Sawa and the executive officer and opened plating that gave this doughty veteran a 10-degree port list. *Kinugasa*'s crew eliminated a fire on the bow in thirty minutes.

A second set of *Enterprise* search planes also found Mikawa. Ensign R. A. Hoogerwerf claimed a near-miss on a heavy cruiser. His wingman, Ensign P. M. Halloran, missed *Maya* with a bomb, but *Maya*'s antiaircraft guns did not miss Halloran's SBD. Halloran clipped *Maya*'s mainmast and crashed into her port side amidships—whether intentionally or not we do not know—igniting about twenty rounds of 4.7-inch shells. *Maya*'s port secondary guns and searchlights were wrecked and thirty-seven of her crew died, but the fire was extinguished.

Based on Gibson's report, Lee's already airborne attack group changed course at 0840 and caught Mikawa about 30 miles west of Rendova Island. Between 1045 and 1100, the seventeen SBDs peeled off into dives that scored misses close aboard *Chokai* and *Isuzu.* Both ships lost two boiler rooms and *Isuzu* her steering control for a time. *Chokai* crewmen contained a fire. Other Dauntlesses secured unusually damaging near-misses that knocked out *Kinugasa*'s engineering plant and rudder and opened more compartments to the sea. Uncontrollable flooding capsized her at 1122 with 511 of her complement. *Makikumo* and *Kazegumo* recovered 146 survivors and then followed the rest of the 8th Fleet to Shortland.

Tanaka's twenty-three-ship troop convoy sallied a second time from Shortland at 1730 on November 13. He and his crews inaugurated the morning of November 14 in high spirits because, recalled Commander Tadashi Yamamoto of *Hayashio,* they "thought that the bombardment groups had succeeded in destroying [the American] planes the night before." As the convoy drew east of New Georgia, radiomen at the Combined Fleet Headquarters picked up plain-language contact reports from American planes. But while dive-bombers mauled Mikawa's men-of-war, at first they barely irked Tanaka. At 0849, Lieutenant (jg) M. D. Carmody and Lieutenant (jg) W. E. Johnson from *Enterprise* found Tanaka's impressive collection of shipping in the Slot. At 0908 they each attacked a transport. Like an earlier trio of SBDs, they missed, and defending fighters shot down Johnson. Lookouts then sighted Lieutenant Commander Lee's group in the distance and the escorting destroyers made smoke, but no major attack developed—yet.

The convoy's good fortune ended emphatically at 1250 when the silvery specks of an attack group moved up the bright-blue fabric of the sky from the southeast: eighteen SBDs headed up by Majors Sailor and Robert Richard and seven TBFs of VT-10 under Lieutenant Coffin. The American pilots inspected three groups of transports and selected one for chastisement. Claims ran to twelve bomb hits divided among three transports; the torpedo planes reported they put two "fish" into one ship and one into another. Japanese records show torpedoes fatally gored *Nagara Maru* and bombs maimed *Sado Maru* and mortally wounded *Canberra Maru. Amagiri* and *Mochizuki* pulled off crews and passengers from *Canberra Maru* and *Nagara Maru* and escorted the damaged *Sado Maru* back to the Shortlands. *Sado Maru*'s most important passenger, General Tanabe, transferred to a destroyer.

The third major strike from Guadalcanal on November 14 departed in several echelons. Lieutenant Commander Lee began his second sortie of the day about 1335 with one other *Enterprise* SBD and seven marines of VMSB-141. They were followed by Lieutenant Richey of VS-10 and three more Marine SBDs of VMSB-141. These contingents found the convoy around 1430 and started a fire on *Brisbane Maru* that burned until she sank. A few minutes after Lee and Richey took off, Lieutenant William I. Martin of VS-10 lifted off with eight more SBDs, which first went hunting for Lieutenant Gibson's mythical "small carrier" before dumping more destruction on the convoy, claiming four hits. After Martin, Ensign Charles Irvine of VS-10 struck a daring note with a solo attack.

Almost as soon as Lee, Richey, Martin, and company completed their runs, the first of two flights of B-17s from Colonel Saunders's 11th Bomb Group droned into sight. The lead flight of seven B-17s divided to attack two ships around 1500, but enjoyed no success. About fifteen minutes later, the second flight of eight Fortresses muscled aside an estimated fifteen Zeros (claiming six) to tumble bombs over the convoy. To Tanaka, one of the indelible images of this day was the sight of all those bombs "wobbling down from high-flying B-17s."

The next major attack originated from *Enterprise*. At 1305, twelve Wildcats buzzed up from her flight deck, followed by the last eight SBDs, armed with 1,000-pound bombs and instructions to put one into every undamaged ship. Having retained only eighteen Wildcats to protect the last operational American carrier in the Pacific, Kinkaid put *Enterprise* on a southerly retirement course. Over the convoy at 1530, Lieutenant Commander James Flatley, the strike group leader, apportioned targets to the SBDs. These skilled pilots crippled *Shinano Maru* and *Arizona Maru,* which shortly afterward were abandoned; *Naganami* and *Makinami* wrested survivors from their hulks. The *Enterprise* fliers then set course for Guadalcanal.

All day long the American airfield complex bustled with fevered activities. Returning pilots taxied with abandon to dispersals, where their planes halted with squealing brakes in gusts of dust. Grunting ground crews mated bombs to empty shackles while fume-enshrouded comrades replenished gasoline and oil. Staff officers huddled with aircrews from three services to absorb the latest intelligence on the convoy's progress and contrive new efforts for its destruction. Bomber pilots found their wingman for the next flight was frequently from a different squadron and, often as not, a different service. News of the size of the convoy and its obvious implications charged the atmosphere at every American position.

The last three strikes of the day by the Cactus Air Force took off and attacked serially. Major Sailor ramrodded five SBDs with three of Lieutenant Coffin's bomb-packing TBFs. They were closely followed by a mixed group of four Navy and Marine SBDs, which in turn were trailed by seven more *Enterprise* SBDs, all from VB-10. Seven VMF-121 Wildcats provided cover, one of them flown by Lieutenant Colonel Bauer, the fighter commander of the Cactus Air Force. These groups successively struck the remaining transports during the period between about 1610 and 1730.

The first attackers had the satisfaction of seeing *Nako Maru* take the plunge, but then the convoy's air cover achieved its only important successes. The 11th Air Fleet managed only thirty-six Zero sorties in defense of the convoy during the entire day. They were supplemented by fourteen of the nimble but underpowered Petes from the R Area Air Force. A cluster of the Zeros found Lieutenant Commander John Thomas's flight of seven VB-10 SBDs without escort and carved it up, shooting down three of the Dauntlesses and impelling two others to turn back because of damage. Thomas and one other pilot pressed on to make attacks. This display was proximate to another air battle at low altitude just above the sprawled survivors of the convoy between three Wildcats bent on strafing and two Zeros. Lieutenant Colonel Bauer destroyed one Zero but was himself shot down. Captain Joseph Foss saw his inspiring leader alive in the water, but Bauer was never seen again. More fortunate was Ensign Jefferson Carroum, pilot of one of the three lost *Enterprise* SBDs. He survived a seventy-three-hour swim and was picked up on November 26. American aircraft losses for November 14 came to five SBDs, all from *Enterprise,* and two Marine Wildcats. Thirteen of the forty-five Zeros sent to defend the convoy failed to regain their base; nine of them fell in combat.

Only darkness ended this day of torment for the convoy. For seven hours, Tanaka's lithe escorts attempted to fend off the chain of air attacks by maneuvering at high speed, staining the sky with antiaircraft fire, and cloaking their charges with smoke screens. In the face of each attack the transports waddled at their best speed and turned individually, shattering all semblance of order. Spray crested columns of water raised by bombs, and fires and smoke foreshortened the borders of visibility during the attacks. But transport after transport was hit, lurching to a halt as fires skittered across decks loaded with ammunition. From his flagship, Tanaka detailed one after another of his destroyers to collect men thronging from sagging decks into a calm sea.

Of the twenty-three ships Tanaka led from Shortland the day before, by sundown of November 14 only nine were near flagship *Hayashio*. Six of the transports were sunk or abandoned, and *Sado Maru* was returning to Shortland with *Amagiri* and *Mochizuki*, bearing between them 1,562 survivors. *Naganami, Makinami, Kawakaze,* and *Suzukaze* were back in the darkness gathering the last of another 3,240 survivors; losses totaled only 450 men, a figure no American flier would have believed. In addition to witnessing the slaughter of his convoy, Tanaka also learned of the approach of an enemy task force. "Prospects looked poor for the operation," laconically commented the worn admiral, who was positive he could not reach Guadalcanal before dawn the next day but uncertain where Mikawa and Kondo had stationed themselves. Tanaka was weighing whether to proceed or retire "to await a more favorable opportunity" when at 1741 the Combined Fleet ordered him to steer for Guadalcanal. By 1815 the admiral re-formed the last four transports with *Hayashio* and five other destroyers immediately at hand. The other four destroyers rejoined one by one upon completing rescue work, but they were so cluttered with survivors that none of them could fight.

During the day, Japanese search planes discovered Lee's six vessels steaming toward Guadalcanal but proved no more adept at ship identification than their American counterparts. At 1455, the first pilot sighted Lee about 100 miles south of Guadalcanal. He correctly classified two-thirds of the unit as destroyers, but he demoted *Washington* and *South Dakota* to "cruisers." Although other aircrews that viewed Lee declared they found battleships accompanied by cruisers (and even carriers), the belief that the Americans numbered two cruisers and four destroyers proved highly contagious. A shadower radioed at 1825 that Lee appeared headed for the convoy, which roused the Combined Fleet to issue a superfluous caution to

Tanaka, who was already maneuvering to assure that he placed Kondo between the convoy and this new threat.

Since 0530, Kondo had been steaming south, initially at reduced speed while refueling. By early afternoon, his strength reached one battleship, two heavy and two light cruisers, and nine destroyers. Six of these ships were veterans of the battle on the 13th. At 1629, *Atago* barely avoided torpedoes fired by submarine *Flying Fish,* and the crew of *Asagumo* received an unwanted thrill when one of these weapons passed under her keel. The ever-alert 4th Fleet radio units monitored *Flying Fish*'s plain-language report of her encounter and notified Kondo.

During the day, Kondo signaled his tactical arrangements and intentions to his subordinates. He would directly command a Bombardment Unit of *Atago* (flag), *Takao,* and *Kirishima.* A Screening Unit under Rear Admiral Kimura with light cruiser *Nagara* and six destroyers would guard the Bombardment Unit. Kondo designated Rear Admiral Hashimoto as commander of the Sweeping Unit. With light cruiser *Sendai* and three destroyers, Hashimoto would take station 9 miles ahead of Kondo and Kimura and comb the waters on both sides of Savo for enemy vessels. Based upon information from search planes, at 1735 Kondo informed his command to expect a clash with "a few" cruisers and destroyers. He stressed that each captain should deal flexibly with any situation that developed, unfettered by any preconceived ideas. At 1900, Kondo affirmed to Tanaka his intentions of clearing a path for the convoy by eliminating any seaborne opposition off Lunga and blasting the airfield. Tanaka was to follow and move the convoy smartly into the anchorage.

Ironically, although Kondo explicitly warned his captains not to harbor presuppositions about the coming battle, Kondo further cultivated one of his own at 2045 when another Japanese plane reported two "cruisers" and four destroyers headed north at 25 knots, 16 miles west-southwest of Cape Esperance. At 2130 an R Area Air Force plane added a dash of complexity to the picture when it announced that a unit of two cruisers and four destroyers, identity unknown, was 50 miles *west* of *Atago.* This was either a phantom or the convoy, but Kondo mentally adjusted his estimate of the situation to allow for the possibility that the Americans might be in two groups after all.

As his ships worked north during the day of November 14, Rear Admiral Willis A. Lee worked on the problem in front of him. Intelligence from search planes and *Flying Fish*'s report led him to expect to meet a bombardment group and a convoy and its covering units. Total enemy strength might be as high as three battleships, eight to ten cruisers, a dozen or more destroyers, and nine transports. Halsey had given him complete freedom of action once Guadalcanal was reached, and Lee determined to take an "excursion" east of Savo, both to assure an early interception and to contrive to confront first any bombardment group and then any convoy covering group. Lee had no opportunity to issue his captains a formal order, so he blinkered his general intentions.

No less troublesome to Lee were the intangible problems accruing from the hasty assembly of his task group. The battleships had never operated together before departing from Noumea on November 11. Their quartet of escorts originated from four different divisions and were attached to Lee solely because they happened to have the most fuel. Their entire experience of maneuvering with each other, and with Lee, consisted of the thirty-hour high-speed run to Guadalcanal. Given the heterogeneous nature of his command, Lee placed it in single column in the order *Walke, Benham, Preston, Gwin, Washington* (flag), and *South Dakota.* However, he ordered a healthy interval of 5,000 yards between the four destroyers and the battleship pair. Lee was gifted with a cool incisive mind and one enormous asset that neither Scott nor Callaghan had possessed: a flagship with SG radar and full appreciation of its valuable capabilities.

The following is a review of the composition of forces:

---

1. JAPANESE
Advanced Force
Vice Adm. Nobutake Kondo

Main Body, Bombardment Unit
Adm. Kondo

BATTLESHIP:

   Kirishima   Capt. Sanji Iwabuchi

HEAVY CRUISERS:

   Cruiser Division 4: *Atago, Takao*
          Screen
          Rear Adm. Susumu Kimura
          (ComDesron 10)

LIGHT CRUISER:

   Nagara

DESTROYERS:

Desdiv 11	Desdiv 61 (-)	Unattached
Shirayuki	Teruzuki	Samidare
Hatsuyuki		Inazuma

Desdiv 9(-)

Asagumo (embarking Rear Adm. Tamotsu Takama, ComDesron 4)

Sweeping Unit
Rear Admiral Shintaro Hashimoto
(ComDesron 3)

LIGHT CRUISER:

Sendai

DESTROYERS:

Desdiv 19: Uranami, Shikinami, Ayanami

Reinforcement Unit
Rear Adm. Raizo Tanaka
(ComDesron 2)
in **Hayashio**

TRANSPORTS:

Kinugasa, Hirokawa, Yamura, Sangetsu Marus

DESTROYERS:

Desdiv 15	Desdiv 31	Desdiv 24
Oyashio	Takanami	Suzukaze
Kuroshio	Naganami	Kawakaze
Kagero	Makinami	Umikaze

---

2. AMERICAN
Task Force 64
Rear Adm. Willis A. Lee

BATTLESHIPS:

Washington	Capt. Glenn B. Davis
South Dakota	Capt. Thomas L. Gatch

Screen

DESTROYERS:

Walke	Cdr. Thomas E. Fraser
Benham	Lt. Cdr. John B. Taylor
Preston	Cdr. Max C. Stormes
Gwin	Lt. Cdr. John B. Fellows Jr.

The following table provides the measure of relative combat power between Lee's two battleships and four destroyers, and Kondo's battleship, four cruisers, and nine destroyers:

	Guns								Torpedo Tubes	
	16"	14"	8"	6"	5.5"	5"	3.9"	3"	21"	24"
American:	18	—	—	—	—	54	—	—	46	—
Japanese:	—	8	20	16	14	71	8	4	—	90

The impending battle makes for an interesting and symbolic match-up, for each commander brought a strong preponderance in his navy's favored weapon. Lee had fewer guns, but immensely more gunnery power. Either American capital ship completely outclassed *Kirishima,* both offensively and defensively. Her broadside weighed less than half that of either *Washington* or *South Dakota* (11,920 pounds versus 24,300 pounds), and there was not a square inch of *Kirishima*—much less of any of the other Japanese vessels present— that was proof against American 16-inch guns, while the vitals of Lee's battleships were immune to 14-inch and lesser shot. But on the other hand, darkness and confined waters yielded optimal conditions for the employment of the abundant Japanese torpedo batteries. Neither *Washington* nor *South Dakota* could shrug off multiple hits by Long Lances, of which Kondo brought ninety, with reloads for all tubes except probably those of *Nagara, Asagumo, Teruzuki,* and *Inazuma.*

THE ENCOUNTERS EAST AND SOUTH OF SAVO: 2200–2357

American sailors noted the dull glow of fires on the western horizon from some of Tanaka's burning transports as Lee took his ships past Cape Esperance to a point about 21 miles northwest of Savo. There at 2110 American prows swung successively to point due east. When the column reached a point 12 miles due north of Savo at 2148, Lee turned them on course 150 degrees, southeast by south. Speed was 17 knots. Ranks of low cirrus clouds marshaled over Iron Bottom Sound, shadowing patches on the calm pane of the sea, and occasional squalls stalked the fringes of the battle area. A heavy scent of vegetation overcame the salty 7-knot sea breeze, reinforcing the claustrophobic feelings engendered in all hands topside by the visible proximity of land in all directions.

Understandably anxious for more knowledge of the tactical situation, Lee requested any late intelligence from Radio Guadalcanal. Not having been assigned a call sign in the haste of sailing, the admiral styled himself by his last name. This produced a stiff reply: "We do not recognize you." To vouchsafe his bona fides, Lee then employed his Naval Academy nickname, confident his friend Vandegrift would recognize it: "Cactus, this is Lee. Tell your boss 'Ching' Lee is here and wants the latest information." Before this ploy brought response, radiomen on *Washington* overheard one of the three skippers of PT boats from Tulagi slithering along in the waters northeast of Savo: "There go two big ones, but I don't know whose they are!" Lee moved expeditiously to enlighten the locals as to his identity and again called radio Guadalcanal: "Refer your big boss about Ching Lee; Chinese, catchee? Call off your boys!" This generated reassurances from the PT officers that they knew Lee and were not after him. Then Lee heard from the shore station the disappointing but candid news "The boss has no additional information." After this interchange, a dispatch, obviously based upon radio intelligence, warned Lee to expect an escorted convoy to arrive off Savo between 0030 and 0230.

At 2200, as Lee swapped radio banter, Kondo split his fourteen ships into three units. Admiral Kimura prepared for independent operations by placing destroyers *Shirayuki, Hatsuyuki, Samidare,* and *Inazuma* in column behind *Nagara* and peeled away from Kondo. Admiral Hashimoto with *Sendai* and three destroyers began to accelerate away from Kondo and Kimura to carry out his sweeping duties. Almost immediately, incredibly keen-eyed lookouts on *Shikinami* were startled to see the distant silhouettes of hostile ships bearing 200 degrees, just west of south. *Uranami* observers discerned the enemy included "new-type cruisers." Hashimoto decided to take *Sendai, Shikinami,* and *Uranami* clockwise around Savo behind the enemy while detaching *Ayanami* to conduct an independent counterclockwise swing to ensure that the route Kondo intended to use for the Bombardment Unit was uncontaminated by other enemy vessels.

By 2231, flagship *Atago* also beheld the enemy, but she and other ships began vexing Kondo with reports of more ship silhouettes in a westerly direction. At 2300, Kondo received a flurry of reports. An R Area Air Force plane belatedly announced it had witnessed Lee make his turn northeast of Savo almost two hours earlier, and identi-

fied the enemy composition as two destroyers followed by two heavy
cruisers or battleships. Timely dispatches from *Sendai* and *Ayanami*
enumerated the enemy as four destroyers and two "cruisers" bearing
south. From all the information reaching him, Kondo concluded
that the units to the west must be Tanaka's Reinforcement Unit and
those to the south enemy. About this same time, Tanaka saw the
main body of the Advanced Force and began maneuvering to maintain visual contact.

At 2307, *Sendai* signaled that the enemy unit had just changed
course to due west. Up to this point, Kondo had been contemplating
taking the Bombardment Unit through the passage south of Savo.
Now, however, this would produce a head-on encounter with the
American detachment, whose composition Kondo firmly determined was four destroyers and two cruisers. Reassessing his ends and
means, Kondo decided the Japanese light forces would first dispose
of the enemy surface unit and then he would bring down the Bombardment Unit to execute his primary mission. Therefore, he
changed course at 2315 with the Bombardment Unit and destroyers
Teruzuki and *Asagumo* to pass north of Savo, and he instructed

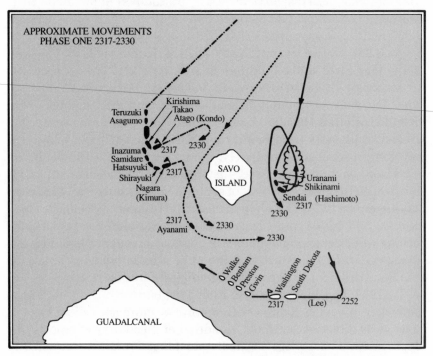

Battleship Action, November 14–15

Hashimoto's Sweeping Unit and Kimura's Screening Unit to follow the enemy around the east side of Savo and engage and sink them. When *Uranami* pinpointed the enemy unit at 2317 as 10 miles southeast of Savo, on course due west at 18 knots, Kondo redirected Kimura to round the west side of Savo.

The American change of course to west actually began at 2252. Shortly after *Washington* swung through the knuckle of water where the destroyers had pivoted, her SG radar picked up returns on Hashimoto's trio at a range of about 9 miles. She tracked the Japanese until 2312, when the main battery director acquired them visually. *South Dakota*'s fire controlmen also had the Japanese in sight, but none of the destroyers did. At 2316, Lee granted permission for his captains to "open fire when you are ready." One minute later, with the range 18,500 yards, *Washington* discharged her first main battery salvo at Hashimoto while her 5-inch guns hung star shells over the enemy. *South Dakota* gunners had their 16-inch rifles laid on the Japanese column and commenced fire less than one minute after the flagship. Spotters on both battleships reported hits. *Washington* radar operators believed one of the "pips" began to flicker as if sinking, while *South Dakota* radiomen heard excited Japanese voices chattering on thirteen stations. Hashimoto's ships were actually unscathed. To keep them that way while awaiting a more favorable moment to attack, the admiral had them lay smoke and wheel around on a northerly heading to open the range. Hashimoto was so wedded to the notion that the largest enemy ships present were cruisers that he evidently convinced himself that the huge columns of water spouting about his ships were created by guns no larger than half their actual caliber.

When the battleships opened fire, Lee's van destroyers were over 2 miles ahead of *Washington* and had just come right to course 300 degrees, approaching a point due south of Savo. None of the four American destroyers mounted an SG radar, and only *Walke* possessed an operational FD fire control radar. This device scented a ship off the *Walke*'s starboard beam on a reciprocal course against the loom of Savo. At 2322, just as the battleships checked fire, the guns of the leading American destroyer began cracking at this new enemy. *Walke*'s target was plucky *Ayanami,* angling in under Savo and preparing to take on the entire American column. *Benham* joined her leader in firing at *Ayanami,* but commendably alert *Preston* lookouts spied Kimura's *Nagara* and her consorts fine off the starboard bow rounding the southwest corner of Savo. *Preston*'s guns sounded the alarm over this new threat about 2327. *Walke* shifted fire to Kimura, as did *Gwin,* which had been attempting to aid the two battleships by firing illumination.

Kimura identified his opponents as three destroyers and a "cruiser." *Nagara*'s 5.5-inch guns and the 5-inch guns of *Ayanami* and the other Japanese destroyers replied effectively to the American challenge. Excellent flashless powder and the backdrop of Savo made the Japanese difficult targets, while Lee's destroyers stood exposed in more open waters. As usual, Japanese torpedomen were not slow to intervene. *Ayanami* launched her Long Lances at 2330. Five minutes later, Kimura authorized the firing of torpedoes and commenced a turn to port. The runs were short.

Even before Japanese torpedoes began to boil around the American destroyers, *Preston* was being heavily hit, probably by *Nagara*'s gunners. One shell struck between the two firerooms, killing all hands in both and heaping firebrick and debris over the amidships section. This hit also toppled the second stack over into the searchlight platform, collapsing it onto the starboard torpedo tubes, ripping open a number of torpedo warheads, and igniting their contents. More hits in the engine rooms and around the after gun mounts turned the area aft of the stacks into "a mass of blazing red-hot wreckage." These shells killed almost everyone from the auxiliary conn aft, including the executive officer. The gunnery officer tried to continue to fight the forward guns, but *Preston* jammed them in train as she began settling by the stern and twisting to starboard. Commander Stormes gave the order to abandon ship at 2336. "Less than a half a minute" later, according to her survivors, *Preston* rolled over on her starboard side and then hung with her bow in the air for ten minutes before she plunged forever. Commander Stormes was among the 117 men (45 percent of the crew) who did not survive their ship.

Sailors on *Gwin,* only 300 yards astern, witnessed these devastating hits on *Preston.* Almost simultaneously at 2332, two shells struck *Gwin* in the after engine room. Torrents of superheated steam drove the crews from that compartment and one handling room; the concussion unlatched the torpedo restraining links, allowing all of *Gwin*'s torpedoes to dangle partly out of their tubes and three of these weapons to slide harmlessly into the sea. Another shell ricocheted into her stern, splitting open two depth charges after *Gwin* heeled to starboard around *Preston*—a course which may have saved her from enemy torpedoes. The other two destroyers were not so fortunate.

Walke was reeling from gunfire hits when a Long Lance impacted just forward of her bridge. The sympathetic detonation of *Walke*'s number two magazine vastly magnified the formidable power of the torpedo's large warhead. The blast seemed to lift the whole ship and shove her to port. The bow snapped off, power and communications failed, the main deck was awash with several inches of oil from ruptured fuel tanks, and flames scampered along what was left of *Walke*'s length. With ammunition exploding and the ship settling rapidly, Commander Fraser ordered her abandoned. Four rafts got off, but as she sank, depth charges exploded, killing more men in the water to bring the death toll to eighty, including Fraser. Another Long Lance struck *Benham* at the extreme bow, à la *O'Brien,* with strikingly similar results. The explosion killed no one, but it tore a chunk from the lower bow, thrust a violent quiver through the hull, and sent a huge wave rolling down the main deck that seriously injured seven men and washed one overboard. *Benham* made a loop to escape gunfire and then gamely resumed course at 10 knots.

Kimura slipped away with little, if any, damage. *Ayanami,* however, paid the forfeit for pressing to within less than 2 miles of the American column. When she opened fire, her gun flashes betrayed her to *Washington,* which had been heretofore unable to see her against the bulk of Savo. Under intense fire, *Ayanami*'s engineering plant sustained damage that resulted in a complete loss of power, leaving her aflame and dead in the water.

South Dakota contributed little to this phase of the battle, because of the first of a series of problems of her own making. At 2330 an error in the operation of engine room switchboards left her without electrical power. Instantly all her search radars stopped revolving and the screens went dark. "The psychological effect on the officers and crew was most depressing. The absence of this gear gave all hands a feeling of being blindfolded," acknowledged Captain Gatch's report. But the practical effect was worse. Without her radars, *South Dakota*'s grasp of the extremely complicated tactical situation evaporated. Kondo had achieved the ultimate in Japanese dispersion tactics: his fourteen ships were divided four ways within a square barely 12 miles on each side that they shared with their adversaries and Savo Island. Exacerbating the confusion inherent in Kondo's tactics were the usual spurious sightings throughout Lee's task force of motor torpedo boats, phantom ships, and "shore batteries" on Savo. Moreover, *South Dakota* also had to worry about ships ahead of her in the column, a serious problem with destroyers flaming and falling out of formation. When *South Dakota*'s power surged back through her circuits at 2336, it reinjected confidence into her crew, but her trials were just beginning.

Captain Davis conned *Washington* to place the fiery stricken destroyers to starboard to keep his ship concealed. His bluejackets found time to drop two rafts for swimming *Walke* survivors. At 2338, topside crewmen on *South Dakota* heard shouts from the water and saw flashlights from life jackets as their ship swept by *Preston* sailors. Unfortunately, *South Dakota* changed course to put the sinking vessels to port, which silhouetted her for the enemy. This maneuver also added to Lee's problems by putting her on *Washington*'s starboard quarter in a blind spot in *Washington*'s radar coverage, leaving *South Dakota* only intermittently visible. Further compounding *South Dakota*'s self-generated difficulties, the restoration of power enabled her main battery to lash out again at Hashimoto at 2340. Turret three, firing dead astern, promptly set three planes on the quarterdeck aflame. Luckily, the next salvo literally blew out the flames on one plane and cuffed the other two over the side.

At heavy cost to themselves, the American destroyers performed a classic mission: thwarting attack on the ships they screened. The two survivors, *Benham* and *Gwin,* both were now hobbled and an impediment to high-speed handling of the task force. Accordingly, at 2348 Lee ordered his remaining destroyers to retire.

All during the actions east and south of Savo, Kondo marked time with his Bombardment Unit. As the battle advanced toward Cape Esperance, Kondo reversed course to a southwesterly heading at 30 knots to remain poised between the enemy and the convoy. Then to award more time to Kimura and Hashimoto and to avoid further anarchy, he changed course to the west and reduced speed to 27 knots. During these maneuvers Kondo witnessed Hashimoto making smoke about 2319, and at 2335 the silhouettes were seen of three hostile destroyers and one "cruiser" to the south. Shortly after settling into the westerly heading, lookouts reported ships off the starboard bow. This gave substance to suspicions Kondo harbored from the confusing search plane findings that another enemy unit might be present. At 2339, he ordered the Bombardment Unit to continue to stand west to confront this new threat, but very soon these dark outlines resolved into the convoy.

Just after the Bombardment Unit turned to course due north at 2350, *Takao* proclaimed the enemy composition as one battleship and three destroyers (Lee's order for his destroyers to retire was only two minutes prior, and thus they had not yet cleared the scene). Lookouts on *Atago* chimed in with news that they also saw what "looked like a battleship." Nonetheless, Kondo continued to discount the possibility that he faced capital ships. Instead he surmised from a dispatch from *Ayanami* at 2350 that the battle had evolved so auspiciously that it was time to shell the airfield. At 2354 he changed course to 130 degrees, toward Lunga Point. At this same time, destroyers *Asagumo* and *Teruzuki* sprang from their previous stations astern to take position ahead of the two heavy cruisers and *Kirishima.*

As Kondo swung the Bombardment Unit toward Henderson Field, he also radioed his intentions to his subordinates. Hashimoto detached *Uranami* to stand by ailing *Ayanami,* and with *Sendai* and *Shikinami* shaped a course for Lunga Point. At 2357, *Nagara* signaled that two enemy battleships bore north of Cape Esperance, but Kondo steadfastly refused to believe that American battleships were present.

THE ACTION WEST OF SAVO, 2357–0140

While Kondo dawdled, at 2335 Lee brought *Washington* to course 282 degrees, just north of west. At the same time, *Washington*'s efficient SG radar picked up the Bombardment Unit and began tracking. *South Dakota* steamed in an unintentional line of bearing, about a mile or more off the flagship's starboard quarter, but another material failure deprived *South Dakota* of her electronic eyes for five critical minutes shortly before midnight. When her SG radar came back on it immediately warned of an enemy unit just forward of the starboard beam less than 3 miles away. This was Kondo, whose own lookouts saw *South Dakota* at 2358 fine off the starboard bow and labeled her a heavy cruiser. One minute later the dark contour sharpened and Japanese lookouts shouted that it was a battleship, but—for the last time—Kondo demurred as to the enemy identity.

Lee's battleships were now about 11 miles west of Savo. Just before turning to place the Americans broadside on a reciprocal course, the Bombardment Unit fired torpedoes at *South Dakota* at short range with an ideal target angle. Then at 0000, November 15, *Atago* opened the shutters of searchlights and adjusted their beams onto *South Dakota.* Only now did the unmistakable high upper deck and tower foremast authenticate her identity to Kondo. Other shafts of light converged on *South Dakota,* and down these bright alleys

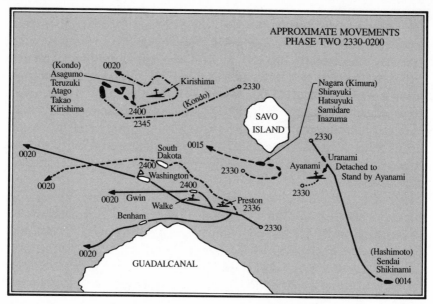

Battleship Action, November 14–15

gunners on all five Japanese ships poured salvo after salvo of shells from 3.9-inch to 14-inch. At 0002, *Asagumo* contributed four more Long Lances to the schools already swimming for *South Dakota.*

Several of *Atago*'s torpedoes exploded prematurely, but observers thought she achieved three to five hits and *Asagumo* two more. In fact, all the Japanese torpedoes missed, but in a span of about four minutes Japanese guns scored twenty-seven hits on *South Dakota.* Armor defeated a 14-inch shell, which caused little damage. The other twenty-six hits centered over *South Dakota*'s superstructure and particularly grouped around her tower foremast. Quite a number perforated her unarmored upperworks without exploding. One of her crewmen recalled how those shells that did detonate produced "a loud crash, a rolling explosion," and then "the sizzling sound that metal fragments make when they crash into cables, guns and the superstructure." While this punishment at no time threatened *South Dakota*'s survival, the cumulative effect of the gunfire damage, in the words of Admiral Lee, was to "render one of our new battleships deaf, dumb, blind and impotent" by knocking out all radios, all but one radar, demolishing radar plot, felling many fire controlmen, and disabling gun directors. *South Dakota*'s main battery got off only four to five salvos for want of data, but the Japanese acknowledged that her four starboard twin 5-inch mounts roared back "very fiercely."

The destruction of *South Dakota* so preoccupied the Bombardment Unit that it completely overlooked the presence of *Washington.* Moreover, the Japanese searchlights conclusively settled the location of both *South Dakota* and her assailants. Now with radar and visual confirmation of the situation, *Washington* apportioned her fire: one pair of twin 5-inch turrets yapped at *Atago,* another 5-inch mount cast out illuminating rounds, and the other starboard pair of 5-inch twins and all nine barrels of the main battery flailed at *Kirishima* at a range of only 8,400 yards. The Japanese battleships was "buried in water columns" and sustained crushing blows from about nine 16-inch shells and perhaps forty or more 5-inch projectiles. These bolts disabled two main battery turrets, ignited internal fires, drilled holes below the waterline, and jammed the rudder. Inrushing water pulled down *Kirishima*'s starboard side, and she began circling to port coughing out dense gouts of smoke.

The repetitive glow of hits and the silence of her main battery convinced the Japanese that they had overwhelmed and sunk *South Dakota.* Beneath powerful illumination from star shells, American projectiles kicked up plumes of water on both sides of flagship *Atago.* She sustained little damage and her sister ship *Takao* none at all, but four minutes of gunfire exchanges persuaded the Japanese to extinguish their searchlights. To open the range, evade gunfire, and come around to a parallel course to again brandish his Long Lances, at 0005 Kondo ordered the Bombardment Unit to put about to port. *Kirishima,* lacking helm control, parted from the Bombardment Unit as she inscribed more staggering loops on the sea. Upon identifying the convoy off the starboard bow, Kondo adjusted the Bombardment Unit to course 270 degrees at about 0009.

When the Japanese abruptly ceased fire there were some twenty-three major fires gnawing toward each other in *South Dakota*'s superstructure. Several converged on Battle II, the alternate conning position, where Commander A. E. Uehlinger, the executive officer, and five other men were stationed. Another shell severed the steam line to the ship's siren, and for a time it looked as if the only question was whether Uehlinger and his shipmates would die first by flames, scalding steam, or suffocating smoke. But they maintained their post as shipmates assaulted the blazes and shut off the steam line. Here as elsewhere the absence or twisted condition of many ladders and the litter of thirty-nine dead or dying and fifty-nine wounded, many of whose life jackets were afire, hindered the fire fighters. Captain Gatch perceived that this damage had transformed his fine ship from an asset to a liability. Therefore at 0010 he decided to retire, "to the great relief of the Task Force commander," wrote Lee.

As the Bombardment Unit came out of its course reversal about 0011, it discerned a battleship about 6 miles away, 15 degrees off the port bow. This was *South Dakota,* dutifully following her flagship northwest. Despite the very unfavorable firing angle, Kondo began to wheel his ships to starboard to launch more torpedoes. Then his lookouts identified a second battleship beyond the first, obviously *Washington.* At 0013, *Atago* and *Takao* each fired eight torpedoes at *Washington* at a range of over 4,000 yards. At the same time Kondo swung the Bombardment Unit to course 300 degrees, to again come broadside with the battleships, and ordered the convoy to turn away. Four minutes after launch, the Japanese thought they hit the trailing battleship. Immediately thereafter they witnessed *South Dakota* haul out of the formation to port and clear the battle area.

Lee commenced this action with six ships. His four destroyers sacrificed themselves foiling Kimura and *Ayanami,* and *South Dakota* inadvertently decoyed the first charge of the Bombardment Unit. Now only Lee's flagship remained, but she was fast, powerful, well protected, and so far undamaged. At 0020, the undaunted admiral ordered her to course 340 degrees to continue the action, noting, "This move by *Washington* appeared to set the whole enemy field in motion to the north and northeast." *Washington*'s lookouts noted flashes off the starboard quarter as Kondo's pursuing cruisers employed their main batteries briefly and *Atago* dispensed three more torpedoes. All of these instruments of destruction missed.

Although stripped of *Kirishima,* Kondo still retained potent torpedo forces. He lacked information, however, as to their whereabouts, so at 0025 he issued a general directive for "all units [to] attack" two enemy battleships 6 miles north of Cape Esperance. Two of the three principal addressees of this message moved to help, though neither could intervene as expeditiously as Kondo would have preferred. Kondo's message put Kimura shortly on a pursuit course, but his Screening Unit both lagged well astern of Kondo and Lee and still struggled to reload torpedo tubes. Tanaka on his own initiative had already detached *Oyashio* and *Kagero* with instructions to attack any American closing on the convoy. He retained his other combat-capable destroyers to provide protection for their four survivor-laden peers and the transports. Kondo's order presumably came as a distinct surprise to its third major recipient, Hashimoto. He was now off Lunga Point, far astern of the westward-moving battle.

Washington's change of heading to 340 degrees put her on a converging course with the Bombardment Unit coming up on her starboard quarter. When Kondo recognized Lee's new heading at 0025, he reduced speed to 24 knots and reiterated his order for all units to engage the enemy as much as possible. At 0028, Kondo believed *Washington* was boring in to reengage, so he increased speed to 30 knots and turned to course 340 degrees—ironically, the same course being steered by Lee. Once again the Japanese thought they saw more torpedo hits—presumably some of those launched by *Atago* at 0020. As the range continued to dwindle, Kondo increased speed to 31 knots and made smoke.

With torpedo reloading completed by 0030, Kimura commenced to pursue *Washington.* Though Kimura remained too distant to present an immediate threat, Lee developed concern at 0033 when he noted *Kagero* and *Oyashio* laying a smoke screen close ahead to starboard. Captain Davis put *Washington* into a sharp starboard swing to avoid the risk of a sudden close-range torpedo attack amid the drifting smoke, and Lee ordered *Washington* to continue the turn to a southerly retirement course. Lee grounded this decision upon the conclusion that the convoy would now be sufficiently delayed to prevent its unloading before daylight and the intervention of the Cactus Air Force.

Upon observing Lee's decampment, Kondo ordered his Bombardment Unit to stop laying smoke. At 0032, Kondo canceled the bombardment. During retirement, Lee held *Washington* well to the west of the tracks of his damaged ships to avoid drawing pursuing Japanese destroyers to them. This precaution was well taken, for *Washington* was now being chased by *Kagero* and *Oyashio* to starboard and all or part of Kimura's contingent from port. As officers on *Kagero* agonized over the identity of *Washington* about 0039, *Oyashio* fired a spread of torpedoes at the galloping American flagship. Six minutes later, *Samidare* uncorked another salvo of Long Lances at the fast-stepping American capital ship from port. Despite the relatively unpromising firing positions of the Japanese destroyers, four or five torpedoes came "uncomfortably close" to *Washington.* Evasive maneuvers took *Washington* alarmingly near Lamon Island, but neither reefs nor warheads touched her hull.

At 0045, Kondo lost sight of Lee and belatedly untethered *Asagumo* and *Teruzuki* from the Bombardment Unit to permit them to join the chase. The Japanese commander now calculated that the coast was literally clear for Tanaka, and that protecting the convoy no longer warranted his presence. Moreover, lingering in these waters would invite attacks from carrier- or land-based planes, and in these circumstances Kondo regarded the preservation of his warships as his most important trust. Therefore, at 0104 Kondo ordered that upon completion of their attacks, all ships should begin a general disengagement to the north. *Atago* and *Takao* formally began their retirement at 0130. The last two Japanese vessels to break contact were *Kagero* and *Nagara,* which had Lee in sight as late as 0140.

When Kondo's explicit order at 0045 for *Kirishima* to retire produced no response, he directed *Asagumo* and *Teruzuki,* and later *Samidare,* to go to her aid. The first two named found *Kirishima* at 0143, 5 miles west of Savo in deep distress. Like her sister ship forty-eight hours earlier, *Kirishima*'s boilers and engines were intact, but seawater sloshed in her steering machinery compartment and the rudder was jammed 10 degrees to starboard. Unlike *Hiei*'s, *Kirishima*'s flooding defied control and her fires refused to be contained. Intense blazes ate toward the magazines, forcing Captain Iwabuchi to order them flooded, but his orders to evacuate the engineering spaces came too late for the men stationed there. With only one screw turning over, speed fell to a crawl. A towline from *Nagara* was declined as *Kirishima*'s soggy hull continued to absorb water. When counterflooding failed to check the increasing heel to starboard, Iwabuchi ordered the crew gathered on the bow, where he supervised the familiar lugubrious rituals. With three banzais the ensign was lowered and the Emperor's portrait transferred to *Asagumo.* Before *Teruzuki* could nudge up alongside it became impossible to stand erect on the upper deck, and at 0325 *Kirishima* rolled over and sank, 11 miles west of Savo. *Asagumo, Teruzuki,* and *Samidare* completed rescue work at 0430 and then headed north.

During this period, another drama played out about 5 miles southeast of Savo. *Uranami* took off most of *Ayanami*'s crew, less about forty killed and missing. Another thirty, including the skipper, stayed with the ship to the last and took a boat to Guadalcanal. The hulk of *Ayanami* sank following two major explosions sometime after 0200.

Happy endings came to two of the damaged American participants, but not *Benham.* Radio contacts about 0215 allayed Lee's fears for the safety of *South Dakota.* At 0900, *South Dakota* rejoined *Washington. Benham* and *Gwin* also exited the battle area separately. *Benham*'s fractured hull amidships creaked and groaned, and her truncated bow cut a wide furrow in the sea. Her crew lightened the ship forward and attempted local repairs of broken framing. At

0300, Lieutenant Commander Taylor evacuated *Benham*'s forward half to reduce the strain on the keel and starboard strakes of plating, which were all that was holding *Benham* together. Taylor described his situation to Lee, who directed the two destroyers to withdraw to Espíritu Santo and authorized Taylor to use his judgment as to abandoning *Benham*. At 0330, *Gwin* joined up with *Benham*. Taylor nursed his fragile command gingerly through calm waters in the forenoon, but rising seas during the afternoon of November 15 doomed *Benham* and nearly her crew. *Gwin* could not come along-side, but excellent seamanship made a tricky boat shuttle work. *Gwin* then tried to scuttle *Benham* with torpedoes and yet again demonstrated the deficiencies in the Mark XV torpedo: the first exploded prematurely, the second missed ahead, the third ran erratically, and the fourth missed astern. Finally, at 1935 *Gwin* hit one of *Benham*'s magazines with a 5-inch shell, sinking her.

By the time Kondo reached Truk, his claims included one "*South Dakota*" Class battleship sunk, one battleship of unknown type "almost certainly sunk," two cruisers and two destroyers "instantly sunk," and two other cruisers which sank more reluctantly. Not everyone wholly accepted these claims. Admiral Ugaki, for one, looked askance at the purported battleship sinkings. Objectively, it must be remarked that once again the samurai seamen displayed remarkable visual acuity at night in sighting Lee over one hour before they first appeared on American radar screens. In the greater Solomons torpedo-jousting tournament, the Long Lances yet again proved superior to their American counterparts, but Japanese performance in this category actually dipped below par by their own high standards—for which the crew of *South Dakota* could be thankful. The proportions tell the tale here: Kondo's torpedomen wielded two-thirds as many launching tubes as Abe's, but Kondo's torpedomen achieved only one-third as many hits. In large measure this disappointment stemmed from difficult firing angles, but the number of reported premature explosions particularly troubled the Japanese. Some suspected a flaw in the exploder; others ventured speculation that the American battleships had some fiendish new "torpedo defense" gear. The failure to sink *South Dakota* by gunfire is not surprising in view of the caliber of the weapons arrayed against her tough armor, and the Japanese were once again caught with ammunition hoists full of bombardment shells when they needed the armor-piercing variety. Overall, however, the inept tactics of Kondo and his subordinates (Kimura excepted) overshadow these material faults. This blundering grew directly from the unshakable notion that they faced a weak group of destroyers and cruisers instead of a powerful group of destroyers and modern fast battleships.

In this battle, 242 American and at least 249 Japanese sailors died, but the exchange of *Walke, Benham,* and *Preston* and moderate damage to *South Dakota* and *Gwin* for the sinking of *Kirishima* and *Ayanami* was very much in Lee's favor and made the result of this battle a clear-cut American victory.[1] To Willis Lee went many accolades. "Audacious planning and execution" marked his operations, commented Halsey, whose own decision to use Lee was itself audacious and a key factor in the success—Kondo consistently rejected the possibility that the enemy would be equally bold in committing battleships to Iron Bottom Sound. Unlike Callaghan, Lee never allowed the action to degenerate into a nautical brawl, because he formulated a workable plan and then adhered to it, even after every ship in his task force except *Washington* was sunk or forced to retire. Lee was never more incisive than in his own evaluation of his success:

> We . . . realized then and it should not be forgotten now, that our entire superiority was due almost entirely to our possession of radar. Certainly we have no edge on the Japs in experience, skill, training or performance of personnel.

To this must be added the tactical formation chosen by Lee, which permitted his destroyers to perform their screening function, and above all the skillful touch of Captain Davis at the conn of *Washington* and the performance of his crew. Regrettably, security concerns

---

[1] Losses were divided as follows:

	Killed	Wounded
South Dakota	39	59
Preston	117	26
Walke	80	48
Benham	0	8
Gwin	6	0
Washington	0	1
Total	242	142

The figure of 249 dead in Kondo's task force includes forty on *Ayanami* and the great majority of the rest, if not all, on *Kirishima.*

masked *Washington*'s vital role and, instead, wholly disproportionate credit went to *South Dakota,* which went stateside for repairs.
Captain Gatch cut a colorful figure, his crew was unquestionably
steadfast and skilled at damage control, but *South Dakota*'s offensive
performance was lackluster.

END OF THE CONVOY

Just before ordering retirement of his forces, Kondo directed Tanaka
to immediately conduct his transports to their anchorage and beach
them. By 0051, Tanaka extracted the convoy from a squall in which
it huddled during the last stages of the action and set it again on
course for Tassafaronga. When Tanaka affirmed his intentions to
beach the ships by radio at 0300, Mikawa interposed his objections
on the grounds that beaching would make the landing of troops and
supplies actually more difficult. To Tanaka this was a further untimely example of the 8th Fleet commander's proclivity to countermand orders without knowledge of local conditions. Yamamoto and
Kondo both clarified these contradictory directives by endorsing
beaching the transports. Around 0400 the last four transports,
Kinugasa Maru, Hirokawa Maru, Yamura Maru, and *Sangetsu
Maru,* ran themselves aground along the coast near Tassafaronga.
By 0430, Tanaka assembled his squadron and started them back for
Shortland. Only *Suzukaze* managed to put any of her soldier survi-
vors ashore.

Floating survivors from *Walke* and *Preston* observed these maneuvers with great interest. Their eventful wavetop vigil was already
marked by the surprise of a submarine surfacing and then a tense
interval under searchlight scrutiny from a Japanese destroyer. The
sight of four explosions marking the demise of *Kirishima* sustained
their morale; spirits surged when the initial glimmers of daylight
brought the first of an assortment of executioners to the enemy
transports.

It was only 0555 when Major Joseph Sailor pushed his SBD over
into a dive on two of the plump hulls stranded near the Poha River.
He and the seven pilots who followed him claimed three hits. Within
ten minutes, *Enterprise*'s visiting squadrons subjected the vessels off
Bunina Point and Doma Reef to similar abuse. Some or all of the six
float planes sent by the Imperial Navy to defend the landing area
sparred ineffectively with the three VS-10 SBDs that plunged down
to claim two hits, while four VT-10 TBFs roared in untouched to add

one more. Two VS-10 SBDs rounded off a check for other new accretions to Guadalcanal's beaches by planting bombs on one transport and in a stack of freshly landed material. When Majors Sailor and Richard returned at 0725 leading nine more SBDs, they parceled bombs between both the transport at Doma Reef and cargo stacked ashore. Four more *Enterprise* SBDs pelted the transports at 0845.

Shore and sea artillery fire augmented the aerial battering. Two 155mm guns of the newly arrived 244th Coast Artillery and a pair of 5-inch guns of the veteran 3d Defense Battalion conducted a successful shoot at the two nearest transports, hitting them repeatedly. But the most spectacular destruction was wrought by destroyer *Meade*. Though originally assigned only the offstage role of escort for cargo ship *Kopara*, Lieutenant Commander Raymond S. Lamb maneuvered his ship and her charge cannily in the face of great uncertainty so as to arrive in Iron Bottom Sound this morning, where *Meade* usurped sea control in waters so recently dominated by capital ships. After tucking *Kopara* into Tulagi harbor, *Meade* stood over to Guadalcanal and promptly lined up her sights on the ship at Doma Cove at 1012. Over the next forty-two minutes, *Meade* pranced up and down the coast stoking up great fires on three ships (the fourth was already well ablaze) and raking the beach with both her 5-inch and 40mm batteries. With his gun crews drooping with exhaustion, Lamb gently eased *Meade* over to the oil patches full of *Walke* and *Preston* survivors and commenced their recovery.

Meade missed two *Walke* survivors, Seaman Dale E. Land and Machinist's Mate Harold Taylor. After two days and nights in the water this duo reached Guadalcanal, deep behind Japanese lines. They began a trek eastward, agonizingly slow because Land lacked shoes and they were compelled to move in the jungle to evade the traffic on the beach. They passed many Japanese bivouacs, close enough to snatch a few scraps of food to supplement a coconut diet, and once heard screams produced by a strafing attack by American aircraft. When they picked up a Japanese rifle and a bandolier of ammunition they became emboldened and took up a sideline in sniper activity, killing a number of Japanese that way. But this practice cost Taylor his life. On December 5, Land crawled to within shouting distance of American lines, where he was found. His naval garb was barely recognizable and he was delirious, with a temperature of 106 degrees, but he recovered.

While *Meade* pried the rest of Land and Taylor's living shipmates from the watery grip of Iron Bottom Sound during the late morning of November 15, the Cactus Air Force was still preying on the carrion left by the convoy. A report placed four of Tanaka's transports drifting but afloat near the Russell Islands. An attack by two VT-8 and two VT-10 TBFs led by Lieutenant Larsen sank one at 1010. A second TBF strike returned with its ordnance rather than wasting it on the remaining gutted hulls. Another four TBFs of Lieutenant Coffin's VT-10 seeded incendiary clusters and 500-pound bombs along the periphery of the beaches now marked by spires of smoke from the grounded transports. Finally at 1350, three VB-10 SBDs hit one of the burning hulks and a nearby ammunition dump, which caused a huge fire that burned for sixteen hours. Two hours after the last strike on the transports, a flight of seven Vals guarded by seven Zeros closed the island. Seven VF-10 Wildcats led by Lieutenant Commander James Flatley intercepted them. The Vals turned back, and Flatley's pilots claimed four Zeros at the cost of one F4F through fuel exhaustion; the pilot was recovered. One Zero was destroyed.

Within hours after the fighting ended around Guadalcanal, both sides began claiming success. The Japanese announced a great battle in which they had sunk eight American cruisers and four or five destroyers and heavily damaged two battleships, three cruisers, and three or four destroyers. They admitted this cost the Imperial Navy one battleship, one cruiser, and three destroyers with forty-one aircraft and "damage" to seven transports. The United States Navy reported sinking one Japanese battleship, five cruisers, five destroyers, and twelve transports in exchange for two light cruisers and six destroyers (apparently word of the loss of Benham was delayed in reaching Washington but was later acknowledged). It is remarkable that both sides were candid about warship losses.

From the gloom of October through initial skepticism at the first accounts of the action, there now broke through a burst of sunny optimism in Washington. Secretary Knox, the former chief public doom-sayer, asserted that there might be more to come, but "We can lick them. I don't qualify that." The death in action of Admirals Scott and Callaghan transfigured them into immediate heroes; both received a posthumous Medal of Honor and the same decorations went to Lieutenant Commanders McCandless and Schonland. The loss of the Sullivan brothers was not revealed until January, when all hope had vanished that any of them could have survived. The Navy did not disclose fully the painful and complex story surrounding the sinking of Juneau. This calamitous tragedy to one family sobered the nation, which had not yet seen long casualty lists. But the fortitude of the Sullivan family in the face of this loss was an indicator of popular resolution.

Whether measured by respective intentions or losses, the Naval Battle of Guadalcanal—or, more properly, the Air-Naval Battle of Guadalcanal—was a decisive American victory. Both sides entered the battle bent on reinforcing Guadalcanal and denying the enemy the same privilege. Admiral Turner hauled 5,529 men and many tons of supplies to Lunga Roads without losing a ship, and put ashore every man and the great majority of supplies. Despite his exceptional tenaciousness, Admiral Tanaka deposited only 2,000 battle-worn men of the 38th Division and pathetically few supplies ashore: 1,500 bags of rice (a four-day supply) and 260 boxes of shells. In accomplishing this, Tanaka lost ten transports Japan could ill spare.

Warship and human losses on both sides were heavy. The battle deprived the United States Navy of two useful light cruisers, seven destroyers, and at least 1,732 sailors, marines, and airmen over three days. The Imperial Navy struck from its list two old but very valuable fast battleships, one veteran heavy cruiser, and three destroyers; around 1,895 Japanese sailors, soldiers, and aviators died. Not only were American naval losses less in tonnage and combat value, they were also much more easily replaced. Twenty-six American and forty Japanese aircraft were lost in this period.

Although the two furious night surface actions dominate by bulk the pages on this battle, the course and the outcome of the struggle were more strongly shaped by the hard-won American air superiority over Guadalcanal and its approaches. The Combined Fleet fully appreciated the danger of the Cactus Air Force and targeted it for neutralization with successive bombardments by battleships and cruisers. The frustration of the original Japanese plan by Callaghan's sacrifice, and of its improvised successor by Lee, permitted the balance of the battle to be swung by American airmen, who accounted for *Kinugasa* and the transports and assured the destruction of *Hiei*.

The Japanese planning erred seriously in the failure to anticipate the possible intervention by *Enterprise* and her air group. This oversight sprang directly from the belief that the remaining American fleet carriers were destroyed at Santa Cruz, and that the only potential sea-based air power would be a few escort carriers. The importance of the contribution by the *Enterprise* air group can scarcely be exaggerated. On the morning of November 13, the Cactus Air Force possessed only thirty-one attack planes (twenty-three SBDs and eight TBFs), but Air Group 10 more than doubled this total with thirty-one SBDs and nine TBFs manned with skilled crews.

Admiral Kinkaid handled *Enterprise* with appropriate circumspection yet extracted full value from Air Group 10 by transferring it to Henderson Field. The Japanese wanted for an air base as handily located in relation to the unfolding action on November 12–15 to similarly exploit *Junyo*'s air group. But the limited participation of *Junyo* and her air group in the battle is only part of a larger deficiency in the Imperial Navy's performance. Her gunners remained equal and her torpedomen superior to those of the United States Navy, but her admirals were decidedly outfought. The fact that—despite advanced warning from radio intelligence—entirely different task forces entered actions within forty-eight hours of one another illustrates that American command performance was not flawless; however, it was markedly superior to that of the Japanese. Among a great many courageous decisions over these tumultuous days, Nimitz gave primacy to Turner's decision to send Callaghan against Abe. Not far behind was Halsey's release of Lee and that flag officer's imperturbable direction of the battleship action. By contrast, the decision (or inertia) that allowed Tanaka's convoy to advance on November 14 without close escort by Mikawa or adequate air cover, to include full-time fighter coverage from *Junyo,* nearly defies comprehension. But even more central to the Japanese failure was the tentativeness of Yamamoto's commitment. The Advanced Force (even in its reduced state), the 11th Air Fleet, and the 8th Fleet brought superior combat power to the area, yet Yamamoto and his subordinates failed to mass that power for decisive results. By contrast, Halsey saw no other way to fight than all-out. By the morning of November 15, Halsey had committed virtually every ship and plane in his command to battle and had suffered grievous losses. But by then the convoy was destroyed and the American grip on Guadalcanal assured.

The Air-Naval Battle of Guadalcanal was a battle that quite probably would not have been fought but for the effects of a change of public information policy by American officials. Ironically, it was decisive for the campaign, and in retrospect, it became clear that it was decisive for the Pacific War as a whole. A Japanese appreciation prepared in late October observed:

It must be said that the success or failure in recapturing Guadalcanal Island, and the vital naval battle related to it, is the fork in the road which leads to victory for them or for us.

That fork was reached at sundown on November 12. By sunrise of November 15 it was clear which path the war was destined to follow.

19

THE BATTLE

OF TASSAFARONGA

"Suitable leadership"

THE LAST ACTION BY THE MATANIKAU

"Now is the time to move in more supplies and to relieve the tried Marine amphibian troops," wrote a staff officer in the CINCPAC daily summary at the conclusion of the Naval Battle of Guadalcanal. Battle fatigue, disease, and short rations had dulled the offensive edge of 1st Marine Division beyond renewal on Guadalcanal. Plans to finally withdraw the division and replace it with Army troops went forth rapidly, but limited shipping resources governed the tempo of replacement. On the logistical front, Halsey took a key step on November 16 when he placed control of cargo discharge and loading at Noumea in Army hands. The skilled and energetic leadership of Brigadier General Raymond E. S. Williamson untied the biggest knot in the American supply line. With the replacement and reinforcement of American ground forces on a sound footing, the agenda next called for the final destruction of the Japanese forces on the island. Events on land and sea during the last two weeks of November illustrated just how difficult that task would be.

Vandegrift remained convinced that no opportunity should be

missed to extend American real estate holdings to the Poha River. In the third week of November he authorized renewal of the offensive aborted by the sea clash. This mission fell naturally to Brigadier General Sebree, who commanded the western sector of the American perimeter. Sebree disposed the veteran 164th Infantry, the 8th Marines, and the two newly landed battalions of the 182d Infantry.

After patrols confirmed that the Japanese had not reoccupied their former line along the Matanikau, Sebree planned his offensive in two steps. First, he would send the two novice battalions of the 182d Infantry across the Matanikau to secure a swath of territory sufficiently west of the Matanikau and south of the coast to gain maneuver room for his other regiments. The line designated for capture ran on a southwesterly axis 2,500 yards inland from Point Cruz. The southern two-thirds of this line followed the trace of a long ridge connecting elevations the Americans arbitrarily labeled Hills 80, 81, and 66. Thereafter, the main attack would commence with all three regiments in a drive to the Poha.

On the morning of November 18, engineers installed a footbridge

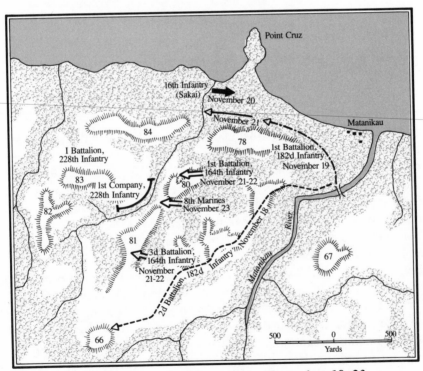

Last Battle at the Matanikau, November 18–23

across the Matanikau under the cover of the 8th Marines. Lieutenant Colonel Bernard B. Twombley pushed his 2d Battalion, 182d Infantry (2/182) over the bridge and up the first rise west of the river, Hill 75. Noon arrived before the unacclimated men of the 182d finished the 2,000-yard march to Hill 66. A small patrol clash that cost the battalion two killed represented the only contact all day.

The following morning, November 19, Lieutenant Colonel Francis F. MacGowan's 1st Battalion, 182d Infantry (1/182) crossed the Matanikau and advanced along the corridor bounded by the coast and a small east-west ridge that ended just southwest of Point Cruz. Company B, 8th Marines guarded the inland flank by moving along the ridge. About 400 yards west of the Matanikau the battalion received its baptism in battle from small enemy groups and skirmished lightly as it moved slowly to a point just east of Point Cruz. Company B traversed the entire ridge and stepped down from its western end (Hill 78), only to be forced back by enemy fire. MacGowan dug his unit in along a 700-yard-long line from the beach to Hill 78 with the inland flank bent back eastward. The Marine company then marched back across the Matanikau to rejoin its parent unit. As darkness fell, a gap of just over 1,000 yards separated the two Army battalions.

Colonel Yoshitsugu Sakai's 16th Infantry Regiment opposed MacGowan. Backed by a few anti-tank guns and mortars, Sakai fielded 700 men fit for combat duty on November 20 along the 400-yard-wide coastal corridor, the only continuously manned sector of the Japanese front. Inland, the Japanese defended only a few key terrain features, generally by company- or battalion-size units dug in on the reverse slopes of ridgelines. The 1st Battalion, 228th Infantry screened the 2,000 yards south of Sakai with its companies widely separated. Beyond the northwest Matanikau fork, Major General Ito coordinated the remainder of the 228th Infantry and the 124th Infantry on a defense line extending to Mount Austen.

During the night of November 19–20, the Japanese tested the 1/182 with their usual infiltration tactics. After a dose of Japanese artillery and mortar fire, part of the 16th Infantry suddenly rapped the left flank of MacGowan's 1/182. The men braced against Hill 78 stood their ground, but those in the coastal flat backpedaled about 400 yards. Sebree and regimental staff officers restored order to the shaken companies. Stiffened by air and artillery support, these units resumed their original posts by 0900 and then advanced up the beach to a position just west of Point Cruz. Another lash of Japanese artillery and mortar fire generated some disorder and straggling

before the battalion rallied into an organized firing line. This thrust
sealed off the Japanese on Point Cruz.

Sebree now decided to insert Colonel Moore's experienced 164th
Infantry into the gap between the two battalions of the 182d and
commence the main assault. After sunset of November 20, the two
battalions of the 182d extended their interior flanks toward each
other. Into the remaining 700-yard-wide gap the 1st Battalion, 164th
Infantry (1/164) drew up on the left of the 1/182, and the 3d Battalion, 164th Infantry (3/164) filled the remaining portion of the line
between the 1/164 and the 2/182. Sebree designated a serpentine
ridge to the northwest, linking Hills 82, 83, and 84, as the objective
of the 164th. A ravine about 200 feet deep and from 50 to 100 yards
wide separated Moore's regiment from this goal. Heavy vegetation
thrived in the ravine itself, but the steep, open upward slopes of the
ridge walls on each side granted superb command for machineguns
sited to fire down the ravine. Elements of the I/228, principally the
1st Company, hunkered in fighting positions in the ravine and on its
slopes in defilade from American artillery and mortar weapons.

On the morning of November 21, murderous enemy fire sent the
assault companies of the 164th to earth after gains of 40 yards or less.
In the coastal flat, layers of small-arm, mortar, and artillery fire
leveled from a web of well-dug-in firing points halted the 1/182. The
battalion reduced Point Cruz but achieved only 100 yards of westward motion. The following day was a grim repetition of these same
events. Sebree waited until the afternoon to alert the 8th Marines to
take up the attack the next day toward Hill 83, thus forcing the
marines to plan without any reconnaissance.

After withdrawal of the front-line companies about 300 yards on
the morning of November 23, one Army and two Marine artillery
battalions and one battery drummed a thirty-minute preparation on
the Japanese lines. The two leading battalions of the 8th Marines
attempted to punch forward with companies in column up an approach picked by map. This proved to be too narrow, with little room
to deploy and none to maneuver; Japanese fire smothered the advance. The Cactus Air Force contributed assistance, and twice
bombs fell around the command post of the 17th Army, slightly
injuring Hyakutake and his chief of staff. One blast destroyed the
only mimeograph machine and scattered papers and supplies, com-
plicating staff work for the rest of the campaign. The Japanese retali-
ated with a few well-laid mortar rounds that fell particularly on the
command posts of 3/164, wounding Lieutenant Colonel Hall and
killing four officers.

Major Nishiyama, the acting commander of the 228th Infantry, noted that his men had deciphered American tactics. They waited in their dugouts until the supporting fires stopped and then emerged to open fire with their weapons and toss grenades. In the face of these ploys and mounting casualties, the American command halted the attack on November 23 and ordered the infantry to dig in along the line of contact from Hill 66 north to Point Cruz. This stalemate would last for over six weeks.

Though limited in scale, this six-day struggle produced major American casualties. Between November 18 and 23, the 164th Infantry lost forty-seven men killed and the 182d Infantry added the names of forty-five soldiers to the fatality lists. Losses in the 8th Marines reached forty-two dead and brought the death toll to 134. A detailed return from the 164th illustrates the type of attrition common to units on Guadalcanal. The regiment arrived on October 13 with 2,818 men, but by November 25 it fielded less than 2,000 fit for combat. Battle deaths accounted for 117. Wounds and illness resulted in the evacuation of 325 men, and the regiment's rear areas harbored another 300 soldiers unfit physically or, in some cases, psychologically for battle.

Japanese losses in this last action along the Matanikau remain undocumented, though very likely they were less than the American total. Commendations went to Colonel Sakai's regiment and First Lieutenant Omasu's 1st Company, 228th Infantry. But by this stage of the campaign, combat caused only a minority of the losses in the 17th Army. A strength return dated November 20 showed that of the 29,117 soldiers landed since August 7, the deduction of those killed, evacuated, or hospitalized because of wounds or illness left only 18,295 still with their units. Of this latter total, those fit by liberal definition for combat duty numbered only 12,775. The survivors of the original garrison (including construction workers) and the Imperial Navy units landed since August 7 added another 2,376 to the aggregate unit strength, but only 550 to the rolls of those fit for combat.

On November 21, Lieutenant General Hitoshi Imamura debarked from a plane at Truk. Imamura represented the physical embodiment of a major change in Japanese command arrangements that underscored the importance of the Southeast Area. Imperial Headquarters recognized that Hyakutake could not effectively control operations on both Guadalcanal and New Guinea. Therefore, it switched jurisdiction over New Guinea operations to Lieutenant General Hatazo Adachi's new 18th Army. To supervise and coordi-

nate the 17th and 18th Armies, Imperial Headquarters appointed
Imamura to lead a new command, the 8th Area Army.[1]

Prior to departing from Tokyo, Imamura received guidance in the
form of a new Central Agreement. Two convictions undergirded the
new compact: first, that the Southeast Area was developing into a
decisive battle; second, that a modest increment in effort would
purchase the victory only narrowly missed in October. The initial
concept framed on November 6 called for the recapture of the Solomons followed by the expulsion of the Allies from New Guinea. The
Naval Battle of Guadalcanal, the destruction of the November convoy, and the approach of MacArthur's forces to Buna on November
16 prompted a scaling-down of these plans. As redrafted on November 18, the Central Agreement limited the objective in New Guinea
to securing "important areas" in preparation for future operations.
The "important areas" essentially comprised air bases at Lae, Salamua, Madang, and Wewak. With the revised orders went additional
forces detailed to the 8th Area Army to include the 6th Infantry
Division from China, the 65th Brigade, and in recognition of the crux
of the problem in the Southeast Area, the 6th Air Division of the
Japanese Army Air Force with 110 aircraft.

The scheme of operations called for expanding airfield facilities,
regaining air superiority, reinforcing the 17th Army, and launching
an attack to seize Guadalcanal about January 20, 1943. In addition
to lifting reinforcements and contributing 135 aircraft, the Imperial
Navy would bar Allied reinforcement of Guadalcanal. Imperial
Headquarters designated this complex of activities the South Pacific
Number 8 Operation. These plans required the diversion to the
Southeast Area of a large amount of shipping from essential occupations critical to Japan's overall war economy.

The allocation of shipping posed strategic problems beyond
Imamura's ken, but at Truk, Imamura confronted a strategic problem of immediate concern. The August landing at Guadalcanal had
served to divert Japanese attention from New Guinea to a new
threat; now MacArthur's forces launched an attack at Buna on New
Guinea in mid-November, which severely jolted Combined Fleet
Headquarters. From Buna, Allied planes would be only 340 miles
from Rabaul, the hub of Japanese operations in the South Pacific and

---

[1] A month later, on December 24, the Imperial Navy created a parallel headquarters
designated the Southeast Area Fleet. Vice Admiral Jinichi Kusaka, the commander of the Base
Air Force (11th Air Fleet), became the leader of the Southeast Area Fleet.

the key to Truk, the premier strategic point in the Pacific. Enemy air bases at Buna threatened Lae and Salamua and challenged Japanese control of the Dampier Strait, the outlet to the Western Pacific and the sea lanes to the Southern Resources Area. Westward thrusts from Buna along the coast of New Guinea would endanger the Philippines and the Netherlands East Indies. To the Combined Fleet staff, the loss of Guadalcanal paled before this host of hazards, and they began incubating plans for abandoning Guadalcanal and shifting priority to operations on New Guinea.

While the Combined Fleet staff fully shared these insights with the Navy Section of Imperial General Headquarters, they confined their discussion with Imamura to the issue of counterattacking at Buna with the 21st Brigade and other elements assigned to the 17th Army heretofore earmarked for the Solomons. Imamura initially declined to adapt this course of action, which implied a reversal of the emphasis contained in his orders. After reflection, however, the 8th Area Army commander authorized the movement of the 21st Brigade to New Guinea for a counterstroke against MacArthur's Buna attack.

Imamura formally assumed command at Rabaul on November 26. His staff commingled officers new to the Southeast Area with four "old hands." One of the latter, Colonel Sugita, presented a paper outlining the current situation which suggested the wisdom of a withdrawal from Guadalcanal. Imamura refused to accept the report formally, and at first the fresh staff officers chided the "old hands" as defeatist. Sugita accepted this rebuff without protest, confident that Imamura and his entourage would soon grasp reality.

A long message carried from Guadalcanal by Major Takahiko Hayashi disclosed to Imamura the status of the 17th Army. Once again the facts were explicitly stated but the implications were left between the lines. The report contained a stinging critique of the support of the Imperial Navy in the critical categories of air operations and throttling American supply lines. But the message stressed an immediate food crisis. The 17th Army's stocks of meat and vegetables stood nearly exhausted, and even rice and barley would be entirely consumed by that very day, November 26.

Other records suggest that Hayashi's account may, if anything, have understated the problem. The units holding the defensive positions on Guadalcanal placed those unable to walk at the dugouts and fighting positions. The few relatively healthy individuals performed all scouting, patrolling, and attacks. Those who could ambulate with the aid of a stick or cane fetched and cooked rations. In the more inland sectors held by the 38th Division, rations had been one-third or less, and by November 26, some units had not been resupplied for six days. On November 21, Major Nishiyama, acting commander of the 228th Infantry, scribbled in his diary that his only food for three or four days had been one dried plum. One of his officers told him:

> Rice. I really want rice. I want to give my men as much as they want. That is the only wish I have. Even when mortars are falling like a squall or the land is reshaped by bombs I don't worry. But I can't stand looking at my men become pale and thin.

Compounding this problem was the lack of medical supplies to counteract the rampant spread of disease, a process exacerbated by the fact that their tactical deployment left the Japanese on sunless and unsanitary reverse slopes.

Resupply of the 17th Army became an urgent concern of the responsible naval commands on November 16. The burgeoning potency of the Cactus Air Force and the current cycle of bright moonlit nights promised to make the costs of immediately resuming the "Rat Transportation" system prohibitive. A search for alternatives led quickly to two new vehicles for moving supplies and a new method of handling supplies by destroyers.

On November 16 the Combined Fleet ordered the Advanced Expeditionary Force to continue a limited program of anti-shipping patrols, but to reassign the bulk of the submarine effort to the new mission of moving foodstuffs to Guadalcanal and Buna. In the next three weeks, sixteen submarines each loaded 20 to 30 tons of supplies at Rabaul for portage to Kamimbo. The presence of aircraft and motor torpedo boats frustrated the first landing effort on November 24. The next night, *I-17* succeeded in landing about 11 tons. Each night thereafter to the end of the month, sailors manhandled 20 to 32 tons of food across narrow submarine decks to landing craft off Kamimbo. Each submarine load represented perhaps a day's worth of food to the 17th Army, but the necessity to move these supplies, almost entirely by hand, many miles through the jungle to the men at the front seriously impaired their value.

Submarine crews detested this duty; their officers derisively labeled this mission a "Marutsu" after the Japanese equivalent of United Parcel Service or Federal Express. It was also dangerous. Almost immediately, submarine *Seadragon* sank *I-4* on November 20. Worse was to come.

A brief digression is appropriate here to recount the activities of those submarines utilized in anti-shipping efforts. *I-21* damaged liberty ship *Edgar Allan Poe* off Noumea on November 9 by a conventional torpedo attack. Unconventional tactics employing midget submarines ported to the scene of action by specifically fitted I-boats commenced on November 7 when midget submarine *Number 11* from *I-20* put one torpedo into auxiliary *Majaba* off Lunga. The Japanese crew survived the counterattack and scuttled their boat; *Majaba* became a floating warehouse at Tulagi. Seven more attempts with the midgets followed between November 11 and December 13, at the price of three crews. Two of these lost crews scored the only other success in this program.

On the morning of November 28, midget *Number 10* from *I-16* fired a torpedo past a screen of five destroyers into naval freighter *Alchiba.* The blast sparked a fire in a hold containing part of *Alchiba*'s explosive brew of aviation gasoline, bombs, and ammunition. *Alchiba*'s skipper, Commander James S. Freeman, ran her aground west of Lunga. While part of her crew off-loaded her perilous cargo, the other portion grappled below with a smoky blaze that burned for four days. As if this were not enough, on December 7 midget *Number 38* from *I-24* hit *Alchiba* with another torpedo, flooding out her engineering spaces. *Alchiba* sat aground for a month; a Navy Department press release announced *Alchiba* as a loss. Freeman and his bluejackets refused to take this verdict. Eventually they repaired *Alchiba* and restored her to service, showing that the spirit in the glamorless part of the Navy fully matched that of the haughty companies of the sleek men-of-war.

The Imperial Navy earnestly desired to replace submarines and destroyers as the haulers of provisions to Guadalcanal and Buna with small motor or sailing craft. Planners envisioned the establishment of three bases between Munda and Guadalcanal and four between Rabaul and Buna. Small vessels would then move at night from one base to the next, where they would be concealed during daylight in hides bristling with antiaircraft weapons. They dubbed this scheme the "Chain Transportation."

The Japanese selected Wickham Anchorage on the small island of Vangunu off the southeast coast of New Georgia as the first base on the Guadalcanal run. On November 27, six destroyers installed 600 men of the 1st Battalion, 229th Infantry at Wickham. Two small vessels, *Kiku Maru* and *Azusa Maru,* loaded the essential complement of antiaircraft weapons, provisions, and another 300 men at Rabaul for movement to Wickham. This attempt ran afoul of an important development in the last fortnight of this eventful month. During this period the Cactus Air Force grew from eighty-five to 188 aircraft by both replacement of exhausted squadrons and the diversification of its armory to include search, antisubmarine, and heavier strike planes. Unchallenged now over Guadalcanal, the Cactus Air Force moved increasingly to extend its mastery to the central Solomons with regular visits to Rekata Bay and Munda.[2] Search planes detected *Kiku Maru* and *Azusa Maru* and strike missions on November 28 and 29 destroyed both of them before they landed more than a small fraction of their cargoes. This seemingly trivial episode left another Japanese detachment short of food, but much more important, it persuaded the Japanese to abandon the entire "Chain Transportation" program.

The limited utility of submarine cargo hauling and the failure of the "Chain Transportation" compelled recourse to the proven mainstay of "Rat Transportation," now with a refinement. Sailors cleaned heavy drums (normally used for oil and gasoline) and half-filled them with 330 pounds of rice and barley. They loaded between 200 and 240 drums, joined in clusters by ropes, on the weather deck of each destroyer. Once off Guadalcanal, the clusters of drums would be shoved overboard close to the landing points and pulled ashore by a central line. This method would require only twenty destroyer runs per month to feed 20,000 men, and drastically reduced the exposure period of each destroyer by minimizing the amount of time spent off Guadalcanal.

The responsibility for the first of five scheduled runs using the new drum method fell on Admiral Tanaka's Reinforcement Unit. At a conference in the midafternoon of November 29, Tanaka explained his intentions to the commanding officers of his reorganized Reinforcement Unit/Destroyer Squadron 2. His command now incorporated the three vessels of Desdiv 31, brand-new ships commissioned between June and August. Of this trio, Tanaka raised his flag on *Naganami*, which, with *Takanami*, became the Screening Unit. They would carry no drums. The admiral attached the remaining ship of Desdiv 31, *Makinami*, to Captain Sato's Desdiv 15 (*Oyashio*, *Kuroshio*, *Kagero*). These four vessels, designated the 1st Transportation Unit, would each drop 240 drums off Tassafaronga. The 2d Transportation Unit comprised the two ships of Desdiv 24, *Suzukaze* and *Kawakaze;* they would each put 200 drums into the water off the

[2]On November 18, Colonel Saunders led the first major strike on Buin by the South Pacific aviators. Fighters intercepted the eleven B-17s, four B-26s, and eight P-38s and forced Saunders's B-17 down off Vella Lavella. Saunders and the other survivors of the crew were rescued by Jack Keenan, a coast watcher, who introduced himself by presenting his card.

mouth of the Umasani River, northwest of Tassafaronga. Weight considerations dictated that the drum-bearing destroyers land their torpedo reloads.

Unease spread among his officers when Tanaka unveiled his tactical configuration for the drum dropping. *Takanami* would take station as a picket abreast the 1st Transportation Unit; flagship *Naganami* would remain back to the northwest with the 2d Transportation Unit. Tanaka offered no reason for this arrangement, though as recent battles illustrated, no guarantee existed that a challenge to the Reinforcement Unit would necessarily emanate from the east rather than the west. Nonetheless, some officers found the absence of the flagship from the traditional position at the head of the column disquieting.

Halsey's forces afloat rebounded rapidly after the bloody clinches of mid-November. King marched to the Joint Chiefs of Staff, in Admiral Leahy's words, "with his sword in his hand" following the Naval Battle of Guadalcanal to demand the release of ships from the Atlantic and Mediterranean to replace losses in the South Pacific. He won immediate authorization to transfer two cruisers, three escort carriers, and five destroyers to Guadalcanal's environs, with more vessels to follow. In the meantime, Halsey's carrier power would be doubled when a new group built around refurbished *Saratoga* joined battered *Enterprise. North Carolina,* her torpedo damage healed, united with Admiral Lee and *Washington* to power a battleship task force; the new *Indiana* soon made it a threesome. On November 24, Rear Admiral Thomas C. Kinkaid received orders to form Task Force 67 to replace Callaghan's shattered unit. His mission: thwart possible new landings.

Like Norman Scott, Kinkaid faced the problem of welding a heterogeneous assortment of ships into a taut instrument fit for night combat. On November 27, Kinkaid took a propitious first step in this direction when he formulated an operations plan reflecting many lessons from recent battle experience. Kinkaid divided Task Force 67 into one destroyer and two cruiser groups, each group led by a ship equipped with SG radar. Radar-equipped destroyers would scout 10,000 yards in front of the task force. Kinkaid intended to exploit his radar advantage with a surprise destroyer torpedo attack. Cruisers would then engage with gunfire from 10,000 to 12,000 yards. The cruiser float planes would fly up to Tulagi, from where they would conduct scouting and illuminating duties in support of the task force.

Before Kinkaid could implement his plan, King detached him for command duty in the North Pacific. Rear Admiral Carleton H. Wright relieved Kinkaid on November 28. On the afternoon of the day following his appointment, Wright adapted Kinkaid's plan and discussed it with his captains. Only a few hours later, Halsey instructed Wright to sortie as soon as possible and take Task Force 67 to Guadalcanal through Lengo Channel so as to arrive off Tassafaronga by 2300, November 30, to intercept a Japanese reinforcement group composed of eight destroyers and six transports. The source of Halsey's information was almost certainly a decoded dispatch transmitted on November 29 alerting the 17th Army to Tanaka's run.

Wright's task force of four heavy and one light cruiser and four destroyers negotiated the minefield at Espíritu Santo at midnight and commenced the 580-mile run for Guadalcanal. Thirty minutes later, Tanaka's eight destroyers departed Shortland. The Japanese admiral crafted his course to evade aerial detection by threading Bougainville Strait on a northerly heading, thence southeast to Roncador Reef before pivoting to the south for the run through Indispensable Strait. Despite this stratagem, an Allied plane shadowed the Reinforcement Unit for about an hour after 0930, November 30. In midafternoon, a Japanese search aircraft warned of twelve enemy destroyers and nine transports off Guadalcanal. At 1430, Tanaka signaled his ships to expect action that night, and if it came, to give priority to "destroy[ing] the enemy without regard for the unloading of supplies."

The aircraft that sighted Tanaka never radioed its findings. Coast watcher Paul Mason, however, from his perch at the southern end of Bougainville, tallied a dozen fewer masts at Shortland on the morning of November 30. Messages relayed this to Wright, and informed him that the enemy might arrive sooner than expected; he might substitute combatant types for transports; or perhaps he would appear only with destroyers. Approaching Lengo Channel after sunset, Wright encountered a small convoy of three transports and three destroyers. Halsey detailed destroyers *Lamson* and *Lardner* from the convoy under Commander Abercrombie (ComDesdiv 9) to join Task Force 67. This move, while well-intentioned, was questionable. Wright possessed neither time nor means to pass the operations and signal plans to them, so he placed Abercrombie at the rear of the formation.

Composition of the two opposing forces was as follows:

1. JAPANESE

Reinforcement Unit (Destroyer Squadron 2)
Rear Adm. Raizo Tanaka
in Naganami

Screen
Naganami, Takanami *(Embarking Capt. Toshio Shimizu, Comdesdiv 31)*

1st Transportation Unit (Desdiv 15)
Capt. Torajiro Sato
Oyashio, Kuroshio, Kagero, Makinami

2d Transportation Unit (Desdiv 24)
Capt. Giichiro Nakahara
Kawakaze, Suzukaze

2. AMERICAN

Task Force 67
Rear Adm. Carleton H. Wright
Task Group 67.2.2, Adm. Wright
in Minneapolis

HEAVY CRUISERS:

Minneapolis	Capt. Charles E. Rosendahl
New Orleans	Capt. Clifford H. Roper
Pensacola	Capt. Frank L. Lowe

Task Group 67.2.3: Rear Adm. Mahlon S. Tisdale in Honolulu

Northampton	Capt. Willard A. Kitts

LIGHT CRUISER:

Honolulu	Capt. Robert W. Hayler

Task Group 67.2.4: Cdr. William M. Cole

DESTROYERS:

Fletcher	Cdr. Cole
Drayton	Lt. Cdr. James E. Cooper
Maury	Lt. Cdr. Gelzer L. Sims
Perkins	Lt. Cdr. Walter C. Reed
Desdiv 9	Cdr. Laurence A. Abercrombie
Lamson	Lt. Cdr. Philip H. Fitzgerald
Lardner	Lt. Cdr. William M. Sweetser

The degree to which the five cruisers and six destroyers of Task Force 67 outclassed the Reinforcement Unit of eight destroyers in gun, though not torpedo, power may be judged from the following table:

	Guns			Torpedo Tubes	
	8″	6″	5″	21″	24″
American:	37	15	68	67	—
Japanese:	—	—	46	—	64

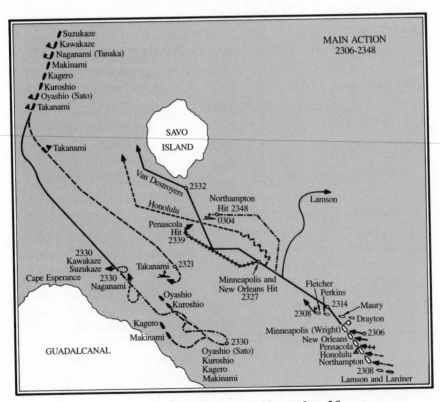

Battle of Tassafaronga, November 30

AMERICAN GUNS, 1845–2327

At 1845, Tanaka marshaled his ships into a line ahead, interval 600 meters, in the order *Takanami, Oyashio, Kuroshio, Kagero, Makinami, Naganami, Kawakaze,* and *Suzukaze.* The Reinforcement Unit penetrated Indispensable Strait at 2140 and sighted Savo Island. At this same moment, Task Force 67 entered the eastern end of Lengo Channel. Wright formed his ships in column in the order *Fletcher, Perkins, Maury, Drayton, Minneapolis, New Orleans, Pensacola, Honolulu, Northampton, Lamson,* and *Lardner.* The cruisers steamed 1,000 yards apart. The four van destroyers led the cruisers by 4,000 yards, but Wright deviated from Kinkaid's plan by failing to deploy any radar pickets.

At 2240, Tanaka's unit intruded into the passage south of Savo with the main column about 3 miles offshore and *Takanami* as a sentinel half again that distance to seaward. Three minutes later, lookouts sighted planes with running lights burning off Savo. These heralded four of Wright's float planes, finally aloft after considerable difficulty in takeoffs because of the light airs at Tulagi. Task Force 67 debouched from Lengo Channel at 2245 and took up course 320 degrees at 20 knots. *Fletcher* and her compatriots moved a position inshore off the flagship's bow. To facilitate search, Wright arrayed his cruisers into a line of bearing on course 280 degrees. Clouds clotted the moonless dome of the sky, making the night very dark. An easterly 16-knot breeze rushed over a sea rippled with slight swells. Surface visibility hovered around 2 miles through American binoculars; Tanaka's lookouts reckoned it at 5.

As SG radar operators on *Minneapolis* watched, Cape Esperance grew an excrescence that enlarged and then detached itself from the landmass. By 2306 the flagship's radar showed two pips bearing 284 degrees and distant 23,000 yards. Wright brought his ships back into a single column at 2308 as radar images multiplied to seven or eight vessels. Aboard Tanaka's destroyers all hands topside except the torpedo tube crews began readying the drums for their swim. The Reinforcement Unit divided into its two transportation units for their respective drop points and reduced speed to 12 knots. At 2312, *Takanami* warned of possible enemy ships in sight bearing almost due east. Other ships confirmed and enlarged this report. At 2316 Tanaka ordered unloading preparations halted and "All ships attack." Consternation reigned on the cluttered afterdecks of the supply-carrying destroyers; some ships kept their drums, but others dumped them. On all ships torpedomen primed their weapons.

Wright brought his ships to 300 degrees by head of column movement at 2314. In the American van destroyers, torpedomen laid tubes out over the port side as radarmen tallied and tracked green blobs marching along the Guadalcanal coast. On *Fletcher,* radar operators discerned the four vessels of the 1st Transportation Unit and *Takanami.* At 2315, with the range 7,000 yards, Commander Cole on *Fletcher* asked permission to fire torpedoes. Wright hesitated two long minutes, then over the TBS commented, "Range on bogies excessive at present." No, replied Cole, the range was satisfactory. Another pause. Then at 2320 Wright granted permission to fire torpedoes. The delay was fatal. During the exchange, *Fletcher*'s targets escaped from an auspicious firing setup with the enemy closing from ahead to, at best, a marginal proposition with the enemy just passing abeam, giving the American torpedoes a long overtaking run.

At 2320, *Fletcher* began releasing ten Mark XV torpedoes in two half-salvos. Next astern, *Perkins* added a spread of eight more. *Maury* lacked an SG radar and thus targets, so she withheld her torpedoes. A similar want of solid data prompted *Drayton* to discharge only two torpedoes toward the enemy contingent—she hoped. Before Cole reported his torpedoes were away—indeed, before all of *Perkins*'s "fish" commenced swimming—Wright issued the open-fire order: "Roger, and I do mean Roger." Almost immediately, the van destroyers began firing star shells followed by service projectiles as they bent into a disengagement course around Savo at 25 knots to clear the stage for the cruiser gunners.

"A brief but furious gun action followed," reported Wright. *Minneapolis* fired her first salvo at 2321, and by 2325 every American cruiser was firing her main battery, creating a romantic portrait of a night naval battle. Wright's heavy cruisers, liveried in blue gray, cleaved high bow waves, rhythmically discharging puffballs of white-yellow flame from 8-inch guns. Secondary batteries spurting illumination and service rounds blinked more rapidly from the waists of their rakish silhouettes. Light cruiser *Honolulu* distinctively flashed like a strobe light as her 6-inch guns cut bright holes in the night. The illuminating rounds worked poorly, because of the heavy overcast, but well enough to outline shimmering walls of water heaving skyward where heavy shells drilled into the soft belly of the sea. In the foreground, intense glows and spark showers betokening hits convinced spotters that they witnessed the disintegration of enemy vessels in this cyclone of fire. Topside sailors sensed little return fire and saw even less, just an occasional muted flash.

Most of this American metal converged as though magnetized to the hull and superstructure of *Takanami.* No mystery surrounds this fact: *Takanami*'s proximity enhanced her radar "signature," and early hits kindled blazes that left her nakedly revealed. She gamely returned fire, which only served to make her the more conspicuous. *Takanami* launched her torpedoes, but within four minutes many hits "incapacitated" her and she glided to a halt wrapped in flames.

While *Takanami* absorbed the attention of Wright's gunners, the rest of the Reinforcement Unit sailed virtually untouched, a fact only dimly perceived by two small groups of Americans. Aviators in float planes noted a group of Japanese destroyers continuing on course to the southeast of the pyre that was *Takanami.* At the same time, *Lardner,* the last ship in Wright's formation, caught glimpses of a group of Japanese destroyers steaming purposefully behind the splashes raised by the cruiser guns. *Lardner* snapped but five rounds at them before they vanished from sight. Those barely seen wraiths hugging Guadalcanal's shore were preparing to counter a deluge of gunfire and avenge *Takanami* with several score Long Lances.

JAPANESE TORPEDOES, 2327–0025

More than halfway back in the Japanese column, flagship *Naganami* radioed Tanaka's order to attack and reversed course to starboard— away from the enemy, an action that later elicited grumbling in wardrooms and mess decks within the squadron. Steadying up on a northwesterly heading, *Naganami* commenced using her guns at 2322 and one minute later began laying smoke. The next two ships astern, Captain Nakahara's Desdiv 24, also reversed course, but to port. From a "favorable firing position," at 2323 *Suzukaze* released eight torpedoes adjusted carefully on the flickering American gun flashes.

At the head of the Japanese column, Captain Torajiro Sato executed one of the most professionally skilled performances of any Imperial Navy destroyer commander during the war. Sato spurned the urgent instinct to immediately ring up all possible speed and reverse course. Instead, he coolly regulated his four ships to moderate speed and maintained the heading down the coast, allowing Wright's cruisers to pass on an opposite course. With their minimum wakes, low silhouettes, and abstinence from gunfire, Sato's destroyers crept down the channel between the walls of splashes and Guadalcanal's coast, unnoted save for a few float plane crewmen and *Lardner.*

Once southeast of the maelstrom around *Takanami,* Sato bent his vessels into sinuous course to close the American column. At 2328, *Kuroshio* dispatched two torpedoes, and one minute later *Oyashio* fired all eight of her Long Lances. *Kuroshio* decanted two more torpedoes as Sato finally began to reverse helm and increase speed. As the Japanese quartet put about, they experienced the optical illusion of the enemy column slowing and then stopping as they drew abreast. During this maneuver, however, *Kagero* and *Makinami* separated from *Oyashio* and *Kuroshio.* Already well to the northwest of Sato, flagship *Naganami* launched her eight torpedoes at 2332, and one minute later *Kawakaze* emptied her eight tubes. *Naganami* began laying smoke before cutting into formation between *Kawakaze* and *Suzukaze.* Thus, in the ten-minute interval between 2323 and 2333, six of Tanaka's destroyers set swimming forty-four powerful Long Lances.

At 2327, *Minneapolis* closed firing keys on her ninth main battery salvo. Wright started for the TBS transmitter to order a turn as he made out three enemy ships within 6,000 yards. Before he got there, two torpedoes, from either *Suzukaze* or *Takanami,* crashed into *Minneapolis*'s forward half within seconds of each other. One warhead found the aviation gasoline storage tanks forward of turret one; the second dispensed death and destruction from fireroom number two. Together they enveloped *Minneapolis* within a broad and lofty arch of flame-crested water. When the arch collapsed, tons of oil-veined ocean smashed down over platforms and decks, rampaging aft in a sloshing stampede, shoving men against bulkheads, wrenching two sailors overboard from the gun deck, and tugging burning gasoline fumes to her stern.

Though *Minneapolis* appeared badly hurt, if not sinking, to "the surprise and gratification of all hands" the main battery spoke again twice before power failed. The bow forward of turret one folded down at a 70-degree angle and blazed; with three firerooms out, the ship rapidly lost way and momentarily lost steering control. But as Captain Rosendahl wrote: "A determination to bring the ship safely to port existed from the first moment of difficulty." Officers and men reflexively began energetic damage-control and weight-jettisoning measures. Within four minutes they extinguished the fire on the forecastle and then quickly halved a list of 4 degrees.

Minneapolis might be saved, but she was a mute spectator for the rest of the battle.

One of the same spread of torpedoes found *New Orleans* barely a half-minute after the flagship was hit. She too had just fired her ninth salvo when her crew saw *Minneapolis* "engulfed in flame" and "demolished" by Long Lances. Then *New Orleans* suffered even more devastating damage. The half ton of Japanese explosive made common cause with some of *New Orleans*'s forward magazines and gasoline storage tanks. A broad fiery spire vaulted heavenward abreast turret one, spinning off whorls of flaming gasoline, oil, and powder. Huge slabs of water and oil crumbled over her superstructure and main deck, in roaring torrents a foot deep. On the bridge, Chaplain Howell M. Forgy recorded: "I opened my eyes to find we were in a cave of fire. . . . The great wall of flame all around me actually dried my sopping uniform in seconds." The blast severed the entire structure forward of turret two from *New Orleans.* With the barrels of turret one pointing skyward, the bow twisted to port, grooving and gouging the hull as it drifted aft to sink off the port quarter. Steering and communications failed on the bridge as *New Orleans* reversed course to starboard.

Pensacola followed next astern in the cruiser column. Lacking the aid of an SG radar, her gunners resorted to cues from illumination provided by *Honolulu* and *Northampton* to find a target. Captain Lowe fought his ship from the sky control platform, leaving the conn in the hands of *Pensacola*'s executive officer, Commander Harry Keeler, Jr. When torpedoes hit *Minneapolis* and *New Orleans,* Keeler concluded their participation was over and swung *Pensacola* to pass them to port—i.e., on the engaged side. *Minneapolis* disproved part of Keeler's thesis by sending her tenth salvo screeching just over *Pensacola*'s stacks.

Keeler's maneuver silhouetted *Pensacola* in front of her burning sisters, but perhaps worse, he returned her to the base course. At 2339, *Pensacola* caught a torpedo abreast the mainmast. A violent shudder slammed Lowe to the deck. All power, communications, and steering failed on the bridge. But aft the injuries were much worse. The warhead released its savage power in a full oil tank, jetting its contents horizontally into the after engine room and living spaces; behind the oil came a gush of water. In its vertical axis the blast pried open the main deck and geysered oil entwined with water as high as the maintop. When the pillar receded it left the mainmast with a skin of oil, which ignited, turning it into a torch within which control crews were burned to death. The hit ripped away the port outer shaft, and the ship took a 13 degree list. The tremendous heat from the fire aft caused oil rising from the ruptured tanks to blaze as soon as it reached the water surface.

Despite the benefit of an SG radar, *Honolulu,* with Admiral Tisdale embarked, initially failed to find a target. About 2325 she located hapless *Takanami,* which *Honolulu*'s fire control men tracked to a dead halt. After *New Orleans* veered out of column, *Pensacola* appeared to slow, but this was not to the taste of Captain Robert W. Hayler. He swerved *Honolulu* to starboard to prevent being silhouetted, bent on 30 knots, and maneuvered radically to evade "torpedo water." *Honolulu*'s gunners concluded a six-minute main battery firing program against a second target, checking when it disappeared behind smoke billowing up from oil fires. The secondary battery continued to issue illumination for another five minutes, but *Honolulu* prudently flashed her fighting lights when she was herself illuminated by a suspected "friend" as she neared Savo.

Just after eight bells, Wright notified Tisdale to take charge of the task force. Tisdale instructed destroyers to stand by cripples and conducted a sweep with *Honolulu* clockwise around Savo. Her radar sniffed four contacts, but these proved to be the van destroyers. These four vessels had circled up Savo's western side after brief participation in the gun action. About 2330, *Fletcher*'s SG radar picked up one or two ships standing northwest toward Cape Esperance, probably Desdiv 24 or *Naganami. Drayton* also acquired them on her SG radar, and her eager torpedo officer persuaded his skeptical skipper to authorize the firing of four torpedoes despite the extreme range. Not surprisingly, they failed to score.

The last cruiser in the American column was *Northampton.* Her fire control radar latched onto a target, almost certainly *Takanami,* and *Northampton*'s 8-inch rifles contributed to the destruction of that vessel. Like *Honolulu, Northampton* sheered right behind the damaged cruisers ahead of her. Unlike *Honolulu, Northampton* did not increase speed, nor did her fire control equipment have the built-in capacity to handle rapid changes of heading. Consequently, *Northampton* returned to the base course, and at 2348, her lookouts sighted two torpedoes from *Kawakaze* close aboard boring in from fine off the port bow. One struck 10 feet below the waterline abreast the after engine room, and four seconds later the second, running virtually on the surface, hit her only 40 feet farther aft. *Honolulu*'s awed executive officer described the scene thus: "A huge smoke and fire cone rose about 250 feet and [*Northampton*] seemed to be aflame instantly." Entangled within and about the fringes of the cone were oil and diesel fuel, which peaked and then splashed into the open hatches of the gun directors and slathered over the mainmast, boat deck, and main deck. The after engine room flooded, and three of four shafts ceased turning. *Northampton* immediately heeled 10 degrees to port, and her single moving propeller wrenched her around to port to a northeasterly heading as she writhed in flames.

At the rear of the American column, *Lamson* and *Lardner* wanted for targets for their guns or torpedoes. As they maneuvered around the damaged cruisers, *Lamson* drew machinegun fire from *New Orleans* and extricated herself by upping speed to 30 knots and violent twists to the east and then west. *Lardner* got the same treatment and hauled out to the east.

Just four minutes before torpedoes struck *Northampton,* Tanaka ordered all his ships to break contact and retire. By this time Captain Sato's ships were the only hail Japanese vessels south of Savo. As *Oyashio* and *Kuroshio* scurried up Guadalcanal's coast, four torpedoes sprang into the water from the latter at 2345. Sato's other pair, *Kagero* and *Makinami,* curved in even closer to the American track. At 2352, *Kagero* loosed four more Long Lances at a "battleship" and one minute later brashly turned on a searchlight to inspect a damaged American cruiser. *Makinami* either failed to clear her torpedo tubes or to find a target and fired no torpedoes during the engagement. When *Takanami* failed to answer radio calls, Tanaka directed *Oyashio* and *Kuroshio* to render assistance to *Takanami* at 0025, December 1.

RESULTS AND REFLECTIONS

Tanaka's order found *Oyashio* and *Kuroshio* west of Savo, where *Oyashio* had just fired two torpedoes at some enemy ships without success. Captain Sato swung back and at 0100 located *Takanami.* The close presence of enemy destroyers, however, compelled Sato to cut short his rescue mission. At about 0130, Captain Toshio Shimizu (ComDesdiv 31) ordered *Takanami* abandoned. Around one hundred men left the ship, but a large explosion and oil fire killed many of them in the water. *Takanami* sank about 0137 with Captain Shimizu and her skipper, Commander Masami Ogura. Of her crew of 244 or so, only thirty-three reached Guadalcanal alive.

It was also toward Guadalcanal that Captain Rosendahl initially pointed *Minneapolis* to prevent her crew from falling into Japanese hands if she sank. When *Minneapolis*'s condition stabilized, Rosendahl conned her to the same berth at Sasapi previously occupied by *Portland.* In view of the fact that two Long Lances hit *Minneapolis,* she sustained amazingly light casualties: thirty-six men entombed in three flooded firerooms, and one of two men washed overboard.

In terms of material damage and human loss, *New Orleans* was much more traumatized than Wright's flagship. The entire ship forward of turret two was gone, as well as every man stationed there and in turret two. Asphyxiating vapors released by the blast rendered untenable the compartment occupied by Lieutenant Commander H. M. Hayter, the damage control officer, and his staff. At Hayter's command, evacuation of that space and the adjacent plotting room began. Most of the enlisted men escaped, but Hayter, who gave his gas mask to a sailor without one, and two other officers perished waiting to leave last. With these deaths the toll reached 183. *New Orleans* struggled to Tulagi, where *Maury* tied up alongside to hold her in position, as all of the cruiser's ground tackle had been amputated.

Pensacola crewmen faced almost equally severe perils from flood and fire. The strong grip of Iron Bottom Sound pulled *Pensacola*'s hull down 13 degrees to port. An ardent and widespread blaze defended the sea-filled compartments from damage control parties. The searing heat boiled the water away in the flooded magazines of turret three and ignited powder and projectiles. A series of these detonations ripped large sections of plating from the barbette and flung them at the fire fighters. In the face of this imminent threat of a massive magazine explosion no one would have questioned an order to abandon ship. But *Pensacola*'s crew refused to give up, and by great good fortune, 150 8-inch shells exploded not in unison, but one by one with heart-stopping reverberations. Destroyer *Perkins* came alongside and proffered fire hoses that helped contain the fire, which was not totally under control for twelve hours. The list was checked and then righted. The one intact fireroom provided sufficient steam to give speeds up to 9 knots on the one operable engine, enabling her to find refuge in Tulagi harbor at 0344. She lost 125 crewmen killed.

There would be no refuge in Tulagi for *Northampton*. Like *Pensacola, Northampton* sailors fought flooding in the teeth of fires that "cooked off" 5-inch ready ammunition. The list reached 16 degrees at 0040 and thirty-five minutes later crossed 23 degrees despite countermeasures. By this time, lubrication failure had stilled the one remaining shaft. At 0130, Japanese guns on Guadalcanal began plunking shells into the water about 1,000 yards shy of *Northampton,* then only about 4 miles northeast of Doma Cove. Kitts ordered everyone off but a salvage crew. *Fletcher* and *Drayton* arrived twenty minutes later and commenced picking up *Northampton* crewmen by the light of the moon that providently broke through the overcast at 0135. By 0200, water pressure failed in the firehoses and with it any hope that the conflagration aft could be mastered. With the list at 35 degrees and increasing fast, Captain Kitts sent all hands over the side. At 0304, *Northampton* twisted onto her beam ends, turned bottom up, and then sank by the stern. Between them, the two destroyers rescued fifty-seven officers and 716 men. Lost with their ship were four officers and forty-six men.

The three crippled cruisers were not out of the woods yet. Inshore mooring and camouflage afforded passive defense against the immediate threat of enemy aircraft. *New Orleans,* for example, said Chaplin Forgy, looked like a "botanical garden." The Cactus Air Force handled the active defense, but the enemy fliers at Rabaul did not come calling. The next step was to make the trio seaworthy. Tulagi, an extremely austere base oriented to the care and maintenance of motor torpedo boats, possessed few tools or materials, but an abundance of heat and disease and misery-bearing mosquitoes and flies. A summons brought artificers from tender *Vestal* and three fleet tugs to help, but the crews performed most of the work. With considerable ingenuity, bluejackets gave coconut logs second careers as false bows for *Minneapolis* and *New Orleans. Minneapolis* tars fought a long battle to regain buoyancy forward, redoubling their efforts after a gas explosion flooded heretofore undamaged compartments. With her ruptured side patched, *Pensacola* cleared Tulagi on December 6; the flagship and *New Orleans* departed on December 12. Repairs and alterations would keep all three out of action for nearly a year.

At this same time the American participants conducted an agonizing review of the action. For none was the matter more painful than Carleton Wright. He had spent thirty years building a record that won him—for forty-eight hours—a coveted independent flag command in combat. It took just over forty minutes from the first radar contact to the last torpedo hit to forever blight his reputation, for Tassafaronga represented not just a defeat, but a humiliation. Put plainly, an inferior, cargo-entangled, and partly surprised destroyer squadron had demolished a superior cruiser-destroyer group. Wright was spared the knowledge that, as awful as it was, it could have been worse: few of the crippled cruisers would have survived had Tanaka's destroyers possessed their reload torpedoes.

Wright manfully shouldered the responsibility and absolved all of his cruiser captains of any blame. Less commendably, Halsey released a good deal of pent-up wrath upon the head of Commander Cole of *Fletcher*. He identified Cole's sins as launching torpedoes at excessive ranges and retiring around Savo instead of "helping" the cruisers. In retrospect, it seems clear that Wright's hesitation spoiled the torpedo attack and Cole's maneuvers precisely paralleled those of Admiral Tisdale in *Honolulu,* who escaped criticism.[3]

Captured survivors identified *Takanami,* but the many vivid "eyewitness" reports by officers of stricken and sinking enemy vessels and disappearing radar pips persuaded Wright and his superiors that the actual score totaled four enemy destroyers sunk and two damaged. This constituted only modest recompense for the loss of *Northampton,* severe damage to three of her sisters, and the deaths of 395 officers and men. These results properly led to a particularly searching probe of material and tactics. Wright praised the gunfire of his cruisers as "very impressive" in volume, but according to a Japanese critique:

> [American] fire was inaccurate, shells [im]properly set for deflection were especially numerous, and it is conjectured that either [American] marksmanship is not remarkable or else the illumination from [their] star shells was not sufficiently effective.

The dean of American naval historians, Samuel Eliot Morison, would cite this as evidence of "abominable" American marksmanship this night. It was certainly ineffective, but the fault rested not in the crews. Later research showed that the relatively slow-firing 8-inch guns and fire control apparatus of the heavy cruisers engaged in this battle were ill-adapted to swatting destroyers at night at moderate range against a land background. Further, as most reports lamented, the fire control radars then in use could not cope with the proximity of land. In a display of some insight on this point, Wright equated one rapid-fire, 6-inch-gunned "light" cruiser like *Honolulu,* with the latest fire control equipment, with "at least" two "heavy" cruisers. The American 8-inch-gunned "treaty cruiser" fought her last night battle in the Solomons at Tassafaronga. This resulted partly by design, but more because of *force majeure*—every one of

---

[3]After a tour of shore duty, Wright again exercised command of a cruiser division at sea during the Kiska landings and the Gilbert operations. It boggles the mind to note, however, that Halsey, Nimitz, and King permitted Wright to be awarded the Navy Cross, the naval service's second-highest award for valor, for his conduct at Tassafaronga.

the thirteen heavy cruisers used around Guadalcanal to date had been sunk or damaged.

The composition of Task Force 67's antagonist, a question coupled to the puzzle over the origins of the enemy torpedoes, baffled Wright and Nimitz. Wright commented that the observed positions of enemy vessels "make it improbable that torpedoes with speed-distance characteristics similar to our own" could have wrought such havoc. Rather than admitting that the Japanese torpedoes enjoyed different (and superior) characteristics, Wright suggested some of the culprits were submarines. Nimitz flatly conceded the superiority of enemy torpedo technique, but he too as yet failed to appreciate the real capabilities of the Long Lance. The inability to recognize this important enemy material superiority even after this dramatic setback plagued American commanders deep into 1943.

As to tactics, everyone could see the obvious undesirability of fighting destroyers with heavy ships in confined waters. Halsey's explicit orders denied Wright the option of bringing Tanaka to battle west of Savo in more open waters. But Halsey, mainly concerned with preventing Japanese reinforcement of Guadalcanal, probably thought the available information only guaranteed an interception off Tassafaronga. In view of the approach course chosen by Tanaka, this may well have been correct.

The postwar criticism of American tactics labeled the failure to use open formations a vice, and the inhibition on independent torpedo attacks by destroyers a sin. The fallacy behind these critiques is twofold. First, merely changing the formation could not cure underlying shortcomings in indoctrination and equipment. Second, even if the basis in indoctrination and equipment had existed, the hasty assembly of Task Force 67 from such disparate sources dictated simple tactical arrangements. Nimitz wisely recognized the institutional rather than individual roots of the defeat. He prescribed a remedy of "training, *training* and MORE TRAINING."

Nimitz also candidly praised the enemy's "energy, persistence and courage." United States naval officers attributed all of these qualities in particular to Raizo Tanaka, who thereafter enjoyed what Americans call a "good press." The many generous tributes paid Tanaka reached their zenith in the account of this battle by Samuel Eliot Morison, who said:

> In many actions of the war, mistakes on the American side were cancelled by those of the enemy; but despite the brief confusion of his destroyers, Tanaka made no mistakes at Tassafaronga.

It will therefore come as a surprise to many readers to discover that not all of Tanaka's subordinates or superiors held him in such high esteem. Critics took him to task over his selection of the approach formation, which, contrary to Imperial Navy tradition, placed his flagship in the center of the column. Once the action began, some charged that *Naganami*'s movements were "not aggressive" and that Tanaka himself neglected to provide "suitable leadership" so that each ship fought individually. These critics attributed the Japanese success to the sacrifice of *Takanami,* which admittedly drew the vast majority of American attention and fire.

To a detached observer this criticism seems overdrawn. The location of *Naganami* was Tanaka's prerogative, and he possessed no objective basis on which to presuppose that major American interference would confront the Reinforcement Unit from the east rather than the west (in the later case the flagship would be better-positioned). Before American gunfire commenced, Tanaka ordered the supply landing plans abandoned and all ships to attack. The counterattack was executed essentially by divisions, not individually, in consonance with sound Imperial Navy doctrine—it was neither necessary nor desirable for Tanaka to attempt to keep his squadron in column. *Naganami*'s use of guns and torpedoes was amply pugnacious, and if she maneuvered alone, then questions should most appropriately be addressed to Captain Nakahara, who went gallivanting off with Desdiv 24 rather than follow *Naganami.* Of course, Tanaka profited from the superb performance of Captain Sato, whom some Japanese viewed as the real hero of the action.

The magnificent performance of the junior officers and crewmen of the torpedoed cruisers left the only bright spot in this otherwise black page in American naval history. With "great determination, ability and resourcefulness," commented Wright, they saved their ships for a better day. At exorbitant expense, Wright and his shipmates did accomplish Halsey's primary goal. None of the supplies carried by the Reinforcement Unit reached the 17th Army on Guadalcanal.

20

THE DECEMBER

DECISION

"It is said if you lose your appetite it is the end"

ON THE SUPPLY LINE

Both sides aimed for major offensives in January; each devoted the days of December to a sequence of preparatory steps. The Japanese mounted interlocking efforts to sustain the forces already on Guadalcanal and to accumulate and position air units. The Americans paced resupply with the replacement of the worn 1st Marine Division by fresh Marine and Army units while simultaneously air and light naval units maintained a counter campaign against Japanese logistical and airfield construction exertions. The American command also inaugurated an effort to annex Mount Austen that provoked some of the most vicious fighting of the campaign. These activities in the Solomons occupied the foreground during December, but in the background a debate convulsed the senior Japanese governmental and service councils in Tokyo that lead to a fateful swing in Japanese strategy. We turn first then to the actions on the supply lines.

Tanaka's failure to deliver supplies on the night of November 30–December 1 enhanced the urgency of the need to reprovision the 17th Army. Destroyers *Arashi, Nowaki,* and *Yugure* brought the

Reinforcement Unit to a total of ten vessels when it cleared Short-land on its second attempt with the drum method at 1300, December 3. A coast watcher alarm and a search plane contact enabled a strike group of eight SBDs and seven TBFs to catch Tanaka's destroyers at twilight 160 miles from their destination. A dozen Petes attempted to pitch into the attack planes, but lost five of their number in exchange for one Wildcat of the escort. Despite pressing their runs to "very close range," according to Tanaka, the SBDs and TBFs inflicted only slight damage on *Makinami* at a cost of one SBD and one Avenger. *Makinami* and her compatriots dumped 1,500 drums at Tassafaronga and regained Shortland safely, but American planes sent all but 310 drums to the depths of Iron Bottom Sound.

The paltry results of this episode resulted in technical refinements of the drum technique, including a limit of 100 per line and a require-ment that the destroyers set their loads adrift as close as possible to shore. In the interval, analysis of the Tassafaronga action convinced the staff of the Combined Fleet that the Reinforcement Unit needed an increased screen. Consequently, new orders detailed *Tanikaze, Urakaze,* and large antiaircraft destroyer *Teruzuki* to join Tanaka. The first two of this trio participated in the third venture with drum delivery on December 7, for which the Reinforcement Unit num-bered twelve vessels (three in the screening role) under Captain Sato of Tassafaronga repute.

Based upon a warning from coast watchers, thirteen SBDs led by Major Joseph Sailor of VMSB-132 confronted Sato at about 1840. A near miss on *Nowaki* killed seventeen men and flooded an engine and boiler room, leaving her without power. She returned to Short-land at the end of a towline from *Naganami,* escorted by *Ariake* and the slightly damaged *Arashi.* On the debit side, a destroyer winged Sailor's Dauntless and then one of eight defending Petes downed him, costing the Cactus Air Force an outstanding leader.

Sato pressed on with the other eight destroyers and met an equal number of PT boats off Savo. *PT 48* and *PT 40* stood athwart the passage between Savo and Cape Esperance; *109* and *43* faced sea-ward between Kokumbona and Cape Esperance; the balance, *59, 36, 37,* and *44* (designated the striking force), stood by concealed in the lee of Savo. One SOC glided overhead as an illuminator. Around 2320, *PT 48* and *PT 40* detected Sato's unit standing into the throat between Savo and Esperance. The boats sought to gain position ahead, but at this juncture *PT 48* lost power on one of her three engines. As she started to withdraw, a second of her power plants failed. She retired toward the south shore of Savo, laying smoke to confuse Japanese gunners, while *PT 40* diverted enemy attentions by outpacing two destroyers in a southeasterly sprint.

The striking force found Sato fifteen minutes later. These four boats decanted a dozen torpedoes, prompting Sato to recoil. During this skirmish, *Kuroshio* and *PT 59* under Lieutenant (jg) John M. Searles, swapped machinegun bursts at about 100 yards, with the result that the PT boat returned to Tulagi after being hit ten times, and her opponent sustained as many casualties. All this action pulled *PT 109* and *PT 43* up to Cape Esperance by 0015. The mere presence of these two boats and the lone SOC caused Sato to abandon a second effort to carry out his mission.

This encounter cast a different light over the date of December 7 in American naval annals, for these upstart young PT sailors achieved the considerable feat of rebuffing the redoubtable Reinforcement Unit without loss, whereas only a week earlier eleven major warships had suffered severely and accomplished no more. Indeed, this night's work represented perhaps the greatest individual success of American PT boats during the war.

Nor were the repercussions of this action limited to a one-night frustration of the Tokyo Express. The following day, General Imamura received what he termed a "bombshell" at a conference with officers from the Combined Fleet, 11th Air Fleet, and 8th Fleet at Rabaul. The Imperial Navy delegation announced intentions to stop all destroyer transportation runs effective immediately. They informed Imamura that if the losses and damage to its screening vessels continued at the pace since mid-November, the Combined Fleet soon would be unable to fight the great decisive battle. In the face of Imamura's protests, the local Navy representatives consented to two more runs of destroyers, one to Guadalcanal and one to Buna. The 8th Area Army took an appeal to Tokyo: without resupply runs by destroyers, the men on Guadalcanal and at Buna would have to be sacrificed.

On this same day, December 8, transports disgorged the last of the Americal Division's three regiments, the 132d Infantry, at Lunga. The next day Vandegrift formally, but without fanfare, turned over command of the American forces on Guadalcanal to Major General Alexander M. Patch of the U.S. Army. Typically, Vandegrift chose to mark this occasion not with a florid speech or general order dwelling on the accomplishments of his division, but with a concise letter that paid generous tribute to the soldiers, sailors, and airmen who had worked, fought, and died side by side with his marines. Nor did he forget the coast watchers, though security requirements obliged him to refer to them guardedly as "our small band of devoted allies who have contributed so vastly in proportion to their numbers."

As these small ceremonies took place, the first echelon of the division, principally the 5th Marines, began embarkation. They were dressed in green dungarees or dirty khaki, often with limbs protruding from shirts chopped back to the shoulders, trousers clipped at the knees, or sleeves and pant legs that ended in fringes of tatters. Knotted laces or pieces of string secured their field boots—"boondockers" to the marines—which listed to the side or leaned back at the heels from wear. A few men sported Japanese footgear. Almost to a man, their bodies were dirty, lean (someone estimated the average weight loss at 20 pounds), wearied to the innermost tissue, and, in too many cases, a playground for malarial parasites. Upon arriving in their boats alongside the ships that were to take them away, the marines were asked to leave as they came, traversing dangling cargo nets. This was far too taxing for some, who had to be hoisted up by the strong arms of healthy sailors.

Many marines made their last act on Guadalcanal a visit to the cemetery that contained most of the division's 650 dead. Many graves bore crude but heartfelt inscriptions: "He died fighting"; "A real Marine"; "Our Buddy." Thirty-one marines would be permanently listed as missing. Another 1,278 marines won Purple Heart Medals for wounds, but around 8,580 wore no decorations for their diseases, principally malaria. About forty-eight hours before their departure, medical officers scrutinized one unidentified regiment (very likely the 5th Marines) and found fully one-third of its members unfit for further combat. This proportion would have been significantly higher were it not for 400 relatively recent replacements. The rest of the division left in two more echelons in December and January. Of the original landing force there remained only the luckless 2d Marines, organically part of the 2d Marine Division, which was only now concentrating at Guadalcanal.

In a flight of editorial naiveté the *New York Times* informed its readers:

> When news comes that the Marines are leaving Guadalcanal for a well-earned rest we know that this is not because they asked to be relieved of their assignment.

This comment would have produced a rude laugh from any member of the 1st Marine Division who read it. But though they had left the island, it would always be figuratively and literally embroidered into the character of the division. On the plane that took Vandegrift from Guadalcanal to Brisbane rode the operations officer, Lieutenant Colonel Merrill Twining, who passed the hours designing a shoulder patch for the division. He chose a diamond of blue with the five stars of the Southern Cross as a background. In the center of the patch he placed a red numeral 1, down the center of which he added the one word that said it all: Guadalcanal.

During the first week of December, provision-bearing Japanese submarines enjoyed more success in evading interference than the Reinforcement Unit. I-boats delivered 20 or more tons on three nights without incident by December 8. But then American radio intelligence, which had issued generalized rather than precise forewarning of runs of the Tokyo Express, succeeded in divining the schedule for the next submarine delivery. Thus in the early hours of December 9, *PT 44* and *PT 59* waited in ambush off Kamimbo when *I-3* surfaced right between them. A torpedo from *PT 59* (Lieutenant Jack M. Searles) eviscerated the big I-boat as she commenced unloading. As a result of this disaster, the Japanese suspended submarine supply hauling.

Eleven destroyers, no fewer than five in the escort role, mustered for the promised additional run of the "Express" on December 11. Tanaka once again put his hand on the helm with his flag in *Teruzuki.* A personal message from Yamamoto underscored the importance of this mission, but other signals enabled American radio intelligence to issue a précis of the composition, timing, and destination of the Reinforcement Unit. This information enabled fourteen dive-bombers under Major Robertshaw to meet Tanaka at extreme range in feeble light about 1855. Despite the absence of defending fighters, the Reinforcement Unit emerged unscathed from the bombing attack and downed one SBD.

Another reception committee awaited Tanaka off Guadalcanal: two PT boats on patrol off Kamimbo and three once again in the handy blind on the southeast side of Savo. The six cargo-laden destroyers cast afloat 1,200 drums off Cape Esperance and began their withdrawal by 0115. From the shadows of Savo, boats *37, 40,* and *48* stalked part of the run, and within seconds of one another, all three boats let fly with torpedoes. One of these struck flagship *Teruzuki* on the port side aft with a shattering blast. The explosion nipped off one propeller shaft and the rudder and ignited a brilliant oil fire that snaked into the ship's interior to set off an after magazine. The torpedo hit also injured Tanaka and knocked him unconscious for a time. The wounded admiral and his staff transferred to *Naganami* at 0133, and *Arashi* took off about 140 men.

This action attracted *PT 44* and *PT 114* from their station off Kamimbo. Lieutenant Frank Freeland took his *PT 44* imprudently close to burning *Teruzuki,* exposing his boat to *Kawakaze* and *Suzukaze.* The first hit crippled the engines of Freeland's craft and set her afire. Moments after Freeland gave the order to abandon ship, a second hit or hits demolished the boat. One of two survivors of the eleven-man crew, Lieutenant (jg) Charles M. Melhorn, reported:

> I dove deep and was still under water when the salvo struck. The concussion jarred me badly, but I kept swimming under water. There was a tremendous explosion, paralyzing me from the waist down. The water around me went red. The life jacket took control and pulled me to the surface. I came up in a sea of fire, the flaming embers of the boat cascading all about me. I tried to get free of the life jacket but couldn't, so I started swimming feebly. I thought the game was up, but the water, which had shot sky-high in the explosion, rained down and put out the fires around me. From the first hit to this point took less than fifteen seconds.

A scuttling order terminated efforts to save *Teruzuki* at 0315. The skipper, the destroyer division commander, and 154 others found refuge at Kamimbo. The rest of the Reinforcement Unit dropped anchor at Shortland at 1130, December 12. Only 220 of the 1,200 drums released off Guadalcanal got to their intended recipients. After this decided success by the weary PT sailors, the Tokyo Express made no further runs to Guadalcanal in 1942.

The travails of the Reinforcement Unit represented the most conspicuous, but not the only significant, Japanese enterprise in the Solomons in December, for they also began replenishing their air power as the first phase of preparation for the new offensive. On December 7 the 11th Air Fleet disposed exactly one hundred operational aircraft (forty-one fighters, thirty-six Bettys, and twenty-three Vals). With the arrival of new aircraft and the repair of currently nonoperational ones, Imperial Headquarters expected the numbers of Zeros and Bettys to reach 168 and 100 respectively by the end of the month. To these would be added 110 aircraft from the Imperial Army's 6th Air Division, which began arriving on December 18.

The 11th Air Fleet staff was acutely aware of a precipitous decline in the skill of the replacement aircrews. On November 19, Admiral Kusaka divided his Bettys into two halves and sent one to Tinian to conduct remedial training. For the same purpose, he routed to Kavieng a significant number of the recently assigned fighter pilots, most of whom had never flown a Zero. In the opinion of Rear Admiral Sakamaki, the chief of staff of the 11th Air Fleet, the latest crop of airmen possessed only a third of the proficiency level of the men they replaced.

The Guadalcanal campaign illustrates that combat power in the air cannot be measured solely by comparing aircraft inventories. Maintenance resources and particularly airfield location and capacity rapidly discounted the raw numbers of aircraft each side fielded. In recognition of these factors, the new Central Agreement accentuated the expansion of the infrastructure of airfields, and on this occasion vigorous action followed good intentions, as it had not on earlier occasions. Construction troops improved existing facilities at Rabaul, Buin, and Shortland and initiated work on the creation of new bases closer to Guadalcanal.[1] The target date for completion of this program was mid-December.

The most important of the new facilities was Munda, on the island of New Georgia only 170 miles from Guadalcanal. As early as November 13, destroyer *Hakaze* landed three companies of the 6th Sasebo Special Naval Landing Force to sweep the area for coast watchers and their native helpers. This party declared Munda adaptable as an airfield. After a small transport installed a rifle battalion at Munda on the nights of November 20 and 21, several small convoys off-loaded the bulk of two battalion-size construction units between November 23 and 27. But as the convoy was returning on November 28, a B-17 hit *Chihaya Maru* and she had to be towed to Rabaul. The following night, a destroyer brought a new commander to Munda, Captain Sanji Iwabuchi, formerly the skipper of *Kirishima*.

These construction units wielded only picks, shovels, hoes, saws, and a few powered tools. To preserve secrecy for as long as possible, they labored mostly at night, and in a clever ruse they left treetops suspended from wires stretched across the projected runway after cutting down the trunks. However, these ploys hoodwinked neither scouts sent by coast watchers nor cameras, and beginning on December 6, Munda attracted daily attention from Allied fliers. Despite these buffetings, work crews readied a rough strip, 1,094 by 44 yards,

---

[1]Japanese officers considered the western end of Guadalcanal among the possible new sites for airfields, but they soon discarded this rather bizarre idea.

with hidden revetments for thirty Zeros by December 14. The addition of a dozen antiaircraft guns, another infantry battalion, and part of the ground echelon of the 252d Air Group completed final preparations for operations by December 19.

On December 23, two dozen Zeros of the 252d Air Group fluttered down to Munda with nine other Zeros in escort. The 252d Air Group lost two planes in a clash over its new base that also cost two Wildcats and a P-39. The following morning, nine SBDs, nine P-39s, four P-38s, and four F4Fs from the Cactus Air Force found four Zeros airborne and the others being readied. The American fighters claimed fourteen Zeros in the air, and the dive-bombers reported mangling the remainder on the ground. Actual losses amounted to two Zeros in the air and eleven "damaged" on the ground.

Christmas Day brought another Japanese setback. Submarine *Seadragon* torpedoed *Nankai Maru,* bearing construction troops for an air base site on Kolombangara, shortly after she stood out of Rabaul. Her escort, *Uzuki,* contrived to collide with the transport, leaving the destroyer immobilized as well. Four more destroyers from Rabaul came to retrieve this duo, but en route back, *Ariake* lost twenty-eight killed in a bombing attack that did serious damage to her armament. The Japanese sought to guard the Munda base with a standing patrol from Buin and flew in five more Zeros on the day after Christmas. But these merely replaced an equal number of Zeros burned out on the ground that day during one of the incessant attacks by the Cactus Air Force.

By December 27, Admiral Kusaka recognized that Munda had become more of a liability than an asset. At the cost of one Betty, the surviving pilots and three flyable Zeros of the 252d Air Group were regathered to Rabaul. This fiasco also compelled the abandonment of a desperate scheme for provisioning the 17th Army. *Patrol Boat 2* had been stripped of armament and loaded with 85 tons of food in readiness for beaching at Kamimbo. But this effort hung contingent on air protection by Zeros at Munda. With the decision to withdraw the fighters, the operation was canceled the same day it was scheduled to take place, December 27. This date marked the end of an equally desperate attempt that began on the 20th to airdrop supplies from Bettys at night to the 17th Army. There is no record of any of this food being recovered. With these failures, the Japanese reactivated their submarine transportation system—also on December 27.

The impact of the inability of the Imperial Navy to deliver provisions in December to the 17th Army was calamitous. Rations in the

38th Division fell to one-sixth for the men in the front line and one-tenth for the others, but even under this regimen the unit consumed all the food landed in December by the 17th. Of the approximately 6,000 men in the division, roughly 30 percent retained the strength to fetch rations for their comrades, but a mere 250 men possessed reasonably full combat capability. In the 2d Division rations likewise diminished far below subsistence levels. Of about 1,000 men in the 4th and 16th Infantry regiments, over two-thirds were sick, injured, or detailed to support those on the line, leaving only 100 to 200 at the front. Unceasing shelling and air attacks took the lives of four to ten men per day per regiment on a good day, and twenty to thirty on a bad day. On December 7, the 8th Area Army notified Tokyo that about fifty men died each day on Guadalcanal. This rate accelerated such that by mid-December, the Sendai Division alone withered by about forty deaths every twenty-four hours.

On December 18, Major Nishiyama of the 228th Infantry recorded in his diary: ". . . orders received to feed men to end of the month on food we have now. This is beyond outrageous." Other diaries portray what one officer termed the "very bottom of the human condition." The entire army was composed of pale wisps of men, with ulcerous skin draped with filthy, sopping clothes. Vast numbers were wracked with fevers, for which there was no medicine. Army headquarters reported they ate tree shoots, coconuts, and grass growing in the rivers. In his diary, Second Lieutenant Yasuo Ko'o, the color bearer of the 124th Infantry, recorded an unfailing formula with which he calibrated the life expectancy of his fellows at the turn of the year:

> Those who can stand—30 days
> Those who can sit up—3 weeks
> Those who cannot sit up—1 week
> Those who urinate lying down—3 days
> Those who have stopped speaking—2 days
> Those who have stopped blinking—tomorrow

"It is said," noted another officer, "if you lose your appetite it is the end." It was in this severely debilitated condition that the 17th Army faced a new American attack.

THE GIFU, PART I

During November, Japanese commanders witnessed the rapidly accelerating deterioration of the combat value and mobility of the 17th Army. They feared a catastrophe if their opponents massed firepower and tanks for a thrust up the coast. Therefore, the 17th Army strived to lure American attention inland by feinting offensive designs. On November 30, one weak company mounted an attack about dusk against the southern rim of the American line on the east bank of the Matanikau. Although the Japanese expended some precious mortar and artillery ammunition to add a tint of seriousness, this turn earned only cursory mention in American records. Meanwhile, Lieutenant General Sano ordered his 38th Engineer Battalion to organize forays by small raiding parties into the American perimeter from Mount Austen. On December 12, a five-man team got away after they destroyed a P-39 and a fuel truck on Fighter Two.

Ironically, no added incentive was required to draw American

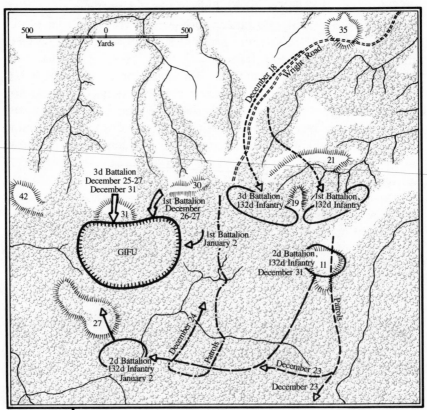

The Gifu, December 18, 1942–January 2, 1943

forces inland. When Patch assumed command on December 9, he believed that expelling the Japanese from Guadalcanal would have to await a cycle of replacement of the 1st Marine Division and reinforcement in the new year. Both he and General Harmon, however, sought to accomplish an essential prelude to that goal with the means at hand. Mount Austen afforded the Japanese excellent observation of all activities within the American perimeter around Lunga Point, from troop movements and deployments through activities at Henderson Field to the arrival and departure of shipping. A limited attack to secure Mount Austen would both deny this fruitful source of intelligence to the Japanese and provide a springboard for a contemplated flanking movement during the offensive slated for January.

Mount Austen is not a single peak but a jumble of abrupt rocky ridges gripped by jungle. The 1,514-foot summit rises about 6 miles southwest of Henderson Field. It marks the end of a ridge that juts up from foothills about 2 miles south of the shore. A census of the lesser crests is difficult because many merge into jungled ridges. The Americans arbitrarily numbered the open crests for reference purposes. West from the summit of Mount Austen sits Hill 27, a small 920-foot rocky plateau barely visible above the jungle. About 750 yards immediately north of Hill 27 rests a grassy area labeled Hill 31, which afforded a good vista of Lunga Point. Hill 31 forms the center of a line of similar open patches, designated from east to west Hills 30-31-42. West of Hill 42 and about 1,500 yards northwest of Mount Austen across the Matanikau are a pair of hilltops (43 and 44) in a grassy area identified from its appearance on aerial photos as the "Sea Horse." Somewhat north and west of the Sea Horse is a matrix of hills (50-51-52-53-53-54-55-57) christened the "Galloping Horse," likewise for its appearance on aerial photos.

Patrols through early December produced no intimations that Mount Austen might harbor substantial forces. But on December 14 a patrol from the 132d Infantry Regiment encountered an organized group of Japanese whose armory included four machineguns and one or two mortars. From this brush and the raid of December 12 intelligence officers apparently deduced a buildup of Japanese strength in the south. As American stirrings in front of Major General Ito's 38th Infantry Group became more pronounced toward mid-December, General Sano turned over his small hoard of reserve food to Ito and arranged the transportation of more supplies to that area. This was none too soon, for on December 16, Patch ordered the 132d Infantry to seize Mount Austen at once.

Colonel Leroy E. Nelson's 132d Infantry, a former Illinois National Guard outfit, only debarked on December 8. Nelson selected Lieutenant Colonel William C. Wright to lead the attack with his 3d Battalion. Lieutenant Colonel Earl F. Ripstra's 1st Battalion would follow Wright. The 105mm howitzers of the 246th Field Artillery Battalion and the 75mm pack howitzers of the 2d Battalion, 10th Marines offered fire support, but a slippery, rough jeep trail whittled along the ridgeline running to Hill 35 constituted the logistical umbilical cord. Beyond that point, native bearers (the "Cannibal Battalion") hand-carried supplies forward. Orders deprived Nelson of the services of his 2d Battalion.

The effort to annex Mount Austen began on December 17 with an uneventful reconnaissance in force up the northeastern slopes by Company L and 110 men of Company K, 132d Infantry. The following day, Company L marched about 1,000 yards southwest of Hill 35 and then pivoted left to enter the jungled slopes leading to Mount Austen's summit. Around 0930, rifle and machinegun fire pinned down the lead elements in heavy vegetation. When the rest of the battalion joined Company L about 1130, it was flagging from its first major exertions in the Guadalcanal heat. Lieutenant Colonel Wright placed artillery fire on the Japanese positions and directed his command to set up a defensive perimeter.

After bombing and strafing by three SBDs and a five-minute artillery preparation on December 19, Wright strode forward to investigate the jungle to the west of his battalion. About 0930, enemy machinegun bullets wounded him; when Wright tried to grenade the enemy position, he sustained mortal wounds. Wright's replacement, Major Louis Franco of the 1st Battalion, could not get forward and take charge until late afternoon. Meanwhile, a patrol recovered Wright's body. Not content with this success, a few Japanese riflemen infiltrated past the forward companies to discompose the command posts of both battalions and to harass the supply parties and engineers on the trail, shortly named Wright Road in honor of the fallen commander. The 3d Battalion achieved no progress all day after Wright's death.

Darkness found the 1st Battalion deployed on the left flank of the 3d Battalion south of Hill 19, and both battalions dug in. During daylight of December 20, more infiltrators or small patrols kept the 132d Infantry edgy by plucking at the flanks and rear. From December 20 to 23, progressively more adventurous American patrolling pushed 1,500 yards south and found neither Japanese nor trails in the jungle, but a 3d Battalion patrol prowled westward as far as Hill

31 on the 23d. Nelson ordered the 3d Battalion to follow the same route to Hill 31 the next day and then attack south toward Hill 27. The 1st Battalion would follow to screen the left flank and protect the supply route that the Japanese constantly nettled.

On December 24 the 3d Battalion reached Hill 31 in the afternoon after brushing back a few enemy riflemen who sought to impede its advance. As the leading elements of the battalion wheeled left to climb the open grassy slopes of Hill 31, dense machinegun fire from well-concealed positions abruptly checked them. All this sound and fury produced no casualties, but Franco thought the hour too late to develop the situation, so he directed the establishment of a defense perimeter for the night.

Franco's men were halted by what proved to be the most strongly fortified Japanese position on Guadalcanal, named by its defenders the Gifu after a prefecture on Honshu. The Gifu sat west of the summit of Mount Austen, sequestered between Hills 31 and 27. Its main line consisted of about forty-five interconnected pillboxes bent into a horseshoe, with the open end to the west, between the two hills. These structures were burrowed into the ground and revetted inside and out with dirt. The walls were two logs thick, the roofs three. Earth and artfully draped foliage covered the 3 feet or so of each emplacement projecting above ground. They were impervious to anything short of a direct hit from a 105mm howitzer.

Each pillbox housed at least one and sometimes two machineguns plus two or three riflemen. The staggered formation of the pillboxes permitted mutual supporting fires, and in front of the main line, the Gifu's creators also prepared positions, frequently under the bases of great mahogany and banyan trees, for riflemen and light machinegunners. Infusing the Gifu with his own exceptional resolution was Major Takeyosho Inagaki, who mustered perhaps 500 to 600 men of his own 2d Battalion, 228th Infantry as well as the 2d Battalion, 124th Infantry.

The first and most difficult problem facing the attackers was simply locating the enemy positions. The dense jungle concealed both emplacements and firing lanes, and the vegetation, as well as the location chosen by the defenders, precluded even the sort of intuitive estimates of enemy positions afforded by more open terrain. Ranges in Guadalcanal's jungles seldom exceeded 30 yards, but at the Gifu it was quite possible, and quite fatal, to trod literally within a few yards of the embrasure of a pillbox without seeing it. The 132d Infantry lacked flamethrowers, and enemy fire kept them from getting close enough to use demolition charges. The Gifu, however, did have vulnerabilities. Its western perimeter was weak, and the defenders lacked the strength to man both the northern perimeter and Hill 27 to the south, thus exposing themselves to being outflanked. The Japanese lacked artillery support, but what they wanted for most was provisions and ammunition of any kind.

Christmas Day and the two days afterward illustrated the formidable character of the Gifu. On the 25th, rifle and machinegun fire from invisible outposts in front of the main line of the Gifu stung back the 3d Battalion. Nelson concluded from this day's events that he faced a perimeter defense. He ordered the 3d Battalion to continue its frontal attack the next day while the 1st Battalion covered the left flank and penetrated 1,000 yards south to launch patrols to find the elusive enemy flanks. Despite air and artillery preparations, on December 26 the 3d Battalion only regained the line of farthest advance from Christmas Day. Machinegun fire snagged Company B's exploration for the Japanese flank. On the third day, Nelson sent the 3d Battalion into a holding attack while swinging the 1st Battalion south and east to strike a flank. However, machinegun fire again checked the 3d Battalion, and the 1st Battalion assembled too far to the west and, instead of hooking into an open flank, it ran headlong into the Gifu, with the usual result.

More patrolling occupied the next two days, December 28 and 29. The 132d identified neither gaps nor open flanks in the Gifu, but on the 29th a patrol found a clear route to Hill 27. This same day the 2d Battalion was finally released for Nelson's use. By now both of the assault battalions were dispirited and physically failing. Between them they had suffered fifty-three killed or missing, 129 wounded, and 131 sick, a total of 313, leaving them with only 1,541 effectives.

With his superiors insistent that Mount Austen must be captured, Nelson now issued a plan to hit the northern and eastern face of the enemy position with respectively the 3d and 1st Battalions while his 2d Battalion captured Hill 27 in a wide envelopment. It took a day longer than planned for Lieutenant Colonel George F. Ferry's 2d Battalion to reach its jump-off point on Hill 11, but on the morning of New Year's Day 1943, the 2d Battalion struck southwest for Hill 27. Though these two crests lay only a mile apart on a map, the actual route scaled and descended precipitous heights that more than trebled the distance to 6,000 yards. The 2d Battalion reached its goal, the southeast slope of Hill 27, by 1600 without loss after brushing back a few riflemen.

This same day, Colonel Nelson was relieved of command—accounts differ as to whether this came at his request or not. His replacement, Lieutenant Colonel Alexander M. George, assumed command in a dramatic fashion calculated to restore confidence. To demonstrate to the men of the 132d the ineffectiveness of Japanese small-arms fire against moving targets, Lieutenant Colonel George, garbed only in shorts and a fatigue cap, walked erect, rifle in hand, the length of his lines. Some Japanese cooperated with George by firing repeatedly but vainly at him.

January 2 found all three battalions of the 132d braced for attack. The 3d Battalion encroached into the jungle south of Hill 31 at a cost of four killed and eighteen wounded. At the same time, the 1st Battalion advanced in column southwest from the ravine between Hills 29 and 30. By the end of the day the companies of the 1st Battalion had closed up on a line confronting the eastern face of the Gifu, at a cost of two killed and four wounded.

The 2d Battalion now reaped the benefits of its difficult march. A strenuous climb from the bivouac beginning at 0630 placed the advanced companies on the crest of Hill 27 at 0907. As the leading skirmishers breasted the hilltop, they surprised and killed the crew of a Japanese field piece, who had been lounging in the shade. The entire battalion was on hand by 1130 and commenced to dig in to defend their gain. The lack of entrenching tools and the rocky soil left this work unfinished when the violent reaction to their success began. First, a small quantity of enemy artillery fire, heavily augmented by mortars, machineguns, and grenade launchers, rippled over the American positions. Then during the afternoon, the 2d Battalion threw back six separate infantry attacks.

With nightfall, the 2d Battalion pulled back off the bare crest to a narrower enclave on the reverse slope of Hill 27. The Japanese pressed around three sides of the position during the night despite abundant supporting artillery fire. At dawn, January 3, the 2d Battalion reoccupied the military crest of Hill 27. That day and the next, the 1st and 3d Battalions sealed the gap between their lines.

The 132d was ordered to dig in and hold its position. Beginning on January 4, George's men clamped a defense line around the northern, eastern, and southern periphery of the Gifu. In twenty-two days on Mount Austen the 132d Infantry Regiment lost 112 killed, three missing, and 272 wounded. These losses, when coupled with the effects of disease and battle exhaustion, rendered the 132d incapable of further offensive action. No record survives of losses among the Gifu's defenders, but Lieutenant Ko'o noted in his diary that everywhere he gazed corpses lay, the freshly dead rotting side by side with already skeletal remains. On New Year's Day the last food was distributed in the Gifu, two crackers and one piece of candy per man.

THE DECISION AT IMPERIAL HEADQUARTERS

The second and third weeks of December produced a momentous change of Japanese strategic policy which now must be addressed. As the reader may recall, after the destruction of the November convoy and the Allied attacks on Buna, the Combined Fleet staff resolved to curtail operations on Guadalcanal in favor of New Guinea. They recognized, however, two major obstacles to the adaptation of their views. First, the writ of the Combined Fleet did not extend to fundamental shifts in national strategy. Second, and perhaps more painful, this reversal of strategy promised to corrode future interservice relations. Basically, the Imperial Navy had induced its sister service to attempt to recapture Guadalcanal thrice; the failure of each effort at least partly stemmed from the Navy's inability to deliver provisions to what the soldiers now pointedly referred to as "Starvation Island." Thus, the Imperial Navy stood on an exceedingly rickety pulpit from which to preach the wisdom of forfeiting the sacrifices already made by the Imperial Army.

Admiral Ugaki hoped the sovereign facts of the situation would soon muster Army officers to the viewpoint of the Imperial Navy without the necessity for protracted and acrimonious debate. This hope was not at all fanciful. As early as November 3, General Hattori heard Colonel Tsuji declare Guadalcanal a lost cause and urge a switch of priority to New Guinea. Strangely, upon his return from his inspection trip to Guadalcanal, Hattori neglected to divulge this opinion to Imperial Headquarters, but on November 19 a staff officer returned to Tokyo from Rabaul with the message that both Tsuji and Sugita regarded the chances for success in the Solomons as slim. Following this report, thoughts of a withdrawal surfaced for the first time within the operations staffs of the Army and Navy Sections. On November 24 and 25, Tsuji appeared at Imperial Headquarters, where he shocked naval officers with his vivid evocation of the situation on Guadalcanal, including trails littered with fly-infested corpses.

The Imperial Army operations staff heard more unsettling news on November 26 when Major Ryuzo Sejima reported that his study of current plans demonstrated that the precipitous decline in unit strength on Guadalcanal meant the proposed January attack by the 38th and 51st Divisions would actually equal a one-division effort. Despite these shadows over current plans, through November the conventional view in Tokyo remained that Japan could still triumph if she snatched back air superiority in the Solomons. The facts underpinning this dogged commitment at the tangible level included Guadalcanal's definite intrinsic value as an airfield site and the fear that extricating the 30,000 men already landed might prove more costly than pressing another assault. But perhaps even more potent were intangible factors. Guadalcanal had gradually acquired an enormous prestige value, and, by an evolutionary process, retaking the island and defeating the first serious Allied counterattack had become the foundation of Japanese strategy, to which many, particularly in the Imperial Army, now clung with the extravagant zeal of the newly converted.

During the first week of December, however, a major battle over the feasibility of essential logistical preparations far eclipsed doubts over current operational plans. As early as mid-October, Imperial Headquarters pledged to the government to transfer 220,000 tons of shipping back to duty supporting Japan's war economy upon completion of the Solomons operations. But after the failed October attack, Imperial Headquarters registered bids for more merchantmen, and the loss of nearly 70,000 tons of high-quality vessels in the abortive November convoy aggravated the situation. To meet the logistical requirements of the mid-November Central Agreement, Imperial General Headquarters requested an added 620,000 tons of shipping, over and above that already under its control. In response to this petition, on November 20 a cabinet meeting sanctioned the transfer of another 290,000 tons to the Army and Navy.

The failure of the cabinet to rubber-stamp the full request of Imperial Headquarters reflected a major difference in perspective. While the struggle in the Southeast Area riveted Imperial General Headquarters, the government focused on the country's long-term war effort, for which shipping was pivotal. On November 21, at a liaison meeting with Imperial Headquarters, Tojo lectured that Japan's minimum steel-production requirements for 1943 were figured at 3.5 million tons. The diversion of the 290,000 tons of cargo capacity authorized the day before would reduce that output to 3 million tons. If the government surrendered the full amount requested by Imperial General Headquarters, Japan's steel production for 1943 would fall to a disastrous 2 million tons.

Despite Tojo's warning, on December 5 the Army Section clamored for more shipping, precipitating a crisis. In the face of a demand for a further 165,000 tons of shipping for the first quarter of 1943, the government buckled to the extent of parting with another 85,000 tons, but Tojo insisted that this was the absolute limit. Officers in the Army Section regarded this partial grant of their demands as tantamount to an order to abandon the Solomons operations. The following night, General Tanaka, chief of the Operations Division, confronted Tojo in a heated face-to-face argument in which Tanaka importuned for reconsideration of the decision on shipping. For this insubordinate and ill-mannered conduct Tanaka paid with his job, but he purchased his objective. On December 10, the 8th Area Army was notified that the government had consented to release of an additional 115,000 tons of shipping by December 20 (over and above that already pledged) as well as a further amount to be determined in January and thereafter. This decision meant Japan's entire war economy would be severely distorted in order to provide the shipping resources to carry out the current plans. From mid-December, staff officers returned to the question of whether those plans could bring success.

The debate over the next two weeks ran simultaneously at Rabaul and Tokyo, but with only limited exchanges between these headquarters. Moreover, while officers frankly discussed most of the pertinent facts, they remained reluctant to pronounce the obvious conclusions. For some time, orders and decisions continued to be based upon the mid-November Central Agreement, although some of these foreshadowed a major change of policy. Further, the extreme secrecy of the discussions resulted in few written records, thus making it difficult to reconstruct these events.

On December 11, Commander Yuji Yamamoto returned to Tokyo from a fact-finding trip to Rabaul. He found the 11th Air Fleet at only half its strength at the start of the war, and, more important, he disclosed that no one at 8th Fleet, 8th Area Army, or the 17th Army exhibited confidence in the current operations. Rather, he detected sentiment for withdrawal from both Guadalcanal and Buna qualified by apprehension that a withdrawal might cost destroyers the Combined Fleet could ill spare. Accompanying Yamamoto was Major Takahiko Hayashi of the 17th Army, who intoned another wrenching firsthand account of the situation on Guadalcanal. These somber reports extended the serious contemplation of withdrawal into the top levels of Imperial General Headquarters.

On December 12, the Army Section of Imperial Headquarters ordered the 8th Area Army to deploy the 51st Division to New

Guinea rather than Guadalcanal. Although a declaration that the Guadalcanal attack remained the main goal accompanied this injunction, Lieutenant Colonel Imoto at the 8th Area Army translated it as a sign that Tokyo was examining the "worse case." He was unsurprised when that same day Captain Shigenori Jin, senior staff officer of the 8th Fleet, approached him with a proposal that they privately begin to examine the possibility of withdrawal from Guadalcanal as well as a renewed offensive. Also on December 12, the Navy Section at Imperial Headquarters advised the Combined Fleet that it agreed that Guadalcanal must be abandoned, and that this conclusion was "understood" by the Army Section. Emboldened by this news on the attitude of the Army Section, on December 14 Commander Watanabe of the Combined Fleet proposed joint deliberations to the 8th Area Army on what to do after an abandonment of Guadalcanal. This, however, the 8th Area Army—still under orders to recapture Guadalcanal—refused to discuss overtly, but Imoto's unofficial exploration continued.

What proved to be the crystallizing event in this process began on December 17. Shortly after Major General Kitsuju Ayabe replaced recently dismissed General Tanaka as the chief of the Operations Division, Colonel Joichiro Sanada relieved Tanaka's deputy, General Hattori. On the aforementioned date, Sanada received orders to discuss future plans with the 8th Area Army at Rabaul. After a brief and rigorously nondiscursive stop at Truk, Sanada, Major Sejima (who had presented the discouraging assessment of current plans on November 26), and one other staff officer reached Rabaul on December 19. There Sanada's party learned that recent local war-gaming disclosed that Allied aircraft would destroy the reinforcement convoys before completion of few, if any, of the necessary logistical preparations. But while Admiral Kusaka bluntly warned that further loss of destroyers might leave the Combined Fleet unable to defend the country and openly urged that strategic priority be shifted to New Guinea, Sanada found that local Army officers preferred circumlocutions. For example, Lieutenant General Ronpei Kato, the chief of staff of the 8th Area Army, sighed that only after he reached Rabaul had he learned of the precipitous decline of the Imperial Navy's air, destroyer, and submarine forces.

Another staff officer, Michio Kato, privately conferred with Sanada and stated that in view of the Navy's situation, the retrieval of Guadalcanal was next to impossible. But rather than blurt out the obvious conclusion, Kato took an oblique track. He professed unease that there were officers who might risk the fate of the nation for fear of endangering their personal reputation. He urged Sanada to "think nothing of himself." General Imamura spoke plainly to Sanada. We cannot talk of withdrawal here, announced Imamura, that was for Imperial Headquarters to contemplate as well as the fate of the nation. But whatever might happen, the general would not countenance an abandonment of the men on Guadalcanal and would strive to evacuate as many as possible. If the news of withdrawal orders leaked out, Imamura cautioned, all of the soldiers on Guadalcanal would commit suicide.

During his return trip, Sanada, with Sejima's aid, formulated a report. Its gist was that current plans to restart an attack on Guadalcanal offered no prospect of success, and correspondingly almost no confidence existed in this venture among local Army and Navy leaders. Sanada pointed out that while the Guadalcanal operation distracted Japan, her position on New Guinea was collapsing, and he advocated giving priority to New Guinea. It was essential to avoid further attrition of aircraft and ships of the Imperial Navy. He urged an immediate withdrawal rather than any temporizing to hold on to Guadalcanal by resupplying for an interval to buy time to develop a new defense line.

Sanada reached Tokyo on December 25 and immediately unveiled his report to Sugiyama and his deputy while Sejima briefed the Operations Division. Somewhat to the surprise of Sanada and Sejima, the proposal to withdraw elicited no objection. Sugiyama, in fact, looked rather relieved. The following day, Sanada made the same presentation to the Navy Section. Here he preached to the converted, for his audience had restudied the proposed operations during Sanada's travels and concluded they offered zero chance of success. Thus, on December 26, Imperial General Headquarters agreed on withdrawal. There remained two steps—the formalization of specific plans and the presentation of the plans to the Emperor.

Between December 27 and 29, staff officers drafted the new plans. The two central conflicts emerged: how to conduct the withdrawal from Guadalcanal and where to set up the new defense line. With respect to the withdrawal, the Imperial Army extracted from the reluctant Imperial Navy a pledge to utilize the maximum feasible number of warships for the evacuation, including destroyers, rather than just barges and small craft. As for the location of the new defense line, the Imperial Army envisioned abandoning everything below the northern Solomons, but the Imperial Navy insisted on protecting the mid-Solomons to keep the Allies, particularly their aircraft, at bay from Rabaul. The ultimate agreement on this point was what often passed as a "compromise" at Imperial Headquarters: each service promised to do as it wished. In this case, the Imperial Navy accepted responsibility for defense of the New Georgia–Santa Isabel area and the Imperial Army would hold the northern Solomons.

At an audience with the Emperor on December 28, General Sugiyama and Admiral Nagano divulged the intent of Imperial Headquarters to order a withdrawal from Guadalcanal and proposed to return on January 4 to present the finished plans. The Emperor responded that he wished not only to be informed of the plans for the withdrawal, but also to learn of the plans for the next step in the war aimed at bringing it to a successful conclusion. He further asked for expedited action.

At 1400 on December 31, Sugiyama and Nagano unfurled the new strategic blueprint for the Emperor. Chastened by the course of the Guadalcanal campaign, the heads of the Imperial Army and Navy vowed more study before operations in the future. The Emperor approved this new strategy, and after the meeting he sent a message to his military chiefs. He had planned to issue a treasured Imperial Rescript upon the recapture of Guadalcanal, but now, even though the struggle would end with Japan quitting the field, he still wished to issue a rescript to acknowledge the heroic sacrifices of his soldiers and sailors. This gesture boldly underscored the significance of the Guadalcanal campaign, and General Sugiyama, for one, found it very moving.

★ ★ ★

21

THE FINAL
OFFENSIVE
BEGINS

*"Our educated guesses are not as reliable
as they have been"*

JANUARY BALANCE SHEETS

On January 3, a delegation from Imperial General Headquarters
issued sweeping new orders at Truk to staff officers from the Southeast Area Fleet, the 8th Area Army, and the Combined Fleet. The
following day the Navy Section of Imperial General Headquarters
formally advised Yamamoto to prepare to secure "important points"
in the Solomons and New Guinea and to withdraw units from Guadalcanal. The new directive clarified the division of operational responsibilities and missions. The Imperial Army would manage the
defense of the northern Solomon Islands to include Shortland, Bougainville, and Buka; the Imperial Navy would exercise parallel authority for the middle Solomons (New Georgia, Santa Isabel).
Yamamoto would expedite reinforcement of Lae, Salamaua, Madang, and Wewak to bolster the Imperial Army's defense of New
Guinea. The Buna garrison, "depending upon the situation," would
withdraw toward Salamaua. The Imperial Army Air Force would
conduct the air battle in New Guinea; the Imperial Navy's Air Force
would fight the air struggle in the Solomons and assist over New

Guinea. Both air services would commit their best efforts to the "KE" Operation, the evacuation of Guadalcanal, set for late January–early February.

By January 9 the Combined Fleet and the 8th Area Army completed an agreement on the "KE" Operation whose basic outline follows: One infantry battalion would be forwarded about January 14 to form the core of the rear guard; twenty-three days' provisions would be stockpiled on Guadalcanal by January 15; the 17th Army would begin a phased withdrawal to the western end of Guadalcanal about January 25–26; upon the completion of the airfield development program, Army and Navy fliers would initiate an air superiority campaign about January 28; the Russell Islands would be secured as a staging area; there would be three lifts on the evacuation featuring destroyers; some men would be transported by landing craft to the Russells for later withdrawal; submarines would be available to pick up anyone who failed to get aboard a destroyer or landing craft; and the target date of completion was February 10. The Japanese also designed an elaborate program of feints to keep the Americans guessing as to their real intentions. To the west there would be a step-up in radio traffic at Java and a night air raid against Port Darwin on Australia's northwest coast. The heavy cruiser *Tone* assumed the central role in a diversion operation east of the Marshalls that would also employ a submarine shelling of Canton Island and fake radio traffic in the Marshalls.

These plans housed a powerful source of internecine strife. Important Army officers viewed the projected use of landing craft and submarines not as a mere prudent provision of redundant means of evacuation, but rather as a thin facade masking an intent to jettison the 17th Army survivors. These suspicions were unfair to Yamamoto, who personally commanded the use of valuable destroyers, and whose subordinates in the Solomons displayed no less dedication in taking great risks on behalf of the starving soldiers on Guadalcanal.

On January 11, the 8th Area Army subjected the evacuation plan to a war game which illuminated dangers and "points needing further study." General Imamura expected the sacrifice of half the destroyers committed to the "KE" Operation. At the Combined Fleet, Commander Watanabe optimistically believed that 80 percent of the 17th Army survivors could be extracted from Guadalcanal. Yamamoto concealed his personal view that only one-third of the 17th Army could be saved at the price of half the destroyers participating in the "KE" Operation.

The January balance sheets on naval, air, and ground forces in the Solomons undoubtedly generated this pessimism in the Japanese command. Yamamoto retained two modern fast battleships, *Yamato* and *Musashi,* and the large carrier *Zuikaku* at Truk. He detailed four heavy cruisers, the two remaining old fast battleships *Kongo* and *Haruna,* and carriers *Junyo* and *Zuiho* to Kondo's Advanced Force to support the "KE" Operation. Destroyer Squadron 2 screened these major units with light cruiser *Jintsu* and nine destroyers. Mikawa's 8th Fleet, which controlled the actual evacuation runs, numbered heavy cruisers *Chokai* and *Kumano,* light cruiser *Sendai,* and twenty-one destroyers.

Unlike Yamamoto, Nimitz held no important units of the Pacific Fleet in reserve. Thus Halsey freely disposed nearly the full panoply of American naval power in the Pacific. By January's end these included carriers *Enterprise* and *Saratoga,* three modern fast battleships, thirteen cruisers, and forty-five destroyers. Halsey's warships also included four old battleships and six escort carriers, but their low speeds circumscribed the utility of both these types in a fleet action.

January brought to completion a restructuring of American air command arrangements and a further influx of strength. Rear Admiral Aubrey W. Fitch remained Commander Aircraft South Pacific, but major shifts took place at the next level of command. General Harmon won the creation of a separate Army Air Forces headquarters, the 13th Air Force, activated on January 13 under command of Brigadier General Nathan F. Twining. At its inauguration, the 13th Air Force included the worn 11th and newer 5th Bomb Groups with eight squadrons of B-17s, two squadrons of B-26s, four fighter squadrons with P-39s, one fighter squadron with P-38s and one with P-40s, one reconnaissance squadron with F5As (modified P-38s), and one transport squadron with C-47s. The authorized strength of the 13th Air Force in bombers and fighters totaled 272, but operational strength on January 22 numbered only ninety-two.

Fitch's other major deputy, Marine Brigadier General Francis Mulcahy, wore two hats as commander of the Second Marine Air Wing and commander of the Cactus Air Force. A return dated January 28 shows 423 land-based Navy and Marine aircraft assigned to the South Pacific. Guadalcanal held only eighty-one of these, but another 195 waited on Espíritu Santo. Elsewhere in the South Pacific or en route were 147 planes. An authoritative figure for the operational number of naval fighters, dive-bombers, and torpedo planes in the South Pacific in the second half of January is not available, but a reasonable estimate would be 153, of which Guadalcanal hosted approximately sixty-five. Fitch also disposed thirty land-based reconnaissance planes and forty-eight Catalinas. The vulnerable Catalinas discovered new roles first in nocturnal patrols and second in the rescue of downed aircrews. VP-12 blazed the way in the former activity and originated the sobriquet "Black Cats" after the paint scheme on their radar-equipped aircraft. A judicious estimate of the effective number of land-based South Pacific aircraft of all services arrayed against the "KE" Operation is about 200. *Enterprise* and *Saratoga* added 161 and six escort carriers another 178 sea-based aircraft, making a grand total of about 539 planes.

The 11th Air Fleet at Rabaul opposed this Allied aerial armada, together with the 6th Air Division of the Imperial Army Air Force. The projected commitment of aircraft numbered 100 Army and 212 Navy planes, including 182 fighters. In addition, sixty-four aircraft of *Zuikaku*'s air group would be temporarily based at Rabaul. Thus aggregate planned land-based strength reached 376. Adding the authorized complement of sixty float planes with the R Area Air Force yields a grand total of 436 planes. The Japanese believed they possessed parity or better in the air over the Solomons, thanks to their interior position. The Imperial Army Air Force estimated that Guadalcanal held about 150 Allied planes. It placed 400–500 Allied aircraft on New Guinea, whereas the actual total hovered about 550, though the daily operational figure reached only 350, and of this total only about thirty heavy bombers could intervene against the evacuation. All total, the "KE" Operation pitted about 436 Japanese planes against about 569 Allied.

The greatest disparity in combat power existed on the ground at Guadalcanal. Patch activated the XIV Corps Headquarters on January 2. By the end of the first week in January the corps fielded 50,666 men. Patch's order of battle included the Americal and 25th Infantry Divisions and the independent 147th Infantry Regiment of the U.S. Army and the 2d Marine Division. Of their constituent ten infantry regiments, three (the 2d Marines and the 164th and the 132d Infantry) lacked the capacity for extended offensive operations. Halsey resisted the redeployment of the 2d Marine Division to free it to prepare for future amphibious offensives "until Army combat efficiency has been demonstrated." No exact strength figures for the 17th Army can be offered for comparison. A fair estimate would be that of the 20,671 soldiers and sailors available on November 20, 1942, about 4,000 to 6,000 had been killed in battle or died of disease or starvation, leaving around 14,000 to 16,000. The 17th Army artillery comprised just *three* operable field pieces; the 2d and 38th Divisions presumably each retained a similarly reduced complement, and there was an ever more severe shortage of ammunition. Patch's artillerymen tended to about 167 weapons ranging from 75mm pack howitzers to 155mm guns, and plentiful stocks of shells.

The failure of American intelligence to unmask Japanese intentions offset much of these material disparities, at least in the short run. Before launching into an exploration of the particulars of this misjudgment, two points must be noted. First, the successive Japanese onslaughts of August, September, October, and November heavily tinted current interpretations. Second, the abrupt Japanese *volte-face* created its own smoke screen. American intelligence officers, working principally from aerial reconnaissance and radio traffic analysis, puzzled over evidence of actions set in motion in December and on into the first days of January in accordance with the now discarded plan for a renewed assault. Not surprisingly, these actions lent verisimilitude to the Japanese cover plan of offensive action.

Turning then to the specifics of information gathering and analysis, during December the concentration of shipping at Rabaul swelled ominously from thirty vessels on December 6 to a high of over a hundred (including one or two cruisers and twenty destroyers) on December 22; it remained at ninety-one on December 30. This pattern, coupled with heavy troop movements to Rabaul, suggested Japanese preparations for another South Pacific offensive, which fitted the expectation at Nimitz's headquarters as December began. Washington lent support for this interpretation on December 10 when the Office of Naval Intelligence predicted that the commander of the 3d (Carrier) Fleet was en route south to command a strike force to coordinate with land-based aircraft with the objective of regaining first air and then sea superiority. Overall, however, the paucity and equivocal nature of the data prompted CINCPAC to acknowledge on December 29: "There is very little known of present enemy deployment and intentions. It is believed that the next major move will be toward Guadalcanal." Staff officers cited Japanese airfield construction in the central Solomons to substantiate the conclusion that Guadalcanal remained the enemy objective. At this same time, they observed that most major combatant vessels of the Imperial Navy were between Truk and Empire waters, and they suspected that about half of the four operational carriers were completing intensive training off Honshu. But given the inherent strategic mobility of sea power, these dispositions told far more about the timing of the next major Japanese initiative than its goal.

On January 1 the Japanese altered their secret communications, and the CINCPAC daily summary noted on January 4 that "as the [Japanese] have changed nearly all ciphers our educated guesses are not as reliable as they have been." During January, intelligence officers extrapolated their "educated guesses" from movements of troops and air reinforcements, the accumulation of sea power, and the concentration and types of headquarters. Vigilant convoy tracking yielded both intelligence and tactical success, though not without cost. On January 9, a large convoy heading for New Guinea hinted a Japanese offensive action in that quarter. Both air units and submarines *Grampus* and *Argonaut* were directed to intercept, but the convoy escorts sank *Argonaut*. In midmonth some analysts divined aggressive intentions from the courses of four convoys from Truk and Rabaul to Shortland. They vectored in submarines *Triton, Swordfish, Gato,* and *Silversides* that ambushed and depleted each of these convoys between January 16 and 20.

Significant information concerning Japanese air power arrived at the beginning and the end of the month. On January 2, analysts suggested that auxiliary carriers were ferrying aircraft to restock the 21st and 26th Air Flotillas at Rabaul. On January 30, a nine-day-old message surrendered its contents to cryptologists, divulging that Rabaul packed 142 planes (forty-one Bettys, eight Nells, fifty-six Zeros, seventeen Vals, twenty reconnaissance) and Buin hosted forty-nine to sixty-nine (fourteen Zeros plus between thirty-five and fifty-five Vals).

The location and character of Japanese headquarters remained a gross indicator of enemy interests, if not his intentions. Only three days into the new year, analysts identified the 8th Area Army Headquarters at Rabaul. By January 8, intelligence officers placed at Truk the commanders of the Combined, 2d, and 4th Fleets, the submarine force, and Battleship Division 3 (*Kongo* and *Haruna*). The habitat of Japanese carriers, however, remained elusive in early January, although the carefully examined "associations" in Japanese radio messages linking 3d Fleet elements with the Southeast Area seemed to presage carrier action in the Solomons. The first solid data came on January 14 when direction-finding fixes pinpointed *Zuikaku* and *Zuiho* of Carrier Division 1 in Empire waters. Analysts also surmised that *Zuikaku*'s battle-damaged sister, *Shokaku,* would soon be operational. On January 20, positive information appeared that Carrier Division 2 had reached Truk on the 19th, though four days later this was amended to read only *Junyo.* A major task force composed of *Zuikaku, Zuiho,* and super-battleship *Musashi* joined her on the 23d. The arrival of this handsome reinforcement, coupled with the sailing and deployment of submarines, suggested major moves afoot. At this same time analysts culled references to the "KE" Operation from recent traffic. The nature of the "KE" Operation remained unknown, but the involved units all seemed to be in the Southeast Area, thus implying that the "KE" Operation would be in the New Guinea or Solomons region.

Radio intelligence analysts promptly branded increased communications traffic in the Marshalls and Gilberts as a deception. They also warned of a possible raid by heavy cruiser *Tone*—note the precise identification—although they miscounted the submarine shelling Canton as two instead of one. Analysts even adjudged the presence of four "fairly definite" carriers at Truk as possibly a part of Japanese deception activities.

While the radio intelligence sources illuminated Japanese capabilities as the new year unreeled, they proved less adept at ferreting out plans. As early as December 30, the team at Melbourne hypothesized that current Japanese moves simply reflected reactions to Allied efforts. Although CINCPAC viewed Japanese aims as aggressive, the daily summary on January 7 admitted:

> It is beginning to seem possible that the Japanese are shifting from [the] offensive to [the] strategic defensive in the New Guinea, New Britain, Solomon area; [the] accumulation of airfields would release [carriers] for operations elsewhere [and the] threat of raids may thus become more real in next month or so.

During the third week of January, CINCPAC continued to accumulate indications of a major Japanese operation in the south, expected at the end of the month. On January 26, the daily CINCPAC intelligence bulletin announced the momentary initiation of a Japanese offensive. This conclusion derived from the fact that current traffic continued to refer to the "KE" Operation, associations by traffic analysts pointing to an offensive in the Solomons or New Guinea and the concentration of commands and forces at Truk, which by now included the headquarters of the Combined, 2d, 3d, and 4th Fleets, the submarine command, both carrier divisions, and the arrival on January 25 of cruisers *Atago* and *Nagara*. Against this background Halsey and Patch orchestrated their tactical operations in January.

THE SLOT BECOMES A TWO-WAY STREET

During January 1943, the Japanese resumed their customary Tokyo Express runs, but for the first time the Slot bore traffic in the other direction. Despite decidedly little success with the drum method in December, the Japanese adhered to this scheme as the new year began, albeit with further refinements. Kapok wrapped around the drums made them buoyant even if strafed. Moreover, the destroyers embarked Army officers who would be released in small landing craft to guarantee that the ropes to which the drums were attached were handed over to reception parties ashore.

On December 30, the 8th Fleet ordered ten destroyers prepared for the resumption of the "reinforcement"—now really resupply— runs. Based upon past experience, the Japanese fully expected the American reception to be fiercer than ever and braced accordingly. They earmarked no fewer than five destroyers for the screening role and fitted them with an extra pair of 13mm machine guns for anti-PT-boat duty. The R Area Air Force drew the assignments of reconnaissance and protection of the anchorage and gained four more float planes from *Chokai, Kumano,* and *Suzuya* for this task. The 11th Air Fleet would contribute night bombing of the American airfields and daylight fighter cover.

Rear Admiral Tomiji Koyanagi, now commanding the Reinforcement Unit, led his ten destroyers from Shortland on January 2 bound for Cape Esperance with food and ammunition. Five B-17s with an equal number of P-38s en route to Buin happened upon Koyanagi and awarded him their attentions without success at 1415. These American aviators, however, raised the hue and cry, and at 1805, nine SBDs, four Wildcats, and five P-38s jumped the Reinforcement Unit. The Japanese began gyrations that Koyanagi wryly likened to a "Bon dance," the ancient ceremonial dance characterized by left and right swinging movements of the Bon Festival of the Lanterns. *Suzukaze* sustained damage from a near-miss and turned back with one sister in escort; two Wildcats and one SBD failed to return; Munda strikes cost another SBD and a B-26. The remainder of Koyanagi's tars pressed on and were seconded by three float planes in skirmishes with no fewer than eleven of the pesky PT boats. The float planes found the wakes of the PT boats easy to see even at 4 miles range and secured for themselves a permanent niche in the Japanese anti-PT repertory after this night. The next day the 17th

Army reported its delight at the results of this run: 540 drums and 250 rubber bags of supplies recovered—about a five-day supply.

The interpretation of Japanese intentions as offensive in character and the enemy's industrious airfield construction activities pointed to the prime importance of Munda. Since the repetitive air bombardments seemed not to have dissuaded the Japanese from the use of this airstrip, though in fact it had been relegated to standby status, Halsey resolved to try a surface-ship bombardment. He synchronized this operation for January 4 with a large troop reinforcement of Guadalcanal. As an overture and postlude to this venture, between January 1 and 6, South Pacific aircraft hammered Buin and Munda while Southwest Pacific aircraft struck at Rabaul.

When seven transports bearing the last echelon of the 25th Division departed Noumea on January 1, they were supported by Lee's Task Force 64 with three fast battleships and four destroyers and Task Force 67 with seven cruisers and five destroyers led by Rear Admiral Walden L. Ainsworth. The transports disgorged their loads on January 4, and at 2000, Ainsworth split his task force in a position southwest of the Russell Islands. Leaving four cruisers and three destroyers behind, Ainsworth turned cruisers *Nashville, St. Louis,* and *Helena* and destroyers *Fletcher* and *O'Bannon* for Munda at 26 knots.

Ainsworth, new to South Pacific operations, displayed careful attention to detail. A radar-equipped Catalina probed ahead of the bombardment unit for enemy vessels, while cruiser float planes served as outguards against enemy interference by sea. Overhead other Catalinas cruised with spotters from the bombardment ships to adjust gunfire. After passing submarine *Grayback,* deployed as a navigational marker, Ainsworth turned his task force broadside to Munda. At 0102, flagship *Nashville* loosed her first salvo and soon went to continuous rapid fire, sending a "stream of tracers looking as though they were playing a hose on the target." At ten-minute intervals, the other two cruisers took up the task of bludgeoning Munda, with the destroyers getting in their licks from 0140. When the gunfire ceased at 0150, the task force was lighter by the weight of just over 4,000 shells, nearly three-quarters 6-inch and the rest 5-inch.

Initially, the Japanese at Munda reported "severe" shelling that destroyed ten buildings and killed or wounded thirty-two men, but in daylight the damage seemed less devastating, and it took only two hours to repair the runway. With news of this intrusion, both the R Area Air Force and the 11th Air Fleet thickened their morning reconnaissance programs to find the American task force, and the latter dispatched fourteen Zeros and four Vals on a dual search and attack mission.

Ainsworth's bombardment unit rejoined the support group at 0900 off Cape Hunter, Guadalcanal. The reunited task force slowed to 10–15 knots to recover float planes and were in that vulnerable posture when the Japanese strike group surprised them at 0936. One pair of Vals made near-misses on *Honolulu,* and the other duo secured a near-miss and a hit on H.M.N.Z.S. *Achilles.* The 550-pound bomb put *Achilles'* number three turret out of commission, killing six and wounding seven of her seamen. Captain C.A.L. Mansergh of *Achilles* signaled that "our fighting efficiency is only slightly reduced and our fighting temper greatly increased." Two of the Vals failed to return; one of these is believed to have been the first victim of the new VT-fuzed 5-inch antiaircraft shell, a device that radically improved the efficiency of large-caliber antiaircraft weapons.[1]

Mechanical frailties, the bombardment of Munda, and subsequent search plane reports on January 6 and 7 influenced the composition and equipment of the reinforcement run of January 10. Defects excluded several old battlers like *Kagero* and *Oyashio,* and a major reshuffle brought more destroyers and Rear Admiral Kimura to take over the Reinforcement Unit. Kimura arrived only on the 10th, however, so Koyanagi led an eight-destroyer "Express," divided equally between transport and escort sections.

A coast watcher sounded the alarm, but too late for intervention by the Cactus Air Force. Nine PT boats waited off Guadalcanal. The two boats on patrol between Doma Cove and Tassafaronga sighted part of the Reinforcement Unit at 0037 on January 11 and closed to attack. When *PT 43* decanted two torpedoes, one tube emitted a bright-red flash from its powder charge, which drew fire that damaged the boat and killed three crewmen. A New Zealand corvette destroyed the hulk of *PT 43* the next day to keep her out of Japanese hands. *PT 40* claimed a hit, as did *PT 112,* but two shells struck and sank the latter boat, though her skipper, Lieutenant Rollin E. Westholm, and her crew survived. One of these two claims represented a hit on *Hatsukaze* that killed eight and wounded twenty-three. She retired at 16 knots with three of her sisters. On the 11th, the 17th

---

[1]The VT or variable-time fuze consisted of a battery-powered radio transmitter that detonated the shell when it came within lethal distance of an aircraft. The earlier mechanical fuzes had to be set prior to firing based upon a very complex prediction as to when the aircraft and shell would meet.

Army announced the recovery of 250 drums with about thirty tons of food, medicine, and ammunition.

PLANS, COMMANDS, AND THE "GALLOPING HORSE"

On January 5, Patch issued his instructions for the first phase of the attack to clear Guadalcanal. The 25th Division intelligence officer described Patch's information on Japanese strength and dispositions as "sketchy." The general character of Japanese positions was somewhat clear, but not the unit identifications or locations. Estimates of Japanese forces varied widely from 7,000 to 10,000, with the high figure still well under the actual total. Moreover, and much less forgivably, the intelligence data contained little inkling of the severely debilitated state of the 17th Army. Aerial reconnaissance constituted the sole source of reasonably full and reliable information that Patch possessed on the area in front of his lines, and he drew his plan primarily from the photographic evidence on the terrain.

Patch declared a line extending south from the beach across Hill 53 and generally about 3,000 yards west of the current positions as the initial XIV Corps objective. In the northern half of the corps front, the 2d Marine Division would push west with its right along the shore. The northwest fork of the Matanikau defined the left boundary of the 2d Marine Division; beyond that lay the 25th Division's zone of action. This division's main axis of advance would also be west, but this unit also drew the job of disposing of the Gifu. Patch, like Vandegrift before him, still worried about the security of the airfields from large- or small-scale Japanese attacks and initially retained the Americal Division's winded regiments plus the 147th Infantry Regiment to guard the airfield sites.

A narrative of the Guadalcanal campaign from January 10 through February 1943 faces the usual complication of intertwined land, air, and sea dimensions. Further, the ground component is exceptionally tangled by the fact that American energies were aimed west at the main body of the 17th Army in two divisional zones and south toward the Gifu while being further differentiated by significant variances in chronology. For purposes of clarity, this account will eschew strict chronology for a topical approach. We begin then with the XIV Corps offensive, which in turn means we must commence with the activities of the 25th Division.

Patch assigned no southern boundary to the 25th Division's zone

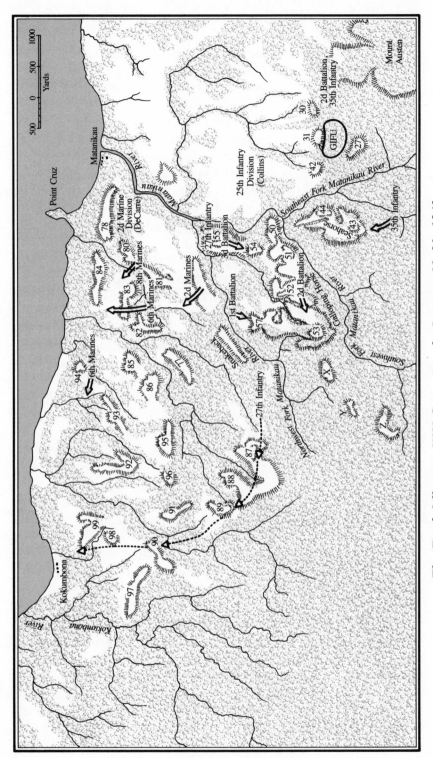

The Final Offensive, XIV Corps Attack, January 10–23, 1943

of action, but practically speaking, the precipitous slopes along the banks of the Lunga south of Mount Austen formed a natural barrier. The deeply eroded forks of the Matanikau severed the 25th Division's territory into three distinct terrain compartments: a large area east of the Matanikau and two smaller areas between the southeast and southwest and the southwest and northwest forks. One main terrain feature dominated each of these compartments. Mount Austen commands the area east of the Matanikau. In the wedge formed by the southeast and southwest forks of the Matanikau are Hills 44 and 43, named the "Sea Horse." Between the southwest and northwest forks is the much larger bare hill mass labeled the "Galloping Horse."

Major General J. Lawton Collins, a gifted forty-five-year-old Louisianian with twenty-five years of soldiering behind him but no battle experience, commanded the 25th Division. Collins devised a scheme of maneuver sophisticated in concept but simple in execution: the 27th Infantry Regiment would seize the Galloping Horse from the north; the 35th Infantry Regiment would contain the Gifu with one battalion while the other two enveloped the Sea Horse from the south; the 27th Infantry would then push south from Hill 53 (the "Horse's Head") to meet the 35th Infantry pressing west from Hill 43. These maneuvers would create "three great pockets . . . [that] could be reduced more or less at leisure." The 27th and 35th Infantry Regiments were regular formations; Collins placed in reserve his third infantry regiment, the 161st, a Washington State National Guard unit.

To sustain his maneuvers, Collins demanded and got a degree of logistical legerdemain achieved at no other time during the campaign so deep into Guadalcanal's interior. The supply officer of the 25th Division boasted that the only maxim controlling the forwarding of provisions to the rifle units was: "Does it work?" The deployment and sustenance of Collins's division trunked from a single treacherous road. The branches to each infantry regiment began as constricted trails partly built with, and hospitable only to, jeeps. Affixed to the end of these trails was a diverse array of innovative means and methods for distributing material to the front line: details from the infantry units themselves; carrying parties of natives; a human-powered boat and barge flotilla up the Matanikau; engineer-rigged elevated cable trolleyways for lifting supplies and lowering casualties; and sleds to negotiate steep inclines. Moreover, on January 13 and 15, B-17s dropped supplies (literally) to the 35th Infantry battalions deep in the interior. However imaginative these methods, ultimately they were profligate of human resources and impinged heavily on tactics. Patch considered landing a regiment at Tassafaronga to trap the Japanese about January 18, but informed Halsey that he held this option in abeyance because of lack of manpower both to handle supplies and to launch an amphibious flanking movement.

In a situation report dispatched on January 5 and 6, the 17th Army alerted Rabaul to the imminence of an American offensive. Despite the hardships of the past eight weeks, Japanese morale retained its amazing flint, but what passed for a defensive scheme rather appears to be an attempt to formalize sheer desperation. According to Colonel Konuma, the basic concept of the defense was simply for each unit to stand unflinchingly at its post. The attackers would naturally infiltrate the many gaps in the Japanese front, but once the two forces became intermingled, the Americans would not be able to exploit their advantages in firepower. At night, the able-bodied Japanese would sally out to prevent the Americans from resupplying their leading elements. Either the attack would bog down completely or the Japanese would force the Americans into a protracted effort to reduce each position, during which the 17th Army expected to be succored by reinforcements. This formula duplicated in miniature the entire Japanese strategic plan for the war. Japanese commands and dispositions remained fundamentally the same as since November: the wasted regiments of the 2d Division manned the narrow coastal corridor and defended the coastline; the 38th Division stretched across the Japanese line to Mount Austen.

The plan of the 27th Infantry to take the Galloping Horse resembled an assault mounted by ants—crawling upward from the hooves of the front and rear legs to the head. In fact, it was dictated by logistical considerations. Two trails led to the regimental zone of action: one ran down the ridgeline west of the Matanikau to Hill 66 opposite the forelegs; the other ran along the high ground east of the Matanikau with an extension to Hill 55 (the hooves of the hind legs). As neither of these paths could sustain the entire regiment, Colonel William A. McCulloch directed the 1st Battalion (Lieutenant Colonel Claude E. Jurney) to move from Hill 66 up the forelegs of the horse while the 3d Battalion (Lieutenant Colonel George E. Bush) jumped off from Hill 55 to move south, up the hind legs, then west with the ultimate objective of the Horse's Head.

The marines reported that a well-dug-in force of Japanese held the "Water Hole" in the valley between the 1st Battalion, 27th Infantry (1/27) and its objective, Hill 57. This area became the target for a massive application of American firepower. Commencing at 0550,

January 10, no fewer than six battalions of guns tossed 92.5 tons of shells into the Water Hole in twenty-five minutes. Then a dozen P-39s each loosed one 500-pound bomb on Hill 53 and a like number of SBDs released three dozen 325-pound depth charges in front of 1/27. At the conclusion of this preparation, Army and Marine units became guarantors of 1/27's flanks. With these preliminaries complete by 0730, three companies of the 1st Battalion advanced in column. After "very slight" resistance from three machineguns, the 1st Battalion gained its objective, Hill 57, at 1140.

The riflemen of Lieutenant Colonel Bush's 3d Battalion, 27th Infantry (3/27) started from Hill 54 at the rear hoof of the Galloping Horse and faced a rugged and elevated, though open, expanse of Guadalcanal. High ground dominated their route at the Horse's body above the forelegs (Hill 52), the neck (soon named Sims's Ridge by the Americans after a fallen officer), and the Horse's Head (Hill 53). An abrupt slope, clifflike in places, marked the length of the Horse's back. Marines described Hill 52 as a "hornet's nest" to Bush, so he designated it as an intermediate objective and planned to seize it with a double envelopment.

At 0635, after the aerial pounding of the Water Hole ceased, the 3d Battalion crossed its line of departure at Hill 54 with Company I on the right and Company L on the left. Company L occupied Hill 51 without opposition, and by 0730 its leading platoon had clambered halfway up Hill 52, where machinegun fire from the left flank halted it. The company experienced confusion lapsing into paralysis, and the company commander contented himself with advising Bush that the terrain rendered impractical the envelopment on the left.

On the battalion's right flank, Company I moved to within 200 yards of the crest of Hill 52, where enemy fire sent it to earth. Bush dispatched his reserve, Company K, to circle around Company I to affect a deeper envelopment to the right while Company L passed into reserve. Meanwhile, he organized a supporting air bombardment mission. After six aircraft dropped depth charges precisely on Hill 52, and an artillery concentration further saturated this height, Company K advanced from the north and northwest side while Company I scaled the eastern side. The assault companies destroyed six machineguns and killed about thirty Japanese on Hill 52. The 3d Battalion achieved its objective by 1625, and halted to prepare to defend its conquests.

Bush was bent on renewing the attack on January 11, but something more elemental than forbidding terrain barriers and stubborn Japanese soldiers stymied him: terrible thirst. A failure in supply planning and execution left most men of the 3d Battalion without any water when the battalion moved out at 0900 after an artillery preparation. The main thrust by two companies toward the Horse's Head came to a standstill in a ravine raked by machineguns. Once halted, mortars assailed them. Here, declaimed Bush, the effects of the lack of water induced an "inertia." Leaders became lethargic, and the led, ever more thirsty and exhausted, rapidly became fewer from heat exhaustion and casualties. In one platoon only ten men remained conscious.

Shortly after noon, Colonel McCulloch sensed that the 3d Battalion had run out of steam. He ordered Lieutenant Colonel Herbert V. Mitchell to pass through the 3d Battalion and continue the attack with his 2d Battalion. During the late afternoon, Mitchell conducted a hasty reconnaissance and issued his orders. Following air and artillery pummeling of the objective, the 2d Battalion attacked from Hill 52 at 0630 on January 12. On the right, Company G gained its goal, the southern meandering of Hill 57, by noon. On the other flank, Company F secured a feature called Exton's Ridge, but was then checked by the Japanese. The defenders likewise halted an attempt by Company E to work around to the south. Company F recoiled and sidestepped to the right to attack Sims's Ridge from the north while Company E plunged frontally against Sims's Ridge. The Japanese stayed Company F about halfway down Sims's Ridge and repulsed Company E.

For January 13, Mitchell drafted a new plan of attack. Company F would pull back off Sims's Ridge and swing wide right to approach the Horse's Head through the cover of the jungle to the north and east. Company E would press down Sims's Ridge and meet Company F at Hill 53, the Horse's Head. While Company F began its maneuver, Company E was checked on Sims's Ridge. With the plan threatening to miscarry, the executive officer of the battalion, Captain Charles W. Davis, volunteered to lead four other men against a knoll at the south end of the ridge that housed machineguns and mortars and was the fulcrum of Japanese resistance. Crawling on their bellies, Davis and his party crept to within 10 yards of the enemy emplacements. Two Japanese grenades came sailing out into their midst but failed to explode. In reply the American party hurled a salvo of eight grenades into the Japanese position. Davis leaped to his feet and fired one shot, whereupon his rifle jammed. With his right hand he drew his pistol and fired at the enemy while with his left he waved the others on with his rifle. This sequence of gestures took place in full view of the Japanese and his own battalion, for the sky perfectly silhouetted Davis on the ridgetop. Collins, who observed the entire action from Hill 52, stated that Davis's bold conduct had "an electrifying effect on the battalion." Company E "came to life" and promptly cleared Sims's Ridge before surging down the Galloping Horse to join Company F at the head. By noon the 27th Infantry held its objective.

THE COASTAL DRIVE

To the north of the 25th Division, the coastal sector assigned the 2d Marine Division sector from Hill 66 to Point Cruz was not active for the first three days of the XIV Corps offensive. On January 12, the Marine division received orders to begin its advance westward. This marked the first action by the division as a whole, although two of its constituent regiments, the 8th and the 2d, had already seen action, and indeed the 2d Marines was vastly overdue for relief. The marines confronted the same ground that had proved impervious to an assault by two reinforced regiments in November: a deep wooded ravine flanked on the east by Hills 80 and 81 and on the west by a ridge peaking at Hills 82, 83, and 84 and commanded by Japanese machineguns expertly sited to place fire seaward perpendicular to the path of any unit attempting to move west. The boundary of the sectors held by the 38th Division and the 2d Division ran across Hill 83 so that the 1st Battalion, 228th Infantry (I/228) faced the left half of the 2d Marine Division front and the remnants of the 4th and the 16th Infantry Regiments confronted the right of the division's front. To nullify the defensive advantages conferred by the terrain, the marines chose to attack in echelon from left (south) to right or, in terms of the ground, from the head of the ravine downward. In this fashion, each unit would maneuver forward clearing a lane so that the next unit on the right could gain the rear of the Japanese positions to its front and attack downhill toward the enemy machinegun emplacements. The commander of the 2d Marine Division, Brigadier General Alphonse DeCarre,[2] aligned his front with the 2d Marines on the left and the 8th Marines on the right (beach) flank. He held the uninitiated 6th Marines in reserve.

---

[2]DeCarre led the 2d Marine Division on Guadalcanal by virtue of an exercise in military punctilio. The actual commander of the division was Major General John Marston, but Marston was senior to Major General Patch. As the Army provided the bulk of the troops on Guadalcanal at this time, Marston remained in New Zealand.

An all-night preparation kept the barrels of Marine artillery and mortar weapons warm before the 1st and 2d Battalions of the 2d Marines began the attack from Hill 66 against elements of the I/228th Infantry at 0500, January 13. The 1st Battalion met mild resistance and achieved its objective by 0730. Japanese mortars fulminated against the 2d Battalion, but it eventually joined its sister battalion. The adjacent 1st Battalion, 8th Marines (I/8) attacked ten minutes later and plunged into a vicious battle in the segment of the ravine to its front between Hills 80 and 81 on the east and 83 and 84 on the west. By nightfall two companies were wired in on their objective, but Company C remained still locked against firm Japanese resistance. The marines renewed their echelon attack on January 14, but accomplished little movement in the center. The 2/8 attempted to assist the 1/8, and 3/8 initiated the first probe of the mouth of the ravine at the coast. As the day ended, the 2d Marines retired to the Lunga perimeter after completing their last combat assignment on Guadalcanal; the 6th Marines stepped forward to replace them. In stark contrast to this major infusion of fresh strength, the 4th Infantry Regiment reported that the arrival of twenty replacements boosted its morale.

The succeeding day, January 15, the 8th Marines encountered heavy resistance from positions bored into the northern slopes of Hills 83 and 84 overlooking the shore. At the coast proper, a tank-supported attack wedged into the Japanese line but failed to smash it. From its enclave on the left of the Marine line, 2/6 pressed north to flank the Japanese in front of the 8th Marines. Sensing the crumbling of his position, General Maruyama sent his chief of staff, Colonel Tamaoki, forward to recommend when to order a withdrawal. Tamaoki pronounced the time as forthwith. Consequently, at 1700, Maruyama directed a retirement of about 1,300 yards. Both front-line regiments characterized their withdrawal as orderly and unpressed, and they reached the reserve position on the morning of the 16th. But the withdrawal came too late for a majority of the men in the 16th and 4th Infantry Regiments ensnared in the rapidly closing Marine net.

On January 17, a Japanese officer noted that the American bombardment "became fiercer and fiercer and the company area was riddled with craters—like a bee's nest." Japanese defenders gave way, and the 6th Marines finished the drive to the beach. The 8th Marines completed the reduction of the ravines to their front by 1400 before passing into reserve. By January 18, the Sendai Division counted only 3,700 mouths to feed and the 4th and 16th Infantry

Regiments, which bore the brunt of the Marine attack, fielded only about eighty men apiece. The marines reported killing 643 Japanese and capturing two between January 13 and 17 inclusive. Over the next several days the 2d Marine Division reshuffled units and scoured its newly won ground for any remaining Japanese units or individuals.

22

THE FINAL

OFFENSIVE

CONTINUES

"Gyokysai"

ORDERS AND OBEDIENCE

For the 17th Army the severe jolts administered by Patch's soldiers and marines packed less seismic impact than the orders delivered by Lieutenant Colonel Kumao Imoto. By January 13, 17th Army Headquarters frankly weighed three options: mount an aggressive defense with the probable consequence of the quick collapse of the army; conduct a cautious defense to prolong the struggle as long as possible; or, as a last resort, launch a massed attack either in the coastal area or inland with the objective of the enemy headquarters. Staff officers christened this last option with the poetic shorthand name *gyokysai*, which may be translated as "gem shattering into pieces." For reasons soon made clear, the 8th Area Army left a request for guidance unanswered. In the interim the 17th Army chose to try to prolong the defense and hold on to a portion of the island.

The Reinforcement Unit loaded passengers as well as provisions for the Tokyo Express run of January 14. Lieutenant Colonel Imoto demanded the duty of carrying the order of the 8th Area Army for the withdrawal from Guadalcanal. The bulk of the transients composed the Yano Battalion, a newly formed unit detailed as the rear guard of the 17th Army. This organization drew approximately 750 men from replacements for the 230th Infantry Regiment and formed them into one machinegun and three rifle companies. A battery of mountain guns numbering another hundred soldiers rounded out the battalion, named after its commander, Major Keiji Yano, a rarity in the Imperial Army, an officer with experience in conducting rear guards. Yano grasped the high importance of his mission, but not its exact nature. Imoto struggled to control his emotions when he witnessed an inspection of the battalion on January 10. He felt certain the entire unit, composed mostly of untrained reservists with an average age of thirty, would perish on Guadalcanal.

Heavy weather shrouded the nine destroyers of the Reinforcement Unit on the passage down the Slot. With assistance from R Area Air Force float planes, the destroyers brushed back PT boats and landed their passengers at Cape Esperance. En route back, a strike group of fifteen SBDs planted bombs that slayed the skipper of *Tanikaze* and damaged her hull and that of *Arashi* at the cost of two Dauntlesses. The escort of seven Wildcats and six P-39s lost one Wildcat and two P-39s in downing three Zeros. A later wave of nine B-17s and fourteen fighters inflicted no damage on the destroyers, but the Army fighter pilots destroyed half of the ten Petes attempting to protect the Reinforcement Unit.

At dawn of January 15th, Imoto and his group began their march to 17th Army Headquarters. Along a trail framed at points with unburied bodies, they passed a stream of empty-handed men headed for Esperance, while in the opposite direction lurched others, each burdened with twenty to forty pounds of supplies. At a muddy dark hospital Imoto blanched at the sight and stench of scores of sick and wounded, most suffering from diarrhea and relieving themselves beside their makeshift beds. Men appealing for water and rations beset Imoto, but most frequently they asked: "Where are the Japanese planes?"

Imoto reached 17th Army Headquarters after dark. General Miyazaki greeted him with the reproach: "How late you come. The attack plan should be given a little earlier." Imoto delivered the withdrawal order as well as the background for this decision to Miyazaki and Konuma, who issued explosions of surprise and indignation. When Imoto finished, his listeners jabbed him with the twin objections that would be voiced over the next several days throughout the 17th Army: (1) the army was in no condition to withdraw and such action would betray those already lost and those persevering in situations "harder than death," i.e., those fighting on in encirclement; (2) the withdrawal of the army would be too costly to Japan in ships and planes—better that the 17th Army sacrifice itself as a last service to the nation. To withdraw the army, snapped Miyazaki, would be "more difficult than to pass over the raging seas." But Imoto countered these arguments with a trump: this was not simply the order of Imperial Headquarters; General Imamura concurred, and the Emperor himself ordained that it be carried out regardless of difficulty.

This exchange, tearful on both sides, continued until dawn, when the sun brought American planes and the "choked sounds of violent fighting." With Miyazaki and Konuma unyielding, Imoto went to Hyakutake. He found the 17th Army commander sitting on a blanket in a hollow beneath a very big tree. After handing over the written orders and a personal letter from Imamura, Imoto reeled out the explanation for the orders to Hyakutake, who listened with eyes closed. At the conclusion of Imoto's presentation, the general spoke in slowly measured words: "The question is very grave. I want to consider the matter quietly and alone for a little while. Please leave me alone until I call for you."

Twice during his period of contemplation Hyakutake huddled with Miyazaki, who cast his lot for *gyokysai*. Finally about noon, January 16, Hyakutake granted Imoto another audience:

> It is a very difficult task for the army to withdraw under existing circumstances. However, the orders of the Area Army, based upon orders of the Emperor, must be carried out at any cost. I cannot guarantee it can be completely carried out.

Despite Hyakutake's acceptance, Imoto encountered an undercurrent of resignation, as when one staff officer remarked that he intended to shave his beard off "so my face will not be ugly in death." Ironically Konuma, who still talked openly of *gyokysai,* took the assignment of issuing the orders to the division headquarters. When he reached the command post of the 38th Division in the early morning of the 18th, Konuma discovered that the division officers had independently concluded the end of their unit was at hand and had set *gyokysai* for the 21st. The staff denounced the orders on much the same lines as Konuma himself had, but Sano quashed this opposition with the comment "You can chose anyplace to die." As Konuma anticipated, the 2d Division Headquarters offered no protest to the withdrawal.

At noon on January 20, the 17th Army disseminated an order for the "KE" Operation built around the cardinal points of supreme secrecy and meticulous coordination. The order listed the mission of the army as a move to Cape Esperance under the cover story of preparing for future offenses. Commencing on the night of January 22–23, the army would begin a pullback in stages during the hours of darkness. The army staff appraised the 38th Division as the more endangered in these maneuvers, so they instructed Sano to break contact with his formation and retire first. The Sendai Division and the Yano Battalion would cover the retirement, moving through each phase line one night after the 38th Division. Those unable to move would be exhorted to "uphold the honor of Imperial Army" by killing themselves, with the assistance of their friends if necessary. During the night of January 20, the 1st Ship Engineer Regiment left for Cape Esperance, assuring that the orders regarding the honor of the Imperial Army were duly carried out. Some of the men too feeble to walk survived because their devoted friends, not strong themselves, carried them away on stretchers.

THE SOUTHERN FRONT

It is time now to turn from the western prongs of the bifurcated American offensive to its complementary southern projections. Collins allocated the 35th Infantry Regiment two diverse assignments in the southern portion of the 25th Division's zone of action: liquidate the Gifu and capture the Sea Horse. To accomplish these tasks, Colonel Robert B. McClure apportioned the Gifu to his 2d Battalion and sent the 3d Battalion after the Sea Horse via a wide envelopment to the south; the 1st Battalion followed the 3d Battalion and would be the regimental reserve. The actions around the Gifu and the Sea Horse are distinct, so it is best to tell them separately.

The 3d Battalion, 124th Infantry and regimental headquarters held Hills 43 and 44, composing the Sea Horse. The survivors of the 1st Battalion, 124th Infantry waited in the valleys to the east. On January 9, the 3d Battalion, 35th Infantry (3/35) reached its jump-off point 1,200 yards south-southwest of Hill 27. At 0635 the next morning, the 3/35 moved out on an azimuth of 210 degrees aiming for a high wooded hill south of Hill 43 and joined to it by a narrow ridge. After a rough march, a small clash with a Japanese supply party, and some impromptu navigational adjustments, the 3d Battalion secured a portion of Hill 43, about 400 yards southwest of the

Sea Horse proper, where the 1st Battalion joined it. By 1300 the next day, January 11, the 3d Battalion captured the Sea Horse, cutting off the Gifu.

On January 12 the 1st Battalion extended the attack westward toward the division objective, but halted at a Japanese strongpoint about 600 yards west of its point of departure. In the event, the enemy unit numbered only a few score, but machinegun bursts and point-blank 70mm gunfire as well as the narrowness of the ridge (about 20 feet wide) and heavy vegetation throttled the advance. For the rest of January 12 and the next two days, both battalions launched patrols with the objectives of finding a route around the Japanese strongpoint or scouring the surrounding low ground for enemy bivouacs. Only after heavy treatment with mortars and artillery did the 1st Battalion smash the opposition in its path on January 15. The next day at 1500, the 1st Battalion reached a ridge overlooking the Matanikau's southwest fork without encountering any resistance. Of the defenders of the Sea Horse, forty men, representing the regimental headquarters (including the colors) and the 1st Battalion, slipped through the encirclement on the 15th, and the survivors of the regimental gun unit made good an escape the next day. McClure's men counted 558 dead, amounting to the rest of the 124th Infantry (less the 2d Battalion), including almost the entire 3d Battalion.

THE GIFU, PART II

To Lieutenant Colonel Ernest Peters's 2d Battalion, 35th Infantry went the unenviable job of reducing the Gifu. By January 9 this single battalion replaced the three of the 132d Infantry and initially deployed along a 2,000-yard arc with Company E and the Reconnaissance Troop of the 25th Division on Hill 27, Company F to their right, and Company G on Hill 31. Company H (less machinegun platoons detached to F and G) set up its mortars and remaining machineguns on Hill 29, while Headquarters Company, about 20 percent of the battalion's strength, portered supplies. There was no reserve.

The 132d tendered to Peters inaccurate and incomplete maps, and an estimate that the Gifu contained just a hundred Japanese and two "known" machineguns—far below the actual figures. Thus, Peters was dealt a difficult hand to being with, and his instructions stripped him of considerable flexibility. Collins and McClure inspected the area from Hill 27 and surmised that the terrain precluded an envelopment of the Gifu from the west between Hills 27 and 31. They dictated to Peters essentially a frontal attack.

For January 10, Peters set a limited objective of advancing the front to better protect the supply trail to Hill 27 and to feel out Japanese dispositions. Each line company set two combat patrols forward, but grenades and gunfire sent each one tumbling back immediately. Peters quickly elevated the estimate of enemy combat power to 400 soldiers and twenty machineguns. Patrol actions likewise consumed the next three days, while in darkness the Japanese tested the 2d Battalion with the customary night infiltrations. Sunrise of January 13 found the 2d Battalion down several notches in alertness and aggressiveness and minus 57 killed or wounded. But the capture of the Sea Horse nearly isolated the Gifu from the rest of the 17th Army. In a last message over a telephone line, Major Inagaki vowed his command would "fight to the last." As an illustration of this pledge, an American report notes that night (italics added):

> . . . a lone Jap raider sneaked up *barefoot* on [the observation post on Hill] 27 trying to knock it out, to do or die. And die he did. No more Jap raider; one body without shoes this morning.

The 14th brought another edition of patrolling, and the roll of Peters's battalion touched the 75 percent mark, now reflecting the ravages of malaria as well as death and wounds. To offset this dilution, the Regimental Anti-Tank Company was placed into the line between Companies F and G. At the same time a decline in sniping and cessation of infiltration through the lines evidenced the wear on Inagaki's men, at least partly generated by a program of irregular shellings of the Gifu nightly with mortars and artillery.

Peters scheduled a general attack for January 15. After a fifteen-minute mortar preparation, three assault companies (G, Anti-Tank, and F) rose along the eastern bulge of the Gifu and started to push west. Here and there small parties wiggled forward, but withering Japanese fire roughly flung most of these units to the ground with an average advance of only 50 yards. A second attempt at 1400 also crumbled. The impact of this day's experience on the battalion may be judged from this comment in the official U.S. Army history:

> About 1630 the battalion executive officer ordered one badly shaken platoon from G Company to withdraw, but as the order was passed verbally along the line, the soldiers misinterpreted it as an order to the entire battalion to retire, and all fell back.

McClure replaced the luckless Peters on January 16 with Major Stanley R. Larsen. A reconnaissance of the position convinced Larsen that the Japanese "had a strong ring of mutually supporting, well-camouflaged pill boxes, covering approximately three-fifths of the circumference of the Gifu." Small combat groups of snipers, a few pillboxes, and light machineguns in shallow foxholes closed the remainder of the perimeter. Larsen recognized that the Japanese had no intention of escaping, but he also saw that the tools in the hands of his infantrymen would not reduce the Gifu without inordinate loss. Based upon his assessment, Larsen elected to extend a closely woven line from Hill 27 to Hill 42 to tightly invest the entire Gifu and to prepare for a massive bombardment of the Gifu on January 17.

While Larsen conducted his survey, a loudspeaker blared a surrender appeal. This activity disgusted the American troops, who were dubious of its effectiveness. These broadcasts, however, did coax five Japanese to respond, all from the 124th Infantry. One later prisoner described how this appeal prompted an extraordinary episode. His company had a meeting, where a general discussion produced a decision not to surrender, because 80 percent or more of the unit was too ill to walk and therefore the ambulatory members of the company believed their sick comrades would perish if the unit laid down its arms. Instead, they elected to die together.

More surrender broadcasts on the 17th delayed the massive artillery bombardment about five hours. Then, after the entire 2d Battalion, except the men on Hill 27, withdrew 300 yards, the snouts of forty-nine howitzers—a dozen 155mm, the rest 105mm—canted skyward and the laborious process began of adjusting each piece to fire into the bowl about 1,000 yards square bounded by Hills 27, 31, 42, and 43. At 1430 all guns "fired for effect," discharging 1,700 shells by 1600, about one every three seconds. The terrific concussion from this barrage left American troops along the eastern side of the pocket dazed for some time after the cease-fire. Prisoners taken over the next ten days were "practically all shell-shocked." But the maximum stunning effect of this concentration was squandered, because the terrain and the lateness of the hour, thanks to the broadcasts, precluded an immediate all-out assault.

On the 18th the attack on the rear of the Gifu got underway. Marches brought three detachments across the west face of the Gifu: Company E, 35th Infantry, Company I, 182d Infantry, and one platoon of Company G, 35th Infantry. This day and the next, the American vise tightened. January 20 passed under a heavy rain with units "feeling for weak spots in the line." That night several small parties of Japanese lost eleven of their number trying to worm through the American lines from the Gifu.

On January 22, the 2d Battalion received precisely the sort of boost it needed to complete the capture of the Gifu. Belated response to requests as early as January 12 resulted in the release of three light tanks. Crews formed from the 25th Division Reconnaissance Squadron manned these vehicles, all originally property of the Marine Corps. Engineers accomplished the considerable feat of scratching a trail to the Gifu for the tanks, but this rigorous climb left only one tank in operational condition. The leader of the Reconnaissance Troop, Captain Teddy Deese, took personal command of this vehicle and at 1040 plunged into the Gifu on the left flank of Company G. One officer and a wedge of fifteen riflemen followed Deese to provide close protection. Deese churned entirely through the position, blasting three pillboxes. He then made a second penetration at 1500, disposing of five more pillboxes, one of which took four 37mm high-explosive shells at close range before it crumbled. When he emerged from the Gifu again, he had breached a gap about 200 yards wide, through which the 2d Battalion surged to occupy a new line beyond the rim of pillboxes.

The response to the crushing effect of the tank attack was not long in coming. At 0230, January 23, an estimated one hundred shouting Japanese armed with hand grenades, pistols, and rifles rushed the American line in the vicinity of the boundary between F and Anti-Tank Companies. A violent but brief twenty-minute skirmish left eighty-five of the Gifu defenders dead and three captured. Inspection of the bodies the next morning revealed Majors Inagaki and Nishihata, the commander of the 2d Battalion, 124th Infantry, eight captains, and fifteen lieutenants. The success of the tank and artillery battering, the enveloping forces, the desperate lunge during the night, and the demoralized state of the few individuals captured convinced Major Larsen that the Gifu was now merely an empty shell. In the morning of January 23, he put his battalion into skirmish line and advanced. By sunset the Americans held custody of the Gifu at a cost of only one wounded.

The names of sixty-four members of the 2d Battalion, 35th Infantry brought the toll of fatalities from the equivalent of five American battalions committed to reducing the Gifu to at least 175. Around the Gifu the 35th Infantry reported it captured forty machineguns, twelve mortars, 200 rifles, and thirty-eight swords and set Japanese deaths at 431. Total Japanese casualties claimed by the 35th Infantry in its operations on the southern flank between January 9 and 26 were 888 killed by the regiment, twenty-nine prisoners, and a further 188 Japanese killed by artillery.

RENEWAL AND READJUSTMENT

By January 17 the first phase of the XIV Corps' western offensive ended. The 25th Division attended to the reduction of the three pockets created by January 15. In the 2d Marine Division sector, the completion of the initial phase of the advance on January 17 coincided with the destruction of the Japanese defenders around Hills 83 and 84.

The annihilation of isolated Japanese detachments from regimental size down to a handful of individuals is a central characteristic of the events over the month after the XIV Corps offensive started. The exceptional scale and severity of the fight for the Gifu earned it examination in detail, and it may be taken as representative of the American perspective of the process. But what of the Japanese perspective? By far the majority of the encircled defenders, like those of the Gifu, perished by disease, starvation, or gunfire and grenades, leaving little more than emaciated corpses and a few scrawled diary entries. The diary of Major Nishiyama, the commander of the 3d Battalion, 228th Infantry Regiment at the Galloping Horse, however, affords a rare insight into the thoughts and conduct of surrounded Japanese soldiers.

On January 12, the 27th Infantry captured the Horse's Head, cutting off Nishiyama's unit. He gathered his survivors, about 200 of his original 600, at the battalion command post for a last stand. There he shared out his last cigarettes and, with tears in his eyes, advised his men to prepare to die. Their calm acceptance of imminent death moved him.

Though the next two days passed with a much-reduced tempo of fighting, Nishiyama's mental anguish waxed. Rain provided the only water for cooking or drinking, and on January 15, he penned a single entry in his diary: "O! Miserable." But the lull gradually transformed the mood of his soldiers. By the 16th, they began to converse of escaping encirclement to move elsewhere where their deaths might be more meaningful. Though Nishiyama admired the spirit animating this choice, he would not openly countenance it, for his last orders had been to hold his position. But in the privacy of his diary Nishiyama debated ordering a withdrawal on his own authority "even at the expense of my honor," something Japanese officers valued more than their lives. He knew a "pretext" could be fabricated, but it would still be a retreat that would dishonor not just himself, but the whole unit. Still vacillating two days later, Nishiyama dispatched a runner to division headquarters, and then in the evening of January 19, General Ito summoned him. Ito sanctioned a withdrawal, though the general disdained to leave personally: "I have already decided what to do." In his last phone conversation with 38th Division Headquarters, Ito informed General Sano to consider him dead as of January 15. With his honor intact, Nishiyama and his 200 survivors succeeded in escaping. The exact circumstances of Ito's death are unknown.

Nishiyama's escape came just in time. As early as January 16, Patch distributed his plan for the next phase of his offensive. He set the corps objective as a line from Hill 87 angled northeast to the beach. Hill 87 and its neighbors, Hills 88 and 89, formed a terrain feature that dominated the Kokumbona area much as Mount Austen did the Lunga Plain. Patch detailed the 2d Marine Division (with only the 6th Marines and 182d Infantry on charge for rifle strength) to secure the corps objective on the right. The 25th Division would again advance in the southern portion of the front and seize its segment of the corps objective (including Hills 87, 88, and 89) by enveloping or turning the enemy right flank. Patch retained four of his ten infantry regiments to guard the airfields and held the 147th Infantry in corps reserve.

In the 25th Division domain, Collins again planned to attack with two regiments abreast. In a subsidiary role, the 27th Infantry on the right would advance astride a narrow ridge called the "Snake" to confront Hill 87 from the east. Collins assumed the Japanese held Hill 87, a dominating terrain feature, in force. The 161st Infantry would mount the principal effort by a deep envelopment from the Galloping Horse to the southwest, capture Hills X, Y, and Z, and adjust its trajectory northwest toward a rise southwest of Hill 87, thus outflanking the latter, and continue on to seize Hills 88 and 89. The 35th Infantry would protect the south flank of the 161st and would continue the extermination—a cruel term for a cruel business—of the Japanese forces already pocketed.

The 2/161st Infantry occupied Hills X and Y by January 21 against minor resistance. To comply with Collins's orders, Colonel Clarence A. Orndorff, the commander of the 161st, planned to detail his 1st Battalion to guard the south flank while a column composed of the 2d and 3d Battalions plunged off Hill Y toward Hill 87. But the 161st had barely begun its movement on January 22 when the situation radically changed, and for that story we must look to the operations of the 27th Infantry.

At sundown of January 21, McCulloch cocked the 27th Infantry to advance on a narrow front with the 1st Battalion as the spearhead followed by the 3d and 2d Battalions in that order. At 0630 on January 22, the four battalions of the 25th Division Artillery began dropping 3,654 rounds (71 tons) of shells on Hills 87, 88, and 89. As an artillery preparation crashed down on Hill 87, the 1st Battalion stepped out in column of companies down the Snake's "back." With the aid of 81mm mortars, the 1st Battalion destroyed three Japanese machineguns attempting to block the advance at the Snake's "tail," and at 0910 the battalion shook out three companies on line to attack Hill 87.

From his position at the division observation post on Hill 49, Collins plainly witnessed the leading elements of the 27th Infantry scrambling up Hill 87 in the face of apparently light opposition. The 1/27 seized Hill 87 by 0940 and, as Collins instantly perceived, an ideal position to take up the main thrust. Accordingly, he ordered the 161st Infantry to permit only its leading battalion to cross from Hill Y to Z while the rest of the regiment turned north to follow along the Snake behind the 27th Infantry and secure its lines of communication. The 27th Infantry would take up the pursuit of the Japanese. Collins started forward to personally contact the 27th Infantry, which had temporarily outrun its wire communications. En route on Hill 66 he met the XIV Corps chief of staff, Brigadier General Robert L. Spragins, who bestowed, in the name of Patch, authority for Collins to continue the drive of the division to Kokumbona as rapidly as possible. Of equal importance, Spragins adjusted the divisional boundaries to place Hills 91, 98, and 99, the elevated stepping-stones in the jungle leading to Kokumbona, in the 25th Division's bailiwick.

Without a pause, 1/27 energetically expanded its success. Company C bounded forward, first to Hill 88 and then to Hill 89 by 1100. As the 1st Battalion organized its positions, at 1400 it received the command to seize Hill 90. After the 3d Battalion came forward and occupied Hills 87, 88, and 89, the 1st Battalion put Companies A and C abreast and shoved off for Hill 90. These companies "shot their way through" a bivouac area in the draw between Hills 89 and 90 and arrived puffing on Hill 90 after ascending its slope on hands and knees. By darkness, the 27th Infantry held a crescent from Hills 90 and 91 in the north to Hill 87 to the southeast, where the 2d Battalion had closed up.

These developments threw Japanese plans into turmoil. After dark on January 22 the 17th Army Headquarters marched to Cape Esperance and the 38th Division began to extricate those units with which it still retained contact. But the thrusts of the 27th Infantry carried them around the flank of the 2d Division and threatened to pinch off the fighting echelon of that formation, as well as the attached Yano Battalion. Although the 2d Division was scheduled to hold its posts until sundown of January 23, reports from staff officers sent to check the situation to the south impelled Maruyama to order his division to pull back at 0500, January 23. Most of the 2d Division units got the word at early dawn and began a withdrawal under fire. But the "Nitto Battalion" of about fifty men from 29th Infantry died at their positions. Maruyama's decision greatly worried and angered the 17th Army Headquarters, but events vindicated him.

On January 23 the 27th Infantry launched a two-pronged attack. The 3d Battalion thrust north on the regiment's right (east) flank toward Hills 98 and 99, while the 1st Battalion on the left (west) flank received the order to take Kokumbona. Initially, artillery and small-arms fire from the 2d Marine Division impacting in front of the 3d Battalion stalled its advance. When this fire halted, the 3d Battalion moved out and soon announced it was on Hill 99. McCulloch then released the 1st Battalion for Kokumbona. The delay in starting allowed the 1st Battalion to probe forward with patrols to the high ground above Kokumbona without incident. The 1st Battalion, with Company E, 2d Battalion attached, moved out in two columns and by 1530 captured Kokumbona. There the battalion organized for all-around defense. In a day and a half, the 1st Battalion had moved 7,000 yards through the jungle and seized the prize of Kokumbona. Between January 10 and 27, the 27th Infantry suffered losses of seven officers and sixty-six men killed.

The capture of Kokumbona generated repercussions both for the Americans fighting along the coast and for the 17th Army's withdrawal plan. For the renewed attack in the northern half of the XIV Corps front, Patch created a unique hybrid Composite Army-Marine Division, with the shortened title of the CAM Division. Its infantry regiments were the 147th, the 182d, and the 6th Marines; its strong artillery component came from both the Americal and the 2d Marine Divisions, and the latter supplied the division headquarters. Although Maruyama could field only eighty men in his 4th Infantry

Regiment and a hundred in the 16th Infantry Regiment, the 3/6 Marines pushing along the beach on January 22 encountered stiff resistance, and its difficulties put a brake on the movement of the adjacent 2/6 and the battalions of the 147th and 182th Infantry that extended the division front inland. The next day, January 23, again saw the inland units rolling westward with the most serious resistance from the terrain while the 6th Marines wore down the elements of the Sendai that had not gotten the word to withdraw or were already cut off. On the 24th, 3/6 contacted the 27th Infantry about 1535 on a ridge just east of Kokumbona, and the last holdouts along the coast were overcome about 1705.

With the linkup of the CAM Division with the 25th Infantry Division the American front narrowed drastically and permanently. The principal reason for this constriction, which negated a large part of the American superiority in combat power, was the terrain. The fringe of level ground along the coast beyond the Poha River much resembles the land between Point Cruz and Kokumbona, with only about 300 to 600 yards separating the surf from a row of coral ridges. Fairly shallow streams with marshy banks extending as much as 200 yards on either side cut this ribbon of ground with "washboard regularity." No bridges spanned either these streams or the many sloughs with boggy borders in between. Coconut trees and thick jungle growth crowd the mean water line and fringe the streams and marshes. The coral ridges reach northward in long fingers to give the ground the aspect of "a narrow defile with the sea on one side and on the other a close series of ridges and woods." To exploit the excellent defensive potential of the terrain, the Japanese exercised their predilection for reverse-slope positions on the ridges from which they could lay fire seaward across the defile. Deep inland envelopments of the type executed by Collins before Kokumbona offered the obvious solution to this tactical problem, but American commanders apparently deemed this maneuver infeasible without a refined logistical gridwork such as the 25th Division developed. The other important reason for this contraction in the western frontage of the XIV Corps was that Patch concurred with the assessment of his superiors on the possibility of yet another Japanese offensive. Therefore, he consistently maintained the equivalent of at least one division around the Lunga airfield complex, and after January 26 he directed Collins, who was eager to push west, to position the 25th Division to repulse an attack on the airfield complex.

The 17th Army placed its withdrawal in full gear, organizing "Coast Defense Units" of the sick but ambulatory to stumble toward

Cape Esperance and Kamimbo with the 38th and 2d Divisions in that order. The Yano Battalion took up positions along the Marmura River on January 25, but the supervisor of the rear guard, Colonel Konuma, on his own initiative pegged the next major delay position along the Bonegi River, where he hoped to make a stand commencing on the east bank that would regain the time lost by the withdrawal forced by the 27th Infantry. Thus the restrained advances of the 27th Infantry on January 24 and 25 that stopped short of the Poha River encountered independent groups of Japanese rather than a coordinated defense. Patch ordered the CAM Division to take up the westward push on January 26. With the 6th Marines again on the right along the coast, the CAM Division advanced and by 1300 on January 26 ran into the positions of the Yano Battalion, which the marines acknowledged put up heavy resistance. Major Yano withdrew grudgingly over the course of January 26 to 28 to a point about half a mile behind (west of) the Marmura. Early on January 29, Yano pulled back across the Bonegi, leaving the tattered remnants of the 2d Infantry Group to face the American advance.

On January 30 the fledgling 147th Infantry took the van of the American advance. About 1000 elements of its leading company crossed the Bonegi, only to be chased back to the east bank. The next day the 147th initiated an envelopment with two companies across the Bonegi inland, but partly through a supply breakdown, the advance stalled again. The Japanese account of the action describes "considerable" losses among the defenders; that night the Japanese extracted their men from the posts at the Bonegi. On February 1 the 147th vaulted the Bonegi after destroyer *Wilson* worked over the Japanese defenses.

AIR AND SEA ACTIONS

Now we must pause for a moment in the narrative of the ground action to update the air and sea contests. American radio intelligence analysts found the Vila-Stanmore area on Kolombangara associated in messages to aviation units on Ballale. Photographic reconnaissance unmasked a nascent air base, and it was also suspected to be a staging point for barges and other small vessels carrying supplies to Munda. Therefore Halsey planned to "pulverize" Vila-Stanmore and destroy Munda air strength trying to interfere; his chosen weapons were surface ships and aircraft. Halsey issued Ainsworth the assignment of conducting another bombardment, this time from

Kula Gulf, the waters of which wash the shores of New Georgia to the southeast and the volcanic cone of Kolombangara to the northwest. The bombardment was prefaced by a busy day for the denizens of Munda, who experienced the heaviest air attacks yet, which cost two Wildcats and an SBD.

Japanese search planes located Ainsworth during the afternoon of January 23, but the cagey admiral feinted effectively as if to give an encore performance off Munda—almost too effectively, for the Japanese readied the Bettys of the 701st and 705st Air Groups, virtuosos in sophisticated night torpedo attack techniques. Fortune permitted Ainsworth to slip away from shadowers as twilight turned to night, leaving the Bettys without a clue as to his whereabouts until his guns flashed in Kula Gulf. Repeating his tactics, Ainsworth left cruisers *Honolulu* and *St. Louis* with three destroyers in support and took flagship *Nashville, Helena,* and destroyers *Nicholas, DeHaven, Radford,* and *O'Bannon* into dangerous Kula Gulf for the shoot.

With a spotter in a Black Cat overhead, at 0200 the cruisers began slamming salvos into the airfield site, expending nearly 2,000 6-inch shells before a half hour passed; together with the destroyer batteries, the cruisers added another 1,500 rounds of 5-inch. According to its Japanese tenants, Kolombangara sustained great material damage that delayed the construction effort, though it killed only five men and wounded only twenty. Meanwhile the R Area Air Force put up eleven float planes to feel for Ainsworth, and thirty Bettys swarmed out from Rabaul. The Americans withdrew, taking full advantage of every rainsquall and applying measured doses of radar-directed 5-inch antiaircraft fire to planes that approached closely. About 0800 the second punch arrived in the form of twenty-four SBDs, seventeen TBFs, and eighteen Wildcats of *Saratoga*'s air group, operating from Guadalcanal. These planes delivered a consignment of 23 tons of bombs and returned to their ship the same day.

Neither Munda nor Vila-Stanmore figured in the Japanese air superiority campaign for the "KE" Operation, whose centerpiece was a joint-service effort of three major daylight attacks set for January 25, 27, and 30. As a prelude and counterpoint to the day effort, a program of night harassment raids of three to ten aircraft to Guadalcanal, Port Moresby, and Espíritu Santo began in mid-January and extended to the middle of February. A solo attack on January 20 by an Emily on Espíritu Santo coincided with the arrival of a delegation of notables, including Secretary of the Navy Knox and Nimitz. When this delegation reached Guadalcanal the next day, their reception included a particularly fierce nocturnal visit by nine

Bettys. This sequence of events was sheer coincidence, but for a time it raised the eyebrows of important personages about the security of American communications.

The core of the first massed day raid since November departed Rabaul at 1015 on January 25. A cocoon of fifty-four Zeros surrounded the eighteen Bettys assigned the live-bait role. Over Buin, twenty-two additional Zeros joined the mission, but weather involuntarily detached eighteen of the escorting fighters. About 15 miles south of the Russells, the Bettys banked around 180 degrees, leaving fifty-eight Zeros, which reached Guadalcanal at 1340. A faltering scramble of the Cactus Air Force succeeded in putting only eight Wildcats and six P-38s into contact with the raiders. A flight of four Wildcats from VMF-121 claimed three Zeros, and a P-38 pilot claimed one more. For once these claims perfectly matched recorded Japanese losses; another six Zeros were "heavily damaged" on landing, and one Betty "failed to return." The Imperial Navy's fliers claimed two Wildcats and one "B-25" for "sure" and two P-38s, one P-39, and one SBD as "probables," but American accounts reflect no losses. Because of weather, few of the Japanese aviators regained Rabaul, most diverting to Buin, and Japanese records refer to "great damage" affecting later operations.

Raid two was the responsibility of the Imperial Army's 6th Air Division. Nine Kawasaki Ki-48 ("Lily") twin-engine light bombers and no fewer than 74 Nakajima Ki-43 ("Oscar") fighters departed Buka and Shortland just before 0900 on January 27, preceded by two Mitsubishi Ki-46 ("Dinah") headquarters reconnaissance planes. The Oscars tangled with a dozen Wildcats, six P-38s, and ten P-40s over Lunga and found themselves battling all the way back to near the Russells. As a result of this action, the defenders lost two each of the P-38s and P-40s and two more P-40s damaged beyond repair; one Wildcat ditched because of fuel starvation. Against these seven aircraft, the 6th Air Division ledgers reflected the loss of six Oscars. While the fighters skirmished, the Lilies dashed in to dump bombs along the Matanikau, with little effect.

The Japanese postponed a third effort, slated for January 29, because of events around Rennell Island that will be covered shortly. They recognized that the air superiority campaign had fallen short of its goals, and the Southeast Area Fleet requested that the "KE" Operation be postponed, but the 8th Area Army adamantly insisted that the evacuation proceed forthwith.

It will be recalled that the Japanese reinstituted submarine supply missions to the 17th Army in late December. On January 8, American radio intelligence analysts made associations between submarine commands and the Guadalcanal garrison that pointed to logistical activities. On the basis of deciphered signals they predicted submarine transportation runs on January 26, 27, and 29. Consequently, on the night of January 29, *Kiwi* and *Moa,* two of the four New Zealand corvettes now operating from Tulagi, were waiting off Kamimbo when Lieutenant Commander G. Bridson's *Kiwi* gained sound contact on *I-1* at about 2105. Two depth charge attacks by *Kiwi* brought the hefty I-boat to the surface for a wild melee with a *Rashomon* quality. Aboard *Kiwi,* an eruption of gunfire of 4-inch and 20mm calibers illuminated the scene as the skipper called for full speed and set course to ram. When these orders drew protest from the chief engineer, Bridson responded, "Shut up! There's a weekend's leave in Auckland dead ahead of us."

Kiwi struck her opponent on the port side, holing her and prompting troops in full packs to jump overboard. As *Kiwi* backed away her gunners ignited the landing barges strapped to the submarine's afterdeck, casting a flickering glow over the tiny arena of combat, which never exceeded a diameter of 150 yards. Bridson conned *Kiwi* for a second essay at ramming ("Hit her again! It'll be a *week's* leave!" he cried). Then *Kiwi* charged in yet again, on Bridson's motto of "Once more for a fortnight!" The third goring sent *Kiwi* rearing up over the submarine and caused a large quantity of diesel oil to spout over the corvette's bow. At this point, ninety minutes after the sound contact, Bridson withdrew his command and turned the action over to *Moa,* which heretofore had stood idle because *Kiwi* and *I-1* were so closely entwined.

Aboard *I-1,* the captain, Lieutenant Commander Eichi Sakamoto, had just raised the periscope when *Kiwi* attacked. The first spread of depth charges knocked out the motors, forcing Sakamoto to blow *I-1*'s ballast tanks. No sooner did the submarine broach than shifting cargo pushed her under again, nosing downward for the bottom, but Sakamoto desperately brought her back to the surface. *I-1*'s gun crews managed to fire a few rounds (*Kiwi* reported two rounds narrowly missed her) before the fusillade of fire from *Kiwi* cut them and Sakamoto down. At this juncture the navigator rushed down the ladder yelling, "Swords! Swords!"—a theme which brought the appropriately accoutered first lieutenant topside. The navigator, a famous swordsman, reemerged topside, edged weapon in hand, and when *Kiwi* came in for another embrace he tried to board the corvette, but only succeeded in gaining a handhold on a rail. By now pandemonium reigned on the I-boat. Imaginary "torpedoes" were seen to miss. The reserve gun crew claimed to have scored a hit on *Kiwi* and sunk her "amid cheers of exaltation from the submarine crew." Defiant rifle fire greeted *Kiwi*'s third ramming. But after nearly ninety minutes of battle, at the "very moment" the first lieutenant decided to run her aground, *I-1* anticipated his order, whereupon the stern sank. Of her company, forty-seven men crawled ashore, where they tore up and buried some of her secret papers, including current code books. *Moa* captured the navigator.

I-1 finally lay twisted to starboard with her bow as far aft as her hydroplanes out of the water. Efforts by survivors to completely sink their boat proved unavailing, as was a bombing attack on February 10. Japanese anxieties over the accessibility of *I-1*'s wreck were confirmed in June when they learned of an article by a thoughtless Australian journalist boasting of the intelligence-gathering work of American divers around *I-1*. The reality was certainly a blow to the Japanese, but not so catastrophic as it might have been. Divers did loot *I-1*'s interior of a "treasure trove" of 200,000 pages of secret documents. This cryptographic material proved valuable in attacking changed editions of JN-25, though much of it was out of date and thus more useful retrospectively than prospectively.

23

OPERATION

"KE"

"With the help of 20,000 souls"

THE BATTLE OF RENNELL ISLAND

In mid to late January, Nimitz and Halsey noted the accumulation of enemy shipping, renewed air activities, and radio intelligence indications pointing to prospective "vigorous operations by the Japanese in the Southern Solomons." They coupled this concern with the projected withdrawal of the 2d Marine Division to more salubrious climes. The last in a series of procrastinations on this matter since late November occasioned King to caustically signal Nimitz and Halsey that the campaign "continues in current status of delay, linger and wait." Thus, to shield movements of troop transports and counter threats of Japanese surface-ship buildups, Halsey deployed virtually the full array of American naval power in the South Pacific. Near sunset of January 29, a carrier group built around *Enterprise* made knots for a rendezvous with the *Saratoga* Group. Task Force 67 (four cruisers and four destroyers) held an intersecting course for a junction with Admiral Lee's Task Force 64 (three battleships and four destroyers). In front of these units sailed two other groups of American vessels. Task Group 62.8 (four transports and four destroyers) maintained a heading to carry it the last 100 miles to Lunga Point via Lengo Channel, and the close cover for TG 62.8, Task Force 18 (six cruisers and six destroyers), then cruised just south of Guadalcanal.

Rear Admiral Richard C. Giffen commanded Task Force 18; he was an officer new to the South Pacific but had considerable sea time in Atlantic and North African waters and was a favorite of King's. A certain rigidity of his mental processes is suggested by the fact that he found Halsey's open-necked shirts and garrison caps repugnant and disdained to appear on his flagship in that uniform. Another manifestation of this trait of much greater consequence is that on this evening Giffen wholly focused upon complying with a directive from Halsey to rendezvous off Cape Hunter at 2100 with Captain Robert Briscoe's four-destroyer "Cactus Striking Force." Once these units merged, Giffen would lead them on a daylight sweep up the Slot as the transports discharged at Lunga Roads on January 30. To keep his appointment, Giffen had detached earlier plodding escort carriers *Suwannee* and *Chenango* and two destroyers so as to up Task Force speed to 24 knots.

During the afternoon the tracks of unidentified aircraft lighted the radar screens in Task Force 18. The escort carriers put up teams of Wildcats and radar-equipped TBFs, but the overcast frustrated their attempts to police the skies, and Giffen refused to break radio silence to provide vectors. Some of these mystery planes bore white star markings of the United States; others bore Rising Sun insignia. In midafternoon, thirty-two Bettys, equally divided between the 701st and 705st Air Groups, lifted from Rabaul runways. One plane returned with mechanical trouble, but the rest cruised southeast, eager to demonstrate their assiduously practiced mastery of a new tactic: night aerial torpedo attacks.

Twilight found Task Force 18 on course 305 degrees zigzagging at 24 knots in an approach formation. Giffen aligned his cruisers in two columns spaced 2,500 yards apart: flagship *Wichita, Chicago,* and *Louisville,* in that order, to starboard and *Montpelier, Cleveland,* and *Columbia* to port. He spread six destroyers along a semicircle 2 miles ahead of the cruiser columns. This disposition was handy for antisubmarine protection and transformation into an arrangement for a surface battle, but very weak from the antiaircraft viewpoint, as it left the after beams and quarters open.

By 1920 the radar plot in *Wichita* resembled a "disturbed hornet's nest." The two Japanese aircraft groups closed from the west but circled around astern of their prey to gain the black backdrop of the eastern sky. At 1919 the sixteen aircraft of the 705st Air Group commenced their attack. Automatic weapons on *Waller* spurted warning as hurtling rotund shadows whipped by her fantail to draw beads on the cruiser columns. One aircraft splashed astern of *Chicago*, leaving a puddle of flaming gasoline. The task force sustained no damage, but a dud torpedo may have struck *Louisville.*

Giffen remained hell-bent on making his rendezvous and altered neither task force speed nor course; at 1930 he even ceased the zigzag. This simplified the task of the second team of Japanese aviators, who placed rows of white flares along each side of the task force like footlights and dropped clusters of float lights glowering in red and green to communicate other information such as speed and composition. With this data in hand, at about 1938 Lieutenant Commander Joji Higai initiated an attack with his fifteen-strong 701st Air Group. The full darkness rendered the gun flashes, tracers, and shell bursts starker than before; the bright bouquets from 5-inch weapons blinded the other gunners. Higai's Betty began to trail flames off *Chicago*'s starboard bow and careened into the sea off her port bow in brilliant flames that "undoubtedly" silhouetted the veteran cruiser. At 1940 a torpedo speared *Chicago* on her starboard side, followed two minutes later by a second Type 95 aerial torpedo; together they halted *Chicago.* A second Betty from this group "failed to return." A third torpedo hit *Wichita,* but it failed to explode.

Giffen did not see fit to change course to 180 degrees and reduce speed to 15 knots until 2008. To maintain concealment, he embargoed his gunners from firing without a definite target. Radar screens remained alive until 2335, but this combination of orders at last succeeded in shaking off a contact-keeping flying boat.

Meanwhile *Chicago* tars checked flooding at an 11-degree list while engineers lighted a boiler and with this power shifted oil to roll *Chicago* back to an even keel. Giffen commissioned *Louisville* to take her motionless sister ship in tow, a tricky assignment in complete darkness ably executed by *Louisville* about midnight.

Daylight of January 30 found *Chicago* creeping southward at 3 knots behind *Louisville* with the rest of Task Force 18 huddled near at hand. Halsey sent destroyer transport *Sands* and tug *Navajo* to join Giffen, and the latter relieved *Louisville.* From early morning to 1400, radar screens again displayed a multiplicity of contacts, some of which represented search planes from Rabaul. Admiral Kusaka learned with gratification of Giffen's withdrawal with a damaged vessel, thus removing a threat to the first run of the "KE" Operation. Figuring *Chicago* would slip beyond the radius of fighter cover from

Guadalcanal that afternoon, Kusaka resolved to launch another air strike in daylight. But here he miscalculated, for from just over the southeastern horizon, escort carriers *Suwannee* and *Chenango* and fleet carrier *Enterprise* shuttled relays of Wildcats to protect *Chicago*.

A shadower Betty left at 1205, ten minutes ahead of the strike, composed of eleven Bettys of the 751st Air Group. A coast watcher enabled Radio Guadalcanal to warn both *Chicago* and *Enterprise* of this threat at 1505. On the carrier, rapid calculation showed the enemy would appear shortly after 1600. Even more deft work by radio intelligence experts permitted Nimitz to advise Giffen of Japanese aircraft shadowing Task Force 18 and of ten enemy submarines deploying south and southeast of Guadalcanal. But Halsey instructed Giffen to make for Efate with the battle-worthy cruisers, and at 1500, Task Force 18 divided, leaving the *Chicago-Navajo* joint venture screened by destroyers *LaVallette, Conway, Frazier, Waller, Edwards,* and *Sands.* The rest of the task force hauled off to the east, stripping *Chicago* of the shield of their formidable antiaircraft batteries and carrying away the force fighter direction officer in *Wichita.*

As a result of the lack of a fighter direction officer with *Chicago,* only four Wildcats remained to guard her. At 1540 they spotted the shadower prowling just ahead of the 751st Air Group and started a chase that dragged them nearly 40 miles before they splashed the snooper. Thus when the attack group sighted *Chicago* at 1606, she lacked aerial defenders. The Japanese initially held course to gain position ahead, but their adversaries interpreted this maneuver as an intent to go for *Enterprise,* then about 40-odd miles southeast of *Chicago.* Fighter directors on the carrier vectored six Wildcats into an interception, and upon spotting them, the Bettys wasted no time in wheeling to port and putting their noses down for high-speed runs at *Chicago.* Only two Wildcats got in among the Bettys before they reached release points.

In the furious seconds that followed—the whole action around *Chicago* lasted but one minute—each Japanese aviator and American sailor registered only snippets of the action. From cockpits and gun positions Japanese fliers witnessed two Wildcats dump three Bettys into the sea; a fourth ignited and veered out to attack a "*Honolulu* Class" light cruiser that interposed herself between their "battleship" target and the attackers. As the Bettys banked and jinked through the circular disposition, antiaircraft gunners deprived the attack group of two more Bettys, and upon emerging from the far side of the ship formation, Wildcats flamed another pair. The four remaining Bettys limped back to Shortland, three with only one propeller turning, and one of these survivors crash-landed.

Chicago sailors could only prepare to put up the best possible antiaircraft barrage. About 1620, eleven Bettys began runs from just forward of the starboard beam. Gunners thought they splashed four of her assailants, but when the firing ceased, five torpedo wakes converged on *Chicago*. At 1624 a torpedo struck forward, tossing debris over the forecastle and bridge. Seconds later, three other warheads ripped open *Chicago*'s already mangled midships. This catastrophic damage impelled Captain Davis to immediately give the order to abandon ship. *Chicago*, said Davis, "rolled slowly over on her starboard side and settled by the stern, with colors flying" at 1643. Six officers and fifty-six men joined *Chicago* in death; there were 1,069 survivors.

The *"Honolulu* Class cruiser" Japanese aviators reported barring the path to *Chicago* was a flattering description of destroyer *La Vallette*, which valiantly turned out to meet the Japanese. To *La Vallette*'s crewmen, it appeared that one section of three Bettys singled out their ship for special attention. One of these tall-tailed torpedo aircraft bored in through a vortex of tracers and, with the port wing and motor ablaze, released a torpedo at a range of only 300 yards. This device or another blasted *La Vallette*'s port side abreast the forward engine room. *La Vallette*'s losses amounted to twenty-one killed or died of wounds. But well-drilled engineers got her underway inside of two minutes after the hit, and she retired. The destruction of nine of the twelve Bettys launched this day brought total losses to twelve. The Japanese would keenly miss Lieutenant Commander Higai, a leading light among the Betty commanders in the Imperial Navy.

For Nimitz the sinking of *Chicago* represented the straw that broke the camel's back in a surfeit of frustrations involving Guadalcanal. His official report of the episode to King categorized *Chicago*'s loss as "especially regrettable because it might have been prevented." These mild words should be interpreted as though uttered through clenched teeth. A long list of errors supported this verdict, prominent among which was Giffen's obsession with keeping a rendezvous to the exclusion of other valid considerations and a very complete assortment of mismanagements of fighter direction, formations, maneuvers, and the escort carriers, together amounting to tactical ineptitude of the first order—all of this compounded by the fact that the new supersecret VT (proximity) fuze equipped these vessels. In a rare outburst of anger, Nimitz vented part of his wrath at his staff, threatening to shoot anyone who announced the loss of *Chicago*.

THE FIRST EVACUATION RUN

In the afternoon of January 31, a decrypted dispatch disclosing the sortie of Kondo's Advanced Force from Truk two days earlier triggered Nimitz to alert his subordinates in the South Pacific to expect a major Japanese operation in their latitudes. The Battle of Rennell Island, however, postponed the beginning of the "KE" Operation to February 1. The instruments selected for the most delicate phases of this project were the Reinforcement Unit and the R Area Air Force. The Reinforcement Unit, which of course was really an evacuation unit, in turn was divided; a Support Unit of heavy cruisers *Chokai* and *Kumano* and light cruiser *Sendai* remained at Kavieng. For the actual troop hauling, twenty-one destroyers gathered at Shortland.

Army officers were assured that the nominated commander of the Reinforcement Unit for the "KE" Operation, Rear Admiral Satsuma Kimura, led the finest flotilla in the Imperial Navy, Destroyer Squadron 10, which habitually guarded the carriers. But on January 19, Kimura sustained injuries when submarine *Nautilus* damaged his flagship, *Akizuki,* off Shortland. Rear Admiral Koyanami replaced Kimura at the head of Destroyer Squadron 10. At this juncture, however, Admiral Kusaka secured the appointment of Rear Admiral Shintaro Hashimoto as commander of the Reinforcement Unit for the "KE" Operation. Koyanami remained with the Reinforcement Unit in a reserve capacity.

The 11th Air Fleet and the 6th Air Division took responsibility for maintaining a daylight Combat Air Patrol over the Reinforcement Unit runs, but at night Hashimoto's sailors relied on the R Area Air Force. The fifty to sixty-odd float planes of the R Area Air Force assumed the roles of sweeping ahead of the Reinforcement Unit and shielding its anchorages from the depredations of American PT Boats.

"KE" Operation plans allocated a critical alternate role to the Russell Islands: if the destroyer effort failed, the 17th Army would be extracted by landing craft via the Russell Islands. Staff officers also hoped the installation of a temporary garrison and base in the Russells would do double duty as a feint. On January 28, six destroyers portered 328 men to the Russells. An attack by thirty-three Cactus Air Force planes on this detachment caused no major damage and only seventeen casualties.

February 1, the first day of the "KE" Operation, began with an exchange of blows by air. Five B-17s with fighter escort rained bombs at Shortland at 0845, with small success. They fended off five Zeros, but four Flying Fortresses, sans escort, that appeared a few minutes later plunged into the aroused defenses, including forty-three more Zeros. Three of the four-engine bombers fell with no return benefit in damage or delay to the "KE" Operation. The Cactus Air Force also lost two SBDs this day in an attack on Munda. Twenty-three Oscars and six Lilies of the 6th Air Division delivered the Japanese aerial counterblow at Guadalcanal. They returned with claims of destroying four "large aircraft" and four fighters at a cost of at least one Oscar.

The next event in this exceedingly busy day concerned more Japanese planes and American shipping. General Patch believed the fall of Kokumbona had finished the Japanese on Guadalcanal unless reinforcements arrived. He feared, however, they might prolong the struggle by a retreat to the south coast. To thwart this possibility, Patch decided to land a reinforced battalion in a blocking position.

Lieutenant Colonel George, the commander of the 132d Infantry, assembled a task force at Lunga built around his 2d Battalion with various attachments, including four 75mm pack howitzers of Battery F, 10th Marines. This contingent loaded themselves and their equipment aboard six newly arrived Landing Craft Tank (LCTs) and destroyer transport *Stringham.* Captain Briscoe's four destroyers of the "Cactus Striking Force" afforded an escort for this expedition. At Nugu Point, *Stringham* installed one company, but news of nearby enemy activity resulted in the shifting of the landing point for the rest of the task force 1.5 miles north to Verahue.

This activity fell under the scrutiny of an Imperial Army reconnaissance pilot who described Briscoe's destroyers as "cruisers," thereby casting the initiative as a challenge to the Reinforcement Unit. To clear the path for the first scheduled run of the "KE" Operation, a strike of thirteen Vals and forty Zeros rose from Buin. At 1443, Radio Guadalcanal issued a "Condition Red" (air raid alert) as destroyers *DeHaven* and *Nicholas* shepherded three returning LCTs 2 miles southeast of Savo. Through a grievous error, the fighter director vectored all scrambled Wildcats to protect *Radford* and *Fletcher* off Verahue.

Aboard *DeHaven,* uncertainty bred a fatal hesitancy. The Condition Red sent her crew to General Quarters. The skipper, Commander Charles E. Tolman, upped speed to 20 knots but then

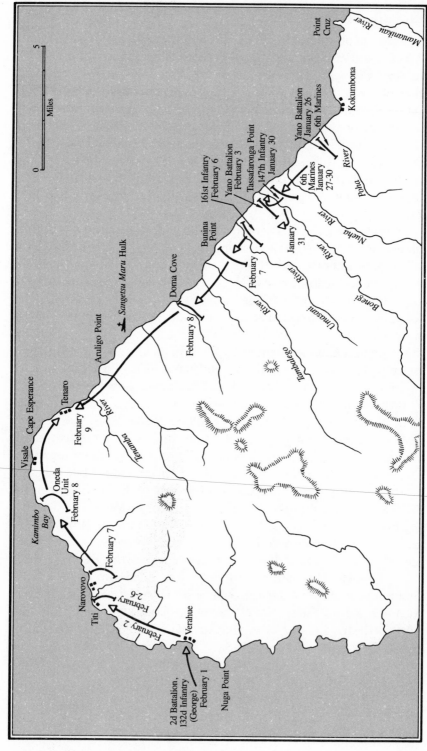

Pursuit and Evacuation, January 26–February 9

ill-advisedly chopped it back to 15, and worse, when the fire control party classified a group of approaching planes as hostile, he initially refused permission to open fire, no doubt because of uncertainty concerning their identity. These actions left *DeHaven* in an exceedingly vulnerable posture when six Vals swooped down on her. At 1453 the first bomb hit *DeHaven* amidships on the port side, causing a "tremendous burst of flame to envelop the central part of the ship." A second bomb hit just aft of the bridge; a third missile caused what appeared to be the explosion of the forward magazine group. Under a gusher of heavy black smoke, *DeHaven* jackknifed and disappeared with 167 officers and men, including Tolman.

Lieutenant Commander Andrew Hill of *Nicholas* barely evaded a similar fate by violent maneuvers at 32 knots as Japanese bombs pounded the water only 20 to 200 feet from the hull and killed two and wounded seven. *Nicholas* claimed three aircraft; defending Wildcats claimed another dozen, but lost three of their number. Actual Japanese losses numbered five Vals and three Zeros. *Nicholas* and the LCTs found only 146 *DeHaven* survivors.

As these preliminaries took place, Hashimoto cleared Shortland at 1130 on February 1 and formed up his twenty destroyers into two columns for the sprint down the Slot. He organized the Reinforcement (Evacuation) Unit as follows:

Cape Esperance Unit
Screen
Rear Adm. Hashimoto in **Makinami**

  1st Unit: *Maikaze, Kawakaze, Kuroshio*
  2d Unit: *Shirayuki, Fumizuki*

Transport Unit
Rear Adm. Koyanami

  Desdiv 10: *Kazegumo, Makikumo, Yugumo, Akigumo*
  Desdiv 17: *Tanikaze, Urakaze, Hamakaze, Isokaze*

Kamimbo Unit
Screen

  Satsuki, Nagatsuki

Transport Unit

  Desdiv 16: *Tokitsukaze, Yukikaze*
  Desdiv 8: *Oshio, Arashio*

A coast watcher sighted the Reinforcement Unit north of Vella LaVella at 1320. The Cactus Air Force put up ninety-two planes in two groups. The first contingent of fifty-one (seventeen TBFs, seventeen SBDs, four P-39s, four P-38s, four P-40s, and five F4Fs) went home with accounts of sinking one destroyer and shooting down seven of the eighteen defending Zeros, at a cost of two TBFs (plus two damaged beyond repair), one SBD, and one P-39. American fliers in the second strike group (eleven TBFs, ten SBDs, twenty F4Fs—forty-one planes in all) eyed the handiwork of their predecessors in one destroyer burning badly and hobbling northwest. All the crews of the second attack group returned to claim two bomb hits and ten Zeros. During the attack, a near-miss rendered Hashimoto's flagship, *Makinami,* unnavigable. Koyanami took charge of the flotilla and detailed *Fumizuki* and *Shirayuki* to stand by *Makinami.* Hashimoto transferred his flag to *Shirayuki* and started after his Reinforcement Unit.

Koyanami joined *Makikumo* and *Yugumo* to the screening detachment to replace *Fumizuki* and *Shirayuki* at 1912. He also set back the schedule of activities by thirty minutes. At about 2000 the screening ships peeled off to conduct a sweep ahead, and as the clock swept up to 2200, the Kamimbo-bound vessels diverged from the remainder. Meanwhile the next hurdles for the Reinforcement Unit, eleven PT boats from Tulagi, assumed their posts in twos and threes off Savo, Cape Esperance, and Doma Cove.

On Guadalcanal, Generals Sano and Miyazaki reached the boarding point at Cape Esperance about 2000. Thousands of men toiling laboriously up muddied trails livened the night. Much shouting accompanied efforts to keep units segregated and to guide those who wandered from the designated area. Miyazaki voiced sharp criticism of the lack of security and preparation. Then he and Sano heard a single rifle shot. They dispatched a staff officer to investigate, who returned to report that one soldier of the 229th Infantry had reached the area supported on the shoulders of two comrades. Unable to move any farther, the exhausted man asked for and received his friends' assistance in committing suicide. Sano further illuminated this incident by explaining that when his division withdrew from the front, those unable to ambulate were helped to kill themselves with the assurance that these would be regarded as deaths in battle. Despite the confusion and the lack of security, the soldiers and sailors completed boarding preparations by 2100, the estimated hour of arrival of the Reinforcement Unit, but minutes passed with no ships in sight. Suddenly the Japanese heard gunfire to seaward, and then they witnessed fires.

All remaining ships of the Reinforcement Unit were panting ahead at 30 knots when Savo Island loomed up at 2210, but thirty-five minutes later so did *PT 48* and *PT 111,* which each uncorked four torpedoes. Lieutenant Lester Gamble, the most successful PT skipper of the Guadalcanal campaign, scurried away in *PT 48* and passed the rest of the night beached on Savo, but Lieutenant John Clagett's *PT 111* took a direct hit from *Kawakaze* at 2254 and became a fireball in which one officer and one man perished.

Off Cape Esperance, Japanese float planes bombed and strafed *PT 59, PT 115,* and *PT 37,* which then became embroiled with what looked like a dozen menacing shadows of destroyers. Ensign Connolly in *PT 115* resolutely bored in to within 500 yards of a target and loosed a pair of torpedoes at it and then emptied his other two tubes at a second target. He evaded gunfire, probably from *Satsuki* and *Nagatsuki,* with a combination of cagey tactics (a speed reduction to suppress his wake) and luck (an opportune rainsquall that also concealed *PT 59*), and waited for dawn on the beach at Savo. Fortune deserted the third member of this patrol. Ensign J. J. Kelly conned his *PT 37* in and fired four torpedoes, but gunfire transformed his command into "a burning inferno of gasoline-soaked mahogany." The only survivor, wounded and burned, was blown through the side of the boat by the explosion that killed all his shipmates.

As *PT 124* and *PT 123* moved in to attack from south of Savo, an unseen and unheard Pete of the R Area Air Force glided down and with remarkable skill or luck planted a bomb squarely on the stern of *PT 123.* Four crewmen died, and the rest abandoned their foreshortened and blazing craft. Lieutenant Clark Faulkner in *PT 124* continued to close in and fired three torpedoes, claiming hits. All these efforts cost three PT boats and fifteen of their sailors.

Another of the R Area Air Force Petes found and began dropping flares over Captain Briscoe's Desron 21, the "Cactus Striking Force," now only three strong after the loss of *DeHaven.* Exactly how Briscoe's trio would harass the eighteen Japanese destroyers present is hard to divine, and the Pete stripped away any chance of the surprise that offered Briscoe's only realistic hope for accomplishing more than getting his ships sunk.

The six transport destroyers reached Esperance at 2240, and at 2400 those similarly employed at Kamimbo began to launch their boats. Sano bid farewell to Imoto and followed the bulk of the surviving members of his division into the landing craft and boats that ferried them to the waiting destroyers. Koyanami described the evacuees:

> [They] wore only the remains of clothes [that were] so soiled their physical deterioration was extreme. Probably they were happy but [they] showed no expression. All had dengue or malaria [and their] diarrhea sent them to the heads. Their digestive organs were so completely destroyed, [we] couldn't give them good food, only porridge.

A report informed Admiral Yamamoto that the evacuees

> . . . were so undernourished that their beards, nails and hair had all stopped growing, their joints looked pitifully large. Their buttocks were so emaciated that their anuses were completely exposed, and on the destroyers that picked them up they suffered from constant and uncontrolled diarrhea.

The last men boarded about 0153 at Kamimbo and five minutes later at Cape Esperance. Because of the delay in the schedule, 1,270 men remained on the beach at Cape Esperance and another 300 at Kamimbo. While this activity unfolded, *Makikumo* chased a PT boat to near Tulagi, but Koyanami recalled her to Cape Esperance. As she headed for the screening area, a large explosion wracked her hull at 0145. The Japanese thought she had collided with a mine, which is entirely probable, for destroyer-minelayers *Tracy, Montgomery,* and *Preble* had inserted 300 of these weapons into the waters from Doma Reef halfway to Cape Esperance. Another possibility is that she ran afoul of one of Lieutenant Faulkner's torpedoes. Whatever the cause, the damage left *Makikumo* without motive means. *Yugumo* took off her crew and scuttled her with torpedoes.

The 11th Air Fleet put eight Bettys over Guadalcanal this night to keep the Cactus Air Force on the ground, but six Dauntlesses managed to take off about midnight. They illuminated the enemy but achieved no hits with their bombs. A final daylight effort about 0800 by the Cactus Air Force also failed to score against the wiggling enemy destroyers, and at noon, the troop bearing members of the Reinforcement Unit reached Bougainville with 4,935 men. *Fumizuki* towed *Makinami* into Shortland thirty minutes later.

THE SECOND AND THIRD EVACUATION RUNS

Sunrise of February 2 found the 17th Army Headquarters savoring the success of the first evacuation run. As a deception, soldiers ignited campfires at Cape Esperance and moved them gradually south toward Tassafaronga the next two nights. Meanwhile the 2d Division began its trek in the opposite direction toward the embarkation points that night. The following day the 8th Area Army ordered that the next lift of soldiers and sailors wait offshore in boats rather than on the beach. This signal fanned skepticism at 17th Army Headquarters over the Imperial Navy's dedication to actually sending its destroyers through the gauntlet three times. Accordingly, the officer in charge of the rear guard, Colonel Matsuda, received instructions contemplating the likelihood that his command would have to make its own way out with landing craft.

Japanese commanders remained extremely concerned about the situation at Marovovo, whither two staff officers departed on the morning of February 3. Lieutenant Colonel George's reinforced battalion-size task force started this day still at Verahue. Around 0910 an American patrol ran into the pair of Japanese staff officers and about 140 men about half a mile from Titi. A brief clash produced casualties on both sides. The Japanese captured two of George's men, who, under interrogation before they were killed, revealed the presence of about 600 of their comrades around Marovovo.

The morning of February 3 found Matsuda's rear guard deployed with about 350 effectives of the Yano Battalion along half a mile of ground an equal distance west of the Bonegi with their inland flank extended by another sixty men, survivors of the 124th Infantry. Matsuda's "main force," consisting of remnants of the Ichiki Detachment and 124th Infantry Regiment plus one section of 15cm howitzers, backstopped this position along the right bank of the Segilau River. With American ground activity by the 147th Infantry limited mainly to patrols, Matsuda found time later in the day to formulate plans for the evacuation of his rear guard. In general, the Japanese colonel intended to contract his forces to Kamimbo and move from there to the Russells by boat.

On February 4, Patch directed the 161st Infantry to take up the advance to Cape Esperance from the 147th Infantry. The latter unit was to creep its lines westward to a point about midway between the Bonegi and Umasani rivers on this date. Matsuda left a detachment of about 128 men under First Lieutenant Miyano on the east bank

of the Segilau River. He also instructed Major Yano to leave a rear
guard of about seventy men and one officer behind in the current
position just west of the Bonegi and to take the rest of his command
to Marovovo. Yano strenuously objected and counterproposed that
the whole battalion remain in place as rear guard, averring that there
was a serious danger the front would be broken with any lesser force.
Yano prepared to defy Matsuda's order and die with his whole
battalion on the Bonegi, but the colonel relented and allowed Yano
to leave only those unable to walk at the Bonegi and to take all others
to the Segilau at 1500. Matsuda's general orders provided for leaving
behind those incapable of walking unaided. Commanders asked the
men still able to fire their weapons to try to delay the American
advance, and then kill themselves when the enemy closed. They
issued each soldier two tablets of mercury bichloride, which brought
a sure but agonizing death. Other soldiers "assisted" those incapable
of firing their weapons in committing suicide. The names of all the
men left behind or helped to die were carefully recorded.

On February 2, 3, and 4, as many as fifteen Bettys canvassed the
sea around Guadalcanal. They found disturbingly strong American
naval detachments, including carriers, gamboling at various points
on the compass near the island. Weather and excessive range frustrated attempts to attack these concentrations with more Betty torpedo bombers, and on February 3, five Bettys failed to return from
an abortive attack, one of which carried Lieutenant Commander
Gen'ichi Mihara, the leader of the 705th Air Group. Despite the
menace of American task forces near the island, a conference between the Southeast Area Fleet and the 8th Area Army on February
3 confirmed the second run of the evacuation effort, in view of the
pressing land situation.

At Yamamoto's order, the Advanced Force detailed *Asagumo* and
Samidare to replace lost *Makikumo* and damaged *Makinami*. Thus
on the morning of February 4, Hashimoto again readied twenty
destroyers, organized as follows:

Cape Esperance Unit
Adm. Hashimoto
Screen

> 1st Unit: *Shirayuki, Kuroshio*
> 2d Unit: *Asagumo, Samidare*
> 3d Unit: *Maikaze, Kawakaze*

Transport Unit
Adm. Koyanami

Desdiv 10: *Yugumo, Kazegumo, Akigumo*
Desdiv 17: *Tanikaze, Urakaze, Hamakaze, Isokaze*

Kamimbo Unit
ComDesdiv 16
Screen

4th Unit: *Satsuki, Fumizuki, Nagatsuki*

Transport Unit

Desdiv 16: *Tokitsukaze, Yukikaze*
Desdiv 8: *Oshio, Arashio*

The Reinforcement Unit departed Shortland at 1130 and took up the accustomed route and formation. Beginning at 1550, twenty-nine Zeros clashed with thirty-three SBDs and TBFs supported by forty-one assorted fighters in two groups attempting to pounce on the score of squirming destroyers. One Zero failed to return, a second "force-landed," and three others were "damaged"; American losses reached eleven (four TBFs, three SBDs, three Wildcats, one P-40). Near-misses crippled *Maikaze,* forcing *Nagatsuki* to tow her to Shortland. Inspection of *Kawakaze* and *Kuroshio* disclosed scratches, but flagship *Shirayuki*'s engines wheezed to a halt at 1925, forcing Hashimoto to transfer his flag again, this time to *Kawakaze.*

At Guadalcanal the clear but moonless night sky buzzed with seven Bettys dispensing flares and bombs over Henderson Field while an equal number of float reconnaissance aircraft sniffed for PT boat activity, but the American motor torpedo boats had shot their bolt and did not sortie. The preparations at the embarkation points proceeded smoothly, with a fresh chop the only serious potential hazard. Just two hours sufficed to embark 3,921 men. Hyakutake and staff boarded *Isokaze,* and Maruyama came over the side of *Hamakaze.* Both transport groups and their screen galloped unmolested back up the Slot, reaching Bougainville by 1250, February 5.

Aboard *Isokaze,* Miyazaki noted that the prone figures of soldiers, basking in the long-denied pleasure of direct sunlight, draped the destroyer's decks, leaving no space to walk. In one corner Miyazaki found a man who had carried the corpse of a friend aboard and was insisting the man still lived.

A coterie of high-ranking officers including Lieutenant General

Moritake Tanabe, deputy chief of staff of the Army Section of Imperial General Headquarters, waited at Bougainville. Miyazaki exchanged wordless salutes, feeling a surge of "painful emotion." When Tanabe approached him, Miyazaki blurted out between tears his desire for an appointment that would give him a death in battle. But Tanabe, also overcome, said: "Everything about this is the responsibility of Imperial Headquarters."

As the Reinforcement Unit collected the second lift of the "KE" Operation, the Yano unit withdrew from the line west of the Bonegi River to the Segilau River. Colonel Matsuda, who now took charge of all Japanese forces on Guadalcanal, departed from the Segilau to shift to Kamimbo. En route, he sent the Oneda Unit (the remnants of the 3d Battalion, 230th Infantry) to the west of Cape Esperance to block any American advance from Marovovo. On reaching Kamimbo at 1700, Matsuda cautiously deployed another unit to fend off George's task force, though the news from that quarter somewhat reassured Matsuda.

Having dealt with the immediate tactical problems, Matsuda turned to the pressing question of how to extricate his rear guard. Only darkly pessimistic forecasts issued from the senior boat engineer officer, Lieutenant Colonel Sakuji Matsuyama, on the prospects for an escape by landing craft. If past experience offered any guide, the enemy fliers would whittle the number of usable boats to a handful by the 7th. Accordingly, signalers tapped a report to Rabaul urging that at least three and preferably four destroyers be detailed for a final run with an adequate number of boats. Any attempt to move the rear guard to the Russells by boat, warned Matsuda, risked "almost sure death." In his diary that night Matsuda confided his doubts that the destroyers would come. Practically speaking, he thought the sacrifice of his 2,000 men would be less of a detriment to Japan than the loss of one destroyer.

Only American idleness on both the south and the west coasts of Guadalcanal projected a ray of hope into the somber picture Matsuda contemplated on February 5. George's task force of the 132d Infantry, after reaching Titi on the 4th, remained there through the 6th. The size of his command and uncertainty as to Japanese intentions enforced caution on George. His unit viewed the energetic Japanese activity offshore on the nights of February 4–5 and the sight of hundreds of collapsible boats and drums adrift the next morning. On the west coast, the 161st Infantry of the 25th Division took up the advance from the 147th. At 1000 on February 6th, the 161st launched a concerted drive that reached the Umasani River.

To solve the logistical obstacles to the advance, the pack mules of the 97th Field Artillery Battalion were detailed to support the 161st Infantry. This experiment did not prosper, for reasons described by Colonel James Dalton, who replaced the ailing Colonel Orndorff as commander of the 161st: "The animals are sensitive to steep slopes, marshes, swift rivers and jungle trails"—which sounds like a symptom complex that could be called Guadalcanalitis.

Despite American inaction on February 5, Matsuda feared that a thrust up the south coast would deprive him of the use of Kamimbo. To keep an alternative in hand, he ordered about one hundred men to move down the west coast to a holding position in the vicinity of the wreck of *Sangetsu Maru,* about 3.5 miles east of Cape Esperance. He shrewdly instructed them to march in daylight and to light bright cooking fires to further his deception plan. About 1735 on February 6, Matsuda received the disheartening news that the Navy might be able to pick up only those men waiting in boats at sea; those remaining would have to make their own way to New Georgia.

Seventeenth Army Headquarters estimated the odds on getting Matsuda's men out as 50 percent. In the evening of February 6, senior Army and Navy commanders conferred. The chief of staff of the 8th Fleet expressed doubts about the prospects for the third effort of the "KE" Operation in light of reports of enemy carriers near Guadalcanal. Colonel Konuma heard this disturbing appraisal and expressed his concern directly to Mikawa, who assured him that the Navy would exert its utmost efforts. Unpacified, Konuma went to see Admiral Hashimoto, who asserted that regardless of the desires or orders of the chief of staff of the 8th Fleet, he would personally see to the evacuation of all men. Hashimoto rebuffed Konuma's request to accompany the run by saying that it would be a blot on the Imperial Navy's record if it could be said that only an Army officer's presence guaranteed the completion of the withdrawal.

On February 7, General Patch went on the record with the opinion that the last two runs of the Tokyo Express had deposited the equivalent of another regiment with some supplies, although he conceded that on return they might have extracted the headquarters of some depleted units. On the west coast, the 161st breasted the Umasani and pressed on about a mile and a half to Bunina with patrols ranging another 1,200 yards to the Tambalego River, still 9 miles from Cape Esperance. During this morning, a leg wound forced George to relinquish command of the task force to Lieutenant Colonel Ferry. The judgment in this command was that the Japanese were withdrawing to Cape Esperance, or they might be evacuating the island. The task force marched toward Marovovo, which their native guides claimed the Japanese had abandoned only thirty minutes before their arrival. According to the Japanese account, there was "severe" shelling of Marovovo this morning, and at about 1240 the detachment defending this locality withdrew despite their orders to hold until dark. Matsuda confronted and chastised them sternly before hustling them back. They returned in time to fire machineguns at the advancing American task force around 1530 about 2,000 yards north of Marovovo. This checked the movement of Ferry's men, who dug in for the night.

For Matsuda, February 7 was the day of decision, and the tension mounted with each hour. Heavy shelling of Marovovo was audible, and then came word of American machinegun fire on Kamimbo. But at sundown twenty-six landing craft still remained operable. Compared to previous experience this seemed like divine intervention. Further evidence of the hand of fortune appeared in near-perfect weather, a mirror-smooth sea, slight wind, and dark-of-moon night. With extra means in hand, Matsuda reorganized the boarding plan to provide for four units of about 500 each. In a hectic forty-five minutes after 2130, the remaining mobile Japanese warriors on Guadalcanal clambered aboard these boats to the accompaniment of the din of American shells slamming into the area of Segilau and in the penumbra of violent fires just to the west. Many men prayed as they waited on the water. The rendezvous time of 2300 passed, but then the soldiers saw the blue recognition lights of approaching destroyers.

Although the second evacuation run passed far more tamely than the first, Yamamoto suspected that major American naval forces lurked just beyond Japanese search plane range south of Guadalcanal. A submarine scouting line combed through these waters without success, and the Advance Force was ordered to close to within 550 miles of Guadalcanal by the morning of February 7 to be ready to support the Reinforcement Unit. For the third run of the "KE" Operation, Hashimoto commanded eighteen destroyers. He again organized them to take off men from two points, but this time from Kamimbo and the Russells. Despite sightings of American carrier and surface unit groups south of San Cristóbal, on February 7 Hashimoto's destroyers tumbled out of Shortland and galloped down the southern rim of the Solomons. An American search plane steered a thirty-six plane strike group (fifteen SBDs, twenty F4Fs, one F5A) to the Reinforcement Unit. Seventeen out of forty-nine Zeros tendered by the 11th Air Fleet as air cover intercepted the attack. At 1755, *Isokaze* took a pair of bombs that straddled the deck around her forward gun mount, killing ten men and starting a fire; she retired in company with *Kawakaze*. *Urakaze* carried on after a near-miss. One Zero failed to return, as did the American F5A.

At Guadalcanal, boats nudged up to the gray destroyer hulls in single file and their occupants climbed to deliverance. At 0003, February 8, 1943, Matsuda received word that boarding was completed. To honor Hashimoto's pledge, sailors rowed boats in along the near shore waters and called out again and again to make sure that no one was left on the beach. By 0132, the boats returned and propellers again began turning. With the wide wakes of a 30-knot speed spreading astern, the Reinforcement Unit left Guadalcanal, and for the last time the Rising Sun fluttered from a surface ship near its blood-soaked shore. Joining the group that picked up the Russells garrison, both contingents retired up the Slot. On the way back, Matsuda signaled the 17th Army: "With the help of 20,000 souls the recovery of 1,972 men from Guadalcanal is reported complete."

Upon reaching Bougainville at 1000, Matsuda formally announced the end of his mission to Hyakutake, adding thanks for the 17th Army's efforts to guarantee the last evacuation run with destroyers. For his part, Hyakutake praised Matsuda's handling of the rear guard. Matsuda reflected that honor had been vouchsafed to the 28th Infantry in the symmetry of the facts that it supplied the first unit to fight on Guadalcanal (Ichiki) and commanded the last withdrawal.

In keeping with the pattern of the campaign, the number of the evacuees in the "KE" Operation is variously recorded, ranging as high as 12,805; but a 17th Army report completed after a thorough investigation on February 22 contains the most authoritative figures. The total given in this document is 10,652, broken down as follows: February 1, 4,935; February 4, 3,921; and February 7, 1,796. Though this number represented double the expectations of Imperial Headquarters, General Tanabe cautioned that it would take a considerable effort and time to make the returnees fit for field duty again, adding that "the months of bitter fighting and loss of many friends has been agony that is very difficult to wipe away."

The returns on the "KE" Operation showed a credit balance on the naval side with the loss of *Makikumo* and major damage to *Makinami, Maikaze,* and *Isokaze* more than balanced by the demise of *Chicago, DeHaven,* and three PT boats as well as damage to *LaVallette.* Air losses between January 25 and February 9 came to at least fifty-six Japanese and fifty-three American aircraft.[1] The 6th Air Division was particularly hard hit, and the 12th Air Wing was reduced to forty aircraft of an original complement of seventy-four (including losses over New Guinea), with a rate of attrition that, if extended, would amount to 100 percent of strength per month.

The Japanese attributed credit for the success of the "KE" Operation to minute planning by the Combined Fleet, careful preparations of all the units involved, and bold and speedy execution by the Reinforcement Unit and the supporting air units. They also paid tribute to the sacrifice of those men left behind, too weak to walk unsupported, who delayed the U.S. pursuit. After receiving word of the return of the Reinforcement Unit on the morning of the 8th, Yamamoto commended all units involved and recalled the Advanced Force.

At dawn of February 8, the members of the task force at Marovovo again observed the seascape littered with small boats and debris from the night's activities. They set off "in fast pursuit" and reached Kamimbo at 1700, having killed five stray Japanese along the way. During these same hours on the western coast, the push of the 161st toward Cape Esperance was punctuated by only sporadic brushes with Japanese soldiers in poor condition living among their own diseased and unburied dead. This dramatic change in the quality of the opposition evidently caused Colonel Dalton of the 161st to venture the opinion that the enemy was not defending or delaying, but was fleeing or had fled. Patch likewise advised Halsey of his conclusion that the last runs of the Tokyo Express were not reinforcing but evacuating the Japanese on Guadalcanal.

On the morning of February 9, the 1st Battalion, 161st Infantry set off at the trot with patrols lightly screening the flanks. This battalion met the 2/132 task force at the village of Tenaro, where Major Butler and Colonel Dalton shook hands at 1650. Patch announced this event thus:

---

[1] Japanese combat losses (fifty-one or fifty-two) were eighteen Zeros (five on the ground), eleven or twelve Oscars (the circumstances of one loss on January 27 are unclear), five Vals, and seventeen Bettys. Recorded operational losses numbered only five Bettys. American combat losses (thirty-nine) included eleven Wildcats, two P-38s, one P-39, five P-40s, one F5A, six SBDs, nine TBFs, three B-17s, and one PBY. An additional fourteen American aircraft became operational losses: ten F4Fs, two P-39s, one P-40, and one B-17.

Total and complete defeat of Japanese forces on Guadalcanal effected 1625 today. . . . [the] Tokyo Express no longer has a terminus on Guadalcanal.

While organized resistance ended on February 9, encounters with isolated individuals and groups of Japanese tapered down through the next several days. Some stragglers lived on in the interior until the last known survivor surrendered in October 1947.

Given the vast disparity in combat power between the severely debilitated 17th Army and Patch's ground forces, as well as the American aerial and sea superiority, the failure to annihilate Hyakutake's command has long been suspect. Hyakutake believed that resolute attacks toward Cape Esperance would have destroyed his army. The failure, if such it was, has two components with respect to the action on the ground. The first of these is the small relative size of the forces engaged in the pincers drive on Cape Esperance. Effectively, after January 25 the American forces normally involved no more than one regiment on the western coast supplemented after February 1 by one reinforced battalion on the southern coast. The second component is the ponderous pace of advance of these forces, which in turn is linked to terrain and logistical factors that have been examined and need no further elaboration. Amphibious hooks, such as Vandegrift repeatedly employed and Patch considered about mid-January, offered the obvious remedy to the terrain and logistical obstacles. But with the full benefit of hindsight, it is more accurate to attribute Patch's decisions in the pursuit of the 17th Army not to a want of skill or imagination, but to a fundamental misreading of Japanese intentions, which was not unique to the commander of the XIV Corps. As Nimitz confessed in his report:

Until the last moment it appeared that the Japanese were attempting a major reinforcement effort. Only skill in keeping their plans disguised and bold celerity in carrying them out enabled the Japanese to withdraw the remanents of the Guadalcanal garrison. Not until all organized forces had been evacuated on 8 February did we realize the purpose of their air and naval dispositions.

24

SUMMARY

AND REFLECTIONS

"Distant on the ear"

After almost exactly six months of struggle, sweat, and blood, the 2,500 square miles of fevered jungle and sunbaked plain called Guadalcanal was in American hands. As both sides recognized, this achievement far exceeded the value of undisputed possession of one Pacific island. In evaluating the costs and the returns, I will reflect first on the strategic decisions that prompted and guided the campaign, then I will make some assessments of the land, sea, and air aspects of the campaign, and finally I will examine the iconography of Guadalcanal both in Japan and in the United States.

Because Guadalcanal followed so shortly upon the Battle of Midway, a degree of haze can easily obscure the contours of the strategic impact of Midway and its relationship to the Guadalcanal campaign. Midway emphatically checked the Japanese strategic offensives in the *Central* Pacific; it thwarted Yamamoto's attempt to create a favorable military and diplomatic situation to negotiate an end to the war in Japan's favor; and material losses at Midway profoundly affected the thinking of the Imperial Navy. Nonetheless, the summer of 1942 found the Imperial Army advancing on Port Moresby, an act that menaced Australia, much as had the thrust checked at the Battle of the Coral Sea. We cannot know with surety whether the Japanese, undistracted by the landing on Guadalcanal, would have seized Port Moresby and whither they might have ventured in the South Pacific once in possession of that critical objective. Indeed, a fundamental critique of their conduct of the war emphasizes their failure to adhere to any limits of advance, or as one officer noted, Japanese strategic objectives and operational concepts found expression in the "language of perimeter versus the reality of overextension." Thus, it must be remembered that after Midway, the Japanese did not uniformly assume a defensive posture to await an expected counterattack against their empire. Quite to the contrary, virtually all senior Japanese officers calculated the Allied counterattack would commence no earlier than 1943 or possibly even later.

Impressive evidence attests to the soundness of these Japanese projections. Although political considerations made inevitable an American offensive in the Pacific before accounts were settled with Germany, it was by no means obvious that this offensive would begin in 1942. Immediately after the Battle of Midway, Nimitz offered no offensive proposal. Moreover, he released a large contingent of his experienced carrier aviators for postings to units training in the United States, a move that left him desperately short of carrier fliers for the Guadalcanal campaign, and one that obviously suggests that CINCPAC anticipated no major operations for some months.

We saw, however, that General MacArthur and Admiral King stomped quickly into territory where Nimitz declined to tread. In King's case, an offensive in the South Pacific fitted Turner's master war plan of March 1942 and would realize an aspiration COMINCH had entertained since at least the dark days of April when he briefed Admiral Ghormley. Sound logic warranted rejection of MacArthur's exceptionally rash plan to leap to Rabaul, but clearly Navy opposition stemmed also from fundamental questions of control of Pacific strategy. King's proposal enjoyed the twin benefits of appearing more realistic than MacArthur's and assuring United States Navy sovereignty over the first American offensive in World War Two.

But what is most impressive in hindsight is not the location but the timing of the first American offensive in the Pacific. There is a natural logic illuminating the desirability of commencing offensive operations in the South or Southwest Pacific Area in view of the availability of land-based, as opposed to carrier-based, planes, not to mention the limited amphibious shipping. Any review of the Guadalcanal campaign must acknowledge that the *timing* of "Watchtower" stemmed wholly from the uncompromising will of Ernest King rather than from a confluence of forces compelling an Allied offensive in the South Pacific in the midsummer of 1942.

King's insistence produced the immense dividend that the assault achieved not only local tactical surprise, but also strategic surprise of the first magnitude. The marines on Guadalcanal reaped the benefit of this surprise not simply on August 7–8, but for an extended period thereafter. Compared to their overall capabilities, the Japanese muted their response to the landing on Guadalcanal for many weeks, essentially because they could not adjust their thinking to take Guadalcanal as a potentially decisive battle. This intangible factor played a key role in sustaining the American grip around Lunga Point during the period of the greatest vulnerability.

But the extraordinarily speedy initiation of "Watchtower" simultaneously spawned an array of flaws, any one of which, not to mention the combination, might have produced a Japanese victory. The shared opinion in Tokyo and at CINCPAC that no Allied offensive was in prospect after Midway rested on a firm objective basis. It is a military axiom that the attacker must possess material superiority over the defender, and oceanic warfare in the broad Pacific places a peculiar cast on this equation. In a felicitous coinage, Churchill dubbed Pacific warfare "triphibious," meaning a composite of sea, air, and land elements. The summer of 1942 found American strength in the Pacific better than even in ground units and land-based air might, but airfield and shipping constraints nullified much of this advantage in the target area. More important, the significant American naval commitments to the Atlantic theater left the Pacific Fleet and its Allied units less than even in combat power with the Imperial Navy. Formidable growth of American forces existed as a future prospect, not an immediate reality when King ordered "Watchtower." Thus King's plan launched a strategic offensive with the Allies in an inferior material position, and one which left a potentially fatal imbalance in one of the legs of the tripod of forces.

As detailed in Chapter 2, a whole series of other deficiencies surrounded the mounting of "Watchtower." The landing force, the amphibious force, and the carrier air support force all represented the abrupt conjunction of untried and unfamiliar units. The tactical plans for the most complex form of military evolution known were forged from skimpy intelligence with tenuous or nonexistent coordination. The command arrangements were awkward, both within the South Pacific theater and in the relations between the South Pacific theater and MacArthur's Southwest Pacific theater. Ghormley does not appear to have understood his mission, and he failed to exercise—or perhaps was denied—a firm hand in guiding the early operations. The absence of preparations for an air garrison for Guadalcanal is astonishing, until one again appreciates that only five weeks separated the orders for "Watchtower" from the landings in the Solomons. The logistical arrangements were so thoroughly precarious that, as Admiral Turner's biographer Admiral George Dyer pointed out, if anyone had grasped their shortcomings, "Watchtower" would never have been attempted.

Had "Watchtower" failed, as readily it might have at any point through mid-November, it is easy to speculate that King would have been dismissed on the grounds that it represented a colossal misjudgment. We may go further to imagine how differently Fletcher's conduct would then appear—would we now say that his decisions represented firm moral courage and that "at least he saved the carriers"? It might well be that critics would all now basically dismiss the entire enterprise as patently doomed from the start—perhaps one of the "lessons" of Guadalcanal is the carelessness with which historical turning points are labeled "inevitable" after the event. It is apparent that all of these factors contributed to the marked oscillations of fortune that both sides experienced and that left victory alternately within the grasp of each combatant. Thus we can see that the outcome hinged ultimately upon the effectiveness of each side at the tactical or operational level, to which we can now turn.

The naval clashes totaled seven, two involving aircraft in the primary role and the rest featuring surface ships. A comparison of losses reveals the following:

COMBATANTS

	Heavy carrier	Light carrier	Battleship	Heavy cruiser	Light cruiser	Destroyer	Submarine
American	2	0	0	6*	2	15	0
Japanese	0	1	2	3	1	11	6

*Includes *Canberra.*

AUXILIARIES

	Transports	Destroyer Conversions
American	1	3
Japanese	13	1

Perhaps more illuminating is the arrangement of the losses by cause:

	Heavy carrier		Light carrier		Battle-ship		Heavy cruiser		Light cruiser		Des-troyer		Sub-marine
	J.	U.S.	J.	U.S.	J.	U.S.	J.	U.S.	J.	U.S.	J.	U.S.	J.
Cause of loss													
Surface ships:	0	0	0	0	1	0	1	5	0	1	6	9	4/5*
Surface ships & aircraft:	0	1	0	0	1	0	0	0	0	0	0	0	0
Submarines:	0	1	0	0	0	0	1	0	0	1	0	1	0
Aircraft:	0	0	1	0	0	0	1	1	1	0	4	3	1/2*
Mines:	0	0	0	0	0	0	0	0	0	0	1	1	0

*I-172 may have been destroyed by a PBY or McCalla.

Of the aerial battles, the Japanese clearly won the Battle of the Santa Cruz Islands; the Americans emerged the victor in the Battle of the Eastern Solomons. In achieving these results the Japanese paid a much higher price in aircraft and aircrews while the United States Navy lost *Hornet,* a far more valuable ship than *Ryujo:*

	Fighters	Dive-bombers	Torpedo planes	Pilots	Crewmen
Eastern Solomons					
American:	12	2	7	6	2
Japanese:	33	23	8	34	28
Santa Cruz					
American:	30	24	15	14	7
Japanese:	27	40	30	69	74
Totals					
American:	42	26	22	20	9
Japanese:	60	63	38	103	102

Note: This table presents only carrier aircraft losses, except for the losses on both sides in the *Ryujo* strike at Guadalcanal during the Battle of the Eastern Solomons. A Judy lost at Santa Cruz is included in the Japanese torpedo plane losses.

It should also be acknowledged that Santa Cruz lurched near to an American disaster rather than simply a defeat, as the Japanese held an opportunity to destroy *Enterprise* as well as *Hornet.*

Fitted on each side of the five surface encounters like bookends were the lopsided Japanese victories at Savo Island and Tassafaronga. These appear the more impressive as the Japanese entered both with much the weaker material strength. The American successes at Cape Esperance and in the Lee-Kondo action came with the balance of forces closer and found the winners in virtually as much disarray as the losers and the losses less disparate. Thus, each side won two of the encounters. The fifth and potentially tiebreaking action, the Battle of Friday the Thirteenth, presents more difficulty in classification: tactically, the significantly larger American personnel and material losses in the nighttime surface-ship action would award the decision to the Japanese, but the material balance in ships was perhaps redressed with the sinking of *Hiei* during the day, and the battle's outcome is difficult to segregate from the fact that it thwarted critical Japanese intentions. The above table reflecting the cause of losses demonstrates that the Japanese gave a lot worse than they got at night, but that American fliers and submariners kept the balance of losses close overall. The Japanese submarines sustained serious losses, but posted considerably more weighty accomplishments than their American counterparts in sinking *Wasp* and disabling *Saratoga* and *North Carolina.*

There is no doubt that intensive study, development, and practice prepared the Japanese effectively for the type of night surface clashes forced upon them by American possession of the airfield at Guadalcanal. It is markedly evident that American equipment was deficient for night battles. The record of the one plain American advantage, radar, is mixed. American management squandered it at Savo Island, the Friday the Thirteenth action, and Tassafaronga. Moreover, Japanese optics achieved sightings prior to any recorded American radar contact at Savo Island and the Lee-Kondo battleship tilt. Radar played a crucial if not decisive role at Cape Esperance, but Goto's errors materially assisted Scott to victory. Only Admiral Lee extracted full benefit from his flagship's electronic equipment, and here we can acknowledge that radar probably made the difference between success and failure—with the campaign hanging in the balance.

While American doctrine for night surface actions suffers in comparison, it is also important to bear in mind two other factors. First, the Japanese participants in these nocturnal encounters normally fought as members of a tactically cohesive division of two to four ships, in stark contrast to the vessels deployed by the United States Navy. The disintegration of American cruiser and destroyer divisional organization was attributed at the time to the demands of convoying multiple small groups of transports to supply Guadalcanal, but in hindsight we must wonder if commanders fully recognized the importance of maintaining tactical cohesion. Second, relatively stable crews with at least one, and frequently more, peacetime training cycles behind them manned the great majority of Imperial Navy ships. For example, thirty Japanese and thirty American destroyers participated in the five surface actions. Of these, twenty-five Japanese ships (83 percent) had been in commission since before the war, while only eighteen (60 percent) of the American ships could claim such background. On the other hand, the intense involvement of Japanese destroyers in reinforcing Guadalcanal wore them down. During Colonel Sanada's trip to Rabaul in December, naval officers privately informed him that the strain had been so great that some destroyer skippers and petty officers had become exhausted and were unable to continue.

The examination of the naval actions brings us inevitably to the question of leadership. The Americans proffered a richness of embarrassments. With striking regularity, almost each month of the struggle produced a relief or a painful exhibit of ineptitude: August, Fletcher's "wound" that permitted his removal from tactical command; September, Noyes's relief for the loss of *Wasp;* October, Ghormley's replacement by Halsey; November, Callaghan's mismanagement that cost his life and those of Admiral Scott and many others; the night of November 30–December 1, Wright's hesitation that lost the Battle of Tassafaronga; and January, Giffen's egregious errors that sank *Chicago.* From the Marine perspective, Admiral Turner ran a neck-and-neck race between the extent to which he assisted or impeded their efforts to hold Guadalcanal. Turner deserves full credit for not becoming defeatist when others did, and any appraisal of his actions must acknowledge three courageous decisions. First, on the morning of August 9 he elected to remain to unload without air cover. Second, he landed the 7th Marines after the loss of *Wasp* and the withdrawal of his carrier cover in September. Third, and most important, he sent Callaghan and Scott against Abe in November.

Deficiencies in leadership, however, played less of a role at the tactical level than the institutional shortcomings left from the interwar period. One of the grand and timeless lessons of the Guadalcanal campaign is the price of a major intellectual failure in doctrine between the wars. The United States Navy anticipated attritional tactics with night torpedo attacks by the Imperial Navy, but its leaders failed to follow up this insight with rigorous programs of material preparation and training to meet this clearly recognized threat. Too many officers ladled on top of this error a "fatal lethargy of mind" as to the capabilities of the Imperial Navy.

Guadalcanal was Halsey's finest hour in the war. His arrival unquestionably bolstered morale at a critical juncture, and no one may underestimate the degree to which morale guides the outcome of any contest. Likewise, we may not fail to notice that Nimitz astutely recognized this factor and used it as the central reason for his relief of Ghormley. Nimitz also earns high marks for his resoluteness in the face of depressing losses and follies by his subordinates. When we look to Halsey's actual management between mid-October and mid-November, however, there is good cause to temper our praise. He exhibited something close to recklessness in provoking the Santa Cruz action, and either he or perhaps his staff failed to smoothly exploit the radio intelligence advantage they possessed at the Naval Battle of Guadalcanal.

On the Japanese side, Admiral Mikawa rendered a virtuoso demonstration of boldness and skill at the Battle of Savo Island. The fact that Imperial Navy destroyers conducted so many successful Tokyo Express runs with so relatively few losses stands as a tribute to the flexibility and consummate professionalism of their commanders and crews. Admirals Hashimoto and Koyanami deserve high marks for the resolute management of the evacuation program. The performance of Admiral Tanaka offers a complex and perhaps cautionary picture. Indeed, it is intriguing to contrast the degree to which the perceived performances of Tanaka and Fletcher colored their reputations after the war. There is good reason to carefully ration the credit due Tanaka for the triumph at the Battle of Tassafaronga, though it is scarcely appropriate to deny him all acclaim for this success. Consciously or unconsciously, many writers allowed the glow of Tassafaronga to place a shine of excellence on all of Tanaka's actions in the war, whether or not they objectively merit such judgment. In Fletcher's case, some historians allowed the troubling chapters of his role at Guadalcanal to tarnish his actions earlier in the war, many of which in this writer's view warrant far more praise than they have received.

Of all the senior naval officers involved, Admiral Yamamoto is the most difficult to judge, because of a paucity of information on his thinking. It is easy to damn him retrospectively for failure either to flatly refuse to become involved in a decisive battle around Guadalcanal or to mass his forces to achieve the victory so plainly in his grasp between mid-September and mid-October. Of these options the latter would appear to be more in keeping with the strategic vision he steered by from Pearl Harbor to Midway—victory by unhinging the will of his materially more powerful opponent. Clearly defeat of the first Allied counterattack on top of Japan's earlier successes would have gone far toward his goal. Yamamoto's failure to select a clear strategy may reflect the degree to which defeat at Midway diminished his own powers of decision and the stunning effect of King's unexpected challenge.

In contrast to the clashes at sea, the actions ashore present a persistent pattern of Japanese failure. The fundamental mistakes were the gross underestimations first of American strength ashore and then of American morale. Despite reports by aviators of as many as twenty transports offshore, staff officers initially estimated only 2,000 or so marines on Guadalcanal. They slowly ratcheted this count upward until it reached 10,000 just before the October offensive, less than half the actual figure. A serious misperception of the durability of American morale paralleled this underestimate of numbers. The conduct and fate of Ichiki exemplified the existence and the cost of both these errors, but Ichiki exhibited commonplace attitudes. These same twin misconceptions undoubtedly played a key role in permitting commanders and staff officers from Tokyo to Rabaul to ignore or minimize gross deficiencies in the logistical arrangements to support the soldiers on Guadalcanal.

Whether because of the general atmosphere of overconfidence or because of negligence, staff work at all levels of the Imperial Army conspicuously failed to include a thorough analysis of the enemy situation. Given the balance of naval forces and the excellence of the Imperial Navy in night fighting, the Americans depended almost absolutely for sustenance on air control mounted from Henderson Field. The crux of American vulnerability was not merely the possession of the earth under Henderson Field, but the capacity to employ that ground as an airfield. Thus, the Japanese only needed to prohibit the use of the field; this did not demand the capture of the field, only that it be brought under either direct small-arms fire or interdiction by artillery. It is interesting to observe that the Imperial Navy recognized this distinction in November when planners thought of moving long-range naval guns ashore to shell the field. Viewing the Marine situation correctly, we see the signal value of the Matanikau action of October 6–9 and the wisdom of establishing defenses at the Matanikau crossings in the face of grave risks.

At the tactical level the story of the campaign reveals a contradiction between common western beliefs as to Japanese society and actual practice. Most westerners think of Imperial Japan as distinctly hierarchical, with superiors commanding and receiving unswerving obedience. Yet at numerous points in the campaign we see Imperial Army officers—Kawaguchi and Oka come immediately to mind— behaving more like independent contractors than officers rigorously adhering to plans issued from above.

The conduct of Vandegrift and his staff gathered ample praise at the time and in the initial postwar assessments, and this account thoroughly validates that verdict. The first sign of this masterful professional performance emerged in the chaotic launching of "Watchtower." The 1st Marine Division conceived the landing plan with precious little assistance from higher commands. While the original directive called for the seizure of "Tulagi and adjacent positions," the 1st Marine Division fixed the airfield on Guadalcanal as a major objective before superior headquarters so directed. When granted some choice as to landing beaches, as at Tulagi and Guadalcanal, the marines elected to land unopposed and maneuver onto their objective. Gavutu-Tanambogo offered no options, and the 1st Parachute Battalion performed no mean feat in securing a foothold when outnumbered and under such tactically unfavorable circumstances.

With the radical change wrought by the Battle of Savo Island, Vandegrift's team accurately assessed their situation and elevated to primary objective the retention of Henderson Field, and later its satellites. Herein the marines suffered the dangerous handicap of dispersion inflicted by the very difficult tactical problem presented in keeping the field secure. The Imperial Army's failure to perceive how small-arms fire or artillery might interdict the field immensely aided the marines, but a parallel failure of Admiral Turner to grasp the vulnerability of the Marine situation and his foot-dragging in adding reinforcements into the original perimeter obstructed the defenders.

With remarkable facility, Vandegrift adjusted his dispositions to stay one step ahead of the 17th Army in each of the attempts to recapture Henderson Field in August, September, and October. The original tactical configuration thwarted Ichiki; the adjustments in September just frustrated Kawaguchi; and the bold decision to employ a perimeter, linear defense averted potential disaster when the immediate estimate of Japanese intentions proved awry in October.

In between these Japanese offensives, the successive jabs at the Matanikau, and occasionally to the east, inflicted important attrition on the Japanese, kept them often off balance, and gave an aggressive edge to the Marine posture. These efforts maintained morale, not in the sense of merely invoking a shibboleth, but because they palpably demonstrated to each marine and soldier that they could strike out at their enemies at a time and place of their choosing rather than constantly await the next move of the Japanese.

The operations of the United States Army units on Guadalcanal present a more mixed picture. The 164th Infantry surmounted adversities that any unit, regular or reserve, would find the stuff of traditions. The 132d Infantry drew a daunting first assignment, and if its overall performance was not lustrous, it was not a disgrace. The operations of the 25th Infantry Division bear detailed study. On the whole, however, the actions on Guadalcanal at the command and staff level show the marines more consistently used imaginative tactics. Indeed, the most serious Marine failure, the action by the Matanikau in September, failed largely because overconfidence permitted an elegant but deeply flawed maneuver scheme to proceed.

Guadalcanal became a trove of experience for the United States Marine Corps and Army. Vandegrift fingered "inadequate physical training and hardening prior to combat" as the greatest problem his command initially faced. The contemporary reports bulge with tactical lessons and comments on jungle fighting as relevant today as when they were first written. One important message from Guadalcanal was the vital necessity of not only combat, but also combat support units. The 1st Marine Division passed the word along that "construction equipment and personnel are not a luxury but an absolute necessity," and the division's engineer pointed out that "a power shovel or a bulldozer is just as important in its own phase of modern warfare as is an artillery piece." Engineers and Seabees kept the airfields open, and the garrison's lifeline open, day to day, come rain or shine, bomb or shell. Nor can we forget how one light tank cracked the Gifu thanks to a triumph of engineering skill.

Among the most interesting aspects of this experience are the judgments on the Imperial Army. Colonel Clifton Cates said the Japanese depended on "courage and cold steel." To American eyes, the Japanese displayed amazing failure to grasp the dominance of automatic weapons and artillery in modern war. As the report of the 1st Marine Division noted, in pursuing their propensity for night attacks, "to preserve direction [the Japanese] followed the conventional practice of moving dense columns of infantry along terrain lines leading to the objective," and these were interdicted "as a matter of course" by deep supporting fires of artillery and mortars. Merritt Edson equated Japanese tactics to "Indian warfare" in the twentieth century. In hindsight, however, we can perceive how the 17th Army did not freely select many plans and tactical choices, but was compelled to them by the strangling effect of American air power and the shrewd countermoves of the 1st Marine Division.

We cannot leave the subject of the Japanese soldiers on Guadalcanal without honoring them for their one supreme virtue, a determination, a courage, far above that of any of the other combatants in World War Two. John B. George, a junior infantry officer who faced the Japanese at the Gifu and later in Burma, wrote:

> . . . most of us who have fought in the Pacific are ready to admit here and now, away from all the convincing firsthand evidence we have seen—mass starvation, untold suffering, shell shock, cannibalism, mass suicide—that for sheer, bloody, hardened steel guts, the stocky and hard-muscled little Jap doughboy has it all over any of us.

In facing defeat, George went on, the Japanese soldier "took it like a man—like a hero. No surrender for him."

Without a doubt, the air struggle produced the most important long-term military effect of the Guadalcanal campaign. Unlike the sea and land contests, however, the air clash took the aspect of a large-scale attritional battle where the outcome is gauged principally in overall crew and aircraft casualties, but here we face two inherent difficulties. First, cumulative loss figures for both sides are arduous to compute and almost impossible to certify as precisely accurate. Second, the raw numbers of Japanese losses alone do not properly convey the significance of the Guadalcanal campaign on Japan's naval aviation.

Neither antagonist maintained one set of master aircraft and crew records in the Solomons but rather both deployed a multiplicity of commands and services. The Japanese employed the carrier commands, the 11th Air Fleet, the R Area Air Force (float planes), and, late in the campaign, the Imperial Army's 6th Air Division. The following table represents the best figures available on Imperial Navy aircraft losses from all causes from August 1 to November 15, 1942:

Command	Type							Totals
	Zeros	Vals	Kates	Bettys	Flying boats	Float planes	Misc.	
Carriers:	81	69	47	0	—	—	1	198
11th Air Fleet:	106	15	—	100	19	—	2	242
R Area Air Force:	—	—	—	—	—	66*	—	46
Totals:	187	84	47	106	18	66	3	506

*Figure includes float planes lost from ships.

American aircraft losses from all causes from August 1 to November 15, 1942, were as follows:

Command	Type									Totals
	F4F	SBD	TBF	P-400/ P-39	PBY	B-17	B-26	C-47/ R4D	Other	
Carriers:	81	63	40	—	—	—	—	—	—	184
Cactus Air Force:	115	66	16	19	—	—	—	—	—	216
Search & Attack:	—	—	—	—	17	18	1	—	—	36
Misc.:	4	5	—	2	—	—	—	3	30*	44
Totals:	200	134	56	21	17	18	1	3	30	480

*Figure includes 20 SOCs (15 at Savo Island, 4 at Cape Esperance, and 1 in the Naval Battle of Guadalcanal), 4 OS2Us, 2 Seagull V, 2 J2Fs, and 2 Hudsons. The F4F, SBD, P-400/P-39 and C-47/R4D figures in the *Misc.* line are operational losses on Espiritu Santo, Efate and other bases.

During the period from November 16, 1942, to February 9, 1943, American losses from all causes were as follows:

Type											
F4F	SBD	TBF	P-39	P-40	P-38	PBY	B-17	B-26	OS2U/ SOC	C-47/ R4D	Other
41	31	10	12	10	6	4	9	4	4	1	2*

*One F5A and one Hudson.

Confirmed Japanese losses in this period numbered 116–117:

Zero	Val	Betty	Oscar	Pete
59	7	25	14–15	11

According to an authoritative statement from Rear Admiral Sakamaki, the chief of staff of the 11th Air Fleet, at least another sixty aircraft must be added to this total just for the period from November 16 to December 24, raising the expenditure to 176–77. The later figure includes some aircraft lost over New Guinea, but is undoubtedly low with respect to float planes. A final total shows Allied losses at 615 planes for the whole campaign; confirmed Japanese losses for the period through November 15 plus a conservative estimate of a wastage of a further 176 to February 9, 1943, yields a final figure of 682. A somewhat different picture is provided when only air combat losses are compared, as American operational losses were much higher for the campaign, largely because of more primitive bases and, at least early on, a somewhat lower overall experience level among the aircrew. In this comparison, Allied losses were 264 aircraft, while Japanese losses reached about 446 aircraft.

Quantification of aircrew casualties is more difficult. American losses included 150 members of the United States Army Air Force and 130 Naval and 140 Marine personnel for a total of 420. Japanese losses exceeded this figure by from two to four times, essentially because more of their missing aircraft contained multiple crewmen and proportionately many fewer of their flight crews survived their aircraft. Moreover, the Japanese losses occurred primarily among their top-quality and best-trained aviation personnel, thus the impact of these losses was far more severe than a simple comparison of the raw numbers of losses to the total available pool would indicate. To take an example, at the beginning of the war the Imperial Navy's air service mustered about 3,500 pilots. Of these, the carrier air groups featured the 600 or so most skilled pilots, with an average of 800 hours of flying time. At Guadalcanal approximately 125 carrier pilots fell, most of whom came from this select band of 600. Further, the severe losses among the Betty-equipped groups deprived the Imperial Navy of another substantial fraction of their most talented airmen. Certainly the comment in December 1942 by Admiral

Sakamaki that the newly arrived crews possessed but a third of the skill of the men they replaced substantiates the devastating qualitative losses sustained by the Imperial Navy's air arm in the course of the campaign.

In addressing the reasons for the outcome of the air campaign we must first divide it into two parts. The initial and decisive phase extended from the date of the landing to the end of the Naval Battle of Guadalcanal. During this period the Japanese enjoyed almost continuous numerical superiority both in seagoing and shore-based aircraft. Thus, their failure may not be ascribed to a disparity in numbers. What did account for this result was their fundamental error of negligently or recklessly accepting battle under serious handicaps. In the fore of these was the lack of an air base closer to Guadalcanal than Rabaul, and later Buka. The 565 miles separating the Japanese aviators from their objective introduced a series of impediments. First, it effectively halved the Zero escort force by precluding the use of the Model 32 Zero. Second, the long, time-consuming flights impelled the Japanese into a routine of operations that simplified the defenders' tasks. Third, the long hauls created excessive wear on aircraft and crews that subtly wore away their numbers and combat effectiveness. Fourth, it turned many damaged aircraft into outright losses—together with their crews.

The Japanese perceived that bases closer to Guadalcanal would cure these ills, but energetic corrective action was conspicuous by its absence. The record suggests that excessive optimism that each monthly attack would triumph restrained efforts, but the lack of an efficient airfield-construction capacity constituted the principal obstacle. An account prepared by Japanese officers and the designer of the Zero fighter plane after the war advanced the proposition that had Japan possessed one-fifth of the airfield-construction capability of the American forces, she would have won the Guadalcanal campaign. A student of the struggle, Thomas Miller, succinctly commented that the Japanese did not lack fighter planes but bulldozers. The Japanese also acknowledged problems with providing a steady stream of replacement aircraft and maintenance crews as contributing factors, but the Americans labored under similar restraints.

From the American perspective, several factors stand out. General Vandegrift stated that he could say "nothing too lavish in praise" of the entire coast watcher organization, and it was in the context of the air campaign that the coast watchers made their greatest contribution. Their warnings, supplemented by radar equipment later, prevented the Wildcat's modest climbing characteristics from fatally undermining the defense of Henderson Field. We must again note that the thirty-five- to forty-minute alerts of impending raids allowed just enough time for the Grumman fighters to achieve the altitudes from which they could effectively intercept the bomber formations and deal defensively with the Zero escorts. Next come the clever dive-and-climb, overhead pass tactics, originated by Major Smith and copied with success by subsequent units, that maximized the Wildcats' capabilities. The sturdiness of the Wildcat earns a place on this list, and the tireless work of the ground crews and supporting personnel who kept the planes of the Cactus Air Force serviceable under appallingly primitive conditions also merits mention.

In the realm of offensive exertions, the 200-mile striking range of the Dauntless SBD dive-bombers emerges in this account as virtually a geographic feature fundamentally controlling the course of the conflict. The day and night attacks by these aircraft enforced the use of destroyers for installation and supply of Japanese land forces on Guadalcanal, thus severely throttling the Imperial Army's capabilities. The work of the Dauntlesses, with the adept assistance of the 67th Fighter Squadron, constricted Japanese operations in daylight on the island and depressed Japanese morale.

Far less satisfactory was the offensive work of the B-17s, which scored hits with less than 1 percent of their bombs. The reasons for this slender contribution acknowledged by Army Air Force historians included the limited number of planes overall, diversions for reconnaissance duties, small bombing formations, aircrew and maintenance crew shortages, adverse weather, inaccurate intelligence, and inadequate facilities. The inability of the Flying Fortresses to hit or sink ships represented a profound doctrinal embarrassment to the Army Air Forces, but the B-17 squadrons made a signal contribution though their reconnaissance work.

In terms of human cost, the Japanese paid the higher toll overall, though not in every category. The Imperial Army put 31,400 men on Guadalcanal, evacuated 740 before the "KE" Operation, and withdrew 9,860, making the fatality total about 20,800, or precisely two-thirds of those who served on the island. The rifle units sustained extremely severe losses. Colonel Obara of the 29th Infantry reported that of the 2,500 men in the regiment, only forty-three were able to walk at the time of the withdrawal, yet battles only accounted for 20 percent of the casualties. To the Imperial Army total must be added about 4,800 naval personnel who served on the island. American ground losses included 1,207 marines and 562 soldiers, for a total of 1,769 (out of about 60,000 committed). For every United States soldier or marine ashore who died, almost three sailors and marines in ship companies perished, 4,911.[1] This writer could not locate definite figures for losses in the Imperial Navy's surface ships and submarines, but a minimum estimate is 3,200, to which may be added another 343 crewmen on the transports assigned to reinforce Guadalcanal. The combined total of killed and permanently missing on land, sea, and air for the United States and Allied forces reached 7,100 (1,769 ground, 4,911 sea, 420 air). The Japanese total falls no lower than 30,343 (25,600 ground, including naval units ashore on Guadalcanal, at least 3,543 sea, and roughly 1,200 air).[2]

The discussion of the operational elements of the campaign draws us back to its overall strategic impact. Quite simply, Guadalcanal was the literal turning point of the war in the Pacific. The Japanese remained on the offensive in the Southeast Area in the summer of 1942, and persisted in an offensive in New Guinea until checked there and forced to focus their attention on the southern Solomons. Moreover, up until the Naval Battle of Guadalcanal the Japanese threatened to crush the attempt of the Allies to move to the offensive. Thus, Guadalcanal, not Midway, represented the actual shift in strategic postures.

But Guadalcanal represented much more than the first milestone along the road to Tokyo. The campaign inflicted irreparable damage on the Imperial Japanese Navy's air arm and severe attrition on her light naval forces. Japanese factories replaced many times over the aircraft losses, but Japan lacked the time or resources to replicate the skilled pilots and crews that perished over and around Guadalcanal. The Imperial Navy's superb destroyer component likewise sustained severe, though not quite so devastating, losses. On August 7 there were sixty-seven modern destroyers in service and another seven commissioned during the campaign, but in that same interval thirteen—almost one in five—were sunk.

---

[1]The figure of 5,041 includes forty-nine marines and ninety-two members of the Australian and New Zealand navies. Therefore, losses among strictly United States Navy personnel were 4,770. If the 130 aviation deaths are included, U.S. Navy fatalities reach an even 4,900. This compares closely to the 4,907 killed or missing at Okinawa, which is regarded as the U.S. Navy's costliest campaign. Proportionate to the forces engaged, however, Guadalcanal was much more bloody. Appendix 3 contains a detailed accounting of Allied naval personnel losses during the campaign.

[2]It should be noted that while the Americans and Japanese were killing each other by the thousands, native casualties were thankfully very light. The death toll from August 6, 1942, to February 9, 1943, reached about forty-three. The worst losses came on August 7 when American carrier planes mistakenly bombed Laulasi village on Malaita, killing about twenty-five people including thirteen children.

These material losses bring us to the question of whether the disparity in forces was such that Japan could never have won the war and that no battle or campaign represented more than one interchangeable episode in an inevitable process. On the naval side, during the period of the campaign each nation commissioned the following warships:

	Heavy carrier	Light carrier	Battleship	Heavy cruiser	Light cruiser	Destroyer	Submarine
U.S.	1	1	1	0	4	62	18
Japan	0	0	0	0	1	7	14

Aircraft production reveals an equally marked divergence. In 1942, the United States turned out 49,445 planes and Japan 8,861. A direct comparison of the ship and aircraft figures must be emphatically qualified by the comment that America deployed a significant majority of her aircraft and a substantial fraction of her warships against Japan's Axis allies. What is less commonly noted when these figures are trotted out, however, is that a different tale is told on the ground. American strategy emphasized industrial production and air and naval might over ground forces. Resource allocation decisions ultimately left the United States Army with only eighty-nine divisions and the Marine Corps with six, for a total of ninety-five, to subdue enemies in Europe and the Pacific. The Japanese fielded 173 such formations in August 1945, albeit almost entirely rifle divisions.

As painful recent experience attests, material factors do not alone dictate victory. Although Japanese strategists as a group possessed a seriously flawed concept of American material might, none of them doubted that Japan would be outgunned. From the outset, they calculated that they could protract the conflict and inflict casualties that would eventually erode the American will to win. As the leading American student of the Imperial Army, Alvin Coox, recently revealed, the apparent vulnerability of American determination not only figured in Japanese war plans, it also steeled the decision-makers to chose war over negotiation:

> . . . Japanese leadership in 1941 gave particular credence to reports of alleged disunity with the United States, especially regarding support for England. Congressional opposition supposedly included Democrats as

well as Republicans, expressed bitter opposition to the policies of President Roosevelt. Gallup polls were reassuring to the Japanese, indicating that the American man in the street opposed involvement in any overseas conflict.

Perhaps the ultimate example of the wide and acrimonious divisions among the American public came in November 1941, when the House of Representatives extended the peacetime draft by a margin of one vote.

Japanese strategists joined impeccable company in doubts about American and Allied will. After the humiliating surrenders at Singapore and then Tobruk, no less a figure than Winston Churchill tearfully, though privately, questioned whether the democratic youth could prevail in battle against the Axis. Later losses at Tarawa shocked the American public, again raising the spector that a war-weary America would ultimately accede to most of Japan's conquests. When we acknowledge that American will was not invulnerable, we can see that in this realm of morale effect lies the other decisive contribution of the Guadalcanal campaign. It conclusively demonstrated that American marines and soldiers could meet the enemy in adversity and prevail. This is why James Jones emphasized the "special qualities" Guadalcanal evoked for his generation.

In the United States, Guadalcanal moved in less than ninety days from total obscurity to legendary status. The fact that this was the first move to retake soil from the detested Japanese guaranteed the distinction, and the absence of major American involvement in competing European or African campaigns until November granted coverage of the campaign ascendancy in the newspapers and on the radio. As the struggle played against a background of months of failure and defeat, and as it generated startling and abrupt twists and dips of fortune, it enjoyed a melodramatic element that riveted the public. To a degree hard to convey adequately to those who did not share this period, the eventual triumph not merely represented a step forward, but vindicated a generation and the nation's faith in itself.

Celebrations of Guadalcanal commenced during the war and never stopped thereafter. Partly this may be ascribed to the special niche World War Two earned in history, but Guadalcanal has been graced by some of the finest of all the works related to this period. First, and still in many respects foremost, came Richard Tregaskis's classic gritty report on the campaign from the landing to late September, *Guadalcanal Diary,* which vaulted to the best-seller lists as soon as it was published. It still reads with a fresh immediacy and is entirely reliable as to any event Tregaskis witnessed. John Hersey's *Into the Valley* provides a narrower angle of vision but contains a timeless glimpse of a small unit in adversity. In this writer's opinion, Samuel Eliot Morrison's major volume on the campaign, *The Struggle for Guadalcanal,* offers the finest example of this master's narrative technique in the whole of his much-acclaimed fifteen-volume series.

The first literary effort to honor Guadalcanal came in James Michener's Pulitzer Prize–winning *Tales of the South Pacific,* in which, however, Guadalcanal was an offstage presence. James Jones transformed his personal experiences in Company F, 27th Infantry, 25th Infantry Division into as fine a novel of the rifleman's war as any extant, *The Thin Red Line.* This book deserves far better recognition than it has yet received.

Guadalcanal provided real-life grist for the celluloid mills, and at least five movies stemmed from the campaign. Richard Tregaskis's immensely popular *Guadalcanal Diary* became in 1943 a successful film, which remains one of the most evocative of the period. Somber tales of sacrifice from the campaign reached the public in *The Fighting Sullivans* in 1944 and in *Pride of the Marines* the following year. The first offered a wrenching story of the loss of the five Sullivan brothers and the second traced the readjustment of a blinded Marine hero. Postwar, *The Gallant Hours* presented James Cagney as Admiral Halsey at the crisis of the struggle. Unfortunately, James Jones's excellent novel suffered the Hollywood treatment in *The Thin Red Line.* John Wayne's *Flying Leathernecks* weaves an account loosely based on the efforts of the Cactus Air Force.

Since Japan ultimately failed at Guadalcanal, it did not become an instant subject of cultural celebration. But it was transformed into a symbol of resolution as the war spiraled downward. For example, in November 1944 a monthly Japanese publication, *Hinode,* contained a large illustration of "exhausted but resolute Japanese soldiers on Guadalcanal." An accompanying verse "spoke of how they ate grass roots, leaves, even dirt, but still retained their indomitable spirit. They held on like gods." The description of the 17th Army's diet is all too true, and no one can deny the "indomitable spirit" of the Japanese soldiers at Guadalcanal. In the decades after 1945, there was no doubt about the significance of Guadalcanal to professional Japanese naval officers. Captain Y. "Tommy" Tamagawa remarked in a conversation with the author:

There were many famous battles in the war—Saipan, Leyte, Okinawa, etc. But after the war we [the professional military] talked only about two, Midway and Guadalcanal.

The Japanese returned to Guadalcanal after the war, as they did to so many battlefields, to claim the bones of their dead. They found that time had cooled the intense enmity of their opponents, and American former soldiers and marines helped them to find the many unmarked graves. On Mount Austen the Japanese erected a graceful memorial to their countrymen who had perished.

In concluding his work on the campaign, Samuel Elliot Morison wrote:

> For us who were there, or whose friends were there, Guadalcanal is not a name but an emotion, recalling desperate fights in the air, furious night naval battles, frantic work at supply or construction, savage fighting in the sodden jungle, nights broken by screaming bombs and deafening explosions of naval shells. Sometimes I dream of a great battle monument on Guadalcanal; a granite monolith on which the names of all who fell and of all the ships that rest in Iron Bottom Sound many be carved. At other times I feel that the jagged cone of Savo Island, forever brooding over the blood-thickened waters of the Sound, is the best monument to the men and ships who here rolled back the enemy tide.

Nearly a half century after the event, veterans of the campaign prevailed in seeing to the erection of an American memorial on Guadalcanal. It will mean much to those who served there, though few of their countrymen will ever be able to view it. But the veterans of the Guadalcanal campaign have something far more valuable than any edifice of stone, of which James Michener wrote immediately after the war:

> They will live a long time, these men of the South Pacific. They had an American quality. They, like their victories, will be remembered as long as our generation lives. After that, like the men of the Confederacy, they will become strangers. Longer and longer shadows will obscure them, until their Guadalcanal sounds distant on the ear like Shiloh and Valley Forge.

Guadalcanal may already "sound distant on the ear"; but while distance is inevitable, immortality is not.

1

FORCES ARRAYED FOR THE LANDING ON GUADALCANAL, AUGUST 7, 1942

ALLIED

Adm. Chester W. Nimitz
Commander in Chief Pacific Fleet and Pacific Ocean Area

Vice Adm. Robert L. Ghormley
Commander South Pacific Area and South Pacific Force

Vice Adm. Frank Jack Fletcher
Commander Expeditionary Force
(Task Force 61)
in Saratoga

Rear Adm. Leigh Noyes
Commander Air Support Force
(Task Group 61.1)
in Wasp

Task Group 61.1.1

CARRIER:

Saratoga			Capt. DeWitt C. Ramsey
Air Group 3	1	SBD-3	Cdr. Harry D. Felt
VF-5	34	F4F-4	Lt. Cdr. Leroy C. Simpler
	1	F4F-7	
VB-3	16	SBD-3	Lt. Cdr. DeWitt W. Shumway
VS-3	17	SBD-3	Lt. Cdr. Louis J. Kirn
VT-8	15	TBF-1	Lt. Harold H. Larsen

Screen

HEAVY CRUISERS:

Minneapolis	Capt. Frank J. Lowry
New Orleans	Capt. Walter S. DeLany

DESTROYERS:

Capt. Samuel B. Brewer
(ComDesron 1)

Phelps		Lt. Cdr. Edward L. Beck
Farragut		Lt. Cdr. Henry D. Rosendal
Worden		Lt. Cdr. William G. Pogue
MacDonough		Lt. Cdr. Erle V. Dennett
Dale		Lt. Cdr. Anthony L. Rorschach

Rear Adm. Thomas C. Kinkaid
(Task Group 61.1.2)

CARRIER:

Enterprise			Capt. Arthur C. Davis
Air Group 6	1	TBF-1	Lt. Cdr. Maxwell F. Leslie
VF-6	36	F4F-4	Lt. Cdr. Louis F. Bauer
	1	F4F-7	
VB-6	17	SDB-3	Lt. Ray Davis
VS-5	18	SBD-3	Lt. Turner F. Caldwell, Jr.
VT-3	14	TBF-1	Lt. Cdr. Charles M. Jett

Screen
Rear Adm. Mahon S. Tisdale
in **Portland**

BATTLESHIP:

North Carolina	Capt. George H. Fort

HEAVY CRUISER:

Portland	Capt. Laurance T. DuBose

LIGHT CRUISER:

Atlanta	Capt. Samuel P. Jenkins

DESTROYERS:

Capt. Edward P. Sauer
(ComDesron 6)

Balch	Lt. Cdr. Harold H. Tiemroth
Maury	Lt. Cdr. Gelzer L. Sims
Gwin	Cdr. John M. Higgins
Benham	Lt. Cdr. Joseph M. Worthington
Grayson	Lt. Cdr. Frederick J. Bell

Rear Adm. Noyes
(Task Group 61.1.3)

CARRIER:

Wasp			Capt. Forrest P. Sherman
Air Group 72	1	TBF-1	Lt. Cdr. Wallace M. Beakley
VF-71	30	F4F-4	Lt. Cdr. Courtney Shands
VS-71	15	SBD-3	Lt. Cdr. John Eldridge, Jr.
VS-72	15	SBD-3	Lt. Cdr. Ernest M. Snowden
VT-7	9	TBF-1	Lt. Henry A. Romberg
Utility	1	J2F-5	

Screen

HEAVY CRUISERS:

San Francisco   Capt. Charles H. McMorris
Salt Lake City   Capt. Ernest G. Small

DESTROYERS:

Capt. Robert G. Tobin
(Comdesron 12)

Lang   Lt. Cdr. John L. Wilfong
Sterett   Cdr. Jesse G. Coward
Aaron Ward   Lt. Cdr. Orville F. Gregor
Stack   Lt. Cdr. Alvord J. Greenacre
Laffey   Lt. Cdr. William E. Hank
Farenholt   Lt. Cdr. Eugene T. Seaward

FUELING GROUP:

Platte   Capt. Ralph H. Henkle
Cimarron   Cdr. Russell M. Ihrig
Kaskaskia   Cdr. Walter L. Taylor
Sabine   Capt. Houston L. Maples
Kanawha   Cdr. Kendall S. Reed

Rear Adm. Richmond Kelly Turner
Commander Amphibious Force South Pacific
(Task Force 62)
in **McCawley**

Rear Adm. V. A. C. Crutchley, RN
Commander Escort
in **Australia**
(Task Group 62.2)

HEAVY CRUISERS:

Australia   Capt. H. B. Farncomb, RAN
Canberra   Capt. Frank E. Getting, RAN
Chicago   Capt. Howard D. Bode

LIGHT CRUISER:

Hobart   Capt. H. A. Showers, RAN

DESTROYERS:

Capt. Cornelius W. Flynn
(ComDesron 4)

Selfridge   Lt. Cdr. Carroll D. Reynolds
Patterson   Cdr. Frank R. Walker
Ralph Talbot   Lt. Cdr. Joseph W. Callahan
Mugford   Lt. Cdr. Edward W. Young
Jarvis   Lt. Cdr. William W. Graham, Jr.
Desdiv 7   Cdr. Leonard B. Austin

Blue	Cdr. Harold N. Williams
Helm	Lt. Cdr. Chester E. Carroll
Henley	Cdr. Robert H. Smith
Bagley	Lt. Cdr. George A. Sinclair

Transport Group X-Ray
(Guadalcanal Transport Group)
Capt. Lawrence F. Reifsnider
Commander Transport Divisions, South Pacific Force
in **Hunter Liggett**

Transport Division "A"
Capt. Paul S. Theiss

American Legion (AP-35)   Capt. Thomas D. Warner
(Regimental Headquarters, 5th Marines, Col. Leroy P. Hunt, and 1st Battalion,
  5th Marines, Lt. Col. William E. Maxwell)
Fuller (AP-14)   Capt. Theiss
(3d Battalion, 5th Marines, Lt. Col. Frederick C. Biebush)
Bellatrix (AK-20)   Cdr. William F. Dietrich
(Misc. troops, including Co. A, 1st Tank Battalion)

Transport Division "B"
Capt. Charles P. McFeaters

Barnett (AP-11)   Capt. W. B. Phillips
(Headquarters, 1st Marines, Col. Clifton B. Cates, and 1st Battalion, 1st
  Marines, Lt. Col. Lenard B. Cresswell)
George F. Elliott (AP-13)   Capt. Watson O. Bailey
(2d Battalion, 1st Marines, Lt. Col. Edwin A. Pollock)
McCawley (AP-10)   Capt. McFeaters
(3d Battalion, 1st Marines, Lt. Col. William N. McKelvy, Jr.)
Libra (AK-53)   Cdr. William B. Fletcher
(Misc. troops, including Headquarters & Service Battery, 3d Battalion, 11th
  Marines)

Transport Division "C"
Capt. Reifsnider

Hunter Liggett (AP-27)   Cdr. Louis W. Perkins, USCG
(Headquarters & Service Battery 5th Battalion, 11th Marines)
Formalhaut (AK-22)   Cdr. J. D. Alvis
(equipment of 1st Engineer Battalion, Maj. James G. Frazer)
Betelgeuse (AK-28)   Cdr. Harry D. Power
(equipment of 3d Defense Battalion)

Transport Division "D"
Capt. Ingolf N. Kiland

Capt. Pat Buchanan
Commander Transport Division 2

Crescent City (AP-40)   Capt. Ingolf N. Kiland
(Regimental Headquarters, 2d Marines, Col. John M. Arthur)
President Hayes (AP-39)   Cdr. Francis W. Benson
(2d Battalion, 2d Marines, Lt. Col. Maj. Orin K. Pressley)

President Adams (AP-38) Cdr. C. W. Brewington
(3d Battalion, 2d Marines, Lt. Col. Robert G. Hunt)
Alhena (AK-26) Cdr. Charles B. Hunt
(3d Battalion, 10th Marines, Lt. Col. Manly L. Curry)

Transport Group Yoke
(Tulagi Transport Group)
Capt. George B. Ashe

Transport Division "E"
Capt. Ashe

Neville (AP-16) Capt. Carlos A. Bailey
(2d Battalion, 5th Marines, Lt. Col. Harold E. Rosecrans)
Heywood (AP-12) Capt. Herbert B. Knowles
(1st Parachute Battalion, Maj. Robert H. Williams, 1st Special Weapons
  Battalion, Maj. Robert Lucky, and Company E, 1st Raider Battalion)
President Jackson (AP-37) Cdr. Charles W. Weitzel
(1st Battalion, 2d Marines, Lt. Col. Robert E. Hill)
Zeilin (AP-9) Capt. Buchanan
(3d Defense Battalion, Col. Robert H. Pepper)

Cdr. Hugh W. Hadley
Commander Transport Division 12

Little (APD-4) Lt. Cdr. J. B. Lofberg
(Headquarters 1st Raider Battalion, Lt. Col. Merritt Edson, and Company A, 1st
  Raider Battalion)
McKean (APD-5) Lt. Cdr. John D. Sweeney
(Company D, 1st Raider Battalion)
Gregory (APD-3) Lt. Cdr. Harry F. Bauer
(Company C, 1st Raider Battalion)
Calhoun (APD-2) Lt. Cdr. E. C. Loughead
(Company B, 1st Raider Battalion)

The transports embarked a total of 475 landing craft divided as follows:

(a) 8 "X" type (30-foot personnel type without ramp)
(b) 303 LCP(L) (36-foot personnel type without ramps, officially "T Boats" prior to
     22 June 42)
(c) 116 LCV or LCPR (36-foot personnel light vehicle type with ramp, officially "TR
     Boats" prior to 22 June 42)
(d) 48 LCM (45-foot medium landing craft with ramp, officially called "WL lighters"
     prior to 22 June 42, and sometimes still called this in contemporary reports)

Fire Support Groups

Task Group 62.3
Fire Support Group L, Capt. Frederick L. Riefkohl

HEAVY CRUISERS:

Vincennes Capt. Riefkohl
Quincy Capt. Samuel N. Moore
Astoria Capt. William G. Greenman

DESTROYERS:

Hull	Lt. Cdr. Richard F. Stout
Dewey	Lt. Cdr. Charles F. Chilling-worth, Jr.
Ellet	Lt. Cdr. Francis H. Gardner
Wilson	Lt. Cdr. Walter H. Price

Task Group 62.4
Fire Support Group M, Rear Adm. Norman Scott

LIGHT CRUISER:

San Juan	Capt. James E. Maher

DESTROYERS:

Monssen	Cdr. Roland N. Smoot
Buchanan	Cdr. Ralph E. Wilson

Task Group 62.5
Minesweeper Group
Cdr. William H. Hartt, Jr.

Hopkins	Lt. Cdr. Benjamin Coe
Trever	Lt. Cdr. Dwight M. Agnew
Zane	Lt. Cdr. Peyton L. Wirtz
Southard	Lt. Cdr. Joe B. Cochran
Hovey	Lt. Cdr. Wilton S. Heald

Rear Adm. John S. McCain
Commander Aircraft South Pacific
(Task Force 63)

AT EFATE:

11th Bomb Group(-)	Col. Laverne G. Saunders		
26th Bomb Squadron	Maj. Allan J. Sewart	5	B-17
VMF-212	Maj. Harold W. Bauer	5	F4F-3A
		4	PBY-5
		3	OS2U

AT ESPÍRITU SANTO:

VMO-251	Lt. Col. John N. Hart	15	F4F-3/3P
VMF-212(-)		11	F4F-3A
98th Bomb Squadron	Maj. Rasmusson	6	B-17
Curtiss (AV-4), VP-23	Lt. James R. Ogden	10	PBY-5
		3	OS2U

AT NEW CALEDONIA:

67th Fighter Squadron	Capt. Dale D. Brannon	38	P-39/400
42d Bomb Squadron	Maj. Ernest R. Manierre	10	B-17
69th Bomb Squadron	Col. Clyde Rich	10	B-26
		2	PBY-5
Number 9 Bomber Squadron, RNZAF(-)		6	Hudsons
		3	OS2U

AT NANDI, FIJIS:

431st Bomb Squadron	Maj. Marion N. Pharr	12	B-17
70th Bomb Squadron	Maj. Leroy L. Stefonowic	12	B-26
70th Fighter Squadron	Maj. Henry Vicellio	17	P-39/400
		6	PBY
Number 9 Bomber Squadron, RNZAF	Sdrn. Ldr. D. E. Grigg	12	Hudsons
Number 4 Bomber Squadron, RNZAF	Sdrn. Ldr. G. N. Roberts	3	Singapores
		9	Vincents

AT NDENI, MALAITA:

MacFarland (AVD-14)	Lt. James O. Cobb		
VP-11			
VP-14	Lt. Leavitt W. Thurlow	6	PBY
(VP-14 in process of withdrawing and primarily engaged in aircraft ferrying)			

AT TONGATABU:

68th Fighter Squadron	1st Lt. Robert M. Caldwell	24	P-39/400

AT SAMOA:

VMF-111	Capt. Daniel W. Torry, Jr.	18	F4F
VMO-151	Maj. Raymond B. Hurst	17	SBC
		10	OS2U

Total

B-17	B-26	P-39/400	F4F	SBC	PBY	Hudsons	Singapores	Vincents	OS2U	
32	22	79	49	17	28	18	3	9	20	= 282

Gen. Douglas MacAtthur
Commander in Chief, Southwest Pacific
(Forces Supporting Guadalcanal Landings Only)

Capt. Ralph W. Christe
Commander Task Force 42
at Brisbane

SUBMARINES:

Submarine Division 201

S-37	Lt. Cdr. Thomas S. Baskett
S-38	Lt. Cdr. Henry G. Munson
S-39	Lt. Cdr. Francis E. Brown
S-40	Lt. Cdr. Francis M. Gambacorta
S-41	Lt. Cdr. Irvin S. Hartman

Submarine Division 51

S-42	Lt. Cdr. Harley K. Nauman
S-43	Lt. Cdr. Edward R. Hannon
S-44	Lt. Cdr. John R. Moore
S-45	Lt. Cdr. Ian C. Eddy
S-46	Lt. Cdr. Ralph C. Lynch, Jr.
S-47	Lt. Cdr. James W. Davis

Maj. Gen. George C. Kenney
Commander, Allied Air Forces Southwest Pacific Area

Aircraft supporting Guadalcanal landings

19th Bomb Group	Lt. Col. Richard Carmichael	16	B-17

Rear Adm. Robert H. English
Commander, Submarines Pacific Fleet
at Pearl Harbor

Submarines deployed to Truk

Drum	Lt. Cdr. Robert H. Rice
Grayling	Lt. Cdr. Eliot Olsen
Greenling	Lt. Cdr. Henry C. Bruton
Grenadier	Lt. Cdr. Bruce L. Carr
Gudgeon	Lt. Cdr. William S. Stovall
Tambor	Lt. Cdr. Stephen H. Ambruster

JAPANESE

Vice Adm. Nishizo Tsukahara
Commander 11th Air Fleet
(Base Air Force)

Rear Adm. Sadayoshi Yamada
Commander 25th Air Flotilla
(5th Air Attack Force)

AT RABAUL:

Tinian Air Group	Capt. Masahisa Saito	24 Zeros
		2 Irving
2d Air Group	Cdr. Sakae Yamamoto	15 Zeros
		16 Vals
Yokohama Air Group	Capt. Shigemune Miyazaki	6 Mavis
14th Air Group (Detachment)		2 Emily
4th Air Group	Capt. Gashi Moritama	32 Betty
Total		97

AT TULAGI:

Yokohama Air Group	Capt. Miyazaki	7 Mavis
		8 Rufe
Total		15

Total

Zero	Val	Betty	Irving	Rufe	Mavis	*Emily*	
39	16	32	2	8	13	2	= 112

Vice Adm. Gunichi Mikawa
Commander 8th Fleet

HEAVY CRUISERS:

Chokai		Capt. Mikio Hayakawa

Rear Adm. Aritomo Goto
Commander Cruiser Division 6

Aoba	Capt. Yonejiro Hisamune
Kinugasa	Capt. Masao Sawa
Furutaka	Capt. Araki Tsutau
Kako	Capt. Yuji Takahashi

LIGHT CRUISERS:

Rear Adm. Mitsuhara Matsuyama
Commander Cruiser Division 18

Yubari	Capt. Masami Ban
Tenryu	Capt. Shinpei Asano

DESTROYERS:

Destroyer Division 29
Oite, Yunagi, Yuzuki, Asakaze
Destroyer Division 30
Mutsuki, Uzuki, Yayoi, Mochisuki

SUBMARINES:

Submarine Squadron 7

TENDER
Jingei

Submarine Division 13
I-121, I-122, I-123
Submarine Division 21
Ro-33, Ro-34
Submarine Squadron 3*
I-11, I-171, I-174, I-176, I-169

*Under orders to support the SN Operation by attacks on the enemy lines of communication and destruction of shipping in the New Caledonia, Fiji, Samoa, Australian east and south coast, and, on further order, New Zealand.

AT GUADALCANAL (2818):

11th Construction Unit	1350 men	Capt. Kanae Monzen
13th Construction Unit	1221 men	Cdr. Tokunaga Okuma
81st Guard Unit and Kure 3d Special Naval Landing Force	247 men	Lt. Yoshio Endo

AT TULAGI (350):

3d Kure Special Naval Landing Force (Detach) (originally 84th Guard or Garrison Unit) 350 men		Cdr. Masaaki Suzuki

AT GAVUTU-TANAMBOGO (536):

Yokohama Air Group (Detach)	342 men	Capt. Shigetoshi Miyazaki
14th Construction Unit	144 men	
One platoon, 3d Kure Special Naval Landing Force	50 men	

8TH FLEET SUPPORT UNITS:

7th Base Force: *SC*s *23, 32;* 85th Communications Unit; 85th Submarine Base Unit

8th Base Force: *MS*s *20, 21;* Submarine Chaser Divisions 21, 31 and 56; Gunboat Division 5; 81st, 82d and 84th Guard Divisions; 8th Submarine Base Unit; 8th Communications Group

8TH FLEET ATTACHED UNITS:

Minelayer *Tsugara;* 3d Kure Special Naval Landing Force; Sasebo 5th Special Naval Landing Force; Seaplane Tender *Kiyokawa Maru;* 10th, 11th, 12th, 13th, 14th, and 15th Airfield and Base Construction Units (some of these attached units were deployed as noted above)

2

ORDER OF BATTLE
OF THE 17TH ARMY
AND STRENGTH RETURN,
20 NOVEMBER 1942

UNIT	STRENGTH ON LANDING	STRENGTH ON 20 NOVEMBER	THOSE CAPABLE OF DUTY	MAJOR EQUIPMENT/ COMMENTS
2d Division				
Division Hdqtrs.:	271	268	100	
Infantry Group Hdqtrs.:	88	76	50	
4th Infantry Regiment:	2,300	725	400	Bn. guns: 3 Machineguns: 8
16th Infantry Regiment:	2,300	1,147	700	Reg. guns: 2 Bn. guns: 4 AT guns: 2 Machineguns: 12
29th Infantry Regiment:	2,330	1,337	780	Reg. guns: 4 Bn. guns: 5 AT guns: 4 Machineguns: 14 Lt. machineguns: 48 Grenade launchers: 44
2d Artillery Regiment (less III Battalion & 4th Battery):	851	766	380	A-4 10cm howitzers: 4 Mt. guns: 5
2d Engineer Regiment:	664	405	240	
Communications Unit:	159	149	100	Telephones: 8 Telephone Wire: 24 km. Type 3 mobile ground radios: 6

UNIT	STRENGTH ON LANDING	STRENGTH ON 20 NOVEMBER	THOSE CAPABLE OF DUTY	MAJOR EQUIPMENT/ COMMENTS
2d Transportation Regiment:	317	306	200	
Medical Unit:	286	281	60	
1st Field Hospital (half):	105	105	50	
4th Field Hospital (half):	78	78	78	
TOTAL:	9,747	5,643	3,138	

38th Division

UNIT	STRENGTH ON LANDING	STRENGTH ON 20 NOVEMBER	THOSE CAPABLE OF DUTY	MAJOR EQUIPMENT/ COMMENTS
Division Hdqtrs.:	89	89	89	
Infantry Group Hdqtrs.:	69	69	69	
228th Infantry Regiment:	2,431	2,411	2,411	Reg. guns: 2 Bn. guns: 4 AT guns: 1 Machineguns: 21
229th Infantry Regiment:	580	575	575	Machinegun: 1 Gun (Reg. or Bn.?): 1
230th Infantry Regiment (less 6th & 7th Companies):	2,300	1,500	800	Insufficient data
38th Mountain Gun Regiment (two batteries):	250	200	120	Mt. gun: 4
38th Engineer Regiment:	520	500	400	Carrying tools & explosives: 500
Communications Unit:	91	91	91	Mobile ground radios: 2 Telephones: 10 Wire: 87 km.
38th Transportation Regiment:	301	301	301	
Medical Unit (half):	85	85	85	
TOTAL:	6,696	5,821	4,921	

35th Brigade

UNIT	STRENGTH ON LANDING	STRENGTH ON 20 NOVEMBER	THOSE CAPABLE OF DUTY	MAJOR EQUIPMENT/ COMMENTS
Brigade Headquarters:	129	107	39	
124th Infantry Regiment:	3,300	1,435	694	
Ichiki Detachment (Kitao Bn.):	1,885	400	65	

UNIT	STRENGTH ON LANDING	STRENGTH ON 20 NOVEMBER	THOSE CAPABLE OF DUTY	MAJOR EQUIPMENT/ COMMENTS
1st Independent Tank Co.:	100	83	40	Tank: 1 "Almost all tanks lost, no crew"
2d Anti-tank Gun Bn. (Hdqtrs. & 1 & 2 Cos.):	123	123	123	Almost all the unit lost, data for 1 Co.
6th Independent Anti-Tank Gun Bn.:	226	167	131	
9th Independent Anti-Tank Gun Bn.:	104	104	104	No weapons, only half the unit landed, rest lost on convoy
4th Artillery Regiment (less 2d Battery):	548	517	420	Guns: 11 Caissons: 13 Trucks: 2
10th Mountain Gun Regiment (Hdqtrs. & 2 Batteries):	442	382	260	Type 41 mt. Guns: 4 (operational)
20th Independent Mountain Gun Regiment:	259	243	100	Mt. guns: 6 (4 operational)
2d Battery, 7th Artillery Regiment:	146	140	120	No operational guns Caissons: 10 (8 operational) Prime movers: 3 (1 operational)
2d Battery, 21st Field Heavy Artillery Regiment:	123	112	73	Year 4 Type 15cm howitzers: 4 (1 operational)
3d Trench Mortar Bn.:	404	404	350	Mortars: 18
38th Antiaircraft Bn.:	416	335	196	Guns operational: ? Guns nonoperational: ?
45th Antiaircraft Bn.:	119	105	50	Equipment: ?
1st Battery, 47th Antiaircraft Bn.:	79	75	40	
39th Field Road Construction Unit:	247	212	100	
TOTAL:	9,150	4,944	2,900	

UNIT	STRENGTH ON LANDING	STRENGTH ON 20 NOVEMBER	THOSE CAPABLE OF DUTY	MAJOR EQUIPMENT/ COMMENTS
Headquarters				
17th Army Hdqtrs.:	26	22	18	Switchboard: 1 Telephones: 20 Wire: 20 km.
88th Independent Wire Communications Company (less one platoon):	147	142	126	Switchboard: 1 Telephones: 21 Wire: 120 km. Phone repair apparatus: 9
3d Independent Radio Communications Platoon:	22	14	4	Type 2 mobile ground radio: 1
6th Independent Radio Communications Platoon:	29	26	15	Not capable of functioning as radio unit
53d Independent Radio Communications Platoon:	28	28	28	Type 2 mobile ground radio: 1
33d Fixed Communications Unit:	25	23	19	Type 2 mobile air-ground radio: 1
44th Fixed Communications Unit:	24	23	19	Type 2 mobile air-ground radio: 1
15th Electrical Communications Regiment (1 Wire Platoon):	56	55	47	
15th Electrical Communications Regiment (1 Radio Platoon):	39	38	30	Type 2 mobile air-ground radio: 1
TOTAL:	396	371	306	
Transportation				
3d Field Transportation Hdqtrs.:	38	38	35	
52d Independent Transportation Company:	192	192	192	

UNIT	STRENGTH ON LANDING	STRENGTH ON 20 NOVEMBER	THOSE CAPABLE OF DUTY	MAJOR EQUIPMENT/ COMMENTS
212th Independent Transportation Company (Detachment):	12	12	12	
76th Line of Communications Hospital (Detachment):	30	30	30	
67th Line of Communications Hospital (Detachment):	15	15	15	
24th Cargo Unit (Detachment):	55	41	21	
17th Army Supply Unit (Detachment):	41	40	40	
TOTAL:	383	358	345	
Ship Units				
1st Ship Unit:	52	52	46	Rifles: 8
2d Ship Unit (Detachment):	5	5	3	
1st Ship Engineer Regiment:	950	318	458	Rifles: 753 Machineguns: 11
2d Ship Engineer Regiment:	305	805	253	Rifles: 251 Machineguns: 2
3d Ship Engineer Regiment:	695	539	103	Rifles: 205 Lt. machineguns: 2
1st Landing Unit	—	—	—	
2d Landing Unit	—	—	—	
1st Ship Artillery Regiment:	440	440	398	Rifles: 23
2d Ship Artillery Regiment:	24	24	4	
Ship Communications Unit:	67	46	40	Rifles: 34
Interim 1st Landing Unit:	104	104	87	
Interim 2d Landing Unit:	103	103	18	Rifles: 27
Shipwrecked Sailors:		315		
TOTAL:	2,745	2,751	1,473	

UNIT	STRENGTH ON LANDING	STRENGTH ON 20 NOVEMBER	THOSE CAPABLE OF DUTY	MAJOR EQUIPMENT/ COMMENTS
Navy Units				
11th Construction Unit:	Soldiers:	137	7	
	Workers:	160	15	
13th Construction Unit:	Soldiers:	60	21	
	Workers:	453	23	
Guard Unit:		93	30	
5th Yokusaka Special Naval Landing Force:		30	2	
4th Maizuru Special Naval Landing Force:		630	200	
Communications Unit:		30	10	
TOTAL:		783	242	
GRAND TOTAL:	29,117	20,671	13,325	

ABBREVIATIONS

AT = anti-tank
Bn. = Battalion
cm = centimeters
Hdqtrs. = Headquarters

km. = kilometers
Lt. = light
Mt. = mountain
Reg. = Regimental

REMARKS

1. Due to insufficient data, these are only approximate figures.

2. The strength as of November 20 is the result of subtraction of the number of dead in combat, the injured in combat, and those hospitalized due to ordinary illness. Therefore, the strength as of November 20 includes those injured in combat and not hospitalized, and those sick and totally incapable of engaging in combat duties.

[Author's note: Cited from "Minami Taiheiyo Homen Sakusen Keika Gaiyo" (General Account of the South Pacific Area Operations). Compiled by the General Staff Office, May 20, 1943.]

3

UNITED STATES AND ALLIED NAVAL CASUALTIES DURING THE GUADALCANAL CAMPAIGN (INCLUDING SHIPBOARD MARINE DETACHMENTS)

DATE	SUNK	DAMAGED/ CASUALTIES	KILLED	WOUNDED
August				
4	Tucker		6	0
		VB-6	2	
Landings on Guadalcanal, Tulagi, and Gavutu-Tananbogo				
7		Mugford	19	32
		San Juan	5	14
8	George F. Elliot		11	13
		Jarvis	15	6
7–8				
Miscellaneous losses				
		Support (Aviation) Force		
		Saratoga & VF-5	5(4 pilots)	3
		Enterprise & VF-6	1	1
		Wasp & VS-71	1	6
		New Orleans	0	1
		Salt Lake City	0	1
		Amphibious Force		
		American Legion	1	6
		Neville	2	0
		Libra	0	1
		McCawley	0	1
		Heywood	0	2
		Fuller	0	1

DATE	SUNK	DAMAGED/ CASUALTIES	KILLED	WOUNDED
		President Jackson	0	3
		Dewey	0	2
		Henley	0	1
		Hovey	0	6
		Hull	0	6
Subtotal losses for amphibious phase:			60	106

August
9
Battle of Savo Island

DATE	SUNK	DAMAGED/ CASUALTIES	KILLED	WOUNDED
		Canberra	85	55
		Chicago	2	21
	Astoria		235 (4 USMC)	190
	Quincy		389 (9 USMC)	147
	Vincennes		342 (4 USMC)	257
		Patterson	10	14
		Ralph Talbot	14	16
Subtotal losses Battle of Savo Island			1,077	700
9 (Day)	Jarvis		233	0
22	Blue		9	20

24
The Battle of the Eastern Solomons

DATE	SUNK	DAMAGED/ CASUALTIES	KILLED	WOUNDED
		Enterprise	74*	63
		North Carolina	1	0
		Grayson	0	13
		Portland	0	1
		Saratoga	0	1
		VF-6	2	2
		VB-6	0	4
		VT-3	2	5
		VF-5	3	0
		VB-3	0	1
		VP-23	1	0

*Includes one VB-6 and six VT-3 personnel on ship.

DATE	SUNK	DAMAGED/ CASUALTIES	KILLED	WOUNDED
Subtotal losses Battle of Eastern Solomons			83	90
30	Colhoun		49	19
31		Saratoga (including VB-3)	0	3
Subtotal other losses August			297	42
Total losses August			1,519	938

September

DATE	SUNK	DAMAGED/ CASUALTIES	KILLED	WOUNDED
5	Little (including ComTransDiv 12)		63	26
	Gregory		25	46
15	Wasp		173 (2 USMC)	175

DATE	SUNK	DAMAGED/ CASUALTIES	KILLED	WOUNDED
		North Carolina	5	4
		O'Brien*	0	7
30		Alhena	5	14

*Lost October 19.

Subtotal losses September			271	272

October

11–12

The Battle of Cape Esperance

	Duncan		48	35
		Boise	107 (7 USMC)	29
		Farenholt	3	40
		Salt Lake City	5	19
		McCalla	0	2
Subtotal Battle of Cape Esperance			163	125

October

15	Meredith		187	57
		Viero	50	10
16		McFarland	18	11
20		Chester	11	20
24		American Legion	0	1
25		Zane	3	9
	Seminole		1	6
	YP-284		0	1

Battle of the Santa Cruz Islands

25–26	Hornet		118 (15 USMC)	142
	Porter		15	8
		Enterprise	44	71
		Smith	57	13
		South Dakota	2	34
		Pensacola	3	14
		Morris	1	0
	DesRon 2			
		Cushing	0	1
		Northampton	0	2
		Juneau	0	1
		Maury	0	1
		Portland	0	11
		San Juan	0	10
		VF-72*	6	1

*Killed includes only losses in air operations October 25–26 for squadrons.

DATE	SUNK	DAMAGED/ CASUALTIES	KILLED	WOUNDED
		VB-8	2	3
		VS-8	0	0
		VT-6	3	1
		VF-10	6	1
		VT-10	5	0
Subtotal Battle of Santa Cruz Islands			262	314
Subtotal other losses October			270	115
Subtotal losses October			695	554
November				
7	*Majaba*		3	9
11	*Betelgeuse*		0	4
Naval Battle of Guadalcanal				
12	*Buchanan*		5	4
	Morris		0	1
	San Francisco		24	45
13	*Barnett*		0	1
Part 1: Night Action of November 13				
13	*Cushing*		72	68
	Laffey		57	114
	Barton		165	31
	Monssen		145	37
	Atlanta		170	103
		Sterrett	29	22
		San Francisco	86 (7 USMC)	85
		Portland	16	10
		Helena	1	13
		Aaron Ward	15	38
Subtotal Part 1, Night Phase			756	516
13 (Day) *Juneau*			683	4
Subtotal Part 1, Night Phase + *Juneau*			1,439	520
14	*VB-10*		7	1
	VF-10		0	1
Naval Battle of Guadalcanal				
Part 2: Night Action of November 14–15				
	Preston		117	26
	Walke		80	48
	Benham		0	8
		Gwin	6	0
		South Dakota	39 (1 USMC)	59
		Washington	0	1
Subtotal Part 2			242	142
Subtotal Naval Battle of Guadalcanal			1,732	715
15	*Meade*		0	1

DATE	SUNK	DAMAGED/ CASUALTIES	KILLED	WOUNDED
		Zeilin	1	0
28		*Alchiba*	0	4
November 30–December 1				
Battle of Tassafaronga				
	Northampton		50	35
		Minneapolis	37	26
		New Orleans	183	20
		Pensacola	125	72
Subtotal Battle of Tassafaronga			395	153
Subtotal other losses November			4	18
Subtotal losses November			2,108	886
December				
7		*Alchiba*	3	6
Subtotal losses December			3	6
1943				
January				
5		*Achilles*	6	7
29		*Moa*	1	0
30–31				
Battle of Rennell Island				
	Chicago		62	50
		LaVallette	22	6
		Montpelier	1	1
		Wichita	0	3
		Sands	0	2
		Chevalier	0	1
		Waller	0	1
Subtotal Battle of Rennell Island			85	64
Subtotal losses January			92	71
February				
2	*DeHaven*		168	39
		Nicholas	2	7
8		*Buchanan*	0	1
Subtotal losses February			170	47

MISCELLANEOUS UNIT LOSSES

Aviation Personnel Operating from or Supporting Guadalcanal

	KILLED	WOUNDED
VS-3	6	0
VT-3	0	1
VF-5	5	4
VT-8	5	8
VF-42	0	1
VF-71	7	2
VF-72	5	3
Patron 11	3	1
Patron 14	0	1
Patron 23	8	0
Patron 91	23	1
Cruiser Scout Ron 6	1	0
Cruiser Scout Ron 9	1	0
Cruiser Scout Ron Detachment Tulagi	7	0
Curtis	1	3
Mackinac	0	1
Escort Scout Ron 11	1	0
Escort Scout Ron 12	2	1
Escort Scout Ron 16	8	0
Escort Scout Ron 20	1	0
Battleship Sdn 1 (flag allowance)	1	0
Scouting Sdn 4-D14	2	0
Subtotal aviation personnel	87	27

NAVAL PERSONNEL ON GUADALCANAL OR IN VICINITY

	KILLED	WOUNDED
1st Marine Division	8	46
1st Marines	1	0
1st Raider Battalion	1	1
1st Raider Regiment	0	2
1st Medical Battalion	0	3
2d Marine Division	19	14
2d Marine Brigade (Battle Pacific Staff)	1	0
2d Marines	1	1
4th Marine Division	1	2
3d Marine Defense Battalion (including 3-inch AA Group)	1	2
5th Marines	5	6
6th Marines	0	1
7th Marines	2	5

8th Marines	0	2
11th Marines	0	2
1st Marine Air Wing	1	0
2d Marine Air Wing	0	1
Marine Air Group 14 (MAG-14)	2	0
CUB 1	5	3
Naval Base Lunga	1	3
Naval Construction Battalion 1	0	1
Naval Construction Battalion 6	12	16
Naval Construction Battalion 18	0	2
Naval Construction Battalion 26	0	5
MTBRon 3	26	12
MTBRon 6 (PT 123)	3	2
Subtotal naval personnel Guadalcanal or vicinity	90	132

MISCELLANEOUS SHIPBOARD PERSONNEL LOSSES

	KILLED	WOUNDED
Bellatrix	0	2
Benham	0	1
Betelgeuse	0	1
Buchanan	0	1
Enterprise	0	1
Farragut	0	1
Growler	3	2
Heywood	0	1
Hornet	0	3
Hull	0	1
Laffey	0	1
Lardner	0	1
McCawley	0	1
Saufley	0	1
YP-346	1	2
Subtotal miscellaneous shipboard losses	4	20

RECAPITULATION

	KILLED	WOUNDED
Loss of *Tucker*	6	0
En route Guadalcanal (VB-6)	2	0
Amphibious Phase	60	106
Battle of Savo Island	1,077	700
Battle of Eastern Solomons	83	90
Other losses August	297	42
Loss of *Wasp*	173	175
Other losses September	98	97
Battle of Cape Esperance	163	125
Battle of Santa Cruz Islands	262	314
Other losses October	270	115
Naval Battle of Guadalcanal, Part I	1,463	565
Naval Battle of Guadalcanal, Part II	242	142
Other Losses November	4	18
Battle of Tassafaronga	395	153
Other losses December	3	6
Battle of Rennell Island	85	64
Other losses January (all RNZN)	7	7
February losses	170	47
Aviation personnel losses (not otherwise listed)	87	27
Personnel on Guadalcanal or in vicinity	90	132
Miscellaneous shipboard losses	4	20
Grand total naval personnel losses	5,041	2,953

The principal source for these figures is the Bureau of Personnel, World War II Casualty List, Books 2 and 3, Naval Historical Center, Washington, D.C. This is supplemented by muster role entries for the Marine detachments aboard cruisers and larger ships for the period at the Marine Corps History Center and by figures from the Australian and New Zealand official histories for losses on *Canberra, Achilles,* and *Moa.* It would appear that the Bureau of Personnel figures understate the total of wounded, but there is no reason to doubt the fatality figures.

4

LOSSES OF PRINCIPAL AIRCRAFT TYPES AUGUST 1, 1942 TO NOVEMBER 15, 1942

1. JAPANESE
11th Air Fleet

	Zero	Val	Betty	Flying Boats	Irving
Air combat:	72	11	95	12	1
Destroyed on the ground:	7	0	0	7	0
Operational:	27	4	5	0	0
Total:	106	15	100	19	1

Carrier Air Groups

	Zero	Val	Kate	Judy
Air combat:	43	58	35	0
Destroyed on ship:	5	0	3	0
Operational:	33	11	9	1
Total:	81	69	47	1

2. AMERICAN

Cactus Air Force and Supporting Units

	F4F	SBD	TBF	P-400, P-39	B-17	B-26	PBY
Air combat:	70	24	2	13	7	0	7
Destroyed on ground:	12	20	7	2	2	0	0
Operational:	33	22	7	4	9	1	10
Total:	115	66	16	19	18	1	17

Carrier Air Groups

	F4F	SBD	TBF
Air combat:	31	11	7
Destroyed on ship:	32	30	10
Operational:	18	22	23
Total:	81	63	40

Source: Compilations from unit records and service department accounting systems by John Lundstrom, James Sawruk, and Richard Frank. A copy of the master list of aircraft losses is held at the Museum of the Pacific War, Nimitz Foundation, Fredericksburg, Texas.

A NOTE ON SOURCES

The research for this narrative was wide ranging. On the allied side, the records ran the gamut from a document titled "The Principles of Indirect Symmetry of Position in Secondary Alphabets and Their Application in the Solution of Polyalphabetic Substitution Ciphers" (sampled lightly) to an index entry at the National Archives Still Photograph Division headed "Guadalcanal: Parties and Picnics" that referred to official photographs of an outing by several Red Cross women and their "fellows" on the wreck of the *Yamazuki Maru* in 1944. Overall, however, fundamental reliance has been placed in documentary sources, rather than contacts with individual campaign participants.

The principal sources for the American side of the Guadalcanal campaign are the original unit and command reports held at the various record repositories. For the Navy, the Operational Archives branch of the Naval History Center in the Washington Navy Yard will contain virtually all the pertinent documents used in this account until 1995 when these records regrettably will be transferred to the National Archives. Marine Corps records were held at, or ordered through, the Marine Corps Historical Center, which is also in the Washington Navy Yard. The voluminous original Army records are held at the Suitland facility of the National Archives in Record Group (RG) 407. Records for the (Army) Air Force were obtained or examined at the Air Force Historical Center at Bolling Air Force Base. Radio intelligence material came from the National Archives.

Given the immense hardships and perils faced by the units that served on Guadalcanal, the loss of many ships, the death of key officers and enlisted men, and the fact that it was the first offensive and therefore many procedures later instituted were not then in effect, it is not surprising that the standard of record keeping in many units was not particularly high. There is certainly no consistent symmetry between the importance of a unit's contribution and the quality or quantity of the surviving documentation. For example, while the carrier *Enterprise* and the 1st Battalion, 7th Marines both played critical roles, the reports of the former are superb, while those of the latter, if they exist at all, are often incredibly terse. Accordingly, I have found letters, diaries and accounts by some journalists to be invaluable sources, and indeed more accurate, than some of the official records, a fair portion of which were prepared at some interval after the event. A special salute is due to Richard Tregaskis, whose *Guadalcanal Diary* is rightly acclaimed as a superb piece of reporting. During the course of my research I had occassion to cross-check his account with numerous other sources, and I found him wonderfully reliable. In fact, the very few instances where I differed from his account stem from a judgment that the source he relied upon was mistaken.

With respect to American air operations, this account profits enormously from the research of Mr. John Lundstrom and Mr. James Sawruk. They not only ferreted out obscure documentary sources, but they also have tirelessly canvassed veterans of the campaign for letters, diaries, and recollections that filled in the large gaps in the conventional records. Their source material is so voluminous, however, that a detailed citation in this account would be prohibitively long.

Japanese material used in this text comes from two basic sources. First in order of magnitude are the four volumes of the Self Defense Agency War History Series pertaining to operations of the Imperial Navy and Imperial Army on and around Guadalcanal. Two of these books cover operations from the perspective of the Imperial Navy and the other two do likewise for the Imperial Army. As these works cover all activities in the Southeast Area, they also recount events on New Guinea. In the case of the Imperial Navy, this is very limited in scope, but the Imperial Army was much more active in that region and the history volumes reflect this fact. Even so, better than 70 percent of the "Army" volumes address the Guadalcanal campaign.

The sources for the Japanese history series include a vast amount of original reports, many of which were not available at the time the well-known "monograph series" was prepared by Japanese officers working for American historians during the occupation of Japan, as well as diaries, memoirs, and various secondary sources. These works are very interesting in their approach, which differs notably from that of American official histories. While chronology is the basic organizing principle, the authors of these works tend to take up the story successively from various command levels, and customarily begin each new section with a recapitulation of events that adds materially to the length of the text and, for this writer at least, quickly becomes irritating. The narrative portions are enlivened considerably with material from diaries and memoirs, but they also contain many verbatim presentations of orders and reports that are normally extremely helpful but sometimes lurch into minutia that becomes very tedious. For example, the Battle of Tassafaronga is covered basically by reprinting in its entirety the "Detailed Battle Report" of Destroyer Squadron 2. In many aspects, the account of Japanese efforts most closely resembles the comprehensive operational narratives drafted by the Office of Naval Intelligence for the U.S. Navy during the war. Information on the American side of operations is handled in concise separate sections that draw basically from Morison, Griffith, and the official histories. Despite these small flaws, there is no doubt that this series is a quantum leap in depth and accuracy over any prior documentation.

Second in volume, though equal or better in value, was the data on air operations generously given to me by Mr. John Lundstrom based upon his research into primary Japanese sources. Mr. Lundstrom has obtained and read most of the Imperial Navy air squadron war diaries (*Kodochushos*) for the period from August to November 15, 1942. These primary records differ in many particulars from the information related in the War History Series. It appears that the War History Series relied upon several reports compiled later, rather than a review of the primary unit documents. Therefore, I have followed Mr. Lundstrom whenever there is a conflict in the sources.

The following abbreviations are used in the notes:

AFHC = Air Force Historical Center
NHC = Naval Historical Center
MCHC = Marine Corps Historical Center

NOTES

CHAPTER 1

Page 3

The First South Pacific Campaign: John B. Lundstrom, *The First South Pacific Campaign Pacific Fleet Strategy December 1941–June 1942* (Annapolis, Md.: Naval Institute Press, 1976) [hereafter Lundstrom, *First South Pacific Campaign*].

Pages 3–6

Biography and character of King: Thomas B. Buell, *Master of Seapower: A Biography of Fleet Admiral Ernest J. King,* Naval Institute Press edition (Boston: Little, Brown, 1980), pp. 7, 9, 11, 25, 34, 36, 52, 89, 91, 93, 118–19 [hereafter Buell, *Master of Seapower*]; Patrick Abbazia, *Mr. Roosevelt's Navy* (Annapolis Md.: Naval Institute Press, 1975), pp. 23–26, 61–62, 69, 134–36 [hereafter Abbazia, *Mr. Roosevelt's Navy*]. Technically, Rear Admiral Alfred L. Johnson initially commanded the "Neutrality Patrol," but he was relieved by Rear Admiral Ellis in a routine change of command before the end of September 1939.

Page 6

Interwar years strategic planning: Grace Person Hayes, *The History of the Joint Chiefs of Staff in World War II: The War Against Japan* (Annapolis, Md.: Naval Institute Press, 1982), pp. 3–6 [hereafter Hayes, *History of the Joint Chiefs of Staff*]; Lundstrom, *First South Pacific Campaign,* p. 13.

Page 6

"Rainbow" series of war plans and initial orders to U.S. Pacific Fleet on outbreak of war: Hayes, *History of the Joint Chiefs of Staff,* pp. 8–13; Lundstrom, *First South Pacific Campaign,* pp. 14–16.

King's new orders to Nimitz: COMINCH to CINCPAC 301740 Dec 41, in the war diary of the Pacific Fleet, p. 121, identified as the CINCPAC Grey Book or as "Captain Steele's Running Estimate and Summary, 7 December 1941 to 31 August 1942" [hereafter Grey Book]; Lundstrom, *First South Pacific Campaign,* p. 19. Subsequent sections of the Grey Book cover the period through the end of the Guadalcanal campaign.

Pages 6, 8

"Arcadia" conference, ABDA, and securing communications to Australia: Hayes, *History of the Joint Chiefs of Staff,* pp. 36–42, 54–55; Lundstrom, *First South Pacific Campaign,* pp. 19–20; Vice Admiral George C. Dyer, *The Amphibians Came to Conquer: The Story of Admiral Richmond Kelly Turner* (Washington, D.C.: U.S. Government Printing Office), Vol. I, p. 234 [hereafter Dyer, *Amphibians Came to Conquer*].

Page 8

U.S. Army Air Force attitudes and plans: Hayes, *History of the Joint Chiefs of Staff,* p. 38; Lundstrom, *First South Pacific Campaign,* pp. 55, 129; and W. F. Craven and J. L. Cate, *The Army Air Forces in World War II,* Vol. I, *Plans and Early Operations (January 1939 to August 1942)* (Chicago: University of Chicago Press, 1948), pp. 47–50 [hereafter Craven and Cate, *Plans and Early Operations*].

Pages 8–9

Naval views on strategy: Hayes, *History of the Joint Chiefs of Staff,* p. 118; Lundstrom, *First South Pacific Campaign,* p. 55; Dyer, *Amphibians Came to Conquer,* pp. 231–32, 239–40; Louis Morton, *United States Army in World War II, The War in the Pacific, Strategy and Command: The First Two Years* (Washington, D.C.: Office of the Chief of Military History, Department of the Army, 1962), p. 219 [hereafter Morton, *Strategy and Command*].

Page 9

Army strategy: Lundstrom, *First South Pacific Campaign,* pp. 50–51; Morton, *Strategy and Command,* pp. 217–18.

Pages 9–10

Creation of chain of island bases: Dyer, *Amphibians Came to Conquer,* pp. 239–44; Lundstrom, *First South Pacific Campaign,* pp. 19, 49; Hayes, *History of the Joint Chiefs of Staff,* p. 57.

Page 10
Conflicts between Navy and Army planners: Dyer, *Amphibians Came to Conquer*, pp. 239–42; Hayes, *History of the Joint Chiefs of Staff* pp. 137–38; Morton, *Strategy and Command*, p. 218.

Pages 10–11
American troops to Australia and New Zealand: Lundstrom, *First South Pacific Campaign*, pp. 28–29, 31, 51–52; Hayes, *History of the Joint Chiefs of Staff*, pp. 57, 59, 84; Dyer, *Amphibians Came to Conquer*, pp. 235, 245. Winston S. Churchill, *The Hinge of Fate* (Boston: Houghton Mifflin, 1950), pp. 155–65 [hereafter Churchill, *Hinge of Fate*].

Page 11
Evidence of American public opinion: Ronald H. Spector, *Eagle Against the Sun* (New York: Free Press, 1985), p. 408 [hereafter Spector, *Eagle Against the Sun*]; Hayes, *History of the Joint Chiefs of Staff*, pp. 24, 32, 150. In a meeting of the Joint Chiefs of Staff on July 10, 1942, General Marshall remarked that a shift of priorities to emphasize the Pacific theater first "would be highly popular throughout the U.S., particularly on the West Coast."

Page 11
"Shipping stranglehold": Churchill, *Hinge of Fate*, p. 189 ("Shipping Stranglehold" is the title of Chapter 11); Hayes, *History of the Joint Chiefs of Staff*, pp. 54, 104–5; W. F. Craven and J. L. Cate, *The Army Air Forces in World War II, Vol. IV, Guadalcanal to Saipan*, p. 27 [hereafter Craven and Cate, *Guadalcanal to Saipan*]. The figures for the troop transport and cargo requirements for the European and Pacific theaters are from Richard M. Leighton and Robert W. Coakley, *United States Army in World War II, The War Department, Global Logistics and Strategy 1940–1943* (Washington, D.C.: Office of the Chief of Military History, Department of the Army, 1955), pp. 386, 390 [hereafter Leighton and Coakley, *Global Logistics and Strategy*].

Page 11
Movement of *Yorktown* south and attitude of CINCPAC: Lundstrom, *First South Pacific Campaign*, pp. 30, 33, 52–53.

Page 12
Proposal for garrisons on Tongatabu and Efate: Hayes, *History of the Joint Chiefs of Staff*, p. 138; Lundstrom, *First South Pacific Campaign*, pp. 49–51; Dyer, *Amphibians Came to Conquer*, 242–43.

Page 12
March 5 meeting: Lundstrom, *First South Pacific Campaign*, p. 52.

Pages 12–13
March 16 Joint Chiefs meeting and garrisons in South Pacific: Hayes, *History of the Joint Chiefs of Staff*, p. 114; Lundstrom, *First South Pacific Campaign*, pp. 54–56; Dyer, *Amphibians Came to Conquer*, pp. 243–44.

Page 13
Turner's March 26 memorandum: Dyer, *Amphibians Came to Conquer*, p. 249; Lundstrom, *First South Pacific Campaign*, p. 57.

Pages 13–14
Command arrangements in the Pacific: Hayes, *History of the Joint Chiefs of Staff*, pp. 88, 96, 98–102; Lundstrom, *First South Pacific Campaign*, pp. 58–60.

Pages 13–14
Creation of South Pacific command and selection of Ghormley: Lundstrom, *First South Pacific Campaign*, p. 60. The process by which Ghormley was selected as the Commander South Pacific Theater has been frequently misstated. Both Buell, *Master of Seapower*, p. 198, and Lundstrom, *First South Pacific Campaign*, p. 87, report that Ghormley was nominated by Nimitz and approved by King at their conference of April 25, 1942. However, this is clearly wrong as Ghormley had been recalled from London and was briefed on April 18, 1942, by King on his new assignment. (Ghormley, "The Tide Turns," unpublished manuscript prepared by Ghormley at the Naval Historical Center, pp. 9–10 [hereafter Ghormley, "Tide Turns"].) Two messages in the Grey Book, COMINCH to CINCPAC 041850 Apr and CINCPAC to COMINCH 051849 Apr, pp. 331–32, show that within the first week of April the exchange between King and Nimitz related in the text occurred. Nimitz's attitude toward Pye, and other officers he inherited from Kimmel, is noted in E. B. Potter, *Nimitz* (Annapolis, Md.: Naval Institute Press, 1976), pp. 45–47 [hereafter Potter, *Nimitz*]. The loyalty of Nimitz to subordinates is attested in Rear Admiral Edwin T. Layton with Captain Roger Pineau and John Costello, *And I Was There* (New York: William Morrow, 1985), p. 391 [hereafter Layton, Pineau, and Costello. *And I Was There*]. The

complex process of flag officer assignments and Secretary Knox's attitudes are well explained in Buell, *Master of Seapower*, pp. 197–98, 319–21, from which the unacceptability of Pye may be easily deduced. Whether Nimitz was aware of Knox's prejudices is not clear. Further, the answer to the interesting question of whether Pye would have been a better choice than Ghormley remains unknown.

Pages 14–15
Ghormley's character and background: Samuel Eliot Morison, *History of United States Naval Operations in World War II, Vol. IV, Coral Sea, Midway and Submarine Actions* (Boston; Little, Brown, 1964), p. 250, note 9 [hereafter Morison, *Coral Sea, Midway and Submarine Actions*]; Potter, *Nimitz*, pp. 45–47; Buell, *Master of Seapower*, p. 198. It is surprising that the literature on U.S. Navy commanders in World War II contains so little detail about Ghormley's personality. What little color there is may be found in Fletcher Pratt, *The Navy's War* (New York: Harper, 1944), p. 210 [hereafter Pratt, *Navy's War*], and by the same author, *The Marine's War* (New York: William Sloane Associates, 1948), p. 5 [hereafter Pratt, *Marine's War*].

Page 15
Ghormley's instructions from King: Ghormley, "Tide Turns," pp. 1, 9–11.

Page 15
"Marshall Memorandum," London trip: Lundstrom, *First South Pacific Campaign*, pp. 126–28; Hayes, *History of the Joint Chiefs of Staff*, pp. 115–16; Dyer, *Amphibians Came to Conquer*, pp. 248, 252.

Pages 15–16
Groundwork for South Pacific offensive: CINCPAC Daily Summary 6 Apr 42, Grey Book, p. 334; Lundstrom, *First South Pacific Campaign*, p. 128; Hayes, *History of the Joint Chiefs of Staff*, p. 139; Dyer, *Amphibians Came to Conquer*, pp. 252–53.

Pages 16–17
Turner's background and character: Turner's official biography, NHC; Dyer, *Amphibians Came to Conquer*, Vol. I, pp. 65–66, 225, 262, 453, Vol. II, pp. 1139–44, 1152–56. The revelation that General Marshall asked for Turner's relief is found in Vol. II, pp. 1167–68.

"a hard man to deal with if you were contrary to his ideas": Maj. Gen. Dewitt Peck, inter-view, Jan–Mar 67 (Oral History Collection, Marine Corps Historical Center), p. 103 [hereafter Peck intvw].

Page 17
Presidential decision to favor "Bolero": Lundstrom, *First South Pacific Campaign*, pp. 128–29, 131, 134–36, 165–67, 171–72; Hayes, *History of the Joint Chiefs of Staff*, p. 120.

Nimitz draws forces back to defend Midway: Lundstrom, *First South Pacific Campaign*, pp. 152–58, 160–61.

Pages 17–18
Tulagi raid proposal: Dyer, *Amphibians Came to Conquer*, pp. 244–45, 257; Lundstrom, *First South Pacific Campaign*, pp. 164, 187–88; Hayes, *History of the Joint Chiefs of Staff*, p. 137.

Page 18
Organization of Imperial General Headquarters: Lundstrom, *First South Pacific Campaign*, pp. 6–7.

Pages 18–19
Differing outlooks of Imperial Army and Navy and strategies: Ibid., pp. 5–6.

Page 19
Japanese emphasize limited scope of war: Lundstrom, *First South Pacific Campaign*, p. 5. Emphasis on the fact that the Japanese planned only a limited war is a main theme of H. P. Willmott, *Empires in Balance: Japanese and Allied Pacific Strategies to April 1942* (Annapolis, Md.: Naval Institute Press, 1982), pp. 24–25 [hereafter Willmott, *Empires in Balance*]. Willmott also illustrates the meticulous planning lavished on the "First Operational Stage," notably in Malaya, pp. 240–42.

Page 19
"First Operational Stage": Lundstrom, *First South Pacific Campaign*, p. 8.

"Second Operational Stage:" Ibid., p. 9.

Page 20
Yamamoto's background and character: Hiroyuki Agawa, *The Reluctant Admiral Yamamoto and the Imperial Navy*, Naval Institute Press edition, translated by John Bestor (Tokyo, New York, and San Francisco: Kodansha International, 1979), pp. 1–2, 6, 8, 17–18, 85–86, 89–90, 158–64 [hereafter Agawa, *Reluctant Admiral*].

Pages 20–21
Organization of the Imperial Navy: Lundstrom, *First South Pacific Campaign,* pp. 7–8.

Page 21
Yamamoto's role in strategic planning: Ibid., pp. 8–9; Agawa, *Reluctant Admiral,* pp. 219–23, 227–32.

Page 21
Inoue's role and personality: Lundstrom, *First South Pacific Campaign,* pp. 9–11, 23–24; Willmott, *Empires in Balance,* p. 63. The quote by Inoue on Japanese politicians and military men is from Agawa, *Reluctant Admiral,* p. 282.

Page 22
"Victory disease": The term appeared in Mitsuo Fuchida and Masatake Okumiya, *Midway: The Battle That Doomed Japan,* edited by Clarke H. Kawakami and Roger Pineau (New York: Ballantine, 1966), p. 210 [hereafter Fuchida and Okumiya, *Midway: The Battle That Doomed Japan*].

Page 22
Extension of defense perimeter: Lundstrom, *First South Pacific Campaign,* pp. 24–25, 38–39, 155.

Lae and Salamaua: Lundstrom, *First South Pacific Campaign,* pp. 39–40.

Page 23
Strategy conflicts at Imperial Headquarters and plans of Admiral Yamamoto: Ibid., pp. 40–47, 65.

Page 23
Yamamoto's plan to capture Hawaii: John J. Stephan, *Hawaii Under the Rising Sun* (Honolulu: University of Hawaii Press, 1984), pp. 89–118 [hereafter Stephan, *Hawaii Under the Rising Sun*].

Page 24
". . . now comes the adult's hour": Agawa, *Reluctant Admiral,* p. 299.

Page 24
Coral Sea battle and results: Lundstrom, *First South Pacific Campaign,* pp. 102–3, 106–13.

Pages 24–25
Midway battle and results: Ibid., pp. 177, 182–84. Japanese carrier aircraft losses from H. P. Willmott, *The Barrier and the Javelin* (Annapolis, Md.: Naval Institute Press, 1983), pp. 104–8 [hereafter Willmott, *Barrier and the Javelin*]. The total of 250 includes

229 in the air groups of the four Japanese carriers in the Striking Force plus 21 Zeros embarked for the proposed Midway garrison.

Pages 25–28
Description of the Bismarck Archipelago and the Solomons: R. W. Robson, *The Pacific Islands Handbook, 1944,* North American Edition (New York: Macmillan, 1945) [hereafter *Pacific Islands Handbook*]; John Miller, Jr., *United States Army in World War II, The War in the Pacific, Guadalcanal: The First Offensive* (Washington, D.C.: U.S. Government Printing Office, reprinted 1978), pp. 4, 24–25, 44 [hereafter Miller, *Guadalcanal: The First Offensive*]; Frank D. Hough, Merle E. Ludwig, and Henry I. Shaw, Jr., *History of United States Marine Corps Operations in World War II, Pearl Harbor to Guadalcanal* (Washington, D.C.: Historical Division, Headquarters, U.S. Marine Corps. U.S. Government Printing Office), pp. 243–45 [hereafter Hough, Ludwig, and Shaw, *Pearl Harbor to Guadalcanal*]; *Rand McNally World Atlas,* Naval Institute Press edition (Chicago, New York, and San Francisco: Rand McNally, 1977); Walter Lord, *Lonely Vigil: Coastwatchers in the Solomons* (New York: Viking, 1977), p. 3 [hereafter Lord, *Lonely Vigil*].

Pages 28–29
Coast watchers: The classic description of this unit is from their leader, Eric Feldt, *The Coast Watchers* (Melbourne: Oxford, 1946), pp. 3–11, 14, 69–70, 84 [hereafter Feldt, *Coast Watchers*]. The quote on native attitudes is on p. 69; Lord, *Lonely Vigil,* pp. 4, 6, 9.

Pages 29–30
Key coast-watching stations: Feldt, *Coast Watchers,* pp. 36–37, 58–63, 78–80, 83; Lord, *Lonely Vigil,* pp. 4–5, 12, 9, 20. Technically, Martin Clemens was a colonial official and a member of the British Solomon Islands Defense Force. According to native reminiscences, Donald Kennedy used a good deal of brutality to enforce obedience. *The Big Death: Solomon Islanders Remember World War II,* Solomon Islands College of Higher Education and the University of the South Pacific (Suva, Fiji Islands: Fiji Times Ltd., 1988), pp. 134–35, 145–46. One native said: "We were afraid of [Kennedy] more than we were of the Japanese."

Page 31
Japanese landing on Tulagi and subsequent developments on Guadalcanal: Lord, *Lonely*

Vigil, pp. 12–13, 16–17, 24–26; Feldt, *Coast Watchers,* p. 82; Martin Clemens, "A Coastwatcher's Diary" (Nicosia, Cyprus: unpublished manuscript, no date), pp. 49–52 [hereafter Clemens MS]. A photocopy of Clemens's manuscript may be found at the Marine Corps Historical Center (MCHC).

CHAPTER 2

Page 32
MacArthur's proposal of June 8 and Navy response: COMSOWESPAC to CINCPAC 080731, 080733, 080735 Jun 42, Grey Book, pp. 557–58; Hayes, *History of the Joint Chiefs of Staff,* pp. 141–43; Morton, *Strategy and Command,* pp. 295–96; Lundstrom, *First South Pacific Campaign,* pp. 188–89.

Pages 32–33
MacArthur's message of June 24 and contemporary plans: Morton, *Strategy and Command,* pp. 296–98; Hayes, *History of the Joint Chiefs of Staff,* p. 144.

Page 33
King's messages of June 24 and 25: COMINCH to CINCPAC 242303, 242306 Jun 42, Grey Book, pp. 602–3; Hayes, *History of the Joint Chiefs of Staff,* pp. 143–44; Morton, *Strategy and Command,* pp. 298–99.

Pages 33–34
Marshall's response to King June 26 and King's reply: Morton, *Strategy and Command,* pp. 299–300; Hayes, *History of the Joint Chiefs of Staff,* pp. 144–45; COMINCH to CINCPAC 271415 Jun 42, COMSOPAC War Diary, 29 Jun 42, p. 19; Dyer, *Amphibians Came to Conquer,* pp. 259–60.

Page 34
MacArthur's outburst of June 28: Morton, *Strategy and Command,* pp. 300–301; Hayes, *History of the Joint Chiefs of Staff,* p. 146.

Pages 34–35
King-Marshall negotiations of June 29–July 1: Morton, *Strategy and Command,* pp. 301–2; Hayes, *History of the Joint Chiefs of Staff,* pp. 145–46.

Pages 34–35
Final plan of July 2: Morton, *Strategy and Command,* pp. 302–3; Hayes, *History of the Joint Chiefs of Staff,* pp. 141, 146–47; Dyer, *Amphibians Came to Conquer,* pp. 260–61. The plan was embodied to the local naval commanders in COMINCH to CINCPAC

022100 (first of seven parts), Grey Book, pp. 605–7.

MacArthur message of July 6: COMSOWES-PAC to COMSOPAC 060130 Jul 42, Grey Book, p. 609.

Page 35
Agreements on Army commander for South Pacific and creation of mobile air forces: Morton, *Strategy and Command,* p. 303; Hayes, *History of the Joint Chiefs of Staff,* pp. 147–48.

Career of General Harmon and opinions on: Miller, *Guadalcanal: The First Offensive,* pp. 22–24; Ghormley, "Tide Turns," pp. 3, 44, 75; General Alexander A. Vandegrift and Robert Asprey, *Once a Marine* (New York: W. W. Norton, 1964), p. 164 [hereafter Vandegrift and Asprey, *Once a Marine*]; Gen. Gerald C. Thomas, USMC (Ret.), interview, Sep 66 (Oral History Collection, Marine Corps Historical Center), pp. 393–94 [hereafter Thomas intvw]. Vandegrift's health was failing at the time his autobiography was drafted and it should be regarded principally as the voice of Asprey. Accordingly, this narrative makes only sparing use of direct quotations from this work.

Page 35
King-Nimitz meeting in San Francisco: Conference notes, Grey Book, pp. 689–94; Hayes, *History of the Joint Chiefs of Staff,* p. 148; Potter, *Nimitz,* pp. 109, 114–15.

Pages 35–36
Diversions mounted for Guadalcanal landings: Kiska Bombardments, Grey Book, pp. 629, 782, 792–93, 820; *Boise*'s raid, Grey Book, pp. 816, 821–22; Makin raid, Grey Book, pp. 828, 830, Maj. Gen. Omar T. Pfeiffer, interview, May–Jun 68 (Oral History Collection, Marine Corps Historical Center), pp. 196–99 [hereafter Pfeiffer intvw]; contribution of British Eastern Fleet, Grey Book, pp. 698–99, 703, Admiralty to CINCPAC 101418 Aug 42, Grey Book, p. 643. It is possible that the *Boise* raid had some effect, as some intercepted and decrypted messages suggested the commander of Carrier Division 2 decided to send some aircraft to Marcus Island (SRH-012, "The Role of Radio-Intelligence in the American Japanese War, August 1941 to August 1942," 4 vols., Vol. IV, pp. 309–12 [hereafter SRH-012].

Pages 35–36
Designation of Guadalcanal as a target: COMSOPAC War Diary 27 Jun 42; CINC-

PAC Daily Summary 5 July, Grey Book, p. 707; Dyer, *Amphibians Came to Conquer,* pp. 272–76; Grey Book, p. 707; Thomas intvw, p. 255. In his interview, General Thomas stated the 1st Marine Division planned a landing on Guadalcanal from the start as that was where they thought most of the Japanese in the area were.

Page 36
Ghormley arrives Noumea and dealings with French: COMSOPAC War Diary 18 May 42; Adm. Ghormley to CINCPAC 160545 Jun 42, COMSOPAC War Diary 16 Jun 42, p. 8; Ghormley, "Tide Turns," pp. 16–18; Morton, *Strategy and Command,* pp. 208–9.

Ghormley's estimate of the situation: Ghormley, "Tide Turns," pp. 19, 11–12, 24, 32, 40; COMSOPAC to CINCPAC 260015 Jun 42, Grey Book, p. 602.

Pages 36–37
Aircraft strengths, types, and dispositions: Commodore Richard W. Bates and Commander Walter D. Innis, "The Battle of Savo Island August 9, 1942, Strategic and Tactical Analysis" (U.S. Naval War College, 1950) [hereafter NWC Analysis]; COMAIRSOPAC to CINCPAC 210900 May 42, Grey Book, p. 522–23; Lundstrom, *First South Pacific Campaign,* p. 170.

Page 37
Establishment of base at Espíritu Santo: Ghormley, "Tide Turns," pp. 20–23; CINCPAC to COMGENSOPAC 230333 May 42, Grey Book, p. 526; COMSOPAC to COMAIRSOPACFOR 022314 Jul 42, Grey Book, p. 605; Commanding General at Efate to COMSOPAC 170530 Jul 42, COMSOPAC War Diary, 18 Jul 42, p. 30; COMGEN EFATE to COMSOPAC 230001 Jul 42, COMSOPAC War Diary 23 Jul 42, p. 41; COMGEN ROSES to COMAIRSOPAC 290800 Jul 42, Grey Book, p. 764.

Page 38
Melbourne meeting of MacArthur and Ghormley and message of July 8: Ghormley, "Tide Turns," pp. 45–51; COMGEN-SOWESPAC to COMINCH 080112 Jul 42, Grey Book, p. 610–13; Hayes, *History of the Joint Chiefs of Staff,* p. 148; Morton, *Strategy and Command,* pp. 306–7.

Pages 38–39
Effectiveness of radio intelligence on May 26: CINCPAC Daily Summary 26 May, Grey Book, p. 543; Lundstrom, *First South Pacific Campaign,* p. 76.

Change of major cryptographic system May 28: CINCPAC Daily Summary 27 May, Grey Book, p. 545; SRH-012, Vol. III, p. 11; Layton, Pineau, and Costello, *And I Was There,* p. 432; W. J. Holmes, *Double Edged Secrets* (Annapolis, Md.: Naval Institute Press), p. 110 [hereafter Holmes, *Double Edged Secrets*]; SRH-012, Vol. IV, p. 437.

Page 39
Preparations to use traffic analysis: SRH-012, Vol. III, pp. 6–12.

Pages 39–40
Basic techniques of traffic analysis: *Hearings Before the Joint Committee on the Investigation of the Pearl Harbor Attack,* Congress of the United States, Seventy-ninth Congress, Second Session, Part 10 (Washington, D.C.: U.S. Government Printing Office, 1946), pp. 4835–36 [hereafter *Pearl Harbor Attack,* Part 10]; Layton, Pineau, and Costello, *And I Was There,* pp. 27, 174; SRH-012, Vol. III, pp. 249–51, 628; Vol. IV, pp. 465, 622; SRH-036, "Radio Intelligence in World War II Tactical Operations in the Pacific Ocean Area, January 1943," pp. 205, 255, 460 [hereafter SRH-036]; SRH-136, "Radio Intelligence in World War II Tactical Operations in the Pacific Ocean Area, December 1942," pp. 594–95 [hereafter SRH-136].

Page 40
Message headings and call signs: Layton, Pineau, and Costello, *And I Was There,* pp. 27, 174. It should be noted that Admiral Layton testified at the Pearl Harbor Hearings that in December 1941 the Japanese were using 12,000 to 15,000 call signs. *Pearl Harbor Attack,* Part 10, p. 4841.

Use of secret serial numbers: SRH-012, Vol. III, p. 309; Vol. IV, pp. 285, 290–91.

Page 40
Structure of Japanese radio communications and use of "association": *Pearl Harbor Attack,* Part 10, p. 4834–35; Layton, Pineau, and Costello, *And I Was There,* p. 182–83.

Pages 40–41
Use of routing information: SRH-012, Vol. III, pp. 249–51, 628; SRH-136, pp. 40, 98.

Page 41
Association of Crudiv 8 and carriers: SRH-012, Vol. IV., pp. 671–72, 787.

Movements of destroyers monitored: SRH-012, Vol. III, pp. 631, 649–50; Vol. IV, p. 612.

Japanese tighten radio security: SRH-012, Vol. III, pp. 487–88; Vol. IV, pp. 8, 143, 166, 191–92, 195, 309, 396, 523, 657; SRH-136, pp. 85, 95.

Page 41
Security breach by *Chicago Tribune*, Walter Winchell, and Congressman Elmer J. Holland: Layton, Pineau, and Costello, *And I Was There*, pp. 454–55; Spector, *Eagle Against the Sun*, pp. 451–52.

Page 41
Other indiscretions: Layton, Pineau, and Costello, *And I Was There*, p. 419; CINC-PAC Daily Summary 2 Feb 43, Grey Book, p. 1386.

Page 42
Difficulties and uncertainties of traffic analysis: *Pearl Harbor Attack*, Part 10, p. 4835, 4838; SRH-012, Vol. IV, p. 61. As to the typical daily traffic, SRH-012, Vol. IV., pp. 707–8, shows that the average from August 1–19 was 505 messages, while on August 7 it was 733.

Page 42
Hazards of using "tendencies": A classic example of the problems of relying on tendencies is illustrated by the fact that estimates prior to Pearl Harbor placed some Japanese carriers in the Mandates because the destroyers that had habitually acted as their plane guards were known to have been transferred to that locale (*Pearl Harbor Attack*, Part 10, p. 4836).

". . . proved or disproved": SRH-012, Vol. III, p. 12.

Time to transmit radio intelligence: SRH-036, pp. 679, 682, for an example.

Page 42
Information gathered on Japanese preparations: SRH-012, Vol. III, pp. 51–57, 64, 67, 140–42, 144, 152, 162, 171–72, 185, 207–8, 212–13, 216–17, 226, 229, 239–40, 261–62, 268, 279–80, 302–05, 332–33, 340, 371–73.

Page 43
July 10 Joint Chiefs of Staff meeting and response to Ghormley MacArthur message of July 8: Hayes, *History of the Joint Chiefs of Staff*, pp. 141, 148–49; Morton, *Strategy and Command*, pp. 307–9; Ghormley, "Tide Turns," pp. 52–53; COMINCH to COMSOPAC 102100, 102118 Jul 42, Grey Book, pp. 615–16; COMSOPAC to CINCPAC 112000 Jul 42, Grey Book, p. 615.

Pages 43–44
Postponement of "FS" Operation and Imperial Army plans: Lundstrom, *First South Pacific Campaign*, pp. 185–86.

Page 44
Organization of 8th Fleet: *Senshi Sosho, Nanto Homen Kaigun Sakusen*, 1, *Gato Dakkai Sakusen Kaishimade*, Boeicho Boei Kenshujo, Senshishitsu, Asagumo Shinbun Sha, September 28, 1971, pp. 372–74 (*War History Series, Southeast Area Navy Operations*, Part I, *Up to the Start of the Guadalcanal Recapturing Operations*, Defense Agency, Defense Research Institute, Office of War History) [hereafter *S.S.*, Vol. 49]; *Senshi Sosho, Minamitaiheiyo Rikugun Sakusen*, 1, *Poto Moresbi–Gato Shoki Sakusen*, Boeicho Boei Kenshujo, Senshishitsu, Asagumo Shinbun Sha, March 25, 1968, pp. 201–11 (*War History Series, South Pacific*, Part I, *Army Operations, Port Moresby–Guadalcanal, Early Operations*, Defense Agency, Defense Research Institute, Office of War History) [hereafter *S.S.*, Vol. 14]; Lundstrom, *First South Pacific Campaign*, p. 186. The dividing line between the Fourth and Eighth fleets was a 285-degree line crossing the equator at 160 degrees east longitude.

Vice Admiral Gunichi Mikawa: *S.S.*, Vol. 49, pp. 404; Captain Toshikazu Ohmae, "The Battle of Savo Island," edited by Roger Pineau, *United States Naval Institute Proceedings*, Vol. 83, No. 12 (December 1957), p. 1264 [hereafter Ohmae, "Battle of Savo Island"].

Pages 44–45
Mikawa concerns and intelligence: *S.S.*, Vol. 49, pp. 428–29, Vol. 14, 210.

Page 45
Briefing by Ohmae and attitudes of local commanders: Ohmae, "Battle of Savo Island," pp. 1265–67.

Activities of 8th Fleet staff and B-17 raids on Guadalcanal: Ohmae, "Battle of Savo Island," p. 1267; Commander Aircraft South Pacific War Diary 31 July–6 Aug 42 [hereafter COMAIRSOPAC War Diary]; Organizational History of the 11th Bombardment Group, Reel B0067, p. 1727 [hereafter 11th BG Hist.], Office of Air Force History, Bolling Air Force Base, Washington, D.C. [hereafter OAFH].

Page 45
Imperial Headquarters radio unit analysis: Ohmae, "Battle of Savo Island," p. 1268.

Page 45
8th Base Force radio unit analysis and disappearance of native workers: *S.S.,* Vol. 14, p. 217; Ohmae, "Battle of Savo Island," p. 1268.

"It is urgently necessary . . .": Griffith, *Battle of Guadalcanal,* p. 23.

Page 46
Alexander Archer Vandegrift: Official Biography, MCHC; Griffith, *Battle of Guadalcanal,* p. 22.

Pages 46–47
Background of 1st Marine Division, 7th Marines to Samoa: 1st Marine Division, Phase I Final Report—Guadalcanal, p. 1, Box 4, File A7-1 [hereafter Final Report, Phase I]; McMillan, *Old Breed,* p. 12; Thomas intvw, pp. 238, 242; Vandegrift and Asprey, *Once a Marine,* p. 100; Griffith, *Battle of Guadalcanal,* pp. 22–23. The Final Report of the 1st Marine Division is divided into five phases plus a supplemental section of comments dated in July 1943. All further citations to the Final Report will be as noted above, keyed to the phase or to the supplemental section cited as Jul 43. All references hereafter to "Box __, File __" are to the system maintained at the Marine Corps Historical Center (MCHC).

Orders for Division to move to New Zealand and Vandegrift's reaction: Final Report, Phase I, pp. 1–2; Vandegrift and Asprey, *Once a Marine,* p. 101; Griffith, *Battle of Guadalcanal,* p. 23.

Page 47
Training of regiments of 1st Marine Division: Final Report, Phase I, p. 1; Thomas intvw, p. 242.

Page 47
Vandegrift assured no combat before January 1, 1943: Final Report, Phase I, p. 2; Griffith, *Battle of Guadalcanal,* p. 23.

Page 47
Movement to New Zealand: Final Report, Phase I, pp. 1–2.

Manpower of 1st Marine Division: Thomas intvw, pp. 229; McMillan, *Old Breed,* p. 12; Final Report, Phase I, p. 6; Clifton B. Cates, "My First at Guadalcanal, 7 Aug to 22 Dec 42," unpublished manuscript, Cates Papers, Marine Corps Historical Center [hereafter Cates, "My First"]. The first portion of Cates's manuscript is not paginated.

U.S. Army acknowledges quality gap of manpower: Robert R. Palmer, Bell I. Wiley, and William R. Keast, *United States Army in World War II, The Army Ground Forces, The Procurement and Training of Ground Combat Troops* (Washington, D.C.: Office of the Chief of Military History, Department of the Army, 1948), pp. 4–5.

Pages 47–48
Griffith's description of "the Old Breed": Griffith, *Battle of Guadalcanal,* pp. 23–24.

Page 48
Movement of 1st Marine Division to New Zealand: Final Report, Phase I, p. 2, Annex A.

Pages 48–49
Vandegrift receives orders: Final Report, Phase I, p. 2, 4; Vandegrift and Asprey, *Once a Marine,* pp. 104–5.

Pages 49–50
Planning begins and intelligence gathering: Final Report, Phase I, pp. 2–3 and Annex E; Griffith, *Battle of Guadalcanal,* p. 27; Herbert Merillat, *The Island* (Boston: Houghton Mifflin, 1944; reprint 1979), pp. 14–15 [hereafter Merillat, *Island*].

Story in *Dominion:* Herbert Christian Merillat, *Guadalcanal Remembered* (New York: Dodd, Mead, 1982), pp. 21–22 [hereafter Merillat, *Guadalcanal Remembered*].

Lost photomap: The story of this incident is from Major John L. Zimmerman, USMCR, "The Guadalcanal Campaign" Historical Division, Headquarters, U.S. Marine Corps, Lancaster Publications, 1949, pp. 14–15 [hereafter Zimmerman, "Guadalcanal Campaign"]. Zimmerman quotes extensively from a 1948 letter of Colonel E. F. Kumpe. In 1942 Kumpe was the commander of the 648th Topographic Battalion and map chief in the Southwest Pacific theater. A copy of this photomap was identified for the author by Mr. George MacGillivray in 1986. It is of such small scale as to have no merit over the "map" used by 1st Marine Division at the time of the landing.

Page 50
Intelligence shortcomings: From respective operations plans, 1st Marine Division Op Plan 7-42, Annex A, Final Report, Phase I, Annex F; Admiral Turner's CTF 62, Op Plan No. A3-42, Serial 0010, 30 July 1942, Annex E; Admiral Ghormley's Commander South Pacific Area and South Pacific Force, A4/A16-3, Serial 0017, Operation Plan 1–42, July 16, 1942, Annex A.

Actual Japanese strength: *S.S.,* Vol. 49, pp. 384–85, 498.

Page 51
Issuing of plans: Final Report, Phase I, Annex F (Op Plan 7–42); Vandegrift and Asprey, *Once a Marine,* p. 111.

Ghormley's plan: Commander South Pacific Area and South Pacific Force, A4/A16-3, Serial 0017, Operation Plan 1–42, July 16, 1942.

Fletcher's plan: Commander Task Force 61, A16-3/0032 N, Operation Order No. 1–42, July 28, 1942.

Turner's schedule and plan: Dyer, *Amphibians Came to Conquer,* p. 270, 289; Commander Task Force 62, Serial 0013, Operation Plan A3-42, July 30, 1942; Thomas intvw, p. 265.

Pages 52–53
Loading of 1st Marine Division: Final Report, Phase I, pp. 5–7 and Annex L; Vandegrift and Asprey, *Once a Marine,* p. 114.

"The essence of combat loading . . .": Merillat, *Guadalcanal Remembered,* p. 33.

Page 53
Scene at Aotea Quay: Griffith, *Battle of Guadalcanal,* p. 32; Merillat, *Guadalcanal Remembered,* p. 32; Vandegrift and Asprey, *Once a Marine,* pp. 102–3, 111, 114; Thomas intvw, pp. 252–53.

Page 53
Delay of landing date and sortie from Wellington: Final Report, Phase I, p. 7; COMSOPAC 160612 Jul 42, Grey Book, p. 620; COMINCH 281830 Jul 42, Grey Book, p. 627; CINCPAC Daily Summaries 15 and 28 July, Grey Book, pp. 771, 783; Ghormley, "Tide Turns," p. 58; Cates, "My First."

Agreement reached for Operation Torch: Hayes, *History of the Joint Chiefs of Staff,* pp. 152–54.

Pages 54–55
Koro Conference: Final Report, Phase I, p. 7; COMSOPAC 311510 Jul 42, COMSOPAC War Diary 31 Jul 42, p. 57; Ghormley, "Tide Turns," pp. 60–61, 64–69; Dyer, *Amphibians Came to Conquer,* pp. 300–302.

Fletcher's background and appearance: Potter, *Nimitz,* p. 185; Lundstrom, *First South Pacific Campaign,* p. 59; Dyer, *Amphibians Came to Conquer;* Vandegrift and Asprey, *Once a Marine,* p. 120. Dyer points out that

Nimitz had been working on Fletcher's promotion since just after the Battle of the Coral Sea. The matter became acute in the weeks leading up to the landing because Rear Admiral Leigh Noyes was senior to Fletcher and by custom would take command of the combined force even though Noyes had no combat experience.

Page 55
Ghormley's response to Fletcher's proposal to withdraw fighter cover: COMSOPAC to CTF 61 020240 Aug 42, Grey Book, p. 631.

Pages 55–56
Ghormley's command position: Dyer, *Amphibians Came to Conquer,* pp. 302–5; COMSOPAC War Diary 9 May 42; CINCPAC to COMSOPAC 272251 Jun 42, COMSOPAC War Diary 28 Jun 42, p. 20; COMINCH 022150 Jul 42, Grey Book, p. 606; CINCPAC to COMSOPAC 092001 Jul 42, COMSOPAC War Diary 10 Jul 42, p. 16; COMSOPAC to CINCPAC 110045 Jul 42, COMSOPAC War Diary 11 Jul 42, p. 17; COMSOPAC to CINCPAC 311510 Jul 42, COMSOPAC War Diary 31 Jul 42, p. 57.

Pages 56–57
Ghormley's perception of his missions: Ghormley, "Tide Turns," pp. 140–42.

Page 57
Koro rehearsal: Final Report, Phase I, p. 7, July 43, p. 2; Vandegrift and Asprey, *Once a Marine,* p. 122; Thomas intvw, pp. 261, 263; Brig. Gen. Samuel B. Griffith, interview, November 1, 1968 (Oral History Collection, Marine Corps Historical Center), p. 81 [hereafter Griffith intvw].

Page 57
"Seldom has an operation . . .": Hough, Ludwig, and Shaw, *Pearl Harbor to Guadalcanal,* p. 248.

Page 58
Strength of 1st Marine Division: Final Report, Phase I, p. 9, gives 19,546, Annex K gives 18,131 (with no figures for the 3d Defense Battalion), Annex M gives 18,134; Phase V, Annex W, gives 19,360. However, all of these reports, with the apparent exception of Annex K, were prepared some time after the landing. The report of Turner's Amphibious Force prepared closer to the events gives 18,722.

Comparative table of naval strengths: Basic source for Imperial Navy is Willmott, *Barrier and the Javelin,* Appendix A, "Nominal Orders of Battle of the Imperial Japanese and U.S. Navies Between 7 December 1941 and 2 September 1945." For the U.S. Navy the same source is used as a base. Pacific Fleet strength for August 7, 1942, is from CINC-PAC War Diary 7 Aug 42. Atlantic Fleet strength is extracted from Samuel Elliot Morison, *History of United States Naval Operations in World War II, The Battle of the Atlantic, September 1939–May 1943,* Appendix VI, "The Atlantic Fleet of the United States Navy, 5 August 1942" (Boston: Little, Brown, 1966).

Page 58
Loss of *Tucker:* U.S.S. *Tucker,* No Serial, 12 August 1942, Subject: Action Report: Espíritu Santo, New Hebrides, Sinking of U.S.S. Tucker.

Turner's thoughts on approaching Guadalcanal: Dyer, *Amphibians Came to Conquer,* p. 318.

CHAPTER 3

Page 59
Japanese garrison of Guadalcanal on August 7, 1942: *S.S.,* Vol. 14, pp. 213–14, 226, Vol. 49, p. 498.

Time of first salvo from *Quincy:* Amphibious Force South Pacific (Task Force 62) War Diary for August 7, 1942 [hereafter TF 62 War Diary].

Reaction of Martin Clemens: Clemens MS, pp. 125–26.

Pages 59–60
Approach of Expeditionary Force: TF 62 War Diary for appropriate dates; Final Report, Phase I, p. 9.

Page 60
Description of Guadalcanal at dawn: Merillat, *Island,* p. 20.

Reaction of Admiral Turner: Dyer, *Amphibians Came to Conquer, Vol. I,* p. 328.

Page 60
Japanese seaplane losses: *S.S.,* Vol. 49, p. 430. The action report from *Wasp's* VF-72 claimed destruction of seven four-engine aircraft off Tanambogo and a total of fifteen Zero float planes between Makambo and a

beach on Halavao, U.S.S. *Wasp,* CV-7, Serial 003, August 14, 1942, Subject: Capture of Tulagi-Guadalcanal Area, 7–8 August 1942 [hereafter *Wasp* Serial 003].

Pages 60–61
Debarking of marines: TF 62 War Diary 7 Aug 42.

"with the smoothness and precision . . .": Final Report, Phase II, p. 1.

Page 61
Scheme of maneuver on Guadalcanal: Ibid., p. 9. This report indicates that the natives told of airfield construction work at Taivu point and therefore the decision was made to land midway between Lunga and Taivu points. The actual landing area, however, is midway between Lunga and Koli points, and it is assumed the report meant Koli Point as the site of the suspected airfield construction.

Pages 61–62
Initial landings on Guadalcanal: Ibid., p. 9, and Annex L, p. 1; 5th Marines Record of Events, Box 6, File A14-1 [hereafter 5th Mar Record of Events].

Page 62
Initial advance inland: Final Report, Phase II, pp. 9–10, and Annex N, pp. 1–3, which contains messages showing that the Japanese disappeared after the initial sighting; Engineer Activities Guadalcanal, p. 2, Box 6, File A34,5-1 [hereafter Engineer Activities Guadalcanal]; 1st Mar Div Op Plan 7–42 (describes Mount Austen as "4 miles south of Lunga Point"): Merillat, *Island,* p. 32; Vandegrift and Asprey, *Once a Marine,* p. 124.

Identity of watercourses between Red Beach and Lunga Point: Clemens MS, p. 150; Miller, *Guadalcanal: The First Offensive,* p. 51, note: Merillat, *Island,* p. 26, note 1.

Pages 62–63
Guadalcanal's rain forest: Basic description is from *Pacific Islands Handbook 1944,* pp. 283–84; Miller, *Guadalcanal: The First Offensive,* p. 25; Vandegrift papers, MCHC, Box 3, File 34; Cates, "My First"; Lieutenant Colonel John B. George, *Shots Fired in Anger* (Washington, D.C.: National Rifle Association, 1981), p. 70.

Page 63
Slowing of advance of 1st and 5th Marines: Final Report. Phase II, p. 10, Annex L, p. 1, Annex M. The missing marine is mentioned in Robert Leckie, *Helmet for My Pillow* (New

York: Bantam, 1979), p. 59 [hereafter Leckie, *Helmet for My Pillow*].

"as if they were about . . .": Vandegrift and Asprey, *Once a Marine*, p. 125.

Pages 63–64
The Marine side of the unloading dispute: Final Report, Phase II, pp. 10–11, Annex N, p. 5, msg 89; Final Report, July 43, pp. 7–8; 1st Marine Division D-3 Journal, 7 Aug 2330, 8 Aug 0242, Box 5, File A7-14 [hereafter 1st Mar Div D-3 Jnl]; Vandegrift and Asprey, *Once a Marine*, p. 124. Griffith, *Battle of Guadalcanal*, pp. 41–42.

The Navy side of the unloading dispute: Dyer, *Amphibians Came to Conquer*, pp. 350–53, which summarizes from the relevant action reports.

Page 64
Radio messages from Tulagi: SRH-012, Vol. III, pp. 544, 648–551, lists several messages. There are several versions of the last message from Tulagi. The text follows Morison, *Struggle for Guadalcanal*, p. 18. The role of these messages in informing Admiral Nimitz is noted in Potter, *Nimitz*, p. 180.

Pages 64–65
Japanese reaction and air counterattacks: *S.S.*, Vol. 49, pp. 430–32, 443–44. A vivid personal account of this raid is found in Saburo Saki with Martin Caldin and Fred Saito, *Samurai* (Garden City, N.Y.: Doubleday, 1957), p. 173 [hereafter Saki, Caldin, and Saito, *Samurai*]. Saki, at p. 177, notes that the Tainan Air Group commander, Lieutenant Commander Nakajima, expected to lose half the A6Ms sent on the flight and urged that only twelve be dispatched. Admiral Yamada wanted to send the whole Tainan Air Group. They compromised at eighteen.

Page 65
Mason's message and word to *Canberra*'s crew: Feldt, *Coast Watchers*, pp. 87–88.

Page 65
Description of G4M Betty: William Green, *Famous Bombers of the Second World War*, Vol. II (Garden City, N.Y.: Hanover House, 1960), pp. 52–54 [hereafter Green, *Famous Bombers of the Second World War*]; Dr. René J. Francillon, *Japanese Navy Bombers of World War Two*, 2d ed. (Garden City, N.Y.: Doubleday, 1970), pp. 37–48 [hereafter Francillon, *Japanese Navy Bombers of World War Two*]; Masatake Okumiya, Jiro Horikoshi,

and Martin Caidin, *Zero* (New York: Ballantine, 1957), p. 228 [hereafter Okumiya, Horikoshi, Caldin, *Zero*].

Pages 65–66
Background of the Zero fighter plane: Jiro Horikoshi, *Eagle of Mitsubishi: The Story of the Zero Fighter*, translated by Shojiro Shindo and Harold N. Wantiez (Seattle: University of Washington Press, 1980); H.P. Willmott, *Zero A6M* (Secaucus, N.J.: Chartwell Books, 1980), p. 30; Robert C. Mikesh and Rikyu Watanabe, *Zero Fighter*, (New York: Crown 1980), p. 27 [hereafter Mikesh and Watanabe, *Zero Fighter*]. Horikoshi designed the Zero fighter, and Mikesh and Watanabe quote from reports of testing of the A6M2 captured in the Aleutians and an F4F-4. The range figures in *Zero Fighter*, p. 31, are 1,930 statue miles or 1,675 nautical miles for the Model 21, and 1,447 and 1,284 respectively for the Model 32. These figures appear to be maximum range, or the distance the aircraft could fly with its fuel load. The term "combat range" noted in the text is a distance an aircraft can fly while executing a combat mission, i.e., a period of time at maximum power in the middle of the flight. According to Ikuhiko Hata and Yasuho Izawa, *Japanese Naval Aces and Fighter Units in World War II*, Naval Institute Press, translated by Don Cyril Graham, (Tokyo: Kantūsha Publishers, 1975), p. 123 [hereafter Hata and Izawa, *Japanese Naval Aces and Fighter Units in World War II*], tests conducted by the 3d Air Group prewar established that the Model 21 could fly 1,200 miles and conduct a twenty-minute air battle. The Model 32 was later modified by adding extra fuel tanks to increase range performance. The amazing fact that the land-based, but not the carrier-based, Zero units did not carry radios was discovered by John Lundstrom. Mr. Shiro Ishikawa, a former pilot who flew many missions to Guadalcanal between August and October 1942, confirmed this fact to the author in conversation in April 1990.

Pages 66–67
Imperial Navy air crew training: Saki, Caidin, and Saito, *Samurai*, pp. 28–34; *United States Strategic Bombing Survey*, Survey No. 62, 1946, "Japanese Air Power," p. 35; R. J. Overy, *The Air War 1939–45* (New York: Stein & Day, 1981), pp. 87, 95.

Page 67
Wildcat virtues: Thomas G. Miller, Jr., *The Cactus Air Force* (New York: Harper & Row,

1969), pp. 4–5 [hereafter Miller, *Cactus Air Force*]; Mikesh and Watanabe, *Zero Fighter*, p. 27.

Page 67
Lack of experience among American carrier pilots: Grey Book, p. 721.

Pages 67–69
American participation in air battle: The basic source is John B. Lundstrom, "Saburo Saki Over Guadalcanal, Part I," *Fighter Pilots in Aerial Combat*, No. 6 (Fall 1982), and Part II of the article with Henry Sakaida in the same publication, No. 7 (Winter 1983). Also consulted were the American action reports: U.S.S. *Enterprise*, CV-6, Serial 0194, 24 August 1942, Subject: Report of Guadalcanal-Tulagi Landings, p. 7 [hereafter *Enterprise* Serial 0194]; U.S.S. *Saratoga*, CV-3/A16-3, Serial 076, 19 August 1942, Subject: Report of Action, Tulagi-Guadalcanal Offensive, August 7–8, 1942; *Wasp* Serial 003.

Time of air attacks: From TF 62 War Diary 7 Aug 42.

Japanese participation in air battles August 7: *S.S.*, Vol. 49, pp. 443–52; Saki, Caidin, and Saito, *Samurai*, p. 184.

Saburo Saki's return flight: Saki, Caidin, and Saito, *Samurai*, pp. 175–98.

Page 69
Damage to *Mugford*: U.S.S. *Mugford*, Serial 028, August 12, 1942, Subject: The Commanding Officer's Report of Engagement with the Enemy in Guadalcanal Area During Period 0345, 7 August to 9 August 1942. Casualty figures are from the Bureau of Personnel Final Report of World War II Casualties, Navy Historical Center. All other naval casualty figures in this narrative are from the same source unless otherwise indicated.

Pages 69–70
Vandegrift issues new orders and situation at dark on Guadalcanal: Final Report, Phase II, p. 10, Annex L, pp. 1–2; Griffith, *Battle of Guadalcanal*, pp. 45.

Page 70
Captain Mouzen attempts counterattack: *S.S.*, Vol. 49, pp. 498–500.

Page 70
Leckie account of facing night in the jungle: Leckie, *Helmet for My Pillow*, p. 69.

Pages 70, 72
Night of August 7–8 on Guadalcanal: Final Report, Phase II, pp. 10–11, Annex N, p. 7, msg 105; Merillat, *Island*, p. 33; Cates, "My First," indicates he contacted only one battalion this night and the other two went on to the slopes of Mount Austen.

Message from General Rupertus: Final Report, Phase II, Annex N. p. 10, msg 1; 1st Mar Div D-3 Jnl 8 Aug 0007.

Page 72
Description of Tulagi and its garrison: Final Report, Phase II, p. 1–2, Annex B (Special map of Tulagi) and Annex D; *S.S.*, Vol. 49, p. 498.

Page 72
Plan of maneuver for Tulagi Group: Final Report, Phase I, p. 4; Phase II, pp. 1–2. These sources say the battalions chosen were the best-trained and oldest-established; Colonel Gerald Thomas called them the "best" (Thomas intvw, p. 255), and Griffith, *Battle of Guadalcanal*, p. 45, correctly adds that they were the most aggressive. For the plan see Annex E, Operations Order 7–42. The Navy units are itemized in Admiral Turner's Operations Order A3-42.

Pages 72–73
Landing on Tulagi: Final Report, Phase II, pp. 2–3, Annex D. pp. 1–2, Annex L, pp. 4–5; 2d Battalion, 5th Marines, Record of Events, pp. 1–2, Box 6, File A16-1 [hereafter 2d Bn, 5th Mar Record of Events]; Griffith, *Battle of Guadalcanal*, p. 46; Merillat, *Island*, pp. 41–42.

Page 73
Resistance encountered on Tulagi: Final Report, Phase II, pp. 2–3.

Page 74
"If they had been good shots . . .": Morison, *Coral Sea, Midway and Submarine Actions*, p. 289.

Page 74
Action during night of August 7–8: Final Report, Phase II, pp. 3–4; Griffith, *Battle of Guadalcanal*, p. 47.

Pages 74–76
Assault on Gavutu: Final Report, Phase I, p. 4, Phase II, Annex C (Map of Gavutu-Tanambogo); ltr Major Charles A. Miller to CMC 9 Feb 49; *S.S.*, Vol. 49, p. 498, for Japanese garrison; 1st Parachute Battalion Action Report, Box 7, File A36-3; Merillat,

Island, p. 46; U.S.S. *Heywood,* AP12/A16-3, Serial 18, August 12, 1942, Subject: U.S.S. Heywood—Report of Action at Solomons Islands, 7–9 August 1942, and Enclosure (A) Boat Wave Commanders Report [hereafter *Heywood* Serial 18]. *Heywood*'s report says she debarked 394 marines for the attack.

Pages 76–77
Description of the fighting on Gavutu and abortive attack on Tanambogo: 1st Parachute Battalion Report; Final Report, Phase II, pp. 5–6; ltr Major Harold R. Thorpe to CMC 19 Jan 49; ltr Colonel Justin G. Duryea to CMC 17 Jan 49; ltr Lt. Col. Wood B. Kyle to CMC 10 Feb 49; Richard W. Johnston. *Follow Me!* (New York: Random House, 1948), pp. 28–29 [hereafter Johnston, *Follow Me*], the last four references for details of Captain Crane's tribulations; Griffith, *Battle of Guadalcanal,* pp. 48–49; Merillat, *Island,* pp. 48–49. The various sources differ as to how many of Captain Crane's boats got ashore. The text follows Kyle's account; Johnston says three got ashore.

Page 77
Turner releases battalions of 2d Marines: Vandegrift and Asprey, *Once a Marine,* p. 125.

Action on Tulagi on August 8: Final Report, Phase II, pp. 4–6.

Page 78
Clearing Tulagi: Griffith, *Battle of Guadalcanal,* pp. 50–51; Final Report, Phase II, p. 4, Annex D, p. 2; Richard Tregaskis, *Guadalcanal Diary* (New York: Random House, 1943), p. 89 [hereafter Tregaskis, *Guadalcanal Diary*]. Prisoners are listed in Annex D, p. 3. One of these reportedly was a laborer.

Page 78
American losses: Readily accessible and reliable American casualty figures for the many ground battles on and around Guadalcanal simply do not exist. The battle on Tulagi is an excellent example of this problem. Marine losses on Tulagi are listed in Final Report, Phase II, p. 4, as three officers and thirty-three enlisted men killed or died of wounds with a further four officers and fifty men wounded. Griffith, *Battle of Guadalcanal,* p. 51, gives losses in the 1st Raider Battalion as forty-seven killed and fifty-two wounded. Griffith also gives the figure of fifty-six casualties in the 2d Battalion, 5th Marines, which intuitively seems high to this writer, and indeed, the report of the 2d Battalion, 5th Marines in Annex L specifically indicates only

one killed and four wounded and mentions "a few" casualties in the mop-up. But an examination of the 2d Bn, 5th Mar Record of Events 12 Aug indicates a report was forwarded that date listing losses as seven killed and nineteen wounded. figures of twenty-four killed and thirty-five wounded, on both Tulagi and Gavutu-Tanambogo. for the 1st and 2d Battalions, 2d Marines may be derived from the data provided in ltr Col. Cornelius P. Van Ness to CMC 12 Jan 49, on overall losses, by subtracting the figures explicitly given for the 3d Battalion.

At the urging of one marine veteran, I tried working from the muster rolls covering the relevant units for August 1942. These records, maintained at the Marine Corps Historical Center, are by company-size units, and although accurate, are very arduous to review because of the format. After working through August 1942 at great expense in time, I abandoned this method, except for certain events, for the rest of the campaign. The text follows the results of my adventure with the muster rolls.

Pages 78–79
Capture of Tanambogo: Final Report, Phase II, pp. 6–7; Griffith, *Battle of Guadalcanal,* pp. 51–52; Merillat, *Island,* pp. 49–50. The tanks were from Company C, 2d Tank Battalion. Final Report erroneously states Lieutenant Sweeney was killed in the tank that was burned out. Merillat, *Island,* pp. 49–50, shows he was in the other tank, and all later sources agree with this version. The story of the sole survivor of the burned-out tank is contained in his own statement in Box 6, File A11-2 and confirmed by the statement of the chaplain of the 3d Battalion, 2d Marines, W. Wyeth Williams, Box 6, File A11-2. Also useful is the report of the 3d Battalion, 2d Marines, Box 6, File A13-1.

Page 79
Losses on Gavutu-Tanambogo: Casualties are from the August 1942 muster rolls of the 1st Parachute Battalion, the 1st and 3d Battalions, 2d Marines, and Company C, 2d Tank Battalion. Naval losses are from the Bureau of Personnel Final Report of World War II Casualties.

". . . the combat assumed . . .": Final Report, Phase II, p. 18.

Pages 79–80
Japanese air unit participation: *S.S.,* Vol. 49, pp. 455–57.

American interception: *Enterprise* Serial 0194.

Quality and quantity of antiaircraft fire: Norman Friedman, *U.S. Naval Weapons* (Annapolis, Md.: United States Naval Institute Press, 1983), pp. 63–67, 76–78, 82–84 [hereafter Friedman, *U.S. Naval Weapons*]; numbers of antiaircraft guns from various ship action reports, for example, *American Legion*, AP35/A12-1, Serial 0525, November 28, 1942, Subject: Report of Action off Guadalcanal Island, August 7–9, 1942; and U.S.S. *Dewey*, DD-349, Serials 148-42 and 157-42, no date, which mention use of Thompson submachine guns, Browning Automatic Rifles, and rifles.

Damage of *Jarvis:* As a result of her subsequent loss, *Jarvis* made no report of this action that survived. The information in the text comes from Commander James C. Shaw, "Jarvis: Destroyer That Vanished," *United States Naval Institute Proceedings*, Vol. 76, No. 2 (February 1950) [hereafter Shaw, "Jarvis: Destroyer That Vanished"]. *Jarvis* lost fourteen men at the time of the torpedo hit and transferred seven wounded crewmen to other vessels, one of whom died.

Loss of *George F. Elliot:* U.S.S. *George F. Elliot*, No Serial, August 13, 1942, Subject: Report of Battle and Abandonment and Loss of George F. Elliot in the Battle of August 8, 1942, and also No Serial, 13 August 1942. Subject: U.S.S. George F. Elliot Abandonment and Loss of in Battle; U.S.S. *Dewey*, Serial 147-42, August 16, 1942, Subject: Action Report of U.S.S. Dewey (349) in the Occupation of Guadalcanal-Tulagi 7–9 August 1942. *Elliot's* reports are quite succinct, and the less creditable details are added in Morison, *Coral Sea, Midway and Submarine Actions*, pp. 295–96.

"blood red": Tregaskis, *Guadalcanal Diary*, p. 53.

Pages 80–81
Advance on Guadalcanal on August 8: Final Report, Phase II, pp. 11–12, Annex L, Annex M; 5th Mar Record of Events, 8 AUG 42; Cates, "My First"; Vandegrift and Asprey, *Once a Marine*, p. 122, for personal reconnaissance.

Page 81
Capture of Japanese installations: Final Report, Phase II, p. 12; Tregaskis, *Guadalcanal Diary*, pp. 55–58; Merillat, *Island*, pp. 35–36.

Page 81
Capture of Japanese cryptographic material: Layton, *And I Was There*, pp. 455–56; Edward Van Der Rhoer, *Deadly Magic* (New York: Scribner, 1978), p. 108 [hereafter Van Der Rhoer, *Deadly Magic*].

Pages 81–82
Assessment of performance of 1st Marine Division: Final Report, Phase II, pp. 15–16, Jul 43, pp. 1–2, 4–7. Griffith, *Battle of Guadalcanal*, pp. 54–55, touches on many of these points.

CHAPTER 4

The fundamental source for this chapter is "The Battle of Savo Island August 9, 1942, Strategical and Tactical Analysis," by Commodore Richard W. Bates and Commander Walter D. Innis (U.S. Naval War College, 1950), referred to herein as NWC Analysis. This excellent work is built around a painstaking reconstruction of the movements of all ships involved in the battle based upon original Allied and Japanese action reports. *S.S.*, Vol. 49, pp. 463–96, contains some very useful additional information. However, as *S.S.* acknowledges, Japanese action reports are suspect as to some movements because of the destruction of *Chokai*'s chart room and certain other failures, such as dead reckoning tracers, on other ships. Bates and Innis overcome these problems by recreating track charts and therefore are more reliable as to certain aspects of the engagement. All Allied action reports were reviewed in detail, as was the three-volume file that constitutes the findings of the inquiry by Admiral Arthur J. Hepburn and its endorsements and associated correspondence. The official title of Admiral Hepburn's report is "Report of Informal Inquiry into Circumstances Attending Loss of U.S.S. Vincennes . . . on Aug. 9, 1942 in the Vicinity of Savo Island," 13 May 1943; hereafter it is referred to as Hepburn Report. Another source that is indispensable for an account, and a spirited defense, of Admiral Turner's decisions is Dyer, *Amphibians Came to Conquer*, Vol. I, pp. 355–402. Dyer also has an interview with Admiral Fletcher that provides some rare insights into that flag officer's thinking. Allied radio intelligence is drawn from SRH-012, Vol. III, covering this period. Last but by no means least, Mr. Robert Cressman of the Naval Historical Center brought to this writer's attention important documents concerning U.S. Navy battle doctrine.

Pages 83–84
Background to American strategic and tactical doctrine: Lundstrom, *First South Pacific Campaign,* p. 13; H. P. Willmott, *Empires in Balance,* pp. 106–17; Peter Hodges and Norman Friedman, *Destroyer Weapons of World War 2,* p. 105.

The frequency and nature of American night battle training immediately before the war are documented in "Annual Report of the Commander-in-Chief United States Pacific Fleet for the Period 1 July 1940 to 30 June 1941," CINCPAC File No. A9/FF12/(05), Serial 01275 A. It is significant that this report notes that Fleet Tactical Boards were currently studying, "with a view to establishing doctrines and standard procedures," "coordinated cruiser-destroyer action in night search and attack." An example of American prewar night gunnery training is contained in "Orders for Gunnery Exercises, United States Navy, Chapter 6 Destroyers F.T.P. 196," Washington, 1940. The serious manner in which President Roosevelt's Atlantic policies impinged on training is explored in Abbazia, *Mr. Roosevelt's Navy,* pp. 145, 251. The shocking fact that *Vincennes* last conducted a night battle practice in February 1941 is confessed in her Serial 0021, 14 August, 1942. Subject: Report of Action Occurring off Savo Island (Guadalcanal–Florida Island) Area—Night of 8/9 August, 1942. Enclosure B, Report of Lt. Cdr. R. R. Craighill, p. 6. [hereafter *Vincennes* Serial 0021].

Page 85
Development of Japanese strategical and tactical doctrine: An overview of developments in Imperial Navy doctrine is contained within the series of articles by Dr. E. Lacroix. "The Development of the 'A Class' Cruisers in the Imperial Japanese Navy," *Warship International,* Vol. XIV, No. 4 (1977), and Vol. XVI, Nos. 1 and 4 (1979), Vol. XVIII, Nos. 1 and 4 (1981), Vol. XX, No. 3 (1983), and Vol. XXI, No. 3 (1984) [hereafter Lacroix, "Development of the 'A Class' Cruisers in the Imperial Japanese Navy"]. Comments on doctrine are in Vol. XVIII, No. 4 (1981), pp. 337, 365–66. Other works containing useful information: Vice Admiral Raizo Tanaka and Roger Pineau, "Japan's Losing Struggle for Guadalcanal," Part I, *United States Naval Institute Proceedings,* Vol. 82, No. 7 (July 1956), p. 698 [Part II of this article is in Vol.

82, No. 8, August 1956; they are cited hereafter as Tanaka, Part I, and Tanaka, Part II, respectively]; Agawa, *Reluctant Admiral,* pp. 173, 179, 195; Gordon W. Prange, *At Dawn We Slept: The Untold Story of Pearl Harbor* (New York: McGraw-Hill, 1981), p. 12. The range of the G4M1 is from Green, *Famous Bombers of the Second World War,* Vol. II, p. 56.

Page 85
Japanese night fighting equipment: Lacroix, "Development of the 'A Class' Cruisers in the Imperial Japanese Navy," No. 4, 1981, pp. 332–33.

Page 86
Japanese torpedo development and performance: U.S. Naval Technical Mission to Japan, Subject: Target Report Japanese Torpedoes and Tubes, 8 Apr 46 (Index No. 0-01-1); Lacroix, "Development of the 'A Class' Cruisers in the Imperial Japanese Navy," No. 4, 1981, pp. 336–37, 364–65; John Campbell, *Naval Weapons of World War Two* (Annapolis, Md.: Naval Institute Press, 1985), pp. 202–8 [hereafter Campbell, *Naval Weapons of World War Two*]. Campbell points out that not all Japanese 24-inch torpedoes were oxygen- rather than air-fueled. There also existed the 24-inch "8th Year Type" (1919) and the 24-inch "Type 90" (1930), both air-fueled, mounted in light cruiser *Nagara* or *Fubuki* Class destroyers.

U.S. torpedo performance: Lieutenant Commander Buford Rowland, USNR, and Lieutenant William B. Boyd, USNR, *U.S. Navy Bureau of Ordnance in World War II* (Washington, D.C.: U.S. Government Printing Office), p. 91. A plain explanation of the defects in American torpedoes has been provided in many works, perhaps best in Clay Blair, Jr., *Silent Victory: The U.S. Submarine War Against Japan,* Vol. I (Philadelphia and New York: Lippincott, 1975), pp. 408–11 [hereafter Blair, *Silent Victory*].

Pages 86–87
Mikawa's decision to form a striking force and radio intelligence: *S.S.,* Vol. 49, pp. 463–64; SRH-012, Vol. III, pp. 121–22.

Page 87
Mikawa orders submarine deployment: NWC Analysis, pp. 46, 51. In response to these orders, on August 7 *I-121* sailed from Rabaul, while *I-123* left Truk and *RO-33* abandoned her patrol area off Australia. *I-122* departed Rabaul on August 8.

Reinforcement Unit formed and loaded on *Meiyo Maru* and *Soya;* sinking of *Meiyo Maru:* Ohmae, "Battle of Savo Island," p. 1269; *S.S.,* Vol. 49, 442; NWC Analysis, pp. 330–31. This ad hoc unit was drawn from the 5th Sasebo and 3d and 5th Kure Special Naval Landing Forces as well as the 81st Garrison Unit.

Page 87
Mikawa and staff analyze situation: Ohmae, "Battle of Savo Island," pp. 1269–70.

Pages 87–88
Mikawa sortie and encounter with *S-38:* NWC Analysis, pp. 47, 68–69; Ohmae, "Battle of Savo Island," p. 1270. Steve Birdsall, *Flying Buccaneers.* (Garden City, N.Y.: Doubleday, 1977), pp. 12–13 [hereafter Birdsall, *Flying Buchaneers*], reports that these B-17s represented a maximum effort strike by the 19th Bomb Group. Originally sixteen aircraft took off but only thirteen reached Rabaul. One was shot down, and the aircraft commander, Captain Harl Pease, received a posthumous award of the Medal of Honor.

Page 88
Efforts of Rabaul search planes: NWC Analysis, pp. 46–49.

Page 88
Searches by cruiser float planes: NWC Analysis, pp. 72–74; Ohmae, "Battle of Savo Island," p. 1271.

Pages 88–89
Information from *Aoba* plane: NWC Analysis, pp. 74–75; Ohmae, "Battle of Savo Island," p. 1271.

Page 89
Mikawa's battle plan: *S.S.,* Vol. 49, pp. 470–71. I have followed this version, which is more complete than that given in NWC Analysis, pp. 75–75.

Passage down New Georgia sound and preparations for battle: Ohmae, "Battle of Savo Island," pp. 1271–72; NWC Analysis, pp. 75–77.

Pages 89–90
Mikawa's order at 1842: Ohmae, "Battle of Savo Island," p. 1272. Slightly differing renditions of this order are given in NWC Analysis, p. 77, and Samuel Eliot Morison, *History of United States Naval Operations in World War II,* Vol. V, *The Struggle for Guadalcanal* (Boston: Atlantic Little, Brown, 1962), p. 22 [hereafter Morison, *Struggle for Guadalcanal*].

Page 90
Air search arrangements: Hepburn Report, p. 5; NWC Analysis, pp. 22–30, Table 2. The boundary line for air search between the theaters was defined precisely; the area to be covered by SOWESPAC was "the water areas southeast of the line Madang-Kapingamarang Islands (1° North, 154°45′ East) and northeast of the line Tagula Island–easternmost point of New Georgia (8°30′ South, 157°55′ East) thence along 158° East Longitude, paying particular attention to the entrances of the Coral Sea from the north and east."

Pages 90–92
Requests by Fletcher and Turner on air search arrangements: NWC Analysis, pp. 26, 53–54. The specific messages were CTF 61 to CTF 63 290857 Jul 42 and CTF 62 to CTF 63 070642 Aug 42.

Page 92
B-17 and *S-38* contact reports: NWC Analysis, pp. 54, 68, *S-38*'s message was contained in COMSOWESPAC to All TFs Pacific 071219 Aug 42, noted in Hepburn Report, p. 9.

Pages 92–93
Air search failure on August 8 in South and Southwest Pacific theaters: NWC Analysis, pp. 97–99. As Dyer, *Amphibians Came to Conquer,* points out p. 365, NWC Analysis places an "or" between the two heavy cruisers and two light cruisers. Dyer uses the version found in the Hepburn Report and COMSOPAC War Diary, and this account does likewise. Morison does not discuss the contents of this report.

Morison described the activities of the first Hudson pilot as follows (*Struggle for Guadalcanal,* p. 25):

> The pilot of this plane, instead of breaking radio silence to report as he had orders to do in an urgent case, or returning to base which he could have done in two hours, spent most of the afternoon completing his search mission, came down at Milne Bay, had his tea, and then reported the contact.

This comment, particularly the phase "had his tea," aroused the ire of the Australian official naval historian George Hermon Gill. According to Mr. Gill, the pilot in question, Sergeant (later Flight Lieutenant) W. J. Stutt of No. 23 Squadron, RAAF, returned to Milne Bay only two hours and sixteen minutes after sighting Mikawa, having attacked two submarines while completing his mission. A jeep picked up Sergeant Stutt and took him immediately to a debriefing, with no delay for any tea. *Royal Australian Navy 1942–1945* (Canberra: Australian War Memorial, 1968), p. 134.

Page 93
Delays in transmitting sighting reports: NWC Analysis, pp. 100–3. When the Hudsons returned to their base at Fall River on New Guinea, their reports were transmitted to Port Moresby and from there to Townsville, Australia (Headquarters, North East Area). Had the importance of the dispatches been recognized at Townsville, they could have been passed directly to Task Force 63 by a special radio link. However, this was not done and instead the messages were sent to Brisbane by RAAF land line to Commander Allied Air Forces SWPAC Area. From there they went by hand to COMSOWESPAC Headquarters, where they were forwarded over Navy land line to Canberra at 080717 (1817 local) and broadcast on Canberra BELLS at 080737 (1837 local). From Canberra they were also sent to Pearl Harbor and were broadcast on FOX at 080743 (1843 local). Turner received them at 1843 and 1845 and Crutchley at 1837 and 1843. FOX and BELLS were the names for the "blind" radio broadcasts from Pearl Harbor and Canberra respectively of orders and information. No receipt from the addressees was required.

Page 93
Fletcher's decision to withdraw: Ibid., pp. 91–95. Fletcher's signal to Noyes about 1630 read: "In view of possibility of torpedo plane attack and reduction in our present fighter strength, I intend to recommend immediate withdrawal of carriers. Do you agree?" CTF 63 Visual Dispatch to CTF 61 080425 Aug 42. Note this message contains no reference to fuel situation. Noyes agreed fifty minutes later.

Page 93
Fletcher's signal to Ghormley: NWC Analysis, p. 92. The message was CTF 61 to COMSOPAC 080707 Aug 42.

Pages 93–94
Challenges to Fletcher's decision to withdraw: These questions are distillations of comments found in NWC Analysis, pp. 92–94, and Morison, *Struggle for Guadalcanal,* pp. 27–28. According to NWC Analysis, p. 93, the reason for Fletcher's belief that he

had lost twenty-one fighters is unclear, since the actual losses totaled only sixteen from all causes, thus leaving him with eighty-three Wildcats.

Page 94
The oil situation in TF 63: NWC Analysis, pp. 93–94, and Dyer. *Amphibians Came to Conquer,* pp. 387–90. A "sea lawyer" might argue that the text of Fletcher's message to Ghormley does not explicitly list oil as a reason for the retirement, but the position and phrasing of the reference to fuel was subject to this interpretation. Whether this was Fletcher's intention is unclear. He did not offer the fuel situation as a reason to retire to Noyes, but did include a request for Noyes's opinion on the wisdom of operating in the same area on the 9th, thus implying that there was sufficient oil on hand for that course of action. On the other hand, the War Diary of Task Force 16 for August 8 contains an entry timed 2330 listing the reasons for the request to withdraw by Fletcher as including the danger of enemy air attack, the reduction in fighter strength, and a "critical fuel situation."

Page 94
Fletcher's response to his critics: Dyer, *Amphibians Came to Conquer,* pp. 391–92; NWC Analysis, p. 94.

Page 95
Warnings of enemy submarines: Hepburn Report, p. 52, notes that on August 7 and 8 at least ten reports were received of submarines in the vicinity or headed to Guadalcanal, for example, CINCPAC 062336 Aug 42, COMSOPAC 071142 Aug 42, and COMSOWESPAC 071930 Aug 42, all of which are contained in Hepburn Report, pp. 8–9.

Submarine alerts and their effect: Hepburn Report, p. 9, CTF 62 to TF 62 080710(-11) Aug 42, and ORANGE BASE 081207(-11) Aug 42. Crutchley noted in his memorandum to Admiral Hepburn that the submarine threat kept his float planes on antisubmarine patrol.

Radio intelligence available and not available to Turner on August 8: SRH-012, Vol. III, pp. 512–13, notes that CINCPAC Summary No. 40 of 060600 Aug 42 showed *Chokai* and *Aoba* at sea and reminded recipients that *Chokai* was the flagship of the 8th Fleet, but that the Commander of the 8th Fleet was still believed to be ashore at Rabaul. Ibid., p. 529, shows CINCPAC Summary No. 26 of 061400 Aug 42 noted *Chokai* at sea, as was

Commander Crudiv 6, who was correctly placed aboard *Aoba*. Ibid., pp. 544–45, CINCPAC Bulletin No. 143, 060245 Aug 42, located Crudiv 6 in the Rabaul area, Crudiv 18 in the Solomons, and *Chokai* in the New Britain area. Ibid., p. 591, CINCPAC Summary No. 28 of 091400 Aug 42, warned that the Commander of the 8th Fleet had put to sea. However, 091400 was 0100(-11), August 10 off Guadalcanal—i.e., after the battle.

A recent book by Edwin T. Layton, with John Costello and Roger Pineau, *And I Was There*, p. 459, claims Turner refused an offer of a special radio intelligence unit for his flagship that might have intercepted messages from Mikawa's float planes betraying Japanese intentions. The example Layton cites appears to be the *Aoba* plane in the morning of August 8, but this plane did not radio a report. The aircraft launched after dark did use their radios, but of course it is speculative to assume that a tactical radio intelligence unit would necessarily have intercepted and read these messages. It may also be relevant to bear in mind that Layton was one of the legion of officers who detested Turner.

Page 95
McCain's warning message on search failures: CTF 63 to CTF 61, 62 081233 Aug 42, in Hepburn Report, p. 10. There is no report by Admiral McCain covering the activities of TF 63 during this period. NWC Analysis, p. 94.

Pages 95–96
Turner's reasoning from the contact reports: Dyer, *Amphibians Came to Conquer*, pp. 364–74; NWC Analysis, p. 87, CTF 62 to COMAIRSOPAC 081055 Aug 42.

Page 96
Turner accused of doing nothing in the face of news of Mikawa's approach: This criticism is one of the themes of Richard F. Newcomb, *Savo: The Incredible Naval Debacle off Guadalcanal* (New York: Holt, Rinehart & Winston, 1961), pp. 82, 86 [hereafter Newcomb, *Savo: The Incredible Naval Debacle off Guadalcanal*]. In the carrier task force, correspondent Clark Lee was told that a small Japanese cruiser-destroyer force had been spotted and to stand by for flying as it had not been decided whether to attack it by air or surface ships. This suggests others reached different conclusions than Turner did on the sighting reports, but does not establish that

Turner's judgment was poor. Clark Lee, *They Call It Pacific* (New York: Viking, 1943), p. 334 (hereafter Lee, *They Call It Pacific*).

Page 96
Turner criticized for ignoring enemy capabilities: This criticism is essentially that of NWC Analysis, p. 90, and Morison, *Struggle for Guadalcanal*, p. 63. Turner's response is in Dyer, *Amphibians Came to Conquer*, pp. 372–74. Turner stated his real error was one of judgment in trusting the description of the composition of the Japanese force in the first contact report, i.e., the two "seaplane tenders."

Pages 96–97
Turner calls conference and Crutchley's and Bode's actions: NWC Analysis, pp. 87–88. Morison, *Struggle for Guadalcanal*, p. 63, criticizes the decision to call the conference, but NWC Analysis, p. 90, Hepburn Report, para. 84, and Dyer, *Amphibians Came to Conquer*, p. 373, call it sound, and this writer agrees.

Page 97
Conference of Turner, Vandegrift, and Crutchley: Vandegrift and Asprey, *Once a Marine*, p. 129; NWC Analysis, pp. 89–90; Final Report, Phase II, p. 13.

Page 97
Crutchley reboards *Australia:* NWC Analysis, pp. 148–49. Crutchley's reasons for his conduct are from "Remarks by CTG 62.6, Night Action off Savo Island, August 9, 1942, to CTF 62. August 11, 1942" in the Hepburn Report file. NWC Analysis observes that this decision probably reflects the debilitating effects of fatigue on Crutchley.

Geography of Guadalcanal-Tulagi water areas: NWC Analysis, p. 3.

Page 98
Intelligence on Japanese forces: Commander Task Force 62 OP-PLAN A3-42, Annex Easy, July 30, 1942. Dyer, *Amphibians Came to Conquer*, p. 316, discusses the reports of the presence of midget submarines in the Solomons.

Pages 98–99
Disposition of screening groups: Crutchley explained the rationale for his dispositions in two memoranda for Admiral Hepburn that may be found in Annex B of the Hepburn Report. Crutchley's battle plan, such as it was, is contained in "CTG 62.6 Special Instructions to Screening Group and Vessels

Temporarily Assigned August 1942." Dyer, *Amphibians Came to Conquer,* pp. 374–78, includes a cogent defense of the dispositions of the cruisers. NWC Analysis, pp. 54–61, is critical of the division of the screen and proposed an alternative of having all cruisers in a single column about 5 miles southeast of Savo, normal (90 degrees) to a line drawn at 125 degrees true from Savo. This would have enabled the Allied cruisers (a) to cross the T of an approaching enemy force; (b) to avoid torpedoes by simple ship's turns; (c) to avoid control problems of a mixed-nationality formation; and (d) to allow maximum concentration of force in a minimum of time against an enemy approaching from the west.

Page 99
Employment of picket destroyers: NWC Analysis, pp. 58–59; Dyer, *Amphibians Came to Conquer,* pp. 378–81. Both agree the picket line should have contained four destroyers, and NWC Analysis says they should have been spaced 5 miles apart.

Page 99
Disposition of flag officers: Dyer, *Amphibians Came to Conquer,* pp. 377–78, quoting from Admiral Turner's letter of August 20, 1950, to DCNO (Admin), Subject: Comments on Morison's Vol. V, pp. 10–11. Turner also expressed his belief that to transfer Scott to *Vincennes* would have impaired Scott's effectiveness because of the sudden shift to a new flagship. Another important reason Turner gave, which gives insight into thinking among naval officers in general, is that Riefkohl and Scott were Naval Academy classmates and Scott, until his recent promotion, had been the junior. Turner was of the opinion that to have replaced Riefkohl, who "was considered a good officer and apparently performing satisfactorily," on his own ship with Scott would have been "a heavy blow to general morale, and would have gone far toward destroying all prospects of Riefkohl's future usefulness and chances of promotion."

Page 100
Japanese Task organization: *S.S.,* Vol. 49, Table 2, "Principal Officers Related to Southeast Area Operations."

Pages 100–101
Allied Task organization: Morison, *Coral Sea, Midway and Submarine Actions,* pp. 270–74.

Page 101
Allied warship particulars: The principal sources are the Navies of the Second World

War Series, H. T. Lenton, *American Battleships, Carriers and Cruisers* (Garden City, N.Y.: Doubleday, 1968), pp. 52–53, 56–57, 64–65 [hereafter Lenton, *American Battleships, Carriers and Cruisers*], H. T. Lenton, *American Fleet and Escort Destroyers,* Vol. I (London: MacDonald, 1971), pp. 61–63 [hereafter Lenton, *American Fleet and Escort Destroyers*]; and H. T. Lenton, *British Cruisers* (Garden City, N.Y.: Doubleday, 1973), pp. 51–59, 86–88. Also important is Alan Raven and John Roberts, *Man of War 1, County Class Cruisers* (Brooklyn, N.Y.: R.S.V. Publishing, 1978), pp. 13–14, 34, for armament of *Australia* and *Canberra.*

Japanese warship particulars: Hansgeorg Jentschura, Dieter Jung, and Peter Mickel, *Warships of the Imperial Japanese Navy, 1869–1945,* translated by Anthony Preston and J. D. Brown (Annapolis, Md.: Naval Institute Press, 1977), pp. 79–81, 83–84, 105, 142–43 [hereafter Jentschura, Jung, and Mickel, *Warships of the Imperial Japanese Navy, 1869–1945*]; Lacroix, "Development of the 'A Class' Cruisers in the Imperial Japanese Navy," *Warship International* No. 4, 1981, pp. 338, 361–62.

Page 102
Weather patterns: NWC Analysis, pp. 3–4.

Message from 25th Air Flotilla and Striking Force formation: Ibid., pp. 77–78, 106; *S.S.,* Vol. 49, pp. 463–64.

Page 103
Sighting of *Blue* and reaction: NWC Analysis, pp. 107–8.

Failure of radar: Ibid., p. 107. According to a report prepared much later in the campaign and addressing the operation of SG radar, a critical problem in radar operation in this era was maintaining a constant frequency tuning between the transmitter and receiver. When these were out of adjustment, performance could fall off as much as 50 percent. This problem was presumably even more troublesome with the earlier SC radars such as those in use at the Battle of Savo Island. It may also be probable that the shock of a ship's own gunfire could slip the radar transmitter and receiver out of adjustment, and this may account for the many stories of targets gradually disappearing from radar screens as if they were sinking. Commander in Chief Pacific Fleet, Pac-90-wb, A16-3/SOL, Serial 00599, 9 March 1943, Subject: Solomons Islands Campaign . . . , p. 11, para. 50.

Page 103
Japanese night-fighting binoculars: Lacroix, "Development of the 'A Class' Cruisers in the Imperial Japanese Navy," No. 4, 1981, p. 333. Lacroix reports the Japanese developed binoculars of 12cm (magnification 20), 15cm (magnification 25), and 18cm (magnification 25).

Pages 103–4
Mikawa maneuvers, *Yunagi* separation: Ibid., pp. 108–9, 117; *S.S.,* Vol. 49, p. 481, gives Lieutenant Seiichi's account. Ohmae, "Battle of Savo Island," p. 1273, gives a differing version of the reasons for *Yunagi's* movements cited in the footnote.

Page 104
Encounter with *Jarvis, Chokai* opens fire: NWC Analysis, pp. 114–18, 122; Ohmae, "Battle of Savo Island," p. 1295. COMAMFORSOPAC to COMSOPACFOR 101305 Aug 42, COMSOPAC War Diary 12 Aug 42, p. 27, says *Jarvis* was proceeding alone without signal apparatus. NWC Analysis, p. 115, points out that the sighting of *Vincennes* at that incredible range may have been false, but the direction was correct.

Page 104
Ralph Talbot's warning: NWC Analysis, p. 90. Crutchley reported that neither *Australia* nor *Canberra* had a TBS voice radio. Lieutenant Commander E. W. Irish, *Chicago's* navigator, stated his ship had no TBS in his interview with Admiral Hepburn (Hepburn Report, Annex I, p. 3), nor does that vessel's action report make any mention of TBS messages.

Pages 104–5
Canberra participation: H.M.A.S. *Canberra,* Report of Commander J. A. Walsh, RAN, Executive Officer, *Canberra,* 12 August 1942, to Rear Admiral Commanding Task Force 44, 12 August 1942, Subject: Loss of H.M.A.S. *Canberra,* and attachments including report of Lt. Cdr. E.J.D. Wright, RAN, Principal Control Officer, *Canberra* [hereafter *Canberra* 12 Aug 42]; NWC Analysis, pp. 118–20, 127–29; Alan Payne, *HMAS Canberra* (Naval Historical Society of Australia, 1973), pp. 82–95, 103–6 [hereafter Payne, *HMAS Canberra*]. The last of these states one rating fired one 8-inch shell during the battle, and Payne's account is very insistent that a torpedo struck *Canberra.*

Pages 105–6
Chicago's participation: NWC Analysis, pp. 120–23, 129–33, 163, 203–6; U.S.S. *Chicago,*

Serial 099, August 13, 1942. Subject: Action Against Enemy Forces Aug. 9, 1942, Guadalcanal-Tulagi Area—Report of. The failure of *Chicago* to report her engagement seems to be well established; however. Admiral Scott's report contains the following strange entry:

> The *Chicago* has reported that at 0115 she, *Canberra, Patterson,* and *Bagley* were engaged in "intermittent gunfire at targets not definitely established." Commander Task Group 62.4, FE24/A16-3, Serial 001, August 13, 1942, Subject: Report of action, Tulagi-Guadalcanal 6-10 August, 1942, p. 6.

Scott's report then goes on to note this action was "neither observed or heard in the *San Juan*" and that his task unit reversed course at the southern end of its patrol line at *0135.* In view of the fact that gunfire broke out about 0143, there is something obviously askew about this portion of Scott's report, but what it is remains mysterious.

Page 106
Bagley's participation: NWC Analysis, pp. 133–35; U.S.S. *Bagley,* Serial 015, August 12, 1942, Subject: Preliminary Report—Night Action Aug. 9, 1942, and Serial 016, August 13, 1942. Night Engagement August 9, 1942, Tulagi-Guadalcanal Area.

Page 107
Patterson's participation: U.S.S. *Patterson,* Serial 001, August 13, 1942, Subject: Engagement with Enemy (Japanese) Surface Ships Night Aug. 8–9 in Savo-Guadalcanal-Tulagi Island Group Solomons; NWC Analysis, pp. 122, 135, 207–9.

Page 107
Split in Japanese formation: NWC Analysis, pp. 120, 162–65. The conclusion reached by NWC Analysis is that the final order of the Western Group of Japanese cruisers was *Yubari, Tenryu,* and *Furutaka, S.S.,* Vol. 49, pp. 480–481, 485, differs in placing them in the order *Yubari, Furutaka,* and *Tenryu,* but this writer finds NWC Analysis more persuasive.

Page 108
Maneuvers of Northern Group and Captain Riefkohl's decisions: NWC Analysis, pp. 138–45.

Page 109
Japanese open fire and gunnery technique: NWC Analysis, pp. 151–56.

Observations of *Kako*'s gunnery officer, Lieutenant Haruyoshi Nishimura: *S.S.,* Vol. 49, p. 489.

Ohmae observations: Ohmae, "Battle of Savo Island," p. 1275.

Chokai's maneuvers: NWC Analysis, p. 158, 215, *S.S.,* Vol. 49. p. 482, insists *Chokai* never lost the lead of the Eastern Group, but NWC Analysis, pp. 161–239, has a mass of convincing evidence that she did.

Pages 110–11
Astoria's mission to Japan: Dyer, *Amphibians Came to Conquer,* pp. 140–47. Poem by Bansui Doi is at p. 355.

Pages 110–11
Astoria's participation: NWC Analysis, pp. 187–95; U.S.S. *Astoria,* CA37/A16-3, Serial 00500, Subject: Battle of SAVO Island—Action Cruisers Task Group 62.3, early morning August 9, 1942—loss of U.S.S. *Astoria,* and particularly enclosures (D), (E), (G), and (H) [hereafter *Astoria* Serial 00500]. The text gives only a sketch of the confusion of *Astoria*'s bridge watch this night.

Pages 111–13
Quincy participation: U.S.S. *Quincy,* Serial CA39/A16-3/(004)/hmc, August 16, 1942, Subject: Report of Engagement the morning of August 9, 1942, off Guadalcanal Island in which the U.S.S. *Quincy* participated (this report was prepared by Lieutenant Commander Harry B. Heneberger, the senior surviving officer); NWC Analysis, pp. 143–44, 152–53, 155–60, 164–65, 178–187, 195–98, 215–20, 235–248, 290–91.

"With great spirit": Ohmae, "Battle of Savo Island," p. 1275.

Statement of Lieutenant Commander John D. Andrews: Enclosure (C), *Quincy* Action Report.

Pages 113–14
Vincennes participation: *Vincennes* Serial 0021 and Serial 0022. August 16, 1942, Subject: Report of Action Between U.S.S. *Vincennes* and Japanese Heavy Cruisers Near Savo Island on Night of 8–9 August 1942; NWC Analysis, pp. 152–59, 171–78, 219, 223–25, 229–35, 289–90. There is a discrepancy between the action report and NWC Analysis in that the former says the ship's after antiaircraft director was blown overboard and the latter says the after main battery director was blown overboard. The text follows the action report, as it is almost inconceivable that the main battery director could have been blown overboard in view of the ship's structure while the loss of the antiaircraft director is quite plausible.

Page 114
Wilson participation: U.S.S. *Wilson,* Serial 008, August 20, 1942, Subject: Action Against Enemy Surface Ships off Savo Island Night of August 8–9, 1942; NWC Analysis, pp. 157, 200–3, 219, 224–25, 251–52, 295–97.

Helm's participation: U.S.S. *Helm,* DD388/A16-3, Serial 125, August 12, 1942. Subject: Night Engagement off Savo Island—Preliminary Report of; NWC Analysis, 155–56, 198–200, 249–50, 295–97.

Pages 114–15
Ralph Talbot's participation: U.S.S. *Ralph Talbot,* A16-3/DD390/03, August 11, 1942, Subject: Preliminary Report of Action, August 8–9, 1942; NWC Analysis, 226–27, 257–59, 264, 299–301. Paul S. Dull, *A Battle History of the Imperial Japanese Navy (1941–1945)* (Annapolis, Md.: Naval Institute Press, 1978), p. 202 [hereafter Dull, *Battle History of the Imperial Japanese Navy*], comments that if *Ralph Talbot* contributed nothing else, she convinced Mikawa of the wisdom of withdrawal, as he could not be certain how many other Allied vessels might still be present.

Page 115
Yunagi's participation: NWC Analysis, pp. 166–67.

Pages 115–16
Mikawa's decision to retire: Ibid., pp. 215–16, 220–223; *S.S.,* Vol. 49, pp. 490–92; Ohmae, "Battle of Savo Island," p. 1276. NWC Analysis points out that this decision was foreshadowed on three occasions. Mikawa's original battle plan stated his intent to be 120 miles from Savo at daybreak, which left little time to annihilate all Allied shipping off Guadalcanal and Tulagi. Twice during the action he declined opportunities to pounce on the transports: once at 0145 after he brushed past the Southern Group, and again at 0200 after he disabled the Northern Group.

Page 116
Withdrawal of striking force and damage assessment: NWC Analysis, pp. 266–68; Ohmae, "Battle of Savo Island," p. 1276; Lacroix. "Development of the 'A Class' Cruisers in the imperial Japanese Navy," No. 3, 1983, p. 239. *S.S.,* Vol. 49, p. 494, gives dam-

age to *Chokai* and notes other hits on Japanese ships were duds.

Page 116
Japanese release news of action and loss of *Kako:* NWC Analysis, pp. 268–70, 337; *S.S.,* Vol. 49, p. 494; Ohmae, "Battle of Savo Island," p. 1277. The time of *Kako*'s torpedoing vary slightly. NWC Analysis gives 0908, *S.S.* gives 0910, and Ohmae says 0907. Japanese news releases are from *New York Times,* August 9, 1942, p. 1., col. 8, and August 10, 1942, p. 48.

Page 117
Table of Japanese casualties: Ohmae, "Battle of Savo Island," p. 1277, supplemented by NWC Analysis, p. 163, which gives higher casualties in *Tenryu,* and Dull, *Battle History of the Imperial Japanese Navy,* p. 203, which gives figures for *Kako*'s losses from the ship's action report. Lacroix, "Development of the 'A Class' Cruisers in the Imperial Japanese Navy," *Warship International* No. 3, 1983, p. 237, gives losses on *Kako* as seventy killed and fourteen wounded and says some of survivors were rescued on August 11 by destroyer *Uzuki.*

Pages 117–18
Loss of *Canberra:* NWC Analysis, pp. 282–85, 287–89, and *Canberra* 12 Aug 42, pp. 2–3 and attachments.

"death warrant": Morison, *Struggle for Guadalcanal,* p. 54.

Page 118
Loss of *Astoria:* NWC Analysis, pp. 291–95; *Astoria* Serial 00500, p. 18 plus enclosures.

"sat dumbly expectant . . .": Clifford Merrill Drury, Captain USNR, *The History of the Chaplin Corps, United States Navy,* Vol. II, *1939–49* (Washington, D.C.: U.S. Government Printing Office), p. 173.

Page 119
Fletcher's retirement: NWC Analysis, pp. 323–27; Dyer, *Amphibians Came to Conquer,* p. 395.

Page 119
Turner's decisions: NWC Analysis, pp. 313–22; War Diary, Amphibious Force South Pacific, 9 Aug. Turner's signal was CTF 62 to CTF 61 081941 Aug 42, and Fletcher's message to Ghormley was CTF 61 to COMSOPAC 090315 Aug 42.

Page 120
Loss of *Jarvis:* NWC Analysis, pp. 272–78, 298; *S.S.,* Vol. 49, pp. 460–61. These accounts differ somewhat, as *S.S.* says *Jarvis* was seen by two planes, one of which reported her as a large destroyer and the other as an *Achilles* Class cruiser. This latter mistaken identification probably was due to her distinctive trunked funnel. Morison discovered the story of *Jarvis*'s loss, and how he did it is told in Shaw, "Jarvis: Destroyer That Vanished." Shaw was an assistant to Morison. Of course there are no American accounts of the end of *Jarvis* and her crew. The comments in the text on the probable fate of any survivors are amply supported by later events in the campaign.

Page 120
Unloading on August 9: Final Report, Phase II, p. 13.

Vandegrift and Asprey, *Once a Marine,* p. 131, acknowledges the outstanding work of the Tulagi Transport Group transports in discharging cargo on August 9, 1942.

Pages 120–21
Assessment of Mikawa's victory: Ohmae, "Battle of Savo Island," pp. 1270, 1278. Ohmae incorporates a separate statement from Mikawa.

Yamamoto's displeasure with Mikawa: *S.S.,* Vol. 49, pp. 491–92.

Ohmae's opinion on role of decisive battle doctrine: Ohmae, "Battle of Savo Island," p. 1277.

Page 121
Allied crew losses: Bureau of Personnel Final Report of World War II Casualties; and Payne, *HMAS Canberra,* which shows her losses included one U.S. Navy officer. Losses among the U.S. Marine detachments for the *Astoria, Vincennes,* and *Quincy* are from the respective muster rolls for August 1942 at the Marine Corps Historical Center. It should be noted that for bureaucratic reasons the Navy's World War II master casualty report does not mention members of ship complements who were marines. Accordingly, to arrive at total casualties for the various naval battles around Guadalcanal the researcher must look at both Navy and Marine Corps records. Shaw, "Jarvis: Destroyer That Vanished," indicates 246 men were lost in *Jarvis,* but the Bureau of Personnel total is 233 based upon subtraction of the fifteen men killed or died of wounds because of the initial aerial torpedo hit on August 8. Morison, *Struggle for Guadalcanal,* p. 63, note 52, gives a total of 1,024 killed.

Pages 121–22
News of Battle of Savo Island: The first official hint of the battle to the American people was contained in the statement of Admiral King on August 10, 1942, that acknowledged the loss of one unnamed U.S. cruiser, *New York Times*, August 11, 1942, p. 1, col. 8. Loss of *Canberra* was made public on August 20 and appeared in the *New York Times* of that date. The withholding of information from U.S. Army and Army Air Force officers is noted by Thomas B. Buell in *Master of Seapower*, pp. 223–24. Navy Department Communiqué Number 147, October 12, 1942, revealed the loss of three U.S. cruisers at Savo, the day before the news of the victory at Cape Esperance was announced in Communiqué Number 149 of October 13, 1943 (*New York Times* of October 13 and 14 respectively). This crude effort at news management provoked comment in the *Times* of October 15, 1942, in an editorial entitled "War Information," p. 22, that stated that the sixty-five-day delay in release of news of the losses "will lead many persons to conclude, however unjustly, that bad news was held up in this case until there was good news to offset it."

Pages 122–23
Orders for inquiry by Admiral Hepburn and conduct of investigation: Memorandum for Admiral, Subject Admiral Hepburn's report on the loss of the U.S.S. *Vincennes*, U.S.S. *Quincy*, U.S.S. *Astoria*, H.M.A.S. *Canberra*, August 9, 1942, near Savo Island—Comment Upon, COMINCH File July 31, 1943, by Captain G. L. Russell, para. 4 [hereafter Russell Memorandum].

Death of Captain Bode: Newcomb, *Savo: The Incredible Naval Debacle off Guadalcanal*, p. 240.

Conclusions of Admiral Hepburn: Hepburn Report, pp. 52–54, paras. 139–144.

Page 123
Nimitz's analysis: Commander in Chief, United States Pacific Fleet, CINCPAC File No. Pac-11-Sn, A17, Serial 00888, Subject: Report of informal inquiry into the circumstances attending the loss of U.S.S. *Vincennes . . .* , para. 6.

Page 123
Captain Russell's analysis: Russell Memorandum, pp. 3–4.

Admiral Turner's final thoughts: These are from an undated memorandum from COMAMPHIBFORSOPAC to CINCPAC,

Subject: Comment on Hepburn Report, p. 10, associated with the Hepburn Report, that contains Turner's observations on Admiral Hepburn's analysis.

CHAPTER 5

Page 124
"Singly or in pairs . . .": Vandegrift and Asprey, *Once a Marine*, pp. 132.

Page 125
Vandegrift and Thomas briefings: Final Report, Phase II, p. 13, Phase III, p. 11; Vandegrift and Asprey, *Once a Marine*, pp. 132–33.

Pages 125–26
Organization of defenses: Final Report, Phase III, pp. 1–2, 5, 10, Annex A; 3d Defense Battalion—Report of Operations, Guadalcanal, pp. 1–4, Enclosure A, p. 7, Box 6, File A32-1 [hereafter 3d Defense Battalion—Report of Operations, Guadalcanal]; Lt. Col. K. W. Benner, interview, Box 6, File A32-2; Griffith, *Battle of Guadalcanal*, pp. 68–69. The details on defense battalion organization are from the D-155 Tables of Organization, MCHC.

Strength of Marine units on Guadalcanal and Tulagi: COMAMPHIBFORSOPAC Serial 0041 15 Aug 42. This writer found no precise statement in Marine records as to how many men remained after Turner's withdrawal.

Page 126–27
Movement and inventory of supplies: Final Report, Phase II, Annex G, pp. 3, 7–9; Phase III, pp. 3–4; Griffith, *Battle of Guadalcanal*, p. 71. There are conflicting data over amount of rations landed before the departure of the transports and the quantity of food captured on Guadalcanal. The extremes are in Final Report, Phase III, which says thirty days, but COMSOPAC to COMINCH 161146 Aug 42, Grey Book, p. 650, says only three days of food were landed. Ghormley's source for this information should have been Turner, but in his COMSOPAC to CINCPAC 131400 Aug 42, COMSOPAC War Diary 14 Aug 42, Ghormley gave figures for rations landed amounting to a twenty-six-day supply on Guadalcanal and four on Tulagi. Merillat, *Island*, pp. 54–55, notes that on August 13, Vandegrift reported there was food on hand for only ten days at two meals per day, and COMSOPAC War Diary 14 Aug 42, p. 36, contains COMGEN GUADALCANAL to COMAMPHIBFOR 131015 that declares

the marines had ten days of rations, including captured supplies. Calculating backward from this message, this would mean about seventeen days of food was on hand when Turner withdrew. A letter from Maj. Harry S. Connors to CMC 14 Feb 49 indicated that his unit (Company E, 2d Battalion, 5th Marines) on Tulagi landed with only three days' rations and received nothing but captured rice and a single 1-gallon can of tomatoes between August 7 and August 21. At the far end of the scale, the official Marine Corps account published in 1958 says there were thirty-seven days of food on hand when Turner departed (Hough, Ludwig, and Shaw, *Pearl Harbor to Guadalcanal,* p. 260).

Page 127

Completion of airfield: RDO Tulagi to RDO Noumea 171000 Aug 42, COMSOPAC War Diary 17 Aug 42, p. 51; Final Report, Phase III, pp. 2–3; 1st Engineer Battalion, Engineer Activities Guadalcanal, pp. 2–4, Box 6, File A34.5-1 [hereafter Engineer Activities Guadalcanal]; Merillat, *Island,* p. 65; Griffith, *Battle of Guadalcanal,* pp. 71; Vandegrift and Asprey, *Once a Marine,* p. 133 (for nickname "Toonerville Trolleys"). Although the heavy equipment of the Engineer battalion was not landed, one R-4 angle-bladed bulldozer property of the Pioneer battalion did get ashore, where it performed "yeoman" service. However, the bulldozer was occupied with other duties during completion of the airfield. Ltr Lt. Col. Henry H. Crockett to CMC 10 Jan 49; ltr Lt. Col. Robert G. Ballance to CMC 12 Feb 49.

Page 127

Naming Henderson Field: The name was proposed by Major Kenneth Weir, the division aviation officer (Thomas intvw, pp. 312–13).

Arrival of Lieutenant Simpson's PBY: Record of Events, 1st Marine Division, August 12, 1942, Box 4, File A7-5.5 [hereafter 1st Mar Div Record of Events]. By December 1, 1942, 2,879 wounded had been evacuated by air, Final Report, Phase V, Annex T (medical).

Pages 127–28

Leisure activities and comic episodes: Griffith, *Battle of Guadalcanal,* pp. 71–72; Cates, "My First"; Merillat, *Island,* pp. 51–52; Gen. Edwin A. Pollack, interview, 14 Apr 73 (Oral History Collection, Marine Corps Historical Center), pp. 127–28 [hereafter Pollack intvw]. Passwords are from the lists contained in the 1st Marine Division D-2 Journal, Vols. I and II, Box 5, Files A7-7, A7-8 [hereafter 1st Mar Div D-2 Jnl].

Pages 128–29

Early air raids: 1st Mar Div Record of Events 9–19 Aug 42; Final Report, Phase III, pp. 2, 5; *S.S.,* Vol. 49 p. 511; Vandegrift and Asprey, *Once a Marine,* p. 135; Engineer Activities Guadalcanal, p. 4; 3d Defense Battalion—Report of Operations, Guadalcanal; Thomas intvw, p. 345.

Pages 129–30

Interception of landing craft moving from Guadalcanal to Tulagi: Tregaskis, *Guadalcanal Diary,* pp. 74–77; Merillat, *Guadalcanal Remembered,* pp. 80–84. Tregaskis and Merillat were riding in the boats; Griffith, *Battle of Guadalcanal,* pp. 72–73, recounts Griffith's personal witnessing of the incident; 2d Bn, 5th Mar Record of Events 12 Aug 42 identifies the firing battery; 1st Mar Div Record of Events 13–18 Aug 42 and Cates, "My First," describe experiences with submarine shellings.

Page 130

Goettge's patrol: Final Report, Phase III, pp. 5–6, Annex A, pp. 3–5; Vandegrift and Asprey, *Once a Marine,* p. 136; Merillat, *Island,* p. 60; 5th Mar Record of Events 13 Aug 42; Tregaskis, *Guadalcanal Diary,* p. 96; McMillan, *Old Breed,* pp. 52–53 (interview with Sergeant Charles C. Arndt, one of the survivors); ltr Col. William J. Whaling to CMC 26 Jan 49 (indicates Whaling found shallow graves in the area whose number matched the total of missing men in the patrol; see also Thomas intvw, pp. 321–23); Zimmerman, "Guadalcanal Campaign," p. 60, note 16 (indicates a piece of clothing with Goettge's name on it was found). The willingness of Japanese prisoners to talk freely and accurately is noted in Zimmerman, "Guadalcanal Campaign," p. 59, note 11, and Miller, *Guadalcanal: The First Offensive,* p. 310. *S.S.,* Vol. 49, p. 530–31, mentions a report of an engagement fitting the circumstances of the Goettge patrol, but has no details.

Pages 130–31

Lieutenant Corry's background: Van Der Rhoer, *Deadly Magic,* pp. 52–53, 110–12. It is extremely doubtful that Vandegrift or Goettge knew of Corry's work in radio intelligence.

Page 131

Clemens and his scouts: 1st Mar Div Record of Events 15 Aug 42; Clemens MS., pp. 138,

141–42, 144, 170, and "Notes on the Guadalcanal Campaign," Comment file, Zimmerman, "Guadalcanal Campaign," MCHC for details on Clemens's arrival and his scout system.

Page 131
Arrival of first APDs: COMSOPAC to CTF 63, COMTRANSDIV 12 120216 Aug 42, Grey Book, p. 646; War Diary, Task Force 62, 15 August 1942; MAG-23, Record of Events for Period 20 August to 16 October 1942, 20 Aug 42, MCHC [hereafter MAG-23 Record of Events]; ltr Col. Charles H. Hayes to CMC 8 Feb 49 (for loading of APDs based upon Hayes's contemporary notes). George Polk performed excellent service on Guadalcanal. After the war he was a correspondent for CBS; he was murdered under mysterious circumstances in Greece in 1948.

Page 131
Arrival of first Japanese reinforcements and situation of original garrison: *S.S.*, Vol. 49, pp. 300, 302.

Pages 131–32
First bombardment of marines on Guadalcanal: 1st Mar Div Record of Events 18–19 Aug 42.

Pages 132–33
First action on the Mantanikau: Final Report, Phase III, pp. 7–8; 5th Mar Record of Events 18–19 Aug 42; Merillat, *Island,* pp. 61–64; *S.S.,* Vol. 49, p. 303. The description of the activities of Company L is based principally upon ltr Lt. Col. Lyman D. Spurlock to CMC 17 Dec 48. Griffith, *Battle of Guadalcanal,* p. 76, contains an excellent analysis. The executive officer of Company L killed in this action, Lieutenant George Mead, was the son of George Mead, founder and owner of the giant Mead Paper Corporation. The younger Mead was a friend of John F. Kennedy, the future President, who visited Mead's grave when he arrived on Guadalcanal in 1943. Mead's obituary, *New York Times,* September 25, 1942, and Joan and Clay Blair, *The Search for JFK* (New York: Berkley, 1976), pp. 99, 173–74.

Page 134
Ghormley's situation and initial directives: COMSOPAC TO CTF 61, 62, 63 090750 Aug 42, Grey Book, p. 640; COMSOPAC to CINCPAC 090830 Aug 42, Grey Book, p. 641; Ghormley, "Tide Turns," p. 104.

Ghormley warns of counterattack and requests for submarine and air support: COM-

SOPAC to TF 62, info COMGEN 1st MARDIV 090950 Aug 42, Grey Book, p. 640; COMSOPAC to COMSOWESPAC 101006 Aug 42. Grey Book, p. 642; COMSOPAC to COMSOWESPAC 121056 Aug 42, Grey Book, p. 647; Ghormley, "Tide Turns," p. 97; CINCPAC Daily Summary 14 Aug 42, Grey Book, p. 825. Commander in Chief, U.S. Pacific Fleet, Pac-9C-wb, A16-3/SOL, Serial 03102, Subject: Solomons Islands Campaign—Action of August 23–25, pp. 15–16, para. 64 [hereafter CINCPAC Serial 03102], indicates Nimitz believed his submarines were more profitably employed at enemy terminals and "focal points," rather than in direct support of the fleet, or by inference of the marines on Guadalcanal. Few marines would have agreed, but the statistics bore out Nimitz's judgment.

Ghormley's orders and initial messages from Vandegrift: COMSOPAC to CTF 61 110206 Aug 42, Grey Book, p. 645. Vandegrift's first message is recorded as COMSOPAC 102230 Aug 42, Grey Book, p. 644, and his request for an additional regiment was relayed as CTF 62 to COMAMPHIBFORSOPAC 110650 Aug 42, Grey Book, p. 645.

Page 134
Intelligence activities: SRH-012, Vol. IV, pp. 67, 72–73, 236, 303–05, 307, 335–36, 396–97; CINCPAC to COMSOPAC 112209 Aug 42, Grey Book, p. 640.

Page 134
Good news to Ghormley: CINCPAC to COMSOPAC 062035 Aug 42, Grey Book, p. 638; COMINCH to CINCPAC 112030 Aug 42, Grey Book, p. 646; COMINCH to CINCLANT 101830 Aug 42, Grey Book, p. 643; COMINCH to CINCPAC 101840 Aug 42, Grey Book, p. 643. In part, the exchange of *Hornet* for *Wasp* was probably based on the fact that *Wasp* needed repairs for an engineering casuality she suffered en route to the South Pacific that had been partly remedied by her crew.

Page 134
Message from Joint Chiefs and Ghormley's reply: COMINCH to COMSOPAC 151951 Aug 42, Grey Book, p. 651; Ghormley, "Tide Turns," p. 108; COMSOPAC to COMINCH 170230 Aug 42, Grey Book, p. 653.

Page 135
Harmon's assessment: Ltr Harmon to Marshall 11 Aug 42, in Miller, *Guadalcanal: The First Offensive,* p. 82.

Doubts grow about Ghormley's handling of the situation: CTF 62 to COMSOPAC 170925 Aug 42, Grey Book, p. 805; CINCPAC Daily Summaries August 19, 20, September 1, Grey Book, pp. 829–30, 1008; COMINCH to CINCPAC 011315 Sep 42, Grey Book, p. 862 (a stronger complaint by King over the inability of Ghormley to stop destroyer bombardments); Ghormley, "Tide Turns," p. 106.

Pages 135–36
Background of logistical problems: Dyer, *Amphibians Came to Conquer,* pp. 401, 405–6, 419; Ghormley, "Tide Turns," pp. 1, 13, 23, 29, 143. Dyer comments that had the logistical problem been understood, it is doubtful that "Watchtower" would have been attempted.

Page 136
Fundamental errors in original setup of South Pacific logistics and Ghormley's selection of his advanced base: Dyer, *Amphibians Came to Conquer,* pp. 405–7, 417; Ghormley, "Tide Turns." pp. 23, 37–39; Leighton and Coakley, *Global Logistics and Strategy,* p. 391; Morton, *Strategy and Command,* pp. 346–47.

Pages 136–37
Advanced base units: These are described in *Building the Navy's Bases in World War II: History of the Bureau of Yards and Docks and the Civil Engineer Corps 1940–1946.* Vol. I (Washington, D.C.: U.S. Government Printing Office, 1947), p. 120. A "Lion" was designed for a Pearl Harbor–size base, a "Cub" was about one-quarter that size. Both could be broken down into component parts. Ghormley's requests are noted in Ghormley, "Tide Turns," pp. 13–14, 36–37; Dyer, *Amphibians Came to Conquer,* p. 422.

Page 137
Situation at Noumea, assistance from Army: Morton, *Strategy and Command,* pp. 345–49; Joseph Bykofsky and Harold Larson, *United States Army in World War II, The Technical Services, The Transportation Corps: Operations Overseas* (Washington, D.C.: U.S. Government Printing Office, 1957), pp. 497–502; Leighton and Coakley, *Global Logistics and Strategy,* pp. 398–406; Dyer, *Amphibians Came to Conquer,* p. 417; Army Air Forces Historical Studies, No. 35, Guadalcanal and the Origins of the Thirteenth Air Force, Prepared by the Assistant Chief of Air Staff, Intelligence Historical Division, July 1945, p. 125 [hereafter 13th AF Hist.]; Craven and

Cates, *Guadalcanal to Saipan,* pp. 74–75; Ghormley, "Tide Turns," pp. 103, 106–7; Vandegrift and Asprey, *Once a Marine,* p. 164.

Page 137
Role of R4Ds/C-47s; Robert Sherrod, *History of Marine Corps Aviation in World War II,* 2d ed. (San Rafael, Calif.: Presidio Press, 1980), pp. 86–87, 111 [hereafter Sherrod, *History of Marine Corps Aviation in World War II*]. This source notes R4Ds of VMJ-253 began regular runs on September 5. They were later joined by VMJ-152. 13th AF Hist., pp. 111–15, reports the 13th Troop Carrier Squadron began operations on October 19 and was joined for a time by the 33d Troop Carrier Squadron, diverted en route to the Southwest Pacific theater in late October and November. The crews of these unarmed and very vulnerable aircraft joked that their motto was "In clouds we trust" (Hanson Baldwin, "Flight to Guadalcanal," *New York Times Magazine,* November 1, 1942). Surprisingly, only five of the Douglas transports were lost during the campaign. One went down on October 20, but the passengers and crew were picked up on October 31 by destroyer *Barton* on D'Entrecasteaux Reef, where they ditched; a second crashed off Lunga Point on November 13 with loss of the crew; and a third disappeared without a trace on January 13, 1943, after taking off from Henderson Field. The other two were lost operationally, but the exact circumstances are not reported.

Pages 137–38
Tactical impact of supply movements: COMSOPAC 160424 Dec 42, Grey Book, p. 1184.

Page 138
Secretary Forrestal's statement: Ghormley, "Tide Turns," pp. 110–11.

Page 138
Failure to have an air garrison ready for Henderson Field: Ltr COMGENSOPAC to CG AAF 15 Sep 42, cited in Miller, *Guadalcanal: The First Offensive,* p. 85; "Estimate: An Offensive for the Capture and Occupation of Tulagi and Vicinity, July 6, 1986," Grey Book, p. 739; Ghormley, "Tide Turns," pp. 104–5; COMAMPHIBFORSOPAC to COMSOPAC 2103335 Jul 42, COMSOPAC War Diary 21 Jul 42, p. 37; COMAIRSOPAC to COMSOPAC 210121 Jul 42, COMSOPAC War Diary 21 Jul 42, p. 37; COMAIRSOPAC to ADMIN of COMCARPACFLT 190749 Jul 42, COMSOPAC

War Diary 23 Jul 42, p. 40; COMAIR-
SOPAC to BUAERO 250811 Jul 42, COM-
SOPAC War Diary 25 Jul 42, p. 48; BUAER
to AIRBAT 261745 Jul 42, COMSOPAC
War Diary 27 Jul 42, p. 51; COMAIR-
SOPAC to COMSOPAC 041436 Aug 42,
COMSOPAC War Diary 4 Aug 42, p. 9;
CINCPAC to COMSOPAC 222211 Jul 42,
COMSOPAC War Diary 22 Jul 42, p. 41.

Pages 138–39
Background of MAG-23 and equipment, personnel, and training of VMF-223 and VMSB-
232: MAG-23 Record of Events; Interview of
Major John Smith USMC . . . in the Bureau
of Aeronautics, 10 November 1942, pp. 1–2
[hereafter Smith intvw]; Interview Lt. Col.
Richard C. Mangrum USMC . . . in the Bureau of Aeronautics, 11 November 1942, pp.
1, 4, 6 [hereafter Mangrum intvw]; Ghormley, "Tide Turns," pp. 104–5; Miller, *Cactus
Air Force,* pp. 21–23.

Page 139
Delay for exchange of pilots: CTF 2.6 to CO-
MAIRSOPAC 130240 Aug 42, COMAIR-
SOPAC to COMSOPAC 140402 Aug 42,
COMSOPAC 150002 Aug 42, COMSOPAC
War Diary 13 Aug 42, pp. 34, 42, 44.

Pages 139–40
Arrival of VMF-223 and VMSB-232 on Gua-
dalcanal: Clemens MS., p. 152; Final Report,
Phase III, pp. 3, 9; Vandegrift and Asprey,
Once a Marine, p. 139; Cates, "My First";
Thomas intvw, p. 328.

CHAPTER 6

This chapter is based on a wide variety of
sources. For the Marine account, Final Report, Phase IV, is the basis, but it is supplemented by unit reports, the works of H. C.
Merillat (*The Island* and *Guadalcanal Remembered*), the Clemens manuscript, and especially the vivid passages in Tregaskis,
Guadalcanal Diary. The foundation of the
Japanese side is *S.S.,* Vol. 14, pp. 250–51,
257, 269–74, 279–84, 289–310. In certain factual matters, however, this writer has found
an account by a survivor of the Ichiki First
Echelon, Mr. Sadanobu Okada, to be more
persuasive than that afforded in *S.S.* Mr.
Okada's story appeared in *Guadalcanal
Echoes,* a publication of the Guadalcanal
Campaign Veterans, in the January, March,
and July 1986 editions.

Pages 141–42
August 7 Liaison Conference: *S.S.,* Vol. 14,
p. 269. Ironically, on August 7 a Lieutenant
Colonel Sugita, who was a specialist on intelligence concerning the United States, lectured at Imperial Headquarters on recent
developments. He concluded that an attack
by American forces on the Pacific front was
less likely than the establishment of air and
naval bases in Far Eastern Soviet territory for
the purpose of attacking Japan by bombing
and submarine warfare. Ibid., p. 271.

Page 142
General Tanaka's misgivings and amplifying
reports: *S.S.,* Vol. 14, pp. 250–51, 257, 270–
71.

Page 142
August 8 Liaison Conference: *S.S.,* Vol. 14,
pp. 272–74.

Pages 142–43
August 10 Central Agreement: *S.S.,* Vol. 14,
pp. 279–80. This directive was Imperial General Headquarters Army Section Instruction
No. 1230.

Page 143
Sources of information changing opinions as
to the Allied situation on Guadalcanal and
Tulagi: *S.S.,* Vol. 14, pp. 280–83.

Information from attaché in Moscow: *S.S.,*
Vol. 14, p. 297; Griffith, *Battle of Guadalcanal,* p. 78.

Pages 143–44
Intelligence from naval and air sources and
report of Lieutenant Commander Matsunaga: *S.S.,* Vol. 14, pp. 283–84.

Pages 143–44
August 12 message of Lieutenant General
Tanabe: Ibid., pp. 289–91. Translation as rendered in Griffith, *Battle for Guadalcanal,*
pp. 78–79.

Pages 144–45
Misgivings among some staff officers at Imperial Headquarters: *S.S.,* Vol. 14, p. 274. Col.
Nishiura revealed his story in correspondence to Brigadier General Griffith (Griffith,
Battle for Guadalcanal, p. 79). Nomonhan is
described in *Nomonhan, Japanese-Soviet Tactical Combat, 1939,* Edward J. Drea, Leavenworth Papers No. 2, Combat Studies
Institute, U.S. Army Command and General
Staff College, Fort Leavenworth, Kansas,
1981.

Page 145
Planning at 17th Army Headquarters: *S.S.*, Vol. 14, pp. 289–91.

Page 145
Ichiki's written orders: *S.S.*, Vol. 14, 295.

Pages 145–46
Ichiki's background: *S.S.*, Vol. 14, pp. 296–97, *S.S.*, acknowledges that Ichiki's attitude was typical in the Imperial Army at this time. Griffith called Ichiki "a distinguished officer with an outstanding record" (*Battle for Guadalcanal*, p. 81). Ichiki's role in China and the Marco Polo Bridge Incident is noted in Edwin P. Hoyt, *Japan's War* (New York: McGraw-Hill, 1986), pp. 307–8, and *Guadalcanal Echoes*, July 1986, p. 2, which also notes the background of the 28th Infantry Regiment.

Page 146
Conversation of Matsumoto and Ichiki: *S.S.*, Vol. 14, p. 297. The source of this information is Colonel Matsumoto and perhaps should be taken with a grain of salt as to how much Matsumoto tried to restrain Ichiki's impetuousness. Matsumoto was the officer who thought that twenty transports might be required to move one American regiment.

Pages 146–47
Arrangements to move Ichiki's unit to Guadalcanal: Tanaka, Part I, pp. 690–91. Details of the conversions of old destroyers to patrol boats *1, 2, 34,* and *35* may be found in Jentschura, Jung, and Mickel, *Warships of the Imperial Japanese Navy, 1869–1945,* pp. 137–38, 141–42. These conversions were not as extensive as those of U.S. Navy APDs.

Page 147
Task organization Ichiki Detachment, First Echelon: *S.S.*, Vol. 14, p. 292.

Page 147
Task organization, Navy: *S.S.*, Vol. 14, p. 519; Tanaka, Part I, p. 690, erroneously listed destroyer *Yamakaze* in this group. *Yamakaze* was sunk on June 25 by submarine *Nautilus*. Dull, *Battle History of the Imperial Japanese Navy*, p. 205, says ten destroyers were sent on this mission, adding *Umikaze, Kawakaze, Suzukaze,* and *Yamakaze* to the list in the text.

Page 147
Landing of Ichiki's First Echelon and initial march: *S.S.*, Vol. 14, pp. 306–7.

Destroyer bombardment and damage to *Hagikaze:* Tanaka, Part I, pp. 690–91; Griffith, *Battle for Guadalcanal,* Chapter 6, note 5. The aircraft that hit *Hagikaze* was piloted by Major James Edmundson, commander of the 431st Bomb Squadron, 11th Bomb Group, according to Eric Hammel, *Guadalcanal: Starvation Island* (New York: Crown, 1987), pp. 142–43 [hereafter Hammel, *Guadalcanal: Starvation Island*). *Kagero* reported an air attack on August 20 that cannot be matched to records reviewed by this writer. These may have been *Wasp* aircraft.

Page 148
American intelligence information on Ichiki: SRH-012, Vol. IV, pp. 352–53, 501–2, 535–36.

Page 148
Nimitz's warning: CINCPAC to COMSOPAC 172047 Aug 42, Grey Book, p. 654.

Relay of intelligence to Vandegrift: These two methods are revealed in COMGEN GUAD to CTF 62 180924 Aug 42, COMSOPAC War Diary 19 Aug 42, p. 57, and COMSOPAC to CTFs 64, 61, 63, 62 100255 Sep 42, COMSOPAC War Diary 10 Sep 42, p. 9. That Vandegrift got word about Nimitz's warning is clear as he in turn alerted Rupertus on Tulagi during the evening of the 18th that an attack on Guadalcanal of Tulagi was possible within forty-eight hours. Vandegrift gave Turner as his source. 1st Mar Div D-3 Jnl 18 Aug 42, entry 10, 1855 hrs.; Vandegrift and Asprey, *Once a Marine,* p. 138.

Pages 148–49
Brush Patrol: Final Report, Phase III, pp. 9–11, Cates, "My First"; ltr Major Charles H. Brush, Jr., to CMC 15 Jan 49; *S.S.*, Vol. 14, pp. 307–8; Sadanobu Okada, "Ichiki on Guadalcanal," *Guadalcanal Echoes,* January 1986, pp. 2, 11; Hammel, *Guadalcanal: Starvation Island,* pp. 157, 162. The postwar Marine official versions (i.e., Zimmerman, "Guadalcanal Campaign," and Hough, Ludwig, and Shaw, *Pearl Harbor to Guadalcanal*) of this episode and Griffith, *Battle for Guadalcanal,* appear to follow an account given by Lieutenant Jackyn in an interview later in the war that this writer could not locate. There is a wide variation among the various contemporaneous records and between them and Lieutenant Jackyn's interview as to the strength of Shibuya's patrol and the losses on both sides, a matter on which *S.S.* is silent. Jackyn reported there were four Japanese officers and thirty men in

the patrol, of whom three escaped, and he put Marine losses at three dead and three wounded. These figures also appear in Final Report, Phase III, p. 9. But the 1st Mar Div Record of Events for August 19, as well as the D-2 and D-3 Journals for that date, give the Japanese unit as four officers and sixteen men with two getting away. Cates, "My First," says there were four officers and eighteen men and gives Marine losses as two slightly wounded. Tregaskis, *Guadalcanal Diary*, p. 125, says there were about twenty-five in the Japanese patrol, of whom eighteen were killed, and these figures are duplicated in Clemens MS., p. 150. (Clemens also says Brush captured prisoners, but none of the other accounts confirm this.) Merillat, *Island*, pp. 68–69, reports there were thirty-five Japanese in the patrol of whom four officers and eighteen men were killed. Marine losses were set at three killed and three wounded. Finally, COMGEN Guad to COMTASK-FOR 62 191530 Aug 42, COMSOPAC War Diary 19 Aug 42, shows a claim of eighteen Japanese dead. After a draft of this chapter was well along, Mr. Okada's story appeared in January 1986. He indicates there were thirty-eight men in the Shibuya patrol and provided a diagram of their formation. According to Mr. Okada, there were only five survivors of the patrol. The text now basically reflects Okada's account.

Page 149

Source of Japanese information on Marine positions: Colonel Gerald Thomas believed the Japanese learned of Marine dispositions by virtue of observation posts on Mount Austen (Thomas intvw, pp. 333–334), and that judgment was joined by Samuel B. Griffith (*Battle for Guadalcanal*, p. 82). However, *S.S.*, Vol. 89, p. 161, mentions the first two observation posts on Mount Austen began operation on September 22, too late to provide Ichiki with any intelligence.

Page 149

Vandegrift assesses situation and elects to await Ichiki: Final Report, Phase III, pp. 10–11; Vandegrift and Asprey, *Once a Marine*, pp. 138–39.

Pages 150–52

Description of the Tenaru and the Marine dispositions: Clemens MS., p. 150; Tregaskis, *Guadalcanal Diary*, p. 136; Final Report, Phase IV, p. 1; Pollock intvw, pp. 129–30; Unit Report No. 13, Combat Group "B"[1st Marines], August 25, 1942, which may be found in the Cates Papers, MCHC, with

Cates, "My First." The fact that the units at the point of impact at the end of the sandbar were one platoon of Company G, 1st Marines and two platoons of Company B Special Weapons Battalion is noted in McMillan, *Old Breed*, p. 61. Merillat, *Island*, p. 70, reports the Company B contingent bore the brunt of the first assault. Strength of these units is assumed to be about the table of organization figure from D-1 and D-85 TOs of 10 Jan 42, MCHC.

Page 151

Ichiki's plan: *S.S.*, Vol. 14, pp. 308–9. Mr. Okada's account gives a different order of march, but *S.S.* follows a copy of the order.

Pages 151–52

Initial indications of Ichiki's approach: Unit Report No. 13. Combat Group "B"[1st Marines], August 25, 1942, with Cates, "My First"; Merillat, *Island*, pp. 69–70; *S.S.*, Vol. 14, pp. 309–10.

"We'll mow 'em down!": Gordon Prange with Donald M. Goldstein and Katherine V. Dillon, *Miracle at Midway* (New York: McGraw-Hill, 1982), p. 35.

Page 152

Ichiki's initial attack: *S.S.*, Vol. 14, p. 309; Okada, "Ichiki on Guadalcanal," *Guadalcanal Echoes*, March 1986, pp. 2,13; Final Report, Phase IV, pp. 1–2; McMillan, *Old Breed*, p. 61 (information from Lieutenant Colonel Pollock); Roger Butterfield, *Al Schmid—Marine* (New York: Farrar & Rinehart, 1944), p. 96 [hereafter Butterfield, *Al Schmid*]. *S.S.* reports Ichiki initially ordered an attack across the lagoon and then the effort at the sandbar. Okada reverses the sequence of these orders, which far more readily matches the American accounts of this action and is followed here.

There is considerable discrepancy in the records over the time of Ichiki's first attack and the presence of a wire fence at the Marine end of the sandbar. Final Report, Phase IV, p. 1, says the attack began at 0310, which is consistent with Unit Report No. 13, Combat Group "B," August 25, 1942. Griffith, *Battle for Guadalcanal*, put it at 0240, a time he was given by a participant. Pollock always insisted the attack was much earlier at about 0118 (Pollock intvw, p. 135). *S.S.*, Vol. 14, p. 310, reports an initial attack "across the river" that was frustrated, following which Ichiki "discovered" the sandbar and ordered an attack there timed at just before daybreak. However, the map on p. 311 shows the time of the "first attack" as 2230, August 20, Tokyo time, which is 0030, August 21, local time. Tregaskis and Clemens were keeping diaries but were in other parts of the perimeter; they noted firing at 0230 and 0210 respectively. 1st Mar Div Record of Events 21 Aug 42 and 1st Mar Div D-3 Jnl 21 Aug 42, item 12, reported the attack started at 0200, and 5th Mar Record of Events 21 Aug recorded firing at 0200 and artillery at 0230. The text simply reflects this writer's judgment that the time of the attack was certainly earlier than 0310 and probably around 0200, but exactly when simply cannot be ascertained from the evidence.

On the second point the record is clearer. Final Report, Phase IV, p. 1, states there was no wire in front of the Marine positions. This statement is plainly rebutted by a number of contemporary sources, including Tregaskis, *Guadalcanal Diary,* p. 136; Cates, "My First"; and Merillat, *Island,* p. 70. Engineer Activities Guadalcanal, p. 5, reports Company C, 1st Engineer Battalion emplaced protective and tactical wire the next day under fire, and this report is supported by ltr Lieutenant Colonel Henry H. Crockett to CMC 10 Jan 49. However, this information must be seen in the light of the fact that what an engineer would consider a wire barrier and what was in front of Lieutenant Colonel Pollack's positions were two different things, and the fact that the engineers arrived after the first attack, which must have damaged if not destroyed the original fence. *S.S.,* Vol. 14, p. 310, also states the attackers ran into a wire fence.

Japanese regard wire fence as electrified: This is inferred from the fact that in October, Japanese intelligence briefings mentioned that survivors of Ichiki's detachment reported American tactics included the use of electrified wire fences in front of their positions. *S.S.,* Vol. 28, p. 108.

Page 152
Story of Marine machinegun crew: Butterfield, *Al Schmid,* pp. 98–103; "Marine Kills 200 and Holds Off Foe," Associated Press, *New York Times,* November 11, 1942. Schmid's story was treated by Hollywood in *Pride of the Marines.*

Japanese position machinegun in abandoned amphibian tractor: Tregaskis, *Guadalcanal Diary,* pp. 138–39; Butterfield, *Al Schmid,* p. 99.

Pages 152–53
Ichiki's first attack checked: Final Report,

Phase IV, p. 2; *S.S.,* Vol. 14, p. 309–10; Merillat, *Island,* p. 70; Pollack intvw, p. 139. Hammel, *Guadalcanal: Starvation Island,* pp. 169–71, shows Pollack committing first one platoon of Company G, but adds that Pollack then ordered the rest of Company G forward. The text follows Pollack's account.

Page 153
Cates calls for artillery support: Cates, "My First"; Final Report, Phase IV, p. 2; Final Report, Phase IV, Annex E, gives time of the first call as 0400 and indicates two concentrations were fired at 0403 and repeated at 0515.

Pages 153–54
Japanese attack along surf: Griffith, *Battle for Guadalcanal,* p. 84; Merillat, *Island,* p. 70.

Aviators awakened: Smith intvw, p. 2.

Pages 153–54
Martin Clemens observations and the story of Sergeant Major Vouza: Clemens MS, pp. 153–55, 160; 1st Mar Div D-2 Jnl 20 Aug 42, Box 5, File A7-7.

Page 154
Marines plan counterattack: Final Report, Phase IV, p. 2; Cates, "My First"; Vandegrift and Asprey, *Once a Marine,* pp. 141–42; Thomas intvw, p. 336. Tregaskis was present and records the conversation when Cates, Thomas, and Cresswell formulated the plan, *Guadalcanal Diary,* pp. 130–31.

"We aren't going to let those people . . .: Tregaskis, *Guadalcanal Diary,* p. 130.

Pages 154–55
Cresswell's battalion launches attack: Final Report, Phase IV, p. 2; Cates, "My First"; ltr Lt. Col. Marion A. Fawcett to CMC 8 Feb 49; Merillat, *Island,* p. 73.

"the customary bayonet attack": Final Report, Phase IV, p. 2.

Page 155
Morning actions of Lieutenant Colonel Pollock's battalion: Tregaskis, *Guadalcanal Diary,* pp. 134–41; ltr Lt. Col. Fawcett to CMC 8 Feb 49; Final Report, Phase IV, p. 3.

Page 155
Attack of tank platoon: Cates, "My First"; Tregaskis, *Guadalcanal Diary,* pp. 142–44; ltr Col. Charles G. Meints to CMC 3 Feb 49.

Cates and Tregaskis make it clear that Cates only authorized Lieutenant Case to make a reconnaissance along the beach, but that Case on his own initiative launched an attack into the grove. It is interesting to note that in Final Report, Phase IV, p. 3, Case is described only as crossing the sand spit and attacking with no reference to the existence or absence of orders while in the subsequent official Marine Corps accounts Case is presented as attacking in accordance with his orders. Final Report, Phase IV, p. 3, says two of these tanks were disabled, but Tregaskis who observed the whole action says only one was disabled, as did Colonel Meints in this letter.

Page 155
" . . . their treads rattling industriously": Tregaskis, *Guadalcanal Diary,* p. 142.

Page 155
"the rear of the tanks looked like meat grinders": Ltr Vandegrift to Holcomb, quoted in Vandegrift and Asprey, *Once a Marine,* p. 142.

End of Ichiki's command and death of Ichiki: Tregaskis. *Guadalcanal Diary,* pp. 144–46; *S.S.,* Vol. 14, p. 310; Okada, "Ichiki on Guadalcanal," *Guadalcanal Echoes,* July 1986.

Page 156
Last efforts of Japanese survivors and Marine response: Clemens MS, p. 156; Griffith, *Battle for Guadalcanal,* pp. 86–87; Cates, "My First"; Tregaskis, *Guadalcanal Diary,* pp. 146–47.

Page 156
Marine losses: Figures for fatalities are from the muster rolls; figures for wounded also include input from Unit Report No. 13, Combat Group "B" [1st Marines], August 25, 1942, with Cates, "My First." The breakdown of American losses was as follows:

Japanese losses: *S.S.,* Vol. 14, p. 310. There is an obvious discrepancy in these figures: 777 "killed" (presumably including the fifteen prisoners of war) and 128 returning to Taivu Point totals 905, while the strength of Ichiki's First Echelon was 917. Moreover, the 128 figure includes individuals present at Taivu Point before Ichiki arrived, and, according to one native report, these numbered eleven (ltr Brush to CMC 15 Jan 49). If it is assumed that 117 members of Ichiki's First Echelon reached Taivu, this would make losses an even 800, including fifteen prisoners. The 900 figure would include losses in Shibuya's patrol, whose bodies would not have been along Alligator Creek ("the Tenaru"). Final Report, Phase IV, p. 3, places Japanese losses at an "estimated" 900. Merillat, *Island,* p. 74, more accurately says that "more than 700" Japanese died at the "Tenaru."

Page 156
Captured equipment: Final Report, Phase IV, p. 3; Merillat, *Island,* p. 75.

Page 157
Churchill's doubts on morale of soldiers of the democracies: *Churchill Taken from the Diaries of Lord Moran* (Boston: Houghton, Mifflin, 1966), pp. 40–41.

"General, I have never heard . . .": Ltr Vandegrift to Holcomb, quoted in Vandegrift and Asprey, *Once a Marine,* p. 142.

Page 157
General contempt in Imperial Army for American infantry units: *S.S.,* Vol. 14, pp. 296–97; Agawa, *Reluctant Admiral,* p. 324.

"This tragedy should have taught the hopelessness of 'bamboo spear' tactics": Tanaka, Part I, p. 691.

	Killed	*Wounded*
2d Battalion, 1st Marines	28	44
1st Battalion, 1st Marines	7 (3)	13 (3)
Weapons Company, 1st Marines	1	0
Headquarters Company, 1st Marines	0	3
1st Special Weapons Battalion	2	6
1st Tank Battalion	0	1
Headquarters, 1st Marine Division	0	3
	38 (41)	70 (73)

The figures in parentheses are for losses in the Brush patrol.

Page 158
". . . part of what happened at the Tenaru . . .": Griffith, *Battle for Guadalcanal,* p. 87.

Retreat of Ichiki survivors to Taivu Point: *S.S.,* Vol. 14, p. 310.

CHAPTER 7

The principal sources for this chapter are the American ship and air unit action reports, *S.S.,* Vol. 49, pp. 545–92, and SRH-012, Vol. IV. Invaluable additional information on aircraft availability, combat actions, and losses was provided by Mr. John Lundstrom and Mr. James Sawruk. Where there is a conflict between the cited reports and information from Mr. Lundstrom and Mr. Sawruk, the latter is followed. As usual, all times given in the text are Zone -11. However, the researcher on this action should note that the American reports are virtually all in Zone -11½; the Japanese kept their customary Zone-9 time. Zone 9 means nine hours ahead of Greenwich time.

Pages 159–60
Reorganization and tactical changes in Combined Fleet: *S.S.,* Vol. 49, pp. 545–46, 561.

Page 161
Sortie of Combined Fleet: Ibid., pp. 541, 549.

Operations of Task Force 61: Commander in Chief, U.S. Pacific Fleet, CINCPAC File Pac-90-wb, A16-3/SOL, Serial 03102, October 24, 1942, Subject: Solomons Islands Campaign—Action of 23–25 August, p. 4, para. 8 [hereafter CINCPAC Serial 03102].

Pages 161–62
American radio intelligence efforts: SRH-012, Vol. IV, pp. 98–99, 102, 105, 114–15, 119, 123, 462–64, 493, 503, 514–15, 652, 671–72, 687, 704–5, 711–13, 745, 747–48, 775–76. The August 21 lineup of the carrier task force named all major units except the two ships of Crudiv 7. The August 22 assessment of the ships in the Advanced Force identified by name every heavy cruiser but missed old light cruiser *Yara* and incorrectly associated battleships *Kongo* and *Haruna* with this command.

Page 162
Japanese search plane work of August 20–21 and strike of August 21: Tanaka, Part I, p. 691; *S.S.,* Vol. 49, pp. 549–50.

Page 162
Clash of VMF-223 and Zeros: MAG-23 Record of Events 21 Aug 42; Smith intvw, pp. 2–3; GUADALCANAL to COMSOPAC-FOR 210900 Aug 42, COMSOPAC War Diary 21 Aug 42; *S.S.,* Vol. 49, pp. 549–50. An SBD of VMSB-232 was lost operationally this day.

Page 163
Kawakaze meets *Blue* and *Henley: S.S.,* Vol. 49, pp. 549–53; Task Force 62 War Diary 21 Aug 42; U.S.S. *Blue.* DD-387, Serial 041, 25 August 1942, Subject: Engagement with enemy surface craft 22 August 1942 and War Damage Report.

Page 163
Decision to try to hurry forward Ichiki's Second Echelon: *S.S.,* Vol. 49, pp. 551–52, 554; *S.S.,* Vol. 14, pp. 324–25; MAG-23 Record of Events 22 Aug 42.

Page 164
Tanaka requests air cover: *S.S.,* Vol. 49, p. 554.

Page 164
Japanese work out compromise on air cover for Tanaka: *Ibid.,* pp. 552–555, 558, 560.

Page 164
Japanese actions and movement August 23: *Ibid.,* pp. 556–57, 559–62.

Pages 164–65
Enterprise search plane contacts: U.S.S. *Enterprise,* CV6/A16-3/(10-MY), Serial 008, September 5, 1942, Subject: Action of August 24, 1942, Including Air Attack on U.S.S. *Enterprise;* Report of, pp. 1–2, part A, paras. 2–3 [hereafter *Enterprise* Serial 008].

PBY contacts: CINCPAC Serial 03102, p. 5, para. 11.

Page 165
Saratoga strike: U.S.S. *Saratoga,* CV3/A16-3/11-gt, Serial 085, September 10, 1942, Subject: Report of Action Against Enemy (Japanese) Forces in Solomons Islands Area on August 24, 1942 [hereafter *Saratoga* Serial 085], Enclosure A, Tactical Situation and Chronological History of Events, p. 1 and Enclosure D, Commander Saratoga Air Group, CSAG/A16-3/Ds, Serial 080, September 5, 1942, Subject: Saratoga Air Group Narrative of Operations for August 23, 1942, and Morning of August 24, 1942 [hereafter CSAG Serial 080].

Tanaka receives permission to turn back: *S.S.,* Vol. 49, p. 557.

PBY sees Tanaka turn and communications failure: Commander Task Force 11, A16-3, Serial 0130N, September 24, 1942, p. 4, para. 3 [hereafter CTF 11 Serial 0130N].

Page 165
"doubting marines": CSAG Serial 080.

Attack by MAG-23: MAG-23 Record of Events 23 Aug 42; Vandegrift and Asprey, *Once a Marine,* p. 144.

Page 165
Fletcher decides to detach *Wasp* for fueling: CTF 11 Serial 0130N, p. 4, para. 3; SRH-012, Vol. IV, p. 777. Bulletins 156 and 159 issued by CINCPAC on August 19 and 22 carried warnings of possible undetected movements by *Shokaku, Zuikaku,* and *Ryujo,* but Fletcher apparently disregarded these (SRH-012, pp. 605, 747–48). The total of sixty-two aircraft on *Wasp* includes sixty-one of her own and one VT-8 TBF temporarily aboard. It does not include the J2F utility plane.

Pages 165–66
End of *Blue:* U.S.S. *Blue,* Serial 040, 25 Aug 42, and War Damage Report; COMDESDIV 7 to CTF 62 211935 Aug 42 and COM-TASKFOR 62 212255 Aug 42, COM-SOPAC War Diary 22 Aug 42, p. 64; TF 62 War Diary 23 Aug 42.

Night of August 23–24 at Guadalcanal: *S.S.,* Vol. 49, pp. 554, 558; CSAG Serial 080; MAG-23 Record of Events 23 Aug 42; 1st Mar Div Record of Events, 24 Aug 42.

Pages 167–72
Japanese task organization: drawn from the text of *S.S.,* Vol. 49, pertaining to this action, the attached Table of Principal Officers, and, for submarine deployments, *Senshi Sosho, Nanto Homen Kaigun Sakusen,* 2, *Gato Tesshu Made,* Boeicho Boei Kenshujo, Senshishitsu, Asagumo Shinbun Sha, August 5, 1975, pp. 62–63 [*War History Series, Southeast Area Navy Operations,* Part 2, *Up to Withdrawal from Guadalcanal,* Defense Agency, Defense Research Institute, Office of War History, hereafter *S.S.,* Vol. 83]. Also of assistance were WDC 160464 and 161709. Mr. John Lundstrom shared the fruits of his research on the names of Japanese air unit commanders and unit strengths and losses. Mr. James Sawruk provided important information on PBY and B-17 operations.

Strength of Japanese air groups: The text follows figures based upon the research of Mr. John Lundstrom in the Japanese air group reports. This source provides somewhat different numbers than those in *S.S.,* Vol. 49, p. 561.

Pages 172–74
American task organization: The text follows the figures provided by Mr. John Lundstrom and Mr. James Sawruk.

Initially, this writer tried to calculate American aircraft availability from the surviving unit reports. This proved inexact at best. Subsequently, Mr. Lundstrom and Mr. Sawruk generously shared their information on these matters, based upon their exhaustive research of the Bureau of Aeronautics card files on individual aircraft and interviews and correspondence with aircrewmen.

Page 166
Japanese Main Body and Advanced Force head southeast: *S.S.,* Vol. 49, p. 566.

Strength of Japanese and American air groups: See notes above on task organization.

Page 166
Characteristics of Aichi D3A1: M. C. Richards and Donald S. Smith, *Aichi D3A ("Val") and Yokoshuka D4Y ("Judy") Carrier Bombers of the IJNAF* (Windsor, England: Profile Publications, 1972), pp. 145–49,; Dr. René J. Francillon, *Japanese Navy Bombers of World War Two,* 2d ed. (Garden City, NY: Doubleday, 1971), pp. 20–30 [hereafter Francillon, *Japanese Navy Bombers of World War Two*].

Characteristics of Douglas SBD: Barrett Tillman, *The Dauntless Dive Bomber of World War Two* (Annapolis, Md.: Naval Institute Press, 1976), pp. 4–16, 216–17; Captain Eric Brown, RN, *Wings of the Navy* (London, New York, and Sydney: Jane's, 1980), pp. 52, 55–59.

Characteristics of Nakajima B5N2: Francillon, *Japanese Navy Bombers of World War Two,* pp. 15–18; Dr. M. F. Hawkins, *The Nakajima BSN "Kate"* (Windsor, England: Profile Publications), pp. 284–92.

Characteristics of Grumman TBF Avenger: Barrett Tillman, *Avenger at War* (New York: Scribner, 1980), pp. 10–17.

Page 175
Shokaku radar: *S.S.,* Vol. 49, pp. 541, 572–73.

Quality of Japanese air groups: Ibid., p. 541.

Quality of American air groups: Grey Book, p. 721.

Pages 175–76
Japanese spread into battle formation: *S.S.,* Vol. 49, pp. 549, 559, 561, 575. Admiral Yamamoto had warned on August 21 that the American carriers might be to the east.

Page 176
Detachment of *Ryujo:* Ibid., pp. 563–64.

Early search plane results: Ibid., pp. 564, 566; CINCPAC Serial 03102, p. 5, para. 14; CTF 11, Serial 0130N, p. 4, para. 3.

Saratoga's attack group returns: CSAG Serial 080; *Saratoga* Serial 085, Enclosure B, p. 1.

American carriers head north at 1130: *Enterprise* Serial 008, p. 2, part A, para. 5; CINCPAC Serial 03012, p. 5, para. 16.

Fletcher orders search by *Enterprise:* CTF 11 Serial 0130N, p. 5, para. 3; *Saratoga* Serial 085, Enclosure A, p. 2.

Page 176
Destruction of Japanese search planes: *Saratoga* Serial 085, Enclosure A, p. 2; *Enterprise* Serial 008, p. 2, part A, para. 6; *S.S.,* Vol. 49, p. 580. American records are confusing on the times of these interceptions. Japanese records show one Betty and one Mavis search plane from Rabaul and Shortland respectively were lost on the morning searches of August 24. These appear to be the planes noted in the *Saratoga* ship and squadron reports. The CEAG Serial 051, p. 6, mentions destruction of a Mavis snooper at "1055," which possibly was the missing Mavis rather than the one claimed by *Saratoga.* Mr. Lundstrom has resolved these mysteries and the text follows his conclusions.

Enterprise search mission at 1239: *Enterprise* Serial 008, p. 3, part A, para. 7.

Pages 176–77
Ryujo launches strike: *S.S.,* Vol. 49, p. 564.

Saratoga radar contact and strike group launched: *Saratoga* Serial 085, Enclosure A, p. 2; CTF 11 Serial 0130N, p. 5, para. 3; Commander *Saratoga* Air Group, CSAG/ A16-3/Ds, August 29, 1942, Serial 078, Subject: *Saratoga* Air Group Narrative of Operations for August 24, 1942, p. 1 [hereafter CSAG Serial 078].

Page 177
Air battle over Guadalcanal: *S.S.,* Vol. 49,

pp. 564–65; MAG-23, Record of Events 24 Aug; Smith intvw, p. 4.

Page 177
Chikuma plane finds U.S. carriers and is destroyed: *S.S.,* Vol. 49, p. 567; CEAG Serial 051, p. 2; Commander Fighting Squadron SIX, VF6/A16-3/Hd, Serial 051, September 1, 1942, Subject: Report of Action—24 August 1942, p. 3 [hereafter VF-6 Serial 051].

Carrier Division 1 launches strikes: *S.S.,* Vol. 49, pp. 567, 569, 574.

Carrier Division 1 heads east and attacked by B-17s: Ibid., pp. 572–73; COMAIRSOPAC War Diary 24 Aug 42; WDC 161709. Five crewmen died in the B-17 that crashed on landing. Although unit reports indicated the B-17 was damaged by antiaircraft fire, subsequent research by a unit historian shows the plane was an operational loss. Mr. James Sawruk brought this to my attention.

Pages 177–78
Reports and attacks by *Enterprise* search aircraft: *Enterprise* Serial 008, p. 3, part A, para. 7, Enclosure E (War Diary 24 Aug 42); CINCPAC Serial 03102, p. 6, para. 18; Commander, Torpedo Squadron 3, VT-3/A9/ A16-3, Serial 022, August 27, 1942, Subject: Report of Action—August 24, 1942, pp. 1–4 [hereafter VT-3 Serial 022]; Commander Scouting Squadron 5, VS-5/A16, Serial 026-c, August 31, 1942, pp. 3–5 [hereafter VS-5 Serial 026-c]; Commander Bombing Squadron 6, FVB-6/A16/nhn, August 31, 1942, Subject: Report of Action, August 24, 1942, pp. 1–3, 7–8 [hereafter VB-6 24 Aug 42].

Attacks on *Maya* and *Shokaku: S.S.,* Vol. 49, pp. 572–73, 575. Losses on *Shokaku* are from WDC 161709.

Page 178
Saratoga planes attack *Ryujo:* CSAG Serial 078; Commander Bombing Squadron 3, VB-3/A16-3, August 27, 1942, pp. 1–2 [hereafter VB-3 27 Aug 42]; Commander Scouting Squadron 3, A16-3/VS3, Serial 019, pp. 1–2 [hereafter VS-3 Serial 019]; Commander Torpedo Squadron 8, VT8/A16-3, August 27, 1942, pp. 1–3 [hereafter VT-8 27 Aug 42]; *S.S.,* Vol. 49, pp. 565–66.

Pages 178–79
Loss of *Ryujo: S.S.,* Vol. 49, pp. 566, 579. It is difficult to fully credit Captain Kato's claim that no bomb hit *Ryujo* in view of the fact that the torpedo planes that attacked her claimed they saw fires already on the ship.

Captain Tameichi Hara of *Amatsukaze* reported that *Ryujo* was hit by two or three bombs near the stern and then "several more," but mentions no torpedo hit. Hara with Fred Saito and Roger Pineau, *Japanese Destroyer Captain* (New York: Ballantine, 1961), pp. 109–10 [hereafter Hara, Saito, and Pineau, *Japanese Destroyer Captain*]. Mr. James Sawruk provided me with a partial translation of an article by Saito Yoshio, "The Tragic Sinking of Carrier *Ryujo* at the Second Battle of the Solomon Sea," which clearly indicates at least three bomb and one torpedo hits. The text follows this source.

Pages 179–80
Personnel losses on *Ryujo:* WDC 161709. Besides the 120 crewmen, one civilian died aboard *Ryujo*, apparently a correspondent. *S.S.,* Vol. 49, gives no loss figures for *Ryujo's* crew. SRH-036, p. 48, shows that it was not until January 10, 1943, that it was clear *Ryujo* was sunk when a dispatch dated November 10 was deciphered revealing this carrier had been removed from the Navy List.

Enterprise 1602 and 1619 radar contacts: *Enterprise* Serial 008, pp. 3–4, part B, paras. 1–4, Enclosure F (Fighter Direction Officers).

U.S. carriers launch fighters: *Enterprise* Serial 008, p. 3, part A, para. 8, p. 4, part B, para. 6; CEAG Serial 051, p. 2; *Saratoga* Serial 085, Enclosure B, p. 1.

Pages 180–81
Breakdown of fighter direction: *Enterprise* Serial 008, p. 4, part B, paras. 5–7, Enclosure F; CINCPAC Serial 03102, p. 8, paras. 28–29.

Page 181
Interception of raid: *Enterprise* Serial 008, Enclosure F; VF-6 Serial 051; Commander Fighting Squadron 5, VF5/A16-3, No Serial, August 24, 1942, Subject: Narrative Report of Action with Enemy on August 24, 1942, in Solomon Islands Area [hereafter VF-5 24 Aug 42]; *Saratoga* Serial 085, Enclosure C, pp. 9–10; CINCPAC Serial 03102, p. 8, para. 29; Eugene Burns, *Then There Was One* (New York: Harcourt, Brace, 1944), pp. 78–79 [hereafter Burns, *Then There Was One*].

Pages 181–82
Preparations to receive attack: *Enterprise* Serial 008, p. 5, part B, para. 8, Enclosure F, p. 1; CINCPAC Serial 03102, p. 8, para. 28, p. 9, para. 32; Edward P. Stafford, *The Big E*

(New York: Random House, 1962), pp. 130–31 [hereafter Stafford, *Big E*]; U.S.S. *Portland,* CA33/A16-3, Serial 059, August 30, 1942, Subject: Air attack made upon U.S.S. *Enterprise* by Japanese August 24, 1942—report of, p. 1, para. 3 [hereafter *Portland* Serial 059].

Page 182
"The enemy planes are directly overhead now!": *Enterprise* Serial 008, p. 5, part B, para. 8.

Enterprise 20mm battery officer sees planes: *Enterprise* Serial 008, p. 6, part C, paras. 1–2, Enclosure B, p. 24; Burns. *Then There Was One,* p. 76.

Japanese attack plan: *S.S.,* Vol. 49, p. 568.

Page 182
Positions of photographers: *Enterprise* Serial 008, Enclosure B, pp. 2–3.

Page 182
"the dives were steep . . .": *Enterprise* Serial 008, p. 5, part B, para. 9.

Portland observations: *Portland* Serial 059, Enclosure B, p. 2.

Pages 182–83
Dive-bombing attack on *Enterprise: Enterprise* Serial 008, pp. 5–6, part B, paras. 9–13, part C, pp. 6–7, paras. 1–7; CINCPAC Serial 03102, pp. 9–11, paras. 34–41; *Portland* Serial 059, Enclosure B, p. 1; U.S.S. *Balch,* War Diary 24 Aug 42 (this is perhaps the best single description of the attack on *Enterprise*); U.S.S. *Atlanta,* CL 51/A16-3/A-9, Serial 050, August 27, 1942, Subject: Action Report, pp. 1–2; Commander Destroyer Squadron 6, War Diary 24 Aug 42; U.S.S. *Maury,* DD410/A16-3, Serial 012, August 29, 1942, Subject: Report of Air Attack on Task Force 16 . . . ; Burns. *Then There Was One,* pp. 76–78. From the reports of the screening vessels, it would appear that about fifteen Vals dived on *Enterprise,* releasing from ten to twelve bombs. *Balch, Maury,* and *Atlanta* indicated that five or six planes fell around the formation during the attack to antiaircraft fire.

Bomb hits on *Enterprise: Enterprise* Serial 008, pp. 7–10, part D, paras. 1–8, Enclosure B, p. 3; Enclosure (War Damage Report).

Page 183
Famous photograph by Marion L. Riley: *Enterprise* Serial 008, Enclosure B, p. 2.

Page 183

Japanese aircraft during withdrawal after attack on *Enterprise:* Commander Destroyer Division 22, A16-3/CDD22, Serial 0088, August 30, 1942, Subject: Reports of action of 24 August 1942, and subsequent events in connection therewith, pp. 4–5 [hereafter ComDesdiv 22 Serial 0088]; CEAG Serial 051, p. 13; VT-3 Serial 022, p. 5; VS-5, Serial 026-c, p. 5.

Pages 183–84

Attack on *North Carolina:* U.S.S. *North Carolina,* BB55/A16-3, Serial 0109, August 26, 1942, Subject: U.S.S. North Carolina—Action of August 24, 1942, report of, pp. 2–4; U.S.S. *North Carolina,* BB55/A16-3/A5-1, Serial 0122, August 30, 1942, Subject: Action of August 24, 1942, p. 8. Mr. Lundstrom and Mr. Sawruk pointed out the most likely explanations for *North Carolina's* comments on a high-altitude bombing attack.

Page 184

Aircraft losses in attack on *Enterprise: S.S.,* Vol. 49, p. 567; Commander Destroyer Squadron 6, A16-3, Serial 0135, August 28, 1942, Subject: Japanese Air Attack on U.S.S. *Enterprise.* . . . pp. 2–3; CEAG Serial 051, p. 3.

"a lull in the action . . ." Commander Frederick Bell, *Condition Red* (New York and Toronto: Longmans, Green, 1943), p. 9 [hereafter Bell, *Condition Red*].

Pages 184–85

Damage control and medical efforts on *Enterprise: Enterprise* Serial 008, pp. 11–12, part F, paras. 1–3; Enclosure B (contains numerous descriptions of individual acts), Enclosure D, especially pp. 17–19; Burns, *Then There Was One,* pp. 78–80.

Page 185

Scene at starboard after 5-inch gun gallery: Lieutenant Frederick Mears, *Carrier Combat* (New York: Ballantine, 1944), p. 121 [hereafter Mears, *Carrier Combat*].

Page 185

Enterprise lands aircraft: *Enterprise* Serial 008, Enclosure E (War Diary 24 Aug).

Pages 185–86

Enterprise steering casualty: *Enterprise* Serial 008, p. 10, part D, para. 9. Burns, *Then There Was One,* pp. 80–86, contains a vivid description of the heroic and skilled actions to return *Enterprise's* rudder to operation.

Page 186

Approach of second Japanese attack group: *S.S.,* Vol. 49, p. 569; *Enterprise* Serial 008, Enclosure F; CINCPAC Serial 03102, p. 13, para. 51; Stafford, *Big E,* p. 141.

Losses in second Japanese attack group and their return to their ships: VS-3 Serial 019, pp. 2–4; *S.S.,* Vol. 49, pp. 569, 574.

Page 186

Japanese decisions at sunset: *S.S.,* Vol. 49, pp. 573–74.

Page 187

Fletcher's withdrawal at sunset: CINCPAC Serial 03102, p. 13, para. 50; *Saratoga* Serial 085, Enclosure A, p. 4.

Pages 187–88

Fates of small strikes from *Enterprise* and *Saratoga: Enterprise* Serial 008, p. 3, part A, para. 9; CEAG Serial 051, pp. 4–5; VT-3, Serial 022, pp. 4–5; VB-3 27 Aug 42, pp. 3–4; VT-8 27 Aug 42, pp. 4–6;

Attack on *Chitose: S.S.,* Vol. 49, pp. 575–76; WDC 160464, 161709 provide basis for deduction that one Pete and three Jakes were destroyed by the bombing.

Page 188

Efforts of Japanese surface combatants and submarines: *S.S.,* Vol. 49, pp. 574–77, 583; ComDesdiv 22 Serial 0088, pp. 6–22. According to Japanese records, destroyer *Maikaze* was bombed by four B-17s at 1750.

Pages 188–89

Maneuvers and orders of convoy on August 24: *S.S.,* Vol. 49, p. 584.

Page 189

Erroneous information and decision to conduct destroyer bombardment and float plane bombing: Ibid., pp. 585–86.

Desdiv 30 bombardment and float plane bombing: Ibid., pp. 584–86; 1st Mar Div Record of Events 25 Aug 42.

Page 189

SBD night attacks: MAG-23 Record of Events 25 Aug 42; *S.S.,* Vol. 49, p. 585.

Captain Yasutake's report: *S.S.,* Vol. 49, p. 586.

Page 190

Guadalcanal SBDs attack convoy: *S.S.,* Vol. 49, pp. 586–87; Tanaka, Part I, pp. 693–94; MAG-23 Record of Events 25 Aug 42; Mangrum intvw, p. 3.

Pages 190–91

Loss of *Mutsuki* and *Kinryu Maru: S.S.,* Vol. 49, pp. 587–88.

"even the B-17s could make a hit once in a while": Commander H. Sekino, interview, *United States Strategic Bombing Survey, Interrogations of Japanese Officials,* Vol. I, p. 31 [hereafter *USSBS Interrogations*]

Page 191

Air raid on Guadalcanal and second strike at convoy: *S.S.,* Vol. 49, p. 588; MAG-23 Record of Events 25 Aug 42; 1st Mar Div Record of Events 25 Aug 42.

Page 191

Losses on *Enterprise: Enterprise* Serial 008, p. 11, part F. The only other fatality in the task force was on *North Carolina.*

Page 191

American aircraft losses: Ibid., p. 11, part E; CEAG Serial 051, pp. 8–10; VF-5 24 Aug 42, p. 2, VT-8 27 Aug 42; COMAIRSOPAC War Diary 23–24 Aug 42. Once again, the information from Mr. Lundstrom and Mr. Sawruk prompted amendments of the figures given in the reports.

Pages 191–92

American analysis of the action: *Enterprise* Serial 008, pp. 11, 13–25, parts F and J; *Saratoga* Serial 085, p. 1, para. 3; Commander Task Force 61, A16-3, Serial 0048N, September 25, 1942; CINCPAC Serial 03102, p. 6, para. 17, p. 15, para. 60, p. 17, para. 70; Commander Cruisers, Pacific Fleet, Serial 0138N, September 24, 1942, Subject: Operations of Carrier Task Forces, p. 3.

Page 192

Radio intelligence failure recognized: SRH-012, Vol. IV, p. 801.

Japanese aircraft losses tabulated: *S.S.,* Vol. 49, pp. 579–80, 592; to these are added the four float planes on *Chitose.*

Pages 192–93

Japanese analysis of the battle: Ibid., pp. 577, 592.

CHAPTER 8

Pages 194–95

Air raid August 26: MAG-23 Record of Events 26 Aug 42; *S.S.,* Vol. 83, p. 40; VMF-223 War Diary 26 Aug 42.

Page 195

Movement of 2d Battalion, 5th Marines to Guadalcanal: 2d Bn, 5th Mar Record of Events 21 Aug 42; Task Force 62 War Diary 21 Aug 42.

Pages 195–97

Kokumbona patrol of 1st Battalion, 5th Marines, August 27–28: The principal source for this account is the well-researched and balanced monograph prepared by a participant, Major Thomas T. Grady, USMC, Operations of the 1st Battalion, 5th Regiment (1st Marine Division) in the Vicinity of Kokumbona, 27–28 August 1942, December 27, 1949, Box 6, File A15-1.5. Also of use were *S.S.,* Vol. 14, pp. 459–60; ltr Major Milton V. O'Connell to CMC 8 Feb 49; Thomas intvw, p. 338; 5th Mar Record of Events; McMillan, *Old Breed,* p. 91; Merillat Diary 8 Sep 42; and muster rolls, 1st Battalion, 5th Marines, MCHC (for casualty figures only). Final Report is misleading in stating that artillery support was provided for the 1st Battalion, 5th Marines, as no direct support for the battalion was physically possible, but Final Report, Phase IV, Annex E, shows seventy-five rounds of 75mm and 105mm were fired in general support across the Matanikau. According to 5th Mar Record of Events, Company I of the regiment patrolled west from the perimeter and hit opposition at 1600.

Page 197

Buildup of Japanese aircraft at Rabaul: *S.S.,* Vol. 14, pp. 420–21, Vol. 83, pp. 36, 38.

Pages 197–98

Creation of R Area Air Force: *S.S.,* Vol. 83, pp. 45–50; Merillat, *Island,* p. 158, for distinction between "Washing Machine Charlie" and "Louie the Louse." Clemens MS, p. 172, notes "Washing Machine Charlie" was also known as "Maytag Charlie." The only record this writer located concerning the B-17 that sank *Patrol Boat 35* was COMSOPAC 032231 Sep 42, in COMSOPAC War Diary 3 Sep 42, p. 2, which indicates an 11th Bomb Group Fortress hit a tanker or seaplane tender at 1100 on 2 September at 7°16' South, 158°3' East and left it stopped in the water. The fifty-two aircraft in the original complement of the R Area Air Force were as follows:

Gamble sinks *I-123:* U.S.S. *Gamble,* Serial 030, 29 Aug 42.

	Type 0 Observation Float Plane "Pete"	Type 95 Observation Float Plane "Dave"	Type 0 or 94 Recon. "Jake" or "Alf"	Type 2 Float Fighter "Rufe"	Total
Chitose	16 Type 0 or 95		7		23
Kamikawa			2	11	13
Sanyo M.	6 Type 0 or 95		2		8
Sanuki M.	8				8
GRAND TOTAL					52

Page 198
Problems in Japanese air buildup: *S.S.,* Vol. 83, pp. 36, 40–41.

Page 198
Major General Kawaguchi's brigade arrives: *S.S.,* Vol. 14, pp. 303–6.

Pages 198–99
Kawaguchi's opinions and Truk meeting August 23: Ibid., pp. 385–87, 395. The picture of Kawaguchi appears in Zimmerman, "Guadalcanal Campaign," p. 85.

Page 199
Revised orders to Kawaguchi, August 26: *S.S.,* Vol. 14, p. 388.

Kawaguchi reaches Rabaul: Ibid., p. 391.

Pages 199–200
Attack on Desdiv 20: *S.S.,* Vol. 83, pp. 24–28, *Vol. 14,* p. 391; MAG-23 Record of Events 28 Aug 42; Burns, *Then There Was One,* p. 101.

Page 200
Reaction to attack on Desdiv 20: *S.S.,* Vol. 83, pp. 26, 29; Vol. 14, pp. 391, 393.

Pages 200–201
Air action of August 29: *S.S.,* Vol. 83, pp. 41–42; MAG-23 Record of Events 29 Aug 42; Robert L. Ferguson, *Guadalcanal: The Island of Fire, Reflections of the 347th Fighter Group* (Blue Ridge Summit, Pa.: Aero, 1987), p. 77 [hereafter Ferguson, *Guadalcanal: The Island of Fire*]; 1st Mar Div Record of Events 29 Aug 42.

Page 201
Kawaguchi recommends use of barges and reinforcement run of August 29–30: *S.S.,* Vol. 14, pp. 393–94; Tanaka, Part I, pp. 694–95; MAG-23 Record of Events 30 Aug 42.

Page 201
Air action of August 30: *S.S.,* Vol. 83, p. 42; MAG-23 Record of Events 30 Aug 42; History of the 67th Fighter Squadron, pp. 26–27 [hereafter 67th FS Hist.]; Smith intvw, pp. 8–10; Ferguson, *Guadalcanal: The Island of Fire,* pp. 78–79, 218–20. Ferguson's account is the best for the role of the Army fighters and resolves conflicts between 67th FS Hist. and Smith intvw.

Pages 201–2
Problems of 67th Fighter Squadron: 67th FS Hist., pp. 25, 27; 13th AF Hist., p. 8. Ltr. Lt. Col. M. E. Carl to CMC 3 Jan 49 and Ltr Col. Richard Mangrum to CMC 7 Feb 49 both insisted the performance problems of the P-400 rested in its engine, but the 67th FS Hist. speaks of the lack of proper equipment to recharge their British-model high-pressure oxygen bottles, limiting altitude to about 14,-000 (the history says: "The planes would struggle up a little higher, but the pilots couldn't do so").

Page 202
Change of mission for P-400: 13th AF Hist., p. 8; COMAIRSOPAC War Diary 29 Sep 42; COMGEN 1ST MARDIV to COMAIRSOPACFOR 020323 Oct 42, COMSOPAC War Diary 2 Oct 42, p. 2.

Page 202

Loss of *Colhoun: S.S.,* Vol. 83, p. 42; U.S.S. *Colhoun,* Serial 301, September 3, 1942, Subject: Loss of U.S.S. *Colhoun;* and No Serial, August 30, 1942, Anti-aircraft action by U.S.S. *Colhoun.*

Page 202

Arrival of rest of MAG-23; MAG-23 Record of Events 30 Aug 42.

Pages 202–3

Japanese conferences and orders, August 30: *S.S.,* Vol. 14, pp. 394–97, Vol. 83, p. 33.

"Nezumi": Van Der Rhoer, *Deadly Magic,* p. 116.

Pages 203–4

Losses of VMF-224 on August 31 and story of Lieutenant Amerine: MAG-23 Record of Events 31 Aug 42; "Marine Flyer, Ex-Kansas Football Star, Kills Four of Foe Behind Their Lines in Solomons," Associated Press, *New York Times,* September 22, 1942, p. 3, col. 3.

Page 204

Torpedoing of *Saratoga:* U.S.S. *Saratoga,* CV3/A16-3, Serial 00111, September 11, 1942; *S.S.,* Vol. 83, p. 65; Lee, *They Call It Pacific,* p. 361; Zenji Orita and Joseph D. Harrington, *I-Boat Captain* (Canoga Park, Calif.: Major Books, 1976), p. 129.

Page 204

"Suitable targets present themselves . . . ": CINCPAC to PACFLT, 190305 Aug 42, COMSOPAC War Diary 19 Aug 42, p. 58.

Page 205

Admiral Tanaka relieved as commander of Reinforcement Unit: Tanaka, Part I, pp. 696–97; *S.S.,* Vol. 83, pp. 31–32; Vol. 14, p. 398.

Kawaguchi reaches Guadalcanal: *S.S.,* Vol. 14, p. 398.

Page 206

Reinforcement run of September 1–2: *S.S.,* Vol. 83, p. 52; MAG-23 Record of Events, 1 Sep. One SBD crashed on takeoff.

Air action of September 2 and return of carrier planes: *S.S.,* Vol. 83, p. 42–43; MAG-23 Record of Events 2 Sep 42.

Reinforcement run of September 2–3; *S.S.,* Vol. 83, p. 52.

Page 206

Arrival of Major General Geiger: MAG-23 Record of Events 3 Sep 42.

Page 206

Background of Geiger: Colonel Roger Willock, USMCR, *Unaccustomed to Fear: A Biography of the Late General Roy S. Geiger* (Princeton, N.J.: Privately published, 1969), pp. 231–34, 242–43; Miller, *Cactus Air Force,* pp. 74–75; interview of Major General Wallace and Brigadier General Bryce by Major John Zimmerman, January 5, 1949; Zimmerman monograph comment file, MCHC.

Pages 206–8

Tactical situation with respect to air defense and detection or raids: Smith intvw, p. 3; Felt, *Coast Watchers,* pp. 92–94; Lord, *Lonely Vigil,* p. 53; "Report on Fighter Direction Cactus, October 8, 1942 to January 1, 1943," Major General Louis Woods Papers, MCHC, Box 9, Entry 52; Mangrum intvw, p. 6. Mr. John Lundstrom furnished information on the bomb loads and tactics of Japanese aircraft.

Effects of Japanese bombs: Torpedo Squadron 8, VT-8/A16/nhn, No Serial, December 1, 1942, p. 4, Part C.

Page 208

U.S. fighter tactics: Smith intvw, pp. 3–6, 10; Interview of Captain J. J. Foss in the Bureau of Aeronautics, 26 April 1943, pp. 1–3, 7, 13–15; Miller, *Cactus Air Force,* p. 72–73, credits Smith with design of fighter tactics.

Pages 208–9

SBD operations: Mangrum intvw, pp. 1, 3, 5–8; Merillat Diary 31 Aug 42.

Pages 209–10

Operational strains on aircrews: MAG-23 Record of Events 20 Aug–16 Oct 42, pp. 12–13; Lt. Gen. Louis Woods, USMC (Ret), interview, May–Jul 68 (Oral History Collection, Marine Corps Historical Center), p. 158 [hereafter Woods intvw]; Miller, *Cactus Air Force,* pp. 69–70; Joseph Foss and Walter Simmons, *Joe Foss Flying Marine* (Zenger Publishing, 1979; reprint of 1st ed., New York: Dutton), pp. 47–48 [hereafter Foss and Simmons, *Joe Foss Flying Marine*].

Page 210

Geiger bombing mission: Geiger Aviation Log, Geiger Papers, MCHC.

Page 211
Tokyo Express run of 4–5 September and loss of *Little* and *Gregory: S.S.,* Vol. 83, p. 42; U.S.S. *Little,* No Serial, 9 Sep 42; *U.S.S. Gregory,* No Serial, 11 Sep 42.

Page 212
"The officers and men serving in these ships . . .": Commander Amphibious Force South Pacific, FE25/L11, Serial 00486, December 13, 1942, Subject: Loss of the U.S.S. *Colhoun* and U.S.S. *Gregory.*

Pages 212–13
Barge convoy to Guadalcanal: *S.S.,* Vol. 14, pp. 399–410; Vol. 83, pp. 43, 57; MAG-23 Record of Events 3–5 Sep 42. According to *S.S.,* Vol. 14, p. 410, no count was recorded of losses on the barge convoy, but at p. 458 a figure of "about 90 dead" is offered.

Page 214
Ghormley requests replacements for Wildcats: COMSOPAC to CINCPAC 270226 Aug 42, Grey Book, p. 811; Ghormley, "Tide Turns," p. 112. Also on August 28 Nimitz was informed of the assignment of a thirty-five plane B-24 group to the Pacific and of the shipment of eighty-six crated fighter planes and pilots (COMINCH TO CINCPAC 171320 Aug 42, Grey Book, p. 573). However, at the same time, General Marshall sternly rejected overtures from General Emmons, the commander of the Hawaiian Department, for still more aircraft to cover the Central Pacific (MARSHALL to CG HAWDEPT, info CINCPAC 270211 Aug 42, Grey Book, p. 812). Ghormley requested P-38s from MacArthur on September 2, but MacArthur pointed out that he had received only about thirty of these aircraft and they were not all assembled or the pilots trained. With only 4 or 5 available, he could spare none. Ghormley, "Tide Turns," p. 118.

Page 214
Forrestal's message: FORRESTAL to SECNAV 301010 Aug 42, Grey Book, p. 664; CINCPAC Daily Summary 30 Aug 42, Grey Book, p. 838.

McCain's message: COMAIRSOPAC 310402 Aug 42, COMSOPAC War Diary 31 Aug 42, pp. 81–82.

Ghormley's view: COMSOPAC to CINCPAC 010305 Sep 42, Grey Book, p. 862; Ghormley, "Tide Turns," p. 117. Nimitz supported these comments in CINCPAC to COMINCH 012331 Sep 42, Grey Book, p. 863.

Page 215
Harmon's request: COMSOPAC to CINCPAC 050730 and 050750 Aug 42, Grey Book, pp. 637–38.

Page 215
Deployment of fifteen air groups: Hayes, *History of the Joint Chiefs of Staff,* pp. 173–85; Morton, *Strategy and Command,* pp. 326–40. It is also of note that the Alaskan theater absorbed a considerable number of planes not under Nimitz's command. As of October 10, there were 146 fighters, fifty medium bombers (including twenty-two of the Royal Canadian Air Force), and twenty-eight heavy bombers with the 11th Air Force. The Navy also contributed twelve Wildcats and thirty-five PBYs (Grey Book, p. 1083).

Page 216
Return of MacArthur's naval units: COMINCH to CINCPAC, COMSOPAC 28 1240 Aug 42, Grey Book, p. 666; COMSOPAC to COMINCH, CINCPAC 290310 Aug 42, Grey Book, p. 666; CINCPAC to COMSOPAC, 302123 Aug 42, Grey Book, p. 667; COMSOPAC to CTFS 61m 17, 18, 44, No Time Group, COMSOPAC War Diary 30 Aug 42, p. 81; Ghormley, "Tide Turns," p. 113.

Page 216
Deployment of 43d Division to South Pacific: COMINCH to CINCPAC 291240 Aug 42, Grey Book, p. 814; CINCPAC Daily Summary 29 Aug 42, Grey Book, p. 838.

Page 216
September 8 orders for amphibious regiment: CINCPAC to COMSOPAC, 081736 Sep 42, Grey Book, p. 870; Ghormley, "Tide Turns," pp. 119–20.

Turner's response: COMAMPHIBFORSOPAC to COMSOPAC 092300 Sep 42, Grey Book, p. 875.

Page 216
Ghormley creates Task Force 64: COMSOPAC 070452 Sep 42, Grey Book, p. 868.

Pages 216–17
King-Nimitz meeting: Conference Notes, September 9, 1942, Grey Book, pp. 1014–26. The reference to relieving Ghormley is on p. 1020.

CHAPTER 9

Page 218
Kawaguchi's strength and intelligence information: *S.S.*, Vol. 14, pp. 398–99, 443.

Pages 218–19
Vandegrift's tactical problems: Final Report, Phase IV, pp. 12–13.

Pages 219–20
Kawaguchi's plans and naval support: *S.S.*, Vol. 14, pp. 443–45; Vol. 83, pp. 102, 116–17.

Page 219
"thus giving repose to the departed souls of the Ichiki Detachment commander and men": Captain William H. Whyte, Jr., USMCR, "The Guadalcanal Campaign—The Japanese Viewpoint," unpaginated, MCHC, Box 9 [hereafter Whyte, "Guadalcanal Campaign"].

Page 220
Erroneous information passed to Navy on date of attack; intelligence on American reinforcements passed to Kawaguchi: *S.S.*, Vol. 14, pp. 444–46, 449. For operations in support of Kawaguchi, the 8th Fleet was organized as follows:

MAIN FORCE
Chokai and *Kagero*

SUPPORT FORCE
Cruiser Division 6 and *Amagiri*

SURPRISE ATTACK FORCE
(Destroyer Squadron 3)

CONVOY FORCE
Two AK and *Shirayuki*

Page 220
Proposal to raid Tasimboko: Final Report, Phase IV, pp. 5–6.

Merritt Edson: Tregaskis, *Guadalcanal Diary*, p. 80; Griffith intvw, p. 86.

Pages 221–22
Execution of Tasimboko raid: Final Report, Phase IV, pp. 5–6 and Annex A; Final Report, Jul 43, p. 11; 1st Mar Div Record of Events 8–9 Sep 42; Report of Operations First Parachute Battalion Solomons Islands Offensive, Tasimboco [sic] Raid 7–8 September 1942, MCHC, Box 6, File A36-1 [hereafter First Parachute Battalion Tasimboko Raid]; MAG-23 Record of Events 8 Sep; Tregaskis, *Guadalcanal Diary*, pp. 207–9; Griffith, *Battle of Guadalcanal*, pp. 108–9;

Interview, Col. Edmund J. Buckley USMCR with Major John L. Zimmerman USMCR, 7 Mar 47; ltr Col. Samuel B. Griffith to CMC 15 Feb 49; *S.S.*, Vol. 14, p. 447. Exactly how many Japanese were around Tasimboko is unclear. Griffith gives a figure of 300. The company Kawaguchi sent to guard his rear was 10th Company, 124th Infantry Regiment.

TF 62 War Diary 8 Sep 42 shows the escorts of *Fuller* and *Bellatrix* were *Hull, Hughes, Zane, Hopkins,* and *Southard.*

Page 222
"It is maddening . . .": Whyte, "Guadalcanal Campaign," quoting Diary Item 1322 USA-FISPA G-2 Rpt. No. 69.

Page 222
Japanese command reaction to Tasimboko raid: *S.S.*, Vol. 14, pp. 448–51. The 11th Air Fleet had dispatched nine Bettys and nine Zeros to Port Moresby.

Page 222
Loss of YP boat: 1st Mar Div Record of Events 9–10 Sep 42.

"This is no motley of Japs": Griffith, *Battle of Guadalcanal*, p. 109.

Pages 222–23
Indications of Kawaguchi's approach: Final Report, Phase IV, p. 6.

Discussion and decision at 1st Marine Division, September 9: Griffith, *Battle of Guadalcanal*, pp. 109–10; Thomas intvw. pp. 355–56; Vandegrift and Asprey, *Once a Marine*, p. 151. Clemens MS, p. 174, says the decision to move the division command post was influenced by an aerial photograph that demonstrated tracks leading to the headquarters area that stuck out like "a sore thumb."

Description of ridge: Merillat, *Island*, p. 93; Merillat, *Guadalcanal Remembered*, p. 129; Report on Operations 1st Parachute Battalion Solomons Islands Offensive Defense of Lunga Ridge, 13–14 September 1942, with accompanying map, MCHC, Box 7, File A36-3 [hereafter 1st Parachute Battalion Defense of Lunga Ridge]; *S.S.*, Vol. 14, pp. 566–67.

Page 223
"impact center": Merillat, *Island,* p. 93.

"profane" arguments: Vandegrift and Asprey, *Once a Marine*, p. 151.

Page 223
Air operations September 8–9: *S.S.,* Vol. 83, p. 94; MAG-23 Record of Events 8–9 Sep 42; 1st Mar Div Record of Events 9 Sep 42.

Page 223
Story of Captain Marion Carl: Miller, *Cactus Air Force,* p. 96.

Pages 223–24
Planning for deployment of III/4: *S.S.,* Vol. 14, pp. 450–52.

Pages 224–25
Kawaguchi's approach march: Ibid., pp. 452–58.

Page 225
Oka's situation and landing of III/4: Ibid., pp. 450, 458–61, Vol. 83, p. 102.

Pages 225–26
Reports of approach of Kawaguchi and deployment of 1st Raiders and 1st Parachutists to the ridge: Final Report, Phase IV, p. 6; Griffith, *Battle of Guadalcanal,* p. 112.

Page 226
Air action September 10: MAG-23 Record of Events 10 Sep 42; *S.S.,* Vol. 83, p. 94.

Movement of VF-5 to Guadalcanal: John Lundstrom discovered the illuminating story of the initiative of Lieutenant Commander Simpler in the deployment of VF-5. The existing documentation is in CINCPAC to COMINCH 012331 Sep 42, COMSOPAC War Diary 2 Sep 42, p. 1; COMSOPAC 111320 Sep 42, COMSOPAC War Diary 11 Sep 42, p. 12; MAG-23 Record of Events 10–11 Sep 42.

Page 226
Air action September 11: MAG-23 Record of Events 11 Sep 42; *S.S.,* Vol. 83, p. 95; 1st Mar Div Record of Events 11 Sep 42; VMF-224 War Diary 11 Sep 42, p. 2. There is a question as to whether the Japanese deliberately sought to bomb the ridge or whether this was pure happenstance.

Page 226
"Marines who clawed a few . . .": Griffith, *Battle of Guadalcanal,* p. 113.

Del Valle prepares artillery: Ibid., p. 115.

Page 227
Turner's visit: 1st Mar Div Record of Events 11 Sep 42; Vandegrift and Asprey, *Once a Marine,* pp. 152–53; Thomas intvw, p. 357;

Ghormley, "Tide Turns," p. 120; TF 62 War Diary 11 Sep 42. A message precisely fitting the description provided by Vandegrift and Thomas is not to be found in the COMSOPAC War Diary. The closest approximation is COMSOPAC to CINCPAC info COMINCH 110516 Sep 42, Grey Book, p. 874. The quote from Turner is from Thomas intvw; a slightly different version is in Vandegrift and Asprey, *Once a Marine,* p. 152. According to Turner, before making his trip he had won tentative agreement from Ghormley to land the 7th Marines near Taivu Point. Amphibious Force South Pacific Force, Office of the Commander, Serial 00195, September 27, 1942. Subject: Report of Operations to land 7th Marines, pp. 2–3 [hereafter AMPHIBFORSOPAC Serial 00195]. COMSOPAC to CINCPAC 040300 Sep 42, Grey Book, p. 865, confirms Turner's report. Twining account: "Head for the Hills," *Marine Corps Gazette,* August 1987. General Twining expressed his views forcefully on the matter in letter to author of February 4, 1990.

Page 228
"moving like a slender white cloud . . .": Tregaskis, *Guadalcanal Diary,* p. 220.

Air raid September 12: *S.S.,* Vol. 83, p. 95 (loss data from Lundstrom); MAG-23 Record of Events 12 Sep 42; Commander Fighting Squadron 5, No Serial, No Date, Subject: Action Reports—Combat in Guadalcanal Area, 12 September to 15 October 1942, 12 Sep 42 [hereafter VF-5 Action Reports Guadalcanal]; 1st Mar Div Record of Events 12 Sep 42.

Loss of three B-17s: 11th BG Hist., Reel B0067, p. 1677; 13th AF Hist., p. 22.

Capture of American aviator and reports reaching Kawaguchi: *S.S.,* Vol. 14, pp. 462–63. The identity and the fate of this flier are not given in *S.S.*

Page 229
Turner's comments to correspondents: Merillat, *Guadalcanal Remembered,* p. 136.

Page 229
Deployment of Edson's forces: 1st Parachute Battalion Defense of Lunga Ridge, Enclosure B (a map mislabeled for September 13, but clearly pertaining to September 12 except for the deployment of Company C of the Raider Battalion); Final Report, Phase IV, p. 7; 1st Mar Div Record of Events 12 Sep 42; Merillat, *Island,* p. 94; Tregaskis, *Guadalcanal Diary,* p. 223; Notes on Interview, Major Houston Stiff, Major John B. Sweeney, Major

Richard S. Johnson, Major William E. Sperling, Platoon Sergeant Pettus with Major John Zimmerman, 4 Feb 49, Zimmerman Comment File [hereafter Zimmerman intvw with Stiff et al.]

Strength of Raiders and Parachutists: figure in text is based on the figures given in 1st Parachute Battalion Tasimboko Raid less the casualties during the raid.

Pages 229, 231
Edson's intentions and orders: Merillat, *Island*, p. 94.

Japanese Navy contingent appears: *S.S.*, Vol. 83, p. 103.

Page 231
Marine view of Japanese attack: Griffith, *Battle of Guadalcanal*, p. 116; Merillat, *Island*, p. 95; Zimmerman intvw with Stiff et al.

Pages 231–32
Japanese experience night of September 12–13: *S.S.*, Vol. 14, pp. 463–67. Addendum 6 of Vol. 14, pp. 558–68, goes into considerable length setting out the evidence on the Japanese side as to what happened on the night of September 12–13. The conclusions are essentially the same as this writer's on events of this most confusing episode.

Pages 232–33
Turner's attitude on departure: Thomas intvw. pp. 361–62 (from which quotes are taken); Vandegrift and Asprey, *Once a Marine*, p. 153. Turner's concept of how the marines ought to go about the business of defending Guadalcanal is set forth unblushingly in his report, AMPHIBFORSOPAC Serial 00195, pp. 2–3. The message Turner dispatched from Guadalcanal read in part as follows (COMAMPHIBFORSOPAC to COMSOPAC 120530 Sep 42, COMSOPAC War Diary 12 Sep 42, p. 14):

> Vandegrift and I agree that control of the north coastal plain requires dispersals along points with troops, and coastal anti-aircraft artillery and additional airfields [but they believe Kukum should be immediately reinforced].

One wonders if this message accurately conveys what Vandegrift believed.

Page 233
Vandegrift meets with Geiger: Vandegrift and Asprey, *Once a Marine*, p. 153.

"They were testing . . .": Griffith, *Battle of Guadalcanal*, pp. 116–17.

Page 233
Marine efforts on morning of September 13: 1st Parachute Battalion Defense of Lunga Ridge, p. 2; Merillat, *Island*, p. 96.

Page 233
Information at Rabaul and reconnaissance flight: *S.S.*, Vol. 14, pp. 475–77; Vol. 83, p. 108. It was not until 1600 that the reconnaissance flight gave Rabaul a definite report that the airfield had not been captured.

Arrival of replacement Wildcats and action with escort of reconnaissance planes: MAG-23 Record of Events 13 Sep 42; VF-5 Action Reports Guadalcanal 13 Sep 42.

Page 234
"We saw one Wildcat . . .": Tregaskis, *Guadalcanal Diary*, pp. 225–26.

Bombing raid September 13: *S.S.*, Vol. 83, p. 98; VMF-223, -224 War Diaries 13 Sep 42; MAG-23 Record of Events 13 Sep 42; VF-5 Action Reports Guadalcanal 13 Sep 42; Miller, *Cactus Air Force*, p. 90; Griffith, *Battle of Guadalcanal*, p. 118.

Pages 234–35
Loss of SBD and arrival of VS-3 and elements of VT-8; MAG-23 Record of Events 13 Sep 42.

Page 235
Oka's report and Kawaguchi's orders: *S.S.*, Vol. 14, p. 468.

Page 235
Edson's defensive scheme: 1st Parachute Battalion Defense of Lunga Ridge, p. 2; Final Report, Phase IV, p. 8; Merillat, *Island*, pp. 96–97; Engineer Activities Guadalcanal, pp. 6–7; ltr Lt. Col. William A. Stiles to CMC 14 Dec 49; Zimmerman intvw. with Stiff et al.; Griffith intvw, pp. 115–16; ltr Col. Samuel B. Griffith to CMC 15 Feb 49.

Page 235
Twining visits Edson's command: McMillan, *Old Breed*, p. 75; Pratt, *Marine's War*, p. 61.

Pages 235, 237
Movements and preparations of 2d Battalion, 5th Marines: Final Report, Phase IV, p. 8; ltr Major Harry S. Connors to CMC 14 Feb 49; ltr Lt. Col. Thomas J. Colley to CMC 14 Feb 49; Griffith, *Battle of Guadalcanal*, p. 116. Griffith says the movement of 2/5 was on

September 12, but Final Report and Major Connors say September 13. It is also unclear from the record on which day Lieutenant Colonel Rosecrans and Major Skinner were injured. Thomas intvw, p. 360, says it was September 12, but 67th FS Hist., pp. 35–37, describes this episode and places it on September 11.

Page 237
Initial Japanese attacks September 13: Final Report, Phase IV, p. 9, Annex E (Artillery), pp. 2–3; Merillat, *Island,* p. 97; 1st Parachute Battalion Defense of Lunga Ridge, p. 4; 1st Mar Div Record of Events 13 Sep 42; *S.S.,* Vol. 14, pp. 471–72.

Page 237
Main attack against first Marine position on the ridge: 1st Parachute Battalion Defense of Lunga Ridge, pp. 4–6; Final Report, Phase IV, pp. 9–10.

"Gas Attack": 1st Parachute Battalion Defense of Lunga Ridge, enclosure (d), Statement of Member of Company A, 1st Parachute Battalion, p. 1; Merillat, *Island,* p. 98; Merillat, *Guadalcanal Remembered,* p. 140.

Page 238
Weight of attack shifts to Company B, 1st Raiders: Final Report, Phase IV, p. 10; Merillat, *Island,* p. 98; 1st Parachute Battalion Defense of Lunga Ridge, p. 6.

Withdrawal and role of Major Bailey: 1st Parachute Battalion Defense of Lunga Ridge, p. 6 and Enclosure D, Statement of Member of Company A, 1st Parachute Battalion (which reveals the story of the "withdraw" rumor).

The actions of the 1st Parachute Battalion this night generated controversy. In his letter to CMC 15 Feb 49, Samuel B. Griffith flatly stated:

> To be historically correct, half the 1st Para Bn "took off" from their positions on the night of 12–13 [Sep.]. Fled, in other words.

Two things may be said with assurance about this comment. First, Griffith apparently confused the night of September 12–13 with the following night, as there was no question about the behavior of the parachutists on September 12–13. Second, Griffith did not personally witness these events, as he was in the jungle to the west of the ridge. When he wrote his own book on the subject he made

no suggestion that the Parachutists bolted, but on the other hand he was also notably reticent about some other episodes during the campaign that were controversial, such as Maxwell's Kokumbona patrol in late August. In a recent account derived in important part from correspondence with participants, Eric Hammel indicated that most of the small Company C of the Parachutists bolted when initially struck by the Japanese and that this was partly responsible for Company B's withdrawal. He adds that both companies "ran headlong" to the rear (*Guadalcanal: Starvation Island,* pp. 229–30). What exactly happened this night is probably impossible to state with complete certainty at this date, but the account in the text follows the report prepared by Captain Torgerson proximate to the event. This admits serious confusion and loss of control, but by no means ignominious flight.

Page 238
Role of 11th Marines: Final Report, Phase IV, Annex E, pp. 2–3; Tregaskis, *Guadalcanal Diary,* p. 228; Merillat, *Guadalcanal Remembered,* p. 139.

Page 238
Attack of II/4: *S.S.,* Vol. 14, pp. 472–73.

Pages 238–39
Defense of the knoll: Final Report, Phase IV, pp. 10–11; 1st Parachute Battalion Defense of Lunga Ridge, pp. 8–11; Vandegrift and Asprey, *Once a Marine,* pp. 154–55; Griffith, *Battle of Guadalcanal,* p. 119; Tregaskis, *Guadalcanal Diary,* pp. 229, 232, 238–39; Merillat, *Island,* p. 101; Clemens MS, p. 176. Gerald Thomas called the commander of the 1st Parachute Battalion a "dud" (Thomas intvw, p. 427).

Page 240
Part of II/4 reaches vicinity of airfield: *S.S.,* Vol. 14, pp. 472–73; Engineer Activities Guadalcanal, p. 7.

Page 240
Attack of P-400s and the scene on the ridge: MAG-23 Record of Events 14 Sep 42; 67th FS Hist., p. 32; Tregaskis, *Guadalcanal Diary,* p. 234.

"With heads lolling . . .": Griffith, *Battle of Guadalcanal,* p. 120.

Page 241
"This powerful battalion . . .": From Kawaguchi's memoirs as quoted in Griffith, *Battle of Guadalcanal,* p. 121.

Page 241
Story of III/124: *S.S.,* Vol. 14, p. 471.

Page 241
Infiltration, death of Major Brown, status of 1st Parachute Battalion, losses in 1st Marines: Merillat, *Island,* p. 99; Griffith, *Battle of Guadalcanal,* p. 120; First Parachute Battalion Defense of Lunga Ridge, p. 8; Hammel, *Guadalcanal: Starvation Island,* pp. 235–36.

Banzais that sounded like a turkey: Tregaskis, *Guadalcanal Diary,* pp. 231–32; Vandegrift and Asprey, *Once a Marine,* p. 155; Griffith, *Battle of Guadalcanal,* p. 120.

Page 242
Attack on 3/1: Final Report, Phase IV, pp. 11–12; *S.S.,* Vol. 14, pp. 470–71. Merillat, *Island,* pp. 102–3, provides the best account of the abortive tank attack.

Page 243
Colonel Oka's attack: *S.S.,* Vol. 14, pp. 473–74; Merillat, *Island,* p. 104; Final Report, Phase IV, p. 12. Final Report appears to be somewhat erroneous about certain details, and the text substantially follows Merillat on this episode.

Page 243
Situation at Japanese headquarters and serial reconnaissance: *S.S.,* Vol. 14, pp. 478–80; Vol. 83, pp. 99–100, 110; VMF-223, -224 War Diaries 14 Sep 42; MAG-23 Record of Events 14 Sep 42.

Page 243
Attack by float planes: *S.S.,* Vol. 83, pp. 99, 101, 110–11; VMF-224 War Diary 14 Sep 42; MAG-23 Record of Events 14 Sep 42; VF-5 Action Reports Guadalcanal 14 Sep 42. On this day heavy cruiser *Myoko* was slightly damaged by fragments from bombs dropped by B-17s as she cruised with the Combined Fleet north of the Solomons. One B-17 failed to return from this mission. *S.S.,* Vol. 83, p. 120; 11th BG Hist., Reel B0067, p. 1677.

Page 244
Air losses: Combat losses totaled from text. During this period one Wildcat, four SBDs, and one P-400 were destroyed on the ground on Guadalcanal. Combat losses also included one each PBY and B-17; one PBY and three B-17s were operational losses during this period, as was one F4F-7 photographic reconnaissance plane.

Page 244
Japanese assessment of Kawaguchi failure: *S.S.,* Vol. 14, pp. 479–82.

"The army had been used to fighting the Chinese": *USSBS Interrogations,* Vol. I, p. 68, interview with Captain Watanabe.

Page 245
Artillery expenditures in Ridge Battle: Final Report, Phase IV, Annex E, p. 3. Final Report, Jul 43, p. 10, comments that the effectiveness of the 105mm howitzer was demonstrated on the night of September 13–14. This weapon won itself a place in the Marine combat team it was to retain for over thirty years and three wars. The 75mm howitzers of the 2d and 3d Battalions, 11th Marines fired 878 rounds in support of the marines holding the east and west flanks.

Page 245
American losses: These figures are drawn from several sources, as the numbers provided by Final Report, Phase IV, are obviously too low. Griffith, *Battle of Guadalcanal,* p. 121, gives what is probably the most accurate accounting of Raider and Parachutist losses. Recorded losses in other units were: 1st Marines (Company B), eighteen dead; 1st Engineer Battalion, five dead, fifteen wounded; 3d Battalion, 1st Marines, four dead; 1st Tank Battalion, four dead; Division Headquarters, one dead. 5th Mar Div Record of Events lists losses as five dead and fifty-five wounded; ltr Major Harry S. Connor to CMC 14 Feb 49 reports his company, E/2/5, lost five killed and nine wounded on September 14 getting into position on the ridge, and Company G had thirty casualties. The figures entered in Merillat, *Island,* p. 105, were contemporaneous to the event and presumably the best.

Page 245
Losses in Kawaguchi's brigade: *S.S.,* Vol. 14, pp. 483–84, 502. The table on pp. 483–84 covers the period from August 13 to October 2.

Pages 245–46
Kawaguchi's retreat: *S.S.,* Vol. 14, pp. 474–75, 500–7; Final Report, Phase IV, p. 14; Whyte, "Guadalcanal Campaign," quoting from Diary Item 1322, USAFISPA G-2 Rpt No. 69; Griffith, *Battle of Guadalcanal,* p. 122. *S.S.,* Vol. 14, p. 480, indicates Kawaguchi received orders from the 17th Army on September 15 to occupy a point west of the Matanikau as close to the airfield as possible, from which point he was to de-

velop intelligence information and attempt to obstruct American air operations while securing the lines of communication to Kamimbo.

Page 246
Imperial Headquarters plans for decisive battle: Ibid., p. 480.

CHAPTER 10

Page 247
Admiral Turner's situation and decision on September 15: Commander, Amphibious Force South Pacific Force, Serial 00195, September 27, 1942. Subject: Report of Operations to Land the 7th Marines, pp. 4–6 [hereafter COMAMPHIBFORSOPAC Serial 00195].

Page 248
I-19 activities: *S.S.,* Vol. 83, pp. 124–26; Orita and Harrington, *I-Boat Captain,* pp. 130–31.

Pages 248–49
Torpedoing of *Wasp:* U.S.S. *Wasp,* P6-1(006), September 24, 1942, Subject: War Damage Report No. 39, U.S.S. *Wasp,* Loss in Action, 15 January 1944. The War Damage Report concludes on p. 7 that human failure accounted for the loss of fire main pressure forward.

Sequence of torpedo hits from *I-19:* Captain Ben W. Blee, USN (Ret.), "Whodunnit?," *United States Naval Institute Proceedings,* Vol. 108/7/953 (July 1982), pp. 42–47. For some time after the war, credit for hits on *North Carolina* and *O'Brien* was given to *I-15,* which was definitely near the scene. However, Blee's article graphically illustrates how Commander Kinashi achieved his successes and sorts out the sequence of hits in the correct order.

Page 248
Torpedoing of *O'Brien:* U.S.S. *O'Brien,* DD415/L11-1, Serial 028, 23 Sep 42, Subject: *O'Brien* DD415—War Damage Report.

Page 249
Torpedoing of *North Carolina:* U.S.S. *North Carolina,* Serial 0128, 26 Sep 42, Subject: Estimated Damage Resulting from Torpedo Hit on September 15, 1942.

Pages 249–50
Ultimate loss of *O'Brien:* U.S.S. *O'Brien,* Serial 01, 26 Oct 42, Subject: Report of Loss of; War Damage Report No. 28, 24 Jun 43,

U.S.S. *O'Brien,* Torpedo Damage and Loss—15 September–19 October 1942, Preliminary Design Section, Bureau of Ships.

Page 250
Criticism of Noyes: Commander in Chief, U.S. Pacific Fleet, CINCPAC File Pac 90-wb, A16-3/Sol, Serial 03168, October 31, 1952, Subject: Solomons Islands Campaign—Torpedoing of Saratoga, Wasp and North Carolina.

Page 250
Noyes response: Commander Task Force 61, No Serial, 21 September 1942, Subject: Report of Operations 8–18 September, and attachments.

Pages 250–51
Effectiveness of Japanese submarines in 1942: Orita and Harrington, *I-Boat Captain,* p. 132, makes the point about the contributions of the Imperial Navy's submarine arm in 1942.

Pages 251–52
Turner's decision to land the 7th Marines and execution: COMAMPHIBFORSOPAC Serial 00195, pp. 6–end; MAG-23 Record of Events 18 Sep 42.

Reinforcement runs of September 16–17, 17–18, and 18–19: *S.S.,* Vol. 83, p. 137; MAG-23 Record of Events 16–17 Sep 42.

Page 252
Japanese commanders shocked by Kawaguchi's failure, recognize significance of Guadalcanal: *S.S.,* Vol. 14, p. 523, Vol. 83, pp. 128–29, 132.

Page 252
Views at Imperial General Headquarters: Ibid., Vol. 14, p. 524, Vol. 83, pp. 132–33.

Pages 252–53
Decisions at Rabaul: Ibid., Vol. 83, pp. 131–32, 137.

Page 253
Reinforcements to 17th Army: Ibid., Vol. 14, pp. 527–27.

Page 253
Sugiyama briefs Emperor and 8th Central Agreement: Ibid., Vol. 14, pp. 525–26, 530–31; Vol. 83, p. 133–34.

Page 254
Staff changes in 17th Army: Ibid., Vol. 14, pp. 531–32.

Pages 254–55
Colonel Konuma's diary entries: *Senshi Sosho, Minamitaiheiyo Rikugun Sakusen,* 2, *Gadarukanaru-Buna Sakusen,* Boeicho Boei Kenshujo, Senshishitsu, Asagumo Shinbun Sha, July 30, 1969, pp. 36–40 (*War History Series, South Pacific Army Operations,* Part 2, *Guadalcanal-Buna Operation,* Defense Agency, Defense Research Institute, Office of War History) [hereafter *S.S.,* Vol. 28].

Page 256
Lack of rest or secure areas, size of perimeter: Merillat, *Island,* pp. 57, 60.

Page 256
"Jungle rot," lack of socks, and monotonous profanity: McMillan, *Old Breed,* pp. 69, 84–85.

Housing boom: Ibid., p. 87; Merillat, *Island,* p. 108.

Start of day on Guadalcanal: Foster Hailey, "Aid to Solomons Is Urged by Fliers," *New York Times,* October 29, 1942, p. 5, col. 3.

Only two daily meals: Although Final Report, Phase IV, p. 16, and Phase V, Annex T, say that after September 18 the garrison was on full rations, there is a very large amount of vehement comment from veterans in the 1st Marine Division that two meals a day remained in effect until the end of the division's participation. See, for example, ltr Col. Frederick L. Wiseman to CMC 17 Dec 48 and ltr Lt. Col. H. D. Adams to CMC 4 Jan 49. Wiseman stated the schedule remained in effect because fires could not be started before dawn and had to be out at sunset.

"rather thin gruel": Mears, *Carrier Combat,* p. 135.

Work details: Ltr Lt. Col. Elmer W. Myers to CMC 7 Feb 48.

Page 257
Vandegrift inspections: Vandegrift and Asprey, *Once a Marine,* p. 180.

Warning flags: Clemens MS, p. 184; John A. DeChant, *Devilbirds* (Washington, D.C.: Zenger Publishing, 1979; reprint of 1947 book), p. 67 [hereafter DeChant, *Devilbirds*]; Feldt, *Coast Watchers,* pp. 94–95.

Watching bombers approach; Colonel Cates fires .45 pistol: Merillat, *Island,* p. 156; Gen. Raymond G. Davis, interview, Feb 77 (Oral History Collection, Marine Corps Historical Center), pp. 121–22.

Description of sound and effects of falling bombs: Mears, *Carrier Combat,* p. 134.

Page 257
Ice plant signs: Clemens MS, p. 169; Griffith, *Battle of Guadalcanal,* p. 99.

Pages 257–58
Lieutenant Commander Simpler's opinion: Narrative by Lt. Cdr. Leroy C. Simpler, U.S.N., Southwest Pacific and Guadalcanal, Air Activities in above theaters of operations, March 8, 1943, p. 4, Naval Historical Center; 13th AF Hist., p. 188.

Importance of sleep: Merillat, *Island,* p. 156.

Bathing: Merillat, *Island,* p. 156; McMillan, *Old Breed,* p. 89.

First mail and ice: Ltr 5 Sep 42, Cates Papers, Box 2, entry 9, MCHC; Foss and Simmons, *Joe Foss Flying Marine,* p. 86.

Page 258
Contributions of Seabees: Engineer Activities Guadalcanal, p. 5; Pratt, *Marines' War,* p. 70.

Page 258
News, rumors, and souvenir industry: Leckie, *Helmet for My Pillow,* passim; "Solomons Menus of Marines Good," Associated Press, *New York Times,* October 15, 1942, p. 5; Vandegrift and Asprey, *Once a Marine,* p. 180; Cates, "My First," pp. 36b, 94.

"While at the first of October . . .": McMillan, *Old Breed,* p. 115.

Page 258
"speculative dread": Leckie, *Helmet for My Pillow,* pp. 79, 84–85.

Pages 258–59
Indications of those approaching limit and rule against running: Merillat, *Island,* pp. 156–57.

"Dead bodies were strewn about the grove . . .": Leckie, *Helmet for My Pillow,* p. 82.

Marine officer requests report of burying bodies: Ltr Colonel Frederick L. Wiseman to CMC 23 Feb 49.

Page 259
"there is no recourse but flight": Leckie, *Helmet for My Pillow,* p. 83.

Page 259
"The men are in good spirits . . .": As quoted in Vandegrift and Asprey, *Once a Marine,* p. 144.

Pages 259–60
Medical problems in 1st Marine Division: Medical Problems, Phase IV, p. 1. Phase V, pp. 3, 5–6, Annex T; Final Report, Jul 43, p. 7; Vandegrift and Asprey, *Once a Marine,* p. 160; McMillan, *Old Breed,* pp. 117–18, 134–35; Miller, *Guadalcanal: The First Offensive,* pp. 225–27.

Page 260
"indescribably wretched" and "Starvation Island": Agawa, *Reluctant Admiral.* p. 338.

"Rice cakes and candies appear in my dreams": Americal Division Intelligence Report, Tab B, File 300-2, Box 5473, RG 407 [hereafter Americal Div Intell Rpt Tab B].

Quality of food: Captain Andrieu D'Albas, *Death of a Navy* (New York: Devin-Adair, 1957), p. 191 [hereafter D'Albas, *Death of a Navy*].

Page 260
"Our bodies are so tired they are like raw cotton": Americal Div Intell Rpt Tab B.

Pages 260–61
Imperial Navy preference for Kamimbo and time to move supplies on Guadalcanal: *S.S.,* Vol. 83, pp. 137, 160.

Aircraft attacks on supply lines: Ibid., p. 161.

"long-nosed planes": Document Translation, 4/19/45, File 214-2, Box 4631, RG 407.

Location of Japanese bivouacs: Operations of the 25th Infantry Division on Guadalcanal, pp. 111, 132, File 325-0.3, Box 7995, RG 407 [hereafter 25th Div Opns].

Page 261
Fate of 11th and 13th Construction Units: *S.S.,* Vol. 83, p. 160.

Pages 261–62
Revised defense plan of 1st Marine Division: Final Report, Phase V, pp. 1–5; Pratt, *Marines' War,* pp. 68–69.

Pages 262–63
Vandegrift makes command changes: Vandegrift and Asprey, *Once a Marine,* p. 161; HQ MarCorp to COMSOPAC 081556 Sep 42, Grey Book, p. 914; Thomas intvw, pp. 281, 373–74; ltrs Vandegrift to Turner 24 Sep 42, Vandegrift to R. C. Kilmartin 18 Sep 42, Vandegrift to W. G. Hawthorne 19 Sep 42, Box 3, file 32, Vandegrift papers, MCHC.

Nine lieutenant colonels were promoted to full colonel, leaving the division seven over in that grade.

Pages 263–64
Formation and tasks of Scout-Snipers: Final Report, Phase IV, p. 14; 1st Mar Div Record of Events 17–18 Sep 42; Merillat, *Island,* pp. 117–18; Merillat diary; Thomas intvw, pp. 378–79.

Page 264
"the weirdest characters . . .": Thomas intvw, pp. 378–79.

Fitch replaces McCain: Ltr McCain to Vandegrift 20 Sep 42, Vandegrift Papers, Box 3, file 32, MCHC: *Vandegrift,* p. 162.

Pages 264–65
Japanese replenish air power: *S.S.,* Vol. 83 pp. 146–48; data developed by John Lundstrom.

Page 265
Strength of Cactus Air Force on September 20 and reinforcements: MAG-23 Record of Events 20 Sep 42, 23 Sep 42.

Page 265
B-17 attacks on Rabaul: *S.S.,* Vol. 83, p. 148.

Page 266
Fitch and Baldwin visit Guadalcanal: Vandegrift and Asprey, *Once a Marine,* pp. 163–64; Hanson W. Baldwin, *New York Times,* November 3, 1942, p. 4.

Page 266
September 20 and 21 runs of Tokyo Express: *S.S.,* Vol. 83, pp. 141–42; MAG-23 Record of Events 20–21 Sep 42.

Page 266
September 24 run of Tokyo Express and decision to stop runs: *S.S.,* Vol. 83, pp. 142–43.

CHAPTER 11

Pages 267–68
Planning at Truk and Rabaul: *S.S.,* Vol. 83, pp. 165–66; Vol. 28, p. 40. Hashimoto wanted thirty destroyers for the Reinforcement Unit.

Page 268
Imperial Army proposes convoy and revised transportation plan: *S.S.,* Vol. 28, p. 40; Vol. 83, pp. 167–68. Plans also included the mining of Tulagi Harbor by Cruiser Division 18, but this was never carried out.

Page 268
Meeting at Truk September 28: *S.S.,* Vol. 83, p. 168.

"thinner than [Mahatma] Gandhi . . .": Agawa, *Reluctant Admiral,* p. 328.

Page 268
Plans for employment of Combined Fleet: *S.S.,* Vol. 83, pp. 168–72.

Warning to Tsuji: *S.S.,* Vol. 83, p. 168; Vol. 28, p. 69.

Page 269
Description of Matanikau: Merillat, *Island,* p. 25; Miller, *Guadalcanal: The First Offensive,* p. 92.

Kawaguchi's plans and activities: *S.S.,* Vol. 14, pp. 506–7.

Page 269
Colonel Oka's actions September 24: Ibid., pp. 507–8.

Pages 269–70
Staff officers report: Ibid., pp. 506, 508.

Page 270
Marine activities after Battle of the Ridge and plans: Final Report, Phase V, p. 5.

Page 270
"loaded with talent": Thomas intvw, p. 421.

"a chin like a bulldozer blade": Clemens MS, p. 236.

Puller's orders: Final Report, Phase V, p. 5; Maj. Charles W. Kelly, Jr., USMCR, to Historical Division, Headquarters, U.S. Marine Corps, 16 May 1944, Subject: Narrative report of action of 1st Battalion, 7th Marines, 23–27 September 1942, p. 1 [hereafter Kelly, Narrative Report]. Lieutenant Colonel Puller made no formal report of this action.

Puller's movement and action September 23–24: Final Report, Phase V, p. 5; Kelly, Narrative Report, p. 1.

Page 270
Events on September 25: *S.S.,* Vol. 14, p. 510; Final Report, Phase V, pp. 5–6; Kelly, Narrative Report, pp. 1–2; 2d Battalion, Fifth Marines Record of Events 25–27 Sep 42, Box 6, File A16-2, MCHC, p. 1 [hereafter 2/5 Record of Events].

Page 271
Encounters of September 26: *S.S.,* Vol. 14, p. 510; 2/5 Record of Events, pp. 1–2, 26 Sep 42; Final Report, Phase V, pp. 5–6.

Pages 271–72
Action along Matanikau, September 27:

Final Report, Phase V, p. 6; 2/5 Record of Events, pp. 2–3; *S.S.,* Vol. 14, p. 510; Merillat, *Island,* pp. 119–20; Hammel, *Guadalcanal: Starvation Island,* p. 261.

"that when it comes to a job . . .": Tregaskis, *Guadalcanal Diary,* p. 251.

Pages 272–73
Air attack September 27: *S.S.,* Vol. 83, p. 148; VMF-223, -224 War Diaries 27 Sep 42; MAG-23 Record of Events 27 Sep 42; VF-5 Action Reports Guadalcanal 27 Sep 42; VF-5 War Diary 27 Sep 42; VT-8 War Diary 27 Sep 42. Lieutenant Turner Caldwell was evacuated this day, ending the tour of *Enterprise*'s Flight 300.

Page 273
Decision to land 1st Battalion, 7th Marines: Final Report, Phase V, pp. 6–7.

Page 273
Action of landing force of 1st Battalion, 7th Marines: Kelly, Narrative Report, pp. 2–7; MAG-23 Record of Events 27 Sep 42; U.S.S. *Monssen* War Diary 27 Sep 42; *S.S.,* Vol. 14, pp. 510–11; Merillat, *Island,* pp. 120–22; Burke Davis, *Marine!: The Life of Chesty Puller* (New York: Bantam, 1964), pp. 121–25 [hereafter Davis, *Marine*]. According to Davis, while Munro was gallantly covering the other boats, one of these craft was only held on the beach by virtue of the fact that Captain Fuller placed a gun to the coxswain's head.

Pages 273–74
American losses: Final Report, Phase V, p. 9; Kelly, Narrative Report, p. 7; 2/5 Record of Events 27 Sep 42, pp. 3–4.

Japanese satisfaction with action: *S.S.,* Vol. 14, p. 511.

Page 274
Analysis of the action: Final Report, Phase V, pp. 8–9; Vandegrift and Asprey, *Once a Marine,* p. 168.

Page 274
"The great lesson however is to be found . . .": Final Report, Phase V, p. 9.

Pages 274–75
Air Action September 28 and Japanese analysis: *S.S.,* Vol. 83, pp. 149–51; VMF-223, -224 War Diaries, 28 Sep 42; MAG-23 Record of Events 28 Sep 42; VF-5 Action Reports Guadalcanal 28 Sep 42.

Pages 275–76
Importance and status of Buin airfield: *S.S.,* Vol. 83, pp. 151–52, 241.

Page 276
Air action September 29: *S.S.,* Vol. 83, p. 151; VMF-223, -224, War Diaries 29 Sep 42; MAG-23 Record of Events 29 Sep 42; VF-5 Action Reports Guadalcanal 29 Sep 42; VF-5 War Diary 29 Sep 42.

Page 276
Arguments at the Joint Chiefs of Staff over aircraft in September: Hayes, *History of the Joint Chiefs of Staff,* pp. 185–87. Arnold, *Global Mission,* p. 338, says he promised one squadron of P-38s and one of heavy bombers on September 16, but conditioned further commitments on the results of his inspection trip.

Arnold's trip to the South Pacific: Arnold, *Global Mission,* pp. 337–41; Thomas M. Coffey, *Hap* (New York: Viking, 1982), pp. 286–89 [hereinafter Coffey, *Hap*]; Potter, *Nimitz,* pp. 189–90.

Page 276
Arnold's visit to 11th Bomb Group and performance of B-17s: Coffey, *Hap,* pp. 89–90; 11th BG Hist., Reel B0067, p. 1724; 13th AF Hist., pp. 23–24, 70; Craven and Cate, *Guadalcanal to Saipan: August 1942 to July 1944,* p. 53.

Page 277
September 28 Noumea meeting: Arnold, *Global Mission,* pp. 347–48; Potter, *Nimitz,* pp. 191–92; Pfeiffer intvw, p. 210.

Arnold's views: Hayes, *History of the Joint Chiefs of Staff,* pp. 186–87; Arnold, *Global Mission,* p. 350; Coffey, *Hap,* pp. 290–91.

Page 277
"So far, the Navy had taken . . .": Arnold, *Global Mission,* p. 342.

Nimitz's trip to Guadalcanal: Potter, *Nimitz,* pp. 192–94; Vandegrift and Asprey, *Once a Marine,* p. 171; Merillat, *Guadalcanal Remembered,* pp. 158–59; Pfeiffer intvw, p. 205.

October 2 meeting of Nimitz and Ghormley: Pfeiffer intvw, pp. 206–7; Ghormley, "Tide Turns," p. 128; Potter, *Nimitz,* p. 195.

Page 277
Nimitz's return to Pearl Harbor and intelligence situation: CINCPAC Daily Summary 6 Oct 42, Grey Book, p. 1079; CINCPAC Daily Summary 30 Sep 42, Grey Book,

p. 1049; Combat Intelligence Unit, 14th Naval District, "Estimate of Enemy Capabilities 1 October," Grey Book, pp. 1071–90.

Page 278
"The enemy is copying our communications methods . . .": Combat Intelligence Unit, 14th Naval District, Estimate of Enemy Capabilities 1 October, p. 3, Grey Book, p. 1073.

"most probably would include . . .": Ibid., p. 7, Grey Book, p. 1077.

Japanese change communications system: CINCPAC Daily Summary 30 Sep 42, Grey Book, p. 1049. Unfortunately, the communications intelligence history for the months of September through November 1942 has not yet been released.

Page 278
Air operations and reinforcement run October 1: *S.S.,* Vol. 83, pp. 173, 178; MAG-23 Record of Events 1 Oct 42.

Pages 278–79
Air operations and reinforcement run October 2: *S.S.,* Vol. 83, pp. 173, 178; VMF-223, -224, War Diaries, 2 Oct 42; MAG-23 Record of Events 2 Oct 42; VF-5 Action Reports Guadalcanal 29 Sep 42; VF-5 War Diary 2 Oct 42.

Page 279
Air operations and reinforcement run of October 3: *S.S.,* Vol. 83, pp. 178–79; VMF-223, -224 War Diaries, 3 Oct 42; MAG-23 Record of Events 3–4 Oct 42; 11th BG Hist., Reel B0067, p. 1728; Lord, *Lonely Vigil,* p. 78; Miller, *Cactus Air Force,* pp. 104–5.

Page 280
Reinforcement run of October 4–5: *S.S.,* Vol. 83, p. 179.

Pages 280–81
American air offensive of October 5: Ghormley, "Tide Turns," pp. 127, 133; U.S.S. *Hornet,* CV8 A16-3, Serial 0023, October 8, 1942, Subject: Report of Action, October 5, 1942; MAG-23 Record of Events 5 Oct 42; CTF 17 to COMSOPAC 062114 Oct 42, Grey Book, p. 940; COMAIRSOPAC War Diary 5 Oct 42; VS-71 War Diary 5 Oct 42; *S.S.,* Vol. 83, p. 175, Vol. 28, p. 74.

Page 281
Reinforcement run of October 5–6: *S.S.,* Vol. 83, p. 175; MAG-23 Record of Events 5–6 Oct 42.

Page 281

Failure of "Ant Transportation": *S.S.,* Vol. 83, pp. 173, 183, Vol. 28, p. 71. The vessels assigned to support the "Ant Transportation" were destroyers *Amagiri* and *Ayanami* and submarines *I-2* and *I-3.*

Pages 281–82

Reinforcement run of October 6–7 and postponement of X-Day: Ibid., Vol. 83, pp. 181–82, 187, Vol. 28, p. 74.

Page 282

Lieutenant General Murayama lands and learns situation: Ibid., Vol. 14, pp. 512–13.

"realize occupation of the [east] bank . . .": Ibid., pp. 512–14.

Page 282

Murayama's orders on October 4: Ibid., Vol. 28, pp. 56–57.

Page 282

Nasu's orders of October 5: Ibid., pp. 60–61.

Pages 282–83

Marine plans for renewed action at Matanikau: Final Report, Phase V, pp. 9–10; Merillat, *Island,* pp. 122–23.

Page 284

Lieutenant Colonel Frisbee briefs John Hersey: John Hersey, *Into the Valley* (New York: Bantam, 1966), pp. 13–14 [hereafter Hersey, *Into the Valley*].

"they look just like dirty-faced little boys . . .": Hersey, *Into the Valley,* p. 64.

Pages 284–85

Action of October 7: Final Report, Phase V, pp. 10–11; 5th Marines Record of Events, Box 6, File A14-1; 3d Battalion, 5th Marines, Unit Report No. 8, Box 6, File A17-1; 2d Battalion, 5th Marines, Misc. Reports, Box 6, File A16-4; Merillat, *Island,* p. 126; 1st Raider Battalion, Box 7, File A38-1.

Japanese account of action October 7: *S.S.,* Vol. 28, pp. 61–63.

Page 285

Reinforcement run October 7–8: *S.S.,* Vol. 83, p. 182. During this day light carrier *Zuiho* flew off thirty Zeros of the 6th Air Group for Rabaul. One was written off in a forced landing at Kavieng and three disappeared in bad weather; twenty-six reached their destination. Ibid., p. 176.

Reinforcement of Cactus Air Force: MAG-23 Record of Events 7 Oct 42.

Pages 285–86

Action of October 8: Final Report, Phase V, p. 11; Merillat, *Island,* pp. 127–28. The details of the very confused fight of the 1st Raiders on October 8 may be found in Hammel, *Guadalcanal: Starvation Island,* pp. 290–92.

Pages 286–87

John Hersey's account of the action of Company H, 2/5: Hersey, *Into the Valley,* pp. 74–93.

Page 287

Marines postpone attack: Final Report, Phase V, p. 11.

Page 287

Japanese reaction on October 8: *S.S.,* Vol. 28, pp. 62–63.

Pages 287–88

Action at mouth of Matanikau, October 8: Ibid., p. 62; 1st Raider Battalion, Box 7, File 38–1.

Marines decide to terminate action: Final Report, Phase V, pp. 11–12.

Page 288

Japanese command on October 8: *S.S.,* Vol. 28, pp. 62–64.

Page 288

Admiral Tsukahara replaced by Admiral Kusaka: *S.S.,* Vol. 83, pp. 175–76.

Page 288

Reinforcement run of October 8–9: *S.S.,* Vol. 83, pp. 154, 175, 182; MAG-23 Record of Events 8–9 Oct 42.

Pages 288–89

Action of October 9: *S.S.,* Vol. 28, p. 64; Final Report, Phase V, pp. 12–13; 1st Battalion, 7th Marines, Box 6, File A21-1.

Page 289

"machine for extermination": Hough, Ludwig, and Shaw, *Pearl Harbor to Guadalcanal,* p. 321.

American losses: Final Report, Phase V, p. 13. Merillat, *Island,* p. 129, gives the same figures.

Japanese losses: Final Report, Phase V, p. 12, which notes diary entry. Cates, "My First," p. 61, quotes a Japanese officer's diary as giving losses as 567 in II/4, about seventy per company (which is contradictory to a total of 567), and as about thirty per company in I/4. COMSOPAC to COMINCH 111336 Oct 42, COMSOPAC War Diary, 11 Oct 42, p. 18, gives Japanese losses for this action as 253 killed.

Page 289
Air action October 9: *S.S.,* Vol. 83, p. 175; VMF-223, -224 War Diaries 9 Oct 42; MAG-23 Record of Events 9 Oct 42.

Pages 289–90
Reinforcement run of October 9–10: *S.S.,* Vol. 83, p. 187; MAG-23 Record of Events 9–10 Oct 42.

Page 290
Situation of R Area Air Force: *S.S.,* Vol. 83, pp. 176–77. On October 6 the R Area Air Force had five float Zeros, twelve Petes, and nine Jakes. These twenty-six aircraft represent exactly half the original total of float planes assigned.

Page 290
Hyukatake arrives and learns of situation: Ibid., Vol. 28, pp. 67, 75–76.

Reinforcement run of October 10–11: Ibid., Vol. 83, p. 187.

Pages 290–91
Japanese reaction to loss of Matanikau position: Ibid., Vol. 28, pp. 37–39.

Page 291
Gurabusu-Koilotumaria raid: Final Report, Phase V, pp. 17–18; 1st Battalion, 2d Marines—Attack on Koilutimaria Gurumbusa Guadalcanal, 20 Oct 42, Box 6, File A12-1: Merillat, *Island,* pp. 131–35; ltr Maj. Harold R. Thorpe to CMC 19 Jan 49; ltr Col. Cornelius P. Van Ness to CMC 12 Jan 49; Clemens MS, pp. 206–7, 220–21.

CHAPTER 12

The principal sources for this chapter are the American after-action reports (except for *Buchanan,* for which her war diary was used); Charles Cook, *The Battle of Cape Esperance* (New York: Crowell, 1968) [hereafter Cook, *Battle of Cape Esperance*]; and *S.S.,* Vol. 83, pp. 188–202.

Pages 292–93
Ghormley's situation and decision to land 164th Infantry Regiment: Ghormley, "Tide Turns," pp. 123–24, 129–130; The Army in the South Pacific, pp. 2–3, 98-USF2-0.1, Box 1606, Record Group 407; Miller, *Guadalcanal: The First Offensive,* Appendix A (General Harmon's important letter of October 6, 1942); COMSOPAC to CG Army SOPAC 070306 Oct 42, Grey Book, p. 891.

Page 293
Support for convoy: Commander in Chief, U.S. Pacific Fleet, CINCPAC File Pac-90-wb, A16-3/Sol, Serial 03791, December 26, 1942. Subject: Solomon Island Campaign, Second Savo Island Action, Night of 11–12 October 1942, pp. 1–2, paras. 3–5 [hereafter CINCPAC Serial 03791].

Page 293
Japanese night battle successes to date: Allied cruisers sunk were *Java, DeRuyther, Perth, Houston, Canberra, Vincennes, Quincy,* and *Astoria.* Allied destroyers sunk were *Piet Hein, Evertsen,* and *Blue.* Destroyer *Jupiter* is sometimes credited to Japanese torpedoes at night, but F. C. Van Oosten, *The Battle of the Java Sea* (Annapolis, Md.: Naval Institute Press, 1976), p. 54 and Appendix 14, contains information that seems to exclude this possibility.

Pages 293–94
Scott's plan: Commander Task Group 64.2, A16-4, Serial 0014, October 22, 1942, Subject: Report of night action 11–12 October, 1942, pp. 2, 7 [hereafter CTG 64.2 Serial 0014], and Enclosures (a) CTF 64 Memorandum Serial 0012 and (B) CTF 64 Memorandum Serial 0013; Cook, *Battle of Cape Esperance,* p. 149. Admiral Scott's report contains this revealing comment:

> A division of forces and dispositions other than column were considered, but it is believed that the column formation is most practical for night action. Without doubt the disposition and maneuvering could be improved with training.

Heavy cruisers *Minneapolis* and *Chester* were also assigned to Scott, but were detached at this time (COMSOPAC 221002 Sep 42, Grey Book, p. 924).

Page 294
Night gunnery practice: CTG 64.2 Serial 0014, p. 7. During one practice on September 30, *San Francisco* collided with *Breese,* and the latter was sent for repairs (Ghormley, "Tide Turns," p. 127).

Scott's flagship selection: Cook, *Battle of Cape Esperance,* p. 25; Norman Friedman,

Naval Radar (Annapolis, Md.: Naval Institute Press, 1981), pp. 83–85, 146–48 [hereafter Friedman, *Naval Radar*].

Page 294

Scott's orders on radar employment: U.S.S. *San Francisco,* CA 38, Serial 003, 31 October 1942, Subject: Action Report—Night Action October 11–12, 1942, pp. 11–12 [hereafter *San Francisco* Serial 003].

Page 295

Maneuvers of TG 64 on October 9–11: CTG 64.2 Serial 0014, p. 1.

Page 295

New Japanese reinforcement and bombardment plan: *S.S.,* Vol. 83, pp. 188–89.

Page 295

Protection for reinforcement run: Ibid., pp. 189–91.

Pages 295–96

Air raids October 11: VMF-223, -224 War Diaries, 11 Oct 42; MAG-23 Record of Events 11 Oct 42; VMF-121 War Diary, 11 Oct 42; Merillat, *Island,* p. 138; *S.S.,* Vol. 83, pp. 189–90. VMF-121 War Diary says the squadron put up thirteen aircraft and lost one with one pilot claiming four bombers. The text follows the account in MAG-23 Record of Events.

Page 296

Nisshin group reported; Scott leads unit in: CTG 64.2 Serial 0014, p. 1; U.S.S. *Salt Lake City,* CA25/A16-3, Serial 0140, October 19, 1942, Subject: Action Against Japanese Naval Surface Units—Night of 11–12 October 1942—Off Savo Island, Solomons Islands—report on, p. 2 [hereafter *Salt Lake City* Serial 0140].

Pages 296–97

American and Japanese task organization: From the American action reports and *S.S.,* Vol. 83, pp. 188–89.

Pages 297–98

Armament comparisons: Navies of the Second World War Series, H. T. Lenton, *American Battleships, Carriers and Cruisers* (Garden City, N.Y.: Doubleday, 1968), pp. 48–49, 56–61; *American Fleet and Escort Destroyers,* Vol. I (London: MacDonald, 1971), pp. 87–89; Lacroix, "Development of the 'A Class' Cruisers in the Imperial Japanese Navy," *Warship International,* No. 4, 1981, pp. 337–43: Jentschura, Jung, and Mickel,

Warships of the Imperial Japanese Navy, 1869–1945, pp. 64, 66, 144–45, 147–48, 150–51.

Page 298

Catapult plane launch: CTG 64.2 Serial 0014, pp. 1–2; *San Francisco* Serial 003, p. 5; *Salt Lake City* Serial 0140, pp. 2, 4; U.S.S. *Helena,* CL50/A16-3. Serial 004, October 20, 1942, Subject: Action off Savo Island, night of 11–12 October, report of, p. 2 [hereafter *Helena* Serial 004]; U.S.S. *Boise,* CL47/ A16-3, Serial 069, 22 October 1942, Subject: Action off Cape Esperance on night of 11–12 October 1942—report of, p. 3; Cook, *Battle of Cape Esperance,* pp. 34–35.

Pages 298–99

Scott's course and speed changes: CTG 64.2 Serial 0014, p. 1.

Weather conditions; *Helena* Serial 004, p. 2; *Boise* Serial 069, p. 2. Typically, the description of the weather in the various action reports contains large and small variances. For example, *Helena* classed the visibility as "poor" while *Salt Lake City* Serial 0140, p. 2, claimed visibility was "high" with surface visibility about 4,000 yards.

Battle formation assumed: CTG 64.2 Serial 0014, p. 2: Commander Destroyer Squadron 12, FC4-12/A16-3, Serial 022. October 23, 1942, Subject: Report of Action off Savo Island, Solomons, Night of 11–12 October, p. 2 [hereafter Desron 12 Serial 022]. Scott's intentions: CTG 64.2 Serial 0014, p. 2.

Page 299

I-26 and Reinforcement Group activities: *S.S.,* Vol. 83, pp. 191–92, 233.

Page 299

Messages from *San Francisco* plane, reaction, and breakdown of *Boise* plane: CTG 64.2 Serial 0014, pp. 1–2; *Salt Lake City* Serial 0140, p. 5; *Boise* Serial 069, p. 3.

Page 299

Scott orders course change and execution: CTG 64.2 Serial 0014, p. 3, U.S.S. *Farenholt,* DD491/A16-3, Serial 003, October 20, 1942. Subject: Report of Action Against Enemy on Night of October 11–12, 1942, p. 1, para. 3 [hereafter *Farenholt* Serial 003], is very firm that the order was for a "column left." *San Francisco* Serial 003, p. 5, also says the order was for "column left." Desron 12 Serial 022, p. 2, reveals how disconcerted Captain Tobin was by the flagship's maneuvers. Scott's report is somewhat vague about the turn, and

Morison accepted what took place as what was intended. However, this account follows Cook, *Battle of Cape Esperance,* pp. 30–41, 71, 147, as to how the execution of the turn went awry.

Page 299
Goto emerges from rainsqualls: *S.S.,* Vol. 83, p. 192.

Pages 299–300
Radar contacts: CTG 64.2 Serial 0014, p. 3; *Helena* Serial 004, p. 2; *Salt Lake City* Serial 0140, pp. 2, 6; *Boise* Serial 069, p. 3. Times in the *Salt Lake City* report run two minutes earlier than those recorded elsewhere prior to the opening of fire and have been adjusted in the text.

Pages 300–301
TBS exchange between Scott and Tobin: *Salt Lake City* Serial 0140, p. 6; CTG 64.2 Serial 0014, p. 3; Desron 12 Serial 022, p. 3.

Page 301
Duncan's maneuvers: U.S.S. *Duncan.* A16-3/(11), Serial 00735, April 26, 1943, Subject: Detailed Report of Action of U.S.S. *Duncan* (485) During Engagement with Japanese Forces off Savo Island, 11–12 October 1942, p. 3 [hereafter *Duncan* Serial 00735].

San Francisco radar contact: *San Francisco,* Serial 003, p. 6.

"Ships visible to the naked eye": *Helena* Serial 004, p. 7.

"What are we going to do, board them?": Cook, *Battle of Cape Esperance,* p. 47.

Page 301
Hoover's request to open fire: *Helena* Serial 004, p. 7; CTG 64.2 Serial 0014, p. 3; *Salt Lake City* Serial 0140, p. 7.

Pages 301–2
Goto's orders, reactions, and mortal injuries: *S.S.,* Vol. 83, pp. 192–94, 198.

Page 302
Distribution of American gunfire: *San Francisco* Serial 003, p. 6; *Boise* Serial 069, pp. 4–5; *Salt Lake City* Serial 0140, p. 7; *Helena* Serial 004, pp. 3, 5; *Farenholt* Serial 003, p. 2; CTG 64.2 Serial 0014, p. 4; CINCPAC Serial 03791, p. 3, paras. 13–14.

The conclusions reached as to "who shot who" are based on an analysis of the relative positions of Goto's and Scott's forces at the opening of fire with the greatest weight at-tached to: (1) the direction each American vessel reported it was firing; (2) the range verified by radar; and (3) agreement that two or more ships shared a target. Much lesser weight is attached to the perceived identity of the target. It is possible that *Salt Lake City* fired at *Fubuki* rather than *Aoba.* Although Morison credits *Helena* with the hits on *Aoba* that wounded Goto, the contents of her report and those of *Boise*'s point fairly clearly to the conclusions in the text.

Page 302
Laffey maneuvers: *Salt Lake City* Serial 0140, p. 8, provides TBS messages from *Laffey* and *McCalla* verifying *Laffey* astern of *McCalla.* See also U.S.S. *McCalla,* DD488/A16-3, Serial 001. October 12, 1942, Subject: Report of Action Off Savo Island on Night of 11–12 October 1942, p. 2 [hereafter *McCalla* Serial 001].

Duncan's lone attack: *Duncan* Serial 00735, pp. 3–4.

Page 302
Scott orders cease-fire: CTF 64.2 Serial 0014, p. 3; *Salt Lake City* Serial 0140, p. 7; *San Francisco* Serial 003, p. 6; Cook, *Battle of Cape Esperance,* p. 72.

Page 302
Firing never halts: CTG 64.2 Serial 0014, p. 3; *Farenholt* Serial 003, p. 2, para. 5; *Salt Lake City* Serial 0140, p. 8.

Exchange between Scott and Tobin: CTF 64.2 Serial 0014, p. 3; Desron 12 Serial 022, pp. 3–4.

Page 303
Japanese actions during respite: *S.S.,* Vol. 83, pp. 194–95; Lacroix, "Development of the 'A Class' Cruisers in the Imperial Japanese Navy," Part VI, pp. 237, 239.

Page 303
Destruction of *Fubuki: S.S.,* Vol. 83, p. 195; *San Francisco* Serial 003, p. 6; *Boise* Serial 069, p. 6; Cook, *Battle of Cape Esperance,* p. 73.

Pages 303–4
"Mystery ship": *San Francisco* Serial 003, p. 7; CTG 64.2 Serial 0014, p. 4; Cook, *Battle of Cape Esperance,* pp. 74–75. Various theories on the identity of this vessel have been sug-gested. One possibility is that there was an unreported third Japanese destroyer with the bombardment group, an idea furthered by Goto's chief of staff, Captain Kijima, who

mentioned the presence of *Murakumo* in a postwar interview. This seems to be firmly contradicted by the contemporary reports and probably was only a confusion of *Murakumo* with *Hatsuyuki* by Kijima. Another possibility is that somehow *Laffey* got herself ahead of the *San Francisco*. No report from *Laffey* survives, but other ships seem to firmly place her at the rear of the column, and her skipper denied making such maneuvers. *Farenholt* did cross ahead of the flagship, but this is believed to have occurred somewhat later. This mystery remains unresolved and is probably unresolvable.

American gunfire damages *Farenholt: Farenholt* Serial 003, pp. 2–3, paras. 6–11; Desron 12 Serial 022, p. 4; *Boise* Serial 069, p. 19; *Helena* Serial 004, pp. 3–4. Captain Tobin stated that *Farenholt* was abreast of *San Francisco* when hit, and *Helena's* report points an accusing finger at *Boise.*

Page 304
Duncan damaged: *Duncan* Serial 00735, pp. 4–5; *Boise* Serial 069, pp. 6–7; *Helena* Serial 004, p. 3; *Salt Lake City* Serial 0140, p. 9; *Buchanan* War Diary 11–12 Oct 42. There is no absolute proof that *Duncan* was hit by "friendly fire"; however, the following facts point firmly to that conclusion: (1) she clearly steamed into the line of fire and was hit from two directions at once; (2) most of the Japanese vessels either fired little, or when they did, their aim was at the main American column; and (3) the relative position of the targets described at various points in the reports of *Helena* and *Boise,* as well as possibly *Salt Lake City* and *Buchanan,* coincide with the known movements of *Duncan.*

Page 304
Furutaka struck by torpedo or shellfire: *S.S.,* Vol. 83, pp. 194–95; *Buchanan* War Diary, 11 Oct 42; CTG 64.2 Serial 0014, p. 4; Lacroix, "Development of the 'A Class' Cruisers in the Imperial Japanese Navy," *Warship International,* No. 4, 1981, p. 237.

"Engaging heavy cruisers": COMTASK Group 64.2 111255 Oct 42; COMSOPAC War Diary 12 Oct 42.

Page 304
"Some shaking down was necessary . . .": CTF 64.2 Serial 0014, p. 4.

Page 305
"This concluded the first phase of the action": Ibid.

Helena and *Boise* sight torpedoes: *Helena* Serial 004, p. 7; *Boise* Serial 069, p. 7; *S.S.,* Vol. 83, p. 195.

"shooting beautifully with twin 8-inch turrets": *Boise* Serial 069, p. 8. The tightness of Japanese salvo patterns is noted in *San Francisco* Serial 003, p. 10.

Page 305
Damage to *Boise: Boise* Serial 069, pp. 8–10, 15, and Enclosure D; CTG 64.2 Serial 0014, p. 4; U.S.S. *Boise* Gunfire Damage October 11–12, 1942, Savo Island, War Damage Report No. 24, January 1943, Bureau of Ships, Navy Department [hereafter *Boise* War Damage Report]. According to *S.S.,* Vol. 83, p. 194, *Furutaka* reported firing thirty-odd 8-inch shells and damaging seriously the "third" ship in the enemy line, presumably *Salt Lake City* and *Aoba* fixed only a few shells. In view of the heavy damage *Furutaka* sustained, it seems fairly clear that *Kinugasa* inflicted the near-fatal damage on *Boise.*

Type 91 shells: Lacroix, "Development of the 'A Class' Cruisers in the Imperial Japanese Navy," *Warship International* No. 1, 1979, p. 60, note 34; *Boise* War Damage Report, p. 11.

Page 306
Captain Small interposes *Salt Lake City* between *Boise* and *Kinugasa: Boise* Serial 069, p. 22, para. 6(d); *Salt Lake City* Serial 0140, pp. 10–12, 16, 23–24; *San Francisco* Serial 003, pp. 7–8; *S.S.,* Vol. 83, p. 198.

Page 306
Scott concludes action: CTG 64.2 Serial 0014, pp. 4–5.

Pages 306–7
"Stand by for further action. The show may not be over": *Salt Lake City* Serial 0140, p. 14.

Reinforcement Group activities: *S.S.,* Vol. 83, p. 191; *Boise* Serial 069, p. 12; CTG 64.2 Serial 0014, p. 7.

Damage control and casualties on *Boise: Boise* Serial 0069, pp. 11–13, 15, Enclosure B, p. 2; War Damage Report No. 24, especially p. 13; CTG 64.2 Serial 0014, p. 5.

Farenholt withdrawal: *Farenholt* Serial 003, p. 3.

Page 307
Aoba withdrawal, loss of *Furutaka: S.S.,* Vol. 83, pp. 194–95.

Page 307
Duncan abandoned: *Duncan* Serial 00735, pp. 5–9.

Scott requests air cover and Japanese air efforts: CTG 64.2 Serial 0014, p. 5; *S.S.,* Vol. 83, pp. 200–1. During search missions this day Betty and a "large seaplane" (either a Mavis or an Emily) were lost.

Pages 307–8
McCalla's search for survivors and efforts to salvage *Duncan:* U.S.S. *McCalla,* DD488/A16-3, Serial 002, 12 October 1942. Subject: Capture of Japanese Survivors After Night Engagement with Enemy and Rescue of Survivors of U.S.S. Duncan; Serial 003, 12 October 1942, Subject: Rescue of Survivors of the U.S.S. Duncan (DD485); Serial 004, 23 October 1942, Subject: Report of Attempted Salvage of U.S.S. Duncan.

Pages 308–9
Trevor and Hovey pick up *Fubuki* survivors: U.S.S. *Hovey* (DMS 11) War Diary 13 Oct 42; U.S.S. *Trevor* (DMS 16) War Diary 13 Oct 42. Cook, *Battle of Cape Esperance,* p. 138, says *Trevor* and *Hovey* picked up 106 survivors. Task Force 62 War Diary 13 Oct 42 says a total of 113 survivors were recovered.

Admiral Mikawa's reaction, efforts to aid Goto's units: *S.S.,* Vol. 83, pp. 195, 200–1. Light cruisers *Sendai* and *Yura* and five destroyers sortied at 0400 to relieve the hard-pressed Japanese forces but did not become involved in the actions of October 12.

Page 309
Loss of *Natsugumo* and *Murakumo: S.S.,* Vol. 83, pp. 201–2; MAG-23 Record of Events 12 Oct 42. According to the Japanese reports, *Murakumo* was hit by a bomb, not a torpedo, and *Natsugumo* was not actually hit by a bomb but only sustained a very near miss. In this instance the text follows American claims that seem more in line with all the evidence.

Pages 309–10
Japanese losses and analysis: *S.S.,* Vol. 83, p. 199; Lacroix, "Development of the 'A Class' Cruisers in the Imperial Japanese Navy," *Warship International* No. 3, 1983, pp. 237, 239; *USSBS, Interrogations,* Vol. II. No. 464, Captain Kunori Kijima. For losses on *Murakumo* and *Natsugumo* see Cook, *Battle of Cape Esperance,* p. 131.

Pages 310–11
American analysis: CTG 64.2 Serial 0014, pp. 6–7, and endorsement by COMSOPAC Serial 00127a, 3 Nov 42; CINCPAC Serial 03791, pp. 5–6, paras. 24–32; *Salt Lake City* Serial 0140, pp. 16, 25.

"This estimate may be on the optimistic side": CTG 64.2 Serial 0014, p. 6; CINCPAC Daily Summary 18 Oct 42, Grey Book, p. 1096.

Publicity for *Boise:* "U.S. 'One-Ship Fleet' Home; Sank 6 of Foe in 27 Minutes," *New York Times,* November 20, 1942, p. 1, col. 5.

"Cape Esperance was a three-sided battle . . .": Cook, *Battle of Cape Esperance,* p. 147.

CHAPTER 13

Page 314
Landing of 164th Infantry Regiment: COMAMPHIBFORSOPAC War Diary 13 Oct 42.

Background of 164th Infantry: Shelby L. Stanton, *Order of Battle U.S. Army World War II* (Novato, Calif.: Presidio Press, 1984), p. 230 [hereafter Stanton, *Order of Battle U.S. Army World War II*]. The problems with National Guard units (state politics, overage and physically unfit officers, inadequate discipline and training) are described in General Omar Bradley and Clay Blair, Jr., *A General's Life* (New York: Simon & Schuster, 1983), pp. 107–8, 110. Isely and Crowl, *Marines and Amphibious War,* p. 151, states the average age in the 164th was ten years older than in the Marine units, which sounds somewhat exaggerated. Many complimentary words about Colonel Bryant Moore may be found in Thomas intvw, pp. 416–17, including the anecdote in the text.

Page 314
Air action 13 October: MAG-23 Record of Events 13 Oct 42; VMF-121 War Diary, 13 Oct 42; 67th FS Hist., p. 40; 13th AF Hist., p. 33; 1st Mar Div D-2, D-3 Jnls 13 Oct 42; "Four Hour 'Hell' on Guadalcanal," *New York Times,* October 25 1942, p. 40 (which notes this was the sixty-first raid of the campaign).

Captain Foss's adventures; Foss and Simmons, *Joe Foss,* pp. 10, 34–36. John Lundstrom examined the relevant Japanese air unit war diaries and these show no Zero losses.

Page 315
Arrangements for High-Speed Convoy: *S.S.,* Vol. 83, pp. 206–8, 216–18, Vol. 28, p. 80.

Another portion of this plan called for seaplane carrier *Chiyoda* to bring up six midget submarines that she had loaded on September 20. She arrived at Shortland on October 8, but further advance of the midget submarines was postponed.

Pages 315–16

Japanese artillery opens fire and atmosphere as darkness approached: *S.S.,* Vol. 28, pp. 98–99; Merillat, *Island,* pp. 140–43; "Four Hour 'Hell' on Guadalcanal," *New York Times,* October 25, 1942, p. 40.

"purple nights": Merillat, *Guadalcanal Remembered,* p. 179.

Page 316

Japanese task organization and arrangements for bombardment: *S.S.,* Vol. 83, pp. 208–11. In addition to these vessels, Desdiv 19 stood by in the passage between Guadalcanal and the Russels (Ibid., p. 214).

Pages 316–17

Japanese task force opens fire: Ibid., pp. 212–13.

3d Defense Battalion 5-inch guns engage: 3d Defense Battalion Report of Operations, Guadalcanal, Box 6, File A32-1, Enclosure B, p. 2, MCHC.

Page 317

"spontaneous cries and shouts . . .": Tanaka Part II, p. 815.

Effects of and reaction to bombardment: Merillat, *Island,* pp. 144–45, 185; Foss and Simmons, *Joe Foss,* p. 49.

"the ground shook with the most awful convulsions": Clemens MS, p. 214.

"Arsenal of the underworld": DeChant, *Devilbirds,* p. 79.

"It seemed as if all the props . . .": Foss and Simmons, *Joe Foss,* p. 37.

". . . and until someone has experienced naval . . .": Vandegrift and Asprey, *Once a Marine,* p. 175.

Page 317

Japanese check fire, then resume: *S.S.,* Vol. 83, p. 213.

"Men were yelling, even crying . . .": Mears, *Carrier Combat,* pp. 145–46; Merillat, *Island,* pp. 144–45.

Page 318

Background on arrival of PT boats: John D. Bulkley, *At Close Quarters* (Washington, D.C.: Naval History Division, U.S. Government Printing Office, 1962), p. 85 [hereafter Bulkley, *At Close Quarters*]; Ghormley, "Tide Turns," p. 130.

Page 318

Attack of PT boats: The best source for this action is Frank D. Johnson, *United States PT-Boats of World War II in Action* (Poole, Dorset: Blandford Press, 1980), pp. 82–95 [hereafter Johnson, *United States PT-Boats of World War II*]. The Japanese side of the action is from *S.S.,* Vol. 83, pp. 213–14, and Tanaka, Part II, p. 815.

Pages 318–19

Rest of night to morning and survey of damage: MAG-23 Record of Events, 14 Oct 42; Merillat, *Island,* p. 159; Vandegrift and Asprey, *Once a Marine,* p. 176; 164th Infantry Regiment, Unit Report No. 1, 164th Infantry, 300-INF-(164)-0.9, Box 5629, RG 407, [hereafter Unit Report No. 1, 164th Infantry]; COMGEN 1st Mar Div to COMSOPAC 160025 Oct 42, Grey Book, p. 949.

Page 319

Japanese reaction to bombardment: *S.S.,* Vol. 83, pp. 215, 218.

Pages 319–20

Morning search and Vandegrift message; MAG-23 Record of Events 14 Oct 42; Vandegrift and Asprey, *Once a Marine,* p. 177; COMGEN 1st Mar Div to COMSOPAC 160025 Oct 42, Grey Book, p. 949.

Deployment of U.S. Navy units: COMSOPAC to CINCPAC 141410 Oct 42, Grey Book, pp. 946–47.

"our position is not favorable": CINCPAC Daily Summary 13 Oct 42, Grey Book, p. 1090.

Page 320

Fitch's efforts: COMAIRSOPAC War Diary 14 Oct 42; Merillat, *Island,* pp. 152–53; Miller, *Cactus Air Force,* pp. 122–23, 129; 67th FS Hist., p. 45.

Page 320

Japanese air raids October 13: VMF-121 War Diary, 13 Oct 42; MAG-23 Record of Events 13 Oct 42; *S.S.,* Vol. 83, pp. 218–19.

Pages 320–21

Colonel Munn addresses 67th Fighter Squadron pilots: 67th FS Hist., p. 44. Miller, *Cactus Air Force,* p. 121, identifies Lieutenant Colonel Munn as the officer.

Page 321

Convoy approach October 14: *S.S.,* Vol. 83, pp. 217–19, Vol. 28, p. 83; MAG-23 Record of Events 14 Oct 42; VMF-121 War Diary 14 Oct 42; VF-5 Action Reports Guadalcanal 14 Oct 42; 67th FS Hist., pp. 44–45; 13th AF Hist., p. 37.

"The arrow has already left the bow": *S.S.,* Vol. 28, p. 83.

Pages 321–22

Arrival of High-Speed Convoy, reinforcement run, and bombardment: *S.S.,* Vol. 83, pp. 217–20; MAG-23 Record of Events 14–15 Oct 42.

Page 322

Dawn sights, early air actions, and repair and fuel effort: 1st Mar Div D-2 & D-3 Jnls 15 Oct 42; MAG-23 Record of Events 15 Oct 42; VF-5 Action Reports Guadalcanal 15 Oct 42; Foss and Simmons, *Joe Foss,* pp. 45–46; Miller, *Cactus Air Force,* pp. 124–25; Merillat, *Island,* p. 148; *S.S.,* Vol. 83, p. 219–20, Vol. 28, p. 84; Woods intvw, p. 162; 13th AF Hist., p. 37.

Page 323

Coordinated attack, Major Cramm's sortie: Miller, *Cactus Air Force,* pp. 125–27; MAG-23 Record of Events 15 Oct 42; VMF-121 War Diary 15 Oct 42; 67th FS Hist., pp. 45–46; Foss and Simmons, *Joe Foss,* pp. 43–44; DeChant, *Devilbirds,* pp. 80–84; *S.S.,* Vol. 83, p. 220, Vol. 28, p. 84 (indicates the hit on *Sasago Maru* was by a bomb). *New York Times,* October 25, 1942, p. 40, gives time. Cramm was awarded a well-earned Navy Cross for his attack.

Page 323

Situation of transports and subsequent air attacks: *S.S.,* Vol. 83, pp. 220–21, Vol. 28, p. 84; Miller, *Cactus Air Force,* p. 128.

Page 324

Last air attack, landing operations halted: MAG-23 Record of Events 15 Oct 42; *S.S.,* Vol. 83, pp. 221–22, Vol. 28, pp. 84–85, 88–89. Strangely, *S.S.* does not give a total figure on the number of troops landed by the convoy. The figure of 4,500, which correlates well with other data, is from Van der Rhoer, *Deadly Magic,* p. 122. The Japanese Campaign in the Guadalcanal Area, 98-USF2-2.01, Box 1616, RG 407, p. 15 [hereafter Japanese Campaign on Guadalcanal], based upon captured documents, gives a figure of about 4,300. The 17th Army History, Box 4631, RG 407, p. 2 [hereafter 17th Army History], likewise based upon captured documents, gives a total of 3,979. 2d Division Information, Box 4631, RG 407, p. 2 [hereafter 2d Division Information], says 2,025 men of the 16th and 29th Infantry Regiments and 2,460 members of other units (total 4,485) were landed by the convoy. The Japanese air raid destroyed one F4F of VF-5 on the ground, which left that unit only one flyable Wildcat. Miller, *Cactus Air Force,* p. 129, also says one VF-5 pilot claimed one A6M in raid of nine escorts, but one F4F of VF-5 was lost, pilot rescued.

Page 324

Losses for October 15: *S.S.,* Vol. 83, p. 221; MAG-23 Record of Events 15 Oct 42; VMF-121 War Diary 15 Oct 42; VF-5 Action Reports Guadalcanal. Once again, important additional data on Japanese air losses were supplied by Mr. John Lundstrom. Six SBDs reached Guadalcanal this day. In an interesting note in the personal diary of Lieutenant H. C. Merillat it was recorded that Marine losses to date were 1,784: thirty-seven officers and 525 men killed and 165 officers and 1,058 men wounded.

Page 325

Loss of *Meredith:* U.S.S. *Meredith,* Compilation Concerning Loss of U.S.S. Meredith 15 Oct 42, No Serial, July 6, 1943; *S.S.,* Vol. 83, p. 229. The decision to scuttle *Vireo* was labeled "disgraceful" in CINCPAC Daily Summary 18 Oct 42, Grey Book, pp. 1096–97.

Page 325

Ordeal of *Meredith* and *Vireo* survivors: Bell, *Condition Red,* pp. 121–52; CTG 63.10 to COMAIRSOPAC 190649 Oct 42, COMSOPAC War Diary 19 Oct 42, p. 43.

Page 326

Renewed bombardment: *S.S.,* Vol. 83, p. 222.

Page 326
Accounting of aircraft losses, air activities October 16: MAG-23 Record of Events, 13–16 Oct 42; Merillat, *Island,* pp. 152–53; 1st Mar Div D-2, D-3 Jnls 16 Oct 42.

Pages 326–27
Attack on *McFarland:* U.S.S. *McFarland,* AVD14/A16-3, Serial 052, December 15, 1942; Merillat, *Island,* pp. 152–53; Foss and Simmons, *Joe Foss,* pp. 50–51; *S.S.,* Vol. 83, pp. 231–32 (which reports the Vals had a Zero escort but gives no loss figures). Japanese loss figures from John Lundstrum.

Page 327
Vandegrift's message and response: COMGEN 1st Mar Div to COMSOPAC 160025 Oct and COMSOPAC to CINCPAC 160440 Oct, Grey Book, p. 949; CINCPAC Daily Summaries 16–18, 21 Oct 42, Grey Book, pp. 1093–99. Nimitz also urged that the 9th Defense Battalion be sent direct to Guadalcanal instead of Efate to relieve the 4th (Daily Summary 18 Oct 42). A dozen B-17s started south on 19 October (Daily Summary 19 Oct 42, pp. 1097–98).

Page 327
Attack by Cardiv 2 aircraft, 1315 bombing raid, and rotation at Guadalcanal: *S.S.,* Vol. 83, pp. 232, 242; VMF-121 War Diary, 17 Oct 42; MAG-23 Record of Events 17 Oct 42; 1st Mar Div Record of Events 17 Oct 42. *S.S.,* shows the Japanese plan provided for diversion of aircraft to Buin or Buka after the raid. The deciphered version of the order had the Japanese going to Buin or Buka to stage for the raid, but correctly gave the scheduled time of the attack. Departure of VS-3 from Guadalcanal, VS-3 War Diary.

Page 327
Vandegrift requests bombardment and execution: COMGEN 1st Mar Div to COMSOPAC 160035 Oct 42, Grey Book, p. 948; Commander Task Unit 64.5.1 (Desron 12), FC4-12/A16-3, Serial 021, October 18, 1942, Subject: Bombardment of this unit of enemy positions on Guadalcanal, October 17, 1942.

Page 328
Additional reinforcement run: *S.S.,* Vol. 83, pp. 221–25, Vol. 28, pp. 87–88.

Pages 328–29
Attack of *Grampus* and deployment of American submarines: *S.S.,* Vol. 83, p. 224;

John D. Alden, *U.S. Submarine Attacks During World War II,* (Annapolis Md.: Naval Institute Press, 1989), p. 20 [hereafter Alden, *U.S. Submarine Attacks*]; Blair, *Silent Victory,* pp. 279–80; COMINCH to CINCPAC 191954 Oct; COMINCH to CINCPAC 201540 Oct; CINCPAC to COMSOPAC 202215 Oct; CINCPAC to COMINCH 202309, Grey Book, pp. 896–97. Blair indicates the submarine that attacked *Yura* was *Sculpin,* but the text follows Alden who attributes the attack to *Grampus.*

Page 329
Loss of *I-22: S.S.,* Vol. 83, pp. 237. *I-22* is recorded as a probable marine casualty (i.e., an operational loss) on "25(4 Nov)Dec" 1942 in the standard reference source, *United States Submarine Losses World War II,* (Washington, D.C.: Naval History Division, 1963), Appendix of Axis Submarine Losses, p. 175 [hereafter *United States Submarine Losses World War II*]. Japanese sources show her last message as on October 4 and the COMAIRSOPAC War Diary shows a PBY-5A attacked a submarine on October 6 at 11°22' South, 162°20' East, a position very close to *I-22*'s last known location. The same source reflects an attack on a submarine on October 28 at 13°15' South, 162°45' East that produced a large oil slick. Detective work by Mr. James Sawruk uncovered the story of Lieutenant King, who was decorated for this attack. The failure of the standard references to mention this is probably attributable to the poor to nonexistent official records of PBY operations at this time.

Pages 329–30
Air raids October 18 and 19: VMF-121 War Diary, 18–19 Oct 42; MAG-23 Record of Events 18–19 Oct 42; Foss and Simmons, *Joe Foss,* p. 56; 1st Mar Div Record of Events 18 Oct 42; *S.S.,* Vol. 83, pp. 242–43. *S.S.* confirms Japanese losses as four Zeros and three bombers with one of each type "force-landed" on October 18. On this date CVE *Unyo* delivered twelve Zeros to Rabaul.

Page 330
Reinforcement run of 19–20 October: *S.S.,* Vol. 83, pp. 225–26; MAG-23 Record of Events 19–20 Oct 42.

Air raid October 20: *S.S.,* Vol. 83, p. 243; VMF-121, War Diary 20 Oct 42; MAG-23 Record of Events 20 Oct 42.

Page 330
Totals of reinforcements to Guadalcanal: *S.S.,* Vol. 83, pp. 226–27, Vol. 28, pp. 86–87. The following figures appear in Vol. 83:

10cm howitzers	2	Tractors (1 by barge)	12
Field antiaircraft guns	3	Ammunition carts	22
75mm field guns	7	"Some light guns"	
75mm mountain guns	5	"Corresponding" amounts	
"Quick Firing" (Anti-tank) guns	18	of ammunition	
75mm regimental guns	14	Provisions	160 tons
70mm battalion guns	13	Field antiaircraft guns	4
Mortars	19	Ammunition	8 tons
		13mm antiaircraft machineguns	3

Page 331
". . . ships of the Navy . . .": Lee, *They Call It Pacific,* p. 324.

Exchange between Nimitz and King at September meeting: Grey Book, p. 1023.

Japanese officers confirm difficulty created by information blackout: This is clear inference in Fuchida and Okumiya, *Midway: The Battle That Doomed Japan,* pp. 78, 101–2.

Page 331
New York Times comments: *New York Times,* August 23, 1942, p. 16, col. 4; October 14, 1942, p. 24; August 26, 1942, p. 18, col. 2.

Page 332
News policy on Guadalcanal and correspondents: Vandegrift and Asprey, *Once a Marine,* p. 150; ltr Cates, 28 Oct 42, Box 2, Entry 9, Cates Papers, MCHC. As the public relations officer of the 1st Marine Division, H. C. Merillat, pointed out to the author, Vandegrift did not have authority to issue communiqués, nor in fact did Admiral Ghormley. That prerogative remained with Admiral Nimitz.

Page 332
Baldwin articles: These appeared in the *New York Times* beginning on September 27, 1942 (with the "nailed the colors to the nest" and "eventual victory" quotes), and September 29, 1942. Other articles appeared as follows: October 23, p. 1, col. 6; October 23, p. 1; October 24, p. 3, col. 5; October 25, p. 1, col. 3; October 26, p. 1, col. 6; October 27, p. 7, col. 1; October 28, p. 6, col. 1; October 29, p. 1, col. 7; October 30, p. 3.

"We have done some of it well . . .": *New York Times,* October 23, 1942, p. 1.

Navy Department changes policy: *New York Times,* October 22, 1942, p. 1, col. 8.

Pages 332–33
"The shadows of a great conflict . . .": *New York Herald Tribune,* October 16, 1942.

". . . Guadalcanal. The name will not die out . . .": *New York Times,* October 16, 1942, p. 18.

Reaction to radio news on Guadalcanal: Merillat, *Island,* p. 155.

"no pink tea": Cates, "My First," p. 40b.

Exchange between reporter and Secretary Knox: *New York Times,* October 17, 1942, p. 1, col. 8.

Page 333
"My forces [are] totally inadequate . . .": COMSOPAC to CINCPAC, info COMINCH 160440 Oct 42, Grey Book, p. 950; Ghormley, "Tide Turns," p. 137.

Decision to relieve Ghormley: Potter, *Nimitz,* pp. 196–97, 222; Hanson Baldwin, *New York Times,* October 23, 1942, p. 1; Layton, Pineau, and Costello, *And I Was There,* pp. 461–62. Foster Hailey, "Halsey Is Known as a Fighting Man," *New York Times,* October 25, 1942, p. 41, comments on the high opinion of Halsey held by American sailors.

Page 334
"Affirmative": Pfieffer intvw, p. 212. Perhaps not surprisingly, the messages between Nimitz and King on the decision to relieve Ghormley do not appear in Grey Book.

Assessment of Ghormley's relief: CINCPAC Daily Summary 18 Oct 42, Grey Book, p. 1096, contains the following comment:

It was felt that Admiral Ghormley had not been successful for several reasons and that the critical situation there required a more aggressive commander.

Vandegrift would later state that he had nothing personal against Ghormley, but that "I simply felt that our drastic situation called for the most positive form of aggressive leadership" (Vandegrift and Asprey, *Once a Marine,* pp. 181–82).

"Remember the enemy is hurt too.": Potter, *Nimitz,* p. 196.

Ghormley's sensitivity to linkage of his relief to Battle of Savo Island: Ghormley, "Tide Turns," p. 139. An example of that linkage may be found in *New York Times,* October 26, 1942, p. 4:

> Admiral Ghormley's removal from command . . . can hardly be termed summary. Ever since the revelation on October 12 that three of our heavy cruisers . . . had been sunk in a night action . . . the public has sensed that a change was due.

Page 335
Halsey receives orders and reaction: Fleet Admiral William F. Halsey and Lieutenant Commander J. Bryan III, *Admiral Halsey's Story* (New York: McGraw-Hill, 1947), pp. 108–9 [hereafter Halsey and Bryan, *Admiral Halsey's Story*].

"a wide mouth held tight . . .": Robert Turnball, "All Out with Halsey," *New York Times Magazine,* December 6, 1942.

Halsey's command character: Peck intvw, p. 121.

Page 335
Halsey's immediate actions: Halsey and Bryan, *Admiral Halsey's Story,* pp. 137–39; Dyer, *Amphibians Came to Conquer,* pp. 421, 443; COMSOPAC to VICE OPNAV 210517 Oct 42, Grey Book, pp. 956–57. Halsey's move ashore received support from de Gaulle via an appeal by King (COMINCH to COMUSNAVFOR Europe 211540 Oct 42, Grey Book, p. 897).

Pages 335–36
Chester torpedoed: U.S.S. *Chester,* CA27, A9/A16-3, Serial 057, October 27, 1942. Chester lost eleven killed and twelve wounded.

Ties-off policy: Halsey and Bryan, *Admiral Halsey's Story,* p. 139.

"the war simply became too complicated for Halsey": Admiral "Jocko" Clark, quoted in

Clark G. Reynolds, *The Fast Carriers: The Forging of an Air Navy* (New York: McGraw-Hill, 1968), p. 387.

"Strike, repeat, strike": Griffith, *Battle of Guadalcanal,* p. 176. Griffith gives the message as "Attack, repeat, attack" and cites his source as "Halsey's message to SoPac Task Forces, October 25, 1942." This writer did not find such a message but COMSOPAC to CTF 61, 64 232350 Oct 42, COMSOPAC War Diary 25 Oct 42, reads "Strike."

CHAPTER 14

Pages 337–39
Japanese planning for the October attack: *S.S.,* Vol. 28, pp. 94, 99–107, 129; Merillat, *Island,* p. 157. It is not clear how many tubes of the 3d Mortar Battalion reached Guadalcanal; probably at least nineteen.

American strength at Guadalcanal and Tulagi: Final Report, Phase V, Annex W, p. 2.

Misinterpretation of copy of British Admiralty chart: Author's correspondence with Mr. George MacGillivray. Mr. MacGillivray served with the 7th Marines on Guadalcanal and after the war worked in mapping for the Central Intelligence Agency.

Page 340
Briefings by General Maruyama and staff officers: *S.S.,* Vol. 28, pp. 107–9.

Page 340
Kawaguchi's "Spirit of the Right Wing": Ibid., p. 109.

Pages 340–41
Hyakutake establishes headquarters and instructions to Colonel Tsuji: Ibid., pp. 107–9.

Pages 341–42
March of the 2d Division between October 16 and 20: Ibid., pp. 114–17, 125–27, 129–32; Japanese Campaign on Guadalcanal, pp. 22, 24. While *S.S.* and a set of captured orders from the 16th Infantry Regiment indicate each soldier was to take twelve days' rations, the Japanese Campaign on Guadalcanal, p. 24 (also largely based on captured documents), says only five days' rations were carried, and this seems in line with subsequent events.

Page 342
17th Army staff begins to study surrender: Ibid., p. 136.

Pages 342–43
General Sumiyoshi's organization and efforts: Ibid., pp. 117–25.

Page 343
American intelligence efforts and command decisions: Final Report, Phase V, pp. 15, 21.

Pages 343–44
Matanikau battle position established: Final Report, Phase V, pp. 13–15.

Page 344
Air action October 21: *S.S.,* Vol. 83, p. 251; VMF-121 War Diary 21 Oct 42; MAG-23 Record of Events 21 Oct 42; 1st Mar Div Record of Events 21 Oct 42. Japanese loss data from John Lundstrom.

Page 344
March of Sendai Division October 21: *S.S.,* Vol. 28, pp. 137–39.

Page 344
Sumiyoshi's orders: *S.S.,* Vol. 28, pp. 146–47.

Holcomb arrives: 1st Mar Div Record of Events 21 Oct 42.

Air action October 22: *S.S.,* Vol. 83, p. 251; MAG-23 Record of Events 22 Oct 42; VMF-121 War Diary, 22 Oct 42; U.S.S. *Nicholas* War Diary 22 Oct 42. Losses among the Val strike are not reflected in *S.S.* Vol. 83. The text follows figures from John Lundstrom.

Pages 344–45
Holcomb's inspection: Vandegrift and Asprey, *Once a Marine,* p. 186.

Page 345
Sendai Division on October 22: Ibid., pp. 138–39.

Hyakutaka orders to Koli Detachment and Sumiyoshi and Sumiyoshi's orders: Ibid., pp. 139, 147.

Vandegrift departs: Vandegrift and Asprey, *Once a Marine,* p. 184.

Command arrangements after Vandegrift departure: According to the official Marine Corps account, General Rupertus took command when Vandegrift departed (Hough, Ludwig, and Shaw, *Pearl Harbor to Guadalcanal,* p. 33). There are grounds to doubt this interpretation. Geiger was clearly the next senior Marine officer, and, indeed, Gerald

Thomas reported that Rupertus assumed command of the ground elements, but had dengue fever and was "terribly sick" (Thomas intvw, p. 431). In fact, as a practical matter Thomas appears to have masterminded the ground defense under the loose supervision of Rupertus and Geiger.

Pages 322–23
Air action October 23: *S.S.,* Vol. 83, p. 252; VMF-121 War Diary 23 Oct 42; MAG-23 Record of Events 23 Oct 42; Miller, *Cactus Air Force,* pp. 139–40; Foss and Simmons, *Joe Foss,* pp. 63–67, 82.

"If you see Zeros, dogfight 'em": Miller, *Cactus Air Force,* p. 139.

Page 346
Sendai Division on October 23: *S.S.,* Vol. 28, pp. 139, 141.

". . . I cannot any longer think . . ." *S.S.,* Vol. 28, p. 141.

Page 346
Aerial photographs: Ibid., pp. 109–11, 115–16. The 76th Army Independent Air Squadron was equipped with six aircraft.

Pages 346–47
Kawaguchi's interpretation of the photographs and actions: Ibid., pp. 142–43.

Page 347
Tsuji's report: Ibid., pp. 141–42.

Kawaguchi's report: Ibid., p. 140.

Page 347
Kawaguchi dismissed and replaced by Shoji: Ibid., pp. 143–45.

Page 347
Position of Left Wing: Ibid., pp. 140–41.

Pages 347–48
Report from Tsuji and decision to postpone attack: Ibid., pp. 141–42.

Page 348
Orders from Yamamoto: Ibid., p. 251.

Page 348
Failure of American reconnaissance efforts to find Sendai Division: Final Report, Phase V, p. 23.

Pages 348–49
Decision to move 2/7 to Matanikau and leave 1/7 alone to guard Sector III of the perimeter: Final Report, Phase V, pp. 22–23; Zim-

merman, "Guadalcanal Campaign," pp. 116–17.

Pages 348–49
Oka's march and problems: *S.S.,* Vol. 28, pp. 121, 147–48.

Page 349
Nakaguma's preparations for an attack at the Matanikau: Ibid., pp. 148–49.

Page 350
"It looks like this is the night": Merillat Diary 23 Oct 42.

Japanese tank attack: Final Report, Phase V, pp. 21–22; Merillat, *Island,* p. 164; Merillat Diary 23 Oct 42; Cates, "My First," pp. 46, 68; *S.S.,* Vol. 28, pp. 149–50; Raymond Suriemont, *Japanese Armor* (Milwaukee: Z & M Enterprises, 1976), pp. 27–28, 34–35. The Japanese Type 97 tanks are sometimes referred to as in the 18-ton class, but they actually weighed only 15 tons, barely less than the U.S. M-3 'light" tank. The presence of Type 95 light tanks is not mentioned in any of the campaign records, but is clearly documented in photograph 80-G-20700 in the Still Photograph Branch, National Archives. Two of these vehicles were authorized for each Japanese tank company.

Page 351
Marine artillery employment: Merillat Diary 23 Oct 42; Merillat, *Island,* p. 165; Final Report, Phase V, p. 22, Annex R (artillery), Marine guns fired 6,164 rounds of 75mm and 2,719 of 105mm.

Page 351
"peps the boys up": Merillat Diary 23 Oct 42.

Action remainder of night and rain: Merillat Diary 23 Oct 42; Merillat, *Island,* p. 165.

McKelvy's losses: Cates, "My First," p. 47.

Page 351
Meeting in Noumea: Vandegrift and Asprey, *Once a Marine,* p. 184; Halsey and Bryan, *Admiral Halsey's Story,* p. 117. The quotes are from Vandegrift.

Page 351
Decision to redeploy 2/7: Final Report, Phase V, p. 23.

Pages 351–52
Lieutenant Colonel Puller's battalion reorganizes defense line and stations outpost: 1st Battalion, 7th Marines, 27 October 1942, Summary of operations of the 1st Battalion,

Seventh Marines, period 24–26 October 1942, Box 6, File A21-1, MCHC [hereafter 1/7 Summary of Operations, period 24–26 October]; Hammel, *Guadalcanal: Starvation Island,* p. 347; Merillat, *Island,* p. 167; Davis, *Marine,* pp. 137–39. The strength of Puller's Battalion for October 24, 1942 is from the unit report of that date, Box 6, File A23-2, MCHC.

Page 351
Indications of Japanese approach from the south: Final Report, Phase V, p. 23.

Pages 351–52
Deployment and approach of Sendai Division: *S.S.,* Vol. 28, pp. 145–46, 152–54.

Pages 352–53
Right Wing advance: Ibid., pp. 153–54.

Pages 353–54
Briggs's outpost: Final Report, Phase V, p. 24; 1/7 Summary of Operations, period 24–26 October; Merillat, *Island,* pp. 167–68, 170–77; Davis, *Marine,* p. 139. Which Japanese unit encountered Sergeant Briggs's platoon is unclear. Although it would seem more logical to suppose that a Left Wing element advanced past the outpost, the report from the Right Wing of a brush about this time seems to confirm that the outpost was first hit by the Right Wing. This episode is only one illustration of the confused maneuvering of the Sendai Division this night. Contemporary reports list four Marines as missing, but Mr. George MacGillivray informed the author that one of these men apparently became intermingled with the Japanese attackers and was found among the dead in front of 1/7.

Pages 353–54
Participation of Right Wing: *S.S.,* Vol. 28, pp. 153–54.

Report Right Wing had captured airfield: Ibid., pp. 139, 155–57.

Page 354
Order of march of Left Wing: Ibid., p. 154.

Confusion in Left Wing and reorganization: Ibid., p. 154.

Advance of III/29 and 11th Company: Ibid., pp. 154–55, 160.

Pages 354–55
Attack of 11th Company: Ibid., pp. 160–61; 1/7 Summary of Operations, period 24–26 October; Hammel, *Guadalcanal: Starvation Island,* pp. 351–52.

Page 355
Attack of 9th Company, heroism of Sergeant Basilone: *S.S.,* Vol. 28, p. 161; Hammel, *Guadalcanal: Starvation Island,* pp. 352–55; Merillat, *Island,* p. 168.

Page 355
"seasoned, well disciplined troops": Unit Report, 1st Battalion, 7th Marines, 26 Oct 42, Box 6, File A21-1, MCHC [hereafter 1/7 Unit Report 26 Oct 42].

Immediate reinforcements of 1/7: Unit History, 164th Infantry Regiment, pp. 1–2, 300-INF (164)-0.2, Box 5626, RG 407, [hereafter 164th Inf Hist.]; 164th Infantry, Report of Battle of Henderson Field, 300-INF (164)-0.3.0, Box 5628, RG 407, [hereafter 164th Inf Henderson Field].

3d Battalion, 164th Infantry committed and march: 164th Inf Hist.; 164th Inf Henderson Field; 1/7 Summary of Operations, period 24–26 October; 1/7 Unit Report 26 Oct 42.

Artillery fire: Cates, "My First," p. 68.

Page 356
Colonel Furimiya reaches front and renews attack: *S.S.,* Vol. 28, pp. 161–62, Appendix III, p. 614. Among the weapons employed by the 3d Machinegun Company was an "automatic gun" of about 20mm. Presumably this was one of the Type 98 20mm antiaircraft automatic cannon.

Page 356
Action along attack front during daylight: 1/7 Summary of Operations, period 24–26 October; Merillat, *Island,* p. 169; *S.S.,* Vol. 28, Appendix III, p. 615.

Page 357
"Dugout Sunday": Merillat, *Island,* p. 177. This day was also referred to as "Red Sunday" (ltr Col. Frederick Wiseman to CMC 17 Dec 48).

Early reconnaissance effort from Rabaul: *S.S.,* Vol. 83, p. 264.

Page 357
American reconnaissance results: MAG-23 Record of Events 25 Oct 42.

Page 358
Deployment of 8th Fleet units in support of 17th Army attack: *S.S.,* Vol. 83, pp. 246–47.

Page 358
Orders and maneuvers of 8th Fleet units early on October 25: Ibid., p. 258.

Page 358
Action of *Trevor* and *Zane:* U.S.S. *Trevor,* Serial 0161, October 27, 1942, Subject: Report of Action October 25, 1942; U.S.S. *Zane,* Serial 0191, 2 Nov 42; *S.S.,* Vol. 83, pp. 258–59.

Pages 358–59
6th Destroyer Division action at Lunga: *S.S.,* Vol. 83, pp. 258–59; MAG-23 Record of Events 25 Oct 42.

Loss of *Seminole* and *YP 284:* Commander Naval Activities Cactus-Ringbolt, ANB/102, A4-1/Sh, No Serial, October 27, 1942, Subject: Loss of U.S.S. *YP 284* and U.S.S. *Seminole.*

Page 359
Early-morning fighter action and adventure of Lieutenant Conger: VMF-121 War Diary 25 Oct 42; MAG-23 Record of Events 25 Oct 42; Foss and Simmons, *Joe Foss,* pp. 70–71; *S.S.,* Vol. 83, p. 264. The identity of the individual Conger rescued is from Hata and Izawa, *Japanese Naval Aces and Fighter Units in World War II,* p. 380. The author met Mr. Ishikawa in April 1990.

Air Raid at 1430: VMF-121 War Diary 25 Oct 42; MAG-23 Record of Events 25 Oct 42; *S.S.,* Vol. 83, p. 264, Vol. 28, p. 164.

Carrier plane attack: *S.S.,* Vol. 83, pp. 265, 280.

Page 360
Merillat notes: Merillat, *Island,* p. 179.

Pages 360–61
Sinking of *Yura: S.S.,* Vol. 83, pp. 259–62; MAG-23 Record of Events 25 Oct 42.

Page 361
Aircraft claims and losses: MAG-23 Record of Events 25 Oct 42; Merillat, *Island,* p. 178; Miller, *Cactus Air Force,* p. 146. Mr. John Lundstrom provided the Japanese loss figures.

5th Marines close gap to 2/7: Final Report, Phase V, p. 23.

"jitterbugging" and "knee high in mud": Merillat Diary 25 Oct 42.

Page 361
Redeployment of 1/7 and 3/164 and reserves: Merillat Diary 25 Oct 42; 1/7 Summary of Operations, period 24–26 October; Lieutenant Colonel Samuel Baglien, "The Second Battle of Henderson Field," *Infantry Journal,* Vol.LIV, No. 5 (May 1944), pp. 25,

27 [hereafter Baglien, "Second Battle of Henderson Field"].

Page 361

Ultra warning: Merillat Diary 25 Oct 42.

"Attempted landing tonight? . . .": Ibid.

Japanese command decisions: *S.S.*, Vol. 28, pp. 156–59, 162.

Page 362

Nasu makes plans and artillery effort: Ibid., p. 162.

Page 362

Character of Japanese attack: 164th Infantry Unit Report No. 1.

Attack of Left Wing: *S.S.*, Vol. 28, pp. 162–63; Merillat, *Island*, pp. 181–82; Final Report, Phase V, p. 24; 1/7 Summary of Operations, period 24–26 October; Baglien, "Second Battle of Henderson Field," pp. 26–28; 164th Inf. Hist., pp. 1–2; correspondence with George MacGillivray (former Weapons Company, 7th Marines). Baglien stated there were four 37mm guns covering the trail, and this was followed by later accounts, including the U.S. Army history volume. However, MacGillivray, who was with the section of two Marine 37mm guns emplaced to cover the trail, points out there were actually two 37mm guns and two .50 caliber machineguns (all from Weapons Company, 7th Marines) commanding this approach.

Page 362

Failure of Right Wing to attack: *S.S.*, Vol. 28, p. 162.

Pages 362–63

Dispositions of 2/7: 2d Battalion, 7th Marines, 26 Oct 42, Summary of Operations of 2d Battalion, 7th Marines, period 25–26 October 1942, Box 6, File A22-1 [hereafter 2/7 Summary of Operations, period 25–26 October]; ltr Col. William R. Williams to CMC 17 Jan 49.

Pages 363–64

Attack on 2/7: 2/7 Summary of Operations, period 25–26 October; Merillat, *Island*, pp. 182–83; Final Report, Phase V, p. 25; McMillan, *Old Breed*, pp. 109–11; *S.S.*, Vol. 28, p. 156.

Page 364

Counterattack led by Major Conoley: Ltr Lt.Col. Odell M. Conoley to CMC 26 Jan 49; ltr Maj. Claude B. Cross to CMC 17 Dec 48; ltr Maj. Robert D. Shine to CMC.

"the situation was in hand": 2/7 Summary of Operations, period 25–26 October; Merillat, *Island*, pp. 183–84.

Page 364

Decision to halt the attack by Hyakutake: *S.S.*, Vol. 28, p. 163.

Pages 364–65

Action along 1/7 front night of October 26–27 and mopping up: Merillat, *Island*, pp. 184–85; *S.S.*, Vol. 28, p. 179.

American casualties: COMSOPAC 280326 Oct 42, Grey Book, p. 963; 1/7 Summary of Operations, period 25–26 October; Unit Report, 2d Battalion, 7th Marines, 26 Oct 42, Box 6, File A22-1; S-1 Journal, 164th Infantry, 300-INF(164)-1.2, RG 407, Box 5630; Unit Report No. 1, 164th Infantry; Cates, "My First," p. 47. As Mr. George MacGillivray pointed out to this writer, the muster rolls of the Marine units provide accurate data on casualties. However, it is an arduous process to review these rolls, and I did not locate easily accessible authoritative statements of Marine losses in my research. Mr. MacGillivray was kind enough to share the fruits of his research on the muster roll totals from which the losses for 1/7 are drawn.

Page 365

Japanese losses: *S.S.*, Vol. 28, p. 163; 164th Inf Henderson Field; Merillat, *Island*, pp. 182–84; Final Report, Phase V, p. 27. Saburo Hayashi in collaboration with Alvin D. Coox, *Kogun: The Japanese Army in the Pacific War* (Quantico, Va.: Marine Corps Association, 1959), p. 60, says 17th Army losses in the October offensive totaled 2,200 dead.

Page 365

17th Army assessment: *S.S.*, Vol. 28, p. 172.

Page 365

Commander Ohmae's assessment: Ibid., pp. 266–67.

Pages 365–66

Colonel Furimiya's fate: Ibid., pp. 614–17; Pratt, *Marine's War*, p. 93.

Page 366

American and Japanese air claims and losses: Data from squadron records, particularly VMF-121 war diary with extensive modifications from research by Mr. James Sawruk and Mr. John Lundstrom.

Pages 366–67
Japense air losses: *S.S.* Vol. 83, p. 265, modified by information from Mr. John Lundstrom.

CHAPTER 15

The principal sources for this chapter are the action reports of the American vessels, squadrons, and commands involved; *S.S.*, Vol. 83, pp. 203–316; and Stafford, *Big E.* Mr. John Lundstrom and Mr. James Sawruk again shared the fruits of their research on aircraft operations and losses during this battle, correcting many errors contained in the Japanese Defense Agency history and the American unit and command reports.

Pages 368–69
Composition and deployment of the Support Force and submarines: *S.S.*, Vol. 83, pp. 203, 244, 313–15. Commander Minoru Genda originated the idea of separating the two carrier divisions by 100 miles. Belote and Belote, *Titans of the Seas,* pp. 160–61.

Page 369
Plans and operations of Support Force in October: *S.S.*, Vol. 83, pp. 202–5, 270 (plan), 226–28, 231 (operations mid-October). Ugaki actually noted in his diary that the two fleets moved "in phase."

Page 370
Reconnaissance, intelligence, and estimates of situation: Ibid., pp. 230, 249–50, 265 (air reconnaissance), 249, 270 (radio intelligence and submarines); 272 (speculation on American trap), 271 (newspaper report); Task Force 16 War Diary 16, 19, 23 Oct 42 [hereafter TF 16 War Diary]; U.S.S. *Enterprise,* CV6/A16-3(10-NY), Serial 0015, 10 Nov 42, Subject: The Battle of Santa Cruz, October 26, 1942—Report of [hereafter *Enterprise* Serial 0015], Section A, para. 2, p. 1 (for activities of *Lamson* and *Mahan*).

Page 370
Concerns over ground and fuel situation; fire on *Hiyo:* *S.S.*, Vol. 83, pp. 232–33, 268–70 (fuel shortage); Vol. 28, pp. 40, 69 (Tsuji warned); Vol. 83, pp. 243–44 (coordination with Army), 250, 273 (*Hiyo* fire). *Hiyo* was escorted by *Isonami* and *Inazuma.* The mishap to *Hiyo* effectively mooted a plan to have aircraft from Carrier Division 2 take up residence on Guadalcanal after the capture of the airfield pending the arrival of a permanent garrison from the 11th Air Fleet.

Page 371
American situation: TF 16 War Diary 24 Oct 42; Commander Task Force 61 (Rear Admiral Kinkaid), A16-3, Serial 0077, 20 Nov 42, Subject: Report of Carrier Action North of the Santa Cruz Islands, 26 October 1942 [hereafter CTF 61 Serial 0077], para. 1, p. 1 (for rendezvous of *Enterprise* and *Hornet* and orders).

Page 371
American intelligence picture: SRNS-0180, 0184, 0188-89, 0191-94.

Page 371
Differences between Carrier Division 1 and Combined Fleet: *S.S.*, Vol. 83, pp. 272, 276–77.

Pages 371–72
Japanese searches and contacts by PBYs: Ibid., pp. 280–81. COMAIRSOPAC War Diary 25 Oct 42 shows six B-17s made attack at 7°5′ South, 163°40′ East.

Pages 372–73
Kinkaid attempts to attack: TF 16 War Diary 25 Oct 42; CTF 61 Serial 0077, para. 3, p. 2; *Enterprise* Serial 0015, Section A, para. 5, p. 2; Commander in Chief, U.S. Pacific Fleet, A16-3/SOL, Serial 00413, January 6, 1943, Subject: Solomons Islands Campaign, Battle of Santa Cruz—26 October 1942 [hereafter CINCPAC Serial 00413], paras. 16–17, p. 5 (for *Enterprise* search-strike). A total of seven planes were reported lost in the *Enterprise* report, but no breakdown is given beyond one F4F. CTF 61 Serial 0077, paras. 3, p. 2, mentions deck crash earlier on October 25, and Fighting Squadron Ten, File No. VF10/A16-3, No Serial, 31 Oct 42, Subject: Fighting Squadron 10 Action Report for October 25 and 26, 1942 [hereafter VF-10 31 Oct], Enclosure (F), shows two F4Fs and three SBDs wrecked in a deck crash on October 25. The totals in the text for losses on October 25 are from Mr. Lundstrom.

Page 373
Japanese air strength: This is very difficult to calculate from available sources. Figures given for establishment strength of the Japanese carriers in *S.S.*, Vol. 83, p. 274, are as follows: *Shokaku* and *Zuikaku* each—twenty-seven Zeros, twenty-seven Vals, eighteen Kates; *Zuiho*—twenty-one Zeros, six Kates; *Junyo*—twenty-one Zeros, eighteen Vals, nine Kates; total—ninety-six Zeros, seventy-two Vals, fifty-one Kates = 219 aircraft. These figures would be subject to revi-

sion based upon operational or combat losses. For example, in the latter category on October 15 *Shokaku* lost one Val and *Zuikaku* two Kates in sinking *Meredith*. The transfusion of strength to *Junyo* from *Hiyo* (three Zeros, one Val, five Kates) plus earlier combat and operational losses adds another variable. These calculations are rendered very suspect when the actual numbers of aircraft used on search and attack missions on October 26 are considered. These latter figures seem to indicate the Val total was less but the Kate total was significantly more than "establishment." The figures in the text, including the order of battle, are from data supplied by Mr. Lundstrom.

The total of American operational aircraft: Figures here are based upon information from Mr. Lundstrom and Mr. Sawruk. It should be noted that *Hornet* Serial 0031 14 Oct 42 indicates her air group was then organized with thirty-two Wildcats, twenty-four SBDs, and twelve TBFs.

Character of American air groups: *Enterprise* Serial 0015, Section J, para. 4, pp. 12–13, describes Air Group 10. Miller, *Cactus Air Force*, p. 149, contains descriptions of all the principal air groups involved; however, the text follows the analysis of Mr. Lundstrom of the Japanese air units.

Page 373
"there is a great likelihood . . .": *S.S.*, Vol. 83, p. 282.

Pages 374–76
Japanese organization: Dull, *Battle History of the Imperial Japanese Navy*, pp. 242–43, supplemented Tables 1 and 2 attached to *S.S.*, Vol. 49, concerning the principal commanders in the Imperial Japanese Navy for the period in question. The text reflects a realignment of Vanguard Force with the 3d Fleet to indicate its actual role. Morison, *Struggle for Guadalcanal*, pp. 206–7, provides the names of some division commanders.

Pages 376–78
Organization of U.S. forces: American action reports and Morison, *Struggle for Guadalcanal*, pp. 204–6, with some modification, particularly with respect to fully listing the vessels in TF 64.

Page 379
Ugaki message: *S.S.*, Vol. 83, p. 282.

PBY activities over Carrier Division 1, the Vanguard Force, and the reaction: Ibid., pp. 282–84, 302; COMAIRSOPAC War Diary

24–26 Oct 42. Miller, *Cactus Air Force*, p. 151, shows three PBYs involved in the night attacks, two making contact. Lieutenant Commander J. O. Cobb of VP-91 (plane 91-P-4) made the attack on *Isokaze* under full radar control. The attack on *Zuikaku* was by plane 51-P-6.

Page 379
American situation and PBY messages: U.S.S. *Hornet*, CV8/A16-3(5), Serial 00100, October 30, 1942, Subject: Report of Action, October 26, 1942, and subsequent loss of U.S.S. *Hornet* [hereafter *Hornet* Serial 00100], para. 5, p. 2; CTF 61 Serial 0077, para. 5, p. 2; *Enterprise* Serial 0015, Section B, para. 2, p. 3.

Page 379
Message from liaison officer on Guadalcanal: *S.S.*, Vol. 83, p. 292.

Japanese dawn searches and maneuvers: *S.S.*, Vol. 83, pp. 284, 292–93, 296. *Zuikaku* and *Shokaku* each launched four Kates and *Zuiho* five. There is an apparent error in the table at p. 309 where only eight Kates are shown as launched on this search mission.

Weather: This is variously described in American action reports, as is frequently the case. This account uses the *Enterprise* Serial 0015, Section B, p. 2, and U.S.S. *Portland*, CA33/A16-3, Serial 071, October 30, 1942, Subject: Air Attack upon U.S.S. *Enterprise* by Japanese, October 26, 1942, report of [hereafter *Portland* Serial 071], para. 4, p. 1. *Portland*'s account also notes that TF 16 took care to use all rainsqualls for concealment.

Page 381
Search activities by the *Enterprise* planes and 0310 PBY report: Scouting Squadron 10, VS10/A16, No Serial, October 29, 1942, Subject: Report of Action, October 16 to 26, 1942 [hereafter VS-10 29 Oct 42], pp. 1–4; Bombing Squadron 10, VB10/A16-4, Serial 01, October 30, 1942 [hereafter VB-10 Serial 01], p. 2; TF 16 War Diary 26 Oct 42, entry 0750. CTF 61 Serial 0077, para. 5, p. 3 (reflects receipt of relay of 0310 PBY message from *Curtis* and Kinkaid's reaction). *Enterprise* Serial 0015, Section B, para. 2, p. 3, confirms that Lee's report was received, and CTF 61 Serial 0077, para. 6, p. 3, states both American carriers got this message. Details of Japanese defenses and *Zuiho*'s damage from *S.S.*, Vol. 83, p. 289. The captain of *Zuiho* is identified in Okumiya, Horikoshi, and Caiden, *Zero*, p. 259. Strong and Irvine reported they attacked at 0730; this account uses the times

given in Japanese reports. All the lost Zeros were from *Zuiho,* and one Kate from this ship on a search mission later in the day was also lost.

Page 382

Details of plane number four's activities and the subsequent actions and decisions: *S.S.,* Vol. 83, pp. 285–86, 293, 296.

Pages 382–83

Details of the first and second strike groups of Carrier Division 1: Ibid., pp. 286, 289–290, and information from Mr. Lundstrom.

Page 383

Organization and composition of the American attack groups: TF 16 War Diary 26 Oct 42; *Enterprise* Serial 0015, Section B, para. 4, p. 3; *Hornet* Serial 00100, para. 7, pp. 2–3, and attached squadron reports. The time of departure of the *Hornet* strike is from Commander Cruiser Division 5, A16-3, Serial 0111, November 2, 1942, Subject: Action Report . . . [hereafter ComCrudiv 5 Serial 0111], Enclosure (A), Chronological Log of Battle . . . , p. 1. *Enterprise* Serial 0015, Enclosure (C) by the air officer, says one F4F of the escort returned with engine trouble, but this is not confirmed in the other reports. Miller, *Cactus Air Force,* p. 152, criticizes the American tactics for this attack and states they "virtually preordained failure."

Pages 383–84

Clash between *Enterprise*'s strike group and the *Zuiho* Zeros: Described in VF-10 31 Oct 42, Enclosure (B); and Torpedo Squadron 10, VT10/A16, No Serial, October 30, 1942, Subject: Action, October 26, 1942, report of [hereafter VT-10 30 Oct 42], pp. 1–3 (from which the quotes are drawn); and *S.S.,* Vol. 83, p. 286. The difficult situation presented to Lieutenant Leppla is well discussed in Miller, *Cactus Air Force,* p. 155.

Pages 384–85

Approach of the first Japanese strike group, the fighter direction problems, and *Enterprise*'s position: *Hornet* Serial 00100, paras. 8–11, pp. 3–4; *Enterprise* Serial 0015, Section B, para. 7, p. 4; Fighting Squadron 72, No Serial, November 2, 1942, Subject: Action Report of October 26, 1942 [hereafter VF-72 2 Nov 42], para. 2(b), pp. 3–5; VF-10 31 Oct 42, Enclosure (I); CINCPAC Serial 00413, para. 30, p. 8; *S.S.,* Vol. 83, p. 287.

Page 385

Description of the attack on *Hornet: Hornet*

Serial 00100, paras. 8–16, pp. 3–5, and particularly Enclosures (D) by the air officer, (E) by the engineer officer, and (H) by the communications officer, together with the article "Carrier Fight Cost Enemy 50 Planes" by reporter Charles McMurty of the Associated Press, which appeared in *New York Times,* November 30, 1942, p. 6. The disposition is described in the report of Destroyer Squadron 2, A16-3, Serial 0279, October 31, 1942, Subject: Report of Action 26 October, 1942 [hereafter Desron 2 Serial 0279], pp. 1–2, with diagram. The sequence of the hits reported here follows the study given in War Damage Report No. 30, 8 July 1943, USS *Hornet* (CV 8), Loss in Action Santa Cruz 26 October 1942, Bureau of Ships, Navy Department [hereafter War Damage Report No. 30], which is at some variance with *Hornet*'s main report, but appears to follow generally Enclosure (D) prepared by the air officer. The Japanese side is from *S.S.,* Vol. 83, pp 287–88.

Pages 385–86

The story of the attack on *Shokaku:* Commander Scouting Squadron 8 and Bombing Squadron 8, A16, No Serial, November 2, 1942, Subject: Action Report of 26 October, with Enemy Japanese Fleet—Solomons Islands Area [hereafter VS/B-8 2 Nov 42]; Commander Bombing Squadron 8, A16-3, No Serial, 29 October 1942, Subject: Action on 26 October 1942 [hereafter VB-8 29 Oct 42], which contains the quote from Lieutenant J. E. Vose; VF-72 2 Nov 42, para. 2(a), pp. 2–3; *S.S.,* Vol. 83, pp. 295, 302. The Japanese were very impressed with the low pullouts of Vose's men, but they thought they had shot down a third of the attackers. *S.S.* says four bombs hit *Shokaku,* but other accounts (such as Okumiya, Horikoshi, and Caiden, *Zero,* p. 260, and D'Albas, *Death of a Navy,* p. 200) have given totals as high as six.

Pages 387–88

Activities of the first group of VT-6 aircraft: Commander Torpedo Squadron 6, No Serial, November 2, 1942, Subject: Action Report for October 26, 1942, of First Division of VT Planes [hereafter VT-6 2 Nov 42]. *Suzuya*'s adventures are in *S.S.,* Vol. 83, p. 297.

Efforts of the *Enterprise* attack group: VS-10 29 Oct 42, p. 4; VF-10 31 Oct 42, Enclosure (B); VT-10 30 Oct 42, pp. 1–3. Japanese side from *S.S.,* Vol. 83, p. 297.

Page 388

Attack on *Chikuma:* Lieutenant J. J. Lynch,

VB8/A16-3, No Serial, 28 October 1942, Subject: Action October 26, 1942, in Solomons Area Against Japanese Forces—Report of; *S.S.*, Vol. 83, p. 297. *Enterprise* Serial 0015, Section J, para. 10, p. 15, points out American bombs were fuzed for only a .01-second delay, which was too short to permit a bomb to penetrate really deep into a ship's vitals.

Efforts of VT-6: Executive Officer, Torpedo Squadron 6, No Serial, October 28, 1942, Subject: Action Report on October 26, 1942, Second Division of VT Planes; *S.S.*, Vol. 83, p. 297.

Pages 388–89

Loss of *Porter:* U.S.S. *Porter,* A16-3, No Serial, October 31, 1942, Subject: U.S.S. *Porter*—Report of Torpedoing; U.S.S. *Shaw,* DD 373/A8, No Serial, November 8, 1942, Subject: Report of U.S.S. *Shaw;* VF-10 31 Oct 42, Enclosure (C); CTF 61 Serial 0077, para. 15, p. 5. Japanese submarine activities are from *S.S.*, Vol. 83, pp. 313–15. The circumstances of the torpedoing of *Porter* have been the subject of some doubt for a long time. *I-21* is credited with sinking *Porter* in Morison, *Struggle for Guadalcanal,* p. 215, and in the generally reliable popular account of Japanese submarine operations, Orita and Harrington, *I-Boat Captain,* p. 137, although Morison concedes Japanese records are not explicit. *Porter's* report contained the interesting theory that the torpedo that sank her came from the TBF that crashed. This seemed highly unlikely to this writer for several reasons, not the least of which was the "sighting" of "two" torpedoes. Mr. James Sawruk, however, worked on this problem for some time and suggested a special check of *S.S.* on the *Porter*. On a second look, Mr. Lundstrom pointed out that *S.S.* says flatly, in the section summarizing American accounts, that no Japanese submarine was in the vicinity of *Porter.* The only remaining question surrounded the fact that "two" torpedoes were seen, but this is explained by the fact that the torpedo was circling.

Page 389

First dive-bombing attack on *Enterprise: Enterprise* Serial 0015, Section B, paras. 8–9, pp. 4–5; *Portland* Serial 071, para. 5, pp. 3–5; U.S.S. *Conynham,* DD 371/Ky, A6/A16-31(C-38), No Serial, November 2, 1942, Subject: Action Report—Air Action with Task Force 16, October 26, 1942, para. 2, p. 1 (which contains a description of the formation at the time of the attack); VF-10 31 Oct 42, Enclosures (C), (D), and (I). See also the

vivid description in Stafford, *Big E,* pp. 165–67. U.S.S. *Pensacola, CA24/A16-3,* Serial 0130, October 31, 1942, Subject: Report of Engagement with Enemy Aircraft on October 26, 1942 [hereafter *Pensacola* Serial 0130], para. 10, p. 4, contains the comment: "The problem of hitting a plane diving on another ship is almost impossible of solution. The ship on which the dive is being made has a much easier problem to solve." The Japanese side is from *S.S.*, Vol. 83, pp. 290–91.

Page 390

Approach of *Zuikaku*'s Kates: *Enterprise* Serial 0015, Section B, para. 10, pp. 5–6; *Portland* Serial 071, para. 5, pp. 5–6; *S.S.*, Vol. 83, pp. 290–91. Lieutenant Vejtasa's exploits are from VF-10 31 Oct 42, Enclosure (D).

Pages 390–91

Story of *Smith:* U.S.S. *Smith,* A16-3/DD 378, Serial 00327, November 2, 1942, Subject: Action Report U.S.S. *Smith* October 26, 1942. The tremendous impression *Smith* made on the rest of the ships in the task force is reflected in the report of Commander Thomas M. Stokes (ComDesdiv 10), who commented that *Smith* was an "inspiration to all that saw her," OF 7-10/A16, Serial 0066, October 27, 1942, Subject: Action Report—Anti-Aircraft Action 26 October 1942 [hereafter Desdiv 10 Serial 0066], para. 8, p. 3.

Page 391

Attack of the *Zuikaku* Kates: Basically the same sources mentioned for pages 00–00 and *S.S.*, Vol. 83, pp. 290–91.

Page 391

Attacks on *Portland* and *San Juan: Portland* Serial 071, para. 5, p. 5; U.S.S. *San Juan,* CL54/A16-3, Serial 004, October 31, 1942, Subject: Report of Action, U.S.S. *San Juan*—October 26, 1942 [hereafter *San Juan* Serial 004], Enclosure A, pp. 2–3. In his endorsement to *Portland's* report, Halsey commented that it showed the Japanese also suffered from defective torpedoes. Nimitz, in CINCPAC Serial 00413, para. 39, p. 10, said he believed the torpedoes had failed to explode because they were launched at short range. Mr. Lundstrom worked out this problem and provided the basis for the conclusion in the text.

Pages 391–92

Problems of *Junyo*'s Val group: *S.S.*, Vol. 83, p. 293. The peculiar tactical situation posed by the weather is explained best in *San Juan*

Serial 004, Enclosure A, p. 8, from which the ceiling figures are taken, and also well described by Lieutenant Pollack in VF-10 31 Oct 42, Enclosure (C). *San Juan* indicated her 5-inch guns were practically useless as even with a 1.2-second fuze setting the shells exploded at 3,000 feet, well above the clouds. The attack on *Enterprise* is from her Serial 0015, Section B, para. 11, p. 6, and U.S.S. *Enterprise,* CV6/L 11-1 (50-B1), November 8, 1942, Subject: War Damage Report, para. 2(b)–(c), pp. 2–14.

Page 392
Incident involving Lieutenant Williams: Stafford, *Big E,* p. 175.

Page 392
Attacks on *San Juan* and *South Dakota: San Juan* Serial 004, Enclosure A, pp. 3–4, 9; U.S.S. *South Dakota* BB57 A 9/A12, November 2, 1942, Serial 0154, Subject: Action Report, October 26, 1942 off Santa Cruz Islands [hereafter *South Dakota* Serial 0154]; U.S.S. *Preston,* DD 379/A16-3, Serial 0391, 31 Oct 1942, Subject: Report of Action— Enemy Air Attack Against Task Force 61 on 26 October 1942 [hereinafter *Preston* Serial 0391], para. 5, p. 2. The quote from Lieutenant Commander Sims is from U.S.S. *Maury,* DD 401/A16-3, Serial 025, November 3, 1942, Subject: Report of Action Against . . ., October 26, 1942 [hereafter *Maury* Serial 025], para. 2, p. 1.

Page 393
Losses and results of *Junyo* attack: *S.S.,* Vol. 83, p. 293.

Page 393
Feat of Daniels and Lindsay: *Enterprise* Serial 0015, Section B, para. 13, pp. 6–7 and Enclosure (A). Mr. Lundstrom pointed out the role of Lieutenant Daniels and supplied the aircraft total.

Kondo's movements and orders as well as those of the Advanced Force: *S.S.,* Vol. 83, pp. 297, 303. *S.S.* notes that after *Chikuma* was bombed, the Vanguard Force took up evasive maneuvers in a northerly direction and it took Kondo a number of repetitions of his orders to get them back on a southeasterly course.

Pages 393–94
Nagumo's situation and decisions: Ibid., pp. 296, 298, 301–2. Captain Arima's proposal is at p. 296.

Page 394
Kakuta's movements and decisions: Ibid., p. 298–99. *Zuikaku*'s movements are at p. 306.

Page 395
Withdrawal of *Enterprise:* CTF 61 Serial 0077, para. 16, p. 5; TF 16 War Diary 26 Oct 42. Miller, *Cactus Air Force,* p. 170, critically examines the reasons listed for withdrawal.

Pages 395–96
Efforts to save *Hornet: Hornet* Serial 00100, paras. 16–24, pp. 5–6, with details of various phases in Enclosures (A), (E), (H), and (J). The work of the destroyers aiding her and the towing problems are from both *Hornet*'s report and Desron 2 Serial 0279, para. 3, pp. 3–4; U.S.S. *Morris,* A16-3/DD 417, Serial 003, October 30, 1942, Subject: U.S.S. *Morris* (DD 417)—Action . . . on October 26, 1942, Report on [hereafter *Morris* Serial 003], paras. 4–7, pp. 3–4; U.S.S. *Mustin,* DD 413/ A16-3, Serial 338, 31 Oct 42, Subject: U.S.S. *MUSTIN . . .* on October 26, 1942 [hereafter *Mustin* Serial 338], Section A, para. 9, pp. 4–7; U.S.S. *Russell,* DD 414/A16-3, Serial 031, October 30, 1942, Subject: Report of Action . . . October 26, 1942 [hereafter *Russell* Serial 031], para. 3, pp. 2–3; U.S.S. *Northampton,* CA26/A16-3, Serial 0109, October 31, 1942, Subject: Report of Action with Enemy [hereafter *Northampton* Serial 0109], para. 3, pp. 2–3.

Page 396
Attack of the *Junyo* Kates: *S.S.,* Vol. 83, p. 299; *Hornet* Serial 00100, para. 24, pp. 6–7; *Northampton* Serial 0109, para. 3, p. 3. During the late morning when aircraft began returning to the immobilized *Hornet* a message was sent by blinker light for them to "Go to *Enterprise.*" Unfortunately the signal was flashed along *Juneau*'s bearing and she understandably assumed the message was for her. She stopped to pick up a plane crew as she began to leave, and Admiral Good did not realize she was leaving the formation permanently until it was too late (U.S.S. *Juneau,* CL52/A16-3, Serial 059, October 30, 1942, Subject: Report of Action on October 26, 1942, para. 3, p. 6; ComCrudiv 5 Serial 0111, para. 1(c) p. 2). The position of the hit on *Hornet* is from War Damage Report No. 30.

Pages 396–97
"A sickly green flash . . .": *Hornet* Serial 00100, Enclosure (E), p. 5.

Page 397
Effects of the third torpedo hit: *Hornet* Serial

00100, para. 24, pp. 6–7; War Damage Report No. 30. CTF 61 Serial 0077 adds that the attack eliminated the possibility of further towing *Hornet,* as it left her with both anchor chains payed out with no power to retrieve them.

Zuikaku's third attack group: *S.S.,* Vol. 83, pp. 299–300.

Page 397
Final abandonment of *Hornet* and attack on *San Diego: Hornet* Serial 00100, paras. 24–29, pp. 6–8; reports from the destroyers involved mentioned in the notes for pages 00–00; U.S.S. *San Diego,* CL53/A16-3, Serial 006, October 30, 1942, Subject: Action with the Enemy October 26, 1942, Report on, para. 1, p. 2.

Page 397
Junyo's third attack: *S.S.,* Vol. 83, p. 300.

Losses on *Hornet: Hornet*'s own report does not contain a final and reliable list of losses among the crew. The figures used here are from the Bureau of Personnel totals compiled after the war, with corrections supplied by Mr. Sawruk, particularly the addition of fifteen members of *Hornet*'s Marine detachment and one member of VT-6 who was killed aboard *Russell.*

Messages reaching Halsey: COMSOPAC War Diary 26–27 Oct 42 contains all these messages. The warning from CINCPAC is from Potter, *Nimitz,* p. 202, and is alluded to in CINCPAC Serial 00413, para. 48, p. 11.

Page 398
Activities of *Mustin* and *Anderson:* Desron 2 Serial 0279, pp. 4–5 (from which times are taken); *Mustin* Serial 338, paras. 9–18, pp. 7–9; U.S.S. *Anderson,* DD 411/A16-3, Serial 0174, October 27, 1942, Subject: Report . . . on October 26, 1942, para. 2, pp. 8–9.

Orders and maneuvers of the Support Force: *S.S.,* Vol. 83, pp. 302–5. The decryption of the order to capture and tow *Hornet* is from Van Der Rhoer, *Deadly Magic,* p. 124.

Page 399
Attack on *Teruzuki:* From Dull, *Battle History of the Imperial Japanese Navy,* pp. 240–41.

Attacks on *Washington:* CTF 64 to COMSOPAC 280133, COMSOPAC War Diary 28 Oct 42, p. 67.

Page 399
Collision of *South Dakota* and *Mahan:*

U.S.S. *Mahan,* DD-364, Serial 0122, 2 Nov 42; TF 16 War Diary 30 Oct 42. The collision occurred at 0406 on October 30 at 24°23′ South, 167°17′ East.

Page 399
Final operations of the Support Force: *S.S.,* Vol. 83, pp. 305–6.

Pages 399–400
Japanese assessment of the results of the battle: *S.S.,* Vol. 83, pp. 306–11. These pages amply reflect the difficulty the Japanese experienced in trying to determine how many American carriers were present from a mass of conflicting evidence. The initial report of the Combined Fleet in the early hours of October 27 asserted American losses included four carriers.

Page 401
"no diminution in the courage . . .": Desron 2 Serial 0279, para. 4(f), pp. 5–6.

Nimitz and King galled by the quick announcement of loss of *Hornet:* CINCPAC to COMINCH 012115 Nov 42, Grey Book, p. 970. In remarks made in November and reported in "Admiral Stresses Unity of Command," *New York Times,* November 16, 1942, p. 7, King attributed the quick release of the news of *Hornet*'s loss to politics—e.g., the desire not to appear to be concealing bad news before the November congressional elections.

Claims for Japanese plane losses: CINCPAC Serial 00413, para. 3. p. 2.

Page 401
American plane and aircrew losses: Sorting out the precise total and mixture of American plane losses is difficult from the contemporaneous reports. A figure of seventy-four aircraft may be found in CINCPAC Serial 00413, para. 6, p. 2, which appears to be higher than the number given in the collective squadron and ship reports. Ultimately, however, research by Mr. Sawruk in the archives of the Bureau of Aeronautics located the figures used in the text. The aircrew losses are more confidently stated. COMAIR-SOPAC War Diary 28 Oct 42 shows a special search recovered Lieutenant Commander Widhelm and his gunner, the only other squadron commander besides Collett shot down. The loss of ship crewmen given in the same paragraph of CINCPAC Serial 00413 is 283 officers and men, which is considerably (and inexplicably) higher than what the contemporary reports reflect or the postwar ac-

counting by the Bureau of Personnel. The total of killed, died of wounds, and missing according to the Bureau of Personnel, with corrections by Mr. Sawruk, were as follows:

Hornet:	118	*Pensacola:*	3
Enterprise:	44	*South Dakota:*	2
Smith:	57	*Morris:*	1
Porter:	15		
	Total: 240		

Pages 401–3
American post-battle analysis: *Enterprise* Serial 0015, Section J; *Hornet* Serial 00100, paras. 30–33, pp. 8–11; the squadron reports (particularly those of VF-10, VF-72, VS-8, and VB-8) noted above, and Kinkaid's endorsements to these reports; CTF 61 Serial 0077, para. 17, pp. 5–6. The quote from Lieutenant Commander Sanchez is from VF-72 2 Nov 42, p. 6. Miller, *Cactus Air Force,* pp. 171–73, also provides an excellent assessment of the American air performance, from which this account benefits. Comments on gunnery performance are from several ships; the estimate that the 5-inch guns accounted for only 5 percent of all planes shot down (with 40mm and 1.1-inch credited with 30 percent and the 20mm with 65 percent) is from *South Dakota* Serial 0154, p. 8, para. 5.

Page 403
"This battle cost us . . .": CINCPAC Serial 00413, para. 89, p. 18.

CHAPTER 16

Page 404
"An atmosphere of tense expectation": "Roosevelt Confers with Naval Chiefs," *New York Times,* October 27, 1942, p. 1, col. 8.

Page 405
"My anxiety about the Southwest Pacific . . .": As quoted in Hayes, *History of the Joint Chiefs of Staff,* p. 193.

Page 405
Responses to President Roosevelt's memorandum and his decision: Ibid., pp. 193–94. Marshall also mentioned ammunition as a limiting factor, but it was not so pressing. King supplied the figure of twenty ships, five less than Marshall estimated. It is not clear whether the President saw the memoranda

from King and Marshall, but Admiral Leahy presumably relayed their contents.

Pages 405–6
Estimate of situation at Imperial Headquarters and impact of American news stories: *S.S.,* Vol. 28, pp. 169–70. On the rationale behind the publication of such information in the American media, the author of *S.S.* asks at p. 170, "What effect were they expecting?"

Page 406
Plans of 17th Army: Ibid., pp. 170, 178, 224–25.

Page 406
Reply of Imperial Headquarters, General Miyazaki's input, and response of 17th Army: Ibid., pp. 170–74. Imperial General Headquarters compared "Bear Height" to the "203 Height," the site of a decisive battle in the Russo-Japanese War.

Pages 406–7
Activities and suffering of the Sendai Division during its retreat: Ibid., pp. 179–80.

Page 407
Quote from Lieutenant Minegishi's diary: Ibid., pp. 180–81.

Page 407
October 29–30 run of the Tokyo Express: *S.S.,* Vol. 83, pp. 343–44; Bulkley, *At Close Quarters,* pp. 87–88. MAG-23 Record of Events 29 Oct 42 shows radio intelligence warned of a run by two or three destroyers that night.

Conference of Miyazaki, Ohmae, and officers of 17th Army, arrival of Tsuji: *S.S.,* Vol. 28, p. 175.

Page 408
Supply calculations of 17th Army and 8th Fleet: Ibid., pp. 176–77, 221, 228–29, Vol. 83, pp. 323–24, 328.

Pages 408–9
Details of planning and atmosphere at the Combined Fleet at this time: Ibid., Vol. 83, pp. 325–29. Comment of Yamamoto is at pp. 325–26. The plan to use naval artillery for shelling led to the creation of the Combined 8th Special Landing Force Unit, composed of the 4th Maizura, 6th Kure, and 7th Yokohama Special Naval Landing Forces. The 4th Meizura was already at Guadalcanal, and the other two were formed on November 20. Armament of these units included 140mm and 120mm guns and 80mm antiair-

craft guns. Rear Admiral Minora Ota commanded the new unit. *S.S.*, Vol. 83, pp. 401–2, 457.

Page 409
American plans for reinforcement and the loss of *President Coolidge:* COMNAVUNIT Button to COMSOPAC 280921 Oct 42, Grey Book, p. 964. Halsey's promise on reinforcements is in COMSOPAC to CINCPAC 290130 Oct 42, Grey Book, p. 965.

Page 409
Arrival and rotation of American squadrons: The condition of the three airfields on Guadalcanal is described in COMARDIV 1 to COMSOPAC 010501 Nov 42, Grey Book, p. 970; VMSB-131, -132, -142, VMF-112 War Diaries for early November.

Page 410
Circumstances of General Geiger's replacement by General Woods and quote from Woods: Miller, *Cactus Air Force*, pp. 176–77.

Page 410
Change of composition and availability of 11th Air Fleet and R Area Air Force: *S.S.*, Vol. 83, pp. 331–32, 336, 339–40, Vol. 28, pp. 225, 232. Figures on American air strength on October 31 are from MAG-23 Record of Events 30 Oct 42 (which gives availability for next day) and 13th AF Hist., p. 49, which states thirty-five of forty-seven B-17s in the South Pacific were operational on October 26 (other information shows no B-17 losses between October 26 and 31).

Page 410
"riches beyond dreams of avarice" and comments on early November action: Vandegrift and Asprey, *Once a Marine*, pp. 192–193.

Pages 410–11
Background of the planning for the offensive: Final Report, Phase V, pp. 27–28, states the plan was made "with a view" toward cutting off the Sendai Division, but the order (Op Ord No. 13–42, 30 Oct 42) lists the sole objective as driving the enemy beyond the Poha to secure the airfield from artillery fire.

Page 411
Japanese situation before the November offensive: *S.S.* Vol. 28, pp. 183–86.

Pages 411–12
November 1 attack on the Matanikau: Final Report, Phase V, p. 28; Merillat, *Island*, pp. 188–90; Engineer Activities Guadalcanal, p.

9; 5th Marines Record of Events; ltr. Lt. Col. W. H. Barba to CMC 29 Jan 49; ltr Maj. Harry S. Connors to CMC 14 Feb 49; ltr Lt. Col. Henry H. Crocket to CMC 10 Jan 49. *S.S.*, Vol. 28, p. 177, shows the 17th Army Headquarters was bombed twice during the day.

Medal of Honor to Anthony Casamento: Biographical files, MCHC; Hammel, *Guadalcanal: Starvation Island*, pp. 377–78.

Page 412
Dissatisfaction with the accomplishments of the 5th Marines and the actual Japanese situation: Merillat, *Guadalcanal Remembered*, p. 217; *S.S.*, Vol. 28, p. 186.

Pages 412–13
Actions on November 2: Final Report, Phase V, p. 28; 5th Marines Record of Events 2 Nov 42; Merillat, *Island*, pp. 191–92; ltr Lt. Col. Lyman D. Spurlock to CMC 27 Jan 49; ltr. Lt. Col. L. W. Walt to CMC, 18 Apr 49; *S.S.*, Vol. 28, p. 186.

Page 414
November 2 run of the Tokyo Express: *S.S.*, Vol. 83, pp. 344–347, Vol. 28, p. 182. The composition of the reinforcement units were: Ko—*Asagumo* (flag); Desdiv 2 with *Murasame, Harusame,* and *Yudachi;* Desdiv 27 with *Shigure, Shiratsuyu, Ariake,* and *Yugure;* Desdiv 11 with *Shirayuki;* Desdiv 6 with *Akatsuki* and *Ikazuchi;* and light cruiser *Tenryu;* Otsu—Desdiv 8 with *Michishio;* Desdiv 19 with *Uranami, Shikanami,* and *Isonami;* and *Mochizuki.* The American reaction is from 1st Mar Div Record of Events 2 Nov 42; Merillat, *Guadalcanal Remembered*, pp. 216–217; MAG-23 Record of Events 2 Nov 42; MAG-14, pp. 2–3 (loss of Lieutenant Commander Eldridge). The warning message was COMSOPAC 010800 Nov 42, COMSOPAC War Diary, 1 Nov 42, p. 1. The activities of Lieutenant Colonel Hanneken's 2/7 are detailed in his 2d Battalion, 7th Marines, Report of Operations, 1–3 Nov 42, 4 Nov 42, pp. 1–2, Box 6, File 22-1. During a halt on the march to the Nalimbiu, a large tree fell, killing two men and injuring four others.

Pages 415–16
Japanese account of the action against Hanneken on November 3: *S.S.*, Vol. 28, pp. 182–83, indicates no comprehensive report remains on this or the subsequent actions near Koli, but that Hanneken definitely only encountered the men landed the night before.

Hanneken's account is from pp. 2–3 of his report.

Page 416
Knowledge and actions of the Marine command: Merillat, *Guadalcanal Remembered,* pp. 218–19.

Page 416
The reduction of the pocket near Point Cruz: Merillat, *Island,* p. 192; ltr. Lt. Col. L. W. Walt to CMC, 18 Apr 49.

Page 416
Japanese deploy reinforcements, strength of 4th Infantry Regiment, and American advance: *S.S.,* Vol. 28, pp. 186–87; Merillat, *Island,* p. 193.

Page 416
Conference between Tamaoki, Tsuji, and Sugita: *S.S.,* Vol. 28, p. 187.

Page 417
General Hattori's impressions and reactions: Ibid., p. 192.

Pages 417–18
Reactions of Vandegrift and his staff: Merillat, *Island,* pp. 197–200 (including quote from Lieutenant Colonel Twining); 1st Battalion, 7th Marines, Summary of Operations of the 1st Battalion, 7th Marines for the period 3–8 November, 1942, both dates inclusive, 9 Nov 42, p. 1, Box 6, File A21-1 [hereafter 1/7 Summary of Operations Koli Point]; ltr Col. Manley L. Curry to CMC 17 Dec 48; and particularly Merillat, *Guadalcanal Remembered,* pp. 218–20. MAG-23 Record of Events 3 Nov 42 provides details of air support for Hanneken. Aircraft sent out included fifteen SBDs, seven P-39/400s, two TBFs, and seven Wildcats. The actions of the Shoji Detachment are from *S.S.,* Vol. 28, p. 182.

Page 418
Conference on morning of November 4: Merillat, *Guadalcanal Remembered,* pp. 224–25.

The Japanese situation on November 4 and the diversion of artillery ammunition: *S.S.,* Vol. 28, pp. 180, 187, 189. P. 189 reports losses in the 4th Infantry Regiment from "late October" through early November as 410 killed, including Nakaguma, and 299 wounded. The strength report for the 4th Infantry Regiment is in 2d Division Information, p. 4, RG 407, Box 4631. The American situation before Kokumbona is from Meril-

lat, *Island,* p. 193. American losses from 1–4 November in this sector are not separately compiled.

Page 420
The situation near Koli Point: Final Report, Phase V, p. 29; Narrative of Operations, Americal Division, At Guadalcanal, p. 2, 300-2, RG 407, Box 5473 [hereafter Narrative of Operations, Americal Division]; 164th Infantry Regiment, Report of Koli Point—Guadalcanal, 300-INF(164)-0.3.0, RG 407, Box 5628 [hereafter 164th Infantry Regiment Koli Point]; 164th Infantry Unit History, 300-INF(164)-0.2, RG 407, Box 5626.

Shelling of Koli Point: Commander in Chief, U.S. Pacific Fleet, PAC-90-wb, A16-3/Sol, Serial 00554, 18 February 1943, Subject: Solomons Islands Campaign—Battle of the Solomons, 11–15 November 1942, p. 4, para. 4 [hereafter CINCPAC Serial 00554].

Pages 420–21
The Aola adventure: Vandegrift and Asprey, *Once a Marine,* p. 192; Clemens MS, p. 231; The Army in the South Pacific, 98-USF2-0.1, p. 3, RG 407, Box 1606 [hereafter Army in the South Pacific]; RDO GUADALCANAL 182223 Nov 42, COMSOPAC War Diary 22 Nov 42, p. 58; COMGEN 1st Mar Div to COMSOPAC 220555 Nov 42, COMSOPAC War Diary 22 Nov 42, p. 58; COMSOPAC 230645 Nov 42, COMSOPAC War Diary 23 Nov 42, p. 60. Task Force 62 War Diary 4 Nov 42 shows the 8th Marines were moved in *Hunter Liggett, President Hayes,* and *Barnett* while the ships detailed to Aola included *Neville, Heywood, Formalhaut, Manley, McKean, Sterett,* and *Gwin.*

Page 421
Action near Koli November 5: 164th Infantry Regiment Koli Point and *S.S.,* Vol. 28, p. 182, describe actions around Koli on November 5. The intramural firefight in the 164th is from General Sebree's interview, cited in Miller, *Guadalcanal: The First Offensive,* p. 198.

Page 421
Air activity of November 5: *S.S.,* Vol. 83, p. 335; MAG-23 Record of Events 5 Nov 42; VMF-121 War Diary 5 Nov 42.

Tokyo Express run of November 5: *S.S.,* Vol. 83, pp. 340, 347–50. The composition of the reinforcement units were: Ko—Desdiv 2 with *Murasame, Harusame,* and *Yudachi;* Desdiv 27 with *Shigure, Shiratsuyu, Ariake,* and *Yugure;* Desdiv 8 with *Arashi* and *Mich-*

ishio; and *Asagumo;* Otsu—Desdiv 11 with *Shirayuki* and *Mochizuki;* Desdiv 19 with *Uranami* (flag), *Shikanami,* and *Isonami;* and light cruiser *Tenryu.* The PT boat action is from Bulkley, *At Close Quarters,* pp. 88–89.

Page 422
American operations on November 6: 164th Infantry Regiment Koli Point provides an account of American operations on November 6–7.

Page 422
Reinforcement run on November 7: *S.S.,* Vol. 83, pp. 340, 350–351; Tanaka, Part II, p. 820. The composition of the "Express" was: Desdiv15 with *Oyashio, Hayashio,* and *Kagero;* Desdiv 24 with *Umikaze, Kawakaze,* and *Suzukaze;* Desdiv 31 with *Makinami, Takanami,* and *Naganami;* and Desdiv 10 with *Yugumo* and *Kazegumo.* American air strike is described in MAG-23 Record of Events 7 Nov 42; MAG-14, p. 3; 67th FS Hist., p. 51; VMF-121 War Diary 7 Nov 42 (which provides the figures on Wildcat strength). Foss and Simmons, *Joe Foss,* pp. 95–98, recounts his adventures, and the PT boat action is from Bulkley, *At Close Quarters,* p. 89.

Page 423
Action on November 8: Same sources as for action on November 6 with the addition of Merillat, *Island,* p. 205, on the command changes. The new commander of the 2/164 was Lieutenant Colonel Ben J. Northridge.

Halsey's visit to Guadalcanal: Vandegrift and Asprey, *Once a Marine,* p. 196; Halsey and Bryan, *Admiral Halsey's Story,* pp. 123–24.

Page 423
Reinforcement run of November 8: *S.S.,* Vol. 83, pp. 351–52, Vol. 28, p. 220. Composition of the Otsu unit was: Desdiv 2 with *Murasame* and *Yudachi;* Desdiv 27 with *Shigure, Shiratsuyu,* and *Yugure;* and *Asagumo, Mochizuki, Arashi,* and *Michishio* with light cruiser *Tenryu* (flag). The PT boat action is from Bulkley, *At Close Quarters,* p. 89.

Page 423
Final action around Koli: Merillat, *Island,* pp. 204–5; 164 Inf Ops Rpt, 31 Oct–16 Nov 42; Final Report, Phase V, pp. 29–30; ltr Lt. Col. John E. Weber to CMC 11 Jan 49; 1/7 Summary of Operations Koli Point; COMGEN 1st MARDIV to COMSOPAC 152246 Nov 42, COMSOPAC War Diary 15 Nov 42, p. 48 (capture of Kawaguchi's effects).

Pages 423–24
Carlson and Shoji: *S.S.,* Vol. 28, pp. 223–24, 307, 312; Report of Operations, 2d Raider Battalion, 20 Dec 42, Box 7, File A39-1, MCHC; Merillat, *Island,* pp. 217–27.

Page 424
The plans and actions for the renewal of the western offensive: Final Report, Phase V, p. 31; 8th Marine Regiment, Report on Operations, undated, pp. 8–9, Box 6, File A24-1 (hereafter 8th Mar Rpt Ops); ltr Col. John M. Arthur to Officer in Charge, Historical Division, Headquarters, U.S. Marine Corps, 11 Oct 45, Box 9 (hereafter ltr Col. J. M. Arthur 11 Oct 45); ltr Col. C. P. Van Ness to CMC 12 Jan 1949. A good description of how the Japanese exploited the defensive advantages of the terrain is in Merillat, *Island,* p. 188. The Japanese side is described in *S.S.,* Vol. 28, pp. 219, 221–23. They reported capturing two mortars and six heavy and light machineguns.

Page 425
Air action and reinforcement run November 10: *S.S.,* Vol. 83, pp. 335, 353; MAG-23 Record of Events 10 Nov 42; Bulkley, *At Close Quarters,* pp. 89–91. The ships involved were Desdiv 10 *(Yugumo, Makigumo,* and *Kazegumo)* plus *Makinami* and *Suzukaze.* The passengers are detailed in *S.S.,* Vol. 28, p. 220.

Page 425
Air attacks November 11: *S.S.,* Vol. 83, p. 335. Loss information from John Lundstrom. The American reaction is itemized in MAG-23 Record of Events 11 Nov 42; 1st Mar Div Record of Events 11 Nov 42; U.S.S. *Zeilin,* AP9/A16-3, Serial 079, November 15, 1942; and VMF-121 War Diary 11 Nov 42 (from which loss figures are taken). VMF-121 lost seven planes and four pilots this day.

Pages 425–26
Renewed American operations on western front: Final Report, Phase V, p. 31; 8th Mar Rpt Ops, pp. 10–11; Merillat, *Island,* p. 203. The Japanese account is from *S.S.,* Vol. 28, pp. 221–23. Ltr Col. Cornelius Van Ness to CMC 12 Jan 49 shows losses in the 2d Marine Regiment between October 31 and November 12 were thirty-five killed, seven missing, and 133 wounded. 8th Mar Rpt Opns shows losses of one killed and fourteen wounded.

Page 426
The emotions of the men ordered to with-

draw from west of the Matanikau: Noted in ltr Col. R. H. Jeschke to CMC 30 Dec 48.

Page 426

"Grand scale offensive"; "reading the mail": CINCPAC Daily Summaries 7 and 10 Nov 42 respectively, Grey Book, pp. 1157, 1160.

Radio intelligence information: SRNS-0203-06, 0211-12, 0214, 2–6, 10–11, 13 Nov 42; SRH-278, 8–9, 12 Nov 42, pp. 0074–75, 0078–79; SRNS-0210, 9 Nov 42.

Page 426

Information Halsey received on November 9: Described in Halsey and Bryan, *Admiral Halsey's Story*, pp. 124–25, and matches CINCPAC to COMSOPAC 092107 Nov 42, Grey Book, pp. 902–3, but there may have been an early message from Nimitz to the same general effect. *S.S.*, Vol. 83, p. 353, indicates this was Combined Fleet Order No. 377. The timing of the convoy was set around the moon phase (Vol. 83, p. 329). The coast watcher report on November 10 is from CINCPAC Daily Summary 10 Nov 42, Grey Book, p. 1159. The estimate that Z-Day was November 13 is in SRNS-0211, 10 Nov 42. The numbers and condition of Halsey's warships are from Halsey and Bryan, *Admiral Halsey's Story*, pp. 124–25, and COMSOPAC to CINCPAC 090347 Nov 42, Grey Book, p. 975. Halsey's orders to Kinkaid are in COMSOPAC to CTF 61 102102 Nov 42, Grey Book, p. 977.

Page 427

Atmosphere in Washington: Described by Assistant Secretary of the Navy James Forrestal to Samuel E. Morison in a 1948 letter quoted in Morison, *Struggle for Guadalcanal*, p. 263.

CHAPTER 17

The sources for this chapter are the American individual ship and higher command reports and *S.S.*, Vol. 83, pp. 350–76. Also of considerable assistance is the Imperial Japanese Navy track chart of the "Third Battle of the Solomon Sea" prepared by the Japanese Defense Agency from the Destroyer Squadron 4 War Diary. This is hereafter referred to as the JDA Track Chart. Some reconciliation of times has been employed in the text around the conclusion that gunfire began at 0148.

Pages 428–29

Characteristics and organization of Tanaka's convoy: *S.S.*, Vol. 83, pp. 350, 355, Vol. 28,

p. 234. I found no figures in either Vol. 28 or Vol. 83 on the total number of soldiers embarked on the transports. The estimate of 7,000 is based on data in Vol. 83, pp. 381, 397–98.

Page 429

Organization and plans of the Combined and 8th Fleets: *S.S.*, Vol. 83, pp. 326–27, 354–58. The Advanced Force left Truk at 1743 on November 9, Destroyer Squadron 4 left Shortland at 1700 on November 11, and Destroyer Division 27 left Shortland at 0000 on November 12 (p. 358).

Pages 429–30

Organization and plans of Admiral Turner: Commander Amphibious Force South Pacific, FE25/A16-3(8), Serial 00469, December 3, 1942, Subject: Report of Operations of Task Force 67 and Task Group 62.4—Reinforcement of Guadalcanal November 8–15, 1942, and Summary of Third Battle of SAVO, pp. 2–4, para. 2, 3, 6–7 (hereafter COMAMPHIBFORSOPAC Serial 00469).

Page 430

Organization of Task Force 16: COMSOPAC 070232 Nov 42, COMSOPAC War Diary 7 Nov 42, p. 18; COMSOPAC to *Pensacola, Preston, Gwin*, 110212 Nov 42, COMSOPAC War Diary 11 Nov 42, p. 29. Destroyer *Clark* was ordered to join Task Force 16 on November 11. COMSOPAC to *Clark* 102312 Nov 42, COMSOPAC War Diary 11 Nov 42, p. 28.

Submarine deployment: CTF 42 to COMSOPAC 121116 Nov 42, COMSOPAC War Diary 12 Nov 42, pp. 32–33; Morison *Struggle for Guadalcanal*, p. 235.

Page 430

Movement of Scott and Turner to Guadalcanal: COMAMPHIBFORSOPAC Serial 00469, pp. 3–7, paras. 4–14.

Source of float plane that saw Scott on November 10: *S.S.*, Vol. 83, p. 341.

Page 430

Southard sinks submarine: U.S.S. *Southard*, DMS10/A16-3/p, Serial 0128, November 22, 1942. Subject: Action Report, Engagement with Submarine, November 10, 1942; COMAMPHIBFORSOPAC Serial 00469, p. 5, para. 8. The identity of this submarine is a matter of dispute. The standard reference work on this subject is the Appendix on Axis Submarine Losses in *United States Sub-*

marine Losses World War II. This appendix lists *Southard's* victim as *I-172* at position 10°13′ South, 161°09′ East; the loss of *I-15* is attributed to *McCalla* on November 2 at position 10°53′ South, 161°50′ East (p. 175). This is consistent with Morison, *Struggle for Guadalcanal,* p. 227.

S.S., Vol. 83, p. 343, notes the Japanese believed *I-172* was sunk on November 27 (no details given). This same source indicates the last contact with *I-15* was on November 3, and she was believed lost by the Japanese on December 5, but adds that U.S. sources list her as sunk by an aircraft on December 16 at 9°10′ South, 159°30′ East. In Orita and Harrington, *I-Boat Captain,* pp. 134–35, the opinion is offered that *I-172* was an operational loss and *Southard's* battle was with *I-15.*

This writer began to doubt the standard American references after review of *Southard's* report, which indicates the submarine she sank broached her forward half and no deck gun was noted. This would strongly suggest the boat was *I-15* rather than *I-172.*

Sinking of *I-172:* COMSOPAC War Diary 5 Nov 42, p. 14; U.S.S. *McCalla,* DD488/A16-3, Serial 019, November 7, 1942, Subject: Action with Enemy Submarine, report of. This report indicates the submarine was sunk on November 3, versus November 2 as reported in the appendix in *American Submarine Losses World War II* noted above. Mr. James Sawruk found information that at 0710 (−11 time) on October 29, a PBY of VP-11 flown by Lieutenant Joseph Hill attacked a submarine west of San Cristóbal in position 13°1′ South, 162°45′ East. The submarine crash-dived, and after two depth charges went off a huge pool of oil formed. Lieutenant Hill was decorated for the attack. I believe this attack must rank at least equally with *McCalla's* as the probable cause of the loss of *I-172.*

Page 430
Action against shore batteries: Commander Amphibious Force South Pacific War Diary 12 Nov 42.

Pages 430–31
Report of Lieutenant Commander Mitzi and reaction at Rabaul and the Combined Fleet: *S.S.,* Vol. 83, pp. 358, 361–62.

Page 431
Air Attack in Lunga Roads: *S.S.,* Vol. 83, p. 336, provides a basic background, but the organization and loss data is from John Lundstrom. COMAMPHIBFORSOPAC

Serial 00469, pp. 7–11, paras. 16–23; U.S.S. *San Francisco,* CA38/A16-3, Serial 0411, November 16, 1942, Subject: Action Report–Air Attack November 12, 1942; U.S.S. *Buchanan,* DD484/A16-3, Serial 00438, 14 Nov 42, Subject: Report of Action Against Enemy—12 November 1942; McCandless, Bruce, Rear Admiral USN (Ret.), "The *San Francisco* Story," *United States Naval Institute Proceedings,* Vol. 84, No. 2 (February 1958), pp. 36–8 [hereafter McCandless, "San *Francisco* Story"] for ship participation; MAG-23 record of events, 12 Nov 42 and VMF-121 War Diary 12 Nov 42 for air action. Wildcat losses were one from VMF-121 and two from 112. U.S.S. *Betelgeuse,* AK28/A16-3, Serial 0203, 16 November 1942, mentions that the ship's passengers joined the gunners with fire ranging from .45 caliber pistols to machineguns. The report goes on to total the cost of every bullet and shell expended, which came to $3,862.33.

Page 432
Arrival of first P-38s and Admiral Fitch's preparations: COMAIRSOPAC War Diary 11–12 Nov 42; 13th AF Hist., p. 56–57.

Total operational aircraft of Cactus Air Force for November 13: 1st Mar Div D-2 Jnl 13 Nov 42, which gives the number of aircraft operational at the start of the day. However, this entry does not mention the eight P-38s that arrived on November 12, and they have been added in the text.

Page 433
Turner's information and plans: COMAMPHIBFORSOPAC Serial 00469, pp. 12–13, paras. 25–28. Besides *Buchanan,* the other escorts Turner took with him were *McCalla, Shaw, Southard,* and *Hovey.* It must be noted that the decision to definitely commit Callaghan was Turner's alone without any specific guidance from Halsey. Moreover, Halsey did not order Task Force 16 to sortie until 1000 on November 11, and at 2000 on 12 November this unit was at 17° 52′ 1″ South, 161° 50′ 4″ East, about 360 miles south of Guadalcanal (COMSOPAC 102102 Nov 42, COMSOPAC War Diary 11 Nov 42, pp. 27–28; U.S.S. *Enterprise,* CV6/A-16-3/ (10-vo), Serial 0019, November 19, 1942, Subject: Action Against Japanese Forces Attempting the Recapture of Guadalcanal, November 13–14, 1942—Report of (Navigator's Report) [Hereafter *Enterprise* Serial 0019]. Admiral Nimitz made it quite clear that the reason why Turner could not count on the assistance of Lee's battleships was the late order to sortie from Noumea (Commander in Chief, U.S.

Pacific Fleet, PAC-90-wb, A16-3/Sol, Serial 00554, 18 February 1943, Subject: Solomons Islands Campaign—Battle of the Solomons, 11–15 Nov 1942, p. 4, para. 9 [hereafter CINCPAC Serial 00554].

Page 433
Turner's selection of Callaghan to command: CTF 67 to CTF 67.4 120133 Nov 42. The text of this message may be found in Commander in Chief, U.S. Pacific Fleet, Pac-90-Wb, A16-3/Sol, Serial 03812, December 26, 1942, Subject: Preliminary Report of Action 12–13 November 1942, p. 3, para. 5 [hereafter CINCPAC Serial 03812]. The official biographies of Scott and Callaghan are at the NHC.

Page 434
Japanese task organization: S.S., Vol. 83, p. 356. Dull, *Battle History of the Imperial Japanese Navy*, pp. 256–57, states that Abe's bombardment unit also carried the operational title of "Volunteer Attack Force" based upon the compound word *Teishin* meaning "bravely (offer) body" or "volunteer." He makes the interesting suggestion that this usage indicates a change of psychology, as prior to this victory was assumed, "but now sailors were being asked to seek death, presaging the 'kamikaze' concept."

Pages 434–35
American task organization: CINCPAC Serial 03812, pp. 1–3, para. 4.

Page 435
Tabular comparison of combat power: Japanese armament from Jentschur, Jung, and Mickel, *Warships of the Imperial Japanese Navy, 1869–1945*, pp. 31–35, 107–8, 145, 147–51. The weight of the 14-inch armor-piercing projectiles is in the table at p. 10. American armament from CINCPAC Serial 03812, pp. 2–3. This table shows *Sterett* fitted with eight instead of her original battery of sixteen torpedo tubes. The weight of American 8-inch projectiles is from Campbell, *Naval Weapons of World War Two*, p. 127.

Page 436
Callaghan's movements and formation: COMAMPHIBFORSOPAC Serial 00469, p. 15, para. 31; the time Callaghan reversed course is from U.S.S. *Sterett*, DD407/A16-3, Serial 005, November 20, 1942, Subject: Report of Action on Night of November 12–13, 1942, p. 2, Part III [hereafter *Sterett* Serial 005]. Radar outfits are itemized in CINCPAC Serial 03812, pp. 1–3, para. 4. However, while this report indicated *Portland* had only

SC-1 radar, that ship's report notes she also had SG radar (U.S.S. *Portland*, CA33/A16-3, Serial 073, November 21, 1942, Subject: Night Action Between Task Force 67.4 and Japanese Forces, November 13, 1942, p. 2, Enclosure (B), p. 2 [hereafter *Portland* Serial 073]).

Additional insight into Callaghan's orders and intentions is provided by Commander Rae E. Arison in a letter to Commander in Chief, U.S. Fleet, A16-3(58857), October 7, 1943, Subject: Report of Operations 12–13 November 1942. Arison, who was *San Francisco*'s navigator, was acting as task force operations officer and was present at a conference in flag plot where the formation was selected. According to Arison:

> This formation was decided upon as the area to be searched was restricted and it was felt that changes of course could be expedited and reversals of course simplified by having the units arranged so that movements could be executed by type divisions thus always maintaining the same basic formation. The tactical units were by destroyer divisions, cruiser divisions, and with the *Atlanta* and *Juneau* operating as independent tactical units.

Page 436
Cushing reenters Lengo Channel at midnight: *Portland* Serial 073, p. 1, para. 4.

Weather in the battle area: S.S., Vol. 83, p. 361; U.S.S. *Helena*, CL50/A16-3, Serial 005, November 15, 1942, Subject: Action off North Coast Guadalcanal Early Morning of November 13, 1942, report of (3d Savo Island Night Action), p. 4 [hereafter *Helena* Serial 005]; *Portland* Serial 073, p. 1, para. 3; *Sterett* Serial 005, p. 2, II(c).

Pages 436–37
Takama rendezvous and formation: S.S., Vol. 83, p. 359.

Page 437
Abe orders: Ibid., p. 359. Abe's pre-battle orders called for Destroyer Squadron 4 to sweep 10 to 15 kilometers ahead of the main body (Ibid., p. 357).

Page 437
Abe's maneuvers, 1700-0125: Ibid., pp. 359–65.

Pages 437–38
Abe's tactical intelligence to 0125: Ibid., p. 361.

Page 438
Helena's radar contact at 0124: *Helena* Serial 005, pp. 4–5. The time given in *Helena*'s account is used in CINCPAC Serial 03812, p. 4, para. 10, and here. Other reports differ as to the time.

Course change to due north: CINCPAC Serial 03812, p. 5, para. 13. There was actually an intermediate course change to 310 degrees from the original course of 280 degrees.

Callaghan's use of TBS and confusion: *Helena* Serial 005, Enclosure (B), TBS Traffic from 1400 to 1800 12 November 1942, pp. 1–4. For the (usual) differing version of TBS transmissions see *Portland* Serial 073, pp. 1–9.

Page 438
Callaghan's intentions: McCandless, "*San Francisco* Story," p. 39, suggests the most likely interpretation of Callaghan's intentions—to place his cruisers athwart the Japanese course to cap Abe's T while releasing both groups of destroyers to make torpedo attacks from the flanks.

Page 438
Commander Stokes's observations: Commander Destroyer Division Ten, No Serial, November 15, 1942, Subject: Engagement with Japanese surface units off Savo Island, about 0200, November 13, 1942, pp. 1–2, para. 3 [hereafter COMDESDIV 10 15 Nov 42]. The times given by Stokes are adjusted in the text.

Yudachi and *Harusame* see *Cushing: S.S.,* Vol. 83, pp. 366. According to Commander Tameichi Hara of *Amatsukaze,* the report of the presence of American warships set off a wild scene on the Japanese battleships as a shift was made from Type 3 bombardment shells to armor-piercing rounds. Here stated that the "decks" of both *Hiei* and *Kirishima* were at one point littered with these shells and thus both ships were highly vulnerable. He also claims they had completed a shift to armor-piercing shells by the time the action was opened. This account was followed by Dull, *Battle History of the Imperial Japanese Navy,* pp. 247–48, and others. There is good reason to question the technical accuracy of this portion of Hara's version, and in any event, it is clear that no shift of ammunition types had been made before fire was opened. Although Hara's account is quite colorful and useful as he presents information he gathered in discussions with other Japanese participants, care must be exercised in evaluating those events of which Hara had no di-

rect knowledge. Hara, Saito, Pineau, *Japanese Destroyer Captain,* pp. 142–51.

Cushing's maneuvers and Stokes's request to fire torpedoes: U.S.S. *Cushing,* A16-3, No Serial, 16 November 1942, Subject: Report of Engagement off Savo Island on November 13, 1942 and Destruction of the U.S.S. Cushing, p. 2, paras. 4–5 [hereafter *Cushing* 16 Nov 42]; *Helena* Serial 005, Enclosure (B), p. 2.

Maneuvers of American column: CINCPAC Serial 03812, p. 5, para. 15; U.S.S. *Atlanta,* File No. A16-3, No Serial, November 20, 1942, Subject: Engagement with Japanese Surface Forces off Guadalcanal Night of 12–13 November 1942, and Loss of U.S.S. Atlanta, pp. 1–2, paras. 4–5 [hereafter *Atlanta* 20 Nov 42]; U.S.S. *San Francisco,* CA38/A16-3, Serial 067, November 16, 1942, Subject: Action Report—Night Action—November 12, 13, 1942, Forwarding of (Enclosure A is actual report), unpaginated [hereafter *San Francisco* Serial 067]; *Cushing* 16 Nov 42, p. 2, para. 5; *Sterett* 20 Serial 005, p. 3, Part III; U.S.S. *O'Bannon,* DD450/ A16, Serial 0134, November 17, 1942, Subject: Report of Engagement with Japanese Units on Morning of November 13, 1942, p. 2, para. 1 and Enclosure (C) [hereafter *O'-Bannon* Serial 0134].

Callaghan's TBS inquiries and orders: *Helena* Serial 005, Enclosure (B), pp. 1–3.

Cushing sights *Nagara: Cushing* 16 Nov 42, p. 2, para. 5.

Page 439
Callaghan's "odd-even" order: CINCPAC Serial 03812, p. 5, para. 17. Criticism of this order may be found in Ibid., p. 9, para. 40, and President, Naval War College (Admiral W. S. Pye), Serial 2238, No Date, Subject: Comments on the Battle of Guadalcanal, Nov. 11–15, 1942, p. 4 [hereafter War College Comments].

Page 440
Yudachi's report and reaction on *Hisi: S.S.,* Vol. 83, pp. 365–66. *S.S.* says there was not sufficient time before the action opened for Destroyer Squadron 10 to change formation, but this is not strictly true. See description of movement of Destroyer Division 6 in text.

Page 440
Abe orders course change and use of *Hiei*'s searchlights: Ibid., p. 366. Because of a three-minute difference in the time of opening fire between the U.S. and Japanese accounts

(0148 versus 0151), the time for Abe's turn in the text is adjusted back to 0145 rather than 0148 as given in *S.S.*.

Page 440

Time of opening fire: this account follows *Helena* Serial 005, pp. 2, 5, 9, which in turn was followed by CINCPAC Serial 03812, p. 5, para. 17. *S.S.*, Vol. 83, p. 366, places the time of opening fire at 0151.

Page 440

Action on *Atlanta*: *Atlanta* 20 Nov 42, pp. 2–4, paras. 4–13, Enclosures A, B, D. That *Akatsuki* torpedoed *Atlanta* has become generally accepted, despite the absence of a report from *Akatsuki*, in view of the fact that the torpedo had to come from a vessel of Destroyer Division 6 and the other two ships apparently made no claim of inflicting this damage.

Page 441

"barroom brawl after the lights had been shot out": attributed to another officer by Lieutenant Commander Charles E. McCombs of *Monssen* in a document in that vessel's individual file, Ship's History Branch, NHC.

Page 441

Cushing's participation: *Cushing* 16 Nov 42, pp. 2–7, paras. 4-20; COMDESDIV 10 15 Nov 42, pp. 2–4, paras. 3–11. The engagement of *Cushing* by *Nagara* and *Yukikaze* is fairly certain based upon Lieutenant Commander Parker's firm identification and the JDA Track Chart.

Pages 441–42

Laffey's participation: U.S.S. *Laffey,* A16-3/ DD459, No Serial, November 14, 1942, Subject: U.S.S. *Laffey,* Battle Report of, [hereafter *Laffey* 14 Nov 42]; additional details are found in "Bridge Blasted from Battleship by U.S. Destroyer off Guadalcanal," *New York Times,* January 13, 1943, p. 1, col. 6, and Eric Hammel, *Decision at Sea* (New York: Crown Publishers, 1988), pp. 213–14 [hereafter Hammel, *Decision at Sea*]. Hammel persuasively argues that *Laffey*'s final struggle was with *Asagumo, Murasame,* and *Samidare.*

Page 442

Sterett's participation: *Sterett* Serial 005, pp. 1–15; Hammel, *Decision at Sea,* p. 159.

Pages 442–43

O'Bannon's participation: *O'Bannon* Serial 0134 and Enclosures (B) and (C); Hammel,

Decision at Sea, pp. 232–33. Hammel clarifies the point that *O'Bannon* passed the sinking bow of *Barton,* not *Laffey.*

Pages 443–45

San Francisco participation: *San Francisco* Serial 067 and particularly McCandless, "San Francisco Story," pp. 40–47, which provides a vivid account of the action from his excellent observation position.

Death of Admiral Scott: *Atlanta* 20 Nov 42, Enclosure (B), pp. 1–5; Pratt, *Navy's War,* p. 267. Admiral Halsey noted in his memoirs that the death of Norman Scott was the greatest personal sorrow he suffered during the entire war. Halsey and Bryan, *Admiral Halsey's Story,* p. 127.

Cease-fire order: *Helena* Serial 005, Enclosure (B), pp. 3–4; *Portland* Serial 073, p. 4; McCandless, "San Francisco Story," p. 41.

Page 444

Portland participation: *Portland* Serial 073, pp. 1–9 and Enclosure (B).

Page 446

Helena participation: *Helena* Serial 005. *Helena*'s damage included one definite and one probable 14-inch hit.

Page 446

Juneau participation: There is no report from this ship for this battle. The most authoritative information is that supplied by Lieutenant (jg) Charles Wang, who was on *Juneau*'s starboard torpedo director during the action. His account is in the transcript at the Naval Historical Center of narrative No. 332 (Lt. (jg) Charles Wang USNR), recorded 29 January 1945, 12 pages [hereafter Wang narrative]. Also of interest is *Helena* Serial 005, Enclosure (C), November 17, 1942, Subject: Report of U.S.S. Juneau Activity from November 11 to 13, 1942, inclusive. This report was prepared by Lieutenant Roger W. O'Neil (MC-V(G), USNR, *Juneau*'s senior survivor.

Pages 446–47

Aaron Ward participation: U.S.S. *Aaron Ward,* DD483/ A16-3(1), Serial 003, November 20, 1942, Subject: U.S.S. *Aaron Ward* (DD483)—Report of Action, Night of November 12–13, 1942, pp. 1–3, Part B [hereafter *Aaron Ward* Serial 003]; Commander Destroyer Squadron 12, FC4-12/A16-3, Serial 0033, November 27, 1942, Subject: Report of Action off Savo Island, November 13, 1942, pp. 1–6 and Enclosures (A)-(C) [hereafter COMDESRON 12 Serial 0033].

Page 447

Barton participation: Senior Surviving Officer, U.S.S. *Barton* (DD599), A16-3/L11, No Serial, November 26, 1942, Subject: U.S.S. *Barton* (DD599), Report of Action of November 12–13, 1942.

Page 447

Monssen participation: U.S.S. *Monssen,* No Serial, 16 November 1942, Subject: U.S.S. *Monssen,* Report of battle of November 13, 1942.

Pages 447–48

Fletcher participation: U.S.S. *Fletcher,* DD445/A16-3, Serial No. (S)-1, November 15, 1942, Subject: Report of Action, pp. 3–6, para. 4–5 [hereafter *Fletcher* Serial (S)-1].

Page 448

Destroyer Squadron 10 participation: *S.S.,* Vol. 83, pp. 367–68. *S.S.* notes that the reports from this unit do not contain times.

Page 448

Nagara and *Yukikaze* participation: Ibid., p. 367; JDA Track Chart.

Page 448

Amatsukaze participation: Hara, Saito, and Pineau, *Japanese Destroyer Captain,* pp. 142–51. Hara claims to have fired eight torpedoes at 0154 and four more at 0159. If so, this was an amazingly rapid reload of one bank of *Amatsukaze*'s torpedo tubes. Based on the JDA Track Chart, it is somewhat difficult to see how *Amatsukaze* closed *San Francisco,* but on the other hand, Hara's description of his action with *Helena* matches *Helena*'s action report rather well, and that source would support Hara's account of his engagement of *San Francisco.* Hara does erroneously claim that *Helena* was sunk in this battle. A very brief description of *Amatsukaze*'s participation is found in *S.S.* Vol. 83, p. 368.

Page 449

Teruzuki's participation: *S.S.,* Vol. 83, pp. 367–68.

Page 449

Destroyer Division 6 participation: Ibid., pp. 367–68; JDA Track Chart. Evidence on whether these ships passed through the American formation may be found in *Atlanta* 20 Nov 42, Enclosure (D), and Pratt, *Navy's War,* p. 267, which contains elaboration by Captain Jenkins on what he saw. At least eight *Akatsuki* survivors were captured after

the battle. Box 8, File C15-4, Enclosure T, MCHC.

Pages 449–50

Yudachi participation: *S.S.,* Vol. 83, p. 366–67. Hara, Saito, Pineau, *Japanese Destroyer Captain,* p. 144, describes *Yudachi* as passing ahead of *Aaron Ward,* which seems quite plausible, as there was probably a large gap between *Aaron Ward* and the ship next ahead (which may have been *Juneau* or *Portland* at this time).

Page 450

Harusame participation: *S.S.,* Vol. 83, p. 367; JDA Track Chart.

Asagumo, Murasame and *Samidare* participation: *S.S.,* Vol. 83, p. 367.

Pages 450–51

Hiei participation: Ibid., p. 366; Lieutenant Commander S. Yunoki, *Hiei*'s main battery control officer, in *USSBS, Interrogations of Japanese Officials,* Vol. I, p. 191.

Kirishima participation: Ibid., p. 366. The single 6-inch hit was reported by Lieutenant Commander Horishi Tokuno, *Kirishima*'s assistant gunnery officer (*USSBS, Interrogations of Japanese Officials,* Vol. I, p. 141).

Page 451

Descriptions of observers ashore: Merillat, *Island,* pp. 207–8; Leckie, *Helmet for My Pillow,* pp. 116–18.

Page 451

Hoover's order at 0226: *Helena* Serial 005, Enclosure (B), p. 4.

Page 452

Yudachi crew removed: *S.S.,* Vol. 83, p. 371.

Kirishima message and Yamamoto reaction: Ibid., pp. 372, 375.

Page 452

Kimura exercises command and conditions on *Hiei:* Ibid., pp. 371–72.

Page 453

Position of American ships east and south of Savo at dawn: *Portland* Serial 073, Enclosure (B), p. 4.

Position of Japanese ships off Savo at dawn: *S.S.,* Vol. 83, pp. 371–72.

Page 453

Hiei engages *Aaron Ward: S.S.,* Vol. 83, p. 372; *Aaron Ward* Serial 007, pp. 4–5, Part B.

Portland sinks *Yudachi* and salvage: *Portland* Serial 073, pp. 5–7, para. 4, Enclosure B, p. 4.

Pages 453–54
Efforts to save *Atlanta:* *Atlanta* 20 Nov 42, pp. 4–6, paras. 14–21. The machinegunning of men in the water by *Bobolink* is noted in Morison, *Struggle for Guadalcanal,* p. 256.

Page 454
Totals of Callaghan's sailors ashore: CINC-PAC Daily Summary 12 Nov 42, Grey Book, p. 1162.

Pages 454–55
Air attacks on *Hiei:* MAG 23 Record of Events 13 Nov 42; VMF-121 War Diary, 13 Nov 42. Headquarters, Marine Aircraft Group 14, 1st Marine Aircraft Wing, Fleet Marine Force, KV14/jhs, December 16, 1942, Subject: Record of Events, Marine Aircraft Group 14, October 16, 1942, to December 16, 1942, pp. 3–4 [hereafter MAG-14 Record of Events]; Marine Air Group 14, FMAW, Cactus, November 18, 1942, Subject: Report of Action on November 13, 14 and 15, p. 1 [hereafter MAG-14 Report 13–15 Nov 42]; Commander Torpedo Squadron 10, VT10/A16-3, Serial 01-42, November 19, 1942. The TBFs from *Enterprise* were originally launched on an offensive sweep with orders to attack any target found and then land on Guadalcanal. These planes (eight TBFs with torpedoes, one TBF with bombs, and six Wildcats) were also launched to clear the flight deck, as *Enterprise*'s number one elevator was out of action because of damage received at Santa Cruz (*Enterprise* Serial 0019, p. 2). *Enterprise*'s air group included thirty-eight Wildcats, thirty-one SBDs, and nine TBFs.

Attacks by B-17s: COMAIRSOPAC to COMSOPAC 130902 Nov 42, COMSOPAC War Diary 13 Nov 42, p. 37.

Pages 454–55
The defensive sorties flown by *Junyo* and the 11th Air Fleet: *S.S.,* Vol. 83, 373. Loss figures are from Mr. John Lundstrom.

Arrival of SOWESPAC P-38s: COMAIR-SOPAC War Diary 14 Nov 42.

Page 455
Efforts to save *Hiei:* *S.S.,* Vol. 83, pp. 372–75.

American radio intelligence monitoring of reports on *Hiei:* Van Der Rhoer, *Deadly Magic,* p. 128.

Page 455
Emperor witnesses last review of Imperial Navy from *Hiei:* Agawa, *Reluctant Admiral,* pp. 200–1. The review took place on October 11, 1940.

Units head north to join Advanced Force: *S.S.,* Vol. 83, p. 371 (Destroyer Squadron 4 and Desdiv 27 ordered north at 0355 and 0325 respectively). Abe returned to find *Hiei* at 0100/14, but the battleship had sunk by that time.

Page 456
Circumstances of loss of *Juneau:* The most vivid account of *Juneau*'s sinking is provided by McCandless, "San Francisco Story," p. 51, from which the quotation is taken. The official accounts are in U.S.S. *Sterett,* DD407/A16-3, Serial 006, November 22, 1942, Subject: Sinking of U.S.S. *Juneau,* report on; *Helena* Serial 005, pp. 3–4, para. 1; and CINCPAC File No. Pac-90-wb, A16-3/Sol, Serial 03719, 20 December 1942, Subject: Action Report—Loss of U.S.S. *Juneau,* November 13, 1942 (enclosed report of *San Francisco*).

CINCPAC Serial 00554, p. 12, para. 56, notes Hoover's message to the B-17 did not get through for unexplained reasons. The account of the activities of the B-17 in the text is based upon letters by Staff Sergeant William E. Entrikin, the radio operator of the plane, which appeared in W. M. Cleveland, editor, *Grey Geese Calling: A History of the 11th Bombardment Group Heavy (H) in the Pacific, 1940–45* (published by 11th Bombardment Group (H) Association, Inc., National Office, P.O. Box 637, Seffner, Fla., 33584), pp. 343–44. Entrikin indicated his crew reported to the operations section of the Cactus Air Force and spoke to Lieutenant Colonel Bauer and one or more others.

I-26 identified as the successful Japanese submarine: *S.S.,* Vol. 83, p. 342.

Page 457
Relief of Captain Hoover and Admiral Halsey's comments: Halsey and Bryan, *Admiral Halsey's Story,* pp. 133–34; Commander South Pacific Area and South Pacific Force, A16-3(11), Serial 00118b November 22, 1942, Subject: Loss of *Juneau,* Circumstances of.

Pages 457–59
Survivor accounts: The story of the men in the water is drawn from the transcripts of the following recorded narratives, which may be

found at the Naval Historical Center: Wang narrative; No. 71, L.E. Zook, Signalman First Class, USN, Battle of Guadalcanal, sinking of U.S.S. *Juneau* off San Cristobal—12 November 1942 [sic], recorded 27 May 1943, 9 pages [hereafter Zook narrative]; No. 12, Signalman Second Class Joseph Hartney U.S.S. *Juneau*, recorded 8 January 1943, 9 pages; and No. 286, Allen Clifton Heyn, GM2/C, U.S.S. *Juneau*, recorded 23 September 1944, 17 pages.

Quotation from Signalman Zook: Zook narrative, p. 6. The individual involved was identified by Zook as J. A. Grycky, Radio Technician Third Class, from Pennsylvania. John Andrew Grycky, from Coatesville, Pennsylvania, is identified in *Combat Connected Naval Casualties, World War II by States, U.S. Navy, Marine Corps, Coast Guard,* Vol. II, *Montana Through Wyoming and Other Areas* (Casualty Section, Office of Public Information, Navy Department, 1946), p. 23.

Page 459
Losses on *Juneau* and other American participants: Bureau of Personnel (see Appendix 3). There were no fatalities on *O'Bannon* or *Fletcher*. The losses on *Juneau* were proportionally the highest of the war of any American warship of cruiser size or above. The only numerically greater losses were on *Arizona* (1,104), *Indianapolis* (880), *Franklin* (772), and *Houston* (696 in battle and 76 POWs = 762). There were no survivors from two United States destroyers (*Erlsall* and *Jarvis*) and thirty-seven submarines.

Pages 459–60
Analysis of American action: CINCPAC Serial 03812, pp. 8–9, paras. 32–43; War College Comments, pp. 4–5 (including quote).

"the men of Cactus lift their battered helmets . . .": COMGEN Cactus to COMSOPAC 150318, Vandegrift Papers, MCHC.

Page 460
Japanese losses: The figures of 255 missing and 297 dead are from *S.S.,* Vol. 83, p. 376. As indicated in the text, these figures seem somewhat low. For example, according to Lieutenant Commander S. Yunoki, *Hiei*'s main battery gunnery officer, losses on his ship alone were about 300. Lieutenant Commander Horishi Tokuno, *Kirishima*'s assistant gunnery officer, stated the losses on *Hiei* were about 450. Both of these statements may be found in *USSBS, Interrogations of Japanese Officials,* Vol. I, pp. 141, 191. D'Albas,

Death of a Navy, p. 216, also says losses on *Hiei* were 450. D'Albas had access to Japanese material in the preparation of his work.

Pages 460–61
Japanese analysis of the action: *S.S.,* Vol. 83, pp. 370, 375–76.

Page 461
Retirement of Abe and Nishida: Hara, Saito, and Pineau, *Japanese Destroyer Captain,* p. 156.

CHAPTER 18
The principal sources for this chapter are the American individual ship and higher command reports and *S.S.,* Vol. 83, pp. 377–97.

Page 462
Yamamoto's orders and Kondo's intentions and plans: *S.S.* Vol. 83, pp. 374, 377, 383–84. Yamamoto postponed Z-Day at 0344 on November 13 and issued orders to Kondo for "sweep and shell" at 1155.

Page 463
Halsey's orders to create Task Force 64 and his decision to commit Lee: COMSOPAC War Diary 13 Nov 42; Halsey and Bryan, *Admiral Halsey's Story,* pp. 128–29. According to COMSOPAC War Diary 13 Nov 42, p. 36, Halsey ordered Task Force 64 formed in COMSOPAC to CTF 16 130505 Nov 42 (1605 local time) and committed Lee in COMSOPAC to CTF 16 130552 Nov 42 (1652 local time). Halsey's previous orders in COMSOPAC to CTF 16 122301 Nov 42 (1001 local time) kept Kinkaid south of 11° 40′ South. COMSOPAC War Diary 13 Nov 42, p. 33.

Page 464
Mikawa and Nishimura conduct bombardment: *S.S.,* Vol. 83, pp. 376–78. Nishimura's cruisers used the 8-inch version of the Type 3 shell. Aircraft losses are from MAG-23 Record of Events 13 Nov 42. COMGEN 1st Mar Div to COMSOPAC 132233 Nov 42 (Grey Book, p. 982) notes this bombardment and indicates only two shells directly hit Fighter One, but lists losses as one SBD, two Wildcats destroyed, and seventeen Wildcats damaged.

PT Boats attack Nishimura: Bulkley, *At Close Quarters,* pp. 92–93.

Page 464
First attack on Mikawa: The American strike

is detailed in MAG-14 Record of Events, p. 4; VMF-121 War Diary 14 Nov 42 shows escort was eight rather than six Wildcats reported in MAG-14 Record of Events. This group claimed two bomb hits on one heavy cruiser (significantly one on the bridge) and three or four torpedo hits. However, the Japanese account of Mikawa's fortunes this morning does not confirm any of this damage (*S.S.*, Vol. 83, p. 378).

Pages 464–65

Enterprise operations November 13–14: U.S.S. *Enterprise,* CV6/A16-3/(10-yo), Serial 0019, November 19, 1942, Subject: Action Against Japanese Forces Attempting the Recapture of Guadalcanal, November 13–14, 1942—Report of, p. 3 [hereafter *Enterprise* Serial 0019].

Page 464

Actions of Lieutenant (jg) Gibson and Ensign Buchanan and attack on *Kinugasa: Enterprise* Serial 0019, pp. 3–4.

Damage to *Kinugasa: S.S.,* Vol. 83, p. 378. Although the earlier Marine dive-bombing attack claimed a hit on the bridge of a heavy cruiser, the time of the bomb hit on *Kinugasa* points to the attack by Lieutenant Gibson.

Attack by ensigns Hoogerwerf and Halloran and crash of Halloran on *Maya: Enterprise* Serial 0019, pp. 4–5; *S.S.,* Vol. 83, p. 378. That Halloran crashed *Maya* is not in American reports, but his was the only plane lost over Mikawa, and Hoogerwerf reported Halloran's target, a "light cruiser," was burning after the attack.

Page 465

Attack by Lieutenant Commander Lee between 1045 and 1100 and sinking of *Kinugasa: Enterprise* Serial 0019, pp. 5–6; *S.S.,* Vol. 83, p. 378; Lacroix, "The Development of the 'A Class' Cruisers in the Imperial Japanese Navy," *Warships International,* No. 3, 1983, p. 239 (details of damage to Mikawa's heavy cruisers). Lacroix also has a photograph of *Maya* after the plane crash at p. 242. Some accounts have suggested *Kinugasa* was the heavy cruiser Lee reported as trailing the formation and on fire and being abandoned. More likely what Lee saw was *Maya* still aflame after being crashed by Halloran. The casualty figures for *Kinugasa* are from Lacroix. *S.S.* is very vague, noting the "whole crew" abandoned, but gives no expli-

cit figures for survivors. Dull, *Battle History of the Imperial Navy,* p. 252, says fifty-one men were lost with *Kinugasa,* and SRH-136, p. 500, shows an intercepted message, dated November 17, 1942 ("Battle Report No. 9, Outer South Seas Force"), indicated *Kinugasa* sank with fifty dead. According to *S.S.,* Mikawa took his vessels to Shortland intending a quick resupply and then a sortie to support the convoy.

Page 465

Tanaka's convoy situation early on November 14: *S.S.,* Vol. 83, p. 379.

Quote from Commander Yamamoto of *Hayashio: USSBS, Interrogations of Japanese Officials,* Vol. II, p. 471.

Contacts and attacks by Lieutenants (jg) Carmody and Johnson: *Enterprise* Serial 0019, p. 4; *S.S.,* Vol. 83, p. 379. It is not clear from American records where the SBDs came from that attacked Tanaka before Carmody and Johnson. Presumably, they were search planes from Guadalcanal.

Pages 465–66

Series of air attacks on the convoy: For the American participation this account principally follows the detailed and contemporaneous reports of *Enterprise*'s squadrons— Commander Air Group 10, U.S.S. *Enterprise,* CV6/AG10, A16(95-as), Serial 006, November 21, 1942; Commander Scouting Squadron 10, VS10/A16, No Serial, November 20, 1942, Subject: Battle Report November 14–15, 1942; Commander Bombing Squadron 10, No Serial, November 20, 1942, Subject: Report of Action November 14–15, 1942; Commander Bombing Squadron 10, VB-10/A16, Serial 082, December 4, 1942, Subject: Report of Action November 14–15, 1942—Supplemental Report; Commander Torpedo Squadron 10, VT10/A16-3, Serial 01-42, November 19, 1942; and Commander Fighting Squadron 10, Serial 029, November 21, 1942, Subject: Report of Action—November 10–17, 1942 [hereafter Air Group 10 ARs]. The Marine participation is covered in MAG-14 Record of Events, p. 4; MAG-14 Report 13–15 Nov 42, p. 1; and VMF-121 War Diary 14 Nov 42.

Japanese account and losses: *S.S.* Vol. 28, p. 236, Vol. 83, p. 379–80; Tanaka, Part II, pp. 821–22. Times of attacks mostly follow the Japanese account. *S.S.,* Vol. 28, pp. 238–39, notes the Imperial Navy sent an urgent message to the 17th Army at 1440, November 14, revealing that the convoy was being severely mauled and requesting immediate shelling of the American airfields. Given the extreme shortage of shells and the poor positioning of its artillery, the 17th Army was able to do little to meet this request, although guns west of the Matanikau and two field pieces of the 20th Mountain Gun Battalion on Mount Austen fired at the airfield complex.

Attack by B-17s and Tanaka's reaction: 13th AF Hist., p. 60; COMAIRSOPAC to COMSOPAC 141358 Nov 42, COMSOPAC War Diary 14 Nov 42; Tanaka, Part II, p. 822.

Pages 467–68
Japanese air defense of convoy: *S.S.,* Vol. 83, p. 379, Vol. 28, p. 236 (which reports only six sorties by Petes). Loss figures are from Mr. John Lundstrom. Japanese claims for enemy aircraft destroyed vary widely between these two volumes. Vol. 28 places claims at twenty-five, whereas Vol. 83 lists claims for three aircraft by ships and seven by defending aircraft for a total of ten. During November 14, the Cactus Air Force received eight of MacArthur's P-38s, ten B-26s of the 70th Bomb Squadron, and five TBFs of VMSB-131 as reinforcements (COMSOPAC War Diary 14 Nov 42, p. 39; COMAIRSOPAC War Diary 14 Nov 42).

Circumstances of loss of Lieutenant Colonel Bauer: Foss and Simmons, *Joe Foss,* pp. 127–28.

Page 468
"Prospects looked poor for the operation": Tanaka, Part II, p. 822.

Orders to Tanaka: *S.S.,* Vol. 83, p. 380.

Page 468
Japanese search plane reports: *S.S.,* Vol. 83, pp. 380–81. The plane that reported Lee at 1525 observed two vessels that "looked like carriers," one battleship and four cruisers.

Page 469
Kondo's maneuvers: Ibid., pp. 384–85. The six vessels that had participated in the action on November 13 were *Kirishima, Nagara, Asagumo, Teruzuki, Inazuma,* and *Samidare. Atago* launched a plane at 1027 on a reconnaissance mission. The plane returned to Rekata Bay.

Submarine attack and report: Ibid., U.S.S. *Flying Fish,* SS229/A16-3, Serial 040, De-

cember 16, 1942, Subject: U.S.S. *Flying Fish* (SS229)—Report of 3d War Patrol, Period from October 27, to December 16, 1942. This attack and the radio report of Kondo is incorrectly credited to submarine *Trout* in Morison, *Struggle for Guadalcanal,* p. 271. *S.S.* indicates that *Asagumo*'s account placed about one hour between the time torpedoes missed *Atago* to the time torpedoes missed her. However, this does not match any American claims for torpedo firing. This writer assumes the times given in *Asagumo*'s report or in *S.S.* were in error and that these two events coincided.

Page 469
Kondo's orders: *S.S.,* Vol. 83, pp. 384–85. The text reflects the grist of instructions issued at 1140, 1255, and 1735.

Page 469
Plane reports at 2045 and 2130: Ibid., pp. 385–86.

Pages 469–70
Lee's plans and orders: Commander Task Force 64, A5/A16-3, 18 Feb 1943, serial 0010, Subject: Report of Night Action, Task Force 64—November 14–15, 1942, p. 7–8, para. 1, 4, 6 [hereafter CTF 64 Serial 0010].

Estimate of Japanese strength: U.S.S. *Washington,* BB56/A16-3(0155), November 27, 1942, Subject: Action Report, Night of November 14–15, 1942, p. 13 [hereafter *Washington* Serial 0155].

Pages 470–71
Composition of Japanese forces: *S.S.,* Vol. 83, p. 384.

Page 471
Composition of American forces: Ship action reports.

Page 472
Table of relative combat power: Japanese armament from Jentschur, Jung, and Mickel, *Warships of the Imperial Japanese Navy, 1869–1945,* pp. 10, 31, 107–9, 144–45, 147–51. American Armament from Robert O. Dulin, Jr., and William H. Garzke, Jr., *Battleships—United States Battleships in World War II* (Annapolis, Md.: Naval Institute Press, 1976), pp. 49, 63, 99, for *Washington* and *South Dakota.* Destroyer armament is from Lenton, *American Fleet and Escort De-*

stroyers, Vol. I, pp. 55–56, 60–61, 76–79. There is some question whether *Preston* had already landed one of her original quintet of 5-inch guns by this time. The table in the text is based upon the assumption that she had not. *Gwin* definitely still had her original five.

Pages 472–73
Lee's approach to the battle area and initial maneuvers: CTF 64 Serial 0010, Enclosure A (Track Chart); *Washington* Serial 0155, p. 6.

Weather in battle area: *Washington* Serial 0155, p. 5; U.S.S. *South Dakota,* BB57/A16-3/(0165), no date, Subject: Action Report, night engagement 14–15 November 1942, with Japanese naval units, off Savo Island, pp. 1–2 [hereafter *South Dakota* Serial 0165]; *S.S.,* Vol. 83, p. 388.

Page 473
Lee's attempts to secure intelligence from Guadalcanal: This matter is covered officially in CTF 64 Serial 0010, Enclosure C, p. 1, but is much more fully fleshed out in Morison, *Struggle for Guadalcanal,* pp. 272–73. Morison's account is based upon his interviews shortly after the battle. *South Dakota* Serial 0165, Enclosure (C), p. 3, adds confirmation to Morison's reconstruction of these events.

Page 473
Information on convoy arrival time from radio intelligence: *South Dakota* Serial 0165, pp. 1, 4.

Maneuvers of Japanese units and sightings just before and at 2200: *S.S.,* Vol. 83, p. 386. Hashimoto originally planned to take *Sendai* and *Ayanami* west of Savo, leaving *Uranami* and *Shikanami* to check the east side.

Pages 473–74
2231 and 2300 reports and Kondo's conclusions: Ibid., p. 386.

Tanaka sights Kondo at 2300: Ibid., p. 380.

Pages 474–75
Kondo's orders after 2307: Ibid., pp. 387–88.

Page 475
Americans change course, open fire at 2317: CTF Serial 0010, Enclosure (C), p. 1; *Washington* Serial 0155, pp. 6–8; *South Dakota* Serial 0165, pp. 2, 4. *South Dakota* reported sighting Hashimoto by radar at 0007 and visually at 0008. Probably because of damage

and loss of records, there are obvious discrepancies in the times given in *South Dakota*'s report. Therefore, this account follows generally the times given in Lee's and *Washington*'s reports.

Hashimoto retires under fire: *S.S.,* Vol. 83, p. 388.

Pages 475–76
Action between American destroyers and *Ayanami* and Kimura: CTF 64 Serial 0010, p. 7, para. 4; U.S.S. *Walke,* DD416/A16, No Serial, November 30, 1942, Subject: Surface Engagement with Japanese Forces, November 15, 1942, report of, pp. 1–2 [hereafter *Walke* 30 Nov 42]; U.S.S. *Benham,* DD397/A16-3, No Serial, 29 Nov. 42, Subject: Report of Action 14–15 November 1942, pp. 1–2, paras. 3–4 [hereafter *Benham* 29 Nov 42]; U.S.S. *Preston,* DD379/A16, No Serial, November 30, 1942, Subject: Surface Engagement with Japanese Forces, November 15, 1942, report of, p. 2 [hereafter *Preston* 30 Nov 42]; U.S.S. *Gwin,* DD433/A16-3, Serial 0047, November 16, 1942, Subject: Report of Night Action 14–15 November 1942, pp. 1–2 [hereafter *Gwin* Serial 0047]; *S.S.,* Vol. 83, p. 388.

SRH-136, pp. 500–1, contains an interesting decrypt of a message from *Ayanami* describing her participation. This shows she claimed sinking one "large cruiser" with torpedoes and one destroyer while setting a second destroyer afire. In turn, American gunfire shot out mounts one and three of *Ayanami*'s main armament, toppled her number one stack, and crippled her steering.

Quality of Japanese flashless powder: CTF 64 Serial 0010, p. 9, para. 8. *Benham* 29 Nov 42, pp. 1–2, para. 3, notes the position of the moon to the south also probably silhouetted the American destroyers.

Page 476
Loss of *Preston: Preston* 30 Nov 42, pp. 2–5. Her crew totaled 262 (fifteen officers and 247 men).

Page 476
Damage to *Gwin: Gwin* Serial 0047, p. 2.

Page 477
Loss of *Walke: Walke* 30 Nov 42, pp. 2–3.

Page 477
Damage to *Benham: Benham* 29 Nov 42, pp. 2–4, paras. 7–10, and Enclosure (B).

Page 477
Damage to *Ayanami: Washington* Serial 0155, pp. 8–9, 19. *S.S.,* Vol. 83, p. 388.

Pages 477–78
South Dakota's difficulties: *South Dakota* Serial 0165, pp. 2, 5–6, 11. Quote on psychological effect of loss of radar on crew is at page 22.

Confusing situation: For examples of spurious reports see *Washington* Serial 0155, pp. 8, 12.

Page 478
Maneuvers of *Washington* and *South Dakota:* Washington Serial 0155, p. 9; *South Dakota* Serial 0165, p. 6.

Aircraft fire on *South Dakota: South Dakota* Serial 0165, pp. 6, 14. The presence of aircraft on *South Dakota* was criticized by Admiral Nimitz; see Commander in Chief Pacific Fleet, PAC-90-wb, A16-3, Serial 00554, Subject: Solomons Islands Campaign—Battle of the Solomons, 11–15 November 1942, p. 21, para. 120 [hereafter CINCPAC Serial 00554].

Page 478
Retirement of destroyers: CTF 64 Serial 0010, p. 3, para. 3, Enclosure (C); *Washington* Serial 0155, p. 9. Admiral Lee gave the time of his order as 2345 in his report, and *Gwin* Serial 0047, p. 3, agrees. However, this account follows Lee's Enclosure (C) (Radio Log) and *Washington*'s report, which show the time of the order was 2348.

Pages 478–79
Kondo's information and orders: *S.S.,* Vol. 83, p. 388–89.

Page 479
Hashimoto's reaction to orders: Ibid., pp. 388, 391.

Page 479
Washington's maneuvers and radar contacts: *Washington* Serial 0155, p. 9.

South Dakota's material failure: *South Dakota* Serial 0165, p. 7.

Page 479
Sightings by Kondo's lookouts and his reaction: *S.S.,* Vol. 83, p. 389. All times for this phase of the action have been reconciled around the benchmark of the time of opening of fire according to Lee and *Washington,* 0000. This is one minute earlier than the time given in the Japanese reports (0001).

Pages 479–80
Position of American battleships at moment fire opened: CTF 64 AR Serial 0010, p. 3, para. 5.

Japanese employ torpedoes, searchlights, and guns: *S.S.,* Vol. 83, p. 389–90. It is not clear if *Takao* fired torpedoes at this time in *S.S.,* but *Teruzuki* definitely did not. Morison, *Struggle for Guadalcanal,* p. 278, says Kimura launched thirty-four torpedoes at *South Dakota* at 2355. *S.S.* contains no mention of this and has Kimura reloading torpedoes for some time after the spreads launched at 2335. Possibly the time given to Morison was wrong and the 2335 launch was mistakenly reported at 2355. CTF 64, Serial 0010, pp. 3–4, para. 5, says three ships illuminated *South Dakota.*

Page 480
Damage to *South Dakota* and its effects: *South Dakota* Serial 0165, pp. 7–8. A fine journalistic account of the experiences of *South Dakota*'s crew is in Sidney Shalett, *Old Nameless* (New York: Appleton-Century, 1943), pp. 106–69. The quote from *South Dakota* crewmen Melvin McSpadden ("a loud crash . . .") is at p. 130.

Quote from Admiral Lee: CTF 64 Serial 0010, p. 8, para. 8.

Fierce reply of *South Dakota*'s secondary battery: *S.S.,* Vol. 83, p. 390.

Page 481
Washington gunnery action: *Washington* Serial 0155, pp. 1, 10, 15, 29.

Damage to *Kirishima: S.S.,* Vol. 83, p. 390, 392. The number of hits on *Kirishima* is given as "six or more" (presumably only counting 16-inch) in *S.S.* The totals given in the text are from Lieutenant Commander Horishi Tokuno, *Kirishima*'s assistant gunnery officer, in *USSBS, Interrogations of Japanese Officials,* Vol. I, p. 142. *Washington* claimed eight hits with her main armament out of seventy-five rounds fired at *Kirishima.*

Page 481
Effects of American star shells and gunfire and Kondo's turn: *S.S.,* Vol. 83, p. 390.

Pages 481–82
Condition of *South Dakota* and Captain Gatch's decision to retire: *South Dakota* Serial 0165, pp. 8, 14–16.

Quote from Admiral Lee: CTF 64 Serial 0010, p. 4, para. 5.

Page 482
Bombardment Unit maneuvers and actions: *S.S.,* Vol. 83, p. 390.

Page 482
Lee continues battle and *Washington* observations: CTF 64 Serial 0010, p. 4, para. 6; *Washington* Serial 0155, p. 11.

Page 482
Bombardment Unit fires main armament and torpedoes: *S.S.,* Vol. 83, p. 390.

Actions of Tanaka and convoy: Ibid., p. 391; Tanaka, Part II, p. 823.

Kondo orders light forces to attack about 0020 and at 0025; response by Kimura and Tanaka: *S.S.,* Vol. 83, p. 391.

Page 482
Kondo maneuvers, lays smoke, turns away: Ibid., p. 391.

Pages 482–83
Lee sees *Oyashio* and *Kagero;* decision to retire: CTF 64 Serial 0010, pp. 4–5, para. 6; *Washington* Serial 0155, p. 11.

Page 483
Kondo's orders at 0032: *S.S.,* Vol. 83, p. 391.

Pages 483–84
Maneuvers of *Washington* during retirement: CTF 64 Serial 0010, p. 5, para. 7; *Washington* Serial 0155, pp. 11–12.

Pursuit of *Washington: S.S.,* Vol. 83, pp. 391–92.

Kondo's decision to retire: Ibid., p. 392.

Page 484
Loss of *Kirishima:* Ibid., pp. 392–93. *S.S.* notes *Kirishima*'s captain reported survivors as sixty-nine officers and 1,031 men, which *S.S.* says is wrong without explaining what the error was. Lieutenant Commander Tokuno (*USSBS Interrogations,* Vol. I, p. 142) says losses on *Kirishima* were about 250 out of 1,400. Jentschur, Jung, and Mickel,

Warships of the Imperial Japanese Navy, 1869–1945 p. 31, gives a nominal complement in this period for all *Kongo* Class battleships as 1,437. Dull, *Battle History of the Imperial Navy,* p. 254, gives Japanese crew losses as 249 killed and eighty-four wounded for the entire battle. His sources were the action reports of *Kirishima, Atago,* and *Nagara* and the Tabular Records of Movements of *Atago, Asagumo, Samidare,* and *Teruzuki.*

Page 484
Loss of *Ayanami: S.S.,* Vol. 83, p. 388.

Pages 484–85
Retirement of *South Dakota* and *Gwin,* loss of *Benham:* CTF 64 Serial 0010, pp. 5–6, paras. 8–9; *South Dakota* Serial 0165, p. 3; *Gwin* Serial 0047, pp. 3–4; *Benham* 29 Nov 42, pp. 4–6, paras. 11–18, and attachments. There is some confusion in the labeling of the enclosures to *Benham*'s report (for example, two different "Enclosure (A)" documents). The conspicuous failure of *Gwin*'s torpedoes is recorded in the report of *Benham*'s executive officer, dated November 19, 1942.

Pages 485–86
Kondo's claims for battle and assessment: *S.S.,* Vol. 83, pp. 395–97.

Page 486
Admiral Nimitz's stamp of approval on Lee: Commander in Chief U.S. Pacific Fleet, CINCPAC File Pac-90-wb, A16-3/SOL, Serial 00617, 18 March 1943, Subject: Report of Night Action, Task Force 64—November 14–15, 1942—Third Battle of Savo Island, p. 1, para. 3.

"Audacious planning and execution:" Commander South Pacific Area and South Pacific Force, A16-3/(90), Serial 00468, Subject: Report of Night Action, Task Force 64—November 14–15, 1942, p. 1, para. 2.

Page 486
"We . . . realized then . . .": CTF 64 Serial 0010, p. 8, para. 7.

Page 487
Tanaka brings convoy into Tassafaronga area: *S.S.,* Vol. 83, pp. 396–97; Tanaka Part II, p. 824.

Page 487
Observations of *Walke* and *Preston* survivors: U.S.S. *Preston,* DD379/A16, No Serial, December 6, 1942, Subject: Addition to Action Report of U.S.S. *Preston;* U.S.S. *Walke,*

DD416/A16-3, No Serial, December 6, 1942, Subject: Addition to Action Report on Surface Engagement with Japanese Forces, November 15, 1942; Senior Officer Present, U.S.S. *Walke* (DD416), No Serial, November 30, 1942, Subject: Report of Action U.S.S. Walke (DD416) November 15, 1942. The last-named mentions the submarine surfacing (not confirmed in *S.S.*, but not improbable) and the illumination of survivors by searchlights.

Pages 487–88
Air attacks on beached and abandoned transports: Air Group 10 ARs; MAG-14 Record of Events, pp. 5–6; MAG-14 Report 13–15 Nov 42, p. 2; MAG 23 Record of Events 15 Nov 42; VMF-121 War Diary 15 Nov 42. One VT-10 TBF was an operational loss in the afternoon. This was the only aircraft lost during the day.

Defensive sorties sent down to protect transports: *S.S.*, Vol. 28, p. 240. No loss figures are given.

Shore-based artillery fire at transports: 1st Mar Div D-2 Journal 15 Nov 42; Miller, *Guadalcanal: The First Offensive*, p. 188 (for 244th Coast Artillery participation); 3d Defense Bn., 5-inch Rpt, p. 4, MCHC, Box 6, A32-1.

Meade activities: U.S.S. *Meade*, DD602/A4-1, Serial 003, November 19, 1942, Subject: Report of Action Against Enemy Transports, Located on Guadalcanal Island, on November 15, 1942. CINCPAC Serial 00554, pp. 18, 24, paras. 107–8, 141, explains and commends Lieutenant Commander Lamb's decisions that brought him to Tulagi this morning.

Story of Land and Taylor: Noted in Morison, *Struggle for Guadalcanal*, pp. 284–85.

Page 489
Public claims of success: Japanese radio broadcasts reported in *New York Times*, November 18, 1942, p. 1, col. 5; American public claims reported in "U.S. Smashes Japanese Fleet in Solomons," *New York Times*, November 17, 1942, p. 1, col. 8, which reflected the contents of U.S. Navy Communiqué 194, 16 Nov 42. Loss of another destroyer (*Benham*) was announced in U.S. Navy Communiqué 198, 22 Nov 42, U.S. Navy Department Communiqués 1-300 and pertinent Press Releases, December 10, 1941, to March 5, 1943, Office of Public Relations, U.S. Navy, Government Printing Office, 1943.

Attitudes in Washington: Potter, *Nimitz*, p. 206.

Page 489
Quote of Secretary Knox: "Joy at Sea Victory," *New York Times*, November 18, 1942, p. 8, col. 2.

Pages 489–90
Announcement of loss of Sullivan brothers: The family was notified on January 12, 1943, and the story was carried in most newspapers over the next several days (*Des Moines Register*, January 15 and 16, 1943, p. 1; *New York Times*, January 13, 1943, p. 10, col. 3, January 15, 1943, p. 7, col. 1). They left a sister, Genevieve, and Albert was survived by a wife and son. The mother of the lost brothers participated in the launching of a destroyer (*The Sullivans*, DD-537) named after her sons.

Troops and supplies landed by Turner: AMPHIBFORSOPAC War Diary 12 Nov 42.

Page 490
Troops and supplies landed by convoy: *S.S.*, Vol. 28, p. 241. Units landed are identified as Headquarters, 229th Infantry Regiment, 2d Battalion, 230th Infantry Regiment, part of the I/229, the 38th Engineer Regiment (actually a battalion-size unit), and the 38th Transportation Regiment (again a battalion).

Page 490
American Casualties Derived as Follows:

Air attack November 12:	29
Surface action November 13 including *Juneau:*	1,439
Surface action November 14–15:	242
Aircrew November 12–15:	22
Total:	1,732

Japanese Casualty Recapitulation Is as Follows:

Surface Action November 13:	552 (at least)
Kinugasa and *Maya* November 14:	548
Convoy November 14:	450
Surface Action November 14–15:	249 (at least)
Aircrew losses November 12–15:	circa 96
Total:	1,895

Aircraft losses are recapitulated as follows:

	American				Japanese			
	F4F	*P-39*	*SBD*	*TBF*	*Zero*	*Pete*	*Jake*	*Betty*
November 12 (Air)	3	2	0		1		1	11
November 13	1		2	1	11			
(Bombardment 13–14)	2		1					
November 14	2		5		13			
November 15	1			1	1	2		
Totals:	8	2	8	2	26	2	1	11
Plus 3 OS2U, 1 SOC, 1 R4D				= 25				= 40

Japanese losses are presented from data provided by John Lundstrom. The second P-39 lost on November 12 was a victim of ground fire. Three OS2Us were destroyed on *South Dakota,* one SOC was lost on November 15, and one R4D was an operational loss off Kukum on November 15. COMGEN 1st MARDIV to COMSOPAC 132233 Nov 42, COMSOPAC War Diary 13 Nov 42, p. 43.

Japanese intelligence estimate prior to the battle: *S.S.,* Vol. 83, p. 330.

Page 491
Nimitz praises Turner: CINCPAC Serial 00554, p. 25, para. 145.

Page 492
"Fork in the road": CINCPAC Serial 00554, p. 25, para. 146.

CHAPTER 19

The principal sources for this chapter are the individual American reports of the events in question. For the battle of Tassafaronga, the Japanese material is extracted largely from *S.S.,* Vol. 83, pp. 431–37, which includes a verbatim reprint of the "Detailed Battle Report" of Destroyer Squadron 2 for this action.

Page 493
"Now is the time . . .": Grey Book, Summary, 15 Nov 42, p. 1168.

Relief of 1st Marine Division: Final Report, Phase V, pp. 33–34; COMSOPAC to CINCPAC 220120 Nov 42, COMSOPAC War Diary 22 Nov 42. The earliest reference to definite plans to relieve the 1st Mar Div is in Harmon to Marshall 031028 Nov 42, COMSOPAC War Diary 3 Nov 42, p. 10.

Halsey transfers management of Noumea to Army control: *Global Logistics and Strategy,*

1941–1943, pp. 402–3. In November, 47,808 short tons of supplies were discharged at Noumea. The figures for December and January were 138,085 tons and 213,982 tons respectively. General Williamson achieved this feat by (1) increasing the labor force; (2) bringing in experienced civilian and military port personnel from New Zealand and the Fijis; and (3) gaining authority for exclusive use of the French Nickel Company's dock for three months.

Pages 494–95
Patrolling and Sebree's scheme of maneuver: Miller, *Guadalcanal: The First Offensive,* pp. 202–3. Miller's sources for this information were an interview with General Sebree, June 19–20, 1943, and an interview with Colonel Paul A. Gavan (G-3 of the Americal Division), November 14, 1946. I was unable to locate these documents in my research, and virtually all of the subsequent citations to Miller in this and the following three chapters pertain to information he obtained in interviews.

Activities of 2/182 on November 18: Report of Operations, Guadalcanal, 182d Inf, 12 Nov 42–30 Jun 43, pp. 2–3, 300-INF(182)-0.3 [hereafter Rpt Ops 182d Inf]; Unit Report No. 5, 182d Inf, 18 Nov 42, 300-INF(182)-0.9; 2/182, S-2 Journal, 18 Nov 42, 300-INF(182)-2.2; Miller, *Guadalcanal: The First Offensive,* p. 204.

Page 495
Activities of 1/182 on November 19: Rpt Ops 182d Inf, p. 3; Unit Report No. 6, 182d Inf, 19 Nov 42, 300-INF(182)-0.9; Americal Division Narrative of Operations, p. 3, 300-2.

Page 495
Japanese dispositions and strength: *S.S.,* Vol. 28, pp. 296–97, 303–5, map at p. 297, and table attached to Vol. 28 showing strength

return of 17th Army for November 20, which is the source for data in Appendix 2.

Page 495
Events of night of November 19–20 and dawn Japanese attack: Americal Division Narrative of Operations, p. 3, 300–2; Unit Report No. 7, 182d Inf, 300-INF(182)-0.9; Col. Paul A. Gavan, Personal Experience Account of ACofS, G-3, Americal Div, p. 1, 300-3.0; Miller, *Guadalcanal: The First Offensive*, p. 205. The reports of the 182d are silent about the events of the morning of November 20 except for the 1/182, S-2 Journal, 20 Nov 42, 300-INF(182)-2.2, and the S-3 Journal, 182d Inf, 20 Nov 42, 300-INF(182)-3.2.

Page 496
Commitment and activities of 164th Infantry, November 20–25: Americal Division Narrative of Operations, p. 3; Report of Matanikau Engagements, 164th Inf, 3 Nov 42–1 Mar 43, 300-INF(164)-0.3.0; 164th Inf, S-1 Journal, 21–25 Nov 42, 300-INF(164)-1.2; Unit Reports 20-26 Nov 42, 164th Inf, 300-INF(164)-0.9; Miller, *Guadalcanal: The First Offensive*, pp. 206–8.

Description of the terrain: Paul A. Gavan, Personal Experience Account of ACofS, G-3, Americal Division, pp. 1–2, 300-3.0.

Japanese account of the fighting: Ibid., pp. 296–97, 307.

Page 496
Activities of 1/182 on November 21 and action of November 22: Americal Division Narrative of Operations, p. 3, 300–2; Unit Reports Nos. 8 and 9, 182d Inf, 300-INF(182)-0.9.

Attack of 8th Marines: Ltrs Lt. Col. John H. Cook to CMC 13 Jan 49 and Col. Hewitt D. Adams to CMC 4 Jan 49, MCHC. The route for the attack was selected by map because there was no time for the Marine commanders to conduct a reconnaissance.

Expenditure of American artillery ammunition: 1st Mar Div Final Rpt V, Arty Annex R, p. 3.

Page 496
Bombing of 17th Army Headquarters: *S.S.*, Vol. 28, pp. 296–98.

Pages 496–97
Mortaring of 3/164: Unit Report NO. 16, 164th Inf, 300INF(164)-0.9, RG 407, Box 5629.

Major Nishiyama notes Japanese tactics: *S.S.*, Vol. 28, p. 306.

Decision to halt attack November 23, exchanges after attack halted: Personal Experience Account of ACofS, G-3, Americal Division, Col. Paul A. Gavan, p. 2, 300-3.0 (Gavan gives date as November 25, but clearly he meant November 23, as the order to withdraw the 1st Mar Div was received on November 23, not 25. Descriptions of subsequent activity may be found in Report of Matanikau Engagements, 164th Inf, 3 Nov 42–1 Mar 43, 300-INF(164)-0.3.0, and ltr Lt. Col. John H. Cook to CMC 13 Jan 49.

American losses: 164th Inf losses from Unit Reports, 20–23 Nov 42; 182d Inf losses from History 182d Inf, 12 Nov 42–30 Jun 43, p. 3, 300-INF(182)-0.2 (list of killed in action); 8th Marines losses from Muster Rolls, MCHC, for November 1942. Total losses for 8th Marines for the month were seventy-seven killed; twenty-eight died between November 24 and 30. The totals for the 182d in its Unit Reports are significantly lower than those given in the unit history.

Data on 164th Infantry attrition: 164th Inf, S-1 Journal, 25 Nov 42; Unit Report No. 1, 164th Inf (for original strength). Miller, *Guadalcanal: The First Offensive*, p. 209, erroneously shows the losses for the 164th as 117 killed from November 19 to 25, whereas the S-1 Journal entry actually indicates this figure is the loss since the regiment reached Guadalcanal.

Page 497
Commendations to Colonel Sakai's regiment and Lieutenant Omasu: *S.S.*, Vol. 28, p. 307. No loss figures for this engagement are given.

17th Army strength return for November 20: Table attached to *S.S.*, Vol. 28, which is source for Appendix 2.

Page 498
Creation of 8th Area Army, appointment of Imamura, creation of Southeast Area Fleet: *S.S.*, Vol. 83, pp. 420–21, 456, Vol. 28, pp. 244–46.

Page 498
New Central Agreement: Ibid., Vol. 83, pp. 399–404, 491–92, Vol. 28, pp. 242–44, 250–51, 267, 270, 285–86, 420. There is a small discrepancy in the totals of aircraft assigned to the 6th Air Division between the accounts in Vol. 28 (IJA) and 83 (IJN). The former says 139 planes and the later says 110. Twenty-eight of the twenty-nine-plane dif-

ference may be accounted for as the aircraft of a light bomber wing which was not officially assigned to the 6th Air Division until December.

Pages 498–99
Changing attitude of the Combined Fleet and the conference with Imamura: *S.S.,* Vol. 83, pp. 418–21, 492–93.

Page 499
Decision to commit the 21st Brigade to New Guinea: Ibid., pp. 424–28. This effort cost the destroyer *Hayashio.*

Page 499
Imamura arrives at Rabaul, formally takes command; reports by Colonel Sugita and Major Hayashi: *S.S.,* Vol. 28, pp. 275, 277, 280–82, 298.

Pages 499–500
Supply situation of the 17th Army on Guadalcanal according to contemporary reports: Ibid., pp. 293, 298, 306, 400.

Page 500
Submarine transportation effort: Ibid., Vol. 83, pp. 407, 442–43, 445–46, Vol. 28, p. 403.

Pages 500–501
Submarine antishipping effort including midget submarine attacks: Ibid., Vol. 83, pp. 341–43.

Damage to *Majaba:* COMAMPHIBFOR-SOPAC War Diary 7 Nov 42; U.S.S. *Bobolink* War Diary 7 Jan 43 (moves *Majaba* to Tulagi); *Dictionary of American Naval Fighting Ships,* Vol. IV, (Washington, D.C.: Navy Department, Office of the Chief of Naval Operations, Naval History Division, 1969), p. 202. The midget sub also fired a torpedo at destroyer *Lansdowne,* which was anchored nearby unloading 81mm mortar ammunition. *Lansdowne* was not hit and got underway within three minutes. One minute later she dropped a pattern of depth charges over the midget sub. U.S.S. *Lansdowne,* DD486/A16-3, Serial 051, November 16, 1942, Subject: Anti-submarine Action, Report of.

Page 501
Alchiba saga: U.S.S. *Alchiba,* AK23/A16-3, Serial 0015, December 15, 1942, Subject: U.S.S. *Alchiba,* Torpedoing of; U.S.S. *Alchiba* (AKA6) Torpedo Damage 28 November 1942 and 7 December 1942, Solomons Islands, War Damage Report No. 40, Bureau of Ships, Navy Department, December 1943. The first torpedoing killed two army passen-

gers and the second two crew members. The Navy Department announced the "loss" of *Alchiba* on December 11 in U.S. Navy Communiqué 216. *U.S. Navy Department Communiqués 1-300 and Pertinent Press Releases, December 10, 1941, to March 5, 1943,* Office of Public Relations, U.S. Navy (Washington, D.C.: U.S. Government Printing Office, 1943).

Page 501
"Chain Transportation" scheme: *S.S.,* Vol. 83, pp. 450–51.

Pages 501–2
Establishment of Wickham base and abandonment of the "Chain Transportation": Ibid., pp. 416, 451. The destroyers making the trip to Wickham on November 27 were *Tanikaze, Urakaze, Inazuma, Arashi, Isonami,* and *Yugure.*

Increasing strength of Cactus Air Force: Totals from 1st Mar Div D-2 Jnl 15 Nov 42 and COMGEN 1ST MARDIV to COMSOPAC 292328 Nov 42, COMSOPAC War Diary 29 Nov 42. On November 19, VMSB-141 ended its tour, having lost 50 percent of its pilots. Individual pilots from VMF-121 left for leave during this period, and VMF-112 got a week's breather in Sidney in December. On November 23, Henderson Field received six Hudsons of the RNZAF 3d Reconnaissance Squadron for search and four OS2Us for antisubmarine work (Sherrod, *History of Marine Corps Aviation,* pp. 119, 121).

November 18 attack on Buin and rescue of Colonel Saunders: 13th AF Hist., p. 65; Lord, *Lonely Vigil,* pp. 94–97.

Page 502
"Drum method" described: *S.S.,* Vol. 83, p. 431, Vol. 28, pp. 400–2. According to the latter source, Admiral Ugaki estimated that no more than one hour would be required at the landing points to off-load the drums. The drums were tied together in clusters of five to ten and each cluster attached to the central line, which was supported at the end by a piece of wood. Total weight of food in a load of 200 drums was 33 tons, and 240 drums carried just under 40 tons. Tanaka, Part II, p. 825, indicates the drums were also loaded with medicines. Two other ideas were examined but not used at this time. One involved waterproof floating bags and the second involved metal cans holding compressed and powdered rations.

Pages 502–3

Tanaka prepares for first run using the drum method: *S.S.*, Vol. 83, pp. 431–33, 436. The commissioning dates of the ships of Desdiv 31 are from Jentschur, Jung, and Mickel, *Warships of the Imperial Japanese Navy, 1869–1945*, p. 150. Morison, *Struggle for Guadalcanal*, p. 301, says Tanaka's squadron had steamed together in peace and war since the summer of 1941. This was but one of a number of errors traceable to the account of this action provided to Morison by Captain Yasumi Toyama, Tanaka's chief of staff. In fact, Desdiv 31 was new (formed August 31, 1942), and Desdiv 24 was only formally assigned to Destroyer Squadron 2 on July 14 and had operated only intermittently with Tanaka since that date. Tanaka, Part I, p. 698, acknowledges the lack of training of his unit by this date.

Page 503

Allied intelligence and the rebuilding of Halsey's forces: Commander in Chief, U.S. Pacific Fleet, Pac-90-1h, A16-3/SOL, Serial 00546, February 15, 1943, Subject: Solomons Islands Campaign, 5th Battle of Savo—30 November 1942, pp. 2–3, paras. 9, 15 [hereafter CINCPAC Serial 00546]; COMSOPAC 230612 Nov 42, COMSOPAC War Diary, 23 Nov 42; COMSOPAC 280022 Nov 42, COMSOPAC War Diary 28 Nov 42. COMSOPAC 230612 also shows that in addition to the units listed in the text, Halsey organized Task Force 65 of battleships *Maryland* and *Colorado*, escort carriers *Nassau* and *Altamaha*, and six destroyers. The ships originally assigned to Task Force 67 were heavy cruisers *New Orleans, Pensacola, Northampton*; light cruisers *Honolulu* and *Helena*; and destroyers *Grayson, O'Bannon, Nicholas, Fletcher, Perkins, Drayton, Maury*, and *Lamson* (Commander Task Force 67, A16-3, Serial 06, December 9, 1942, Subject: Report of Action off Cape Esperance, Night of November 30, 1942, p. 1, para. 3 [hereafter CTF 67 Serial 06]).

"with his sword in his hand": Leahy, *I Was There*, p. 119. Ships transferred were listed in COMINCH to CINCPAC 171255 Nov 42.

Page 503

Kinkaid's plan: CTF 67 Serial 06, Enclosures (D)-(F) (Copies of CTF 67, A16-3/CTF67, Serial 01, November 27, 1942, Operations Plan 1–42).

Pages 503–4

Wright replaces Kinkaid: CINCPAC Serial 00546, p. 3, para. 15; CTF 67 Serial 06, p. 1, para. 3.

Halsey's orders to Wright: CINCPAC Serial 00546, p. 3, paras. 16, 17; CTF 67 Serial 06, pp. 1–2, paras. 4–5. The information provided Wright could only have come from a decrypt, and the content of the intelligence passed to Wright parallels almost exactly the information sent to the 17th Army on Guadalcanal from the 8th Fleet at Rabaul (*S.S.*, Vol. 83, p. 432).

Wright sorties: CTF 67 Serial 06, p. 2, para. 6; Commander Task Unit 67.2.3 (Rear Admiral Tisdale), A16-3, Serial 042, December 6, 1942, Subject: Report of Action—Night of November 30–December 1, 1942, p. 1, para. 1 [hereafter CTF 67.2.3 Serial 042].

Page 504

Tanaka sorties and daylight run: *S.S.*, Vol. 83, p. 433.

Page 504

Information to Wright and joining of *Lamson* and *Lardner:* CTF 67 Serial 06, pp. 3–4, paras. 5, 9–10.

Page 505

Composition of Reinforcement Unit: *S.S.*, Vol. 83, pp. 431–32, 436; Tanaka, Part II, p. 825–27.

Page 505

Composition of Task Force 67: From CTF 67 Serial 06, p. 1, para. 2, and the individual ship action reports.

Pages 506–7

Tabular comparison of combat power: Lenton, *American Battleships, Carriers and Cruisers*, pp. 48–49, 52–53, 56–57, 60–61; Lenton, *American Fleet and Escort Destroyers*, Vol. 1, pp. 54–56, 61–63, 105–9.

Japanese forces: From Jentschur, Jung, and Mickel, *Warships of the Imperial Japanese Navy, 1869–1945*, pp. 146–50.

Tanaka takes up approach formation and sights Savo: *S.S.*, Vol. 83, p. 433.

Wright enters Lengo Channel and assumes battle formation: CTF 67 Serial 06, pp. 3, 5, paras. 6, 7, 11–12.

Page 507

Tanaka enters passage south of Savo: *S.S.*, Vol. 83, p. 433.

Status of Task Force 67 float planes: CTF 67 Serial 06, p. 14, para. 47; U.S.S. *Minneapolis,*

CA36/A16-3/(0247), 6 December 1942, Subject: U.S.S. *Minneapolis* Action Report for 30 November–1 December 1942, Enclosure (C) (aircrew report) [hereafter *Minneapolis* Serial 0247]. The latter document indicates that four aircraft became airborne: two from *Minneapolis* and one each from *New Orleans* and *Honolulu.*

Wright clears Lengo Channel and maneuvers: CTF 67 Serial 06, p. 5, paras. 12–13; CTF 67.2.3 Serial 042, p. 1, para. 2. Times are reconciled.

Weather and visibility: *S.S.,* Vol. 83, p. 433; CTF 67, Serial 06, p. 5, para. 12; U.S.S. *Honolulu* CL48/A16-3(C142), December 4, 1942, Subject: Action Report—Engagement off Savo Island, Night of November 30th–December 1st 1942—U.S.S. *Honolulu,* p. 5, para. 13 [hereafter *Honolulu* Serial C142].

Initial radar contacts: *Minneapolis* Serial 0247, p. 3, para. 5, Enclosure (B), p. 2; CTF 67 Serial 06, p. 5, paras. 13–14.

Page 507
Takanami sights Wright, Tanaka reacts: *S.S.,* Vol. 83, pp. 433–35.

Page 508
Orders to American destroyers to launch torpedoes: Wright's account in the text of his main report on the firing of torpedoes by his van destroyers is terse. He simply states that Commander Cole asked for permission to fire torpedoes at 2317 and that it was granted (CTF 67 Serial 06, pp. 5–6, para. 16). The account in the text is derived from the report of Admiral Tisdale (CTF 67.2.3 Serial 042, Communications Log), Admiral Wright's own Enclosure (B) (Communications Log), and Commander Cole's report (U.S.S. *Fletcher* DD445/A16-3 Serial No. (S)-3, December 3, 1942, Subject: Action Report [hereafter *Fletcher* Serial (S)-3]). These latter reports all reflect a five-minute interval between the original request by Cole and Wright's actual authorization to fire torpedoes, though they vary somewhat on the exact times. The times in the text are reconciled around the fact that it is fairly certain that the American cruisers opened fire at 2321.

Page 508
Van destroyers launch torpedoes: *Fletcher* Serial (S)-3; U.S.S. *Perkins,* DD377/A16(01854), December 1, 1942, Subject: Report of Action, Night of November 30, 1942 [hereafter *Perkins* Serial 01854]; U.S.S. *Maury,* DD401/A16-3, Serial 026, Decem-

ber 3, 1942, Subject: Report of Action with Japanese Surface Forces the Night of November 30–December 1, 1942, off Savo Island [hereafter *Maury* Serial 026]; U.S.S. *Drayton,* DD366, A16-3, Serial (057), December 3, 1942, Subject: Action Report, Night of 30 November–1 December, off Northeast Coast of Guadalcanal [hereafter *Drayton* Serial 057]; CTF 67 Serial 06, pp. 5–6, para. 16. The quote of Wright is at p. 2 of *Fletcher*'s report.

Page 508
"A brief but furious gun action followed": CTF 67 Serial 06, p. 6, para. 17; CTF 67.2.3 Serial 042, p. 1, para. 3. Description of scene is based on comments in various action reports and the account of Chaplin Howell M. Forgy of *New Orleans* in . . . *And Pass the Ammunition* (New York: Appleton-Century, 1944), p. 186 [hereafter Forgy, *And Pass the Ammunition*].

Page 509
Destruction of *Takanami: S.S.,* Vol. 83 p. 437, which contains the report of Lieutenant (jg) Eda, *Takanami*'s navigator. He stated that *Takanami* launched her torpedoes at 2323.

Observations by aviators and *Lardner:* CTF 67 Serial 06, Enclosure (A), *Minneapolis* Serial 0247, Enclosure (C); U.S.S. *Lardner* DD487/A16-3, December 8, 1942, Subject: Report of Night Surface Action, November 30–December 1, 1942 [hereafter *Lardner* 8 Dec 42].

Pages 509–10
Tanaka's destroyers launch torpedoes between 2323 and 2333: *S.S.,* Vol. 83, pp. 435–36. Also instructive is the track chart at p. 434. Dull, *Battle History of the Imperial Japanese Navy,* p. 265, says *Naganami* received a fragment hit on a funnel at about 2333 with "minor casualties."

Page 510
Minneapolis torpedoed: CTF 67 Serial 06, p. 6, para. 19; *Minneapolis* Serial 0247, pp. 5–7, 13–14, paras. 10–14, 31. Only torpedoes from *Takanami* or *Suzukaze* could have hit *Minneapolis* (and *New Orleans*) in view of the launch times. Time-distance factors would favor *Takanami,* particularly as according to the Japanese track chart (as opposed to that in Morison, *Struggle for Guadalcanal,* between pp. 291–92) she was firing from ahead of the American column. But this is not completely clear, and *Takanami* was a new ship under heavy fire while veteran *Suzukaze* was under little, if any, distraction.

Page 511
New Orleans torpedoed: U.S.S. *New Orleans,* CA32/A12-1/(637), December 4, 1942, Subject: U.S.S. *New Orleans,* Action Report Covering Night Action November 30–December 1, 1942, pp. 1–6 [hereafter *New Orleans* Serial 637]. A vivid personal account of *New Orleans's* ordeal is provided by Chaplain Forgy in Forgy, *And Pass the Ammunition,* pp. 179–219. The "cave of fire" quote is at p. 190.

Pages 511–12
Pensacola torpedoed: U.S.S. *Pensacola,* CA24/A16-3/(0178), December 4, 1942, Subject: Report of Engagement with Enemy on the Night of November 30–December 1, 1942, pp. 2–4, paras. 4–13 and Enclosure (A) [hereafter *Pensacola* Serial 0178]. The time of the torpedoing is given as 2339 in CTF 67 Serial 06, p. 7, para. 21. *Pensacola* was probably struck by torpedoes from *Oyashio* or *Kuroshio.*

Page 512
Honolulu's maneuvers and Admiral Tisdale's actions: *Honolulu* Serial C142; CTF 67.2.3 Serial 042, pp. 2–3, paras. 5–8; CTF 67, Serial 06, p. 6, para. 19.

Page 512
Van destroyers maneuver, *Drayton* fires torpedoes: *Drayton* Serial 057; *Fletcher* Serial (S)-3; *Perkins* Serial 01854; *Maury* Serial 026.

Pages 512–13
Northampton torpedoed: U.S.S. *Northampton,* CA26/A16-3, Serial 06, December 5, 1942, Subject: Report of Action with the enemy and resultant sinking of *U.S.S. Northampton,* pp. 1–3 [hereafter *Northampton* Serial 06]; and U.S.S. *Northampton* (CA26), Loss in Action 30 November 1942 [sic] Battle of Lunga Point, War Damage Report No. 41, Preliminary Design Section, Bureau of Ships, Navy Department, 10 March 1944 [hereafter War Damage Report No. 41]. The limitation on *Northampton's* ability to maneuver is from CTF 67.2.3, Serial 042, pp. 3–4, para 12; quote from executive officer of *Honolulu* is from *Honolulu* Serial C142, Enclosure (A), p. 1. CTF 67 Serial 06, p. 7, para. 27, says *Northampton* was torpedoed at 2349. Based upon the angle of approach, the torpedoes that hit *Northampton* came from either *Naganami* or *Kawakaze,* most likely the latter. Morison, *Struggle for Guadalcanal,* p. 306, attributes these hits to *Oyashio* based upon a launch time of 2339, but *S.S.,* Vol. 83, p. 436, says *Oyashio* fired her

torpedoes at 2329, which does not work out in terms of time-distance for hits on *Northampton.*

Page 513
Lamson and *Lardner:* U.S.S. *Lamson,* DD367/A16-3, Serial 00242, December 3, 1942, Subject: Action Report, Night of 30 November–1 December 1942, Solomons Islands Area [hereafter *Lamson* Serial 00242]; *Lardner* 8 Dec 42. That *New Orleans* fired on these vessels is confirmed in her report, *New Orleans* Serial 637, p. 4.

Tanaka orders retirement and assistance for *Takanami: S.S.,* Vol. 83, p. 437.

Pages 513–14
Efforts to rescue *Takanami's* crew and her sinking: *S.S.,* Vol. 83, pp. 435, 437.

Losses on *Takanami: S.S.,* Vol. 83, gives no loss figures. Dull, *Battle History of the Imperial Japanese Navy,* p. 265, reports 211 men were lost with *Takanami,* and Grey Book, Summary 1 Dec 42, p. 1179, notes twenty-six survivors of *Takanami* landed on Guadalcanal.

Minneapolis moves to Tulagi: *Minneapolis* Serial 0247, pp. 8–14, paras. 17–21.

Page 514
New Orleans moves to Tulagi: *New Orleans* Serial 637, pp. 3–8. The sacrifice of Lieutenant Commander Hayter is described in Forgy, *And Pass the Ammunition,* pp. 212–13, and Morison, *Struggle for Guadalcanal,* pp. 309–10.

Page 514
Pensacola moves to Tulagi: *Pensacola* Serial 0178, pp. 3–7, paras. 9–22.

Pages 514–15
Loss of *Northampton: Northampton* Serial 06, p. 3–15; War Damage Report No. 41; *Fletcher* Serial (S)-3.

Page 515
Salvage activities at Tulagi: U.S.S. *Minneapolis,* CA36/A9/L11-1, Serial 00106, 15 March 1943, Subject: Report of *Minneapolis* War Damage and Damage Control Measures, resulting from action on night of 30 November–1 December 1942; U.S.S. *New Orleans* (CA32) Torpedo Damage Lunga Point 30 November 1942, War Damage Report No. 38, Bureau of Ships, Navy Department, 1 November 1943; U.S.S. *Pensacola,* CA24/L11-1/Serial 0263, December 27, 1942, Sub-

ject: Fire on board U.S.S. Pensacola; U.S.S. *Portland* (CA33) Gunfire and Torpedo Damage Battle of Guadalcanal 13 November 1942, U.S.S. *Pensacola* (CA24) Torpedo Damage Battle of Lunga Point 30 November 1942, War Damage Report No. 35, Preliminary Design Section, Bureau of Ships, Navy Department, 1 March 1944. The date *Pensacola* left Tulagi is given in her War Diary 6 Dec 42.

Page 515
Post battle analysis: CTF 67 Serial 06, pp. 8–11, 15–18, paras. 28–29, 31–33, 36–37, 50, 53, 55–56; CINCPAC Serial 00546, pp. 11–16, paras. 54–77.

Page 516
Award of Navy Cross to Wright: Wright's official biography, NHC.

Criticism of Cole: COMSOPAC A16-3/(90) Serial 00411, February 20, 1942, Subject: Report of Action off Cape Esperance, Night of November 30, 1942, p. 1, paras. 3–4. Morison pointed out the fallacies in the charges against Cole (Morison, *Struggle for Guadalcanal,* p. 313, note 27). It is well to remember in this context the rewards for *Lamson* and *Lardner* when they attempted to assist the U.S. cruisers.

Page 517
Japanese critique: "Battle of Tassafaronga," ATIS 16086, quoted in Morison, *Struggle for Guadalcanal,* p. 313.

Gunnery problems of the American heavy cruisers: These are illuminated in Norman Friedman, *U.S. Cruisers: An Illustrated Design History* (Annapolis, Md.: United States Naval Institute Press, 1984), pp. 313, 347.

Page 517
". . . mistakes on the American side were cancelled by those of the enemy . . .": Morison, *Struggle for Guadalcanal,* p. 315.

Page 518
Criticism of Tanaka: *S.S.,* Vol. 83, p. 436.

CHAPTER 20

The principal sources for this chapter are the American unit and higher command reports, SRH-136, pp. 4–10; *S.S.,* Vol. 83, pp. 334–36, 406, 410–14, 422–23, 429–30, 440–61, 472, 480–81, 492–97, Vol. 28, pp. 271–96, 302–320, 396–97, 405–14, 419–444, 475–77.

Pages 519–20
Reinforcement run of December 3: *S.S.,* Vol. 83, pp. 440–41, and Tanaka, Part II, p. 828, for Japanese side. *Ariake* was detailed to the Support Force at the same time the other destroyers were sent to the Reinforcement Unit. Air action from VMSB-132, War Diary 3 Dec 42 and MAG-14 Record of Events, p. 7. SRH-136, pp. 4, 150, notes a dispatch from CINCPAC predicted the landing that night, but it was sent out a half hour after the intercept took place. An earlier message, however, afforded a general warning of the run, which a coast watcher confirmed at 1300. Tanaka discloses that after this run he met with Admiral Mikawa on December 4 and recommended evacuation of the island.

Pages 520–21
Reinforcement run of December 7: *S.S.,* Vol. 83, pp. 441–42; Tanaka, Part II, p. 828–29; SRH-136, pp. 5–6, 242, 244 (for intelligence aspects); and VMSB-132 War Diary, 7 Dec 42; MAG-14 Record of Events, p. 7. Tanaka moved his flag to *Teruzuki,* but the reason he did not lead this run is not reported. The American description of the PT boat action is found in Motor Torpedo Boat Squadron 2, No Serial, 9 December 1942, Memorandum for Commanding General, Cactus, Subject: PT operations, night of 7–8 December 1942. In this writer's view, the complete frustration of Sato's mission this night must rank higher than any individual sinking achieved by American PT boats during the war.

Page 521
Conference at Rabaul and "bombshell": *S.S.,* Vol. 83, pp. 443–45, Vol. 28, pp. 408–9. Vol. 28 notes that the Imperial Navy had lost ten destroyers since late October and expected to build only eleven in fiscal year 1943 and ten the following fiscal year; p. 288 notes a bitter message from the 17th Army on December 9 complaining that only one out of five drums launched were recovered since November 30 and protesting the failure of Captain Sato's ships to launch any drums after a "small battle" with PT boats.

Page 521
Arrival of 132d Infantry and change of command: COMAMPHIBFORSOPAC War Diary 8 Dec 42; Final Report, Phase V, p. 34. Miller, *Guadalcanal: The First Offensive,* pp. 213, reports that the task of selecting an Army officer to command on Guadalcanal was delegated to General Harmon, who chose Patch.

Page 522
Condition of 1st Marine Division at departure: Merillat, *Island,* pp. 236–40; Merillat, *Guadalcanal Remembered,* pp. 249–51; Leckie, *Helmet for My Pillow,* pp. 130–33; Cates, "My First," pp. 97–98; McMillan, *Old Breed,* pp. 134–40; Final Report, Phase V, Annex T, Medical Problems, p. 8. The casualty figures for the 1st Marine Division are from Hough, Ludwig, and Shaw, *Pearl Harbor to Guadalcanal,* p. 359, and exclude totals from attached units such as the 3d Defense Battalion, 1st Raider Battalion, 1st Parachute Battalion, and others.

Page 522
Departure order of 1st Marine Division: Final Report, Phase V, p. 34; Commander in Chief, U.S. Pacific Fleet, CINCPAC File Pac-90-wb, A16-3, Serial 00599, 9 March 1943, Subject: Solomons Islands Campaign . . . , pp. 3, 7, paras. 9, 28 [hereafter CINCPAC Serial 00599]; TF 62 War Diary 15 Dec 42, 5 Jan 43.

boat participation from Johnson, *United States PT-Boats of World War II,* pp. 108–10. According to *S.S.,* Vol. 28, p. 405, when informed that only 220 drums had been recovered, Admiral Ugaki questioned whether this was correct or whether the 17th Army was hoarding. Dull, *Battle History of the Imperial Japanese Navy,* p. 267, reports *Arashi* and *Naganami* rescued 138 members of *Teruzuki*'s crew.

Page 524
"I dove deep and was still under water . . .": As reported in Morison, *Struggle for Guadalcanal,* p. 320.

Pages 524–25
Status of Japanese air power in December: *S.S.,* Vol. 83, pp. 422–23, 458, 460, Vol. 28, pp. 262, 285. According to Sakamaki, forty-four of the sixty new fighter pilots lacked any experience with Zeros.

The organization and distribution of the 11th Air Fleet in early December follows:

Location	Units	Operational Aircraft
Rabaul:	701st Air Group	26 Bettys
	705th Air Group	
	252d Air Group	17 Zeros
	582d Air Group (less Val detachment)	2 Vals
Buin:	204th Air Group	12 Zeros
	582d Air Group (Val detachment only)	18 Vals
	Hiyo Detachment (until December 15)	
Kavieng:	751st Air Group	24 Bettys
	253d Air Group	4 Zeros

Page 522
"When news comes that . . .": *New York Times,* January 23, 1943, p. 12.

Page 523
Creation of patch for 1st Marine Division: McMillan, *Old Breed,* pp. 143–44.

Submarine transportation and destruction of *I-3: S.S.,* Vol. 83, pp. 442–43; SRH-0136, pp. 7–8, 10; Johnson, *United States PT-Boats of World War II,* p. 108.

Pages 523–24
Reinforcement run of December 11: Japanese participation from *S.S.,* Vol. 83, pp. 442, 446–48, Vol. 28, p. 405, and Tanaka, Part *II,* p. 829. American air unit participation from VMSB-132 War Diary, 11 Dec 42, MAG-14 Record of Events, pp. 7–8. Intelligence aspects are from SRH-136, pp. 6, 41, 43. PT

In addition to these there were also five flying boats and twelve float planes available.

On December 1 the 707th Air Group was disbanded and survivors absorbed into the 705th Air Group. Yamamoto ordered the carrier air groups back to Japan for refitting in November. However, the shortage of aircraft at Rabaul resulted in *Hiyo*'s detachment remaining there through the middle of December, and subsequently *Junyo*'s air group was sent to Wewak. Organization from *S.S.,* Vol. 83, p. 423, 458. Strength figures are from *S.S.,* Vol. 28, pp. 407–8, and are for "late December," at which time there were also thirteen Zeros at Munda.

The 1st Air Group of the 6th Air Division arrived at Rabaul on December 18 with forty-five Type 1 ("Oscar") fighters. Naval aviators criticized these aircraft as lacking in range and firepower. Their pilots (as were the other aircrews in the 6th Air Division) were also inexperienced in over-water operations. *S.S.,* Vol. 83, p. 461, Vol. 28, p. 397.

Page 525
Importance of airfields: *S.S.,* Vol. 28, p. 262.

Page 525
Creation of Munda airfield: *S.S.,* Vol. 83, pp. 334, 336, 412, 429–30, 452–54. The 22d Construction Unit was lifted to Munda in a small convoy of *Chihaya Maru, Jini Maru,* and *Houn Maru* escorted by two destroyers and a patrol boat. They landed on the nights of November 23 and 24. On the 27th, *Sanso Maru* and *Chihaya Maru* returned with the rest of the 22d Construction Unit and the Army 10th Airfield Construction Unit. Other work produced a 1,400-by-80-meter airstrip at Shortland and a 1,000-by-40-meter field on New Ireland. Ibid., pp. 410–11, 459.

Pages 525–26
Detection of construction activity at Munda: Feldt, *Coast Watchers,* p. 110; Sherrod, *History of Marine Corps Aviation in World War II,* p. 123. The latter source says aerial cameras detected the airfield; the former claims the discovery was made by native scouts. The Japanese were quite envious of the speed with which American engineers constructed air bases with the aid of their equipment. By contrast the first mechanized construction battalion the Japanese organized (the 11th) lost all its equipment in a ship sunk by an American submarine off Rabaul (*S.S.,* Vol. 28, pp. 282, 396–97).

Page 526
Regular bombing attacks on Munda after discovery of airfield: CINCPAC Serial 00599, p. 4, para. 14.

Page 526
Arrival and withdrawal of 252d Air Group: *S.S.,* Vol. 83, pp. 452, 455.

Kolombangara air base and torpedoing of *Nankai Maru,* damage to *Uzuki* and *Ariake:* *S.S.,* Vol. 83, pp. 453–55; Alden, *U.S. Submarine Attacks During World War II,* p. 26. On December 17, *Bandung Maru* was en route to Munda when sunk by *Grouper* (Alden, *U.S. Submarine Attacks During World War II,* p. 24). The loss of eighteen antiaircraft guns and twenty-four large antiaircraft machineguns with this ship was described as "quite a shock" (*S.S.,* Vol. 83, p. 406). B-17 attacks on Rabaul resulted in damage to two ships each on December 10 and 25; on December 26 they sank one trans-

port and blew the bow off destroyer *Tachikaze* (*S.S.,* Vol. 83, p. 459, Vol. 28, p. 406).

Page 526
Cancellation of plan to beach *Patrol Boat 2:* *S.S.,* Vol. 83, p. 451.

Attempt at aerial resupply and restart of submarine transportation: *S.S.,* Vol. 83, pp. 448–50, Vol. 28, pp. 411, 414. According to the G-2 Daily Summary of the Americal Division for December 22 (300-2.6, RG 407, Box 5498), American observers spotted about forty parachutes in an open field about 3 miles southwest of Doma Cove. It was speculated that their location was unknown to the Japanese and they were strafed. This is the only record of the attempted supply drop I could locate.

Pages 526–27
Supply situation of 17th Army: *S.S.,* Vol. 28, pp. 302, 313–14, 318–20, 423–25, 475–76. About December 17 the chief of staff of the 17th Army informed Imperial Headquarters that units on Guadalcanal lost 50 percent of their effectiveness each month (Vol. 28, p. 296). A captured order from the 229th Infantry Regiment refers to emergency court-martial procedures against those caught stealing food with "drastic punishment." G-2 Combat Experience Report, Americal Division, Tab C (300-2, RG 407, Box 5473).

Page 528
Japanese concerns and activities late November to mid-December: *S.S.,* Vol. 28, pp. 307–9; 13th AF Hist., p. 161. The 8th Company, 124th Infantry mounted the November 30 attack. The Americal Division G-3 Journal for 1800, 30 November, to 1800, 1 December (300-3.2, Box 5508, RG 407), indicates that the 3d Battalion, 8th Marines "repulsed" an attack by "15–20" enemy soldiers about 2000. The activities of the raiding parties organized by the 38th Engineer Regiment are given considerable coverage in *S.S.,* Vol. 28, pp. 308–9. Two parties of one officer and four men each left on December 6. The party of Second Lieutenant Nakazawa made the successful attack of December 12. The party lead by Second Lieutenant Terazawa also claimed a successful attack, and both of these patrols returned between December 14 and 15. A third patrol lead by First Lieutenant Ono left December 15 and vanished. Probably three members of this patrol were killed on December 28 by soldiers of the Americal Division based on an entry on December 29 in the G-2 Daily Summary, Gua-

dalcanal, American Division, 7 Dec 42–14 Jan 43 (300-2.6, RG 407, Box 5499).

Page 529

Background to decision to take Mount Austen: The Army in the South Pacific, pp. 5–6, 98-USAFISPA-0.1; 13th AF Hist., p. 149; Miller, *Guadalcanal, The First Offensive,* pp. 232–33.

Page 529

Description of Mount Austen area: The basic source is Miller, *Guadalcanal: The First Offensive,* Maps X–XI and pp. 233–35, which give precise elevations of some heights. Also of interest is Col. Manley L. Curry to CMC 17 Dec 48.

Page 529

Patrols of Mount Austen and estimate of enemy intentions: Unit Rpts, 2–4, 132d Inf (300-INF(132)-0.9, RG 407, Box 5616.); Memo, Assit Div Cmdr American Div, G-3 Jnl File, American Div 15 Dec 42 (300-3.3, RG 407, Boxes 5513–18); 132d Inf Hist., p. 5 (300-INF(132)-0.1, RG 407, Box 5613).

General Sano releases supplies: *S.S.,* Vol. 28, p. 313.

Patch orders 132d to take Mount Austen: Open Memo No. 3, Headquarters, U.S. Forces in Cactus, 16 Dec 42, G-3 Jnl, American Div, 16 Dec 42.

Page 530

Background and plans of 132d Infantry: 132d Inf Hist., pp. 1–5; 132d Inf Opn Memo No. 3, 16 Dec 42, 132d Inf Msgs and Ords (300-INF(132)-0.12, RG 407, Box 5618); Task Force 62 War Diary 8, 10 Dec 42; History of 246th Field Artillery Battalion, 300-FA(246)-0.1, RG 407, Box 5594; Miller, *Guadalcanal: The First Offensive,* pp. 237–38. The majority of the 132d landed December 8 with the 1st Battalion following two days later. The final decision not to release the 2d Battalion for Colonel Nelson's use was not made until December 21. Msg, Asst Div Cmdr to CO 132d Inf, 1440, 132d Inf Jnl, 21 Dec (300-INF(132)-0.7, RG 407, Box 5624).

Page 530

Activities of December 17–18: Unit Rpts 5 & 6 (and overlays), 132d Inf; 132d Inf Msgs, 1100 & 1249, 18 Dec 42, 132d Inf Jnl; 132d Inf Hist., p. 5 (the dates in this source are in error, i.e., events of December 18 are given as December 17, etc.).

Page 530

December 19: Unit Rpt 7 (and overlay), 132d Inf; 132d Inf Hist., pp. 5–6 (again events of December 19 are given as December 18); Narrative of Operations, American Division, p. 4 (300-2, RG 407, Box 4573); G-3 Periodic Report, 15–31 December, American Division (300-3.1, RG 407, Box 5506); Miller, *Guadalcanal: The First Offensive,* p. 239. Details on the death of Lieutenant Colonel Wright are from Robert C. Muehrcke, editor, *Orchids in the Mud: Personal Accounts by Veterans of the 132d Infantry Regiment 1941–45* (Chicago: J. S. Printing, 1985), pp. 112–116 [hereafter Muehrcke, *Orchids in the Mud*]. Miller, *Guadalcanal: The First Offensive,* p. 239, incorrectly identifies Major Franco as a lieutenant colonel and the executive officer of the 3d Battalion. Franco was executive officer of the 1st Battalion and had to make his way forward to take command, which accounts for the delay.

Pages 530–31

Activities of December 20–23: Unit Rpts 8–11, 132d Inf (and overlays); 132d Inf Hist., p. 6; Msg Assist Div Cdr Amer Div to CO 132d Inf, 1440, 21 Dec 42, 132d Inf Jnl; CO 132d to CO 3d Bn 2000 23 Dec 42, 132d Inf Jnl 23 Dec 42.

Action on December 24: Unit Rpt 12, 132d Inf (and overlay); 132d Inf Hist., p. 6.

Page 531

Description of Gifu defenses: Amer Div Int Rpt Tab A; Captain Gerald H. Shea, "Lessons from Guadalcanal," *Infantry Journal,* July 1943, pp. 9–10; George, *Shots Fired in Anger,* pp. 70, 104–5, 315–20; Miller, *Guadalcanal: The First Offensive,* pp. 243–44. American sources say seventy-five pillboxes, but Miller, citing an interview with Lieutenant Colonel Stanley Larsen, says about forty-five. Miller also indicates there were no defenses on Hill 27, but George recounts finding cut fire lanes.

Pages 531–32

The Gifu's defenders: *S.S.,* Vol. 28, p. 475 and map p. 320. The total number of soldiers under Inagaki's command is uncertain, and the text reflects an estimate. Inagaki's battalion originally was probably about 600 strong. According to a captured document, the 124th Infantry had a total of 888 men in the Mount Austen area on December 8, of whom 227 were "sick." Some members of II/124 were in the Gifu, but probably not more than 200. G-2 Daily Summary, Guadalcanal, American Division, 11 Jan 43.

Page 532
Activities of December 25–27: Unit Rpts 13–15, 132d Inf; 132d Inf Hist., pp. 6–7; Msg CO 132d Inf to CO 1st Bn, 0725, 26 Dec 42, 132d Inf Jnl; Miller, *Guadalcanal: The First Offensive*, p. 245.

Page 532
Patrolling December 28–29: Unit Rpts 16–17, 132d Inf (and overlays); 132d Inf Hist., p. 7; 132d Inf Jnl 30 Dec 42.

Events of December 30 1942, to January 1, 1943: Unit Rpts 18–20, 132d Inf; 132d Inf. Hist., p. 7; 132d Inf FO No. 1, 30 Dec 42, 132d Inf Orders and Msgs; 132d Inf Jnl 1 Jan 43; Personal Experience Account of ACofS, G-3, Americal Division, p. 4 (300-3.0, Box 5506, RG 407).

Pages 532–33
Lieutenant Colonel George takes command of 132d Inf: 132d Inf Jnl 1 Jan 43; 132d Inf Hist., p. 7; Miller, *Guadalcanal: The First Offensive*, p. 249; Muehrcke, *Orchids in the Mud*, pp. 131–32. The 132d Inf Hist. and Miller say Nelson requested his own relief; Muehrcke quotes an individual who observed Nelson before and after the conference resulting in his relief and implies Nelson was removed for cause. Miller gives George's rank as colonel, but contemporary reports all list him as a lieutenant colonel. George had organized and commanded the Americal Division's unique jeep-mounted Mobile Combat Reconnaissance Squadron.

Page 533
Attack of January 2, 1943: Unit Rpt 21, 132d Inf. (and overlay); 132d Inf Hist., pp. 7–8; Miller, *Guadalcanal: The First Offensive*, pp. 250–51.

Pages 533–34
End of action at Gifu: Unit Rpts 22–23, 132d Inf.; 132d Inf. Hist., pp. 8–9.

Comments from Lieutenant Ko'o: *S.S.*, Vol. 28, pp. 476–77.

Page 534
Ugaki's appraisal of position of Imperial Navy with respect to proposed withdrawal: Ibid., pp. 426–27.

Page 534
Tsuji's comments to Hattori in November: Ibid., p. 420. Hattori feared the fall of Rabaul would follow the fall of Guadalcanal and was not sure a withdrawal was a practical possibility.

Page 534
Staff officer returns from Rabaul to Tokyo and Tsuji talks: Ibid., p. 421, Vol. 83, pp. 492–93. According to the latter source, in mid-November Commander Yuji Yamamoto of the operations department of the Navy Section approached Lieutenant Colonel Imoto in the Army Section and began informal discussion of a withdrawal from Guadalcanal.

Pages 534–35
Major Sejima study and attitudes at Imperial General Headquarters: Ibid., Vol. 28, pp. 272–73, 420–22.

Pages 535–36
The crisis over the shipping situation: Ibid., pp. 271–75.

Page 536
Features of discussion in late December: Ibid., p. 419.

Page 536
Reports of Commander Yamamoto and Major Hayashi: Ibid., Vol. 83, pp. 494–95.

Pages 536–37
Orders and events of December 12–16: Ibid., Vol. 28, pp. 290, 428–29, 432–33, Vol. 83, p. 495.

Pages 537–38
Colonel Sanada's trip to Rabaul: Ibid., Vol. 83, pp. 480–1, 493, 495, Vol. 28, pp. 288, 429–31, 436–37. For purposes of the war games at the 8th Area Army, it was assumed that the Allies could field 360 aircraft (160 B-17s, the rest other types) in New Guinea and the Solomons, which Japan could oppose with 190 in the Solomons. The most that could be achieved by Japan under this scenario was a temporary air superiority over Guadalcanal, and only if the Allies failed to reinforce the island from carriers or Espíritu Santo.

Page 538
Colonel Sanada's report and reaction: Ibid., Vol. 28, pp. 438–40, Vol. 83, pp. 495–96.

Pages 538–39
New plans worked out between December 27 and 29: Ibid., Vol. 83, p. 496–97, Vol. 28, pp. 440–41. The war game of December 27 showed only one-third or less of the planned force could be landed on Guadalcanal, while it was thought that the attack could not succeed without 70–80 percent of two divisions.

Page 539
Meetings with the Emperor on December 28 and 31: Ibid., Vol. 83, p. 497, Vol. 28, pp. 442–44.

CHAPTER 21

Pages 540–51
Delivery and contents of orders to headquarters at Truk and Rabaul: *S.S.,* Vol. 83, pp. 497–98, 500–2, *S.S.,* Vol. 28, p. 451. Imperial Headquarters sent Yamamoto Navy Section Instructions No. 184 on the "KE" Operation and parallel orders to the 8th Area Army. These directives officially discarded the Central Agreement of November 18.

Page 541
Agreement on "KE" Operation between the Combined Fleet and 8th Area Army: *S.S.,* Vol. 83, pp. 504–5; Vol. 28, pp. 458–59.

Program of feints: Ibid., Vol. 83, pp. 507, 510, 553.

Page 541
Strife over means of evacuation: Ibid., Vol. 28, p. 458, Vol. 83, pp. 503–04.

Page 541
Japanese anticipate great difficulty in evacuation operation: Ibid., Vol. 28, pp. 455, Vol. 83, p. 503; Agawa, *Reluctant Admiral,* p. 339.

Page 542
Japanese naval strength: *S.S.,* Vol. 83, p. 552, Vol. 28, p. 407. These figures are modified in

which contains the dispositions of all naval vessels in the Pacific; also of interest is COMSOPAC 090432 Jan 43 and 100352 Jan 43, Grey Book, pp. 1368–69. Eight of Halsey's destroyers and four elderly destroyer-minesweepers were organized into a pool for escorting supply ships and transports. According to the "Estimate of Situation, Solomons Islands" in the Grey Book, p. 1282, Halsey had forty-eight of the sixty-three available destroyers in the southern Pacific. The transfer of the old battleships *Maryland, Colorado, New Mexico,* and *Mississippi* to the South Pacific was to balance possible Japanese employment of capital ships in any renewed offensive based on the November example, and to offset the severe losses of heavy cruisers (CINCPAC 030521 Dec 42, Grey Book, p. 1180).

Pages 542–43
American air command arrangements and strength: Command File World War II, Location of United States Naval Aircraft, 28 January 1943 (Navy and Marine aircraft); Craven and Cate, *Guadalcanal to Saipan,* pp. 81, 86, 113; 13th AF Hist., pp. 105–06, 153, 166–70; Richard C. Knott, *Black Cat Raiders of WW II* (Annapolis, Md.: Nautical and Aviation Publishing Company of America, 1981), pp. 85–95; Sherrod, *History of Marine Corps Aviation,* pp. 119–127 and Appendix IX (unravels the complicated story of Marine squadron deployments to Guadalcanal during January). Mulcahy replaced Brigadier General Louis Woods on December 26.

Army Air Force aircraft allocations for the South Pacific ordered by the Joint Chiefs of Staff were not met as of December 30, 1942, as the following table shows:

Type	Authorized	Actually on hand	Difference
Heavy bombers	72	47	−25
Medium bombers	52	26	−26
Fighters	150	158	+8
	274	231	−43

(Graven and Cate, *Guadalcanal to Saipan,* p. 113, footnote.)

the text to reflect the actual rather than planned deployments for the "KE" Operation.

Page 542
American naval strength: The principal source is War Diary, Commander in Chief, United States Pacific Fleet, 25 January 1943,

By January 8, 1943, only nineteen of the original thirty-five B-17 crews remained with the 11th Bomb Group. The last of these crews were withdrawn on March 28 and the group received a well-deserved Presidential Unit Citation for its work during the Guadalcanal campaign. The figures for availability of the 13th Air Force on January 22 are from

COMSOPAC 271210 Jan 43, Grey Book, p. 1374. According to CINCPAC Serial 00599, p. 2, para. 6, and COMSOPAC 260612 Dec 42, Grey Book, p. 1189, the capacity of Guadalcanal to handle aircraft was limited by the gasoline storage facilities, so much so that Halsey sent eighteen B-17s, nine B-26s, and eight P-38s to MacArthur for temporary operations from SOWESPAC against Rabaul. On December 26 there were 161 aircraft of all types at Guadalcanal (CINCPAC Daily Summary, 26 Dec 42, Grey Book, p. 1258).

Page 543
Japanese air strength: *S.S.*, Vol. 83, pp. 500, 505–6, 540, Vol. 28, p. 459. These sources provide conflicting figures: Vol. 83, p. 500, says planned commitment of Navy aircraft was 190 and Army aircraft was 164, whereas pp. 505–6 says the Navy total was 212 and the Army total was 100. This later set of numbers is used because these were recorded nearer to the start of the "KE" Operation; they also agree with Vol. 28, p. 459. Figures for the R Area Air Force are from Vol. 83, p. 537.

Page 543
Imperial Army estimate of Allied air strength: Ibid., Vol. 28, p. 463.

Information on the strength of the 5th Air Force on New Guinea: Birdsall, *Flying Buccaneers,* pp. 49–50; Kenn C. Rust, *Fifth Air Force Story* (Temple City, Calif.: Historical Aviation Album, 1973), p. 8. According to these sources the 5th Air Force possessed about 537 aircraft of which "no more than" 350 were operational. Only the fifty-five B-17s and sixty B-24s of the 43d and 90th Bomb Groups respectively could reach Rabaul and the Solomons, but because of the programs of maintenance and modification and the daily reconnaissance demands only twenty-seven to twenty-nine of these were available for strikes.

American ground organization and strength: Miller, *Guadalcanal: The First Offensive,* p. 218 (for activation of XIV Corps Headquarters); Strength Reports, Headquarters, XIV Corps, 320.2 (1-7-43), Subject: Strength Report (300-1.17, Box 5472, RG 407); COMSOPAC to CINCPAC 011136 Jan 43, Grey Book, p. 1211. Miller points out that as late as February 1, the XIV Corps Headquarters numbered only eleven officers and two enlisted men.

Pages 543–44
17th Army strength and equipment: *S.S.,*

Vol. 28, attached table 1 for figures as of November 20, 1942. The data on available artillery is from Vol. 28, p. 469. The American artillery figures are based upon table of organization strengths (twelve guns per battalion), which, so far as this writer can ascertain, were met in all cases. Each of the divisions deployed on Guadalcanal had four battalions of artillery, and under XIV Corps control were the 97th Field Artillery Battalion (pack mule), a separate battery of three 155mm guns (Battery F, 244th Coast Artillery Regiment), a separate battery of 155mm howitzers (Battery A, 1st Amphibious Corps), and one battery with British 25-pounder field howitzers (Provisional Battery K, 246th Field Artillery Battalion, originally attached to the separate 147th Infantry Regiment). Of this total of 167 weapons, the equivalent of one battalion was split between Tulagi and Koli Point. Not included in these figures are antiaircraft and coast defense pieces. Sources: Stanton, *Order of Battle U.S. Army World War II,* pp. 29–31; 13 Dec Artillery Strength, Strength Reports—New Caledonia and Guadalcanal—American Division, 1 Jun 42–11 Mar 43, 300-1.17; Miller, *Guadalcanal: The First Offensive,* p. 174 and Appendix E.

Pages 544–46
Intelligence gathering and analysis: Radio Intelligence December 1942, SRH-0136, pp. 11, 18–19, 67, 72, 79; Radio Intelligence January 1943, SRH-036, pp. 2–5, 8–11, 14–15, 17, 18, 21–22, 23–26, 30, 33, 35–36, 39, 43, 59–61, 63, 66–68, 71–72, 74, 76, 79, 90, 125, 145–51, 390–94, 402–07, 431–34, 520; CINCPAC Daily Summaries for November 30, December 1, 3, 5–6, 9, 12–13, 15, 20–22, 27–30, and January 1–4, 7, 14, 17, 19, 22, 24–31, Grey Book, pp. 1179, 1212, 1214–1216, 1246–48, 1250, 1253–54, 1259–68, 1271, 1276, 1338, 1340, 1342, 1349–56; COMINCH to CINCPAC 102220 Dec 42, ONI Intelligence Bulletin Number One, Grey Book, p. 1198; COMSOPAC 310836 Dec 42, Grey Book, p. 1208; Van Der Rhoer, *Deadly Magic,* p. 132. According to SRH-036, p. 229, a decrypted dispatch showed that *Argonaut* was sunk by *Maikaze.*

Pages 547–48
Reinforcement run of January 2, 1943: *S.S.,* Vol. 83, pp. 511–12, Vol. 28, p. 484, and Ito and Pineau, *The End of the Imperial Japanese Navy,* p. 80, for Japanese account; intelligence aspects, SRH-036, p. 1; air action from VMSB-233 War Diary, 2 Jan 43; Commander in Chief Pacific Fleet, Pac-90-wb, A16-3/SOL, Serial 00599, 9 March 1943,

Subject: Solomons Islands Campaign . . . , pp. 5–6, paras. 21, 23 [hereafter CINCPAC Serial 00599]. Loss of B-26: History of 70th Bombardment Squadron (Medium), p. 8, Reel A0560, p. 0296, AFHC. On January 7, two B-26s from the 69th Bombardment Squadron were shot down on a mission to Munda. Historical Record of the 69th Bombardment Squadron (Medium) from January 1942 to July 1, 1943, p. 12, Reel A0558, p. 1242, AFHC.

PT boat participation: Bunkley, *At Close Quarters*, p. 99. The organization of the Reinforcement Unit was as follows:

SCREEN

Naganami, Kawakaze, Suzukaze, Makinami, Arashi

TRANSPORTS

Oyashio, Kuroshio, Kagero, Isonami, Ikazuchi

Pages 547–49

Ainsworth's bombardment of Munda: Basic sources are CINCPAC Serial 00599, pp. 7–12, paras. 26–62, and Oliver A. Gillespie, *Official History of New Zealand in the World War 1939–45, The Pacific* (Wellington, New Zealand: War History Branch, Department of Internal Affairs, 1952), p. 241 [hereafter Gillespie, *The Pacific*]. Also consulted were TF 67 to COMSOPAC 050405 Jan 43, Grey Book, p. 1360 (quote from Captain Mannergh); *S.S.*, Vol. 83, pp. 527–29. Information on the VT fuze is from Friedman, *U.S. Naval Weapons*, p. 88.

Pages 549–50

Reinforcement run of January 10: *S.S.*, Vol. 83, pp. 512–13; intelligence aspects, SRH-036, pp. 2, 48; PT activities, Commander Motor Torpedo Boat Flotilla and Base Tulagi, 13 January 1943, Subject: Report of Motor Torpedo Boat Activities on the night of 10–11 January 1943, local date (Enclosure E to CINCPAC Serial 00618); losses on *Hatsukaze* from decrypted dispatch in SRH-036, p. 265. Organization of the Reinforcement Unit was as follows:

SCREEN

Kawakaze, Kuroshio, Hatsukaze, Tokitsukaze

TRANSPORTS

Arashi, Asashio, Oshio, Makinami

Page 550

Patch's information sources: 25th Div Opns

Rpt, p. 15; Informal Report on Combat Operations, XIV Corps, 15 Sep 43, Tab A, p. 2 (214-0, RG 407, Box 4620). Also of importance is Annex No. 2 to Field Order No. 1, Headquarters, 25th Inf Div, 8 Jan 43.

Pages 550, 552

General Patch's plans: Headquarters XIV Corps, 5 Jan 1943, Subject: Letter of Instructions, in Miller, *Guadalcanal: The First Offensive*, Appendix B.

Page 552

Biographical data on Major General Collins: Miller, *Guadalcanal: The First Offensive*, p. 255.

Plans of 25th Division: 25th Div Opns Rpt, pp. 4–7, 25.

Pages 552–53

Logistical support of the XIV Corps offensive: 25th Div Opns Rpt, pp. 17, 19–20, 31, 43–44, 97–98, 113–14, 148, 154, 161; 13th AF Hist., p. 154.

Patch contemplates then discards amphibious flanking movement: COMSOPAC to CINCPAC, COMINCH 011136 Jan 43, Grey Book p. 1211; Notes on Noumea conference 23 January, Grey Book, p. 1343. Patch also gave a shortage of landing craft as a reason for his decision.

Page 553

Japanese prepare to receive attack: *S.S.*, Vol. 28, pp. 470–71.

Page 553

Plans of the 27th Infantry Regiment: 25th Div Opns, pp. 25–26.

Page 554

Operations of 1st Battalion, 27th Infantry on January 10 and artillery bombardment: 25th Div Opns Rpt, pp. 8, 27, 30–31, 39, 136, 139; After Action Report, Guadalcanal, 25th Division Artillery, 1 Jan–10 Feb 43, p. 3 (325-ART-0.3, RG 407, Box 8055); 13th AF Hist., p. 153; 2d Mar Div D-3 Periodic Report 10 Jan 43, Box 5, File A8-4.

Page 554

Operations of 3d Battalion, 27th Infantry on January 10–11: 25th Div Opns Rpt, pp. 27, 32–36; Activities of the 3d Battalion, 27th Infantry for the Period Jan 10–27, 1943, pp. 1–3 (325-INF(27)-7-0.3., RG 407, Box 8134).

Pages 554–56

Operations of 2d Battalion, 27th Infantry on

January 11–13: 25th Div Opns Rpt, pp. 27–28, 38, 46.

Pages 556–57
Attack of 2d Marine Division: Basic sources are the 2d Marine Division D-3 Periodic Reports 10–20 Jan 1943, Box 5, File A8-4, and D-2 Periodic Reports for the same dates, Box 5, file A8-1. Other Marine sources are 6th Marine Regiment, Report of Operations, Guadalcanal, Box 6, File A18-2; 3d Battalion, 6th Marines, Record of Events Guadalcanal, Box 6, File A20-1; 8th Marine Regiment, Unit Report, Guadalcanal, Box 6, File A24-2.

Japanese dispositions: *S.S.,* Vol. 28, p. 474 (map).

Japanese account of coastal fighting: Ibid., pp. 480–82, 501–5.

Quotation of Japanese officer, January 17: Translations of Captured Enemy Documents (98-USF2-2.9, RG 407, Box 1622).

Japanese losses as reported by 2d Marine Division: XIV Corps, G-2 Summary, 19 Jan 43, p. 3 (214-2.6, RG 407).

CHAPTER 22

Page 559
17th Army assesses situation: *S.S.,* Vol. 28, p. 472.

Pages 559–60
January 14 run of Reinforcement Unit: Ibid., pp. 459–62 for background on Lieutenant Colonel Imoto's mission and Yano Battalion; Vol. 83, pp. 513–14, for Imperial Navy role. American air participation and radio intelligence from VMF-121 War Diary, 15 Jan 43, Narrative History of 12th Fighter Squadron, 22 Mar 45, Reel A0722, AFHC, and SRH-036, pp. 301–4. Radio intelligence provided a general warning of an impending run, but no direct details. The 6th Air Division provided morning air cover for the Reinforcement Unit.

Page 560
Lieutenant Colonel Imoto marches to 17th Army Headquarters: *S.S.,* Vol. 28, pp. 462, 485–86.

Pages 560–61
Imoto delivers orders and response at 17th Army Headquarters: Ibid., pp. 487–90; Griffith, *Battle of Guadalcanal,* pp. 238–40. Griffith's narrative profits greatly from correspondence with Lieutenant Colonel Imoto, who added many details concerning these events, from which the direct quotes are taken.

Pages 561–62
Delivery of orders to 2d and 38th Divisions: *S.S.,* Vol. 28, pp. 492–94.

Page 562
Plans of 17th Army for the withdrawal: Ibid., pp. 506–10.

Page 562
1st Ship Engineers begin withdrawal: Ibid., p. 514.

Pages 562–63
The capture of the Sea Horse: American unit activities from 25th Div Opns Rpt, pp. 69–77, 100–1. Japanese participation from *S.S.,* Vol. 28, pp. 320 (map), 477, 496, 500.

Page 563
35th Infantry report of enemy casualties: 35th Infantry Activities, January 9–26, 1943, S-2 Periodic Reports, 35th Inf (325-INF(35)-2.1, RG 407, Box 8164). This later report included seventy-six Japanese described as killed by artillery or mortars. In addition, the 1st and 3d Battalions captured seventeen.

Pages 563–64
Initial deployment and orders for 2d Battalion, 35th Infantry: 25th Div Opns Rpt, pp. 79–80, 97, 102.

Page 564
Operations on January 10–12: Ibid., p. 80; 35th Inf Unit Jnl & File 12 Jan 43 (325-INF(35)-0.7, RG 407, Box 8136).

Page 564
Events of January 13–14: 25th Div Opns Rpt, p. 81; 35th Inf Unit Jnl 13–14 Jan 43; *S.S.,* Vol. 28, pp. 477–78.

Pages 564–65
Attack of January 15 and relief of Lieutenant Colonel Peters: 25th Div Opns Rpt, pp. 81–83; 35th Inf Unit Rpt 16 Jan; Miller, *Guadalcanal: The First Offensive,* pp. 295–96. Contemporary reports show Larsen as a major, not a lieutenant colonel as reported by Miller; see, for example, 35th Inf Unit Jnl & File 19 Jan 43.

Page 565
Surrender broadcasts of January 16–17; Captain John A. Burden, "Report of Broadcast

propaganda experiment from Hills 43, 44 and 32," in Americal Div G-2 Jnl Rpts 19 Jan 43 (300-2.3, RG 407, Box 5481); 25th Div Opns Rpt, p. 83, 87.

Page 565
Bombardment of January 17: 25th Div Opns Rpt, pp. 84, 87, 92–94; 64th FA Bn Hist Jan–Dec 43, pp. 2–5 (325-FA(64)-0.1, RG 407, Box 8102).

Pages 565–66
Actions on January 18–21: 25th Div Opns Rpt, pp. 84–85.

Page 566
Tank attack at the Gifu: Ibid., pp. 85–87, 102–3; 25th Reconnaissance Troop Mechanized, Activation to July 7, 1943, pp. 9–10 (325-CAV-0.1, RG 407, Box 8097); 25th Division G-3 Jnl & File 23 Jan 43, entry 28 (325-3.2, 8036–37, Boxes RG 407).

Page 566
Events of January 23: 25th Div Opns Rpt, pp. 85–86; and Miller, *Guadalcanal: The First Offensive,* p. 305 (citing an interview with Major Larsen).

Pages 566–67
Casualties and captured material at the Gifu: 25th Div Opns Rpt, p. 88.

Total claims of 35th Infantry: 35th Infantry Activities, January 9–26, 1943, S-2 Periodic Reports, 35th Inf (325-INF(35)-2.1, RG 407, Box 8164).

Pages 567–68
Major Nishiyama's account: *S.S.,* Vol. 28, pp. 478–80. Descriptions of mop-up operations of encircled Japanese detachments are found in 25th Div Opns Rpt, pp. 74, 77, 105–6. Basically these consisted of trail blocks and patrols.

Page 568
General Patch's plans: XIV Corps Field Order No. 1, 16 January 1943, reprinted as Appendix C, Miller, *Guadalcanal: The First Offensive;* 25th Div Opns Rpt, p. 9. Patch's order merely stated the Americal Division would detail one infantry regiment to the 2d Marine Division, and the 182d Infantry was selected.

Page 568
25th Division plans: 25th Div Opns Rpt, p. 9.

Pages 568–69
Operations of 161st Infantry: Ibid., p. 106–7.

Pages 569–70
Advance of 27th Infantry and change of plans January 22: Ibid., pp. 9–10, 49–50, 53, 55, 58–59, 63, 136.

Page 570
Japanese plans disrupted: *S.S.,* Vol. 28, pp. 515–17.

Pages 570
Advance to Kokumbona January 23: 25th Div Opns Rpt, pp. 50–51, 53, 55–56, 59.

Pages 570–71
Attack of CAM Division January 22–24: 2d Marine Division, D-3 Periodic Reports from 22–24 Jan 1943, Box 5, File A8-4, and D-2 Periodic Reports for same dates, Box 5, File A8-1.

Maruyama reports January 22 strength of 4th and 16th Infantry Regiments: *S.S.,* Vol. 28, p. 514.

Pages 570–71
Junction of 25th and CAM Divisions: 25th Div Opns Rpt, pp. 51, 56, 59.

Page 571
Description of the terrain beyond Kokumbona: Ibid., p. 108.

Pages 571–72
25th Division directed to prepare to defend against new Japanese offensive aimed at the airfields: Ibid., p. 10.

Page 572
Japanese withdrawal and rear-guard fighting January 25 to February 1: *S.S.,* Vol. 28, 519–31.

Account from advancing American units: 2d Marine Division, D-3 Periodic Reports from 26–30 Jan 1943, Box 5, File A8-4, and D-2 Periodic Reports for same dates, Box 5, File A8-1; 147th Infantry Regiment History, 1942–45, pp. 12–15 (INRG-147-0.1, RG 407, Box 21171).

Page 572
Bombardment by *Wilson:* U.S.S. *Wilson,* Serial None, February 10, 1943, Subject: Report of action against enemy forces on Guadalcanal, January 31, 1943, Enclosure to Commander in Chief Pacific Fleet, Pac-90-wb, Serial 00712, April 17, 1943, Subject: Solomons Islands Campaign—Fall of Guadalcanal, period 25 January to 10 February 1943 [hereafter CINCPAC Serial 00712].

Pages 572–73

Bombardment of Kolumbangara: Primary source is Commander in Chief Pacific Fleet, Pac-90-1h, Serial 00618, March 19, 1943, Subject: Solomons Islands Campaign, from 6 January 1943 through Villa Bombardment, paras. 22–40 [hereafter CINCPAC Serial 00618]; SRH-036, pp. 6–7, 58, for radio intelligence role. Japanese information from *S.S.,* Vol. 83, pp. 540–42.

Pages 573–74

Plans for air superiority campaign and night bombing effort: *S.S.,* Vol. 28, pp. 462–63, 465, Vol. 83, pp. 538–40, 549–50. According to Vol. 83, pp. 549–50, the night raids cost two Bettys. A day raid to Port Moresby on January 20 by twenty-three Bettys and forty-three Zeros cost one of the latter.

Bombing of party including Secretary Knox and Admiral Nimitz: Potter, *Nimitz,* pp. 215–16.

Page 574

Raid of January 25: *S.S.,* Vol. 83, p. 550; Vol. 28, p. 465. American participation: SENAV Guad to COMAIRSOPAC 250639 Jan 43, Grey Book, p. 1372; VMF-121 War Diary 25 Jan 43.

Page 574

Raid of January 27: *S.S.,* Vol. 28, p. 562, and Vol. 83, p. 551, for 6th Air Division activities. The Japanese organization for this strike was as follows:

with the colorful details from Hashimoto); SRH-036, pp. 5–6, 43–44, 46, 77–78 (for contribution of radio intelligence); Commander Naval Base, Cactus, A16-3, Serial 0068, February 5, 1943, Subject: HMNZS KIWI and MOA—Submarine Action, Night of 29–30 January 1943, and Halsey, *Admiral Halsey's Story,* pp. 148–49 (for story of *Kiwi* and *Moa,* with the colorful details from Halsey); Gillespie, *The Pacific,* p. 243 (shows one dead on *Moa*); CINCPAC Serial 00712, para. 42, p. 10; Van Der Rhoer, *Deadly Magic,* p. 130, and Holmes, *Double Edged Secrets,* p. 124 (indicate the captured secret documents were of greater use retrospectively than prospectively, but Layton, Pineau, and Costello, *And I Was There,* p. 473, says the documents greatly assisted in keeping track of additive groups in changes in JN-25). The last-named source identifies the submarine as *I-23,* one of the large number of small errors that characterize this work.

CHAPTER 23

Pages 577–78

Backround to Battle of Rennell Island: CINCPAC Serial 00712, p. 3–4, para. 5–8. Admiral Halsey basically deployed all his major units except the four old and slow battleships of Battleship Division 4 (*Maryland,* and *Colorado*) and Battleship Division 3 (*New Mexico* and *Mississippi*).

Strike Leader:	Lt. Col. Shuichi Okamoto
Scouting element:	2 Mitsubishi Ki. 46, Type 100 Dinah, Headquarters reconnaissance planes of the 76th Independent Chutai
Bombers:	9 Nakajima Ki. 48 Type 99 Lilly light bombers of the 45th Sentai
Fighters:	74 Nakajima Ki. 43 Type 1 Oscars
	36 from the 1st Sentai
	33 from the 11th Sentai
	5 from the Headquarters of the 12th Air Wing

Vol. 83 gives total number of Oscars participating in the raid as fifty-nine. American participation: SENAV Guad to COMAIRSOPAC 280838 Jan 43, Grey book, p. 1374.

6th Air Division takes over responsibility for air superiority campaign: *S.S.,* Vol. 83, p. 551.

Pages 575–76

Sinking of *I-1:* Ibid., pp. 522–23, and Hashimoto, *Sunk,* pp. 63–66 (for Japanese side,

Admiral King's signal: COMINCH to CINCPAC info COMSOPAC 311405 Jan 43, Grey Book, p. 1376.

Page 578

Giffen as favorite of King: Buell, *Master of Sea Power,* p. 147.

Giffen's attitudes toward Halsey's uniform directives: Task Force 18 War Diary 5, 10 Jan 43.

"Cactus Striking Force": This unit was created by Halsey on January 10 to be based at Guadalcanal with the mission of coordinating with PT boats and small craft against the Japanese destroyer and submarine transportation efforts and to conduct bombardments. It was nominally composed of destroyers *Balch, Nicholas, Radford, O'Bannon,* and *Fletcher.* COMSOPAC 100352 Jan 43, COMSOPAC to CTF 67 100042 Jan 43, Grey Book, p. 1369.

Pages 578-79
American account of the action the night of January 29-30: Drawn from CINCPAC Serial 00712; Commander Task Force 18, A16-3/FE24-18, Serial 0010, 19 February 1943, Subject: Action Report—Task Force 18, January 29-30, 1943, pp. 1-5 [hereafter CTF 18 Serial 0010]; Commander Cruiser Division 12, FB3-12/A1603, Serial 001, February 2, 1943; U.S.S. *Chicago,* Secret Ltr., February 3, 1943, Subject: Preliminary report of action of 29 and 30 January, 1943, with Japanese aircraft off Guadalcanal Island, pp. 1-3 [hereafter *Chicago* 3 Feb 43]; U.S.S. *Louisville,* CA28/A16-3, Serial 011, February 3, 1943, Subject: Japanese Air Attack of January 29, 1943, Report of; U.S.S. *Wichita,* CA45/A16-3/A9, Serial 002, 1 February 1943; U.S.S. *Columbia,* CL56/A16-3, Serial 005, January 31, 1943, Subject: Night Anti-Aircraft Action . . .; U.S.S. *Cleveland,* Serial 007, February 1, 1943; U.S.S. *LaVallette,* DD448/A16-3/tg, Serial 0-6, February 6, 1943, Subject: Action Report . . . [hereafter *LaVallette* Serial 0-6]; U.S.S. *Waller,* Serial CF0006, February 14, 1943.

Japanese account of the action the night January 29-30: Drawn from *S.S.,* Vol. 83, pp. 542-44. Although it is possible that the Betty that crashed off *Chicago*'s port bow was the other plane that "failed to return," it seems far more likely that it was Higai's, as his fellow pilots observed his loss and claimed he crashed an enemy ship, which would be an easy mistake to make in these circumstances and close to what he actually did.

Pages 579-81
The American account of the day action of January 30: Drawn from CTF 18, Serial 0010, pp. 6-7; *Chicago* 3 Feb 43, pp. 3-5; CINCPAC Serial 00712, p. 9, para. 37; U.S.S. *Enterprise,* Serial 003, February 3, 1943; SRH-036, pp. 86-87, 89, 639, 642, 651; Charles McMurtry, "Heroic Fight Made by Doomed Chicago," *New York Times,* February 21, 1943, p. 4; U.S.S. *LaVallette,* DD448/A16-3/tg, Serial 0-7, February 8, 1943, Subject: Action Report; U.S.S. *Navajo* Serial 07, January 30, 1943; U.S.S. *Waller,* Serial 0005, February 14, 1943.

Japanese account of the day action of January 30: *S.S.,* Vol. 83, pp. 544-45.

Page 581
Nimitz's reaction to loss of *Chicago:* CINCPAC Serial 00712, pp. 16-17, para. 82-83; Potter, *Nimitz,* p. 219.

Page 582
Warning of sailing of Advanced Force: SRH-036, pp. 23, 90.

Delay in start of "KE" Operation: *S.S.,* Vol. 83, p. 555.

Page 582
Organization and command of the Reinforcement Unit: Ibid., pp. 534-36, 551, Vol. 28, pp. 466-67, 562-64. Vol. 83 notes Hashimoto had established a good reputation in his previous work in the Reinforcement Unit and that Commander Ohmae belived that Admiral Kusaka expressly asked for Hashimoto as he had great confidence in him. Technically, *Sendai* was flagship of Desron 3 and part of the Reinforcement Unit, but she was sent to Kavieng with the heavy cruisers. Apparently, *Swordfish* was not aware that she had torpedoed *Akizuki* (U.S.S. *Swordfish,* SS-193, Seventh War Patrol Report).

Page 582
Organization and role of aviation units: *S.S.,* Vol. 83, pp. 537-38, Vol. 28, pp. 562-63. The establishment of the R Area Air Force on 1 February was:

Kamikawa Maru:	7 Type 0 (Jake) reconnaissance planes
	3 Type 0 (Pete) observation planes
Kunikawa Maru:	12 Type 0 (Pete) observation planes
Sanyo Maru:	5 Type 0 (Jake) reconnaissance planes
	5 Type 0 (Pete) observation planes
802d Air Group:	12 Type 0 (Rufe) float fighters
958th Air Group:	16 Type 0 (Pete) observation planes
Total:	60 (12 Jakes, 12 Rufes, 36 Petes)

In addition to these aircraft, six Type 94 reconnaissance planes were contributed by *Suyuza* and *Sendai* and another three came from the Advanced Force.

Occupation of the Russell Islands: *S.S.,* Vol. 83, p. 538, Vol. 28, p. 462. The ships detailed for this run were *Tokitsukaze, Kuroshio, Shirayuki, Urakaze, Hamakaze,* and *Kawakaze.*

Pages 582–83

B-17 attacks on Shortland and Munda attack: VMSB-234 War Diary, 1 Feb 43; Grey Book, Summary 31 Jan 43, p. 1356; *S.S.,* Vol. 28, p. 563. In preparation for the "KE" Operation the Japanese positioned at Buin a large force of Zeros from the 204th, 253d, and 582d Air Groups and *Zuikaku.* The 582d Air Group also included a Val unit. At the same time the 252d Air Group with Zeros was deployed to Shortland. The interception of the B-17s on February 1 included five Zeros of the 253d Air Group, twelve from the 204th, fourteen of the 582d, and seventeen of the 252d (*S.S.,* Vol. 83, p. 557).

Page 583

"Air Superiority" attack on Guadalcanal: *S.S.,* Vol. 28, p. 563, Vol. 83, p. 558. The loss of the Oscar over or in connection with the strike at Guadalcanal is inferred from loss information supplied to the author by Mr. John Lundstrom and Mr. James Sawruk.

Planning and organization of Marovovo task force: Gavan Personal Experience Account, p. 5, 300-3.0 and 132d Infantry Regimental History, pp. 10–11. The task force commander was Lieutenant Colonel Alexander George, and the Units were 2d Battalion, 132d Infantry; Anti-Tank Company, 132d Infantry; Company M, 132d Infantry (less .50 caliber machinegun platoon); one platoon, Company K, 132d Infantry; Battery F, 10th Marines; one platoon, 65th Engineers; and detachments of medical, communications, and service personnel.

Pages 583, 585

Sinking of *DeHaven* and attack on *Nicholas:* U.S.S. *DeHaven,* A16-3(2) (DD469)—Loss of, February 5, 1943; CINCPAC Serial 00712, pp. 9–11, 20–21, paras. 39–49, 101, 105; U.S.S. *Nicholas,* A16-3/A9, Serial No. 04, February 3, 1943; *New York Times,* February 24, 1943, p. 8; Grey Book, Summary 1 Feb 43, p. 1385; VMF-112, -122 War Diaries, 1 Feb 43; *S.S.,* Vol. 83, p. 558. The Japanese strike group originally had fifteen Vals of the 582d Air Group, but two returned early. The

escort comprised nineteen Zeros from *Zuikaku* and twenty-one from the 582d Air Group.

Pages 585–86

Reinforcement Unit on first evacuation run: *S.S.,* Vol. 83, pp. 556–61. Of the twenty-one destroyers at Shortland, only *Yugure* did not participate in this run.

Page 586

Air attacks on Reinforcement Unit February 1: VMSB-131, -234, VGS-11, -12, -16 War Diaries 1 Feb 43; SENAV Guad to CO-MAIRSOPAC, 040845 Feb 43, Grey Book, p. 1417. The VMSB-131 War Diary shows that two TBFs that returned were scrapped.

Pages 586–87

Attack by PT boats: Commander Motor Torpedo Boat Flotilla One, Serial 15, 2 February 1943, Subject: Report of Motor Torpedo Boat Activities on the Night of 1–2 February 1943; Johnson, *United States PT-Boats of World War II,* p. 112. Once again Johnson contains additional information drawn from interviews.

17th Army gathers at boarding points: *S.S.,* Vol. 28, pp. 537–38.

"a burning inferno of gasoline-soaked mahogany": Johnson, *United States PT-Boats of World War II,* p. 112.

Page 587

Briscoe's "Cactus Striking Force": CINC-PAC Serial 00712, pp. 11–12, paras. 51–56.

Pages 587–88

Boarding of first lift: *S.S.,* Vol. 28, p. 538.

Descriptions of conditions of evacuated members of the 17th Army: *S.S.,* Vol. 83, pp. 560–61; Agawa, *Reluctant Admiral,* p. 338.

Page 588

Loss of *Makikumo: S.S.,* Vol. 83, p. 560; Johnson, *United States PT-Boats of World War II,* p. 112. The Japanese attribute the loss of *Makikumo* to mines, but Johnson argues that Lieutenant Faulkner's torpedoes did her in.

Page 589

17th Army evaluates first run, orders fire ruse, and receives order of 8th Area Army: *S.S.,* Vol. 28, pp. 539–40.

Page 589

Marovovo Task Force and skirmish outside Titi: 132d Infantry Regiment Hist., pp. 11–

12; Muehrcke, *Orchids in the Mud,* p. 175; *S.S.,* Vol. 28, p. 541. Muehrcke reports the loss of two men of the 132d on February 5, but other sources say the 3d.

Page 589
Situation on February 3 along north coast: *S.S.,* Vol. 28, p. 539; 147th Infantry, Unit Report 3 Feb 43, Box 6, file A28-1, MCHC.

Matsuda's plans: *S.S.,* Vol. 28, p. 545.

Page 589–90
Orders to 161st Infantry and position of 147th Infantry: 25th Div Rpt Opns, p. 108.

Page 590
Japanese activities on Guadalcanal on February 4: *S.S.,* Vol. 28, pp. 546–48.

Pages 590–91
Background and preparations for second evacuation run: Ibid., Vol. 83, pp. 562–63.

Pages 591–92
Japanese account of second evacuation run: Ibid., pp. 562–66, Vol. 28, pp. 542–43.

Air attacks on second evacuation run: VMSB-233, -234, VGS-11, -12, -16, War Diaries 4 Feb 43.

Page 592
Scene on arrival at Bougainville: *S.S.,* Vol. 28, p. 543. The specific debarkation point on Bougainville is reported as Eleventa, but this writer could not identify this location.

Page 592
Matsuda's movements and orders February 5: Ibid., pp. 549–51, 468.

Pages 592–93
Marovovo Task Force: 132d Infantry Regiment Hist., p. 12.

Page 593
161st Infantry: 25th Div Rpt Opns, p. 109.

Colonel Dalton's description of mules: Ibid., p. 118.

Matsuda on February 5 and 6: *S.S.,* Vol. 28, pp. 551–53.

Page 593
17th Army Headquarters and Colonel Konuma: *S.S.,* Vol. 28, pp. 544, 556–57.

Page 593
Patch's assessment of situation: CG Cactus to COMSOPAC 081115 Feb 43, Grey Book, p. 1419.

Action of 161st Infantry: 25th Div Rpt Opns, p. 109.

Pages 593–94
Marovovo Task Force: 132d Infantry Regiment Hist., p. 12.

Page 594
Matsuda directs activities of February 7: *S.S.* Vol. 28, pp. 557–58, 560.

Pages 594–95
Reinforcement Unit on third evacuation run: Ibid., Vol. 83, pp. 566–68. Losses on *Isokaze* from Dull, *Battle History of the Imperial Japanese Navy,* p. 268. On Yamamoto's order, Admiral Kondo led Crudivs 4 and 5, *Nagara, Hatsuyuki, Onami,* and *Shigure* south.

Air attacks on third evacuation run: VMSB-144, 234, VGS-11, -12, -16, War Diaries 7 Feb 43.

Page 595
Boarding of Matsuda's command: *S.S.,* Vol. 28, p. 560.

Page 595
Arrival of last lift at Bougainville: Ibid., pp. 560–61.

Number of evacuees: Ibid., Vol. 83, pp. 568–69 (giving Imperial Navy figures as 12,-805), Vol. 28, pp. 569–70.

Page 595
Tanabe message to Imperial General Headquarters: Ibid., Vol. 28, p. 543.

Pages 595–96
Naval and air losses: Drawn from text. The statistics on the 12th Air Wing are from *S.S.,* Vol. 28, p. 565.

Page 596
Japanese analysis of "KE" Operation: *S.S.,* Vol. 83, pp. 569–70.

Page 596
Link-up of Marovovo Task Force and 161st Infantry February 8 and 9: 132d Infantry Regiment Hist., pp. 12–13; 25th Div Rpt Opns, p. 109–10. Both the 132d and the 161st Infantry claim to have reached Tenaru first.

Page 597
Last-known Japanese soldier surrenders: McMillan, *Old Breed,* p. 140.

Hyukatake's judgment on final American op-
ertions: Miller, *Guadalcanal: The First Offensive.* p. 349.

Page 597
Admiral Nimitz's assessment: CINCPAC Serial 00712, para. 81, p. 16.

CHAPTER 24

Page 599
Japanese critique of strategy: Saburo Hayashi
in collaboration with Alvin D. Coox, *Kogun:
The Japanese Army in the Pacific War* (Quantico, Va.: Marine Corps Association, 1959),
p. 65.

"the language of perimeter . . .": Alvin Coox,
"The Effectiveness of the Japanese Military
Establishment in the Second World War," in
*Military Effectiveness, Vol. III, The Second
World War,* edited by Allan R. Millett and
Williamson Murray (Boston: Allen & Unwin,
1988), p. 28 [hereafter Coox, "Effectiveness
of the Japanese Military Establishment in the
Second World War"].

Nimitz releases carrier aviators: John B,
Lundstrom, *The First Team* (Annapolis,
Md.: Naval Institute Press, 1984), p. 436.

Pages 600–601
Dyer on logistics: Dyer, *Amphibians Came to
Conquer,* Vol. I, pp. 401, 405–6, 419.

Pages 601–2
American and Australian losses: Carriers
Wasp, Hornet; heavy cruisers *Quincy, Vin-
cennes, Astoria,* HMAS *Canberra, Northamp-
ton, Chicago;* light cruisers *Atlanta, Juneau;*
destroyers *Tucker, Jarvis, Blue, O'Brien,
Duncan, Meredith, Porter, Barton, Laffey,
Cushing, Monssen, Walke, Preston, Benham,
DeHaven;* transport *George F. Elliot;* de-
stroyer conversions *Colhoun, Little, Gregory.*

Japanese losses: Carrier *Ryujo;* battleships
Hiei, Kirishima; heavy cruisers *Kako,
Furutaka, Kinugasa;* light cruiser *Yura;* de-
stroyers *Mutsuki, Asagiri, Fubuki,
Murakumo, Natsugumo, Akatsuki, Yudachi,
Ayanami, Takanami, Teruzuki, Makikumo;*
submarines *I-123, I-22, I-172, I-15, I-3, I-1;*
transports *Sasago Maru, Azumasan Maru,
Kyushu Maru, Nagara Maru, Canberra
Maru, Brisbane Maru, Shinano Maru, Ari-
zona Maru, Kinugasa Maru, Hirokawa Maru,
Yamura Maru, Sangetsu Maru;* destroyer
conversion *Patrol Boat 35.*

Certain classifications, inclusions, and exclu-
sions in this list need amplification. When the
U.S. Navy modified a number of World War
I vintage destroyers into the roles of fast
transports, it also reclassified them as auxiliary ships as opposed to combatants. This
reflected both a change in their mission and
especially their armament, for the ships lost
their torpedo tubes. Thus, I have placed *Colhoun, Little,* and *Gregory* in the auxiliary category rather than the destroyer list.
Similarly, the Imperial Navy modified some
old destroyers into escort vessels and reclassified them as patrol boats. Although *Patrol
Boat 35* remained a combatant, she was more
comparable to the U.S. fast transports, so I
placed her accordingly.

Only one U.S. submarine was lost during the
period of the campaign, *Argonaut,* on January 10, 1943. She was en route from Pearl
Harbor to Brisbane, where she was to carry
out special duties supporting guerrillas for
MacArthur (Blair, *Silent Victory,* pp. 346–
47). As noted in the text, she was lost trying
to intercept a convoy heading from Rabaul to
New Guinea. In view of her assignment and
the specific circumstances of her sinking, like
Morison, I have not listed her with the American losses in the campaign. Along these same
principles, Japanese naval vessels lost in conjunction with actual operations around New
Guinea are not on the list (i.e., light cruiser
Tenryu, destroyers *Hayashio, Yayoi,* submarines *RO-33* and *I-4*).

Pages 603–4
Comparison of peacetime training:

AMERICAN

Prewar Commission (18):

Savo Island: *Blue, Ralph Talbot, Patterson,
Bagley, Wilson, Helm, Jarvis, Monssen*
Cape Esperance: None
Friday the Thirteenth: *Cushing, Sterett, Monssen*
Battleship Action 14–15 Nov: *Walke, Benham, Preston*
Tassafaronga: *Maury, Drayton, Perkins, Lamson*

Wartime Commission (12):

Savo Island: *Buchanan*
Cape Esperance: *Buchanan, Farenholt, Laffey,
Duncan, McCalla*
Friday the Thirteenth: *Laffey, O'Bannon, Aaron Ward,
Barton, Fletcher*
Battleship Action 14–15 Nov: *Gwin*
Tassafaronga: *Fletcher, Lardner*
Buchanan and *Laffey* participated in two actions.

JAPANESE
Prewar Commission (25):

Savo Island: *Yunagi*
Cape Esperance: *Fubuki, Hatsuyuki, Asagumo, Natsugumo, Yamagumo, Murakumo, Shirayuki*
Friday the Thirteenth: *Yudachi, Harusame, Akatsuki, Inazuma, Ikazuchi, Yukikaze, Amatsukaze, Asagumo, Murasame, Samidare*
Battleship Action 14–15 Nov: *Inazuma, Shirayuki, Hatsuyuki, Asagumo, Samidare, Uranami, Shikinami, Ayanami, Oyashio, Kagero*
Tassafaronga: *Kuroshio, Oyashio, Kagero, Kawakaze, Suzukaze*

Wartime Commission (5):

Savo Island: None
Cape Esperance: *Akizuki*
Friday the Thirteenth: *Teruzuki*
Battleship Action 14–15 Nov: *Teruzuki*
Tassafaronga: *Takanami, Naganami, Makinami*
Asagumo participated in three battles and *Inazuma, Shirayuki, Hatsuyuki, Samidare, Oyashio,* and *Kagero* in two.

Page 604
Information to Colonel Sanada: *S.S.,* Vol. 28, pp. 436–37.

Page 608
"inadequate physical training . . .": Final Report, Jul 43, p. 6.

"Indian fighting": Hersey, *Into the Valley,* p. 15.

Page 609
"most of us who have fought in the Pacific . . .": George, *Shots Fired in Anger,* p. 320.

"took it like a man—like a hero . . .": Ibid., p. 236.

Page 610
Tables of losses from August 1 to November 15: These were compiled from the records of all American units and commands and the Japanese Defense Agency history volumes, with invaluable assistance from the research of Mr. John Lundstrom and Mr. James Sawruk. The totals reflect losses from both combat and operational causes of all aircraft employed in missions directly connected to or supporting the Guadalcanal campaign. August 1 is selected as the commencing date rather than August 7 because preliminary operations began at least this early, both with B-17s attacking Guadalcanal and carrier planes protecting the assault convoy.

The Japanese figures do not include any aircraft lost in support of operations on New Guinea. The totals are notably lower than those found in the United States Strategic Bombing Survey for the period of August to November 1942, when by far and away the main combat theater was the Solomons and New Guinea.

	Zeros	Vals & Kates	Bettys	Flying boats	Float planes	Total
Combat	344	197	125	12	136	814
Operational	238	44	60	8	61	411
TOTALS	582	241	185	20	197	1,225

United States Strategic Bombing Survey, No. 62, Japanese Air Power, Exhibit D.

Page 608
"construction equipment and personnel . . .": Final Report, Phase III, pp. 12–13.

"A power shovel or bulldozer . . .": Engineer Activities Guadalcanal, p. 15.

"courage and cold steel": Cates, "My First," p. 48.

Japanese failure to grasp dominance of automatic weapons and artillery, propensity for night attacks: Final Report, Phase IV, p. 18; Jul 43, p. 11.

This discrepancy is puzzling, but I am confident that my totals for losses from the Japanese carriers and in the 11th Air Fleet are quite accurate. In fact, my figures for Bettys and flying boats are reasonably close to those given in the Strategic Bombing Survey; the differences are in the numbers for Zeros, Vals, Kates, and float planes. In this context, I must emphasize that the totals I have for float plane losses are quite suspect. My information is spotty and it appears that this type of aircraft was subject to a high rate of operational attrition not always mentioned in *S.S.*

We have one very enlightening and authoritative contemporary statement from a Japanese officer that verifies the data for the 11th Air Fleet. On December 30, 1942, Rear Admiral Sakamaki, the chief of staff of the 11th Air Fleet, spoke to Admiral Ugaki. According to Ugaki's diary, Sakamaki related that between August 7 and the end of October 11, Air Fleet losses amounted to 236 planes, including those destroyed on the ground. My figure for the 11th Air Fleet for this period is 238 (101 Zeros, ninety-eight Bettys, nineteen Vals, nineteen flying boats, and one reconnaissance plane). It appears that Sakamaki's figures included all losses in this interval and incorporate thirty-five planes lost over and around New Guinea (sixteen Zeros, fifteen Bettys, and four Vals).

counting Branch, Office of the Adjutant General, Reports Control Symbol CsCap (OT) 87, p. 94 [hereafter Army Battle Casualties and Nonbattle Deaths in World War II]; Hough, Ludwig, and Shaw, *Pearl Harbor to Guadalcanal,* p. 374; Navy Department, Bureau of Personnel, Casualty List World War II, Books 2 and 3. Army Air Force losses include a handful of ground crew men; the other branches are all aviators.

Japanese aircrew losses: *S.S.* contains no specific comment on this point. The text reflects a best guess as to Japanese aviation personnel losses. The table on carrier plane losses just in the two carrier battles yields 205 fatalities. The 11th Air Fleet losses through November 15 shows the following crews aboard lost aircraft:

	Zero	Val	Betty	
Planes:	106	15	100	
Crew per plane:	1	2	7	
Total:	106	30	700	(836)
Other losses:	Flying boats	Float planes	Misc.	
Planes:	19	66	2	
Crew per plane:	9	2	2	
Total:	171	132	4	(307)
Carrier planes not lost in carrier battles:	Zeros	Kates		
Planes:	19	9		
Crew per plane:	1	2		
Total:	19	18	(37)	

Pages 610–11

Loss figures for period November 16, 1942, to February 9, 1943: The data on American losses are extracted from the same sources as above. Between November 1 and December 24, Sakamaki indicated 11th Air Fleet losses totaled 159; however, most of these were fighters on defensive missions. Subtracting ninety-nine aircraft lost between November 1–15, or accounted for in the period from November 16 to December 24, from Sakamaki's total of 159 yields a difference of sixty planes. Once again, float plane losses are presumably incomplete.

Page 611

American aircrew losses: Army Battle Casualties and Nonbattle Deaths in World War II, Final Report, 7 December 1941–31 December 1946, Prepared by the Statistical and Ac-

This gives a total of 1,180 crew members at risk. Assuming 60 percent of these men were lost places fatalities at 708. Adding this figure to crew losses in the two carrier battles raises the total to 913, just for the period through November 15. Support for the estimated percentage of losses may be found from the fact that a recent study of Imperial Navy fighter operations, Hata and Izawa, *Japanese Naval Aces and Fighter Units in World War II,* Appendix B, shows that 104 pilots (57 percent) died of the 187 at risk in Zeros lost on operations connected to the Guadalcanal campaign between August 7 and November 15, 1942. The only firm statement I located on total Imperial Navy losses in this category is found in Masanori Ito with Roger Pineau, *The End of the Imperial Japanese Navy* (New York: Macfadden, 1965), p. 84, which says Japanese losses in the campaign reached 893 planes and 2,362 airmen. This would tend to suggest that the aircrew figures derived above are conservative.

Page 611
Imperial Navy aircrew availability at the start of the war: United States Strategic Bombing Survey, No. 62, Japanese Air Power, p. 35.

Page 612
Lack of construction capacity: Okumiya, Horikoshi, and Caidin, *Zero,* p. 206.

Importance of bulldozer: Miller, *Cactus Air Force,* p. 208.

Page 612
"nothing too lavish in praise:" Vandegrift and Asprey, *Once a Marine,* p. 137.

Page 613
B-17 performance: 13th AF Hist., pp. 74–77; Craven and Cate, *Guadalcanal to Saipan,* pp. 90–91.

Page 613
Imperial Army losses: *S.S.,* Vol. 28, pp. 569–70.

Colonel Obara's comments: Interview, Col. Obara, Shigetaka, p. 3, NHC.

UNIT

	17th Army Hdqtrs.	2d Div.	38th Div.	35th Bde.	Ichiki Det.	17th Army direct cmd. units	Supply units
A. Landed	192	10,318	7,646	3,545	2,108	4,248	815
B. Withdrawn	142	2,647	2,473	618	264	1,666	480
C. A - B	50	7,671	5,173	2,927	1,844	2,582	335
D. Killed in action	17	2,334	4,562	—	4,886	—	—
E. Died of wounds	1	1,179	186	—	393	—	—
F. Disease deaths	—	2,551	136	—	1,027	—	—
G. Missing	—	1,131	119	—	1,107	—	—

Note: The figures in D–G beneath the Ichiki Det. are combined totals for the 35th Bde., Ichiki Det. and 17th Army direct command units.

UNIT

	17th Army (less ship units)	Ship units	Navy	Total
A. Landed	28,872	2,486 (318)	—	31,358 (318)
B. Withdrawn	8,290	1,527	848	10,665
C. A - B	20,582	—	—	—
D. Killed in action	—	723 (307 crews)	—	12,507
E. Died of wounds	—	172 (36 crews)	—	1,931 (36)
F. Disease deaths	—	485	—	4,203
G. Missing	—	—	—	2,497

Total Losses: 21,138

Page 614

U.S. Army losses: Basic figures are from Army Battle Casualties and Nonbattle Deaths in World War II, Final Report, 7 December 1941–31 December 1946, p. 94. This report lists 527 deaths in the combat divisions, 150 deaths in Air Force units, and thirty-five in "other units." The text groups the combat division and "other unit" fatalities. Miller, *Guadalcanal: The First Offensive*, p. 350, gives slightly different figures for Army losses in the combat divisions: 334 in the Americal Division and 216 in the 25th Division for a total of 550. The source cited by Miller for the Americal Division (Casualty Reports Guadalcanal, Americal Division, RG 407, File 300-1.16) gives the following breakdown of casualties:

U.S. Marine Corps losses: Hough, Ludwig, and Shaw, *Pearl Harbor to Guadalcanal*, p. 374. This source lists 1,152 marines killed and fifty-five missing among the nonaviation units. It refers to a tabulation in Appendix D that works out to 1,364 killed or missing in the other units, assuming aviation losses remain 140 (fifty-five killed or died of wounds and eighty-five missing). I chose the lower figure as it comports more closely with losses itemized by units. It is not explicitly clear if the figures in the official Marine Corps history include losses among personnel assigned to shipboard detachments. For purposes of my accounting, I assumed they did not.

Naval personnel losses: see Appendix 3.

Unit	Killed, Died of Wounds, or Missing		Wounded	
	Officers	*Enlisted*	*Officers*	*Enlisted*
164th Infantry	22	127	10	432
132d Infantry	8	113	17	255
182d Infantry	8	55	11	261
Subtotal	38	295	38	948
Other Units	6	15	7	?
Americal Division	44	310	45	948+

It will be noted that the figures in the tables do not match the total given in the narrative of the report (346 deaths) or the figure cited by Miller.

For the 25th Division the Report of Operations, p. 162, gives a total of 216 deaths. A detailed breakdown is not given but the following figures for the infantry are of interest:

Figures for U.S. Navy losses at Okinawa: Roy E. Appleman, James M. Burns, Russell A. Gugeler, and John Stevens, *United States Army in World War II, The War in the Pacific, Okinawa: The Last Battle*, (Washington, D.C.: Historical Division, Department of the Army, 1948), p. 473.

Unit	Killed		Wounded		
	Officers	*Enlisted*	*Officers*	*Enlisted*	*Total*
27th Infantry	7	66	—	—	73+
161th Infantry	5	24	3	52	84
35th Inf. (2d Bn only)		64		42	104
Total		166			

Sources: 27th Inf Reg, Operations Report Guadalcanal, RG 407, file 325-Inf (27) −0.3; 35th Inf, Report of Operations 25th Division, p. 88; 161th Inf Hist. December 30, 1942–July 1, 1943, RG 407, file 325-Inf (161)−0.1

Page 614
Known Japanese naval personnel losses:

	Event	Killed	
9 Aug	Savo Island	129	
19 Aug	*Hagikaze* damaged	33	
24 Aug	Eastern Solomons, *Ryujo* sunk	120	
	Shokaku damaged	6	
	Chitose damaged, 14 wounded		
25 Aug	*Mutsuki* sunk	40	
28 Aug	SBD attacks on destroyers		
	Asagiri sunk (circa 120); *Yugiri* (32) and	154	
	Shirakumo (2) damaged		
28 Aug	*I-123* sunk	75	
2 Sep	*Patrol Boat 35* sunk, 52 survivors	50?	
2 Sep	*Tsugaru*	14	
24 Sep	*Umikaze* and *Urakaze* damaged	14	"casualties"
2 Oct	*Tenryu* damaged	30	"casualties"
10 Oct	*Nowaki* damaged	30	"casualties"
12 Oct	Cape Esperance	454	
25 Oct	*Akatsuki* and *Ikazuchi*	6	
	Yura sunk, *Akizuki* damaged	?	
26 Oct	Santa Cruz: *Chikuma* damaged	192	
	Zuiho (?) and *Shokaku* (?) damaged	?	
? Oct	*I-22* sunk	95	
2 Nov	*I-15* sunk	94	
7 Nov	*Naganami* and *Takanami* damaged;	17	"casualties"
12 Nov	*I-172* sunk	70	
12–15 Nov	Naval Battle of Guadalcanal	1,352	
11 Nov–13 Dec	3 Midget sub crews	6	
1 Dec	Tassafaronga; *Takanami* sunk	211	
7 Dec	*Nowaki* damaged	17	
9 Dec	*I-3* sunk	68	
11 Dec	*Teruzuki* sunk	?	
26 Dec	*Ariake* damaged	28	
15 Jan	*Tanikaze* damaged	1	(at least)
28 Jan	Run to Russells, 6 destroyers	17	"casualties"
29 Jan	*I-1* sunk	21	
1 Feb	1st evacuation run, *Makigumo* sunk	?	
4 Feb	2d evacuation run, *Maikaze* damaged	?	
7 Feb	3d evacuation run, *Isokaze* damaged	10	
Grand Total		3,176	definite
		108	"casualties"

I rounded these figures to 3,200.

The figures are from *S.S.*, supplemented with data from Jentschur, Jung, and Mickel, *Warships of the Imperial Japanese Navy, 1869–1945;* Lacroix, "Development of the 'A Class' Cruisers in the Imperial Japanese Navy"; and Dorr Carpenter and Norman Polmar, *Submarines of the Imperial Japanese Navy* (Annapolis, Md.: Naval Institute Press, 1986). Obviously, there is considerable room for addition in the spaces marked "?" The figure of 343 crewmen in transports is from the above table for Imperial Army losses.

Native casualties: Hugh Laracy and Geoffrey White, "Taem Blong Fact: World War II in Melanesia," *'O'O A Journal of Solomon Islands Studies,* Number 4, 1988, Appendix B, which appears to itemize native losses.

Page 614
Ships commissioned for U.S. Navy, August 7, 1942 to February 9, 1943: Norman Friedman, *U.S. Aircraft Carriers: An Illustrated Design History* (Annapolis, Md.: Naval Institute Press, 1983), pp. 412–13; Norman Fried-

man, *U.S. Battleships: An Illustrated Design History* (Annapolis, Md.: Naval Institute Press, 1985), p. 421; Norman Friedman, *U.S. Cruisers: An Illustrated Design History* (Annapolis, Md.: Naval Institute Press, 1984), p. 452; Norman Friedman, *U.S. Destroyers: An Illustrated Design History* (Annapolis, Md.: Naval Institute Press, 1982), pp. 440–48; John D. Alden, *The Fleet Submarine in the U.S. Navy* (Annapolis, Md.: Naval Institute Press, 1979), Appendix 8.

Ships commissioned for Imperial Navy, August 7, 1942, to February 9, 1943: Jentschur, Jung, and Mickel, *Warships of the Imperial Japanese Navy, 1869–1945,* passim.

Aircraft production in 1942 in United States and Japan: René J. Francillon, *Japanese Aircraft of the Pacific War* (Annapolis, Md.: Naval Institute Press, 1987), p. 10. Figures are from the United States Strategic Bombing Survey.

Pages 615–16
Totals of divisions: Shelby L. Stanton, *Order of Battle U.S. Army, World War II* (Novato, Calif.: Presidio Press, 1984), p. 3; Coox, "Effectiveness of the Japanese Military Establishment in the Second World War," p. 18. The American total of eighty-nine Army divisions included sixteen armored, five airborne, one mountain, and sixty-seven infantry (including the 1st Cavalry Division, which fought as infantry). All six Marine divisions were infantry, though each had a well-integrated tank battalion. The Japanese lost a number of divisions prior to August 1945, but at that time had 169 infantry and four armored in existence. Of these, twenty-four served in the Kwantung Army, seven divisions occupied Korea, and twenty-three, including one armored, held large tracts of China. The great majority of the rest defended Japan proper, a fact often overlooked in discussions of invading Japan.

". . . Japanese leadership in 1941 . . . :" Coox, "Effectiveness of the Japanese Military Establishment in the Second World War," p. 24.

Page 617
"exhausted but resolute . . . :" John W. Dower, *War Without Mercy,* (New York: Pantheon Books, 1986), p. 249.

Page 618
"There were many famous battles . . . :" Capt. Y. (Tommy) Tamagawa with author, March 1981.

"For us who were there . . . :" Morison, *The Struggle for Guadalcanal,* p. 373.

Page 618
"They will live . . . :" James Michener, *Tales of the South Pacific,* (New York: Fawcett Crest, 1973), p. 12.

ABDA area, 8, 13
Abe, Hiroaki, 168, 462, 485, 491, 604
  Friday the Thirteenth Battle and, 429,
    431–38, 440, 441, 451, 452, 455–56,
    460
  Santa Cruz Islands Battle and, 369, 375,
    381, 383, 386–88, 393
Abe, Toshio, 167
Abercrombie, Laurence A., 504, 505
Adachi, Hatazo, 497
Adams, Dudley, 68
Adams, Robert L., 114
aerial photographs, 346, 365
Agnew, Lieutenant Commander, 358
Ainsworth, Warden L., 548–49
  Vila-Stanmore bombarded by, 572–73
air cover for supplies to Guadalcanal, 138
aircraft, shortage of, 138–39, 198
air raids, Japanese, 80, 226, 234, 243, 314,
    320, 323, 421
  of August 7th, 64–66, 67–69
  Cates and, 257
  Japanese tactics in, 275–76
  radar warning of, 295–96
  "Tokyo Express" and, 274–82
air superiority campaign, 573–74
Alderman, John C., 326
Alligator Creek, see Tenaru River
Amerine, Richard, 203
Andrew, John D., 112–13
Anibe, Yuji, 168
Ant Transportation, 267–68, 328
  cancellation of, 281
ANZAC Area, 10, 13
Aola expedition, 420–21
Arcadia Conference, 6–8
Ariga, Kosaku, 168
Arima, Masafumi, 167, 186, 394
Arima, Tokikichi, 169
Arison, Rae E., 444
Arita, Yuzo, 199–200
Arnold, Henry H., 12, 13, 34, 138
  Ghormley and, 276
  on Navy logistics, 277
  on reinforcements, 215–16
  South Pacific tour by, 276–77
Arthur, John M., 424–25
Asakura, Bunji, 169
Asano, Shinpei, 100
Ashe, George B., 72

Atlantic Fleet, U.S., 5
Australia, 8–9, 10–11, 12, 13, 25, 28, 37,
    45, 50, 56, 541, 598
Ayabe, Kitsuju, 537

Bailey, Kenneth D., 73
  death of, 272
  in Edson's Ridge Battle, 238–40
  Medal of Honor awarded to, 245
Baldinus, Lawrence, 190, 231
Baldwin, Hanson, 266, 332, 333
Ban, Masami, 100
Banta, Shepard, 241–42
barge convoy, 205, 213, 219
  Kawaguchi's insistence on, 198–99, 201,
    203, 212
Barnes, D. C., 181
Basilone, John, 355
Battle of Guadalcanal, The (Griffith), viii
Bauer, Harold F., 320, 327, 345
  shot down, 467
Bauer, Harry, F., 211
Bauer, Louis H., 173
Beach Blue, 72, 73
Beach Red, 61, 62, 63, 70, 126
Beakley, Wallace M., 173
Bear Height, 406
Beck, Edward L., 172
Bell, Frederick J., 173, 184
Bell, G. A., 319
Biebush, Frederick C., 243
Blue Base, 400n
Bode, Howard D., 97, 100, 106, 117, 122
Bofors 40mm antiaircraft gun, 389, 402–3
Bolero, Operation, 15, 17
"Bombardment, The," 313, 316–21, 330,
    337
  Clemens on, 317
  effectiveness of, 319
  Geiger and, 319, 322–23
  164th Infantry Regiment and, 319
  Vandegrift and, 317, 320
"bone heap," 162, 360
Borneo Campaign, 199
Bouterse, M. J., 118
Bowen, Robert O., 284, 412
Boyd, D. H., 304
Boyer, Randolph B., 377
Brannon, Dale D., 174, 201, 213, 432
Brewer, C. E., 181

Brewer, Charles F., 180
Brice, William O., 409
Bridson, G., 575
Briggs, Ralph, 352–54
Briscoe, Robert, 578, 583, 587
British Solomon Islands Protectorate, 72
Brown, Robert S., 241
Brush, Charles H., 148–49, 151
Brush-Shibuya skirmish, 148–49, 157
Buchanan, R. M., 464
Buckley, Edmund J., 130
Buin airfield, 267–68, 295, 502n, 545, 548
   Yamamoto and, 275–76
Buna, 498–99, 500, 540
Bush, George E., 553–55
Bushido warrior code, 158
Butler, Major, 596
Butler, Smedley, 46

"Cactus," see Guadalcanal
Cactus Air Force, 267, 275, 280, 281, 285,
   289, 296, 314–15, 366–67, 496, 501–2,
   542
   compositional changes of, 409–10
   first aircraft arrival of, 139–40
   pilot stress in, 209–10
Cactus Air Force, The (Miller), viii
Cactus Express, 210, 210n
Cagney, James, 617
Caldwell, Turner, 187
Calhoun, Admiral, 457
Callaghan, Daniel J., 56n, 454, 459,
   460–63, 470, 486, 490, 503, 604
   death of, 444, 451
   Friday the Thirteenth Battle and,
      434–36, 436n, 438, 441,
   Medal of Honor awarded to, 489
   "odd-even" order of, 439–40, 442
   seniority of, 433n
   Turner's appointment of, 433
   Watchtower and, 54–55
Callahan, Joseph W., 100, 114–15
"Cannibal Battalion," 530
Cape Esperance, Battle of, 292–312, 436,
   610
   armaments contrasted in, 297–98
   assessment of, 309–12, 603
   Boise damaged in, 304–7
   Bombardment Group in, 296
   casualties in, 309, 310
   Duncan sunk in, 307–8
   8th Japanese Fleet and, 309–10
   Fubuki sunk in, 303
   Furutaka sunk in, 307
   Goto in, 296, 299, 301–4, 306–7, 309–11
   Helena in, 294, 297–303, 305, 310, 311
   initial formations in, 299
   Japanese Cruiser Division 6 in, 295, 308
   Japanese failures in, 298–99, 309–10
   Kinugasa in, 296, 299, 305–8

Nimitz's assessment of, 403
onset of, 299–301
opposing forces in, 296–297
radar and, 294–95, 299, 301, 603
radio intelligence in, 294
Reinforcement group in, 295, 296, 301,
   306, 310
San Francisco in, 294, 297–99, 301–2,
   303–4, 306
Scott in, 294–95, 296–97, 299–306,
   310–11, 312
Carl, Marion, 223, 279
Carlson's Raiders, 423
Carmody, M. D., 465
Carroll, Chester E., 101, 114
Carroum, Jefferson, 467
Casamento, Anthony, 412n
Case, Leo B., 155
casualties:
   aircrew, 611–12
   in Cape Esperance Battle, 309, 310
   in convoy and capital ship actions, 486,
      490
   in Eastern Solomons Battle, 191–93
   in Edson Ridge Battle, 244–46
   of 1st Marine Division, 522
   in Friday the Thirteenth Battle, 459, 460
   on Gavutu-Tanambogo, 78–79
   at the Gifu, 566–67
   health problems and, 259–60
   in Henderson Field Battle, 351, 364–65
   in initial landings, 78–79
   in Japanese 4th Infantry Regiment, 365
   at Kokumbona, 570
   in last Matanikau Battle, 497
   in Matanikau October battles, 273–74
   in Mount Austen Battle, 532, 533–34
   in Santa Cruz Islands Battle, 400–401
   in Savo Island Battle, 117n, 121n
   in 17th Army, 497
   in 164th Infantry Regiment, 164–65
   in Tassafaronga Battle, 514
   in Tenaru River Battle, 156
   total Japanese, 613–14
   total U.S., 614
   on Tulagi, 78–79
Cates, Clifton B., 51, 140, 333, 608
   air raids and, 257
   initial landings, 62, 69–70, 80
   in Tenaru River Battle, 153–55
cattle stampede incident, 128
Cecil, Charles P., 377
Centipede Height, 406
Central Agreements, 18, 142–43, 525, 535,
   536
   revisions of, 253–54, 267, 498
Chain Transportation, 501–2
Chambers, Justice, 74
Champagne, Joseph D. R., 350
Chicago Tribune, 41, 331

China, 18, 145n–46n
Christie, Ralph, 329
Churchill, Winston, 6, 10, 11, 12, 157, 600, 616
CINCPAC (Commander in Chief Pacific Fleet), Nimitz's appointment as, 5, 13
CINCPOA (Commander in Chief Pacific Ocean Area), Nimitz's appointment as, 13
Clagett, John, 587
Clemens, Martin, 30–31, 49, 59, 148, 150, 154, 208, 221, 222, 224, 348, 420
   on "The Bombardment," 317
   on Puller, 270
   Tenaru Battle observed by, 153
   Vandegrift and, 131
Coast Guard, U.S., 273n
coast watchers, 28–31, 194, 200, 206–7, 208, 272, 274, 279, 313, 426, 502n, 504, 520, 525, 549, 580, 586
   Vandegrift on, 521–22, 612
code-breaking, see radio intelligence
Coffin, Albert, 454, 465, 467, 489
Cole, William M., 378, 435, 505, 508
   Halsey's criticism of, 516
Collett, John A., 376, 384, 401
Collins, J. Lawton, 552, 556, 562, 563–64, 568, 571
combat flying, in Guadalcanal campaign, 209–10
Combined Chiefs of Staff, 14
COMINCH (Commander in Chief U.S. Fleet), King's appointment as, 5
Commander South Pacific War Diary, 433n
Conger, J. E., 359, 359n
Connolly, Ensign, 587
Conoley, Odell M., 364
convoy and capital ship actions, 462–92, 603
   assessment of, 490–92
   Ayanami sunk in, 484, 486
   Benham sunk in, 484–86
   Bombardment Unit in, 469, 470, 473, 474, 478–83
   casualties in, 486, 490
   comparison of forces in, 472
   composition of forces in, 463, 470–71
   convoy's end in, 487–89
   Enterprise and, 463–67, 487, 490–91
   Junyo in, 462, 491
   Kimura in, 469–70, 473, 477–78, 482–83, 485–86
   Kirishima in, 469, 470, 472, 479, 486n, 487
   Kondo and, 462–63, 468–70, 472, 474–75, 477, 478–79, 481–87
   Lee and, 463, 465, 468, 471–75, 477, 479–86, 490
   Lee's success in, 486–87

Mikawa and, 462–65
   Nagara in, 469, 470, 472, 473, 475–76, 479, 484
   Preston sunk in, 476, 486
   radar in, 470, 475, 477, 479, 480
   radio intelligence in, 473, 479
   R Area Air Force and, 467, 469, 473–74
   Tanaka and, 465, 466, 468–69, 471, 472, 474, 482, 483, 487, 489, 490–91
   Task Force 64 in, 463, 471–72
   U.S. aerial attacks in, 465–68, 487–89
   Walke sunk in, 477, 486
   Washington in, 463, 468, 470–73, 475, 477–79
Cook, Charles, 311
Cooke, Charles M., 38
Cooley, Colonel, 308–9
Cooper, James E., 505
Cooper, William G., 297, 378
Coox, Alvin, 615–16
Coral Sea, Battle of the, 24, 31, 41n, 43, 54, 67, 93, 384, 401, 598–99
cordon defense, 261–63, 607
Corry, Ralph, 130–31
Coward, Jesse G., 174, 435, 442
Craig, John R., 328
Cram, Jack, 323
Crane, Edward J., 72, 77
Creehan, Edward P., 395, 396–97
Cresswell, Lenard B., 154, 155, 156
Crouter, Mark, 432, 444–45
Crutchley, Victor A. C., 51, 54, 100
   Hepburn's report and, 122–23
   pre-battle dispositions of, 97–99
   Savo Island Battle and, 105n, 107n, 108, 113
   Savo Island Battle prelude and, 93
   Turner's meeting with, 96–97
cryptanalysis, see radio intelligence
Cub One, 131
Cub supply detachments, 137
Curry, Manley T., 418
Curtin, John, 10–11, 41n
Custer, Steven, 129

daily existence, in Guadalcanal campaign, 256–61
Dalton, James, 593, 596
Daniel, Henry C., 377
Daniels, James, 393, 395
d'Argenlieu, Georges, 36
Dauntless SBD dive-bomber, 166
Davidson, Walter B., 111
Davis, Arthur C., 173, 182, 186
Davis, Charles W., 555–56, 581
Davis, Glenn B., 378, 471, 478, 483, 486
Davis, Leonard, 289
Davis, Ray, 173, 178, 320, 322, 324
DeCarre, Alphonse, 556

Decisive Battle Doctrine, 83
Deese, Teddy, 566
Defense Agency, Japanese, 253n
de Gaulle, Charles, 36
Delany, Walter S., 172
del Valle, Pedro A., 51, 226–27, 263
dengue fever, 259
Dennett, Erle V. E., 172
Diamond, Lee, 152
Dibb, R.A.M., 181
Diving Shell, 306n
Dobbin, John, 309
Domei news agency, 116
Dominion, 49
Doolittle, James, 14
Doolittle raid, 14, 24
DuBose, Laurance T., 173, 376, 434, 444,
    445, 453
Durr, C. G., 248
Dyer, George, 601

Eastern Solomons, Battle of, 159–93, 194,
    382
  air searches in, 176–77
  assessment of, 191–93, 602
  Blue sunk in, 165–66
  carrier battle in, 166–88
  casualties in, 191–93
  composition of forces in, 167–74
  convoy battle in, 188–91
  Enterprise in, 164, 173, 175–87, 189,
    191–93
  Fletcher and, 165, 172, 187, 193
  Japanese carrier deployment in, 175–76
  Japanese 2d Fleet in, 160, 162, 166,
    169–70, 175–76, 178, 187, 188, 193
  Japanese 3d Fleet in, 160, 161, 164,
    166–68, 176, 178, 193
  Japanese 11th Air Fleet in, 171–72,
    193
  Kirishima in, 168, 176–77
  Nagara in, 168, 176, 177
  Nagumo in, 164, 167, 175, 186, 193
  new Japanese tactics for, 159–60
  North Carolina in, 173, 182, 183–84,
    187
  preludes to, 159–66
  radar in, 163, 174–75, 179–80, 186
  radio discipline in, 180, 192
  radio intelligence in, 161
  Ryujo in, 160, 161–62, 165, 166, 168,
    176–79, 187, 188, 190, 192
  Saratoga in, 165, 166, 172, 175–81, 187,
    188, 189
  Shokaku in, 160, 161–62, 165, 166, 167,
    175–78, 182, 183, 186
  67th Fighter Squadron in, 174
  Tanaka and, 162, 164–65, 166, 170,
    188–89, 190, 193
  Task Force 61 in, 172–74
  Turner in, 163, 166
  U.S. readiness for, 175
  Wasp in, 162, 165, 173, 191, 192–93
  Yamamoto and, 159, 193
  Zuikaku in, 161–62, 165–67, 176–78,
    180, 182, 184, 191
Edison, Charles, 5
Edson, Merritt A., 73, 128, 220, 413, 415,
    609
  deep advance opposed by, 418
  Edson's Ridge Battle and, 223–26,
    229–33, 235–40
  5th Marine Regiment commanded by,
    263
  Matanikau Battles and, 271–73, 284
  Medal of Honor awarded to, 245
  Tasimboko raid and, 221–22
Edson's Ridge, Battle of, 218, 223–46,
    262
  air losses in, 244
  Bailey in, 238–40
  casualties in, 244–46
  Edson and, 223–26, 229–33, 235–40
  1st Parachute Battalion in, 225, 229,
    235–39, 241, 245
  1st Pioneer Battalion in, 229, 235
  1st Raiders in, 225, 229, 231–33, 235,
    237–39, 245
  gas attack scare in, 237
  Griffith in, 235
  Imperial General Headquarters and, 224,
    244, 246
  Japanese march in, 224–25
  jungle in, 224, 231–32, 244
  Kawaguchi and, 218–19, 223–25,
    228–29, 231–35, 240–41, 242, 243,
    244–46
  Kuma Battalion and, 219, 224, 229, 232,
    242, 245, 246
  lull after, 265
  Oka in, 229, 232, 235, 243, 246
  67th Fighter Squadron in, 240
  tanks in, 242
  Thomas in, 220, 222–23, 233
  Turner and, 229, 232–33
  Turner-Vandegrift meeting and, 227–28
  U.S. artillery in, 237–39
  Vandegrift and, 223, 233, 242, 243
Eisenhower, Dwight D., 9
El Alamein, Battle of, 404
Elder, R. M., 187
Eldridge, John, 173, 275, 330, 361, 414
  Natsugumo sunk by, 309
  Nisshin attacked by, 280
  Yura attacked by, 360
Eliot, George Fielding, 49
Ellis, Hayne, 5
Emmons, Delos, 276
Enright, William K., 412
Exton's Ridge, 555

Farncomb, H. B., 100
Faulkner, Clark, 587, 588
Feldt, Eric, 28–29
Fellows, John B., Jr., 471
Felt, Harry D., 165, 172, 176–77, 178–79
Ferry, George F., 532, 593–94
Fighter One air field, 223, 240, 322, 357, 410, 464
Fighter Two air field, 410, 528
Fighting Sullivans, The (film), 617
Fike, Charles L., 139
Fink, Christian, 190, 200
First South Pacific Campaign, 3, 25
Fitch, Aubrey, 329, 378, 457, 542
    aircraft available to, 543
    airlift organized by, 320
    McCain replaced by, 264
    Vandegrift visited by, 266
Fitzgerald, Philip H., 505
Flatley, James H., Jr., 376, 384–85, 402, 466, 489
Fletcher, Frank J., 51, 52, 56, 135, 138, 601, 604, 605
    air searches and, 176–77
    carriers withdrawn by, 93–94, 96, 119
    critics answered by, 94
    Eastern Solomons Battle and, 165, 172, 187, 193
    enigmatic conduct of, 204–5
    Ghormley and, 133–34
    King and, 54
    Nimitz's support for, 54
    pre-landing conference and, 54–55, 56n
    Savo Island Battle prelude and, 90, 92
    wounded, 204
Flying Leathernecks (film), 617
Flynn, Cornelius W., 174
Fontana, Paul, 409
food:
    crisis in, 499–500
    shortage of, 260–61
    on "Tokyo Express," 261
Forgy, Howell M., 511, 515
Forrestal, James, 138, 214
Fort, George H., 173
Foss, Joseph, 314, 316, 317, 329, 346, 361, 422, 467
Fox, Douglas H., 377, 435
Franco, Louis, 530, 531
Fraser, Thomas E., 471, 477
Freeland, Frank, 524
Freeman, James S., 501
Friday the Thirteenth, Battle of, 428–61
    Abe and, 429, 431–38, 440, 441, 452, 455–56, 460
    aftermath of, 451–59
    Akatsuki sunk in, 449
    assessment of, 459–61, 603

Atlanta sunk in, 453–54
B Area Air Force and, 437
Barton sunk in, 446–48
Callaghan and, 434–36, 438, 441
casualties in, 459, 460
comparison of forces in, 433–35
Enterprise and, 426–27, 430, 454
formations' disintegration in, 441
Helena in, 430, 434, 436, 438, 446, 448–51, 456–57, 459, 460
Hiei in, 429, 434, 437–38, 440–41, 443–51
Hiei sunk in, 456
Japanese 8th Fleet and, 429, 431
Japanese forces in, 429, 434
Japanese formation in, 437
Japanese gunnery advantage in, 435
Jenkins in, 434, 439–40, 444n, 449, 453–54
Juneau in, 430, 434, 436, 446, 448, 450, 456–57, 460
Junyo in, 429, 454
Kirishima in, 429, 434, 438, 440–42, 444–45, 448, 451, 455, 460, 462
Laffey sunk in, 441–42
Monssen sunk in, 447
Nagara in, 429, 434, 437, 439–42, 444, 446, 448, 452
radar in, 436, 438, 446, 447, 460, 603
radio intelligence in, 432–33, 455
results of, 461
San Francisco in, 430, 433, 434, 436, 438, 445, 446, 448–49
Scott in, 430, 433, 434, 436, 459
U.S. command arrangements in, 436
U.S. radio discipline in, 438, 460
Frisbee, Julian, 284
"FS" Operation, 23, 43
Fujimori, Yasuo, 171
Fujimoto, Tsutau, 171
Fujita, Isamu, 167
Funabashi, Masatoshi, 425
Furimiya, Colonel, 356, 361, 365–66
Futami, Akisaburo, 145, 200, 244, 254, 274

Gaines, Richard K., 376
Galer, Robert E., 139, 202, 226, 279
Gallant Hours, The (film), 617
"Galloping Horse," 529, 552, 567
    U.S. assault on, 553–55
Gallup polls, 616
Gamble, Lester, 587
Gardner, Francis H., 173
gas attack scare, 237
Gatch, Thomas L., 376, 471, 481–82, 487
    on effect of radar failure, 477
    wounded, 393
Gavutu-Tanambogo, 72, 81, 125, 414, 607
    casualties on, 78–79
    U.S. landings on, 74–79

Geiger, Roy S., 223, 326, 345, 360
  Bombardment and, 319, 322–23
  Henderson Field arrival of, 206
  night flying prohibited by, 321
  personnel problem faced by, 209–10
  Vandegrift and, 233
  Woods as replacement for, 410
General Signal Procedure, 301
Genung, J., 257
George, Alexander M., 533, 583, 589, 592, 593
George, John B., 609
Germany, Nazi, 6, 8, 11, 41, 53
Germany First strategy, 6, 8
  Marshall's opposition to, 43
Getting, Frank E., 100, 105
Ghormley, Robert L., 34, 43, 48, 49, 52, 53, 90, 131, 172, 233, 251, 266, 304, 422, 433, 599, 605
  air offensive of, 280–81
  air power commanded by, 36–37
  Arnold and, 276
  career and personality of, 14
  carrier withdrawal and, 93, 94, 119
  command position of, 55–56
  command problems of, 214–18
  failure of, 600–601
  Fletcher and, 133–34
  Halsey's replacement of, 333–36, 604
  Harmon's correspondence with, 292–93
  Joint Chiefs of Staff and, 134–35
  King and, 216–17
  MacArthur and, 37–38, 134, 334
  Nimitz and, 55–56, 216–17, 226, 277, 292
  pre-landing conference and, 54–55
  priorities as understood by, 56–57
  psychological state of, 334
  on reinforcements, 214–15
  responsibilities of, 214
  Savo Island Battle and, 133–34
  supply difficulties and, 136–38
  Task Force 64 created by, 216–17
  Vandegrift and, 227–28
  Watchtower plan of, 50–51
Gibson, Robert D., 464–66
Giffen, Richard C.:
  in Rennell Island Battle, 579–81, 604
  rigid personality of, 578
Gifu, The, 528–32, 550, 562–66, 609
  casualties at, 566–67
  description of, 531
  tank breakthrough at, 566, 608
  vulnerability of, 531–32
Goettge, Frank, 50, 132
  patrol of, 130–31, 143
Good, Howard H., 377
Goss, Angus, 77
Goto, Aritomo, 100, 170, 295, 438, 603
  in Cape Esperance Battle, 296, 299, 301–4, 306–7, 309–11

  mortally wounded, 302, 307
  in Savo Island Battle, 109–10
Grady, Thomas, 196
Graham, Lieutenant Commander, 120
Great Britain, 9, 15, 27, 84n
  Indian Ocean demonstration by, 35
Greenacre, Alvord J., 174
Greenman, William G., 101, 110–11, 118–19
Gregor, Orville F., 174, 378, 435
Griffith, Samuel B., viii, 149n, 158
  battlefield described by, 240
  in Edson Ridge Battle, 235
  1st Raider Battalion commanded by, 263
  Old Breed described by, 47–48
  wounded, 272
Group "X-ray," 60
Group "Yoke," 60, 72
Grumman F4F Wildcat, 37, 60, 68, 612–13
  shortage of, 138–39
  Zero compared with, 65–67, 94
Grumman TBF Avenger, 166, 174
Guadalcanal, 81
  first Japanese troops on, 31
  geography of, 26–27
  Japanese name for, 261
  psychological value of, 214–15
  terrain of, 62–63, 571
  U.S. memorial on, 618
Guadalcanal campaign:
  combat flying in, 209–10
  comparison of losses in, 601–2
  daily existence in, 256–61
  end of organized resistance in, 597
  interwar period and, 604–5
  Japanese failure in, 606–8
  Japanese tactics in, 608–9
  Japanese withdrawal decision in, 538
  maps and, 50, 63, 143
  Midway Battle and, 598
  Morison on, 618
  naval aviation in, 608–12
  New Guinea campaign as influence on, 498–99
  planning of, 32–36
  public information policy and, 331
  public perception of, 266, 616
  results of, 614–16
  strategic impact of, 614
  Task One of, 34, 35
  Task Three of, 34
  Task Two of, 34
  U.S. naval leadership in, 604–5
Guadalcanal Diary (Tregaskis), 616–17
Guadalcanal landings:
  air strip captured in, 81
  Beach Red in, 61, 62, 63, 70, 126
  casualties in, 78–79
  Cates in, 62, 69–70, 80
  cattle stampede incident after, 128

of 1st Marine Regiment, 61–63
of 7th Marine Regiment, 233, 247,
    251–52, 604
Henderson Field completed after, 127
initial, 79–82
Japanese reaction to, 141–44
success and failure of, 81–82
supply shortage after, 126–27
surprise achieved in, 600
timing of, 599–600
U.S. perimeter built after, 125–26, 127
Vandegrift and, 61, 63, 69, 70, 72, 80, 82
Yamamoto's reaction to, 64
see also Watchtower, Operation
Guadalcanal Remembered (Merillat), 237n
Guthrie, Richard A., 377

Haberman, Roger, 323
Hadley, Hugh W., 211
Hall, Robert, 355, 361, 362, 496
Hallelujah Night, 128
Halloran, P. M., 465
Halsey, William F. "Bull," 56n, 333, 345,
    430, 433, 454, 457, 462, 463, 491, 493,
    503, 516n, 518, 542, 546, 553, 596
Aola expedition and, 420
Cagney's portrayal of, 617
Cole criticized by, 516
Ghormley replaced by, 333–36, 604
Guadalcanal visit of, 422–23
King's approval of, 334
Kinkaid and, 371, 426–27
on Lee's performance, 486
morale and, 605
Munda bombardment and, 548
Ndeni operation cancelled by, 335, 420
Nimitz's appointment of, 333–34
reinforcements and, 409, 411
Rennell Island Battle and, 577–80
Santa Cruz Islands Battle and, 371, 376,
    397–99
Vandegrift and, 351, 422
Vila-Stanmore bombardment ordered by,
    572
Wright instructed by, 504
Hank, William E., 297, 301, 434, 441
Hanneken, Colonel:
in Henderson Field Battle, 361, 363, 364
in Matanikau Battles, 288–89, 351–52,
    414–18
Hara, Chuichi, 168, 176, 375
Hara, Tameichi, 168, 448–49
Hardison, Osborne B., 376, 391
Hardy, Bert W., 132
Harmer, R. E., 181
Harmon, Millard F., 35, 137, 215, 277,
    351, 529, 542
Ghormley's correspondence with, 292–93
Guadalcanal plan criticized by, 138
Watchtower Operation doubted by, 135

Hart, B. H. Liddell, 58
Hartwig, Glenn R., 377
Harwood, Bruce L., 179, 275
in KE Operation, 593–95
Konuma and, 593
Hashimoto, Shintaro, 199, 211, 266,
    281–82, 330, 469, 471, 473, 474–75,
    478, 479, 482, 582, 586, 605
Reinforcement Unit as organized by,
    585, 590–91
Tanaka replaced by, 205
"Tokyo Express" and, 267, 279
Hatano, Commander, 170
Hattori, Taksuhiro, 254–55, 416, 534, 537
17th Army visited by, 417
Hawkins, William B., 132
Hay, Kenneth D., 29, 31
Hayakawa, Mikio, 100, 104, 116, 170
Hayashi, Takahiko, 499, 536
Hayes, Charles H., 131
Hayler, Robert W., 505, 512
Hayter, H. M., 514
health problems, 259–61, 522, 564
Henderson, Loftus, 127
Henderson Field, 127, 135, 140, 163, 256,
    267, 269, 274, 275, 277, 288, 607,
    612
air control and, 606
artillery fire on, 315–16
bombed runways of, 314
"bone heap" on, 162, 360
early warnings and, 206–7
Geiger's arrival at, 206
tactical significance of, 218–19
see also air raids, Japanese; Henderson
    Field, Battle for
Henderson Field, Battle for, 337–367
aerial photographs and, 346, 365
air battle losses in, 366–67
assessment of, 365–66
casualties in, 351, 364–65
final Japanese assaults in, 361–64
1st Marine Division and, 365, 366
1st Marine Regiment in, 343, 348
5th Marine Regiment in, 343, 348, 361,
    364
Hanneken in, 361, 363, 364
"horseshoe" in, 344, 348, 350–52, 361
Hyakutake and, 339–45, 348, 364
imbalance of firepower in, 338–39, 351
Japanese 2d (Sendai) Division and,
    337–42, 346–48, 351–56, 361–62, 364,
    372, 379
Japanese order of battle in, 340
Japanese planning and preparations for,
    337–43, 344–48, 349–50
jungle marches in, 344, 348, 353
Kawaguchi in, 340, 346–48, 365
Left Wing Unit in, 340, 341, 342, 345,
    346, 347, 353–54, 361–62, 364

Henderson Field (*cont'd*)
  Maruyama and, 340–42, 344, 345,
    347–49, 352, 361–62, 364–66
  Matsumoto's planning of, 337–40
  Mikawa and, 357–58, 360
  Nakaguma in, 342–43, 345, 349–51
  Nasu in, 347, 354, 356
  naval action during, 357–61
  Oka and, 342–43, 344, 345, 349–50, 351,
    361, 363, 365
  Puller in, 349, 352–54, 355–56, 361, 362,
    365, 366
  radio intelligence in, 361
  Right Wing Unit in, 340, 342, 348, 353,
    362, 364, 366
  17th Army and, 337–42, 345–48, 354,
    362, 364–66
  7th Marine Regiment in, 343, 348–49,
    352, 362
  tanks in, 342*n*, 343, 350
  Tsuji and, 337, 340–41, 346–47, 348,
    349, 364
  U.S. planning for, 343–44, 348, 351
  Vandegrift and, 343–44
  Yura sunk during, 360–61
Heneberger, Harry B., 112–13
Hepburn, Arthur J., 122
Hersey, John, 284, 285–87, 332, 617
Heyn, Allen C., 458–59
Hiedka, Saneyasu, 384
Higai, Joji, 579, 581
high-speed convoy, 267–68, 313, 314, 328,
    330
  composition of, 315
  Matanikau Battles as influence on, 315
  offloading of, 321–22, 340, 341
  preparations for, 316
  Tanaka and, 316
  Yamamoto and, 316, 319, 326
Hill, Andrew, 585
Hill, Robert E., 73, 291
Hill 11, 532
Hill 27, 529–33, 562–65
Hill 29, 533, 563
Hill 30, 529, 533
Hill 31, 529–31, 533, 563–65
Hill 35, 530
Hill 42, 529, 565
Hill 43, 529, 552, 562–63, 568
Hill 44, 529, 552, 562
Hill 49, 569
Hill 50, 529
Hill 51, 529, 554
Hill 52, 529, 554–56
Hill 53, 529, 550, 552–55
Hill 54, 529, 554
Hill 55, 529, 553
Hill 57, 529, 553–55
Hill 66, 494, 495, 496, 553, 556–57,
    569

Hill 75, 495
Hill 78, 495
Hill 80, 494, 556, 557
Hill 81, 494, 556, 557
Hill 82, 496, 556
Hill 83, 496, 556, 557, 567
Hill 84, 496, 556, 557, 567
Hill 87, 568–70
Hill 88, 568–69
Hill 89, 568–69
Hill 90, 569–70
Hill 91, 569
Hill 98, 569, 570
Hill 99, 569, 570
Hill 121, 74, 76, 78
Hill 148, 74, 76
Hill 208, 73
Hill 281, 72, 74, 77
Hill X, 568
Hill Y, 568–69
Hill Z, 568, 569
Hinode, 617
Hirohito, Emperor of Japan, 18, 144, 224,
    253, 365, 456, 538, 561
  Imperial Rescript of, 539
  Kawaguchi's failure explained to, 253
Hiroyasu, Colonel, 362
Hisamune, Yonejiro, 100, 170, 296
*History of United States Naval Operations
    in World War II* (Morison), viii
Hitler, Adolf, 5
Holcomb, Harold R., 173, 259, 263
Holcomb, Thomas, 47, 157, 351
  front-line tour of, 344–45
Hoogerwerf, R. A., 465
Hoover, Gilbert C., 297, 301, 378, 434,
    451
  Juneau's sinking and, 456–57
Hopkins, Harry, 53
Horihasi, Takeshi, 243
Horii, Tomitaro, 22
Horikoshi, Jiro, 65, 66
Horton, W. W., 53
House of Representatives, U.S., 41
  draft extended by, 616
Hubbard, Harry, 325
Hubbard, Joseph C., 444
Hunt, Leroy P., 51, 52, 130, 195, 196,
    263
Hunt, R. G., 78, 81
Hunter, George P., 172
Hyakutake, Harukichi, 43, 254, 417, 424,
    597
  evacuation of, 591, 595
  Guadalcanal arrival of, 289–90, 338
  Guadalcanal orders of, 143, 146, 157
  Henderson Field Battle and, 339–45,
    348, 364
  Imoto's interviews with, 561
  Kawaguchi's failure as received by, 244

Konuma and, 339
New Guinea operations and, 497
Tanabe's message to, 144
wounded, 496

Ichiki, Kiyoano, 143, 147, 148, 159, 163,
    170, 198, 331, 415, 418, 606, 607
    background of, 145–46
    death of, 156
    Matsumoto's briefing of, 145–46
    Shibuya's firefight as viewed by, 149
    Tenaru River Battle and, 151–53,
        155
Ichimaru, Rinsosuke, 264
Ichimaru, Toshinosuke, 410
Ijuin, Matsuji, 169
Imajuku, Geichiro, 375, 383
Imajuku, Shigeichiro, 167
Imamura, Hitoshi, 497–98, 499, 521, 538,
    541, 561
Imazato, Hiroshi, 171
Imoto, Kumao, 537, 559, 560–61, 587
    Hyakutake's interviews with, 561
Imperial General Headquarters, Japanese,
    144, 290, 400, 499, 524
    Central Agreements of, 18, 142–43,
        253–54, 267, 498, 525, 535, 536
    command rearranged by, 497–98
    Edson Ridge Battle and, 224, 244, 246
    Guadalcanal withdrawal arranged by,
        538
    Guadalcanal withdrawal orders issued
        by, 540
    liaison studies convened by, 141–42
    reinforcements by, 253–55
    revised plans of, 252–55
    shipping debate in, 535–36
    strategic policy change and, 534–39
    U.S. media influence on, 405
    U.S. strengths underestimated by,
        338
Imperial Rescript, 539
Inagaki, Takeyosho, 531, 564, 566
information policy, public, 330–33, 491
"ink-spot" strategy, 227–28
Inoue, Shigeyoshi, 18, 21–22, 23, 31
Into the Valley (Hersey), 332, 617
Irikiin, Yoshiaki, 374, 396
Iron Bottom Sound, 113, 166, 453
Irvine, Charles B., 381–82, 466
Ishii, Shizue, 169
Ishikawa, Nobuo, 171
Ishikawa, Shiroamao, 359, 359n
Ishimoto (intelligence agent), 153–54, 291
Island, The (Merillat), 237n
Ito, General, 324, 328, 421, 425, 495, 529
    death of, 568
Ito, Lieutenant, 287
Iwabuchi, Sanji, 168, 434, 470, 484, 525
Iwahashi, Toru, 169

J2F amphibious biplane, 285
Jachym, Joseph, 148
James, Capers, 263
Japan, 6, 11, 18, 84n
    aircraft production in, 615
    air power doctrine of, 66–67
    China and, 145–46
    steel production in, 535–36
    Western perception of, 607
Jenkins, Samuel P., 173, 378
    in Friday the Thirteenth Battle, 434,
        439–40, 444n, 449, 453–54
Jensen, H. M., 181
Jeschke, Richard H., 424
Jett, Charles M., 173
Jin, Shigenori, 537
Johnson, D. M., 181
Johnson, W. E., 465
Joint Board, of Army and Navy, 6
Joint Chiefs of Staff, 12, 13, 14, 38
    campaign planning and, 34, 43
    Ghormley and, 134–35
    Guadalcanal reinforcements and, 215,
        276
    King and, 216–17, 503
    Pestilence operation as defined by, 56
    Roosevelt's memorandum to, 404–5
Jones, James, vii, 617
Jones, Wilbur G., 377
Joshima, Takaji, 198
Jurney, Claude E., 553

KA, Operation, 198, 253
Kakuta, Kakuji, 370, 374, 393–94, 398
Kamiyama, Masao, 170
Kaneda, Kiyoshi, 169
Kate torpedo bomber, 166
Kato, Michio, 537–38
Kato, Ronpei, 537
Kato, Tadao, 168, 178–79
Katsumata, Jiro, 346, 354–55
Katsumi, Motoi, 168
Kawaguchi, Kiyotaki, 143, 202, 247, 418,
    421, 423, 607
    assault plan of, 219
    barge convoys and, 198–99, 201, 203,
        212
    Edson Ridge Battle and, 218–19, 223–25,
        228–29, 231–35, 240–41, 242, 243,
        244–46
    8th Fleet support of, 219–20
    failure of, 252–54
    Guadalcanal arrival of, 205
    in Henderson Field Battle, 340, 346–48,
        365
    Maruyama message of, 347
    Matanikau Battles and, 269–70, 282, 290
    replacement of, 347
    17th Army and, 198, 201, 203, 218, 220,
        222, 223, 282

Kawaguchi (cont'd)
  Tanaka's conference with, 202–3
  Tasimboko Raid and, 221–22
  withdrawal ordered by, 245
Keeler, Harry, Jr., 511
Keenan, Jack, 502n
Kelly, Charles W., Jr., 273, 352
Kelly, J. J., 587
Kennedy, Donald, 29, 206
Kenny, General, 277
KE Operation:
  air battles during, 582–85, 594–95
  air superiority campaign in, 573–74
  basic outline of, 541
  combat losses in, 595–96, 596n
  DeHaven sunk during, 585
  8th Area Army and, 541, 574, 589–90
  8th Fleet and, 542, 593
  feints planned for, 541
  first evacuation in, 582–88
  Hashimoto in, 593–95
  Japanese forces available for, 542,
    543–44
  La Vallette damaged during, 581
  Makikumo sunk during, 588
  Nimitz on, 597
  numbers evacuated in, 595
  PT-37 sunk during, 587
  PT-111 sunk during, 587
  PT-123 sunk during, 587
  Reinforcement Unit in, 582, 583–87,
    590–92, 594–95
  Rennell Island Battle and, 582
  second evacuation run in, 589–92
  success of, 596
  third evacuation run in, 589, 592–97
  U.S. forces available against, 542–43
  U.S. intelligence failure and, 544–46
  Yamamoto and, 588, 590, 594, 596
Kijima, Kikunori, 307, 309
Kikkawa, Kiyoshi, 449–50
Kimmell, Husband E., 6, 14
Kimura, Masatomi, 168
Kimura, Satsuma, 168, 375, 549, 582
  in convoy-capital ship action, 469–70,
    473, 477–78, 482–83, 485–86
  in Friday the Thirteenth Battle, 434,
    448, 452
  in KE Operation, 582
Kinashi, Takaichi Kinashi, 171, 248
King, Ernest Joseph, 31, 57, 134, 136, 160,
    292, 401, 405, 516n, 577, 578, 581,
    601, 606
  career and personality of, 4–5
  COMINCH appointment of, 5
  Fletcher and, 54
  Ghormley and, 216–17, 503
  Ghormley's command as defined by,
    55–56
  Halsey approved by, 334

  Hepburn's report and, 123
  Joint Chiefs of Staff and, 503
  Kinkaid reassigned by, 503–4
  Lexington group formed by, 10–11
  London visit of, 53
  Nimitz's conferences with, 35, 36, 331
  Pacific strategy and, 8, 9, 12–17, 43
  reinforcements and, 215
  target priorities of, 329
  Watchtower Operation and, 599–600
King, W., 329
"King Board," 5
Kinkaid, Thomas C., 51, 54, 172, 336, 463,
    464, 466
  on Bofors gun, 403
  Halsey and, 426–27
  Halsey's orders to, 371
  King's reassignment of, 503–4
  operations plan of, 503, 507
  Santa Cruz Islands Battle and, 371, 372,
    376, 379, 381, 388–89, 395, 397–99,
    401–2
  Wright's replacement of, 503–4
Kirn, Louis J., 172, 251, 280, 309, 321
  friendly fire on, 234–35
  Guadalcanal departure of, 328
  Minegumo attacked by, 281
  Shikinama attacked by, 266
Kitts, Willard A., III, 377, 505, 515
Knox, Frank, 15, 333, 489
  Guadalcanal visited by, 573–74
Koga, Magotaro, 168
Kokumbona, 413, 583
  capture of, 570
Kokusho, Yukichi, 219, 232, 237
Komatsu, Teruhisa, 171, 375
Kondo, Nobutake, 160, 164, 169, 187, 188,
    193, 429, 542, 582
  convoy-capital ship actions and, 462–63,
    468–70, 472, 474–75, 477, 478–79,
    481, 482–84, 486, 487
  damage claims of, 485
  failure of, 485–86
  plans of, 469, 473
  Santa Cruz Islands Battle and, 368, 369,
    370, 373, 374, 380, 382, 393–94, 398,
    399
Konig, R. H., 187
Konishi, Kaname, 167
Konuma, Norio, 348, 553, 572
  diary of, 254–55
  Hashimoto and, 593
  Hyakutake and, 339
  Mikawa and, 593
  withdrawal order as viewed by, 560–61
Ko'o, Yasuo, 527, 533–34
Koyanagi, Tomiji, 547, 549
Koyanami, Admiral, 582, 586, 605
  evacuees described by, 588
Kozai, Hirai, 170

Kuramoto, Major, 152
Kurita, Takeo, 316, 318, 319, 324, 374
Kurojima, Kameto, 255
Kusaka, Jinichi, 288, 345, 376, 498n, 524–25, 526, 537, 582
　Rennell Island Battle and, 579–80

Lamb, Raymond S., 488
Land, Dale E., 488
Larsen, Harold H., 172, 187, 235, 309, 489
Larsen, Stanley R., 565, 566
League of Nations, 6
Leahy, William, 503
Leary, Herbert F., 10, 13, 33
Leckie, Robert, 70, 258
　battlefield described by, 258
　sea battle described by, 451
Lee, Clark, 331
Lee, James R., 376, 381, 464, 466
Lee, Willis A., 371, 399, 479–87, 503, 548, 577, 603
　convoy-capital ship actions and, 463, 465, 468, 471–75, 477, 479, 482–86, 490
　destroyers withdrawn by, 478–79
　Halsey on performance of, 486
　nickname used by, 473
　plans of, 469–70
　on South Dakota's damage, 480, 482
　Vandegrift and, 473
Lee-Kondo action, see convoy and capital ship actions; Kondo, Nobutake
Leppla, John, 384
Leslie, Dale, 273
Leslie, Maxwell F., 173, 187, 188
Lindsay, Robin, 393, 395
Lindsey, John D., 162
Lion supply detachments, 137
Lofberg, Gus B., 211
London Naval Treaty (1930), 84n
Long Lance torpedoes, 85–86, 101n, 104, 106, 163, 399, 435, 447, 472, 476, 477, 480, 483, 485, 509, 510, 514, 517
"Louie the Louse," 197–98, 231, 316–17
Lowe, Frank L., 377, 505, 511
Lowry, Frank J., 172
Lundstrom, John, 3
Lynch, Lieutenant, 388

MacArthur, Douglas, x, 13, 17, 43, 50, 90, 142, 198, 216, 251, 265, 276, 455n, 599
　Ghormley and, 134
　Ghormley's conference with, 37–38, 334
　New Guinea campaign of, 498–99
MacArthur-Ghormley message, 38
McCain, John S., 51, 52, 127, 164, 174, 227
　air search and, 90, 92, 95

air search failure and, 123
　description of, 36
　Fitch's replacement of, 264
　in pre-landing conference, 54
　on Guadalcanal reinforcements, 214
McCandless, Bruce, 445, 456, 489
McClure, Robert B., 562, 563–65
McCombs, Charles E., 435, 447
McCulloch, William A., 553, 555, 569, 570
McDougal, David S., 284, 287
MacFarland, Donald S., 29, 31
MacGowan, Francis F., 495
McInerney, Francis X., 172
McKean, William, 49
McKelvy, William J., 242, 352
　"horseshoe" defended by, 344, 348, 351
McLarney, E. P., 239
McMillan, George, vii
McMorris, Charles H., 174, 297, 378
Maher, James E., 101, 174, 377
malaria, 259–61, 522, 564
　in 1st Marine Division, 259–60, 351
　see also health problems
Mandates, 6, 20, 42, 44, 370
Mangrum, Richard C., 139–40, 174, 189, 190, 212, 257, 315
　operations routine of, 209
Mansergh, C.A.L., 549
maps, 50, 63, 143, 339
Marchant, William S., 26, 30
Marco Polo Bridge Incident, 145–46
Mark 13 torpedo, 174
Mark XV torpedo, 85–86, 435, 485, 508
Marshall, George C., 9, 12, 13–14, 15, 17, 53, 135, 276, 405
　Germany First strategy opposed by, 43
　reinforcements and, 215
Marshall Memorandum, 15
Marston, John, 556n
Martin, William I., 466
Maruyama, Masao, 279, 557, 570–71, 591
　chronic illness of, 365
　Furimiya's message to, 366
　Guadalcanal arrival of, 282
　Henderson Field Battle and, 340–42, 344, 345, 347–49, 352, 361–62, 364–66
　Kawaguchi's message to, 347
　Matanikau Battles and, 287–88
　reserves needed by, 364
Mason, Charles P., 377, 385, 396, 397
Mason, Paul, 65, 206, 431, 504
Matanikau, battles of the:
　assessment of, 274
　casualties in last action of, 497
　Edson and, 271–73, 284
　1st Marine Division and, 282–83
　1st Marine Raider Battalion in, 270, 271–74, 284, 287

Matanikau (*cont'd*)
  5th Marine Regiment in, 129, 132–33,
    283–84, 287
  7th Marine Regiment in, 270, 283–85,
    287, 289
  8th Marine Regiment in, 494–97
  Hanneken in, 288–89, 351–52, 414–18
  high speed convoy influenced by, 315
  Japanese 4th Infantry Regiment in, 269,
    287–90
  Kawaguchi and, 269–70, 282, 290
  last action of, 493–97
  Maruyama and, 287–88
  Nakaguma in, 284–85, 287, 411, 416
  Nasu in, 282, 284, 287–88
  October, 267, 269–74, 282–91, 606–7
  October casualties in, 273–74
  Oka and, 269, 271, 273, 274
  164th Infantry Regiment in, 494, 496–97
  one-log bridge in, 271, 283–85, 287
  puller and, 270–71, 273, 289
  Scout-Snipers in, 283–85, 287–89
  September, 132–33, 154, 608
  stalemate after, 497
  "Tokyo Express" and, 274–82
  Vandegrift and, 270, 274, 283, 287
Matsubara, Takisaburo, 170
Matsuda, Colonel, 589–90, 592–95
Matsumoto, Hiroshi, 142, 222, 224, 243,
    254, 354
  Henderson Field Battle planning and,
    337–40
  Ichiki briefed by, 145–46
Matsunaga, Lieutenant Commander, 144
Matsuyama, Mitsuhara, 100
Matsuyama, Sakuji, 592
Maxwell, William E., 61, 195–97
Mead, George H., Jr., 132
Mears, Frederick, 317–18
Medal of Honor, 273n, 314n, 327, 355,
    364, 412n
  Bailey awarded, 245
  Callaghan awarded, 489
  Edson awarded, 245
  Scott awarded, 489
Melhorn, Charles M., 524
Merillat, H. C., 237n, 360, 361, 451
Mesley, Lieutenant Commander, 105n
Michener, James, 617, 618
midget submarines, 321–22, 501
Midway, Battle of, 31, 38, 41, 67, 93, 93,
    331, 401, 402
  Guadalcanal campaign and, 598, 614,
    618
  Imperial Navy affected by, 115, 142,
    193, 382–83, 387, 598
  Japanese 3d Fleet in, 25
  Nimitz and aftermath of, 599
  Yamamoto and, 23, 24–25, 606

Mihara, Gen'ichi, 590
Mikawa, Gunichi, 44–45, 90, 92, 95, 100,
    163, 166, 170, 189, 198, 251, 281,
    308, 312, 322, 369, 429, 468, 491,
    542
  assessment of, 605
  battle plan of, 89
  convoy-capital ship action and, 462–65
  flawed victory of, 121
  float planes used by, 197
  formation used by, 311
  Henderson Field Battle and, 357–58, 360
  Konuma and, 593
  Murakami and, 200
  in Savo Island Battle, 102–4, 106–7,
    109, 112, 115
  surprise achieved by, 120–21, 122, 123
  Tanaka and, 487
  U.S. landings as viewed by, 86–89
  weather as used by, 102
  withdrawal ordered by, 116
Miller, Charles A., 76, 77
Miller, Robert C., 332
Miller, Thomas G., Jr., viii, 210n, 612
Minegishi, Keijiro, 407
Mitchell, Herbert V., 555
Mitsubishi G3M (Nell) bomber, 85
Mitsubishi G4M (Betty) bomber, 67–68,
    85, 206–7
Mitzi, Lieutenant Commander, 431, 437
Miyano, Lieutenant, 589–90
Miyazaki, Shigetoshi, 31, 74, 78
Miyazaki, Shu'ichi, 330, 370, 407
  aerial photographs and, 346
  diary of, 321
  evacuation by, 586, 591–92
  Futami replaced by, 254
  Sugita and, 416
  38th Infantry Division and, 406, 408
  withdrawal opposed by, 560–61
Miyazaki, Takeharu, 171
Miyoshi, Teruhiko, 169
Mizuno, Eishi, 219, 242
Montgomery, Allen, 318
Monzen, Kanae, 31, 59, 70, 131–32, 196,
    225
Moore, Bryant E., 313–14, 496
Moore, John R., 116
Moore, Samuel N., 101, 111–12
morale:
  daily existence and, 256, 257
  of 11th Air Fleet, 410
  enemy bombardment and, 139–40,
    209–10, 351
  Halsey and, 605
  Japanese, 608, 613
  passivity and, 195, 463
  radio broadcasts and, 333, 342
  in 17th Army, 553

of U.S. pilots, 201–2
of U.S. troops, 606, 616
Moran, Edward J., 297, 299, 305, 307
Moret, Paul, 410
Mori, Tomoichi, 169
Morinaga, Masahiko, 171
Morison, Samuel Eliot, viii, 93, 105n, 117,
    210, 516, 617
    on Guadalcanal campaign, 618
    on Tanaka, 517–18
Morrell, Rivers J., 213
Mount Austen, 519, 552
    casualties on, 532, 533–34
    fighting on, 530–31
    Japanese memorial on, 618
    terrain of, 529
Mulcahy, Francis, 542
Munda airfield:
    fiasco at, 525–26
    U.S. bombardment of, 548–49
Munn, J. C. "Toby," 320–21
Munro, Douglas A., 273
Munson, Henry G., 87
Murakami, Binichi, 168
Murakami, Yonosuke, 200, 201, 205
Murata, Shigeharu, 167, 375, 382, 401
Murray, George D., 371, 377, 395–96,
    397–98
Myhre, F.B.T., 307–8

Nabeshima, Shunsaku, 169
Nagano, Osami, 18, 19, 142, 144, 539
Nagumo, Chuichi, 23, 160
    in Eastern Solomons Battle, 164, 167,
        175, 186, 193
    Indian Ocean sortie of, 24, 44, 186
    at Midway, 24, 186
    in Santa Cruz Islands Battle, 368–69,
        372, 374, 379–83, 393–94
Nakagawa, Minoru, 167
Nakaguma, Colonel:
    death of, 420
    in Henderson Field Battle, 342–43, 345,
        349–51
    in Matanikau battles, 284–85, 287, 411,
        416
Nakahara, Giichiro, 168, 505, 509, 518
Nakai, Makoto, 171
Nakajima, Kehei, 354
Nakasugi, Seiji, 168
Naoi, Toshio, 168
Nasu, Yumio, 341, 345, 346
    death of, 362
    Guadalcanal arrival of, 278
    in Henderson Field Battle, 347, 354, 356
    Left Wing Unit commanded by, 340
    in Matanikau Battles, 282, 284, 287–88
    Ohmae's opinion of, 365
National Geographic, 277

National Guard, U.S., 313, 530, 552
Naval Battle of Guadalcanal, 605, 610,
    612, 614; see also convoy and capital
    ship actions; Friday the Thirteenth,
    Battle of
naval code, Japanese, 81
    see also radio intelligence
Naval General Staff, Japanese, 252
Naval Intelligence, U.S. Office of, 544
Navy, Imperial:
    aircraft lost by, 609–12
    air crews lost by, 611–12
    air groups renumbered by, 410
    air power and, 197
    Decisive Battle Doctrine of, 83
    destroyers used as transports by, 199
    "Diving Shell" developed by, 306n
    Midway Battle's impact on, 598
    night fighting expertise of, 84–85
    sea lift controversy of, 408
    submarine deployment of, 248
    supplies and, 261
    supply by destroyer terminated by, 521
    total commitment of, 252
    traditionalism of, 66, 84
    U.S. navy compared to, 603–4
    warship losses acknowledged by, 489
Navy, U.S.:
    aircraft lost by, 610
    Arnold on logistics of, 277
    Imperial Navy compared to, 603–4
    leadership of, 604–5
    media and, 331–33
    night fighting ability of, 84–85
    radar used by, 294n
    radio monitoring by, 148
    Savo Island Battle as viewed by,
        121–23
    "treaty cruisers" of, 516–17
    warship losses acknowledged by, 489
Navy Department, U.S., 14, 42n, 501
    War Plans Division of, 38
Navy List, Japanese, 179
Navy's War, The (Pratt), 444n
Ndeni operation, 133–34
    Halsey's cancellation of, 335, 420
    Turner and, 292–93, 420
Nelson, Leroy E., 530–31, 532–33
Netherlands East Indies, 499
Neutrality Patrol, 5, 84
New Guinea, 26, 33, 34, 45, 278, 537, 538,
    540–41, 545, 546, 611, 614
    MacArthur's campaign in, 498–99
New York Herald Tribune, 332–33
New York Times, 266, 331, 332, 333, 404,
    522
New Zealand, 8–9, 10–11, 44, 46, 52, 53,
    56
Nezumi operation, 202

Nimitz, Chester W., x, 31, 134, 138, 148, 172, 370, 401, 409, 491, 516*n*, 542, 574
  assessment of, 605
  Cape Esperance Battle assessed by, 403
  Chicago sinking as viewed by, 581
  CINCPAC appointment, 5, 6
  CINCPOA appointment of, 13
  Fletcher's promotion urged by, 54
  Ghormley and, 55–56, 216–17, 226, 277, 292
  Halsey appointed by, 333–34
  Japanese torpedoes unappreciated by, 517
  on KE Operation, 597
  King's conference with, 35, 36, 331
  Midway aftermath and, 599
  Pacific Fleet message of, 204
  Pacific strategy and, 12–15
  pilot training and, 139, 175
  radio intelligence and, 398, 544, 573, 577, 580, 582, 605
  Savo Island Battle as assessed by, 123
  South Pacific tour of, 276–77, 292
  submarines and, 94–95, 329
  Tulagi and, 33, 64
  Vandegrift and tour of, 277
  Wasp sinking investigated by, 250
Nishida, Masao, 168, 434, 440, 452, 455, 461
Nishihata, Major, 566
Nishimura, Shoji, 168, 375, 429, 463–64
Nishino, Kozo, 171
Nishiura, Susumu, 144–45
Nishiyama, Major, 497, 500, 527, 567–68
Nishizawa, Hiroyoshi, 64
Noble, Christopher, 377
Norita, Sadatoshi, 171
North Africa, invasion of, 215, 216
Notomi, Kenjiro, 168, 176
Notomo, Tameteru, 167
Noumea, 136–37
Noyes, Leigh, 51, 67, 93, 119, 173, 604
  Wasp sinking and, 248, 249–50
Number 8 Operation, 498

Obara, Colonel, 613
Obayashi, Sueo, 375, 382
odd-even order, 439–40, 442
Ofstie, Ralph, 277
Ogura, Masami, 513
Ohmae, Toshikazu, 45, 109, 116, 121, 365, 407, 415
Oka, Akinosuka, 411, 607
  barge convoy of, 203, 212–13, 219, 225
  in Edson's Ridge Battle, 229, 232, 235, 243, 246
  Henderson Field Battle and, 342–43, 344, 345, 349–50, 351, 361, 363, 365

  Matanikau battles and, 269, 271, 273, 274
Okamura, Norinaga, 59
Okuma, Tokunaga, 31
"Old Breed," 47–48
Omasu, Lieutenant, 497
Omori, Sentaro, 374
O'Neil, Roger W., 456, 459
one-log bridge, 271, 283–85, 287
Orndorff, Clarence A., 568, 593
Ota, Toshio, 64
over-claiming, 314*n*–15*n*

P-400 fighter, 37, 202
Pacific Fleet, U.S., 20, 24, 172–74
  Nimitz's message to, 204
Pacific Islands Yearbook, 49
Pacific Ocean Campaign Plan, 15–16
Paige, Mitchell, 363–64
Parker, Edward N., 434, 441
Parker, Edwin B., Jr., 377, 383, 387
passwords, 128
Patch, Alexander M., 137, 351, 529, 544, 546, 553, 556*n*, 559, 568, 572, 583, 589, 593
  assault plan of, 550
  CAM Division created by, 570
  U.S. victory as announced by, 596–97
  Vandegrift replaced by, 521–22
Pate, Randolph M., 52
Patterson, Robert, 322
Pearl Harbor attack, 3, 20–21, 23
Pepper, Robert H., 126, 343
Perry, Benjamin F., 377
"Pestilence," Operation, 35
  Joint Chiefs of Staff definition of, 56
Peters, Ernest, 563–65
Petersen, Wallis F., 377
Philippines, 6, 8, 13, 16, 18, 499
pillboxes, at the Gifu, 531
Pistol Pete, 319
Pogue, William G., 172
Polk, George W., 131
Pollock, Edwin A., 150, 153, 156
Powell, William K., 183
Prange, Gordan, 151*n*
Pratt, Fletcher, 444*n*
Pratt, Malcolm, 130
Price, Walter H., 101
Pride of the Marines (film), 617
PT Boats, 425, 464, 473, 560, 582, 588, 591, 596
  first action of, 318
  Reinforcement Unit attacks by, 520–21, 523–24, 547, 549, 586–87
  submarine sunk by, 523
  Tenryu skirmish of, 423
public information policy, 330–33, 491
Puller, Lewis B. "Chesty," 417, 420
  Clemens on, 270

in Henderson Field Battle, 349, 352–54, 355–56, 361, 362, 365, 366
Matanikau Battles and, 270–71, 273, 289
wounded, 422
Purple Heart Medal, 522
Pye, William S., 14, 459–60

radar, 103, 111, 207, 278, 313, 431, 503
air raid warning by, 295–96
assessment of, 603
Cape Esperance Battle and, 294–95, 299, 301, 603
in convoy-capital ship action, 470, 475, 477, 479, 480
in Eastern Solomons Battle, 163, 174–75, 179–80, 186
in Friday the Thirteenth Battle, 436, 438, 446, 447, 460, 603
Japanese, capture of, 81
in Santa Cruz Islands Battle, 384, 385, 390, 391, 392
Savo Island Battle and, 99, 603
Scott and, 294
South Dakota's, 477–78, 479
in Tassafaronga Battle, 507–9, 511–12, 516, 603
of U.S. Navy, 294n
visual means vs., 103
see also SG radar
radio broadcasts, 333, 342
radio discipline, 180, 192
Radio Guadalcanal, 473, 580, 583
radio intelligence, 214, 281, 328, 407, 414, 426, 523, 546
in Cape Esperance Battle, 294
in convoy-capital ship action, 473, 491
in Eastern Solomons Battle, 161
in Friday the Thirteenth Battle, 432–33, 455
in Henderson Field Battle, 361
Japanese, 278, 369–70
Japanese logistics and, 574–75
Nimitz and, 398, 544, 573, 577, 580, 582, 605
overview of, 38–43
in Santa Cruz Islands Battle, 369–70, 398
U.S. Navy monitoring and, 148
Vila-Stanmore and, 572
Radio Tulagi, 64
Radke, A., 110
Rainbow Five plan, 6
Ramsey, DeWitt C., 172
Ramsey, Donald J., 122, 377
Rat operation, 202
Rat Transportation, 266, 267, 268, 500, 502
Read, Jack, 29, 79, 206, 279
Read, Robert F., 182, 183
Red Base, 400n
Reed, Walter C., 505

Register, Francis R., 180
Reifsnider, Lawrence F., 63
reinforcement shuttles, 199–202
Reinforcement Unit, 547, 549, 559, 560
continued efforts of, 519–21
11th Air Fleet and, 295–96, 594–95
Hashimoto's organization of, 585, 590–91
in KE Operation, 582, 583–87, 590–92, 594–95
PT Boat attacks on, 523–24, 547, 549
supply by, 502, 504, 505, 507, 509, 518, 519–20
Tassafaronga Battle and, 502, 504, 507, 509, 578
Rennell Island, Battle of, 577–81
Chicago sunk in, 581, 604
Giffen in, 579–81, 604
Halsey and, 577–80
KE Operation affected by, 582
Kusaka and, 579–80
Reynolds, Carroll D., 174
Rhoades, F. Ashton "Snowy," 29, 31
Richard, Robert, 410, 465, 488
Richardson, David C., 181, 228
Richey, Lieutenant, 466
Riduka, Frank, 391
Riefkohl, Frederick L., 97, 99, 101, 108–9, 113, 114, 122, 123
Rigaud, Charles A., 285–87
Ringer, Wilfred, 130
Ripstra, Earl F., 530
River Base, 400n
Rivers, John, 152
Roberts, David G., 377
Robertshaw, Major, 523
Rodee, Walter F., 377
Rogers, Otho, 273
Romberg, Henry A., 173
Roosevelt, Franklin D., 3, 5, 10, 11, 12, 15, 17, 53, 84, 616
Joint Chiefs memorandum of, 404–5
Roosevelt, James, 35
Roper, Clifford H., 505
Rorschach, Anthony L., 172
Rosecrans, Harold E., 73
Rosendahl, Charles E., 505, 510, 513–14
Round-up, Operation, 15
Runyon, Donald E., 181
Rupertus, William B., 48, 51, 72, 75, 77, 418, 420, 421, 422
Russell, G. L., 123
Russo-Japanese War, 85

Sailor, Joseph, 409, 425, 464, 465, 467, 487–88
death of, 520
Saito, Hiroshi, 110
Sakai, Saburo, 64, 67, 68–69
Sakai, Yoshitsugu, 495, 497

Sakakibara, Lieutenant, 158
Sakamaki, Munetaka, 145, 525, 611–12
Sakamoto, Eichi, 575
Sanada, Joichiro, 537, 538, 604
Sanchez, Henry G., 377, 388, 402
Sano, Tadayoshi, 425, 528, 529, 561, 568, 586, 588
Santa Cruz Islands, Battle of, 368–403, 605
    Abe and, 369, 375, 381, 383, 386–88, 393
    aircraft losses in, 400–401
    assessment of, 399–403, 602
    casualties in, 400–401
    Enterprise in, 370–73, 376, 379, 383–85, 388–93, 395–96, 399, 400n, 401–2
    Halsey and, 371, 376, 397–99
    Hornet in, 369–71, 373, 377, 379, 383–88, 389, 390, 391–92, 394–99, 400n, 401, 402
    Hornet sunk in, 398–99
    Japanese Carrier Division 1 in, 368–69, 372, 374–75, 379, 382, 388, 394, 397
    Japanese 11th Air Fleet in, 376
    Japanese force composition in, 368–69, 374–76
    Japanese fuel problems in, 370, 399
    Japanese 2d Fleet in, 368, 372, 374, 382, 398
    Japanese superiority in, 373
    Japanese 3d Fleet in, 368, 374, 375
    Junyo in, 368, 370–72, 374, 391–97, 399
    Kinkaid and, 371, 372, 376, 379, 381, 388–89, 395, 397–99, 401–2
    Kondo and, 368, 369, 370, 373, 374, 380, 382, 393–94, 398, 399
    Nagumo in, 368–69, 372, 374, 379–83, 393–94
    Porter sunk in, 388–90
    radar in, 384, 385, 387, 390, 391, 392
    radio intelligence in, 369–70, 398
    Shokaku in, 368–69, 374, 382–83, 387, 390, 394, 395, 396, 401
    South Dakota in, 371, 376, 389, 391, 392–93, 399
    Support Fleet in, 368–70, 372, 379, 399
    U.S. intelligence estimates in, 371
    Vanguard Force in, 369, 372, 379–81, 386–87, 393, 398
    Yamamoto and, 368, 373, 374, 398, 399
    Zuiho in, 369, 375, 381–82, 384, 388, 394, 400–401
    Zuikaku in, 368–69, 375, 379, 382–83, 390, 393, 394–97, 400
Sasaki, Hanmazu, 171
Sasaki, Seigo, 169
Sato, Kiichiro, 168
Sato, Masao, 375
Sato, Shiro, 169

Sato, Torajiro, 147, 169, 422, 505, 513, 518, 520–21
    in Tassafaronga Battle, 502, 509–10
Sato, Yasuo, 169
Sauer, Edward P., 173
Saunders, LaVerne "Blondie," 37, 174, 276, 466, 502n
Sautot, Governor, 36
Savo Island, Battle of, 83–123, 217, 251, 293, 311, 312, 331, 605, 607, 610
    aerial reconnaissance in, 88–89, 90–93, 123
    aftermath of, 117–120
    Allied material superiority in, 101
    assessment of, 120–23, 603
    Astoria in, 108–11, 113
    Astoria sunk in, 118–19
    Canberra in, 104–7, 109
    Canberra sunk in, 117–18
    Chicago in, 105–7, 109
    Chokai in, 86–88, 103–5, 107, 108, 109–11, 112, 113, 114, 116
    composition of forces in, 100–101
    Crutchley and, 105n, 107n, 108, 113
    Goto in, 109–10
    Hepburn's report on, 122–23
    Japanese casualties in, 117n
    Japanese Cruiser Division 6 in, 86–87, 110, 116
    Japanese Cruiser Division 18 in, 86, 106–8
    Japanese formation in, 102–3
    Jarvis sunk in, 120
    Kinugasa in, 100, 103, 106–7, 111, 113, 116
    Mikawa in, 102–4, 106–7, 109, 112, 115
    Mikawa withdraws from, 116
    Naval War College Analysis, 87n, 94n, 105n
    night fighting tactics in, 84–86
    Nimitz's assessment of, 123
    Northern Group, U.S. in, 98–99, 101, 107–8
    prewar strategy and, 83–84
    Quincy in, 104, 108, 109, 111–14
    Quincy sunk in, 113
    radar and, 99, 603
    Scott in, 97–99, 101
    Southern Group, U.S. in, 97, 98, 100, 104–7, 108, 109
    torpedoes used in, 85–86
    Turner and prelude to, 90, 92, 93, 94–96, 99
    Turner on, 123
    U.S. carriers and, 93–94, 119
    U.S. casualties in, 121n
    U.S. Navy reaction to, 121–23
    U.S. preparations and, 89–101
    U.S. screening patrols prior to, 97–99

Vincennes in, 104, 107, 109, 113
Vincennes sunk in, 114
weather and, 102
Yamamoto's reaction to, 121
Sawa, Masao, 100, 116, 170, 296, 303, 464
Sawruk, James, 389*n*
Schinka, Joseph, 182
Schmid, Albert A., 152
Schonland, Herbert E., 445, 489
Scott, Norman, 97, 174, 249, 320, 470, 503, 603, 604
  battle discontinued by, 306
  battle plan of, 293–94
  in Cape Esperance Battle, 294–95, 296–97, 299–306, 310–11, 312
  death of, 443–44
  flagship of, 293
  in Friday the Thirteenth Battle, 430, 433, 434, 436, 459
  Medal of Honor awarded to, 489
  radars ordered off by, 294
  in Savo Island Battle, 97–99, 101
  seniority and, 433*n*
SCR air warning radar, 207
Sea Horse, 529, 552, 562–64
Searles, John M., 318, 521, 523
Searles, Robert L., 318
Seaward, Eugene T., 174, 297
Sebree, General, 422, 423, 494–96
  offensive as planned by, 494
Second South Pacific Campaign, 3, 25
Seiichi, Okada, 100
Sejima, Ryuzo, 534–35, 537, 538
Seki, Mamoru, 167, 177, 180, 189, 374, 383, 390, 401
Semba, Shigeo, 167
SG radar, 294, 300, 436, 438, 447, 470, 475, 479, 503, 507–8, 511–12
Shands, Courtney, 173
sharks:
  Juneau survivors attacked by, 458–59
  Meredith and *Viero* survivors attacked by, 325
Shaw, R. C., 178
Sherman, Forrest P., 119, 173, 249
Sherman, James F., 151
Shibayama, Kazuo, 170
Shibuya, Captain, 148–49, 157
Shichiji, Tsuneo, 171
Shiga, Yoshio, 374, 391–92, 397
Shimizu, Toshio, 505, 513
Shingo, Hideki, 167, 374
Shinohara, Tamao, 86
Shirane, Ayao, 167, 375
Shoji, Colonel, 347, 353–54, 362, 406, 421–24
Short History of Japan, A, 128
Shoup, David, 424
Shoup, F. E., 118
Showers, H. A., 101

Shumway, DeWitt W., 172
Silver Star Medal, 154
Simpler, Leroy C., 172, 226, 257–58, 276, 323, 326
Simpson, Rodger W., 377
Simpson, W. S., 127
Sims, Arthur, 420
Sims, Gelzer L., 173, 377, 393, 505
Sims's Ridge, 555, 556
Sinclair, George A., 100
Singapore, 616
Singer, Jack, 249
Singletary, Wesley S., 325
Sino-Japanese War, 85
Sledgehammer, Operation, 15, 53
Slot, the, 206, 212, 280, 547
Small, Ernest G., 174, 297, 300
Smedberg, William R., 378
Smith, Herschel A., 184
Smith, John L., 139, 162, 174, 201, 202, 223, 279
  aerial combat tactics of, 207–8
Smith, Leo R., 202
Smith, William A., 186
Smoot, Roland N., 101, 173
SN Operation, 31
Snowden, Ernest M., 173
Solomon Islands, geography of, 26–27
Soma, Shohei, 167
Soucek, Apollo, 396
Southerland, James J., 67–68
South Pacific Sea Battle, *see* Cape Esperance, Battle of
Soviet Union, 15, 18
Spragins, Robert L., 569
Spruance, Raymond, 56*n*, 402
Spurlock, Lyman D., 132–33, 154
Stafford, Richard Y., 291
Stalingrad, Battle of, 404
Stark, Harold R., 4
steel production, shipping vs., 535–36
Stephan, John J., 24
Stimson, Henry L., 12
Stokes, Thomas M., 377, 434, 438
Stormes, Max C., 377, 471, 476
Stover, E. T., 322
Strong, Stockton B., 173, 381–82
Struggle for Guadalcanal, The (Morison), 617
submarines, 328–29, 500–502
  Imperial Navy deployment of, 248
  midget, 321–22, 501
  Nimitz and, 329
  supply by, 500–502, 523, 574–75
Suenaga, Naoji, 170
Sugita, Colonel, 340, 342, 413, 418, 499, 534
  Miyazaki and, 416
Sugitani, Nagahide, 170
Sugiyama, Hajime, 18, 142, 144–45, 253, 255, 538–39

Sullivan, Albert, 457, 459, 489–90
Sullivan, Francis, 457, 459, 489–90
Sullivan, George, 457, 458, 459, 489–90
Sullivan, Joseph, 457, 459, 489–90
Sullivan, Madison, 457, 459, 489–90
Sumiyoshi, Tadashi, 339, 342–43, 344, 345, 348, 349, 411
Sumrall, H. M., 180
Sunderland, General, 277
supply:
    drum method of, 501–2, 520, 547
    Ghormley and, 136–38
    after Guadalcanal landings, 126–27
    Imperial Navy and, 261
    Japanese problem in, 408
    Japanese 38th Division and, 499–500, 526–27
    Reinforcement Unit and, 502, 504, 505, 507, 509, 518, 519–20
    of 17th Army, 408, 500, 518, 519
    by submarines, 500–502, 523, 574–75
    tactics as affected by, 137–38
    U.S. Army control of, 493
    U.S. difficulties in, 126–27, 135–38
    see also "Tokyo Express"
Suzuki, Masaaki, 72
Suzuki, Masakane, 441
Suzuki, Yasuatsu, 169
Sweeney, John B., 238
Sweeny, R. J., 78–79
Sweetser, Willard M., 378, 505
Swenson, Lyman K., 377, 434, 446, 456

Tachibana, Masao, 170
tactics:
    air raid, 275–76
    improvised, 77–78
    Japanese, 73–74, 159–60
    supply as influence on, 137–38
    in Tassafaronga Battle, 517–18
    torpedoes as influence on, 86
Takagi, Takeo, 169
Takahashi, Kameshiro, 167
Takahashi, Lieutenant, 131, 133
Takahashi, Sadamu, 167, 177, 186, 193, 375
Takahashi, Yuji, 100
Takama, Tamotsu, 169, 315, 357, 358, 360–61, 434, 436, 437, 450, 452, 470
    U.S. air attack as viewed by, 323–24
Takamatsu, Etsuo, 213
Takayanagi, Gihachi, 167
Tales of the South Pacific (Michener), 617
Tamagawa, Y. "Tommy," 617–18
Tamaoki, Colonel, 339, 340, 341, 344, 347, 406, 557
Tamura, Masao, 219, 238–39, 240, 411, 413
Tanabe, Moritake, 145, 255, 290, 465, 591–92, 595
    Hyakutake message of, 144

Tanabe, Suketomo, 428
Tanaka, Ichiro, 375, 397
Tanaka, Kikumatsu, 168
Tanaka, Raizo, 146, 147, 157, 159, 199, 200, 201, 326, 374, 422, 428–29, 432, 452, 519–20
    attack ordered by, 507–8
    convoy and capital ship actions and, 465, 466, 468–69, 471, 472, 474, 482, 483, 487, 489, 490–91
    criticism of, 517–18
    Eastern Solomons Battle and, 162, 164–65, 166, 170, 188–89, 190, 193
    Hashimoto's replacement of, 205
    High Speed Convoy and, 316
    Kawaguchi's conference with, 202–3
    Mikawa and, 487
    Morison on, 517–18
    Tassafaronga Battle and, 502–3, 504, 505, 507–9, 513, 517, 605
    wounded, 523–24
Tanaka, Shin'ichi, 142, 255, 537
    Tojo's argument with, 536
tanks:
    in Edson's Ridge Battle, 242
    at the Gifu, 566, 608
    in Henderson Field Battle, 342n, 343, 350
    in Tenaru River Battle, 154–56
    Tregaskis's description of, 155
    Type 95, 350
    Type 97, 350
Tasimboko Raid, 218, 220–22
Task One, *see* Watchtower, Operation
Task Two, 134
Tassafaronga, Battle of, 493, 502–18, 604, 605
    aftermath of, 513–16
    casualties in, 514
    composition of forces in, 505–6
    fatal delay in, 508
    1st Transportation Unit in, 502–3, 505, 508
    2d Transportation Unit in, 502, 505
    Japanese torpedo segment of, 509–13
    Minneapolis torpedoed in, 510–11
    New Orleans in, 505, 507, 511–12, 514, 515
    Northampton sunk in, 514–15
    Pensacola torpedoed in, 511–12
    radar in, 507–9, 511–12, 516, 603
    Reinforcement Unit in, 502, 504, 505, 507, 509, 518
    results of, 517–18, 603
    Sato in, 502, 509–10
    tactics in, 517–18
    Takanami sunk in, 513
    Tanaka and, 502–3, 504, 505, 513, 517, 605
    Tanaka's attack order in, 507–8

Tanambogo, *see* Gavutu-Tanambogo
Task Force 67 in, 503–7, 517
  U.S. command change in, 512
  U.S. review of, 515–16
  Wright and, 504, 505, 507, 508, 510,
    514, 517, 518
Taylor, Edmund B., 297, 301, 302, 304,
    307, 485
Taylor, Harold, 488
Taylor, John B., 378, 471
Tenaru River, Battle of, 150–58, 259, 262
  assessment of, 157–58
  casualties in, 156
  Cates in, 153–55
  Clemens's observation of, 153
  Ichiki and, 151–53, 155
  psychological products of, 156–57
  tanks in, 154–56
  Thomas and, 154
  Vandegrift and, 154, 155, 157
Terrell, W. R., 58*n*
Thin Red Line, The (Jones), vii, 617
Thomas, Gerald, 125, 140, 263, 270, 316,
    413, 418
  in Edson's Ridge Battle, 220, 222–23,
    233
  Ghormley-Vandegrift message and,
    227–28
  Tenaru River Battle and, 154
Thomas, James A., 376
Thomas, John, 467
Tiemroth, Harold H., 173
Timboe, Arthur C., 423
Tisdale, Mahlon S., 173, 376, 505, 516
  Wright seconded to, 512
Tobin, Robert G., 174, 300–301, 302, 306,
    435, 436*n*, 446
Tobruk, 616
Tojo, Hideki, 18, 144–45, 254, 535
  Tanaka's argument with, 536
"Tokyo Express," 205, 210, 247, 260, 266,
    267–68, 295, 321, 414, 422–23, 521,
    523, 524, 547, 559, 593, 596–97, 605
  air raids and, 274–82
  food carried by, 261
  Hashimoto and, 267, 279
  Matanikau Battles and, 274–82
  17th Army and, 315, 324, 328, 330, 421
Tolman, Charles E., 583–85
Topper, James R., 110
Torch, Operation, 53, 404, 405
Torgerson, Harry L., 78, 237, 238, 239,
    241
torpedoes, 105, 109, 113, 114, 116
  Long Lance, 85–86, 101*n*, 104, 106, 163,
    399, 435, 447, 472, 476, 477, 480, 483,
    485, 509, 510, 514, 517
  Mark 13, 174
  Mark XV, 85–86, 435, 485, 508
"Torpedo Junction," 335

Toshima, Shunichi, 170
treaty cruisers, 516–17
Tregaskis, Richard, 220, 222, 233, 238,
    241, 272, 332, 616–17
  tanks described by, 155
True, Arnold E., 377, 401
Truesdell, William H., 110
Tsuji, Masanobu, 254, 269, 290, 370,
    407–8, 416, 534
  Henderson Field Battle and, 337,
    340–41, 346–47, 348, 349, 364
  Yamamoto's meeting with, 268
Tsukahara, Nishizo, 44, 64, 163, 164, 170,
    171, 288
Tsukamoto, Moritaro, 169
Tsutau, Araki, 100, 170, 296, 303, 309–10
Tulagi, 60, 64, 81, 125, 338*n*
  casualties on, 78–79
  1st Marine Raider Battalion on, 72–74,
    77–78
  initial U.S. landings on, 72–74
Turner, Richmond Kelly, 13, 38, 50, 51,
    52, 58, 77, 110, 119, 120, 127, 131,
    134, 138, 212, 216, 277, 313, 334, 420,
    425, 431–32, 435, 436, 457, 490, 491,
    599, 604, 607
  background and personality of, 16–17
  Callaghan appointed by, 433
  Canberra ordered destroyed by, 117–18
  convoys planned by, 429–30
  Crutchley's meeting with, 96–97
  in Eastern Solomons Battle, 163, 166
  Edson's Ridge Battle and, 229, 232–33
  errors of, 96, 99
  Ghormley-Vandegrift message and,
    227–28
  Guadalcanal Island as viewed by, 60
  Guadalcanal recommended as objective
    by, 35–36
  at Halsey's conference, 351
  Hepburn's report and, 122–23
  "ink spot" strategy of, 227–28
  Japanese radar and, 81
  Ndeni operation and, 292–93, 420
  pre-landing conference and, 54
  on Savo Island Battle, 123
  Savo Island Battle prelude and, 90, 92,
    93, 94–96, 99
  7th Marine Regiment and, 247, 251
  transports withdrawn by, 124–25
  Vandegrift's meeting with, 96–97
  war plan of, 15–16
  Wasp and, 247–48
  Watchtower rehearsal and, 57
Tuttle, W. B., 420
Twining, Merrill B., 49, 156, 228*n*, 235,
    263, 350, 413, 417, 418
  shoulder patch designed by, 523
Twining, Nathan F., 542
Twombley, Bernard B., 495

"Two-Ocean Navy Act" (1940), 20
Type 3 shells, 316
Type 95 light tank, 350
Type 97 tank, 350

Uehlinger, A. E., 481
Uesugi, Yoshitake, 167
Ugaki, Tamaki, 169, 265, 310, 379, 398, 431, 485, 534
Ultra code, 42
United States, 10, 18, 53, 84n, 405
  aircraft production in, 615
  Japanese perception of, 615–16
  public information policy of, 330–33, 491

Val dive-bomber, 166
Vandegrift, Archer, 51, 52, 53, 94, 119, 132, 134, 135, 137, 148, 165, 195, 206, 216, 251, 259, 304, 327, 328, 338n, 350, 366, 409, 417, 418, 420, 424, 459, 493–94, 523, 550, 597
  artillery fire and, 315–16
  assessment of, 607–8
  Baldwin's conversation with, 266
  "The Bombardment" and, 317, 320
  Brush's firefight aftermath and, 149
  Clemens and, 131
  on coast watchers, 521–22, 612
  completion of airfield and, 127
  cordon defense by, 261–63
  Edson's Ridge Battle and, 223, 233, 242, 243
  1st Marine Division reorganized by, 46–47
  5th Marine Regiment and, 196
  7th Marine Regiment and, 46, 227–28
  Fitch's visit to, 266
  forces commanded by, 48–49
  Geiger and, 233
  Ghormley's message to, 227–28
  on Halsey, 422
  Halsey and, 351
  Henderson Field Battle and, 343–44
  initial landings and, 61, 63, 69, 70, 72, 80, 82
  inspections by, 257
  Lee and, 473
  Matanikau Battles and, 270, 274, 283, 287
  Maxwell relieved by, 196–97
  media and, 332
  Nimitz's inspection tour and, 277
  November offensive planned by, 411
  Patch's replacement of, 521–22
  patrols ordered by, 129–30
  perimeter defense created by, 219
  personal reconnaissance by, 81
  pilots greeted by, 140
  pre-landing conference and, 54
  Scout-Sniper unit created by, 263–64
  subordinates described by, 124–25
  Tasimboko Raid and, 220–21
  Tenaru River Battle and, 154, 155, 157
  Turner's meeting with, 96–97
  Watchtower rehearsal and, 57
Vejtasa, Stanley W., 390
Victory Disease, 22
Vila-Stanmore, 572–73
Vorse, Lieutenant, 180–81
Vose, James E., 377, 387
Vouza, Jacob, 131
  ordeal of, 153–54
VT (variable time) fuze, 549, 581

Wakabayashi, Kazuo, 163, 170
Wakiya, Colonel, 225
Walker, Frank R., 100, 106–7, 117
Wallace, William J., 202
Walsh, J. A., 105n, 117
Walt, Lewis, 412, 414
War Department, U.S., 12, 134
Warlick, William W., 174
War Plans Division, 13, 14
"Washing Machine Charlie," 197
Washington Naval Treaty (1922), 84n
Watanabe, Kusukichi, 219, 241, 537, 541
Watchtower, Operation, 35, 37, 607
  Callaghan and, 54–55
  flaws in, 600–601
  Ghormley's plan for, 50–51
  Guadalcanal incorporated in, 36
  Harmon's distrust of, 135
  King and, 599–600
  loading problems in, 52–53
  planning and, 50–52
  pre-landing conference for, 54–55
  reconnaissance and, 49–50
  rehearsal for, 57
  surprise achieved in, 59
  Torch Operation as priority vs., 53
  Turner and rehearsal of, 57
  U.S. feints in, 35
  Vandegrift and rehearsal for, 57
Water Hole, 553–54
Wavell, Archibald, 8
Wayne, John, 617
Weems, G. T., 308
Wells, Erskine, 414
Westholm, Rollin E., 549
Whaling, William J., 133, 235–37, 264, 361
Widhelm, William J., 377, 383, 386–88, 402
Wilfong, John L., 174
Wilkinson, Edwin, 435, 443
Williams, Brad, 392
Williams, Harold N., 100
Williams, Robert H., 75
Williamson, Raymond E. S., 493
Willmott, H. P., 254

Willoughby, Charles A., 50
Wilson, Ralph E., 101, 174, 297
Winchell, Walter, 41
Wood, Hunter, Jr., 377, 390–91
Woodruff, William, 322
Woods, Louis, 206, 322
  Geiger replaced by, 410
Worthington, Joseph M., 173
Wright, Carleton H., 172, 504
  fatal delay by, 508, 604
  Halsey's instructions to, 504
  Kinkaid replaced by, 503–4
  Navy Cross awarded to, 516*n*
  responsibility shouldered by, 515–16
  Tassafaronga Battle and, 504, 505, 507, 510, 514, 517, 518
  Tisdale given command by, 512
Wright, William C., 530

Yamada, Sadayoshi, 64, 79, 120, 121, 171
Yamada, Yusuke, 357, 358–59
Yamagata, Seizo, 172
Yamaguchi, Masao, 374
Yamamoto, Isoroku, 18, 167, 244, 288, 325, 327, 328, 348, 359–60, 426, 430, 452, 455–56, 462, 487, 523, 540, 541, 598
  assessment of, 605–6
  Buin airfield and, 275–76
  career and personality of, 19–20
  convoy failure and, 491
  Eastern Solomons Battle and, 159, 193
  Guadalcanal landings as viewed by, 64
  High Speed Convoy and, 316, 319, 326
  KE Operation and, 588, 590, 594, 596
  Midway Battle and, 23, 24–25
  opportunities of, 250–51
  Pearl Harbor attack and, 20–21, 23
  Santa Cruz Islands Battle and, 368, 373, 374, 398, 399
  Savo Island Battle as viewed by, 121
  17th Army plan and, 408
  Tsuji's meeting with, 268
  X-Day delayed by, 282
Yamamoto, Tadashi, 465
Yamamoto, Yuji, 536
Yamazaki, Shigeaki, 171
Yamazumi, Teijiro, 169
Yano, Keiji, 560, 572, 590
Yasutake, Shiro, 170, 189, 190
Yokota, Minoru, 171, 204, 298
Yokoi, Minoru, 170
Yoshida, Masayoshi, 167
Yoshitomi, Setsuzo, 171
Young, Cassin, 434, 443, 444

Z, Operation, 20
Zero fighter, 49, 275, 612
  Grumman F4F Wildcat compared with, 65–66, 67, 94
Zook, Lester, 458

INDEX OF MILITARY UNITS

(INDEXED BY UNIT SIZE)

Japan

IMPERIAL ARMY

8th Area Army, 536–37, 540, 545, 559
death rate reported by, 527
forces diverted to New Guinea by, 499
KE Operation and, 541, 574, 589–90
resupply and, 521
17th Army commanded by, 497–98
6th Air Division attached to, 498
17th Army, 42, 87, 142, 143, 233, 244,
  252, 253n, 268, 281, 289, 290, 319,
  405–9, 413, 423, 499, 504, 536, 541,
  564, 570, 574, 582, 589, 593, 595, 597,
  607, 617
aerial photographs ignored by, 346
casualties in, 497
coastal defense units organized by,
  571–72
debilitated condition of, 526–28, 543–44,
  550
8th Area Army command of, 497–98
evacuation of, *see* KE Operation
expanded headquarters of, 254–55
Hattori's visit to, 417
headquarters bombed, 496
Henderson Field Battle and, 337–42,
  345–48, 354, 362, 364–66
Ichiki detachment and, 145, 158, 163
Kawaguchi and, 198, 201, 203, 218, 220,
  222, 223, 282
maps used by, 339n
morale in, 553
Port Moresby, effort of, 43–45
supply drums recovered by, 547–48,
  549–50
supply problems of, 408, 500, 518, 519
38th Division attached to, 253
"Tokyo Express" and, 315, 324, 328,
  330, 421
withdrawal orders received by, 559–62
Yamamoto and, 408
Y-Day delays by, 369–72
18th Army, 143, 497–98
2d Infantry (Sendai) Division, 222, 251,
  252–53, 254, 279, 290, 421, 553, 557
attack by, 351–56
death rate in, 527
debilitated condition of, 338, 417, 527

in final offensive, 553, 556, 562, 571
Henderson Field Battle and, 337–42,
  346–48, 354, 361–62, 364, 372, 379
jungle march of, 344, 348
reduced artillery complement of, 544
retreat of, 404–9, 416, 418
withdrawal of, 570, 571–72, 589
withdrawal orders received by, 561
6th Infantry Division, 498
38th Infantry Division, 251, 255, 338, 362,
  417, 421, 425, 490, 529, 535, 568
artillery complement of, 544
controversy on use of, 406
in final offensive, 553, 556, 561–62,
  570–72
Miyazaki and, 406, 408
17th Army joined by, 253
supply shortage of, 499–500, 526–27
51st Infantry Division, 406, 408, 535,
  536–37
Sendai Division, *see* 2d Infantry (Sendai)
  Division
2d Ship Group, 428
21st Independent Mixed Brigade, 406, 408,
  499
35th Infantry Brigade, 143, 144, 145, 198
65th Infantry Brigade, 498
2d Artillery Regiment, 2d Battalion of,
  406–7
7th Engineer Construction Regiment, 147
4th Field Heavy Artillery Regiment, 315
4th Infantry Regiment (Aoba Detachment),
  143, 144, 343, 416
casualties in, 365
debilitated condition of, 527
in final offensive, 556–58, 570–71
in Matanikau Battles, 269, 287–90
reduced strength of, 338, 411, 570–71
resupply of, 266, 278
1st Battalion of, 251, 284–85, 349, 411,
  420n
2d Battalion of, 203, 211, 219, 224,
  231–32, 238, 240, 245, 285, 287, 289,
  411, 420n
3d Battalion of, 223–24, 225, 235, 243,
  244, 284–86, 342, 364, 411, 418
16th Infantry Regiment, 282, 315, 340,
  347, 348, 362, 365, 495, 527, 571
in final offensive, 556–58

28th Infantry Regiment (Ichiki Detachment), 143, 144, 156, 158, 595
   reputation of, 145–46
   2d Battalion of, 147
29th Infantry Regiment, 282, 340, 364, 365, 613
   1st Battalion of, 288, 354
   2d Battalion of, 356
   3d Battalion of, 354, 356
124th Infantry Regiment, 203, 339, 425, 495, 527, 565, 589
   1st Battalion of, 199, 201, 219, 224, 231–32, 237, 238, 240, 282, 562–63
   2d Battalion of, 213, 219, 225, 244, 269, 270, 273, 282, 531, 563, 566
   3d Battalion of, 199, 219, 224, 231–32, 241, 269, 282, 340, 342, 347, 562
144th Infantry Regiment, 22
228th Infantry Regiment, 338, 362, 421, 497, 500, 527
   1st Battalion (Koli Detachment) of, 340, 345, 357, 362, 495, 496
   2d Battalion of, 531
   3d Battalion of, 567
229th Infantry Regiment, 586
   1st Battalion of, 428, 501
230th Infantry Regiment, 315, 347, 415, 560
   1st Battalion of, 354
   2d Battalion of, 428
   3d Battalion of, 340, 592
1st Ship Engineer Regiment, 562
8th Tank Regiment, 253
Kuma Battalion, 219, 224, 229, 232, 242, 245, 246, 269, 270–71, 278
Nankai Detachment, 222, 253
Nitto Battalion, 570
Oneda Unit, 592
Shoji Detachment, 414, 418, 423–24
South Seas Detachment, 21–22
Yano Battalion, 559–60, 562, 570, 572, 589, 592
2d Anti-tank Gun Battalion, 342n, 413, 416
2d Engineer Battalion, 362
38th Engineer Battalion, 340, 528
20th Mountain Gun Battalion, 407
3d Mortar Battalion, 340
11th Construction Unit, 31, 59, 70, 151, 261
13th Construction Unit, 31, 59, 261
14th Construction Unit, 74
39th Field Road Construction Unit, 413
1st Independent Tank Company, 315, 343, 349, 350

IMPERIAL ARMY AIR UNITS

6th Air Division, 524, 543, 582–83, 590, 609
   attached to 8th Area Army, 498
   raid by, 574
76th Army Independent Air Squadron, 346

IMPERIAL NAVY

Southeast Area Fleet, 498n
1st Fleet, 20
2d Fleet, 20
   in Eastern Solomons Battle, 160, 162, 166, 169–70, 175–76, 178, 187, 188, 193
   radio intelligence and, 545, 546
   in Santa Cruz Islands Battle, 368, 372, 374, 382, 398
3d (Carrier) Fleet, 20, 22
   in Eastern Solomons Battle, 160, 161, 164, 166–68, 176, 178, 193
   Indian Ocean sortie of, 23–24
   at Midway Battle, 25
   radio intelligence and, 40, 544–46
   in Santa Cruz Islands Battle, 368, 374, 375
4th Fleet (Inner South Seas Force), 20, 21, 40, 42, 44, 45, 545, 546
5th Fleet (Northern Force), 20
6th Fleet (Advanced Expeditionary Force), 20, 171, 369, 375–76, 500
8th Fleet (Outer South Seas Force), 42, 44, 45, 142, 163, 164, 199, 201, 243, 251–53, 254, 269, 358, 369, 426, 463, 465, 487, 491, 521, 536, 537, 547
   Cape Esperance Battle and, 309–10
   in Eastern Solomons Battle, 170–71, 189
   Friday the Thirteenth Battle and, 429, 431
   Ichiki Detachment and, 146, 158
   Kawaguchi supported by, 219–20, 222
   KE Operation and, 542, 593
   radio intelligence and, 95
   sea lift computations by, 408
8th Base Force, 42, 45, 87, 143–44
Carrier Division 1, 160, 161, 325
   in Santa Cruz Islands Battle, 368–69, 372, 374–75, 379, 382, 388, 394, 397
Carrier Division 2, 324, 327, 360, 368, 374, 545
Carrier Division 11(-), 169
Battleship Division 3, 374, 545
Battleship Division 11, 168, 375, 425, 429, 434, 450
Cruiser Division 4, 169, 374, 462, 470
Cruiser Division 5, 169, 374
Cruiser Division 6, 44, 95, 100, 101n, 148, 170
   in Cape Esperance Battle, 295, 308
   in Savo Island Battle, 86–87, 110, 116
   U.S. air search and, 90, 92
Cruiser Division 7, 168, 375
Cruiser Division 8, 41, 375

Cruiser Division 8(-), 168
Cruiser Division 18, 44, 95, 100
  in Savo Island Battle, 86, 106–8
Destroyer Squadron 2, 146, 148, 170, 374,
    398, 422, 428, 471, 502, 505, 542
Destroyer Squadron 3, 199, 471
Destroyer Squadron 4, 169, 315, 357, 429,
    431, 432, 434, 436, 437–38, 439, 450,
    452, 460, 471
Destroyer Squadron 6, 44n
Destroyer Squadron 10, 168, 375, 429, 434,
    448, 460, 470, 582
Destroyer Division 2, 170, 434, 452
Destroyer Division 4, 147, 168, 375
Destroyer Division 6, 357, 434, 448, 459
Destroyer Division 7(-), 167
Destroyer Division 8, 585, 591
Destroyer Division 9, 279, 297
Destroyer Division 9(-), 471
Destroyer Division 10, 167, 375, 422, 585,
    591
Destroyer Division 11, 199, 201, 278, 296,
    471
Destroyer Division 15, 147, 169, 170, 374,
    422, 471, 502, 505
Destroyer Division 16, 167, 168, 375, 434,
    585, 591
Destroyer Division 17, 147, 168, 170, 375,
    448, 585, 591
Destroyer Division 19, 330, 357, 471
Destroyer Division 20, 199
Destroyer Division 24, 170, 200, 201,
    205, 266, 374, 471, 502, 505, 509,
    512, 518
Destroyer Division 27, 429, 431, 434,
    437–38, 452
Destroyer Division 30, 170, 189
Destroyer Division 31, 374, 471, 502, 505,
    513
Destroyer Division 61(-), 434, 471
Submarine Squadron 1, 171, 188, 376
Submarine Squadron 2, 375–76
Submarine Squadron 3, 171
Submarine Squadron 7, 44, 87, 171
Submarine Division 2, 171, 376
Submarine Division 4, 171
Submarine Division 6, 376
Submarine Division 7, 375
Submarine Division 11, 171, 376
Submarine Division 13, 171
4th Fleet Communications Unit, 394, 469

Ships

Akagi, 20
Akatsuki, 321, 357, 359, 429, 434, 440,
    446, 447, 460, 461
  sinking of, 449
Akebono, 167
Akigumo, 167, 279, 375, 399, 585, 591

Akizuki, 167, 280, 288, 297, 315, 357, 360,
    582
Amagiri, 199, 200, 203, 251, 322, 466, 468
Amatsukaze, 168, 176, 179, 375, 429, 434,
    446, 448–49, 450, 460, 461
Aoba, 88, 95, 100, 103, 105, 107, 109–10,
    111, 114, 116, 170, 296, 299, 301–3,
    304, 306, 307, 308, 309n
Arashi, 147, 252, 375, 429, 463, 464,
    519–20, 524, 560, 585, 591
Arashio, 279, 429, 463, 464, 585, 591
Ariake, 315, 323, 407, 520, 526
Arizona Maru, 466
Asagiri, 199–200, 210
Asagumo, 279, 297, 308, 321, 429, 434,
    436, 437, 441–42, 449, 450, 451, 452,
    469, 470, 472, 474, 479, 480, 483, 484,
    590
Asashio, 429
Atago, 169, 193n, 374, 429, 462, 469, 470,
    473, 478, 479–80, 481, 482, 483, 484,
    546
Ayanami, 280, 429, 471, 473, 474, 475–76,
    477, 479, 482, 486n
  sinking of, 484, 486
Azumasan Maru, 315, 323, 324
Azusa Maru, 501–2
Boston Maru, 170, 190
Brisbane Maru, 466
Canberra Maru, 466
Chihaya Maru, 525
Chikuma, 41, 161, 168, 176, 177,
    192n–93n, 369, 375, 388, 400, 401
Chitose, 169, 188, 192n, 193, 198, 243,
    281, 295, 299
Chokai, 44, 95, 100, 101n, 170, 322, 429,
    463, 465, 542, 547, 582
  damage sustained by, 116
  in Savo Island Battle, 86–88, 102–5, 107,
    108, 109–11, 112, 113, 114, 116
Daifuku Maru, 170, 190
Fubuki, 231, 251, 278, 280, 296, 299, 304,
    308, 309n
  sinking of, 303
Fumizuki, 585, 586, 588, 591
Furutaka, 100, 102, 104, 105, 106–7, 108,
    112, 113–14, 115, 170, 296, 299,
    302–3, 304, 308, 309, 311–12
  sinking of, 307
Hagikaze, 147
Haguro, 169, 193n
Hakaze, 525
Hamakaze, 147, 266, 375, 585, 591
Haruna, 316, 317, 319n, 369, 374, 429,
    462–63, 542, 545
Harusame, 170, 279, 315, 361, 429, 434,
    436, 437, 438, 443, 449, 450
Hatsukaze, 167, 375
Hatsuyuki, 211, 278, 296, 299, 303, 307,
    308, 471, 473

Hayashio, 169, 279, 316, 374, 465, 468, 471
Hiei, 84n, 168, 176, 177, 375, 409, 452–53, 460, 461, 462, 484, 490
   aerial assault on, 454–55
   11th Air Fleet defense of, 454–55
   in Friday the Thirteenth Battle, 429, 434, 437–38, 440, 441, 443–51
   sinking of, 456
Hirokawa Maru, 471, 487
Hiyo, 322, 327, 368, 370–71, 374, 396
Ikazuchi, 321, 357, 359, 429, 434, 440, 449, 460
Inazuma, 374, 429, 434, 440, 447, 449, 471, 472, 473
Isokaze, 170, 375, 379, 585, 591, 595
Isonami, 374
Isuzu, 316, 317, 374, 398, 463, 465
I-1, 375
   destruction of, 575–76
I-2, 375
I-3, 375
   sinking of, 523
I-4, 376
   sinking of, 500
I-5, 376
I-7, 375
I-9, 171
I-11, 164, 171
I-15, 171, 188, 249, 376, 399
   sinking of, 430
I-16, 501
I-17, 164, 171, 188, 376, 500
I-19, 171
   Wasp sunk by, 247–49
I-20, 501
I-21, 376, 399, 500–501
I-22, 329
I-24, 376, 399, 501
I-26, 171, 298, 310, 456
   Juneau sunk by, 456
   Saratoga torpedoed by, 203–4
I-31, 376
I-121, 171
I-122, 129, 143, 171
I-123, 129, 143, 171, 201
I-172, 376
I-174, 171, 376
I-175, 171, 376
I-176, 335, 376
Jinjei, 171
Jintsu, 146, 148, 159, 170, 190, 192, 231, 542
Junyo, 169, 322, 327, 426, 542, 545–46
   in convoy-capital ship actions, 462, 491
   in Friday the Thirteenth Battle, 429, 454
   in Santa Cruz Islands Battle, 368, 370–72, 374, 391–97, 399
Kagero, 147, 166, 170, 191, 266, 374, 382, 471, 482, 483, 484, 502, 505, 507, 510, 513, 549

Kako, 100, 102, 105, 106, 107, 109, 111, 112, 113, 114
   sinking of, 116–17
Katauragi Maru, 329
Kawakaze, 163, 170, 252, 316, 374, 468, 471, 502–3, 505, 507, 510, 512, 524, 585, 590–91, 595
Kazegumo, 167, 375, 429, 463, 465, 585, 591
Kiku Maru, 501–2
Kinryu Maru, 147, 170, 190–92
Kinugasa, 170, 322, 414, 429, 463, 490
   bombing of, 464
   in Cape Esperance Battle, 296, 299, 305–8
   capsized, 465
   in Savo Islands Battle, 100, 102, 106–7, 111, 113, 116
Kinugasa Maru, 471, 487
Kirishima, 375, 409, 525
   in convoy-capital ship actions, 469, 470, 472, 479, 486n, 487
   in Eastern Solomons Battle, 168, 176–77
   in Friday the Thirteenth Battle, 429, 434, 438, 440–42, 444–45, 448, 451, 455, 460, 462
   heavily damaged, 481
   sinking of, 484, 486
Komura, 168
Kongo, 316, 317, 319n, 369, 374, 429, 452, 462–63, 542, 545
Kumano, 168, 176, 375, 429, 542, 547, 582
Kuroshio, 169, 279, 316, 374, 471, 502, 505, 507, 510, 513, 521, 585, 590–91
Kyushu Maru, 315, 323, 324
Maikaze, 168, 279, 375, 585, 590, 591, 595
Makikumo, 167, 279, 375, 399, 429, 463, 465, 586, 590, 595
   sinking of, 588
Makinami, 316, 374, 382, 466, 468, 471, 502, 505, 507, 510, 513, 520, 586, 588, 590, 595
Maya, 169, 178, 326, 374, 382, 398, 429, 463, 465
Meiyo Maru, 87–88
Michishio, 429, 463
Mikuma, 115
Minegumo, 279, 281
Mochizuki, 189, 191, 322, 423, 466
Mogami, 115
Murakumo, 211, 278, 280, 297, 308–9
Murasame, 170, 279, 281, 315, 421, 429, 434, 436, 437, 441–42, 449, 450, 451, 452
Musashi, 266, 542, 545–46
Mutsu, 169, 187–88, 370
Mutsuki, 170, 189, 191, 192
Myoko, 169, 326, 374, 382, 398

Naganami, 316, 318, 374, 422, 466, 471, 502–3, 505, 507, 509, 510, 512, 518, 520, 524

Nagara, 375, 398, 546
in convoy-capital ship actions, 469, 470, 472, 473, 475–76, 479, 484
in Eastern Solomons Battle, 168, 176, 177
in Friday the Thirteenth Battle, 429, 434, 437, 439–42, 444, 446, 448, 452

Nagara Maru, 466
Nagatsuki, 585, 587, 591
Nako Maru, 467
Nankai Maru, 315, 323, 526
Natsugumo, 279, 281, 297, 308, 309
Nisshin, 268, 279–81, 288, 295, 296, 298, 299, 308, 321
Nowaki, 168, 279, 290, 519–20
Number 10 (midget submarine), 501
Number 11 (midget submarine), 501
Number 38 (midget submarine), 501
Oite, 131
Oshio, 585, 591
Oyashio, 169, 316, 374, 471, 482, 483, 502, 505, 507, 510, 513, 549
Patrol Boat 1, 146–47, 171, 190, 201
Patrol Boat 2, 146–47, 171, 190, 526
Patrol Boat 34, 146–47, 171, 201
Patrol Boat 35, 146–47, 171, 198
Patrol Boat 36, 198
Ryujo, 134, 602
in Eastern Solomons Battle, 160, 161–62, 165, 166, 168, 176–79, 187, 188, 190, 192
sinking of, 179

Sado Maru, 315, 466, 468
Sakido Maru, 315
Samidare, 170, 315, 321, 361, 429, 434, 436, 437, 441–42, 449, 450, 451, 452, 471, 473, 483, 484, 590
Sangetsu Maru, 471, 487, 593
Sasago Maru, 315, 323, 324
Satsuki, 585, 591
Sendai, 211, 222, 231, 233, 251–52, 321, 357, 414, 429, 469, 471, 473, 474, 479, 542, 582
Shigure, 280, 315, 407, 429, 434
Shikinami, 205, 231, 266, 279, 471, 473, 479
Shinano Maru, 466
Shirakumo, 199, 200, 203
Shiratsuyu, 315, 357, 429, 434
Shirayuki, 266, 278, 280, 297, 308–9, 321–22, 471, 473, 585, 586, 590–91
Shoho, 24
Shokaku, 23, 24, 134, 198, 429, 545
Eastern Solomons Battle and, 160, 161–62, 165, 166, 167, 175, 176, 177, 178, 182, 183, 186

in Santa Cruz Islands Battle, 368–69, 374, 382–83, 387, 390, 394, 395, 396, 401

Soya, 87
Suzanami, 251, 266
Suzukaze, 170, 191, 231, 251, 252, 316, 374, 468, 471, 487, 502–3, 505, 507, 509, 510, 524, 547
Suzuya, 168, 176, 177, 375, 388, 463, 547
Taiyo, 167
Takanami, 316, 374, 422, 471, 502–3, 505, 507–10, 512, 516, 518
sinking of, 513
Takao, 169, 374, 398, 429, 462, 469, 470, 478, 481, 482, 484
Tanikaze, 147, 168, 375, 388, 520, 560, 585, 591
Tatsuta, 281, 289–90, 357
Tenryu, 86, 100, 101n, 102, 106, 107, 109, 112, 113–15, 278, 414, 421, 429, 463
PT Boat skirmish of, 423
Teruzuki, 369, 375, 387, 399, 401, 429, 434, 441, 449, 452, 471, 472, 474, 479, 484, 520, 523
sinking of, 524
Tokitsukaze, 168, 176, 179, 375, 585, 591
Tone, 41, 168, 176, 178–79, 375, 382, 387–88, 429, 546
Tsugaru, 87, 205–6, 357
Umikaze, 170, 252, 266, 316, 374, 471
Urakaze, 147, 266, 375, 388, 520, 585, 591, 595
Uranami, 266, 279, 330, 471, 473, 474, 479, 484
Ushio, 167, 251, 266
Uzuki, 170, 526
Yamagumo, 297
Yamato, 167, 266, 316, 368, 370, 374, 542
Yamura Maru, 471, 487
Yayoi, 170, 189
Yubari, 86, 100, 102, 107, 109, 113, 115
Yudachi, 203, 211, 266, 315, 361, 429, 434, 436, 437, 438, 440, 443, 446, 448, 449–50, 452, 460, 461
sinking of, 453
Yugiri, 199–200
Yugumo, 167, 375, 429, 463, 585, 586, 588, 591
Yugure, 429, 434, 519–20
Yukikaze, 375, 429, 434, 441, 448, 452, 455, 585, 591
Yunagi, 87, 89, 100, 101n, 102–4, 114, 115, 120, 163
Yura, 169, 321, 328, 357, 358
sinking of, 360–61
Zuiho, 426, 429, 542, 545–46
in Santa Cruz Islands Battle, 369, 375, 381–82, 384, 388, 394, 400–401
Zuikaku, 23, 134, 160, 198, 429, 542, 543, 545–46

Zuikaku (cont'd)
  Eastern Solomons Battle and, 161–62,
    165–67, 180, 182, 184, 191
  in Santa Cruz Islands Battle, 368–69,
    375, 379, 382–83, 390, 393, 394–97,
    400

IMPERIAL NAVY AVIATION

R Area Air Force, 251, 290, 295, 321, 322,
    324, 422, 543, 582, 609
  aircraft lost by, 367, 610
  convoy-capital ship actions and, 467,
    469, 473–74
  creation of, 198
  Friday the Thirteenth Battle and, 437
  rebuilding of, 410
  reconnaissance by, 547–49, 573, 587
1st Air Fleet, *see* 3d (Carrier) Fleet
11th Air Fleet (Base Air Force), 20, 44,
    45, 64, 158, 162, 164, 188, 194, 213,
    222, 272, 278, 288, 315, 321, 326, 344,
    371, 372, 408, 421, 425, 426, 431, 467,
    491, 498n, 521, 536, 543, 547, 548–49,
    582, 588, 609
  aircraft lost by, 610–11
  air superiority effort of, 408–9
  altered composition of, 410
  decline of aircraft crew quality in,
    524–25
  in Eastern Solomons Battle, 171–72, 193
  ground crew shortage in, 198
  Hiei defended by, 454–55
  losses by, 324, 367
  radios lacked by, 66
  Reinforcement Unit and, 295–96, 594–95
  in Santa Cruz Islands Battle, 376
  U.S. air power as assessed by, 345
21st Air Flotilla, 264, 410, 545
25th Air Flotilla (5th Air Attack Force),
    42, 45, 64, 87, 89, 102, 120, 171, 244,
    264–65, 376
26th Air Flotilla (6th Air Attack Force),
    172, 265, 376, 410, 545
2d Air Group, 171
3d Air Group, 264
4th Air Group, 65, 120, 171, 265
6th Air Group, 172
14th Air Group, 171
31st Air Group, 265, 345
252d Air Group, 410, 526
701st Air Group, 573, 578–79
705th Air Group, 573, 578–79, 590
751st Air Group, 580
956th Air Group, 410
Kanoya Air Group, 264
Kisarazu Air Group, 172
Misawa Air Group, 79, 120, 172
Tainan Air Group, 64, 67, 171
Takao Air Group, 265

Yokohama Air Group, 60, 74, 78, 171, 265
12th Air Wing, 596

IMPERIAL NAVY LAND UNITS

Special Duty Group (Radio Intelligence),
    45
3d Kure Special Naval Landing Force, 72,
    74
4th Maizuru Special Naval Landing Force,
    281, 288, 289, 315, 330
5th Yokosuka Special Naval Landing
    Force, 131, 147, 159, 170
5th Sasebo Special Naval Landing Force,
    42
6th Sasebo Special Naval Landing Force,
    525

United States

ARMY

XIV Corps, 550, 556, 567, 570, 597
  activation of, 543
  contraction of frontage of, 571
25th Infantry Division, 327, 543, 548, 592,
    608, 617
  in final offensive, 556, 562, 563, 567–69
  logistics employed by, 552–53, 571
  zone of action of, 550–52
32d Infantry Division, 11
37th Infantry Division, 11, 17
41st Infantry Division, 10
43d Infantry Division, 216, 409
American Division, 9, 17, 293, 521, 543,
    550, 570
CAM Division, 570, 571, 572
27th Infantry Regiment, 617
  1st Battalion of, 553–54, 569, 570
  2d Battalion of, 555, 569–70
  3d Battalion of, 553–55, 569, 570
  in final offensive, 552, 567–72
  Galloping Horse assaulted by, 553–55
  Kokumbona captured by, 570
35th Infantry Regiment, 552, 568
  1st Battalion of, 562–63
  2d Battalion of, 562–66
  3d Battalion of, 562–63
132d Infantry Regiment, 521, 529, 543,
    563, 583, 592, 608
  1st Battalion of, 530–33
  2d Battalion of, 530, 532–33, 583, 596
  3d Battalion of, 530–33
147th Infantry Regiment, 420, 543, 550,
    568, 570–72, 583, 589, 592
161st Infantry Regiment, 552, 589, 592–93
  1st Battalion of, 568–69, 596
  2d Battalion of, 568–69
  3d Battalion of, 568–69
164th Infantry Regiment, 293, 354,
    418–20, 543

assessment of, 608
"Bombardment" and, 319
casualties in, 164–65
character of, 313–14
envelopment movement by, 421, 423
Guadalcanal arrival of, 343
landing of, 313
in last Matanikau battle, 494, 496–97
1st Battalion of, 418–20, 424, 496
2d Battalion of, 362, 421, 422, 423
3d Battalion of, 355, 362, 421, 422, 496
172d Infantry Regiment, 409
182d Infantry Regiment, 430, 494, 497,
   565, 568, 570, 571
1st Battalion of, 495
2d Battalion of, 495
3d Battalion of, 430
244th Coast Artillery Battalion, 488
97th Field Artillery Battalion, 593
246th Field Artillery Battalion, 530

ARMY AIR FORCE

13th Air Force, 542
5th Bomb Group, 276–77, 542
11th Bomb Group, 37, 45, 90, 174, 276,
   280, 454, 466, 542
23d Bomb Squadron, 277
31st Bomb Squadron, 277
69th Bomb Squadron, 432
70th Bomb Squadron, 432
72d Bomb Squadron, 276
67th Fighter Squadron, 295, 326, 422, 613
in Eastern Solomons Battle, 174
in Edson's Ridge Battle, 240
Guadalcanal arrival of, 163
Munn's lecture to, 320–21

MARINE CORPS

1st Marine Division, vii, 17, 53, 131, 233,
   350, 413, 609
casualties sustained by, 522
character of, 522–23
elements of, 48–49
enemy strength estimate of, 50
fatigue of, 493
Henderson Field Battle and, 365, 366
importance of engineers to, 608
malaria in, 259–60, 351
Matanikau battles and, 282–83
ordered to New Zealand, 46–47
replacement of, 277, 519, 522–23, 529
revised defense plan of, 261
Watchtower plans of, 36, 51, 607
2d Marine Division, 48, 522, 543, 555,
   556n, 577
coastal drive by, 556–58, 567–68, 570
1st Marine Regiment, 48, 61, 62, 63, 70,
   241, 261, 343, 348
airfield seized by, 80–81

cattle stampede and, 128
in Guadalcanal Group, 51
in Henderson Field Battle, 343, 348
landing of, 61–63
1st Battalion of, 125, 154, 264
2d Battalion of, 150–52
3d Battalion of, 150, 242, 344, 412
2d Marine Regiment, 51, 77, 125, 411, 414,
   416, 424, 522, 543, 556–58
in final offensive, 556–58
U.S. departure of, 48–49
1st Battalion of, 72–73, 291, 416, 418,
   424, 557
2d Battalion of, 77, 78, 418, 424, 557
3d Battalion of, 78, 283, 285, 343, 361,
   362, 411
5th Marine Regiment, 47, 69, 125, 261,
   411, 413, 418
document captured by, 417
Edson moved to, 263
in first Matanikau Battle, 129, 132–33
in Guadalcanal Group, 51
in Henderson Field Battle, 343, 348, 361,
   364
Lunga crossed by, 81
replacement of, 522
in second Matanikau battle, 283–84,
   287
U.S. departure of, 48
Vandegrift and, 196
1st Battalion of, 61–62, 63, 70, 195–97,
   283, 412, 413
2d Battalion of, 61, 72, 73, 74, 77, 78,
   125, 129–30, 195, 235, 237, 240,
   270–72, 274, 284, 285, 412, 413
3d Battalion of, 62, 243, 284, 413, 416
6th Marine Regiment, 556, 568, 570, 572
2d Battalion of, 557, 571
3d Battalion of, 571
7th Marine Regiment, 46n, 48, 195, 261,
   417, 421
in Henderson Field Battle, 343, 348–49,
   352, 362
landing of, 233, 247, 251–52, 604
in Matanikau battles, 270, 283–85, 287,
   289
Turner and, 247, 251
Vandegrift and, 46, 227–28
1st Battalion of, 270, 272–74, 289, 349,
   420, 423
2d Battalion of, 288–89, 348, 352, 361,
   363–65, 414, 415, 423
3d Battalion of, 283, 344, 348, 352, 363,
   411
8th Marine Regiment, 292, 423
in final offensive, 556–57
in Kokumbona drive, 424
landing of, 409, 417–18, 420
in last Matanikau battle, 494–97
1st Battalion of, 557

8th Marine Regiment (*cont'd*)
  2d Battalion of, 557
  3d Battalion of, 424–25, 557
10th Marine Regiment, 351, 583
  2d Battalion of, 530
  3d Battalion of, 418
11th Marine Regiment, 47, 128, 130, 238, 245, 318, 411
  1st Battalion of, 251
  2d Battalion of, 126, 351
  3d Battalion of, 126, 153, 351
  5th Battalion of, 126, 245, 351
3d Defense Battalion, 48, 126, 231, 257, 343, 488
1st Marine Amphibian Tractor Battalion, 261
1st Marine Engineer Battalion, 229, 235, 237, 240, 261, 412
1st Marine Raider Battalion, 17, 47, 48, 211, 263
  in Edson's Ridge Battle, 225, 229, 231–33, 235, 237–39, 245
  Griffith in command of, 263
  in Matanikau battles, 270, 271–74, 284, 287
  in Tasimboko Raid, 220–22
  Tulagi landings of, 72–74, 77–78
2d Marine Raider Battalion (Carlson's Raiders), 35, 420, 423
4th Marine Replacement Battalion, 430
1st Parachute Battalion, 48, 72, 75, 79, 220, 252, 607
  in Edson's Ridge Battle, 225, 229, 235–39, 241, 245
  in Tasimboko Raid, 221–22
1st Pioneer Battalion, 63, 78, 127, 261
  in Edson's Ridge Battle, 229, 235
1st Special Weapons Battalion, 157
1st Tank Battalion, 343
Marine Scout-Sniper unit (Whaling Group), 348, 352, 411, 412, 413, 416, 418
  in Matanikau Battles, 283–85, 287–89
  Vandegrift's creation of, 263–64

MARINE AVIATION

First Marine Air Wing, 206, 279, 313
Second Marine Air Wing, 542
Marine Air Group 11, 409
Marine Air Group 14, 327
Marine Air Group 23, 135, 138–40, 202, 209, 326
VMF-112, 409–10
VMF-121, 289, 295, 309, 314, 322, 323, 329, 359, 467, 574
VMF-212, 139, 327, 329
VMF-223, 139, 162, 174, 205, 223, 226, 243, 295–96
VMF-224, 139, 202, 203, 205, 226, 243, 295–96, 309, 326

VMSB-131, 410, 432, 454, 464
VMSB-132, 409, 414–15, 422, 464, 520
VMSB-141, 309, 319, 322, 466
VMSB-142, 410, 432, 454
VMSB-231, 139, 202, 273, 326
VMSB-232, 139, 174, 257, 315
1st Marine Aviation Engineer Battalion, 430

NAVY

Task Force, 11, 172
Task Force 16, 173, 371, 376–77, 389, 430, 433, 463
Task Force 17, 371, 377
Task Force 18, 173–74
  Rennell Island Battle and, 578–80
Task Force 44 (MacArthur's Navy), 44, 51, 216
Task Force 61, 51, 93, 94n, 161, 371, 376
  in Eastern Solomons Battle, 172–74
Task Force 62, 100
Task Force 63, 51, 174, 378
Task Force 64, 293, 297, 371, 378, 548, 577
  in convoy-capital ship action, 463, 471–72
  Ghormley's creation of, 216–17
Task Force 67, 548, 577
  in Tassafaronga Battle, 503–7, 517
Task Group 62.4, 430
Task Group 62.8, 577–78
Task Group 67.1, 430
Task Group 67.2.2, 505
Task Group 67.2.3, 505
Task Group 67.2.4, 505
Task Group 67.4, 430, 434
Cruiser Division 4, 376
Cruiser Division 5, 377
Destroyer Squadron 1, 172
Destroyer Squadron 4, 174
Destroyer Squadron 6, 173
Destroyer Squadron 12, 174, 297, 300, 435, 436n
Destroyer Squadron 21, 587
Destroyer Division 2, 172
Destroyer Division 9, 504, 505
Destroyer Division 10, 377, 434
Destroyer Division 15, 174
Destroyer Division 22, 173
Motor Torpedo Boat Squadron 3, 318
Submarine Squadron 2, 329
Combat Intelligence Unit, 277–78
Malaria Control Unit, 260
3d Naval Construction Battalion, 37

Ships

Aaron Ward, 174, 307, 328, 378, 435, 436, 446–47, 450, 453, 454, 459
Achilles (New Zealand), 549

Alchiba, 324, 501
Anderson, 377, 398–99
Argonaut, sinking of, 545
Argonne, 56, 277, 335
Astoria, 98–99, 101, 121*n*
  in Savo Island Battle, 108–11, 113
  sinking of, 118–19
Athena, 163
Atlanta, 173, 378
  in Friday the Thirteenth Battle, 430,
    433, 434, 436, 438–40, 448, 449, 459,
    460
  San Francisco fire upon, 443–44
  sinking of, 453–54
Australia (Australia), 96, 97, 98, 100,
  107*n*, 122
Bagley, 98, 100, 106, 114, 118
Balch, 173, 186
Ballard, 459
Barton, 377, 435, 436, 443, 459
  sinking of, 446–48
Bellatrix, 221, 324, 325
Benham, 173, 378, 470, 471, 475, 477, 478,
  486*n*, 489
  sinking of, 484–86
Betelgeuse, 430
Blue, 99, 100, 103, 104, 117–18, 120, 163,
  210
  sinking of, 165–66
Bobolink, 453, 454
Boise, 35, 294, 297–300, 302, 303, 306*n*,
  310, 311
  damaged, 304–7
Buchanan, 75, 78, 98, 101, 174, 297, 298,
  304, 431, 433
Canberra (Australia), 65, 97, 98, 100, 121,
  601
  in Savo Island Battle, 104–7, 109
  sinking of, 117–18
Chenango, 578, 580
Chester, 335
Chicago, 97, 98, 100, 117, 121*n*, 124–25,
  595–96
  in Rennell Island Battle, 578–81
  in Savo Island Battle, 105–7, 109
  sinking of, 581, 604
  torpedoed, 579
Cleveland, 578
Colhoun, 131, 202, 212
Columbia, 578
Conway, 580
Conyngham, 377
Crescent City, 430
Curtiss, 90, 378, 381
Cushing, 377, 434, 436, 438, 439, 441,
  442–43, 448, 449, 451, 453, 459
Dale, 172
DeHaven, 573, 583, 587, 596
  sinking of, 585
Drayton, 505, 507, 508, 512, 515

Duncan, 297, 298, 301–4, 305, 310, 311
  sinking of, 307–8
Edgar Allan Poe, 501
Edwards, 580
Ellet, 118, 173
Enterprise, 24, 51, 67, 68, 69, 80, 94*n*, 95,
  335, 503, 542, 543, 577, 580, 603
  bomb hit on, 392
  convoy-capital ship action and, 463–67,
    487, 490–91
  in Eastern Solomons Battle, 164, 173,
    175, 176, 177–78, 179, 180, 181–86,
    187, 189, 191–93
  Friday the Thirteenth Battle and,
    426–27, 430, 454
  in Santa Cruz Islands Battle, 370–73,
    376, 379, 383–85, 388–93, 395–96,
    399, 400*n*, 401–2
Farenholt, 174, 297, 298, 300–301, 302,
  303–4, 305, 306, 307, 310, 311
Farragut, 172
Fletcher, 378, 435, 436, 446, 447–48, 505,
  507, 508, 512, 515, 516, 548, 583
Flying Fish, 469–70
Fomalhaut, 162–63
Frazier, 580
Fuller, 221
Gamble, 201
Gato, 545
George F. Elliot, 80
Grampus, 328–29, 545
Grayback, 548
Grayson, 173, 183, 188, 325
Gregory, 131, 211–12
Gwin, 325, 470, 471, 476, 478, 484, 485,
  486
Helena, 378, 420, 548, 573
  in Cape Esperance Battle, 294, 297–303,
    305, 310, 311
  in Friday the Thirteenth Battle, 430,
    434, 436, 438, 446, 448–51, 456–57,
    459, 460
Helm, 99, 101, 114, 163
Henley, 163, 165, 210
Hobart (Australia), 98, 101
Holland, 329
Honolulu, 505, 507, 508, 511, 512, 516,
  549, 573
Hornet, 14, 24, 134, 247, 248, 250, 251,
  280–81, 293, 320, 325, 326, 328, 602,
  603
  bombing of, 385–86
  fatal hit on, 396–97
  fighter direction by, 385, 402
  in Santa Cruz Islands Battle, 369–71,
    373, 377, 379, 383–88, 389, 390,
    391–92, 394–99, 400*n*, 401, 402
  sinking of, 398–99
Hovey, 308, 326, 430
Hughes, 377

Hull, 80
Indiana, 503
Jamestown, 324
Jarvis, 80, 103, 105, 115, 121n
   sinking of, 120
Juneau, 377, 385, 396
   in Friday the Thirteenth Battle, 430,
      434, 446, 448, 450, 460
   ordeal of survivors of, 457–59
   sinking of, 456–57
   Sullivan brothers on, 457, 459, 489–90
Kiwi (New Zealand), 575–76
Kopara, 200–201, 488
Laffey, 297, 298, 301, 302, 434, 436, 443,
    449, 450, 451, 459
   sinking of, 441–42
Lamson, 370, 504, 505, 507, 512
Lang, 174
Lansdowne, 249, 378
Lardner, 328, 378, 430, 504, 505, 507, 509,
    510, 512
LaVallette, 580, 596
   sinking of, 581
Lexington, 4, 11, 22, 24, 93
Libra, 430
Little, 131, 211–12
Long Island, 139, 162
Louisville, 578–79
McCalla, 297, 298, 302, 306, 307, 308,
    310n, 378
   I-15 and, 430, 602
McCawley, 293, 430, 431
MacDonough, 172, 204
McFarland, 90, 326–27
McKean, 131, 220
Mackinac, 90, 378
Mahan, 370, 377, 399
Majaba, 501
Manley, 220
Maury, 173, 377, 392, 505, 507, 508, 514
Meade, 488–89
Meredith, 324, 325, 332
Minneapolis, 172
   in Tassafaronga Battle, 505, 507–8,
    513–15
   torpedoed, 510–11
Moa (New Zealand), 575–76
Monssen, 75, 98, 101, 173, 204, 273, 435,
    436, 446, 450, 453, 459
   sinking of, 447
Montgomery, 588
Montpelier, 578
Morris, 377, 395, 396
Mugford, 69
Mustin, 377, 395, 398–99
Nashville, 548, 573
Nautilus, 582
Navajo, 579, 580
Neville, 72, 76

New Orleans, 172
   in Tassafaronga Battle, 505, 507, 512,
    514, 515
   torpedoed, 511
Nicholas, 324, 325, 345, 573, 583, 585
Northampton, 377, 385, 396, 430, 505, 507,
    511, 516
   sinking of, 514–15
   torpedoed, 512–13
North Carolina, 503, 603
   in Eastern Solomons Battle, 173, 182,
    183–84, 187
   torpedoed, 248–50
O'Bannon, 435, 436, 438, 442–43, 456,
    548, 573
O'Brien, 248, 250, 332, 477
Patterson, 98, 100, 104, 106–7, 109, 111,
    117–18, 121n
Pensacola, 377, 385, 396, 430, 505, 507,
    514, 515
   torpedoed, 511–12
Perkins, 505, 507, 508, 514
Phelps, 172
Porter, 377
   sinking of, 388–90
Portland, 173, 182, 376, 389, 391, 430,
    434, 436, 444, 445, 450, 459, 514
   Yudachi sunk by, 453
Preble, 588
President Adams, 430
President Coolidge, 409
President Jackson, 430
Preston, 377, 393, 470, 471, 475, 478,
    486n, 487, 488
   sinking of, 476, 486
Prince of Wales (Great Britain), 80, 85
PT 36, 520
PT 37, 423, 520, 523
   sinking of, 587
PT 38, 318
PT 39, 421, 423
PT 40, 520–21, 523, 549
PT 43, 520–21
   sinking of, 549
PT 44, 520, 523
   sinking of, 524
PT 48, 520–21, 523, 587
PT 59, 520–21, 587
   I-3 sunk by, 523
PT 60, 318
PT 61, 423
PT 109, 520–21
PT 111:
   sinking of, 587
PT 112, 549
PT 114, 524
PT 115, 587
PT 123:
   sinking of, 587

PT 124, 587
Quincy, 60, 98–99, 101, 121*n*
  in Savo Island Battle, 104, 108, 109, 111–14
  sinking of, 113
Radford, 573, 583
Ralph Talbot, 99, 100, 103, 104, 114–15, 121*n*
Repulse (Great Britain), 85
Russell, 377, 395
S-38, 87–88, 91
S-44:
  Kako sunk by, 116
St. Louis, 548, 573
Salt Lake City, 174, 294, 297–98, 300, 302, 305–6, 310
San Diego, 377, 397, 430
Sands, 579, 580
San Francisco, 174, 249, 420, 451, 456, 459
  aerial attack on, 431–32
  Atlanta fired upon by, 443–44
  in Cape Esperance Battle, 294, 297–99, 301–2, 303–4, 306
  in Friday the Thirteenth Battle, 430, 433, 434, 436, 438, 445, 446, 448–49
San Juan, 75, 78, 98, 101, 174, 377, 385, 389, 391, 392–93
Saratoga, 51, 52, 54, 67, 94*n*, 119, 120, 226, 234, 235, 275, 503, 542, 543, 573, 577, 603
  Eastern Solomons Battle and, 165, 166, 172, 175, 176–77, 178–81, 187, 188, 189
  torpedoed, 203–4, 250
Seadragon:
  I-4 sunk by, 500
  Nankai Maru torpedoed by, 526
Selfridge, 118, 174
Seminole, 359
Shaw, 377, 389
Silversides, 545
Smith, 377, 390–91
Southard, 326, 430
South Dakota, 134, 399, 430
  in convoy-capital ship actions, 463, 468, 470–72, 475, 479–82, 484–87
  damaged, 480
  Lee on, 480, 482
  radar failures of, 477–78, 479
  in Santa Cruz Islands Battle, 371, 376, 389, 391, 392–93, 399
  withdrawal of, 481–82
Stack, 174
Sterett, 174, 420, 435, 436, 442–43, 446, 456, 459
Stringham, 583
Sturgeon, 329
Suwanee, 578, 580

Swordfish, 545
Tracy, 588
Trevor, 308, 358
Triton, 545
Tucker, 58
Vestal, 515
Vincennes, 84, 98–99, 101, 121*n*
  in Savo Island Battle, 104, 107, 109, 113
  sinking of, 114
Vireo, 324–25
Wakefield, 48
Walke, 470, 471, 475–78, 486*n*, 487, 488
  sinking of, 477, 486
Waller, 579, 580
Washington, 293, 328, 371, 378, 399, 430, 503
  in convoy-capital ship actions, 463, 468, 470–73, 475, 477–79, 481–84, 486–87
Wasp, 51, 60, 68, 76, 88, 94*n*, 119, 134, 275, 404, 604
  in Eastern Solomons Battle, 162, 165, 173, 192, 193*n*
  sinking of, 247–49, 250, 603
  Turner and, 247–48
Wichita, 578, 579, 580
William Ward Burrows, 200–201, 207
Wilson, 99, 101, 109, 114, 572
Worden, 172
Yorktown, 11, 22, 24, 30, 93, 250
YP 284, 359
YP 298, 220
YP 346, 220
Zane, 358
Zeilin, 293, 425, 430

NAVAL AVIATION

Air Group 8, 377
Air Group 10, 373, 376, 402, 491
VB-3, 172
VB-6, 68, 173, 324, 409–10
VB-8, 377, 388
VB-10, 376, 464, 467, 489
VF-5, 67–68, 172, 203, 226, 228, 234, 235, 243, 257, 272, 276, 322, 326, 345
VF-6, 67, 69, 173
VF-10, 376, 388, 489
VF-71, 173
VF-72, 60, 377
VP-11, 90, 174, 430*n*
VP-12 (Black Cats), 543
VP-14, 90, 174
VP-23, 90, 174, 192*n*
VP-72, 174
VS-3, 172, 234–35, 275, 328
VS-5, 68, 173
VS-8, 377
VS-10, 376, 466, 487–88

VS-71, 68, 173, 275, 280, 309, 330, 360,
410, 414–15
VS-72, 173
VT-3, 173
VT-6, 377

VT-7, 173
VT-8, 172, 235, 275, 280, 309, 422, 489
VT-10, 376, 384, 454, 464, 465, 466,
487–88, 489
Utility Unit 1, 173

A B O U T   T H E   A U T H O R

RICHARD B. FRANK was born in Kansas in 1947. His life long interest in naval and military history began when he read a volume of Samuel Eliot Morison's *History of United States Naval Operations in World War II* at age ten. Upon graduation from the University of Missouri in 1969, he was commissioned in the United States Army, in which he served almost four years, including a tour of duty in the Republic of Vietnam as an aerorifle platoon leader with the 101st Airborne Division. In 1976 he completed his studies at Georgetown Law Center in Washington, D.C., and the following year initiated research for this narrative, including extensive work with a Japanese translator on the massive Japanese Defense Agency War History series. Mr. Frank is currently a member of the Board of Veterans Appeals and lives in Virginia with his wife and daughter.